Safety Symbols

These symbols appear in laboratory activities. They warn of possible dangers in the laboratory and remind you to work carefully.

Safety Goggles Wear safety goggles to protect your eyes in any activity involving chemicals, flames or heating, or glassware.

Lab Apron Wear a laboratory apron to protect your skin and clothing from damage.

Breakage Handle breakable materials, such as glassware, with care. Do not touch broken glassware.

Heat-Resistant Gloves Use an oven mitt or other hand protection when handling hot materials such as hot plates or hot glassware.

Plastic Gloves Wear disposable plastic gloves when working with harmful chemicals and organisms. Keep your hands away from your face, and dispose of the gloves according to your teacher's instructions.

Heating Use a clamp or tongs to pick up hot glassware. Do not touch hot objects with your bare hands.

Flames Before you work with flames, tie back loose hair and clothing. Follow instructions from your teacher about lighting and extinguishing flames.

No Flames When using flammable materials, make sure there are no flames, sparks, or other exposed heat sources present.

Corrosive Chemical Avoid getting acid or other corrosive chemicals on your skin or clothing or in your eyes. Do not inhale the vapors. Wash your hands after the activity.

Poison Do not let any poisonous chemical come into contact with your skin, and do not inhale its vapors. Wash your hands when you are finished with the activity.

Fumes Work in a ventilated area when harmful vapors may be involved. Avoid inhaling vapors directly. Only test an odor when directed to do so by your teacher, and use a wafting motion to direct the vapor toward your nose.

Sharp Object Scissors, scalpels, knives, needles, pins, and tacks can cut your skin. Always direct a sharp edge or point away from yourself and others.

Animal Safety Treat live or preserved animals or animal parts with care to avoid harming the animals or yourself. Wash your hands when you are finished with the activity.

Plant Safety Handle plants only as directed by your teacher. If you are allergic to certain plants, tell your teacher; do not do an activity involving those plants. Avoid touching harmful plants such as poison ivy. Wash your hands when you are finished with the activity.

Electric Shock To avoid electric shock, never use electrical equipment around water, or when the equipment is wet or your hands are wet. Be sure cords are untangled and cannot trip anyone. Unplug equipment not in use.

Physical Safety When an experiment involves physical activity, avoid injuring yourself or others. Alert your teacher if there is any reason you should not participate.

Disposal Dispose of chemicals and other laboratory materials safely. Follow the instructions from your teacher.

Hand Washing Wash your hands thoroughly when finished with the activity. Use antibacterial soap and warm water. Rinse well.

General Safety Awareness When this symbol appears, follow the instructions provided. When you are asked to develop your own procedure in a lab, have your teacher approve your plan before you go further.

PEARSON
Prentice
Hall

Boston, Massachusetts
Upper Saddle River, New Jersey

PRENTICE HALL Science Explorer

Physical Science

Program Resources

Student Edition
StudentExpress™ with Interactive Textbook
Teacher's Edition
All-in-One Teaching Resources
Color Transparencies
Guided Reading and Study Workbook
Laboratory Manual
Consumable and Nonconsumable Materials Kits
Computer Microscope Lab Manual
Inquiry Skills Activity Books
Progress Monitoring Assessments
Test Preparation Workbook
Test-Taking Tips With Transparencies
Teacher's ELL Handbook
Reading Strategies for Science Content

Program Technology Resources

TeacherExpress™ CD-ROM
Interactive Textbooks Online
PresentationExpress™ CD-ROM
Student Edition on Audio CD
ExamView® Computer Test Bank CD-ROM
Lab zone™ Easy Planner CD-ROM
Probeware Lab Manual With CD-ROM
Computer Microscope and Lab Manual
Materials Ordering CD-ROM
Discovery Channel School® Video and DVD Library
Lab Activity Video and DVD Library
Web Site at PHSchool.com

Spanish Resources for Modular Series

Spanish Student Edition
Spanish Guided Reading and Study Workbook
Spanish Teaching Guide With Tests

Acknowledgments appear on pages 840–842, which constitute an extension of this copyright page.

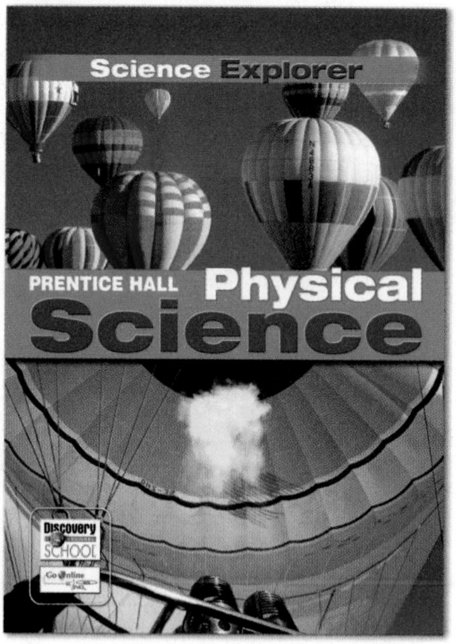

Cover
Hot-air balloons float because air expands as it is heated. The heated air within a rising balloon is less dense than the surrounding air.

PEARSON Prentice Hall

ISBN 0-13-190123-0
3 4 5 6 7 8 9 10 10 09 08 07 06

Program Authors

Michael J. Padilla, Ph.D.
Professor of Science Education
University of Georgia
Athens, Georgia

Michael Padilla is a leader in middle school science education. He has served as an author and elected officer for the National Science Teachers Association and as a writer of the National Science Education Standards. As lead author of Science Explorer, Mike has inspired the team in developing a program that meets the needs of middle grades students, promotes science inquiry, and is aligned with the National Science Education Standards.

Ioannis Miaoulis, Ph.D.
President
Museum of Science
Boston, Massachusetts

Originally trained as a mechanical engineer, Ioannis Miaoulis is in the forefront of the national movement to increase technological literacy. As dean of the Tufts University School of Engineering, Dr. Miaoulis spearheaded the introduction of engineering into the Massachusetts curriculum. Currently he is working with school systems across the country to engage students in engineering activities and to foster discussions on the impact of science and technology on society.

Martha Cyr, Ph.D.
Director of K–12 Outreach
Worcester Polytechnic Institute
Worcester, Massachusetts

Martha Cyr is a noted expert in engineering outreach. She has over nine years of experience with programs and activities that emphasize the use of engineering principles, through hands-on projects, to excite and motivate students and teachers of mathematics and science in grades K–12. Her goal is to stimulate a continued interest in science and mathematics through engineering.

Book Authors

David V. Frank, Ph.D.
Head, Department of Physical Sciences
Ferris State University
Big Rapids, Michigan

T. Griffith Jones, Ph.D.
Science Department Chair
P. K. Yonge Developmental Research School
College of Education—University of Florida
Gainesville, Florida

John G. Little
Science Teacher
St. Mary's High School
Stockton, California

Beth Miaoulis
Technology Writer
Sherborn, Massachusetts

Steve Miller
Science Writer
State College, Pennsylvania

Jay M. Pasachoff, Ph.D.
Professor of Astronomy
Williams College
Williamstown, Massachusetts

Camille Wainwright, Ph.D.
Professor of Science Education
Pacific University
Forest Grove, Oregon

Contributing Writers

Linda Blaine
Science Teacher
Millbrook High School
Raleigh, North Carolina

Rose-Marie Botting
Science Teacher
Broward County School District
Fort Lauderdale, Florida

Mary Sue Burns
Science Teacher
Pocahontas County High School
Dunmore, West Virginia

Edward Evans
Former Science Teacher
Hilton Central School
Hilton, New York

Mark Illingworth
Teacher
Hollis Public Schools
Hollis, New Hampshire

Thomas L. Messer
Science Teacher
Foxborough Public Schools
Foxborough, Massachusetts

Thomas R. Wellnitz
Science Instructor
The Paideia School
Atlanta, Georgia

Consultants

Reading Consultant

Nancy Romance, Ph.D.
Professor of Science Education
Florida Atlantic University
Fort Lauderdale, Florida

Mathematics Consultant

William Tate, Ph.D.
Professor of Education and Applied Statistics and Computation
Washington University
St. Louis, Missouri

Reviewers

Content Reviewers

Paul Beale, Ph.D.
Department of Physics
University of Colorado
Boulder, Colorado

Jeff Bodart, Ph.D.
Chipola Junior College
Marianna, Florida

Michael Castellani, Ph.D.
Department of Chemistry
Marshall University
Huntington, West Virginia

Eugene Chiang, Ph.D.
Department of Astronomy
University of California – Berkeley
Berkeley, California

Charles C. Curtis, Ph.D.
Department of Physics
University of Arizona
Tucson, Arizona

Daniel Kirk-Davidoff, Ph.D.
Department of Meteorology
University of Maryland
College Park, Maryland

Diane T. Doser, Ph.D.
Department of Geological Sciences
University of Texas at El Paso
El Paso, Texas

R. E. Duhrkopf, Ph.D.
Department of Biology
Baylor University
Waco, Texas

Michael Hacker
Co-director, Center for Technological Literacy
Hofstra University
Hempstead, New York

Michael W. Hamburger, Ph.D.
Department of Geological Sciences
Indiana University
Bloomington, Indiana

Alice K. Hankla, Ph.D.
The Galloway School
Atlanta, Georgia

Donald C. Jackson, Ph.D.
Department of Molecular Pharmacology, Physiology, & Biotechnology
Brown University
Providence, Rhode Island

Jeremiah N. Jarrett, Ph.D.
Department of Biological Sciences
Central Connecticut State University
New Britain, Connecticut

David Lederman, Ph.D.
Department of Physics
West Virginia University
Morgantown, West Virginia

Becky Mansfield, Ph.D.
Department of Geography
Ohio State University
Columbus, Ohio

Elizabeth M. Martin, M.S.
Department of Chemistry and Biochemistry
College of Charleston
Charleston, South Carolina

Joe McCullough, Ph.D.
Department of Natural and Applied Sciences
Cabrillo College
Aptos, California

Robert J. Mellors, Ph.D.
Department of Geological Sciences
San Diego State University
San Diego, California

JJoseph M. Moran, Ph.D.
American Meteorological Society
Washington, D.C.

David J. Morrissey, Ph.D.
Department of Chemistry
Michigan State University
East Lansing, Michigan

Philip A. Reed, Ph.D.
Department of Occupational & Technical Studies
Old Dominion University
Norfolk, Virginia

Scott M. Rochette, Ph.D.
Department of the Earth Sciences
State University of New York, College at Brockport
Brockport, New York

Laurence D. Rosenhein, Ph.D.
Department of Chemistry
Indiana State University
Terre Haute, Indiana

Ronald Sass, Ph.D.
Department of Biology and Chemistry
Rice University
Houston, Texas

George Schatz, Ph.D.
Department of Chemistry
Northwestern University
Evanston, Illinois

Sara Seager, Ph.D.
Carnegie Institution of Washington
Washington, D.C.

Robert M. Thornton, Ph.D.
Section of Plant Biology
University of California
Davis, California

John R. Villarreal, Ph.D.
College of Science and Engineering
The University of Texas – Pan American
Edinburg, Texas

Kenneth Welty, Ph.D.
School of Education
University of Wisconsin–Stout
Menomonie, Wisconsin

Edward J. Zalisko, Ph.D.
Department of Biology
Blackburn College
Carlinville, Illinois

Tufts University Content Reviewers

Faculty from Tufts University in Medford, Massachusetts, developed *Science Explorer* chapter projects and reviewed the student books.

Astier M. Almedom, Ph.D.
Department of Biology

Wayne Chudyk, Ph.D.
Department of Civil and Environmental Engineering

John L. Durant, Ph.D.
Department of Civil and Environmental Engineering

George S. Ellmore, Ph.D.
Department of Biology

David L. Kaplan, Ph.D.
Department of Chemical Engineering

Samuel Kounaves, Ph.D.
Department of Chemistry

David H. Lee, Ph.D.
Department of Chemistry

Douglas Matson, Ph.D.
Department of Mechanical Engineering

Karen Panetta, Ph.D.
Department of Electrical Engineering and Computer Science

Jan A. Pechenik, Ph.D.
Department of Biology

John C. Ridge, Ph.D.
Department of Geology

William Waller, Ph.D.
Department of Astronomy

Teacher Reviewers

David R. Blakely
Arlington High School
Arlington, Massachusetts

Jane E. Callery
Two Rivers Magnet Middle School
East Hartford, Connecticut

Melissa Lynn Cook
Oakland Mills High School
Columbia, Maryland

James Fattic
Southside Middle School
Anderson, Indiana

Dan Gabel
Hoover Middle School
Rockville, Maryland

Wayne Goates
Eisenhower Middle School
Goddard, Kansas

Katherine Bobay Graser
Mint Hill Middle School
Charlotte, North Carolina

Darcy Hampton
Deal Junior High School
Washington, D.C.

Karen Kelly
Pierce Middle School
Waterford, Michigan

David Kelso
Manchester High School Central
Manchester, New Hampshire

Benigno Lopez, Jr.
Sleepy Hill Middle School
Lakeland, Florida

Angie L. Matamoros, Ph.D.
ALM Consulting, Inc.
Weston, Florida

Tim McCollum
Charleston Middle School
Charleston, Illinois

Bruce A. Mellin
Brooks School
North Andover, Massachusetts

Ella Jay Parfitt
Southeast Middle School
Baltimore, Maryland

Evelyn A. Pizzarello
Louis M. Klein Middle School
Harrison, New York

Kathleen M. Poe
Fletcher Middle School
Jacksonville, Florida

Shirley Rose
Lewis and Clark Middle School
Tulsa, Oklahoma

Linda Sandersen
Greenfield Middle School
Greenfield, Wisconsin

Mary E. Solan
Southwest Middle School
Charlotte, North Carolina

Mary Stewart
University of Tulsa
Tulsa, Oklahoma

Paul Swenson
Billings West High School
Billings, Montana

Thomas Vaughn
Arlington High School
Arlington, Massachusetts

Susan C. Zibell
Central Elementary
Simsbury, Connecticut

Safety Reviewers

W. H. Breazeale, Ph.D.
Department of Chemistry
College of Charleston
Charleston, South Carolina

Ruth Hathaway, Ph.D.
Hathaway Consulting
Cape Girardeau, Missouri

Douglas Mandt
Science Education Consultant
Edgewood, Washington

Activity Field Testers

Nicki Bibbo
Witchcraft Heights School
Salem, Massachusetts

Rose-Marie Botting
Broward County Schools
Fort Lauderdale, Florida

Colleen Campos
Laredo Middle School
Aurora, Colorado

Elizabeth Chait
W. L. Chenery Middle School
Belmont, Massachusetts

Holly Estes
Hale Middle School
Stow, Massachusetts

Laura Hapgood
Plymouth Community Intermediate School
Plymouth, Massachusetts

Mary F. Lavin
Plymouth Community Intermediate School
Plymouth, Massachusetts

James MacNeil, Ph.D.
Cambridge, Massachusetts

Lauren Magruder
St. Michael's Country Day School
Newport, Rhode Island

Jeanne Maurand
Austin Preparatory School
Reading, Massachusetts

Joanne Jackson-Pelletier
Winman Junior High School
Warwick, Rhode Island

Warren Phillips
Plymouth Public Schools
Plymouth, Massachusetts

Carol Pirtle
Hale Middle School
Stow, Massachusetts

Kathleen M. Poe
Fletcher Middle School
Jacksonville, Florida

Cynthia B. Pope
Norfolk Public Schools
Norfolk, Virginia

Anne Scammell
Geneva Middle School
Geneva, New York

Karen Riley Sievers
Callanan Middle School
Des Moines, Iowa

David M. Smith
Eyer Middle School
Allentown, Pennsylvania

Gene Vitale
Parkland School
McHenry, Illinois

Contents

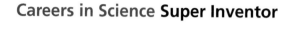

Physical Science

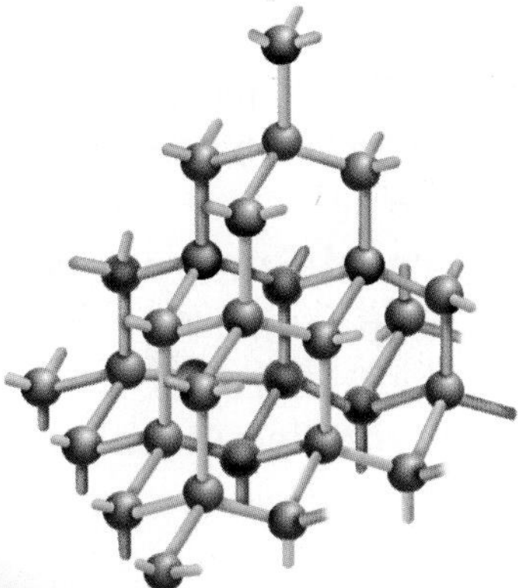

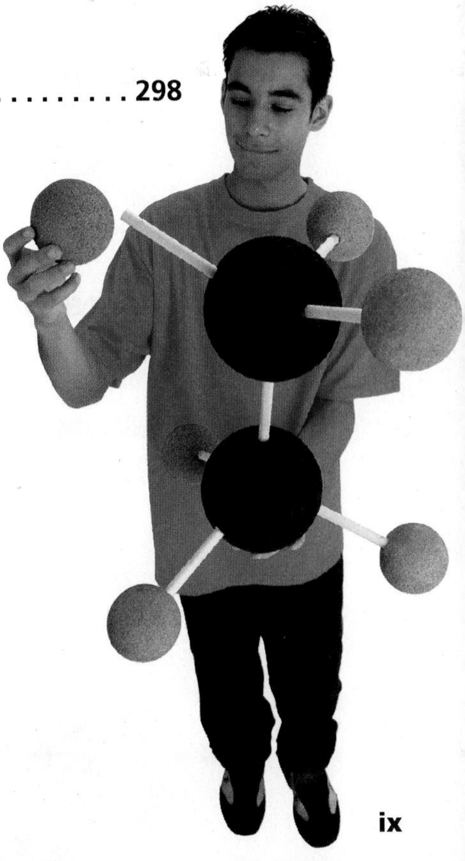

Unit 2 Motion, Forces, and Energy

Unit 3 Sound and Light

Unit 4 Electricity and Magnetism

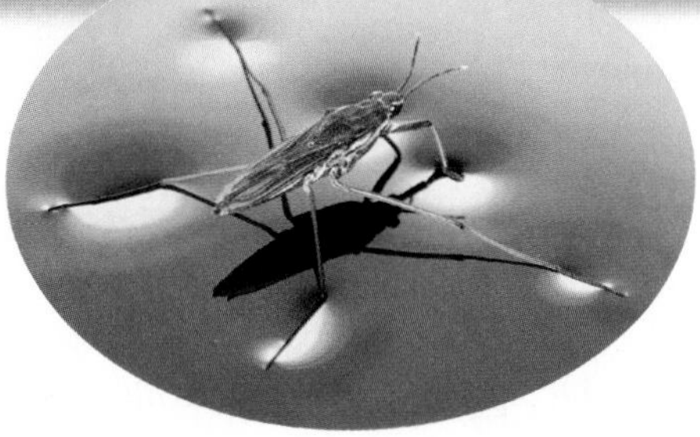

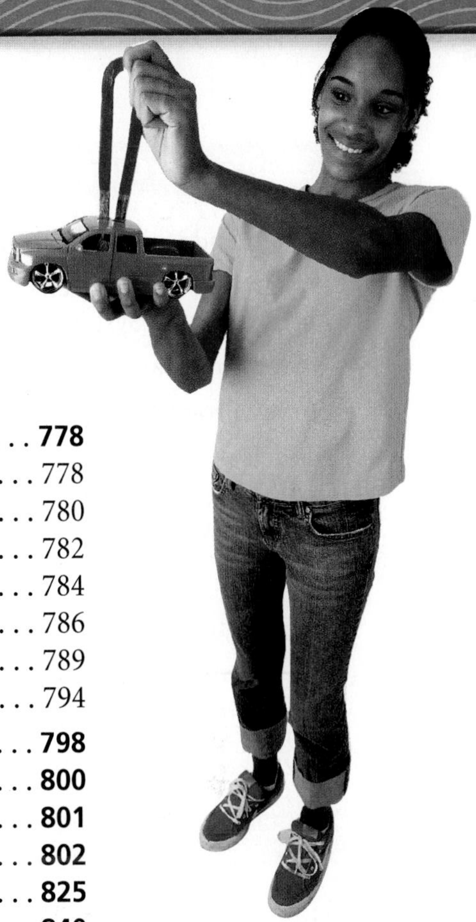

Reference Section

Discovery Channel School

VIDEO

Enhance understanding through dynamic video.

Preview Get motivated with this introduction to the chapter content.

Field Trip Explore a real-world story related to the chapter content.

Assessment Review content and take an assessment.

Go Online

Web Links

Get connected to exciting Web resources in every lesson.

SCI LINKS™ NSTA Find Web links on topics relating to every section.

Active Art Interact with selected visuals from every chapter online.

Planet Diary® Explore news and natural phenomena through weekly reports.

Science News® Keep up to date with the latest science discoveries.

Interactive Textbook

Experience the complete textbook online and on CD-ROM.

Activities Practice skills and learn content.

Videos Explore content and learn important lab skills.

Audio Support Hear key terms spoken and defined.

Self-Assessment Use instant feedback to help you track your progress.

Activities

Lab zone™ Chapter Project — Opportunities for long-term inquiry

Lab zone Discover Activity — Exploration and inquiry before reading

Lab zone Try This Activity — Reinforcement of key concepts

Lab zone Skills Activity — Practice of specific science inquiry skills

Lab zone **Labs** In-depth practice of inquiry skills and science concepts

Lab zone At-Home Activity — Quick, engaging activities for home and family

Math Point-of-use math practice

Analyzing Data

Sample Problems

Math Skills

Math Practice

• Tech & Design • Design, build, test, and communicate

active art Illustrations come alive online

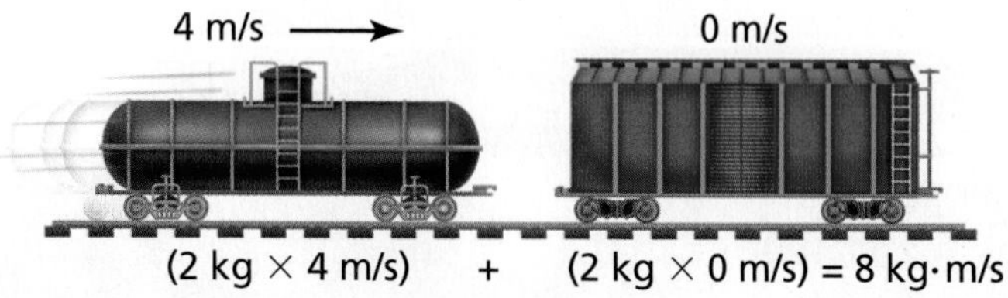

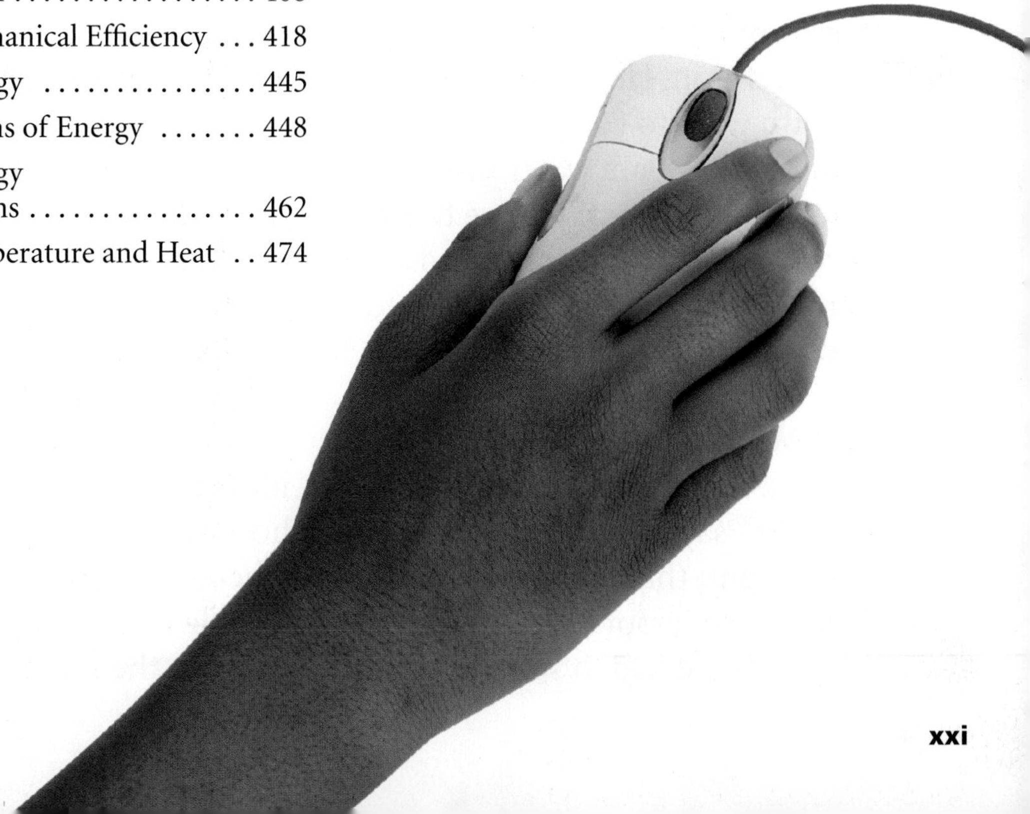

Careers in **Science**

Do you recognize this invention by Lonnie Johnson?

Super Inventor

Engineer Lonnie Johnson was working on a new invention. He was experimenting with ways to cool the inside of a refrigerator with plain water instead of with harmful chemicals. As he tested his cooling system with a homemade nozzle in his bathroom sink, he noticed that he could blast a stream of water across the room. He stepped back and thought, "Wouldn't it be great if . . .?"

"That sink nozzle was the idea for a super squirter," says Lonnie. But to make a water gun that could store enough energy to shoot a stream of water forcefully, he had to solve an engineering problem. How could he get a high-pressure water stream from a toy that a child could operate? How could he make the water shoot out in almost the same way that water comes out of a fire hydrant?

Recently, Lonnie set up his own company. He invents new devices to solve tough problems in science and engineering. But he also puts his ideas to work to invent new toys and household products. Lonnie says that whether you're working on a space vehicle or a toy, the process of inventing is much the same.

Talking With Lonnie Johnson

What kind of kid were you?

I was always interested in how things work—in building and making things. My favorite toy was my erector set. I also liked those plastic building blocks. I used to take my brother's and sister's toys apart to see how they worked. And I used to repair stuff. If there was something broken around the house, like a lamp, I'd try to repair it. I learned from my father, too. He would work on his cars at home and that fascinated me. I was learning about machines by watching and helping him.

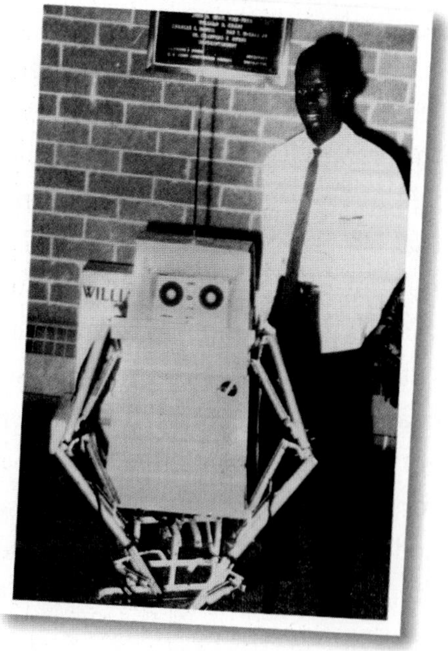

In high school, Lonnie won first place in a national science-fair competition with a homemade remote-control robot, which he called "Linex."

How did you get interested in engineering?

The whole interest in building and fixing stuff—I guess that's where the seed came from. Repairing a broken lamp isn't all that different from inventing a super new toy. You need to be able to imagine how something works in your head, to see all the machine parts and how they'd work together—that's the basic skill. I'm usually pretty good at imagining how machines could be put together and work, whether they're big or small, simple or complex.

Career Path

Lonnie Johnson grew up in Alabama. He attended Tuskegee University and received a B.S. in mechanical engineering, an M.S. in nuclear engineering, and an honorary Ph.D. in science. He worked for the Jet Propulsion Laboratory in Pasadena, California. Now Lonnie owns his own company in Georgia.

Do you solve problems all in your head? Or do you experiment?

I do both. It depends on the problem. Sometimes, just getting started is the key. You start building and putting things together, and other things reveal themselves along the way as you work.

For example, I have a long-term project I'm working on. I want to make a new kind of engine that's friendly to the environment, an engine that will make electricity from heat. In science, we call that a thermionic engine (from *therm,* the Greek root for "heat," and *ion*, an atom with an electrical charge). My first idea was a mechanical engine, one with moving parts. But we faced some real challenges when we tried to make it. So now I've got an engine idea that has no moving parts. I'm very excited about this particular solution. But I had to build the mechanical engine to realize that I needed to come up with a different engine.

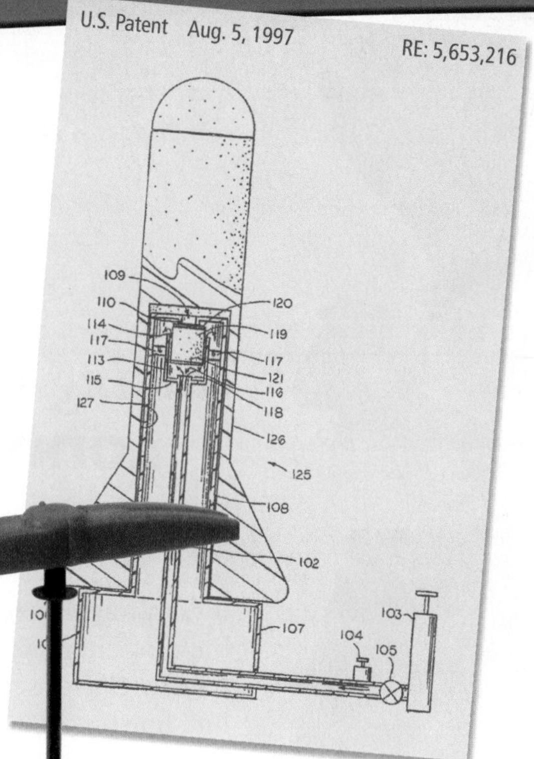

What happens if you get stuck?

When you have a problem you can't solve, you put it on hold. It sits there in the back of your mind. Then when you're doing something else, you find a clue.

I try to make that work in my company as well as inside my own head. We've got a toy side of the company that's very creative. The other side of the company is more hard science. We take the technology from the science side and use it in thinking up new toys. If you learn about how water works under pressure, you can invent a refrigerator, or a way to heat houses, or make a super squirt gun. There's a lot of crossing back and forth. I have a lot of fun.

This toy rocket is powered by pumped air. The U.S. patent for Lonnie's rocket is shown above.

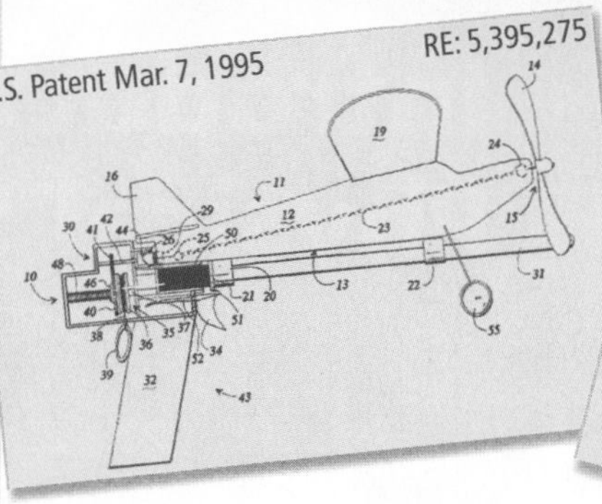

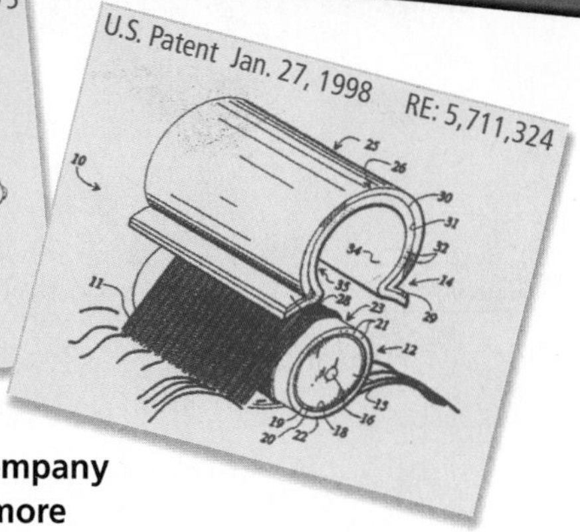

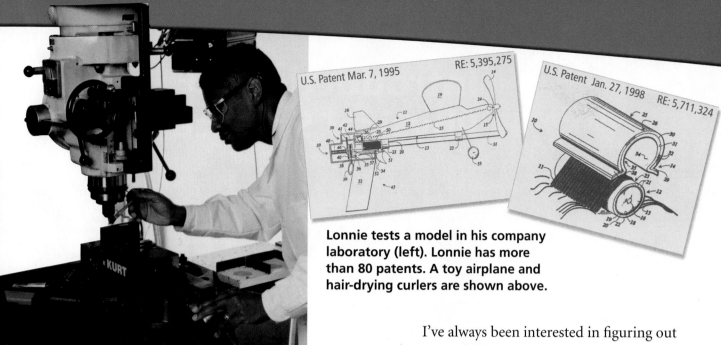

Lonnie tests a model in his company laboratory (left). Lonnie has more than 80 patents. A toy airplane and hair-drying curlers are shown above.

? How do you get started on an invention?

You ask the question: What would be a great thing to have? You develop an overall idea. Then you define it by thinking of the specific problems that need to be solved.

Think about model rockets. I used to build model rockets when I was a kid. I'd order them through the mail, assemble them, and launch them. After a while, I made my own. I went to the library and found a book on how to build them. But those rockets used explosive chemicals for fuel. I wanted to make toy rockets that were cleaner and safer. So now I've invented rockets that use pumped air and water for power.

? Is inventing hard?

If you can focus and work for a long time, you get very good at what you do. Problem solving is a process. There can be so many pieces to the puzzle. It's like a jigsaw puzzle. Sometimes all the pieces are there. Yet you can't even see them at first. But if you get your hands in and touch them and start working on it, you can start feeling the shapes. You start to understand how the pieces fit together.

I've always been interested in figuring out how to make things go and in working with new and different sources of power. When I was an engineer at NASA, I worked on the nuclear power source for the Galileo spacecraft. But I've also worked on powering toys with water and air, and making toy planes fly with rubber bands. The basic ideas are the same.

The trick is to keep working at it. Know what you're aiming for and keep looking for new solutions. Following through is also key to my philosophy: Believe in yourself and persevere. That's what I tell kids whenever I get the chance.

Writing in Science

Career Link Lonnie says the first step in an invention is the idea. Think of something that would be "a great thing to have," such as a toy or gadget. As an inventor, write a paragraph that describes your idea. Then, in a second paragraph, identify clearly some of the "little problems" you'll need to solve to make your idea work. (Remember, you don't need to know what the solutions will be.)

Go Online
PHSchool.com
For: More on this career
Visit: PHSchool.com
Web Code: cgb-6000

Chapter 1

Introduction to Physical Science

Chapter Preview

1 What Is Physical Science?
Discover *How Does a Ball Bounce?*
At-Home Activity *Quantitative or Qualitative?*

2 Scientific Inquiry
Discover *Can You Make a Shadow Disappear?*
Skills Activity *Classifying*
Analyzing Data *Car Travel*
Active Art *The Nature of Inquiry*
At-Home Activity *Which Falls Fastest?*

3 Science Laboratory Safety
Discover *Where Is the Safety Equipment in Your School?*
Skills Lab *Swing Time*

4 What Is Technology?
Discover *Why Redesign?*
Active Art *Technology Design Process*
Try This *Watch Ideas Take Off*

Interactive Textbook

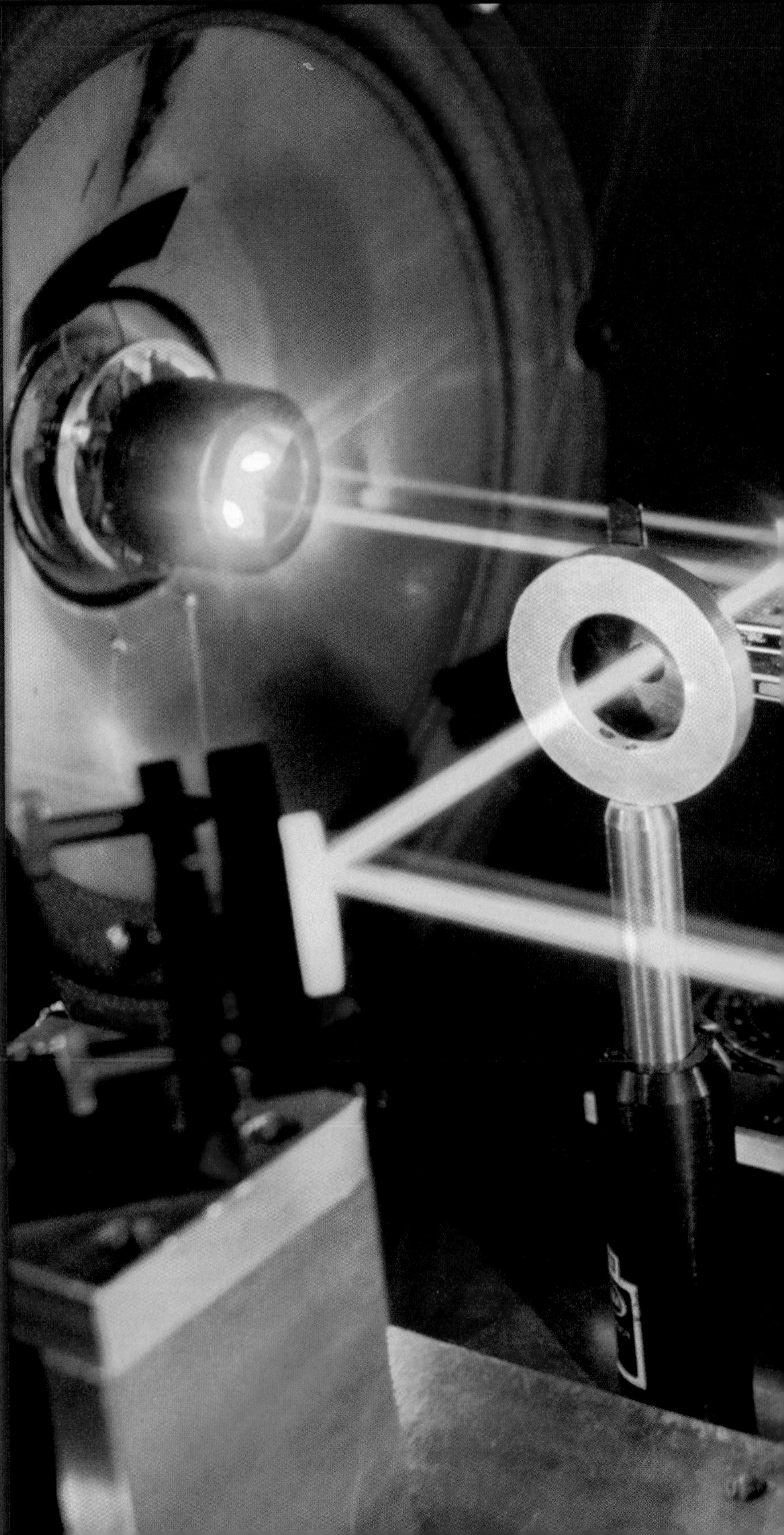

Lasers are used in many technology products, from supermarket scanners to audio equipment. ▶

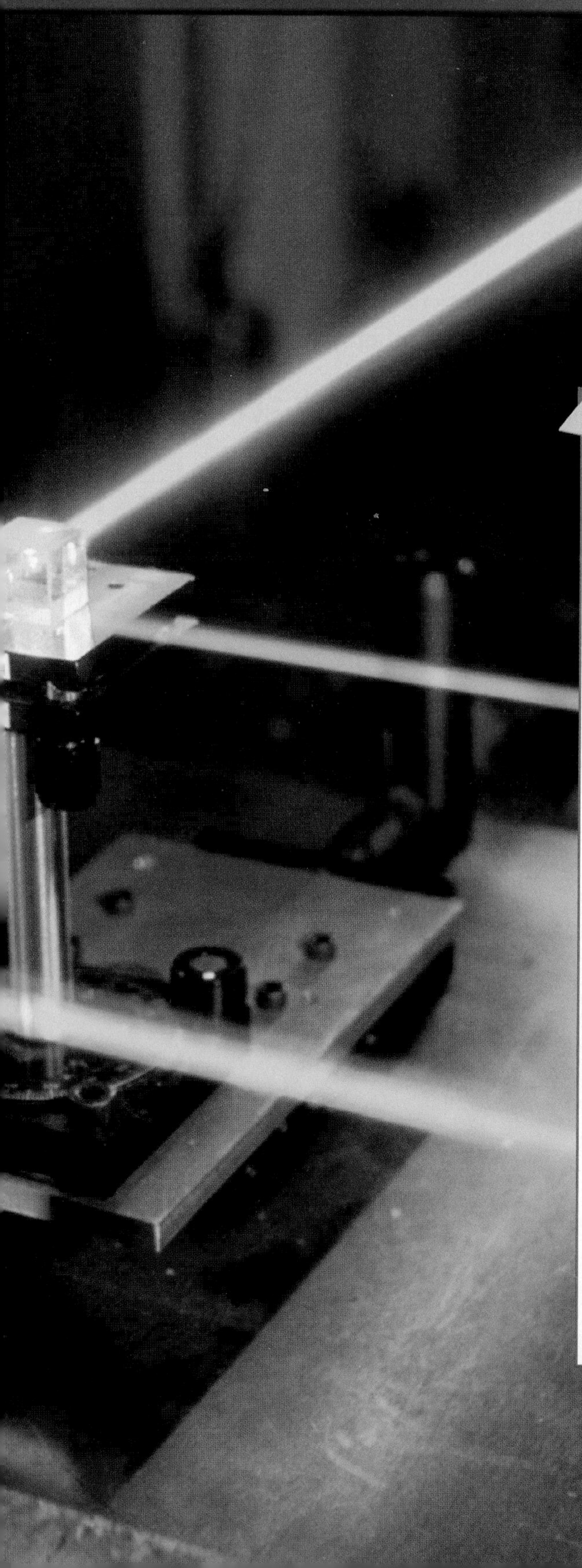

Discovery Channel School

Technology and Engineering

▶ Video Preview
Video Field Trip
Video Assessment

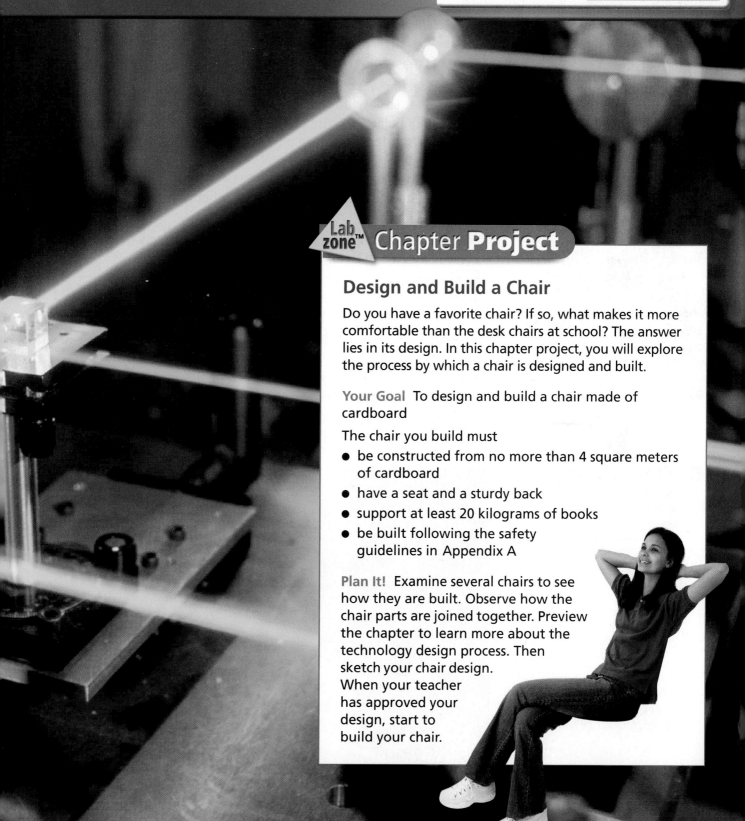

Lab zone™ Chapter **Project**

Design and Build a Chair

Do you have a favorite chair? If so, what makes it more comfortable than the desk chairs at school? The answer lies in its design. In this chapter project, you will explore the process by which a chair is designed and built.

Your Goal To design and build a chair made of cardboard

The chair you build must

- be constructed from no more than 4 square meters of cardboard
- have a seat and a sturdy back
- support at least 20 kilograms of books
- be built following the safety guidelines in Appendix A

Plan It! Examine several chairs to see how they are built. Observe how the chair parts are joined together. Preview the chapter to learn more about the technology design process. Then sketch your chair design. When your teacher has approved your design, start to build your chair.

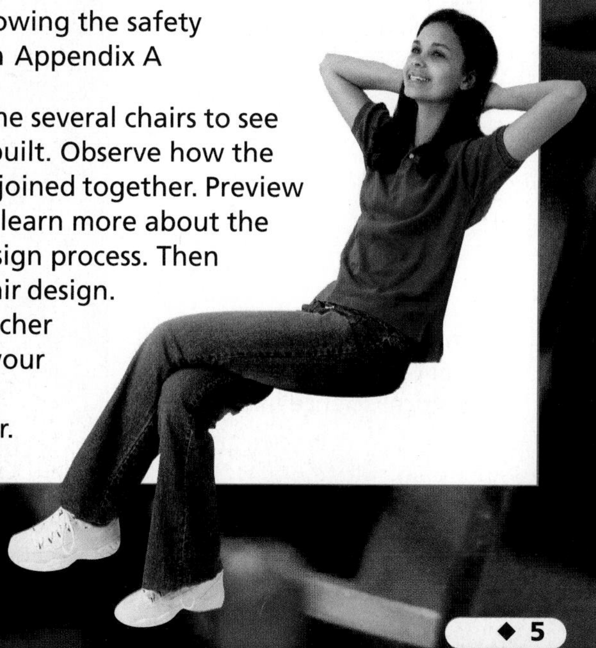

Section 1

What Is Physical Science?

Reading Preview

Key Concepts

- What skills do scientists use to learn about the world?
- What do physical scientists study?

Key Terms

- science • observing
- qualitative observation
- quantitative observation
- inferring • predicting
- chemistry • physics

Target Reading Skill

Using Prior Knowledge Before you read, look at the section headings to see what this section is about. Then write what you know about physical science in a graphic organizer like the one below. As you read, write what you learn.

What You Know
1. Physical science includes the study of motion. 2.

What You Learned
1. 2.

Lab zone Discover Activity

How Does a Ball Bounce?

1. Your teacher will give you three balls and a meter stick. Hold the meter stick with the zero end touching the floor.
2. Hold one ball beside the top of the meter stick so it doesn't touch. Drop the ball. Have a partner record the height of the first bounce.
3. Repeat Step 2 twice using the same ball.
4. Repeat Steps 2 and 3 for each of the other balls.

Think It Over

Predicting Can you use your data to predict accurately how each ball will bounce in the future? Explain.

As you walk around an amusement park, you may wonder how the rides work. How does a ferris wheel spin? How do the bumper cars work? What makes the neon lights so colorful? Why don't people fall out of the roller coaster as it completes a loop? These are all questions that physical science can help to answer. The designers of amusement parks must know a great deal about physical science to make sure that visitors experience fun and thrills while staying safe.

An amusement park is a great place to observe physical science in action. ▶

How Scientists Think

Physical science is one type of science. **Science** is a way of learning about the natural world by gathering information. Science includes all of the knowledge gained by exploring nature. To think and work like a scientist, you need to use the same skills that they do. **Scientists use the skills of observing, inferring, and predicting to learn more about the natural world.**

Go Online
PHSchool.com
For: More on scientific thinking
Visit: PHSchool.com
Web Code: cgd-6011

Observing Like everyone else, scientists observe things. **Observing** means using one or more senses to gather information. Your senses include sight, hearing, touch, taste, and smell. Each day of your life, you observe things that help you decide what to eat, what to wear, and whether to stay inside or go out.

Scientists usually make observations in a careful, orderly way. They make both qualitative and quantitative observations. **Qualitative observations** are descriptions that don't involve numbers or measurements. Noticing that a ball is round, that milk smells sour, that honey tastes sweet, or that a car is moving is a qualitative observation. **Quantitative observations** are measurements. You make a quantitative observation when you measure your height or weight. In science, observations may also be called evidence, or data.

Inferring Have you ever bumped into a bumper car that wasn't moving? What happened? If your bumper car was moving fast enough, it made the other bumper car move when they bumped. You might then say that if an object is standing still, one way to make it move is to hit it with another moving object.

When you explain your observations, you are **inferring,** or making an inference. Inferences are based on reasoning from what you already know. You make inferences all the time without thinking about it. For example, your teacher gives lots of surprise quizzes. So if your teacher walks into the room carrying a stack of paper, you may infer that the pages contain a quiz. But inferences are not always correct. The papers could be announcements to be taken home.

Reading Checkpoint What are inferences based on?

FIGURE 1 Inferring
When you explain or interpret your observations, you are making an inference. Inferring *How do you think these young women obtained the stuffed bear? Explain your reasoning.*

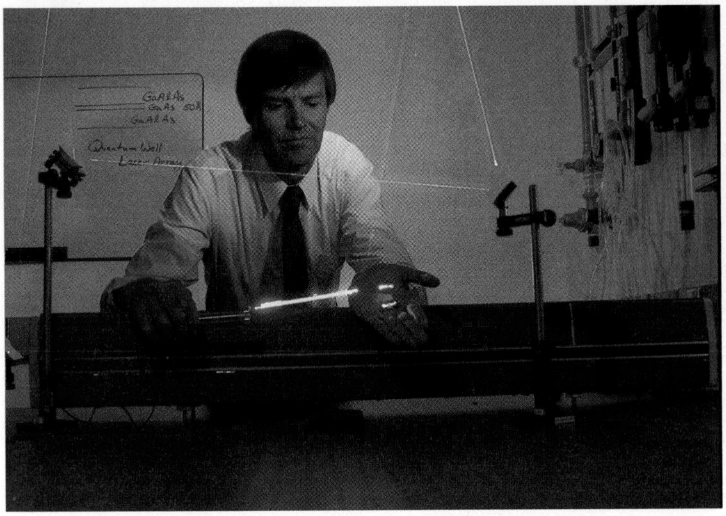

▲ This physicist is experimenting with lasers.

▲ A chemist is removing a liquid from a flask.

FIGURE 2

Careers in Physical Science

People who work in physical science study changes in matter and energy. Physicists, chemists, and engineers are examples of people who work in physical science.

Predicting Every day, people make statements about the future. Before a soccer game, for example, you might predict, "We're going to win big!" **Predicting** means making a forecast of what will happen in the future based on past experience or evidence. Saying your team will win is a prediction if it is based on the records of the two teams. It is a guess if it is not based on any data.

Predicting is important in science, too. For example, some scientists predict the weather based on past experience and current information.

The Study of Matter and Energy

Physical science is the study of matter, energy, and the changes they undergo. Matter is all around you. It is anything that has mass and occupies space. Energy is the ability to do work or cause change. An amusement park ride uses energy as it moves. Physical science is divided into two main areas: chemistry and physics.

Chemistry is the study of the properties of matter and how matter changes. When you study chemistry, you will learn about the particles that make up matter and why different forms of matter have different properties. You will find out how matter can change and why. For example, you'll learn why some materials burn while others do not.

Physics is the study of matter and energy and how they interact. When you study physics, you will learn about motion and forces and how they are related. You will also learn about the different forms of energy and the physical laws that govern energy. Other topics you will study in physics include sound, light, electricity, and magnetism.

▲ Two engineers are installing communications equipment on a mountaintop.

All of the people shown in Figure 2 work in some area of physical science. Some careers involve scientific research. Other careers, such as photographer, piano tuner, or firefighter, require that you understand physical science.

You may be thinking that physical science is important only if you work in careers like these. But you use physical science all the time. For example, when you put on sunglasses to protect your eyes from bright sunlight, or you blow on a spoonful of soup to cool it down, you are using physical science. In this book, you will find out about many more everyday events that involve physical science.

Reading Checkpoint **What is physics?**

Section 1 Assessment

Target Reading Skill **Using Prior Knowledge** Review your graphic organizer and revise it based on what you just learned in the section.

Reviewing Key Concepts

1. a. **Listing** Name three skills that scientists use to learn more about the natural world.
   b. **Comparing and Contrasting** How do observing and inferring differ?
   c. **Classifying** Is this statement an observation or an inference? *It must be raining outside.* Explain.
2. a. **Defining** What is physical science?
   b. **Identifying** What are the two main areas of physical science?
   c. **Inferring** How would a knowledge of physical science be useful to a musician? To a photographer?

Lab zone **At-Home Activity**

Quantitative or Qualitative? Look around your room at home. Write down three qualitative and three quantitative observations. How do these two types of observations differ from one another?

Section 2 Scientific Inquiry

Reading Preview

Key Concepts

- How do scientists investigate the natural world?
- What role do models, laws, and theories play in science?

Key Terms

- scientific inquiry
- hypothesis • variable
- manipulated variable
- responding variable
- controlled experiment
- data • communicating
- scientific law • scientific theory

Target Reading Skill

Building Vocabulary After you read this section, reread the paragraphs that contain definitions of Key Terms. Use all the information you have learned to write a definition of each Key Term in your own words.

Lab zone Discover Activity

Can You Make a Shadow Disappear?

1. Using a piece of clay as a base, set up a straw so that it stands up straight.
2. Shine a flashlight on the straw from as many directions as you can. Observe the different shadows you create. Record your observations.
3. Determine whether you can make the shadow disappear while using the light. If you can, describe how you did it.

Think It Over

Posing Questions If you had a meter stick among your materials, what are two other questions you could investigate?

Have you ever made shadow puppets on a wall? Shadows are produced when something blocks light from shining on a surface. Making shadow puppets might make you wonder about light and shadows. Your curiosity can be the first step in scientific inquiry. **Scientific inquiry** refers to the different ways scientists study the natural world. It is the ongoing process of discovery in science.

Just like you, scientists often find that being curious is the first step in scientific inquiry. Scientists have other habits of mind as well: honesty, open-mindedness, skepticism, and creativity. Honesty means reporting observations truthfully. Open-mindedness is accepting new and different ideas. Skepticism is being doubtful about information presented without evidence. Creativity involves coming up with new ways to solve problems.

A shadow puppet ▼

The Process of Inquiry

Scientific inquiry does not always occur in the same way. But, certain processes are often involved. **The processes that scientists use in inquiry include posing questions, developing hypotheses, designing experiments, collecting and interpreting data, drawing conclusions, and communicating ideas and results.**

Posing Questions Suppose you want to learn more about light and shadows. You might ask, Does the size of a shadow depend on the distance between the light and the object? How is a shadow affected by the light's position? Will you get shadows if you have several light sources?

All those questions about light and shadows are scientific questions because you can answer them by making observations. Not all questions are scientific, however. For example, suppose you ask, "Which is the most interesting photo in a photography contest?" The answer to that question is based on personal opinion, not on evidence. Scientific inquiry cannot answer questions based on opinions, values, or judgments.

Developing Hypotheses Scientific inquiry moves forward when ideas can be tested. For example, suppose you want to find out how the distance between the object and the light affects the size of a shadow. Your first step might be to develop a hypothesis (plural: *hypotheses*). A **hypothesis** is a possible answer to a scientific question or explanation for a set of observations. For example, you may say: *Changing the distance between an object and a light source changes the size of the object's shadow.*

It is important to realize that your hypothesis is not a fact. It is only one possible way to answer a question. But in science, a hypothesis must be testable by observation or experiment. In that way, information can be collected that may or may not support the hypothesis. Many trials are needed before a hypothesis can be accepted as true.

Reading Checkpoint **What is a hypothesis?**

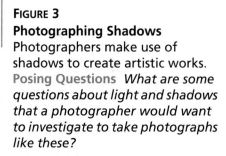

Lab zone **Skills Activity**

Classifying

Which of the following questions can be answered by scientific inquiry?

- Is running a better sport than swimming?
- Does running make your muscles stronger than swimming does?
- Which brand of running shoes looks best?

How did you make your decision in each case?

FIGURE 3
Photographing Shadows
Photographers make use of shadows to create artistic works.
Posing Questions *What are some questions about light and shadows that a photographer would want to investigate to take photographs like these?*

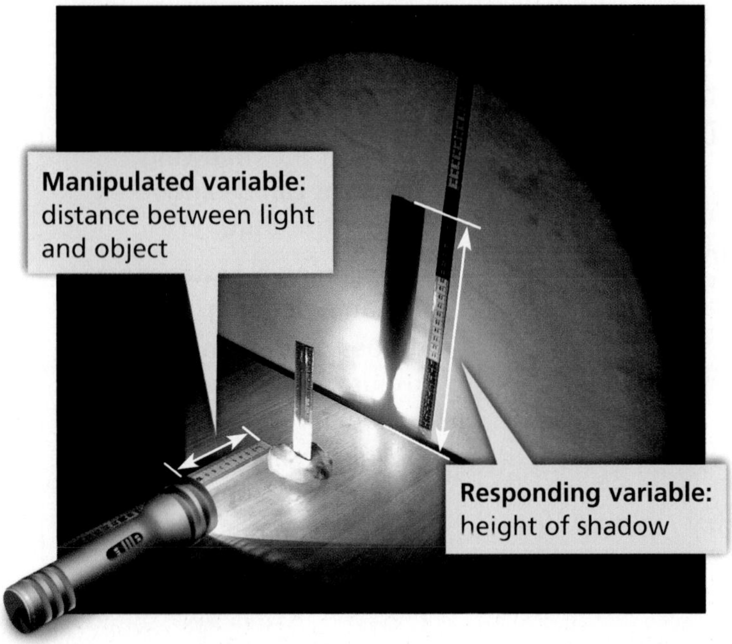

FIGURE 4
Investigating Shadows
This photo shows the setup for an experiment to test how the distance between an object and a light source affects the size of the object's shadow. What is the manipulated variable in the experiment?

Designing an Experiment Scientists can test a hypothesis by designing an experiment. They begin to plan their experiment by first examining all the variables. **Variables** are factors that can change in an experiment. In a well-designed experiment, only one variable is purposely changed. The variable that is changed is the **manipulated variable** (or independent variable). The variable that is expected to change because of the manipulated variable is the **responding variable** (or dependent variable).

Look at Figure 4. For your hypothesis about shadows, the manipulated variable is the distance between the light source and the object. The responding variable is the height of the shadow.

To be sure that changes in the manipulated variable are causing the changes in the responding variable, scientists change only one variable at a time. All the other variables must be controlled—that is, kept constant. Figure 4 shows some variables that need to be controlled in your shadow experiment: the type of light, the height and angle of the light, and the distance between the object and the wall. An investigation in which all variables except one remain the same is called a **controlled experiment.**

Shadow Experiment

Distance Between Object and Light (cm)	Height of Shadow (cm)
10	32
15	27
20	25
25	23
30	22
35	21
40	20

Change in Shadow Height

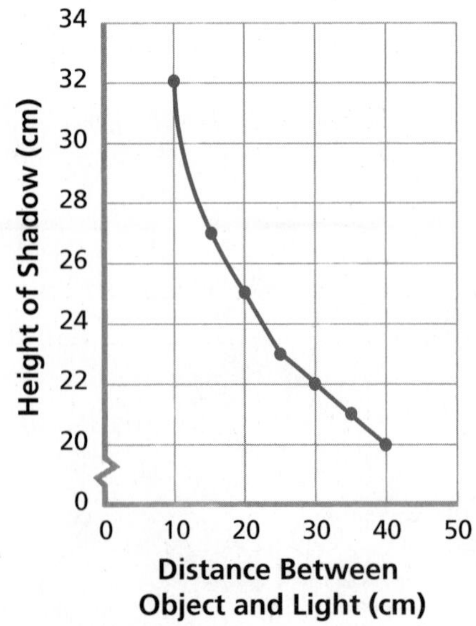

FIGURE 5 Showing Experimental Results
The results of the shadow experiment are shown here as a data table and as a graph. Interpreting Graphs *What relationship do the data show?*

Math Analyzing Data

Car Travel

The graph shows the distance a car travels in a one-hour period. Use the graph to answer the questions below.

1. **Reading Graphs** What variable is plotted on the horizontal axis? What variable is plotted on the vertical axis?
2. **Interpreting Data** How far does the car travel in the first 10 minutes? In the first 40 minutes?
3. **Interpreting Data** How long does it take the car to travel 30 km? 60 km?
4. **Predicting** Use the graph to predict how far the car would travel in 120 minutes. Assume the car continues to travel at the same speed.
5. **Graphing** Draw a graph of a car moving at a steady speed of 30 kilometers per hour for a one-hour period. What is the relationship between the steepness of the graph lines and the speed of the cars?

Distance Traveled by Car

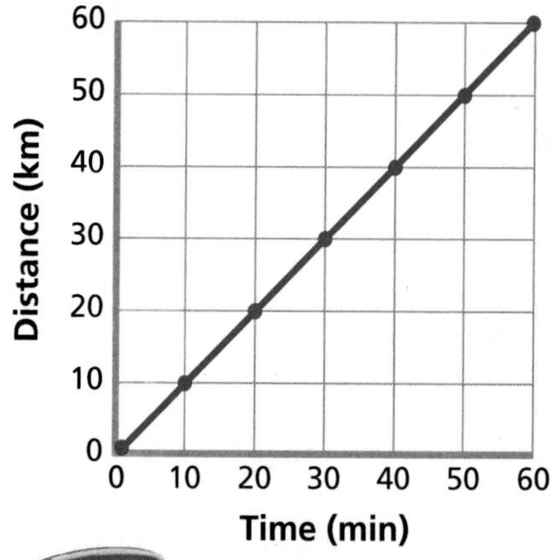

Collecting and Interpreting Data Before scientists begin an experiment, they usually create a data table for recording their data. **Data** are the facts, figures, and other evidence gathered through observations. A data table provides an organized way to collect and record observations. Figure 5 shows a data table that you might have made during your shadow experiment.

Recall that observations can be qualitative or quantitative. Data can also be qualitative or quantitative. Qualitative data can be recorded as notes in a journal or log. Scientists make it easier to share quantitative data by using the same system of measurement, called the International System of Units (SI). Notice that the data table uses centimeters (cm), an SI unit of length. You can learn more about measuring with SI in the Skills Handbook at the end of this book.

After the data are collected, they need to be interpreted, or explained. Graphs are a useful way to view quantitative data because they can reveal trends or patterns in the data. Look at the graph in Figure 5. It shows that as the distance between the object and the light increased, the height of the shadow decreased in a regular way. You can learn more about using data tables and graphs in the Skills Handbook.

Reading Checkpoint Why do scientists use the SI system?

Drawing Conclusions After scientists interpret their data, they draw a conclusion about their hypothesis. A conclusion states whether or not the data support the hypothesis. For the data in the shadow experiment, you would conclude that the height of a shadow decreases as the light is moved farther away from an object.

Communicating An important part of scientific inquiry is communicating. **Communicating** is sharing ideas and conclusions with others through writing and speaking. It is also sharing the process you used in your inquiry. When a scientist shares the design of an experiment, others can repeat that experiment to check the results. Scientists often communicate by giving talks at scientific meetings, exchanging information on the Internet, or publishing articles in scientific journals.

Communicating information about scientific discoveries often leads to new questions, new hypotheses, and new investigations, as you can see in Figure 6. Scientific inquiry is a process with many paths. Work may go forward or even backward when testing out new ideas.

Go Online
active art

For: The Nature of Inquiry activity
Visit: PHSchool.com
Web Code: cgp-6012

FIGURE 6
The Nature of Inquiry
There is no set path that a scientific inquiry must follow.

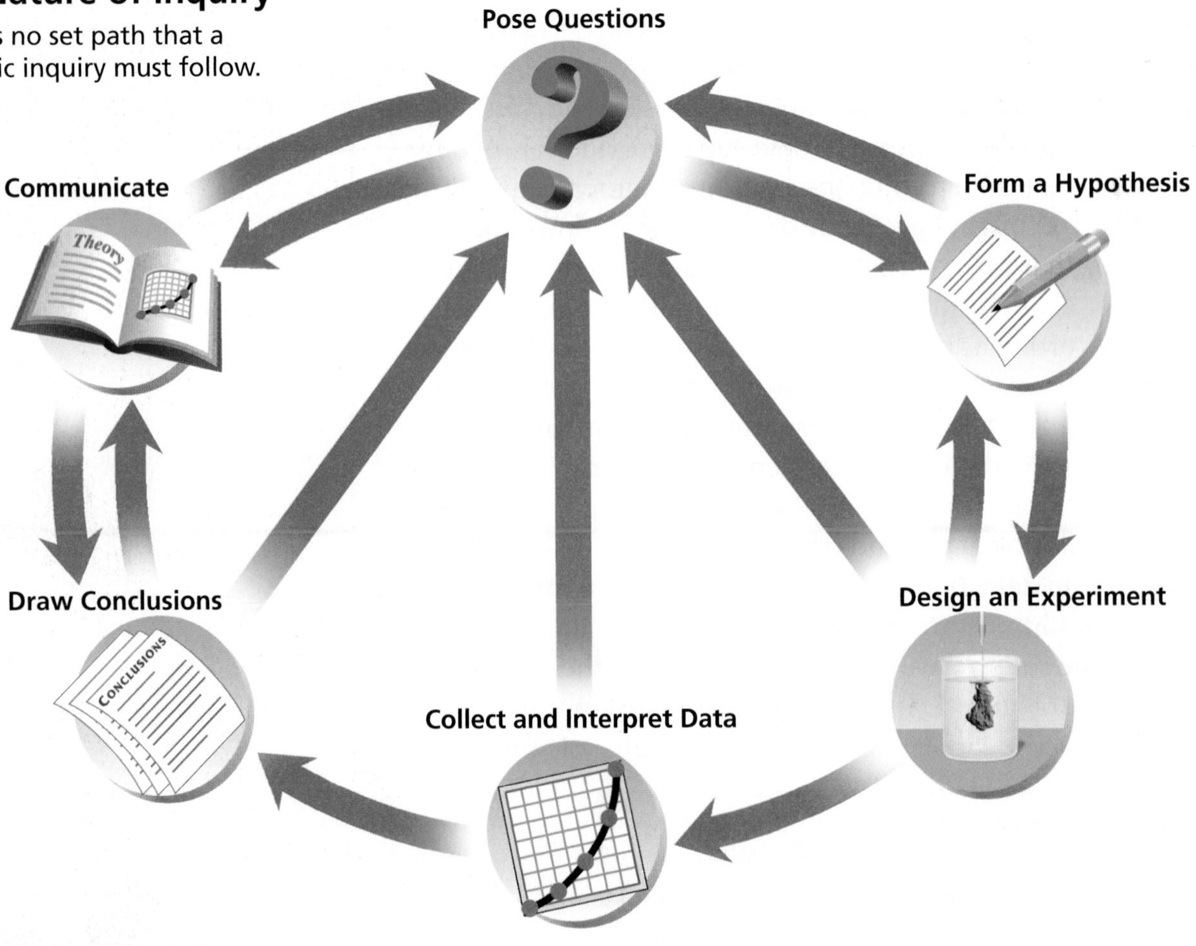

FIGURE 7
A Scientific Law
According to the law of gravity, this sky diver will eventually land back on Earth.

How Science Develops

Today, the amount of scientific knowledge is huge. It covers topics ranging from matter's smallest particles to the whole universe. How did that knowledge develop? Over the years, as scientists studied the natural world, they did more than collect facts. They developed more complete explanations for their observations. **Scientists use models and develop laws and theories to increase people's understanding of the natural world.**

Scientific Models Sometimes, it may be impossible to observe certain objects and scientific processes. So a scientist will make a model. A model is a picture, diagram, computer image, or other representation of an object or process. Physical models, such as a representation of the solar system, may look like the real thing. Other models can be generated by computers, such as the flight plan of a space vehicle. Still others can be mathematical equations or words that describe how something works. Certain models, such as models of atoms (the particles that make up matter), have been especially important in building up our understanding of science.

Scientific Laws Have you ever heard someone say "What goes up must come down"? When scientists repeatedly observe the same result in specific circumstances, they may develop a scientific law. A **scientific law** is a statement that describes what scientists expect to happen every time under a particular set of conditions.

A scientific law describes an observed pattern in nature without attempting to explain it. You can think of a scientific law as a rule of nature. For example, the law of gravity states that all objects in the universe attract each other. This law has been verified over and over again.

Reading Checkpoint **What is a scientific law?**

Scientific Theories In some cases, many observations can be connected by one explanation. This can lead to the development of a scientific theory. A **scientific theory** is a well-tested explanation for a wide range of observations or experimental results. For example, according to the atomic theory, all substances are composed of tiny particles called atoms. The atomic theory helps explain many observations, such as why water freezes or boils at certain temperatures, and why it can dissolve many other materials.

Scientists accept a theory only when there is a large body of evidence that supports it. However, future evidence may not suport the theory. If that happens, scientists may modify the theory or discard it altogether. This illustrates the ever-growing and exciting nature of scientific knowledge.

FIGURE 8
A Scientific Theory
Based on observations of sunsets and sunrises, ancient people theorized that the sun revolved around Earth. New evidence led scientists to abandon that ancient theory. Today, scientists know that Earth, along with the other planets in the solar system, revolves around the sun.

Section 2 Assessment

Target Reading Skill Building Vocabulary Use your definitions to help you answer the questions below.

1. a. **Defining** What is scientific inquiry?
   b. **Listing** Name six processes that are often involved in scientific inquiry.
   c. **Inferring** How can an experiment that disproves a hypothesis be useful?
2. a. **Defining** What is a scientific theory? A scientific law?
   b. **Comparing and Contrasting** How do scientific theories differ from scientific laws?
   c. **Classifying** The students who conducted the shadow length experiment concluded that their results supported their hypothesis. Can their supported hypothesis be called a scientific theory? Why or why not?

Lab zone At-Home Activity

Which Falls Fastest? Design an experiment to determine which falls fastest—an unfolded sheet of paper, a sheet of paper folded in fourths, or a crumpled sheet of paper. Be sure to develop a hypothesis, design a controlled experiment, and collect data. Do your data support your hypothesis? Discuss your results with a family member.

Section 3

Science Laboratory Safety

Reading Preview

Key Concepts

- Why is preparation important when carrying out scientific investigations?
- What should you do if a lab accident occurs?

Target Reading Skill

Previewing Visuals Before you read, preview Figure 10. Then write two questions that you have about the figure in a graphic organizer like the one below. As you read, answer your questions.

Safety in the Lab

Q. Why are safety goggles necessary in the lab?
A.
Q.

Lab zone Discover Activity

Where Is the Safety Equipment in Your School?

1. Look around your classroom or school for any safety-related equipment.
2. Draw a floor plan of the room or building and clearly label where each item is located.

Think It Over

Predicting Why is it important to know where safety equipment is located?

Suppose you and your family decide to go rock climbing. What plans should you make? You'll need to bring rope, some snacks to eat, and water to drink. But you'll also need to plan for everyone's safety.

For the climb to go smoothly, you'll want to make sure that everyone has the proper clothing and safety gear, such as helmets, harnesses, and climbing shoes. You'll check to see whether the equipment is in good condition. You'll also want to make sure that everyone follows proper procedures and knows their role as others take their turn climbing.

FIGURE 9
Climbing Safely
Climbing rocks safely requires careful preparation and the use of proper equipment.

Safety in the Lab

Good preparation is as important to a scientific investigation as it is to rock climbing. **Good preparation helps you stay safe when doing science activities in the laboratory.**

Thermometers, balances, and glassware are some of the equipment you will use in science labs. Do you know how to use these items? What should you do if something goes wrong? Thinking about these questions ahead of time is an important part of being prepared.

Preparing for the Lab Preparing for a lab should begin the day before you will perform the lab. It is important to read through the procedure carefully and make sure you understand all the directions. Also, review the general safety guidelines in Appendix A, including those related to the specific equipment you will use. If anything is unclear, be prepared to ask your teacher about it before you begin the lab.

FIGURE 10
Safety in the Lab
Good preparation for an experiment helps you stay safe in the laboratory. **Observing** *List three precautions each student is taking while performing the labs.*

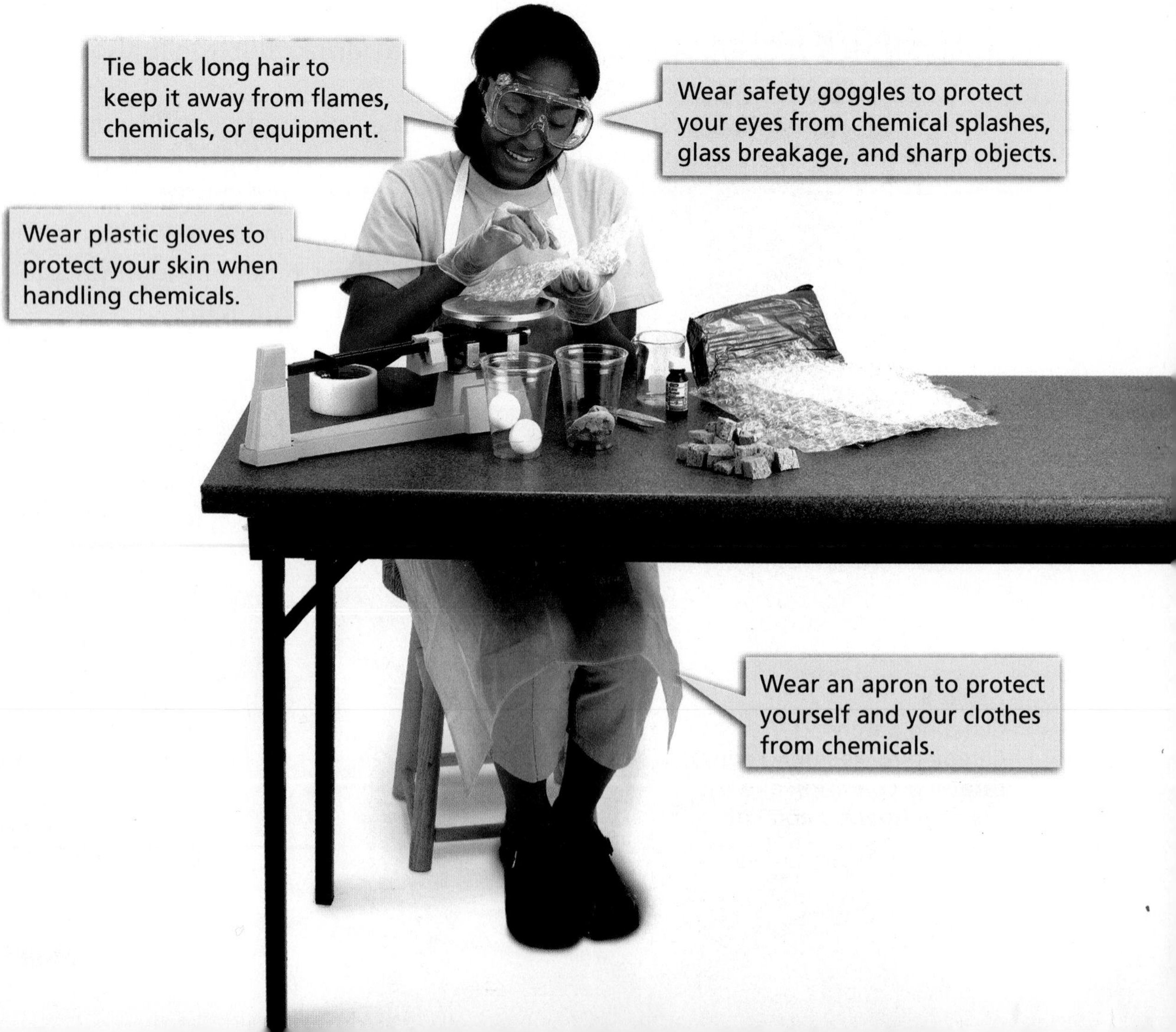

Tie back long hair to keep it away from flames, chemicals, or equipment.
Wear safety goggles to protect your eyes from chemical splashes, glass breakage, and sharp objects.
Wear plastic gloves to protect your skin when handling chemicals.
Wear an apron to protect yourself and your clothes from chemicals.

Performing the Lab Whenever you perform a science lab, your chief concern must be the safety of yourself, your classmates, and your teacher. The most important safety rule is simple: Always follow your teacher's instructions and the textbook directions exactly. You should never try anything on your own without asking your teacher first.

Labs and activities in this textbook series include safety symbols like those at the right. These symbols alert you to possible dangers in performing the lab and remind you to work carefully. They also identify any safety equipment that you should use to protect yourself from potential hazards. The symbols are explained in detail in Appendix A. Make sure you are familiar with each safety symbol and what it means.

Another thing you can do to make your lab experience safe and successful is to keep your work area clean and organized. Also, do not rush through any of the steps. Finally, always show respect and courtesy to your teacher and classmates.

Reading Checkpoint **What is the most important safety rule?**

Wear heat-resistant gloves when handling hot objects.
Keep your work area clean and uncluttered.
Make sure electric cords are untangled and out of the way.
Wear closed-toe shoes when working in the laboratory.

Safety Symbols

- **Safety Goggles**
- **Lab Apron**
- **Breakage**
- **Heat-Resistant Gloves**
- **Plastic Gloves**
- **Heating**
- **Flames**
- **No Flames**
- **Corrosive Chemical**
- **Poison**
- **Fumes**
- **Sharp Object**
- **Animal Safety**
- **Plant Safety**
- **Electric Shock**
- **Physical Safety**
- **Disposal**
- **Hand Washing**
- **General Safety Awareness**

In Case of Emergency

ALWAYS NOTIFY YOUR TEACHER IMMEDIATELY

Injury	What to Do
Burns	Immerse burns in cold water.
Cuts	Cover cuts with a clean dressing. Apply direct pressure to the wound to stop bleeding.
Spills on Skin	Flush the skin with large amounts of water.
Foreign Object in Eye	Flush the eye with large amounts of water. Seek medical attention.

FIGURE 11
In Case of Emergency
These first-aid tips can help guide your actions during emergency situations. Remember, always notify your teacher immediately if an accident occurs.

End-of-Lab Procedures Your lab work does not end when you reach the last step in the procedure. There are important things you need to do at the end of every lab.

When you have completed a lab, be sure to clean up your work area. Turn off and unplug any equipment and return it to its proper place. It is very important that you dispose of any waste materials properly. Some wastes should not be thrown in the trash or poured down the drain. Follow your teacher's instructions about proper disposal. Finally, be sure to wash your hands thoroughly after working in the laboratory.

In Case of an Accident

Good preparation and careful work habits can go a long way toward making your lab experiences safe ones. But, at some point, an accident may occur. A classmate might accidentally knock over a beaker or a chemical might spill on your sleeve. Would you know what to do?

When any accident occurs, no matter how minor, notify your teacher immediately. Then, listen to your teacher's directions and carry them out quickly. Make sure you know the location and proper use of all the emergency equipment in your lab room. Knowing safety and first-aid procedures beforehand will prepare you to handle accidents properly. Figure 11 lists some first-aid procedures you should know.

Section 3 Assessment

Target Reading Skill Previewing Visuals Refer to your questions and answers about Figure 10 to help you answer Question 1 below.

Reviewing Key Concepts

1. a. Listing List two things you should do ahead of time to prepare for a lab.
   b. Interpreting Diagrams Suppose a lab included the safety symbols below. What do these symbols mean? What precautions should you take?

   c. Making Judgments Should everyone take time to prepare for a lab when several students work together in a group? Explain.
2. a. Reviewing During a lab activity you get a cut and start to bleed. What is the first thing you should do?
   b. Sequencing List in order the next steps you would take to deal with your injury.
   c. Making Judgments Some people feel that most accidents can be prevented with careful preparation and safe behavior. Do you agree or disagree with this viewpoint? Explain your reasoning.

Writing in Science

Safety Poster Make a poster of one of the safety rules in Appendix A to post in your lab. Be sure to include the safety symbol, clear directions, and additional illustrations.

Lab zone **Skills Lab**

Swing Time

Problem

Does the swing of a pendulum take longer for an object of greater mass?

Skills Focus

graphing, interpreting data

Materials

- stand with clamp
- large paper clip
- ruler
- string, 50 cm in length
- stopwatch
- 5 metal washers
- safety goggles

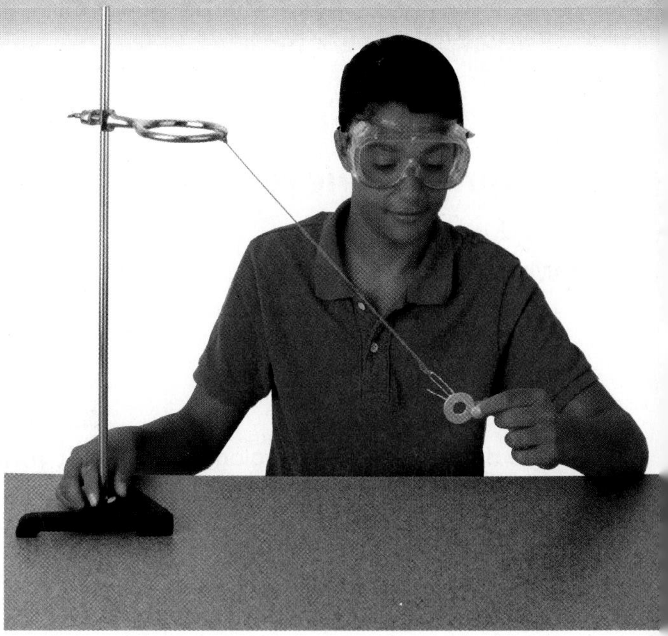

Procedure

1. Read the whole procedure. Write a hypothesis describing how the mass of washers attached to a pendulum will affect the time of its swing. Then create a data table like the one below.
2. Put on your safety goggles. Tie one end of a string to a clamp on a stand. Tie the other end to a large paper clip. Pull out one side of the paper clip to serve as a hook.
3. Place a metal washer on the hook and let it hang down. If necessary, raise the clamp so that the washer swings freely.
4. Pull the washer back so that the string makes an angle of about 45° with the stand. Have your partner measure the height of the washer above the table top. Record this height as the starting position of the washer.
5. Release the washer gently, without pushing it. During a complete swing, the washer will move from its starting position and return back again.

Data Table

Number of washers	Time for 10 swings (s)	Average time per swing (s)
1		
2		

6. Record the time for 10 swings to the nearest tenth of a second. Then divide that time by 10 to find the average time for one swing.
7. Repeats Steps 5 and 6, increasing the mass each time by adding a washer. Make sure that you always start the swing at the same height.

Analyze and Conclude

1. **Graphing** Graph your results. (*Hint:* Place the number of washers on the horizontal axis and the average time per swing on the vertical axis.)
2. **Interpreting Data** Use the graph to decide if your data support your hypothesis.
3. **Drawing Conclusions** What conclusion can you draw from this experiment?
4. **Communicating** In a paragraph, explain how this experiment enabled you to test your hypothesis.

Design an Experiment

Design an experiment to test how the average time for a pendulum swing changes when the mass of the washers is constant but the length of the string changes. *Obtain your teacher's approval before carrying out this experiment.*

Section 4

• Tech & Design •

What Is Technology?

Reading Preview

Key Concepts

- What are the steps in the technology design process, and what is involved in each step?
- What are the parts of a technological system?
- How do society and technology impact each other?

Key Terms

- technology
- engineer
- brainstorming
- constraint
- trade-off
- prototype
- troubleshooting
- system

Target Reading Skill

Sequencing As you read, make a flowchart that shows the steps in the technology design process. Put each step of the process in a separate box in the flowchart in the order in which it occurs.

The Technology Design Process

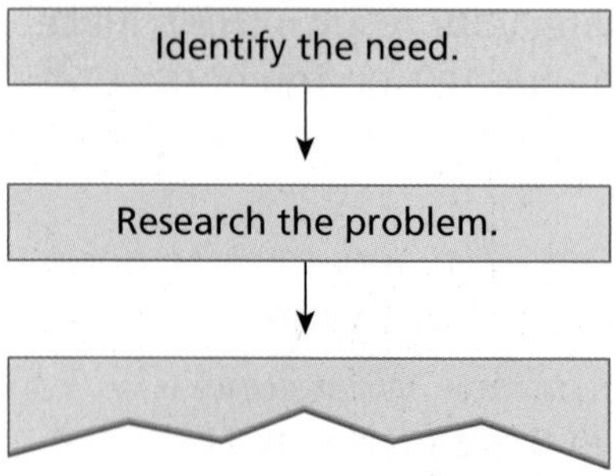
Identify the need.
Research the problem.

Lab zone Discover Activity

Why Redesign?

1. Use the materials your teacher gives you to design and construct a boat out of aluminum foil. Your goal is to make a boat that will float and carry as many pennies as possible.
2. Test your aluminum-foil boat against those of two other students to see how well your design works.
3. Based on your observations in Step 2, change the design of your boat, if necessary. Build a new boat and test it again.

Think It Over

Problem Solving What problems did you identify by testing your boat? How did you improve upon your original boat's design?

What comes to mind when you hear the word "mouse"? Perhaps you imagine a tiny furry animal? Or perhaps you might think of the device that sends signals from your hand to a computer. Where did this modern mouse come from?

The computer mouse is the result of technology. Technology is closely related to science, but the two activities have different goals. **Technology** is a way of changing the natural world to meet human needs or solve problems. By contrast, the goal of science is a study of the natural world in order to understand it.

People who work in a field in technology are called engineers. An **engineer** is someone who is trained to use both technological and scientific knowledge to solve practical problems. Engineers often follow a set of steps called the technology design process.

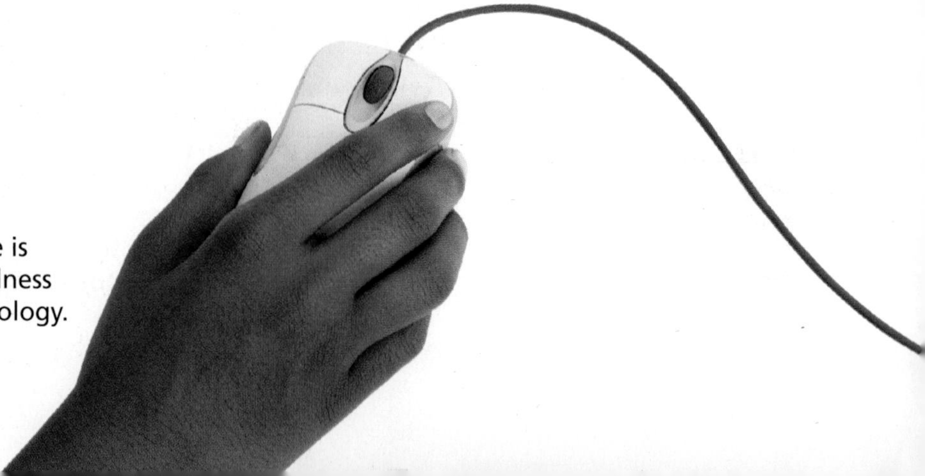

FIGURE 12
The Computer Mouse
The design of a mouse is important to its usefulness and success as a technology.

Technology Design Process

The technology design process, like scientific inquiry, does not always follow rigid steps. **Often, engineers follow a common process: They identify a need, research the problem, design a solution, build and evaluate a prototype, troubleshoot and redesign, and communicate the solution.** Figures 13 and 14 show some of the steps in this process.

Go Online
active art

For: Technology Design Process activity
Visit: PHSchool.com
Web Code: cgp-6032

Identifying a Need Engineers designed the first mouse for use with large, complex computers. Early versions had several problems. They were expensive. Dirt easily became trapped in the mechanism, preventing the mouse from working. Also, the mouse often "slipped," meaning that the cursor didn't move when the mouse moved.

Imagine that you are an engineer on the team that is redesigning the original mouse. As your first step, you must decide exactly what need you are trying to fulfill. When engineers identify a need, they clearly define the problem they are trying to solve.

Researching the Problem What is the next stage? After defining a problem, engineers need to research it fully. That may include performing experiments related to the technology they are designing.

In gathering information about the mouse, the engineers discovered that the ball inside the mouse was held in place by a complex system of sensitive, costly parts. Too much pressure on the ball made it slip frequently. Any bit of dirt or dust would jam up the system. To fix it, the entire mouse had to be taken apart, and each part had to be cleaned separately.

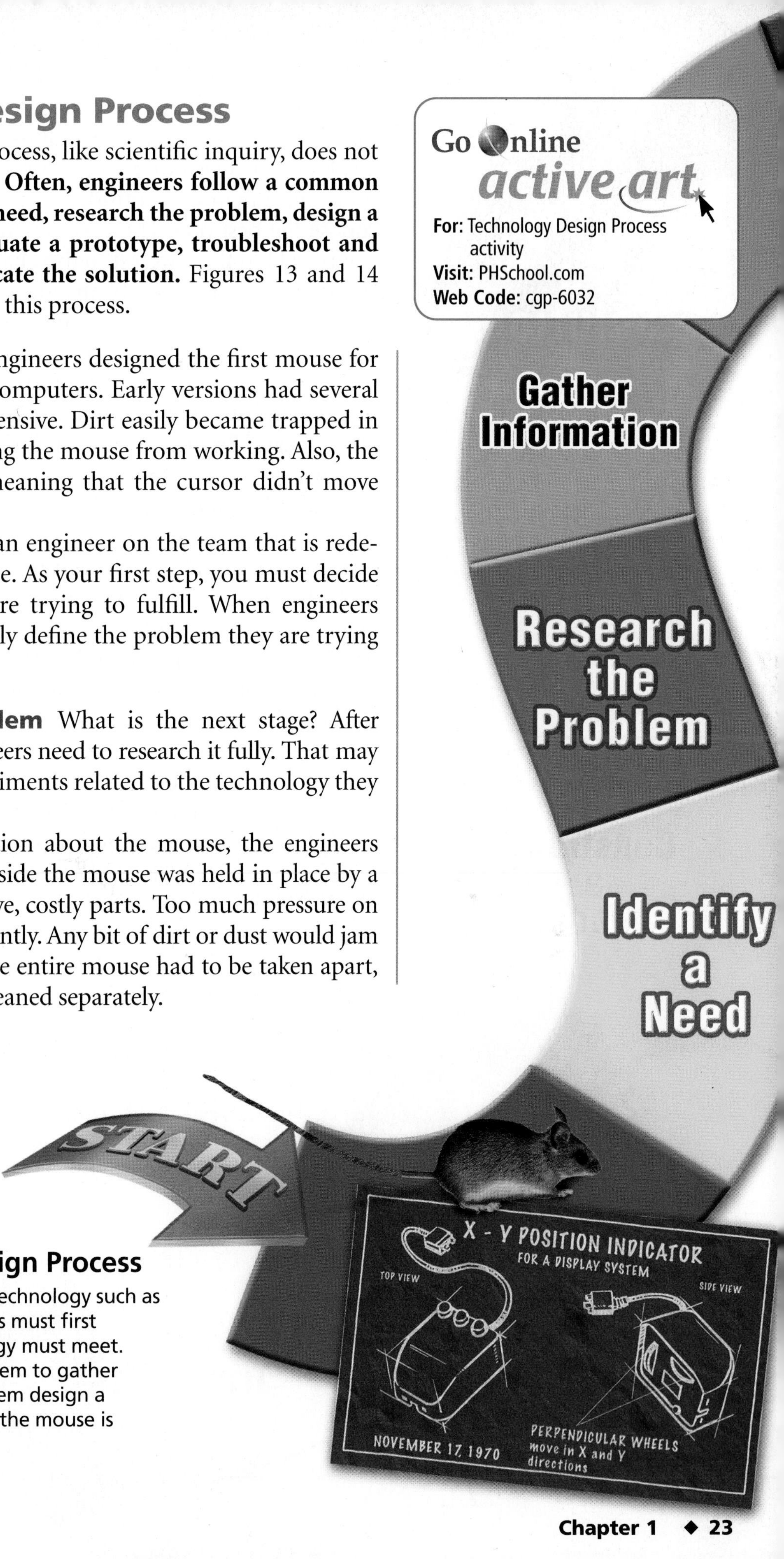

FIGURE 13
The Technology Design Process
In designing a new piece of technology such as a computer mouse, engineers must first identify needs that technology must meet. They then research the problem to gather infomation that may help them design a solution. An early design for the mouse is shown at right.

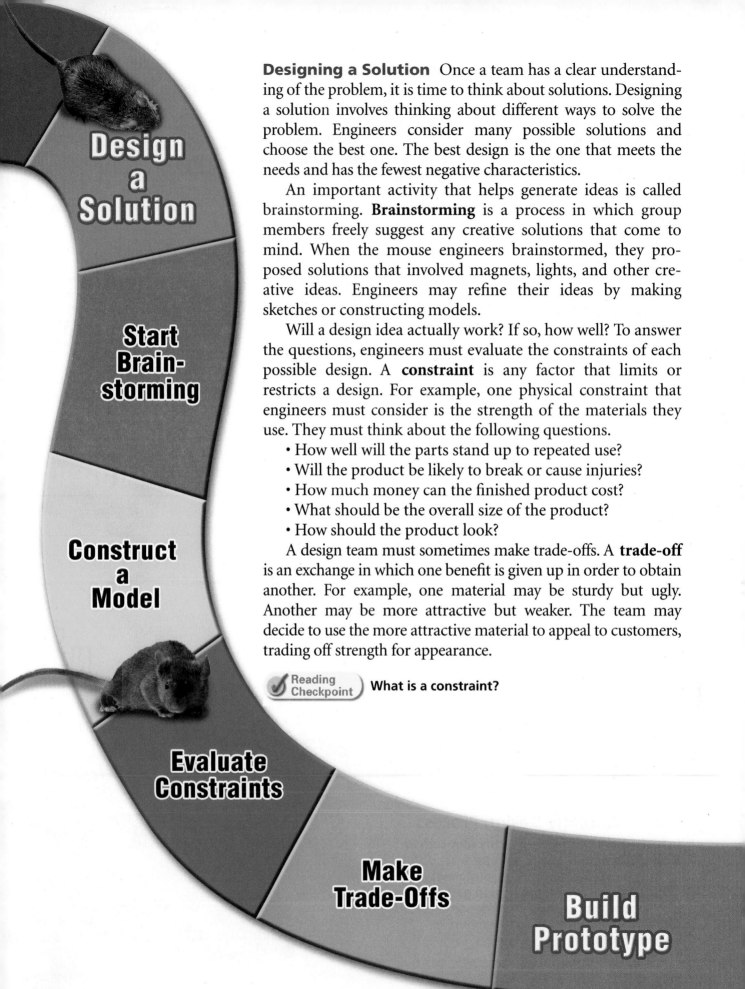

Designing a Solution Once a team has a clear understanding of the problem, it is time to think about solutions. Designing a solution involves thinking about different ways to solve the problem. Engineers consider many possible solutions and choose the best one. The best design is the one that meets the needs and has the fewest negative characteristics.

An important activity that helps generate ideas is called brainstorming. **Brainstorming** is a process in which group members freely suggest any creative solutions that come to mind. When the mouse engineers brainstormed, they proposed solutions that involved magnets, lights, and other creative ideas. Engineers may refine their ideas by making sketches or constructing models.

Will a design idea actually work? If so, how well? To answer the questions, engineers must evaluate the constraints of each possible design. A **constraint** is any factor that limits or restricts a design. For example, one physical constraint that engineers must consider is the strength of the materials they use. They must think about the following questions.

- How well will the parts stand up to repeated use?
- Will the product be likely to break or cause injuries?
- How much money can the finished product cost?
- What should be the overall size of the product?
- How should the product look?

A design team must sometimes make trade-offs. A **trade-off** is an exchange in which one benefit is given up in order to obtain another. For example, one material may be sturdy but ugly. Another may be more attractive but weaker. The team may decide to use the more attractive material to appeal to customers, trading off strength for appearance.

Reading Checkpoint **What is a constraint?**

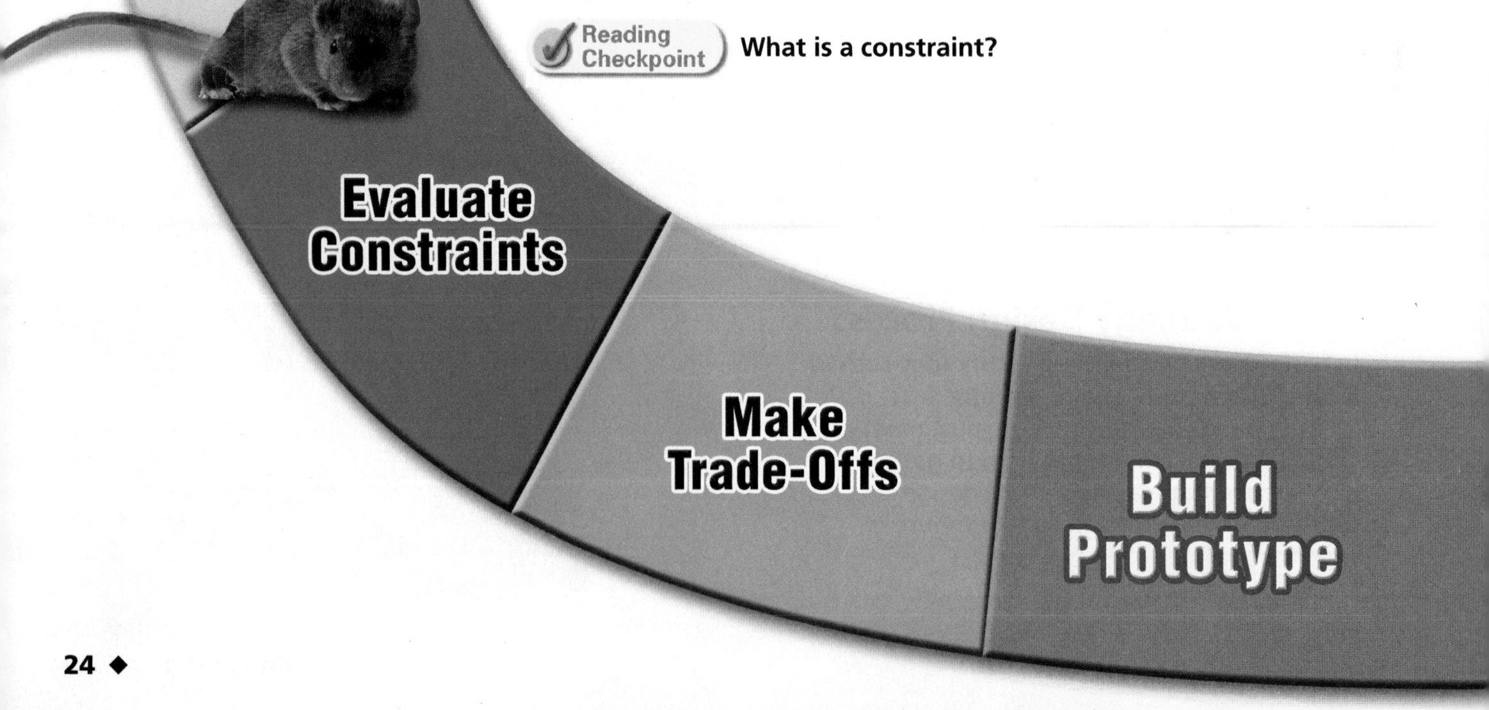

Building a Prototype The next phase of the process is to build and test a prototype. A **prototype** is a working model used to test a design. Some prototypes are full size and made of the materials proposed for the final product. Today, many prototypes are completely "virtual," or computer generated.

The engineers designed many tests to study the new mouse. They designed a machine that kept the mouse working all day. They found that after the equivalent of three years of use, the mouse showed only minor problems in performance.

Troubleshooting and Redesigning The next stage in the design process is to identify the causes of any problems and to redesign the product to address the problems. The process of analyzing a design problem and finding a way to fix it is called **troubleshooting.** Figure 14 shows some problems the mouse team discovered.

Communicating the Solution The team will want to share its accomplishments! In the last stage of the technology design process, engineers must communicate to consumers how a product meets their needs. They must also communicate with those involved in bringing the product to consumers.

Through effective communication, information about the mouse reached the public, and the mouse became increasingly popular over the next few years. Decades later, the mouse is still the most popular method of moving a cursor around a computer screen.

Lab zone **Try This Activity**

Watch Ideas Take Off

In this activity, you will model some stages of the design process.

1. With a team of three or four classmates, brainstorm some ideas for a new product that would keep shoelaces from constantly untying.
2. Evaluate each idea, and discuss the constraints and trade-offs you might have to make.
3. Sketch the design solution the team has agreed on.

Predicting After selecting a design solution, what do you think is the next step your team should take?

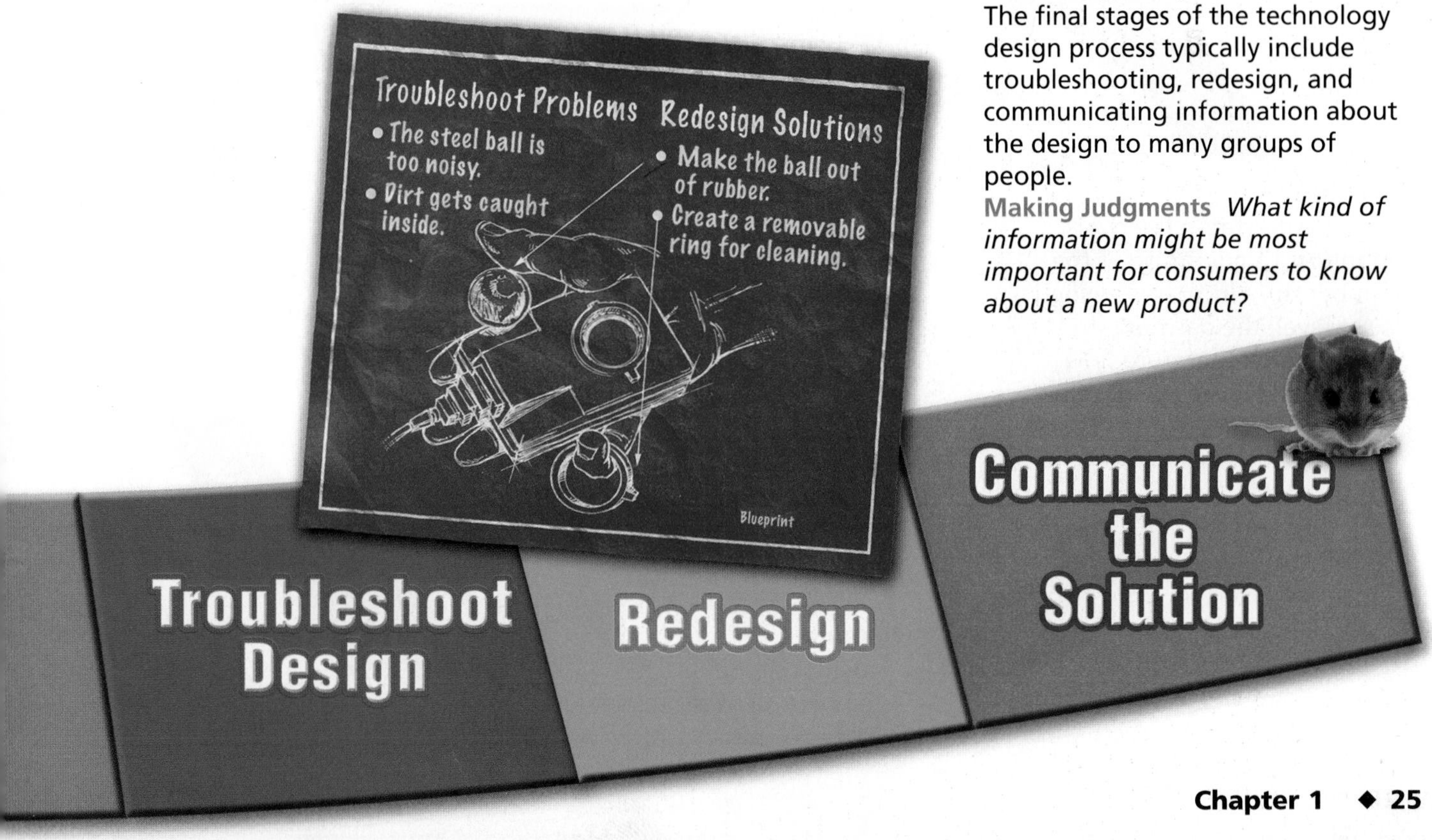
Troubleshoot Problems
• The steel ball is too noisy.
• Dirt gets caught inside.
Redesign Solutions
• Make the ball out of rubber.
• Create a removable ring for cleaning.
Blueprint
Troubleshoot Design
Redesign
Communicate the Solution

FIGURE 14
Final Design Stages
The final stages of the technology design process typically include troubleshooting, redesign, and communicating information about the design to many groups of people.
Making Judgments *What kind of information might be most important for consumers to know about a new product?*

Discovery Channel School

Technology and Engineering

Video Preview

▶ Video Field Trip

Video Assessment

Technology as a System

When you hear the word *system*, what comes to mind? Maybe you think of your school system or the circulatory system in your body. All **systems** have one thing in common: They are made of parts that work together.

Technology products can be thought of as systems, too. **A technological system includes a goal, inputs, processes, outputs, and, in some cases, feedback.** Figure 15 describes these in one familiar technological system—an oven.

Technological systems are designed to achieve a particular goal, or purpose. An input is something that is put into a system in order to reach that goal. The process is a sequence of actions that the system undergoes. An output is a result or product. If the system works correctly, the output should match the goal. Some technological systems have an additional component, called feedback. Feedback is information a system uses to monitor the input, process, and output so that the system can adjust itself to meet the goal.

Reading Checkpoint **What do all systems have in common?**

FIGURE 15

The Oven as a System

An oven is a technological system. Input, process, output, and feedback are all involved in achieving the goal of cooking food—such as tasty cookies!

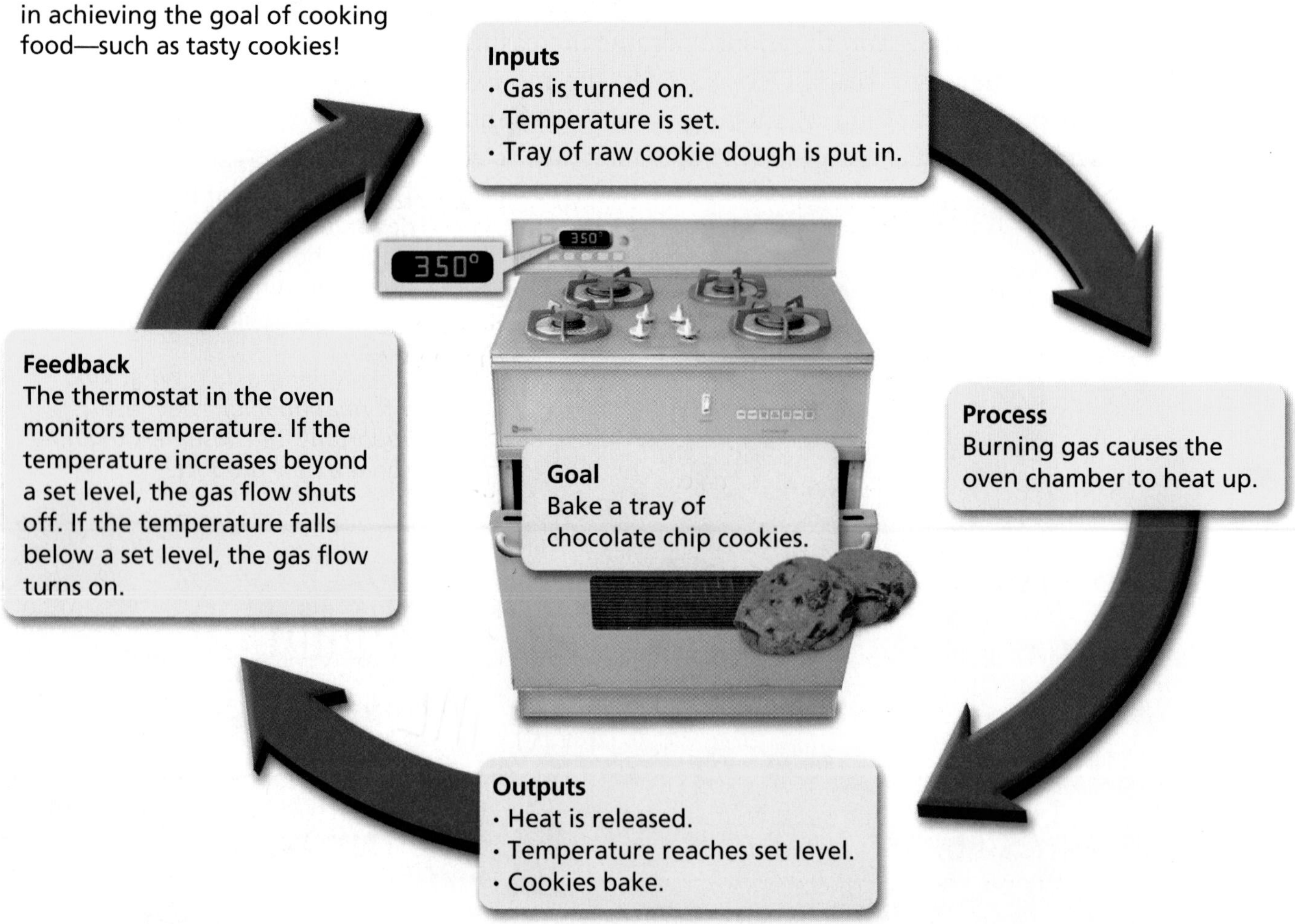

Inputs
• Gas is turned on.
• Temperature is set.
• Tray of raw cookie dough is put in.
350°
Process
Burning gas causes the oven chamber to heat up.
Goal
Bake a tray of chocolate chip cookies.
Outputs
• Heat is released.
• Temperature reaches set level.
• Cookies bake.
Feedback
The thermostat in the oven monitors temperature. If the temperature increases beyond a set level, the gas flow shuts off. If the temperature falls below a set level, the gas flow turns on.

Technology and Society

Technology has always been a part of human history. During the Stone Age, people used stones to make tools. Spears, axes, and spades enabled them to hunt animals and grow crops. The food supply became more stable. People no longer needed to wander in search of food. They began to settle in one place.

The situation in the Stone Age is one example of how technology can affect society. The term *society* refers to any group of people who live together in an area, large or small, and have certain things in common, such as a form of government. **Throughout history, from the Stone Age to the Information Age today, technology has had a large impact on society.** Today cellular phones, satellites, and high-speed Internet connections allow people to share information quickly around the world.

Technological advances have done much to move societies forward through the centuries. However, technology has both good and bad impacts. Often, the negative effects are unintentional. They may not be recognized until long after the technology has been put to use.

In deciding whether to use a particular technology, people must analyze its possible risks and benefits. Analyzing risks involves evaluating the possible problems of a technology. These risks are compared to the expected advantages, or benefits, of the technology.

FIGURE 16
Spreading Technology
This Kenyan tribesman uses a cellular phone to communicate with friends and family while out in his fields.

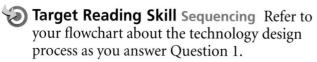

Section 4 Assessment

Target Reading Skill Sequencing Refer to your flowchart about the technology design process as you answer Question 1.

Reviewing Key Concepts

1. a. Describing List the stages in the technology design process. Briefly describe each stage.
   b. Explaining What are design constraints? Give two examples of constraints that should be considered when designing a cellular phone.
   c. Making Judgments A team working on a new bicycle seat design must choose between a comfortable but costly material and a less expensive but uncomfortable material. Which trade-off would you make? Explain.
2. a. Reviewing What four components do all technological systems include? What fifth component do some systems have?
   b. Applying Concepts An alarm clock is a technological system. Identify each major component of this system.
3. a. Listing List five examples of common technologies that influence society today.
   b. Drawing Conclusions Do you think that technology had a greater impact on society in the past than it has today? Explain.

Writing in Science

How-To Paragraph Think about the computer mouse you use most often. Suppose your team has just finished designing this mouse model. Write step-by-step instructions explaining how to use the mouse to move a cursor on a computer screen. Include a sketch.

Chapter 1 Study Guide

1 What Is Physical Science?

Key Concepts

- Scientists use the skills of observing, inferring, and predicting to learn more about the natural world.
- Physical science is the study of matter, energy, and the changes that matter and energy undergo.

Key Terms

science
observing
qualitative observations
quantitative observations
inferring
predicting
chemistry
physics

2 Scientific Inquiry

Key Concepts

- The processes that scientists use in inquiry include posing questions, developing hypotheses, designing experiments, collecting and interpreting data, drawing conclusions, and communicating ideas and results.
- Scientists use models and develop laws and theories to increase people's understanding of the natural world.

Key Terms

scientific inquiry
hypothesis
variable
manipulated variable
responding variable
controlled experiment
data
communicating
scientific law
scientific theory

3 Science Laboratory Safety

Key Concepts

- Good preparation helps you stay safe when doing science activities in the laboratory.
- When any accident occurs, no matter how minor, notify your teacher immediately. Then, listen to your teacher's directions and carry them out quickly.

4 What Is Technology?

Key Concepts

- Often engineers follow a common process: They identify a need, research the problem, design a solution, build and evaluate a prototype, troubleshoot and redesign, and communicate the solution.
- A technological system includes a goal, inputs, processes, outputs, and, in some cases, feedback.
- Throughout history, from the Stone Age to the Information Age today, technology has had a large impact on society.

Key Terms

technology
engineer
brainstorming
constraint
trade-off
prototype
troubleshooting
system

Review and Assessment

Go Online PHSchool.com
For: Self-Assessment
Visit: PHSchool.com
Web Code: cka-1010

Organizing Information

Comparing and Contrasting Copy the Venn diagram comparing science and technology onto a separate sheet of paper. Then complete it and add a title. (For more on Comparing and Contrasting, see the Skills Handbook.)

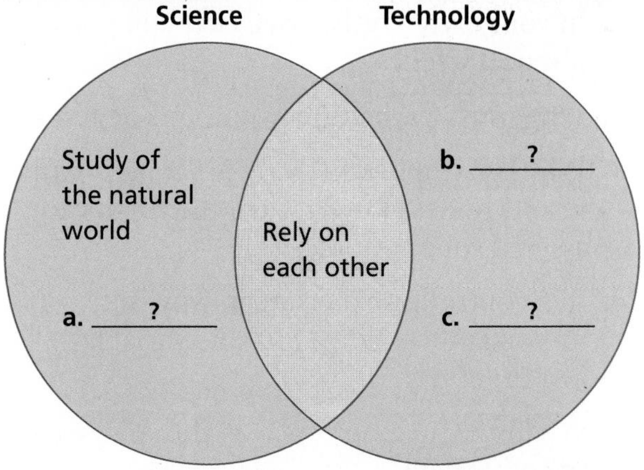

Reviewing Key Terms

Choose the letter of the best answer.

1. A logical interpretation based on reasoning from prior experience is called
   a. scientific inquiry.
   b. a prediction.
   c. an inference.
   d. an observation.
2. Scientific inquiry often begins with
   a. collecting data.
   b. designing an experiment.
   c. posing questions.
   d. communicating results.
3. In an experiment where you change only the temperature, temperature is the
   a. responding variable.
   b. manipulated variable.
   c. hypothesis.
   d. controlled variable.
4. In the event that a glass beaker breaks during a lab, the first thing you should do is
   a. wash your hands.
   b. clean up the broken glass.
   c. alert your teacher.
   d. obtain another beaker.
5. Any factor that limits or restricts a design is called a
   a. trade-off. **b.** system.
   c. prototype. **d.** constraint.

If the statement is true, write *true*. If it is false, change the underlined word or words to make the statement true.

6. A quantitative observation doesn't involve numbers or measurements.
7. A scientific law is a well-tested explanation for a wide range of observations or experimental results.
8. Data are the facts, figures, and other evidence gathered through observations.
9. Science is a way of changing the natural world to meet human needs or solve problems.
10. Brainstorming is the process of analyzing a design problem and finding a way to fix it.

Writing in Science

News Report Choose a technology product with which you are familiar. Imagine that you are a news reporter covering the product's first introduction to the public. Write a 30-second informative report to be broadcast on the news.

Discovery Channel School
Technology and Engineering
Video Preview
Video Field Trip
▶ Video Assessment

Review and Assessment

Checking Concepts

11. In your own words, briefly explain what physical science is.

12. Why must a scientific hypothesis be testable?

13. Why is it important to report experimental results honestly even when the results go against your hypothesis?

14. In a controlled experiment, why is it important to change just one variable at a time?

15. What role do graphs play in the analysis of scientific data?

16. What are three things you should do when preparing for a lab?

17. Why is building a prototype an important part of the technology design process?

18. What is the role of feedback in a technological system?

Thinking Critically

19. Making Judgments Why do you think that, as a general precaution, you should never bring food or drink into the laboratory?

20. Classifying For the system shown below, identify the input, process, and output.

Car moves forward

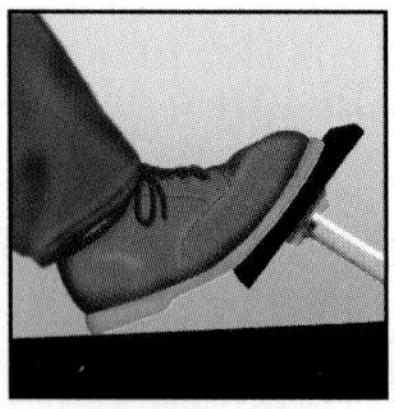

Driver steps on gas pedal

Gas makes engine run

21. Problem Solving Your team is designing a new computer keyboard. From prototype tests, you learn that the keyboard successfully reduces hand strain, but that it breaks easily. Users also complained about the keyboard's appearance. How would you proceed?

22. Relating Cause and Effect How might a scientist who tracks hurricanes depend on satellite technology? How might satellite engineers depend on the work of scientists?

Applying Skills

Use the table to answer Questions 23–26.

This table provides data on the types of trains in the United States in 1900 and 1960.

Number of Trains in Use in the United States, 1900 and 1960

Type	1900	1960
Steam trains	37,463	374
Electric trains	200	498
Diesel trains	0	30,240

23. Interpreting Data What kinds of trains existed in the United States in 1900? In 1960?

24. Calculating How did the number of steam trains change between 1900 and 1960? How did the number of electric and diesel trains change over that period?

25. Inferring Which type of train met people's needs best in 1960? What is your evidence?

26. Drawing Conclusions Based on this table, what can you conclude about the progress of train technology between 1900 and 1960?

Lab zone Chapter Project

Performance Assessment Before testing your chair, explain to your classmates why you designed your chair the way you did. How did you join the pieces of cardboard together? How did you address the design constraints? When you test your model, examine how steady your chair is while supporting 20 kilograms of books. How could you improve your chair's design?

Standardized Test Prep

Test-Taking Tip

Eliminating Incorrect Answers

When answering a multiple-choice question, you can often eliminate some answer choices because they are clearly incorrect. By doing this, you increase your odds of choosing the correct answer.

Sample Question

Which of the following is usually the first stage in the technology design process?

A communicate about the design solution
B identify a need
C redesign the product to address any problems
D build a prototype

Answer

The correct answer is **B**. You can eliminate **A** and **C** because these steps typically occur near the end of the technology design process. Of the remaining choices, **B** occurs first.

Choose the letter of the best answer.

1. What would be the best way to tell which brand of paper towels is the "strongest when wet"?
A Compare television commercials that demonstrate the strength of paper towels.
B Tear different brands of towels when they are wet to feel which seems strongest.
C Compare how much weight each brand of towel can hold when wet before it breaks.
D Conduct a survey of consumers, professional cooks, and restaurant staff.

2. Engineers have designed a car with a new engine and body design. Which of the following trade-offs would have a negative effect on public safety?
F choosing lower-cost materials over good results in crash tests
G choosing the appearance of the car seats over their comfort
H choosing to install a more powerful music system over a better air-conditioning system
J choosing a more powerful engine over better gas mileage

The graph below compares how well two different brands of insulated mugs retain heat. Use the graph and your knowledge of science to answer Questions 3–4.

Comparing Insulated Mugs

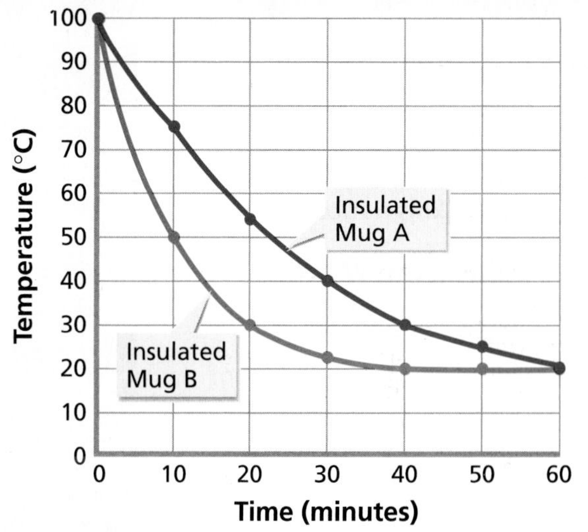

3. What was the manipulated variable in this experiment?
A the temperature of the water
B the location of the insulated mug
C the brand of insulated mug
D the length of time the water was allowed to cool

4. What conclusion can you draw from this experiment?
F There is no difference between Brand A and Brand B.
G Brand A keeps water warmer than Brand B.
H Brand B keeps water warmer than Brand A.
J Brand B seems to add heat to the water.

Constructed Response

5. Suppose that a newly designed robot automatically scans products at checkout lines in supermarkets. The cost to install a robot at a cash register is less than the cost of hiring a cashier. Describe some of the risks and benefits that this new technology might have on society.

Chapter 2

Introduction to Matter

Chapter Preview

Interactive Textbook

This "junk sculpture" of an armadillo is made entirely of metal can lids.

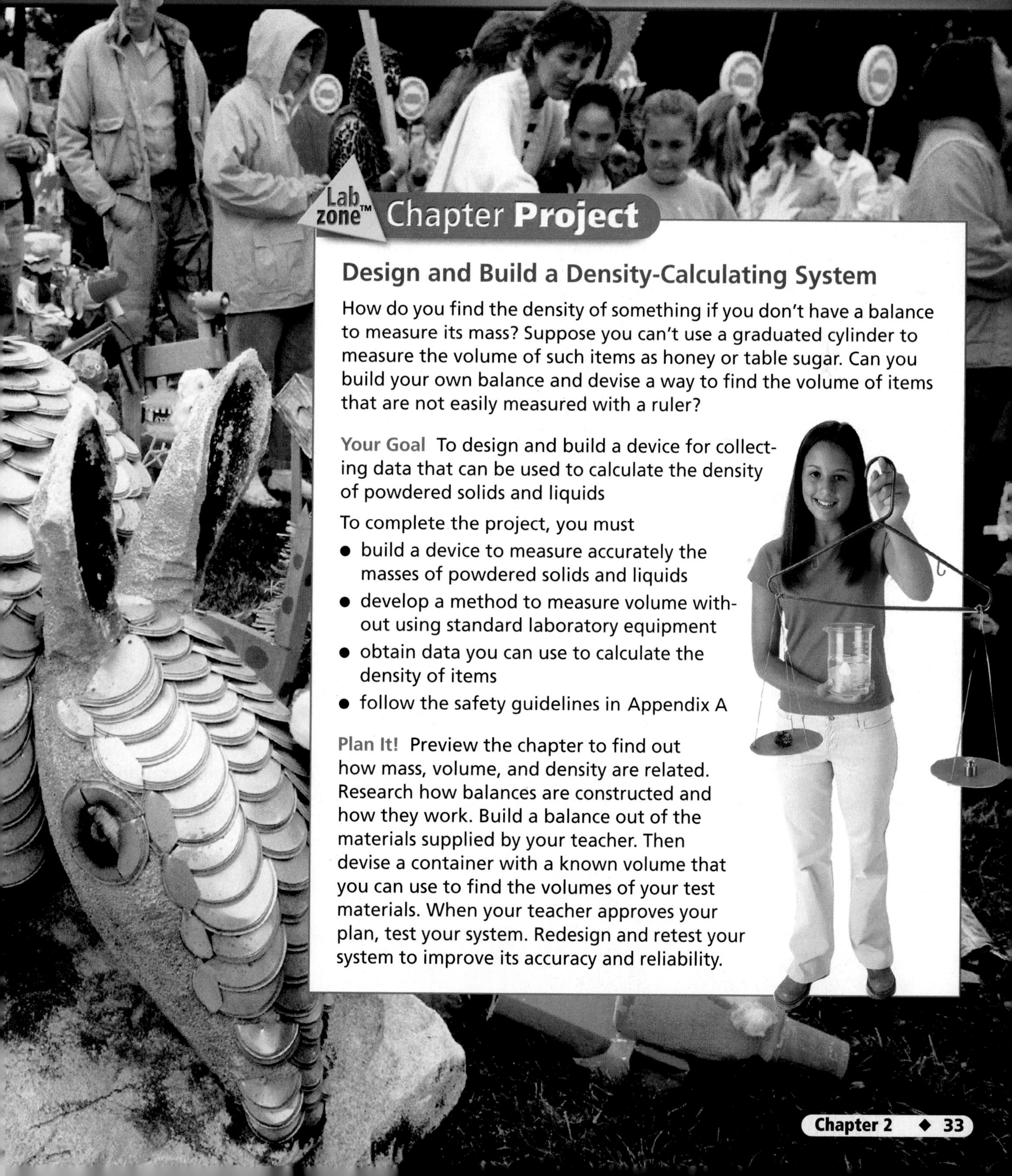

Lab zone™ Chapter **Project**

Design and Build a Density-Calculating System

How do you find the density of something if you don't have a balance to measure its mass? Suppose you can't use a graduated cylinder to measure the volume of such items as honey or table sugar. Can you build your own balance and devise a way to find the volume of items that are not easily measured with a ruler?

Your Goal To design and build a device for collecting data that can be used to calculate the density of powdered solids and liquids

To complete the project, you must

- build a device to measure accurately the masses of powdered solids and liquids
- develop a method to measure volume without using standard laboratory equipment
- obtain data you can use to calculate the density of items
- follow the safety guidelines in Appendix A

Plan It! Preview the chapter to find out how mass, volume, and density are related. Research how balances are constructed and how they work. Build a balance out of the materials supplied by your teacher. Then devise a container with a known volume that you can use to find the volumes of your test materials. When your teacher approves your plan, test your system. Redesign and retest your system to improve its accuracy and reliability.

Section 1

Describing Matter

Reading Preview

Key Concepts

- What kinds of properties are used to describe matter?
- What are elements, and how do they relate to compounds?
- What are the properties of a mixture?

Key Terms

- matter • chemistry
- substance • physical property
- chemical property • element
- atom • chemical bond
- molecule • compound
- chemical formula • mixture
- heterogeneous mixture
- homogeneous mixture
- solution

Target Reading Skill

Building Vocabulary

A definition states the meaning of a word or phrase by telling its most important feature or function. After you read the section, use what you have learned to write a definition of each Key Term in your own words.

Lab zone Discover Activity

What Is a Mixture?

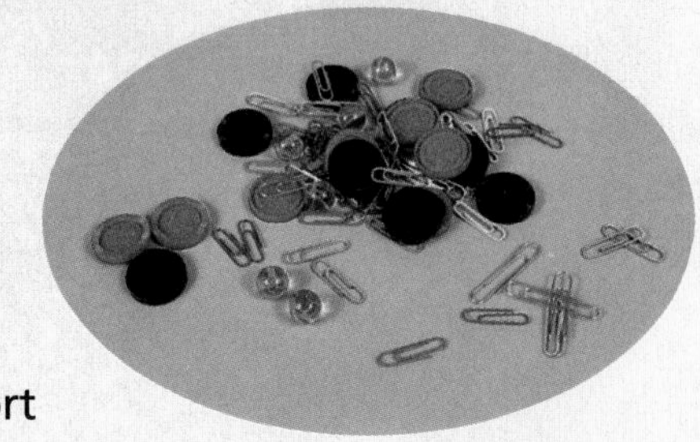

1. Your teacher will give you a handful of objects, such as checkers, marbles, and paper clips of different sizes and colors.
2. Examine the objects. Then sort them into at least three groups. Each item should be grouped with similar items.
3. Describe the differences between the unsorted handful and the sorted groups of objects. Then make a list of the characteristics of each sorted group.

Think It Over

Forming Operational Definitions The unsorted handful of objects represents a mixture. Your sorted groups represent substances. Using your observations, infer what the terms *mixture* and *substance* mean.

You have probably heard the word *matter* many times. Think about how often you hear the phrases "As a matter of fact, ..." or "Hey, what's the matter?" In science, this word has a specific meaning. **Matter** is anything that has mass and takes up space. All the "stuff" around you is matter, and you are matter too. Air, plastic, metal, wood, glass, paper, and cloth—all of these are matter.

▼ **Paper, ceramic, wood, metal, and foam are all forms of matter.**

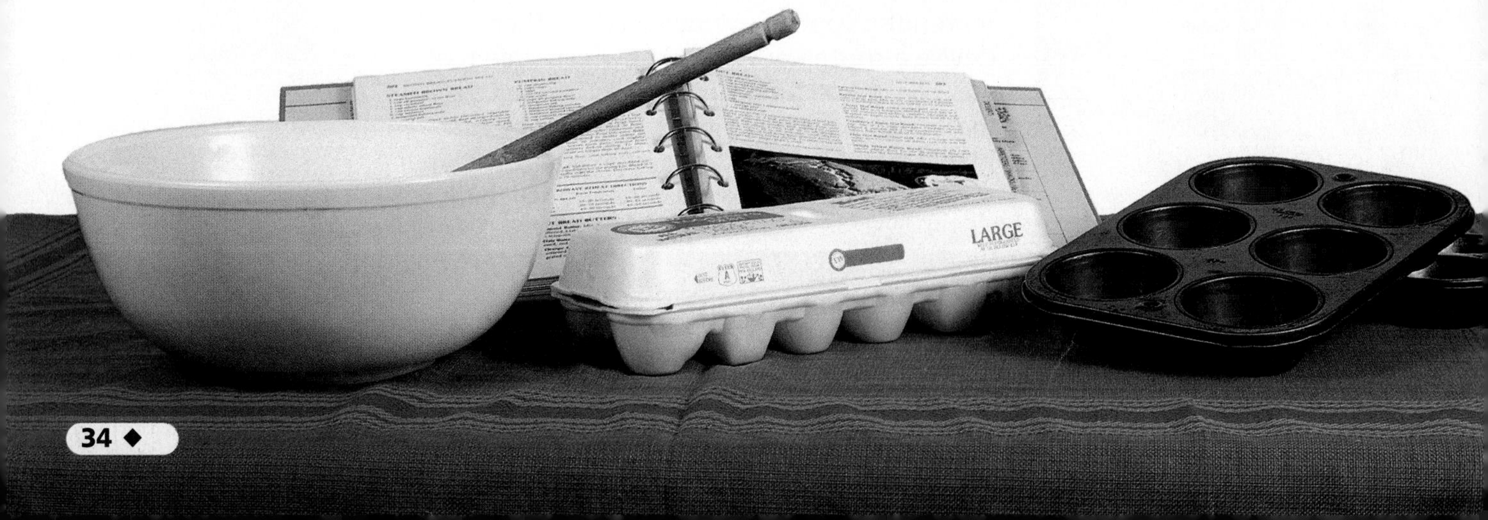

Properties of Matter

Even though air and plastic are both matter, no one has to tell you they are different materials. Matter can have many different properties, or characteristics. Materials can be hard or soft, rough or smooth, hot or cold, liquid, solid, or gas. Some materials catch fire easily, but others do not burn. **Chemistry** is the study of the properties of matter and how matter changes.

The properties and changes of any type of matter depend on its makeup. Some types of matter are substances and some are not. In chemistry, a **substance** is a single kind of matter that is pure, meaning it always has a specific makeup—or composition—and a specific set of properties. For example, table salt has the same composition and properties no matter where it comes from—seawater or a salt mine. On the other hand, think about the batter for blueberry muffins. It contains flour, butter, sugar, salt, blueberries, and other ingredients shown in Figure 1. While some of the ingredients, such as sugar and salt, are pure substances, the muffin batter is not. It consists of several ingredients that can vary with the recipe.

Every form of matter has two kinds of properties—physical properties and chemical properties. A physical property of oxygen is that it is a gas at room temperature. A chemical property of oxygen is that it reacts with iron to form rust. You'll read more about physical and chemical properties in the next two pages.

FIGURE 1
Substances or Not?
Making muffin batter involves mixing together different kinds of matter. The batter itself is not a pure substance. **Classifying** *Why are salt, sugar, and baking soda pure substances?*

Pure Substances
Table salt, table sugar, and baking soda are pure substances.

Not Substances
Flour, baking powder, milk, eggs, and fruit are not pure substances.

FIGURE 2

Physical Properties

The physical properties of matter help you identify and classify matter in its different forms.

Applying Concepts *Why is melting point a physical property?*

▲ **Physical State**
Above 0°C, these icicles of solid water will change to liquid.

◄ **Texture and Color**
Bumpy texture and bright colors are physical properties of this hungry chameleon.

▲ **Flexibility**
Metal becomes a shiny, flexible toy when shaped into a flat wire and coiled.

Lab zone **Skills Activity**

Interpreting Data

Melting point is the temperature at which a solid becomes a liquid. Boiling point is the temperature at which a liquid becomes a gas. Look at the data listed below. Identify each substance's physical state at room temperature (approximately 20°C). Is it a gas, a liquid, or a solid? Explain your conclusions.

Substance	Melting Point (°C)	Boiling Point (°C)
Water	0	100
Ethanol	–117	79
Propane	–190	–42
Table salt	801	1,465

Physical Properties of Matter A **physical property** is a characteristic of a pure substance that can be observed without changing it into another substance. For example, a physical property of water is that it freezes at a temperature of 0°C. When liquid water freezes, it changes to solid ice, but it is still water. Hardness, texture, and color are some other physical properties of matter. When you describe a substance as a solid, a liquid, or a gas, you are stating another physical property. Whether or not a substance dissolves in water is a physical property, too. Sugar will dissolve in water, but iron will not. Stainless steel is mostly iron, so you can stir sugar into your tea with a stainless steel spoon.

Physical properties can be used to classify matter. For example, two properties of metals are luster and the ability to conduct heat and electricity. Some metals, such as iron, can be attracted by a magnet. Metals are also flexible, which means they can be bent into shapes without breaking. They can also be pressed into flat sheets and pulled into long, thin wires. Other materials such as glass, brick, and concrete will break into small pieces if you try to bend them or press them thinner.

FIGURE 3
Chemical Properties

The chemical properties of different forms of matter cannot be observed without changing a substance into a new substance.

◀ **New Substances, New Properties** Gases produced during baking create spaces in freshly made bread.

◀ **Flammability** Wood fuels a fire, producing heat, gases, and ash.

Ability to React ▶ Iron can form rust, turning a once shiny car into a crumbling relic.

Chemical Properties of Matter Unlike physical properties of matter, some properties can't be observed just by looking at or touching a substance. A **chemical property** is a characteristic of a pure substance that describes its ability to change into different substances. To observe the chemical properties of a substance, you must try to change it to another substance. Like physical properties, chemical properties are used to classify substances. For example, a chemical property of methane (natural gas) is that it can catch fire and burn in air. When it burns, it combines with oxygen in the air and forms new substances, water and carbon dioxide. Burning, or flammability, is a chemical property of methane as well as the substances in wood or gasoline.

One chemical property of iron is that it will combine slowly with oxygen in air to form a different substance, rust. Silver will react with sulfur in the air to form tarnish. In contrast, a chemical property of gold is that it does *not* react easily with oxygen or sulfur. Bakers make use of a chemical property of the substances in bread dough. With the help of yeast added to the dough, some of these substances can produce a gas, which causes the bread to rise.

Reading Checkpoint **What must you do in order to observe a chemical property of a substance?**

FIGURE 4
Examples of Elements
Some elements have familiar uses. Many elements are solids at room temperature, but some are gases or liquids.

Tungsten wire

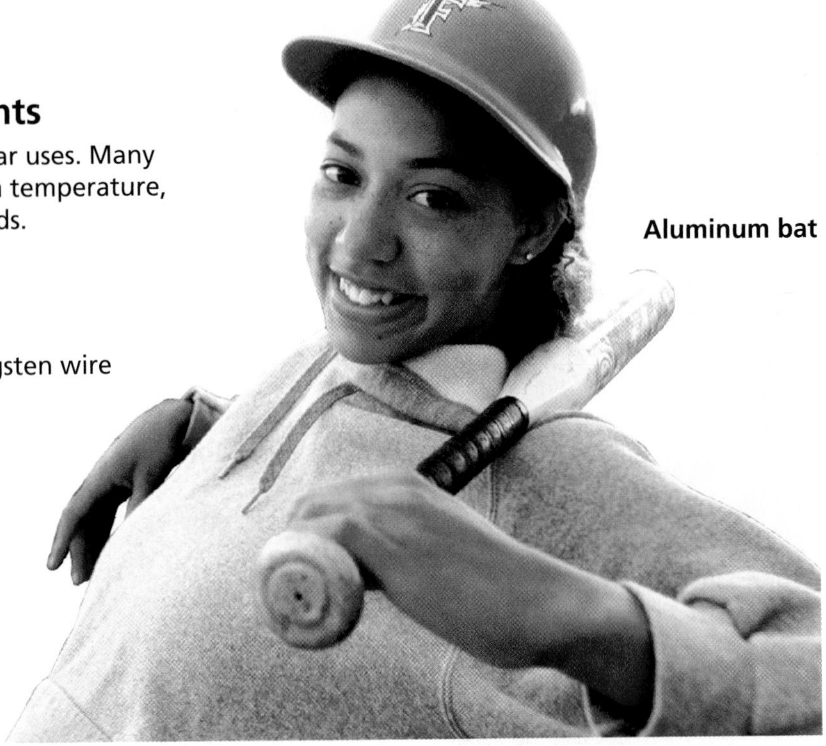
Aluminum bat

Copper coating on pennies

Elements

What is matter made of? Why is one kind of matter different from another kind of matter? Educated people in ancient Greece debated these questions. Around 450 B.C., a Greek philosopher named Empedocles proposed that all matter was made of four "elements"—air, earth, fire, and water. He thought that all other matter was a combination of two or more of these four elements. The idea of four elements was so convincing that people believed it for more than 2,000 years.

What Is an Element? In the late 1600s, experiments by the earliest chemists began to show that matter was made up of many more than four elements. Now, scientists know that all matter in the universe is made of slightly more than 100 different substances, still called elements. An **element** is a pure substance that cannot be broken down into any other substances by chemical or physical means. **Elements are the simplest substances.** Each element can be identified by its specific physical and chemical properties.

You are already familiar with some elements. Aluminum, which is used to make foil and outdoor furniture, is an element. Pennies are made from zinc, another element. Then the pennies are given a coating of copper, also an element. With each breath, you inhale the elements oxygen and nitrogen, which make up 99 percent of Earth's atmosphere. Elements are often represented by one- or two-letter symbols, such as C for carbon, O for oxygen, and H for hydrogen.

Go Online
SCI LINKS NSTA
For: Links on describing matter
Visit: www.SciLinks.org
Web Code: scn-1111

Particles of Elements—Atoms What is the smallest possible piece of matter? Suppose you could keep tearing a piece of aluminum foil in half over and over again. Would you reach a point where you have the smallest possible piece of aluminum? The answer is yes. Since the early 1800s, scientists have known that all matter is made of atoms. An **atom** is the basic particle from which all elements are made. Different elements have different properties because their atoms are different. Experiments in the early 1900s showed that an atom is made of even smaller parts. Look at the diagram of a carbon atom in Figure 5. The atom has a positively charged center, or nucleus, that contains smaller particles. It is surrounded by a "cloud" of negative charge. You will learn more about the structure of atoms in Chapter 3.

When Atoms Combine Atoms of most elements have the ability to combine with other atoms. When atoms combine, they form a **chemical bond**, which is a force of attraction between two atoms. In many cases, atoms combine to form larger particles called **molecules** (MAHL uh kyoolz)—groups of two or more atoms held together by chemical bonds. A molecule of water, for example, consists of an oxygen atom chemically bonded to two hydrogen atoms. Two atoms of the same element can also combine to form a molecule. Oxygen molecules consist of two oxygen atoms. Figure 6 shows models of three molecules. You will see similar models throughout this book.

Reading Checkpoint **What is a molecule?**

FIGURE 5
Modeling an Atom
Pencil "lead" is made of mostly graphite, a form of carbon. Two ways to model atoms used in this book are shown here for carbon.

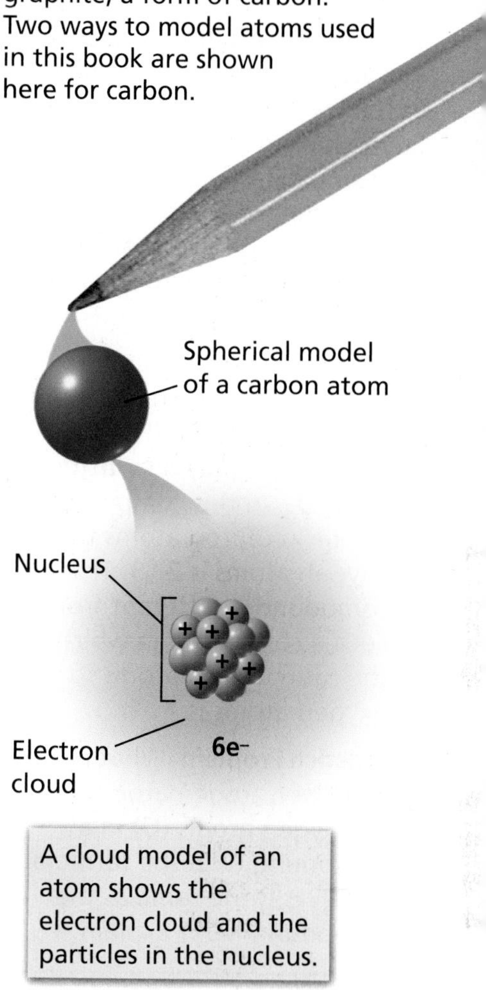

FIGURE 6
Modeling Molecules
Models of molecules often consist of colored spheres that stand for different kinds of atoms.
Observing *How many atoms are in a molecule of carbon dioxide?*

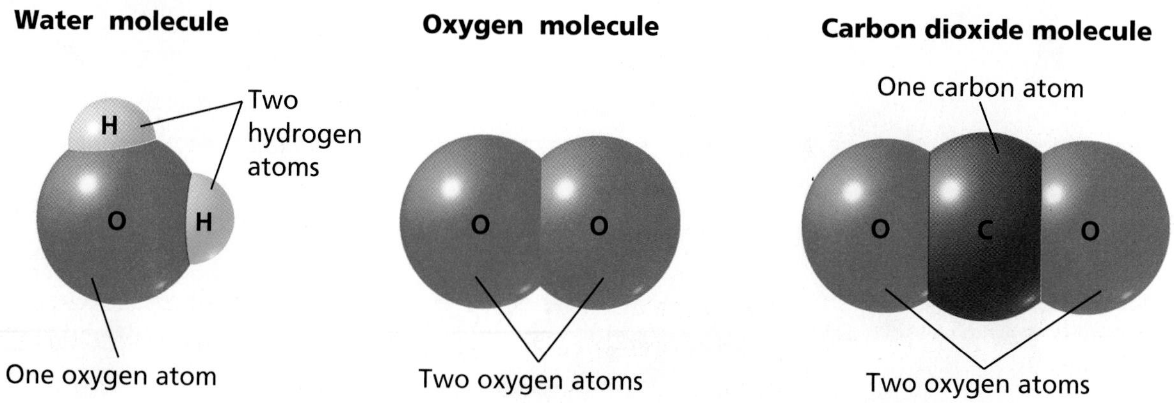

Math Skills

Ratios A ratio compares two numbers. It tells you how much you have of one item compared to how much you have of another. For example, a cookie recipe calls for 2 cups of flour to every 1 cup of sugar. You can write the ratio of flour to sugar as 2 to 1, or 2 : 1.

The chemical formula for rust, a compound made from the elements iron (Fe) and oxygen (O), may be written as Fe_2O_3. In this compound, the ratio of iron atoms to oxygen atoms is 2 : 3. This compound is different from FeO, a compound in which the ratio of iron atoms to oxygen atoms is 1 : 1.

Practice Problem What is the ratio of nitrogen atoms (N) to oxygen atoms (O) in a compound with the formula N_2O_5? Is it the same as the compound NO_2? Explain.

Compounds

All matter is made of elements, but most elements in nature are found combined with other elements. A **compound** is a pure substance made of two or more elements chemically combined in a set ratio. A compound may be represented by a **chemical formula,** which shows the elements in the compound and the ratio of atoms. For example, part of the gas you exhale is carbon dioxide. Its chemical formula is CO_2. The number *2* below the symbol for oxygen tells you that the ratio of carbon to oxygen is 1 to 2. (If there is no number after the element's symbol, the number *1* is understood.) If a different ratio of carbon atoms and oxygen atoms are seen in a formula, you have a different compound. For example, carbon monoxide—a gas produced in car engines—has the formula CO. Here, the ratio of carbon atoms to oxygen atoms is 1 to 1.

When elements are chemically combined, they form compounds having properties that are different from those of the uncombined elements. For example, the element sulfur is a yellow solid, and the element silver is a shiny metal. But when silver and sulfur combine, they form a compound called silver sulfide, Ag_2S. You would call this black compound *tarnish.* Table sugar ($C_{12}H_{22}O_{11}$) is a compound made of the elements carbon, hydrogen, and oxygen. The sugar crystals do not resemble the gases oxygen and hydrogen or the black carbon you see in charcoal.

Reading Checkpoint **What information does a chemical formula tell you about a compound?**

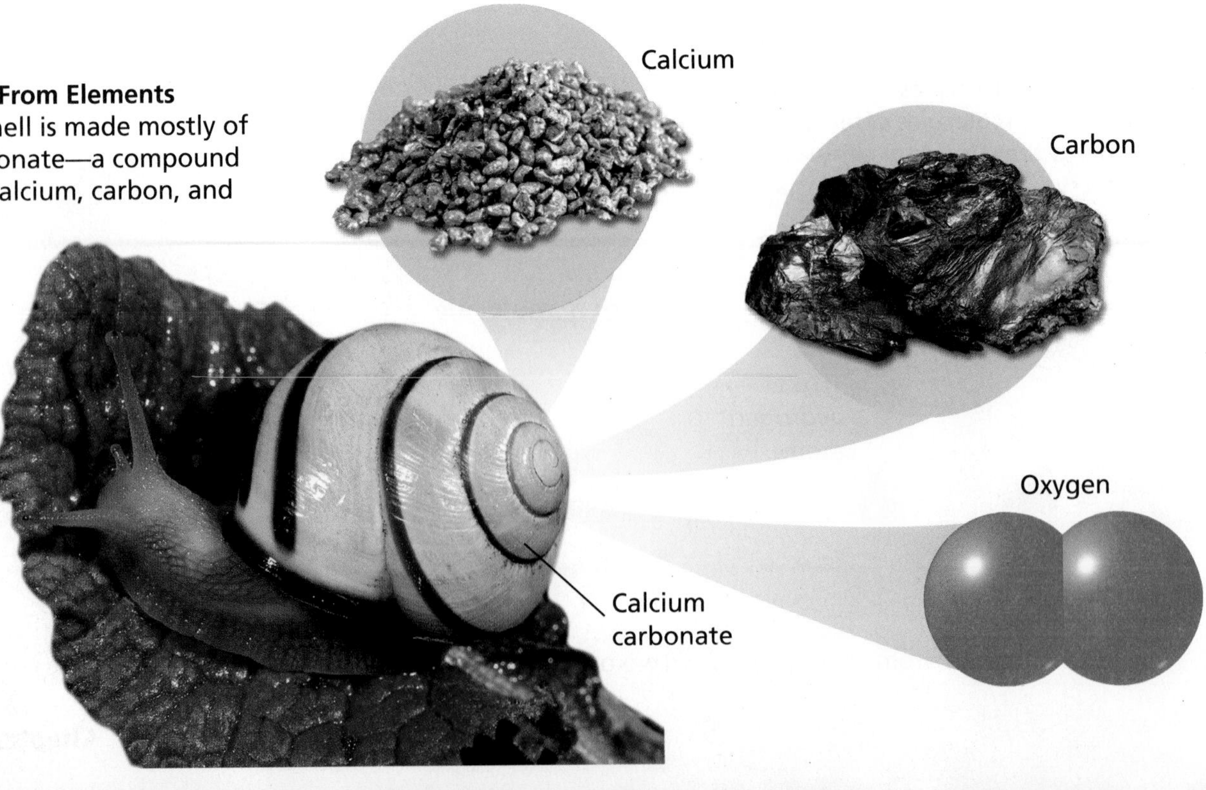

FIGURE 7
Compounds From Elements
This snail's shell is made mostly of calcium carbonate—a compound made from calcium, carbon, and oxygen.

Mixtures

Elements and compounds are pure substances, but most of the materials you see every day are not. Instead, they are mixtures. A **mixture** is made of two or more substances—elements, compounds, or both—that are together in the same place but are not chemically combined. Mixtures differ from compounds in two ways. **Each substance in a mixture keeps its individual properties. Also, the parts of a mixture are not combined in a set ratio.**

Think of a handful of moist soil such as that in Figure 8. If you look at the soil through a magnifier, you will find particles of sand, bits of clay, maybe even pieces of decaying plants. If you squeeze the soil, you might force out a few drops of water. A sample of soil from a different place probably won't contain the same amount of sand, clay, or water.

FIGURE 8
Heterogeneous Mixture
Soil from a flowerpot in your home may be very different from the soil in a nearby park.
Interpreting Photographs
What tells you that the soil is a heterogeneous mixture?

Heterogeneous Mixtures A mixture can be heterogeneous or homogeneous. In a **heterogeneous mixture** (het ur uh JEE nee us), you can see the different parts. The damp soil described above is one example of a heterogeneous mixture. So is a salad. Just think of how easy it is to see the pieces of lettuce, tomatoes, cucumbers, and other ingredients that cooks put together in countless ways and amounts.

Homogeneous Mixtures The substances in a **homogeneous mixture** (hoh moh JEE nee us), are so evenly mixed that you can't see the different parts. Suppose you stir a teaspoon of sugar into a glass of water. After stirring for a little while, the sugar dissolves, and you can no longer see crystals of sugar in the water. You know the sugar is there, though, because the sugar solution tastes sweet. A **solution** is an example of a homogeneous mixture. A solution does not have to be a liquid, however. Air is a solution of nitrogen gas (N_2) and oxygen gas (O_2), plus small amounts of a few other gases. A solution can even be solid. Brass is a solution of the elements copper and zinc.

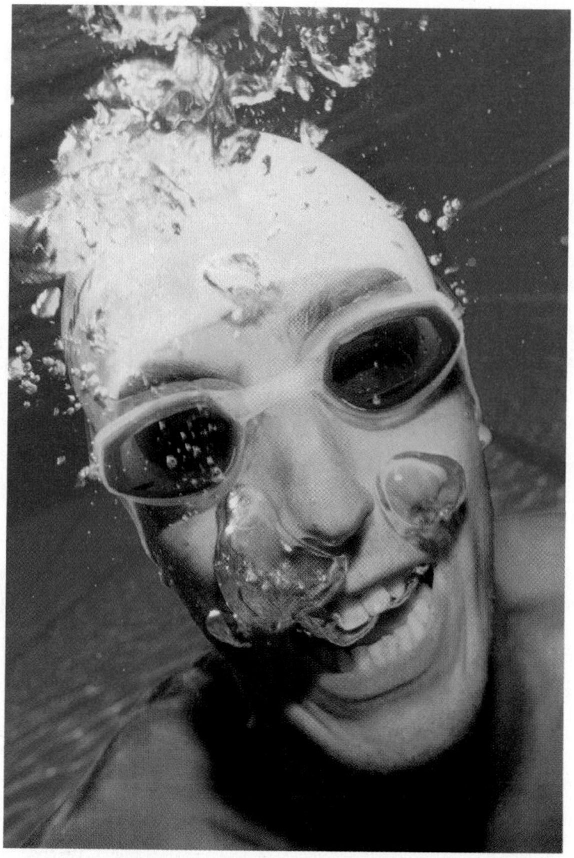

FIGURE 9
Homogeneous Mixture
A swimmer blows bubbles of air—a homogeneous mixture of gases.

FIGURE 10

Separating a Mixture

The different physical properties of iron, sulfur, and table salt help in separating a mixture of these substances.

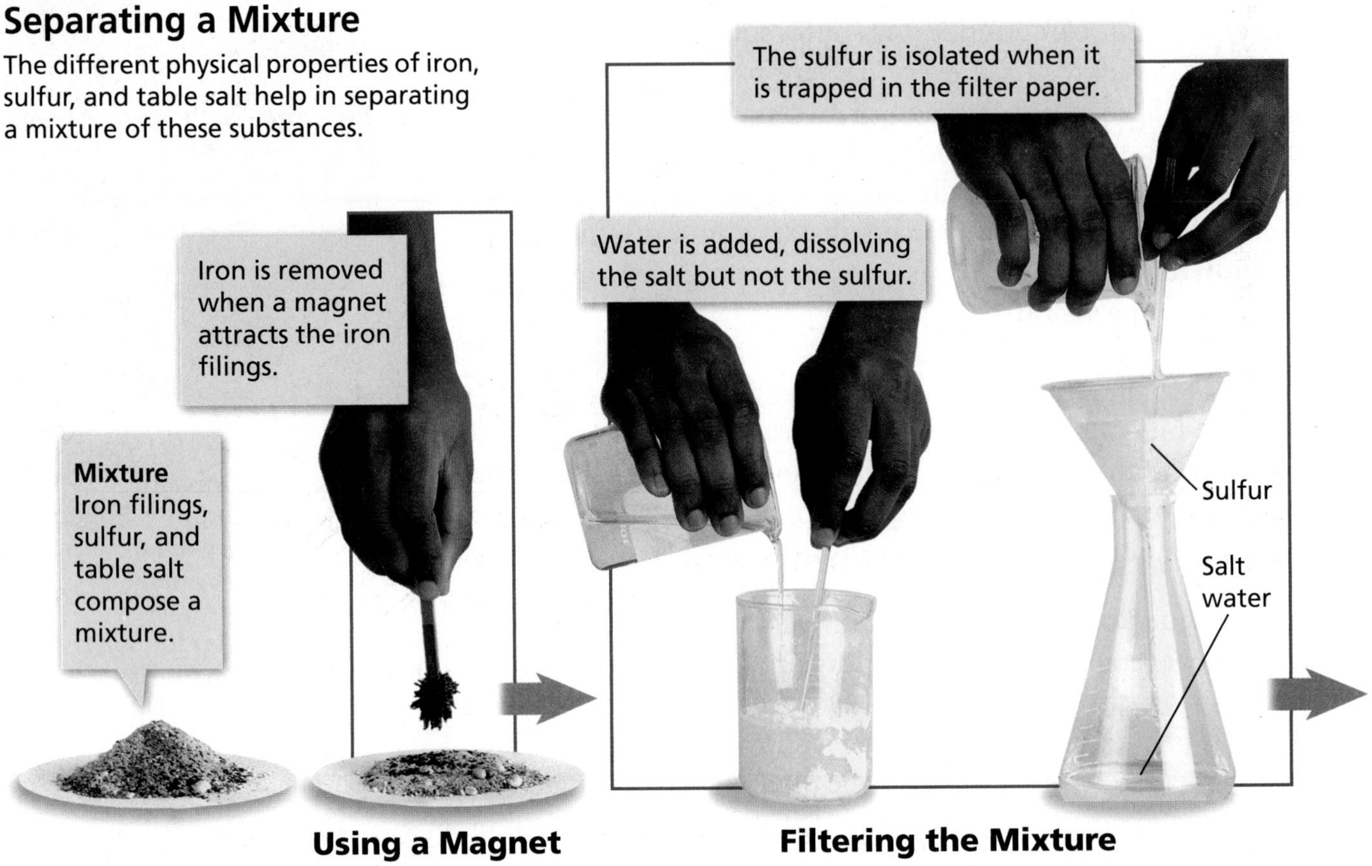

Mixture
Iron filings, sulfur, and table salt compose a mixture.
Iron is removed when a magnet attracts the iron filings.
Water is added, dissolving the salt but not the sulfur.
The sulfur is isolated when it is trapped in the filter paper.
Sulfur
Salt water
Using a Magnet
Filtering the Mixture

Separating Mixtures Compounds and mixtures differ in yet another way. A compound can be difficult to separate into its elements. But, a mixture is usually easy to separate into its components because each component keeps its own properties. Figure 10 illustrates a few of the ways you can use the properties of a mixture's components to separate them. These methods include magnetic attraction, filtration, distillation, and evaporation.

In the Figure, iron filings, powdered sulfur, and table salt start off mixed in a pile. Iron is attracted to a magnet, while sulfur and salt are not. Salt can be dissolved in water, but sulfur will not dissolve. So, pouring a mixture of salt, sulfur, and water through a paper filter removes the sulfur.

Now the remaining solution can be distilled. In distillation, a liquid solution is boiled. Components of the mixture that have different boiling points will boil away at different temperatures. As most of the water boils in Figure 10, it is cooled and then collected in a flask. Once the remaining salt water is allowed to dry, or evaporate, only the salt is left.

Discovery CHANNEL SCHOOL™

Introduction to Matter

Video Preview
▶ Video Field Trip
Video Assessment

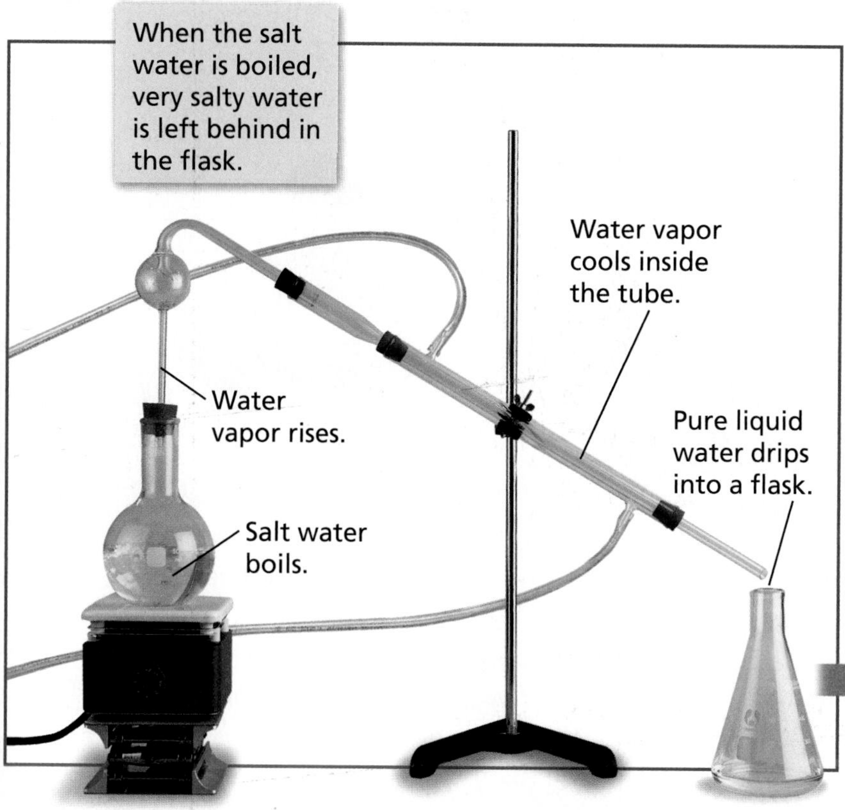

When the salt water is boiled, very salty water is left behind in the flask.
Water vapor cools inside the tube.
Water vapor rises.
Pure liquid water drips into a flask.
Salt water boils.

Distilling a Liquid Solution

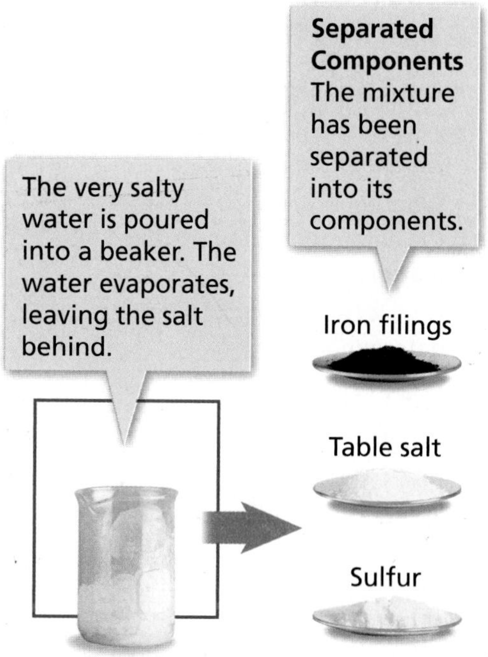

Evaporation

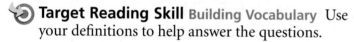

Section 1 Assessment

Target Reading Skill **Building Vocabulary** Use your definitions to help answer the questions.

Reviewing Key Concepts

1. a. Explaining What is the difference between chemical properties and physical properties?

b. Classifying A metal melts at 450°C. Is this property of the metal classified as chemical or physical? Explain your choice.

c. Making Judgments Helium does not react with any other substance. Is it accurate to say that helium has no chemical properties? Explain.

2. a. Reviewing How are elements and compounds similar? How do they differ?

b. Applying Concepts Plants make a sugar compound with the formula $C_6H_{12}O_6$. What elements make up this compound?

3. a. Identifying How does a heterogeneous mixture differ from a homogeneous mixture?

b. Drawing Conclusions Why is it correct to say that seawater is a mixture?

c. Problem Solving Suppose you stir a little baking soda into water until the water looks clear again. How could you prove to someone that the clear material is a solution, not a compound?

Math Practice

4. Ratios Look at the following chemical formulas: H_2O_2 and H_2O. Do these formulas represent the same compound? Explain.

Section 2 Measuring Matter

Reading Preview

Key Concepts

- What is the difference between weight and mass?
- What units are used to express the amount of space occupied by matter?
- How is the density of a material determined?

Key Terms

- weight • mass
- International System of Units
- volume • density

Target Reading Skill

Asking Questions Before you read, preview the red headings. In a graphic organizer like the one below, ask a *what* or *how* question for each heading. As you read, write the answers to your questions.

Weight and Mass

Question	Answer
How are weight and mass different?	Weight is a measure of . . .

Lab zone Discover Activity

Which Has More Mass?

1. Your teacher will provide you with some small objects. Look at the objects, but do not touch them.
2. Predict which object is lightest, which is second lightest, and so on. Record your predictions.
3. Use a triple-beam balance to find the mass of each object.
4. Based on the masses, list the objects from lightest to heaviest.

Think It Over

Drawing Conclusions How did your predictions compare with your results? Are bigger objects always heavier than smaller objects? Why or why not?

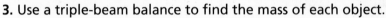

Here's a riddle for you: Which weighs more, a pound of feathers or a pound of sand? If you answered "a pound of sand," think again. Both weigh exactly the same—one pound.

There are all sorts of ways to measure matter, and you use these measurements every day. Scientists rely on measurements as well. In fact, scientists work hard to make sure their measurements are as accurate as possible.

Weight and Mass

Suppose you want to measure your weight. To find the weight, you step on a scale like the one shown in Figure 11. Your body weight presses down on the springs inside the scale. The more you weigh, the more the springs compress, causing the pointer on the scale to turn farther, giving a higher reading. However, your scale would not indicate the same weight if you took it to the moon and stepped on it. You weigh less on the moon, so the springs of the scale would not be compressed as much by your weight.

FIGURE 11
Measuring Weight
If you stood on this scale on the moon, it would show that your weight there is less than on Earth.

Weight Your **weight** is a measure of the force of gravity on you. On Earth, all objects are attracted toward the center of the planet by the force of Earth's gravity. On another planet, the force of gravity on you may be more or less than it is on Earth. On the moon, you would weigh only about one-sixth of your weight on Earth.

Go Online
PHSchool.com
For: More on measuring matter
Visit: PHSchool.com
Web Code: cgd-1012

Mass Why do you weigh less on the moon than on Earth? The force of gravity depends partly on the mass of an object. The **mass** of an object is the measurement of the amount of matter in the object. If you travel to the moon, the amount of matter in your body—your mass—does not change. But, the mass of the moon is much less than the mass of Earth, so the moon exerts much less gravitational force on you. **Unlike weight, mass does not change with location, even when the force of gravity on an object changes.** For this reason scientists prefer to measure matter by its mass rather than its weight. The mass of an object is a physical property.

Equating Units of Mass
1 kg = 1,000 g 1 g = 0.001 kg

Units of Mass To measure the properties of matter, scientists use a system called the **International System of Units.** This system is abbreviated "SI" after its French name, *Système International.* The SI unit of mass is the kilogram (kg). If you weigh 90 pounds on Earth, your mass is about 40 kilograms. Although you will see kilograms used in this textbook, usually you will see a smaller unit—the gram (g). There are exactly 1,000 grams in a kilogram. A nickel has a mass of 5 grams, and a baseball has a mass of about 150 grams.

Reading Checkpoint **What is the SI unit of mass?**

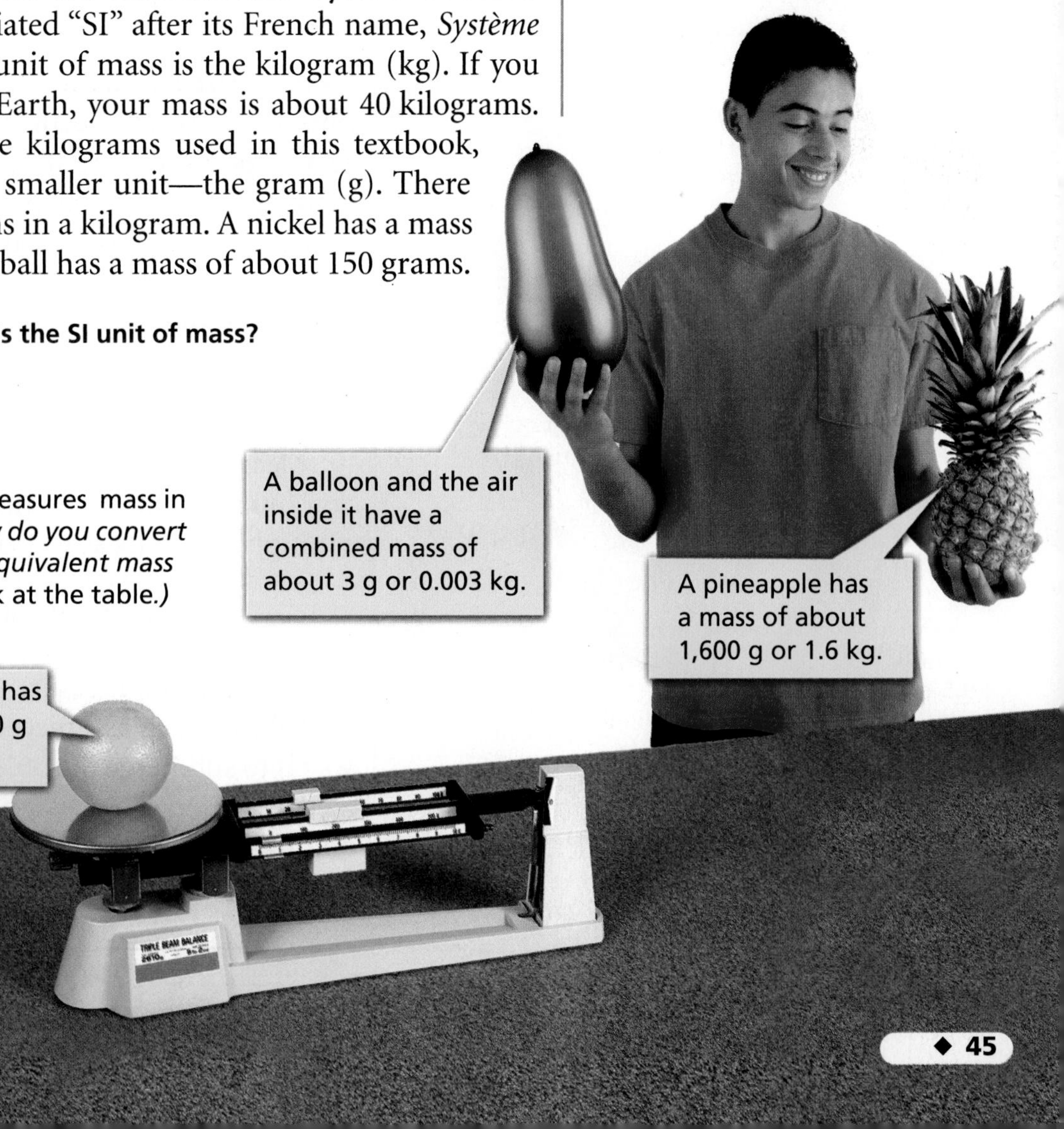
A balloon and the air inside it have a combined mass of about 3 g or 0.003 kg.
A pineapple has a mass of about 1,600 g or 1.6 kg.
An average orange has a mass of about 230 g or 0.23 kg.
TRIPLE BEAM BALANCE

FIGURE 12
Measuring Mass
A triple-beam balance measures mass in grams. Calculating *How do you convert a mass in grams to the equivalent mass in kilograms? (Hint:* Look at the table.*)*

Volume

You learned in Section 1 that all matter has mass and takes up space. The amount of space that matter occupies is called its **volume.** It's easy to see that solids and liquids take up space. Gases have volume, too. Watch a balloon as you blow into it. You're actually increasing the volume of gas in the balloon with your breath.

Units of Volume **Common units of volume include the liter (L), milliliter (mL), and cubic centimeter (cm^3).** Some plastic soda bottles hold 1 liter of liquid. Volumes smaller than a liter are usually given in milliliters. A milliliter is one one-thousandth of a liter and is exactly the same volume as 1 cubic centimeter. A teaspoonful of water has a volume of about 5 milliliters, and an ordinary can of soda contains 355 milliliters of liquid. In the laboratory, volumes of liquid are usually measured with a graduated cylinder.

Equating Units of Volume
1 L = 1,000 mL
1 mL = 0.001 L
1 mL = 1 cm^3

Calculating Volume The volumes of solid objects are usually expressed in cubic centimeters. Suppose you want to know the volume of a rectangular object, such as the brick shown in Figure 13. First, you measure the brick's length, width, and height (or thickness). Then, you multiply these values.

Volume = Length × Width × Height

Measurements always have units. So, when you multiply the three measurements, you must multiply the units as well as the numbers.

Units = cm × cm × cm = cm^3

How can you measure the volume of an irregular object, such as a piece of fruit or a rock? One way is to submerge the object in water in a graduated cylinder. The water level will rise by an amount that is equal to the volume of the object in milliliters.

Reading Checkpoint **How are milliliters related to cubic centimeters?**

FIGURE 13
Finding Volume
The volume of a regular solid can be found by measuring its dimensions and multiplying the values.
Interpreting Tables *What volume of water in milliliters would this brick displace if submerged?*

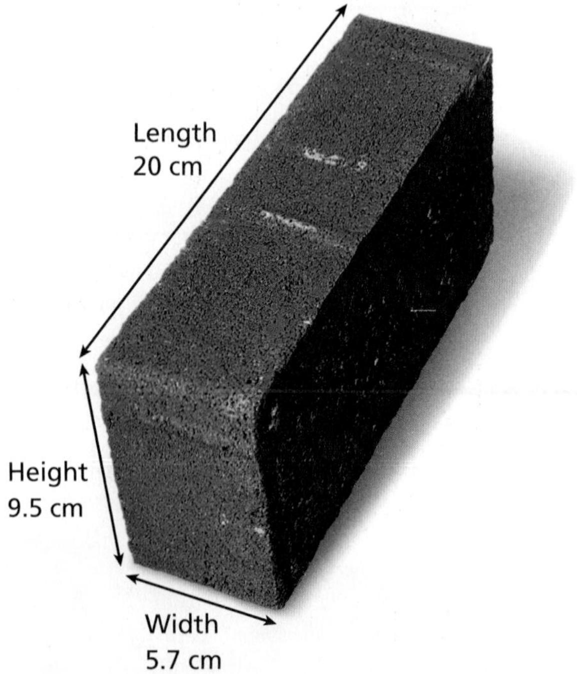

Volume = 20 cm x 9.5 cm x 5.7 cm
= 1,083 cm^3

Density

Samples of two different materials may have the same volume, but they don't necessarily have the same mass. Remember the riddle about the sand and the feathers? A kilogram of sand takes up much less space than a kilogram of feathers. The volumes differ because sand and feathers have different densities—an important property of matter. **Density** relates the mass of a material in a given volume. Often, density is expressed as the number of grams in one cubic centimeter. For example, the density of water at room temperature is stated as "one gram per cubic centimeter (1 g/cm^3)." This value means that every gram of water has a volume of 1 cm^3. Notice that the word *per* is replaced by the fraction bar in the units of density. **The bar tells you that you can determine the density of a sample of matter by dividing its mass by its volume.**

$$\text{Density} = \frac{\text{Mass}}{\text{Volume}}$$

Math Sample Problem

Calculating Density

A small block of wood floats on water. It has a mass of 200 g and a volume of 250 cm^3. What is the density of the wood?

1 Read and Understand

What information are you given?

Mass of block = 200 g

Volume of block = 250 cm^3

2 Plan and Solve

What quantity are you trying to calculate?

The density of the block = ■

What formula contains the given quantities and the unknown quantity?

$$\text{Density} = \frac{\text{Mass}}{\text{Volume}}$$

Perform the calculation.

$$\text{Density} = \frac{\text{Mass}}{\text{Volume}} = \frac{200 \text{ g}}{250 \text{ cm}^3} = 0.80 \text{ g/cm}^3$$

3 Look Back and Check

Does your answer make sense?

The density is lower than 1.0 g/cm^3, which makes sense because the block can float.

Math Practice

1. A sample of liquid has a mass of 24 g and a volume of 16 mL. What is the density of the liquid?
2. A piece of solid metal has a mass of 43.5 g and a volume of 15 cm^3. What is the density of the metal?

FIGURE 14
Density Layers
The density of water is less than corn syrup but greater than vegetable oil.

Sinking or Floating? Suppose you have a solid block of wood and a solid block of iron. When you drop both blocks into a tub of water, you can see right away that the wood floats and the iron sinks. You know the density of water is 1 g/cm^3. Objects with densities greater than that of water will sink. Objects with lesser densities will float. So, the density of this wood is less than 1 g/cm^3. The density of the iron is greater than 1 g/cm^3.

Watch a bottle of oil-and-vinegar salad dressing after it has been shaken. You will see oil droplets rising above the vinegar. Finally, the oil forms a separate layer above the vinegar. What can you conclude? You're right if you said that the oil is less dense than vinegar.

Using Density Density is a physical property of a substance. So, density can be used to identify an unknown substance. For example, suppose you were hiking in the mountains and found a shiny, golden-colored rock. How would you know if the rock was really gold? Later at home, you could look up the density of gold at room temperature. Then measure the mass and volume of the rock and find its density. If the two densities match, you would have quite a find!

Reading Checkpoint **Why does the oil in some salad dressings rise to the top of the bottle?**

Section 2 Assessment

Target Reading Skill Asking Questions Use the answers you wrote in your graphic organizer about the headings to answer the questions below.

Reviewing Key Concepts

1. a. Defining What is mass?

b. Explaining Why is mass more useful than weight for measuring matter?

2. a. Identifying What property of matter is measured in cubic centimeters?

b. Comparing and Contrasting How are milliliters related to liters?

c. Calculating A plastic box is 15.3 cm long, 9.0 cm wide, and 4.5 cm high. What is its volume? Include units in your answer.

3. a. Listing What measurements must you make to find the density of a sample of matter?

b. Explaining How can you determine whether a solid object is more dense or less dense than water?

c. Problem Solving Propose a way to determine the density of air.

Math Practice

4. Calculating Density A piece of metal has a volume of 38 cm^3 and a mass of 277 g. Calculate the density of the metal, and identify it based on the information below.

Iron	7.9 g/cm^3	Tin	7.3 g/cm^3
Lead	11.3 g/cm^3	Zinc	7.1 g/cm^3

Making Sense of Density

Problem

Does the density of a material vary with volume?

Skills Focus

drawing conclusions, measuring, controlling variables

Materials

- balance
- water
- paper towels
- metric ruler
- graduated cylinder, 100-mL
- wooden stick, about 6 cm long
- ball of modeling clay, about 5 cm wide
- crayon with paper removed

Procedure

1. Use a balance to find the mass of the wooden stick. Record the mass in a data table like the one shown above right.
2. Add enough water to a graduated cylinder so that the stick can be completely submerged. Measure the initial volume of the water.
3. Place the stick in the graduated cylinder. Measure the new volume of the water.
4. The volume of the stick is the difference between the water levels in Steps 2 and 3. Calculate this volume and record it.
5. The density of the stick equals its mass divided by its volume. Calculate and record its density.
6. Thoroughly dry the stick with a paper towel. Then carefully break the stick into two pieces. Repeat Steps 1 through 5 with each of the two pieces.
7. Repeat Steps 1 through 6 using the clay rolled into a rope.
8. Repeat using the crayon.

Data Table

Object	Mass (g)	Volume Change (cm^3)	Density (g/cm^3)
Wooden stick			
Whole			
Piece 1			
Piece 2			
Modeling clay			
Whole			
Piece 1			
Piece 2			
Crayon			
Whole			
Piece 1			
Piece 2			

Analyze and Conclude

1. **Measuring** For each object you tested, compare the density of the whole object with the densities of the pieces of the object.
2. **Drawing Conclusions** Use your results to explain how density can be used to identify a material.
3. **Controlling Variables** Why did you dry the objects in Step 6?
4. **Communicating** Write a paragraph explaining how you would change the procedure to obtain more data. Tell how having more data would affect your answers to Questions 1 and 2 above.

Design an Experiment

Design an experiment you could use to determine the density of olive oil. With your teacher's permission, carry out your plan.

Section 3

Changes in Matter

Reading Preview

Key Concepts

- What is a physical change?
- What is a chemical change?
- How are changes in matter related to changes in energy?

Key Terms

- physical change
- chemical change
- law of conservation of mass
- energy • temperature
- thermal energy
- endothermic change
- exothermic change

Target Reading Skill

Relating Cause and Effect A cause makes something happen. An effect is what happens. As you read, identify two effects caused by a chemical change. Write the information in a graphic organizer like the one below.

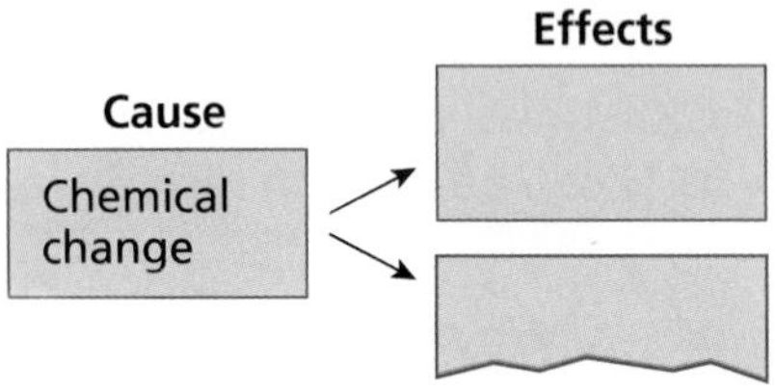

Lab zone Discover **Activity**

Is a New Substance Formed?

1. Obtain a piece of chalk about the size of a pea. Observe it and record its properties.
2. On a piece of clean paper, crush the piece of chalk with the back of a metal spoon. Describe the changes that occur.
3. Place some of the crushed chalk into the bowl of the spoon. Add about 8 drops of vinegar. Describe what happens.

Think It Over

Drawing Conclusions Chalk is mostly a single substance, calcium carbonate. Do you think a new substance was formed when the chalk was crushed? Do you think a new substance was formed when vinegar was added? Provide evidence for your answers.

You look up from the sand sculpture you and your friends have been working on all afternoon. Storm clouds are gathering, and you know the sand castle may not last long. You pull on a sweatshirt to cover the start of a sunburn and begin to pack up. The gathering of storm clouds, the creation of sand art, and your sunburn are examples of changes in matter. Chemistry is mostly about changes in matter. In this section, you will read about some of those changes.

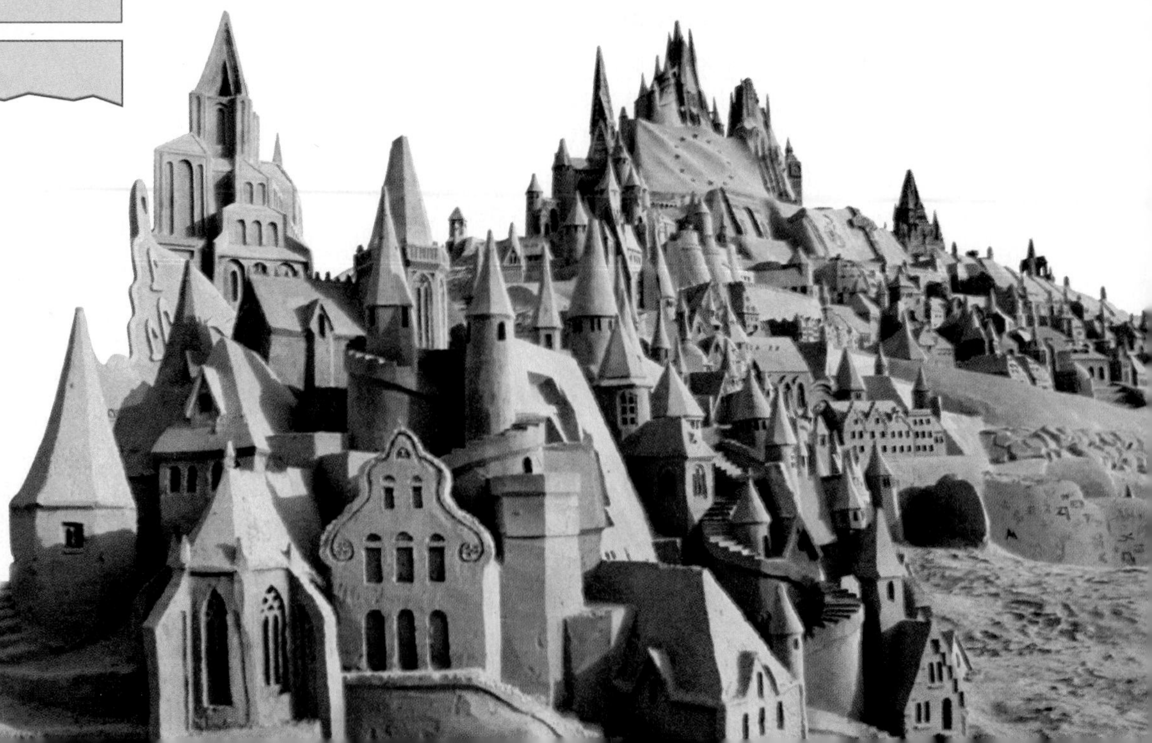

Sand has been ▶ transformed into art.

Physical Change

In what ways can matter change? A **physical change** is any change that alters the form or appearance of matter but does not make any substance in the matter into a different substance. For example, a sand artist may change a formless pile of sand into a work of art. However, the sculpture is still made of sand. **A substance that undergoes a physical change is still the same substance after the change.**

Changes of State As you may know, matter occurs in three familiar states—solid, liquid, and gas. Suppose you leave a small puddle of liquid water on the kitchen counter. When you come back two hours later, the puddle is gone. Has the liquid water disappeared? No, a physical change happened. The liquid water changed into water vapor (a gas) and mixed with the air. A change in state, such as from a solid to a liquid or from a liquid to a gas, is an example of a physical change.

Changes in Shape or Form Is there a physical change when you dissolve a teaspoon of sugar in water? To be sure, you would need to know whether or not the sugar has been changed to a different substance. For example, you know that a sugar solution tastes sweet, just like the undissolved sugar. If you pour the sugar solution into a pan and let the water dry out, the sugar will remain as a crust at the bottom of the pan. The crust may not look exactly like the sugar before you dissolved it, but it's still sugar. So, dissolving is also a physical change. Other examples of physical changes are bending, crushing, breaking, chopping, and anything else that changes only the shape or form of matter. The methods of separating mixtures—filtration and distillation—that you read about in Section 1 also involve physical changes.

Reading Checkpoint **Why is the melting of an ice cube called a physical change?**

FIGURE 15
Change of State
At room temperature, the element iodine is a purple solid that easily becomes a gas.
Classifying *Why is the change in the iodine classified as a physical change?*

FIGURE 16
Change in Form
Crushing aluminum soda cans doesn't change the aluminum into another metal (left). When table sugar dissolves in a glass of water, it is still sugar (right).

Lab zone Skills Activity

Inferring

Make a list of changes in matter that you observe during a single day. These changes may occur in your environment (such as changes in the weather), as a result of people's activities (such as cooking or driving a car), or in other situations. Try to classify each change on your list as a physical change or a chemical change. Then briefly explain your choice.

Chemical Change

A second kind of change occurs when a substance is transformed into a different substance. A change in matter that produces one or more new substances is a **chemical change,** or a chemical reaction. In some chemical changes, a single substance simply changes to one or more other substances. For example, when hydrogen peroxide is poured on a cut on your skin, it breaks down into water and oxygen gas.

In other chemical changes, two or more substances combine to form different substances. For example, iron metal combines with oxygen from the air to form the substance iron oxide, which you call rust. **Unlike a physical change, a chemical change produces new substances with properties different from those of the original substances.**

Examples of Chemical Change One familiar chemical change is the burning of natural gas on a gas stove. Natural gas is mostly the compound methane, CH_4. When it burns, methane combines with oxygen in the air and forms new substances. These new substances include carbon dioxide gas, CO_2, and water vapor, H_2O, which mix with air and are carried away. Both of these new substances can be identified by their properties, which are different from those of the methane. The chemical change that occurs when fuels such as natural gas, wood, candle wax, and gasoline burn in air is called combustion. Other processes that result in chemical change include electrolysis, oxidation, and tarnishing. The table in Figure 17 describes each of these kinds of chemical changes.

FIGURE 17
Four examples of chemical change are listed in the table.
Interpreting Photographs *What fuel is undergoing combustion in the photograph?*

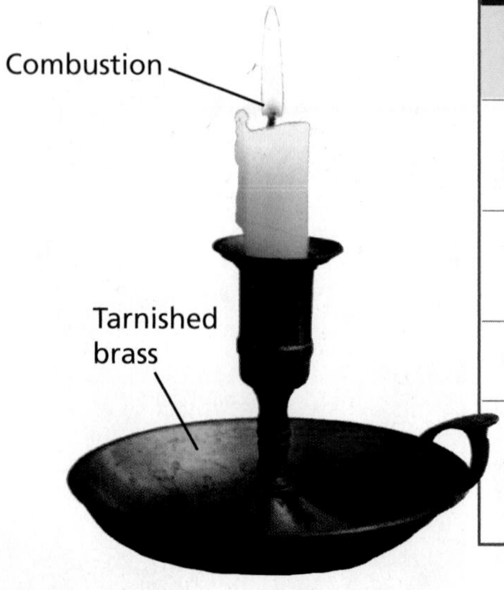

Examples of Chemical Change

Chemical Change	Description	Example
Combustion	Rapid combination of a fuel with oxygen; produces heat, light, and new substances	Gas, oil, or coal burning in a furnace
Electrolysis	Use of electricity to break a compound into elements or simpler compounds	Breaking down water into hydrogen and oxygen
Oxidation	Slow combination of a substance with oxygen	Rusting of an iron fence
Tarnishing	Slow combination of a bright metal with sulfur or another substance, producing a dark coating on the metal	Tarnishing of brass

Conservation of Mass A candle may seem to "go away" when it is burned, or water may seem to "disappear" when it changes to a gas. However, scientists long ago proved otherwise. In the 1770s, a French chemist, Antoine Lavoisier, carried out experiments in which he made accurate measurements of mass both before and after a chemical change. His data showed that no mass was lost or gained during the change. The fact that matter is not created or destroyed in any chemical or physical change is called the **law of conservation of mass.** Remember that mass measures the amount of matter. So, this law is sometimes called the law of conservation of matter.

Suppose you could collect all the carbon dioxide and water produced when methane burns, and you measured the mass of all of this matter. You would find that it equaled the mass of the original methane plus the mass of the oxygen that was used in the burning. No mass is lost, because during a chemical change, atoms are not lost or gained, only rearranged. A model for this reaction is shown in Figure 19.

Reading Checkpoint **Why is combustion classified as a chemical change?**

FIGURE 18
Using Methane
Natural gas, or methane, is the fuel used in many kitchen ranges. When it burns, no mass is lost.

Go Online active art

For: Conserving Matter activity
Visit: PHSchool.com
Web Code: cgp-1013

FIGURE 19
Conserving Matter
The idea of atoms explains the law of conservation of matter. For every molecule of methane that burns, two molecules of oxygen are used. The atoms are rearranged in the reaction, but they do not disappear.

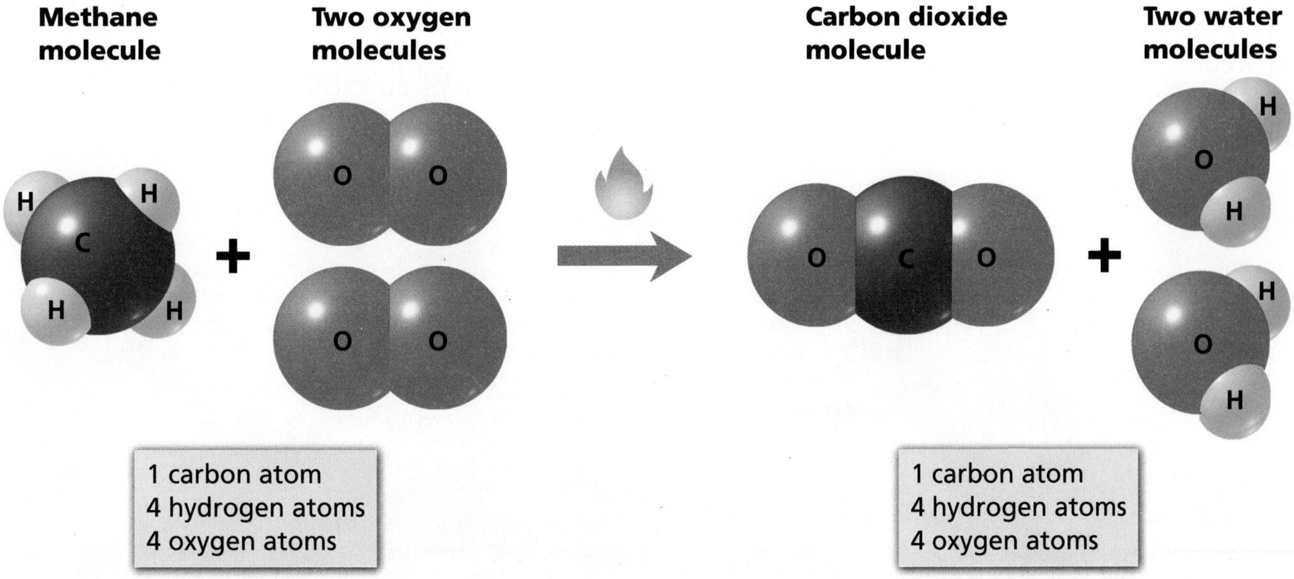

FIGURE 20
Flow of Thermal Energy
Thermal energy from a hot cup of cocoa can warm cold hands on a chilly day.
Developing Hypotheses *How will the flow of thermal energy affect the cocoa?*

Matter and Thermal Energy

Do you feel as if you are full of energy today? **Energy** is the ability to do work or cause change. **Every chemical or physical change in matter includes a change in energy.** A change as simple as bending a paper clip takes energy. When ice changes to liquid water, it absorbs energy from the surrounding matter. When candle wax burns, it gives off energy.

Temperature and Thermal Energy Think of how it feels when you walk inside an air-conditioned building from the outdoors on a hot day. Whew! Did you exclaim about the change in temperature? **Temperature** is a measure of the average energy of random motion of particles of matter. The particles of gas in the warm outside air have greater average energy of motion than the particles of air in the cool building.

Thermal energy is the total energy of all of the particles in an object. Most often, you experience thermal energy when you describe matter—such as the air in a room—as feeling hot or cold. Temperature and thermal energy are not the same thing, but temperature is related to the amount of thermal energy an object has. Thermal energy always flows from warmer matter to cooler matter.

Thermal Energy and Changes in Matter When matter changes, the most common form of energy released or absorbed is thermal energy. For example, ice absorbs thermal energy from its surroundings when it melts. That's why you can pack food and drinks in an ice-filled picnic cooler to keep them cold. The melting of ice is an **endothermic change,** a change in which energy is taken in. Changes in matter can also occur when energy is given off. An **exothermic change** releases energy. Combustion is a chemical change that releases energy in the form of heat and light. You've taken advantage of an exothermic change if you've ever warmed your hands near a wood fire.

FIGURE 21
An Endothermic Change
An iceberg melting in the ocean absorbs thermal energy from the surrounding water.

Math Analyzing Data

Comparing Energy Changes

A student observes two different chemical reactions, one in beaker A and the other in beaker B. The student measures the temperature of each reaction every minute. The student then plots the time and temperature data and creates the following graph.

1. **Reading Graphs** What do the numbers on the *x*-axis tell you about the length of the experiment?
2. **Comparing and Contrasting** How did the change in temperature in beaker B differ from that in beaker A?
3. **Interpreting Data** Which reaction is exothermic? Explain your reasoning.
4. **Calculating** Which reaction results in a greater change in temperature over time?

Energy of Two Reactions

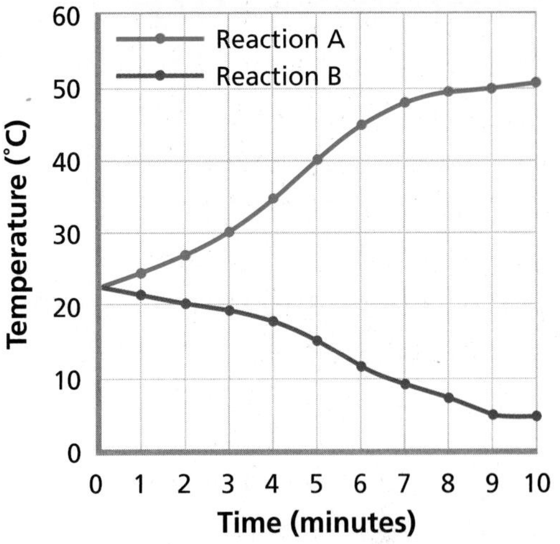

Section 3 Assessment

Target Reading Skill

Relating Cause and Effect Refer to your graphic organizer about chemical change to help you answer Question 2 below.

Reviewing Key Concepts

1. a. Listing Identify three different kinds of physical change that could happen to a plastic spoon.

b. Making Judgments Which of the following processes is not a physical change: drying wet clothes, cutting snowflakes out of paper, lighting a match from a matchbook?

2. a. Defining What evidence would you look for to determine whether a chemical change has occurred?

b. Applying Concepts Why is the electrolysis of water classified as a chemical change but the freezing of water is not?

c. Problem Solving Explain why the mass of a rusted nail would be greater than the mass of the nail before it rusted. Assume that all the rust is still attached to the nail. (*Hint:* The nail rusts when exposed to the air.)

3. a. Reviewing What is thermal energy?

b. Explaining How can you tell whether one glass of water has more thermal energy than another, identical glass of water?

c. Inferring How might you cause an endothermic chemical change to begin and keep going?

Writing in Science

Persuasive Letter Write a letter to persuade a friend that a change in temperature does not necessarily mean that a chemical change has occurred.

Transporting Hazardous Chemicals

Each year, millions of tons of hazardous substances criss-cross the country by truck and rail. These substances can be poisonous, flammable, and even explosive. The chemical industry tries to make the transport of hazardous substances safe, and problems are rare. But when spills do happen, these compounds can damage the environment and threaten human lives. How can hazardous substances be transported safely?

Why Do People Transport Hazardous Substances?

Useful products are made from the hazardous materials that trucks and trains carry. For example, CDs are made from plastics. To produce plastics, manufacturers use compounds such as benzene and styrene. Benzene fumes are poisonous and flammable. Styrene can explode when exposed to air. Public health experts say it is important to find safe substitutes for dangerous substances. But finding alternatives is difficult and expensive.

What Are the Risks?

Since 2000, the number of accidents in the United States involving hazardous chemical releases has dropped steadily from more than 350 to less than 20 in 2003. Still, public health experts say that some substances are too hazardous to transport on roads and railroads. An accidental release near a city could harm many people.

Some people say that vehicles carrying hazardous substances should be restricted to isolated roads. However, many factories that use the chemical compounds are located in cities. Chemicals often must be transported from where they are made to where they are used. For example, trucks and trains must transport gasoline to every neighborhood and region of the country.

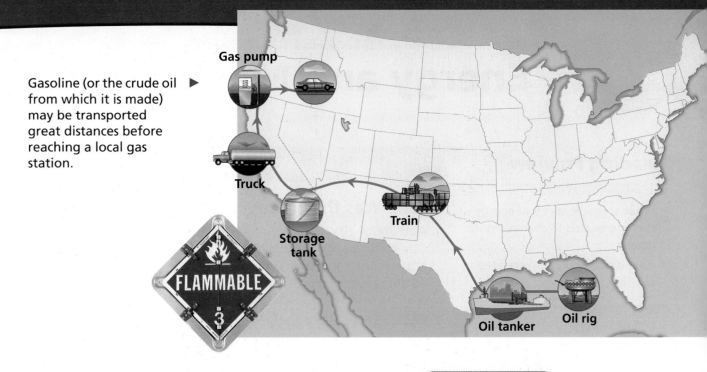

Gasoline (or the crude oil from which it is made) may be transported great distances before reaching a local gas station. ▶

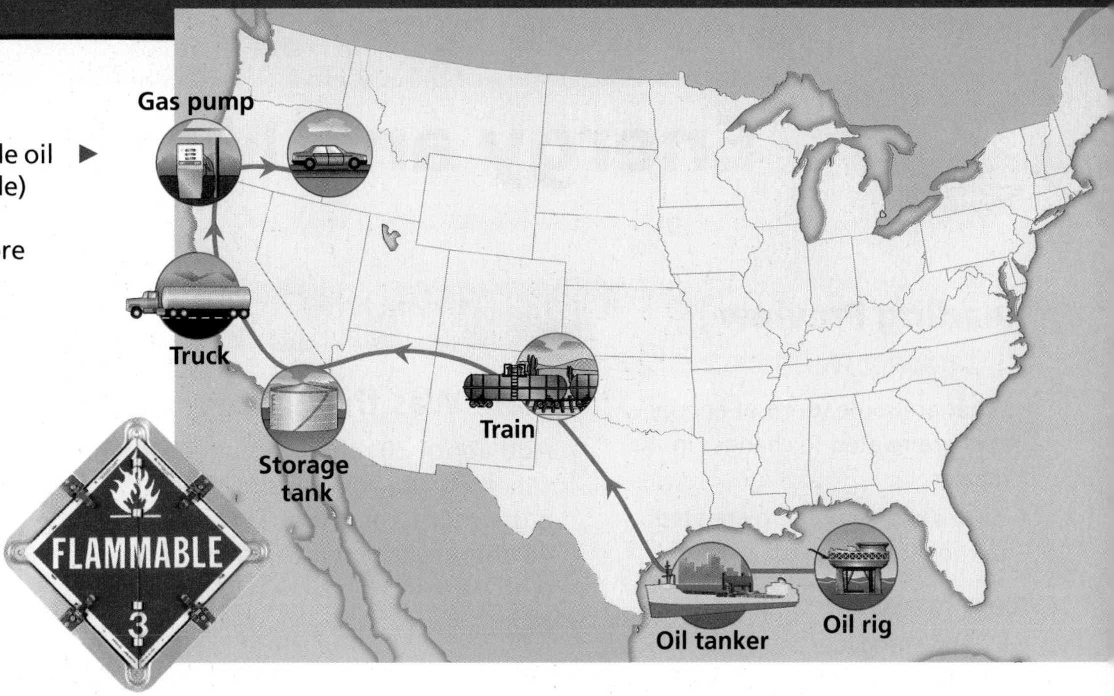

How Should Transportation Be Regulated?

Manufacturers that use hazardous chemicals say that there already are adequate laws. The Hazardous Materials Transportation Act (1975, revised in 1994) requires carriers of hazardous substances to follow strict labeling and packaging rules. They must keep records of what they carry and where they travel. Local emergency officials in communities near transportation routes must also be trained to handle accidents involving these substances.

On the other hand, public health experts say there are not enough inspectors to check all trucks and trains and make sure rules are followed. But hiring more inspectors would cost additional tax money.

You Decide

1. Identify the Problem
In your own words, explain the problem of safely transporting hazardous substances.

2. Analyze the Options
Examine the pros and cons of greater regulation of the transport of hazardous substances. In each position, consider the effects on chemical industries and on the public.

3. Find a Solution
You are the emergency planning director in your city. Create regulations for transporting hazardous substances through your community.

Go Online
PHSchool.com

For: More on transporting hazardous chemicals
Visit: PHSchool.com
Web Code: cgh-1010

Section 4

Integrating Physics

Energy and Matter

Reading Preview

Key Concepts

- What are some forms of energy that are related to changes in matter?
- How is chemical energy related to chemical change?

Key Terms

- kinetic energy
- potential energy
- chemical energy
- electromagnetic energy
- electrical energy • electrode

Target Reading Skill

Identifying Main Ideas As you read Forms of Energy, write the main idea in a graphic organizer like the one below. Then write three supporting details that give examples of the main idea.

Main Idea

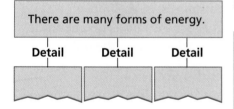

There are many forms of energy.

Detail	Detail	Detail

Lab zone Discover Activity

Where Was the Energy?

1. Add about 20 mL of tap water to an empty soda can. Measure the temperature of the water with a thermometer. (*Hint*: Tilt the can about 45 degrees to cover the bulb of the thermometer with water.)
2. Bend a paper clip into the shape shown in the photograph.
3. Stick a small ball of modeling clay into the center of an aluminum pie pan. Then stick the straight end of the paper clip into the ball.
4. Place one mini marshmallow on the flat surface formed by the top of the paper clip. Light the marshmallow with a match.
5. Use tongs to hold the can about 2 cm over the burning marshmallow until the flame goes out.
6. Measure the water temperature.

Think It Over

Drawing Conclusions How can you account for any change in the water's temperature? What evidence of a chemical change did you observe? What forms of energy were released when the marshmallow burned? Where did the energy come from?

Like matter, energy is never created or destroyed in chemical reactions. Energy can only be transformed—that is, changed from one form to another.

Forms of Energy

How do you know when something has energy? You would probably say that a basketball flying toward the hoop has energy because it is moving, and you'd be right. You can be sure that the player who threw the ball also has energy. Maybe you would mention light and heat from a burning candle. Again you would be right.

Energy is all around you, and it comes in many forms. **Forms of energy related to changes in matter may include kinetic, potential, chemical, electromagnetic, electrical, and thermal energy.**

Near the top of the track, the slow-moving car has more potential energy than kinetic energy.

The car's kinetic energy increases as it gains speed on the downward track.

FIGURE 22
Energy Changes
The thrills of a roller coaster ride start with the transformation of potential energy into kinetic energy. **Applying Concepts** *Where did the potential energy of the car come from?*

Kinetic Energy and Potential Energy In Section 3, you learned that energy is the ability to do work or cause change. All matter has energy of at least one form. **Kinetic energy** is the energy of matter in motion. A rolling bowling ball has kinetic energy and can do work by knocking down bowling pins. If you drop the bowling ball on your toe, you'll experience the work done by the kinetic energy of the falling ball. Even though you can't see them, the smallest particles of matter have kinetic energy because they are in constant, random motion. Recall from Section 3 that the kinetic energy of particles contributes to the thermal energy of a substance.

Suppose you push your bike to the top of a hill. That action takes energy, doesn't it? But the energy isn't wasted. In a way, it is now stored in you and in the bike. This stored energy will change to kinetic energy as you enjoy an exciting coast back down the hill. As you went up the hill, you increased the potential energy of both you and the bike. **Potential energy** is the energy an object has because of its position. When a diver climbs up to a diving board, she increases her potential energy. When you stretch a rubber band, your action gives potential energy to the rubber band to snap back and do work.

Lab zone Try This **Activity**

Dropping the Ball

1. Work with a partner. Using a meter stick as a guide, hold a ball about 0.5 m off the floor. Let go of the ball and note how high it bounces.
2. Repeat Step 1 from heights of 1 m, 1.5 m, and 2 m.

Inferring When does the ball have the most potential energy? When does it have the most kinetic energy?

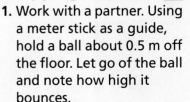

Go Online SCiLINKS NSTA

For: Links on matter and energy
Visit: www.SciLinks.org
Web Code: scn-1114

Chemical Energy The internal energy stored in the chemical bonds between atoms is a form of potential energy that is sometimes called **chemical energy**. When a chemical change occurs, these bonds are broken and new bonds are formed. If the change is exothermic, some of the chemical energy is transformed and released in a variety of other forms. As you read in Section 3, one of those forms is often thermal energy.

Electromagnetic Energy You probably know that energy reaches Earth in the form of sunlight. Energy from the sun can increase the temperature of the surface of a sidewalk or change your skin by burning it. Visible light is one example of **electromagnetic energy,** a form of energy that travels through space as waves. Radio waves, infrared "rays" from heat lamps, the waves that heat food in a microwave oven, ultraviolet rays, and X-rays are other types of electromagnetic energy.

Chemical changes can give off electromagnetic energy, such as the light from a wood fire. Also, both chemical and physical changes in matter may be *caused* by electromagnetic energy. For example, a microwave oven can change a frozen block of spaghetti and sauce into a hot meal—a physical change.

FIGURE 23
Electrolysis of Water
Electrical energy can be used to break down water, H_2O, into its elements. Bubbles of oxygen gas and hydrogen gas form at separate electrodes.
Drawing Conclusions *Why is the volume of hydrogen formed twice that of oxygen?*

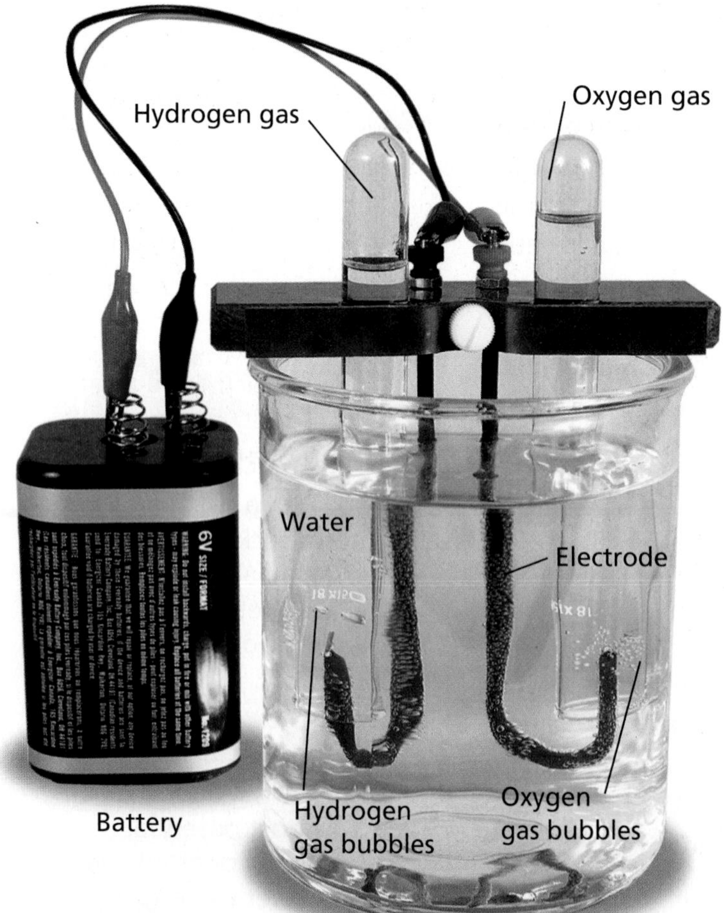

Electrical Energy Recall from Section 1 that an atom consists of a positively charged nucleus surrounded by a negatively charged cloud. This "cloud" symbolizes moving, negatively charged particles called electrons. **Electrical energy** is the energy of electrically charged particles moving from one place to another. Electrons move from one atom to another in many chemical changes.

Electrolysis—a chemical change you first read about in Section 3—involves electrical energy. In electrolysis, two metal strips called **electrodes** are placed in a solution, but the electrodes do not touch. Each electrode is attached to a wire. The wires are connected to a source of electrical energy, such as a battery. When the energy begins to flow, atoms of one kind lose electrons at one electrode in the solution. At the other electrode, atoms of a different kind gain electrons. New substances form as a result.

Reading Checkpoint **Where is chemical energy stored?**

Transforming Energy

The burning of a fuel is a chemical change that transforms chemical energy and releases it as thermal energy and electromagnetic energy. When you push a bike (and yourself) up a hill, chemical energy from foods you ate is transformed into the kinetic energy of your moving muscles. Similarly, other forms of energy can be transformed, or changed, *into* chemical energy. **During a chemical change, chemical energy may be changed to other forms of energy. Other forms of energy may also be changed to chemical energy.**

One of the most important energy transformations on Earth that involves chemical energy is photosynthesis. During photosynthesis, plants transform electromagnetic energy from the sun into chemical energy as they make molecules of sugar. These plants, along with animals and other living things that eat plants, transform this chemical energy once again. It becomes the energy needed to carry out life activities. The carrots you have for dinner may supply the energy you need to go for a walk or read this book.

Reading Checkpoint **What type of energy transformation occurs during photosynthesis?**

FIGURE 24
Photosynthesis
Photosynthesis is a series of chemical changes in which plants convert electromagnetic energy from the sun into chemical energy.

Section 4 Assessment

Target Reading Skill Identifying Main Ideas Use your graphic organizer to help you answer Question 1 below.

Reviewing Key Concepts

1. a. Listing What are six forms of energy related to changes in matter?
   b. Classifying Which form of energy is represented by a book lying on a desk? Which form of energy is represented by a book falling off a desk?
   c. Making Generalizations What happens to energy when matter undergoes a chemical or physical change?
2. a. Reviewing What happens to chemical energy during a chemical change?
   b. Relating Cause and Effect What are the two main forms of energy given off when paper burns, and where does the energy come from?
   c. Sequencing Describe the energy changes that link sunshine to your ability to turn a page in this book.

Lab zone At-Home Activity

Tracking Energy Changes
Volunteer to help cook a meal for your family. As you work, point out energy transformations, especially those that involve chemical energy. Explain to a family member what chemical energy is and what other forms of energy it can be changed into. Talk about energy sources for cooking and other tools and appliances used to prepare food. Try to identify foods that change chemically when they are cooked.

Lab zone **Skills Lab**

Isolating Copper by Electrolysis

Problem

How can electrical energy be used to isolate copper metal?

Skills Focus

making models, inferring, observing, interpreting data

Materials

- glass jar, about 250 mL
- two metal paper clips • 6-volt battery
- index card
- wires with alligator clips or a battery holder with wires
- copper chloride solution (0.6 *M*), 100 mL

Procedure

1. Unbend a paper clip and make a hook shape as shown in the diagram. Push the long end through an index card until the hook just touches the card.
2. Repeat Step 1 with another paper clip so that the paper clips are about 3 cm apart. The paper clips serve as your electrodes.

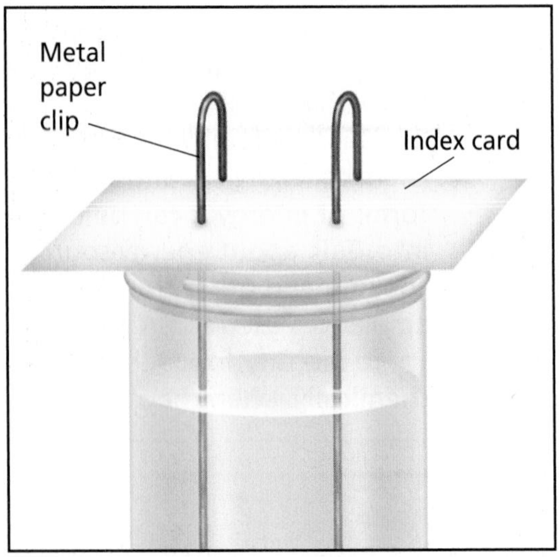

3. Pour enough copper chloride solution into a jar to cover at least half the length of the paper clips when the index card is set on top of the jar. **CAUTION:** *Copper chloride solution can be irritating to the skin and eyes. Do not touch it with your hands or get it into your mouth. The solution can stain skin and clothes.*
4. Place the index card on top of the jar. If the straightened ends of the paper clips are not at least half covered by the copper chloride solution, add more solution.
5. Attach a wire to one pole of a battery. Attach a second wire to the other pole. Attach each of the other ends of the wires to a separate paper clip, as shown in the diagram. Do not allow the paper clips to touch one another.
6. Predict what you think will happen if you allow the setup to run for 2 to 3 minutes. (*Hint:* What elements are present in the copper chloride solution?)
7. Let the setup run for 2 to 3 minutes or until you see a deposit forming on one of the electrodes. Also look for bubbles.
8. Disconnect the wires from both the battery and the paper clips. Bring your face close to the jar and gently wave your hand toward your nose. Note any odor.
9. Note whether the color of the solution has changed since you began the procedure.

10. Note the color of the ends of the electrodes.
11. Discard the solution as directed by your teacher, and wash your hands.

Analyze and Conclude

1. **Making Models** Make a labeled diagram of your laboratory setup. Indicate which electrode is connected to the positive (+) side of the battery and which is connected to the negative (–) side.
2. **Inferring** Based on your observations, what substances do you think were produced at the electrodes? On which electrode was each substance produced? Recall that one of the substances was a solid you could see and the other was a gas you could smell.
3. **Observing** Compare the properties of the substances produced to those of the copper chloride in solution.
4. **Interpreting Data** If the color of the solution changed, how can you explain the change?
5. **Inferring** Based on your observations, does electrolysis produce a chemical change? Explain your reasoning.
6. **Communicating** Write a paragraph describing what you think happened to the copper chloride solution as the electric current flowed through it.

Design an Experiment

What do you think would happen if you switched the connections to the battery without disturbing the rest of the equipment? Design an experiment to answer this question. *Obtain your teacher's permission before carrying out your investigation.*

Chapter 2 Study Guide

1 Describing Matter

Key Concepts

- Every form of matter has two kinds of properties—physical properties and chemical properties.
- Elements are the simplest substances.
- When elements are chemically combined, they form compounds having properties that are different from those of the uncombined elements.
- Each substance in a mixture keeps its individual properties. Also, the parts of a mixture are not combined in a set ratio.

Key Terms

matter
chemistry
substance
physical property
chemical property
element
atom
chemical bond
molecule
compound
chemical formula
mixture
heterogeneous mixture
homogeneous mixture
solution

2 Measuring Matter

Key Concepts

- Unlike weight, mass does not change with location, even when the force of gravity on an object changes.
- Common units of volume include the liter (L), milliliter (mL), and cubic centimeter (cm^3).
- Volume = Length × Width × Height
- You can determine the density of a sample of matter by dividing its mass by its volume.

$$\text{Density} = \frac{\text{Mass}}{\text{Volume}}$$

Key Terms

weight
mass
International System of Units
volume
density

3 Changes in Matter

Key Concepts

- A substance that undergoes a physical change is still the same substance after the change.
- Unlike a physical change, a chemical change produces new substances with properties different from those of the original substances.
- Every chemical or physical change in matter includes a change in energy.

Key Terms

physical change
chemical change
law of conservation of mass
energy
temperature
thermal energy
endothermic change
exothermic change

4 Energy and Matter

Key Concepts

- Forms of energy related to changes in matter include kinetic, potential, chemical, electromagnetic, electrical, and thermal energy.
- During a chemical change, chemical energy may be changed to other forms of energy. Other forms of energy may also be changed to chemical energy.

Key Terms

kinetic energy
potential energy
chemical energy
electromagnetic energy
electrical energy
electrode

Review and Assessment

Go Online
PHSchool.com
For: Self-Assessment
Visit: PHSchool.com
Web Code: cga-1010

Organizing Information

Concept Mapping Copy the concept map about matter onto a separate sheet of paper. Then complete the map by adding in the correct missing words or phrases. (For more on Concept Mapping, see the Skills Handbook.)

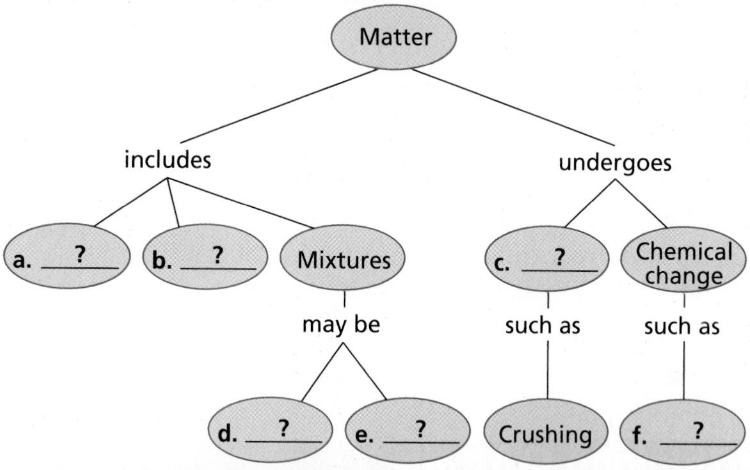

Reviewing Key Terms

Choose the letter of the best answer.

1. The ability to dissolve in water and to conduct electricity are examples of
   a. physical properties.
   b. chemical changes.
   c. chemical properties.
   d. chemical bonding.
2. Water is an example of
   a. an element.
   b. a homogeneous mixture.
   c. a compound.
   d. a heterogeneous mixture.
3. Density relates the mass of a material to the material's
   a. temperature. **b.** volume.
   c. weight. **d.** length.
4. New substances are always formed when matter undergoes a
   a. change in shape.
   b. physical change.
   c. change in temperature.
   d. chemical change.
5. Chemical energy is the potential energy of
   a. temperature.
   b. bonds between atoms.
   c. electricity.
   d. light.

If the statement is true, write *true*. If it is false, change the underlined word or words to make the statement true.

6. Energy is anything that has mass and takes up space.
7. A mixture is made of two or more elements that are chemically combined.
8. The weight of an object changes if the force of gravity changes.
9. Energy is taken in during an exothermic change.
10. Light is an example of electromagnetic energy.

Writing in Science

How-to Paragraph Suppose you are preparing for a long journey on the ocean or in space. Write a journal entry that describes your plan for having fresh, drinkable water throughout your entire trip.

Discovery Channel School
Introduction to Matter
Video Preview
Video Field Trip
▶ Video Assessment

Review and Assessment

Checking Concepts

11. What are three ways that compounds and mixtures differ?

12. What two quantities do you need to measure in order to determine the density of an object?

13. What can you infer about the density of a material if a sample of it floats in water?

14. How do you know that the burning of candle wax is an exothermic change?

15. What is kinetic energy? Give an example of a use of kinetic energy that you saw today.

Thinking Critically

16. **Classifying** Which of the following is a solution: pure water, clear lemon soda, cereal and milk in a bowl? Explain how you know.

17. **Making Judgments** Which measurement shown in the diagram is not needed to find the volume of the box? Explain.

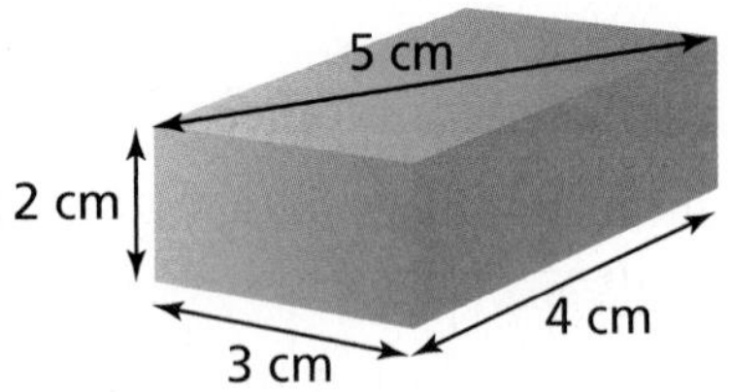

18. **Inferring** Ice has a lower density than liquid water. How does the volume of a kilogram of water change when it freezes to ice?

19. **Problem Solving** Suppose you dissolve some table salt in a glass of water. How could you prove to someone that the dissolving was a physical change, not a chemical change?

Math Practice

20. **Ratios** The elements phosphorus and oxygen form a compound with the formula P_2O_5. What is the ratio of phosphorus atoms to oxygen atoms in the compound?

21. **Calculating Density** A piece of magnesium metal has a mass of 56.5 g and a volume of 32.5 cm^3. What is the density of the magnesium?

Applying Skills

Use the information and the diagrams below to answer Questions 22–25. Some questions may have more than one answer.

Each diagram below represents a different kind of matter. Each ball represents an atom. Balls of the same color represent the same kind of atom.

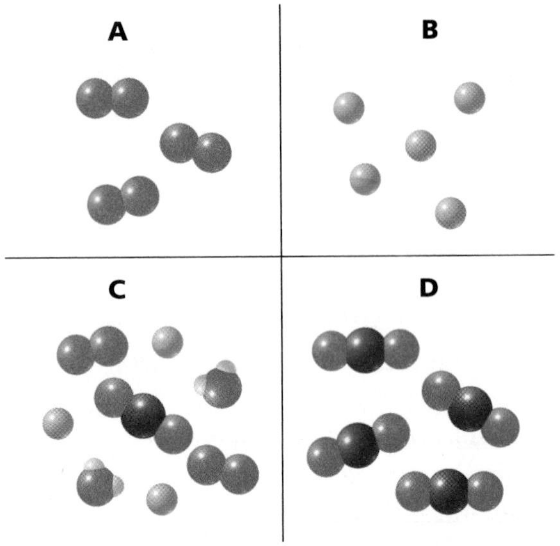

22. **Interpreting Diagrams** Which diagrams represent a single element? Explain.

23. **Classifying** Which diagrams represent pure substances? Explain.

24. **Interpreting Data** How do the molecules in diagram A differ from those in diagram D?

25. **Interpreting Diagrams** Which diagram represents a mixture? Explain.

Lab zone Chapter Project

Performance Assessment Present a brief summary of your experience with building your density-calculating system. Describe the most difficult part of construction. What steps were easiest? Defend the accuracy and reliability of your system, and describe its limitations.

Standardized Test Prep

Test-Taking Tip

Anticipating the Answer

You may be able to figure out the answer to a question before looking at the answer choices. After thinking of your own answer, compare it with the choices provided. Select the answer that most closely matches your own. This strategy can be especially useful for questions that test vocabulary. Try to answer the question below before looking at the answer choices.

Sample Question

Which two pieces of laboratory equipment would be most useful for measuring the mass and volume of a rectangular aluminum block?

A metric ruler and stopwatch
B balance and metric ruler
C thermometer and graduated cylinder
D balance and stopwatch

Answer

The correct answer is **B**. Mass is measured with a balance. The volume of a rectangular solid is found by multiplying length × width × height, which are measured with a metric ruler. Choices **A** and **D** each contain only one of the necessary pieces of equipment. A stopwatch measures time. In Choice **C**, the graduated cylinder measures volume, but a thermometer measures temperature, not mass.

Choose the letter of the best answer.

A scientist did an experiment, described by the words and symbols below, to demonstrate the law of conservation of mass. Use the information and your knowledge of science to answer Questions 1 to 2.

hydrogen + oxygen → water + energy

1. The scientist found that 2 grams of hydrogen reacted completely with 16 grams of oxygen. What was the total mass of water produced?

A 8 grams **B** 14 grams
C 18 grams **D** 32 grams

2. Which pair of terms best describes the type of change that occurred in the reaction?

F chemical and exothermic
G chemical and endothermic
H physical and exothermic
J physical and endothermic

3. What is the best title for the chart below?

?	
Helium	Colorless; less dense than air
Iron	Attracted to a magnet; melting point of 1,535°C
Oxygen	Odorless; gas at room temperature

A The Periodic Table of the Elements
B Gases Found in Air
C Chemical Properties of Some Compounds
D Physical Properties of Some Elements

4. Which diagram best represents a mixture of two kinds of gas molecules?

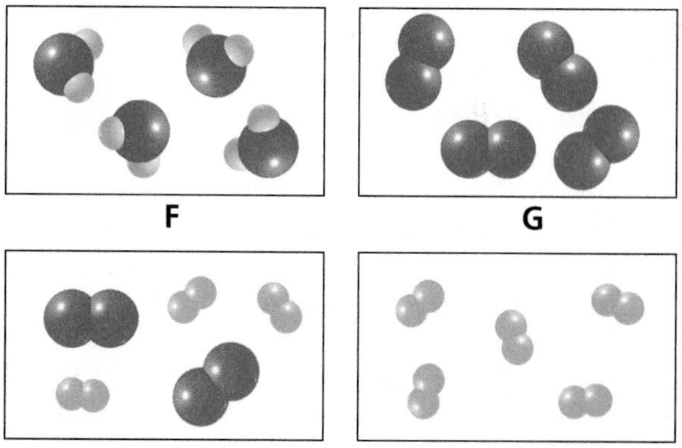

5. The density of a substance equals its mass divided by its volume. The density of sulfur is 2.0 g/cm^3. What is the mass of a sample of sulfur that has a volume of 6.0 cm^3?

A 3.0 g **B** 4.0 g
C 8.0 g **D** 12 g

Constructed Response

6. Describe three forms of energy related to changes in matter and provide an example of each.

Chapter 3

Solids, Liquids, and Gases

Chapter Preview

Interactive Textbook

This Japanese macaque soaks in a hot spring. In and around the spring, water exists as a liquid, solid, and gas.

Discovery Channel School

Solids, Liquids, and Gases

▶ Video Preview
Video Field Trip
Video Assessment

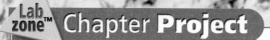

Lab zone™ Chapter Project

A Story of Changes in Matter

In this chapter, you will learn how particles of matter change from a solid to a liquid to a gas. As you read this chapter, you will build a model that shows these changes.

Your Goal To create a skit or cartoon that demonstrates how particles of matter behave as they change from a solid to a liquid to a gas and then from a gas to a liquid to a solid

To complete the project, you must

- describe what happens to the particles during each change of state
- outline your skit or cartoon in a storyboard format
- illustrate your cartoon or produce your skit

Plan It! With a group of classmates, brainstorm a list of the properties of solids, liquids, and gases. You'll be working on this project as you study this chapter. When you finish Section 2, describe the particles in solids, liquids, and gases, and begin preparing a storyboard. Add information when you finish Section 3, and complete your cartoon or skit at the end of the chapter. Finally, present your completed skit or cartoon to the class.

Section 1 States of Matter

Reading Preview

Key Concepts

- What are the characteristics of a solid?
- What are the characteristics of a liquid?
- What are the characteristics of a gas?

Key Terms

- solid • crystalline solid
- amorphous solid • liquid
- fluid • surface tension
- viscosity • gas

Target Reading Skill

Building Vocabulary A definition states the meaning of a word or phrase by telling about its most important feature or function. After you read the section, reread the paragraphs that contain definitions of Key Terms. Use all the information you have learned to write a definition of each Key Term in your own words.

Lab zone Discover Activity

What Are Solids, Liquids, and Gases?

1. Break an antacid tablet (fizzing type) into three or four pieces. Place them inside a large, uninflated balloon.
2. Fill a 1-liter plastic bottle about halfway with water. Stretch the mouth of the balloon over the top of the bottle, taking care to keep the tablet pieces inside the balloon.
3. Jiggle the balloon so that the pieces fall into the bottle. Observe what happens for about two minutes.
4. Remove the balloon and examine its contents.

Think It Over

Forming Operational Definitions Identify examples of the different states of matter—solids, liquids, and gases—that you observed in this activity. Define each of the three states in your own words.

It's a bitter cold January afternoon. You are practicing ice hockey moves on a frozen pond. Relaxing later, you close your eyes and recall the pond in July, when you and your friends jumped into the refreshing water on a scorching hot day. Was the water in July made of the same water you skated on this afternoon? Perhaps, but you're absolutely certain that solid water and liquid water do not look or feel the same. Just imagine trying to swim in an ice-covered pond in January or play hockey on liquid water in July!

FIGURE 1
A Wintry Solid
As a solid, water makes a great surface for ice hockey.
Observing *What useful property does the frozen water have here?*

Your everyday world is full of substances that can be classified as solids, liquids, or gases. (You will read about a less familiar form of matter, called plasma, in a later chapter.) Solids, liquids, and gases may be elements, compounds, or mixtures. Gold is an element. Water is a compound you've seen as both a solid and a liquid. Air is a mixture of gases. Although it's easy to list examples of these three states of matter, defining them is more difficult. To define solids, liquids, and gases, you need to examine their properties. The familiar states of matter are defined not by what they are made of but mainly by whether or not they hold their volume and shape.

Solids

What would happen if you were to pick up a solid object, such as a pen or a comb, and move it from place to place around the room? What would you observe? Would the object ever change in size or shape as you moved it? Would a pen become larger if you put it in a bowl? Would a comb become flatter if you placed it on a tabletop? Of course not. A **solid** has a definite shape and a definite volume. If your pen has a cylindrical shape and a volume of 6 cubic centimeters, then it will keep that shape and volume in any position and in any container.

FIGURE 2
Liquid Lava, Solid Rock
Hot, liquid lava flows from a volcano. When it cools to a solid, new rock will be formed.

FIGURE 3
Behavior of Solid Particles
Particles of a solid vibrate back and forth but stay in place.

Particles in a Solid The particles that make up a solid are packed very closely together. In addition, each particle is tightly fixed in one position. **This fixed, closely packed arrangement of particles causes a solid to have a definite shape and volume.**

Are the particles in a solid completely motionless? No, not really. The particles vibrate, meaning that they move back and forth slightly. This motion is similar to a group of people running in place. The particles that make up a solid stay in about the same position, but they vibrate in place.

Types of Solids In many solids, the particles form a regular, repeating pattern. These patterns create crystals. Solids that are made up of crystals are called **crystalline solids** (KRIS tuh lin). Salt, sugar, and snow are examples of crystalline solids. When a crystalline solid is heated, it melts at a specific temperature.

In **amorphous solids** (uh MAWR fus), the particles are not arranged in a regular pattern. Plastics, rubber, and glass are amorphous solids. Unlike a crystalline solid, an amorphous solid does not melt at a distinct temperature. Instead, it may become softer and softer or change into other substances.

Reading Checkpoint **How do crystalline and amorphous solids differ?**

FIGURE 4
Types of Solids
Solids are either crystalline or amorphous.

◀ Quartz is a crystalline solid. Its particles are arranged in a regular pattern.

◀ Butter is an amorphous solid. Its particles are not arranged in a regular pattern.

Liquids

A **liquid** has a definite volume but no shape of its own. Without a container, a liquid spreads into a wide, shallow puddle. Like a solid, however, a liquid does have a constant volume. If you gently tried to squeeze a water-filled plastic bag, for example, the water might change shape, but its volume would not decrease or increase. Suppose that you have 100 milliliters of milk in a pitcher. If you pour it into a tall glass, you still have 100 milliliters. The milk has the same volume no matter what shape its container has.

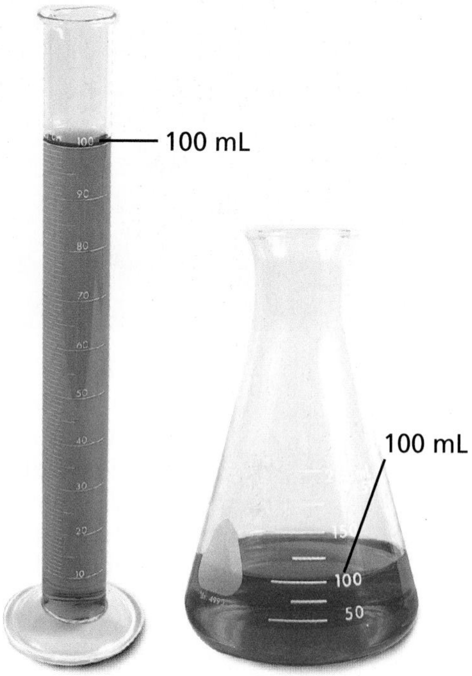

FIGURE 5
Equivalent Volumes
A liquid takes the shape of its container but its volume does not change.

Particles in a Liquid In general, the particles in a liquid are packed almost as closely as in a solid. However, the particles in a liquid move around one another freely. You can compare this movement to the way you might move a group of marbles around in your hand. In this comparison, the solid marbles serve as models for the particles of a liquid. The marbles slide around one another but stay in contact. **Because its particles are free to move, a liquid has no definite shape. However, it does have a definite volume.** These freely moving particles allow a liquid to flow from place to place. For this reason, a liquid is also called a **fluid,** meaning "a substance that flows."

FIGURE 6
Behavior of Liquid Particles
Particles in a liquid are packed close together but move freely, allowing liquids to flow.
Comparing and Contrasting *How are liquids and solids alike? How do they differ?*

FIGURE 7
Surface Tension
Water beads up on a leaf due to attractions between the water molecules. Surface tension in water is strong enough to support the weight of an insect.

Lab zone Try This **Activity**

As Thick as Honey

You can compare the viscosity of two liquids.

1. Place on a table a clear plastic jar almost filled with honey and another clear plastic jar almost filled with vegetable oil. Make sure that the tops of both jars are tightly closed.
2. Turn the jars upside down at the same time. Observe what happens.
3. Turn the two jars right-side up and again watch what happens.

Drawing Conclusions Which fluid has a greater viscosity? What evidence leads you to this conclusion?

Properties of Liquids One characteristic property of liquids is surface tension. **Surface tension** is the result of an inward pull among the molecules of a liquid that brings the molecules on the surface closer together. Perhaps you have noticed that water forms droplets and can bead up on many surfaces, such as the leaf shown in Figure 7. That's because water molecules attract one another strongly. These attractions cause molecules at the water's surface to be pulled slightly toward the water molecules beneath the surface.

Due to surface tension, the surface of water can act like a sort of skin. For example, a sewing needle floats when you place it gently on the surface of a glass of water, but it quickly sinks if you push it below the surface. Surface tension enables the water strider in Figure 7 to "walk" on the calm surface of a pond.

Another property of liquids is **viscosity** (vis KAHS uh tee)—a liquid's resistance to flowing. A liquid's viscosity depends on the size and shape of its particles and the attractions between the particles. Some liquids flow more easily than others. Liquids with high viscosity flow slowly. Honey is an example of a liquid with a particularly high viscosity. Liquids with low viscosity flow quickly. Water and vinegar have relatively low viscosities.

Reading Checkpoint **What property of liquids causes water to form droplets?**

Gases

Like a liquid, a gas is a fluid. Unlike a liquid, however, a **gas** can change volume very easily. If you put a gas in a closed container, the gas particles will either spread apart or be squeezed together as they fill that container. Take a deep breath. Your chest expands, and your lungs fill with air. Air is a mixture of gases that acts as one gas. When you breathe in, air moves from your mouth to your windpipe to your lungs. In each place, the air has a different shape. When you breathe out, the changes happen in reverse.

What about the volume of the air? If you could see the particles that make up a gas, you would see them moving in all directions. The particles are no longer limited by the space in your body, so they move throughout the room. **As they move, gas particles spread apart, filling all the space available. Thus, a gas has neither definite shape nor definite volume.** You will read more about the behavior of gases in Section 3.

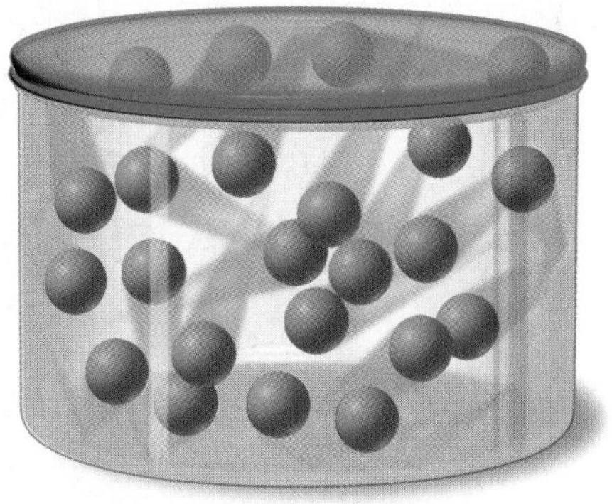

FIGURE 8
Modeling Gas Particles
The particles of a gas can be squeezed into a small volume.
Predicting *What will happen if the container lid is removed?*

Reading Checkpoint **How does breathing demonstrate that gases are fluids?**

Section 1 Assessment

Target Reading Skill

Building Vocabulary Use your definitions to help answer the questions below.

Reviewing Key Concepts

1. a. **Listing** What are the general characteristics of solids?

b. **Comparing and Contrasting** How do crystalline solids differ from amorphous solids?

c. **Drawing Conclusions** A glass blower can bend and shape a piece of glass that has been heated. Is glass a crystalline or an amorphous solid? Explain.

2. a. **Describing** How may liquids be described in terms of shape and volume?

b. **Explaining** How do the positions and movements of particles in a liquid help to explain the shape and volume of the liquid?

c. **Relating Cause and Effect** Explain why a sewing needle can float on the surface of water in a glass.

3. a. **Reviewing** What determines the shape and volume of a gas inside a container?

b. **Applying Concepts** Use what you know about the particles in a gas to explain why a gas has no definite shape and no definite volume.

Lab zone At-Home Activity

Squeezing Liquids and Gases Show your family how liquids and gases differ. Fill the bulb and cylinder of a turkey baster with water. Seal the end with your finger and hold it over the sink. Have a family member squeeze the bulb. Now empty the turkey baster. Again, seal the end with your finger and have a family member squeeze the bulb. Did the person notice any difference? Use what you know about liquids and gases to explain your observations.

Section 2

Changes of State

Reading Preview

Key Concepts

- What happens to a substance during changes between solid and liquid?
- What happens to a substance during changes between liquid and gas?
- What happens to a substance during changes between solid and gas?

Key Terms

- melting
- melting point
- freezing
- vaporization
- evaporation
- boiling
- boiling point
- condensation
- sublimation

Target Reading Skill

Outlining As you read, make an outline about changes of state. Use the red headings for the main ideas and the blue headings for the supporting ideas.

Changes in State

I. Changes Between Solid and Liquid
   A. Melting
   B.
II. Changes Between Liquid and Gas

Lab zone Discover Activity

What Happens When You Breathe on a Mirror?

1. Obtain a hand mirror. Clean it with a dry cloth. Describe the mirror's surface.
2. Hold the mirror about 15 cm away from your face. Try to breathe against the mirror's surface.
3. Reduce the distance until breathing on the mirror produces a visible change. Record what you observe.

Think It Over

Developing Hypotheses What did you observe when you breathed on the mirror held close to your mouth? How can you explain that observation? Why did you get different results when the mirror was at greater distances from your face?

Picture an ice cream cone on a hot summer day. The ice cream quickly starts to drip onto your hand. You're not surprised. You know that ice cream melts if it's not kept cold. But why does the ice cream melt?

Particles of a substance at a warmer temperature have more thermal energy than particles of that same substance at a cooler temperature. You may recall that thermal energy always flows as heat from a warmer substance to a cooler substance. So, when you take ice cream outside on a hot summer day, it absorbs thermal energy from the air and your hand. The added energy changes the ice cream from a solid to a liquid.

Increased thermal energy turns an ice cream cone into a gooey mess! ▶

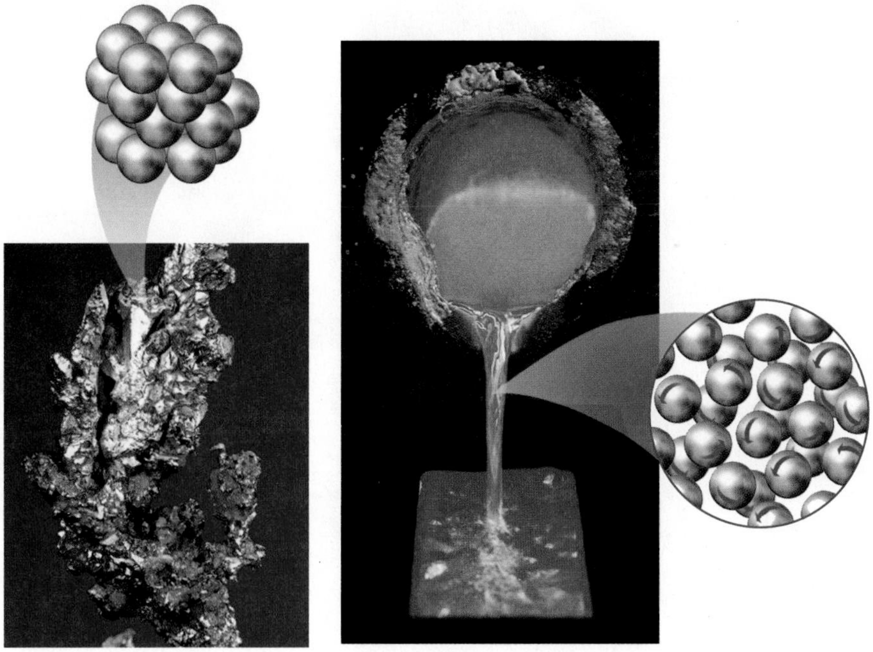

Solid silver

Liquid silver

FIGURE 9
Solid to Liquid
In solid silver, atoms are in a regular, cubic pattern. Atoms in liquid (molten) silver have no regular arrangement.
Applying Concepts *How can a jewelry maker take advantage of changes in the state of silver?*

Changes Between Solid and Liquid

How does the physical state of a substance relate to its thermal energy? Particles of a liquid have more thermal energy than particles of the same substance in solid form. As a gas, the particles of this same substance have even more thermal energy. A substance changes state when its thermal energy increases or decreases sufficiently. A change from solid to liquid involves an increase in thermal energy. As you can guess, a change from liquid to solid is just the opposite: It involves a decrease in thermal energy.

Melting The change in state from a solid to a liquid is called **melting.** In most pure substances, melting occurs at a specific temperature, called the **melting point.** Because melting point is a characteristic property of a substance, chemists often compare melting points when trying to identify an unknown material. The melting point of pure water, for example, is 0°C.

What happens to the particles of a substance as it melts? Think of an ice cube taken from the freezer. The energy to melt the ice comes mostly from the air in the room. At first, the added thermal energy makes the water molecules vibrate faster, raising their temperature. **At its melting point, the particles of a solid substance are vibrating so fast that they break free from their fixed positions.** At 0°C, the temperature of the ice stops increasing. Any added energy continues to change the arrangement of the water molecules from ice crystals into liquid water. The ice melts.

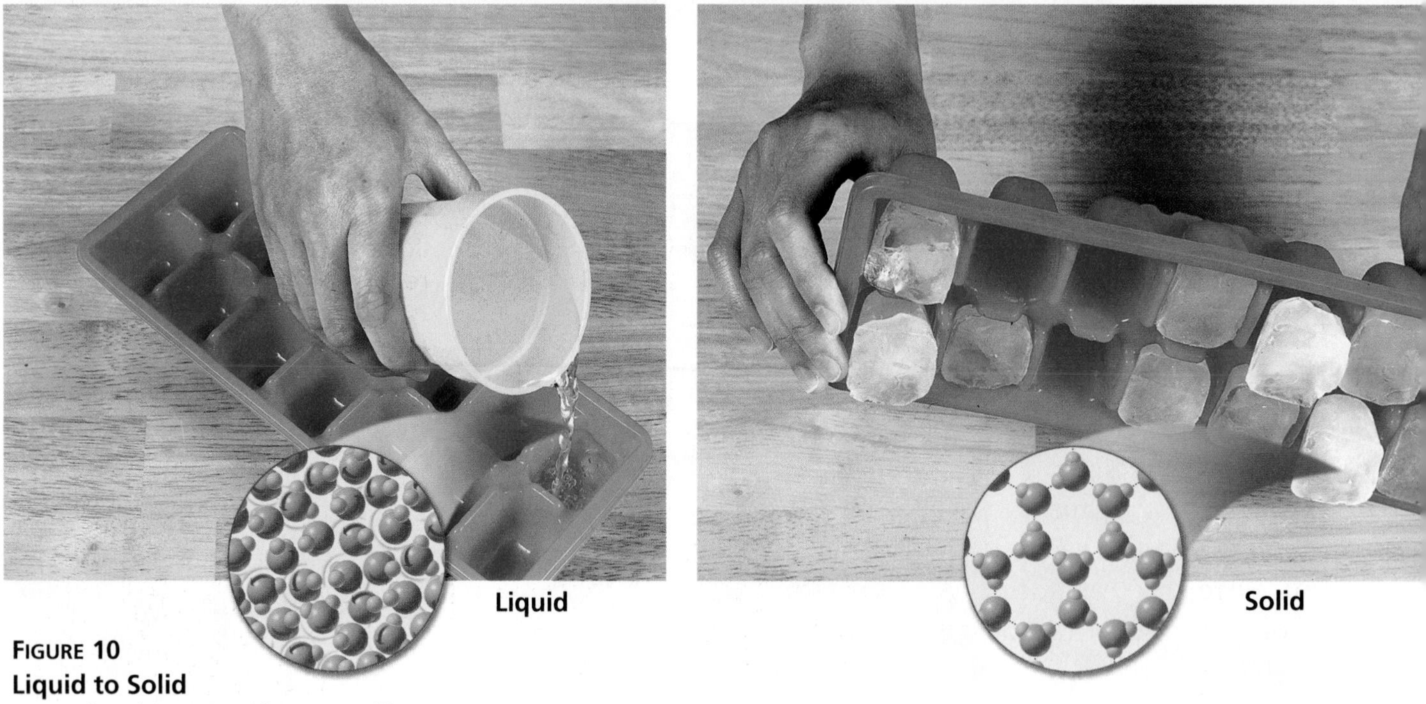

FIGURE 10
Liquid to Solid
Just a few hours in a freezer will change liquid water into a solid.

Freezing The change of state from liquid to solid is called **freezing.** It is just the reverse of melting. **At its freezing temperature, the particles of a liquid are moving so slowly that they begin to form regular patterns.**

When you put liquid water into a freezer, for example, the water loses energy to the cold air in the freezer. The water molecules move more and more slowly as they lose energy. Over time, the water becomes solid ice. When water begins to freeze, its temperature remains at 0°C until freezing is complete. The freezing point of water, 0°C, is the same as its melting point.

Reading Checkpoint **What happens to the particles of a liquid as they lose more and more energy?**

Changes Between Liquid and Gas

Have you ever wondered how clouds form, or why rain falls from clouds? And why do puddles dry up after a rain shower? To answer these questions, you need to look at what happens when changes occur between the liquid and gas states.

The change from a liquid to a gas is called **vaporization** (vay puhr ih ZAY shun). **Vaporization takes place when the particles in a liquid gain enough energy to form a gas.** There are two main types of vaporization—evaporation and boiling.

Evaporation Vaporization that takes place only on the surface of a liquid is called **evaporation** (ee vap uh RAY shun). A shrinking puddle is an example. Water in the puddle gains energy from the ground, the air, or the sun. The added energy enables some of the water molecules on the surface of the puddle to escape into the air, or evaporate.

Lab zone Try This Activity

Keeping Cool

1. Wrap the bulbs of two alcohol thermometers with equal amounts of gauze.
2. Lay the thermometers on a paper towel on a table.
3. Use a medicine dropper to put 10 drops of water on the gauze surrounding the bulb of one thermometer.
4. Using rubbing alcohol rather than water, repeat step 3 with the second thermometer.
5. Read the temperatures on the two thermometers for several minutes.

Interpreting Data Which liquid evaporates faster? Explain your answer.

Boiling Another kind of vaporization is called boiling. **Boiling** occurs when a liquid changes to a gas below its surface as well as at the surface. You see the results of this process when the boiling liquid bubbles. The temperature at which a liquid boils is called its **boiling point.** As with melting points, chemists use boiling points to help identify an unknown substance.

Boiling Point and Air Pressure The boiling point of a substance depends on the pressure of the air above it. The lower the pressure, the less energy needed for the particles of the liquid to escape into the air. In places close to sea level, the boiling point of water is 100°C. In the mountains, however, air pressure is lower and so is water's boiling point. In Denver, Colorado, where the elevation is 1,600 meters above sea level, water boils at 95°C.

FIGURE 11
Evaporation and Boiling
Liquids can vaporize in two ways. Interpreting Diagrams *How do these processes differ?*

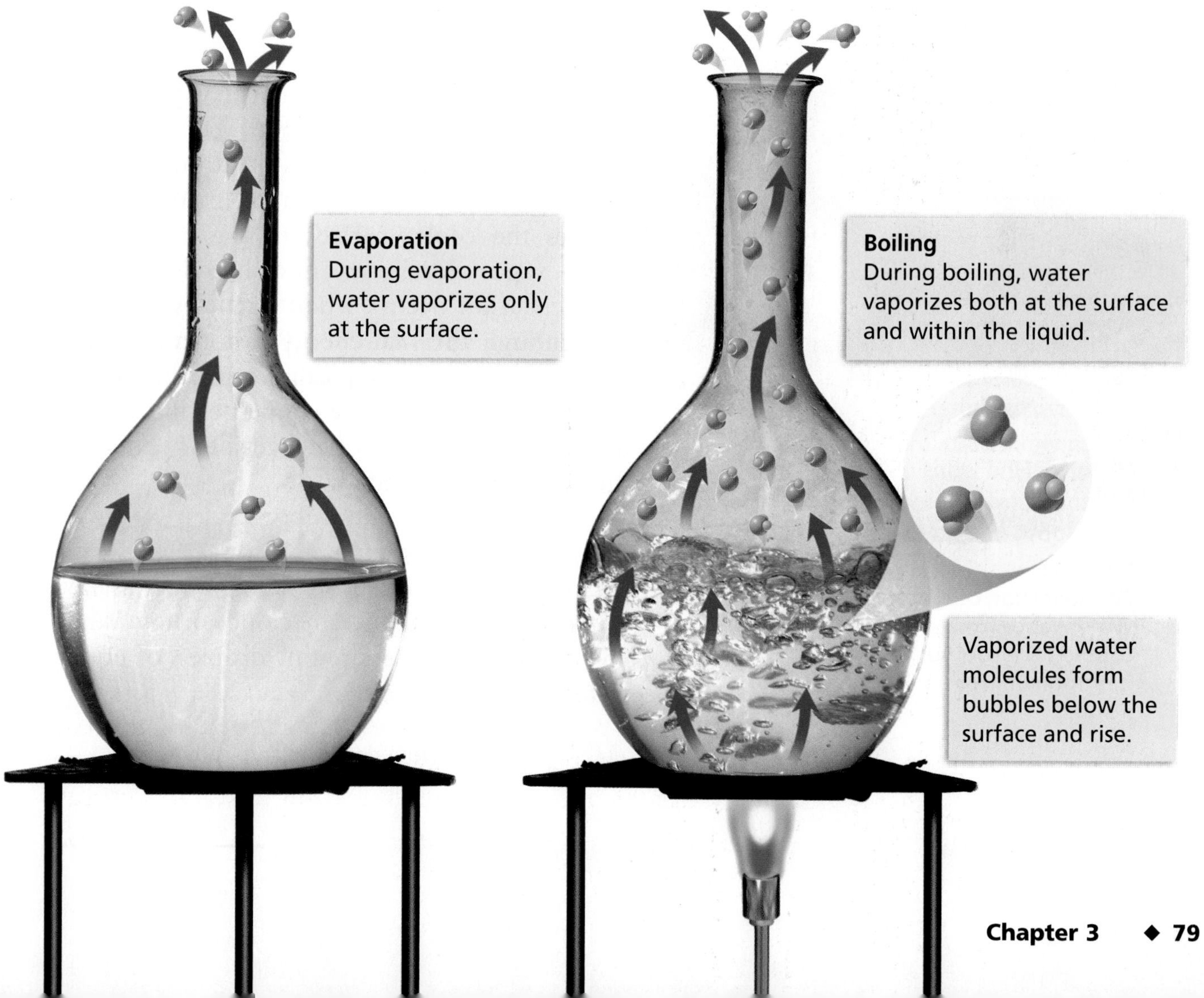

Evaporation
During evaporation, water vaporizes only at the surface.
Boiling
During boiling, water vaporizes both at the surface and within the liquid.
Vaporized water molecules form bubbles below the surface and rise.

Math Analyzing Data

Temperature and Changes of State

A beaker of ice at −10°C was slowly heated to 110°C. The changes in the temperature of the water over time were recorded. The data were plotted on the graph shown here.

1. **Reading Graphs** What two variables are plotted on the graph?
2. **Reading Graphs** What is happening to the temperature of the water during segment C of the graph?
3. **Interpreting Data** What does the temperature value for segment B represent? For segment D?
4. **Drawing Conclusions** What change of state is occurring during segment B of the graph? During segment D?

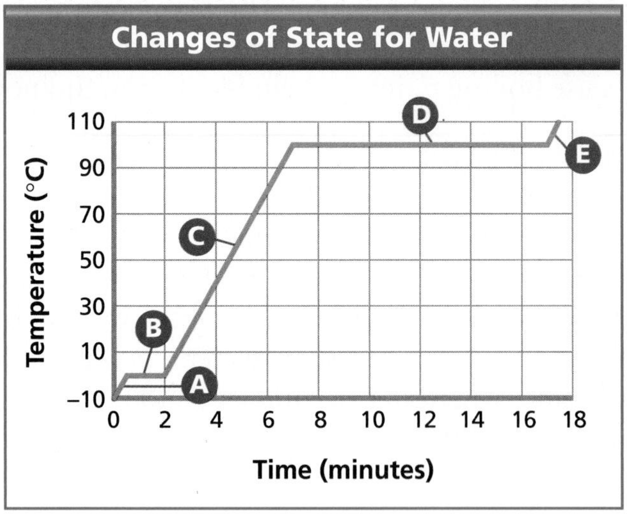

5. **Inferring** In which segment, A or E, do the water molecules have more thermal energy? Explain your reasoning.

FIGURE 12
Condensation of Water
Water vapor from a hot shower contacts the cool surface of a bathroom mirror and condenses into a liquid.

Condensation The opposite of vaporization is called **condensation.** One way you can observe condensation is by breathing onto a mirror. When warm water vapor in your breath reaches the cooler surface of the mirror, the water vapor condenses into liquid droplets. **Condensation occurs when particles in a gas lose enough thermal energy to form a liquid.** For example, clouds typically form when water vapor in the atmosphere condenses into liquid droplets. When the droplets get heavy enough, they fall to the ground as rain.

You cannot see water vapor. Water vapor is a colorless gas that is impossible to see. The steam you see above a kettle of boiling water is not water vapor, and neither are clouds or fog. What you see in those cases are tiny droplets of liquid water suspended in air.

Reading Checkpoint **How do clouds typically form?**

Changes Between Solid and Gas

If you live where the winters are cold, you may have noticed that snow seems to disappear even when the temperature stays well below freezing. This change is the result of sublimation. **Sublimation** occurs when the surface particles of a solid gain enough energy that they form a gas. **During sublimation, particles of a solid do not pass through the liquid state as they form a gas.**

One example of sublimation occurs with dry ice. Dry ice is the common name for solid carbon dioxide. At ordinary atmospheric pressures, carbon dioxide cannot exist as a liquid. So instead of melting, solid carbon dioxide changes directly into a gas. As it changes state, the carbon dioxide absorbs thermal energy. This property helps keep materials near dry ice cold and dry. For this reason, using dry ice is a way to keep temperature low when a refrigerator is not available. When dry ice becomes a gas, it cools water vapor in the nearby air. The water vapor then condenses into a liquid, forming fog around the dry ice.

FIGURE 13
Dry Ice
When solid carbon dioxide, called "dry ice," sublimates, it changes directly into a gas. **Predicting** *If you allowed the dry ice to stand at room temperature for several hours, what would be left in the glass dish? Explain.*

Reading Checkpoint **What physical state is skipped during the sublimation of a substance?**

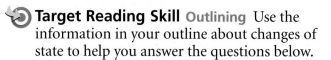

Section 2 Assessment

Target Reading Skill **Outlining** Use the information in your outline about changes of state to help you answer the questions below.

Reviewing Key Concepts

1. a. **Reviewing** What happens to the particles of a solid as it becomes a liquid?
   b. **Applying Concepts** How does the thermal energy of solid water change as it melts?
   c. **Making Judgments** You are stranded in a blizzard. You need water to drink, and you're trying to stay warm. Should you melt snow and then drink it, or just eat snow? Explain.
2. a. **Describing** What is vaporization?
   b. **Comparing and Contrasting** Name the two types of vaporization. Tell how they are similar and how they differ.
   c. **Relating Cause and Effect** Why does the evaporation of sweat cool your body on a warm day?
3. a. **Identifying** What process occurs as pieces of dry ice gradually get smaller?
   b. **Interpreting Photos** What is the fog you see in the air around the dry ice in Figure 13? Why does the fog form?

Writing in Science

Using Analogies Write a short essay in which you create an analogy to describe particle motion. Compare the movements and positions of people dancing with the motions of water molecules in liquid water and in water vapor.

Lab zone **Skills Lab**

Go Online
PHSchool.com
For: Data sharing
Visit: PHSchool.com
Web Code: cgd-1022

Melting Ice

Problem

How does the temperature of the surroundings affect the rate at which ice melts?

Skills Focus

predicting, interpreting data, inferring

Materials

- stopwatch or timer
- thermometer or temperature probe
- 2 plastic cups, about 200 mL each
- 2 stirring rods, preferably plastic
- ice cubes, about 2 cm on each side
- warm water, about 40°C–45°C
- water at room temperature, about 20°C–25°C

Procedure

1. Read Steps 1–8. Based on your own experience, predict which ice cube will melt faster.
2. In your notebook, make a data table like the one below.
3. Fill a cup halfway with warm water (about 40°C to 45°C). Fill a second cup to the same depth with water at room temperature.
4. Record the exact temperature of the water in each cup. If you are using a temperature probe, see your teacher for instructions.
5. Obtain two ice cubes that are as close to the same size as possible.
6. Place one ice cube in each cup. Begin timing with a stopwatch. Gently stir each cup with a stirring rod until the ice has completely melted.
7. Observe both ice cubes carefully. At the moment one of the ice cubes is completely melted, record the time and the temperature of the water in the cup.
8. Wait for the second ice cube to melt. Record its melting time and the water temperature.

Data Table

Cup	Beginning Temperature (°C)	Time to Melt (s)	Final Temperature (°C)
1			
2			

Analyze and Conclude

1. **Predicting** Was your prediction in Step 1 supported by the results of the experiment? Explain why or why not.
2. **Interpreting Data** In which cup did the water temperature change the most? Explain.
3. **Inferring** When the ice melted, its molecules gained enough energy to overcome the forces holding them together as solid ice. What is the source of that energy?
4. **Communicating** Write a paragraph describing how errors in measurement could have affected your conclusions in this experiment. Tell what you would do differently if you repeated the procedure. (*Hint*: How well were you able to time the exact moment that each ice cube completely melted?)

Design an Experiment

When a lake freezes in winter, only the top turns to ice. Design an experiment to model the melting of a frozen lake during the spring. *Obtain your teacher's permission before carrying out your investigation.* Be prepared to share your results with the class.

Section 3

Gas Behavior

Reading Preview

Key Concepts

- What types of measurements are useful when working with gases?
- How are the volume, temperature, and pressure of a gas related?

Key Terms

- pressure
- Boyle's law
- Charles's law

Target Reading Skill

Asking Questions Before you read, preview the red headings. In a graphic organizer like the one below, ask a *what* or *how* question for each heading. As you read, write the answers to your questions.

Gases

Question	Answer
What measurements are useful in studying gases?	Measurements useful in studying gases include . . .

Lab zone **Discover Activity**

How Can Air Keep Chalk From Breaking?

1. Stand on a chair and drop a piece of chalk onto a hard floor. Observe what happens to the chalk.
2. Wrap a second piece of chalk in wax paper or plastic food wrap. Drop the chalk from the same height used in Step 1. Observe the results.
3. Wrap a third piece of chalk in plastic bubble wrap. Drop the chalk from the same height used in Step 1. Observe the results.

Think It Over

Inferring Compare the results from Steps 1, 2, and 3. What properties of the air in the bubble wrap accounted for the results in Step 3?

How do you prepare a hot-air balloon for a morning ride? First, you inflate the balloon, using powerful air fans. Then you heat the air inside with propane gas burners. But the balloon and its cargo won't begin to rise until the warmer air inside is less dense than the air outside the balloon. How does this change occur? How can you keep the balloon floating safely through the atmosphere? How can you make it descend when you are ready to land? To answer these and other questions, you would need to understand the relationships between the temperature, pressure, and volume of a gas.

Before a flight, a hot-air balloon is filled with air. ▶

Measuring Gases

How much helium is in the tank in Figure 14? If you don't know the mass of the helium, you may think that measuring the volume of the tank will give you an answer. But gases easily contract or expand. To fill the tank, helium was compressed—or pressed together tightly—to decrease its volume. When you use the helium to fill balloons, it fills a total volume of inflated balloons much greater than the volume of the tank. The actual volume of helium you get, however, depends on the temperature and air pressure that day. **When working with a gas, it is helpful to know its volume, temperature, and pressure.** So what exactly do these measurements mean?

Volume You know that volume is the amount of space that matter fills. Volume is measured in cubic centimeters (cm^3), milliliters (mL), liters (L), and other units. Because gas particles move and fill the space available, the volume of a gas is the same as the volume of its container.

Temperature Hot soup, warm hands, cool breezes—you are familiar with matter at different temperatures. But what does temperature tell you? Recall that the particles within any substance are constantly moving. Temperature is a measure of the average energy of random motion of the particles of a substance. The faster the particles are moving, the greater their energy and the higher the temperature. You might think of a thermometer as a speedometer for molecules.

Even at ordinary temperatures, the average speed of particles in a gas is very fast. At room temperature, or about 20°C, the particles in a typical gas travel about 500 meters per second—more than twice the cruising speed of a jet plane!

FIGURE 14
How Much Helium?
A helium tank the height of this girl can fill over 500 balloons!
Interpreting Photos *How is the helium in the tank different from the helium in the balloons?*

Pressure Gas particles constantly collide with one another and with the walls of their container. As a result, the gas pushes on the walls of the container. The **pressure** of the gas is the force of its outward push divided by the area of the walls of the container. Pressure is measured in units of pascals (Pa) or kilopascals (kPa). (1 kPa = 1,000 Pa.)

$$\text{Pressure} = \frac{\text{Force}}{\text{Area}}$$

The firmness of a gas-filled object comes from the pressure of the gas. For example, the air inside a fully pumped basketball has a higher pressure than the air outside. This higher pressure is due to a greater concentration of gas particles inside the ball than in the surrounding air. (Concentration is the number of particles in a given unit of volume.)

When air leaks out of a basketball, the pressure decreases and the ball becomes softer. Why does a ball leak even when it has a tiny hole? The higher pressure inside the ball results in gas particles hitting the inner surface of the ball more often. Therefore, gas particles inside the ball reach the hole and escape more often than gas particles outside the ball reach the hole and enter. Thus, many more particles go out than in. The pressure inside drops until it is equal to the pressure outside.

Reading Checkpoint **What units are used to measure pressure?**

Math Skills

Using Formulas

Pressure can be calculated using the formula below. Force is measured in newtons (N). If area is measured in square meters (m^2), pressure is expressed in pascals (Pa).

$$\text{Pressure} = \frac{\text{Force}}{\text{Area}}$$

For example, a machine exerts a force of 252 N on a piston having an area of 0.430 m^2. What is the pressure on the piston in Pa?

$$\text{Pressure} = \frac{252 \text{ N}}{0.430 \text{ m}^2}$$

$$= 586 \text{ Pa}$$

Practice Problem A trash compactor exerts a force of 5,600 N over an area of 0.342 m^2. What pressure does the compactor exert in Pa?

FIGURE 15

A Change in Pressure

A punctured basketball deflates as the gas particles begin to escape.

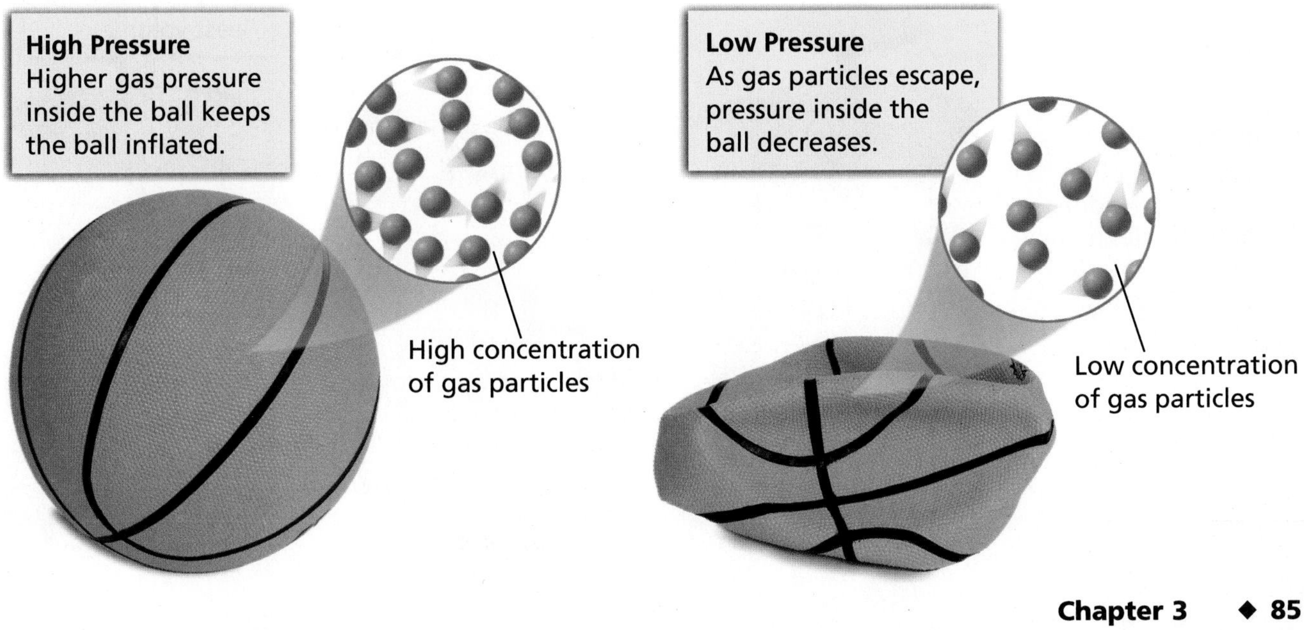
High Pressure
Higher gas pressure inside the ball keeps the ball inflated.
High concentration of gas particles
Low Pressure
As gas particles escape, pressure inside the ball decreases.
Low concentration of gas particles

FIGURE 16
Inflating a Tire
A bicycle pump makes use of the relationship between the volume and pressure of a gas.

Pressure and Volume

Suppose you are using a bicycle pump. By pressing down on the plunger, you force the gas inside the pump through the rubber tube and out the nozzle into the tire. What will happen if you close the nozzle and then push down on the plunger?

Boyle's Law The answer to this question comes from experiments done by the scientist Robert Boyle in an effort to improve air pumps. In the 1600s, Boyle measured the volumes of gases at different pressures. **Boyle found that when the pressure of a gas at constant temperature is increased, the volume of the gas decreases. When the pressure is decreased, the volume increases.** This relationship between the pressure and the volume of a gas is called **Boyle's law.**

Boyle's Law in Action Boyle's law plays a role in research using high-altitude balloons. Researchers fill the balloons with only a small fraction of the helium gas that the balloons can hold. As a balloon rises through the atmosphere, the air pressure around it decreases and the balloon expands. If the balloon were fully filled at takeoff, it would burst before it got very high.

Boyle's law also applies to situations in which the *volume* of a gas is changed. Then the *pressure* changes in the opposite way. A bicycle pump works this way. As you push on the plunger, the volume of air inside the pump cylinder gets smaller and the pressure increases, forcing air into the tire.

Reading Checkpoint **What could cause a helium balloon to burst as it rises in the atmosphere?**

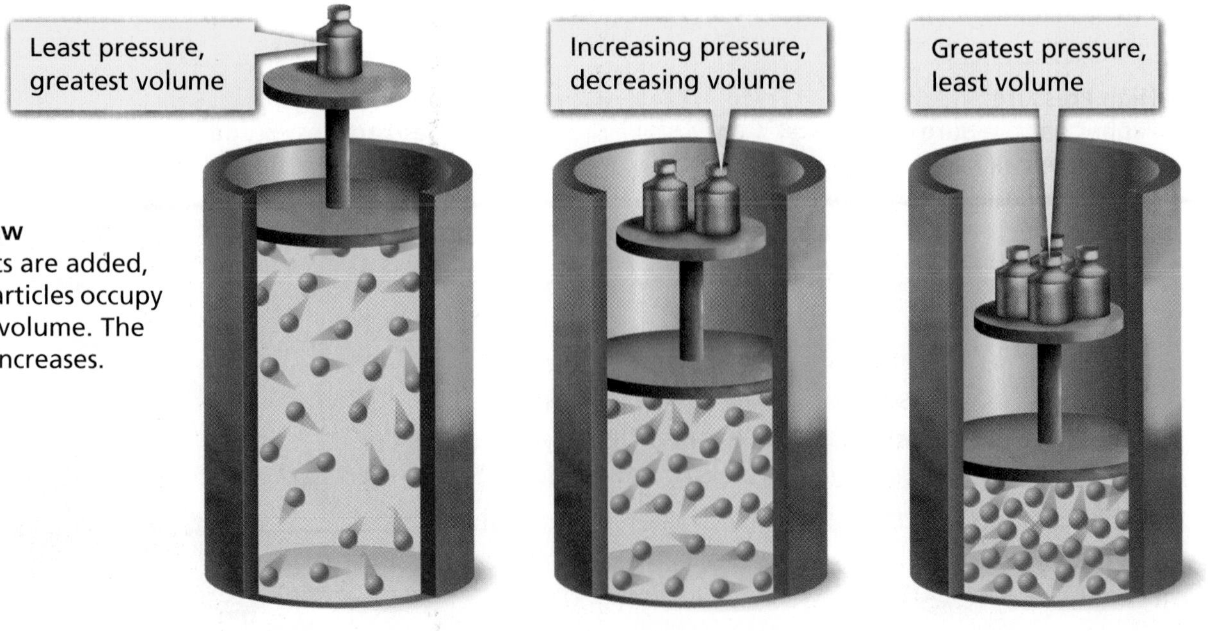

FIGURE 17
Boyle's Law
As weights are added, the gas particles occupy a smaller volume. The pressure increases.

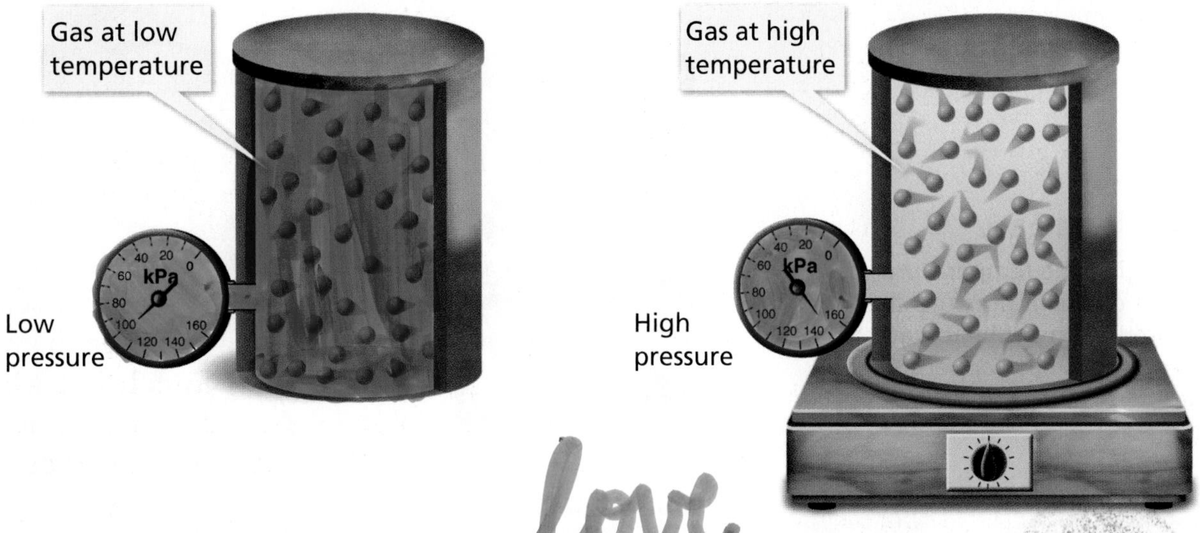

FIGURE 18
Gas Pressure and Temperature
When a gas is heated, the particles move faster and collide more with each other and with the walls of their container. The pressure of the gas increases.

Pressure and Temperature

If you dropped a few grains of sand onto your hand, you would hardly feel them. But what if you were caught in a sandstorm? Ouch! The sand grains fly around very fast, and they would sting if they hit you. The faster the grains travel, the harder they hit your skin.

Although gas particles are much smaller than sand grains, a sandstorm is a good model for gas behavior. Like grains of sand in a sandstorm, gas particles travel individually and at high speeds (but randomly). The faster the gas particles move, the more frequently they collide with the walls of their container and the greater the force of the collisions.

Increasing Temperature Raises Pressure Recall from Section 2 that the higher the temperature of a substance, the faster its particles are moving. Now you can state a relationship between temperature and pressure. **When the temperature of a gas at constant volume is increased, the pressure of the gas increases. When the temperature is decreased, the pressure of the gas decreases.** (*Constant volume* means that the gas is in a closed, rigid container.)

Pressure and Temperature in Action Have you ever looked at the tires of an 18-wheel truck? Because the tires need to support a lot of weight, they are large, heavy, and stiff. The inside volume of these tires doesn't vary much. On long trips, especially in the summer, a truck's tires can become very hot. As the temperature increases, so does the pressure of the air inside the tire. If the pressure becomes greater than the tire can hold, the tire will burst. For this reason, truck drivers need to monitor and adjust tire pressure on long trips.

Go Online
active art
For: Gas Laws activity
Visit: PHSchool.com
Web Code: cgp-1023

Discovery Channel School
Solids, Liquids, and Gases
Video Preview
Video Field Trip
Video Assessment

FIGURE 19

Charles's Law

Changing the temperature of a gas at constant pressure changes its volume in a similar way.

Inferring *What happens to the gas particles in the balloon as the gas is warmed?*

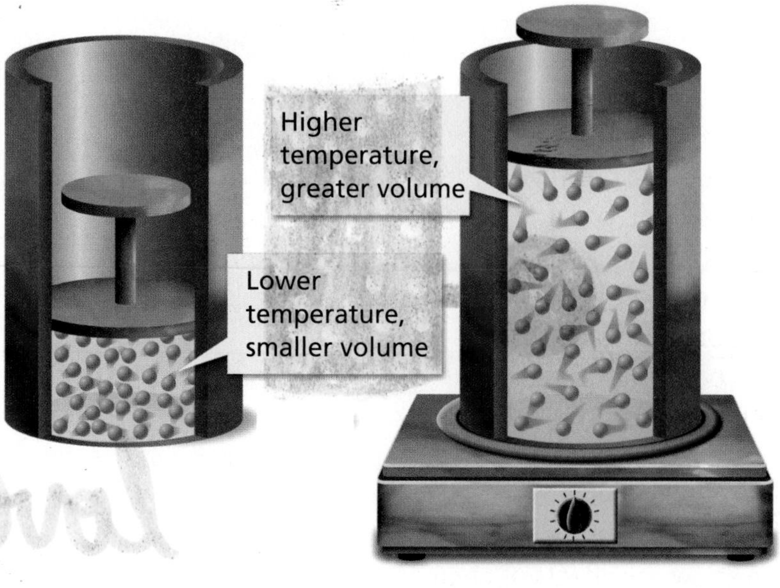

▲ A gas-filled balloon is at room temperature.

▲ The balloon is lowered into liquid nitrogen at −196°C.

▲ The balloon shrinks as gas volume decreases.

Volume and Temperature

In the late 1700s, French scientist Jacques Charles helped start a new sport. He and others took to the skies in the first hydrogen balloons. Charles's interest in balloon rides led him to discover how gas temperature and volume are related.

Charles's Law Jacques Charles examined the relationship between the temperature and volume of a gas that is kept at a constant pressure. He measured the volume of a gas at various temperatures in a container that could change volume. (A changeable volume allows the pressure to remain constant.) **Charles found that when the temperature of a gas is increased at constant pressure, its volume increases. When the temperature of a gas is decreased at constant pressure, its volume decreases.** This principle is called **Charles's law.**

Charles's Law in Action In Figure 19, you can see the effects of Charles's law demonstrated with a simple party balloon. Time-lapse photos show a balloon as it is slowly lowered into liquid nitrogen at nearly −200°C, then removed. The changes to the balloon's volume result from changes in the temperature of the air inside the balloon. The pressure remains more or less constant because the air is in a flexible container.

▲ When removed from the nitrogen, the gas warms and the balloon expands.

▲ The balloon is at room temperature again.

Now think again about a hot-air balloon. Heating causes the air inside the balloon to expand. Some of the warm air leaves through the bottom opening of the balloon, keeping the pressure constant. But now, the air inside is less dense than the air outside the balloon, so the balloon begins to rise. If the pilot allows the air in the balloon to cool, the reverse happens. The air in the balloon contracts, and more air enters through the opening. The density of the air inside increases, and the balloon starts downward.

Boyle, Charles, and others often described the behavior of gases by focusing on only two factors that vary at a time. In everyday life, however, gases can show the effects of changes in pressure, temperature, and volume all at once. People who work with gases, such as tire manufacturers and balloonists, must consider these combined effects.

Reading Checkpoint **What factor is kept unchanged when demonstrating Charles's law?**

FIGURE 20
Hot-Air Balloon
Balloonists often use a propane burner to heat the air in a balloon.

Section 3 Assessment

Target Reading Skill **Asking Questions** Use the answers to the questions you wrote about the headings to help you answer the questions below.

Reviewing Key Concepts

1. a. Defining How is gas pressure defined?

b. Describing Describe how the motions of gas particles are related to the pressure exerted by the gas.

c. Relating Cause and Effect Why does pumping more air into a basketball increase the pressure inside the ball?

2. a. Reviewing How does Boyle's law describe the relationship between gas pressure and volume?

b. Explaining Explain why increasing the temperature of a gas in a closed, rigid container causes the pressure in the container to increase.

c. Applying Concepts Suppose it is the night before a big parade, and you are in charge of inflating the parade balloons. You just learned that the temperature will rise 15°C between early morning and the time the parade starts. How will this information affect the way you inflate the balloons?

Math Practice

3. Using Formulas Suppose the atmosphere exerts a force of 124,500 N on a kitchen table with an area of 1.5 m^2. What is the pressure in pascals of the atmosphere on the table?

Section 4

Integrating Mathematics

Graphing Gas Behavior

Reading Preview

Key Concepts

- What type of relationship does the graph for Charles's law show?
- What type of relationship does the graph for Boyle's law show?

Key Terms

- graph
- origin
- directly proportional
- vary inversely

Target Reading Skill

Previewing Visuals Before you read, preview Figure 23. In a graphic organizer like the one below, write questions that you have about the diagram. As you read, answer your questions.

Graphing Charles's Law

Q. What is the relationship between gas volume and temperature?

A.

Q.

Lab zone Discover Activity

Can You Graph Gas Behavior?

Temperature (°C)	Pressure (kPa)
0	8
5	11
10	14
15	17
20	20
25	23

1. In an experiment, the temperature of a gas at a constant volume was varied. Gas pressure was measured after each 5°C change. Use the data in this table and follow Steps 2–4 to make a graph.
2. Show temperature on the horizontal axis with a scale from 0°C to 25°C. Show pressure on the vertical axis with a scale from 0 kPa to 25 kPa. (1 kPa = 1,000 Pa.)
3. For each pair of measurements, draw a point on the graph.
4. Draw a line to connect the points.

Think It Over

Drawing Conclusions What happens to the pressure of a gas when the temperature is increased at constant volume?

Graphs are a way to tell a story with data. A **graph** is a diagram that tells how two variables, or factors that change, are related. If you did the activity above, you made a graph that helped you understand how the pressure of a gas changes when its temperature is changed. In this section, you will learn how to make and interpret graphs that relate these and other properties of gases.

A graph consists of a grid set up by two lines, one horizontal and one vertical. Each line, or axis, is divided into equal units. The horizontal axis, or *x*-axis, shows the manipulated variable. The vertical axis, or *y*-axis, shows the responding variable. Each axis is labeled with the name of the variable, the unit of measurement, and a range of values.

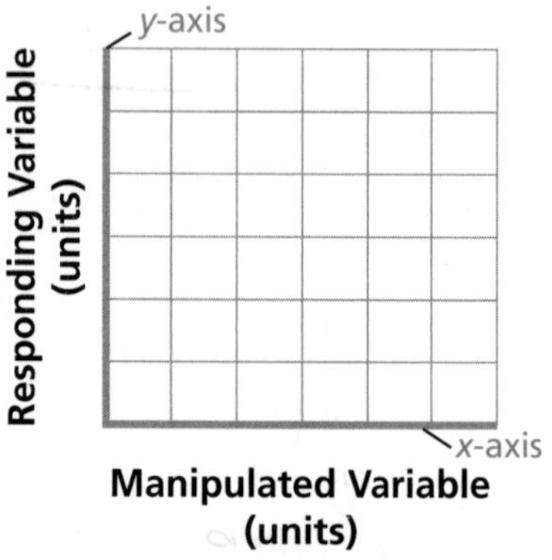

FIGURE 21
Making a Graph
The *x*-axis (horizontal) and the *y*-axis (vertical) form the "backbone" of a graph.

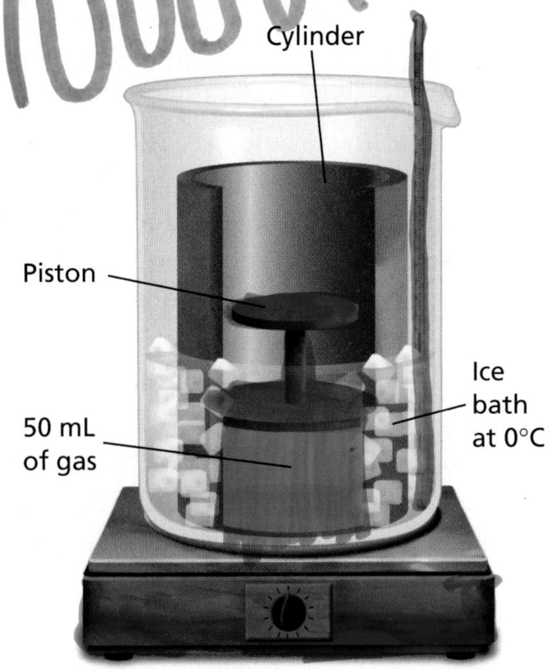

Temperature (°C)	Temperature (K)	Volume (mL)
0	273	50
10	283	52
20	293	54
30	303	56
40	313	58
50	323	60
60	333	62
70	343	63
80	353	66
90	363	67
100	373	69

FIGURE 22
Temperature and Gas Volume
As the temperature of the water bath increases, the gas inside the cylinder is warmed by the water. The data from the experiment are recorded in the notebook table.
Calculating *How do you convert Celsius degrees to kelvins?*

Temperature and Volume

Recall that Charles's law relates the temperature and volume of a gas that is kept at a constant pressure. You can explore this relationship by doing an experiment in which you change the temperature of a gas and measure its volume. Then you can graph the data you have recorded and interpret the results.

Collecting Data As you can see from the cutaway view in Figure 22, the gas in the experiment is in a cylinder that has a movable piston. The piston moves up and down freely, which allows the gas to change volume and keep the same pressure. To control the temperature of the gas, the cylinder is placed in a water bath.

The experiment begins with an ice-water bath at 0°C and the gas volume at 50 mL. Then the water bath is slowly heated. Gradually, the temperature increases from 0°C to 100°C. Each time the temperature increases by 10°C, the volume of the gas in the cylinder is recorded.

You'll notice a second set of temperatures listed in the table in Figure 22. Scientists often work with gas temperatures in units called kelvins. To convert from Celsius degrees to kelvins (K), add 273. The kelvin temperatures will be used to graph the data.

[redacted] **What units do scientists use to measure gas temperatures?**

Go [redacted]nline
SCI LINKS NSTA
For: Links on gases
Visit: www.SciLinks.org
Web Code: scn-1124

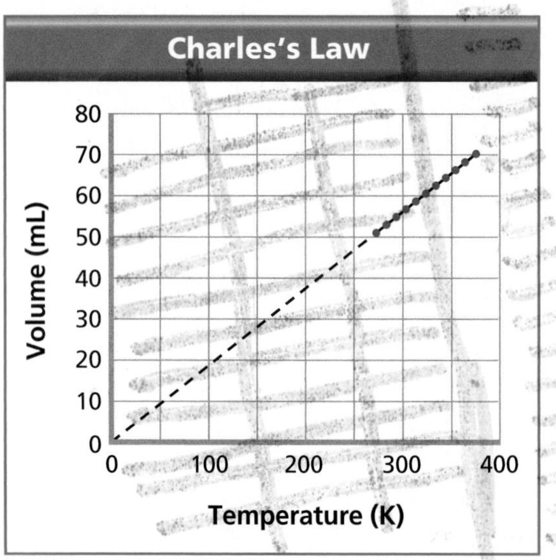

FIGURE 23
Graphing Charles's Law
A graph of the data from Figure 22 shows the relationship known as Charles's law. The dotted line predicts how the graph would look if the gas could be cooled further.

Graphing the Results Look at the graph in Figure 23. It appears as if the line would continue downward if data could be collected for lower temperatures. Such a line would pass through the point (0, 0), called the **origin.** When a graph of two variables is a straight line passing through the origin, the variables are said to be **directly proportional** to each other. **The graph of Charles's law shows that the volume of a gas is directly proportional to its kelvin temperature under constant pressure.**

In reality, the line on the graph cannot be extended as far as the origin. Remember that if a gas is cooled enough, it will condense into a liquid. After that, the volume would no longer change much. However, the line that results from the data represents a relationship that is directly proportional.

Pressure and Volume

A different experiment can show how gas pressure and volume are related when temperature is kept constant. Recall that this relationship is called Boyle's law.

Collecting Data The gas in this experiment is also contained in a cylinder with a movable piston. A gauge indicates the pressure of the gas inside the cylinder. The experiment begins with the volume of the gas at 300 mL. The pressure of the gas is 20 kPa. Next, the piston is pushed into the cylinder, making the gas volume smaller. The pressure of the gas is recorded after each 50-mL change in volume. Temperature remains constant.

FIGURE 24
Pushing on the top of the piston decreases the volume of the gas. The pressure of the gas increases. The data from the experiment are recorded in the notebook table.
Predicting *What would happen if you pulled up on the piston?*

Graphing the Results In this pressure-volume experiment, the manipulated variable is volume. Volume is shown on the scale of the horizontal axis from 0 mL to 300 mL. The responding variable is pressure. Pressure is shown on the scale of the vertical axis from 0 kPa to 120 kPa.

As you can see in Figure 25, the plotted points lie on a curve. Notice that the curve slopes downward from left to right. Also notice that the curve is steep at lower volumes and becomes less steep as volume increases. When a graph of two variables forms this kind of curve, the variables are said to **vary inversely** with one another. Such a relationship means that when one variable goes up, the other variable goes down in a regular way. **The graph for Boyle's law shows that the pressure of a gas varies inversely with its volume at constant temperature.**

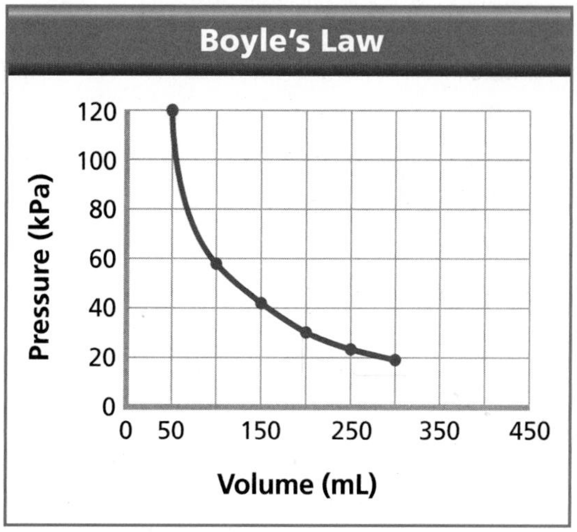

FIGURE 25
This graph of the data from Figure 24 shows the relationship between pressure and volume known as Boyle's law.

Reading Checkpoint **What is the manipulated variable in the pressure-volume experiment?**

Section 4 Assessment

Target Reading Skill Previewing Visuals Refer to your questions and answers about Figure 23 to help you answer Question 1 below.

Reviewing Key Concepts

1. a. Classifying What term describes the relationship illustrated by the graph in Figure 23?
   b. Relating Cause and Effect How does the volume of a gas change when its temperature is increased at constant pressure?
   c. Predicting Suppose the temperature of the gas is increased to 400 kelvins (127°C). Use Figure 23 to predict the volume of the gas at this temperature.
2. a. Classifying What is the relationship between the pressure and the volume of a gas?
   b. Estimating Use the graph in Figure 25 to estimate the gas pressure when the gas volume is 125 mL.
   c. Comparing and Contrasting Compare and contrast the Charles's law and Boyle's law graphs. How can you tell the difference between a graph in which one variable is directly proportional to another and a graph in which two variables vary inversely?

Lab zone At-Home Activity

Finding Graphs Look for graphs in your newspaper or in magazines. Point out to members of your family which variable is the manipulated variable and which is the responding variable for each graph. Then compare any line graphs you have found to the graphs in this section. Which of your graphs show two variables that are directly proportional to each other? Do any show variables that vary inversely?

Lab zone **Skills Lab**

It's a Gas

Problem

How does the pressure you exert on a syringe affect the volume of the air inside it?

Skills Focus

graphing, predicting, interpreting data, drawing conclusions

Materials

- strong plastic syringe (with no needle), at least 35-cm^3 capacity
- modeling clay
- 4 books of uniform weight

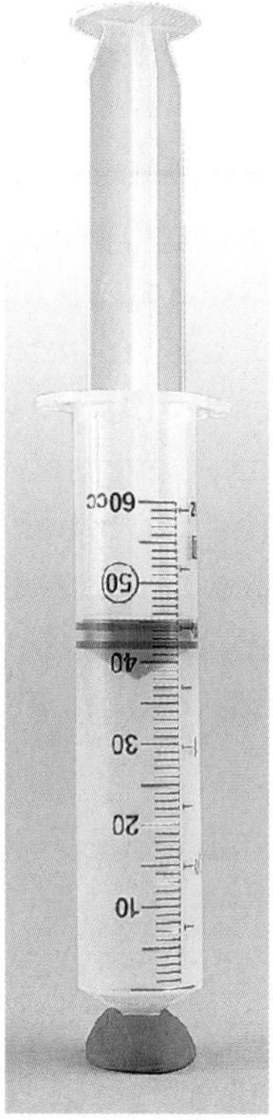

Procedure

1. Make a data table in your notebook like the one below.
2. Lift the plunger of the syringe as high as it will move without going off scale. The volume inside the syringe will then be as large as possible.
3. Seal the small opening of the syringe with a piece of clay. The seal must be airtight.
4. Hold the syringe upright with the clay end on the table. With the help of a partner, place one book on top of the plunger. Steady the book carefully so it does not fall.
5. With the book positioned on the plunger, read the volume shown by the plunger and record it in your data table.
6. Predict what will happen as more books are placed on top of the plunger.
7. Place another book on top of the first book resting on the plunger. Read the new volume and record it in your data table.
8. One by one, place each of the remaining books on top of the plunger. After you add each book, record the volume of the syringe in your data table.
9. Predict what will happen as books are removed from the plunger one by one.
10. Remove the books one at a time. Record the volume of the syringe in your data table after you remove each book.

Data Table			
Adding Books		Removing Books	
Number of Books	Volume (cm^3)	Number of Books	Volume (cm^3)
0		4	
1		3	
2		2	
3		1	
4		0	

Analyze and Conclude

1. **Graphing** Make a line graph of the data obtained from Steps 5, 7, and 8. Show volume in cubic centimeters (cm^3) on the vertical axis and number of books on the horizontal axis. Title this Graph 1.
2. **Graphing** Make a second line graph of the data obtained from Step 10. Title this Graph 2.
3. **Predicting** Did the results you obtained support your predictions in Steps 6 and 9? Explain.
4. **Interpreting Data** Compare Graph 2 with Graph 1. How can you explain any differences in the two graphs?
5. **Drawing Conclusions** What does Graph 1 tell you about how the volume of a gas changes with increasing pressure?
6. **Communicating** Write a paragraph explaining how the volume of the gas changed as books were added one by one. Base your explanation on what was happening to the gas particles in the syringe.

Design an Experiment

How could you use ice and warm water to show how the temperature and volume of a gas are related? Design an experiment to test the effect on the volume of a gas when you change its temperature. *Obtain your teacher's permission before carrying out your investigation.*

Chapter 3 Study Guide

1 States of Matter

Key Concepts

- A fixed, closely packed arrangement of particles causes a solid to have a definite shape and volume.
- Because its particles are free to move, a liquid has no definite shape. However, it does have a definite volume.
- As they move, gas particles spread apart, filling the space available. Thus, a gas has neither definite shape nor definite volume.

Key Terms

solid
crystalline solid
amorphous solid
liquid
fluid
surface tension
viscosity
gas

2 Changes of State

Key Concepts

- At its melting point, the particles of a solid substance are vibrating so fast that they break free from their fixed positions.
- At its freezing temperature, the particles of a liquid are moving so slowly that they begin to form regular patterns.
- Vaporization takes place when the particles in a liquid gain enough energy to form a gas.
- Condensation occurs when particles in a gas lose enough thermal energy to form a liquid.
- During sublimation, particles of a solid do not pass through the liquid state as they form a gas.

Key Terms

melting
melting point
freezing
vaporization
evaporation
boiling
boiling point
condensation
sublimation

3 Gas Behavior

Key Concepts

- When working with a gas, it is helpful to know its volume, temperature, and pressure.
- $\text{Pressure} = \dfrac{\text{Force}}{\text{Area}}$
- Boyle found that when the pressure of a gas at constant temperature is increased, the volume of the gas decreases. When the pressure is decreased, the volume increases.
- When the temperature of a gas at constant volume is increased, the pressure of the gas increases. When the temperature is decreased, the pressure of the gas decreases.
- Charles found that when the temperature of a gas is increased at constant pressure, its volume increases. When the temperature of a gas is decreased at constant pressure, its volume decreases.

Key Terms

pressure
Boyle's law
Charles's law

4 Graphing Gas Behavior

Key Concepts

- A graph of Charles's law shows that the volume of a gas is directly proportional to its kelvin temperature under constant pressure.
- A graph of Boyle's law shows that the pressure of a gas varies inversely with its volume at constant temperature.

Key Terms

graph
origin
directly proportional
vary inversely

Review and Assessment

Go Online PHSchool.com
For: Self-Assessment
Visit: PHSchool.com
Web Code: cga-1020

Organizing Information

Comparing and Contrasting Copy the graphic organizer about solids, liquids, and gases onto a separate piece of paper. Complete the table and add a title. (For more on Comparing and Contrasting, see the Skills Handbook.)

State of Matter	Shape	Volume	Example (at room temperature)
a. ___?___	Definite	b. ___?___	Diamond
Liquid	c. ___?___	Definite	d. ___?___
Gas	e. ___?___	Not definite	f. ___?___

Reviewing Key Terms

Choose the letter of the best answer.

1. A substance with a definite volume but no definite shape is a(n)
   a. crystalline solid.
   b. liquid.
   c. gas.
   d. amorphous solid.
2. Unlike solids and liquids, a gas will
   a. keep its volume in different containers.
   b. keep its shape in different containers.
   c. expand to fill the space available to it.
   d. have its volume decrease when the temperature rises.
3. The process in which a gas cools and becomes a liquid is called
   a. evaporation.
   b. sublimation.
   c. boiling.
   d. condensation.
4. According to Boyle's law, the volume of a gas increases when its
   a. pressure increases.
   b. pressure decreases.
   c. temperature falls.
   d. temperature rises.
5. The vertical axis of a graph shows the
   a. responding variable.
   b. manipulated variable.
   c. constant factors.
   d. same variable as the *x*-axis.

If the statement is true, write *true*. If it is false, change the underlined word or words to make the statement true.

6. Rubber and glass, which become softer as they are heated, are examples of <u>crystalline solids</u>.
7. When you see steam, fog, or clouds, you are seeing water in the <u>liquid</u> state.
8. A substance changes from a solid to a liquid at its <u>boiling point</u>.
9. The <u>volume</u> of a gas is the force of its outward push divided by the area of the walls of the container.
10. According to <u>Boyle's law</u>, the volume of a gas varies inversely with its pressure.

Writing in Science

Explanation Write an introduction to a safety manual for deep-sea divers who use compressed air (scuba) tanks. Explain what air pressure is and what happens to gas molecules when air is compressed.

Discovery Channel School

Solids, Liquids, and Gases
Video Preview
Video Field Trip
▶ Video Assessment

Review and Assessment

Checking Concepts

11. Describe the motion of particles in a solid.

12. Why are both liquids and gases called fluids?

13. Compare and contrast liquids with high and low viscosities.

14. How is the thermal energy of a substance related to its physical state?

15. Describe four examples of changes in state.

16. What happens to water molecules when water is heated from 90°C to 110°C?

17. What happens to the gas particles when the air in an inflated ball leaks out?

18. How does heating a gas in a rigid container change its pressure?

Math Practice

19. **Using Formulas** A skier exerts a force of 660 N on the snow. The surface area of the skis contacting the snow is about 0.20 m^2. What is the pressure in Pa of the skier on the snow?

Thinking Critically

20. **Relating Cause and Effect** Explain why placing a dented table-tennis ball in boiling water is one way to remove the dent in the ball. (Assume the ball has no holes.)

21. **Applying Concepts** When you open a solid room air freshener, the solid slowly loses mass and volume. How do you think this happens?

22. **Interpreting Data** Use the table below that shows the volume and pressure of a gas to predict how a graph of the data would look.

Volume (cm^3)	Pressure (kPa)
15	222
21	159
31	108
50	67

Applying Skills

Use the table to answer Questions 23–25.

The data table tells how much mass of a compound dissolves in 100 mL of water as the temperature of the water is increased. Use the data to construct and interpret a graph.

Temperature (°C)	Mass of Compound Dissolved (g)
0	37
10	47
20	56
30	66
40	75

23. **Graphing** Label each axis of your graph with the appropriate variable, units, and range of values. Then plot the data in a line graph.

24. **Interpreting Data** What does the graph show about the effect of temperature on the amount of the compound that will dissolve in water?

25. **Predicting** Assume the amount of the compound dissolved continues to increase as the water is heated. Predict how many grams will dissolve at 50°C.

Lab zone Chapter Project

Performance Assessment If you prepared a cartoon, read the captions to the class and discuss the illustrations. If you prepared a skit, perform the skit in front of the class. After you finish your presentation, invite the class to ask questions about your project. Be prepared to share the decisions you made in creating your presentation.

Standardized Test Prep

Test-Taking Tip

Interpreting Line Graphs

A line graph expresses a relationship between two variables. When answering a question related to a line graph, keep the following tips in mind. Read the question carefully. Also, read the title of the graph. It may help you identify what information is given in the graph. Examine the labels on each axis to determine what data are plotted on the graph and identify the scale of each axis. Once you have chosen your answer, check it against the graph.

Sample Question

The graph in Question 3 represents the changes in a 1.0-kg sample of a crystalline solid as it absorbs energy at a constant rate. What is the melting point of the substance?

A 0°C
B 40°C
C 80°C
D 200°C

Answer

The correct answer is **C.** Choice **A** is not shown on the graph. At 40°C **(B)**, the substance is a solid. At 200°C **(D)**, the substance is in the process of changing from a liquid to a gas.

Choose the letter of the best answer.

1. A wet towel is hanging on a clothesline in the sun. The towel dries by the process of

A boiling. **B** condensation.
C evaporation. **D** sublimation.

2. The pressure of a confined gas equals the force pushing on the surface divided by the area of the surface.

$$\text{Pressure} = \frac{\text{Force}}{\text{Area}}$$

What is the pressure if a force of 1,000 N acts on an area of 5.0 m^2?

F 200 Pa **G** 500 Pa
H 2,000 Pa **J** 5,000 Pa

3. The graph below shows changes in 1 kg of a solid as energy is added.

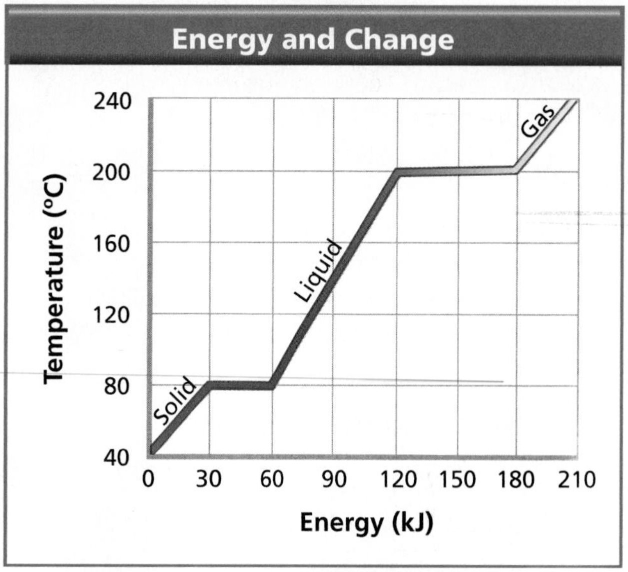

Based on the graph, what is the total amount of energy absorbed by the substance as it changes from a solid at 40°C to a gas?

A 30 kJ
B 60 kJ
C 120 kJ
D 180 kJ

4. A gas at constant temperature is confined to a cylinder with a movable piston. The piston is slowly pushed into the cylinder, decreasing the volume of the gas. The pressure increases. What are the variables in this experiment?

F temperature and time
G time and volume
H volume and pressure
J pressure and temperature

Constructed Response

5. Spray cans filled with gas usually have a warning printed on their labels that say, "Store in a cool place." Explain the danger in storing the can near a source of heat. Describe the motion of the gas molecules in the can when they gain thermal energy.

Chapter 4

Elements and the Periodic Table

Chapter Preview

1. **Introduction to Atoms**
   Discover *What's in the Box?*
   Try This *How Far Away?*
   At-Home Activity *Modeling Atoms*

2. **Organizing the Elements**
   Discover *Which Is Easier?*
   Skills Activity *Classifying*
   Active Art *Periodic Table*

3. **Metals**
   Discover *Why Use Aluminum?*
   Analyzing Data *Melting Points in a Group of Elements*
   At-Home Activity *Everyday Metals*
   Consumer Lab *Copper or Carbon? That Is the Question*

4. **Nonmetals and Metalloids**
   Discover *What Are the Properties of Charcoal?*
   Try This *Show Me the Oxygen*
   At-Home Activity *Halogen Hunt*
   Skills Lab *Alien Periodic Table*

5. **Radioactive Elements**
   Discover *How Much Goes Away?*
   Skills Activity *Predicting*
   Active Art *Radioactive Tracers*

interactive Textbook

Just as each spice in this Turkish bazaar has its own bin, every element has its own place in the periodic table.

Discovery Channel School

Elements and the Periodic Table

▶ Video Preview
Video Field Trip
Video Assessment

Lab zone™ Chapter **Project**

Survey Properties of Metals

Chemists have a system for organizing the elements. There are more than 100 elements, and as you will learn in this chapter, about 80 of them are classified as metals. In this project, you will examine more closely the physical and chemical properties of metals.

Your Goal To survey the properties of several samples of metallic elements

To complete the project, you must

- interpret what the periodic table tells you about your samples
- design and conduct experiments that will allow you to test at least three properties of your metals
- compare and contrast the properties of your sample metals
- follow the safety guidelines in Appendix A

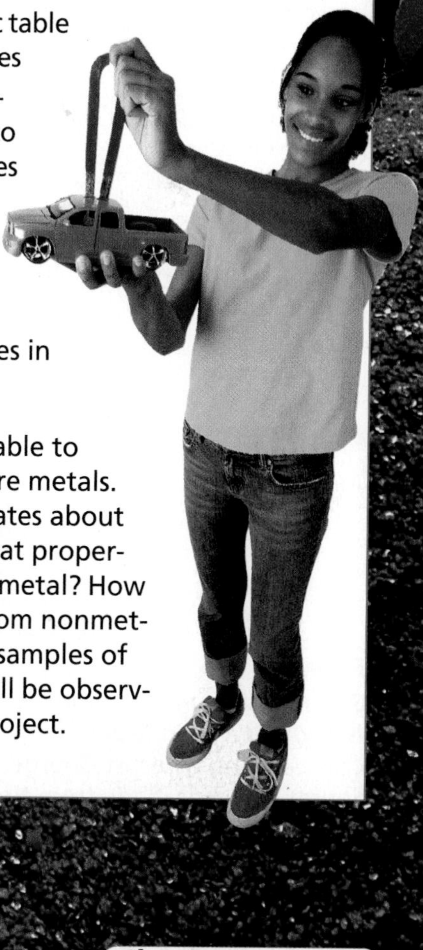

Plan It! Study the periodic table to determine which elements are metals. Brainstorm with your classmates about the properties of metals. What properties allow you to recognize a metal? How do you think metals differ from nonmetals? Your teacher will assign samples of metals to your group. You will be observing their properties in this project.

Section 1

Introduction to Atoms

Reading Preview

Key Concepts

- How did atomic theory develop and change?
- What is the modern model of the atom?

Key Terms

- atom
- electron
- nucleus
- proton
- energy level
- neutron
- atomic number
- isotope
- mass number

Target Reading Skill

Previewing Visuals Before you read, preview Figure 7. Then write two questions you have about the diagram in a graphic organizer like the one below. As you read, answer your questions.

Structure of an Atom

Q. What particles are in the center of an atom?
A.
Q.

Lab zone Discover Activity

What's in the Box?

1. Your teacher will give you a sealed box that contains an object. Without opening the box, move the box around to find out as much as you can about the object.
2. Make a list of your observations about the object. For example, does the object slide or roll? Is it heavy or light? Is it soft or hard? Is the object round or flat?
3. Think about familiar objects that could give you clues about what's inside the box.

Think It Over

Inferring Make a sketch showing what you think the object looks like. Tell how you inferred the properties of the object from indirect observations.

Glance at the painting below and you see people enjoying an afternoon in the park. Now look closely at the circled detail of the painting. There you'll discover that the artist used thousands of small spots of color to create these images of people and the park.

Are you surprised that such a rich painting can be created from lots of small spots? Matter is like that, too. The properties of matter that you can observe result from the properties of tiny objects that you cannot see. As you learned earlier, the tiny objects that make up all matter are atoms.

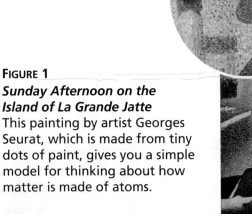

FIGURE 1
Sunday Afternoon on the Island of La Grande Jatte
This painting by artist Georges Seurat, which is made from tiny dots of paint, gives you a simple model for thinking about how matter is made of atoms.

Development of Atomic Models

If you could look into an atom, what might you see? Figuring out what atoms are made of hasn't been easy. Because atoms are so small, studying them is a bit like trying to solve the mystery of the sealed box in the Discover activity. Ideas about the shape and structure of atoms have changed many times.

The first people to think about the nature of matter were the ancient Greeks. Around the year 430 B.C., a Greek philosopher named Democritus proposed the idea that matter is formed of small pieces that could not be cut into smaller parts. He used the word *atomos*, which means "uncuttable," for these smallest possible pieces. In modern terms, an **atom** is the smallest particle of an element.

The ancient Greeks did not prove the existence of atoms because they did not do experiments. In science, ideas are just ideas unless they can be tested. The idea of atoms began to develop again in the 1600s. This time, however, people did do experiments. As a result, atomic theory began to take shape. **Atomic theory grew as a series of models that developed from experimental evidence. As more evidence was collected, the theory and models were revised.**

Dalton's Atomic Theory Using evidence from many experiments, John Dalton, an English chemist, inferred that atoms had certain characteristics. He began to propose an atomic theory and model for atoms. The main ideas of Dalton's theory are summarized in Figure 2. With only a few changes, Dalton's atomic theory is still accepted today.

Go Online
PHSchool.com

For: More on atomic structure
Visit: PHSchool.com
Web Code: cgd-2011

FIGURE 2 Dalton Model
Dalton thought that atoms were like smooth, hard balls that could not be broken into smaller pieces.

Summary of Dalton's Ideas

- All elements are composed of atoms that cannot be divided.
- All atoms of the same element are exactly alike and have the same mass. Atoms of different elements are different and have different masses.
- An atom of one element cannot be changed into an atom of a different element. Atoms cannot be created or destroyed in any chemical change, only rearranged.
- Every compound is composed of atoms of different elements, combined in a specific ratio.

FIGURE 3
Thomson Model
Thomson suggested that atoms had negatively charged electrons embedded in a positive sphere.

Thomson and Smaller Parts of Atoms Through a series of experiments around the start of the twentieth century, scientists discovered that atoms are made of even smaller parts. In 1897, another British scientist, J. J. Thomson, found that atoms contain negatively charged particles. Yet, scientists knew that atoms themselves had no electrical charge. So, Thomson reasoned, atoms must also contain some sort of positive charge.

Thomson proposed a model like the one in Figure 3. He described an atom that consisted of negative charges scattered throughout a ball of positive charge—something like raisins or berries in a muffin. The negatively charged particles later became known as **electrons.**

Rutherford and the Nucleus In 1911, one of Thomson's students, Ernest Rutherford, found evidence that countered Thomson's model. In an experiment diagrammed in Figure 4, Rutherford's research team aimed a beam of positively charged particles at a thin sheet of gold foil. They predicted that, if Thomson's model were correct, the charged particles would pass right through the foil in a straight line. The gold atoms would not have enough positive charge in any one region to strongly repel the charged particles.

Reading Checkpoint **Where were the electrons located in Thomson's model of an atom?**

FIGURE 4
Rutherford's Gold Foil Experiment
Rutherford was surprised that a few particles were deflected strongly. This led him to propose an atomic model with a positively charged nucleus.

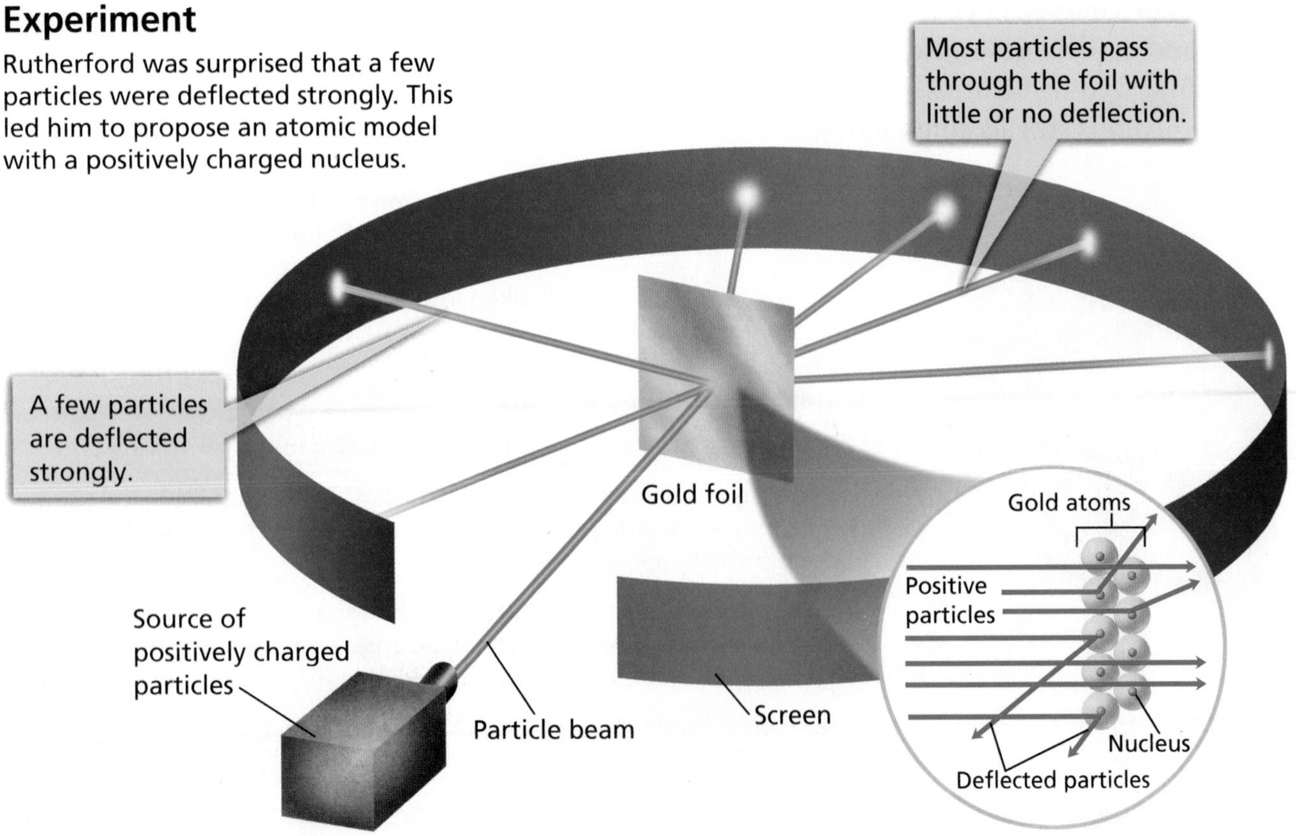

Rutherford's team observed that most of the particles passed through the foil undisturbed, as expected. But, to their surprise, a few particles were deflected strongly. Since like charges repel each other, Rutherford inferred that an atom's positive charge must be clustered in a tiny region in its center, called the **nucleus** (NOO klee us). Any particle that was deflected strongly had been repelled by a gold atom's nucleus.

Scientists knew from other experiments that electrons had almost no mass. Therefore, they reasoned that nearly all of an atom's mass must also be located in the tiny, positively charged nucleus. In Rutherford's model of the atom, the atom was mostly empty space with electrons moving around the nucleus in that space. Work by other scientists later suggested that the nucleus was made of one or more positively charged particles. Rutherford named these positively charged particles in the nucleus of an atom **protons.**

Bohr's Model In 1913, Niels Bohr, a Danish scientist and a student of both Thomson and Rutherford, revised the atomic model again. Bohr showed that electrons could have only specific amounts of energy, leading them to move in certain orbits. The series of orbits in Bohr's model resemble planets orbiting the sun or the layers of an onion, as shown in Figure 6.

A Cloud of Electrons In the 1920s, the atomic model changed again. Scientists determined that electrons do not orbit the nucleus like planets. Instead, electrons can be anywhere in a cloudlike region around the nucleus. The "cloud" is a visual model. It symbolizes where electrons are likely to be found. An electron's movement is related to its **energy level,** or the specific amount of energy it has. Electrons of different energy levels are likely to be found in different places.

FIGURE 5
Rutherford Model
According to Rutherford's model, an atom was mostly empty space. **Making Models** *How is a fruit with a pit at its center a simple model for Rutherford's idea?*

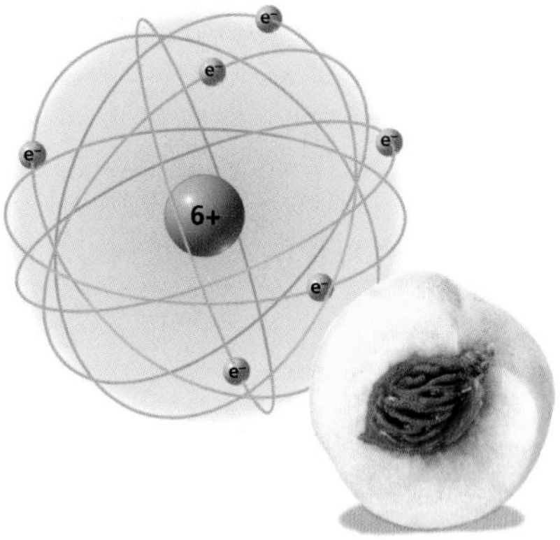

FIGURE 6
Later Atomic Models
Through the first part of the twentieth century, atomic models continued to change.

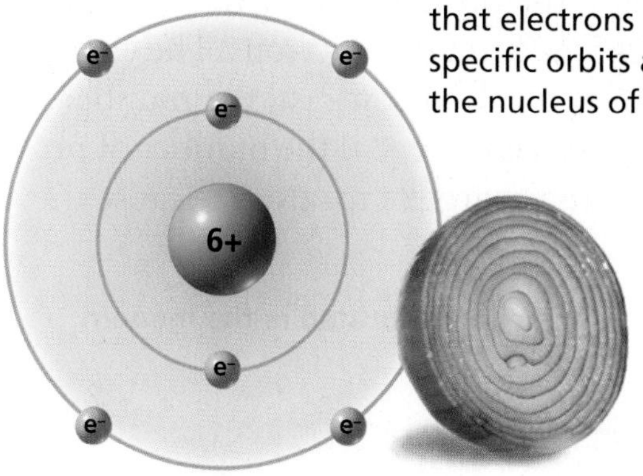

▼ **Bohr Model**
Niels Bohr suggested that electrons move in specific orbits around the nucleus of an atom.

◀ **Cloud Model**
According to the cloud model, electrons move rapidly in every direction around the nucleus.

FIGURE 7
Modern Model of an Atom
This model of a carbon atom consists of protons and neutrons in a nucleus that is surrounded by a cloud of electrons.

Relating Cause and Effect *What effect do the neutrons in the nucleus have on the atom's electric charge? Explain.*

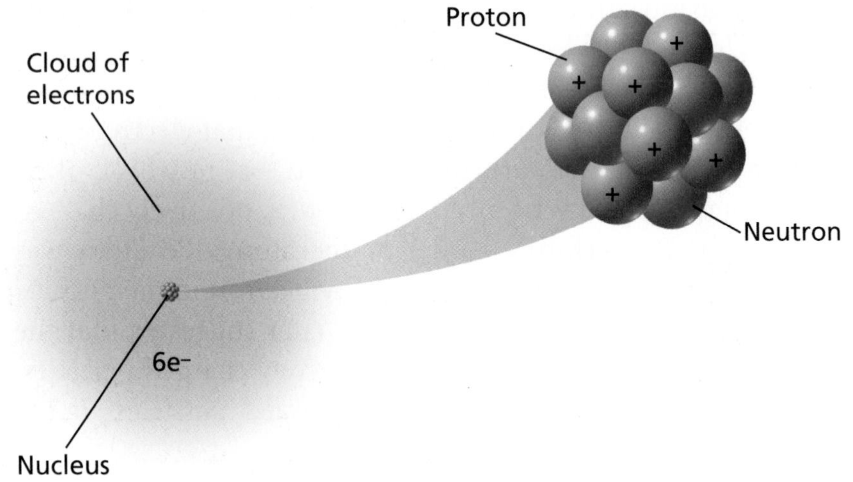

Lab zone Try This Activity

How Far Away?

1. On a piece of paper, make a small circle no bigger than a dime. The circle represents the nucleus of an atom.
2. Measure the diameter of the circle in centimeters.
3. Now predict where the outer edge of this model atom would be. For example, would the outer edge be within the edges of the paper? Your desk? The classroom? The school building?

Calculating The diameter of an actual atom can be 100,000 times that of its nucleus. Calculate the diameter of your model atom. How close was your prediction in Step 3 to your calculation? (*Hint:* To understand the scale of your answer, change the units of measurement from centimeters to meters.)

The Modern Atomic Model

In 1932, British scientist James Chadwick discovered another particle in the nucleus of atoms. This new particle was hard to detect because it has nearly the same mass as a proton. Since it was electrically neutral, the particle was called a **neutron.**

Chadwick's discovery led to an adjustment in the atomic model. This model, pictured in Figure 7, has not changed much since the 1930s. **The modern model describes an atom as consisting of a nucleus that contains protons and neutrons, surrounded by a cloudlike region of moving electrons.** New research continues to provide data that support this model.

Particle Charges Look closely at the model of the carbon atom in Figure 7. Protons are shown in the diagram by a plus sign (+), and electrons are shown by the symbol e^-. If you count the number of protons and electrons, you'll see there are six of each. In an atom, the number of protons equals the number of electrons. As a result, the positive charge from the protons equals the negative charge from the electrons. The charges balance, making the atom neutral. In contrast, the number of neutrons in an atom does not have to equal the number of protons. Neutrons don't affect the charge of an atom because they have no charge.

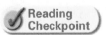

Reading Checkpoint **Where are the electrons located in the modern model of an atom?**

Particles in an Atom				
Particle	Symbol	Charge	Relative Mass (amu)	Model
Proton	p^+	1+	1	
Neutron	n	0	1	
Electron	e^-	1–	$\frac{1}{1,836}$	

FIGURE 8
Each particle in an atom has a unique symbol. In this book, protons, neutrons, and electrons may also be represented by the colored models shown in the table.

Comparing Particle Masses Although electrons may balance protons charge-for-charge, they can't compare when it comes to mass. It takes almost 2,000 electrons to equal the mass of just one proton. On the other hand, a proton and a neutron are about equal in mass. Together, the protons and neutrons make up nearly all the mass of an atom.

Figure 8 compares the charges and masses of the three atomic particles. Atoms are too small to be described easily by everyday units of mass, such as grams or kilograms. Sometimes scientists use units known as atomic mass units (amu). A proton or a neutron has a mass equal to about one amu.

Scale and Size of Atoms Looking back at the modern model (Figure 7), you may see that most of an atom's volume is the space in which the electrons move. In contrast, the nucleus seems tiny. But no image can be drawn in a book that would show how small the nucleus really is compared to an entire atom. To picture the scale of an atom, imagine that the nucleus were the size of an eraser on a pencil. If you put this "nucleus" on the pitcher's mound of a baseball stadium, the electrons could be as far away as the top row of seats!

In reality, atoms themselves are amazingly small. The tiniest visible speck of dust may contain 10 million billion atoms. Because they are so small, atoms are hard to study. Today's powerful microscopes can give a glimpse of atoms, as shown in Figure 9. But they do not show the structure of atoms or how they might work. Models, such as those shown in this book, are helpful in learning more about atoms.

FIGURE 9
Imaging Atoms
This image was made by a scanning tunneling microscope. It shows a zigzag chain of cesium atoms (red) on a background of gallium and arsenic atoms (blue). The colors were added to the image.

Atomic Number Every atom of an element has the same number of protons. For example, the nucleus of every carbon atom has 6 protons. Every oxygen atom has 8 protons, and every iron atom has 26 protons. This unique number of protons in the nucleus of an atom is an element's **atomic number.** Atomic number identifies an element. Carbon's atomic number is 6, oxygen's is 8, and iron's is 26.

FIGURE 10 Isotopes
Atoms of all isotopes of carbon contain 6 protons and 6 electrons, but they differ in their number of neutrons. Carbon-12 is the most common isotope.
Interpreting Diagrams *Which isotope of carbon has the largest mass number?*

Isotopes and Mass Number Although all atoms of an element have the same number of protons, their number of neutrons can vary. Atoms with the same number of protons and a different number of neutrons are called **isotopes** (EYE suh tohps). Three isotopes of carbon are illustrated in Figure 10. Each carbon atom has 6 protons and 6 electrons. But the number of neutrons is 6, 7, or 8.

An isotope is identified by its **mass number,** which is the sum of the protons and neutrons in the nucleus of an atom. The most common isotope of carbon has a mass number of 12 (6 protons + 6 neutrons) and may be written as "carbon-12." Two other isotopes are carbon-13 and carbon-14. Although these carbon atoms have different mass numbers, all carbon atoms react the same way chemically.

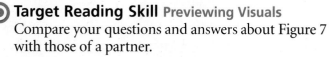

Section 1 Assessment

Target Reading Skill Previewing Visuals Compare your questions and answers about Figure 7 with those of a partner.

Reviewing Key Concepts

1. a. **Reviewing** In general, why did atomic theory change with time?
   b. **Describing** Describe Bohr's model of the atom. What specific information did Bohr contribute to scientists' understanding of the atom?
   c. **Comparing and Contrasting** How is the modern atomic model different from Bohr's model?
2. a. **Reviewing** What are the three main particles in the modern model of an atom?
   b. **Relating Cause and Effect** Why do atoms have no electric charge even though most of their particles have charges?
   c. **Explaining** What is atomic number, and how is it used to distinguish one element from another?
   d. **Applying Concepts** The atomic number of the isotope nitrogen-15 is 7. How many protons, neutrons, and electrons make up an atom of nitrogen-15?

Lab zone At-Home Activity

Modeling Atoms Build a three-dimensional model of an atom to show to your family. Use beads, cotton, small candies, clay, and other simple materials. Describe the parts of your model, and explain what makes atoms of different elements different from one another.

Section 2

Organizing the Elements

Reading Preview

Key Concepts

- How did Mendeleev discover the pattern that led to the periodic table?
- What information about elements does the periodic table provide?
- How are elements created?

Key Terms

- atomic mass • periodic table
- period • group
- chemical symbol
- plasma • nuclear fusion

Target Reading Skill

Asking Questions Before you read, preview the red headings. In a graphic organizer like the one below, ask a *what* or *how* question for each heading. As you read, write the answers to your questions.

Patterns in the Elements

Question	Answer
What pattern of elements did Mendeleev discover?	Patterns appeared when . . .

Lab zone Discover Activity

Which Is Easier?

1. Make 4 sets of 10 paper squares, using a different color for each set. Number the squares in each set from 1 through 10.
2. Place all of the squares on a flat surface, numbered side up. Don't arrange them in order.
3. Ask your partner to name a square by color and number. Have your partner time how long it takes you to find this square.
4. Repeat Step 3 twice, choosing different squares each time. Calculate the average value of the three times.
5. Rearrange the squares into four rows, one for each color. Order the squares in each row from 1 to 10.
6. Repeat Step 3 three times. Calculate an average time.
7. Trade places with your partner and repeat Steps 2 through 6.

Think It Over

Inferring Which average time was shorter, the one produced in Step 4 or Step 6? Why do you think the times were different?

You wake up, jump out of bed, and start to get dressed for school. Then you ask yourself a question: Is there school today? To find out, you check the calendar. There's no school today because it's Saturday.

The calendar arranges the days of the month into horizontal periods called weeks and vertical groups called days of the week. This arrangement follows a repeating pattern that makes it easy to keep track of which day it is. The chemical elements can also be organized into something like a calendar. The name of the "chemists' calendar" is the periodic table.

◄ **A calendar organizes the days of the week into a useful, repeating pattern.**

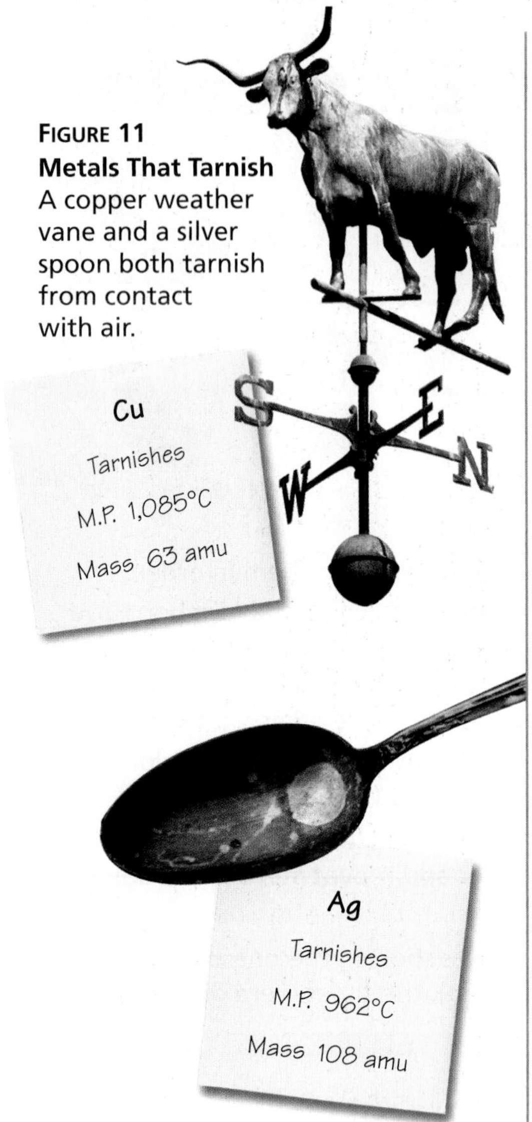

FIGURE 11
Metals That Tarnish
A copper weather vane and a silver spoon both tarnish from contact with air.

Patterns in the Elements

By 1869, a total of 63 elements had been discovered. A few were gases. Two were liquids. Most were solid metals. Some reacted explosively as they formed compounds. Others reacted more slowly. Scientists wondered if the properties of elements followed any sort of pattern. A Russian scientist, Dmitri Mendeleev (men duh LAY ef), discovered a set of patterns that applied to all the elements.

Mendeleev's Work Mendeleev knew that some elements have similar chemical and physical properties. For example, both fluorine and chlorine are gases that irritate the lungs and form similar compounds. Silver and copper, shown in Figure 11, are both shiny metals that tarnish if exposed to air. Mendeleev thought these similarities were important clues to a hidden pattern.

To find that pattern, Mendeleev wrote each element's melting point (M.P.), density, and color on individual cards. He also included the element's atomic mass and the number of chemical bonds it could form. The **atomic mass** is the average mass of all the isotopes of an element. Mendeleev tried various arrangements of cards. **He noticed that a pattern of properties appeared when he arranged the elements in order of increasing atomic mass.**

Mendeleev's Periodic Table Mendeleev found that the properties of elements repeated. After fluorine (F), for instance, the next heaviest element he knew was sodium (Na). (Neon had not yet been discovered.) But sodium reacted with water the same way that lithium (Li) and potassium (K) did. So he placed the cards for these elements into a group. He did the same with other similar elements.

Reading Checkpoint **What properties do silver and copper share?**

FIGURE 12
Metals That React With Water
Lithium and sodium both react with water. **Interpreting Photographs** *Which metal reacts more vigorously with water?*

			Ti=50	Zr=90	?=180.
			V=51	Nb=94	Ta=182.
			Cr=52	Mo=96	W=186.
			Mn=55	Rh=104,4	Pt=197,4
			Fe=56	Ru=104,4	Ir=198.
			Ni=Co=59	Pl=106,6	Os=199.
H=1			Cu=63,4	Ag=108	Hg=200.
	Be=9,4	Mg=24	Zn=65,2	Cd=112	
	B=11	Al=27,4	?=68	Ur=116	Au=197?
	C=12	Si=28	?=70	Sn=118	
	N=14	P=31	As=75	Sb=122	Bi=210
	O=16	S=32	Se=79,4	Te=128?	
	F=19	Cl=35,5	Br=80	I=127	
Li=7	Na=23	K=39	Rb=85,4	Cs=133	Tl=204
		Ca=40	Sr=87,6	Ba=137	Pb=207.
		?=45	Ce=92		
		?Er=56	La=94		
		?Yt=60	Di=95		
		?In=75,6	Th=118?		

FIGURE 13
Mendeleev's Periodic Table
When Mendeleev published his first periodic table, he left question marks in some places. Based on the properties and atomic masses of surrounding elements, he predicted that new elements with specific properties would be discovered.

Predicting New Elements Mendeleev found that arranging the known elements strictly by increasing atomic mass did not always group similar elements together. So, he moved a few of his element cards into groups where the elements did have similar properties. After arranging all 63 elements, three blank spaces were left. Mendeleev predicted that the blank spaces would be filled by elements that had not yet been discovered. He even predicted the properties of those new elements.

In 1869, Mendeleev published the first periodic table. It looked something like the one shown in Figure 13. Within 16 years, chemists discovered the three missing elements—scandium, gallium, and germanium. Their properties are close to those that Mendeleev had predicted.

The Modern Periodic Table In the **periodic table** used today, the properties of the elements repeat in each period—or row—of the table. (The word *periodic* means "in a regular, repeated pattern.") The periodic table has changed a little since Mendeleev's time. New elements were added as they were discovered. Also, an important change occurred in the early 1900s. In 1913, Henry Moseley, a British scientist, discovered a way to measure the positive charge on an atom's nucleus—in other words, the atomic number. Not long after, the table was rearranged in order of atomic number, not atomic mass. As a result, a few of the elements shifted position, and some of the patterns of properties became more regular. An up-to-date version of the table appears on the next two pages.

FIGURE 14
Periodic Table of the Elements

The periodic table includes over 100 elements. Many of the properties of an element can be predicted by its position in the table.

Go Online *active art*
For: Periodic Table activity
Visit: PHSchool.com
Web Code: cgp-1032

Key

C	Solid
Br	Liquid
H	Gas
Tc	Not found in nature

Symbol
One- or two-letter symbols identify most elements. Some periodic tables also list the names of the elements.

Period | Group

Period	1	2	3	4	5	6	7	8	9
1	1 H Hydrogen 1.0079								
2	3 Li Lithium 6.941	4 Be Beryllium 9.0122							
3	11 Na Sodium 22.990	12 Mg Magnesium 24.305							
4	19 K Potassium 39.098	20 Ca Calcium 40.08	21 Sc Scandium 44.956	22 Ti Titanium 47.90	23 V Vanadium 50.941	24 Cr Chromium 51.996	25 Mn Manganese 54.938	26 Fe Iron 55.847	27 Co Cobalt 58.933
5	37 Rb Rubidium 85.468	38 Sr Strontium 87.62	39 Y Yttrium 88.906	40 Zr Zirconium 91.22	41 Nb Niobium 92.906	42 Mo Molybdenum 95.94	43 Tc Technetium (98)	44 Ru Ruthenium 101.07	45 Rh Rhodium 102.91
6	55 Cs Cesium 132.91	56 Ba Barium 137.33	71 Lu Lutetium 174.97	72 Hf Hafnium 178.49	73 Ta Tantalum 180.95	74 W Tungsten 183.85	75 Re Rhenium 186.21	76 Os Osmium 190.2	77 Ir Iridium 192.22
7	87 Fr Francium (223)	88 Ra Radium (226)	103 Lr Lawrencium (262)	104 Rf Rutherfordium (261)	105 Db Dubnium (262)	106 Sg Seaborgium (263)	107 Bh Bohrium (264)	108 Hs Hassium (265)	109 Mt Meitnerium (268)

Lanthanides

57 La Lanthanum 138.91	58 Ce Cerium 140.12	59 Pr Praseodymium 140.91	60 Nd Neodymium 144.24	61 Pm Promethium (145)	62 Sm Samarium 150.4

Actinides

89 Ac Actinium (227)	90 Th Thorium 232.04	91 Pa Protactinium 231.04	92 U Uranium 238.03	93 Np Neptunium (237)	94 Pu Plutonium (244)

To make the table easier to read, the lanthanides and the actinides are printed below the rest of the elements. Follow the blue shading to see how they fit in the table.

Key

- Metal
- Metalloid
- Nonmetal
- Properties not established

Atomic Mass
Atomic mass is the average mass of an element's atoms. Atomic masses in parentheses are those of the most stable isotope.

Atomic Number
The atomic number is the number of protons in an atom's nucleus.

Many periodic tables include a zigzag line that separates the metals from the nonmetals.

10	11	12	13	14	15	16	17	18
								2 He Helium 4.0026
			5 B Boron 10.81	6 C Carbon 12.011	7 N Nitrogen 14.007	8 O Oxygen 15.999	9 F Fluorine 18.998	10 Ne Neon 20.179
			13 Al Aluminum 26.982	14 Si Silicon 28.086	15 P Phosphorus 30.974	16 S Sulfur 32.06	17 Cl Chlorine 35.453	18 Ar Argon 39.948
28 Ni Nickel 58.71	29 Cu Copper 63.546	30 Zn Zinc 65.38	31 Ga Gallium 69.72	32 Ge Germanium 72.59	33 As Arsenic 74.922	34 Se Selenium 78.96	35 Br Bromine 79.904	36 Kr Krypton 83.80
46 Pd Palladium 106.4	47 Ag Silver 107.87	48 Cd Cadmium 112.41	49 In Indium 114.82	50 Sn Tin 118.69	51 Sb Antimony 121.75	52 Te Tellurium 127.60	53 I Iodine 126.90	54 Xe Xenon 131.30
78 Pt Platinum 195.09	79 Au Gold 196.97	80 Hg Mercury 200.59	81 Tl Thallium 204.37	82 Pb Lead 207.2	83 Bi Bismuth 208.98	84 Po Polonium (209)	85 At Astatine (210)	86 Rn Radon (222)
110 Ds Darmstadtium (269)	111 *Uuu Unununium (272)	112 *Uub Ununbium (277)		114 *Uuq Ununquadium				

*Name not officially assigned

63 Eu Europium 151.96	64 Gd Gadolinium 157.25	65 Tb Terbium 158.93	66 Dy Dysprosium 162.50	67 Ho Holmium 164.93	68 Er Erbium 167.26	69 Tm Thulium 168.93	70 Yb Ytterbium 173.04
95 Am Americium (243)	96 Cm Curium (247)	97 Bk Berkelium (247)	98 Cf Californium (251)	99 Es Einsteinium (252)	100 Fm Fermium (257)	101 Md Mendelevium (258)	102 No Nobelium (259)

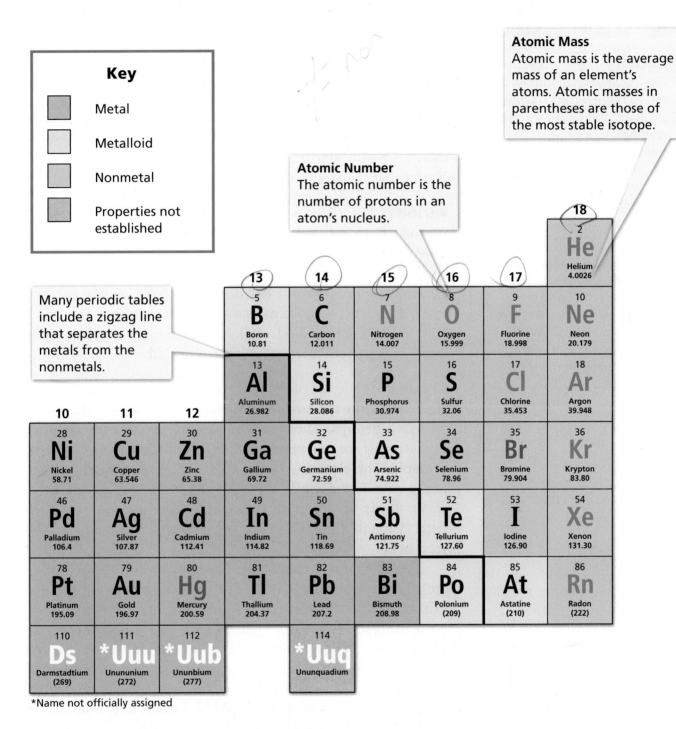

Lab zone Skills Activity

Classifying

Choose any ten elements and assign them letters from *A* to *J*. On an index card for each element, write the letter for the element and list some of its properties. You may list properties that you learn about in this chapter or properties presented in another reference source.

Exchange cards with a classmate. Can you identify each element? Can you identify elements that have similar properties? Which properties are most helpful in identifying elements?

Organization of the Periodic Table

The properties of an element can be predicted from its location in the periodic table. This predictability is the reason that the periodic table is so useful to chemists. Knowing how the table is organized can make the table useful to you, too.

Remember that the periodic table is arranged by atomic number. Look over the entire table in Figure 14 on the previous two pages, starting at the upper left with hydrogen (H). Notice that the atomic numbers increase from left to right.

Periods The table is organized in horizontal rows called **periods.** A period contains a series of different elements, just as a week on a calendar has a series of different days. From left to right, the properties of the elements change in a pattern. For example, elements on the left side of the table are highly reactive metals. Less reactive metals are in the middle of the table. Next come the metalloids, followed by the nonmetals on the right. This pattern is repeated in each period.

Groups As a result of the repeating pattern of properties, the elements of the modern periodic table fall into 18 vertical columns, or **groups.** These groups—sometimes known as families—consist of elements with similar characteristics. For example, The elements in Group 1 are metals that react violently with water, while the elements in Group 2 react with water slowly or not at all. Group 17 elements react violently with elements from Group 1, but Group 18 elements rarely react at all.

The elements known as the lanthanides and the actinides are part of Periods 6 and 7. But these elements are usually printed below the others, and they are not part of the 18 groups already described. Figure 15 shows a different form of the periodic table. It includes the lanthanides and actinides where they would fit, according to their atomic numbers. If you wanted to show more than an element's symbol, this version of the periodic table would be hard to fit in a book!

FIGURE 15
An Expanded Periodic Table
If the lanthanides and actinides were placed within the body of the periodic table, they would increase the number of groups to 32.

1	H																															He
2	Li	Be																									B	C	N	O	F	Ne
3	Na	Mg																									Al	Si	P	S	Cl	Ar
4	K	Ca															Sc	Ti	V	Cr	Mn	Fe	Co	Ni	Cu	Zn	Ga	Ge	As	Se	Br	Kr
5	Rb	Sr															Y	Zr	Nb	Mo	Tc	Ru	Rh	Pd	Ag	Cd	In	Sn	Sb	Te	I	Xe
6	Cs	Ba	La	Ce	Pr	Nd	Pm	Sm	Eu	Gd	Tb	Dy	Ho	Er	Tm	Yb	Lu	Hf	Ta	W	Re	Os	Ir	Pt	Au	Hg	Tl	Pb	Bi	Po	At	Rn
7	Fr	Ra	Ac	Th	Pa	U	Np	Pu	Am	Cm	Bk	Cf	Es	Fm	Md	No	Lr	Rf	Db	Sg	Bh	Hs	Mt	Ds	Uuu	Uub		Uuq				

Reading an Element's Square The periodic table has one square for each element. **In this book, each square includes the element's atomic number, chemical symbol, name, and atomic mass.** Other periodic tables may include more information, and some may include less. Look again at the large periodic table shown earlier in this section and find the square for iron. That square is reproduced below in Figure 16. The first entry in the square is the number 26, the atomic number for iron. Recall that the atomic number tells you that every iron atom has 26 protons in its nucleus. Because it has 26 protons, an iron atom also has 26 electrons.

Just below the atomic number are the letters Fe—the **chemical symbol** for iron. Most chemical symbols contain either one or two letters. Often, an element's symbol is an abbreviation of the element's name in English. For example, zinc's symbol is Zn, the symbol for calcium is Ca, and the symbol for silicon is Si. Other elements, especially those that were known in ancient times, have symbols that are abbreviations of their Latin names. For example, the Latin name of sodium is *natrium,* so its symbol is Na. The Latin name of potassium is *kalium,* so its symbol is K. The symbol Au for gold stands for *aurum.* Fe for iron stands for *ferrum,* and Pb for lead stands for *plumbum.*

Average Atomic Mass The last number in the square is the average atomic mass. For iron, this value is 55.847 amu. The atomic mass is an average because most elements consist of a mixture of isotopes. For example, iron is a mixture of four isotopes. About 92 percent of iron atoms are iron-56 (having 30 neutrons). The rest are a mixture of iron-54, iron-57, and iron-58. The average atomic mass of iron is determined from the combined percentages of all its isotopes.

Reading Checkpoint **Why is the atomic mass of an element an average?**

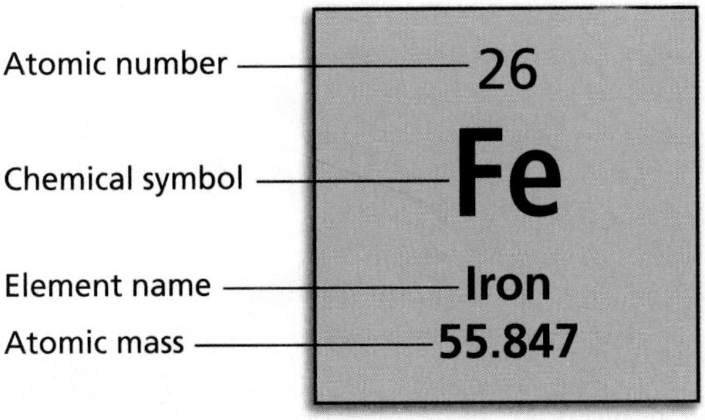

FIGURE 16
Iron
Bok choy is a green, leafy vegetable used in Asian cooking. It is rich in iron.
Interpreting Diagrams *What does atomic number 26 in the square tell you about iron?*

Discovery Channel School

Elements and the Periodic Table

Video Preview
▶ Video Field Trip
Video Assessment

How Elements Form in Stars

You have learned that elements are the simplest substances from which other forms of matter are made. Do you wonder where the elements come from? The answer might surprise you: stars! By studying the sun and other stars, scientists have formed hypotheses about the origins of matter on Earth.

Matter in the Sun Like many other stars, the sun is made mostly of one element—hydrogen. This hydrogen exists at tremendously high pressures and at temperatures as hot as 15 million degrees Celsius. At these extremes, matter does not exist as solid, liquid, or gas. Instead, it is **plasma,** a state of matter that consists of a gas-like mixture of free electrons and nuclei of atoms that have been stripped of electrons.

Remember that atomic nuclei contain protons, which are positively charged. So the atoms that are stripped of their electrons in a plasma are positively charged nuclei. Usually positive charges repel one another. But in stars, the pressure is so high that nuclei are squeezed close together and collide.

New Elements from Fusion When colliding nuclei have enough energy, they can join together, as shown in Figure 17. **Nuclear fusion** is a process in which two atomic nuclei combine, forming a larger nucleus and releasing huge amounts of energy. **Nuclear fusion, which occurs in stars on a huge scale, combines smaller nuclei into larger nuclei, creating heavier elements.** In the sun, different isotopes of hydrogen fuse, producing nuclei of helium. The energy produced in this reaction is the most important source of energy in the sun.

FIGURE 17
Nuclear Fusion
During nuclear fusion, two atomic nuclei collide and fuse.
Applying Concepts *How can nuclear fusion result in the production of a different element?*

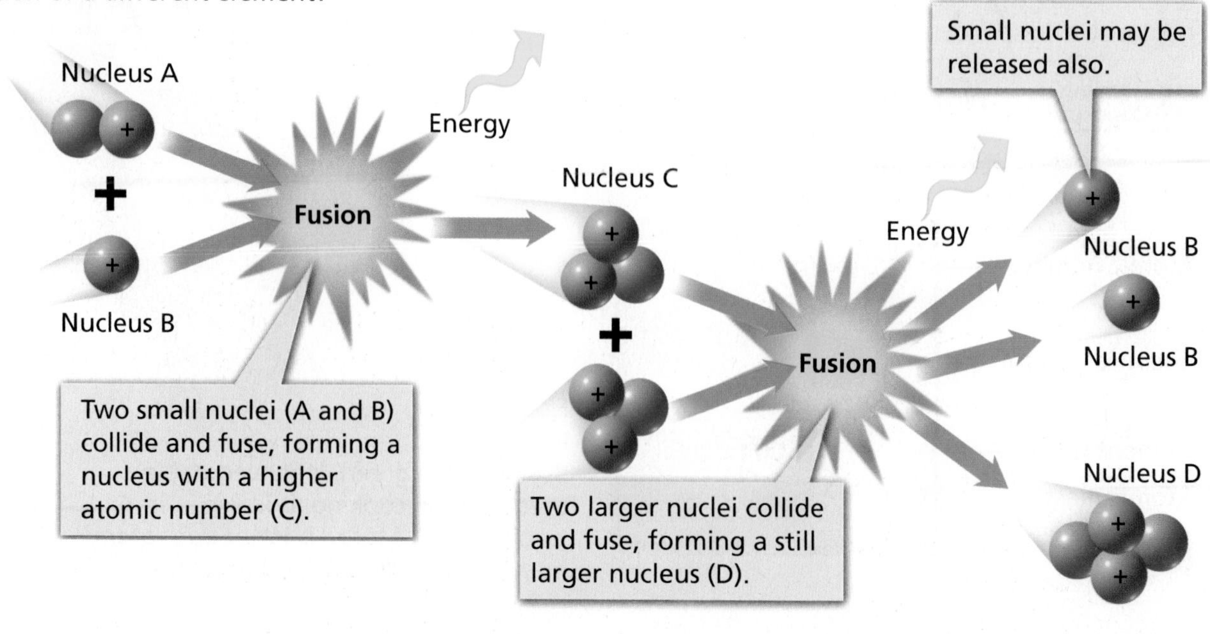

Nucleus A
+
Nucleus B
Fusion
Energy
Two small nuclei (A and B) collide and fuse, forming a nucleus with a higher atomic number (C).
Nucleus C
+
Fusion
Energy
Two larger nuclei collide and fuse, forming a still larger nucleus (D).
Small nuclei may be released also.
Nucleus B
Nucleus B
Nucleus D

As helium builds up in the sun's core, other fusion reactions occur. Over time, two or more helium nuclei can fuse, forming beryllium. Another helium nucleus can fuse with a beryllium nucleus, forming carbon, and so on. Stars the size of the sun do not contain enough energy to produce elements heavier than oxygen. But larger stars do. These stars are hot enough to produce elements such as magnesium and silicon. In more massive stars, fusion continues until the core is almost all iron.

In the final hours of the most massive stars, scientists have observed an event called a supernova. The star explodes, producing temperatures up to 1 billion degrees Celsius. A supernova provides enough energy to create the heaviest elements. These elements are blown off into space as the star burns out.

Most astronomers agree that the matter in the sun and its planets originally came from a gigantic supernova that occurred billions of years ago. If so, this means that the matter all around you was created in a star, and all matter on Earth is a form of stardust.

FIGURE 18
Supernova
The Crab Nebula is the supernova of a massive star first observed on Earth in A.D. 1054 by Chinese astronomers.
Making Generalizations *What elements may have formed in this supernova that would not have formed in a smaller star?*

Reading Checkpoint **Where are elements heavier than iron produced?**

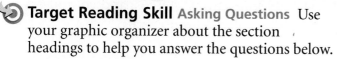

Section 2 Assessment

Target Reading Skill **Asking Questions** Use your graphic organizer about the section headings to help you answer the questions below.

Reviewing Key Concepts

1. a. Reviewing In what order did Mendeleev arrange the elements in the first periodic table?
b. Explaining What pattern did Mendeleev discover when he arranged the elements?
c. Comparing and Contrasting Describe two differences between Mendeleev's periodic table and the modern periodic table.

2. a. Identifying List three kinds of information about an element that can be found in a square of the periodic table.
b. Interpreting Tables What element has 47 protons in its nucleus?
c. Making Generalizations Why aren't the atomic masses of most elements whole numbers?

3. a. Identifying What is the process that produces elements in stars?
b. Explaining How are the elements beryllium, carbon, and oxygen produced in stars like the sun?
c. Developing Hypotheses Earth has abundant amounts of iron, but also has many elements heavier than iron. Form a hypothesis to explain the presence of these heavier elements.

Writing in Science

Advertisement Write an advertisement that you could use to sell copies of Mendeleev's periodic table to chemists in 1869. Be sure to emphasize the benefits of the table to the chemical profession. Remember that the chemists have never seen such a table.

Section 3

Metals

Reading Preview

Key Concepts

- What are the physical properties of metals?
- How does the reactivity of metals change across the periodic table?
- How are elements that follow uranium in the periodic table produced?

Key Terms

- metal • malleable • ductile
- conductivity • reactivity
- corrosion
- alkali metal
- alkaline earth metal
- transition metal
- particle accelerator

Target Reading Skill

Using Prior Knowledge Before you read, write what you know about metals in a graphic organizer like the one below. As you read, write what you learn.

What You Know
1. Metals are shiny.
2.

What You Learned
1.
2.

Lab zone Discover Activity

Why Use Aluminum?

1. Examine several objects made from aluminum, including a can, a disposable pie plate, heavy-duty aluminum foil, foil-covered wrapping paper, and aluminum wire.
2. Compare the shape, thickness, and general appearance of the objects.
3. Observe what happens if you try to bend and unbend each object.
4. For what purpose is each object used?

Think It Over

Inferring Use your observations to list as many properties of aluminum as you can. Based on your list of properties, infer why aluminum was used to make each object. Explain your answer.

Metals are all around you. The cars and buses you ride in are made of steel, which is mostly iron. Airplanes are covered in aluminum. A penny is made of zinc coated with copper. Copper wires carry electricity into lamps, stereos, and computers. It's hard to imagine modern life without metals.

Properties of Metals

What is a metal? Take a moment to describe a familiar metal, such as iron, copper, gold, or silver. What words did you use—*hard, shiny, smooth*? Chemists classify an element as a **metal** based on its properties. Look again at the periodic table. All of the elements in blue-tinted squares to the left of the zigzag line are metals.

Physical Properties **The physical properties of metals include shininess, malleability, ductility, and conductivity.** A **malleable** (MAL ee uh bul) material is one that can be hammered or rolled into flat sheets and other shapes. A **ductile** material is one that can be pulled out, or drawn, into a long wire. For example, copper can be made into thin sheets and wire because it is malleable and ductile.

Conductivity is the ability of an object to transfer heat or electricity to another object. Most metals are good conductors. In addition, a few metals are magnetic. For example, iron (Fe), cobalt (Co), and nickel (Ni) are attracted to magnets and can be made into magnets like the one in Figure 19. Most metals are also solids at room temperature. However, one metal—mercury (Hg)—is a liquid at room temperature.

Chemical Properties The ease and speed with which an element combines, or reacts, with other elements and compounds is called its **reactivity.** Metals usually react by losing electrons to other atoms. Some metals are very reactive. For example, sodium (Na) reacts strongly when exposed to air or water. To prevent a reaction, sodium and metals like it must be stored under oil in sealed containers. By comparison, gold (Au) and platinum (Pt) are valued for their *lack* of reactivity and because they are rare.

The reactivities of other metals fall somewhere between those of sodium and gold. Iron, for example, reacts slowly with oxygen in the air, forming iron oxide, or rust. If iron is not protected by paint or plated with another metal, it will slowly turn to reddish-brown rust. The destruction of a metal through this process is called **corrosion.**

Reading Checkpoint What are three physical properties of metals?

FIGURE 19
Properties of Metals
Metals have certain physical and chemical properties. **Classifying** *Categorize each of the properties of metals that are shown as either physical or chemical.*

Magnetism ▲
Many metals are attracted to magnets.

▼ Malleability
Gold can be pounded into coins.

Reactivity ▶
This iron chain is coated with rust after being exposed to air.

◀ Potassium is highly reactive with air, so it is stored in oil.

Bananas are a good source of potassium in a healthful diet. ▶

▲ The reactions of some compounds containing potassium help get fireworks off the ground.

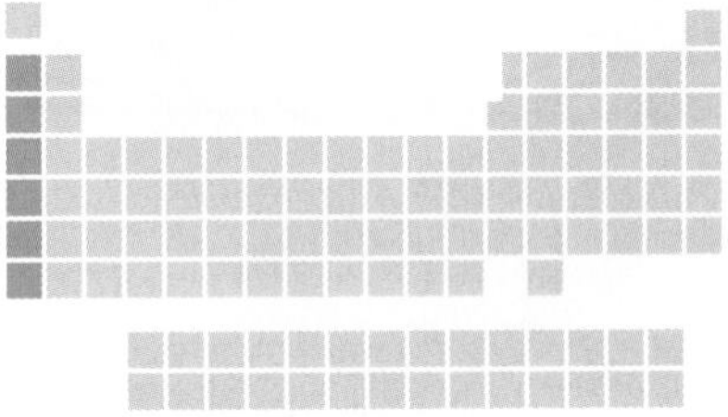

FIGURE 20
Alkali Metals

Potassium is an alkali metal. Making Generalizations *What characteristics do other Group 1 elements share with potassium?*

Metals in the Periodic Table

The metals in a group, or family, have similar properties, and these family properties change gradually as you move across the table. **The reactivity of metals tends to decrease as you move from left to right across the periodic table.**

Alkali Metals The metals in Group 1, from lithium to francium, are called the **alkali metals.** Alkali metals, listed in Figure 20, react with other elements by losing one electron. These metals are so reactive that they are never found as uncombined elements in nature. Instead, they are found only in compounds. In the laboratory, scientists have been able to isolate alkali metals from their compounds. As pure, uncombined elements, some of the alkali metals are shiny and so soft that you can cut them with a plastic knife.

The two most important alkali metals are sodium and potassium. Sodium compounds are found in large amounts in seawater and salt beds. Your diet includes foods that contain compounds of sodium and potassium, elements important for life. Another alkali metal, lithium, is used in batteries and some medicines.

Alkaline Earth Metals Group 2 of the periodic table contains the **alkaline earth metals.** Each is fairly hard, gray-white, and a good conductor of electricity. Alkaline earth metals react by losing two electrons. These elements are not as reactive as the metals in Group 1, but they are more reactive than most other metals. Like the Group 1 metals, the Group 2 metals are never found uncombined in nature.

The two most common alkaline earth metals are magnesium and calcium. Mixing magnesium and a small amount of aluminum makes a strong but lightweight material used in ladders, airplane parts, automobile wheels, and other products. Calcium compounds are an essential part of teeth and bones. Calcium also helps muscles work properly. You get calcium compounds from milk and other dairy products, as well as from green, leafy vegetables.

▲ Without calcium, muscles and bones cannot grow and function.

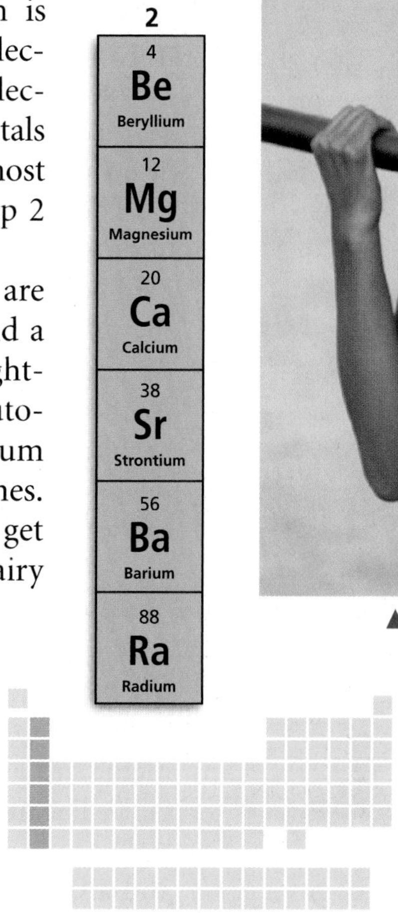

FIGURE 21
Alkaline Earth Metals
Calcium is one of the Group 2 elements.

Math Analyzing Data

Melting Points in a Group of Elements

The properties of elements within a single group in the periodic table often vary in a certain pattern. The following graph shows the melting points of Group 1 elements (alkali metals) from lithium to francium.

1. **Reading Graphs** As you look at Group 1 from lithium to francium, describe how the melting points of the alkali metals change.
2. **Predicting** If element number 119 were synthesized, it would fall below francium in Group 1 of the periodic table. Predict the approximate melting point of new element 119.
3. **Interpreting Data** Room temperature is usually about 22°C. Human body temperature is 37°C. Which of the alkali metals are liquids at room temperature? Which might melt if you could hold them in your hand?

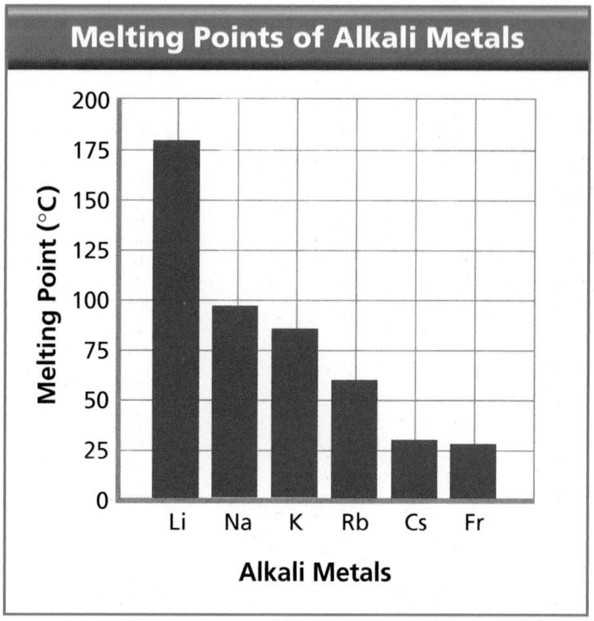

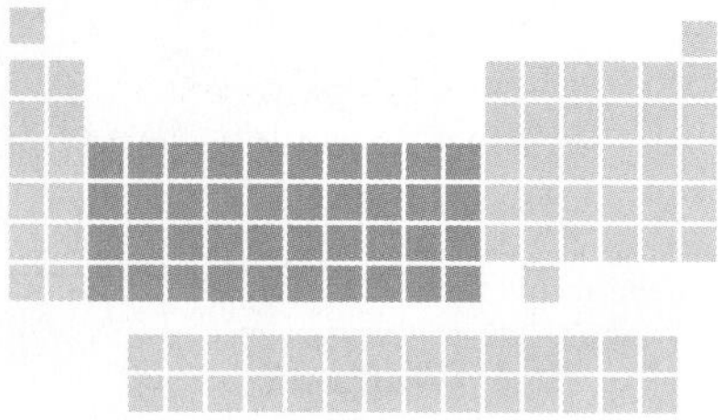

Transition Metals The elements in Groups 3 through 12 are called the **transition metals.** The transition metals include most of the familiar metals, such as iron, copper, nickel, silver, and gold. Most of the transition metals are hard and shiny. All of the transition metals are good conductors of electricity. Many of these metals form colorful compounds.

The transition metals are less reactive than the metals in Groups 1 and 2. This lack of reactivity is the reason ancient gold coins and jewelry are as beautiful and detailed today as they were thousands of years ago. Even when iron reacts with air and water, forming rust, it sometimes takes many years to react completely. Some transition metals are important to your health. For example, you would not survive without iron. It forms the core of a large molecule called hemoglobin, which carries oxygen in your bloodstream.

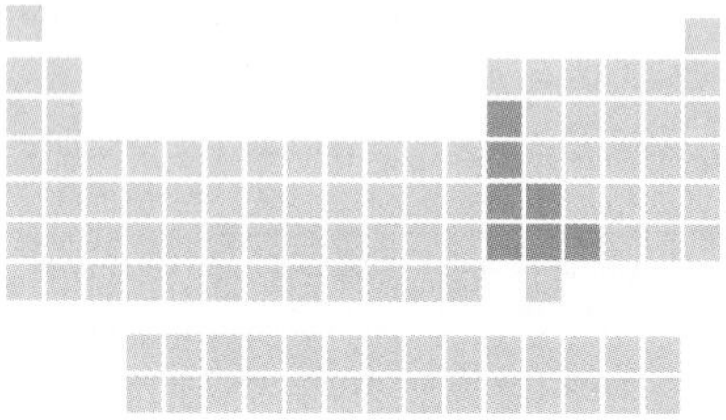

Metals in Mixed Groups Only some of the elements in Groups 13 through 15 of the periodic table are metals. These metals are not nearly as reactive as those on the left side of the table. The most familiar of these metals are aluminum, tin, and lead. Aluminum is the lightweight metal used in beverage cans and airplane bodies. A thin coating of tin protects steel from corrosion in some cans of food. Lead was once used in paints and water pipes. But lead is poisonous, so it is no longer used for these purposes. Now, its most common uses are in automobile batteries and weights for balancing tires.

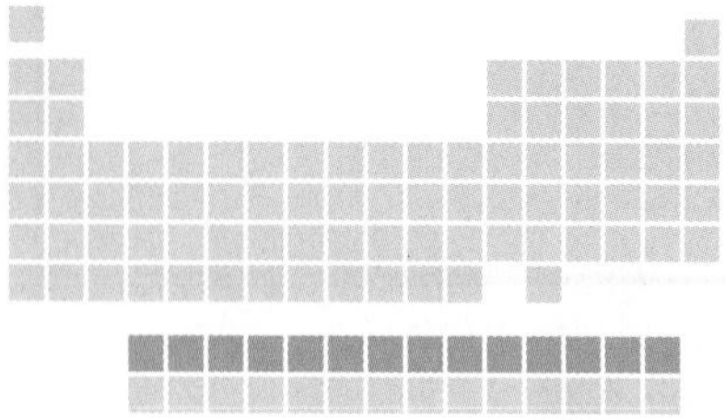

Lanthanides Two rows of elements are placed below the main part of the periodic table. This makes the table more compact. The elements in the top row are called the lanthanides (LAN thuh nydz). Lanthanides are soft, malleable, shiny metals with high conductivity. They are mixed with more common metals to make alloys. An alloy is a mixture of a metal with at least one other element, usually another metal. Different lanthanides are usually found together in nature. They are difficult to separate from one another because they all share very similar properties.

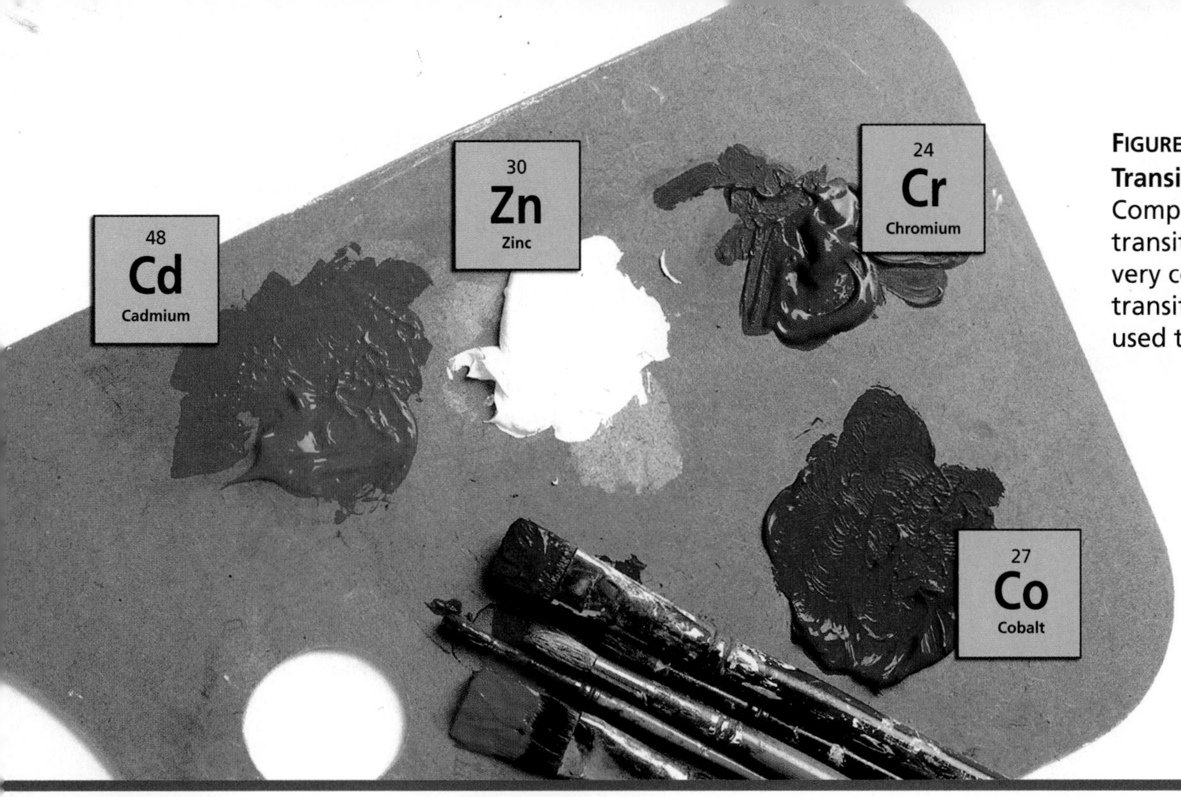

FIGURE 22
Transition Metals
Compounds made with transition metals can be very colorful. Several transition metals are used to make paints.

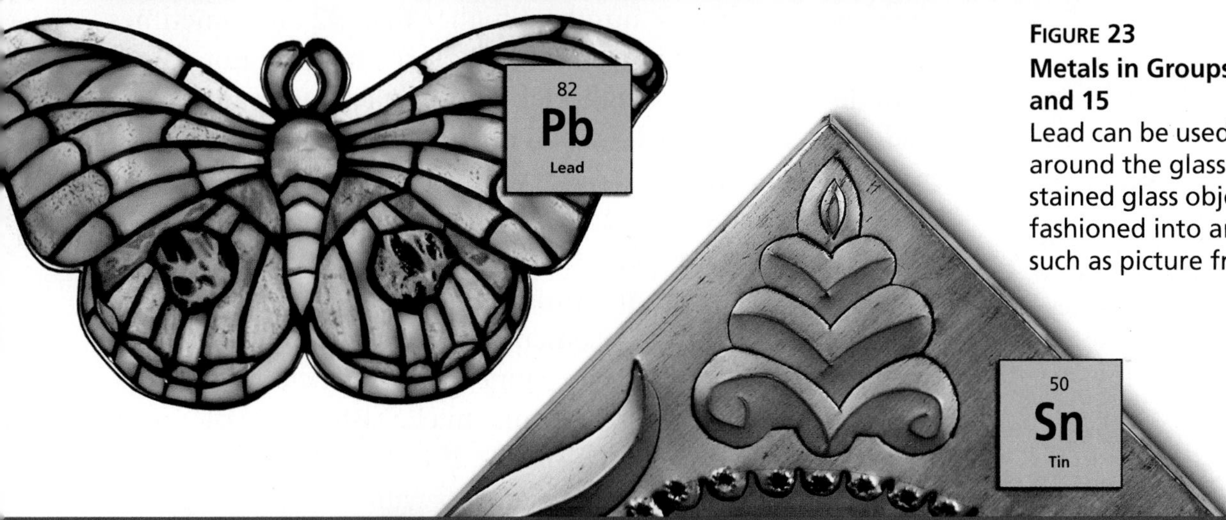

FIGURE 23
Metals in Groups 13, 14, and 15
Lead can be used in the borders around the glass sections in stained glass objects. Tin can be fashioned into artistic objects, such as picture frames.

FIGURE 24
Lanthanides
Neodymium is used in manufacturing the tiny speakers inside stereo headphones.

Actinides The elements below the lanthanides are called actinides (AK tuh nydz). Of the actinides, only actinium (Ac), thorium (Th), protactinium (Pa), and uranium (U) occur naturally on Earth. Uranium is used to produce energy in nuclear power plants. All of the elements after uranium were created artificially in laboratories. The nuclei of these elements are very unstable, meaning that they break apart very quickly into smaller nuclei. In fact, many of these elements are so unstable that they last for only a fraction of a second after they are made.

Reading Checkpoint **Where are the actinides located in the periodic table?**

FIGURE 25
Mars Exploration Rover
Curium, one of the actinide elements, is used as a source of high-energy particles that heat and provide power for certain scientific equipment aboard the Mars Exploration Rover.
Posing Questions *Based on this information, write a question about curium.*

Synthetic Elements

Elements with atomic numbers higher than 92 are sometimes described as synthetic elements because they are not found naturally on Earth. **Instead, elements that follow uranium are made—or synthesized—when nuclear particles are forced to crash into one another.** For example, plutonium is made by bombarding nuclei of uranium-238 with neutrons in a nuclear reactor. Americium-241 (Am-241) is made by bombarding plutonium nuclei with neutrons.

To make even heavier elements (with atomic numbers above 95), scientists use powerful machines called particle accelerators. **Particle accelerators** move atomic nuclei faster and faster until they have reached very high speeds. If these fast-moving nuclei crash into the nuclei of other elements with enough energy, the particles can sometimes combine into a single nucleus. Curium (Cm) was the first synthetic element to be made by colliding nuclei. In 1940, scientists in Chicago synthesized curium by colliding helium nuclei with plutonium nuclei.

In general, the difficulty of synthesizing new elements increases with atomic number. So, new elements have been synthesized only as more powerful particle accelerators have been built. For example, German scientists synthesized element 112 in 1996 by accelerating zinc nuclei and crashing them into lead. Element 112, like other elements with three-letter symbols, has been given a temporary name and symbol. In the future, scientists around the world will agree on permanent names and symbols for these elements.

Reading Checkpoint **Which elements are described as synthetic elements and why?**

Go Online
SCI LINKS NSTA
For: Links on metals
Visit: www.SciLinks.org
Web Code: scn-1133

Americium-241 is produced in nuclear reactors. It is widely used in smoke detectors.

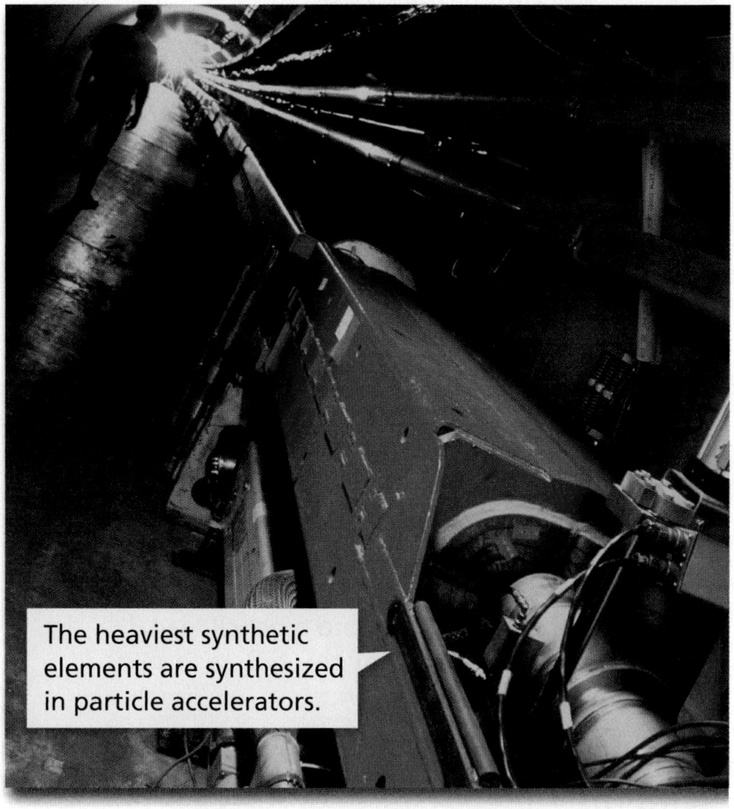

The heaviest synthetic elements are synthesized in particle accelerators.

FIGURE 26
Synthetic Elements
Synthetic elements are not found naturally on Earth.

Section 3 Assessment

Target Reading Skill **Using Prior Knowledge** Review your graphic organizer about metals and revise it based on what you learned in the section.

Reviewing Key Concepts

1. a. **Defining** What properties of metals do the terms *conductivity* and *ductility* describe?
   b. **Classifying** Give an example of how the ductility of metal can be useful.
   c. **Inferring** What property of metals led to the use of plastic or wood handles on many metal cooking utensils? Explain.
2. a. **Identifying** What family of elements in the periodic table contains the most reactive metals?
   b. **Applying Concepts** What area of the periodic table is the best place to look for a metal that could be used to coat another metal to protect it from corrosion?
   c. **Predicting** If scientists could produce element 120, what predictions would you make about its reactivity?
3. a. **Describing** Describe the general process by which new elements are synthesized.
   b. **Applying Concepts** How is plutonium made?

Lab zone At-Home Activity

Everyday Metals Make a survey of compounds in your home that contain metals. Look at labels on foods, cooking ingredients, dietary supplements, medicines, and cosmetics. Also look for examples of how metals are used in your home, such as in cookware and wiring. Identify for your family the ways that the properties of metals make them useful in daily life.

Lab zone **Consumer Lab**

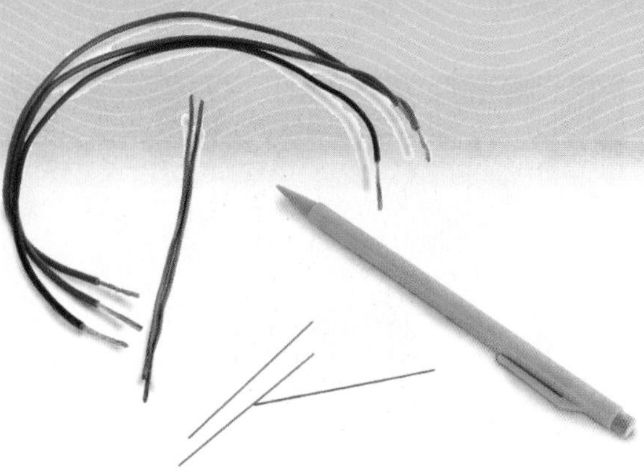

Copper or Carbon? That Is the Question

Problem

Materials scientists work to find the best materials for different products. In this lab, you will look for an answer to the following problem: How do the properties of copper and graphite determine their uses? You will compare the properties of a copper wire and a pencil lead. Pencil lead is made mostly of graphite, a form of the nonmetal element carbon.

Skills Focus

observing, classifying, controlling variables, drawing conclusions

Materials

- 1.5-V dry cell battery
- 250-mL beaker • stopwatch
- flashlight bulb and socket
- 3 lengths of insulated wire
- thin copper wire with no insulation, about 5–6 cm long
- 2 graphite samples (lead from a mechanical pencil), each about 5–6 cm long
- hot plate
- water

Procedure

1. Fill a 250-mL beaker about three-fourths full with water. Heat it slowly on a hot plate. Let the water continue to heat as you complete Part 1 and Part 2 of the investigation.

PART 1 Physical Properties

2. Compare the shininess and color of your copper and graphite samples. Record your observations.
3. Bend the copper wire as far as possible. Next, bend one of the graphite samples as far as possible. Record the results of each test.

PART 2 Electrical Conductivity

4. Place a bulb into a lamp socket. Use a piece of insulated wire to connect one pole of a dry cell battery to the socket, as shown in the photo below.
5. Attach the end of a second piece of insulated wire to the other pole of the dry cell battery. Leave the other end of this wire free.
6. Attach the end of a third piece of insulated wire to the other pole of the lamp socket. Leave the other end of this wire free.

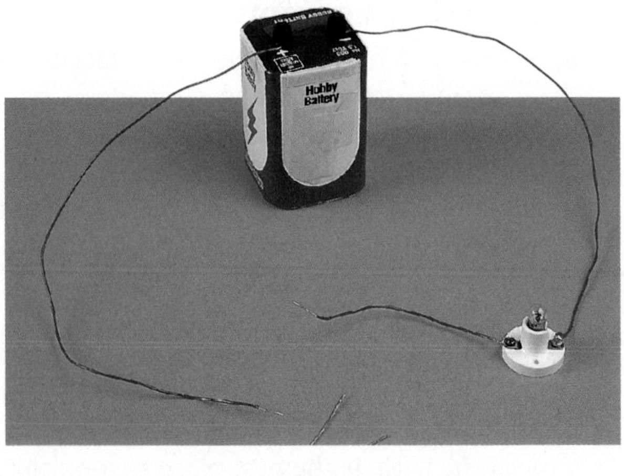

7. Touch the free ends of the insulated wire to the ends of the copper wire. Record your observations of the bulb.
8. Repeat Step 7 using a graphite sample instead of the copper wire.

PART 3 Heat Conductivity

9. Turn off the hot plate.
10. Hold one end of a graphite sample between the fingertips of one hand. Hold one end of the copper wire between the fingertips of the other hand. **CAUTION:** *Be careful not to touch the beaker.*
11. Dip both the graphite and copper wire into the hot water at the same time. Allow only about 1 cm of each piece to reach under the water's surface. From your fingertips to the water, the lengths of both the graphite sample and the copper wire should be approximately equal.
12. Time how long it takes to feel the heat in the fingertips of each hand. Record your observations.

Analyze and Conclude

1. **Observing** Compare the physical properties of copper and graphite that you observed.
2. **Classifying** Based on the observations you made in this lab, explain why copper is classified as a metal.
3. **Controlling Variables** In Step 11, why was it important to use equal lengths of copper wire and graphite?
4. **Drawing Conclusions** Which of the two materials, graphite or copper, would work better to cover the handle of a frying pan? Explain your choice.
5. **Communicating** Write a paragraph explaining why copper is better than graphite for electrical wiring. Include supporting evidence from your observations in this lab.

More to Explore

Research other uses of copper in the home and in industry. For each use, list the physical properties that make the material a good choice.

Section 4

Nonmetals and Metalloids

Reading Preview

Key Concepts

- What are the properties of nonmetals?
- How are the metalloids useful?

Key Terms

- nonmetal
- diatomic molecule • halogen
- noble gas • metalloid
- semiconductor

Target Reading Skill

Using Prior Knowledge Before you read, write what you know about the properties of nonmetals and metalloids in a graphic organizer like the one below. As you read, write what you learn.

What You Know
1. Nonmetals are not shiny. 2.

What You Learned
1. 2.

Lab zone Discover Activity

What Are the Properties of Charcoal?

1. Break off a piece of charcoal and roll it between your fingers. Record your observations.
2. Rub the charcoal on a piece of paper. Describe what happens.
3. Strike the charcoal sharply with the blunt end of a fork. Describe what happens.
4. When you are finished with your investigation, return the charcoal to your teacher and wash your hands.

Think It Over

Classifying Charcoal is a form of the element carbon. Would you classify carbon as a metal or a nonmetal? Use your observations from this activity to explain your answer.

Life on Earth depends on certain nonmetal elements. The air you and other animals breathe contains several nonmetals, including oxygen. And all living organisms are made from compounds of the nonmetal carbon. Yet, while many compounds containing nonmetals are useful to life, some nonmetals by themselves are poisonous and highly reactive. Still other nonmetals are completely unreactive. Compared to metals, nonmetals have a much wider variety of properties. However, nonmetals do have several properties in common.

These bears, the grass behind them, and all life on Earth are based on carbon, a nonmetal. ▶

FIGURE 27
Physical Properties of Nonmetals

Nonmetals have properties that are the opposite of metals.
Comparing and Contrasting *Contrast the properties of these nonmetals with those of metals.*

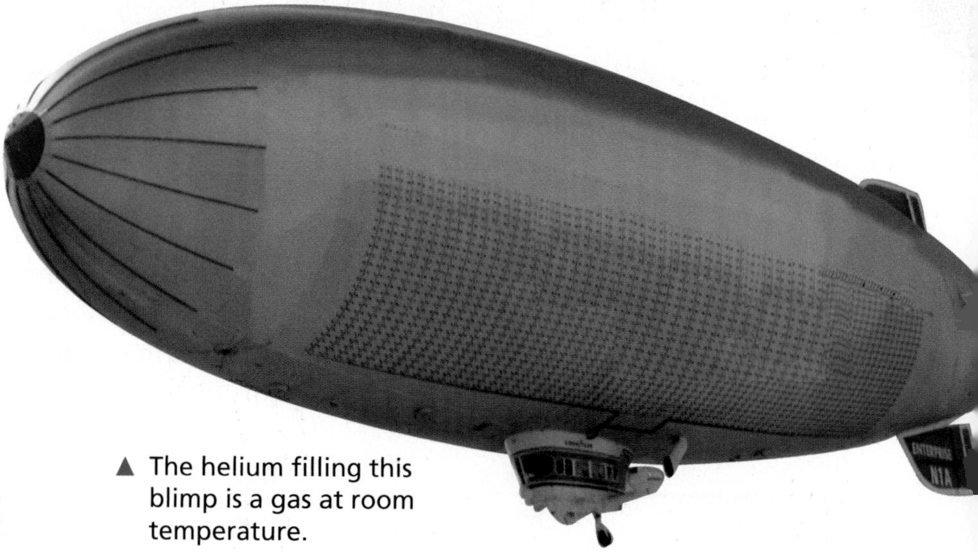

▲ The helium filling this blimp is a gas at room temperature.

◀ Sulfur crumbles into a powder.

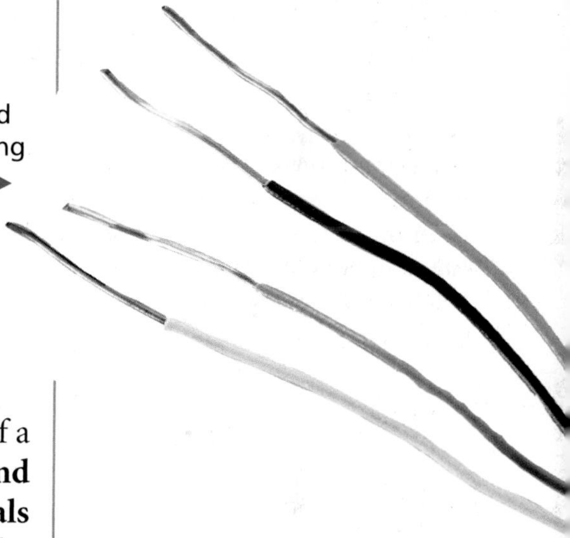

Nonmetals are good insulators. Carbon compounds are found in the plastic insulating these copper wires. ▶

Properties of Nonmetals

A **nonmetal** is an element that lacks most of the properties of a metal. **Most nonmetals are poor conductors of electricity and heat and are reactive with other elements. Solid nonmetals are dull and brittle.** Look at the periodic table again. All of the elements in green-tinted boxes are nonmetals. Many of the nonmetals are common elements on Earth.

Physical Properties Ten of the 16 nonmetals are gases at room temperature. The air you breathe is mostly a mixture of two nonmetals, nitrogen (N) and oxygen (O). Other nonmetal elements, such as carbon (C), iodine (I), and sulfur (S), are solids at room temperature. Bromine (Br) is the only nonmetal that is liquid at room temperature.

Look at examples of nonmetals in Figure 27. In general, the physical properties of nonmetals are the opposite of those of the metals. Solid nonmetals are dull, meaning not shiny, and brittle, meaning not malleable or ductile. If you hit most solid nonmetals with a hammer, they break or crumble into a powder. Nonmetals usually have lower densities than metals. And nonmetals are also poor conductors of heat and electricity.

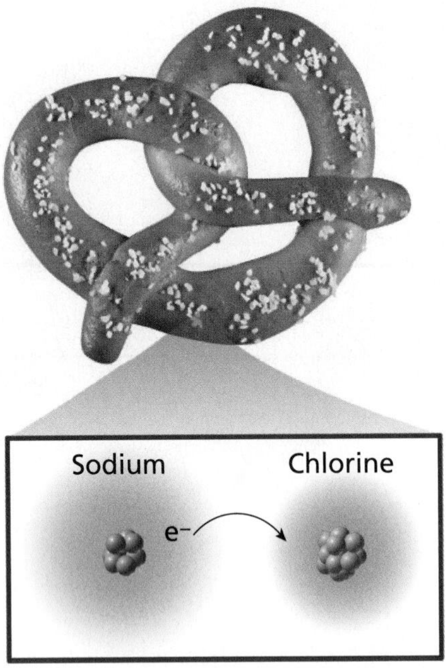

FIGURE 28
Reactions of Nonmetals
The table salt on a pretzel is mined from deposits found on Earth. The same compound can also be formed from a reaction between the metal sodium and the nonmetal chlorine.

Chemical Properties Most nonmetals are reactive, so they readily form compounds. In fact, fluorine (F) is the most reactive element known. Yet, Group 18 elements hardly ever form compounds.

Atoms of nonmetals usually gain or share electrons when they react with other atoms. When nonmetals and metals react, electrons move from the metal atoms to the nonmetal atoms, as shown by the formation of salt, shown in Figure 28. Another example is rust—a compound made of iron and oxygen (Fe_2O_3). It's the reddish, flaky coating you might see on an old piece of steel or an iron nail.

Many nonmetals can also form compounds with other nonmetals. The atoms share electrons and become bonded together into molecules.

Reading Checkpoint **In which portion of the periodic table do you find nonmetals?**

Families of Nonmetals

Look again at the periodic table. Notice that only Group 18 contains elements that are all nonmetals. In Groups 14 through 17, there is a mix of nonmetals and other kinds of elements.

The Carbon Family Each element in the carbon family has atoms that can gain, lose, or share four electrons when reacting with other elements. In Group 14, only carbon is a nonmetal. What makes carbon especially important is its role in the chemistry of life. Compounds made of molecules containing long chains of carbon atoms are found in all living things.

Most of the fuels that are burned to yield energy contain carbon. Coal, for example, is mostly the element carbon. Gasoline is made from crude oil, a mixture of carbon compounds with chains of 5 to 50 or more carbon atoms in their molecules.

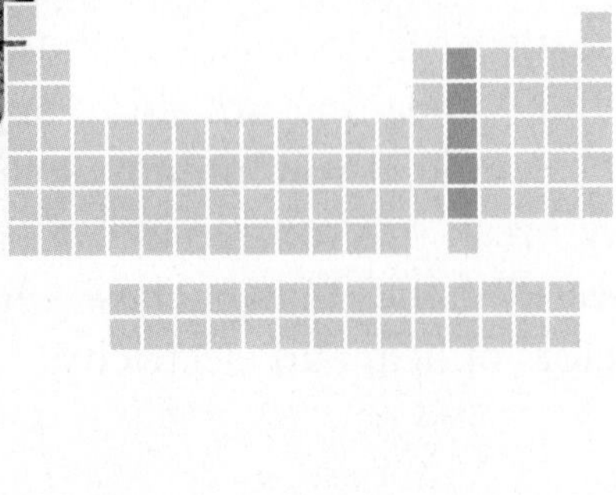

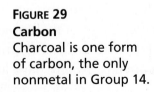

FIGURE 29
Carbon
Charcoal is one form of carbon, the only nonmetal in Group 14.

The Nitrogen Family Group 15, the nitrogen family, contains two nonmetals, nitrogen and phosphorus. These nonmetals usually gain or share three electrons when reacting with other elements. To introduce yourself to nitrogen, take a deep breath. The atmosphere is almost 80 percent nitrogen gas (N_2). Nitrogen does not readily react with other elements, so you breathe out as much nitrogen as you breathe in.

Nitrogen is an example of an element that occurs in nature in the form of diatomic molecules, as N_2. A **diatomic molecule** consists of two atoms. In this form, nitrogen is not very reactive. Although living things need nitrogen, most of them are unable to use nitrogen from the air. However, certain kinds of bacteria can use this nitrogen to form compounds. This process is called nitrogen fixation. Plants can then take up these nitrogen compounds formed in the soil by the bacteria. Farmers also add nitrogen compounds to the soil in the form of fertilizers. Like all animals, you get the nitrogen you need from the food you eat—from plants, or from animals that ate plants.

Phosphorus is the other nonmetal in the nitrogen family. Phosphorus is much more reactive than nitrogen, so phosphorus in nature is always found in compounds. A compound containing phosphorus is used to make matches, because it can react with oxygen in the air.

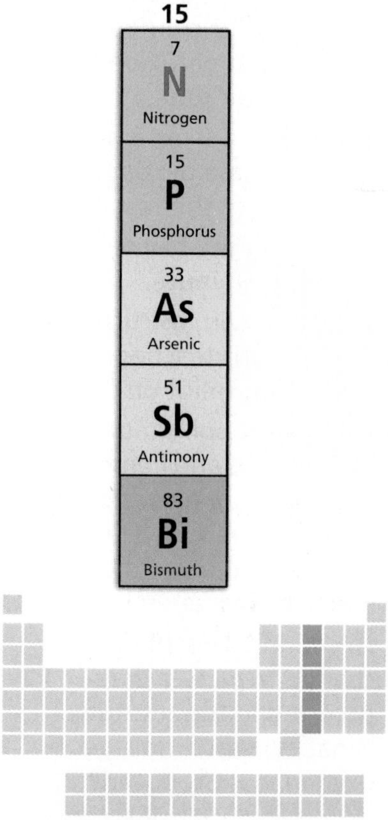

FIGURE 30

The Nitrogen Family

Nitrogen and phosphorus are grouped in the same family of the periodic table, Group 15. **Making Generalizations** *How do atoms of both these elements change when they react?*

▼ Nitrogen is a key ingredient of fertilizers.

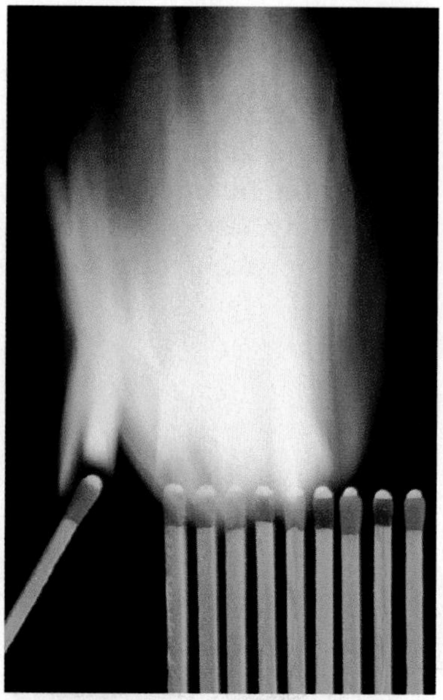

▲ Match heads contain a highly reactive phosphorus compound that ignites easily.

Lab zone Try This Activity

Show Me the Oxygen

How can you test for the presence of oxygen?

1. Pour about a 3-cm depth of hydrogen peroxide (H_2O_2) into a test tube.
2. Add a pea-sized amount of manganese dioxide (MnO_2) to the test tube.
3. Observe the test tube for about 1 minute.
4. When instructed by your teacher, set a wooden splint on fire.
5. Blow the splint out after 5 seconds and immediately plunge the glowing splint into the mouth of the test tube. Avoid getting the splint wet.

Observing Describe the change in matter that occurred in the test tube. What evidence indicates that oxygen was produced?

The Oxygen Family Group 16, the oxygen family, contains three nonmetals—oxygen, sulfur, and selenium. These elements usually gain or share two electrons when reacting with other elements.

You are using oxygen right now. With every breath, oxygen travels into your lungs. There, it is absorbed into your bloodstream, which distributes it all over your body. You could not live without a steady supply of oxygen. Like nitrogen, the oxygen you breathe is a diatomic molecule (O_2). In addition, oxygen sometimes forms a triatomic (three-atom) molecule, which is called ozone (O_3). Ozone collects in a layer in the upper atmosphere, where it screens out harmful radiation from the sun. However, ozone is a dangerous pollutant at ground level because it is highly reactive.

Because oxygen is highly reactive, it can combine with almost every other element. It also is the most abundant element in Earth's crust and the second-most abundant element in the atmosphere. (The first is nitrogen.)

Sulfur is the other common nonmetal in the oxygen family. If you have ever smelled the odor of a rotten egg, then you are already familiar with the smell of some sulfur compounds. Sulfur is used in the manufacture of rubber for rubber bands and automobile tires. Most sulfur is used to make sulfuric acid (H_2SO_4), one of the most important chemicals used in industry.

FIGURE 31

The Oxygen Family

Oxygen and sulfur are the most common of the three nonmetals in Group 16. **Interpreting Tables** *What is the atomic number of each Group 16 element?*

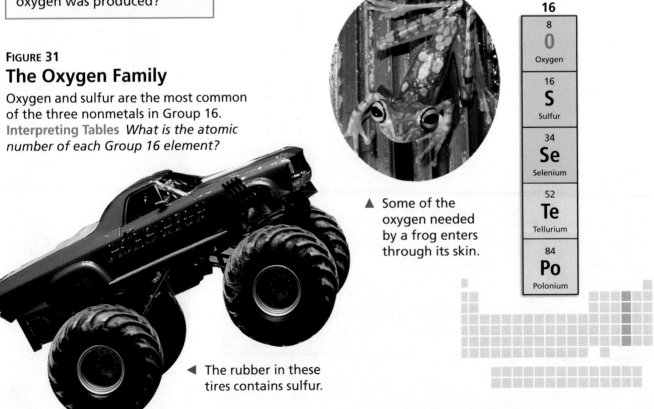

▲ Some of the oxygen needed by a frog enters through its skin.

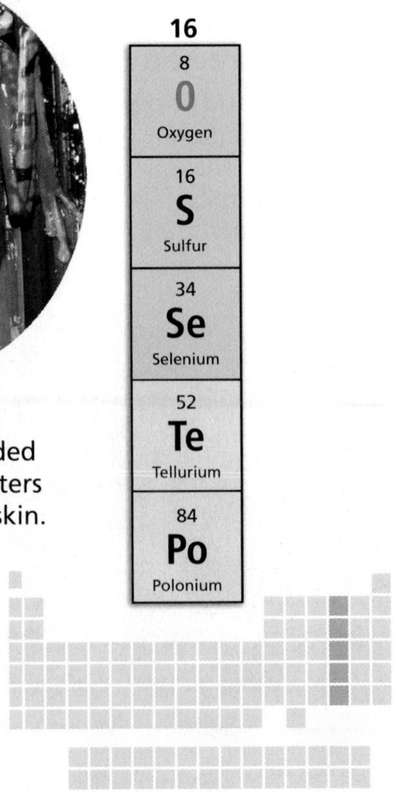

◄ The rubber in these tires contains sulfur.

The Halogen Family Group 17 contains fluorine, chlorine, bromine, iodine, and astatine. These elements are also known as the **halogens,** which means "salt forming." All but astatine are nonmetals, and all share similar properties. A halogen atom typically gains or shares one electron when it reacts with other elements.

All of the halogens are very reactive, and the uncombined elements are dangerous to humans. Fluorine is so reactive that it reacts with almost every other known substance. Even water and powdered glass will burn in fluorine. Chlorine gas is extremely dangerous, but it is used in small amounts to kill bacteria in water supplies.

Though the halogen elements are dangerous, many of the compounds that halogens form are quite useful. Compounds of carbon and fluorine make up the nonstick coating on cookware. Small amounts of fluorine compounds that are added to water supplies help prevent tooth decay. Chlorine is one of the elements in ordinary table salt (the other is sodium). Another salt of chlorine, calcium chloride, is used to help melt ice on roads and walkways. Bromine reacts with silver to form silver bromide, which is used in photographic film.

Go Online
SCI LINKS NSTA
For: Links on nonmetals
Visit: www.SciLinks.org
Web Code: scn-1134

FIGURE 32
The Halogens
The Group 17 elements are the most reactive nonmetals. Atoms of these elements easily form compounds by sharing or gaining one electron with atoms of other elements.

▲ Fluorine-containing compounds are found in toothpaste.

◀ Bromine is highly reactive, and will burn skin on contact.

FIGURE 33 The Noble Gases
Electricity makes the Group 18 elements glow brightly inside glass tubes. **Applying Concepts** *Why are neon and the other noble gases so unreactive?*

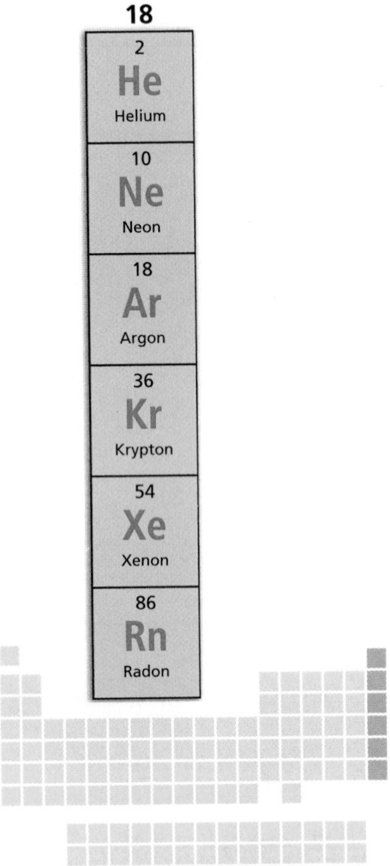

The Noble Gases The elements in Group 18 are known as the **noble gases.** They do not ordinarily form compounds because atoms of noble gases do not usually gain, lose, or share electrons. As a result, the noble gases are usually unreactive. Even so, scientists have been able to form some compounds of the heavy noble gases (Kr, Xe) in the laboratory.

All the noble gases exist in Earth's atmosphere, but only in small amounts. Because they are so unreactive, the noble gases were not discovered until the late 1800s. Helium was discovered by a scientist who was studying not the atmosphere but the sun.

Have you made use of a noble gas? You have if you have ever purchased a floating balloon filled with helium. Noble gases are also used in glowing electric lights. These lights are commonly called neon lights, even though they are often filled with argon, xenon, or other noble gases.

Hydrogen Alone in the upper left corner of the periodic table is hydrogen—the element with the simplest and smallest atoms. Each hydrogen atom has one proton and one electron. Some hydrogen atoms also have neutrons. Because the chemical properties of hydrogen differ very much from those of the other elements, it really cannot be grouped into a family. Although hydrogen makes up more than 90 percent of the atoms in the universe, it makes up only 1 percent of the mass of Earth's crust, oceans, and atmosphere. Hydrogen is rarely found on Earth as a pure element. Most hydrogen is combined with oxygen in water (H_2O).

Reading Checkpoint **Why were the noble gases undiscovered until the late 1800s?**

FIGURE 34
Importance of Hydrogen
Water is a compound of hydrogen and oxygen. Without liquid water, life on Earth would be impossible.

The Metalloids

Along the border between the metals and the nonmetals are seven elements called metalloids. These elements are shown in the yellow squares in the periodic table. The **metalloids** have some characteristics of both metals and nonmetals. All are solids at room temperature. They are brittle, hard, and somewhat reactive.

The most common metalloid is silicon (Si). Silicon combines with oxygen to form silicon dioxide (SiO_2). Ordinary sand, which is mostly SiO_2, is the main component of glass. A compound of boron (B) and oxygen is added during the process of glassmaking to make heat-resistant glass. Compounds of boron are also used in some cleaning materials.

The most useful property of the metalloids is their varying ability to conduct electricity. Whether or not a metalloid conducts electricity can depend on temperature, exposure to light, or the presence of small amounts of impurities. For this reason, metalloids such as silicon, germanium (Ge), and arsenic (As) are used to make semiconductors. **Semiconductors** are substances that can conduct electricity under some conditions but not under other conditions. Semiconductors are used to make computer chips, transistors, and lasers.

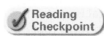

Reading Checkpoint **What is the most common metalloid, and where is it found?**

FIGURE 35 Silicon
A silicon computer chip is dwarfed by an ant, but the chip's properties as a semiconductor make it a powerful part of modern computers.

Section 4 Assessment

Target Reading Skill **Using Prior Knowledge** Review your graphic organizer about nonmetals and metalloids, and revise it based on what you learned in the section.

Reviewing Key Concepts

1. a. **Reviewing** What physical and chemical properties are found among the nonmetals?
   b. **Making Generalizations** What happens to the atoms of most nonmetals when they react with other elements?
   c. **Comparing and Contrasting** How do the physical and chemical properties of the halogens compare with those of the noble gases?
2. a. **Identifying** Where in the periodic table are the metalloids found?
   b. **Describing** What are three uses of metalloids?
   c. **Applying Concepts** What property makes certain metalloids useful as "switches" to turn a small electric current on and off?

Lab zone At-Home Activity

Halogen Hunt Identify compounds in your home that contain halogens. Look at labels on foods, cooking ingredients, cleaning materials, medicines, and cosmetics. The presence of a halogen is often indicated by the words *fluoride, chloride, bromide,* and *iodide* or the prefixes *fluoro-, chloro-, bromo-,* and *iodo-*. Show your family these examples and describe properties of the halogens.

Lab zone **Skills Lab**

Alien Periodic Table

Problem

Imagine that inhabitants of another planet send a message to Earth that contains information about 30 elements. However, the message contains different names and symbols for these elements than those used on Earth. Which elements on the periodic table do these "alien" names represent?

Skills Focus

drawing conclusions, classifying, interpreting data, inferring

Materials

- ruler
- periodic table from text for reference

Procedure

1. Copy the blank periodic table on the next page into your notebook.
2. Listed below are data on the chemical and physical properties of the 30 elements. Place the elements in their proper position in the blank periodic table.

Alien Elements

The noble gases are **bombal** (Bo), **wobble** (Wo), **jeptum** (J), and **logon** (L). Among these gases, wobble has the greatest atomic mass and bombal the least. Logon is lighter than jeptum.

The most reactive group of metals are **xtalt** (X), **byyou** (By), **chow** (Ch), and **quackzil** (Q). Of these metals, chow has the lowest atomic mass. Quackzil is in the same period as wobble.

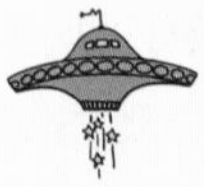

Apstrom (A), **vulcania** (V), and **kratt** (Kt) are nonmetals whose atoms typically gain or share one electron. Vulcania is in the same period as quackzil and wobble.

The metalloids are **ernst** (E), **highho** (Hi), **terriblum** (T), and **sississ** (Ss). Sississ is the metalloid with the greatest atomic mass. Ernst is the metalloid with the lowest atomic mass. Highho and terriblum are in Group 14. Terriblum has more protons than highho. **Yazzer** (Yz) touches the zigzag line, but it's a metal, not a metalloid.

The lightest element of all is called **pfsst** (Pf). The heaviest element in the group of 30 elements is **eldorado** (El). The most chemically active nonmetal is apstrom. Kratt reacts with byyou to form table salt.

The element **doggone** (D) has only 4 protons in its atoms.

Floxxit (Fx) is important in the chemistry of life. It forms compounds made of long chains of atoms. **Rhaatrap** (R) and **doadeer** (Do) are metals in the fourth period, but rhaatrap is less reactive than doadeer.

Magnificon (M), **goldy** (G), and sississ are all members of Group 15. Goldy has fewer electrons than magnificon.

Urrp (Up), **oz** (Oz), and **nuutye** (Nu) all gain 2 electrons when they react. Nuutye is found as a diatomic molecule and has the same properties as a gas found in Earth's atmosphere. Oz has a lower atomic number than urrp.

The element **anatom** (An) has atoms with a total of 49 electrons. **Zapper** (Z) and **pie** (Pi) lose two electrons when they react. Zapper is used to make lightweight alloys.

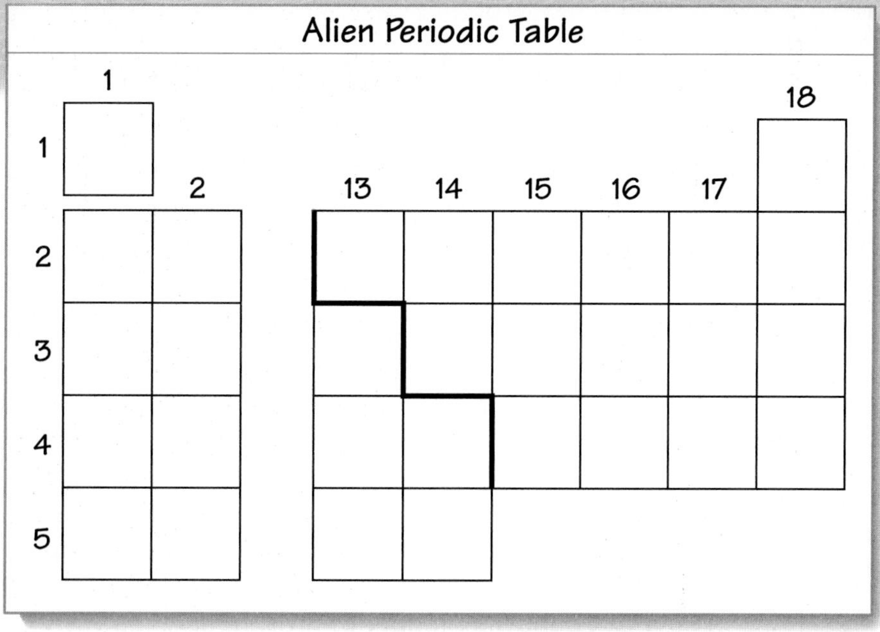

Analyze and Conclude

1. **Drawing Conclusions** List the Earth names for the 30 alien elements in order of atomic number.
2. **Classifying** Were you able to place some elements within the periodic table with just a single clue? Explain using examples.
3. **Interpreting Data** Why did you need two or more clues to place other elements? Explain using examples.
4. **Inferring** Why could you use clues about atomic mass to place elements, even though the table is now based on atomic numbers?
5. **Communicating** Write a paragraph describing which groups of elements are not included in the alien periodic table. Explain whether or not you think it is likely that an alien planet would lack these elements.

More to Explore

Notice that Period 5 is incomplete on the alien periodic table. Create names and symbols for each of the missing elements. Then, compose a series of clues that would allow another student to identify these elements. Make your clues as precise as possible.

▼ **Radio telescopes in New Mexico**

Section 5

Integrating Technology

Radioactive Elements

Reading Preview

Key Concepts

- How was radioactivity discovered?
- What types of particles and energy can radioactive decay produce?
- In what ways are radioactive isotopes useful?

Key Terms

- radioactive decay
- radioactivity
- alpha particle
- beta particle
- gamma radiation
- tracer

Target Reading Skill

Building Vocabulary A definition states the meaning of a word or phrase by explaining its most important feature or function. After you read the section, reread the paragraphs that contain definitions of Key Terms. Use all the information you have learned to write a definition of each Key Term in your own words.

Lab zone Discover Activity

What Happens When an Atom Decays?

1. Using green beads to represent protons and purple beads to represent neutrons, make a model of a beryllium-8 nucleus. Your model should contain 4 protons and 4 neutrons.
2. Beryllium-8 is an unstable isotope of the element beryllium. Its atoms can undergo decay by losing a particle made of two protons and two neutrons. Remove the appropriate number of beads from your model to represent this process.
3. Count the number of protons and neutrons left in your model.

Think It Over

Drawing Conclusions What element does your nuclear model now represent? How do you know? What is the mass number of the new model nucleus?

What if you could find a way to turn dull, cheap lead metal into valuable gold? More than a thousand years ago, many people thought it was a great idea, too. They tried everything they could think of. Of course, nothing worked. There is no chemical reaction that converts one element into another. Even so, elements do sometimes change into other elements. A uranium atom can become a thorium atom. Atoms of carbon can become atoms of nitrogen. (But lead never changes into gold, unfortunately!) How is it possible for these changes to happen?

FIGURE 36
Trying to Make Gold From Lead
This painting from 1570 shows people trying to change lead into gold. No such chemical reaction was ever accomplished.

Radioactivity

Remember that atoms with the same number of protons and different numbers of neutrons are called isotopes. Some isotopes are unstable; that is, their nuclei do not hold together well. In a process called **radioactive decay,** the atomic nuclei of unstable isotopes release fast-moving particles and energy.

FIGURE 37
Radiation From Uranium
As with Becquerel's discovery, radiation from the uranium-containing mineral has exposed the photographic film.

Discovery of Radioactivity **In 1896, the French scientist Henri Becquerel discovered the effects of radioactive decay quite by accident while studying a mineral containing uranium.** He observed that with exposure to sunlight, the mineral gave off a penetrating energy that could expose film. Becquerel assumed that sunlight was necessary for the energy release. So, when the weather turned cloudy, he put away his materials in a dark desk drawer, including a sample of the mineral placed next to a photographic plate wrapped in paper. Later, when Becquerel opened his desk to retrieve these items, he was surprised to discover an image of the mineral sample on the photographic plate. Sunlight wasn't necessary after all. Becquerel hypothesized that uranium spontaneously gives off energy, called radiation, all the time. But if so, what was the source of the energy?

Becquerel presented his findings to a young researcher, Marie Curie and her husband, Pierre. After further study, the Curies concluded that a reaction was taking place within the uranium nuclei. **Radioactivity** is the name that Marie gave to this spontaneous emission of radiation by an unstable atomic nucleus.

Polonium and Radium Marie Curie was surprised to find that some minerals containing uranium were even more radioactive than pure uranium. Suspecting that the minerals contained small amounts of other, highly radioactive elements, the Curies set to work. They eventually isolated two new elements, which Marie named polonium and radium.

Reading Checkpoint **What did Marie Curie call the energy that is spontaneously released by uranium?**

FIGURE 38 Marie Curie
Marie Curie, her husband Pierre, and Henri Becquerel pioneered the study of radioactive elements.

FIGURE 39
Radioactive Decay
Radioactive elements give off particles and energy during radioactive decay. **Interpreting Diagrams** *Which type of radioactive decay produces a negatively charged particle?*

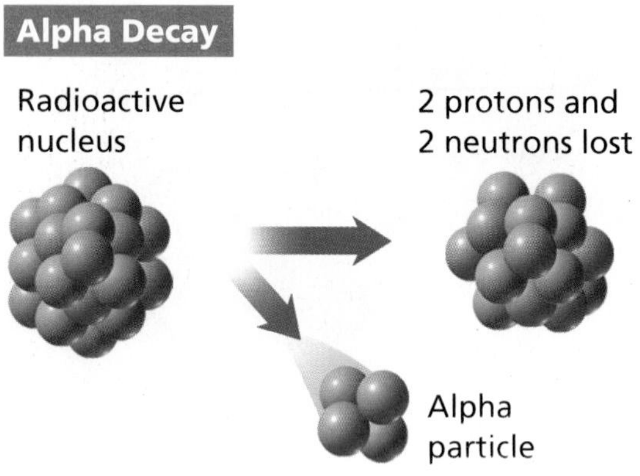

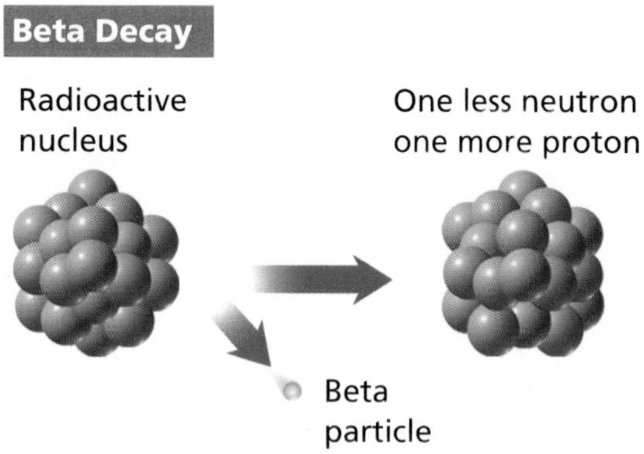

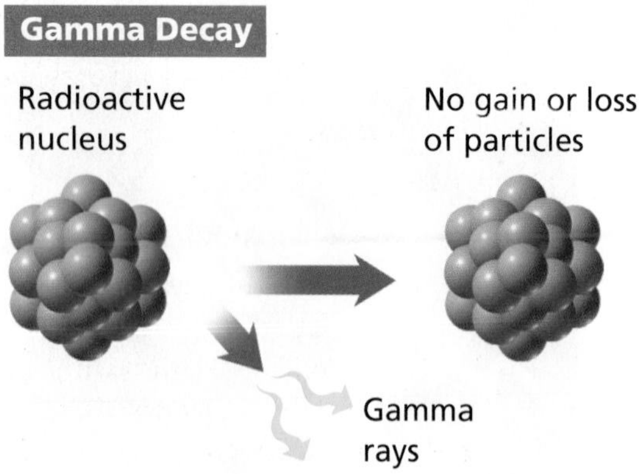

Types of Radioactive Decay

There are three major forms of radiation produced during the radioactive decay of an unstable nucleus. **Natural radioactive decay can produce alpha particles, beta particles, and gamma rays.** The particles and energy produced during radioactive decay are forms of nuclear radiation.

Alpha Decay An **alpha particle** consists of two protons and two neutrons and is positively charged. It is the same as a helium nucleus. The release of an alpha particle by an atom decreases the atomic number by 2 and the mass number by 4. For example, a thorium-232 nucleus decays to produce an alpha particle and a radium-228 nucleus.

Beta Decay Some atoms are unstable because they have too many neutrons. During beta decay, a neutron inside the nucleus of an unstable atom changes into a negatively charged beta particle and a proton. A **beta particle** is a fast-moving electron given off by a nucleus during radioactive decay. The new proton remains inside the nucleus. That means that the nucleus now has one less neutron and one more proton. Its mass number remains the same but its atomic number increases by 1. For example, a carbon-14 nucleus decays to produce a beta particle and a nitrogen-14 nucleus.

Gamma Radiation Alpha and beta decay are almost always accompanied by gamma radiation. **Gamma radiation** consists of high-energy waves, similar to X-rays. Gamma radiation (also called gamma rays) has no charge and does not cause a change in either the atomic mass or the atomic number.

Effects of Nuclear Radiation Although alpha particles move very fast, they are stopped by collisions with atoms. In Figure 40, you can see that alpha particles are blocked by a sheet of paper. Alpha radiation can cause an injury to human skin that is much like a bad burn.

FIGURE 40

The Penetrating Power of Nuclear Radiation

The three types of nuclear radiation were named based on how easily each one could be blocked. Alpha, beta, and gamma are the first three letters of the Greek alphabet. **Inferring** *Which type of nuclear radiation is the most penetrating?*

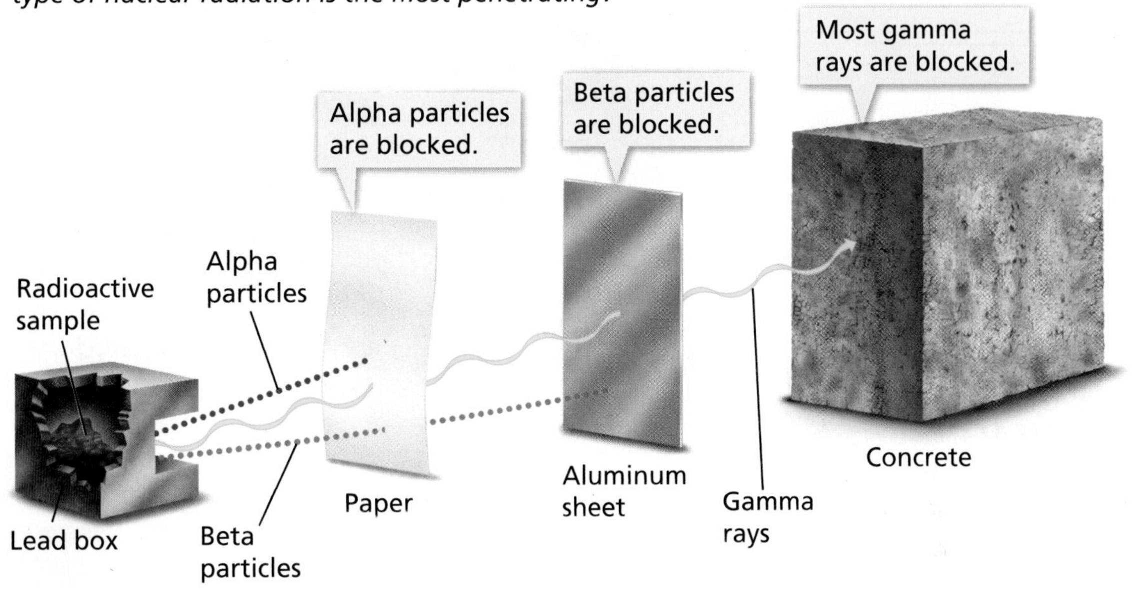

Beta particles are much faster and more penetrating than alpha particles. They can pass through paper, but they are blocked by an aluminum sheet 5 millimeters thick. Beta particles can also travel into the human body and damage its cells.

Gamma rays are the most penetrating type of radiation. You would need a piece of lead several centimeters thick or a concrete wall about a meter thick to stop gamma rays. They can pass right through a human body, delivering intense energy to cells and causing severe damage.

Reading Checkpoint **How can alpha radiation affect the body?**

Using Radioactive Isotopes

Radioactive isotopes have many uses in science and industry. In some cases, the energy released by radioactive isotopes is itself useful. Nuclear power plants, for example, harness this energy to generate electricity. In other cases, radiation is useful because it can be easily detected. **Uses of radioactive isotopes include tracing the steps of chemical reactions and industrial processes, and diagnosing and treating disease.**

Lab zone Skills Activity

Predicting

Look at the table of radioactive isotopes below.

Isotope	Type of Decay
Uranium-238	Alpha
Nickel-63	Beta
Iodine-131	Beta
Radium-226	Alpha

With the help of a periodic table, predict the element that forms in each case. Explain your reasoning.

Go Online
active art
For: Radioactive Tracers activity
Visit: PHSchool.com
Web Code: cgp-1044

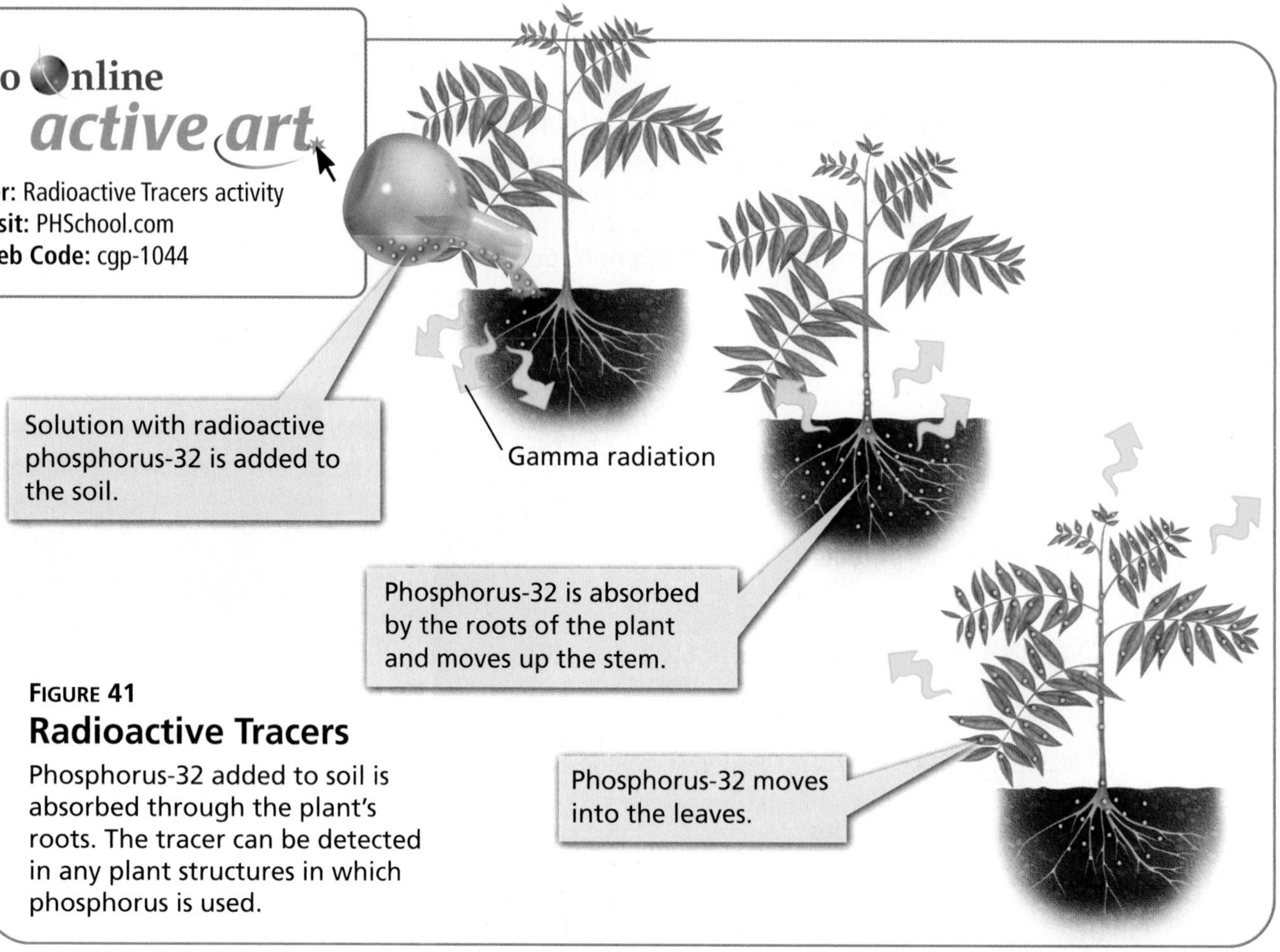

Solution with radioactive phosphorus-32 is added to the soil.
Gamma radiation
Phosphorus-32 is absorbed by the roots of the plant and moves up the stem.
Phosphorus-32 moves into the leaves.

FIGURE 41
Radioactive Tracers
Phosphorus-32 added to soil is absorbed through the plant's roots. The tracer can be detected in any plant structures in which phosphorus is used.

Uses in Science and Industry Like a lighthouse flashing in the night, a radioactive isotope "signals" where it is by emitting radiation that can be detected. **Tracers** are radioactive isotopes that can be followed through the steps of a chemical reaction or an industrial process. Tracers behave the same way as nonradioactive forms of an element. For example, phosphorus is used by plants in small amounts for healthy growth. As shown in Figure 41, a plant will absorb radioactive phosphorus-32 added to the soil just as it does the nonradioactive form. Radiation will be present in any part of the plant that contains the isotope. In this way, biologists can learn where and how plants use phosphorus.

In industry, tracers are used to find weak spots in metal pipes, especially oil pipelines. When added to a liquid, tracers can easily be detected if they leak out of the pipes. Gamma rays can pass through metal and be detected on a photographic film. By looking at the gamma-ray images, structural engineers can detect small cracks in the metal of bridges and building frames. Without these images, a problem might not be discovered until a disaster occurs.

Reading Checkpoint **What is a tracer?**

Uses in Medicine Doctors use radioactive isotopes to detect medical problems and to treat some diseases. Tracers injected into the body travel to organs and other structures where that chemical is normally used. Using equipment that detects radiation, technicians make images of the bone, blood vessel, or organ affected. For example, tracers made with technetium-99 are used to diagnose problems in the bones, liver, kidneys, and digestive system.

In a process called radiation therapy, radioactive elements are used to destroy unhealthy cells. For example, iodine-131 is given to patients with tumors of the thyroid gland—a gland in the neck that controls the rate at which nutrients are used. Because the thyroid gland uses iodine, the radioactive iodine-131 collects in the gland. Radiation from this isotope destroys unwanted cells in the gland without serious effects on other parts of the body.

Cancer tumors of different kinds often are treated from outside the body with high-energy gamma rays. Many hospitals use cobalt-60 for this purpose. When gamma radiation is directed toward a cancer tumor, it causes changes that kill the cancer cells.

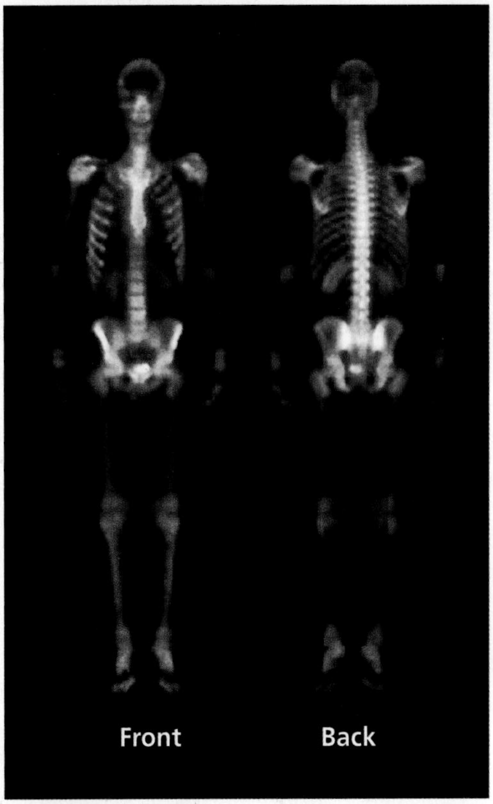

FIGURE 42
Radioactive Isotopes in Medicine
Front and back body scans of a healthy patient were made using a radioactive isotope.

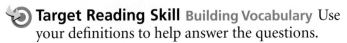

Section 5 Assessment

Target Reading Skill Building Vocabulary Use your definitions to help answer the questions.

Reviewing Key Concepts

1. a. Identifying Under what circumstances did Becquerel first notice the effects of radioactivity?
   b. Interpreting Photographs Look at the photo in Figure 37. Explain in your own words what happened.
   c. Applying Concepts How did Becquerel's work lead to the discovery of two new elements?
2. a. Listing What are three products of radioactive decay?
   b. Comparing and Contrasting Contrast the penetrating power of the three major types of nuclear radiation.
   c. Predicting Predict the identity and mass number of the nucleus formed during the beta decay of magnesium-28.
3. a. Explaining How can radioactive isotopes be used as tracers?
   b. Relating Cause and Effect How is the use of radioactive isotopes in treating some forms of cancer related to certain properties of gamma radiation?

Writing in Science

Firsthand Account Suppose you could go back in time to interview Henri Becquerel on the day of his discovery of radioactivity. From his perspective, write an account of the discovery.

Chapter 4 Study Guide

1 Introduction to Atoms

Key Concepts

- Atomic theory grew as a series of models that developed from experimental evidence. As more evidence was collected, the theory and models were revised.
- The modern model describes an atom as consisting of a nucleus that contains protons and neutrons, surrounded by a cloudlike region of moving electrons.

Key Terms

atom
electron
nucleus
proton
energy level
neutron
atomic number
isotope
mass number

2 Organizing the Elements

Key Concepts

- Mendeleev noticed that a pattern of properties appeared when he arranged the elements in order of increasing atomic mass.
- The properties of an element can be predicted from its location in the periodic table.
- Each square in the periodic table includes the element's atomic number, chemical symbol, name, and atomic mass.
- Nuclear fusion, which occurs in stars on a huge scale, combines smaller nuclei into larger nuclei, creating heavier elements.

Key Terms

atomic mass
periodic table
period
group
chemical symbol
plasma
nuclear fusion

3 Metals

Key Concepts

- The physical properties of metals include shininess, malleability, ductility, and conductivity.
- The reactivity of metals tends to decrease from left to right across the periodic table.
- Synthetic elements are made when nuclear particles are forced to crash into one another.

Key Terms

metal
malleable
ductile
conductivity
reactivity
corrosion
alkali metal
alkaline earth metal
transition metal
particle accelerator

4 Nonmetals and Metalloids

Key Concepts

- Most nonmetals are poor conductors of heat and electricity and are reactive with other elements. Solid nonmetals are dull and brittle.
- The most useful property of the metalloids is their varying ability to conduct electricity.

Key Terms

nonmetal
diatomic molecule
halogen
noble gas
metalloid
semiconductor

5 Radioactive Elements

Key Concepts

- In 1896, the French scientist Henri Becquerel discovered radioactive decay quite by accident while studying a mineral containing uranium.
- Natural radioactive decay can produce alpha particles, beta particles, and gamma rays.
- Uses of radioactive isotopes include tracing the steps of chemical reactions and industrial processes, and diagnosing and treating disease.

Key Terms

radioactive decay
radioactivity
alpha particle
beta particle
gamma radiation
tracer

Review and Assessment

Go Online
PHSchool.com
For: Self-Assessment
Visit: PHSchool.com
Web Code: cka-1040

Organizing Information

Concept Mapping Copy the concept map about the periodic table onto a sheet of paper. Then complete it and add a title. (For more on Concept Mapping, see the Skills Handbook.)

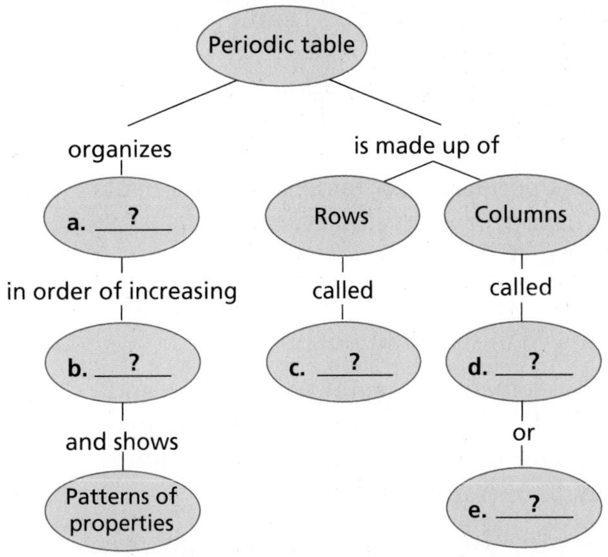

Reviewing Key Terms

Choose the letter of the best answer.

1. The atomic number of an atom is determined by the number of
   a. protons. **b.** electrons.
   c. neutrons. **d.** isotopes.
2. In the modern periodic table, elements are arranged
   a. according to atomic mass.
   b. according to atomic number.
   c. in alphabetical order.
   d. according to the number of neutrons in their nuclei.
3. Inside the sun, nuclear fusion creates helium nuclei from
   a. oxygen nuclei.
   b. beryllium nuclei.
   c. carbon nuclei.
   d. hydrogen nuclei.
4. Of the following, the group that contains elements that are the most reactive is the
   a. alkali metals.
   b. alkaline earth metals.
   c. carbon family.
   d. noble gases.
5. Unlike metals, many nonmetals are
   a. good conductors of heat and electricity.
   b. malleable and ductile.
   c. gases at room temperature.
   d. shiny.
6. Unstable atomic nuclei that release fast-moving particles and energy are
   a. radioactive.
   b. alloys.
   c. isotopes.
   d. alpha particles.

Writing in Science

News Report Imagine you are writing an article for a space magazine about the life cycle of a star. Which elements are produced in a star at different stages? How are these elements distributed into space?

Discovery Channel School

Elements and the Periodic Table
Video Preview
Video Field Trip
▶ Video Assessment

Review and Assessment

Checking Concepts

7. What discoveries about the atom did Rutherford make from his team's experiments?
8. How do two isotopes of an element differ from one another? How are they similar?
9. Use the periodic table to name two elements that have properties similar to those of chlorine (Cl).
10. Why are elements heavier than oxygen *not* produced in stars like the sun?
11. Of the elements oxygen (O), zinc (Zn), and iodine (I), which one is likely to be a poor conductor of electricity and a brittle solid at room temperature?
12. What properties of radioactive isotopes make them useful?

Thinking Critically

13. **Comparing and Contrasting** List the three kinds of particles that make up atoms, and compare their masses and their locations in an atom.
14. **Applying Concepts** Below is a square taken from the periodic table. Identify the type of information given by each labeled item.

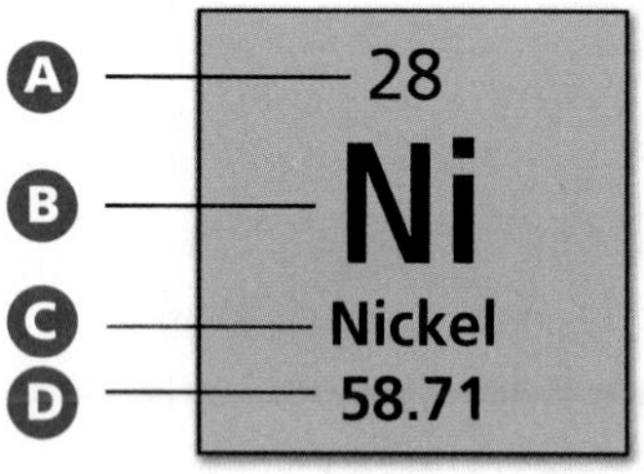

15. **Relating Cause and Effect** Why is extremely high pressure required to cause atomic nuclei to crash into one another in stars?
16. **Predicting** Using the periodic table, predict which element—potassium, iron, or aluminum—is most reactive. Explain.
17. **Inferring** What property of the materials used in computer chips makes them useful as switches that turn electricity on and off?

Applying Skills

Use the diagram to answer the questions.

The diagram below shows the first few steps of the radioactive decay of uranium-238.

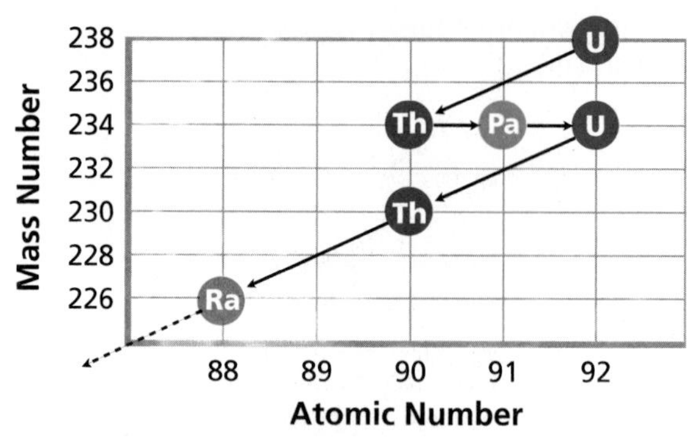

18. **Reading Graphs** What do the numbers on the *x*-axis and *y*-axis tell you about atomic particles in the nuclei of the isotopes?
19. **Interpreting Data** How many elements are in the diagram? How many different isotopes of each element are there?
20. **Classifying** What type of radioactive decay resulted in uranium-238 becoming thorium-234? How do you know?
21. **Interpreting Diagrams** Describe how thorium-234 is changed into uranium-234.
22. **Inferring** How do you know from the diagram that thorium-230 is radioactive?
23. **Posing Questions** What information would you need to have in order to extend the graph to show how radon-226 changes?

Lab zone Chapter Project

Performance Assessment Display the chart showing the metals you studied. Be ready to discuss which properties are common to all metals. Describe other properties of metals you could not test. List all the properties that could be used to find out whether an unknown element is a metal.

Standardized Test Prep

Test-Taking Tip

Reading All the Answer Choices

In answering a multiple-choice question, always read *every* answer choice before selecting the answer you think is correct. In some cases, all of the responses may be true statements, but only one answers the question correctly. In the sample question below, for example, you are asked why a carbon atom is heavier than the total mass of its protons and electrons. Each answer choice is a statement. If you look at each answer choice by itself, it expresses something that is correct. However, only one of the answer choices explains why a carbon atom is heavier than the total mass of its protons and electrons.

Sample Question

Why is the mass of a carbon atom greater than the total mass of its protons and electrons?

A The mass of a proton is greater than the mass of an electron.
B A proton is positively charged and an electron is negatively charged.
C Most of the atom's volume is the sphere-shaped cloud of electrons.
D One or more neutrons in the nucleus add mass to the atom.

Answer

The correct answer is **D**. With the exception of some hydrogen atoms, every atom contains one or more neutrons. The mass of a neutron is about the same as that of a proton. Choices **A, B,** and **C** are true statements about the subatomic particles that make up every atom. However, none of the statements answers the question.

Choose the letter of the best answer.

1. Elements that are gases at room temperature are likely to be classified as which of the following?
A metals
B nonmetals
C metalloids
D unreactive

2. Which property of aluminum makes it a suitable metal for soft drink cans?
F It has good electrical conductivity.
G It can be hammered into a thin sheet (malleability).
H It can be drawn into long wires (ductility).
J It can reflect light (shininess).

Use the table below to answer Questions 3–5.

8 **O** Oxygen 15.999	9 **F** Fluorine 18.998	10 **Ne** Neon 20.179
16 **S** Sulfur 32.06	17 **Cl** Chlorine 35.453	18 **Ar** Argon 39.948

3. Which element has an atomic number of 18?
A hydrogen
B oxygen
C fluorine
D argon

4. An atom of fluorine has 10 neutrons. What is the total number of other subatomic particles in this atom?
F 9 protons and 9 electrons
G 9 protons and 19 electrons
H 10 protons and 10 electrons
J 19 protons and 19 electrons

5. Which combination of elements represents part of a group, or family, of the periodic table?
A oxygen, fluorine, and neon
B sulfur, chlorine, and argon
C fluorine and chlorine
D oxygen and chlorine

Constructed Response

6. Describe the modern model of the atom. Your discussion should include the three main types of particles that make up an atom and the charge and location of each. Include an explanation of the overall charge on an atom.

Chapter 5

Atoms and Bonding

Chapter Preview

1 Atoms, Bonding, and the Periodic Table
Discover *What Are the Trends in the Periodic Table?*
Active Art *Periodic Table*
Science and History *Discovery of the Elements*
At-Home Activity *Looking for Elements*
Skills Lab *Comparing Atom Sizes*

2 Ionic Bonds
Discover *How Do Ions Form?*
Skills Activity *Interpreting Data*
Try This *Crystal Clear*
Skills Lab *Shedding Light on Ions*

3 Covalent Bonds
Discover *Can Water and Oil Mix?*
Analyzing Data *Comparing Molecular and Ionic Compounds*
At-Home Activity *Laundry Chemistry*

4 Bonding in Metals
Discover *Are They "Steel" the Same?*
Try This *What Do Metals Do?*

Interactive Textbook

Each water molecule in this computer model consists of two hydrogen atoms (clear) bonded to one oxygen atom (red).

Atoms and Bonding

▶ Video Preview
Video Field Trip
Video Assessment

Lab zone™ Chapter **Project**

Models of Compounds

In this chapter, you will learn how atoms of elements react with one another to form compounds. When they form compounds, the atoms become chemically bonded to each other. In this project, you will create models of chemical compounds.

Your Goal To make models demonstrating how atoms bond in ionic compounds and in molecular compounds

To complete the project, you must

- select appropriate materials to make models of atoms
- indicate the number of bonds each atom forms
- use your model atoms to compare compounds that contain ionic bonds with compounds that contain covalent bonds
- follow the safety guidelines in Appendix A

Plan It! Brainstorm with some classmates about materials you can use to represent different atoms and chemical bonds. Look ahead in the chapter to preview ionic and covalent bonding. Think about how you will show that ionic and covalent bonding are different. You may need to find some small, but highly visible, objects to represent electrons. Be ready to display your models and explain what they show.

Section 1

Atoms, Bonding, and the Periodic Table

Reading Preview

Key Concepts

- How is the reactivity of elements related to valence electrons in atoms?
- What does the periodic table tell you about atoms and the properties of elements?

Key Terms

- valence electron
- electron dot diagram
- chemical bond

Target Reading Skill

Identifying Main Ideas As you read *How the Periodic Table Works*, write the main idea in a graphic organizer like the one below. Then write three supporting details that give examples of the main idea.

Main Idea

The number of valence electrons in atoms affects the reactivity of elements.

Detail	Detail	Detail

Lab zone Discover **Activity**

What Are the Trends in the Periodic Table?

1. Examine the periodic table of the elements that your teacher provides. Look in each square for the whole number located above the symbol of the element. As you read across a row from left to right, what trend do you see?
2. Now look at a column from top to bottom. What trend do you see in these numbers?

Think It Over

Interpreting Data Can you explain why one row ends and a new row starts? Why are certain elements in the same column?

Why isn't the world made only of elements? How do the atoms of different elements combine to form compounds? The answers to these questions are related to electrons and their energy levels. And the roadmap to understanding how electrons determine the properties of elements is the periodic table.

Valence Electrons and Bonding

You learned earlier about electrons and energy levels. An atom's **valence electrons** (VAY luns) are those electrons that have the highest energy level and are held most loosely. **The number of valence electrons in an atom of an element determines many properties of that element, including the ways in which the atom can bond with other atoms.**

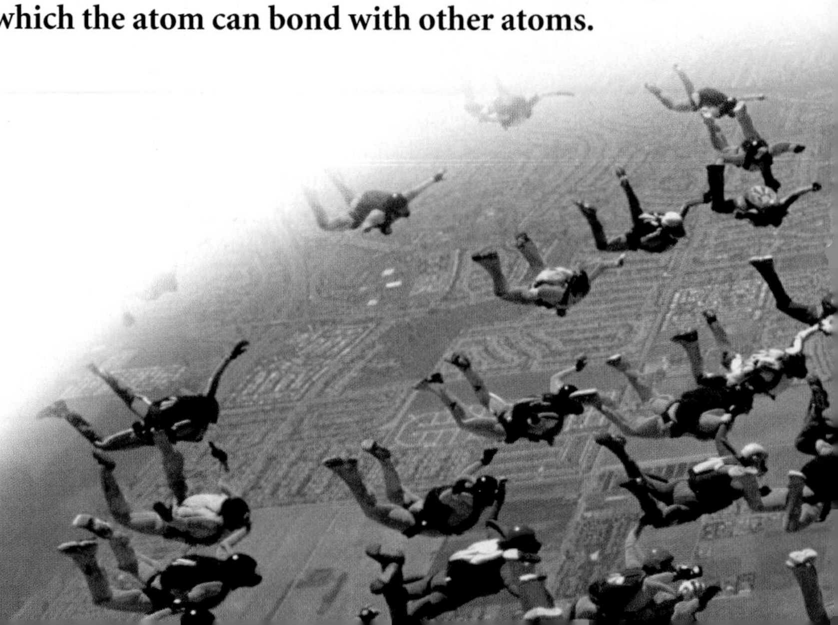

FIGURE 1
Valence Electrons
Skydivers in the outer ring are less securely held to the group than are members of the inner ring. Similarly, valence electrons are more loosely held by an atom than are electrons of lower energy levels.

Electron Dot Diagrams Each element has a specific number of valence electrons, ranging from 1 to 8. Figure 2 shows one way to depict the number of valence electrons in an element. An **electron dot diagram** includes the symbol for the element surrounded by dots. Each dot stands for one valence electron.

Chemical Bonds and Stability Atoms of most elements are more stable—less likely to react—when they have eight valence electrons. For example, atoms of neon, argon, krypton, and xenon all have eight valence electrons and are very unreactive. These elements do not easily form compounds. Some small atoms, such as helium, are stable with just two valence electrons in their first and only energy level.

Atoms usually react in a way that makes each atom more stable. One of two things can happen: Either the number of valence electrons increases to eight (or two, in the case of hydrogen). Or, the atom gives up loosely held valence electrons. Atoms that react this way can become chemically combined, that is, bonded to other atoms. A **chemical bond** is the force of attraction that holds two atoms together as a result of the rearrangement of electrons between them.

Chemical Bonds and Chemical Reactions When atoms bond, electrons may be transferred from one atom to another, or they may be shared between the atoms. In either case, the change results in a chemical reaction—that is, new substances form. Later in this chapter, you will learn which elements are likely to gain electrons, which are likely to give up electrons, and which are likely to share electrons. You will also learn how the periodic table of the elements can help you predict how atoms of different elements react.

Reading Checkpoint **What information does an electron dot diagram show?**

FIGURE 2
Electron Dot Diagrams
An atom's valence electrons are shown as dots around the symbol of the element. Notice that oxygen atoms have six valence electrons. Predicting *How many more electrons are needed to make an oxygen atom stable?*

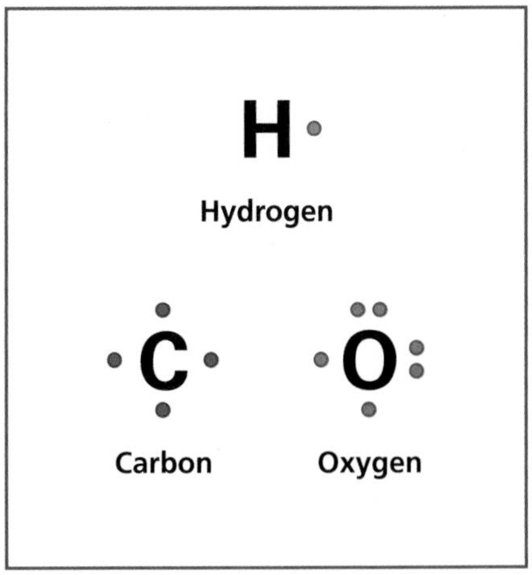

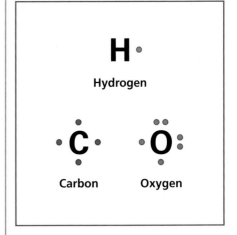

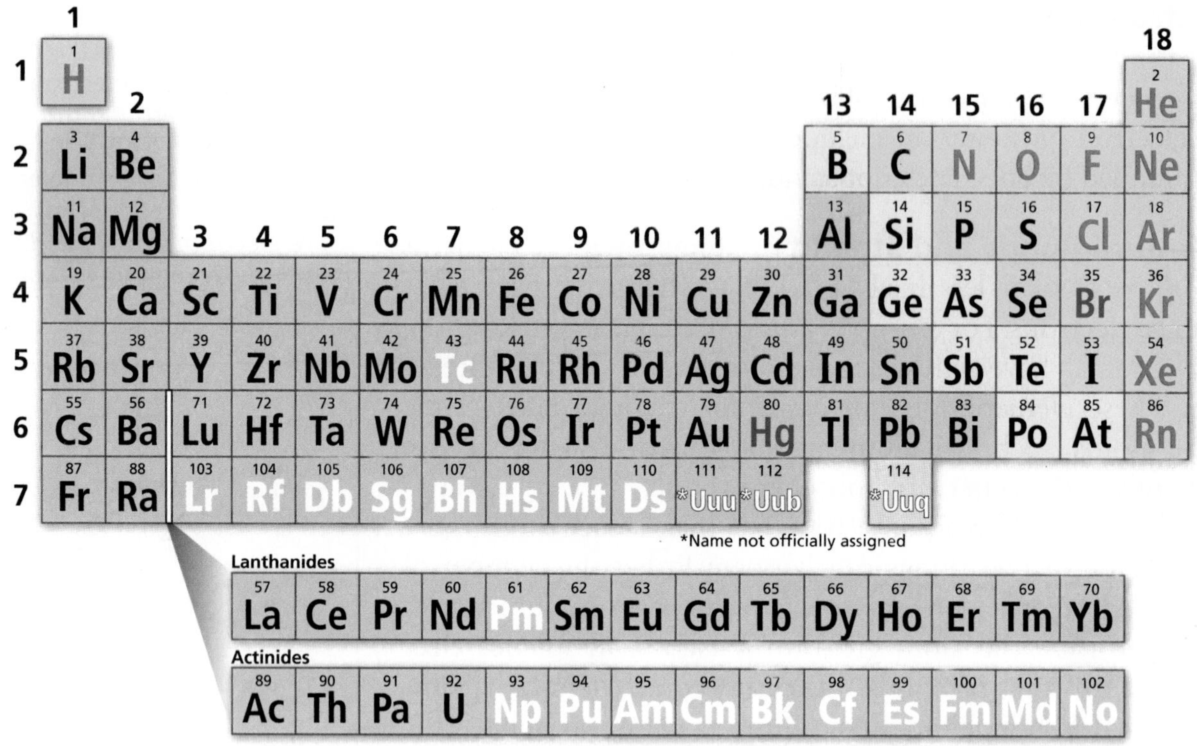

FIGURE 3
Periodic Table of the Elements
The periodic table is a system used worldwide for organizing the elements. Clues to an element's properties relate to its position in the table.

Go Online
active art

For: Periodic Table activity
Visit: PHSchool.com
Web Code: cgp-1032

How the Periodic Table Works

Recall that the periodic table is organized by atomic number—the number of protons in the nucleus of an atom. **The periodic table gives you information about the arrangement of electrons in atoms.** If you know the number of valence electrons that atoms of different elements have, you have a clue as to which elements combine and how.

Relating Periods and Groups Look at Figure 3 and think about how atoms change from left to right across a period, or row. As the atomic number increases, the number of electrons also increases. A period ends when the highest energy level has eight electrons. Valence electrons of atoms in the next period are of a higher energy level. This repeating pattern means that the elements within a group, or column, always have the same number of valence electrons.

Figure 4 compares the electron dot diagrams of elements in Periods 2 and 3. Notice that each element has one more valence electron than the element to its left. For example, Group 1 elements have one valence electron. The elements in Group 2 have two. Elements in Group 13 have three valence electrons, elements in Group 14 have four, and so on. (Elements in Groups 3 to 12 follow a slightly different pattern.) **The elements within a group have similar properties because they all have the same number of valence electrons in their atoms.**

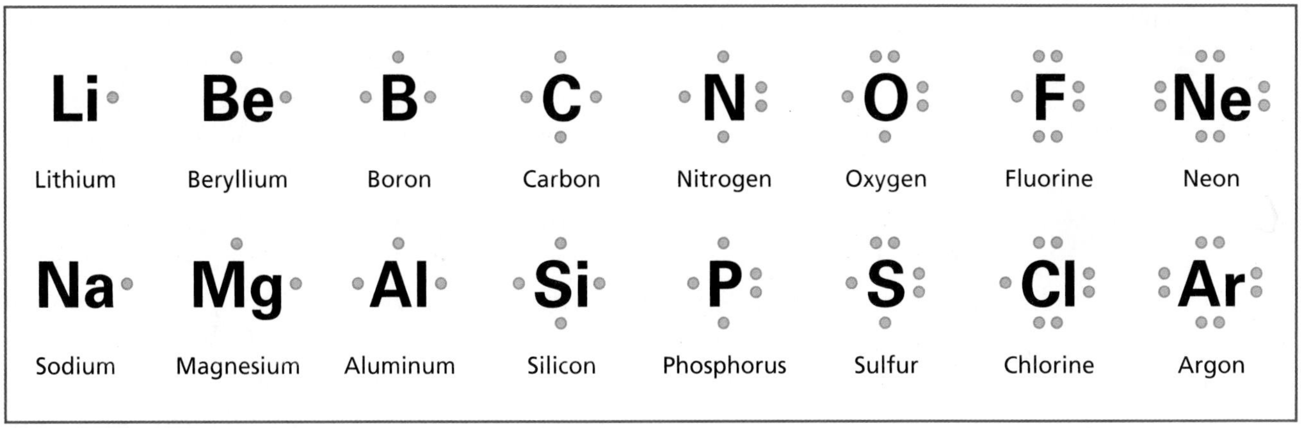

FIGURE 4
Patterns of Valence Electrons
After the number of valence electrons reaches 8, a new period begins.

Noble Gases The Group 18 elements are the noble gases. Atoms of these elements have eight valence electrons, except for helium, which has two. As you have read, atoms with eight valence electrons (or two, in the case of helium) are stable. Such atoms are unlikely to transfer electrons to other atoms or to share electrons with other atoms. As a result, noble gases do not react easily with other elements. Even so, chemists have been able to make noble gases form compounds with a few other elements.

Reactive Nonmetals and Metals Now look at the elements in the column just to the left of the noble gases. The elements in Group 17, the halogens, have atoms with seven valence electrons. A gain of just one more electron gives these atoms the stable number of eight electrons, as in the noble gases. As a result, the halogens react easily with other elements whose atoms can give up or share electrons.

At the far left side of the periodic table is Group 1, the alkali metal family. Atoms of the alkali metals have only one valence electron. Except for lithium, the next lowest energy level has a stable set of eight electrons. (Lithium atoms have a stable set of two electrons at the next lowest energy level.) Therefore, alkali metal atoms can become chemically more stable by losing their one valence electron. This property makes the alkali metals very reactive.

Reading Checkpoint **How are atoms of the elements in Group 1 similar?**

FIGURE 5
Reactivity of Chlorine
Chlorine is so reactive that steel wool burns when exposed to the chlorine gas in this jar.
Relating Cause and Effect *Why is chlorine so reactive?*

Discovery Channel School

Atoms and Bonding

Video Preview
▶ Video Field Trip
Video Assessment

Other Metals Look at the elements in Groups 2 through 12 of the periodic table. Like the Group 1 elements, these elements are metals. Most have one, two, or three valence electrons. They react by losing these electrons, especially when they combine with oxygen or one of the halogens.

How reactive a metal is depends on how easily its atoms lose valence electrons. Some metals, such as those in Group 2 (the alkaline earth metals), lose electrons easily and are almost as reactive as the alkali metals of Group 1. Other metals, such as platinum (Pt) in Group 10 and gold (Au) in Group 11, are unreactive. In general, the reactivity of metals decreases from left to right across the periodic table. Among Groups 1 and 2, reactivity increases from top to bottom.

Science and **History**

Discovery of the Elements

In 1869, Dmitri Mendeleev published the first periodic table. At that time, 63 elements were known. Since then, scientists have discovered or created about 50 new elements.

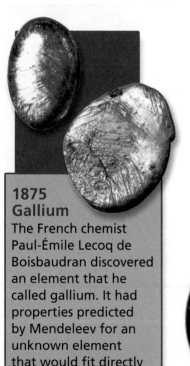

1875
Gallium
The French chemist Paul-Émile Lecoq de Boisbaudran discovered an element that he called gallium. It had properties predicted by Mendeleev for an unknown element that would fit directly below aluminum in the periodic table.

1894
Argon, Neon, Krypton, and Xenon
British chemist William Ramsay discovered an element he named argon, after the Greek word for "lazy." The name fits because argon does not react with other elements. Ramsay looked for other nonreactive gases and discovered neon, krypton, and xenon.

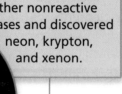

1898
Polonium and Radium
Polish chemist Marie Curie started with three tons of uranium ore before she eventually isolated a few grams of two new elements. She named them polonium and radium.

1830 1865 1900

Other Nonmetals Elements in the green section of the periodic table are the nonmetals. Notice that, unlike the metals, most nonmetals are gases at room temperature. Five nonmetals are solids, and one is a liquid. All of the nonmetals have four or more valence electrons. Like the halogens, other nonmetals become stable when they gain or share enough electrons to have a set of eight valence electrons.

The nonmetals combine with metals usually by gaining electrons. But nonmetals can also combine with other nonmetals by sharing electrons. Of the nonmetals, oxygen and the halogens are highly reactive. In fact, fluorine is the most reactive element known. It even forms compounds with some of the noble gases.

Writing in Science

Research and Write Select three elements that interest you and find out more about them. Who identified or discovered the elements? How did the elements get their names? How are the elements used? To answer these questions, look up the elements in reference books.

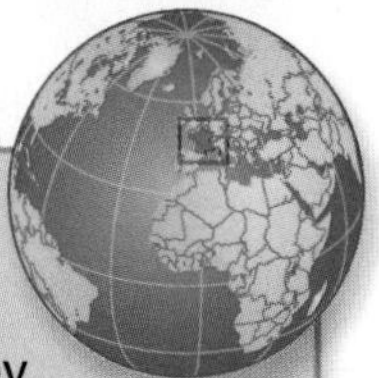

1939
Francium
Although Mendeleev predicted the properties of an element he called "eka-cesium," the element was not discovered until 1939. French chemist Marguerite Perey named her discovery francium, after the country France.

1941
Plutonium
American chemist Glenn Seaborg was the first to isolate plutonium, which is found in small amounts in uranium ores. Plutonium is used as fuel in certain nuclear reactors. It has also been used to power equipment used in space exploration.

1997
Elements 101 to 109
The International Union of Pure and Applied Chemists (IUPAC) agreed on names for elements 101 to 109. Many of the names honor scientists, such as Lise Meitner, shown here in 1946. All of the new elements were created in laboratories, and none is stable enough to exist in nature.

2003 to Present
Darmstadtium
Element 110, first created in the mid-1990s, is named darmstadtium. Research to produce and study new synthetic elements continues.

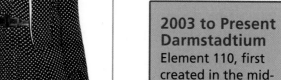

1935 — 1970 — 2005

◀ The quartz movement of the watch

FIGURE 6
A Metalloid at Work
This quartz-movement watch keeps time with a small quartz crystal, a compound made of the metalloid silicon and the nonmetal oxygen. The crystal vibrates at about 32,000 vibrations per second when a voltage is applied.

Metalloids Several elements known as metalloids lie along a zigzag line between the metals and nonmetals. The metalloids have from three to six valence electrons. They can either lose or share electrons when they combine with other elements. So, depending on the conditions, these elements can behave as either metals or nonmetals.

Hydrogen Notice that hydrogen is located above Group 1 in the periodic table. It is placed there because it has only one valence electron. However, hydrogen is considered to be a nonmetal. It is a reactive element, but its properties differ greatly from those of the alkali metals.

Reading Checkpoint **Why is hydrogen grouped above the Group 1 elements even though it is not a metal?**

Section 1 Assessment

Target Reading Skill Identifying Main Ideas Use your graphic organizer to help you answer Question 2 below.

Reviewing Key Concepts

1. a. **Defining** What are valence electrons?
   b. **Reviewing** What role do valence electons play in the formation of compounds from elements?
   c. **Comparing and Contrasting** Do oxygen atoms become more stable or less stable when oxygen forms compounds? Explain.
2. a. **Summarizing** Summarize how the periodic table is organized, and tell why this organization is useful.
   b. **Explaining** Why do the properties of elements change in a regular way across a period?
   c. **Relating Cause and Effect** How reactive are the elements in Group 18? Explain this reactivity in terms of the number of valence electrons.

Lab zone At-Home Activity

Looking for Elements Find some examples of elements at home. Then locate the elements on the periodic table. Show your examples and the periodic table to your family. Point out the positions of the elements on the table and explain what the periodic table tells you about the elements. Include at least two nonmetals in your discussion. (*Hint:* The nonmetals may be invisible.)

Lab zone **Skills Lab**

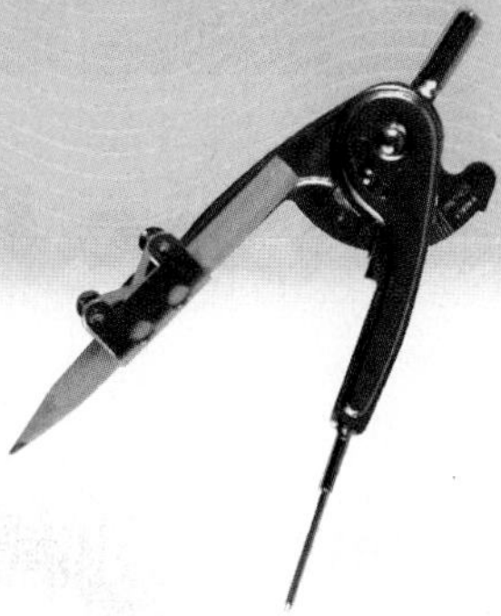

Comparing Atom Sizes

Problem

How is the radius of an atom related to its atomic number?

Skills Focus

making models, graphing, interpreting data

Materials

- drawing compass
- metric ruler
- calculator
- periodic table of the elements

Procedure

1. Using the periodic table as a reference, predict whether the size (radius) of atoms will increase, remain the same, or decrease as you go from the top to the bottom of a group, or family, of elements.
2. The data table lists the elements in Group 2 in the periodic table. The atomic radius of each element is given in picometers (pm). Copy the data table into your notebook.
3. Calculate the relative radius of each atom compared to beryllium, the smallest atom listed. Do this by dividing each radius by the radius of beryllium. (*Hint:* The relative radius of magnesium would be 160 pm divided by 112 pm, or 1.4.) Record these values, rounded to the nearest tenth, in your data table.
4. Using a compass, draw a circle for each element with a radius that corresponds to the relative radius you calculated in Step 3. Use centimeters as your unit for the radius of each circle. **CAUTION:** *Do not push the sharp point of the compass against your skin.*
5. Label each model with the symbol of the element it represents.

Data Table

Atomic Number	Element	Radius (pm)*	Relative Radius
4	Be	112	1
12	Mg	160	
20	Ca	197	
38	Sr	215	
56	Ba	222	

**A picometer (pm) is one billionth of a millimeter.*

Analyze and Conclude

1. **Making Models** Based on your models, was your prediction in Step 1 correct? Explain.
2. **Graphing** Make a graph of the data given in the first and third columns of the data table. Label the horizontal axis *Atomic Number.* Mark the divisions from 0 to 60. Then label the vertical axis *Radius* and mark its divisions from 0 to 300 picometers.
3. **Interpreting Data** Do the points on your graph fall on a straight line or on a curve? What trend does the graph show?
4. **Predicting** Predict where you would find the largest atom in any group, or family, of elements. What evidence would you need to tell if your prediction is correct?
5. **Communicating** Write a paragraph explaining why it is useful to draw a one- to two-centimeter model of an atom that has an actual radius of 100 to 200 picometers.

More to Explore

Look up the atomic masses for the Group 2 elements. Devise a plan to model their relative atomic masses using real-world objects.

Section 2

Ionic Bonds

Reading Preview

Key Concepts

- What are ions, and how do they form bonds?
- How are the formulas and names of ionic compounds written?
- What are the properties of ionic compounds?

Key Terms

- ion • polyatomic ion
- ionic bond • ionic compound
- chemical formula • subscript
- crystal

Target Reading Skill

Previewing Visuals Before you read, preview Figure 9. Then write two questions that you have about the diagram in a graphic organizer like the one below. As you read, answer your questions.

Formation of an Ionic Bond

Q. What is an ionic bond?
A.
Q.

Lab zone Discover Activity

How Do Ions Form?

1. Place three pairs of checkers (three red and three black) on your desk. The red represent electrons and the black represent protons.
2. Place nine pairs of checkers (nine red and nine black) in a separate group on your desk.
3. Move a red checker from the smaller group to the larger group.
4. Count the number of positive charges (protons) and negative charges (electrons) in each group.
5. Now sort the checkers into a group of four pairs and a group of eight pairs. Repeat Steps 3 and 4, this time moving two red checkers from the smaller group to the larger group.

Think It Over

Inferring What was the total charge on each group before you moved the red checkers (electrons)? What was the charge on each group after you moved the checkers? Based on this activity, what do you think happens to the charge on an atom when it loses electrons? When it gains electrons?

You and a friend walk past a market that sells apples for 40 cents each and pears for 50 cents each. You have 45 cents and want an apple. Your friend also has 45 cents but wants a pear. You realize that if you give your friend a nickel, she will have 50 cents and can buy a pear. You will have 40 cents left to buy an apple. Transferring the nickel gets both of you what you want. Your actions model, in a simple way, what can happen between atoms.

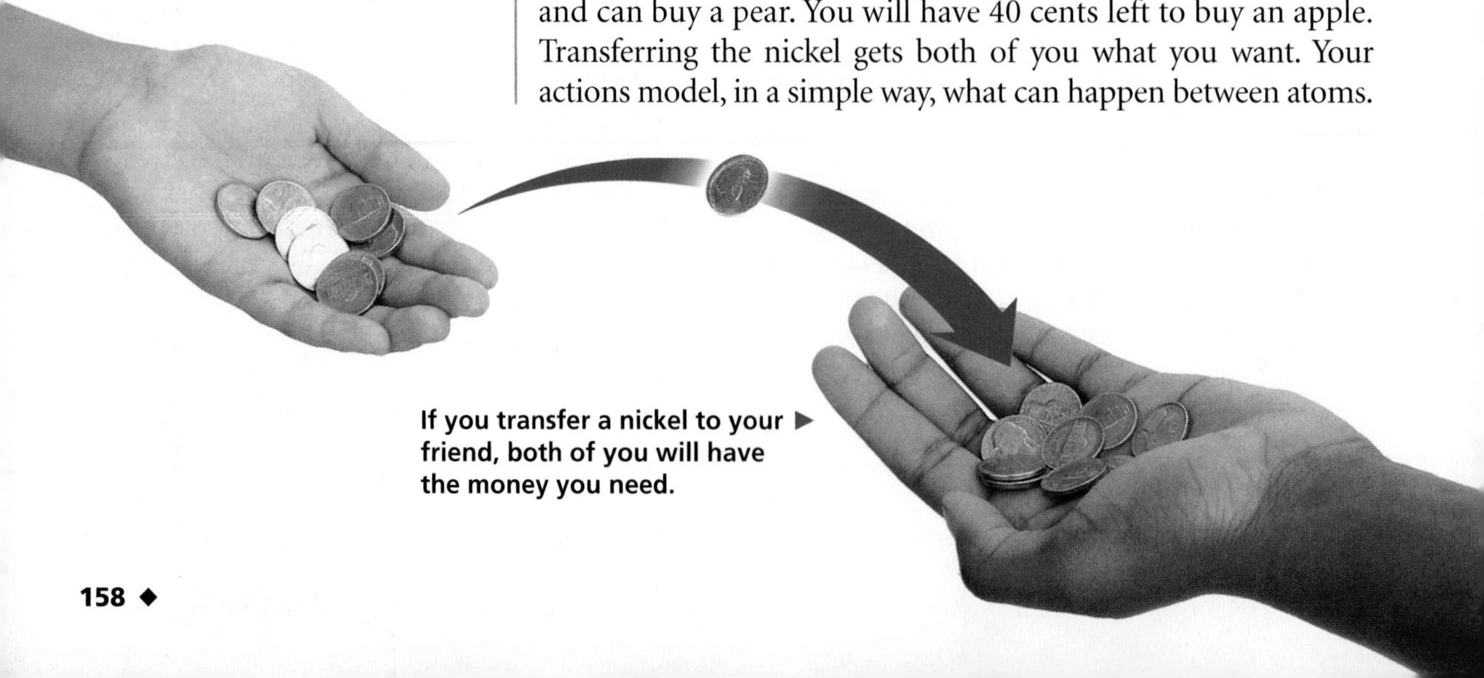

If you transfer a nickel to your friend, both of you will have the money you need. ▶

FIGURE 7
How Ions Form
When an atom loses one of its electrons, it becomes a positively charged ion. The atom that gains the electron becomes a negatively charged ion.

Ions and Ionic Bonds

Atoms with five, six, or seven valence electrons usually become more stable when this number increases to eight. Likewise, most atoms with one, two, or three valence electrons can lose electrons and become more stable. When these two types of atoms combine, electrons are transferred from one type of atom to the other. The transfer makes both types of atoms more stable.

How Ions Form An **ion** (EYE ahn) is an atom or group of atoms that has an electric charge. **When an atom loses an electron, it loses a negative charge and becomes a positive ion. When an atom gains an electron, it gains a negative charge and becomes a negative ion.** Figure 8 lists some ions you will often see in this book. Use this table as a reference while you read this section and other chapters.

Polyatomic Ions Notice in Figure 8 that some ions are made of several atoms. For example, the ammonium ion is made of nitrogen and hydrogen atoms. Ions that are made of more than one atom are called **polyatomic ions** (pahl ee uh TAHM ik). The prefix *poly* means "many," so *polyatomic* means "many atoms." You can think of a polyatomic ion as a group of atoms that reacts as a unit. Like other ions, polyatomic ions have an overall positive or negative charge.

Reading Checkpoint How does an ion with a charge of 2+ form?

Ions and Their Charges

Name	Charge	Symbol or Formula
Lithium	1+	Li^+
Sodium	1+	Na^+
Potassium	1+	K^+
Ammonium	1+	NH_4^+
Calcium	2+	Ca^{2+}
Magnesium	2+	Mg^{2+}
Aluminum	3+	Al^{3+}
Fluoride	1–	F^-
Chloride	1–	Cl^-
Iodide	1–	I^-
Bicarbonate	1–	HCO_3^-
Nitrate	1–	NO_3^-
Oxide	2–	O^{2-}
Sulfide	2–	S^{2-}
Carbonate	2–	CO_3^{2-}
Sulfate	2–	SO_4^{2-}
Phosphate	3–	PO_4^{3-}

FIGURE 8
Ions are atoms that have lost or gained electrons. **Interpreting Tables** *How many electrons does a sulfur atom gain when it becomes a sulfide ion?*

Ionic Bonds Look at Figure 9 to see how sodium atoms and chlorine atoms combine to form sodium chloride (table salt). Notice that sodium has one valence electron and chlorine has seven valence electrons. When sodium's valence electron is transferred to chlorine, both atoms become ions. The sodium atom becomes a positive ion (Na^+). The chlorine atom becomes a negative ion (Cl^-).

Because oppositely charged particles attract, the positive Na^+ ion and the negative Cl^- ion attract each other. An **ionic bond** is the attraction between two oppositely charged ions. **Ionic bonds form as a result of the attraction between positive and negative ions.** A compound that consists of positive and negative ions, such as sodium chloride, is called an **ionic compound.**

FIGURE 9

Formation of an Ionic Bond

Reactions occur easily between metals in Group 1 and nonmetals in Group 17. Follow the process below to see how an ionic bond forms between a sodium atom and a chlorine atom.

Relating Cause and Effect *Why is sodium chloride electrically neutral?*

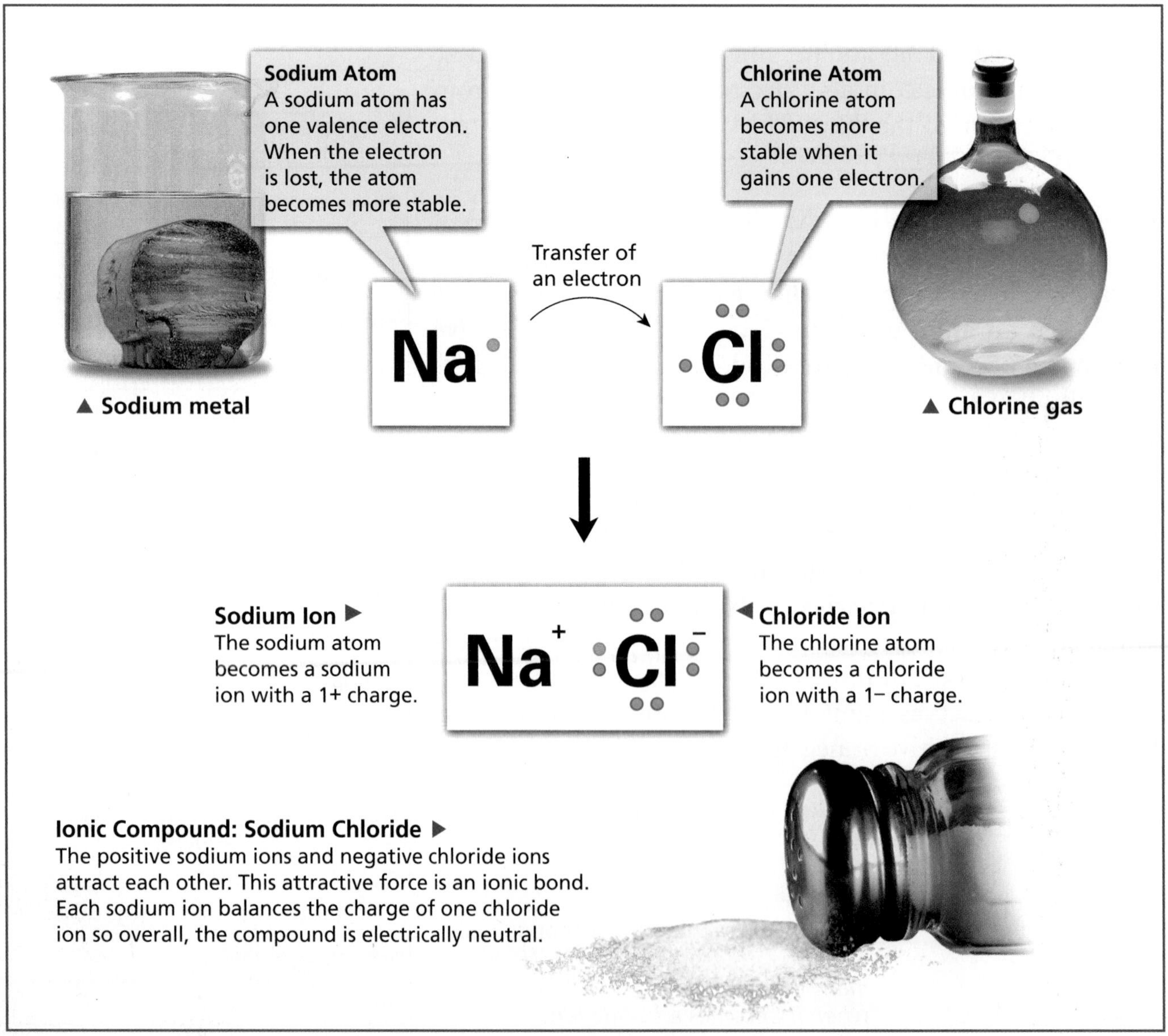

Sodium Atom
A sodium atom has one valence electron. When the electron is lost, the atom becomes more stable.
Chlorine Atom
A chlorine atom becomes more stable when it gains one electron.
Transfer of an electron
Na
Cl
▲ Sodium metal
▲ Chlorine gas
Sodium Ion ▶
The sodium atom becomes a sodium ion with a 1+ charge.
Na+ Cl−
◀ Chloride Ion
The chlorine atom becomes a chloride ion with a 1– charge.
Ionic Compound: Sodium Chloride ▶
The positive sodium ions and negative chloride ions attract each other. This attractive force is an ionic bond. Each sodium ion balances the charge of one chloride ion so overall, the compound is electrically neutral.

Chemical Formulas and Names

Compounds can be represented by chemical formulas. A **chemical formula** is a combination of symbols that shows the ratio of elements in a compound. For example, the formula for magnesium chloride is $MgCl_2$. What does the formula tell you?

Formulas of Ionic Compounds From Figure 8 you know that the charge on the magnesium ion is 2+. **When ionic compounds form, the ions come together in a way that balances out the charges on the ions. The chemical formula for the compound reflects this balance.** Two chloride ions, each with a charge of 1− will balance the charge on the magnesium ion. That's why the formula of magnesium chloride is $MgCl_2$. The number "2" is a subscript. A **subscript** tells you the ratio of elements in the compound. For $MgCl_2$, the ratio of magnesium ions to chloride ions is 1 to 2.

If no subscript is written, the number 1 is understood. For example, the formula NaCl tells you that there is a 1 to 1 ratio of sodium ions to chloride ions. Formulas for compounds of polyatomic ions are written in a similar way. For example, calcium carbonate has the formula $CaCO_3$.

Naming Ionic Compounds Magnesium chloride, sodium bicarbonate, sodium oxide—where do these names come from? **For an ionic compound, the name of the positive ion comes first, followed by the name of the negative ion.** The name of the positive ion is usually the name of a metal. But, a few positive polyatomic ions exist, such as the ammonium ion (NH_4^+). If the negative ion is a single element, as you've already seen with sodium chloride, the end of its name changes to *-ide*. For example, MgO is named magnesium oxide. If the negative ion is polyatomic, its name usually ends in *-ate* or *-ite*, as in Figure 8. The compound NH_4NO_3, named ammonium nitrate, is a common fertilizer for gardens and crop plants.

Reading Checkpoint **What is the name of the ionic compound with the formula K_2S?**

Lab zone Skills Activity

Interpreting Data

Use the periodic table and Figure 8 to identify the charges of the ions in each ionic compound listed below. Then write the formula for each compound.

- sodium bromide
- lithium oxide
- magnesium sulfide
- aluminum fluoride
- potassium nitrate
- ammonium chloride

How did you know how many of each ion to write in the formula?

FIGURE 10
Calcium Carbonate
The white cliffs of Dover, England, are made of chalk formed from the remains of tiny sea organisms. Chalk is mostly an ionic compound, calcium carbonate.

Lab zone Try This Activity

Crystal Clear

Can you grow a salt crystal?

1. Add salt to a jar containing about 200 mL of hot tap water and stir. Keep adding salt until no more dissolves and it settles out when you stop stirring.
2. Tie a large crystal of coarse salt into the middle of a piece of thread.
3. Tie one end of the thread to the middle of a pencil.
4. Suspend the other end of the thread in the solution by laying the pencil across the mouth of the jar. Do not allow the crystal to touch the solution.
5. Place the jar in a quiet, undisturbed area. Check the size of the crystal over the next few days.

Observing Does the salt crystal change size over time? What is its shape? What do you think is happening to the ions in the solution?

Properties of Ionic Compounds

Table salt, baking soda, and iron rust are different compounds with different properties. You wouldn't want to season your food with either iron rust or baking soda. However, these compounds are alike in some ways because they are all ionic compounds. **In general, ionic compounds are hard, brittle crystals that have high melting points. When dissolved in water or melted, they conduct electricity.**

Ionic Crystals Figure 11 shows a chunk of halite, or table salt, NaCl. Pieces of halite have sharp edges, corners, flat surfaces, and a cubic shape. Equal numbers of Na^+ and Cl^- ions in solid sodium chloride are attracted in an alternating pattern, as shown in the diagram. The ions form an orderly, three-dimensional arrangement called a **crystal.**

In an ionic compound, every ion is attracted to ions of opposite charge that surround it. It is attracted to ions above, below, and to all sides. The pattern formed by the ions remains the same no matter what the size of the crystal. In a single grain of salt, the crystal pattern extends for millions of ions in every direction. Many crystals of ionic compounds are hard and brittle, due to the strength of their ionic bonds and the attractions among all the ions.

High Melting Points What happens when you heat an ionic compound such as table salt? When you heat a substance, its energy increases. When ions have enough energy to overcome the attractive forces between them, they break away from each other. In other words, the crystal melts to a liquid. Because ionic bonds are strong, a lot of energy is needed to break them. As a result, ionic compounds have high melting points. They are all solids at room temperature. Table salt must be heated to 801°C before the crystal melts.

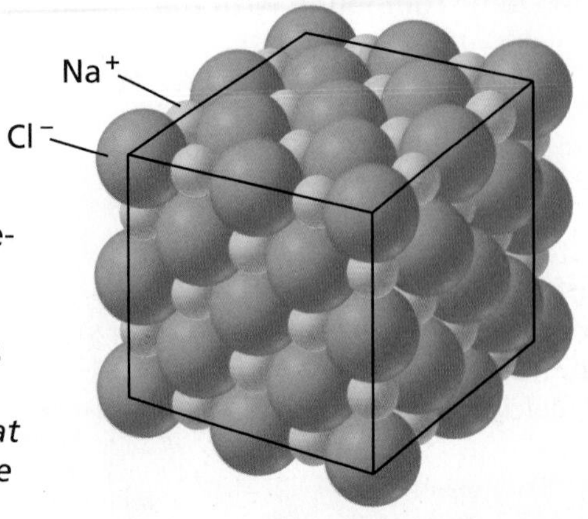

FIGURE 11
Ionic Crystals
The ions in ionic compounds are arranged in specific three-dimensional shapes called crystals. Some crystals have a cube shape like these crystals of halite, or sodium chloride.
Making Generalizations *What holds the ions together in the crystal?*

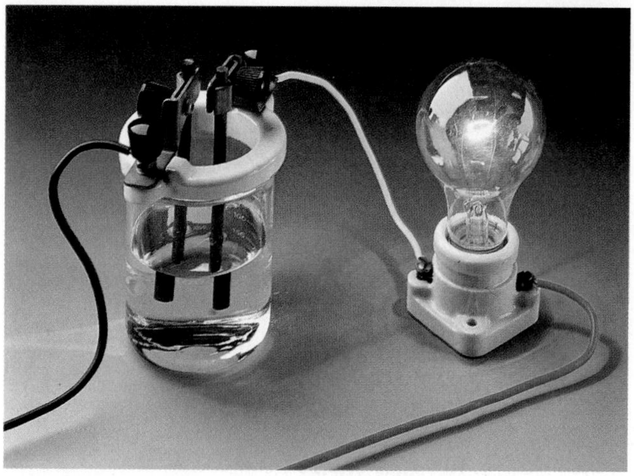

FIGURE 12
Ions in Solution
A solution of sodium chloride conducts current across the gap between the two black rods of a conductivity tester. As a result, the bulb lights up.

Electrical Conductivity Electric current is the flow of charged particles. When ionic crystals dissolve in water, the bonds between ions are broken. As a result, the ions are free to move about, and the solution conducts current. Likewise, after an ionic compound melts, the ions are able to move freely, and the liquid conducts current. In contrast, ionic compounds in solid form do not conduct current well. The ions in the solid crystal are tightly bound to each other and cannot move from place to place. If charged particles cannot move, there is no current.

Reading Checkpoint What is a crystal?

Go Online SCI LINKS NSTA

For: Links on ionic compounds
Visit: www.SciLinks.org
Web Code: scn-1213

Section 2 Assessment

Target Reading Skill Previewing Visuals Compare your questions and answers about Figure 9 with those of a partner.

Reviewing Key Concepts

1. a. **Reviewing** What are the two basic ways in which ions form from atoms?
   b. **Comparing and Contrasting** Contrast sodium and chloride ions, including how they form. Write the symbol for each ion.
   c. **Relating Cause and Effect** What holds the ions together in sodium chloride? Indicate the specific charges that are involved.
2. a. **Identifying** What information is given by the formula of an ionic compound?
   b. **Explaining** The formula for sodium sulfide is Na_2S. Explain what this formula means.
   c. **Applying Concepts** Write the formula for calcium chloride. Explain how you determined this formula.
3. a. **Listing** List three properties of ionic compounds.
   b. **Making Generalizations** Relate each property that you listed to the characteristics of ionic bonds.

Writing in Science

Firsthand Account Pretend that you are the size of an atom, observing a reaction between a potassium atom and a fluorine atom. Write an account of the formation of an ionic bond as the atoms react. Tell what happens to the valence electrons on each atom and how each atom is changed by losing or gaining electrons.

Lab zone **Skills Lab**

Shedding Light on Ions

Problem

What kinds of compounds produce ions in solution?

Skills Focus

controlling variables, interpreting data, inferring

Materials

- 2 dry cells, 1.5 V
- small light bulb and socket
- 4 lengths of wire with alligator clips on both ends
- 2 copper strips

(or conductivity probe)

- distilled water
- small beaker
- small plastic spoon
- sodium chloride
- graduated cylinder, 100-mL
- sucrose
- additional materials supplied by your teacher

Procedure

1. Make a conductivity tester as described below or, if you are using a conductivity probe, see your teacher for instructions. Then make a data table in your notebook similar to the one above.

Data Table	
Sample	Observations
Tap water	
Distilled water	
Sodium chloride	
Sodium chloride in water	

2. Pour about 50 mL of tap water into a small beaker. Place the copper strips in the beaker. Be sure the strips are not touching each other. Attach the alligator clip of the free end of one wire to a copper strip. Do the same with the other wire and the other copper strip. Record your observations.
3. Disconnect the wires from the copper strips. Take the strips out of the beaker, and pour out the tap water. Dry the inside of the beaker and the copper strips with a paper towel.
4. Pour 50 mL of distilled water into the beaker. Reconnect the conductivity tester and test the water as in Step 2. Keep the copper strips about the same distance apart as in Step 2. Record your observations.
5. Use 3 spoonfuls of sodium chloride to make a small pile on a clean piece of paper. Dry off the copper strips of the conductivity tester and use it to test the conductivity of the sodium chloride. Record your observations.

Making a Conductivity Tester

A. Use wire with alligator clips to connect the positive terminal of a dry cell to a lamp socket. **CAUTION:** *The bulb is fragile and can break.*

B. Similarly connect another wire between the negative terminal of the cell and the positive terminal of the second cell.

C. Connect one end of a third wire to the negative terminal of the second dry cell.

D. Connect one end of a fourth wire to the other terminal of the lamp socket.

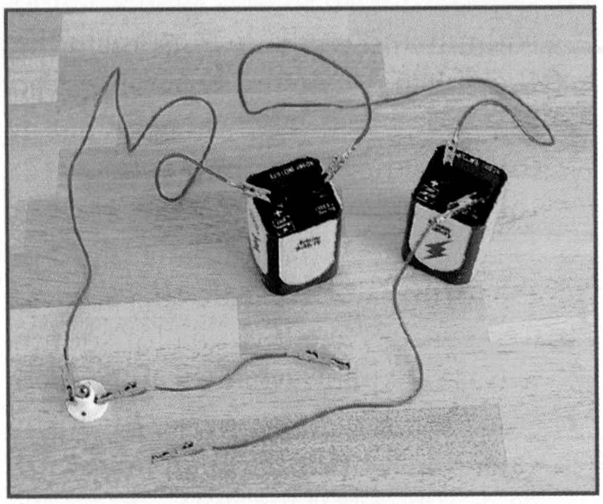

6. Add 1 spoonful of sodium chloride to the distilled water in the beaker. Stir with the spoon until the salt dissolves. Repeat the conductivity test and record your observations.
7. Disconnect the conductivity tester and rinse the beaker, spoon, and copper strips with distilled water. Dry the beaker as in Step 3.
8. Test sucrose (table sugar) in the same ways that you tested sodium chloride in Steps 4 through 7. Test additional materials supplied by your teacher.
    - If the material is a solid, mix 1 spoonful of it with about 50 mL of distilled water and stir until the material dissolves. Test the resulting mixture.
    - If the substance is a liquid, simply pour about 50 mL into the beaker. Test it as you did the other mixtures.

Analyze and Conclude

1. **Controlling Variables** Why did you test both tap water and distilled water before testing the sodium chloride solution?
2. **Interpreting Data** Could you have used tap water in your tests instead of distilled water? Explain.
3. **Drawing Conclusions** Based on your observations, add a column to your data table indicating whether each substance produced ions in solution.
4. **Inferring** Sodium chloride is an ionic compound. How can you account for any observed differences in conductivity between dry and dissolved sodium chloride?
5. **Communicating** Based on your observations, decide whether or not you think sucrose (table sugar) is made up of ions. Explain how you reached your answer, using evidence from the experiment.

Design an Experiment

Design an experiment to test the effects of varying the spacing between the copper strips of the conductivity tester. *Obtain your teacher's permission before carrying out your investigation.*

Section 3

Covalent Bonds

Reading Preview

Key Concepts

- What holds covalently bonded atoms together?
- What are the properties of molecular compounds?
- How does unequal sharing of electrons occur, and how does it affect molecules?

Key Terms

- covalent bond
- molecule
- double bond
- triple bond
- molecular compound
- polar bond
- nonpolar bond

Target Reading Skill

Asking Questions Before you read, preview the red headings. In a graphic organizer like the one below, ask a *what* or *how* question for each heading. As you read, answer your questions.

Covalent Bonds

Question	Answer
How do covalent bonds form?	Covalent bonds form when...

Lab zone Discover Activity

Can Water and Oil Mix?

1. Pour water into a small jar that has a tight-fitting lid until the jar is about a third full.
2. Add an equal amount of vegetable oil to the jar. Cover the jar tightly.
3. Shake the jar vigorously for 20 seconds. Observe the contents.
4. Allow the jar to sit undisturbed for 1 minute. Observe again.
5. Remove the top and add 3 drops of liquid detergent. Cover the jar and repeat Steps 3 and 4.

Think It Over

Forming Operational Definitions Based on your observations, write an operational definition of *detergent.* How might your observations relate to chemical bonds in the detergent, oil, and water molecules?

Uh oh, you have a big project due in English class next week! You need to write a story and illustrate it with colorful posters. Art has always been your best subject, but writing takes more effort. Luckily, you're working with a partner who writes well but doesn't feel confident in art. If you each contribute your skills, together you can produce a high-quality finished project.

FIGURE 13
Sharing Skills
One student is a skilled artist, while the other is a skilled writer. By pooling their skills, the students can complete their project.

How Covalent Bonds Form

Just as you and your friend can work together by sharing your talents, atoms can become more stable by sharing electrons. The chemical bond formed when two atoms share electrons is called a **covalent bond.** Covalent bonds usually form between atoms of nonmetals. In contrast, ionic bonds usually form when a metal combines with a nonmetal.

Electron Sharing Recall that the noble gases are not very reactive. In contrast, all other nonmetals, including hydrogen, can bond to other nonmetals by sharing electrons. Most nonmetals can even bond with another atom of the same element, as is the case with fluorine in Figure 14. When you count the electrons on each atom, count the shared pair each time. By sharing electrons, each atom has a stable set of eight. **The force that holds atoms together in a covalent bond is the attraction of each atom's nucleus for the shared pair of electrons.** The two bonded fluorine atoms form a molecule. A **molecule** is a neutral group of atoms joined by covalent bonds.

How Many Bonds? Look at the electron dot diagrams in Figure 15. Count the valence electrons around each atom. Except for hydrogen, the number of covalent bonds that nonmetal atoms can form equals the number of electrons needed to make a total of eight. Hydrogen needs only two electrons.

For example, oxygen has six valence electrons, so it can form two covalent bonds. In a water molecule, oxygen forms one covalent bond with each of two hydrogen atoms. As a result, the oxygen atom has a stable set of eight valence electrons. Each hydrogen atom can form one bond because it needs only a total of two electrons to be stable. Do you see why water's formula is H_2O, instead of H_3O, H_4O, or just HO?

FIGURE 14
Sharing Electrons
By sharing electrons in a covalent bond, each fluorine atom has a stable set of eight valence electrons.

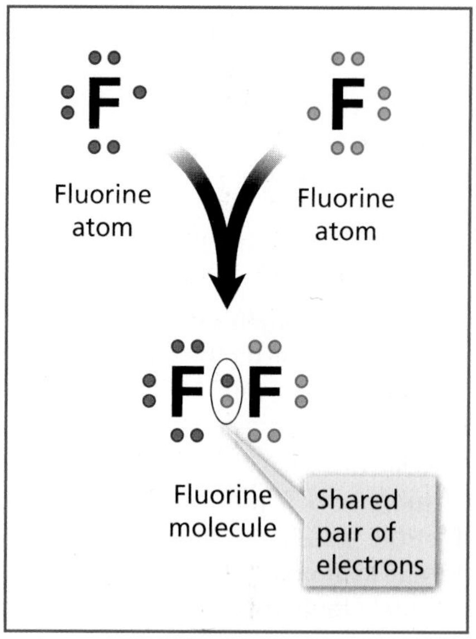

FIGURE 15
Covalent Bonds
The oxygen atom in water and the nitrogen atom in ammonia each have eight valence electrons as a result of forming covalent bonds with hydrogen atoms.
Interpreting Diagrams *How many covalent bonds can a nitrogen atom form?*

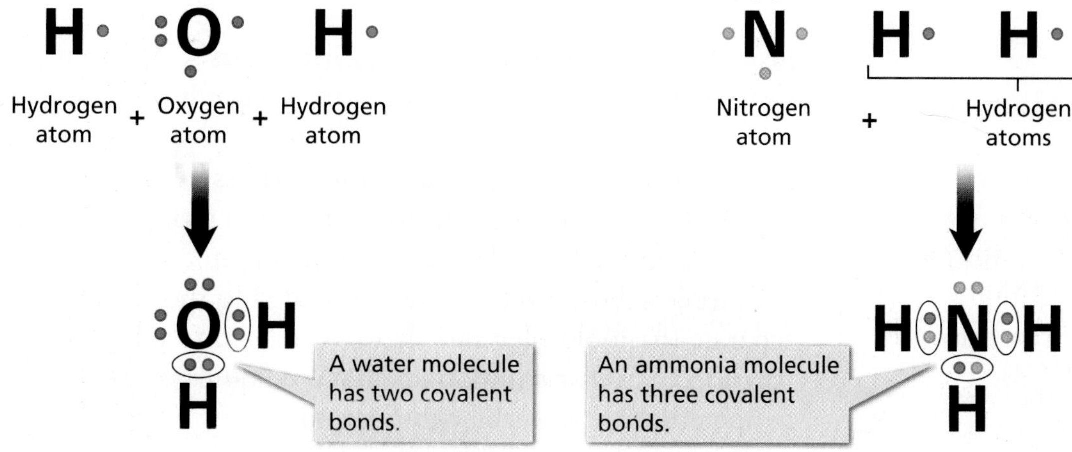

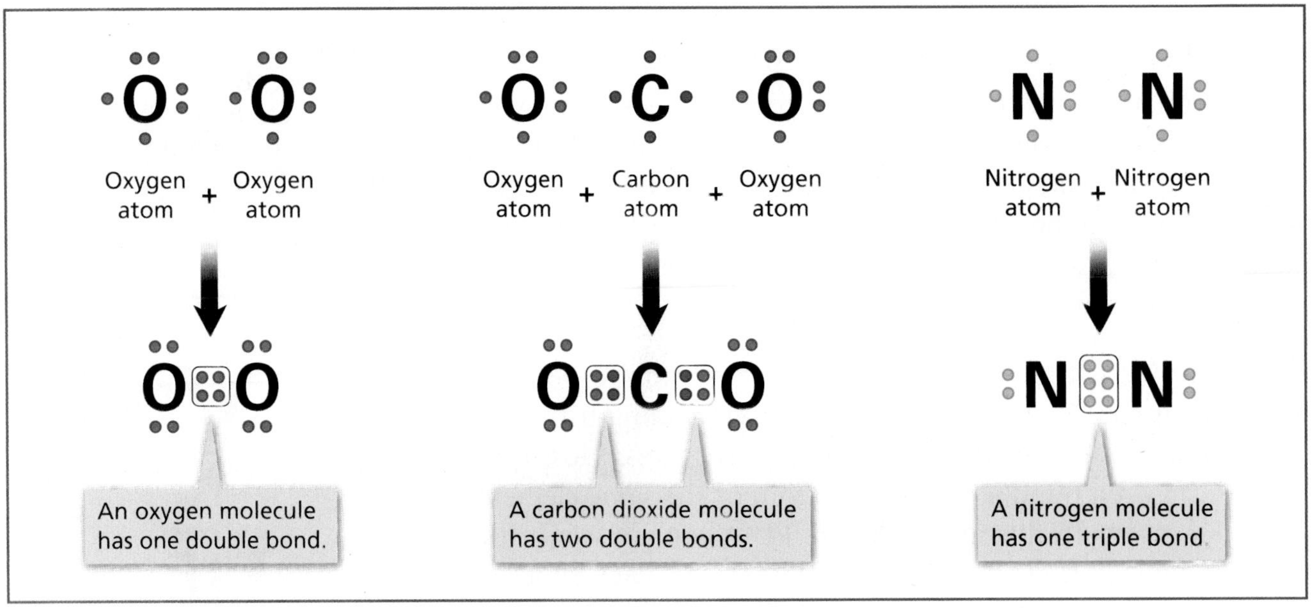
Oxygen atom
+
Oxygen atom
An oxygen molecule has one double bond.
Oxygen atom
+
Carbon atom
+
Oxygen atom
A carbon dioxide molecule has two double bonds.
Nitrogen atom
+
Nitrogen atom
A nitrogen molecule has one triple bond.

FIGURE 16
Double and Triple Bonds
Double and triple bonds can form when atoms share more than one pair of electrons.
Interpreting Diagrams *In a nitrogen molecule, how many electrons does each nitrogen atom share with the other?*

Double Bonds and Triple Bonds Look at the diagram of the oxygen molecule (O_2) in Figure 16. What do you see that's different? This time the two atoms share two pairs of electrons, forming a **double bond.** In a carbon dioxide molecule (CO_2), carbon forms a double bond with each of two oxygen atoms. Elements such as nitrogen and carbon can form **triple bonds** in which their atoms share three pairs of electrons.

Reading Checkpoint **What is the difference between a double bond and a triple bond?**

Molecular Compounds

A **molecular compound** is a compound that is composed of molecules. The molecules of a molecular compound contain atoms that are covalently bonded. Molecular compounds have very different properties than ionic compounds. **Compared to ionic compounds, molecular compounds generally have lower melting points and boiling points, and they do not conduct electricity when dissolved in water.**

Low Melting Points and Boiling Points Study the table in the Analyzing Data box on the next page. It lists the melting points and boiling points for a few molecular compounds and ionic compounds. In molecular solids, forces hold the molecules close to one another. But, the forces between molecules are much weaker than the forces between ions in an ionic solid. Compared with ionic solids, less heat must be added to molecular solids to separate the molecules and change the solid to a liquid. That is why most familiar compounds that are liquids or gases at room temperature are molecular compounds.

Go Online SCI LINKS NSTA
For: Links on molecular compounds
Visit: www.SciLinks.org
Web Code: scn-1214

Math Analyzing Data

Comparing Molecular and Ionic Compounds

The table compares the melting points and boiling points of a few molecular compounds and ionic compounds. Use the table to answer the following questions.

1. **Graphing** Create a bar graph of just the melting points of these compounds. Put the molecular compounds on the left and the ionic compounds on the right. Arrange the bars in order of increasing melting point. The *y*-axis should start at −200°C and go to 900°C.
2. **Interpreting Data** Describe what your graph reveals about the melting points of molecular compounds compared to those of ionic compounds.
3. **Inferring** How can you account for the differences in melting points between molecular compounds and ionic compounds?
4. **Interpreting Data** How do the boiling points of the molecular and ionic compounds compare?

Melting Points and Boiling Points of Molecular and Ionic Compounds

Substance	Formula	Melting Point (°C)	Boiling Point (°C)
Methane	CH_4	–182.4	–161.5
Rubbing alcohol	C_3H_8O	–89.5	82.4
Water	H_2O	0	100
Zinc chloride	$ZnCl_2$	290	732
Magnesium chloride	$MgCl_2$	714	1,412
Sodium chloride	NaCl	800.7	1,465

Molecular compound   Ionic compound

5. **Predicting** Ammonia's melting point is −78°C and its boiling point is −34°C. Is ammonia a molecular compound or an ionic compound? Explain.

Poor Conductivity Most molecular compounds do not conduct electric current. No charged particles are available to move, so there is no current. Materials such as plastic and rubber are used to insulate wires because these materials are composed of molecular substances. Even as liquids, molecular compounds are poor conductors. Pure water, for example, does not conduct electric current. Neither does table sugar or alcohol when they are dissolved in pure water.

Unequal Sharing of Electrons

Have you ever played tug of war? If you have, you know that if both teams pull with equal force, the contest is a tie. But what if the teams pull on the rope with unequal force? Then the rope moves toward the side of the stronger team. The same is true of electrons in a covalent bond. **Atoms of some elements pull more strongly on shared electrons than do atoms of other elements. As a result, the electrons are pulled more toward one atom, causing the bonded atoms to have slight electrical charges.** These charges are not as strong as the charges on ions.

FIGURE 17
Nonpolar and Polar Bonds
Fluorine forms a nonpolar bond with another fluorine atom. In hydrogen fluoride, fluorine attracts electrons more strongly than hydrogen does, so the bond formed is polar.

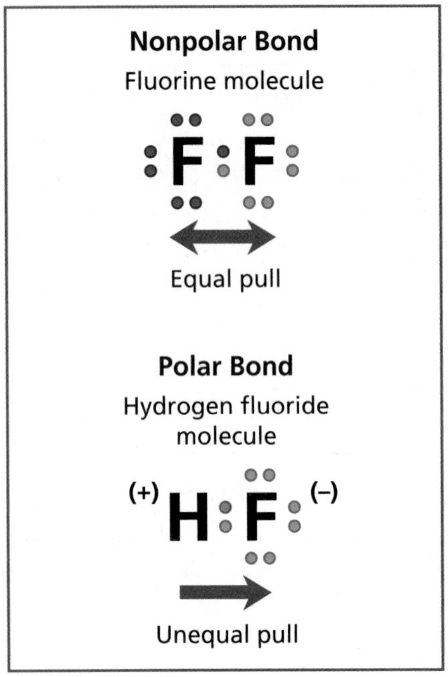

Polar Bonds and Nonpolar Bonds The unequal sharing of electrons is enough to make the atom with the stronger pull slightly negative and the atom with the weaker pull slightly positive. A covalent bond in which electrons are shared unequally is called a **polar bond.** Of course, if two atoms pull equally on the electrons, neither atom becomes charged. A covalent bond in which electrons are shared equally is a **nonpolar bond.** Compare the bond in fluorine (F_2) with the bond in hydrogen fluoride (HF) in Figure 17.

Polar Bonds in Molecules It makes sense that a molecule with nonpolar bonds will itself be nonpolar. But a molecule may contain polar bonds and still be nonpolar overall. In carbon dioxide, the oxygen atoms attract electrons much more strongly than carbon does. So, the bonds between the oxygen and carbon atoms are polar. But, as you can see in Figure 18, a carbon dioxide molecule has a shape like a straight line. So, the two oxygen atoms pull with equal strength in opposite directions. In a sense, the attractions cancel out, and the molecule is nonpolar.

In contrast, other molecules that have polar covalent bonds are themselves polar. In a water molecule, the two hydrogen atoms are at one end of the molecule, while the oxygen atom is at the other end. The oxygen atom attracts electrons more strongly than do the hydrogen atoms. As a result, the oxygen end has a slight negative charge and the hydrogen end has a slight positive charge.

Attractions Between Molecules If you could shrink small enough to move among a bunch of water molecules, what would you find? The negatively charged oxygen ends of the polar water molecules attract the positively charged hydrogen ends of nearby water molecules. These attractions pull water molecules toward each other. In contrast, there is little attraction between nonpolar molecules, such as carbon dioxide molecules.

FIGURE 18
Nonpolar and Polar Molecules
A carbon dioxide molecule is a nonpolar molecule because of its straight-line shape. In contrast, a water molecule is a polar molecule because of its bent shape.
Interpreting Diagrams *What do the arrows in the diagram show?*

Nonpolar Molecule
Carbon dioxide

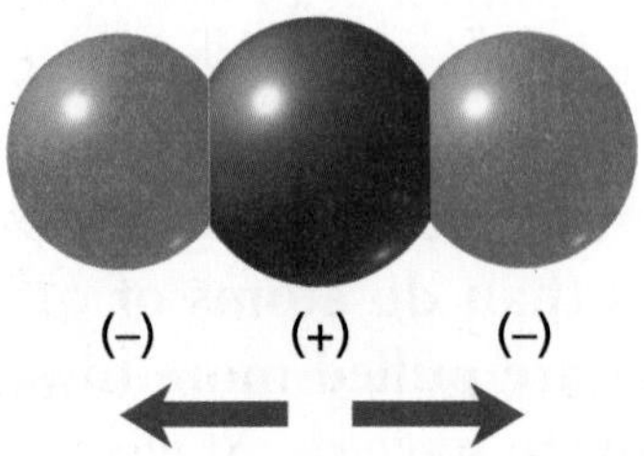

Opposite pulling cancels

Polar Molecule
Water

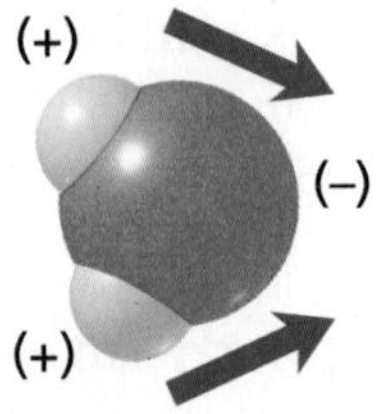

Electrons pulled toward oxygen

The properties of polar and nonpolar compounds differ because of differences in attractions between their molecules. For example, water and vegetable oil don't mix. The molecules in vegetable oil are nonpolar, and nonpolar molecules have little attraction for polar water molecules. On the other hand, the water molecules are attracted more strongly to one another than to the molecules of oil. Thus, water stays with water, and oil stays with oil.

If you did the Discover activity, you found that adding detergent helped oil and water to mix. This is because one end of a detergent molecule has nonpolar covalent bonds. The other end includes an ionic bond. The detergent's nonpolar end mixes easily with the oil. Meanwhile, the charged ionic end is attracted to polar water molecules, so the detergent dissolves in water.

Reading Checkpoint **Why is water (H_2O) a polar molecule but a fluorine molecule (F_2) is not?**

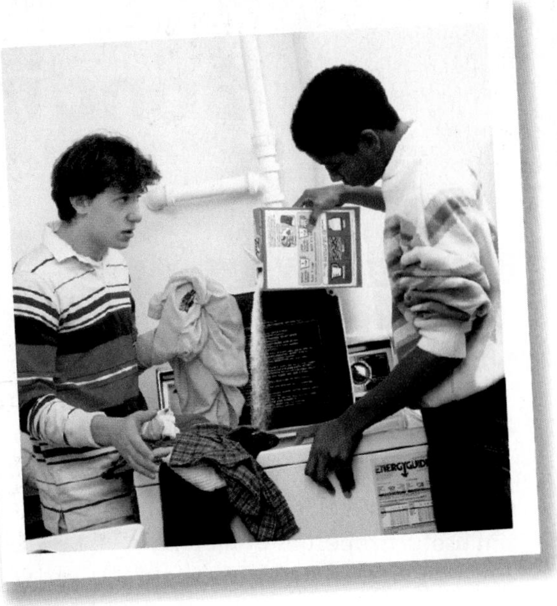

FIGURE 19
Getting Out the Dirt
Most laundry dirt is oily or greasy. Detergents can mix with both oil and water, so when the wash water goes down the drain, the soap and dirt go with it.

Section 3 Assessment

Target Reading Skill **Asking Questions** Use the answers to the questions you wrote about the headings to help you answer the questions below.

Reviewing Key Concepts

1. a. **Identifying** What is the attraction that holds two covalently bonded atoms together?
   b. **Inferring** A carbon atom can form four covalent bonds. How many valence electrons does it have?
   c. **Interpreting Diagrams** What is a double bond? Use Figure 16 to explain how a carbon dioxide molecule has a stable set of eight valence electrons for each atom.
2. a. **Reviewing** How are the properties of molecular compounds different from those of ionic compounds?
   b. **Relating Cause and Effect** Why are most molecular compounds poor conductors of electricity?
3. a. **Reviewing** How do some atoms in covalent bonds become slightly negative or slightly positive? What type of covalent bonds do these atoms form?
   b. **Comparing and Contrasting** Both carbon dioxide molecules and water molecules have polar bonds. Why then is carbon dioxide a nonpolar molecule while water is a polar molecule?
   c. **Predicting** Predict whether carbon dioxide or water would have a higher boiling point. Explain your prediction in terms of the attractions between molecules.

Lab zone At-Home Activity

Laundry Chemistry Demonstrate the action of soaps and detergents to your family. Pour some vegetable oil on a clean cloth and show how a detergent solution can wash the oil away better than water alone can. Explain to your family the features of soap and detergent molecules in terms of their chemical bonds.

Section 4

• Tech & Design •

Bonding in Metals

Reading Preview

Key Concepts

- How do the properties of metals and alloys compare?
- How are metal atoms bonded in solid metal?
- How does metallic bonding result in useful properties of metals?

Key Terms

- alloy
- metallic bond

Target Reading Skill

Relating Cause and Effect As you read, identify the properties of metals that result from metallic bonding. Write the information in a graphic organizer like the one below.

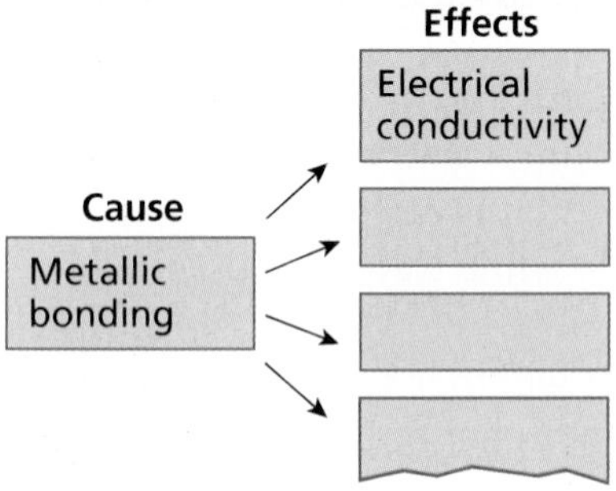

Lab zone Discover Activity

Are They "Steel" the Same?

1. Wrap a cut nail (low-carbon steel), a wire nail (high-carbon steel), and a stainless steel bolt together in a paper towel.
2. Place the towel in a plastic bag. Add about 250 mL of salt water and seal the bag.
3. After one or two days, remove the nails and bolt. Note any changes in the metals.

Think It Over

Developing Hypotheses What happened to the three types of steel? Which one changed the most, and which one changed the least? What do you think accounts for the difference?

Why would you choose metal to cover the complex shape of the building in Figure 20? You couldn't cover the building with brittle, crumbly nonmetals such as sulfur or silicon. What physical properties make metal an ideal material for making furniture, musical instruments, electrical wire, pots and pans, eating utensils, and strong beams for buildings? Why do metals have these physical properties?

FIGURE 20
Metal in Architecture
The Guggenheim Museum in Bilbao, Spain, makes dramatic use of some properties of metals. The museum's shiny outer "skin" is made of the lightweight metal titanium, which can be pressed into large, thin, flexible sheets.

FIGURE 21
Brass Trumpet
Brass is an alloy of the elements copper and zinc. **Observing** *What are some metallic properties of brass that you can see here?*

Metals and Alloys

You know a piece of metal when you see it. It's usually hard and shiny. At room temperature, most metals are solids. They can be hammered flat or drawn out into thin wire. Electronics such as stereos, computers, and MP3 players have metal parts because metals conduct electric current well. However, very few of the "metals" you use every day are made of one element. Instead, metals are usually used in the form of an alloy. An **alloy** is a mixture made of two or more elements that has the properties of metal. In every alloy, at least one of the elements is a metal. **Alloys are generally stronger and less likely to react with air or water than are the pure metals from which they are made.**

Physical Properties The properties of an alloy can differ greatly from those of its individual elements. But depending on how they are mixed, alloys also retain many of the physical properties of metals. For example, pure gold is shiny, but it is soft and easily bent. For that reason, gold jewelry and coins are made of an alloy of gold mixed with a harder element, such as copper or silver. These gold alloys are much harder than pure gold but still retain their beauty and shine. Even after thousands of years, objects made of gold alloys still look exactly the same as when they were first made.

Chemical Properties Iron is an extremely strong metal that would be good for making tools. However, iron objects rust when they are exposed to air and water. For this reason, iron is often alloyed with one or more other elements to make steel. Tools made of steel are nearly as strong as iron but resist rust much better. For example, forks and spoons made of stainless steel can be washed over and over again without rusting. That's because stainless steel—an alloy of iron, carbon, nickel, and chromium—does not react with air and water as iron does.

Reading Checkpoint **Why is most jewelry made of gold alloys rather than pure gold?**

FIGURE 22
Gold and Steel
This pipe wrench is made of steel. The necklace is made of gold alloys.

Lab zone Try This Activity

What Do Metals Do?

1. Your teacher will give you pieces of different metals. Examine each metal and try changing its shape by bending, stretching, folding, or any other action you can think of.
2. Write down the properties that are common to these metals. Write down the properties that are different.
3. What properties make each metal suitable for its intended use?

Inferring What properties must aluminum have in order to be made into foil?

Metallic Bonding

The properties of solid metals and their alloys can be explained by the structure of metal atoms and the bonding between those atoms. Recall that most metals have 1, 2, or 3 valence electrons. When metal atoms combine chemically with atoms of other elements, they usually lose valence electrons, becoming positively charged metal ions. Metals lose electrons easily because their valence electrons are not strongly held.

The loosely held electrons in metal atoms result in a type of bonding that is characteristic of metals. Like many solids, metals exist as crystals. The metal atoms are very close together and in specific arrangements. These atoms are actually positively charged ions. Their valence electrons are free to drift among the ions. Each metal ion is held in the crystal by a **metallic bond**—an attraction between a positive metal ion and the electrons surrounding it. Look at Figure 23. **A metal or metal alloy consists of positively charged metal ions embedded in a "sea" of valence electrons.** The more valence electrons an atom can add to the "sea," the stronger the metallic bonds will be.

Reading Checkpoint **What is a metallic bond?**

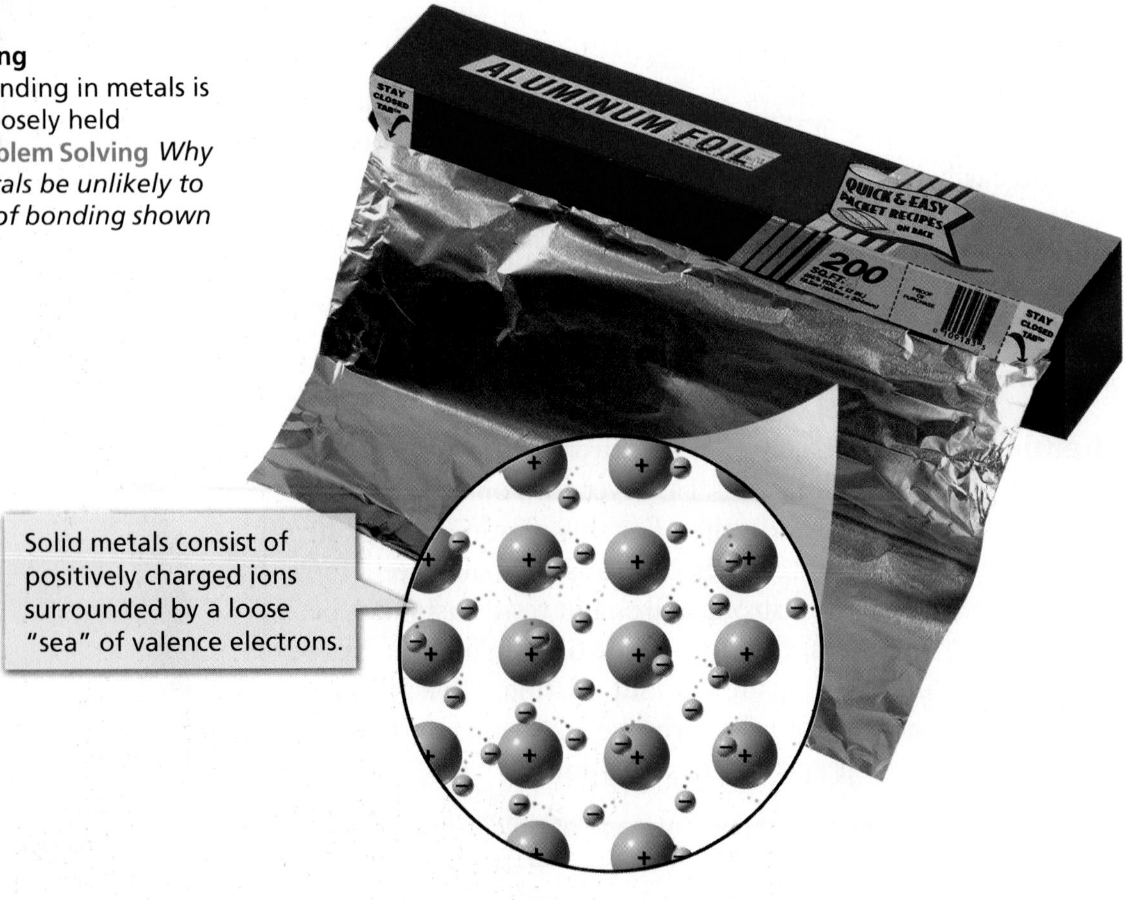

ALUMINUM FOIL
QUICK & EASY PACKET RECIPES ON BACK
200
Solid metals consist of positively charged ions surrounded by a loose "sea" of valence electrons.

FIGURE 23
Metallic Bonding
The type of bonding in metals is the result of loosely held electrons. **Problem Solving** *Why would nonmetals be unlikely to have the type of bonding shown here?*

Metallic Properties

Suppose that you placed one hand on an unheated aluminum pan and the other hand on a wooden tabletop. The aluminum pan would feel cooler than the tabletop even though both are at the same temperature. You feel the difference because aluminum conducts heat away from your hand much faster than wood does. Metal fins called a "heat sink" are used inside many electronics to cool their insides. However, a metal's ability to conduct heat would not be very useful if the metal couldn't be bent or hammered into a useful shape.

Metallic bonding explains many of the common physical properties of metals and their alloys. **The "sea of electrons" model of solid metals explains the ease with which they can change shape, their ability to conduct electric current, their luster, and their ability to conduct heat.**

Changes in Shape Most metals are flexible and can be reshaped easily. They can be stretched, pushed, or compressed into different shapes without breaking. Metals act this way because the positive ions are attracted to the loose electrons all around them rather than to other metal ions. These ions can be made to change position, as shown in Figure 24. However, the metallic bonds between the ion and the surrounding electrons keep the metal from breaking.

Because the metal ions move easily, metals are ductile, which means that they can be bent easily and pulled into thin strands or wires. Metals are also malleable—able to be rolled into thin sheets, as in aluminum foil, or beaten into complex shapes.

Go Online
SCiLINKS NSTA

For: Links on metallic bonding
Visit: www.SciLinks.org
Web Code: scn-1215

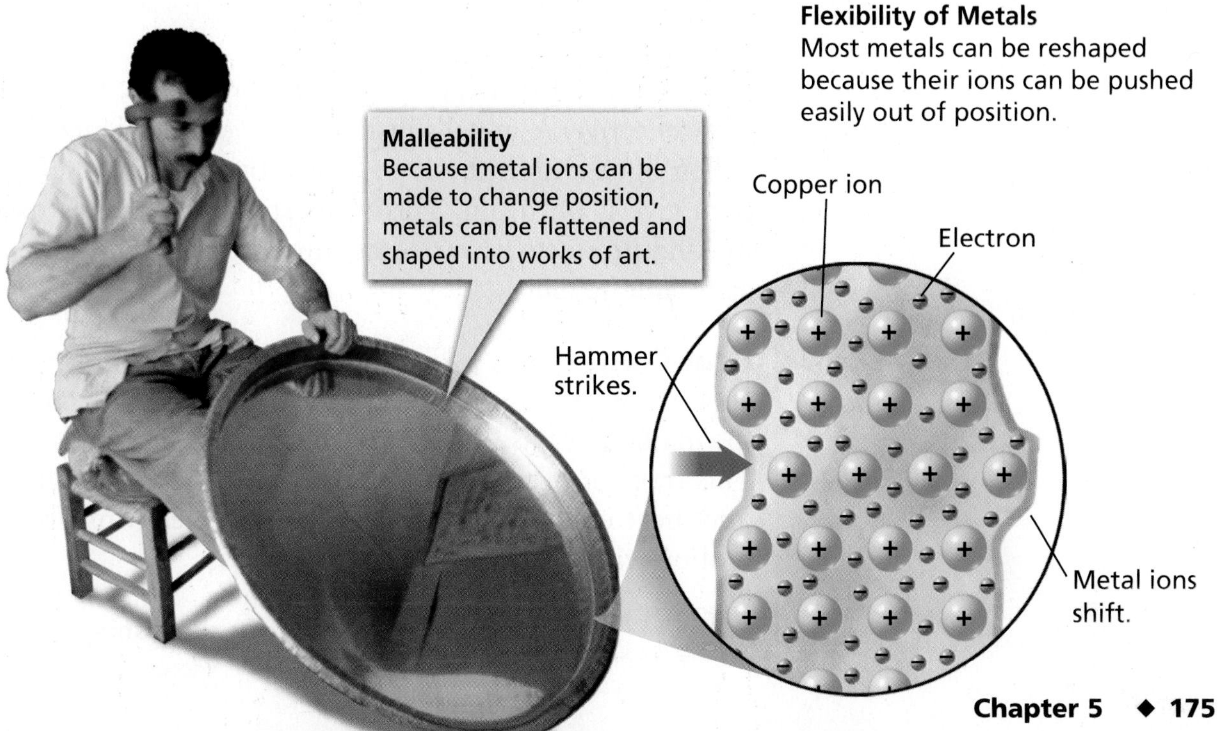
Malleability
Because metal ions can be made to change position, metals can be flattened and shaped into works of art.
Copper ion
Electron
Hammer strikes.
Metal ions shift.

FIGURE 24
Flexibility of Metals
Most metals can be reshaped because their ions can be pushed easily out of position.

FIGURE 25

Conductivity and Luster of Metals

The unique properties of metals result from the ability of their electrons to move about freely.

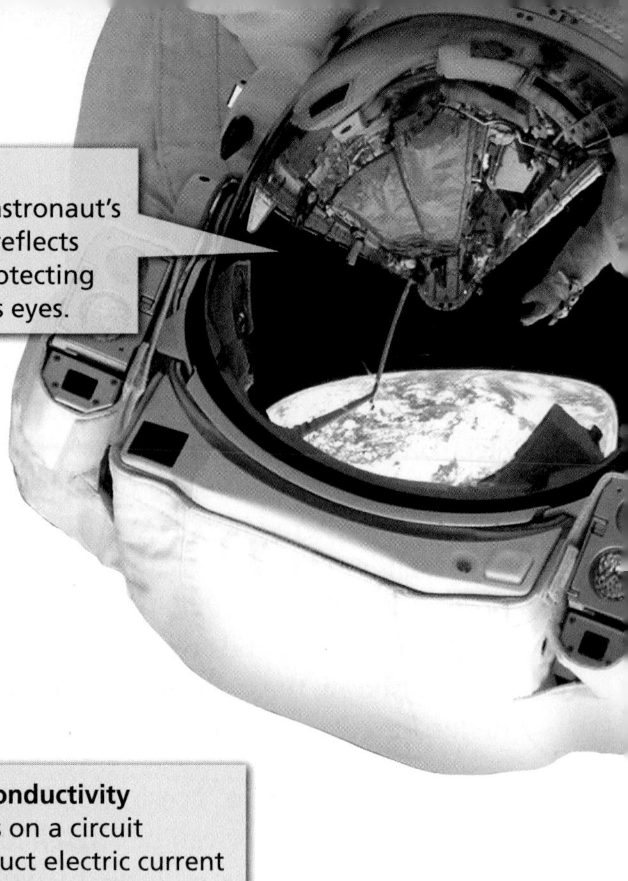
Luster
Gold in an astronaut's face shield reflects sunlight, protecting the wearer's eyes.

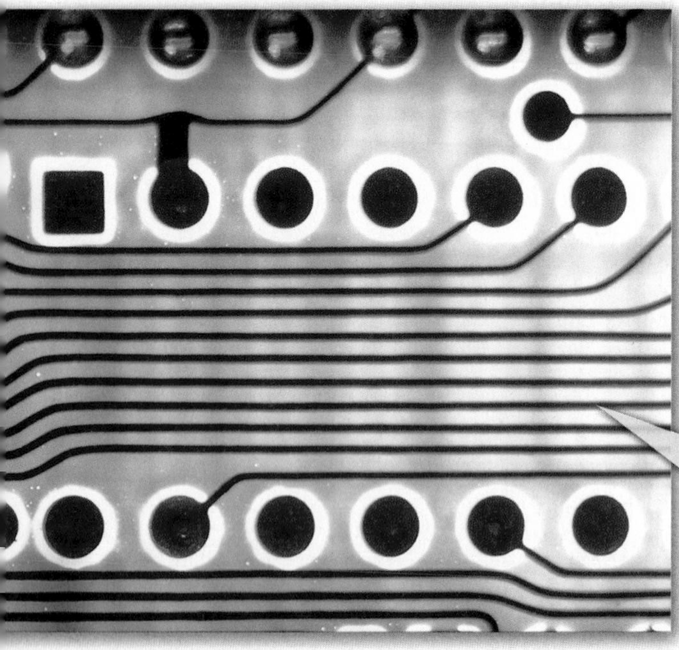
Electrical Conductivity
Metal strips on a circuit board conduct electric current throughout the circuit.

Electrical Conductivity You may recall that when charged particles are free to move an electric current is possible. Metals conduct current easily because the electrons in a metal can move freely among the atoms. When connected to a device such as a battery, there is a current into the metal at one point and out at another point.

Luster Polished metals exhibit luster, that is, they are shiny and reflective. A metal's luster is due to its valence electrons. When light strikes these electrons, they absorb the light and then give it off again. This property makes metals useful for making products as varied as mirrors, buildings, jewelry, and astronaut helmets.

Heat Conductivity Thermal energy travels through materials as the greater motion of the particles in the warmer parts of the material is passed along to the particles in the cooler parts. This transfer of thermal energy is known as heat. Metals conduct heat easily because of the valence electrons' freedom of motion within a metal or metal alloy.

Reading Checkpoint **Why are metals and their alloys shiny?**

Heat Conductivity
Metal fins cool a motorcycle engine by conducting heat to the outside.

Section 4 Assessment

Target Reading Skill **Relating Cause and Effect** Refer to your graphic organizer about metallic properties to help you answer Question 3 below.

Reviewing Key Concepts

1. a. **Defining** What is an alloy?
   b. **Reviewing** From what pure metals is stainless steel made?
   c. **Comparing and Contrasting** Compare and contrast the general properties of alloys and pure metals.
2. a. **Describing** What is a metallic bond?
   b. **Relating Cause and Effect** Explain how metal atoms form metallic bonds. What role do the valence electrons play?
   c. **Comparing and Contrasting** Review what you learned earlier about ionic bonds. How does a metallic bond differ from an ionic bond?
3. a. **Listing** Name four properties of metals. What accounts for these properties?
   b. **Applying Concepts** Why is it safer to use a nonmetal mixing spoon when cooking something on a stove?

Writing in Science

Product Label Choose a familiar metal object and create a "product label" for it. Your label should describe at least two of the metal's properties and explain why it exhibits those properties. You can include illustrations on your label as well.

Chapter 5 Study Guide

1 Atoms, Bonding, and the Periodic Table

Key Concepts

- The number of valence electrons in an atom of an element determines many properties of that element, including the ways in which the atom can bond with other atoms.
- The periodic table gives you information about the arrangement of electrons in atoms.
- The elements within a group have similar properties because they all have the same number of valence electrons in their atoms.

Key Terms

valence electron
electron dot diagram
chemical bond

2 Ionic Bonds

Key Concepts

- When an atom loses an electron, it becomes a positive ion. When an atom gains an electron, it becomes a negative ion.
- Ionic bonds form as a result of the attraction between positive and negative ions.
- When ionic compounds form, the charges on the ions balance out.
- Ionic compounds are hard, brittle crystals that have high melting points and conduct electricity when dissolved in water.

Key Terms

ion
polyatomic ion
ionic bond
ionic compound
chemical formula
subscript
crystal

3 Covalent Bonds

Key Concepts

- The force that holds atoms together in a covalent bond is the attraction of each atom's nucleus for the shared pair of electrons.
- Molecular compounds have low melting and boiling points and do not conduct electricity.
- In polar covalent bonds, the bonded atoms have slight electrical charges.

Key Terms

covalent bond
molecule
double bond
triple bond
molecular compound
polar bond
nonpolar bond

4 Bonding in Metals

Key Concepts

- Alloys are generally stronger and less likely to react with air or water than are the pure metals from which they are made.
- A metal or metal alloy consists of positively charged metal ions in a "sea" of valence electrons.
- The "sea of electrons" model of solid metals explains the ease with which they can change shape, their ability to conduct electric current, their luster, and their ability to conduct heat.

Key Terms

alloy
metallic bond

Review and Assessment

Go Online PHSchool.com
For: Self-Assessment
Visit: PHSchool.com
Web Code: cka-1050

Organizing Information

Comparing and Contrasting Copy the graphic organizer about chemical bonds onto a separate sheet of paper. Then complete it. (For more on Comparing and Contrasting, see the Skills Handbook.)

Types of Chemical Bonds

Feature	Ionic Bond	Polar Covalent Bond	Nonpolar Covalent Bond	Metallic Bond
How Bond Forms	a. ?	Unequal sharing of electrons	b. ?	c. ?
Charge on Bonded Atoms?	Yes; positive or negative	d. ?	e. ?	Yes; positive
Example	f. ?	g. ?	O_2 molecule	h. ?

Reviewing Key Terms

Choose the letter of the best answer.

1. Valence electrons in an atom are those that are
   a. held most loosely.
   b. of the lowest energy level.
   c. always easily lost.
   d. never easily lost.
2. An electron dot diagram shows an atom's number of
   a. protons. **b.** electrons.
   c. valence electrons. **d.** chemical bonds.
3. On the periodic table, elements with the same number of valence electrons are in the same
   a. square. **b.** period.
   c. block. **d.** group.
4. When an atom loses or gains electrons, it becomes a(n)
   a. ion. **b.** formula.
   c. crystal. **d.** subscript.
5. A covalent bond in which electrons are shared unequally is a
   a. double bond. **b.** triple bond.
   c. polar bond. **d.** nonpolar bond.
6. The metal atoms in stainless steel are held together by
   a. ionic bonds. **b.** polar bonds.
   c. covalent bonds. **d.** metallic bonds.

If the statement is true, write *true*. If it is false, change the underlined word or words to make the statement true.

7. A <u>chemical bond</u> is a force of attraction between two atoms.
8. A <u>polyatomic ion</u> is made up of more than one atom.
9. A neutral group of atoms joined by covalent bonds is <u>an ion</u>.
10. <u>An alloy</u> is a mixture of elements that has the properties of a metal.

Writing in Science

Travel Brochure Pretend you have just visited a city modeled on the periodic table. Write a travelogue about how the "city" is organized. Be sure to describe some of the elements you visited and how they are related to their neighbors.

Discovery Channel School

Atoms and Bonding
Video Preview
Video Field Trip
▶ Video Assessment

Review and Assessment

Checking Concepts

11. Which element is less reactive, an element whose atoms have seven valence electrons or an element whose atoms have eight valence electrons? Explain.
12. Why do ionic compounds generally have high melting points?
13. The formula of sulfuric acid is H_2SO_4. How many atoms of hydrogen, sulfur, and oxygen are in one molecule of sulfuric acid?
14. How is the formation of an ionic bond different from the formation of a covalent bond?
15. Why is the covalent bond between two atoms of the same element a nonpolar bond?
16. Explain how metallic bonding causes metals to conduct electric current.

Thinking Critically

17. **Making Generalizations** What information does the organization of the periodic table tell you about how reactive an element may be?
18. **Classifying** Classify each molecule below as either a polar molecule or a nonpolar molecule. Explain your reasoning.

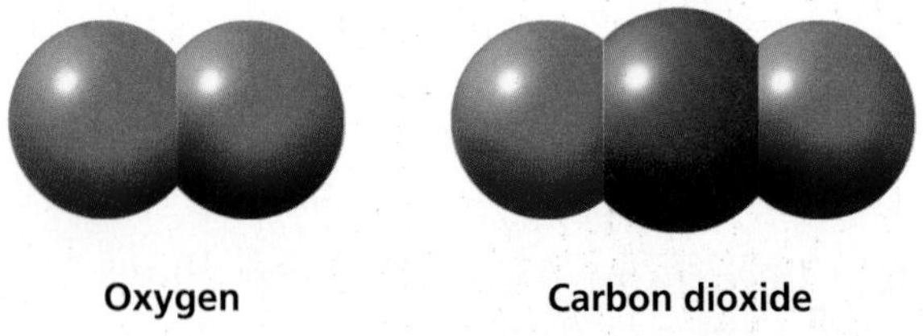

19. **Relating Cause and Effect** Many molecular compounds with small molecules are gases at room temperature. Water, however, is a liquid. Use what you know about polar and nonpolar molecules to explain this difference. (*Hint:* Molecules of a gas are much farther apart than molecules of a liquid.)
20. **Applying Concepts** Why does a metal horseshoe bend but not break when a blacksmith pounds it into shape?

Applying Skills

Use the electron dot diagrams below to answer Questions 21–25.

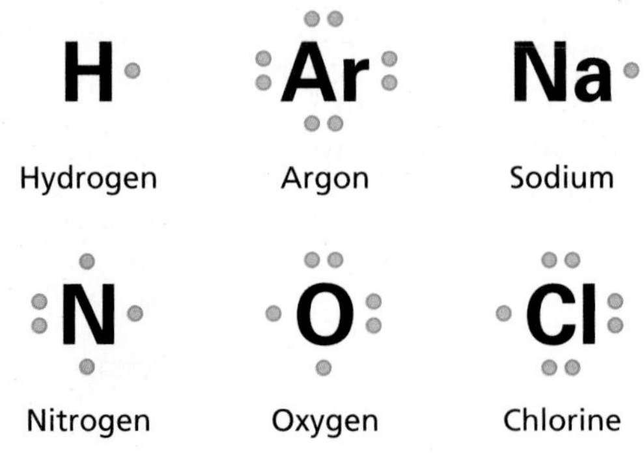

21. **Predicting** When nitrogen and hydrogen combine, what will be the ratio of hydrogen atoms to nitrogen atoms in a molecule of the resulting compound? Explain.
22. **Inferring** Which of these elements can become stable by losing one electron? Explain.
23. **Drawing Conclusions** Which of these elements is least likely to react with other elements? Explain.
24. **Interpreting Diagrams** Which of these elements would react with two atoms of sodium to form an ionic compound? Explain.
25. **Classifying** What type of bond forms when two atoms of nitrogen join to form a nitrogen molecule? When two atoms of oxygen join to form an oxygen molecule?

Lab zone Chapter Project

Performance Assessment Present your models to the class, telling what the parts of each model represent. Explain why you chose particular items to model the atoms and chemical bonds. Which kind of bonds were easier to show? Why? What more would you like to know about bonding that could help improve your models?

Standardized Test Prep

Test-Taking Tip

Interpreting Diagrams

When answering a question related to a diagram, examine the diagram carefully. Read any titles or labels included. Be sure you understand the meanings of the symbols used. For example, in the diagram below, the dots represent valence electrons. Study the diagram and answer the sample question.

Sample Question

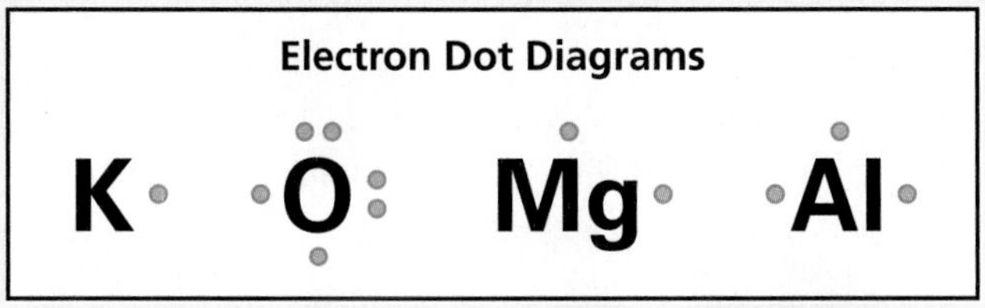

Which element is the most likely to lose two electrons and form an ion with a charge of 2+?

A potassium (K)
B oxygen (O)
C magnesium (Mg)
D aluminum (Al)

Answer

The correct answer is **C**. Atoms with low numbers of valence electrons are likely to lose electrons. Potassium, magnesium, and aluminum all have low numbers of valence electrons, but only magnesium will lose two electrons, producing an ion with a 2+ charge.

Choose the letter of the best answer.

Use the electron dot diagrams above to answer Questions 1–3.

1. Oxygen has 6 valence electrons, as indicated by the 6 dots around the letter symbol "O." Based on this information, how many covalent bonds could an oxygen atom form?

A six
B three
C two
D none

2. If a reaction occurs between potassium (K) and oxygen (O), what will be the ratio of potassium ions to oxide ions in the resulting compound, potassium oxide?

F 1 : 1 **G** 1 : 2
H 2 : 1 **J** 2 : 2

3. The element boron (B) is directly above aluminum (Al) on the periodic table. Which statement about boron is true?

A Boron is in the same period as aluminum and has two valence electrons.
B Boron is in the same group as aluminum and has two valence electrons.
C Boron is in the same period as aluminum and has three valence electrons.
D Boron is in the same group as aluminum and has three valence electrons.

4. The chemical formula for a glucose molecule is $C_6H_{12}O_6$. The subscripts represent the

F mass of each element.
G number of atoms of each element in a glucose molecule.
H total number of bonds made by each atom.
J number of valence electrons.

5. An ice cube (solid H_2O) and a scoop of table salt (NaCl) are left outside on a warm, sunny day. Which best explains why the ice cube melts and the salt does not?

A The attractive forces between molecules of H_2O are much weaker than those between ions in NaCl.
B NaCl can dissolve in H_2O.
C The mass of the H_2O was less than the mass of the NaCl.
D NaCl is white and H_2O is colorless.

Constructed Response

6. In a working light bulb, a thin tungsten wire filament that is wound in a coil conducts electric current. Describe two properties that make the metal tungsten a good material for the filament of a light bulb. Indicate how the type of bonding in tungsten contributes to these properties.

Chapter 6

Chemical Reactions

Chapter Preview

1 Observing Chemical Change
- **Discover** *What Happens When Chemicals React?*
- **Skills Activity** *Classifying*
- **Try This** *Mostly Cloudy*
- **Analyzing Data** *Energy in Chemical Changes*
- **Skills Lab** *Where's the Evidence?*

2 Describing Chemical Reactions
- **Discover** *Do You Lose Anything?*
- **Try This** *Still There*
- **Active Art** *Balancing Equations*
- **Analyzing Data** *Balancing Chemical Equations*
- **Technology and Society** *Air Bags*

3 Controlling Chemical Reactions
- **Discover** *Can You Speed Up or Slow Down a Reaction?*
- **Skills Lab** *Temperature and Enzyme Activity*

4 Fire and Fire Safety
- **Discover** *How Does Baking Soda Affect a Fire?*

Interactive Textbook

Sparks fly as sodium metal reacts with water. ▶

Discovery Channel School

Chemical Reactions

▶ Video Preview
Video Field Trip
Video Assessment

Lab zone™ Chapter **Project**

Design and Build a Closed Reaction Chamber

When water evaporates, it is not destroyed or lost. In fact, matter is never created or destroyed in either a physical change or a chemical reaction. In this chapter project, you will design and build a closed structure in which a chemical reaction can occur. You will use the chamber to confirm that matter is not created or destroyed in a chemical reaction.

Your Goal To design and build a closed chamber in which sugar can be broken down

Your structure must

- be made of materials that are approved by your teacher
- be built to specifications agreed upon by the class
- be a closed system so the masses of the reactants and products can be measured
- be built following the safety guidelines in Appendix A

Plan It! Before you design your reaction chamber, find out how sugar can be broken down. Next, brainstorm with classmates to determine the safety features of your chamber. Then choose materials for your structure and sketch your design. When your teacher has approved your design, build and test your structure.

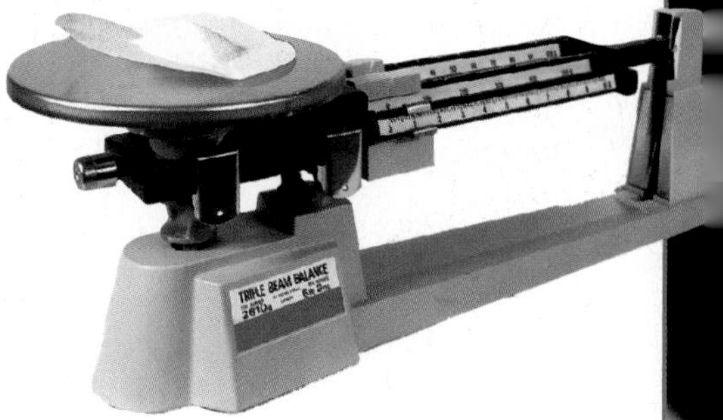

Section 1

Observing Chemical Change

Reading Preview

Key Concepts

- How can matter and changes in matter be described?
- How can you tell when a chemical reaction occurs?

Key Terms

- matter • chemistry
- physical property
- chemical property
- physical change
- chemical reaction • precipitate
- endothermic reaction
- exothermic reaction

Target Reading Skill

Asking Questions Before you read, preview the red headings. In a graphic organizer like the one below, ask a *what* or *how* question for each heading. As you read, write the answers to your questions.

Properties and Changes of Matter

Question	Answer
What are physical properties of matter?	Physical properties are . . .

Lab zone Discover Activity

What Happens When Chemicals React?

1. Put on your safety goggles. Place 2 small spoonfuls of baking soda into a clear plastic cup.
2. Holding the cup over a large bowl or sink, add about 125 mL of vinegar. Swirl the cup gently.
3. Look at the material in the cup. What changes do you see? Feel the outside of the cup. What do you notice about the temperature?
4. Carefully fan the air above the liquid toward you. What do you smell?

Think It Over

Observing What changes did you detect using your senses of smell and touch?

Picture yourself toasting marshmallows over a campfire. You see the burning logs change from a hard solid to a soft pile of ash. You hear popping and hissing sounds from the fire as the wood burns. You smell smoke. You feel the heat on your skin. Finally, you taste the results. The crisp brown surface of the toasted marshmallow tastes quite different from the soft white surface of a marshmallow just out of its bag. Firewood, skin, and marshmallows are all examples of matter. **Matter** is anything that has mass and takes up space. The study of matter and how matter changes is called **chemistry.**

Chemical change can lead to a treat. ▶

Properties and Changes of Matter

Part of studying matter is describing it. When you describe matter, you explain its characteristics, or properties, and how it changes. **Matter can be described in terms of two kinds of properties—physical properties and chemical properties. Changes in matter can be described in terms of physical changes and chemical changes.**

Properties of Matter A **physical property** is a characteristic of a substance that can be observed without changing the substance into another substance. The temperature at which a solid melts is a physical property. For example, ice melts at a temperature of zero degrees Celsius. Color, hardness, texture, shine, and flexibility are some other physical properties of matter. The ability of a substance to dissolve in water and how well it conducts heat and electricity are examples of still more physical properties of matter.

A **chemical property** is a characteristic of a substance that describes its ability to change into other substances. To observe the chemical properties of a substance, you must change it to another substance. For example, when magnesium burns, it combines with oxygen in the air, forming a new substance called magnesium oxide. People who make objects out of magnesium must be careful because the metal can catch fire. Burning is only one type of chemical property. Other examples of chemical properties are tarnishing and rusting.

FIGURE 1
Properties of Water
This geyser gives off hot water and water vapor, which condenses into a visible cloud in the cold air. The temperatures at which water boils and freezes are physical properties of water.
Predicting *How will the snow change when spring arrives?*

Chemical Properties of Water
• Made of hydrogen atoms and oxygen atoms in a 2 to 1 ratio
• Does not burn
• Reacts with some metals
Physical Properties of Water
• Clear, colorless liquid at room temperature
• Boils at 100°C
• Freezes at 0°C

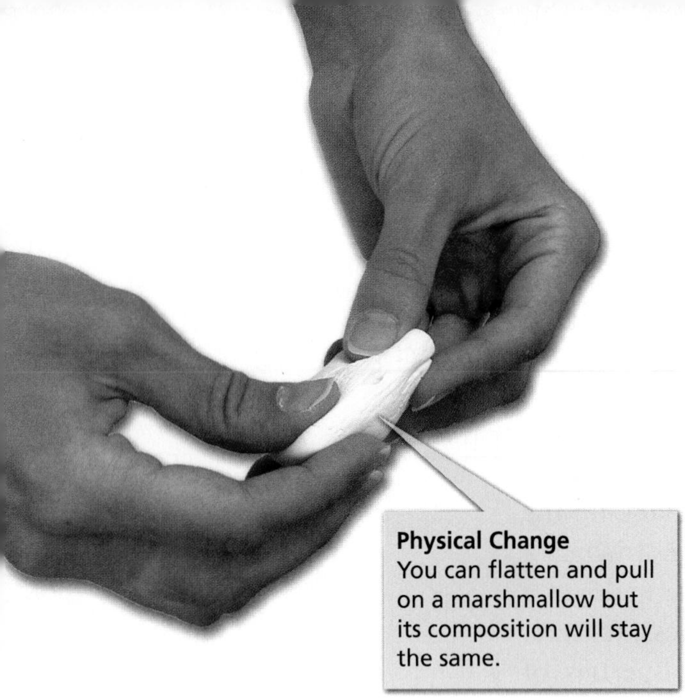

Physical Change
You can flatten and pull on a marshmallow but its composition will stay the same.

Chemical Change
If you toast a marshmallow, the sugars and other substances will cook or burn, producing a crust made of new substances.

FIGURE 2
Changes in Matter
Matter can undergo both physical change and chemical change.

Lab zone Skills Activity

Classifying

Classify each of the following changes as either a chemical change or a physical change. Explain your reasoning for each case.

- A piece of metal is heated to a high temperature and changes to a liquid.
- When two solutions are poured into the same container, a powdery solid forms and settles to the bottom.
- Water left in a dish overnight has disappeared by the next day.
- A blacksmith hammers a piece of red-hot iron into the shape of a knife blade.

Changes of Matter You probably have seen solid water (ice) change to liquid water. Water is the same substance, whether it is frozen or liquid. Therefore, changing from a solid to a liquid is a physical change. A **physical change** is any change that alters the form or appearance of a substance but that does not make the substance into another substance. You cause a physical change when you squash a marshmallow. The shape of the marshmallow changes but not the taste! It's still made of the same compounds that have the same properties. Other examples of physical changes are bending, crushing, breaking, cutting, and anything else that changes only the shape or form of matter. Braiding your hair is another example of a physical change.

Sometimes when a change occurs in a substance, the substance itself is changed. For example, the brown crust on a toasted marshmallow is the result of sugar changing to different substances in a mixture called caramel. A change in matter that produces one or more new substances is a chemical change, or **chemical reaction.** The burning of gasoline in a car's engine is a chemical change. The new substances formed end up as the car's exhaust.

Reading Checkpoint **What kind of change occurs when you toast the outside of a marshmallow?**

Bonding and Chemical Change **Chemical changes occur when bonds break and new bonds form.** As a result, new substances are produced. You may recall that atoms form bonds when they share or transfer electrons. The reaction pictured in Figure 3 involves both the breaking of shared bonds and a transfer of electrons.

Oxygen gas (O_2) in the air consists of molecules made of two oxygen atoms that share electrons. These bonds are broken when oxygen reacts with magnesium metal (Mg). Each magnesium atom transfers two of its electrons to an oxygen atom. The oxygen atom becomes a negative ion, and the magnesium atom becomes a positive ion.

You can probably guess what happens next. You may recall that oppositely charged ions attract. An ionic bond forms between the Mg^{2+} ions and the O^{2-} ions. The ionic compound magnesium oxide (MgO) is produced, and energy is released. Magnesium oxide—a white, crumbly powder—has properties that differ from those of either shiny magnesium or oxygen gas. For example, while magnesium melts at about 650°C, it takes temperatures of more than 2,800°C to melt magnesium oxide!

Go Online
SCILINKS NSTA
For: Links on chemical changes
Visit: www.SciLinks.org
Web Code: scn-1221

FIGURE 3
Bonding and Chemical Change
As magnesium burns, bonds between atoms break and new bonds form. The reaction gives off energy. **Interpreting Diagrams** *Why does the oxygen ion have a 2– charge?*

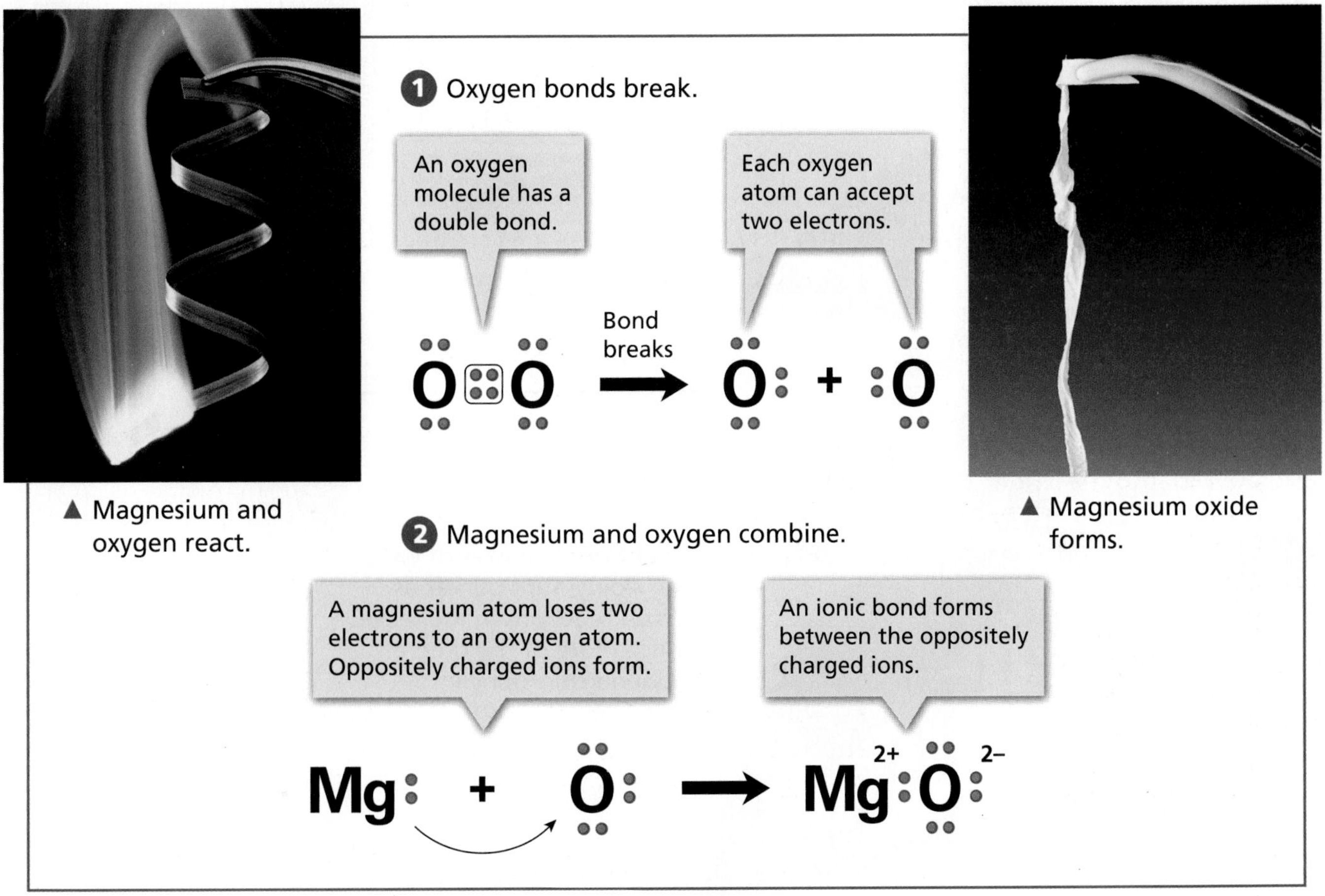

1 Oxygen bonds break.
An oxygen molecule has a double bond.
Each oxygen atom can accept two electrons.
Bond breaks
2 Magnesium and oxygen combine.
A magnesium atom loses two electrons to an oxygen atom. Oppositely charged ions form.
An ionic bond forms between the oppositely charged ions.
2+
2–

▲ Magnesium and oxygen react.

▲ Magnesium oxide forms.

Evidence for Chemical Reactions

Look at the photograph below of the beaker. Even without reading the caption, you probably could guess it shows a chemical reaction. But how do you know? How can you tell when a chemical reaction occurs? **Chemical reactions involve two main kinds of changes that you can observe—formation of new substances and changes in energy.**

Changes in Properties One way to detect chemical reactions is to observe changes in the properties of the materials involved. Changes in properties result when new substances form. What kinds of changes should you look for? Look at Figure 4. First, a color change may signal that a new substance has formed. Second, a solid may appear when two solutions are mixed. A solid that forms from solution during a chemical reaction is called a **precipitate** (pree SIP uh tayt).

FIGURE 4

Evidence for Chemical Reactions

Many kinds of change provide evidence that a chemical reaction has occurred.
Applying Concepts *What other evidence might tell you a chemical reaction has occurred?*

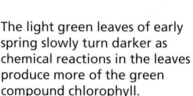

Two clear liquids react, ▲ forming a precipitate.

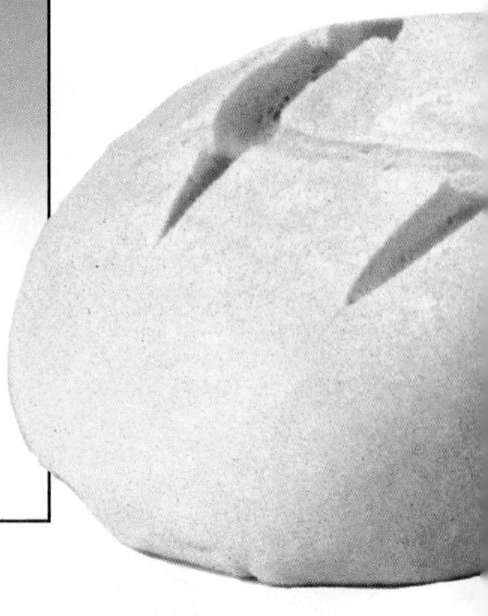

◀ The light green leaves of early spring slowly turn darker as chemical reactions in the leaves produce more of the green compound chlorophyll.

Third, a gas might be produced from solids or liquids. If the reaction occurs in a liquid, you may see the gas as bubbles. Finally, other kinds of observable changes in properties can also signal a chemical reaction. For example, moist bread dough forms a dry, porous solid after baking.

Although you may observe a property change in matter, the change does not always indicate that a chemical reaction has taken place. Sometimes physical changes give similar results. For example, when water boils, the gas bubbles you see are made of molecules of water, just as the original liquid was. The sign of a chemical reaction is that one or more new substances are produced. For example, when an electric current is passed through water during electrolysis, two gases are produced, hydrogen gas (H_2) and oxygen gas (O_2).

Reading Checkpoint **How is a precipitate evidence for a chemical reaction?**

Lab zone Try This Activity

Mostly Cloudy

1. Put on your safety goggles and apron.
2. Pour about 5 mL of limewater into a plastic cup.
3. Pour an equal amount of plain water into another plastic cup.
4. Add about 5 mL of carbonated water to each of the cups.

Drawing Conclusions In which cup do you think a chemical reaction occurred? What evidence supports your conclusion?

A golden loaf of bread with its crunchy crust has very different properties from the soft dough that went into the oven. ▼

Oxygen bubbles that form during photosynthesis collect on the leaves of a plant. ▼

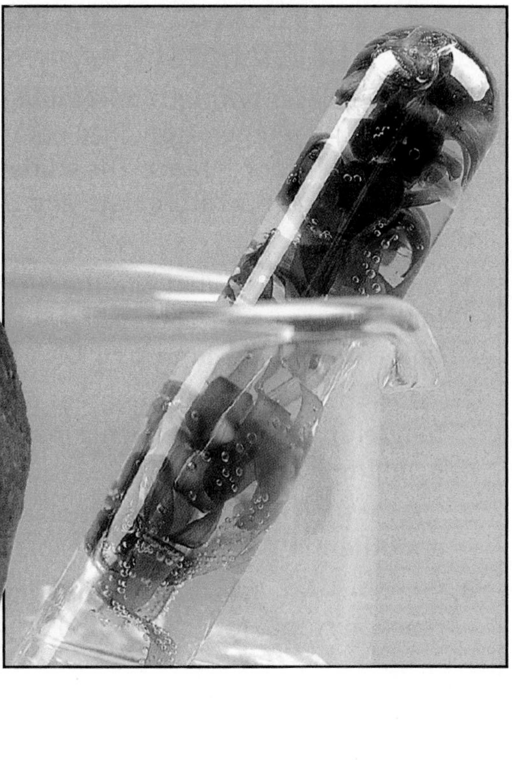

FIGURE 5
An Endothermic Reaction
Energy must be added continuously to fry an egg. Making Generalizations *In terms of energy, what kind of reaction usually occurs when food is cooked?*

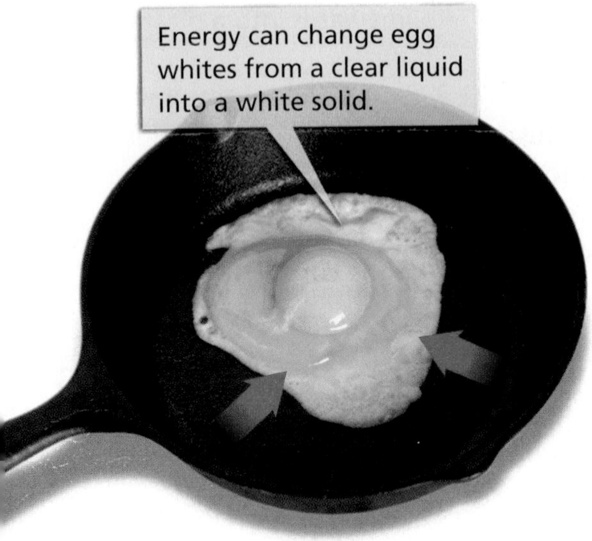

Energy can change egg whites from a clear liquid into a white solid.

Changes in Energy From your everyday experience, you know about various types of energy, such as heat, light, and electricity. As matter changes, it can either absorb or release energy. A change in energy occurs during a chemical reaction. Some reactions absorb energy, while others release energy. One common indication that energy has been absorbed or released is a change in temperature.

If you did the Discover activity, you observed that the mixture became colder. When baking soda (sodium bicarbonate) reacts with vinegar, the reaction takes heat from the solution, making it feel cooler. This kind of reaction is an example of an endothermic reaction. An **endothermic reaction** (en doh THUR mik) is a reaction in which energy is absorbed. However, endothermic reactions do not always result in a decrease in temperature. Many endothermic reactions occur only when heat is constantly added. For example, the reactions that occur when you fry an egg are endothermic.

Math Analyzing Data

Energy in Chemical Changes

A student places two substances in a flask and measures the temperature once per minute while the substances react. The student plots the time and temperature data and creates the graph at right.

1. Reading Graphs What was the temperature in the flask at 4 minutes? When was the first time the temperature was 6°C?
2. Calculating How many degrees did the temperature drop between 2 minutes and 5 minutes?
3. Interpreting Data Is the reaction endothermic or exothermic? Explain.
4. Inferring At what temperature did the reaction stop? How can you tell?

Energy of a Chemical Reaction

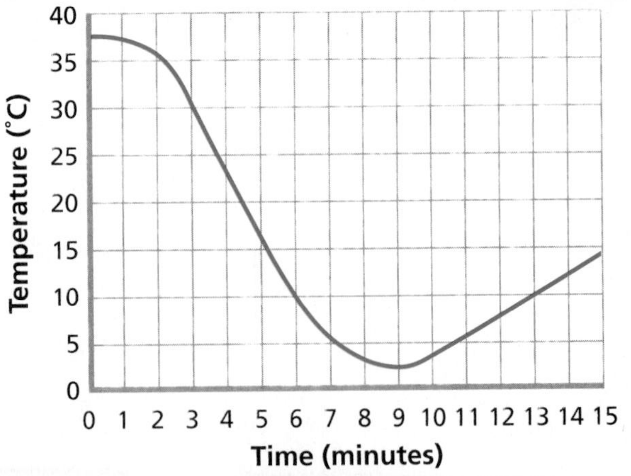

5. Drawing Conclusions Suppose the temperature in the flask increased instead of decreased as the reaction occurred. In terms of energy, what kind of reaction would it be? Explain.

FIGURE 6
An Exothermic Reaction
Enough energy is released by the burning of airplane fuel to keep a plane moving fast enough to fly.

In contrast, the reaction between fuel and oxygen in an airplane engine releases energy, mostly in the form of heat. The heat causes gases in the engine to expand. The expansion and movement of the gases out of the plane exerts a force that moves the plane forward. A reaction that releases energy in the form of heat is called an **exothermic reaction** (ek soh THUR mik). You will learn more about energy and chemical changes in Section 3.

Reading Checkpoint **What is an endothermic reaction?**

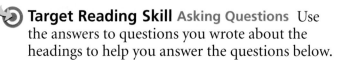

Section 1 Assessment

Target Reading Skill Asking Questions Use the answers to questions you wrote about the headings to help you answer the questions below.

Reviewing Key Concepts

1. a. Explaining What is the difference between the physical properties and the chemical properties of a substance?
   b. Posing Questions When silver coins are found in ancient shipwrecks, they are coated with a black crust. What question could you ask to help you decide whether the silver underwent a chemical change or a physical change? Explain.
   c. Making Generalizations In terms of chemical bonds and electrons, what kinds of changes occur between atoms when substances undergo chemical reactions?
2. a. Listing What are five kinds of evidence you can use to determine if a chemical reaction has occurred?
   b. Interpreting Photographs How do the properties of the cooked egg shown in Figure 5 differ from the properties of a raw egg?
   c. Comparing and Contrasting How are endothermic and exothermic reactions the same? How are they different?

Writing in Science

Persuasive Letter Imagine you have a pen pal who is studying chemistry just like you are. Your pen pal claims the change from liquid water to water vapor is a chemical change. Write a brief letter that might convince your pen pal otherwise.

Lab zone **Skills Lab**

Where's the Evidence?

Problem

What are some signs that a chemical reaction has taken place?

Skills Focus

observing, predicting, drawing conclusions

Materials

- 4 small plastic cups
- birthday candles
- 2 plastic spoons
- sugar
- tongs
- clay
- matches
- sodium carbonate (powdered solid)
- graduated cylinder, 10 mL
- aluminum foil, about 10-cm square
- dilute hydrochloric acid in a dropper bottle
- copper sulfate solution
- sodium carbonate solution

Procedure

Preview the steps for each reaction and copy the data table into your notebook.

PART 1

1. Put a pea-sized pile of sodium carbonate into a clean plastic cup. Record in the data table the appearance of the sodium carbonate.
2. Observe a dropper containing hydrochloric acid. Record the appearance of the acid. **CAUTION:** *Hydrochloric acid can burn you or anything else it touches. Wash spills immediately with water.*
3. Make a prediction about how you think the acid and the sodium carbonate will react when mixed. Record your prediction.
4. Add about 10 drops of hydrochloric acid to the sodium carbonate. Swirl to mix the contents of the cup. Record your observations.

PART 2

5. Fold up the sides of the aluminum foil square to make a small tray.
6. Use a plastic spoon to place a pea-sized pile of sugar into the tray.
7. Carefully describe the appearance of the sugar in your data table.

Data Table

Reaction	Observations Before Reaction	Predictions	Observations During Reaction	Observations After Reaction
1. Sodium carbonate (powder) + hydrochloric acid				
2. Sugar + heat				
3. Copper sulfate + sodium carbonate solutions				

8. Secure a small candle on your desktop in a lump of clay. Carefully light the candle with a match only after being instructed to do so by your teacher. **CAUTION:** *Tie back long hair and loose clothing.*
9. Predict what you think will happen if you heat the sugar. Record your prediction.
10. Use tongs to hold the aluminum tray. Heat the sugar slowly by moving the tray gently back and forth over the flame. Make observations while the sugar is heating.
11. When you think there is no longer a chemical reaction occurring, blow out the candle.
12. Allow the tray to cool for a few seconds and set it down on your desk. Record your observations of the material left in the tray.

PART 3

13. Put about 2 mL of copper sulfate solution in one cup. **CAUTION:** *Copper sulfate is poisonous and can stain your skin and clothes. Do not touch it or get it in your mouth.* Put an equal amount of sodium carbonate solution in another cup. Record the appearance of both liquids.
14. Write a prediction of what you think will happen when the two solutions are mixed.
15. Combine the two solutions and record your observations. **CAUTION:** *Dispose of the solutions as directed by your teacher.*
16. Wash your hands when you have finished working.

Analyze and Conclude

1. Predicting How do the results of each reaction compare with your predictions?
2. Observing How did you know when the reaction in Part 1 was over?
3. Interpreting Data What was the evidence of a chemical reaction in Part 1? In Part 2?
4. Drawing Conclusions Was the reaction in Part 2 endothermic or exothermic? Explain.
5. Observing Was the product of the reaction in Part 3 a solid, a liquid, or a gas? How do you know?
6. Drawing Conclusions How do you know if new substances were formed in each reaction?
7. Communicating Make a table or chart briefly describing each chemical change in this lab, followed by the evidence for the chemical change.

More to Explore

Use your observation skills to find evidence of chemical reactions involving foods in your kitchen. Look for production of gases, color changes, and formation of precipitates. Share your findings with your classmates.

Section 2 Describing Chemical Reactions

Reading Preview

Key Concepts

- What information does a chemical equation contain?
- What does the principle of conservation of mass state?
- What must a balanced chemical equation show?
- What are three categories of chemical reactions?

Key Terms

- chemical equation
- reactant • product
- conservation of mass
- open system • closed system
- coefficient • synthesis
- decomposition • replacement

Target Reading Skill

Building Vocabulary Using a word in a sentence helps you think about how best to explain the word. After you read the section, reread the paragraphs that contain definitions of Key Terms. Use all of the information you have learned to write a meaningful sentence using each Key Term.

Lab zone Discover Activity

Do You Lose Anything?

1. Place about two dozen coins on a table. Sort them into stacks of pennies, nickels, dimes, and quarters.
2. Count and record the number of coins in each stack. Calculate and record the value of each stack and the total of all stacks combined.
3. Mix all the coins together and then divide them randomly into four unsorted stacks.
4. Again calculate the value of each stack and the total amount of money. Count the total number of each type of coin.
5. Repeat Steps 3 and 4.

Think It Over

Making Models What happened to the total value and types of coins when you rearranged them? Did rearranging the coins change the properties of any coin? If you think of the coins as each representing a different type of atom, what does this model tell you about chemical reactions?

You look at your cellular phone display and read the message "U wan2 gt pza 2nite?" You reply "No. MaB TPM. CUL8R." These messages are short for saying "Do you want to get some pizza tonight?" and "No. Maybe tomorrow afternoon (P.M.). See you later."

Cellular phone messages use symbols and abbreviations to express ideas in shorter form. A type of shorthand is used in chemistry too. "Hydrogen molecules react with oxygen molecules to form water molecules" is a lengthy way to describe the reaction between hydrogen and oxygen. And writing it is slow. Instead, chemists often use chemical equations in place of words.

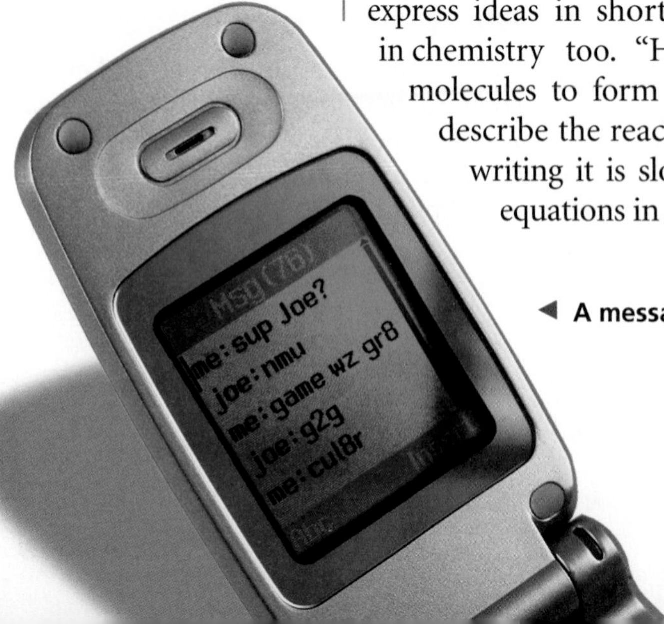

◄ A message on a cellular display

What Are Chemical Equations?

A **chemical equation** is a short, easy way to show a chemical reaction, using symbols instead of words. Although chemical equations are shorter than sentences, they contain more information. **Chemical equations use chemical formulas and other symbols instead of words to summarize a reaction.**

Formulas in an Equation All chemical equations use formulas to represent the substances involved in a reaction. You may recall that a chemical formula is a combination of symbols that represents the elements in a compound. For example, CO_2 is the formula for carbon dioxide. The formula tells you that this compound is made up of the elements carbon and oxygen and each molecule has 1 carbon atom and 2 oxygen atoms. Figure 7 lists formulas of other compounds that may be familiar to you.

Structure of an Equation All chemical equations have a common structure. A chemical equation tells you the substances you start with in a reaction and the substances you get at the end. The substances you have at the beginning are called the **reactants.** When the reaction is complete, you have new substances called the **products**.

The formulas for the reactants are written on the left, followed by an arrow. You read the arrow as "yields." The formulas for the products are written on the right. When there are two or more reactants, they are separated by plus signs. In a similar way, plus signs are used to separate two or more products. Below is the general plan for a chemical equation.

Reactant + Reactant ⟶ Product + Product

The number of reactants and products can vary. Some reactions have only one reactant or product. Other reactions have two, three, or more reactants or products. In Figure 8, you can see the equation for a reaction that occurs when limestone ($CaCO_3$) is heated. Count the number of reactants and products, and familiarize yourself with the parts of the equation.

FIGURE 7
The formula of a compound identifies the elements in the compound and the ratios in which their atoms are present.

Formulas of Familiar Compounds

Compound	Formula
Water	H_2O
Carbon dioxide	CO_2
Propane	C_3H_8
Sugar (sucrose)	$C_{12}H_{22}O_{11}$
Rubbing alcohol	C_3H_8O
Ammonia	NH_3
Sodium chloride	NaCl
Baking soda	$NaHCO_3$

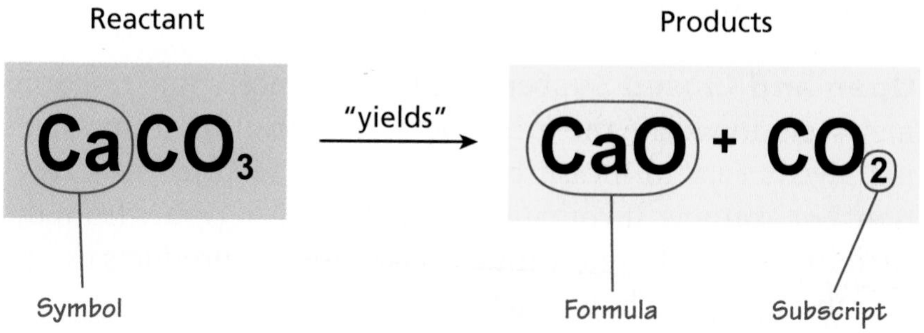

FIGURE 8
A Chemical Equation
Like a building, a chemical equation has a basic structure.
Interpreting Diagrams *What does the subscript 3 in the formula for calcium carbonate tell you?*

$$Fe + S \rightarrow FeS$$

Iron Sulfur Iron Sulfide

FIGURE 9
Conservation of Mass
Mass is conserved in chemical reactions.

Conservation of Mass

Look closely at the values for mass in Figure 9. Iron and sulfur can react to form iron sulfide. The photograph represents a principle first demonstrated by the French chemist Antoine Lavoisier in 1774. This principle is called **conservation of mass,** and it states that during a chemical reaction, matter is not created or destroyed. All the atoms present at the start of the reaction are present at the end.

Modeling Conservation of Mass Think about what happens when classes change at your school during the day. A class is made of a group of students and a teacher together in a room. When the bell rings, people from each class move from room to room, ending up in different classes. The number of people in the school has not changed. But their arrangement has.

Now imagine that all the students and teachers are atoms, each class is a molecule, and the changing of classes is a chemical reaction. At the end of the reaction, the same atoms are present, but they are grouped together differently. The amount of matter does not change. **The principle of conservation of mass states that in a chemical reaction, the total mass of the reactants must equal the total mass of the products.**

Open and Closed Systems At first glance, some reactions may seem to violate the principle of conservation of mass. It's not always easy to measure all the matter involved in a reaction. For example, if you burn a match, oxygen comes from the surrounding air. But how much? Likewise, the products escape into the air. Again, how much?

Lab zone Try This Activity

Still There

1. Measure the mass of a collection of bolts, each with a nut attached to it.
2. Remove all the nuts from the bolts. Measure the total mass of the nuts. Then do the same with the bolts. Add these values.
3. Rearrange your collection, putting two or three nuts on one bolt, one nut on another bolt, and so on. You can even leave a few pieces unattached.
4. Measure the total mass again. Compare this figure with the totals from Steps 1 and 2.

Making Models How does your activity model the idea of conservation of mass?

A burning match is an example of an open system. In an **open system**, matter can enter from or escape to the surroundings. The burned out fire in Figure 10 is another example of an open system. If you want to measure all the matter before and after a reaction, you have to be able to contain it. In a **closed system**, matter is not allowed to enter or leave. The pear decaying under glass in Figure 10 is a closed system. So is a chemical reaction inside a sealed plastic bag.

Reading Checkpoint **What is a closed system?**

FIGURE 10

Open and Closed Systems

A wood fire is an open system because gases escape into the air. A pear in a glass dome is a closed system because the reactants and products are contained inside the dome.
Problem Solving *What masses would you need to measure before and after a wood fire to show conservation of mass?*

Open System
Except for the ash, products of the wood fire have escaped up the chimney or into the room.

Closed System
The total mass of the pear and the substances produced during its decay are contained by the glass dome.

Fresh pear

Decayed pear

Go Online
active art

For: Balancing Equations activity
Visit: PHSchool.com
Web Code: cgp-2022

Balancing Chemical Equations

The principle of conservation of mass means that the same number of atoms exists in the products as in the reactants. **To describe a reaction accurately, a chemical equation must show the same number of each type of atom on both sides of the equation.** Chemists say an equation is balanced when it accurately represents conservation of mass. How can you write a balanced chemical equation?

❶ Write the Equation Suppose you want to write a balanced chemical equation for the reaction between hydrogen and oxygen that forms water. To begin, write the correct formulas for both reactants and product.

$$H_2 + O_2 \longrightarrow H_2O$$

Reactants   Products

Place the reactants, H_2 and O_2, on the left side of the arrow, separated by a plus sign. Then write the product, H_2O, on the right side of the arrow.

❷ Count the Atoms Count the number of atoms of each element on each side of the equation. You find two atoms of oxygen in the reactants but only one atom of oxygen in the product.

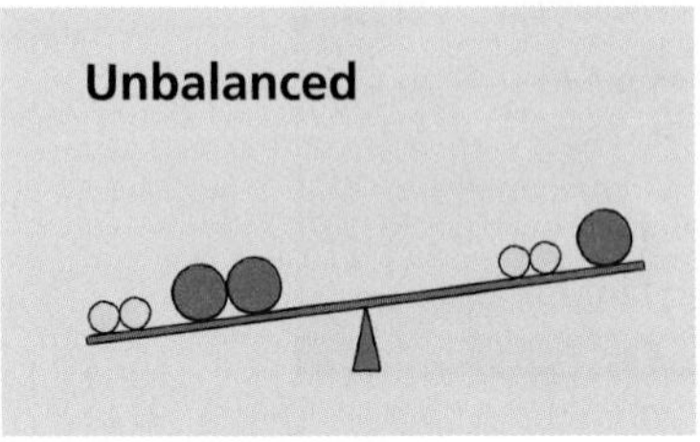

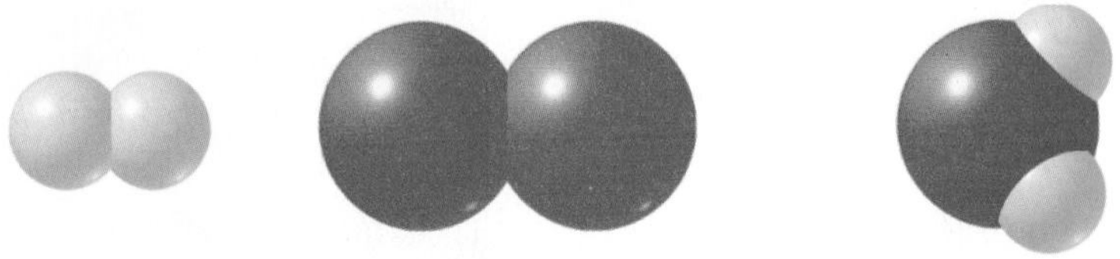

2 hydrogen atoms + 2 oxygen atoms ⟶ 1 oxygen atom, 2 hydrogen atoms

How can you get the number of oxygen atoms on both sides to be the same? You cannot change the formula for water to H_2O_2 because H_2O_2 is the formula for hydrogen peroxide, a completely different compound. So, how can you show that mass is conserved?

❸ Use Coefficients to Balance Atoms To balance the equation, use coefficients. A **coefficient** (koh uh FISH unt) is a number placed in front of a chemical formula in an equation. It tells you how many atoms or molecules of a reactant or a product take part in the reaction. If the coefficient is 1, you don't need to write it.

Balance the number of oxygen atoms by writing the coefficient 2 for water. That's like saying "2 × H_2O." Now there are two oxygen atoms—one in each molecule of water.

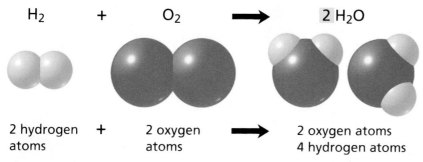

H_2 + O_2 → **2** H_2O

2 hydrogen atoms + 2 oxygen atoms → 2 oxygen atoms, 4 hydrogen atoms

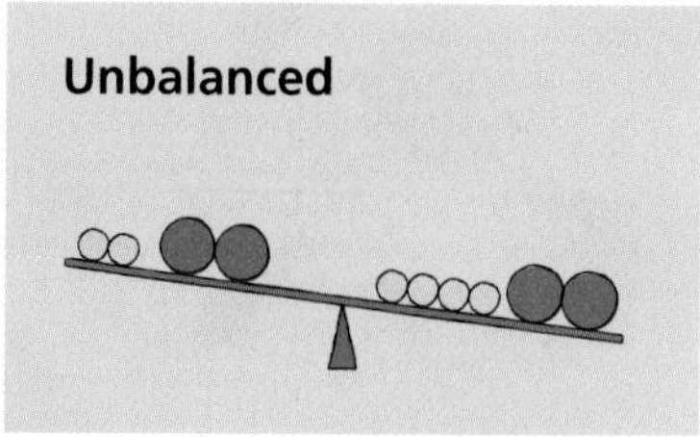

Balancing the oxygen atoms throws off the hydrogen atoms. There are now two hydrogen atoms in the reactants and four in the product. How can you balance the hydrogen? Try doubling the number of hydrogen atoms on the left side of the equation by writing the coefficient 2 for hydrogen.

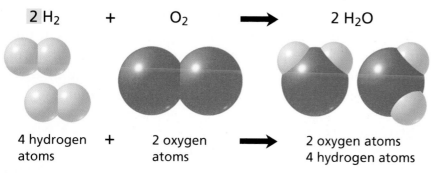

2 H_2 + O_2 → 2 H_2O

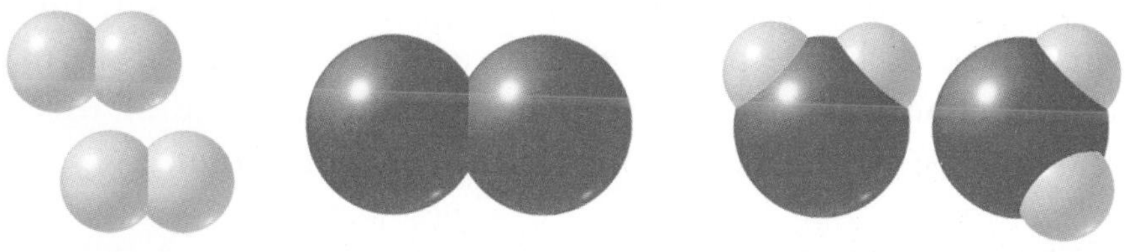

4 hydrogen atoms + 2 oxygen atoms → 2 oxygen atoms, 4 hydrogen atoms

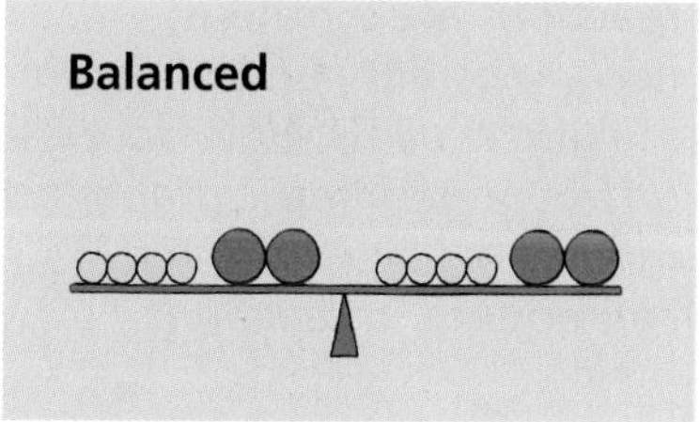

4 Look Back and Check The equation is balanced. It tells you that two molecules of hydrogen react with one molecule of oxygen to yield two molecules of water. Count the atoms in the balanced equation again to see that the equation is correct.

Math Analyzing Data

Balancing Chemical Equations

Magnesium metal (Mg) reacts with oxygen gas (O_2) forming magnesium oxide (MgO). To write a balanced equation for this reaction, first write the equation using the formulas of the reactants and products. Then, count the number of atoms of each element.

1. **Balancing Chemical Equations** Balance the equation for the reaction of sodium metal (Na) with oxygen gas (O_2), forming sodium oxide (Na_2O).
2. **Balancing Chemical Equations** Balance the equation for the reaction of tin (Sn) with chlorine gas (Cl_2), forming tin chloride ($SnCl_2$).

Balancing Equations

1. Write the Equation
   $Mg + O_2 \rightarrow MgO$
2. Count the Atoms
   $Mg + O_2 \rightarrow MgO$
   1 2 1 1
3. Use Coefficients to Balance the Atoms
   $Mg + O_2 \rightarrow 2\,MgO$
   2 2
   $2\,Mg + O_2 \rightarrow 2\,MgO$
   2 2 2 2
4. Look Back and Check

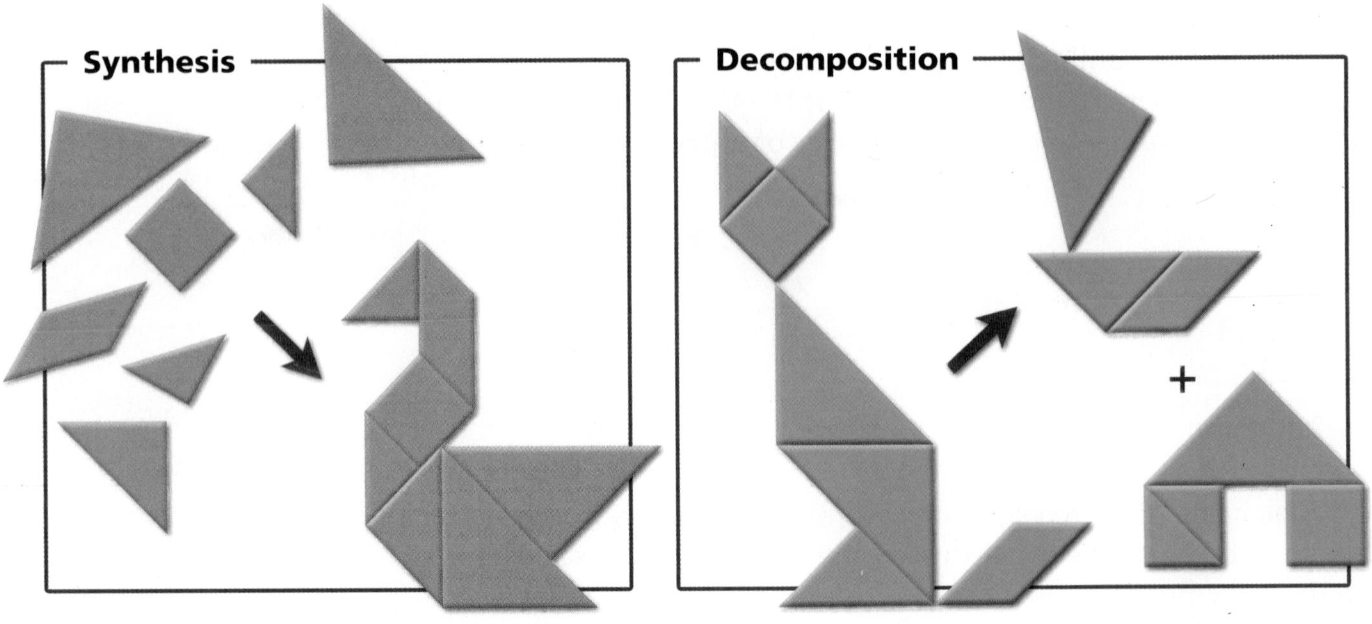

FIGURE 11

Types of Reactions

Three categories of chemical reactions are synthesis, decomposition, and replacement.
Making Models *How do these different geometric shapes act as models for elements and compounds in reactions?*

Classifying Chemical Reactions

Substances may combine to make a more complex substance. They may break apart to make simpler substances. Or, they may even exchange parts. In each case, new substances form. **Many chemical reactions can be classified in one of three categories: synthesis, decomposition, or replacement.**

Synthesis Have you ever listened to music from a synthesizer? You can hear many different notes and types of sounds combined to make music. To synthesize is to put things together. In chemistry, when two or more elements or compounds combine to make a more complex substance, the process is called **synthesis** (SIN thuh sis). The reaction of hydrogen and oxygen to make water is a synthesis reaction.

Decomposition In contrast to a synthesis reaction, a process called **decomposition** breaks down compounds into simpler products. You may have a bottle of hydrogen peroxide (H_2O_2) in your house to clean cuts. If you keep such a bottle for a very long time, you'll have water instead. The hydrogen peroxide decomposes into water and oxygen gas.

$$2\ H_2O_2 \longrightarrow 2\ H_2O + O_2$$

Replacement When one element replaces another in a compound, or when two elements in different compounds trade places, the process is called **replacement.** Look at this example:

$$2\ Cu_2O + C \longrightarrow 4\ Cu + CO_2$$

Copper metal can be obtained by heating copper oxide with carbon. The carbon takes the place of copper.

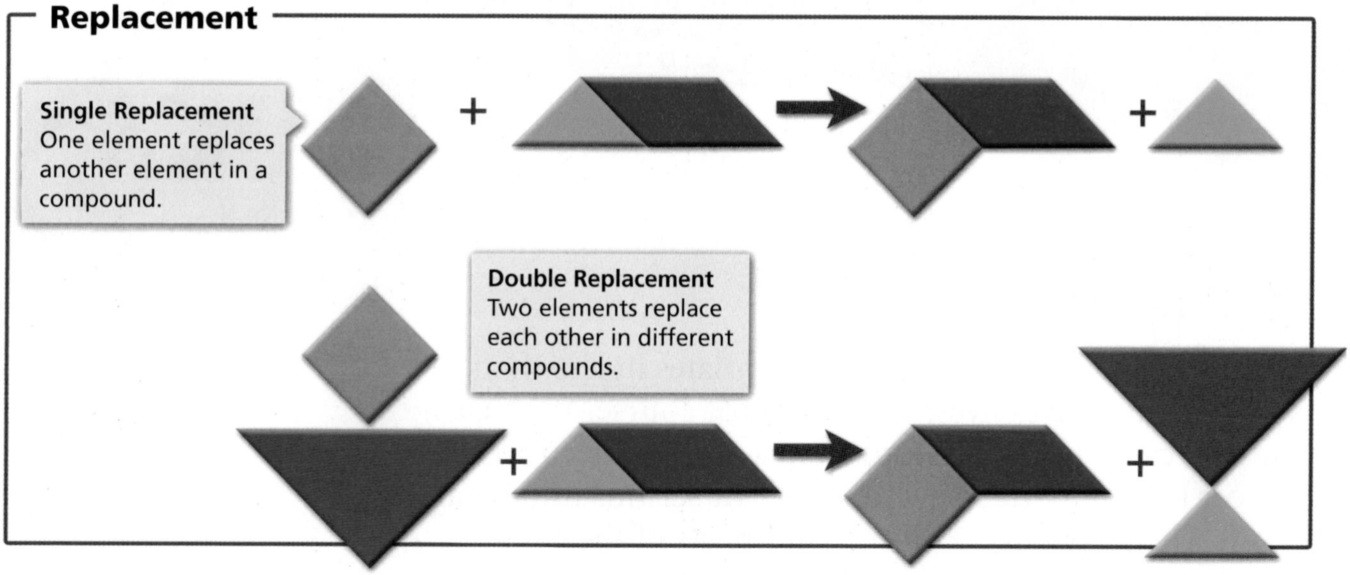
Replacement
Single Replacement
One element replaces another element in a compound.
Double Replacement
Two elements replace each other in different compounds.

The reaction between copper oxide and carbon is called a *single* replacement reaction because one element, carbon, replaces another element, copper, in the compound. In a *double* replacement reaction, elements in one compound appear to "trade places" with elements in another compound. The following reaction is an example of a double replacement:

$$FeS + 2\,HCl \longrightarrow FeCl_2 + H_2S$$

Use Figure 11 to help you track what happens to elements in different types of chemical reactions.

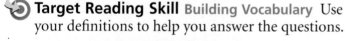

Section 2 Assessment

Target Reading Skill **Building Vocabulary** Use your definitions to help you answer the questions.

Reviewing Key Concepts

1. a. Identifying What do the formulas, arrow, and plus signs in a chemical equation tell you?

b. Comparing and Contrasting How are reactants and products treated the same in a chemical reaction? How are they treated differently?

2. a. Summarizing In your own words, state the meaning of the principle of conservation of mass.

b. Applying Concepts If the total mass of the products of a reaction is 250 g, what was the total mass of the reactants?

3. a. Reviewing What are three types of chemical reactions?

b. Inferring What is the smallest possible number of products in a decomposition reaction?

c. Classifying Classify the following reaction:

$$P_4O_{10} + 6\,H_2O \longrightarrow 4\,H_3PO_4$$

Math Practice

Balance the following equations:

4. $Fe_2O_3 + C \longrightarrow Fe + CO_2$

5. $SO_2 + O_2 \longrightarrow SO_3$

Technology and **Society** • Tech & Design •

Air Bags

What moves faster than 300 km/h, inflates in less than a second, and saves lives? An air bag, of course! When a moving car is suddenly stopped in a crash, objects inside the car keep moving forward. Death or serious injury can result when passengers hit the hard parts of the car's interior. Air bags, working with seat belts, can slow or stop a person's forward motion in a crash.

How Do Air Bags Increase Safety?

Before front air bags became a requirement in the 1990s, seat belts were the only restraints for passengers in cars. Seat belts do a great job of keeping people from flying forward in a crash, but even with seat belts, some movement takes place. Air bags were designed as a second form of protection. They provide a buffer zone between a person and the steering wheel, dashboard, or windshield.

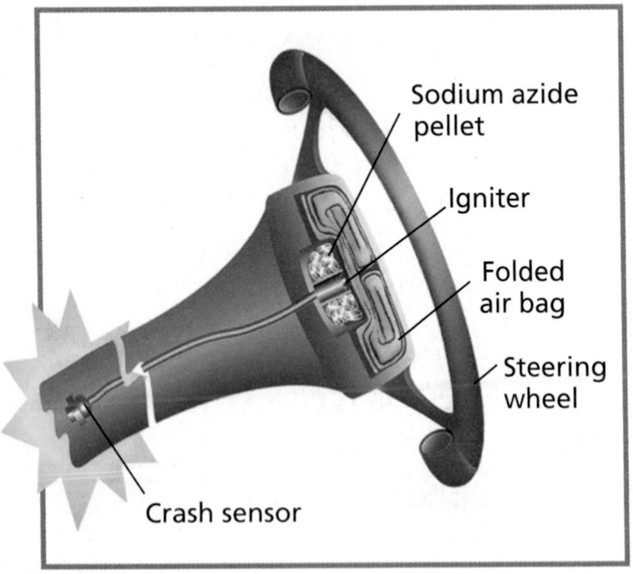

Collision Detected
The crash sensor is located toward the front of the car. The sensor detects an impact and sends a signal to the air bag igniter to start the chemical reaction.

$2\ NaN_3 \longrightarrow 2\ Na + 3\ N_2$

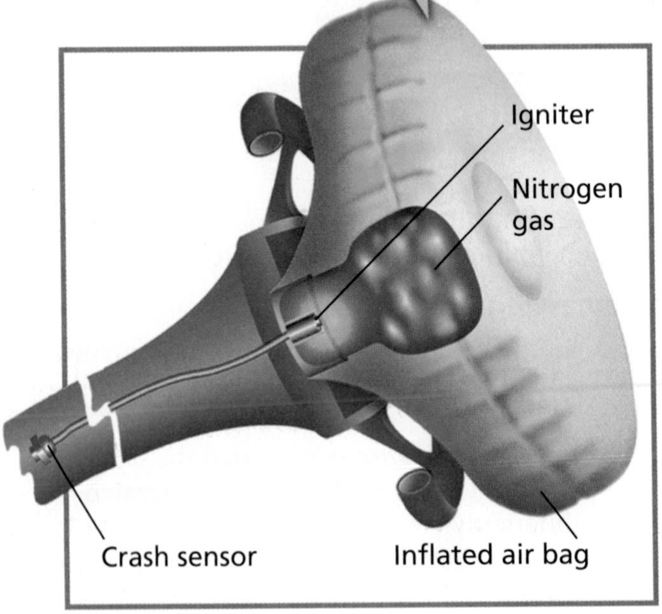

Air Bag Inflates
Pellets of a compound called sodium azide (NaN_3) are heated, causing a rapid decomposition reaction. This reaction releases sodium metal (Na) and nitrogen gas (N_2), which inflate the air bag in about 30 milliseconds.

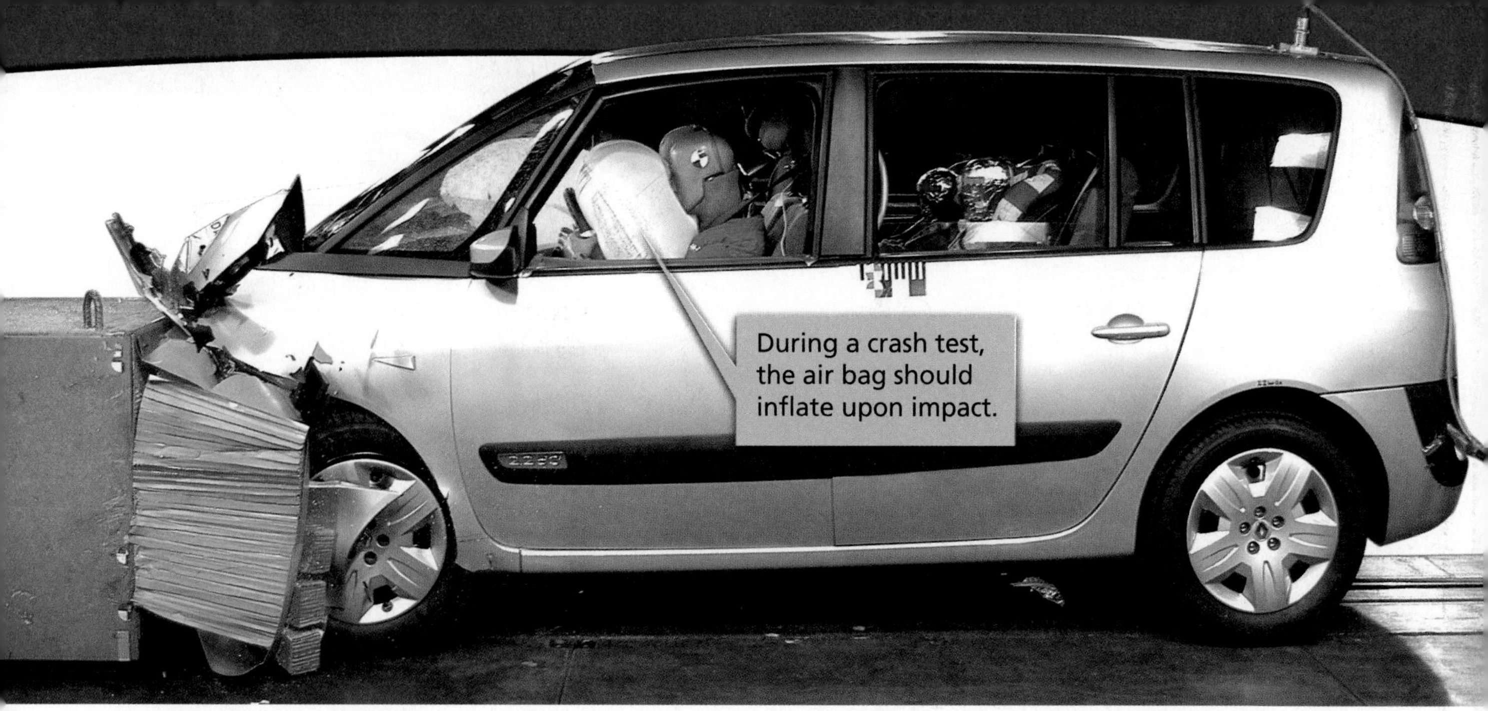

During a crash test, the air bag should inflate upon impact.

▲ Car manufacturers must test their vehicles to verify that they meet minimum government safety standards. New cars are required to have air bags on both the driver and passenger sides.

Cushion or Curse?

Air bags save hundreds of lives each year. However, if your body is too close to the air bag when it inflates, the impact of the expanding bag may do more harm than good. Since 1990, more than 200 people, including 140 children, have been killed by air bags inflating close to them. Air bags are designed for adults but pose a risk to smaller, lightweight adults and children. That is why children should never ride in a front seat. They are safer in the back seat without air bags than in the front seat with air bags.

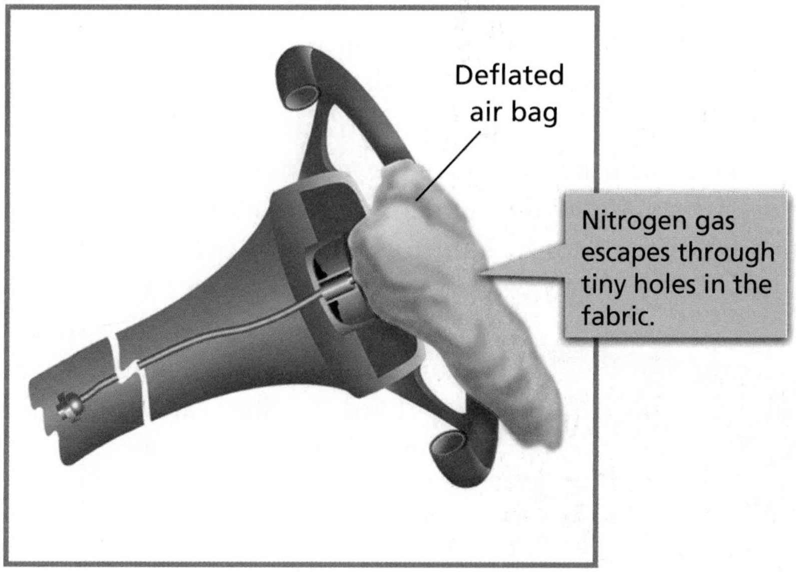

Air Bag Deflates
Tiny holes in the fabric of the air bag allow some of the nitrogen gas to escape, so the bag starts to deflate by the time a person makes contact with it. In this way, the air bag provides a deflating cushion that slows forward movement.

Weigh the Impact

1. Identify the Need
Air bags are called supplemental restraint systems. Why is it so important to restrain people in a collision?

2. Research
Use the Internet to learn how air bags are being changed, added, and redesigned to improve their safety and effectiveness.

3. Write
Choose one type of new air bag technology and summarize it in a few short paragraphs.

Go Online PHSchool.com
For: More on air bags
Visit: PHSchool.com
Web Code: cgh-2020

Section 3

Controlling Chemical Reactions

Reading Preview

Key Concepts

- How is activation energy related to chemical reactions?
- What factors affect the rate of a chemical reaction?

Key Terms

- activation energy
- concentration
- catalyst
- enzyme
- inhibitor

Target Reading Skill

Relating Cause and Effect As you read, identify the factors that can cause the rate of a chemical reaction to increase. Write the information in a graphic organizer like the one below.

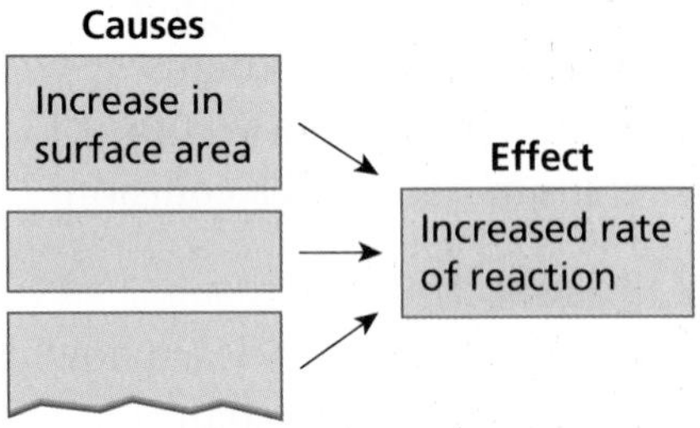

Lab zone Discover Activity

Can You Speed Up or Slow Down a Reaction?

1. Put on your safety goggles and lab apron.
2. Obtain three 125-mL solutions of vitamin C and water—one at room temperature, one at about 75°C, and one chilled to between 5°C and 10°C.
3. Add 3 drops of iodine solution to each container and stir each with a clean spoon. Compare changes you observe in the solutions.
4. Clean up your work area and wash your hands.

Think It Over

Inferring What conclusion can you make about the effect of temperature on the reaction of iodine and vitamin C?

With a splintering crash, a bolt of lightning strikes a tree in the forest. The lightning splits the tree and sets fire to the leaves on the ground below it. The leaves are dry and crisp from drought. The crackling fire burns a black patch in the leaves. The flames leap to nearby dry twigs and branches on the ground. Soon, the forest underbrush is blazing, and the barks of trees start burning. Miles away in an observation tower, a ranger spots the fire and calls in the alarm—"Forest fire!"

Forest fires don't just happen. Many factors contribute to them—lightning and drought to name just two. But, in general, wood does not always burn easily. Yet, once wood does begin to burn, it gives off a steady supply of heat and light. Why is it so hard to start and maintain some chemical reactions?

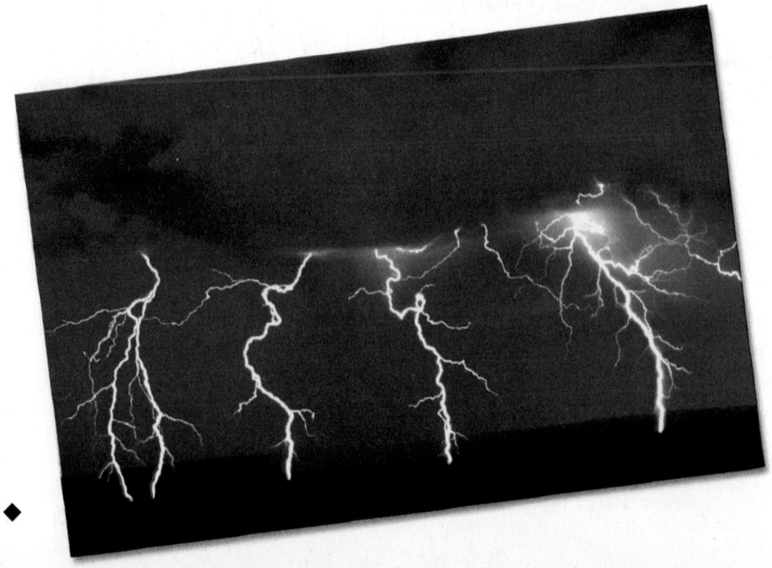

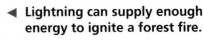

◀ **Lightning can supply enough energy to ignite a forest fire.**

FIGURE 12
Modeling Activation Energy
The rock at the top of this hill cannot roll down the hill until a small push gets it going.
Making Models *How is this cartoon a kind of model for the role of activation energy in a chemical reaction?*

Energy and Reactions

To understand why it can be hard to start some chemical reactions, look at Figure 12. The rock at the top of the hill can fall over the cliff, releasing energy when it crashes into the rocks at the bottom. Yet it remains motionless until it's pushed over the small hump.

Activation Energy Every chemical reaction is like that rock. A reaction won't begin until the reactants have enough energy to push them "over the hump." The energy is used to break the chemical bonds of the reactants. Then, the atoms begin to form the new chemical bonds of the products. The **activation energy** is the minimum amount of energy needed to start a chemical reaction. **All chemical reactions need a certain amount of activation energy to get started.**

Consider the reaction in which hydrogen and oxygen form water. This reaction gives off a large amount of energy. But if you just mix the two gases together, they can remain unchanged for years. For the reaction to start, a tiny amount of activation energy is needed—even just an electric spark. Once a few molecules of hydrogen and oxygen react, the rest will quickly follow because the first few reactions provide activation energy for more molecules to react. Overall, the reaction releases more energy than it uses. Recall from Section 1 that this type of reaction is described as exothermic.

Reading Checkpoint **What is the function of a spark in a reaction between hydrogen gas and oxygen gas?**

Chemical Reactions

Video Preview
▶ Video Field Trip
Video Assessment

Exothermic and Endothermic Reactions Every chemical reaction needs activation energy to get started. Whether or not a reaction needs still more energy from the environment to keep going depends on if it is exothermic or endothermic.

Exothermic reactions follow the pattern you can see in the first diagram in Figure 13. The dotted line marks the energy of the reactants before the reaction begins. The peak in the graph shows the activation energy. Notice that at the end of the reaction, the products have less energy than the reactants. This difference results in a release of heat. The burning of fuel, such as wood, natural gas, or oil, is an example of an exothermic reaction. People can make use of the heat that is released to warm their homes and cook food.

Now look at the graph of an endothermic reaction on the right of Figure 13. Endothermic reactions also need activation energy to get started. But, in addition, they need energy to keep going. Notice that the energy of the products is higher than that of the reactants. This difference tells you that the reaction must absorb energy to continue.

When you placed baking soda in vinegar in the Discover activity in Section 1, the thermal energy already present in the solution was enough to start the reaction. The reaction continued by drawing energy from the solution, making the solution feel colder. But most endothermic reactions require a continuous source of heat to occur. For example, baking bread requires added heat until the baking process is completed.

Reading Checkpoint **In what type of reaction do the reactants have less energy than the products?**

FIGURE 13
Energy Changes in Chemical Reactions
Both exothermic and endothermic reactions need energy to get started. **Reading Graphs** *What does the peak in the curve in each graph represent?*

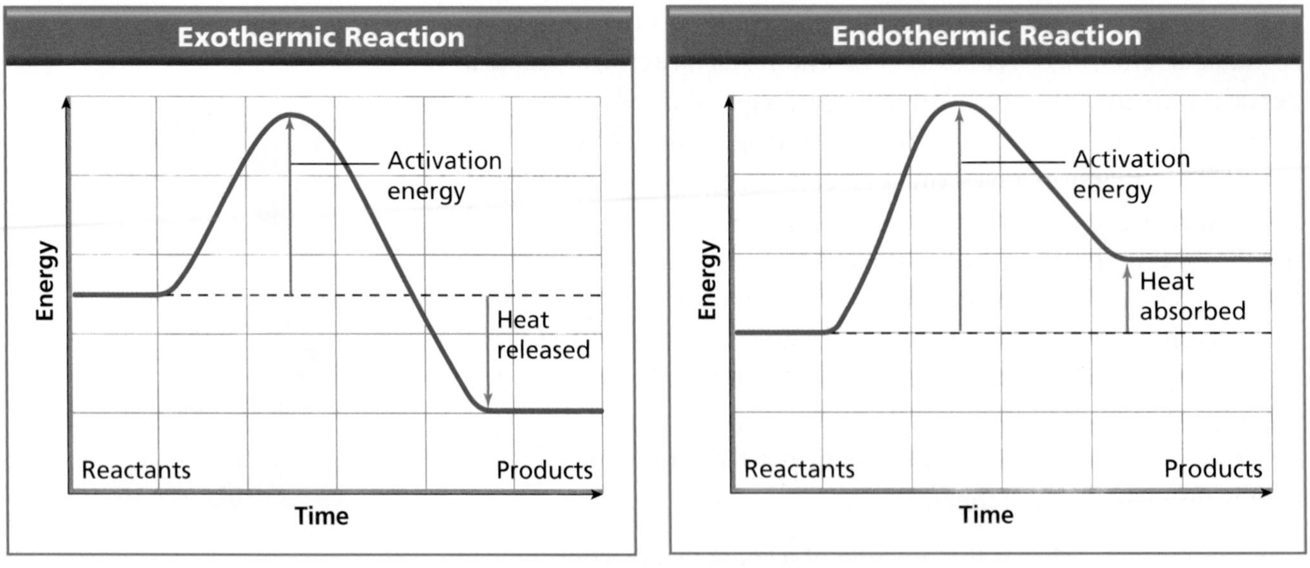

Rates of Chemical Reactions

Chemical reactions don't all occur at the same rate. Some, like explosions, are very fast. Others, like the rusting of metal, are much slower. Also, a particular reaction can occur at different rates depending on the conditions.

If you want to make a chemical reaction happen faster, you need to get more reactant particles together more often and with more energy. To slow down a reaction, you need to do the opposite. **Chemists can control rates of reactions by changing factors such as surface area, temperature, and concentration, and by using substances called catalysts and inhibitors.**

Surface Area Look at Figure 14. The wreckage used to be a grain elevator. It exploded when grain dust ignited in the air above the stored grain. Although the grain itself doesn't react violently in air, the grain dust can. This difference is related to surface area. When a chunk of solid substance reacts with a liquid or gas, only the particles on the surface of the solid come into contact with the other reactant. But if you break the solid into smaller pieces, more particles are exposed and the reaction happens faster. Sometimes, speeding up a reaction this way is dangerous. Other times, increasing surface area can be useful. For example, chewing your food breaks it into smaller pieces that your body can digest more easily and quickly.

Lab zone Skills Activity

Interpreting Data

1. Measure the length and width of a face of a gelatin cube.
2. Calculate the area of that face of the cube.
   Area = length × width
3. Repeat for each of the other five faces. Then add the six values to get the total surface area.
4. Using a plastic knife, cut the cube in half. Add the surface areas of the two pieces to get a new total.

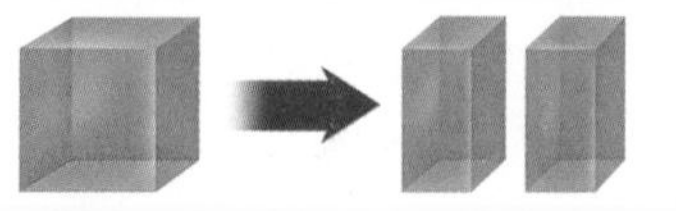

5. How did the original total surface area compare with the total area after the cube was cut?
6. Predict the total surface area if you cut each cube in two again. If you have time, test your prediction.

FIGURE 14
Surface Area and Reaction Rate
Grain dust reacts explosively with oxygen. Minimizing grain dust in a grain elevator can help prevent an accident like the one shown here.

Temperature Another way to increase the rate of a reaction is to increase its temperature. When you heat a substance, its particles move faster. Faster-moving particles increase the reaction rate in two ways. First, the particles come in contact more often, which means there are more chances for a reaction to happen. Second, faster-moving particles have more energy. This increased energy causes more particles of the reactants to get over the activation energy "hump."

In contrast, reducing temperature slows down reaction rates. For example, milk contains bacteria, which carry out thousands of chemical reactions as they live and reproduce. At room temperature, those reactions happen faster and milk spoils more quickly. You store milk and other foods in the refrigerator because keeping foods cold slows down those reactions, so your foods stay fresh longer.

Concentration A third way to increase the rate of a chemical reaction is to increase the concentration of the reactants. **Concentration** is the amount of a substance in a given volume. For example, adding a small spoonful of sugar to a glass of lemonade will make it sweet. But adding a large spoonful of sugar makes the lemonade sweeter. The glass with more sugar has a greater concentration of sugar molecules.

Increasing the concentration of reactants supplies more particles to react. Compare the two reactions of acid and magnesium metal in Figure 15. The test tube on the left has a lower concentration of acid. This reaction is slower than the one on the right, where the acid concentration is higher. You see evidence for the increased rate of reaction in the greater amount of gas bubbles produced.

Reading Checkpoint **Why may an increase in temperature affect the rate of a chemical reaction?**

FIGURE 15
Concentration and Reaction Rate
Bubbles of hydrogren gas form when magnesium reacts with acid.
Relating Cause and Effect *What makes the reaction faster in the test tube on the right?*

Catalysts Another way to control the rate of a reaction is to change the activation energy needed. A **catalyst** (KAT uh list) is a material that increases the rate of a reaction by lowering the activation energy. Although catalysts affect a reaction's rate, they are not permanently changed by a reaction. For this reason catalysts are not considered reactants.

Many chemical reactions happen at temperatures that would kill living things. Yet, some of these reactions are necessary for life. The cells in your body (as in all living things) contain biological catalysts called **enzymes** (EN zymz). Your body has thousands of different enzymes. Each one is specific—it affects only one chemical reaction.

As shown in Figure 16, enzymes provide a surface on which reactions can take place. By bringing reactant molecules close together, the enzyme lowers the activation energy needed. In this way, enzymes make chemical reactions that are necessary for life happen at a low temperature.

Inhibitors Sometimes a reaction is more useful when it can be slowed down rather than speeded up. A material used to decrease the rate of a reaction is an **inhibitor.** Most inhibitors work by preventing reactants from coming together. Usually they combine with one of the reactants either permanently or temporarily. Inhibitors include preservatives added to food products to prevent them from becoming stale or spoiling.

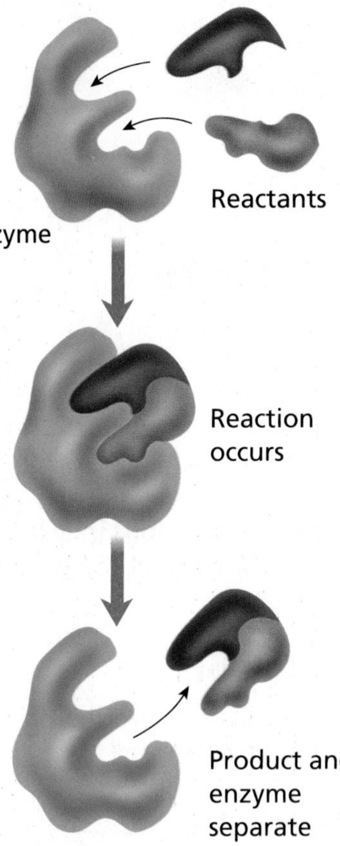

FIGURE 16
Enzyme Action
After a reaction, an enzyme molecule is unchanged.

Section 3 Assessment

Target Reading Skill Relating Cause and Effect Use the information in your graphic organizer about speeding up chemical reactions to help you answer Question 2 below.

Reviewing Key Concepts

1. a. Defining What is activation energy?
   b. Describing What role does activation energy play in chemical reactions?
   c. Making Generalizations Look at the diagram in Figure 13, and make a generalization about activation energy in exothermic and endothermic reactions.
2. a. Identifying What are four ways that chemists can control the rates of chemical reactions?
   b. Applying Concepts Which would react more quickly in a chemical reaction: a single sugar cube or an equal mass of sugar crystals? Explain.

Lab zone At-Home Activity

Comparing Reaction Rates Place an iron nail in a plastic cup. Add enough water to almost cover the nail. Place a small piece of fine steel wool in another cup and add the same amount of water. Ask family members to predict what will happen overnight. The next day, examine the nail and steel wool. Compare the amount of rust on each. Were your family's predictions correct? Explain how surface areas affect reaction rates.

Lab zone **Skills Lab**

Temperature and Enzyme Activity

Problem

Catalase is an enzyme that speeds up the breakdown of hydrogen peroxide into water and oxygen gas. Hydrogen peroxide is a poisonous waste product of reactions in living things. How does temperature affect the action of the enzyme catalase?

Skills Focus

calculating, interpreting data, drawing conclusions

Materials

- forceps
- stopwatch
- test tube with a one-hole stopper
- 0.1% hydrogen peroxide solution
- filter paper disks soaked in liver preparation (catalase enzyme) and kept at four different temperatures (room temperature, 0–4°C, 37°C, and 100°C)
- container to hold water (beaker or bowl)

Procedure

1. Form a hypothesis that predicts how the action of the catalase enzyme will differ at the different temperatures to be tested.

Data Table		
Temperature (°C)	Time (sec)	Average Time for Class (sec)

2. Fill a container with water. Then fill a test tube with 0.1% hydrogen peroxide solution until the test tube is overflowing. Do this over a sink or the container of water.
3. Make a data table similar to the one shown.
4. Moisten the small end of a one-hole stopper with water.
5. Using forceps, remove a filter paper disk soaked in liver preparation (catalase enzyme) that has been kept at room temperature. Stick it to the moistened end of the one-hole stopper.
6. Your partner should be ready with the stopwatch for the next step.
7. Place the stopper firmly into the test tube, hold your thumb over the hole, and quickly invert the test tube. Start the stopwatch. Put the inverted end of the test tube into the container of water, as shown in the photograph, and remove your thumb.

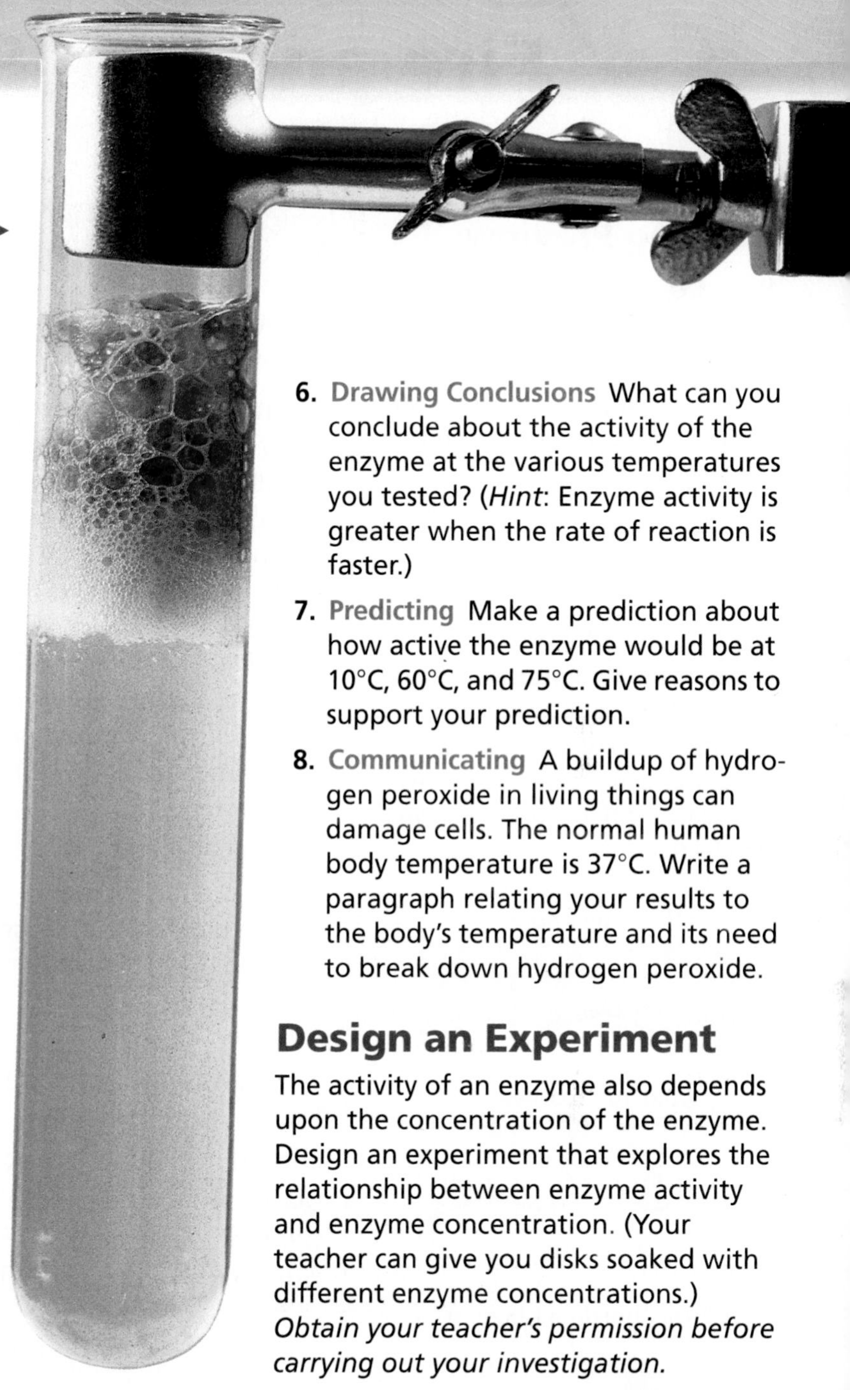

Catalase from blood reacts ▶ with hydrogen peroxide.

8. Observe what happens to the filter paper inside the test tube. Record the time it takes for the disk to rise to the top. If the disk does not rise within 2 minutes, record "no reaction" and go on to Step 9.
9. Rinse the test tube and repeat the procedure with catalase enzyme disks kept at 0°C, 37°C, and 100°C. **CAUTION:** *When you remove the disk kept in the hot water bath, do not use your bare hands. Avoid spilling the hot water.*

Analyze and Conclude

1. **Observing** What makes the disk float to the top of the inverted test tube?
2. **Calculating** Calculate the average time for each temperature based on the results of the entire class. Enter the results in your data table.
3. **Graphing** Make a line graph of the data you collected. Label the horizontal axis (*x*-axis) "Temperature" with a scale from 0°C to 100°C. Label the vertical axis (*y*-axis) "Time" with a scale from 0 to 30 seconds. Plot the class average time for each temperature.
4. **Interpreting Data** What evidence do you have that your hypothesis from Step 1 is either supported or not supported?
5. **Interpreting Data** How is the time it takes the disk to rise to the top of the inverted tube related to the rate of the reaction?
6. **Drawing Conclusions** What can you conclude about the activity of the enzyme at the various temperatures you tested? (*Hint*: Enzyme activity is greater when the rate of reaction is faster.)
7. **Predicting** Make a prediction about how active the enzyme would be at 10°C, 60°C, and 75°C. Give reasons to support your prediction.
8. **Communicating** A buildup of hydrogen peroxide in living things can damage cells. The normal human body temperature is 37°C. Write a paragraph relating your results to the body's temperature and its need to break down hydrogen peroxide.

Design an Experiment

The activity of an enzyme also depends upon the concentration of the enzyme. Design an experiment that explores the relationship between enzyme activity and enzyme concentration. (Your teacher can give you disks soaked with different enzyme concentrations.) *Obtain your teacher's permission before carrying out your investigation.*

Go Online
PHSchool.com
For: Data sharing
Visit: PHSchool.com
Web Code: cgd-2023

Section 4

Integrating Health

Fire and Fire Safety

Reading Preview

Key Concepts

- What are the three things necessary to maintain a fire?
- Why should you know about the causes of fire and how to prevent a fire?

Key Terms

- combustion • fuel

Target Reading Skill

Using Prior Knowledge Before you read, write what you know about fire safety in a graphic organizer like the one below. As you read, continue to write in what you learn.

What You Know
1. A fire needs fuel to burn. 2.

What You Learned
1. 2.

Lab zone Discover Activity

How Does Baking Soda Affect a Fire?

1. Put on your safety goggles.
2. Secure a small candle in a holder or a ball of clay. After instructions from your teacher, use a match to light the candle.
3. Place a beaker next to the candle. Measure 1 large spoonful of baking soda into the beaker. Add about 100 mL of water and stir. Add about 100 mL of vinegar.
4. As soon as the mixture stops foaming, tip the beaker as if you are pouring something out of it onto the flame. **CAUTION:** *Do not pour any liquid on the candle.*
5. Observe what happens to the flame.

Think It Over

Developing Hypotheses The gas produced in the beaker was carbon dioxide, CO_2. Based on the results of this experiment, develop a hypothesis to explain what you observed in Step 5.

The call comes in. Fire! A blaze has been spotted in a warehouse near gasoline storage tanks. Firefighters scramble aboard the ladder truck and the hose truck. Lights flash, sirens blare, and traffic swerves to clear a path for the trucks. The firefighters know from their training that fire is a chemical reaction that can be controlled—but only if they reach it in time.

Firefighters battle a blaze. ▼

Understanding Fire

Fire is the result of **combustion,** a rapid reaction between oxygen and a substance called a fuel. A **fuel** is a material that releases energy when it burns. Common fuels include oil, wood, gasoline, natural gas, and paper. Combustion of these types of fuel always produces carbon dioxide and water. When fuels don't burn completely, products such as smoke and poisonous gases may be produced.

The Fire Triangle Although a combustion reaction is very exothermic and fast, a fire cannot start unless conditions are right. **The following three things are necessary to start and maintain a fire—fuel, oxygen, and heat.**

You probably know that oxygen is one of the gases in air. About 20 percent of the air around you is composed of oxygen gas. If air can reach the fuel, so can oxygen. A large fire can create a strong draft that pulls air toward it. As the air around the flame is heated, it rises rapidly. Cooler air flows toward the fire, replacing the heated air and bringing a fresh supply of oxygen. If you stand in front of a fire in a fireplace, you can feel the air flow toward the fire.

Heat is a part of the fire triangle. Fuel and oxygen can be together, but they won't react until something provides the activation energy to start combustion. This energy can come from a lighted match, an electric spark, or the heat from a stove. Once combustion starts, the heat released supplies more activation energy to keep the reaction going.

Once started, a fire can continue burning as long as all components of the fire triangle are available. Coal in abandoned mines under the town of Centralia, Pennsylvania, started burning in 1962. The coal is still burning. Many old airshafts lead into the tunnels. Because some airshafts cannot be located and sealed, air continues to flow into the mines, supporting the fire. Heat and poisonous gases coming up from the fire through cracks in the ground made living in Centralia difficult. Everyone eventually moved away. No one knows how long this fire will continue to burn.

Reading Checkpoint **What is heat's role in starting a fire?**

FIGURE 17
The Fire Triangle
The fire triangle can be controlled in the grill below. If any point of the fire triangle is missing, a fire will not continue.
Applying Concepts *How would closing the lower air vents affect the fire?*

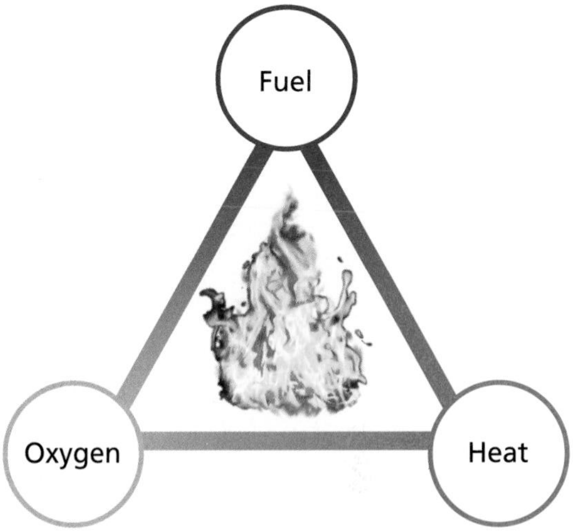

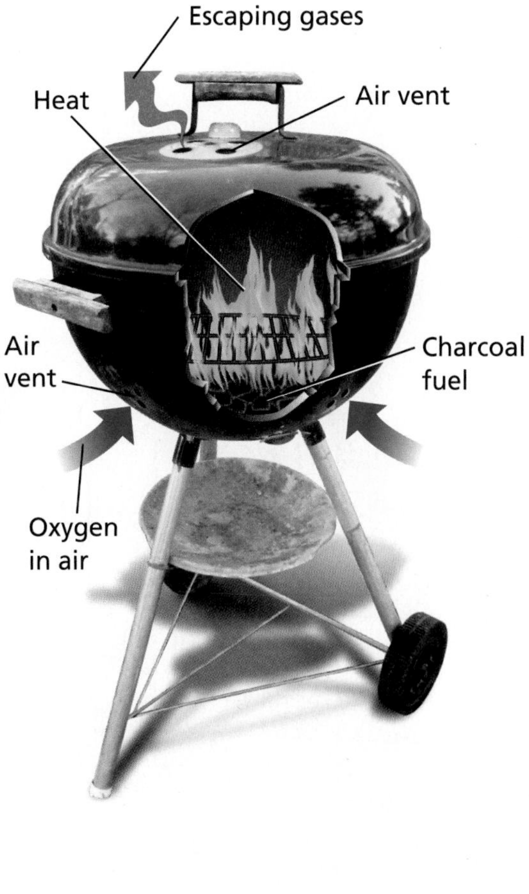

Go Online
SCI LINKS NSTA
For: Links on fire safety
Visit: www.SciLinks.org
Web Code: scn-1224

Controlling Fire Use your knowledge of chemical reactions to think of ways to control a fire. What if you remove one part of the fire triangle? For example, you can get the fuel away from the flames. You can also keep oxygen from getting to the fuel. Finally, you can cool the combustion reaction.

How do firefighters usually fight fires? They use hoses to spray huge amounts of water on the flames. Water removes two parts of the fire triangle. First, water covers the fuel, which keeps it from coming into contact with oxygen. Second, evaporation of the water uses a large amount of heat, causing the fire to cool. Without heat, there isn't enough energy to continue the combustion. Therefore, the reaction stops.

Home Fire Safety

Every year, fire claims thousands of lives in the United States. **If you know how to prevent fires in your home and what to do if a fire starts, you are better prepared to take action.** You may save your home or even your life! The most common sources of home fires are small heaters, cooking, and faulty electrical wiring. The fires that cause the most deaths start from carelessness with cigarettes.

Fighting Fires You can fight a small fire by using what you know about the fire triangle. For example, carbon dioxide gas can smother a fire by preventing contact between the fuel and oxygen in the air. Therefore, you can put out a small fire on the stove by throwing baking soda on it. Baking soda decomposes when heated and releases carbon dioxide gas. Or, you can use the cover of a saucepan to cut off the flow of oxygen.

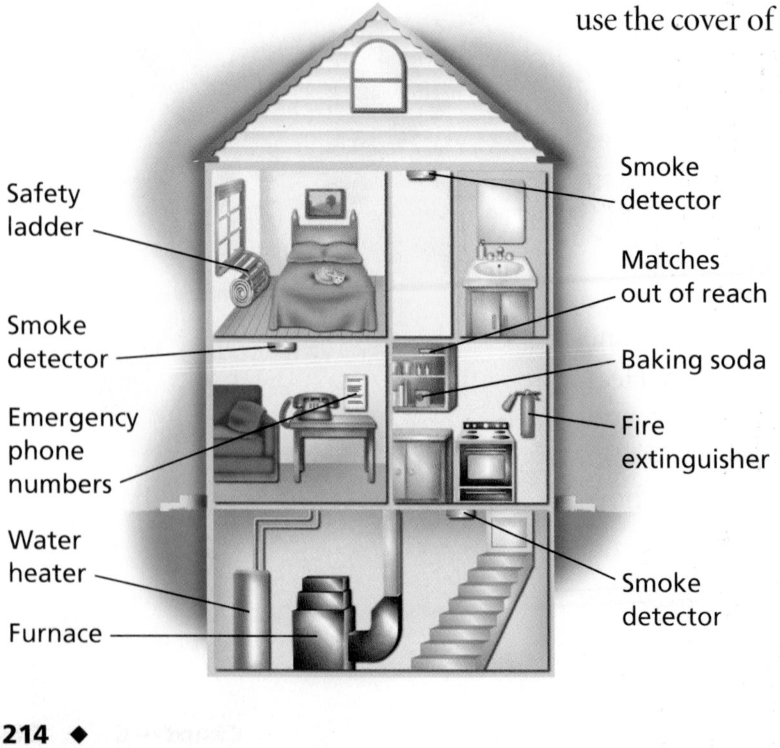

FIGURE 18
A Fire-Safe House
This fire-safe house has many fire-prevention and fire safety features. **Inferring** *Why are smoke detectors located on every floor?*

A small fire is easy to control. You can cool a match enough to stop combustion just by blowing on it. A small fire in a trash can may be doused with a pan of water. If the fire spreads to the curtains, however, even a garden hose might not deliver enough water to put it out.

One of the most effective ways to fight a small fire is with a fire extinguisher. But a fire that is growing as you fight it is out of control. If a fire is out of control, there is only one safe thing to do—get away from the fire and call the fire department.

Preventing Trouble The best form of fire safety is prevention. Figure 18 shows some features of a fire-safe house. You can also check your home to be sure that all flammable items are stored safely away from sources of flames, such as the kitchen stove. Fires can be dangerous and deadly, but many fires can be prevented if you are careful. Understanding the chemistry of fire gives you a way to reduce risk and increase your family's safety.

Reading Checkpoint **How does baking soda put a fire out?**

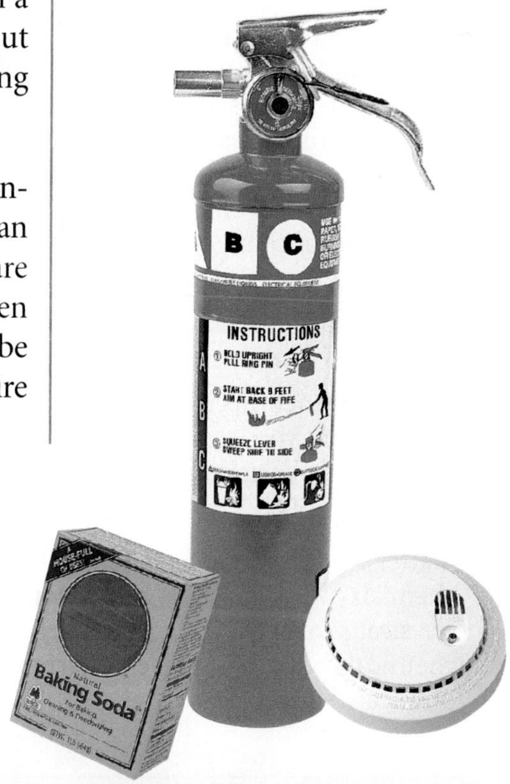

FIGURE 19
Fire-Prevention Devices
Fire extinguishers and baking soda can be used to interrupt the fire triangle. Smoke detectors can help you identify a fire and escape to safety.

Section 4 Assessment

Target Reading Skill **Previewing Visuals** Review your graphic organizer and revise it based on what you just learned in the section.

Reviewing Key Concepts

1. a. **Listing** What three things are required for combustion?
   b. **Explaining** How does the fire triangle help you control fire?
   c. **Applying Concepts** To stop a forest fire, firefighters may remove all the trees in a strip of land that lies in the path of the fire. What part of the fire triangle is affected? Explain.
2. a. **Reviewing** Why is it important to know about the causes of fire and how to prevent fires?
   b. **Identifying** What are the three most common causes of home fires?
   c. **Problem Solving** Choose one common cause of home fires. Describe measures that can be taken to prevent fires of this type.

Lab zone At-Home Activity

Family Safety Plan Work with your family to formulate a fire safety plan. How can fires be prevented in your home? How can fires be put out if they occur? Is there a functioning smoke detector on each floor of the home, especially near the bedrooms? How can the fire department be contacted in an emergency? Design a fire escape route. Make sure all family members know the route as well as a meeting place outside.

Chapter 6 Study Guide

1 Observing Chemical Change

Key Concepts

- Matter can be described in terms of two kinds of properties—physical properties and chemical properties. Changes in matter can be described in terms of physical changes and chemical changes.
- Chemical changes occur when bonds break and new bonds form.
- Chemical reactions involve two main kinds of changes that you can observe—formation of new substances and changes in energy.

Key Terms

matter
chemistry
physical property
chemical property
physical change
chemical reaction
precipitate
endothermic reaction
exothermic reaction

2 Describing Chemical Reactions

Key Concepts

- Chemical equations use chemical formulas and other symbols instead of words to summarize a reaction.
- The principle of conservation of mass states that, in a chemical reaction, the total mass of the reactants must equal the total mass of the products.
- To describe a reaction accurately, a chemical equation must show the same number of each type of atom on both sides of the equation.
- Many chemical reactions can be classified in one of three categories: synthesis, decomposition, or replacement.

Key Terms

chemical equation
reactant
product
conservation of mass
closed system
open system
coefficient
synthesis
decomposition
replacement

3 Controlling Chemical Reactions

Key Concepts

- All chemical reactions need a certain amount of activation energy to get started.
- Chemists can control rates of reactions by changing factors such as surface area, temperature, and concentration, and by using substances called catalysts and inhibitors.

Key Terms

activation energy
concentration
catalyst
enzyme
inhibitor

4 Fire and Fire Safety

Key Concepts

- The following three things are necessary to start and maintain a fire—fuel, oxygen, and heat.
- If you know how to prevent fires in your home and what to do if a fire starts, you are better prepared to take action.

Key Terms

combustion
fuel

Review and Assessment

Go Online
PHSchool.com
For: Self-Assessment
Visit: PHSchool.com
Web Code: cga-2020

Organizing Information

Concept Mapping Copy the chemical reactions concept map onto a separate sheet of paper. Then complete it and add a title. (For more on Concept Mapping, see the Skills Handbook.)

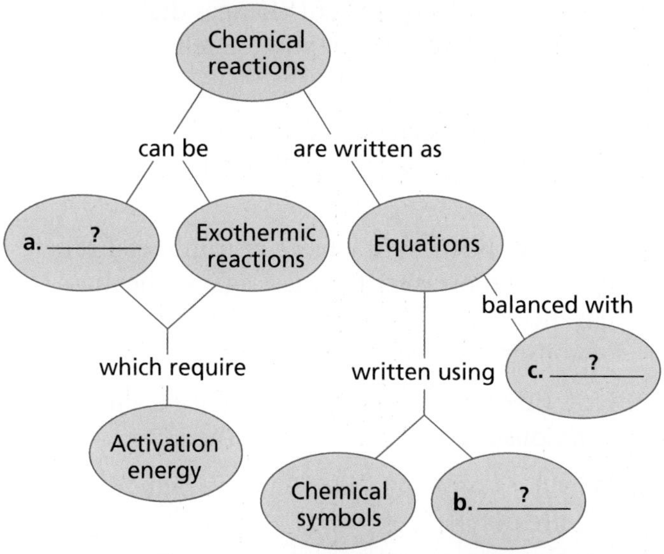

Reviewing Key Terms

Choose the letter of the best answer.

1. Which of the following is *not* a physical property?
   a. flexibility
   b. ability to catch fire
   c. melting point
   d. ability to conduct electricity
2. A chemical reaction that gives off heat is likely to be
   a. endothermic.
   b. a precipitate.
   c. a physical change.
   d. exothermic.
3. You can balance a chemical equation by changing the
   a. subscripts.
   b. coefficients.
   c. reactants.
   d. products.
4. A chemical reaction in which two elements combine to form a compound is called a
   a. synthesis reaction.
   b. replacement reaction.
   c. decomposition reaction.
   d. precipitation reaction.
5. The activation energy of a chemical reaction
   a. is supplied by a catalyst.
   b. is released at the end.
   c. starts the reaction.
   d. changes with time.
6. A chemical reaction in which a fuel combines rapidly with oxygen is a (an)
   a. inhibited reaction.
   b. combustion reaction.
   c. enzyme reaction.
   d. endothermic reaction.

Writing in Science

Explanation You are a writer for a children's book about chemistry. Write a paragraph that young children would understand that explains the concept of "activation energy." Be sure to use examples, such as the burning of wood or gas.

Discovery Channel School

Chemical Reactions
Video Preview
Video Field Trip
▶ Video Assessment

Review and Assessment

Checking Concepts

7. What are the two kinds of changes that occur in matter? Describe how you can tell one from the other.

8. Why can't you balance a chemical equation by changing the subscripts of the reactants or the products?

9. You find the mass of a piece of iron metal, let it rust, and measure the mass again. The mass has increased. Does this violate the principle of conservation of mass? Explain.

10. How do enzymes in your body make chemical reactions occur at safe temperatures?

11. Why does spraying water on a fire help to put the fire out?

12. How are inhibitors useful in controlling chemical reactions?

Thinking Critically

13. **Problem Solving** Steel that is exposed to water and salt rusts quickly. If you were a shipbuilder, how would you protect a new ship? Explain why your solution works.

14. **Classifying** The following are balanced equations for chemical reactions. Classify each of the equations as synthesis, decomposition, or replacement.

a. $2\ Al + Fe_2O_3 \longrightarrow 2\ Fe + Al_2O_3$
b. $2\ Ag + S \longrightarrow Ag_2S$
c. $CaCO_3 \longrightarrow CaO + CO_2$
d. $2\ NO + O_2 \longrightarrow 2\ NO_2$

15. **Relating Cause and Effect** Firefighters open doors very carefully because sometimes a room will burst violently into flames when the door is opened. Based on your knowledge of the fire triangle, explain why this happens.

16. **Inferring** Some statues are made of materials that can react in acid rain and begin to dissolve. It has been observed that statues with smooth surfaces are dissolved by acid rain much slower than statues with very detailed carvings. Explain this observation.

Math Practice

Balance the chemical equations in Questions 17–20.

17. $MgO + HBr \longrightarrow MgBr_2 + H_2O$

18. $N_2 + O_2 \longrightarrow N_2O_5$

19. $C_2H_4 + O_2 \longrightarrow CO_2 + H_2O$

20. $Fe + HCl \longrightarrow FeCl_2 + H_2$

Applying Skills

Use the energy diagram to answer Questions 21–23.

The two graphs below represent the same chemical reaction under different conditions.

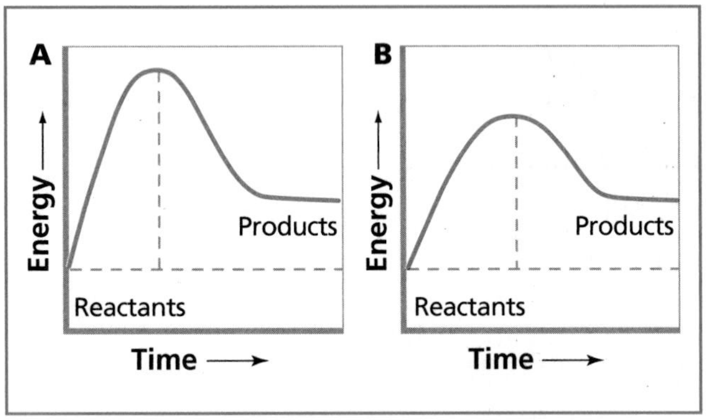

21. **Interpreting Data** How does the energy of the products compare with the energy of the reactants?

22. **Classifying** Tell whether this reaction is exothermic or endothermic.

23. **Applying Concepts** What change in condition might account for the lower "hump" in the second graph? Explain.

Lab zone Chapter Project

Performance Assessment Make a poster of your test results. Display your reaction chamber for the class. Discuss how your chamber was built to the specifications agreed upon by the class. Describe its safety features. Based on your results, rate how effectively your chamber works as a closed system.

Standardized Test Prep

Test-Taking Tip

Watching for Qualifiers

Many multiple-choice questions use qualifiers such as the words *best, except for, most,* and *least.* For example, you might be asked what is the *best* method for determining the density of a liquid. When you answer that kind of question, you need to read all the answer choices very carefully. Some of the answers may be correct, but not the best answer. In another question you may be told that a particular condition is satisfied by all the answer choices *except for* one. If you read the question too quickly, you may miss this two-word qualifier. In this type of question, the incorrect statement is actually the correct answer choice.

Sample Question

Each chemical equation below is correctly balanced *except for*

A $NaOH + HCl \longrightarrow NaCl + H_2O$
B $SO_3 + H_2O \longrightarrow H_2SO_4$
C $AgNO_3 + H_2S \longrightarrow Ag_2S + HNO_3$
D $Fe + H_2SO_4 \longrightarrow FeSO_4 + H_2$

Answer

The correct answer is **C.** A balanced chemical equation shows the same number of each type of atom on both sides of the equation. The left side of the equation shows a total of 1 Ag, 1 N, 3 O, 2 H, and 1 S. The right side shows 1 N and 3 O, but 2 Ag and only 1 H, so the equation is not balanced.

Choose the letter of the best answer.

1. Which of the following is the *best* evidence for a chemical reaction?
A gas bubbles
B formation of a new substance
C change of state
D change in temperature

2. Which shows a balanced chemical equation for the decomposition of aluminum oxide (Al_2O_3)?
F $Al_2O_3 \longrightarrow 2\,Al + O_2$
G $Al_2O_3 \longrightarrow 2\,Al + 3\,O_2$
H $2\,Al_2O_3 \longrightarrow 4\,Al + O_2$
J $2\,Al_2O_3 \longrightarrow 4\,Al + 3\,O_2$

Base your answers to Questions 3 and 4 on the diagram below. The diagram represents molecules of two different elements that are gases. The elements react chemically to produce a third gas.

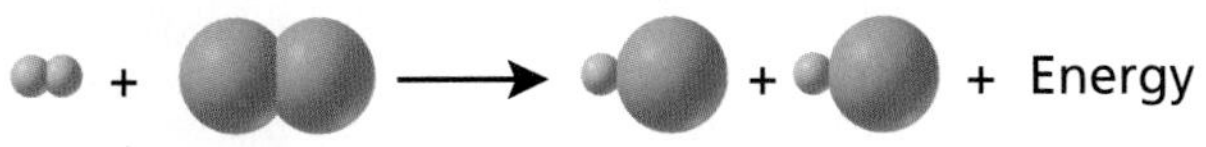

3. The diagram represents a(n)
A endothermic reaction in which energy is released.
B exothermic reaction in which energy is absorbed.
C exothermic reaction in which energy is released.
D reaction in which energy is destroyed.

4. What can be inferred from the diagram?
F Matter is not created or destroyed in a chemical reaction.
G The rate of a reaction depends on the surface area of the reactants.
H A gas molecule always consists of two identical atoms.
J The product is carbon monoxide gas.

Constructed Response

5. Zinc metal (Zn) reacts with hydrochloric acid (HCl) to produce hydrogen gas (H_2) and zinc chloride ($ZnCl_2$). A scientist has powdered zinc and a chunk of zinc of equal mass. Available in the lab are dilute HCl and concentrated HCl. Which combination of zinc and acid would react most quickly? Explain why the combination you chose would make the reaction occur most quickly.

Chapter 7

Acids, Bases, and Solutions

Chapter Preview

Interactive Textbook

Solutions containing transition metal compounds are often very colorful. ▶

Acids, Bases, and Solutions

▶ Video Preview
Video Field Trip
Video Assessment

Lab zone™ Chapter **Project**

Make Your Own Indicator

As you learn about acids and bases in this chapter, you can make your own solutions that will tell you if something is an acid or a base. Then you can use your solutions to test for acids and bases among substances found in your home.

Your Goal To make acid-base indicators from flowers, fruits, vegetables, or other common plant materials

To complete the project, you must

- make one or more indicators that will turn colors in acids and bases
- use your indicators to test a number of substances
- compare your indicators to a standard pH scale
- rank the tested substances according to their pH
- follow the safety guidelines in Appendix A

Plan It! Brainstorm with your classmates about foods, spices, flowers, or other plant materials that have definite, deep colors. Think about fruits and vegetables you may find in a supermarket. These materials may make good candidates for your indicators.

Section 1

Understanding Solutions

Reading Preview

Key Concepts

- What are the characteristics of solutions, colloids, and suspensions?
- What happens to the particles of a solute when a solution forms?
- How do solutes affect the freezing point and boiling point of a solvent?

Key Terms

- solution • solvent • solute
- colloid • suspension

Target Reading Skill

Identifying Main Ideas As you read the *What is a Solution?* section, write the main idea in a graphic organizer like the one below. Then write supporting details that further explain the main idea.

Main Idea

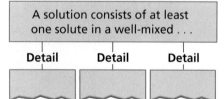

A solution consists of at least one solute in a well-mixed . . .

Detail | Detail | Detail

Lab zone Discover Activity

What Makes a Mixture a Solution?

1. Put about 50 or 60 milliliters of water into a plastic cup. Add a spoonful of pepper and stir well.
2. To a similar amount of water in a second cup, add a spoonful of table salt. Stir well.
3. Compare the appearance of the two mixtures.

Think It Over

Observing What is the difference between the two mixtures? What other mixtures have you seen that are similar to pepper and water? That are similar to table salt and water?

Imagine a hot summer day. You've been outdoors and now you're really thirsty. A tall, cool glass of plain tap water would taste great. But exactly what is tap water?

Tap water is more than just water. It's a mixture of pure water (H_2O) and a variety of other substances, such as chloride, fluoride, and metallic ions. Gases, such as oxygen and carbon dioxide, are also dissolved in tap water. The dissolved substances give tap water its taste.

What Is a Solution?

Tap water is one example of a mixture called a solution. A **solution** is a well-mixed mixture that contains a solvent and at least one solute. The **solvent** is the part of a solution present in the largest amount. It dissolves the other substances. The **solute** is the substance that is present in a solution in a smaller amount and is dissolved by the solvent. **A solution has the same properties throughout. It contains solute particles (molecules or ions) that are too small to see.**

Solutions With Water In many common solutions, the solvent is water. Sugar in water, for example, is the starting solution for flavored soft drinks. Adding food coloring gives the drink color. Dissolving carbon dioxide gas in the mixture produces a fizzy soda. Water dissolves so many substances that it is often called the "universal solvent."

Life depends on water solutions. Nutrients used by plants are dissolved in water in the soil. Sap is a solution that carries sugar dissolved in water to tree cells. Water is the solvent in blood, saliva, and tears. Reactions in cells take place in solution. To keep cells working, you must replace the water you lose in sweat and urine—two other water solutions.

Solutions Without Water Many solutions are made with solvents other than water, as you can see in Figure 1. For example, gasoline is a solution of several different liquid fuels. You don't even need a liquid solvent to make solutions. A solution may be made of any combination of gases, liquids, or solids.

Discovery Channel School

Acids, Bases, and Solutions

Video Preview
▶ Video Field Trip
Video Assessment

Reading Checkpoint **What solvent is essential to living things?**

Examples of Common Solutions

Solute	Solvent	Solution
Gas	Gas	Air (oxygen and other gases in nitrogen)
Gas	Liquid	Soda water (carbon dioxide in water)
Liquid	Liquid	Antifreeze (ethylene glycol in water)
Solid	Liquid	Dental filling (silver in mercury)
Solid	Liquid	Ocean water (sodium chloride and other compounds in water)
Solid	Solid	Brass (zinc and copper)

FIGURE 1
Solutions can be made from any combination of solids, liquids, and gases.
Interpreting Photos *What are the solutes and solvent for stainless steel?*

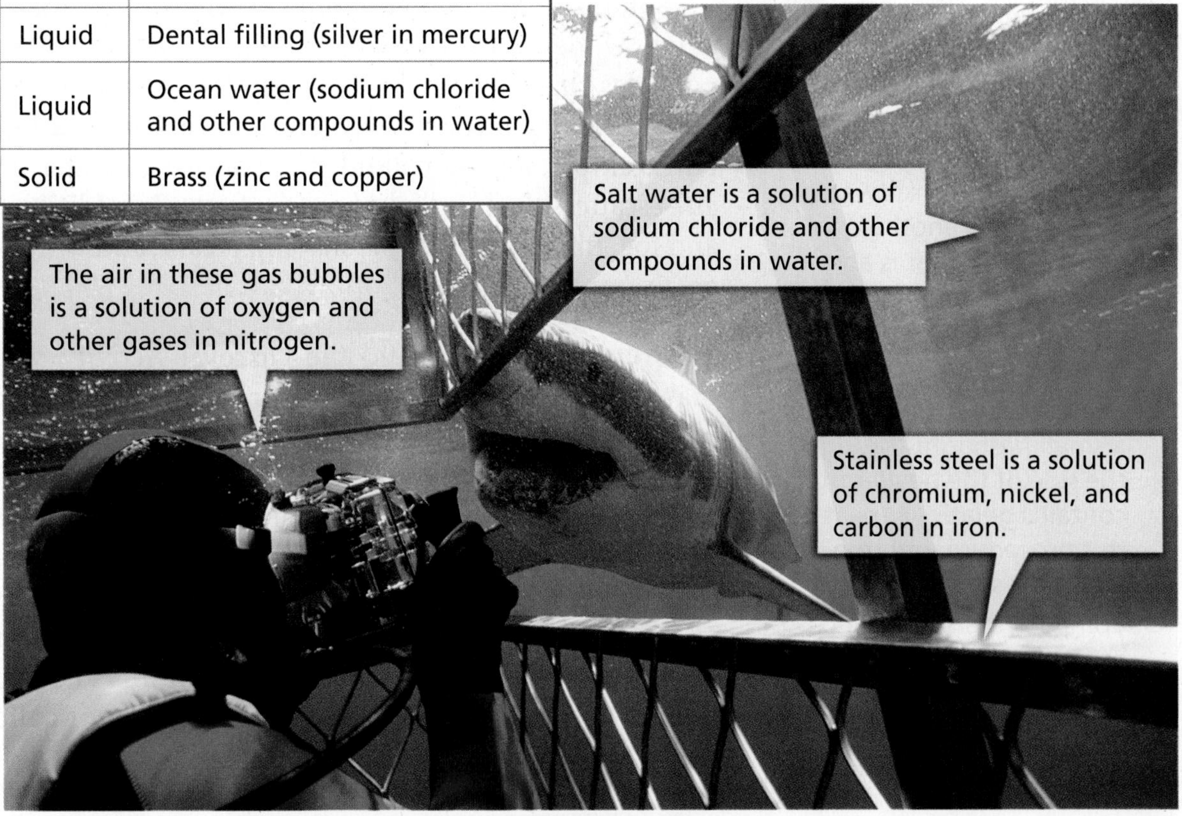

Salt water is a solution of sodium chloride and other compounds in water.
The air in these gas bubbles is a solution of oxygen and other gases in nitrogen.
Stainless steel is a solution of chromium, nickel, and carbon in iron.

FIGURE 2
Comparing Three Mixtures
Solutions are different from colloids and suspensions.
Interpreting Photographs *In which mixture can you see the particles?*

Solution
In a solution of glass cleaner, particles are uniformly distributed and too small to scatter light.
Colloid
Fats and proteins in milk form globular particles that are big enough to scatter light, but are too small to be seen.
Suspension
Suspended particles of "snow" in water are easy to see.
PHILADELPHIA

Colloids and Suspensions

Not all mixtures are solutions. Colloids and suspensions are mixtures that have different properties than solutions.

Colloids Have you ever made a gelatin dessert? To do so, you stir powdered gelatin in hot water until the two substances are uniformly mixed. The liquid looks like a solution, but it's not. Gelatin is a colloid. A **colloid** (KAHL oyd) is a mixture containing small, undissolved particles that do not settle out.

Solutions and colloids differ in the size of their particles and how they affect the path of light. **A colloid contains larger particles than a solution. The particles are still too small to be seen easily, but are large enough to scatter a light beam.** For example, fog—a colloid that consists of water droplets in air—scatters the headlight beams of cars. In addition to gelatin and fog, milk, mayonnaise, shaving cream, and whipped cream are examples of colloids.

Suspensions If you did the Discover Activity, you noticed that no matter how much you stir pepper and water, the two never really seem to "mix" completely. When you stop stirring, you can still see pepper flakes floating on the water's surface and collecting at the bottom of the cup. Pepper and water make a suspension. A **suspension** (suh SPEN shun) is a mixture in which particles can be seen and easily separated by settling or filtration. **Unlike a solution, a suspension does not have the same properties throughout. It contains visible particles that are larger than the particles in solutions or colloids.**

Reading Checkpoint **Which kind of mixture has the largest particles?**

Lab zone Try This Activity

Scattered Light

1. Pour 50 mL of a gelatin-and-water mixture into a small, clean glass beaker.
2. Pour 50 mL of a saltwater solution into another clean beaker that is about the same size.
3. Compare the appearance of the two liquids.
4. In a darkened room, shine a small flashlight through the side of the beaker that contains gelatin. Repeat this procedure with the saltwater solution.
5. Compare the appearance of the light inside the two beakers.

Inferring What evidence tells you that gelatin is a colloid?

Particles in a Solution

Why do solutes seem to disappear when you mix them with a solvent? If you had a microscope powerful enough to look at the mixture's particles, what would you see? **When a solution forms, particles of the solute leave each other and become surrounded by particles of the solvent.**

Ionic and Molecular Solutes Figure 3 shows what happens when an ionic solid mixes with water. The positive and negative ions are attracted to the polar water molecules. Water molecules surround each ion as it leaves the surface of the crystal. As each layer of the solid is exposed, more ions can dissolve.

However, not every substance breaks into ions when it dissolves in water. A molecular solid, such as sugar, breaks up into individual neutral molecules. The polar water molecules attract the slightly polar sugar molecules. This causes the sugar molecules to move away from each other. But covalent bonds within the molecules are not broken.

Solutes and Conductivity You have a water solution, but you don't know if the solute is salt or sugar. How could you find out? Think about what you learned about the electrical conductivity of compounds. A solution of ionic compounds in water conducts electricity, but a water solution of molecular compounds may not. You could test the conductivity of the solution. If no ions are present (as in a sugar solution), electricity will not flow.

Reading Checkpoint **Which kind of solution conducts electricity?**

Go Online
active art

For: Salt Dissolving in Water activity
Visit: PHSchool.com
Web Code: cgp-2031

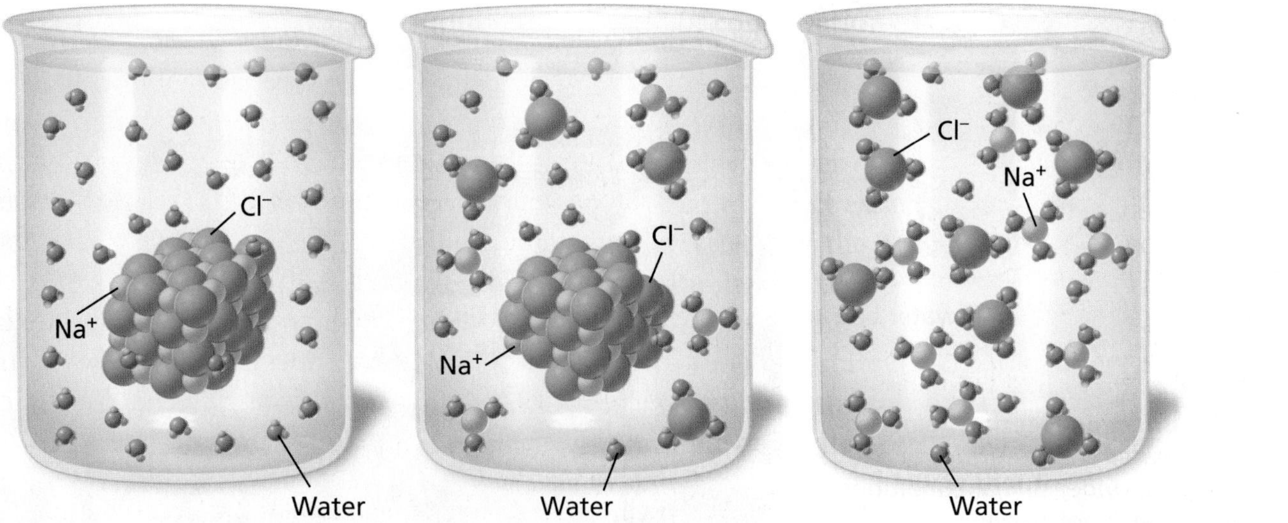

FIGURE 3
Salt Dissolving in Water
When an ionic solid—like table salt—dissolves, water molecules surround and separate the positive and negative ions. Notice that the sodium ions attract the oxygen ends of the water molecules.

Skills Activity

Designing Experiments

How does the mass of a solute affect the boiling temperature of a given volume of water? Design an experiment using a solute, water, a balance, a hot plate, and a thermometer.

What variables should remain constant in your experiment? What is the manipulated variable? What will be the responding variable?

With approval from your teacher, do the experiment.

Effects of Solutes on Solvents

The freezing point of water is 0°C, and the boiling point is 100°C. These statements are true enough for pure water under everyday conditions, but the addition of solutes to water can change these properties. **Solutes lower the freezing point and raise the boiling point of a solvent.**

Lower Freezing Points Solutes lower the freezing point of a solvent. When liquid water freezes, water molecules join together to form crystals of solid ice. Pure water is made only of water molecules that freeze at 0°C. In a salt solution, solute particles are present in the water when it freezes. The solute particles make it harder for the water molecules to form crystals. The temperature must drop lower than 0°C for the solution to freeze. Figure 4 illustrates the particles in pure water and in a saltwater solution.

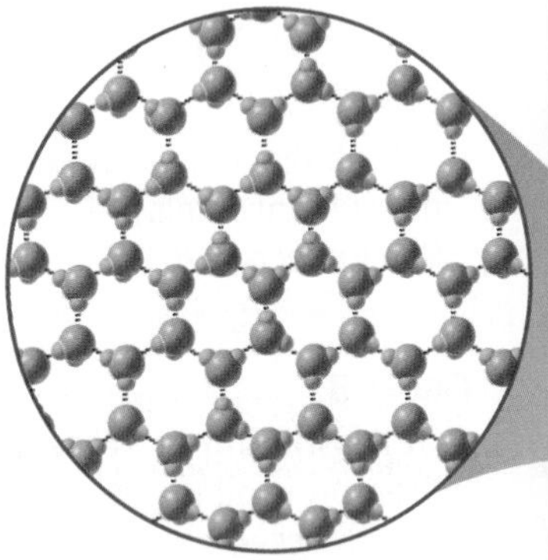
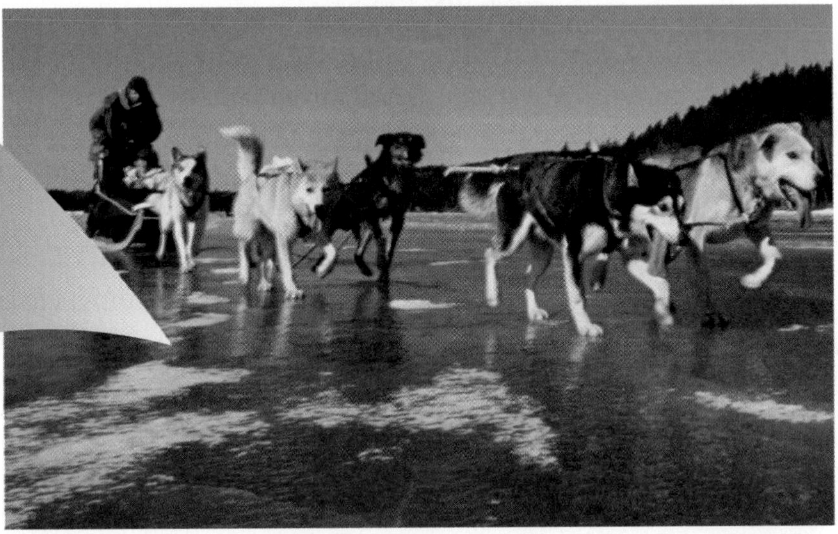

Freshwater lake ▶

Solute particles

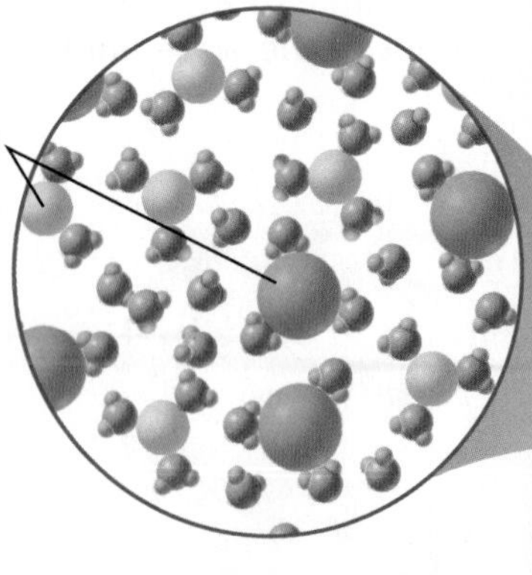
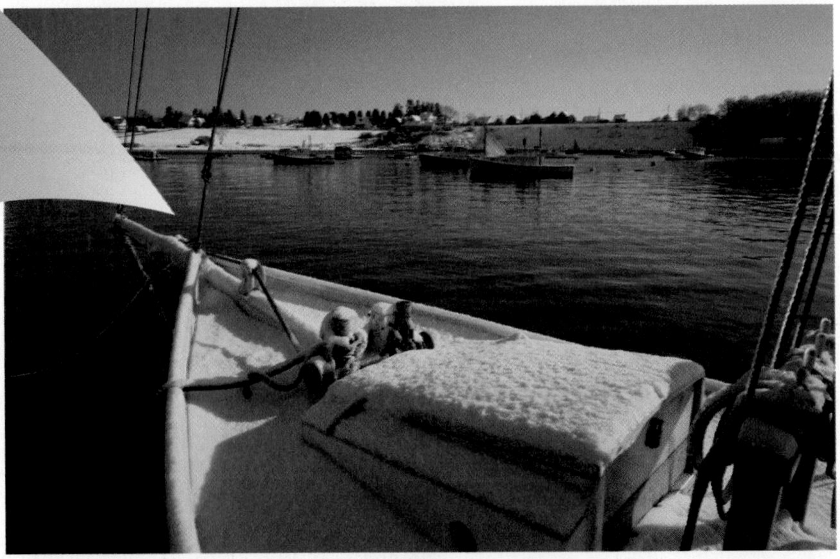

Saltwater bay ▶

FIGURE 4
Salt's Effect on Freezing Point
Fresh water on the surface of a lake is frozen. Under similar conditions, salt water is not frozen.

Higher Boiling Points Solutes raise the boiling point of a solvent. To see why, think about the difference between the molecules of a liquid and those of a gas of the same substance. In a liquid, molecules are moving close to each other. In a gas, they are far apart and moving more rapidly. As the temperature of a liquid rises, the molecules gain energy and escape into the air. In pure water, all the molecules are water. But in a solution, some of the particles are water molecules and others are particles of solute. The presence of the solute makes it harder for the water molecules to escape, so more energy is needed. The temperature must go higher than 100°C for the water to boil.

Car manufacturers make use of the effects of solutes to protect engines from heat and cold. The coolant in a car radiator is a solution of water and another liquid called antifreeze. (Often the antifreeze is ethylene glycol.) The mixture of the two liquids has a higher boiling point and lower freezing point than water alone. Because this solution can absorb more of the heat given off by the running engine, risk of damage to the car from overheating is greatly reduced. The risk of damage from freezing in very cold weather is also reduced.

FIGURE 5
Calling Solutes to the Rescue?
This couple might have prevented their car from overheating by using the proper coolant in the radiator.
Relating Cause and Effect *Explain how coolant works.*

Reading Checkpoint **Does salt water have a lower or higher freezing point than pure water?**

Section 1 Assessment

Target Reading Skill Identifying Main Ideas
Use your graphic organizer to help you answer Question 1 below.

Reviewing Key Concepts

1. a. Defining What is a solution?
   b. Comparing and Contrasting How are solutions different from colloids and suspensions?
   c. Inferring Suppose you mix food coloring in water to make it blue. Have you made a solution or a suspension? Explain.
2. a. Reviewing What happens to the solute particles when a solution forms?
   b. Sequencing Describe as a series of steps what happens to sugar molecules when they dissolve in water.
3. a. Summarizing What effects do solutes have on a solvent's freezing and boiling points?
   b. Relating Cause and Effect Why is the temperature needed to freeze ocean water lower than the temperature needed to freeze the surface of a freshwater lake?
   c. Applying Concepts Why does salt sprinkled on icy roads cause the ice to melt?

Lab zone At-Home Activity

Passing Through With a family member, mix together a spoonful each of sugar and pepper in about 100 mL of warm water in a plastic container. Pour the mixture through a coffee filter into a second container. Ask your family member what happened to the sugar. Let the water evaporate overnight. Describe the difference between a solution and a suspension.

Lab zone Design Your Own Lab

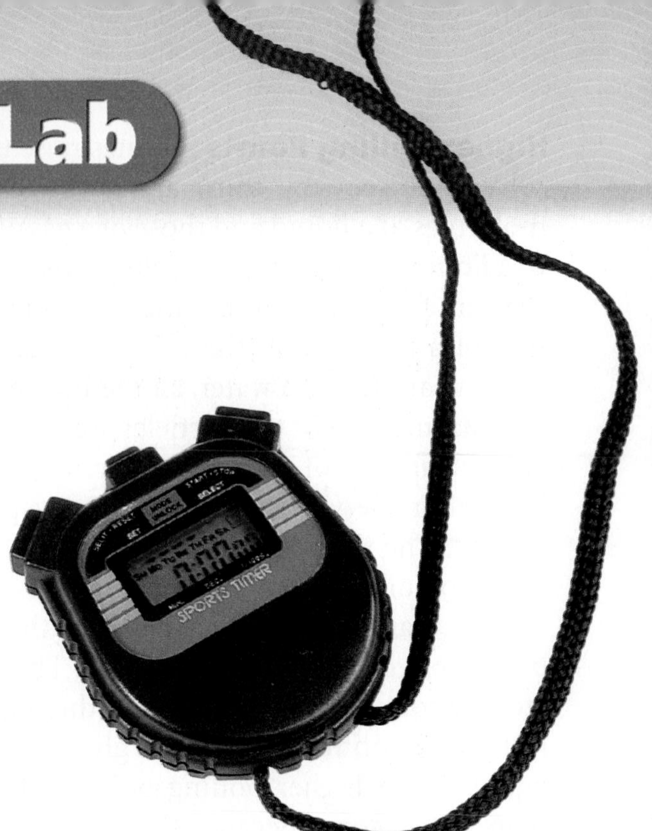

Speedy Solutions

Problem

How can you control the rate at which certain salts dissolve in water?

Skills Focus

controlling variables, drawing conclusions, designing experiments

Materials

- spoon
- solid stoppers, #4
- thermometers
- hot plate
- balance
- stirring rods
- ice
- timer or watch
- test tube rack
- test tubes, 25 × 150 mm
- coarse, rock, and table salt
- graduated cylinders and beakers, various sizes

Design a Plan

1. Make a list of all the variables you can think of that could affect the speed at which sodium chloride dissolves in water.
2. Compare your list with your classmates' lists, and add other variables.
3. Choose one variable from your list to test.
4. Write a hypothesis predicting the effect of your chosen variable on the speed of dissolving.
5. Decide how to work with your choice.
   - If you choose temperature, you might perform tests at 10°C, 20°C, 30°C, 40°C, and 50°C.
   - If you choose stirring, you might stir for various amounts of time.
6. Plan at least three tests for whichever variable you choose. Remember to control all other variables.
7. Write down a series of steps for your procedure and safety guidelines for your experiment. Be quite detailed in your plan.
8. As part of your procedure, prepare a data table in which to record your results. Fill in the headings on your table that identify the manipulated variable and the responding variable. (*Hint:* Remember to include units.)

Data Table

Manipulated Variable	Dissolving Time		
	Test 1	Test 2	Test 3

9. Have your teacher approve your procedure, safety guidelines, and data table.
10. Perform the experiment.

Analyze and Conclude

1. **Controlling Variables** Which is the manipulated variable in your experiment? Which is the responding variable? How do you know which is which?
2. **Controlling Variables** List three variables you held constant in your procedure. Explain why controlling these variables makes your data more meaningful.
3. **Graphing** Make a line graph of your data. Label the horizontal axis with the manipulated variable. Label the vertical axis with the responding variable. Use an appropriate scale for each axis and label the units.
4. **Drawing Conclusions** Study the shape of your graph. Write a conclusion about the effect of the variable you tested on the speed at which salt dissolves in water.
5. **Drawing Conclusions** Does your conclusion support the hypothesis you wrote in Step 4 of your Plan? Explain.
6. **Designing Experiments** What advantage would there be in running your tests a second or third time?
7. **Predicting** If you switched procedures with another student who tested the same variable as you, do you think you would get the same results? Explain why or why not.
8. **Communicating** Write an e-mail to a friend explaining how your results relate to what you have learned about particles and solubility.

More to Explore

Choose another variable from the list you made in Steps 1 and 2 of your Plan. Repeat the process with that variable. Of the two variables you chose, which was easier to work with? Explain.

Section 2

Concentration and Solubility

Reading Preview

Key Concepts

- How is concentration measured?
- Why is solubility useful in identifying substances?
- What factors affect the solubility of a substance?

Key Terms

- dilute solution
- concentrated solution
- solubility
- saturated solution
- unsaturated solution
- supersaturated solution

Target Reading Skill

Building Vocabulary As you read, carefully note the definition of each Key Term. Also note other details in the paragraph that contains the definition. Use all this information to write a meaningful sentence using the Key Term.

Lab zone Discover Activity

Does It Dissolve?

1. Put half a spoonful of soap flakes into a small plastic cup. Add about 50 mL of water and stir. Observe whether the soap flakes dissolve.
2. Clean out the cup. Repeat the test for a few other solids and liquids provided by your teacher.
3. Classify the items you tested into two groups: those that dissolved easily and those that did not.

Think It Over

Drawing Conclusions Based on your observations, does the physical state (solid or liquid) of a substance affect whether or not it dissolves in water? Explain.

Have you ever had syrup on your pancakes? You probably know that it's made from the sap of maple trees. Is something that sweet really made in a tree? Well, not exactly.

Concentration

The sap of a maple tree and pancake syrup differ in their concentrations. That is, they differ in the amount of solute (sugar) dissolved in a certain amount of solvent (water). The sap is a **dilute solution,** a mixture that has only a little solute dissolved in a certain amount of solvent. The syrup, on the other hand, is a **concentrated solution**—one that has a lot of solute dissolved in the solvent.

Making Maple Syrup ▼

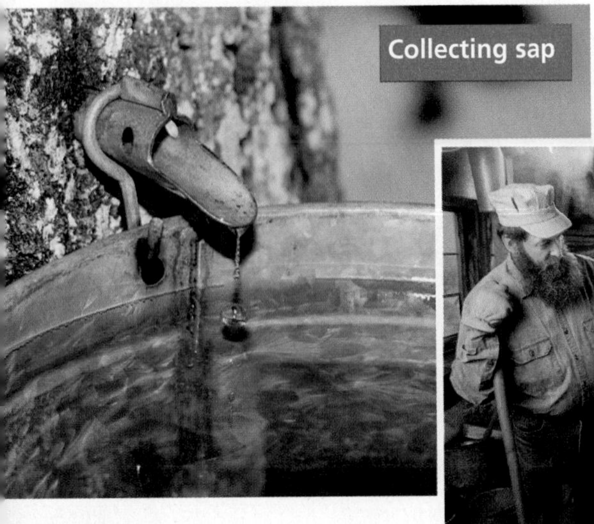
Collecting sap

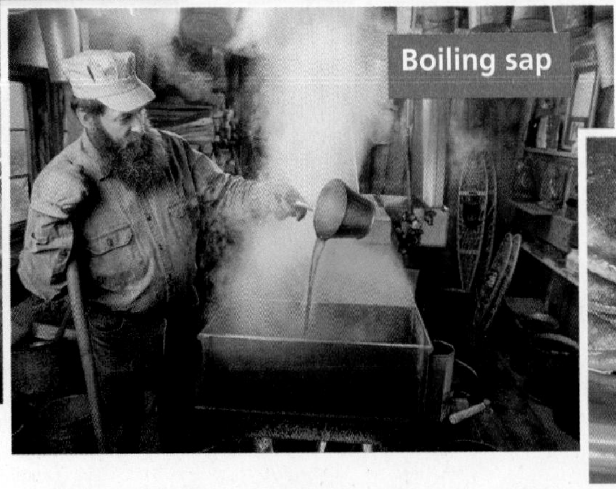
Boiling sap

Syrup

Changing Concentration You can change the concentration of a solution by adding more solute. You can also change it by adding or removing solvent. For example, fruit juices are sometimes packaged as concentrates, which are concentrated solutions. In making the concentrate, water was removed from the natural juice. When you make juice from the concentrate, you add water, making a dilute solution.

Measuring Concentration You know that maple syrup is more concentrated than maple sap. But you probably do not know the actual concentration of either solution. **To measure concentration, you compare the amount of solute to the amount of solvent or to the total amount of solution.**

Often, the method used to describe concentration depends on the type of solution. For example, you might measure the mass of a solute or solvent in grams. Or you might measure the volume of a solute or solvent in milliliters or liters. You can report concentration as the percent of solute in solution by volume or mass.

Reading Checkpoint **How can you change the concentration of a solution?**

Math Skills

Calculating a Concentration

To calculate the concentration of a solution, compare the amount of solute to the amount of solution and multiply by 100 percent.

For example, if a solution contains 10 grams of solute dissolved in 100 grams of solution, then its concentration can be reported as 10 percent.

$$\frac{10\text{ g}}{100\text{ g}} \times 100\% = 10\%$$

Practice Problem A solution contains 12 grams of solute dissolved in 36 grams of solution. What is the concentration of the solution?

Solubility

If a substance dissolves in water, a question you might ask is, "How much can dissolve?" Suppose you add sugar to a glass of iced tea. Is there a limit to how "sweet" you can make the tea? The answer is yes. At the temperature of iced tea, several spoonfuls of sugar are about all you can add. At some point, no matter how much you stir the tea, no more sugar will dissolve. **Solubility** is a measure of how much solute can dissolve in a solvent at a given temperature.

When you've added so much solute that no more dissolves, you have a **saturated solution.** If you add more sugar to a saturated solution of iced tea, the extra sugar just settles to the bottom of the glass. On the other hand, if you can continue to dissolve more solute, you still have an **unsaturated solution.**

FIGURE 6
Dissolving Sugar in Tea
At some point, this boy will not be able to dissolve any more sugar in his tea.
Applying Concepts *What term describes how much sugar can dissolve in a solvent?*

Solubility in 100 g of Water at 0°C	
Compound	**Solubility (g)**
Carbon dioxide (CO_2)	0.348
Baking soda ($NaHCO_3$)	6.9
Table salt ($NaCl$)	35.7
Table sugar ($C_{12}H_{22}O_{11}$)	180

FIGURE 7
Each compound listed in the table dissolves in water, but in different amounts.
Interpreting Tables *Which compound is the most soluble? Which is the least soluble?*

Working With Solubility The solubility of a substance tells you how much solute you can dissolve before a solution becomes saturated. Solubility is given for a specific solvent (such as water) under certain conditions (such as temperature). Look at the table in Figure 7. It compares the solubility of some familiar compounds. In this case, the solvent is water and the temperature is 0°C. From the table, you can see that 6.9 grams of baking soda will dissolve in 100 grams of water at 0°C. But the same mass of water at the same temperature will dissolve 180 grams of table sugar!

Using Solubility **Solubility can be used to help identify a substance because it is a characteristic property of matter.** Suppose you had a white powder that looked like table salt or sugar. You wouldn't know for sure whether the powder is salt or sugar. And you wouldn't use taste to identify it. Instead, you could measure its solubility in water at 0°C and compare the results to the data in Figure 7.

Reading Checkpoint **What does the solubility of a substance tell you?**

Lab zone Skills Activity

Predicting

Make a saturated solution of baking soda in water. Add one small spoonful of baking soda to about 250 mL of cool water. Stir until the baking soda dissolves. Continue adding baking soda until no more dissolves. Keep track of how much baking soda you use. Then predict what would happen if you used warm water instead. Make a plan to test your prediction. With approval from your teacher, carry out your plan. Did your results confirm your prediction? Explain.

Factors Affecting Solubility

Which dissolves more sugar: iced tea or hot tea? You have already read that there is a limit to solubility. An iced tea and sugar solution quickly becomes saturated. Yet a hot, steaming cup of the same tea can dissolve much more sugar before the limit is reached. The solubilities of solutes change when conditions change. **Factors that affect the solubility of a substance include pressure, the type of solvent, and temperature.**

Pressure Pressure affects the solubility of gases. The higher the pressure of the gas over the solvent, the more gas can dissolve. To increase the carbon dioxide concentration in soft drinks, the gas is added under high pressure. Opening the bottle or can reduces the pressure. The escaping gas makes the sound you hear.

Scuba divers are aware of the effect of pressure on gases. Air is about 80 percent nitrogen. When divers breathe from tanks of compressed air, nitrogen from the air dissolves in their blood in greater amounts as they descend. This occurs because the pressure underwater increases with depth. If divers return to the surface too quickly, nitrogen bubbles come out of solution and block blood flow. Divers double over in pain, which is why this condition is sometimes called "the bends."

FIGURE 8
Pressure Changes Solubility
Opening a shaken bottle of soda water may produce quite a spray as dissolved gas comes out of solution.

Solvents Sometimes you just can't make a solution because the solute and solvent are not compatible. Have you ever tried to mix oil and vinegar, which is mostly water, to make salad dressing? If you have, you've seen how the dressing quickly separates into layers after you stop shaking it. Oil and water separate because water is a polar compound and oil is nonpolar. Polar compounds and nonpolar compounds do not mix very well.

For liquid solutions, the solvent affects how well a solute dissolves. The expression "like dissolves like" gives you a clue to which solutes are soluble in which solvents. Ionic and polar compounds usually dissolve in polar solvents. Nonpolar compounds do not usually dissolve in polar solvents. If you work with paints, you know that water-based (latex) paints can be cleaned up with just soap and water. But cleaning up oil-based paints may require a nonpolar solvent, such as turpentine.

FIGURE 9
Solvents and Solubility
Try as she might, this girl cannot get oil and vinegar to stay mixed. Nonpolar and polar compounds don't form solutions with each other.

Math Analyzing Data

Temperature and Solubility

The solubility of the compound potassium nitrate (KNO_3) varies in water at different temperatures.

1. **Reading Graphs** At which temperature shown in the graph is KNO_3 least soluble in water?
2. **Reading Graphs** Approximately what mass of KNO_3 is needed to saturate a water solution at 40°C?
3. **Calculating** About how much more soluble is KNO_3 at 40°C than at 20°C?
4. **Interpreting Data** Does solubility increase at the same rate with every 20°C increase in temperature? Explain.

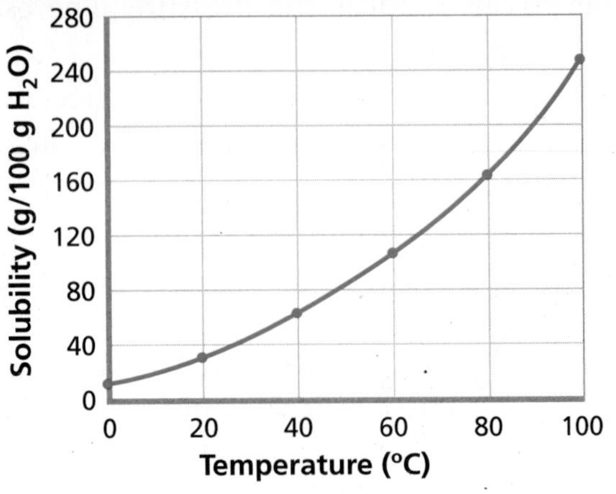

Temperature For most solids, solubility increases as the temperature increases. That is why the temperature is reported when solubilities are listed. For example, the solubility of table sugar in 100 grams of water changes from 180 grams at 0°C to 231 grams at 25°C to 487 grams at 100°C.

Cooks use this increased solubility of sugar when they make desserts such as rock candy, fudge, or peanut brittle. To make peanut brittle, you start with a mixture of sugar, corn syrup, and water. At room temperature, not enough of the required sugar can dissolve in the water. The mixture must be heated until it begins to boil. Nuts and other ingredients are added before the mixture cools. Some recipes call for temperatures above 100°C. Because the exact temperature can affect the result, cooks use a candy thermometer to check the temperature.

Unlike most solids, gases become less soluble when the temperature goes up. For example, more carbon dioxide will dissolve in cold water than in hot water. Carbon dioxide makes soda water fizzy when you pour it into a glass. If you open a warm bottle of soda water, carbon dioxide escapes the liquid in greater amounts than if the soda water had been chilled. Why does warm soda taste "flat"? It contains less gas. If you like soda water that's very fizzy, open it when it's cold!

FIGURE 10
Temperature Changes Solubility
Some hard candy is made by cooling a sugar water solution. **Interpreting Photographs** *Why does sugar form crystals when the solution is cooled?*

FIGURE 11
A Supersaturated Solution
Dropping a crystal of solute into a supersaturated solution (left) causes the excess solute to rapidly come out of solution (center). Soon, the formation of crystals is complete (right).

When heated, a solution can dissolve more solute than it can at cooler temperatures. If a heated, saturated solution cools slowly, sometimes the extra solute will remain dissolved. A **supersaturated solution** has more dissolved solute than is predicted by its solubility at the given temperature. When you disturb a supersaturated solution by dropping in a crystal of the solute, the extra solute will come out of solution.

Reading Checkpoint **As temperature increases, what happens to the solubility of a gas?**

Go Online
SCI LINKS NSTA
For: Links on solubility
Visit: www.SciLinks.org
Web Code: scn-1232

Section 2 Assessment

Target Reading Skill **Building Vocabulary** Use your sentences about the Key Terms to help answer the questions.

Reviewing Key Concepts

1. a. Reviewing What is concentration?
b. Describing What quantities are compared when the concentration of a solution is measured?
c. Applying Concepts Solution A contains 50 g of sugar. Solution B contains 100 g of sugar. Can you tell which solution has a higher sugar concentration? Explain.

2. a. Defining What is solubility?
b. Explaining How can solubility help you identify a substance?
c. Calculating Look back at the table in Figure 7. At 0°C, about how many times more soluble in water is sugar than salt?

3. a. Listing What are three factors that affect solubility?
b. Summarizing How does temperature affect the solubility of most solids?
c. Relating Cause and Effect When you heat water and add sugar, all of the sugar dissolves. When you cool the solution, some sugar comes out of solution. Explain.

Math Practice

4. Calculating a Concentration What is the concentration of a solution that contains 45 grams of sugar in 500 grams of solution?

5. Calculating a Concentration How much sugar is dissolved in 500 grams of a solution if the solution is 70 percent sugar by mass?

Section 3

Describing Acids and Bases

Reading Preview

Key Concepts

- What are the properties of acids and bases?
- Where are acids and bases commonly used?

Key Terms

- acid
- corrosive
- indicator
- base

Target Reading Skill

Asking Questions Before you read, preview the red headings. In a graphic organizer like the one below, ask a *what* question for each heading. As you read, write the answers to your questions.

Describing Acids and Bases

Question	Answer
What is an acid?	An acid is . . .

Lab zone Discover Activity

What Colors Does Litmus Paper Turn?

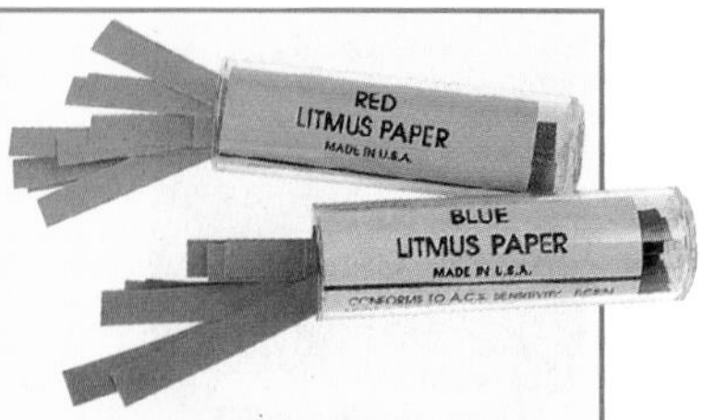

1. Use a plastic dropper to put a drop of lemon juice on a clean piece of red litmus paper. Put another drop on a clean piece of blue litmus paper. Observe.
2. Rinse your dropper with water. Then test other substances the same way. You might test orange juice, ammonia cleaner, tap water, vinegar, and solutions of soap, baking soda, and table salt. Record all your observations.
3. Wash your hands when you are finished.

Think It Over

Classifying Group the substances based on how they make the litmus paper change color. What other properties do the items in each group have in common?

Did you have any fruit for breakfast today—perhaps an orange, an apple, or fruit juice? If so, an acid was part of your meal. The last time you washed your hair, did you use shampoo? If your answer is yes, then you may have used a base.

You use many products that contain acids and bases. In addition, the chemical reactions of acids and bases even keep you alive! What are acids and bases—how do they react, and what are their uses?

Properties of Acids

What is an acid, and how do you know when you have one? In order to identify an acid, you can test its properties. **Acids** are compounds whose characteristic properties include the kinds of reactions they undergo. **An acid is a substance that tastes sour, reacts with metals and carbonates, and turns blue litmus paper red.** Some common acids you may have heard of are hydrochloric acid, nitric acid, sulfuric acid, carbonic acid, and acetic acid.

◀ Lemons are acidic.

Sour Taste If you've ever tasted a lemon, you've had first-hand experience with the sour taste of acids. Can you think of other foods that sometimes taste sour, or tart? Citrus fruits—lemons, grapefruits, oranges, and limes—are acidic. They all contain citric acid. Other fruits (cherries, tomatoes, apples) and many other types of foods contain acids, too.

Although sour taste is a characteristic of many acids, it is not one you should use to identify a compound as an acid. Scientists never taste chemicals in order to identify them. Though acids in sour foods may be safe to eat, many other acids are not.

Reactions With Metals Do you notice the bubbles in Figure 12? Acids react with certain metals to produce hydrogen gas. Not all metals react this way, but magnesium, zinc, and iron do. When they react, the metals seem to disappear in the solution. This observation is one reason acids are described as **corrosive,** meaning they "eat away" at other materials.

The metal plate in Figure 12 is being etched with acid. Etching is one method of making printing plates that are then used to print works of art on paper. To make an etching, an artist first coats a metal plate with an acid-resistant material—often beeswax. Then the design is cut into the beeswax with a sharp tool, exposing some of the metal. When the plate is treated with acid, the acid eats away the design in the exposed metal. Later, ink applied to the plate collects in the grooves made by the acid. The ink is transferred to the paper when the etching is printed.

FIGURE 12
Etching With Acid
Metal etching takes advantage of the reaction of an acid with a metal. Lines are cut in a wax coating on a plate. Here, hydrochloric acid eats away at the exposed zinc metal, forming bubbles you can see in the close-up. **Applying Concepts** *What gas forms in this reaction?*

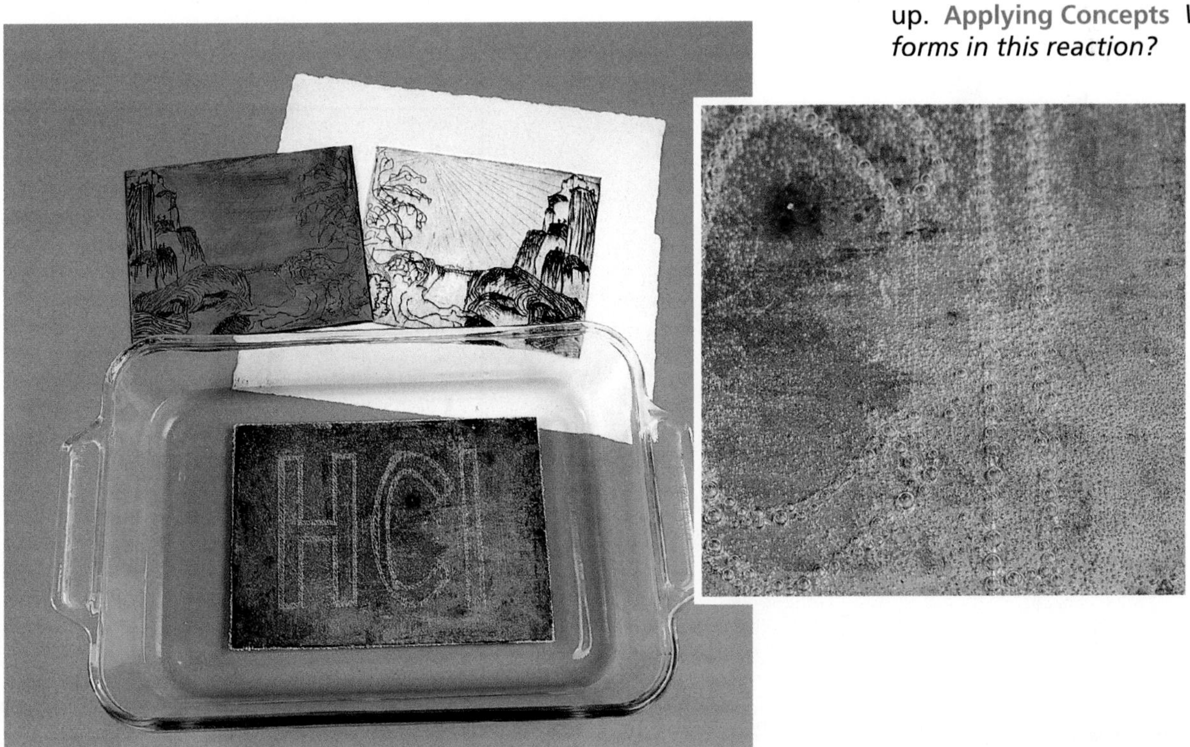

Reactions With Carbonates Acids also react with carbonate ions in a characteristic way. Recall that an ion is an atom or a group of atoms that has an electric charge. Carbonate ions contain carbon and oxygen atoms bonded together. They carry an overall negative charge (CO_3^{2-}). One product of an acid's reaction with carbonates is the gas carbon dioxide.

Geologists, scientists who study Earth, use this property of acids to identify rocks containing certain types of limestone. Limestone is a compound that contains the carbonate ion. If a geologist pours dilute hydrochloric acid on a limestone rock, bubbles of carbon dioxide appear on the rock's surface.

Reactions With Indicators If you did the Discover activity, you used litmus paper to test several substances. Litmus is an example of an **indicator,** a compound that changes color when in contact with an acid or a base. Look at Figure 13 to see what happens to litmus paper as it is dipped in a solution containing acid. Vinegar, lemon juice, and other acids turn blue litmus paper red. Sometimes chemists use other indicators to test for acids, but litmus is one of the easiest to use.

Properties of Bases

Bases are another group of compounds that can be identified by their common properties. **A base is a substance that tastes bitter, feels slippery, and turns red litmus paper blue.** Bases often are described as the "opposite" of acids. Common bases include sodium hydroxide, calcium hydroxide, and ammonia.

FIGURE 13
The Litmus Test
Litmus paper is an easy way to identify quickly whether an unknown compound is an acid or a base. **Inferring** *What can you infer about a liquid that does not change the color of blue litmus paper?*

FIGURE 14
Bases in Soaps
If you give a dog a sudsy bath, bases in the soap could make your hands feel slippery.

Bitter Taste Have you ever tasted tonic water? The slightly bitter taste is caused by the base quinine. Bases taste bitter. Soaps, some shampoos, and detergents taste bitter too, but you wouldn't want to identify these as bases by a taste test!

Slippery Feel Picture yourself washing a dog. As you massage the soap into the dog's fur, you notice that your hands feel slippery. This slippery feeling is another characteristic of bases. But just as you avoid tasting a substance to identify it, you wouldn't want to touch it. Strong bases can irritate or burn your skin. A safer way to identify bases is by their other properties.

Reactions With Indicators As you might guess, if litmus paper can be used to test acids, it can be used to test bases, too. Look at Figure 13 to see what happens to a litmus paper as it is dipped in a basic solution. Bases turn red litmus paper blue. Like acids, bases react with other indicators. But litmus paper gives a reliable, safe test. An easy way to remember which color litmus turns for acids or bases is to remember the letter *b*. **B**ases turn litmus paper **bl**ue.

Other Reactions of Bases Unlike acids, bases don't react with carbonates to produce carbon dioxide. At first, you may think it is useless to know that a base doesn't react with certain chemicals. But if you know what a compound doesn't do, you know something about it. For example, you know it's not an acid. Another important property of bases is how they react with acids. You will learn more about these reactions in Section 4.

Reading Checkpoint **What is one safe way to identify a base?**

Go Online SCiLINKS NSTA
For: Links on acids and bases
Visit: www.SciLinks.org
Web Code: scn-1233

FIGURE 15

Uses of Acids

Acids play an important role in our nutrition and are also found in valuable products used in homes and industries.

Acids in the Home ▶
People often use dilute solutions of acids to clean brick and other surfaces. Hardware stores sell muriatic (hydrochloric) acid, which is used to clean bricks and metals.

Acids and Food ▼
Many of the vitamins in the foods you eat are acids.

Tomatoes and oranges contain ascorbic acid, or vitamin C.

Folic acid, needed for healthy cell growth, is found in green leafy vegetables.

Acids and Industry ▼
Farmers and manufacturers depend on acids for many uses.

Sulfuric acid is used in car batteries, to refine petroleum, and to treat iron and steel.

Nitric acid and phosphoric acid are used to make fertilizers for crops, lawns, and gardens.

Uses of Acids and Bases

Where can you find acids and bases? Almost anywhere. You already learned that acids are found in many fruits and other foods. In fact, many of them play important roles in the body as vitamins, including ascorbic acid, or vitamin C, and folic acid. Many cell processes also produce acids as waste products. For example, lactic acid builds up in your muscles when you make them work hard.

Manufacturers, farmers, and builders are only some people who depend on acids and bases in their work. **Acids and bases have many uses around the home and in industry.** Look at Figure 15 and Figure 16 to learn about a few of them. Many of the uses of bases take advantage of their ability to react with acids.

Reading Checkpoint **What vitamin is an acid?**

FIGURE 16
Uses of Bases

The reactions of bases make them valuable raw materials for a range of products.

Bases and Industry ▲
Mortar and cement are manufactured using the bases calcium oxide and calcium hydroxide. Gardeners sometimes add calcium oxide to soil to make the soil less acidic for plants.

Bases in the Home ▶
Ammonia solutions are safe to spray with bare hands, but gloves must be worn when working with drain cleaners.

Drain cleaners contain sodium hydroxide (lye).

You can't mistake the odor of household cleaning products made with ammonia.

Bases and Food ▼
Baking soda reacts with acids to produce carbon dioxide gas in baked goods. Without these gas bubbles, this delicious variety of breads, biscuits, cakes, and cookies would not be light and fluffy.

Section 3 Assessment

Target Reading Skill Asking Questions Work with a partner to check the answers in your graphic organizer.

Reviewing Key Concepts

1. a. Listing What are four properties of acids? Of bases?
   b. Describing How can you use litmus paper to distinguish an acid from a base?
   c. Applying Concepts How might you tell if a food contains an acid as one of its ingredients?
2. a. Reviewing What are three practical uses of an acid? Of a base?
   b. Making Generalizations Where are you most likely to find acids and bases in your own home? Explain.
   c. Making Judgments Why is it wise to wear gloves when spreading fertilizer in a garden?

Writing in Science

Wanted Poster A bottle of acid is missing from the chemistry lab shelf! Design a wanted poster describing properties of the missing acid. Also include descriptions of tests a staff member from the chemistry lab could *safely* perform to determine if a bottle that is found actually contains acid. Add a caution on your poster that warns people *not* to touch any bottles they find. Instead, they should notify the chemistry lab.

Section 4

Acids and Bases in Solution

Reading Preview

Key Concepts

- What kinds of ions do acids and bases form in water?
- What does pH tell you about a solution?
- What happens in a neutralization reaction?

Key Terms

- hydrogen ion (H^+)
- hydroxide ion (OH^-)
- pH scale • neutralization • salt

Target Reading Skill

Previewing Visuals When you preview, you look ahead at the material to be read. Preview Figure 21. Then write two questions that you have about the diagram in a graphic organizer like the one below. As you read, answer your questions.

Neutralization

Q. What is a neutral solution?
A.
Q.

Go Online PHSchool.com

For: More on pH scale
Visit: PHSchool.com
Web Code: cgd-2034

Lab zone Discover Activity

What Can Cabbage Juice Tell You?

1. Using a dropper, put 5 drops of red cabbage juice into each of three separate plastic cups.
2. Add 10 drops of lemon juice (an acid) to one cup. Add 10 drops of ammonia cleaner (a base) to another. Keep the third cup for comparison. Record the colors you see.
3. Now add ammonia, 1 drop at a time, to the cup containing lemon juice. Keep adding ammonia until the color no longer changes. Record all color changes you see.
4. Add lemon juice a drop at a time to the ammonia until the color no longer changes. Record the changes you see.

Think It Over

Forming Operational Definitions Based on your observations, what could you add to your definitions of acids and bases?

A chemist pours hydrochloric acid into a beaker. Then she adds sodium hydroxide to the acid. The mixture looks the same, but the beaker becomes warm. If she tested the solution with litmus paper, what color would the paper turn? Would you be surprised if it did not change color at all? If exactly the right amounts and concentrations of the acid and the base were mixed, the beaker would hold nothing but salt water!

Acids and Bases in Solution

How can two corrosive chemicals, an acid and a base, produce something harmless to the touch? To answer this question, you must know what happens to acids and bases in solution.

Acids What do acids have in common? Notice that each formula in the list of acids in Figure 17 begins with hydrogen. The acids you will learn about in this section produce one or more hydrogen ions and a negative ion in solution with water. A **hydrogen ion** (H^+) is an atom of hydrogen that has lost its electron. The negative ion may be a nonmetal or a polyatomic ion. Hydrogen ions are the key to the reactions of acids.

Important Acids and Bases			
Acid	**Formula**	**Base**	**Formula**
Hydrochloric acid	HCl	Sodium hydroxide	$NaOH$
Nitric acid	HNO_3	Potassium hydroxide	KOH
Sulfuric acid	H_2SO_4	Calcium hydroxide	$Ca(OH)_2$
Carbonic acid	H_2CO_3	Aluminum hydroxide	$Al(OH)_3$
Acetic acid	$HC_2H_3O_2$	Ammonia	NH_3
Phosphoric acid	H_3PO_4	Calcium oxide	CaO

FIGURE 17
The table lists some commonly encountered acids and bases.
Making Generalizations *What do all of the acid formulas in the table have in common?*

Acids in water solution separate into hydrogen ions (H^+) and negative ions. In the case of hydrochloric acid, for example, hydrogen ions and chloride ions form:

$$HCl \xrightarrow{\text{water}} H^+ + Cl^-$$

Now you can add to the definition of acids you learned in Section 3. **An acid is any substance that produces hydrogen ions (H^+) in water.** These hydrogen ions cause the properties of acids. For instance, when you add certain metals to an acid, hydrogen ions interact with the metal atoms. One product of the reaction is hydrogen gas (H_2). Hydrogen ions also react with blue litmus paper, turning it red. That's why every acid gives the same litmus test result.

Bases The formulas of bases give you clues to what ions they have in common. You can see in the table in Figure 17 that many bases are made of positive ions combined with hydroxide ions. The **hydroxide ion (OH^-)** is a negative ion, made of oxygen and hydrogen. When bases dissolve in water, the positive ions and hydroxide ions separate. Look, for example, at what happens to sodium hydroxide:

$$NaOH \xrightarrow{\text{water}} Na^+ + OH^-$$

Not every base contains hydroxide ions. For example, the gas ammonia (NH_3) does not. But in solution, ammonia is a base that reacts with water to form hydroxide ions.

$$NH_3 + H_2O \longrightarrow NH_4^+ + OH^-$$

Notice that in both reactions, there are negative hydroxide ions. **A base is any substance that produces hydroxide ions (OH^-) in water.** Hydroxide ions are responsible for the bitter taste and slippery feel of bases, and turn red litmus paper blue.

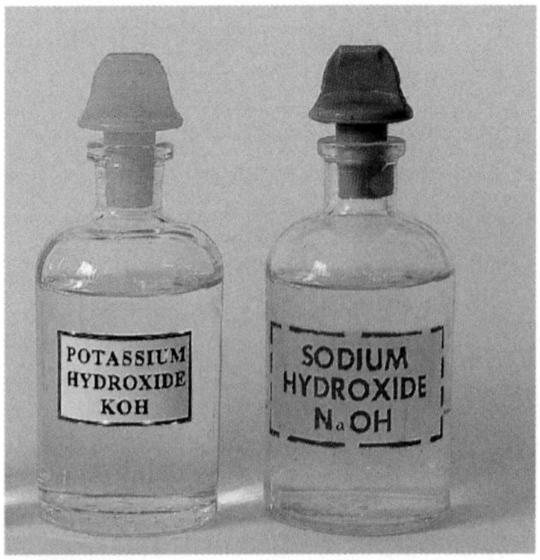

FIGURE 18
Comparing Bases
Many bases are made of positive ions combined with hydroxide ions.

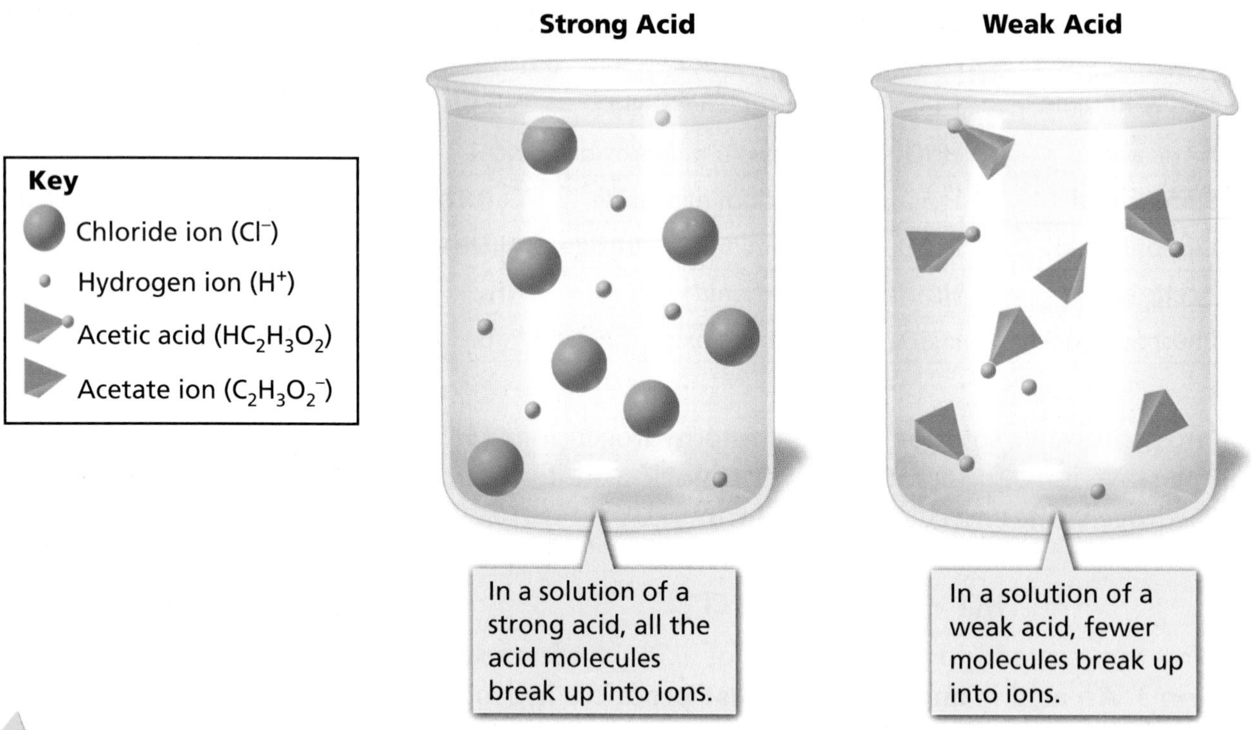
Key
Chloride ion (Cl^-)
Hydrogen ion (H^+)
Acetic acid ($HC_2H_3O_2$)
Acetate ion ($C_2H_3O_2^-$)
Strong Acid
Weak Acid
In a solution of a strong acid, all the acid molecules break up into ions.
In a solution of a weak acid, fewer molecules break up into ions.

FIGURE 19
Acids in Solution
Strong acids and weak acids act differently in water. Hydrochloric acid (left) is a strong acid. Acetic acid (right) is a weak acid.

Lab zone Try This Activity

pHone Home

1. Select materials such as fruit juices, soda water, coffee, tea, and antacids. If the sample is solid, dissolve some in a cup of water. Use a liquid as is.
2. Predict which materials are most acidic or most basic.
3. Using a plastic dropper, transfer a drop of one sample onto a fresh strip of pH test paper.
4. Compare the color of the strip to the pH test scale on the package.
5. Repeat for all your samples, rinsing the dropper between tests.

Interpreting Data List the samples from lowest to highest pH. Did any results surprise you?

Strength of Acids and Bases

Acids and bases may be strong or weak. Strength refers to how well an acid or a base produces ions in water. As shown in Figure 19, the molecules of a strong acid react to form ions in solution. With a weak acid, very few molecules form ions. At the same concentration, a strong acid produces more hydrogen ions (H^+) than a weak acid does. Examples of strong acids include hydrochloric acid, sulfuric acid, and nitric acid. Most other acids, such as acetic acid, are weak acids.

Strong bases react in a water solution in a similar way to strong acids. A strong base produces more hydroxide (OH^-) ions than does an equal concentration of a weak base. Ammonia is a weak base. Lye, or sodium hydroxide, is a strong base.

Measuring pH Knowing the concentration of hydrogen ions is the key to knowing how acidic or basic a solution is. To describe the concentration of ions, chemists use a numeric scale called pH. The **pH scale** is a range of values from 0 to 14. It expresses the concentration of hydrogen ions in a solution.

Figure 20 shows where some familiar substances fit on the pH scale. Notice that the most acidic substances are at the low end of the scale. The most basic substances are at the high end of the scale. You need to remember two important points about pH. **A low pH tells you that the concentration of hydrogen ions is high. In contrast, a high pH tells you that the concentration of hydrogen ions is low.** If you keep these ideas in mind, you can make sense of how the scale works.

You can find the pH of a solution by using indicators. The student in Figure 20 is using indicator paper that turns a different color for each pH value. Matching the color of the paper with the colors on the test scale tells how acidic or basic the solution is. A pH lower than 7 is acidic. A pH higher than 7 is basic. If the pH is 7, the solution is neutral. That means it's neither an acid nor a base. Pure water has a pH of 7.

Using Acids and Bases Safely Strength determines, in part, how safe acids and bases are to use. People often say that a solution is weak when they mean it is dilute. This could be a dangerous mistake! Even a dilute solution of hydrochloric acid can eat a hole in your clothing. An equal concentration of acetic acid, however, will not. In order to handle acids and bases safely, you need to know both their pH and their concentration.

Reading Checkpoint How would a weak base differ from an equal concentration of a strong base?

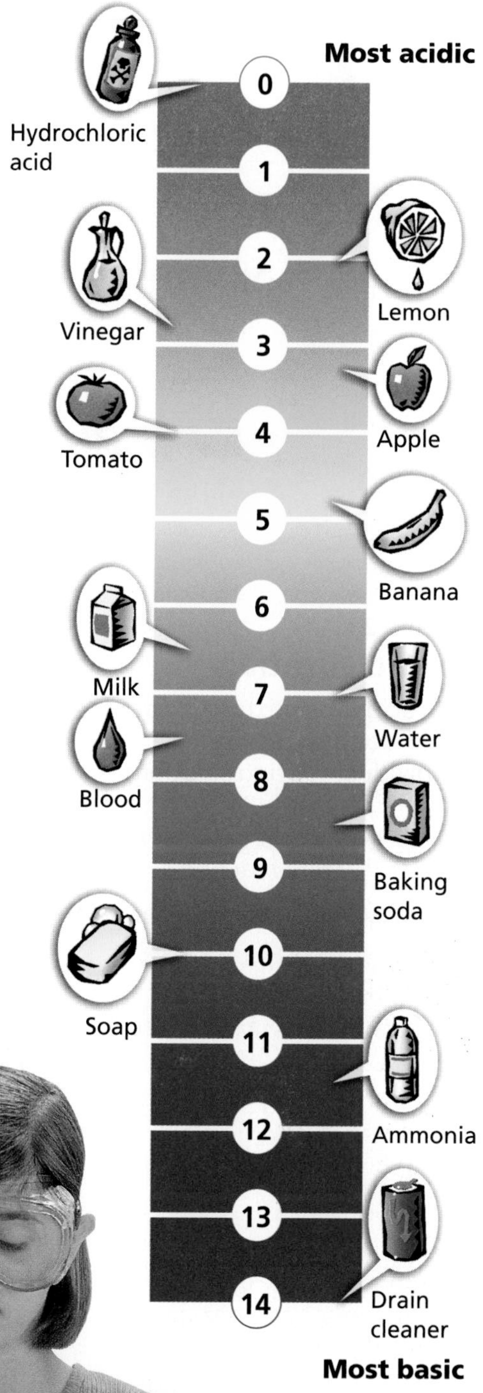

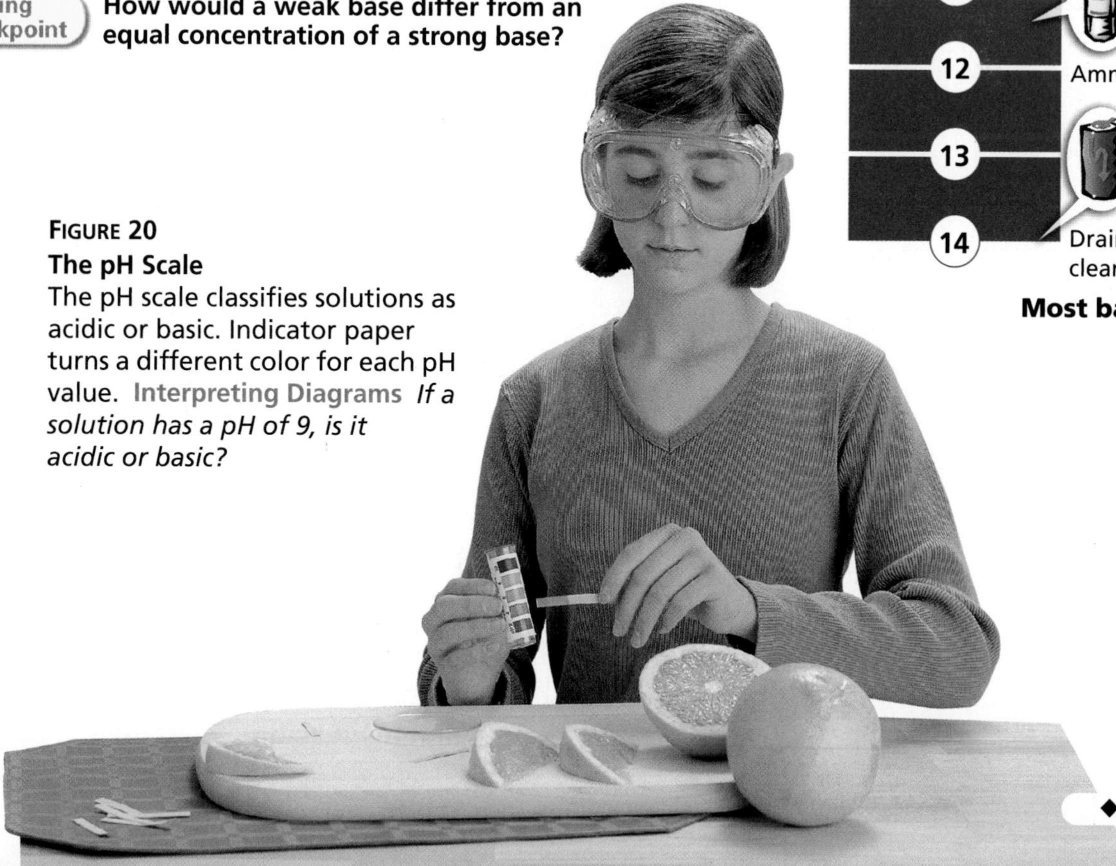

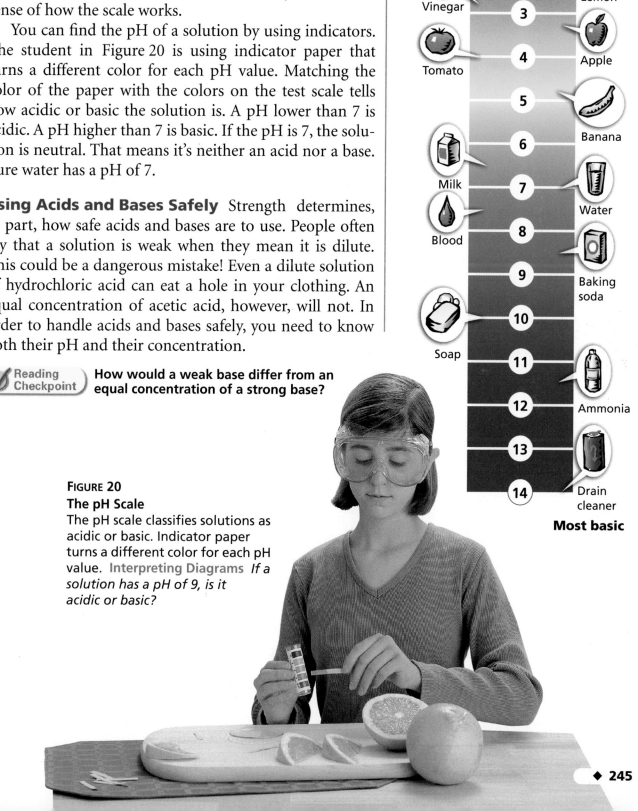

FIGURE 20
The pH Scale
The pH scale classifies solutions as acidic or basic. Indicator paper turns a different color for each pH value. **Interpreting Diagrams** *If a solution has a pH of 9, is it acidic or basic?*

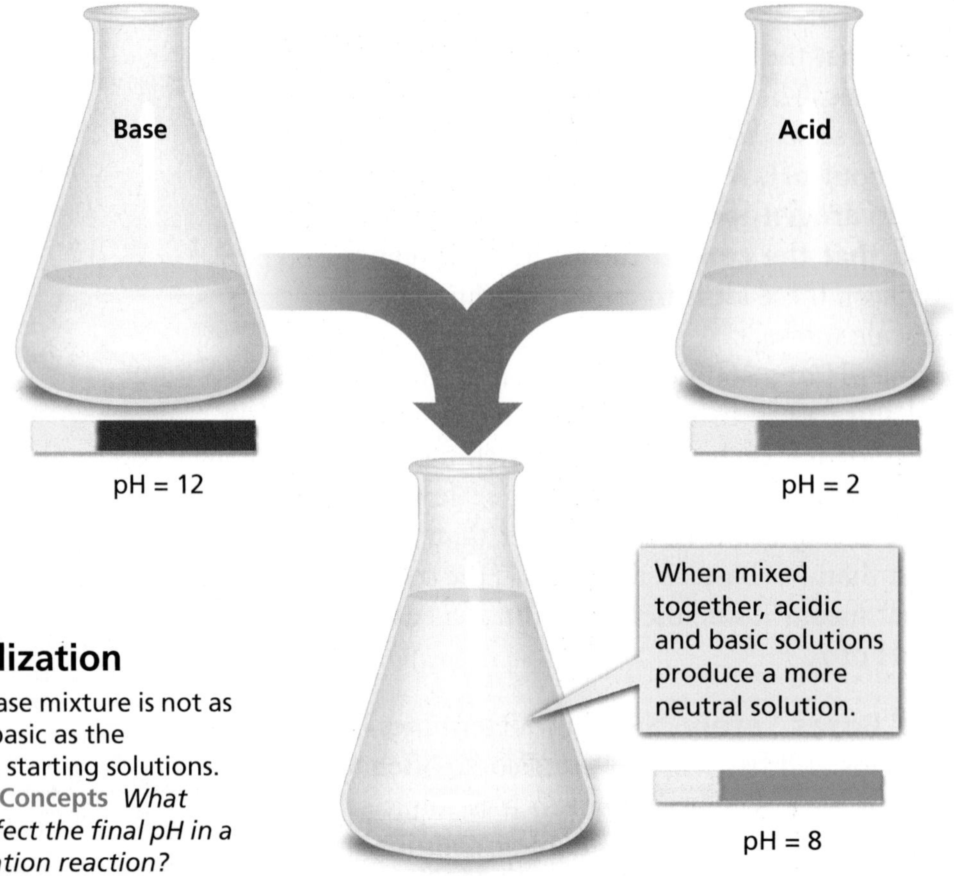

FIGURE 21
Neutralization
An acid-base mixture is not as acidic or basic as the individual starting solutions.
Applying Concepts *What factors affect the final pH in a neutralization reaction?*

Acid-Base Reactions

The story at the start of this section describes a chemist who mixed hydrochloric acid with sodium hydroxide. She got a solution of table salt (sodium chloride) and water.

$$HCl + NaOH \longrightarrow H_2O + Na^+ + Cl^-$$

If you tested the pH of the mixture, it would be close to 7, or neutral. In fact, a reaction between an acid and a base is called **neutralization** (noo truh lih ZAY shun).

Reactants After neutralization, an acid-base mixture is not as acidic or basic as the individual starting solutions were. Sometimes an acid-base reaction even results in a neutral solution. The final pH depends on such factors as the volumes, concentrations, and identities of the reactants. For example, some acids and bases react to form products that are not neutral. Also, common sense tells you that if only a small amount of strong base is reacted with a much larger amount of strong acid, the solution will remain acidic.

Products "Salt" may be the familiar name of the stuff you sprinkle on food. But to a chemist, the word refers to a specific group of compounds. A **salt** is any ionic compound that can be made from the neutralization of an acid with a base. A salt is made from the positive ion of a base and the negative ion of an acid.

Look at the equation for the reaction of nitric acid with potassium hydroxide:

$$HNO_3 + KOH \longrightarrow H_2O + K^+ + NO_3^-$$

One product of the reaction is water. The other product is potassium nitrate (KNO_3), a salt. **In a neutralization reaction, an acid reacts with a base to produce a salt and water.** Potassium nitrate is written in the equation as separate K^+ and NO_3^- ions because it is soluble in water. Some salts, such as potassium nitrate, are soluble. Others form precipitates because they are insoluble. Look at the table in Figure 22 to see a list of some common salts and their formulas.

Reading Checkpoint **What is a salt?**

Common Salts

Salt	Uses
Sodium chloride $NaCl$	Food flavoring; food preservative
Potassium iodide KI	Additive in "iodized" salt that prevents iodine deficiency
Calcium chloride $CaCl_2$	De-icer for roads and walkways
Potassium chloride KCl	Salt substitute in foods
Calcium carbonate $CaCO_3$	Found in limestone and seashells
Ammonium nitrate NH_4NO_3	Fertilizer; active ingredient in cold packs

FIGURE 22
Each salt listed in this table can be formed by the reaction between an acid and a base.

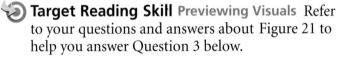

Section 4 Assessment

Target Reading Skill **Previewing Visuals** Refer to your questions and answers about Figure 21 to help you answer Question 3 below.

Reviewing Key Concepts

1. a. **Identifying** Which element is found in all the acids described in this section?
   b. **Describing** What kinds of ions do acids and bases form in water?
   c. **Predicting** What ions will the acid HNO_3 form when dissolved in water?
2. a. **Reviewing** What does a substance's pH tell you?
   b. **Comparing and Contrasting** If a solution has a pH of 6, would the solution contain more or fewer hydrogen ions (H^+) than an equal volume of solution with a pH of 3?
   c. **Making Generalizations** Would a dilute solution of HCl also be weak? Explain.
3. a. **Reviewing** What are the reactants of a neutralization reaction?
   b. **Explaining** What happens in a neutralization reaction?
   c. **Problem Solving** What acid reacts with KOH to produce the salt KCl?

Lab zone **At-Home Activity**

pH Lineup With a family member, search your house and refrigerator for the items found on the pH scale shown in Figure 20. Line up what you are able to find in order of increasing pH. Then ask your family member to guess why you ordered the substances in this way. Use the lineup to explain what pH means and how it is measured.

The Antacid Test

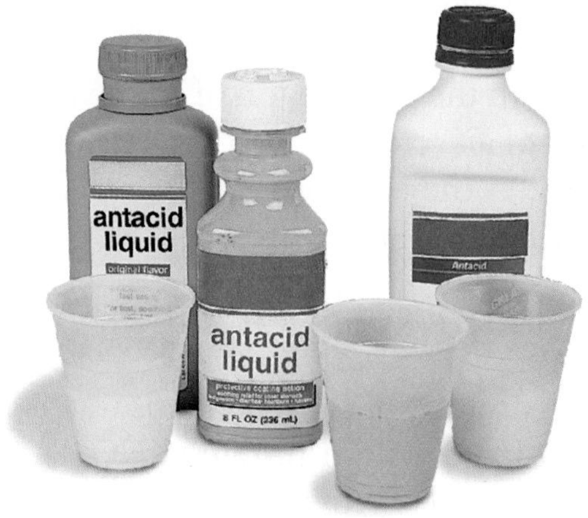

Problem

Which antacid neutralizes stomach acid with the smallest number of drops?

Skills Focus

designing experiments, interpreting data, measuring

Materials

- 3 plastic droppers
- small plastic cups
- dilute hydrochloric acid (HCl), 50 mL
- methyl orange solution, 1 mL
- liquid antacid, 30 mL of each brand tested

Procedure

PART 1

1. Using a plastic dropper, put 10 drops of hydrochloric acid (HCl) into one cup. **CAUTION:** *HCl is corrosive. Rinse spills and splashes immediately with water.*
2. Use another plastic dropper to put 10 drops of liquid antacid into another cup.
3. In your notebook, make a data table like the one below. Record the colors of the HCl and the antacid.

Data Table		
Substance	Original Color	Color With Indicator
Hydrochloric Acid		
Antacid Brand A		
Antacid Brand B		

4. Add 2 drops of methyl orange solution to each cup. Record the colors you see.
5. Test each of the other antacids. Discard all the solutions and cups as directed by your teacher.

PART 2

6. Methyl orange changes color at a pH of about 4. Predict the color of the solution you expect to see when an antacid is added to a mixture of methyl orange and HCl.
7. Design a procedure for testing the reaction of each antacid with HCl. Decide how many drops of acid and methyl orange you need to use each time.
8. Devise a plan for adding the antacid so that you can detect when a change occurs. Decide how much antacid to add each time and how to mix the solutions to be sure the indicator is giving accurate results.
9. Make a second data table to record your observations.
10. Carry out your procedure and record your results.
11. Discard the solutions and cups as directed by your teacher. Rinse the plastic droppers thoroughly.
12. Wash your hands thoroughly when done.

Analyze and Conclude

1. Designing Experiments What is the function of the methyl orange solution?
2. Interpreting Data Do your observations support your predictions from Step 6? Explain why or why not.
3. Inferring Why do you think antacids reduce stomach acid? Explain your answer, using the observations you made.
4. Controlling Variables Explain why it is important to use the same number of drops of HCl in each trial.
5. Measuring Which antacid neutralized the HCl with the smallest number of drops? Give a possible explanation for the difference.
6. Calculating If you have the same volume (number of drops) of each antacid, which one can neutralize the most acid?
7. Drawing Conclusions Did your procedure give results from which you could draw conclusions about which brand of antacid was most effective? Explain why or why not.
8. Communicating Write a brochure that explains to consumers what information they need to know in order to decide which brand of antacid is the best buy.

Design an Experiment

A company that sells a liquid antacid claims that its product works faster than tablets to neutralize stomach acid. Design an experiment to compare how quickly liquid antacids and chewable antacid tablets neutralize hydrochloric acid. *Obtain your teacher's permission before carrying out your investigation.*

Section 5

Integrating Life Science

Digestion and pH

Reading Preview

Key Concepts

- Why must your body digest food?
- How does pH affect digestion?

Key Terms

- digestion
- mechanical digestion
- chemical digestion

Target Reading Skill

Sequencing A sequence is the order in which a series of events occurs. As you read, make a flowchart that shows the sequence of changes in pH as food moves through the digestive system.

pH During Digestion

At a pH near 7, enzymes in the mouth start to break down carbohydrates.

↓

At a pH near 2, stomach enzymes break down proteins.

↓

(blank box)

Lab zone Discover Activity

Where Does Digestion Begin?

1. Obtain a bite-sized piece of crusty bread.
2. Chew the bread for about one minute. Do not swallow until after you notice a change in taste.

Think It Over

Inferring How did the bread taste before and after you chewed it? How can you explain the change in taste?

You may have seen commercials like the following: A man has a stomachache after eating spicy food. A voice announces that the problem is excess stomach acid. The remedy is an antacid tablet.

Ads like this one highlight the role of chemistry in digestion. You need to have acid in your stomach. But too much acid is a problem. Other parts of your digestive system need to be basic. What roles do acids and bases play in the digestion of food?

What Is Digestion?

Foods are made mostly of water and three groups of compounds: carbohydrates, proteins, and fats. Except for water, your body can't use foods in the form they are in when you eat them. **Foods must be broken down into simpler substances that your body can use for raw materials and energy.**

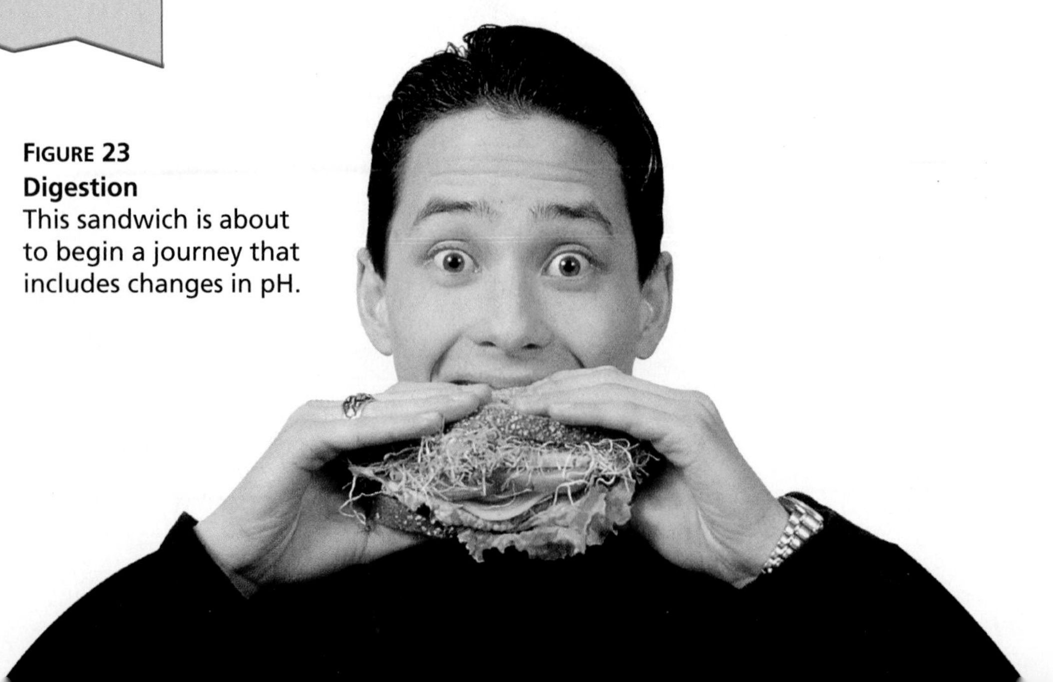

FIGURE 23
Digestion
This sandwich is about to begin a journey that includes changes in pH.

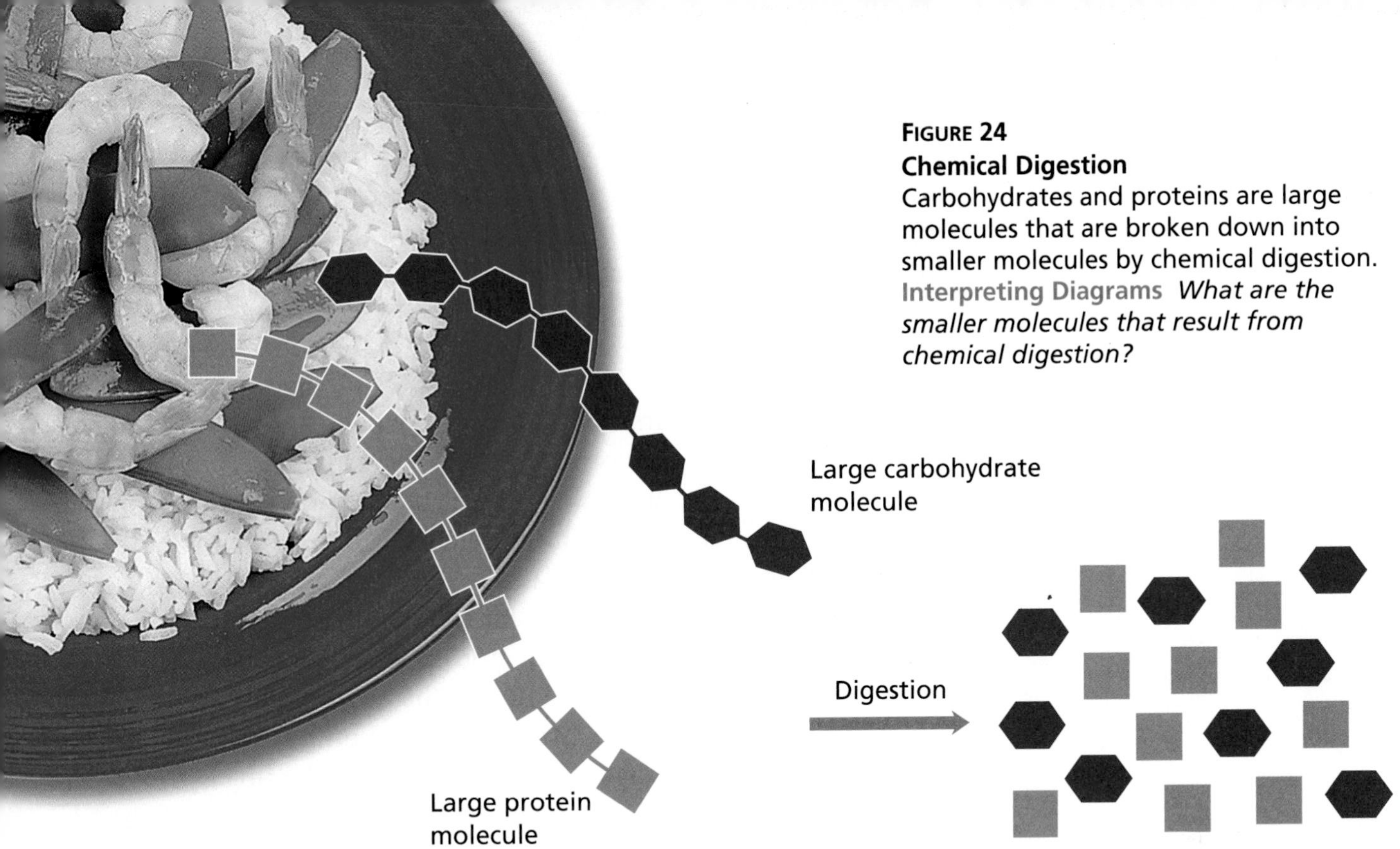

FIGURE 24
Chemical Digestion
Carbohydrates and proteins are large molecules that are broken down into smaller molecules by chemical digestion.
Interpreting Diagrams *What are the smaller molecules that result from chemical digestion?*

The process of **digestion** breaks down the complex molecules of foods into smaller molecules. Digestion has two parts—mechanical and chemical.

Mechanical Digestion **Mechanical digestion** is a physical process in which large pieces of food are torn and ground into smaller pieces. The result is similar to what happens when a sugar cube is hit with a hammer. The size of the food is reduced, but the food isn't changed into other compounds.

Chemical Digestion **Chemical digestion** breaks large molecules into smaller ones. Look at Figure 24 to see what happens to large carbohydrate and protein molecules during chemical digestion. They are broken down into much smaller molecules. Some molecules are used by the body to get energy. Others become building blocks for muscle, bone, skin, and other organs.

Chemical digestion takes place with the help of enzymes. You may recall that enzymes are catalysts that speed up reactions in living things. Enzymes require just the right conditions to work, including temperature and pH. **Some digestive enzymes work at a low pH. For others, the pH must be high or neutral.**

Reading Checkpoint **What happens to foods during chemical digestion?**

pH in the Digestive System

A bite of sandwich is about to take a journey through your digestive system. Figure 25 shows the main parts of the human digestive system. As you read, trace the food's pathway through the body. Keep track of the pH changes that affect the food molecules along the way.

Your Mouth The first stop in the journey is your mouth. Your teeth chew and mash the food. The food also is mixed with a watery fluid called saliva. Have you ever felt your mouth water at the smell of something delicious? The odor of food can trigger production of saliva.

What would you expect the usual pH of saliva to be? Remember that saliva tastes neither sour nor bitter. So you're correct if you think your mouth has a pH near 7, the neutral point.

Saliva contains amylase (AM uh lays), an enzyme that helps break down the carbohydrate starch into smaller sugar molecules. Amylase works best when the pH is near 7. You can sense the action of this enzyme if you chew a piece of bread. After about two minutes in your mouth, the starch is broken down into sugars. The sugars make the bread taste sweet.

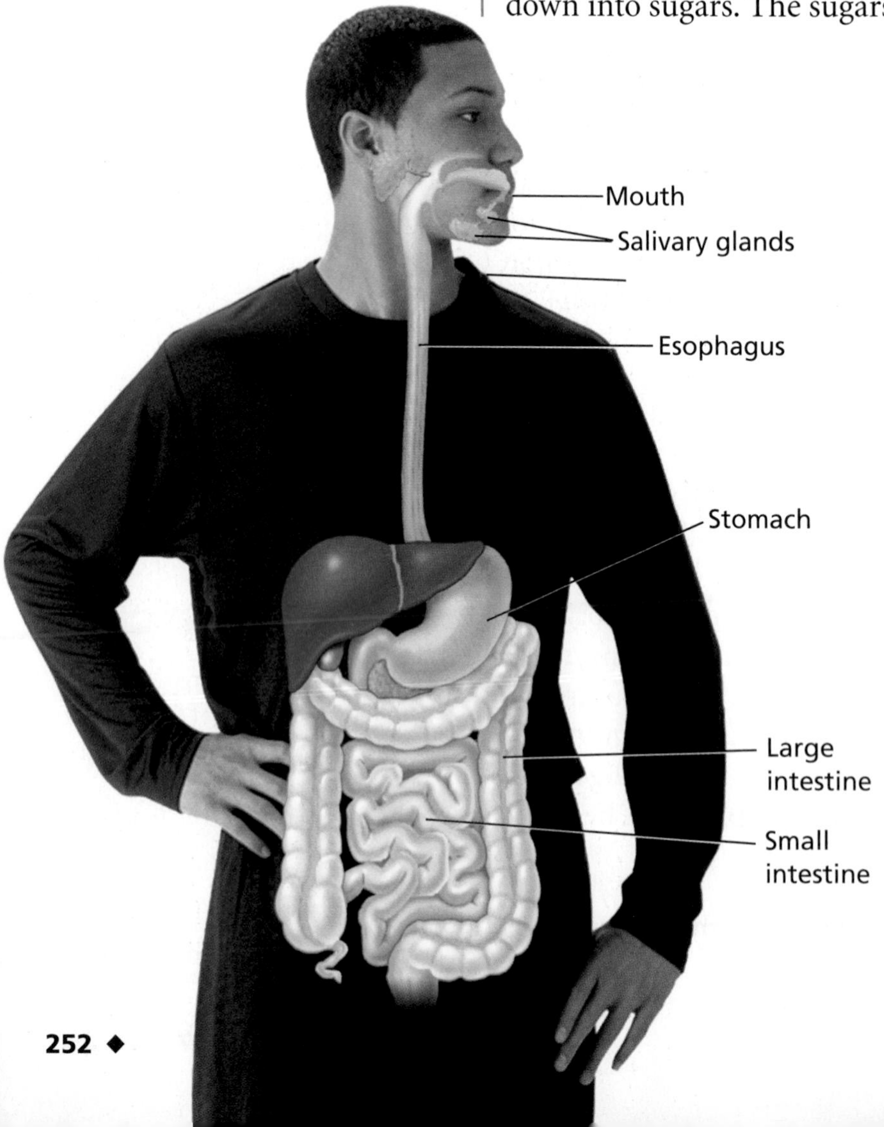

FIGURE 25
Foods are exposed to several changes in pH as they move through the digestive system.
Relating Cause and Effect *Why do certain digestive enzymes work only in certain parts of the digestive system?*

pH Changes During Digestion	
Organ	**pH**
Mouth	7
Stomach	2
Small intestine	8

Your Stomach Next, the food is swallowed and arrives in your stomach, where mechanical digestion continues. Also, chemical digestion begins for foods that contain protein, such as meat, fish, and beans. Cells in the lining of your stomach release enzymes and hydrochloric acid. In contrast to the near-neutral pH of your mouth, the pH here drops to a very acidic level of about 2.

The low pH in your stomach helps digestion take place. Pepsin is one enzyme that works in your stomach. Pepsin helps break down proteins into small molecules called amino acids. Most enzymes work best in a solution that is nearly neutral. But pepsin is different. It works most effectively in acids.

Your Small Intestine Your stomach empties its contents into the small intestine. Here, digestive fluid containing bicarbonate ions (HCO_3^-) surrounds the food. This ion creates a slightly basic solution, with a pH of about 8. At this slightly basic pH, enzymes of the small intestine work best. These enzymes complete the breakdown of carbohydrates, fats, and proteins.

By now, the large food molecules from the sandwich have been split up into smaller ones. These smaller molecules pass through the walls of the small intestine into your bloodstream and are carried to the cells that will use them.

Reading Checkpoint **What acid do the cells in the lining of your stomach release?**

Go Online SciLinks NSTA

For: Links on digestion and pH
Visit: www.SciLinks.org
Web Code: scn-1235

Section 5 Assessment

Target Reading Skill Sequencing Refer to your flowchart about the digestive system as you answer Question 2.

Reviewing Key Concepts

1. a. Reviewing What are the two parts of digestion?
   b. Comparing and Contrasting How do these two processes differ?
   c. Inferring People who have lost most of their teeth may have trouble chewing their food. How does this affect their digestive process?
2. a. Listing What is the pH in your mouth? Stomach? Small intestine?
   b. Sequencing Arrange the three body locations in part (a) from least acidic to most acidic.
   c. Applying Concepts Why are pH variations in different parts of the digestive system important to the process of digestion?

Writing in Science

News Report Suppose you are a news reporter who can shrink down in size and be protected from changes in the environment with a special suit. You are assigned to accompany a bite of food as it travels through the digestive system. Report your findings in a dramatic but accurate way. Include a catchy headline.

Chapter 7 Study Guide

1 Understanding Solutions

Key Concepts

- A solution has the same properties throughout. It contains solute particles that are too small to see.
- A colloid contains larger particles than a solution. The particles are still too small to be seen easily, but are large enough to scatter a light beam.
- Unlike a solution, a suspension does not have the same properties throughout. It contains visible particles that are larger than the particles in solutions or colloids.
- When a solution forms, particles of the solute leave each other and become surrounded by particles of the solvent.
- Solutes lower the freezing point and raise the boiling point of a solvent.

Key Terms

solution
solvent
solute
colloid
suspension

2 Concentration and Solubility

Key Concepts

- To measure concentration, you compare the amount of solute to the amount of solvent or to the total amount of solution.
- Solubility can be used to help identify a substance because it is a characteristic property of matter.
- Factors that affect the solubility of a substance include pressure, the type of solvent, and temperature.

Key Terms

dilute solution
concentrated solution
solubility
saturated solution
unsaturated solution
supersaturated solution

3 Describing Acids and Bases

Key Concepts

- An acid is a substance that tastes sour, reacts with metals and carbonates, and turns blue litmus paper red.
- A base is a substance that tastes bitter, feels slippery, and turns red litmus paper blue.
- Acids and bases have many uses around the home and in industry.

Key Terms

acid
corrosive
indicator
base

4 Acids and Bases in Solution

Key Concepts

- An acid is any substance that produces hydrogen ions (H^+) in water.
- A base is any substance that produces hydroxide ions (OH^-) in water.
- A low pH tells you that the concentration of hydrogen ions is high. In contrast, a high pH tells you that the concentration of hydrogen ions is low.
- In a neutralization reaction, an acid reacts with a base to produce a salt and water.

Key Terms

hydrogen ion (H^+)
hydroxide ion (OH^-)
pH scale
neutralization
salt

5 Digestion and pH

Key Concepts

- Foods must be broken down into simpler substances that your body can use for raw materials and energy.
- Some digestive enzymes work at a low pH. For others, the pH must be high or neutral.

Key Terms

digestion
mechanical digestion
chemical digestion

Review and Assessment

Go Online
PHSchool.com
For: Self-Assessment
Visit: PHSchool.com
Web Code: cga-2030

Organizing Information

Concept Mapping Copy the concept map about solutions onto a sheet of paper. Then complete it and add a title. (For more on Concept Mapping, see the Skills Handbook.)

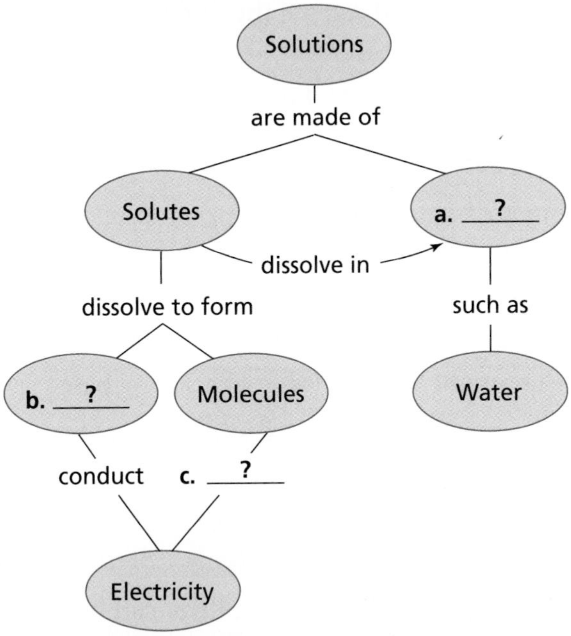

Reviewing Key Terms

Choose the letter of the best answer.

1. Sugar water is an example of a
   a. suspension.
   b. solution.
   c. solute.
   d. colloid.
2. A solution in which more solute may be dissolved at a given temperature is a(n)
   a. neutral solution.
   b. unsaturated solution.
   c. supersaturated solution.
   d. saturated solution.
3. A compound that changes color when it contacts an acid or a base is called a(n)
   a. solute.
   b. solvent.
   c. indicator.
   d. salt.
4. A polyatomic ion made of hydrogen and oxygen is called a
   a. hydroxide ion.
   b. hydrogen ion.
   c. salt.
   d. base.
5. Ammonia is an example of a(n)
   a. acid. **b.** salt.
   c. base. **d.** antacid.
6. The physical part of digestion is called
   a. digestion.
   b. mechanical digestion.
   c. chemical digestion.
   d. solubility.

Writing in Science

Product Label Suppose you are a marketing executive for a maple syrup company. Write a description of the main ingredients of maple syrup that can be pasted on the syrup's container. Use what you've learned about concentration to explain how dilute tree sap becomes sweet, thick syrup.

Discovery Channel School

Acids, Bases, and Solutions
Video Preview
Video Field Trip
▶ Video Assessment

Review and Assessment

Checking Concepts

7. Explain how you can tell the difference between a solution and a clear colloid.
8. Describe at least two differences between a dilute solution and a concentrated solution of sugar water.
9. Tomatoes are acidic. Predict two properties of tomato juice that you would be able to observe.
10. Explain how an indicator helps you distinguish between an acid and a base.
11. What might be a pH value of a strong base?
12. What combination of acid and base can be used to make the salt sodium chloride?

Thinking Critically

13. **Applying Concepts** A scuba diver can be endangered by "the bends." Explain how the effects of pressure on the solubility of gases is related to this condition.
14. **Relating Cause and Effect** When you heat tap water on the stove, you can see tiny bubbles of oxygen form. They rise to the surface long before the water begins to boil. Explain what causes these bubbles to appear.
15. **Drawing Conclusions** You have two clear liquids. One turns blue litmus paper red and one turns red litmus paper blue. If you mix them and retest with both litmus papers, no color changes occur. Describe the reaction that took place when the liquids were mixed.
16. **Comparing and Contrasting** Compare the types of particles formed in a water solution of an acid with those formed in a water solution of a base.
17. **Problem Solving** Fill in the missing salt product in the reaction below.

$$HCl + KOH \longrightarrow H_2O + \underline{?}$$

18. **Predicting** Suppose a person took a dose of antacid greater than what is recommended. Predict how this action might affect the digestion of certain foods.

Math Practice

19. **Calculating a Concentration** If you have 1,000 grams of a 10 percent solution of sugar water, how much sugar is dissolved in the solution?
20. **Calculating a Concentration** The concentration of an alcohol and water solution is 25 percent alcohol by volume. What is the volume of alcohol in 200 mL of the solution?

Applying Skills

Use the diagram to answer Questions 21–24.

The diagram below shows the particles of an unknown acid in a water solution.

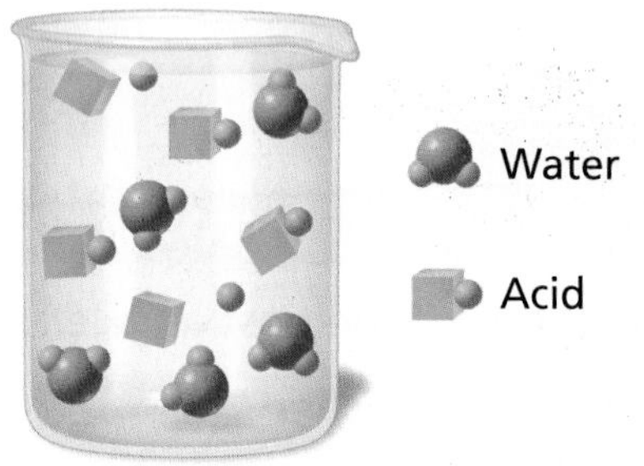

21. **Interpreting Diagrams** How can you tell that the solution contains a weak acid?
22. **Inferring** Which shapes in the diagram represent ions?
23. **Making Models** Suppose another unknown acid is a strong acid. Make a diagram to show the particles of this acid dissolved in water.
24. **Drawing Conclusions** Explain how the pH of a strong acid compares with the pH of a weak acid of the same concentration.

Lab zone Chapter Project

Performance Assessment Demonstrate the indicators you prepared. For each indicator, list the substances you tested in order from most acidic to least acidic. Would you use the same materials as indicators if you did this project again? Explain.

Standardized Test Prep

Test-Taking Tip

Eliminating Incorrect Answers

When answering a multiple choice question, you can often eliminate some answer choices because they are clearly incorrect. By doing so, you increase your odds of choosing the correct answer.

Sample Question

A scientist observes that an unknown solution turns blue litmus paper red and reacts with zinc to produce hydrogen gas. The unknown solution is most likely

A a colloid. **B** an acid.
C a base. **D** a suspension.

Answer

The correct answer is **B**. You can eliminate **A** and **D** because indicators, such as litmus paper, are used to determine whether a substance is an acid or a base. You have now narrowed your choices to **B** and **C**. **C** is incorrect because bases turn red litmus paper blue and do not react with metals to produce hydrogen gas.

Choose the letter of the best answer.

1. Which of the following pH values indicates a solution with the highest concentration of hydrogen ions?
A pH = 1
B pH = 2
C pH = 7
D pH = 14

2. A small beaker contains 50 milliliters of water at 20°C. If three sugar cubes are placed in the beaker, they will eventually dissolve. Which action would speed up the rate at which the sugar cubes dissolve?
F Use less water initially.
G Transfer the contents to a larger beaker.
H Cool the water and sugar cubes to 5°C.
J Heat and stir the contents of the beaker.

Use the graph below and your knowledge of science to answer Question 3.

Solubility of Potassium Chloride (KCl)

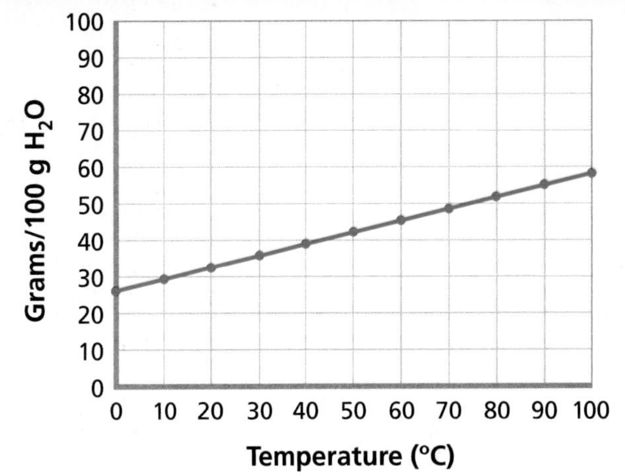

3. If 30 grams of KCl are dissolved in 100 grams of water at 50°C, the solution can be best described as
A saturated.
B supersaturated.
C unsaturated.
D soluble.

4. Which safety procedures should be followed when using acids and bases in the laboratory?
F Wear an apron and safety goggles.
G Dispose of chemical wastes properly.
H Wash your hands before leaving the lab.
J all of the above

Constructed Response

5. Salt water is a solution of table salt (the solute) and water (the solvent). Describe a laboratory procedure that could be used to determine the concentration of salt in a sample of salt water. Indicate all measurements that must be made. (*Hint:* Remember that the concentration of a solution can be expressed as a ratio of the mass of the solute to the mass of the solution.)

Chapter

8

Carbon Chemistry

Chapter Preview

❶ **Properties of Carbon**
Discover *Why Do Pencils Write?*
Active Art *Carbon Bonding*

❷ **Carbon Compounds**
Discover *What Do You Smell?*
Try This *Dry or Wet?*
Analyzing Data *Boiling Points of Hydrocarbons*
Skills Activity *Classifying*
At-Home Activity *Mix It Up*
Skills Lab *How Many Molecules?*

❸ **Polymers and Composites**
Discover *What Did You Make?*
Skills Activity *Calculating*
Tech & Design in History *The Development of Polymers*
Technology and Society *Polyester Fleece*

❹ **Life With Carbon**
Discover *What Is in Milk?*
Try This *Alphabet Soup*
Try This *Like Oil or Water?*
Consumer Lab *Are You Getting Your Vitamins?*

Interactive Textbook

Butterflies, flowers, and all other living things contain carbon compounds. ▶

Discovery Channel School

Carbon Chemistry

▶ Video Preview
Video Field Trip
Video Assessment

Lab zone™ Chapter **Project**

Check Out the Fine Print

All the foods you eat and drink contain carbon compounds. In this project, you will look closely at the labels on food packages to find carbon compounds.

Your Goal To identify carbon compounds found in different foods

To complete the project you must

- collect at least a dozen labels with lists of ingredients and nutrition facts
- identify the carbon compounds listed, as well as substances that do not contain carbon
- interpret the nutrition facts on labels to compare amounts of substances in each food
- classify compounds in foods into the categories of polymers found in living things

Plan It! Brainstorm with your classmates about what kinds of packaged foods you want to examine. After your teacher approves your plan, start collecting and studying food labels.

Section 1

Properties of Carbon

Reading Preview

Key Concepts

- How is carbon able to form such a huge variety of compounds?
- What are four forms of pure carbon?

Key Terms

- diamond
- graphite
- fullerene
- nanotube

Target Reading Skill

Using Prior Knowledge Before you read, look at the section headings and visuals to see what this section is about. Then, write what you know about carbon in a graphic organizer like the one below. As you read, continue to write in what you learn.

What You Know
1. Carbon atoms have 6 electrons. 2.

What You Learned
1. 2.

Lab zone Discover Activity

Why Do Pencils Write?

1. Tear paper into two pieces about 5 cm by 5 cm. Rub the two pieces back and forth between your fingers.
2. Now rub pencil lead (graphite) on one side of each piece of paper. Try to get as much graphite as possible on the paper.
3. Rub together the two sides covered with graphite.
4. When you are finished, wash your hands.

Think It Over

Observing Did you notice a difference between what you observed in Step 3 and what you observed in Step 1? How could the property of graphite that you observed be useful for purposes other than writing?

Open your mouth and say "aah." Uh-oh, you have a small cavity. Do you know what happens next? Your tooth needs a filling. But first the dentist's drill clears away the decayed part of your tooth.

Why is a dentist's drill hard enough and sharp enough to cut through teeth? The answer has to do with the element carbon. The tip of the drill is covered with diamond chips. Diamond is a form of carbon and the hardest substance on Earth. Because the drill tip is made of diamonds, a dentist's drill stays sharp and useful. To understand why diamond is such a hard substance, you need to take a close look at the carbon atom and the bonds it forms.

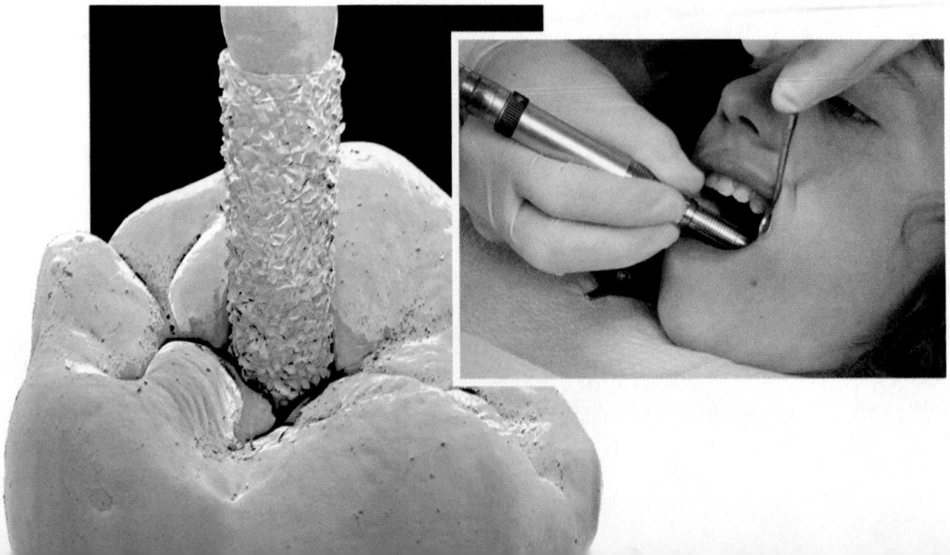

FIGURE 1
Uses of Carbon
This colorized photo shows the tip of a dentist's drill (yellow). The tip is made of diamond and is strong enough to bore into a tooth (blue).

FIGURE 2
Carbon Atoms and Bonding
Carbon atoms and the bonds between them can be modeled in several ways.

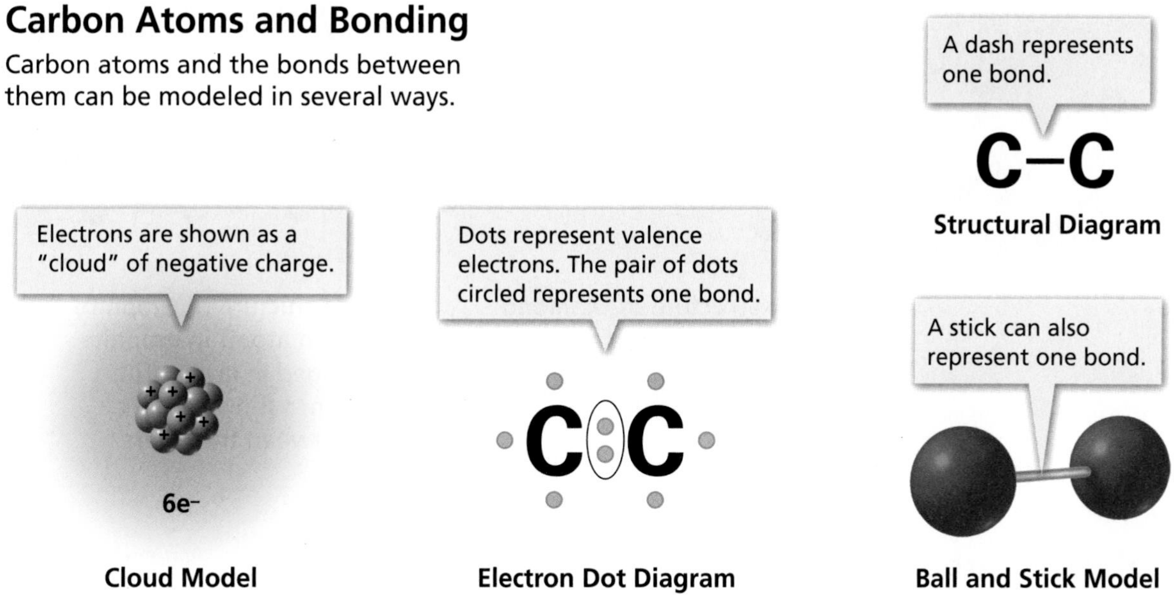

A dash represents one bond.
C–C
Structural Diagram
Electrons are shown as a "cloud" of negative charge.
6e⁻
Cloud Model
Dots represent valence electrons. The pair of dots circled represents one bond.
Electron Dot Diagram
A stick can also represent one bond.
Ball and Stick Model

Carbon Atoms and Bonding

Recall that the atomic number of carbon is 6, which means that the nucleus of a carbon atom contains 6 protons. Surrounding the nucleus are 6 electrons. Of these electrons, four are valence electrons—the electrons available for bonding.

As you have learned, a chemical bond is the force that holds two atoms together. A bond between two atoms results from changes involving the atoms' valence electrons. Atoms gain, lose, or share valence electrons in a way that makes the atoms more stable. A carbon atom can share its valence electrons with other atoms, forming covalent bonds. Figure 2 shows ways that covalent bonds between atoms may be represented.

Atoms of most elements form chemical bonds. Carbon, however, is unique. **Few elements have the ability of carbon to bond with both itself and other elements in so many different ways. With four valence electrons, each carbon atom is able to form four bonds.** So, it is possible to form molecules made of thousands of carbon atoms. By comparison, hydrogen, oxygen, and nitrogen can form only one, two, or three bonds, respectively, and cannot form such long chains.

As you can see in Figure 3, it is possible to arrange the same number of carbon atoms in different ways. Carbon atoms can form straight chains, branched chains, and rings. Sometimes, two or more carbon rings can even join together.

Reading Checkpoint **What happens to a carbon atom's valence electrons when it bonds to other atoms?**

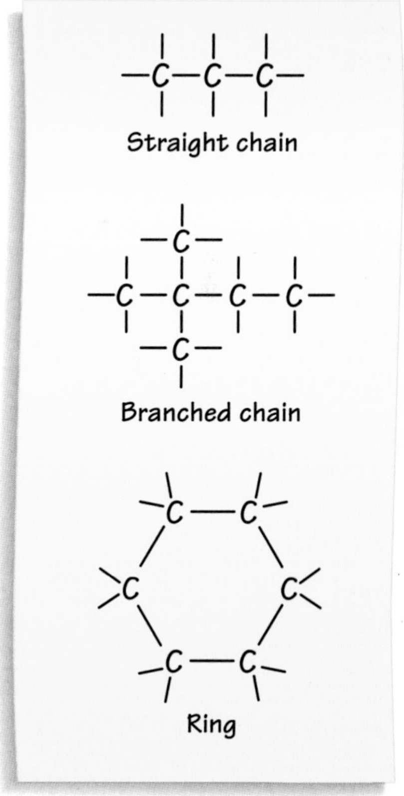

FIGURE 3
Arrangements of Carbon Atoms
Carbon chains and rings form the backbones for molecules that may contain other atoms.

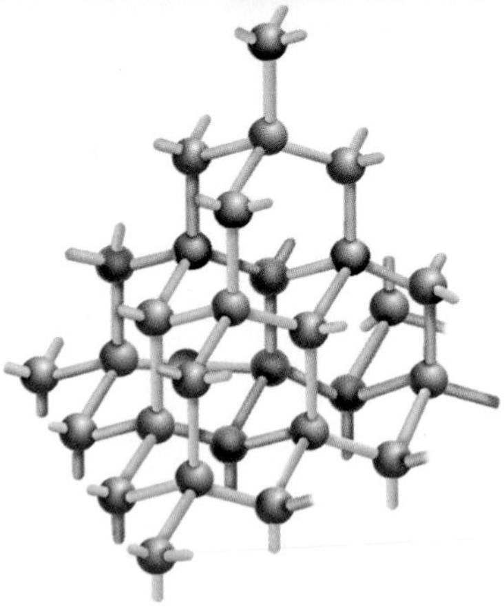

Crystal Structure of Diamond The carbon atoms in a diamond are arranged in a crystal structure.

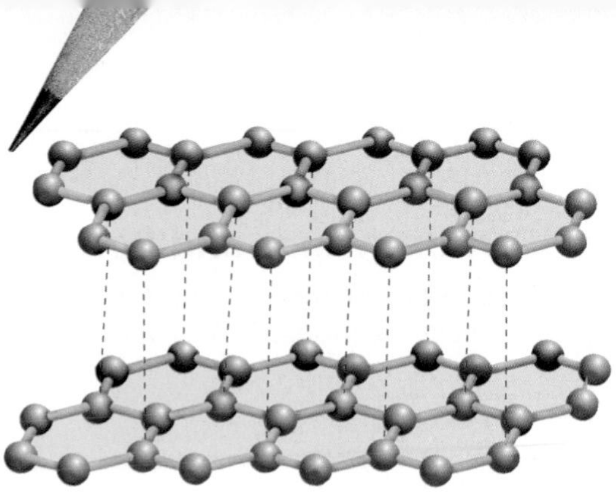

Layered Structure of Graphite The carbon atoms in graphite are arranged in layers. The dashed lines show the weak bonds between the layers.

FIGURE 4

Forms of Pure Carbon

Pure carbon exists in the form of diamond, graphite, fullerenes, and nanotubes. The properties of each form result from the unique repeating pattern of its carbon atoms. **Interpreting Diagrams** *Which form of carbon has a crystal structure?*

Forms of Pure Carbon

Because of the ways that carbon forms bonds, the pure element can exist in different forms. **Diamond, graphite, fullerenes, and nanotubes are four forms of the element carbon.**

Diamond The hardest mineral, **diamond,** forms deep within Earth. At very high temperatures and pressures, carbon atoms form diamond crystals. Each carbon atom is bonded strongly to four other carbon atoms. The result is a solid that is extremely hard and nonreactive. The melting point of diamond is more than 3,500°C—as hot as the surface temperatures of some stars.

Diamonds are prized for their brilliance and clarity when cut as gems. Industrial chemists are able to make diamonds artificially, but these diamonds are not considered beautiful enough to use as gems. Both natural and artificial diamonds are used in industry. Diamonds work well in cutting tools, such as drills.

Graphite Every time you write with a pencil, you leave a layer of carbon on the paper. The "lead" in a lead pencil is actually mostly **graphite,** another form of the element carbon. In graphite, each carbon atom is bonded tightly to three other carbon atoms in flat layers. However, the bonds between atoms in different layers are very weak, so the layers slide past one another easily.

If you run your fingers over pencil marks, you can feel how slippery graphite is. Because it is so slippery, graphite makes an excellent lubricant in machines. Graphite reduces friction between the moving parts. In your home, you might use a graphite spray to help a key work better in a sticky lock.

Reading Checkpoint **Why is diamond such a hard and nonreactive substance?**

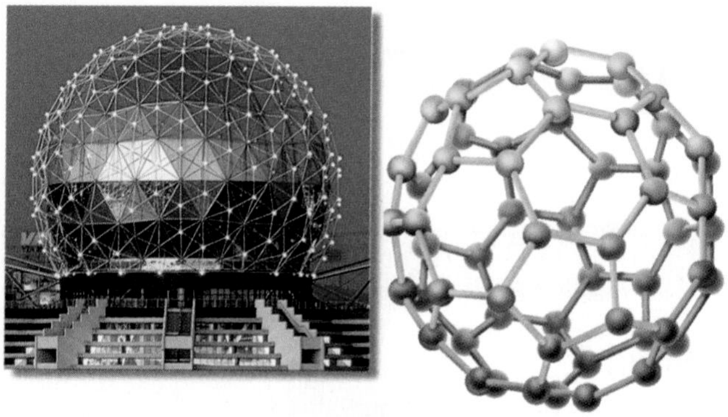

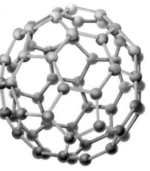

Spherical Structure of a Fullerene
The carbon atoms in a fullerene form a sphere that resembles a geodesic dome.

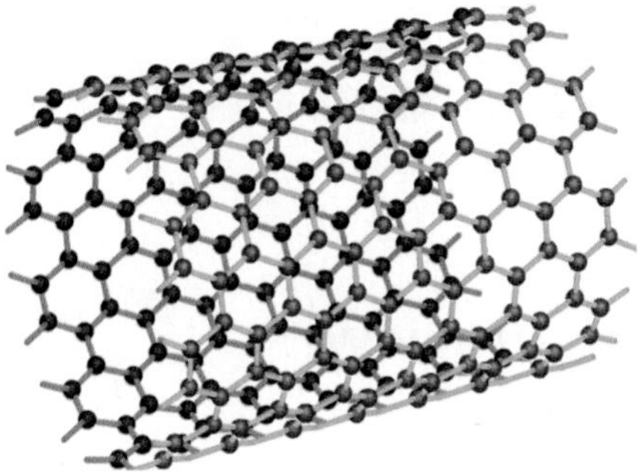

Cylindrical Structure of a Nanotube
The carbon atoms in a nanotube are arranged in a cylinder.

Fullerenes and Nanotubes In 1985, scientists made a new form of carbon. It consists of carbon atoms arranged in the shape of a hollow sphere. This form of carbon was named a **fullerene** (FUL ur een), for the architect Buckminster Fuller, who designed dome-shaped buildings called geodesic domes. One type of fullerene has been nicknamed "buckyballs."

In 1991, yet another form of carbon was made—the nanotube. In a **nanotube,** carbon atoms are arranged in the shape of a long, hollow cylinder—something like a sheet of graphite rolled into a tube. Only a few nanometers wide in diameter, nanotubes are tiny, light, flexible, and extremely strong. Nanotubes are also good conductors of electricity and heat.

Scientists are looking for ways to use the unique properties of fullerenes and nanotubes. For example, chemists are studying how fullerenes and nanotubes may be used to deliver medicine molecules into cells. Nanotubes may also be used as conductors in electronic devices and as super-strong cables.

Go Online
active art
For: Carbon Bonding activity
Visit: PHSchool.com
Web Code: cgp-2041

Section 1 Assessment

Target Reading Skill Using Prior Knowledge Review your graphic organizer and revise it based on what you learned in this section.

Reviewing Key Concepts

1. a. Identifying How many bonds can a carbon atom form?
   b. Explaining What bonding properties of carbon allow it to form so many different compounds?
2. a. Listing List the four forms of pure carbon.
   b. Describing Describe the carbon bonds in graphite.
   c. Relating Cause and Effect How do the differences in carbon bonds explain why graphite and diamonds have different properties?

Writing in Science

Explanation Draw electron dot diagrams for a straight carbon chain and a branched chain. Then, write an explanation of what you did to show how the carbons are bonded.

Section 2

Carbon Compounds

Reading Preview

Key Concepts

- What are some properties of organic compounds?
- What are some properties of hydrocarbons?
- What kind of structures and bonding do hydrocarbons have?
- What are some characteristics of substituted hydrocarbons, esters, and polymers?

Key Terms

- organic compound
- hydrocarbon
- structural formula
- isomer
- saturated hydrocarbon
- unsaturated hydrocarbon
- substituted hydrocarbon
- hydroxyl group
- alcohol
- organic acid
- carboxyl group
- ester
- polymer
- monomer

Target Reading Skill

Outlining As you read, make an outline about carbon compounds. Use the red headings for the main ideas and the blue headings for supporting ideas.

Lab zone Discover Activity

What Do You Smell?

1. Your teacher will provide you with some containers. Wave your hand toward your nose over the top of each container.
2. Try to identify each of the odors.
3. After you record what you think is in each container, compare your guesses to the actual substance.

Think It Over

Developing Hypotheses Develop a hypothesis to explain the differences between the smell of one substance and another.

Imagine that you are heading out for a day of shopping. Your first purchase is a cotton shirt. Then you go to the drug store, where you buy a bottle of shampoo and a pad of writing paper. Your next stop is a hardware store. There, you buy propane fuel for your camping stove. Your final stop is the grocery store, where you buy olive oil, cereal, meat, and vegetables.

What do all of these purchases have in common? They all are made of carbon compounds. Carbon atoms act as the backbone or skeleton for the molecules of these compounds. Carbon compounds include gases (such as propane), liquids (such as olive oil), and solids (such as cotton). Mixtures of carbon compounds are found in foods, paper, and shampoo. In fact, more than 90 percent of all known compounds contain carbon.

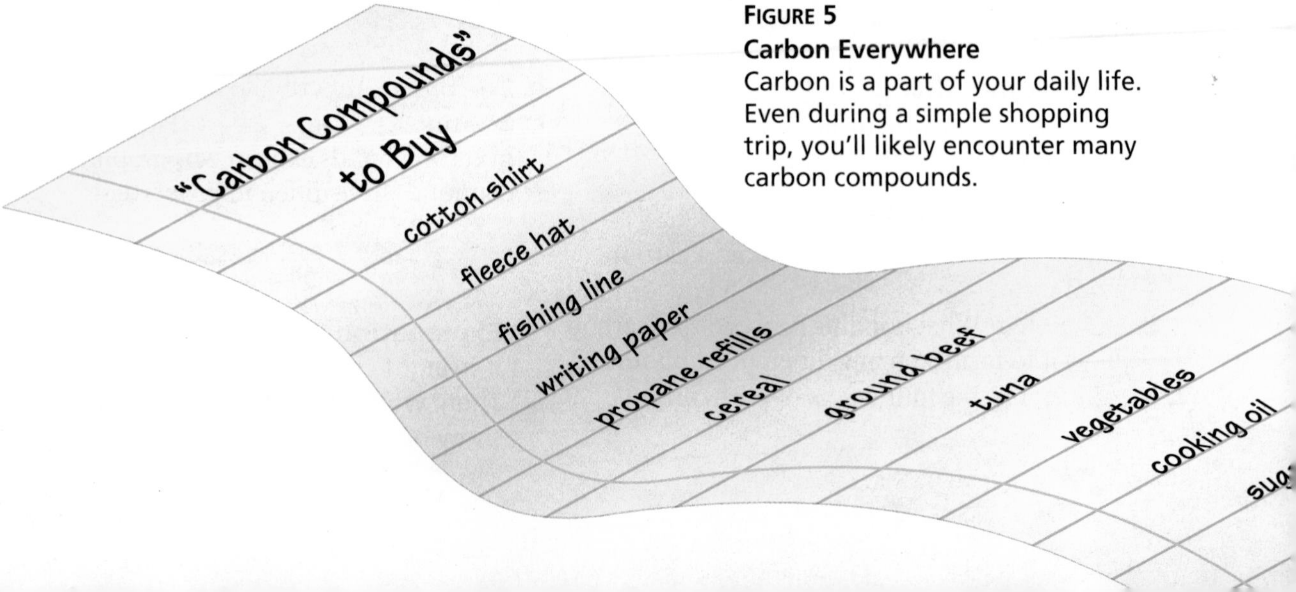

FIGURE 5
Carbon Everywhere
Carbon is a part of your daily life. Even during a simple shopping trip, you'll likely encounter many carbon compounds.

FIGURE 6
Where Organic Compounds Are Found
These three lists represent only a few of the places where organic compounds can be found. Organic compounds are in all living things, in products from living things, and in human-made materials.

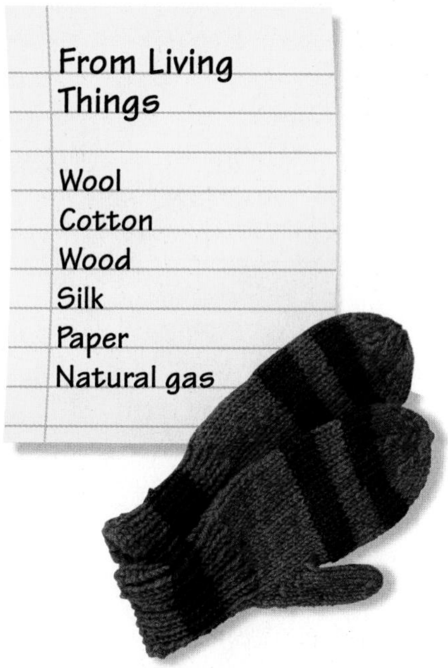

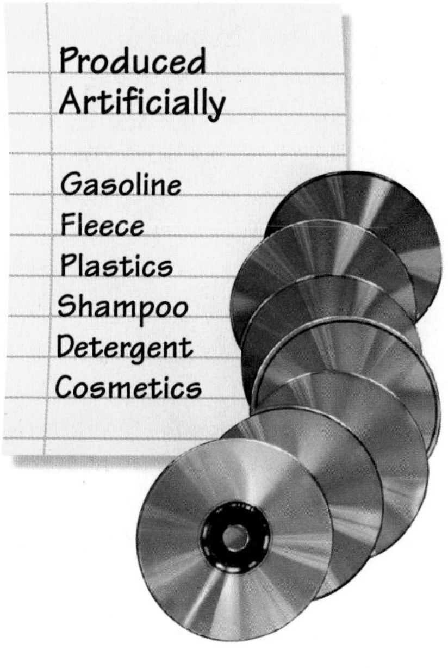

Organic Compounds

Carbon compounds are so numerous that they are given a specific name. With some exceptions, compounds that contain carbon are called **organic compounds.** This term is used because scientists once thought that organic compounds could be produced only by living things. (The word *organic* means "of living things.") Today, however, scientists know that organic compounds also can be found in products made from living things and in materials produced artificially in laboratories and factories. Organic compounds are part of the solid matter of every organism on Earth. They are part of products that are made from organisms, such as paper made from the wood of trees. Plastics, fuels, cleaning solutions, and many other such products also contain organic compounds. The raw materials for most manufactured organic compounds come from petroleum, or crude oil.

Many organic compounds have similar properties in terms of melting points, boiling points, odor, electrical conductivity, and solubility. Many organic compounds have low melting points and low boiling points. As a result, they are liquids or gases at room temperature. Organic liquids generally have strong odors. They also do not conduct electricity. Many organic compounds do not dissolve well in water. You may have seen vegetable oil, which is a mixture of organic compounds, form a separate layer in a bottle of salad dressing.

Reading Checkpoint **What is an organic compound?**

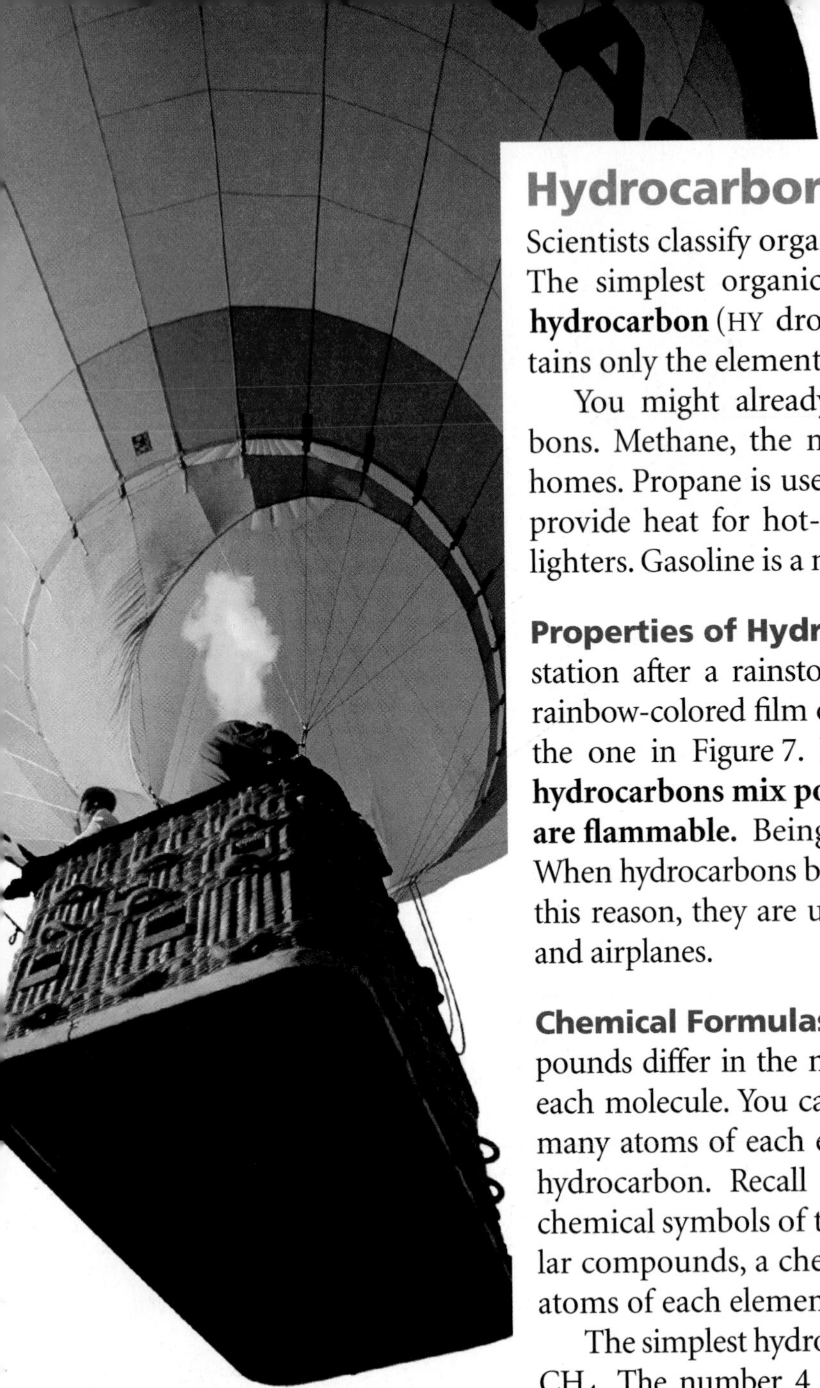

Hydrocarbons

Scientists classify organic compounds into different categories. The simplest organic compounds are the hydrocarbons. A **hydrocarbon** (HY droh KAHR bun) is a compound that contains only the elements carbon and hydrogen.

You might already recognize several common hydrocarbons. Methane, the main gas in natural gas, is used to heat homes. Propane is used in portable stoves and gas grills and to provide heat for hot-air balloons. Butane is the fuel in most lighters. Gasoline is a mixture of several different hydrocarbons.

Properties of Hydrocarbons Have you ever been at a gas station after a rainstorm? If so, you may have noticed a thin rainbow-colored film of gasoline or oil floating on a puddle, like the one in Figure 7. **Like many other organic compounds, hydrocarbons mix poorly with water. Also, all hydrocarbons are flammable.** Being flammable means that they burn easily. When hydrocarbons burn, they release a great deal of energy. For this reason, they are used as fuel for stoves, heaters, cars, buses, and airplanes.

Chemical Formulas of Hydrocarbons Hydrocarbon compounds differ in the number of carbon and hydrogen atoms in each molecule. You can write a chemical formula to show how many atoms of each element make up a molecule of a specific hydrocarbon. Recall that a chemical formula includes the chemical symbols of the elements in a compound. For molecular compounds, a chemical formula also shows the number of atoms of each element in a molecule.

The simplest hydrocarbon is methane. Its chemical formula is CH_4. The number 4 indicates the number of hydrogen atoms (H). Notice that the 4 is a subscript. Subscripts are written lower and smaller than the letter symbols of the elements. The symbol for carbon (C) in the formula is written without a subscript. This means that there is one carbon atom in the molecule.

FIGURE 7
Hydrocarbons
Hydrocarbons contain only the elements carbon and hydrogen. From the fuel that heats the air in hot-air balloons (above) to multicolored oil slicks (below right), hydrocarbons are all around you.
Making Generalizations *What properties of hydrocarbons do the hot-air balloon and oil slick demonstrate?*

A hydrocarbon with two carbon atoms is ethane. The formula for ethane is C_2H_6. The subscripts in this formula show that an ethane molecule is made of two carbon atoms and six hydrogen atoms.

A hydrocarbon with three carbon atoms is propane (C_3H_8). How many hydrogen atoms does the subscript indicate? If you answered eight, you are right.

Reading Checkpoint **What is a hydrocarbon?**

Structure and Bonding in Hydrocarbons

The properties of hydrocarbon compounds are related to the compound's structure. **The carbon chains in a hydrocarbon may be straight, branched, or ring-shaped.** If a hydrocarbon has two or more carbon atoms, the atoms can form a single line, that is, a straight chain. In hydrocarbons with four or more carbon atoms, it is possible to have branched arrangements of the carbon atoms as well as straight chains.

Lab zone Try This Activity

Dry or Wet?

Petroleum jelly is manufactured from hydrocarbons.

1. Carefully coat one of your fingers in petroleum jelly.
2. Dip that finger in water. Also dip a finger on your other hand in water.
3. Inspect the two fingers, and note how they feel.
4. Use a paper towel to remove the petroleum jelly, and then wash your hands thoroughly.

Inferring Compare how your two fingers looked and felt in Steps 2 and 3. What property of hydrocarbons does this activity demonstrate?

Structural Formulas To show how atoms are arranged in the molecules of a compound, chemists use a structural formula. A **structural formula** shows the kind, number, and arrangement of atoms in a molecule.

Figure 8 shows the structural formulas for molecules of methane, ethane, and propane. Each dash (—) represents a bond. In methane, each carbon atom is bonded to four hydrogen atoms. In ethane and propane, each carbon atom is bonded to at least one carbon atom as well as to hydrogen atoms. As you look at structural formulas, notice that every carbon atom forms four bonds. Every hydrogen atom forms one bond. There are never any dangling bonds. In other words, both ends of a dash are always connected to something.

FIGURE 8
Structural Formulas
Each carbon atom in these structural formulas is surrounded by four dashes representing four bonds. **Interpreting Diagrams** *In propane, how many hydrogen atoms is each carbon bonded to?*

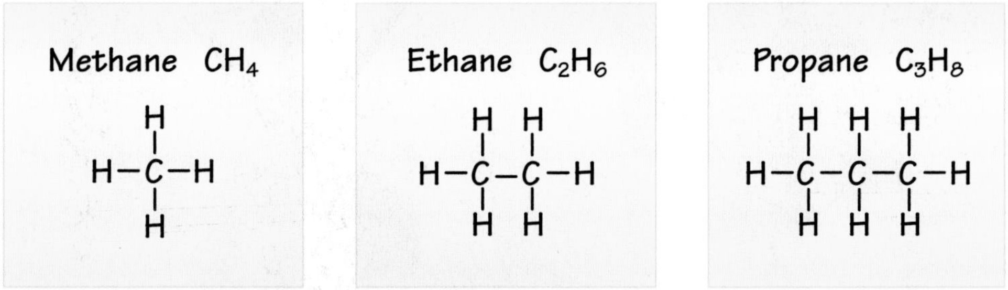

Math Analyzing Data

Boiling Points of Hydrocarbons

The graph shows the boiling points of several hydrocarbons. (*Note:* Some points on the *y*-axis are negative.)

Use the graph to answer the following questions.

1. **Reading Graphs** Where is 0°C on the graph?
2. **Interpreting Data** What is the approximate boiling point of C_3H_8? C_5H_{12}? C_6H_{14}?
3. **Calculating** What is the temperature difference between the boiling points of C_3H_8 and C_5H_{12}?
4. **Drawing Conclusions** At room temperature (about 22°C), which of the hydrocarbons are gases? How can you tell?

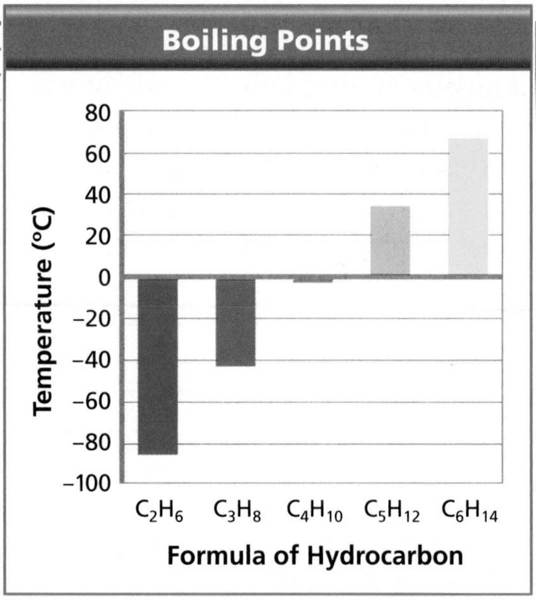

Isomers Consider the chemical formula of butane: C_4H_{10}. This formula does not indicate how the atoms are arranged in the molecule. In fact, there are two different ways to arrange the carbon atoms in C_4H_{10}. These two arrangements are shown in Figure 9. Compounds that have the same chemical formula but different structural formulas are called **isomers** (EYE soh murz). Each isomer is a different substance with its own characteristic properties.

Notice in Figure 9 that a molecule of one isomer, butane, is a straight chain. A molecule of the other isomer, isobutane, is a branched chain. Both molecules have 4 carbon atoms and 10 hydrogen atoms, but the atoms are arranged differently in the two molecules. And these two compounds have different properties. For example, butane and isobutane have different melting points and boiling points.

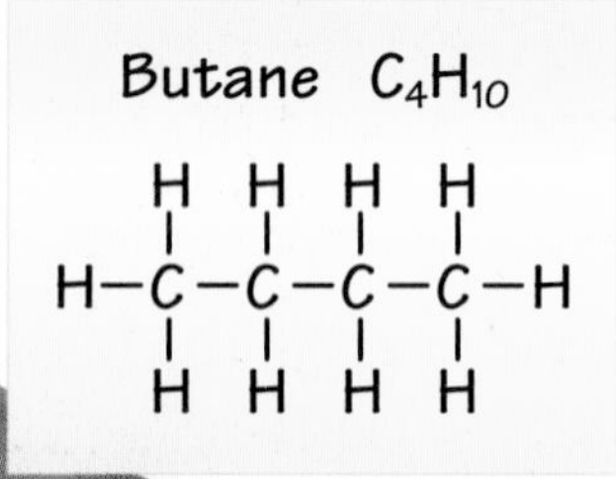

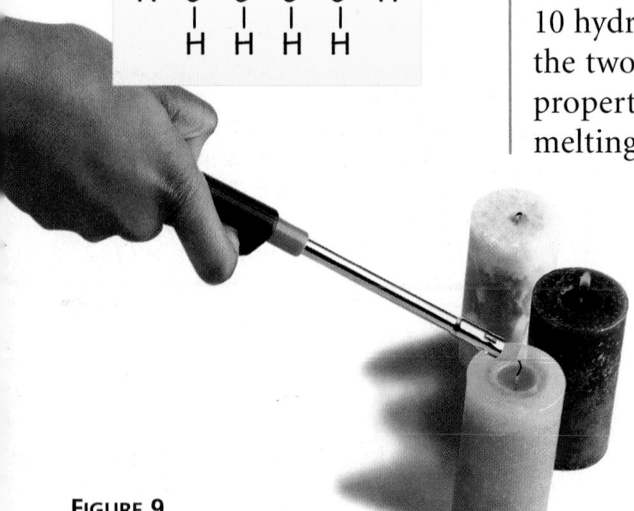

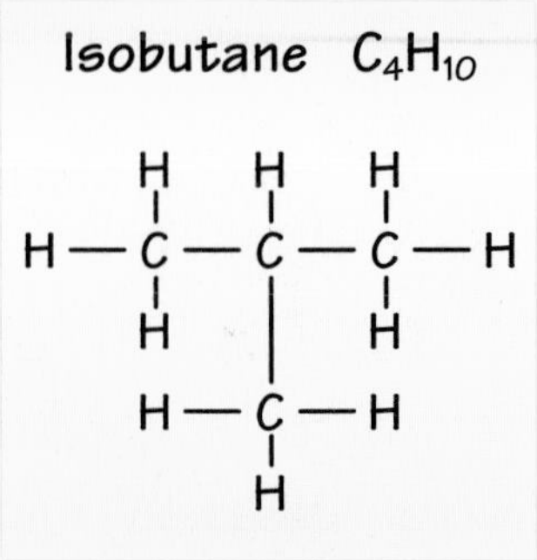

FIGURE 9
Isomers
C_4H_{10} has two isomers, butane and isobutane. **Applying Concepts** *Which isomer is a branched chain?*

Double Bonds and Triple Bonds So far in this section, structural formulas have shown only single bonds between any two carbon atoms (C−C). A single dash means a single bond. **In addition to forming a single bond, two carbon atoms can form a double bond or a triple bond.** A carbon atom can also form a single or double bond with an oxygen atom. Structural formulas represent a double bond with a double dash (C=C). A triple bond is indicated by a triple dash (C≡C).

Saturated and Unsaturated Hydrocarbons A hydrocarbon can be classified according to the types of bonds between its carbon atoms. If there are only single bonds, it has the maximum number of hydrogen atoms possible on its carbon chain. These hydrocarbons are called **saturated hydrocarbons.** You can think of each carbon atom as being "saturated," or filled up, with hydrogens. Hydrocarbons with double or triple bonds have fewer hydrogen atoms for each carbon atom than a saturated hydrocarbon does. They are called **unsaturated hydrocarbons.**

Notice that the names of methane, ethane, propane, and butane all end with the suffix *-ane*. In general, a chain hydrocarbon with a name ending in *-ane* is saturated, while a hydrocarbon with a name ending in *-ene* or *-yne* is unsaturated.

The simplest unsaturated hydrocarbon with one double bond is ethene (C_2H_4). Many fruits produce ethene gas. Ethene gas helps the fruit to ripen. The simplest hydrocarbon with one triple bond is ethyne (C_2H_2), which is commonly known as acetylene. Acetylene torches are used in welding.

Reading Checkpoint **What is the difference between saturated and unsaturated hydrocarbons?**

Lab zone Skills Activity

Classifying

Determine whether each of the following hydrocarbons contains single, double, or triple bonds. (*Hint*: Remember that carbon forms four bonds and hydrogen forms one bond.)

C_2H_6	C_3H_8
C_2H_4	C_3H_4
C_2H_2	C_4H_{10}

FIGURE 10
Unsaturated Hydrocarbons
Ethene gas (C_2H_4), which causes fruits such as apples to ripen, has one double bond. Acetylene (C_2H_2), the fuel in welding torches, has one triple bond.

Go Online
SCiLINKS™ NSTA

For: Links on carbon compounds
Visit: www.SciLinks.org
Web Code: scn-1242

Substituted Hydrocarbons

Hydrocarbons contain only carbon and hydrogen. But carbon can form stable bonds with several other elements, including oxygen, nitrogen, sulfur, and members of the halogen family. **If just one atom of another element is substituted for a hydrogen atom in a hydrocarbon, a different compound is created.** In a **substituted hydrocarbon,** atoms of other elements replace one or more hydrogen atoms in a hydrocarbon. Substituted hydrocarbons include halogen-containing compounds, alcohols, and organic acids.

Compounds Containing Halogens In some substituted hydrocarbons, one or more halogen atoms replace hydrogen atoms. Recall that the halogen family includes fluorine, chlorine, bromine, and iodine.

One compound, Freon (CCl_2F_2), was widely used as a cooling liquid in refrigerators and air conditioners. When Freon was found to damage the environment, its use was banned in the United States. However, a very hazardous compound that contains halogens, trichloroethane ($C_2H_3Cl_3$), is still used in dry-cleaning solutions. It can cause severe health problems.

Alcohols The group —OH can also substitute for hydrogen atoms in a hydrocarbon. Each —OH, made of an oxygen atom and a hydrogen atom, is called a **hydroxyl group** (hy DRAHKS il). An **alcohol** is a substituted hydrocarbon that contains one or more hydroxyl groups.

Most alcohols dissolve well in water. They also have higher boiling points than hydrocarbons with a similar number of carbons. Therefore, the alcohol methanol (CH_3OH) is a liquid at room temperature, while the hydrocarbon methane (CH_4) is a gas. Methanol, which is extremely toxic, is used to make plastics and synthetic fibers. It is also used in solutions that remove ice from airplanes.

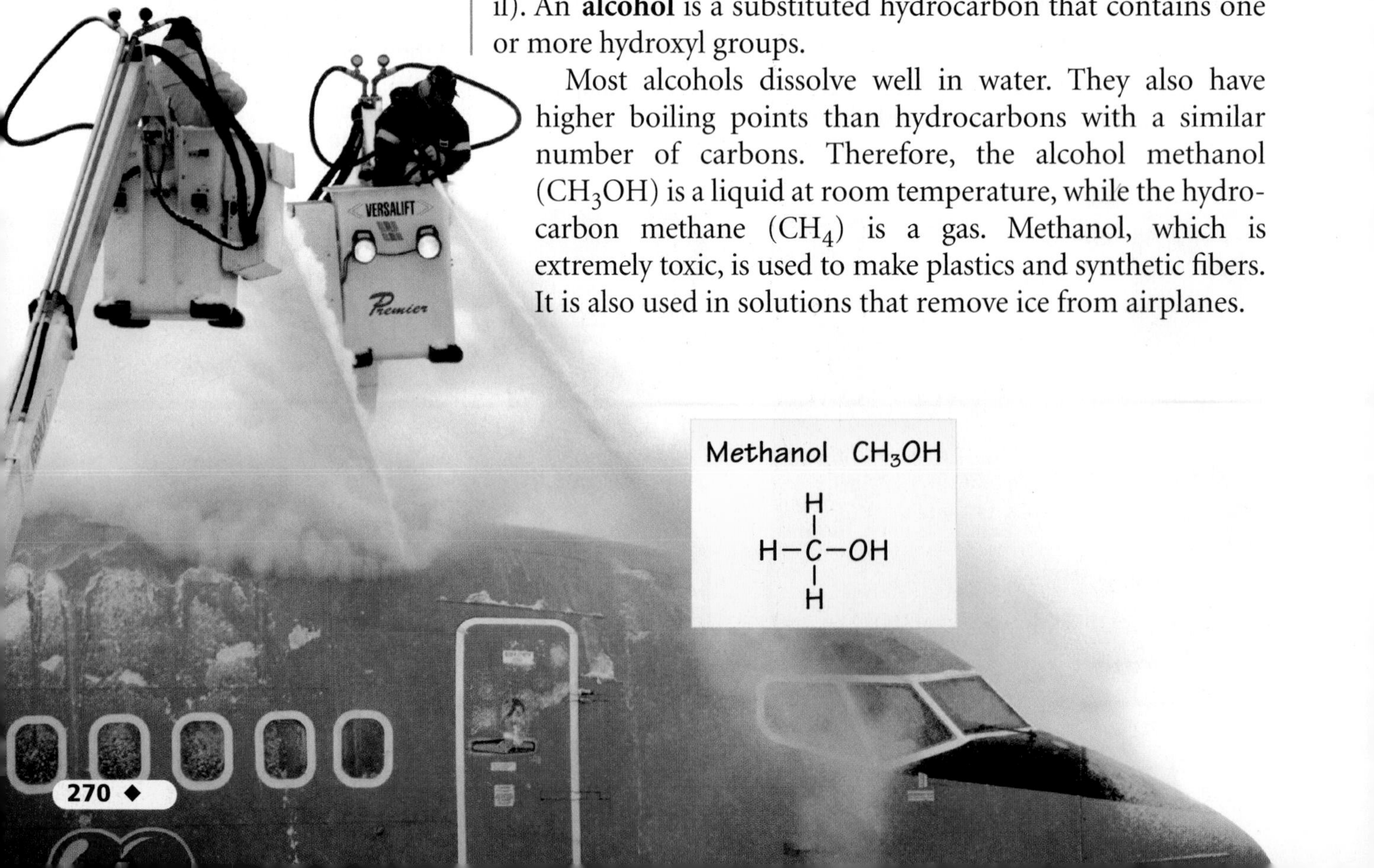

FIGURE 11
Alcohol
Methanol is used for de-icing an airplane in cold weather.
Classifying *What makes methanol a substituted hydrocarbon?*

Methanol CH_3OH

FIGURE 12
Organic Acid
Formic acid is the simplest organic acid. It is the acid produced by ants and is responsible for the pain caused by an ant bite.

When a hydroxyl group is substituted for one hydrogen atom in ethane, the resulting alcohol is ethanol (C_2H_5OH). Ethanol is produced naturally by the action of yeast or bacteria on the sugar stored in corn, wheat, and barley. Ethanol is a good solvent for many organic compounds that do not dissolve in water. It is also added to gasoline to make a fuel for car engines called "gasohol." Ethanol is used in medicines and is found in alcoholic beverages. The ethanol used for industrial purposes is unsafe to drink. Poisonous compounds such as methanol have been added. The resulting poisonous mixture is called denatured alcohol.

Organic Acids Lemons, oranges, and grapefruits taste a little tart or sour, don't they? The sour taste of many fruits comes from citric acid, an organic acid. An **organic acid** is a substituted hydrocarbon that contains one or more carboxyl groups. A **carboxyl group** (kahr BAHKS il) is written as —COOH.

You can find organic acids in many foods. Acetic acid (CH_3COOH) is the main ingredient of vinegar. Malic acid is found in apples. Butyric acid makes butter smell rancid when it goes bad. Stinging nettle plants make formic acid (HCOOH), a compound that causes the stinging feeling. The pain from ant bites also comes from formic acid.

Esters

If you have eaten wintergreen candy, then you are familiar with the smell of an ester. An **ester** is a compound made by chemically combining an alcohol and an organic acid. **Many esters have pleasant, fruity smells.** Esters are responsible for the smells of pineapples, bananas, strawberries, and apples. If you did the Discover activity, you smelled different esters. Other esters are ingredients in medications, including aspirin and the local anesthetic used by dentists.

FIGURE 13
Esters
Strawberries contain esters, which give them a pleasant aroma and flavor.

FIGURE 14
Monomers and Polymers
This chain of plastic beads is somewhat like a polymer molecule. The individual beads are like the monomers that link together to build a polymer.
Comparing and Contrasting *How do polymers differ from monomers?*

Polymers

A very large molecule made of a chain of many smaller molecules bonded together is called a **polymer** (PAHL ih mur). The smaller molecules are called **monomers** (MAHN uh murz). The prefix *poly-* means "many," and the prefix *mono-* means "one." **Organic compounds, such as alcohols, esters, and others, can be linked together to build polymers with thousands or even millions of atoms.**

Some polymers are made by living things. For example, sheep grow coats of wool. Cotton fibers come from the seed pods of cotton plants. And silkworms make silk. Other polymers, called synthetic polymers, are made in factories. If you are wearing clothing made from polyester or nylon, you are wearing a synthetic polymer. Any plastic item you use is most certainly made of synthetic polymers.

Reading Checkpoint **What is a monomer?**

Section 2 Assessment

Target Reading Skill Outlining Work with a partner to check the answers in your graphic organizer.

Reviewing Key Concepts

1. a. Listing List properties common to many organic compounds.
   b. Applying Concepts You are given two solid materials, one that is organic and one that is not organic. Describe three tests you could perform to help you decide which is which.
2. a. Identifying What are some properties of hydrocarbons?
   b. Comparing and Contrasting How are hydrocarbons similar? How are they different?
3. a. Reviewing What are three kinds of carbon chains found in hydrocarbons?
   b. Describing Compare the chemical and structural formulas of butane and isobutane.
   c. Problem Solving Draw a structural formula for a compound called butene. In terms of bonding, how does butene differ from butane?
4. a. Defining What is a substituted hydrocarbon?
   b. Classifying What kinds of substituted hydrocarbons react to form an ester?
   c. Drawing Conclusions What do you think the term *polyester fabric* refers to?

Lab zone At-Home Activity

Mix It Up You can make a simple salad dressing to demonstrate one property of organic compounds. In a transparent container, thoroughly mix equal amounts of a vegetable oil and a fruit juice. Stop mixing, and observe the oil and juice mixture for several minutes. Explain your observations to your family.

Lab zone **Skills Lab**

How Many Molecules?

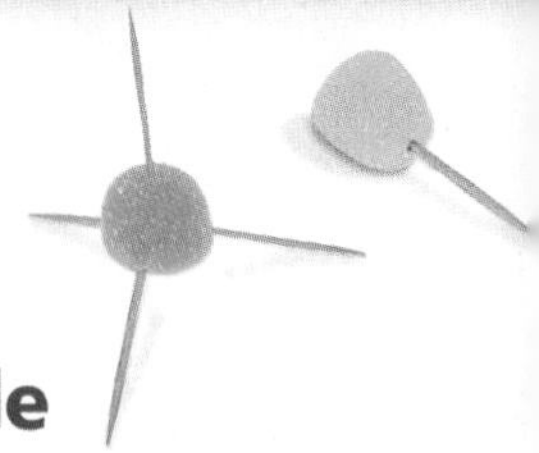

Problem

In this lab you will use gumdrops to represent atoms and toothpicks to represent bonds. How many different ways can you put the same number of carbon atoms together?

Skills Focus

making models

Materials

- toothpicks
- multicolored gumdrops
- other materials supplied by your teacher

Procedure

1. You will need gumdrops of one color to represent carbon atoms and gumdrops of another color to represent hydrogen atoms. When building your models, always follow these rules:
   - Each carbon atom forms four bonds.
   - Each hydrogen atom forms one bond.

   CAUTION: *Do not eat any of the food substances in this experiment.*
2. Make a model of CH_4 (methane).
3. Now make a model of C_2H_6 (ethane).
4. Make a model of C_3H_8 (propane). Is there more than one way to arrange the atoms in propane? (*Hint:* Are there any branches in the carbon chain or are all the carbon atoms in one line?)
5. Now make a model of C_4H_{10} (butane) in which all the carbon atoms are in one line.
6. Make a second model of butane with a branched chain.
7. Compare the branched-chain model with the straight-chain model of butane. Are there other ways to arrange the atoms?
8. Predict how many different structures can be formed from C_5H_{12} (pentane).
9. Test your prediction by building as many different models of pentane as you can.

Analyze and Conclude

1. **Making Models** Did any of your models have a hydrogen atom between two carbon atoms? Why or why not?
2. **Observing** How does a branched chain differ from a straight chain?
3. **Drawing Conclusions** How many different structures have the formula C_3H_8? C_4H_{10}? C_5H_{12}? Use diagrams to explain your answers.
4. **Predicting** If you bend a straight chain of carbons, do you make a different structure? Why or why not?
5. **Communicating** Compare the information you can get from models to the information you can get from formulas like C_6H_{14}. How does using models help you understand the structure of a molecule?

More to Explore

Use a third color of gumdrops to model an oxygen atom. An oxygen atom forms two bonds. Use the rules in this lab to model as many different structures for the formula $C_4H_{10}O$ as possible.

Section 3 • Tech & Design •

Polymers and Composites

Reading Preview

Key Concepts

- How do polymers form?
- What are composites made of?
- What benefits and problems relate to the use of synthetic polymers?

Key Terms

- protein
- amino acid
- plastic
- composite

Target Reading Skill

Asking Questions Before you read, preview the red headings. In a graphic organizer like the one below, ask a *how* or *why* question for each heading. As you read, write the answers to your questions.

Question	Answer
How do polymers form?	Polymers form when chemical bonds link . . .

Lab zone Discover Activity

What Did You Make?

1. Look at a sample of borax solution and write down the properties you observe. Do the same with white glue.
2. Put about 2 tablespoons of borax solution into a paper cup.
3. Stir the solution as you add about 1 tablespoon of white glue.
4. After 2 minutes, record the properties of the material in the cup. Wash your hands when you are finished.

Think It Over

Observing What evidence of a chemical reaction did you observe? How did the materials change? What do you think you made?

Delectable foods and many other interesting materials surround you every day. Have you ever wondered what makes up these foods and materials? You might be surprised to learn that many are partly or wholly polymers. Recall that a polymer is a large, complex molecule built from smaller molecules joined together in a repeating pattern.

The starches in pancakes and the proteins in meats and eggs are natural polymers. Many other polymers, however, are manufactured or synthetic. These synthetic polymers include plastics and polyester and nylon clothing. Whether synthetic or natural, most polymers rely on the element carbon for their fundamental structures.

FIGURE 15
Polymers
The clothing, boots, goggles, and helmet worn by this climber are all made of polymers.

Forming Polymers

Food materials, living things, and plastic have something in common. All are made of organic compounds. Organic compounds consist of molecules that contain carbon atoms bonded to each other and to other kinds of atoms. Carbon is present in several million known compounds, and more organic compounds are being discovered or invented every day.

Carbon's Chains and Rings Carbon's unique ability to form so many compounds comes from two properties. First, carbon atoms can form four covalent bonds. Second, as you have learned, carbon atoms can bond to each other in straight and branched chains and ring-shaped groups. These structures form the "backbones" to which other atoms attach.

Hydrogen is the most common element found in compounds with carbon. Other elements include oxygen, nitrogen, phosphorus, sulfur, and the halogens—especially chlorine.

Carbon Compounds and Polymers Molecules of some organic compounds can bond together, forming larger molecules, such as polymers. Recall that the smaller molecules from which polymers are built are called monomers. **Polymers form when chemical bonds link large numbers of monomers in a repeating pattern.** A polymer may consist of hundreds or even thousands of monomers.

Many polymers consist of a single kind of monomer that repeats over and over again. You could think of these monomers as linked like the identical cars of a long passenger train. In other cases, two or three monomers may join in an alternating pattern. Sometimes links between monomer chains occur, forming large webs or netlike molecules. The chemical properties of a polymer depend on the monomers from which it is made.

Reading Checkpoint What are the patterns in which monomers come together to form polymers?

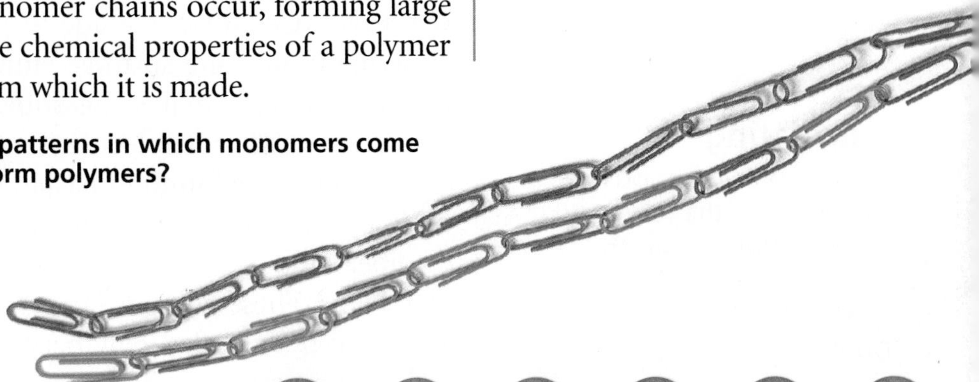

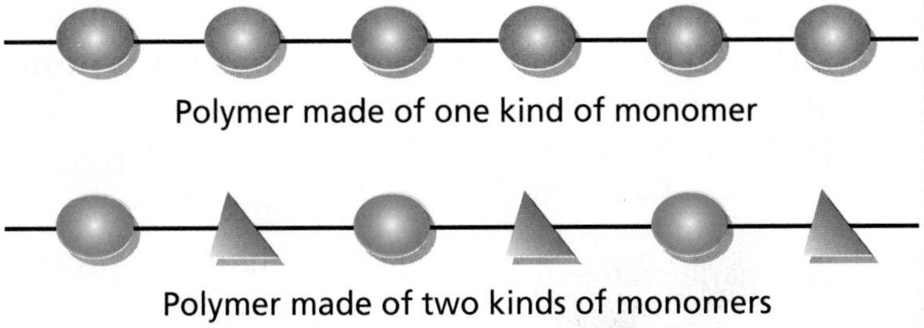

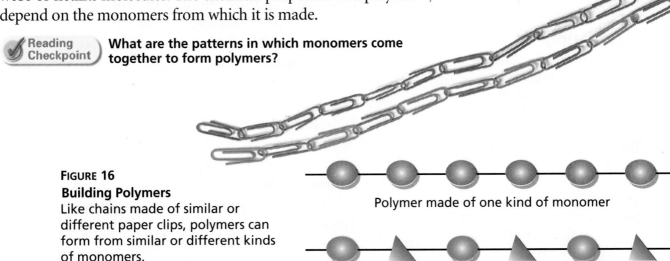

FIGURE 16
Building Polymers
Like chains made of similar or different paper clips, polymers can form from similar or different kinds of monomers.

FIGURE 17
Natural Polymers
Cellulose, the proteins in snake venom, and spider's silk are three examples of natural polymers.

▲ The cellulose in fruits and vegetables serves as dietary fiber that keeps the human digestive system healthy.

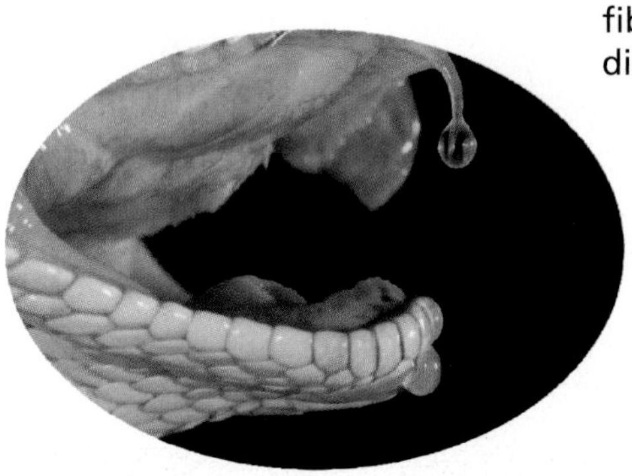

▲ Snake venom is a mixture containing approximately 90 percent proteins.

A spider's web is a silken polymer that is one of the strongest materials known. ▶

Polymers and Composites

Polymers have been around as long as life on Earth. Plants, animals, and other living things produce many natural materials made of large polymer molecules.

Natural Polymers Cellulose (SEL yoo lohs) is a flexible but strong natural polymer found in the cell walls of fruits and vegetables. Cellulose is made in plants when sugar molecules are joined into long strands. Humans cannot digest cellulose. But plants also make digestible polymers called starches, formed from sugar molecules that are connected in a different way. Starches are found in pastas, breads, and many vegetables.

You can wear polymers made by animals. Silk is made from the fibers of the cocoons spun by silkworms. Wool is made from sheep's fur. These polymers can be woven into thread and cloth. Your own body makes polymers, too. For example, your fingernails and muscles are made of polymers called proteins. Within your body, **proteins** are formed from smaller molecules called amino acids. An **amino acid** is a monomer that is a building block of proteins. The properties of a protein depend on which amino acids are used and in what order. One combination builds the protein that forms your fingernails. Yet another combination forms the protein that carries oxygen in your blood.

Lab zone Skills Activity

Calculating

Sit or stand where you have a clear view of the room you are in. Slowly sweep the room with your eyes, making a list of the objects you see. Do the same sweep of the clothes you are wearing. Check off those items on your list made (completely or partly) of natural or synthetic polymers. Calculate the percent of items that were *not* made with polymers.

Synthetic Polymers Many polymers you use every day are synthesized—or made—from simpler materials. The starting materials for many synthetic polymers come from coal or oil. **Plastics,** which are synthetic polymers that can be molded or shaped, are the most common products. But there are many others. Carpets, clothing, glue, and even chewing gum can be made of synthetic polymers.

Figure 18 lists just a few of the hundreds of polymers people use. Although the names seem like tongue twisters, see how many you recognize. You may be able to identify some polymers by their initials printed on the bottoms of plastic bottles.

Compare the uses of polymers shown in the figure with their characteristics. Notice that many products require materials that are flexible, yet strong. Others must be hard or lightweight. When chemical engineers develop a new product, they have to think about how it will be used. Then they synthesize a polymer with properties to match.

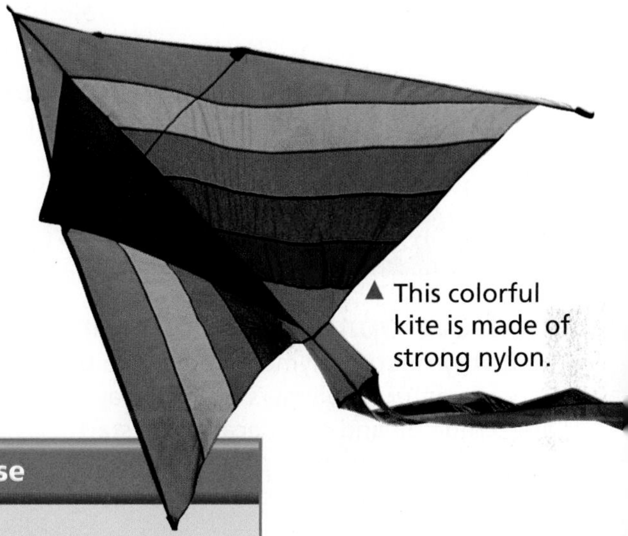

▲ This colorful kite is made of strong nylon.

Some Synthetic Polymers You Use

Name	Properties	Uses
Low-density polyethylene (LDPE)	Flexible, soft, melts easily	Plastic bags, squeeze bottles, electric wire insulation
High-density polyethylene (HDPE)	Stronger than LDPE; higher melting temperatures	Detergent bottles, gas cans, toys, milk jugs
Polypropylene (PP)	Hard, keeps its shape	Toys, car parts, bottle caps
Polyvinyl chloride (PVC)	Tough, flexible	Garden hoses, imitation leather, plumbing pipes
Polystyrene (PS)	Lightweight, can be made into foam	Foam drinking cups, insulation, furniture, "peanut" packing material
Nylon	Strong, can be drawn into flexible thread	Stockings, parachutes, fishing line, fabric
Teflon (polytetrafluoroethylene)	Nonreactive, low friction	Nonstick coating for cooking pans

FIGURE 18
The properties of synthetic polymers make them ideal starting materials for many common objects.
Applying Concepts *Which synthetic polymer would you use to make a cover for a picnic table?*

Comparing Polymers Synthetic polymers are often used in place of natural materials that are too expensive or wear out too quickly. Polyester and nylon fabrics, for example, are frequently used instead of wool, silk, and cotton to make clothes. Laminated countertops and vinyl floors replace wood in many kitchens. Other synthetic polymers have uses for which there is no suitable natural material. Compact discs, computer parts, artificial heart valves, and even bicycle tires couldn't exist without synthetic polymers.

Composites Every substance has its desirable and undesirable properties. What would happen if you could take the best properties of two substances and put them together? A **composite** combines two or more substances in a new material with different properties.

• Tech & Design in History •

The Development of Polymers

The first synthetic polymers were made by changing natural polymers in some way. Later, crude oil and coal became the starting materials. Now, new polymers are designed regularly in laboratories.

1839
Synthetic Rubber
Charles Goodyear invented a process that turned natural rubber into a hard, stretchable polymer. It did not get sticky and soft when heated or become brittle when cold, as natural rubber does. Bicycle tires were an early use.

1869
Celluloid
Made using cellulose, celluloid became a substitute for ivory in billiard balls and combs and brushes. It was later used to make movie film. Because celluloid is very flammable, other materials have replaced it for almost all purposes.

1909
Bakelite
Bakelite was the first commercial polymer made from compounds in coal tar. Bakelite doesn't get soft when heated, and it doesn't conduct electricity. These properties made it useful for handles of pots and pans, for telephones, and for parts in electrical outlets.

1800 1850 1900

By combining the useful properties of two or more substances in a composite, chemists can make a new material that works better than either one alone. **Many composite materials include one or more polymers.** The idea of putting two different materials together to get the advantages of both was inspired by the natural world. Many synthetic composites are designed to imitate a common natural composite—wood.

Wood is made of long fibers of cellulose, held together by another plant polymer called lignin. Cellulose fibers are flexible and can't support much weight. Lignin is brittle and would crack under the weight of the tree branches. But the combination of the two polymers makes a strong tree trunk.

Reading Checkpoint **Why is wood a composite?**

Writing in Science

Research and Write Find out more about the invention of one of these polymers. Write a newspaper headline announcing the invention. Then write the first paragraph of the news report telling how the invention will change people's lives.

1934
Nylon
A giant breakthrough came with a synthetic fiber that imitates silk. Nylon replaced expensive silk in women's stockings and fabric for parachutes and clothing. It can also be molded to make objects like buttons, gears, and zippers.

1971
Kevlar
Kevlar is five times stronger than steel. Kevlar is tough enough to substitute for steel ropes and cables in offshore oil rigs but light enough to use in spacecraft parts. It is also used in protective clothing for firefighters and police officers.

2002
Light-Emitting Polymers
Discovered accidentally in 1990, light-emitting polymers (LEPs) are used commercially in products such as MP3 audio players and electric shavers with display screens. LEPs give off light when exposed to low-voltage electricity. Newer, more colorful LEPs may be useful as flexible monitors for computers, TV screens, and watch-sized phones.

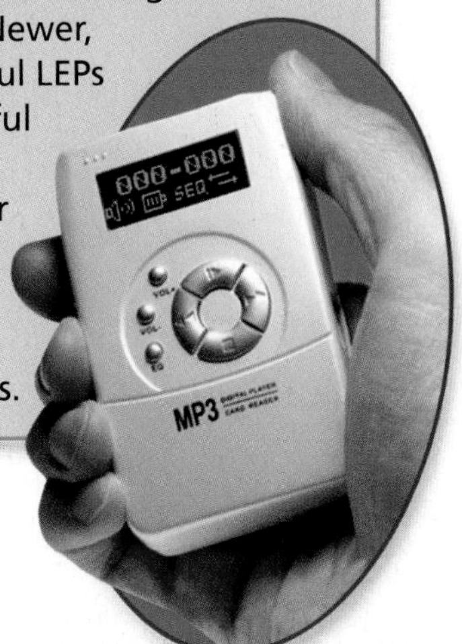

1950 2000 2050

FIGURE 19
Synthetic Composites
The composites in the fishing rod above make it flexible so that it will not break when reeling in a fish. Fiberglass makes the snowboard at right both lightweight and strong.

Uses of Composites The idea of combining the properties of two substances to make a more useful one has led to many new products. Fiberglass composites are one example. Strands of glass fiber are woven together and strengthened with a liquid plastic that sets like glue. The combination makes a strong, hard solid that can be molded around a form to give it shape. These composites are lightweight but strong enough to be used as a boat hull or car body. Also, fiberglass will not rust as metal does.

Many other useful composites are made from strong polymers combined with lightweight ones. Bicycles, automobiles, and airplanes built from such composites are much lighter than the same vehicles built from steel or aluminum. Some composites are used to make fishing rods, tennis rackets, and other sports equipment that needs to be flexible but strong.

Reading Checkpoint **What are two examples of composites?**

Too Many Polymers?

You can hardly look around without seeing something made of synthetic polymers. They have replaced many natural materials for several reasons. **Synthetic polymers are inexpensive to make, strong, and last a long time.**

But synthetic polymers have caused some problems, too. Many of the disadvantages of using plastics come from the same properties that make them so useful. **For example, it is often cheaper to throw plastics away and make new ones than it is to reuse them. As a result, plastics increase the volume of trash.**

Go Online
PHSchool.com

For: More on polymers
Visit: PHSchool.com
Web Code: cgd-1041

One of the reasons that plastics last so long is that most plastics don't react very easily with other substances. As a result, plastics don't break down—or degrade—into simpler materials in the environment. In contrast, natural polymers do. Some plastics are expected to last thousands of years. How do you get rid of something that lasts that long?

Is there a way to solve these problems? One solution is to use waste plastics as raw material for making new plastic products. You know this idea as recycling. Recycling has led to industries that create new products from discarded plastics. Bottles, fabrics for clothing, and parts for new cars are just some of the many items that can come from waste plastics. A pile of empty soda bottles can even be turned into synthetic wood. Look around your neighborhood. You may see park benches or "wooden" fences made from recycled plastics. Through recycling, the disposal problem is eased and new, useful items are created.

Reading Checkpoint **Why do plastic materials often increase the volume of trash?**

FIGURE 20
Recycling Plastics
Plastics can be recycled to make many useful products. This boardwalk, for example, is made of recycled plastics. Making Judgments *What advantages or disadvantages does this material have compared to wood?*

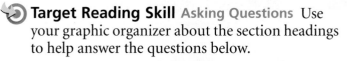

Section 3 Assessment

Target Reading Skill Asking Questions Use your graphic organizer about the section headings to help answer the questions below.

Reviewing Key Concepts

1. a. Defining What are polymers made of?
   b. Identifying What properties enable carbon atoms to form polymers and so many other compounds?
   c. Interpreting Diagrams How do the two kinds of polymers modeled in Figure 16 differ?
2. a. Reviewing Distinguish between natural polymers, synthetic polymers, and composites.
   b. Classifying Make a list of polymers you can find in your home. Classify them as natural or synthetic.
   c. Drawing Conclusions Why are composites often more useful than the individual materials from which they are made?
3. a. Listing List two benefits and two problems associated with the use of synthetic polymers.
   b. Making Judgments Think of something plastic that you have used today. Is there some other material that would be better than plastic for this use?

Writing in Science

Advertisement You are a chemist. You invent a polymer that can be a substitute for a natural material such as wood, cotton, or leather. Write an advertisement for your polymer, explaining why you think it is a good replacement for the natural material.

Technology and Society

• Tech & Design •

Polyester Fleece

Would you go hiking in the freezing Antarctic wearing a bunch of plastic beverage bottles? If you are like most serious hikers, you would. Polyester fleece is a lightweight, warm fabric made from plastic, including recycled soda bottles. The warmth of the fabric is due to its ability to trap and hold air. Polyester fleece is easy to wash and requires less energy to dry than wool or goose down.

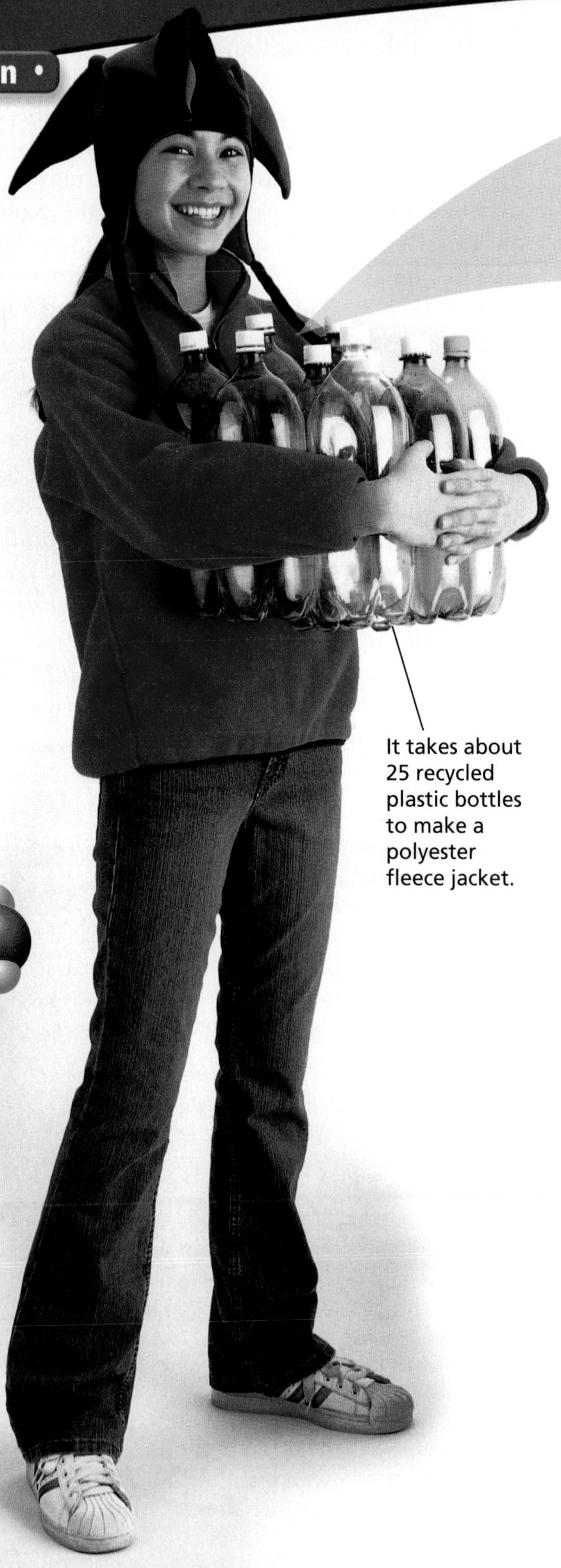

It takes about 25 recycled plastic bottles to make a polyester fleece jacket.

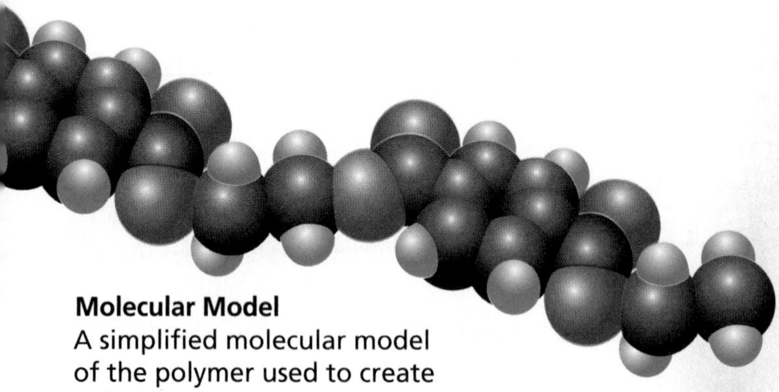

Molecular Model
A simplified molecular model of the polymer used to create polyester fleece is shown here. The molecules form long, straight chains.

Making Polyester Fleece

Polyethylene terephthalate, or PET, is the polymer that is used to make polyester fleece. The first step in the process is creating the polyester fiber or thread. It can be made from raw materials or recycled PET plastic. The thread is then knit into fabric, which can be dyed or printed. It is then dried and "napped." In the napping process, the fibers are first raised and then clipped to an even height. This process increases the amount of air the fabric can hold, which helps keep you warm in cold weather.

Properties of Polyester Fleece

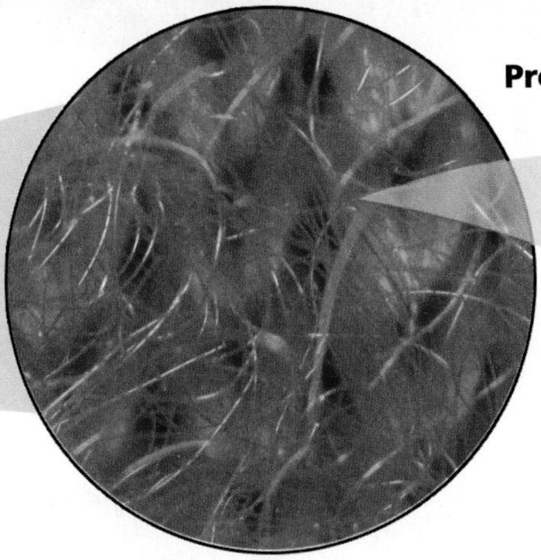

▲ **Fleece Fabric**
Similar to yarn in a sweater, fleece fibers are knit together to create a stretchy, dense fabric that is soft, lightweight, and durable.

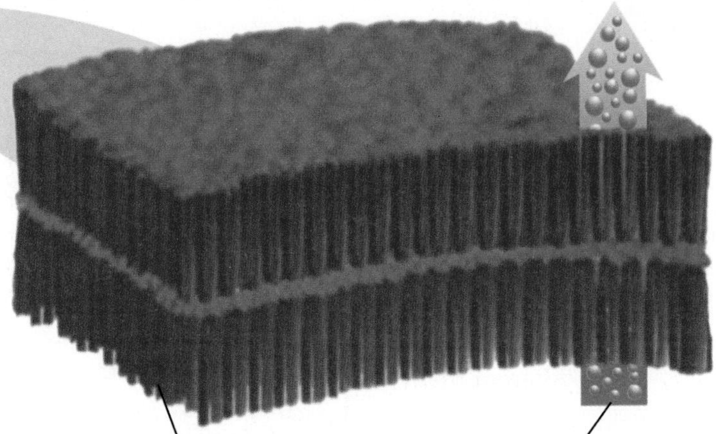
Air pockets between fibers trap body heat.
Moisture from the body passes through the fabric.

Polyester Fleece and the Environment

Making polyester fleece fabric uses water and energy, like other fabric-making processes. Using recycled materials to create polyester fleece saves energy and reduces wastes. One trade-off involves the safety of workers in the fleece factories. The clipping process creates dust particles in the air that workers then breathe. Some companies that produce fleece are developing technology that should reduce dust in the workplace, as well as technologies that conserve and reuse energy and water.

1

Plastic Bottle Granules
PET plastic bottles are chipped to create granules like those shown here. The granules can be used in making polyester fleece.▼

Weigh the Impact

1. **Identify the Need**
   What are some benefits of using polyester fleece to make clothing and blankets?
2. **Research**
   Use the Internet to find companies that make or sell polyester fleece made from recycled plastic. Identify ways in which this form of recycling helps the environment.
3. **Write**
   Create a pamphlet to encourage your classmates to recycle plastics. Describe how PET plastic can be used to create polyester fleece.

Go Online PHSchool.com
For: More on polyester fleece
Visit: PHSchool.com
Web Code: cgh-1040

Life With Carbon

Reading Preview

Key Concepts

- What are the four main classes of organic compounds in living things?
- How are the organic compounds in living things different from one another?

Key Terms

- carbohydrate • glucose
- complex carbohydrate
- starch • cellulose • lipid
- fatty acid • cholesterol
- nucleic acid • DNA • RNA
- nucleotide

Target Reading Skill

Asking Questions Before you read, preview the red headings. In a graphic organizer like the one below, ask a *what* question for each heading. As you read, write the answers to your questions.

Life With Carbon

Question	Answer
What is a carbohydrate?	A carbohydrate is . . .

Lab zone Discover Activity

What Is in Milk?

1. Pour 30 mL of milk into a plastic cup.
2. Pour another 30 mL of milk into a second plastic cup. Rinse the graduated cylinder. Measure 15 mL of vinegar and add it to the second cup. Swirl the two liquids together and let the mixture sit for a minute.
3. Set up two funnels with filter paper, each supported in a narrow plastic cup.
4. Filter the milk through the first funnel. Filter the milk and vinegar through the second funnel.
5. What is left in each filter paper? Examine the liquid that passed through each filter paper.

Think It Over

Observing Where did you see evidence of solids? What do you think was the source of these solids?

Have you ever been told to eat all the organic compounds on your plate? Have you heard how eating a variety of polymers and monomers contributes to good health? What? No one has ever said those things to you? Well, maybe what you really heard was something about eating all the vegetables on your plate, or eating a variety of foods to give you a healthy balance of carbohydrates, proteins, fats, and other nutrients. All these nutrients are organic compounds, which are the building blocks of all living things.

A bowl of soup contains a variety of nutrients. ▼

Foods provide organic compounds, which the cells of living things use, change, or store. **The four classes of organic compounds required by living things are carbohydrates, proteins, lipids, and nucleic acids.** Carbohydrates, proteins, and lipids are nutrients. Nutrients (NOO tree unts) are substances that provide the energy and raw materials the body needs to grow, repair worn parts, and function properly.

Carbohydrates

A **carbohydrate** (kahr boh HY drayt) is an energy-rich organic compound made of the elements carbon, hydrogen, and oxygen. The word *carbohydrate* is made of two parts: *carbo-* and *-hydrate*. *Carbo-* means "carbon" and *-hydrate* means "combined with water." If you remember that water is made up of the elements hydrogen and oxygen, then you should be able to remember the three elements in carbohydrates.

Simple Carbohydrates The simplest carbohydrates are sugars. You may be surprised to learn that there are many different kinds of sugars. The sugar listed in baking recipes, which you can buy in bags or boxes at the grocery store, is only one kind. Other sugars are found naturally in fruits, milk, and some vegetables.

One of the most important sugars in your body is the monomer **glucose.** Its chemical formula is $C_6H_{12}O_6$. Glucose is sometimes called "blood sugar" because the body circulates glucose to all body parts through blood. The structural formula for a glucose molecule is shown in Figure 21.

The white sugar that sweetens cookies, candies, and many soft drinks is called sucrose. Sucrose is a more complex molecule than glucose and has a chemical formula of $C_{12}H_{22}O_{11}$.

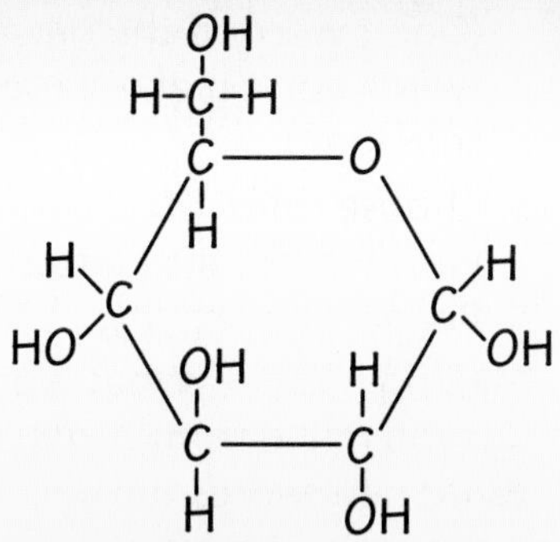

Glucose $C_6H_{12}O_6$

FIGURE 21
Carbohydrates
The honey made by honeybees contains glucose, a simple carbohydrate. **Applying Concepts** *What are some other examples of foods that contain carbohydrates?*

Lab zone Try This **Activity**

Alphabet Soup

Here's how you can model the rearrangement of amino acids in your body.

1. Rearrange the letters of the word *proteins* to make a new word or words. (Don't worry if the new words don't make sense together.)
2. Choose three other words with ten or more letters. Repeat the activity.

Making Models What words did you make from *proteins*? What new words did you make from the words you chose? How does this activity model the way your body uses proteins in food to make new proteins?

Complex Carbohydrates When you eat plants or food products made from plants, you are often eating complex carbohydrates. Each molecule of a simple carbohydrate, or sugar, is relatively small compared to a molecule of a complex carbohydrate. A **complex carbohydrate** is a polymer made of smaller molecules that are simple carbohydrates bonded to one another. As a result, just one molecule of a complex carbohydrate may have hundreds of carbon atoms.

Two of the complex carbohydrates assembled from glucose molecules are starch and cellulose. **Starch and cellulose are both polymers built from glucose, but the glucose molecules are arranged differently in each case.** Having different arrangements means that starch and cellulose are different compounds. They serve different functions in the plants that make them. Your body also uses starch very differently from the way it uses cellulose.

Starch Plants store energy in the form of the complex carbohydrate **starch.** You can find starches in food products such as bread, cereal, pasta, rice, and potatoes.

The process of breaking large molecules, such as starch, into smaller ones involves chemical reactions that occur during digestion. The body digests the large starch molecules from these foods into individual glucose molecules. The body then breaks apart the glucose molecules, releasing energy in the process. This energy allows the body to carry out its life functions.

Cellulose Plants build strong stems and roots with the complex carbohydrate **cellulose** and other polymers. Most fruits and vegetables are high in cellulose. So are foods made from whole grains. Even though the body can break down starch, it cannot break down cellulose into individual glucose molecules. Therefore the body cannot use cellulose as an energy source. In fact, when you eat foods with cellulose, the molecules pass through you undigested. However, this undigested cellulose helps keep your digestive tract active and healthy. Cellulose is sometimes called fiber.

Reading Checkpoint What foods are high in cellulose?

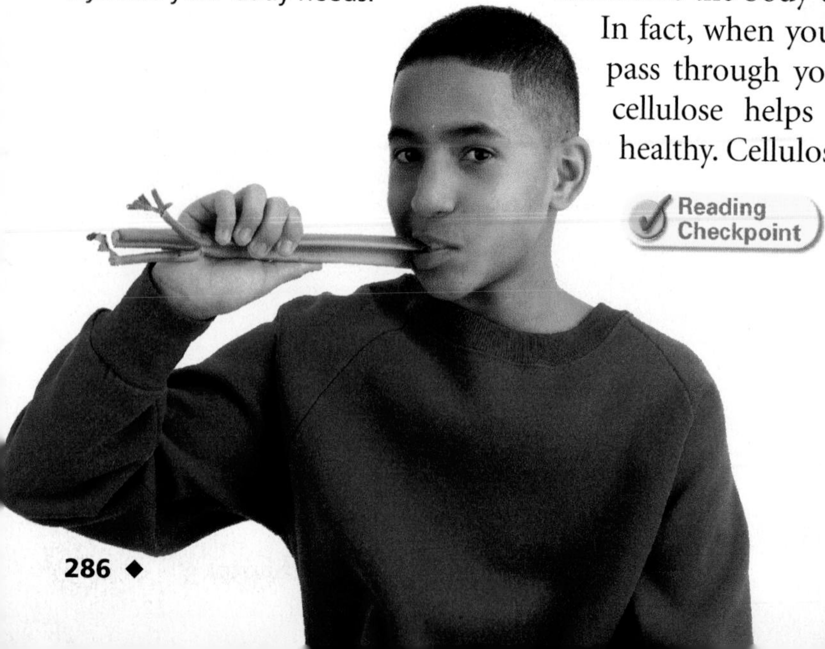

FIGURE 22
Cellulose
Cellulose, found in celery and other vegetables, is a carbohydrate your body needs.

Proteins

If the proteins in your body suddenly disappeared, you would not have much of a body left! Your muscles, hair, skin, and fingernails are all made of proteins. A bird's feathers, a spider's web, a fish's scales, and the horns of a rhinoceros are also made of proteins.

Chains of Amino Acids As you have learned, proteins are polymers formed from combinations of monomers called amino acids. There are 20 kinds of amino acids found in living things. **Different proteins are made when different sequences of amino acids are linked into long chains.** Since proteins can be made of combinations of amino acids in any order and number, a huge variety of proteins is possible.

The structure of an amino acid is shown in Figure 23. Each amino acid molecule has a carboxyl group (—COOH). The *acid* in the term *amino acid* comes from this part of the molecule. An amino group, with the structure $—NH_2$, is the source of the *amino* half of the name. The remaining part of the molecule differs for each kind of amino acid.

Food Proteins Become Your Proteins Some of the best sources of protein include meat, fish, eggs, and milk or milk products. If you did the Discover activity, you used vinegar to separate proteins from milk. Some plant products, such as beans, are good sources of protein as well.

The body uses proteins from food to build and repair body parts and to regulate cell activities. But first the proteins must be digested. Just as starch is broken down into glucose molecules, proteins are broken down into amino acids. Then the body reassembles those amino acids into thousands of different proteins that can be used by cells.

Reading Checkpoint **What are good sources of dietary protein?**

FIGURE 23
Amino Acids
Alanine and serine are two of the 20 amino acids in living things. Each amino acid has a carboxyl group (—COOH) and an amino group ($—NH_2$).

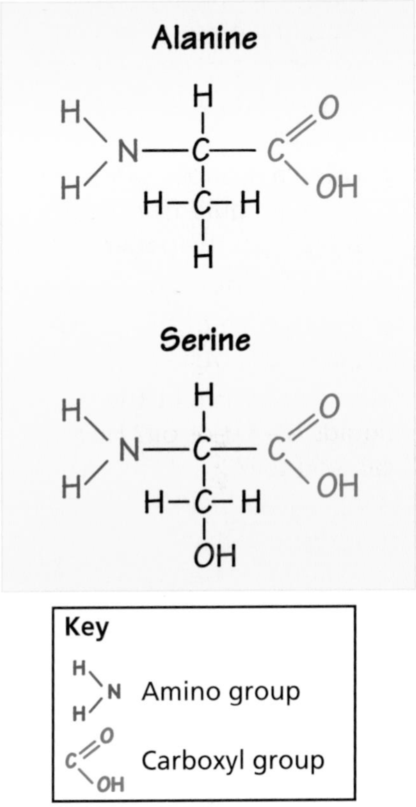

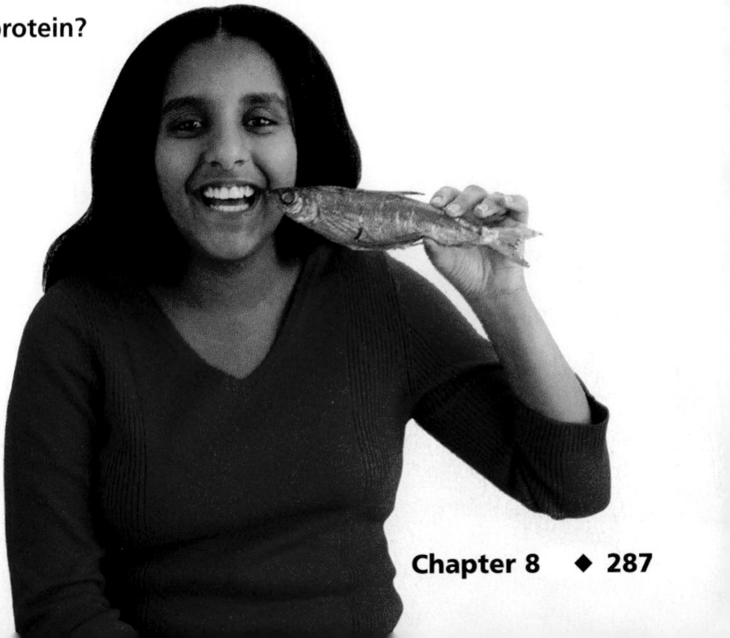

FIGURE 24
Proteins
Your body needs proteins, which are available in fish and meat. **Drawing Conclusions** *How are amino acids related to proteins?*

Lab zone **Try This Activity**

Like Oil or Water?

Oils mix poorly with water. They also do not evaporate very quickly when exposed to air.

1. Obtain a piece of brown paper and some samples of liquids provided by your teacher.
2. Using a dropper, place one drop of liquid from each sample on the paper.
3. Wait 5 minutes.
4. Note which of the liquids leaves a spot.

Inferring Which of the liquids is a fat or oil? How can you tell?

Lipids

The third class of organic compounds in living things is lipids. Like carbohydrates, **lipids** are energy-rich compounds made of carbon, oxygen, and hydrogen. Lipids include fats, oils, waxes, and cholesterol. **Gram for gram, lipids release twice as much energy in your body as do carbohydrates.** Like hydrocarbons, lipids mix poorly with water.

Fats and Oils Have you ever gotten grease on your clothes from foods that contain fats or oils? Fats are found in foods such as meat, butter, and cheese. Oils are found in foods such as corn, sunflower seeds, peanuts, and olives.

Fats and oils have the same basic structure. Each fat or oil is made from three **fatty acids** and one alcohol named glycerol. There is one main difference between fats and oils, however. Fats are usually solid at room temperature, whereas oils are liquid. The temperature at which a fat or an oil becomes a liquid depends on the chemical structure of its fatty acid molecules.

You may hear fats and oils described as "saturated" or "unsaturated." Like saturated hydrocarbons, the fatty acids of saturated fats have no double bonds between carbon atoms. Unsaturated fatty acids are found in oils. Monounsaturated oils have fatty acids with one double bond. Polyunsaturated oils have fatty acids with many double bonds. Saturated fats tend to have higher melting points than unsaturated oils have.

Cholesterol Another important lipid is **cholesterol** (kuh LES tuh rawl), a waxy substance found in all animal cells. The body needs cholesterol to build cell structures and to form compounds that serve as chemical messengers. Unlike other lipids, cholesterol is not a source of energy. The body produces the cholesterol it needs from other nutrients. Foods that come from animals—cheese, eggs, and meat—also provide cholesterol. Plants do not produce cholesterol.

Although cholesterol is often found in the same foods as saturated fats, they are different compounds. An excess level of cholesterol in the blood can contribute to heart disease. So can saturated fats. And saturated fats can affect the level of cholesterol in the blood. For this reason it is wise to limit your intake of both nutrients.

Reading Checkpoint **What are sources of cholesterol in the diet?**

FIGURE 25
Fats and Oils
Foods that contain fats and oils include peanut butter, butter, cheese, corn, and olives.

FIGURE 26
The Molecules of Life
Complex carbohydrates, proteins, lipids, and nucleic acids are all large organic molecules. They are built of smaller molecules linked in different patterns. **Applying Concepts** *What are the building blocks of proteins?*

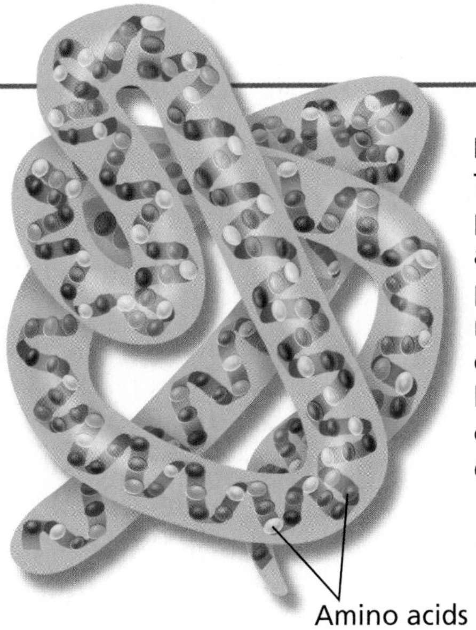

Proteins
The building blocks of proteins are amino acids. Although protein chains are never branched, each chain can twist and bend, forming complex three-dimensional shapes.

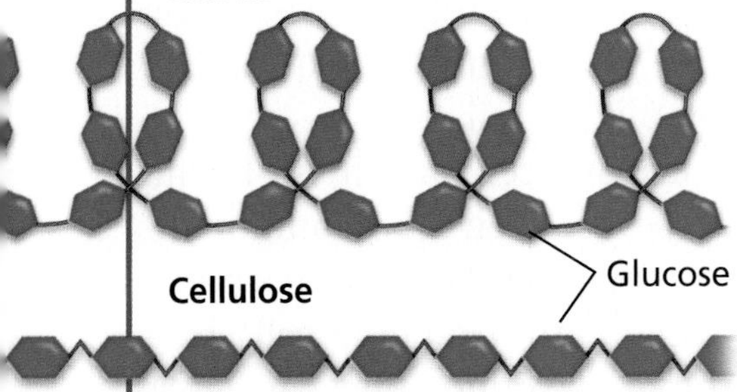

Complex Carbohydrates
Complex carbohydrates are polymers of simple carbohydrates. Starch and cellulose, both made of glucose, differ in how their molecules are arranged.

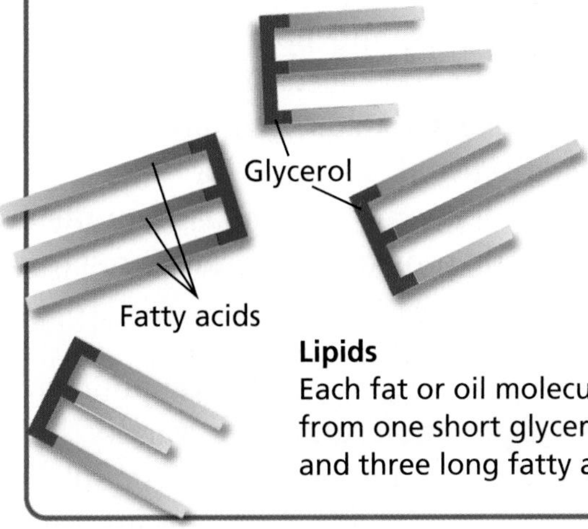

Lipids
Each fat or oil molecule is made from one short glycerol molecule and three long fatty acids.

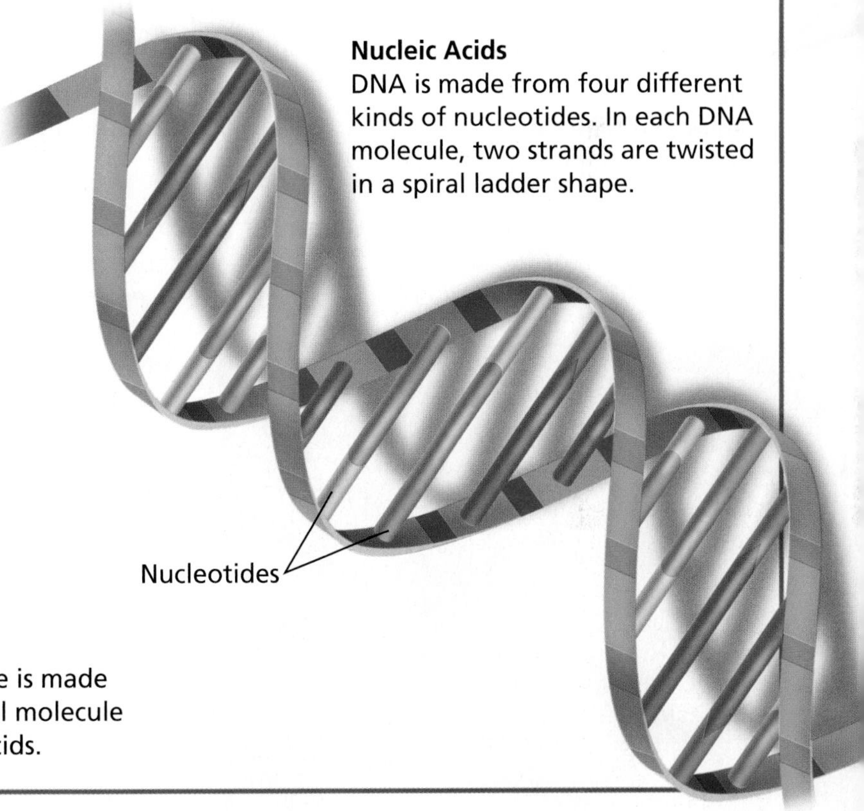

Nucleic Acids
DNA is made from four different kinds of nucleotides. In each DNA molecule, two strands are twisted in a spiral ladder shape.

Nucleic Acids

The fourth class of organic compounds in living things is nucleic acids. **Nucleic acids** (noo KLEE ik) are very large organic molecules made up of carbon, oxygen, hydrogen, nitrogen, and phosphorus. You have probably heard of one type of nucleic acid—**DNA,** deoxyribonucleic acid (dee ahk see ry boh noo KLEE ik). The other type of nucleic acid, ribonucleic acid (ry boh noo KLEE ik), is called **RNA.**

Discovery Channel School

Carbon Chemistry

Video Preview
▶ Video Field Trip
Video Assessment

Nucleotides DNA and RNA are made of different kinds of small molecules connected in a pattern. The building blocks of nucleic acids are called **nucleotides** (NOO klee oh tydz). In even the simplest living things, the DNA contains billions of nucleotides! There are only four kinds of nucleotides in DNA. RNA is also built of only four kinds of nucleotides, but the nucleotides in RNA differ from those in DNA.

DNA and Proteins **The differences among living things depend on the order of nucleotides in their DNA.** The order of DNA nucleotides determines a related order in RNA. The order of RNA nucleotides, in turn, determines the sequence of amino acids in proteins made by a living cell.

Remember that proteins regulate cell activities. Living things differ from one another because their DNA, and therefore their proteins, differ from one another. The cells in a hummingbird grow and function differently from the cells in a flower or in you. When living things reproduce, they pass DNA and the information it carries to the next generation.

Reading Checkpoint **What are the building blocks of nucleic acids?**

FIGURE 27
Vitamins and Minerals
Sources of vitamins and minerals include fruits, vegetables, nuts, meats, and dairy products.
Observing *Which of these foods can you identify in the painting?*

Other Compounds in Foods

Carbohydrates, proteins, and lipids are not the only compounds your body needs. Your body also needs vitamins, minerals, water, and salts. **Unlike the nutrients discussed so far, vitamins and minerals are needed only in small amounts.** They do not directly provide you with energy or raw materials.

Vitamins Vitamins are organic compounds that serve as helper molecules in a variety of chemical reactions in your body. For example, vitamin C, or ascorbic acid, is important for keeping your skin and gums healthy. Vitamin D helps your bones and teeth develop and keeps them strong.

Minerals Minerals are elements in the form of ions needed by your body. Unlike the other nutrients discussed in this chapter, minerals are not organic compounds. Minerals include calcium, iron, iodine, sodium, and potassium. They are important in many body processes.

If you eat a variety of foods, you will probably get the vitamins and minerals you need. Food manufacturers add some vitamins and minerals to packaged foods to replace vitamins and minerals that are lost in food processing. Such foods say "enriched" on their labels.

Sometimes manufacturers add extra vitamins and minerals to foods to "fortify," or strengthen, the nutritional value of the food. For example, milk is usually fortified with vitamin A and vitamin D.

Water Although water, H_2O, is not an organic compound, it is a compound that your body needs to survive. In fact, you would be able to survive only a few days without fresh water. Water makes up most of your body's fluids, including about 90 percent of the liquid part of your blood.

Nutrients and other important substances are dissolved in the watery part of the blood and carried throughout the body. Many chemical reactions, such as the breakdown of nutrients, take place in water. Wastes from cells dissolve in the blood and are carried away.

Reading Checkpoint What is a vitamin?

Go Online NSTA SCiLINKS

For: Links on organic compounds
Visit: www.SciLinks.org
Web Code: scn-1243

Section 4 Assessment

Target Reading Skill **Asking Questions** Review your graphic organizer and revise it based on what you just learned in the section.

Reviewing Key Concepts

1. a. **Naming** What are the four main classes of organic compounds required by living things?
   b. **Classifying** To what class of organic compounds does each of the following belong: glucose, RNA, cholesterol, cellulose, and oil?
   c. **Making Generalizations** How is each class of organic compounds used by the body?
2. a. **Identifying** What are the building blocks of complex carbohydrates?
   b. **Comparing and Contrasting** Compare the building blocks found in complex carbohydrates with those found in proteins.
   c. **Making Judgments** Would it matter if you ate foods that provided only carbohydrates but not proteins? Explain your reasoning.

Writing in Science

Advertisement Collect several food advertisements from magazines and watch some TV commercials. What do the ads say about nutrients? What do they emphasize? What do they downplay? Choose one ad and rewrite it to reflect the nutritional value of the product.

Lab zone **Consumer Lab**

Are You Getting Your Vitamins?

Problem

Fruit juices contain vitamin C, an important nutrient. Which juice should you drink to obtain the most vitamin C?

Skills Focus

controlling variables, interpreting data, inferring

Materials

- 6 small cups
- 6 plastic droppers
- starch solution
- iodine solution
- vitamin C solution
- samples of beverages (orange juice, apple juice, sports drink, fruit-flavored drink)

Procedure

PART 1 Vitamin C Test

1. Using a plastic dropper, place 25 drops of tap water into one of the small cups. Add 2 drops of starch solution.
2. Add 1 drop of iodine solution to the cup. **CAUTION:** *Iodine solution can stain skin or clothing.* Observe the color of the mixture. Save this cup to use for comparison in Step 4.
3. Using a fresh dropper, place 25 drops of vitamin C solution into another cup. Add 2 drops of starch solution.
4. Add 1 drop of iodine solution to the cup and swirl. Continue adding iodine a drop at a time, swirling after each drop, until you get a dark blue color similar to the color obtained in Step 2. Record the number of iodine drops.
5. Save the cup from Step 4 and use it for comparison during Part 2.

PART 2 Comparison Test

6. Make a data table in your notebook similar to the one on the next page.
7. Which beverage sample do you think has the most vitamin C? Which do you think has the least? Rank your beverage samples according to your predictions.

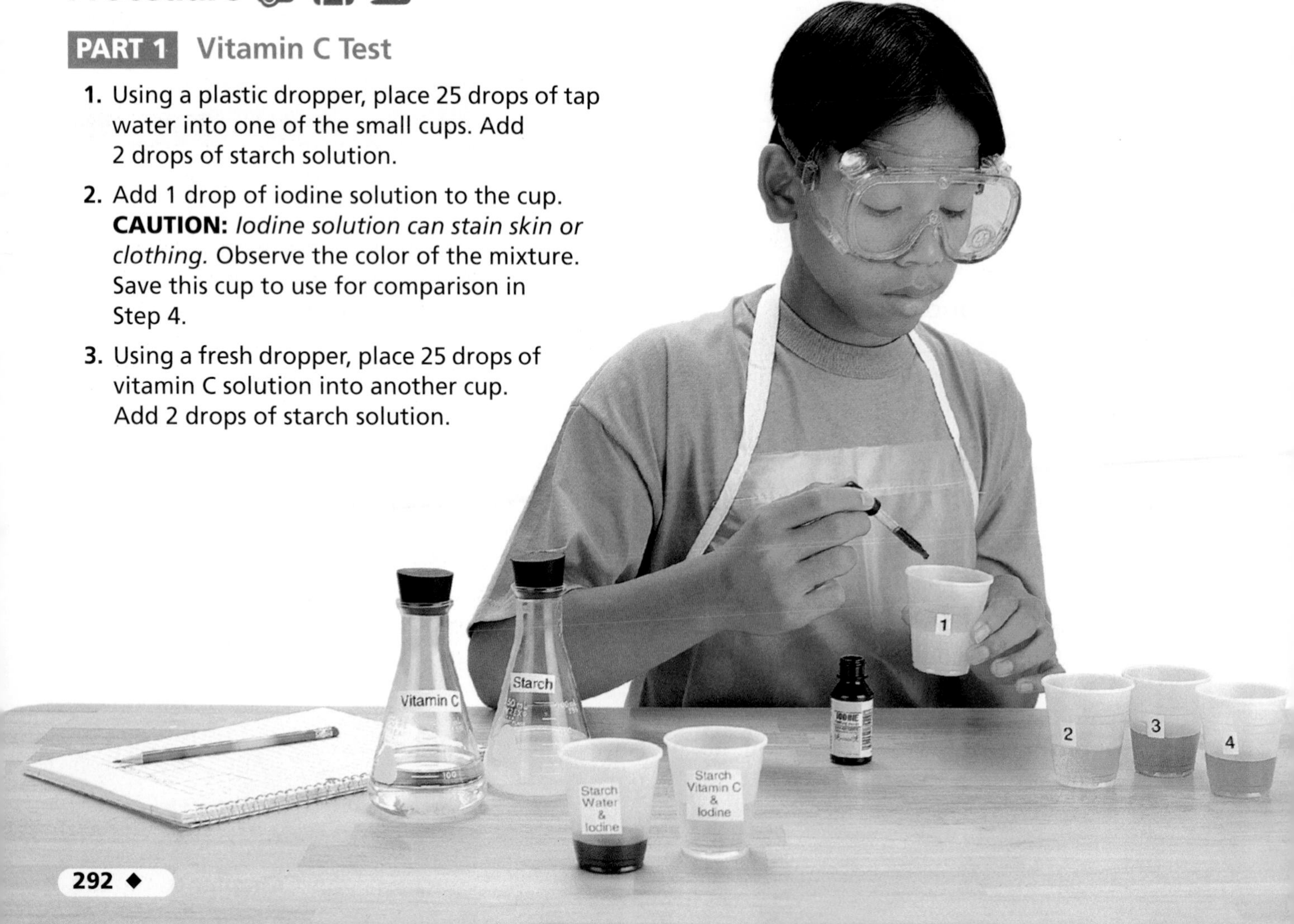

Data Table			
Test Sample	Drops of Iodine	Predicted Rank	Actual Rank
Vitamin C			
Orange juice			
Apple juice			
Sports drink			
Fruit-flavored drink			

8. Adapt the procedure from Part 1 so you can compare the amount of vitamin C in your beverage samples to the vitamin C solution.
9. Carry out your procedure after your teacher approves.

Analyze and Conclude

1. **Controlling Variables** What was the purpose for the test of the mixture of starch and water in Step 2?
2. **Controlling Variables** What was the purpose for the test of the starch, water, and vitamin C in Step 4?
3. **Drawing Conclusions** What do you think caused differences between your data from Step 2 and Step 4?
4. **Controlling Variables** Why did you have to add the same amount of starch to each of the beverages?
5. **Predicting** What would happen if someone forgot to add the starch to the beverage before they began adding iodine?
6. **Measuring** Of the four drinks you tested, which took the most drops of iodine before changing color? Which took the fewest?
7. **Interpreting Data** Which beverage had the most vitamin C? Which had the least? How do you know?
8. **Inferring** When you tested orange juice, the color of the first few drops of the iodine faded away. What do you think happened to the iodine?
9. **Communicating** If a beverage scored low in your test for vitamin C, does that mean it isn't good for you? Write a paragraph in which you explain what other factors might make a beverage nutritious or take away from its nutrient value.

Design an Experiment

Foods are often labeled with expiration dates. Labels often also say to "refrigerate after opening." Design an experiment to find out if the vitamin C content of orange juice changes over time at different temperatures. *Obtain your teacher's permission before carrying out your investigation.*

Chapter 8 Study Guide

1 Properties of Carbon

Key Concepts

- Few elements have the ability of carbon to bond with both itself and other elements in so many different ways. With four valence electrons, each carbon atom is able to form four bonds.
- Diamond, graphite, fullerenes, and nanotubes are four forms of the element carbon.

Key Terms

diamond
graphite
fullerene
nanotube

2 Carbon Compounds

Key Concepts

- Many organic compounds have similar properties in terms of melting points, boiling points, odor, electrical conductivity, and solubility.
- Hydrocarbons mix poorly with water. Also, all hydrocarbons are flammable.
- The carbon chains in a hydrocarbon may be straight, branched, or ring-shaped. In addition to forming a single bond, two carbon atoms can form a double bond or a triple bond.
- If just one atom of another element is substituted for a hydrogen atom in a hydrocarbon, a different compound is created.
- Many esters have pleasant, fruity smells.
- Organic compounds, such as alcohols, esters, and others, can be linked together to build polymers with thousands or even millions of atoms.

Key Terms

organic compound
hydrocarbon
structural formula
isomer
saturated hydrocarbon
unsaturated hydrocarbon
substituted hydrocarbon
hydroxyl group
alcohol
organic acid
carboxyl group
ester
polymer
monomer

3 Polymers and Composites

Key Concepts

- Polymers form when chemical bonds link large numbers of monomers in a repeating pattern.
- Many composite materials include one or more polymers.
- Synthetic polymers are inexpensive to make, strong, and last a long time.
- It is often cheaper to throw plastics away and make new ones than it is to reuse them. As a result, plastics increase the volume of trash.

Key Terms

protein
amino acid
plastic
composite

4 Life With Carbon

Key Concepts

- The four classes of organic compounds required by living things are carbohydrates, proteins, lipids, and nucleic acids.
- Starch and cellulose are both polymers built from glucose, but the glucose molecules are arranged differently in each case.
- Different proteins are made when different sequences of amino acids are linked into long chains.
- Gram for gram, lipids release twice as much energy in your body as do carbohydrates.
- The differences among living things depend on the order of nucleotides in their DNA.
- Vitamins and minerals are needed only in small amounts.

Key Terms

carbohydrate
glucose
complex carbohydrate
starch
cellulose
lipid
fatty acid
cholesterol
nucleic acid
DNA
RNA
nucleotide

Review and Assessment

Go Online PHSchool.com
For: Self-Assessment
Visit: PHSchool.com
Web Code: cka-1080

Organizing Information

Comparing and Contrasting Copy the Venn Diagram comparing proteins and nucleic acids onto a separate sheet of paper. Then complete it and add a title. (For more on Comparing and Contrasting, see the Skills Handbook.)

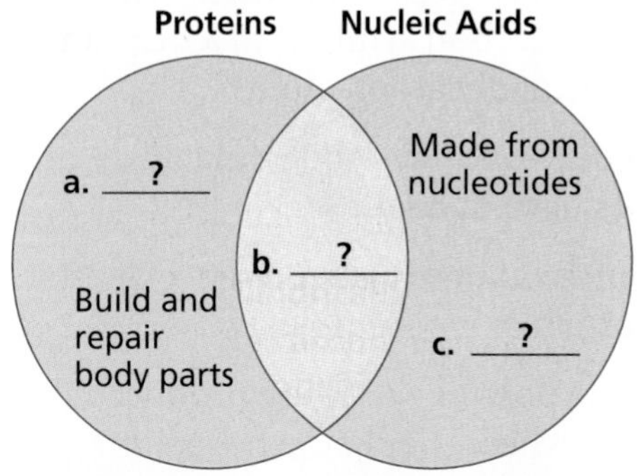

Reviewing Key Terms

Choose the letter of the best answer.

1. A form of carbon in which the carbon bonds are arranged in a repeating pattern similar to a geodesic dome is
   a. a fullerene.
   b. graphite.
   c. diamond.
   d. a nanotube.
2. A compound that contains only hydrogen and carbon is defined as
   a. a monomer.
   b. an isomer.
   c. a hydrocarbon.
   d. a polymer.
3. Fiberglass is a type of
   a. polymer.
   b. alloy.
   c. ceramic.
   d. composite.
4. The smaller molecules from which cellulose is made are
   a. glucose.
   b. amino acids.
   c. nucleotides.
   d. fatty acids.
5. Cholesterol is a type of
   a. nucleic acid.
   b. carbohydrate.
   c. lipid.
   d. cellulose.

If the statement is true, write *true*. If it is false, change the underlined word or words to make the statement true.

6. Because the bonds between layers of carbon atoms are weak, layers of <u>fullerenes</u> slide easily past one another.
7. Hydrocarbons that contain only single bonds are said to be <u>unsaturated hydrocarbons.</u>
8. An <u>organic acid</u> is characterized by one or more hydroxyl groups.
9. <u>Plastics</u> are synthetic polymers that can be molded or shaped.
10. Proteins are made up of long chains of <u>amino acids.</u>

Writing in Science

Web Site You are writing a feature article on carbon for a chemistry Web site. In your article, describe four forms of the element carbon. Include in your descriptions how the carbon atoms are arranged and how the bonds between the carbon atoms affect the properties of the substance. Include any helpful illustration.

Discovery Channel School

Carbon Chemistry
Video Preview
Video Field Trip
▶ Video Assessment

Review and Assessment

Checking Concepts

11. What does a dash represent when written between two carbon symbols in a diagram of a chain or ring of carbon atoms?
12. What do diamonds, graphite, fullerenes, and nanotubes have in common?
13. How would you notice the presence of esters in a fruit such as a pineapple?
14. Name some polymers that are produced in nature. Tell where they come from.
15. Starch and cellulose are both complex carbohydrates. How does your body treat these compounds differently?
16. Compare and contrast the fatty acids in fats that are solid at room temperature with fatty acids in oils that are liquids.

Thinking Critically

17. **Relating Cause and Effect** What features of the element carbon allow it to form the "backbone" of such a varied array of different compounds?
18. **Applying Concepts** Which of the diagrams below represents a saturated hydrocarbon? Which represents an unsaturated hydrocarbon? Explain your answer.

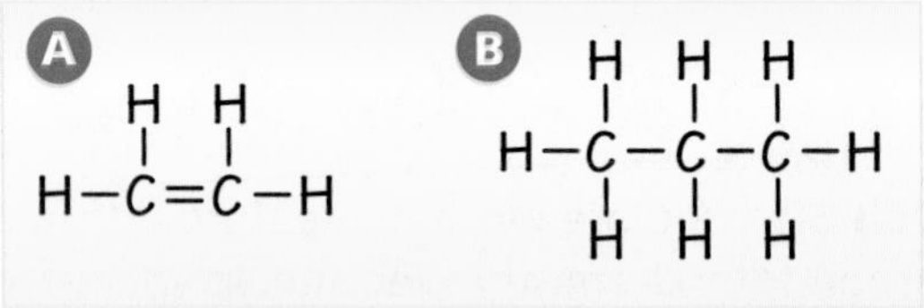

19. **Making Judgments** The plastic rings that hold beverage cans together are sometimes hazardous to living things in the ocean. Do you think companies that make soft drinks should be allowed to continue using plastic rings? Consider what could replace them.
20. **Posing Questions** Glucose and fructose are both simple carbohydrates with the formula $C_6H_{12}O_6$. What else do you need to know about glucose and fructose to decide if they should be considered different compounds?

Applying Skills

Use the following structural formulas to answer Questions 21–25.

A

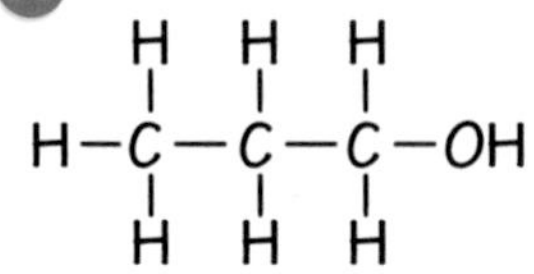

B

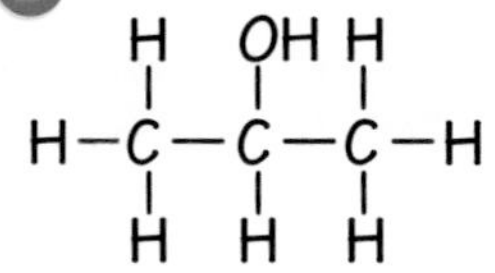

21. **Classifying** Which type of substituted hydrocarbons are compounds A and B? What information in the structural formulas did you use to decide your answer?
22. **Observing** What is the correct subscript for the carbon atoms (C) in the chemical formula that corresponds to each structural formula?
23. **Inferring** Are compounds A and B isomers? How can you tell?
24. **Predicting** Would you expect these two compounds to have identical properties or different properties? Explain.
25. **Problem Solving** What kind of compound would result if an organic acid were chemically combined with compound A? What properties would you expect the new compound to have?

Lab zone Chapter Project

Performance Assessment Display your data table classifying compounds in foods, along with the labels from which you collected your data. Point out the nutrients that are found in almost all foods and the nutrients found in only a few.

Standardized Test Prep

Test-Taking Tip

Choosing Among Similar Answers

Sometimes two or more answer choices in a multiple choice question are almost identical. If you do not read each choice carefully, you may select an incorrect answer. In the sample question below, the four chemical formulas given as answer choices are very similar. Examine each formula carefully before selecting your answer. Drawing a diagram of each formula may also help you see the differences between the answer choices.

Sample Question

Which chemical formula represents a saturated hydrocarbon with 2 carbon atoms?

A C_2H_2
B C_2H_4
C C_2H_6
D CH_4

Answer

The correct answer is **C.** A saturated hydrocarbon has only single bonds and, thus, has the maximum number of hydrogen atoms on its carbon chain. Only choices **C** and **D** represent saturated hydrocarbons. CH_4, however, has only one carbon atom while C_2H_6 has two.

Choose the letter of the best answer.

1. The formula $C_5H_{11}OH$ represents an
A amino acid.
B organic acid.
C alcohol.
D ester.

2. Material X is an organic compound that mixes poorly with water and is highly flammable. Of the following choices, material X is most likely a(n)
F carbohydrate.
G ester.
H alcohol.
J hydrocarbon.

Use the structural diagrams below and your knowledge of science to answer Questions 3–5.

1
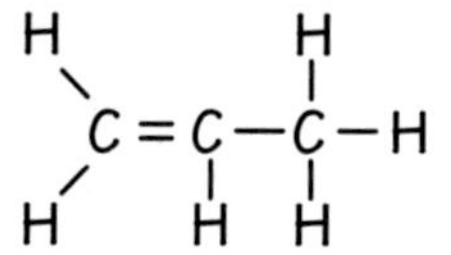

2
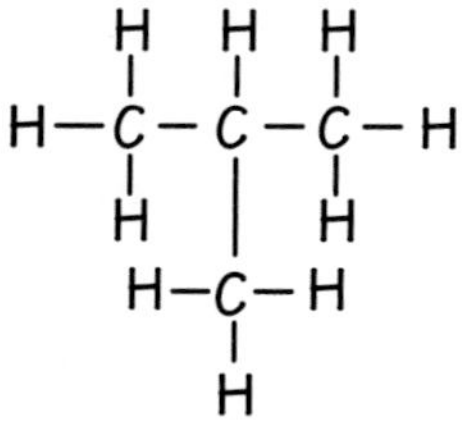

3
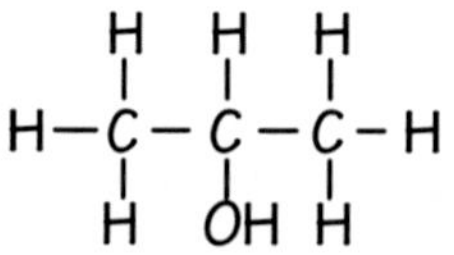

4
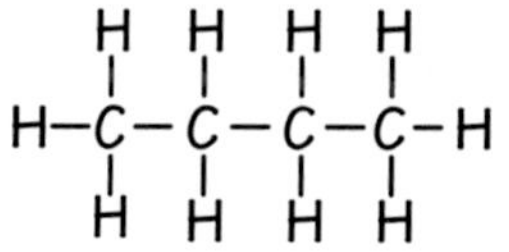

3. Isomers are organic compounds having the same chemical formula, but different structural formulas. Which pair of compounds are isomers?
A 1 and 2 **B** 1 and 3
C 2 and 3 **D** 2 and 4

4. Which structural diagram represents an unsaturated hydrocarbon?
F 1 **G** 2
H 3 **J** 4

5. What is the ratio of carbon atoms to hydrogen atoms in the compound represented by 1?
A 1 to 9
B 9 to 1
C 3 to 6
D 6 to 3

Constructed Response

6. Explain why carbohydrates, lipids, and proteins are important parts of a well-balanced diet.

Interdisciplinary **Exploration**

Soap—The Dirt Chaser

What slippery substance

- makes things cleaner, fresher, brighter?
- can you put on your head and on your floors?
- rids your hands of germs?

It's soap, which is a cleaner made from materials that are found in nature. People figured out how to make soap by heating natural fats or oils, alkali (a chemical they got from wood ashes), and water. Detergent is also a cleaner. It's similar to soap, but made from manufactured materials.

In a year, the average American uses about 11 kilograms of soap just to keep clean! Some of that soap is used for baths and showers. Soap is also used by medical experts to clean wounds and prevent infection.

In your home you use soaps and detergents to clean dishes, laundry, windows, floors, and much more. Even factories use soaps in the process of making products such as rubber, jewelry, aluminum, antifreeze, leather, and glossy paper.

So, if you lived without soap, you and your surroundings would be a lot dirtier! You would look and feel quite different. You may just owe your way of life to soap!

Car Wash
Young workers apply soap to this windshield.

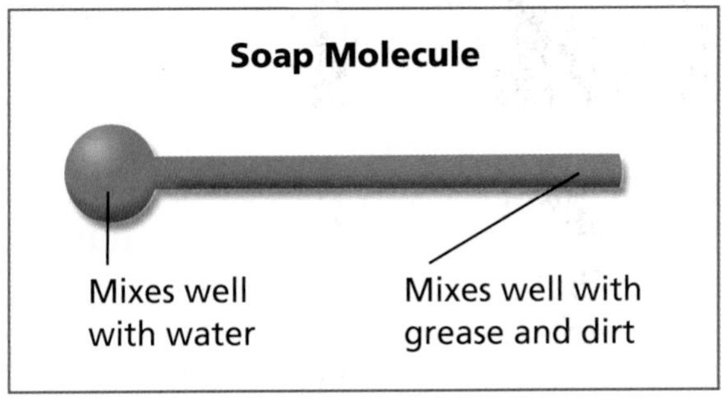

Soap Molecules
These molecules help loosen dirt. Water washes away the dirt.

How Soap Works

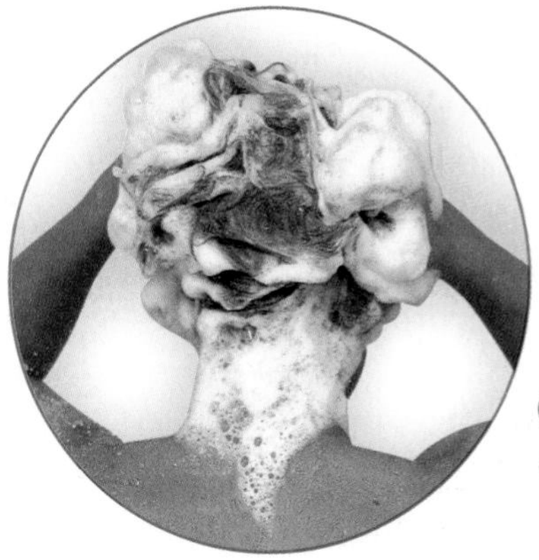

1 You rub shampoo and water into your hair.

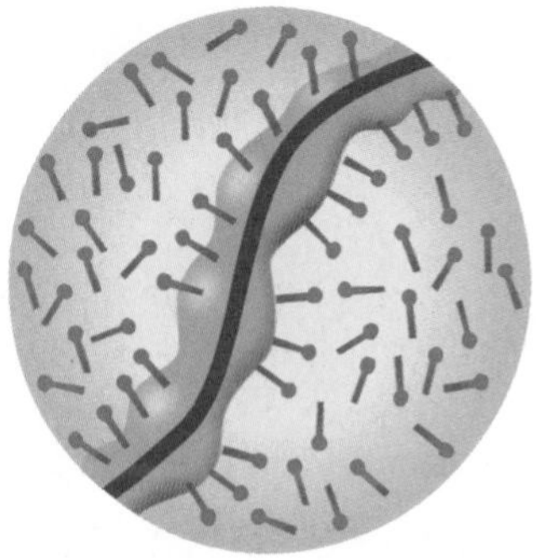

2 Soap molecules in shampoo loosen the grease and dirt on your hair.

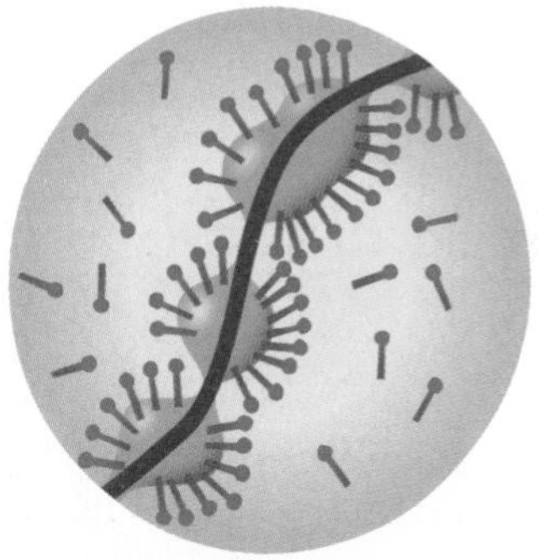

3 Soap molecules break the dirt into tiny pieces.

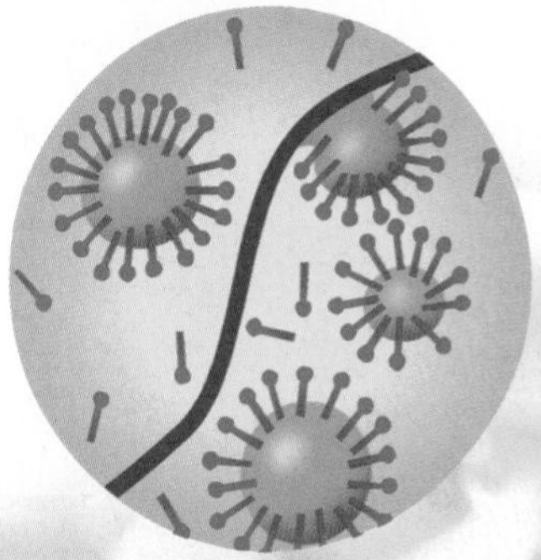

4 Water carries away the dirt surrounded by soap molecules.

Wash the Dirt Away

Soap manufacturers claim that their products can wash away the dirt from the dirtiest clothes. How does that work? First, you need to wet the clothes with water that contains soap. The soap then spreads out and soaks into the material.

Each molecule of soap is shaped like a tiny tadpole. The tail-like end is similar to a hydrocarbon molecule. It mixes poorly with water, but it mixes well with dirt and grease. The large end, on the other hand, mixes well with water. When you wash, the soap molecules surround the dirt and break it up into tiny pieces that water can wash away.

Some dirt is difficult to dissolve. It takes longer for the soap molecules to loosen it. In these cases, rubbing, scrubbing, and squeezing may help to lift the dirt.

Some water, called hard water, has minerals dissolved in it—calcium, magnesium, and iron. In hard water, soap forms deposits, called scum. Scum doesn't dissolve and is difficult to wash away. It keeps clean hair from being shiny and leaves a "bathtub ring."

The invention of detergents helped solve the problem of scum and stubborn stains. For many cleaning tasks, detergent is more effective than soap. Detergent also dissolves in cold water more easily than soap.

Chemistry of Soap

How is soap made? It's the product of heating two types of compounds—an acid and a base. Acids and bases are compounds that have physical and chemical properties opposite to each other. An acid tastes sour. Grapefruits, pickles, and vinegar have acids in them. A base has properties that make it taste bitter and feel slippery. Bases and acids combine to neutralize each other.

Natural fats and oils are the source of the acids in soapmaking. Fats and oils are polymers, made of three fatty acid monomers and an alcohol called glycerol.

In soapmaking, the fatty acids combine with an alkali solution (made of bases). The mixture is processed using water and heat. The resulting chemical reaction is called *saponification.* Saponification produces the main material of soaps, called "neat" soap. The glycerol left over, also called glycerin, is pumped away.

The difference between solid and liquid soaps depends on the alkali that's added. In a solid soap, the alkali solution is the base sodium hydroxide. In liquid soaps, the alkali solution is the base potassium hydroxide.

Making Soap Using the Continuous Process

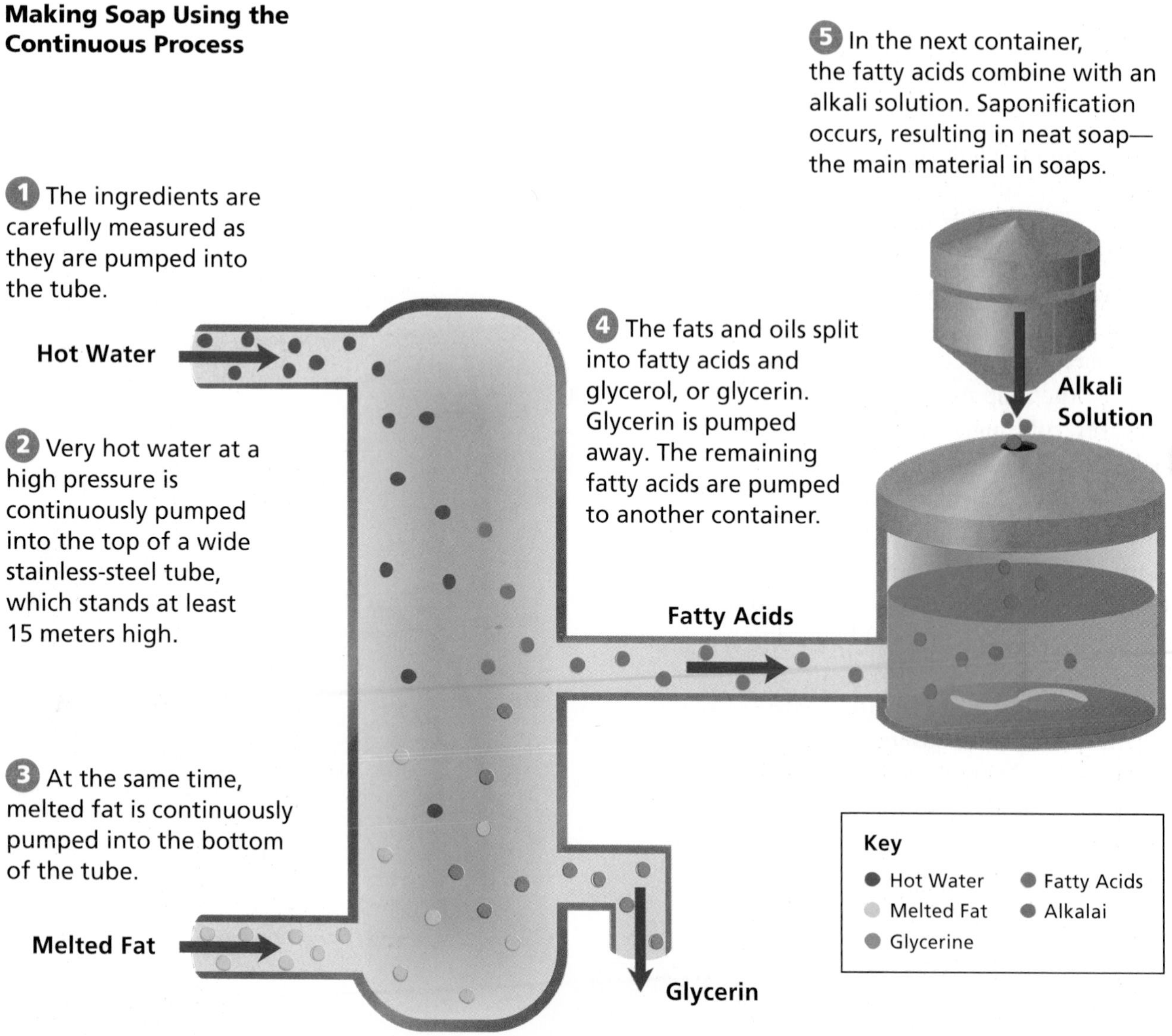

5 In the next container, the fatty acids combine with an alkali solution. Saponification occurs, resulting in neat soap—the main material in soaps.
1 The ingredients are carefully measured as they are pumped into the tube.
Hot Water
2 Very hot water at a high pressure is continuously pumped into the top of a wide stainless-steel tube, which stands at least 15 meters high.
3 At the same time, melted fat is continuously pumped into the bottom of the tube.
Melted Fat
4 The fats and oils split into fatty acids and glycerol, or glycerin. Glycerin is pumped away. The remaining fatty acids are pumped to another container.
Alkali Solution
Fatty Acids
Glycerin
Key
Hot Water
Melted Fat
Glycerine
Fatty Acids
Alkalai

Soapmaking

After saponification occurs, neat soap is poured into molds. Other ingredients are sometimes added at this stage. Then the bars are stamped with a brand name or design and wrapped for shipment.

To make cosmetic soaps, an additional process called milling is needed. The neat soap is poured into large slabs instead of into molds. When the slab cools, several sets of rollers press and crush it. This process makes finer, gentler soaps that people can use on their face and hands.

At this stage, a variety of other ingredients can be added, such as scents, colors, or germicides (to kill bacteria). Air can be whipped into soap to make it float. Soapmakers compete to find the combination of ingredients that will be most attractive and smell pleasant to customers.

Science Activity

Make your own soap, using lard, baking soda, water, and salt.

- Prepare a solution of baking soda by dissolving 5 grams in 10 milliliters of water.
- Mix the baking soda solution with 20 grams of lard in a 400-milliliter glass beaker.
- Boil gently on a hot plate for 20 minutes. Stir continuously while the mixture is boiling.
- Let the mixture cool. Transfer to a plastic beaker. Place in an ice water bath for 5–10 minutes. Stir.
- Make a saturated salt solution by dissolving 20 grams in 25 milliliters of water. Add to the mixture. Stir.
- Remove soap curdles by pouring through cheesecloth. Drain any liquid. Put soap into a dish to dry and harden.
- Put a portion of soap into warm water and stir. Observe the bubbles.
- Test with litmus paper to see if it is acid or base. (Blue litmus paper turns red in an acid. Red litmus paper turns blue in a base.)

6 Neat soap is poured into molds and allowed to harden. Before neat soap is made into bars, flakes, or powdered soap, other optional ingredients such as abrasives (scrubbing agents) can be added.

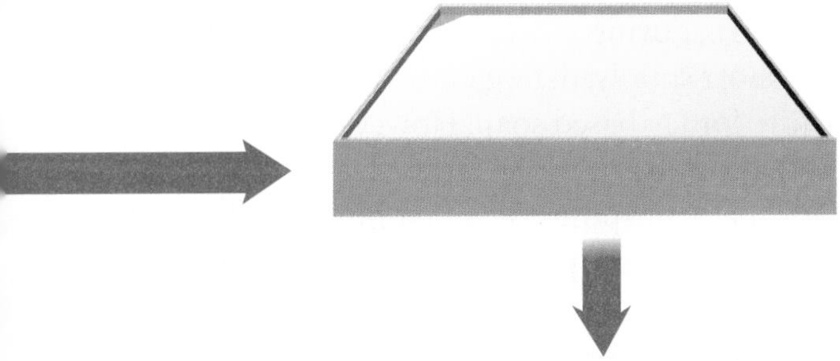

7 Cosmetic soaps require an additional process. After the neat soap cools, it goes through the milling process. The soap is fed through rollers that crush it. Perfumes and other ingredients can be added at this stage.

8 The finished soap is pressed, cut, stamped, and wrapped for shipment.

The Development of Soap

People have made soap for at least 2,300 years. The ancient Babylonians, Arabs, Greeks, Romans, and Celts made soap and sometimes traded it. The English word comes from "saipo," the Celts' name for soap. But these early cultures used soap primarily as a hair dye or a medicine, not as a cleaner! Only in the period from A.D. 100–199 did soap become known as a cleaning agent.

Soapmaking in Western Europe began about A.D. 100. First France was a leading producer, then Italy by 700, and Spain by 800. England didn't begin making soap until about 1200. But even then, most people didn't use soap for bathing.

Around 1790, Nicolas Leblanc, a French scientist, discovered that alkali could be made from common table salt and water. After that, soap could be made more easily and sold for profit.

Cutting Soap
This illustration shows that cutting soap required strength and precision.

In North America beginning around 1650, colonists made their own soap. Families would make up to a year's supply for their own use. Then around 1800, some people started collecting waste fats and ashes from their neighbors and making soap in large quantities. Soon bars of soap were sold from door to door.

In 1806, William Colgate, a soap and candle maker, started a business called Colgate and Company. His company produced soap and another cleaner, toothpaste. Today, nearly all soap is made in factories using large machinery.

The first detergent was produced in Germany around 1916, during World War I. Because fats were in short supply, detergent was meant to be a substitute for fat-based soap. However, people found that detergent was a better cleaner than soap for many purposes. The first household detergents appeared in the United States in 1933.

Soap Ad
This Lenox Soap advertisement is from 1898.

Social Studies Activity

Create a time line of important events in the history of soapmaking. Find photos or make illustrations for the time line. Include the following events:

- early uses and users of soap
- beginning of the soapmaking industry
- early North American soapmaking
- first detergent

Before they discovered soap, what do you think people in earlier times used as a cleaner?

Colonial Soapmaking

Making soap in North America in the 1600s was an exhausting, unpleasant process. For months, colonists saved barrels of ashes from their wood fires. Then they poured hot water over the ashes. An alkali solution, called lye, dripped out of a spigot in the bottom of the barrel.

In a large kettle over a roaring outdoor fire, they boiled the alkali solution with fat, such as greases, which they had also saved. They had to keep the fire high and hot and stir the mixture for hours. When it was thick, they ladled the liquid soap into shallow boxes. Families made soap in the spring and sometimes again in the fall.

The following passage is from the novel *The Iron Peacock* by Mary Stetson Clarke. The story takes place in 1650 in Massachusetts Bay Colony. In the passage, two large supports hold a crossbar where the pot is hung over the fire. The women stir the pot with a homemade tool.

The next morning was fair, the air washed sparkling clear. Duncan built a fire under the framework. Maura measured the grease, adding a quantity of lye. Ross and Duncan placed the crossbar under the handle of the pot and raised it until it rested on the supports. Maura took up a long wooden bar with a shorter one set at right angles to it, and began stirring the contents of the pot.

"We'll be back at noon to lend you a hand," said Duncan.

Maura and Joanna took turns stirring the soap. When Maura judged it to be of the right consistency, they let the fire die down.

After the men had lifted the pot off the fire, Joanna and Maura ladled the thick brown liquid into boxes lined with old pieces of cloth.

It cooled quickly into thick cream-colored slabs. Maura would cut it into cakes in a few days, when it was solid enough to handle. Then she would stack the bars in a dry place where the air could circulate around them until the soap had seasoned enough for use.

Colonial Soapmaking
Soapmaking was an all-day process done at home.

Language Arts Activity

Reread the passage and list the steps for making soap. Think of a process or activity that you know well. It can be packing for a trip or preparing for a party. Jot down the steps and number them. Then, write a description of the process. Include steps and details so that a reader unfamiliar with your activity would know how to do it.

Mathematics

A Year's Supply of Soap

What would you do if you had to make a year's supply of your own soap, using modern ingredients? You probably buy the soap you use from a store. But it is still possible to make soap yourself by using the right ingredients and following specific instructions.

Soap recipes are as varied and numerous as food recipes. You can make soap using the oil from avocados, hazelnuts, or sunflower seeds. To add natural scents, you might include rose, cinnamon, cloves, lavender, lemon, mint, grapefruit, pine, rose, vanilla, or something else.

Colors might come from beetroot, cocoa, goldenrod, licorice, paprika, or even seaweed. You can even include "scrubbers" such as cornmeal, oatmeal, or poppy seeds!

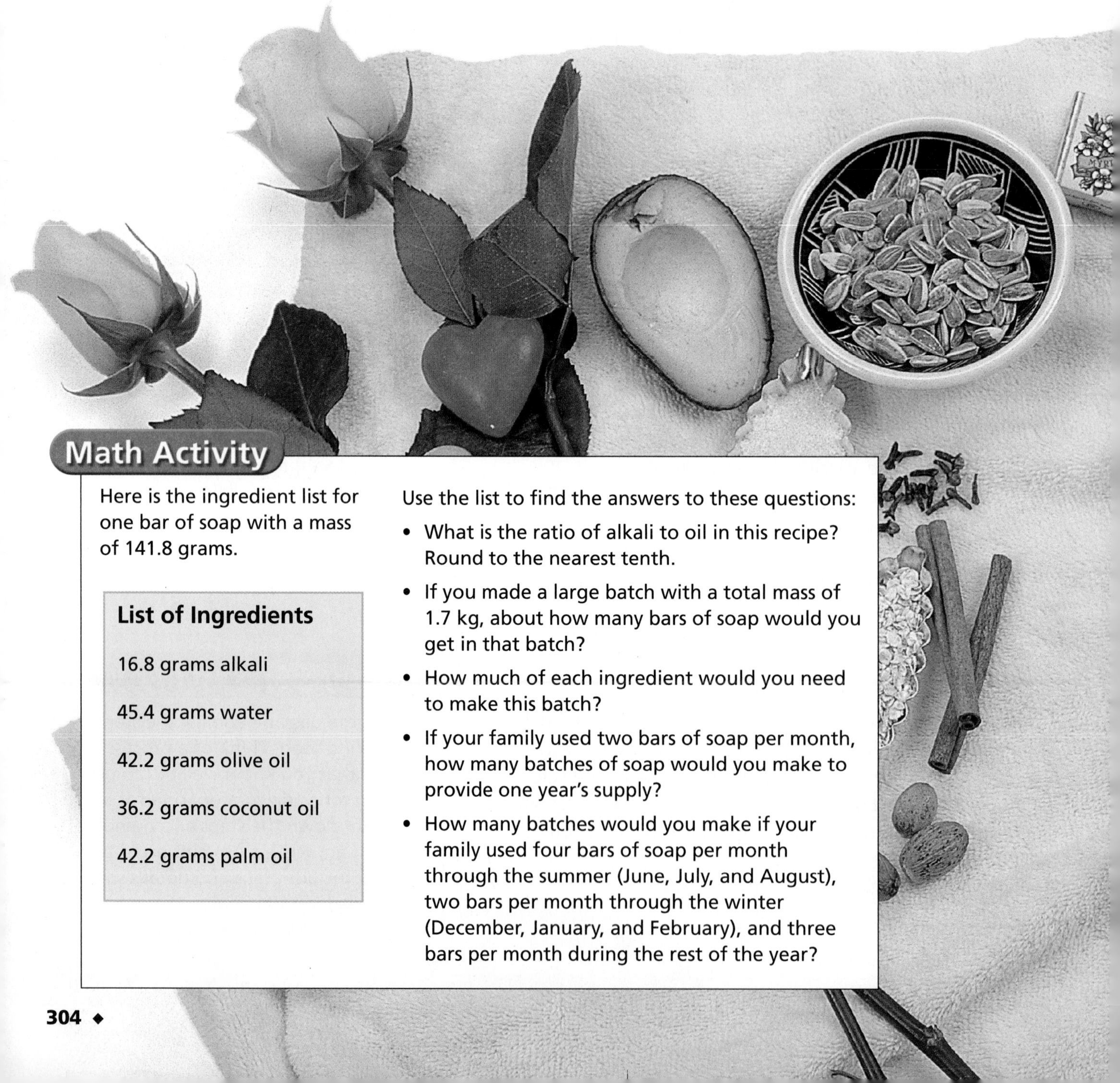

Math Activity

Here is the ingredient list for one bar of soap with a mass of 141.8 grams.

List of Ingredients
16.8 grams alkali
45.4 grams water
42.2 grams olive oil
36.2 grams coconut oil
42.2 grams palm oil

Use the list to find the answers to these questions:

- What is the ratio of alkali to oil in this recipe? Round to the nearest tenth.
- If you made a large batch with a total mass of 1.7 kg, about how many bars of soap would you get in that batch?
- How much of each ingredient would you need to make this batch?
- If your family used two bars of soap per month, how many batches of soap would you make to provide one year's supply?
- How many batches would you make if your family used four bars of soap per month through the summer (June, July, and August), two bars per month through the winter (December, January, and February), and three bars per month during the rest of the year?

Tie It Together

Soap Study

Organize a class project to survey and test soaps and soap products that are on the market today. Work in small groups. Choose one kind of cleaner to study, such as bar soaps, dishwashing detergents, laundry detergents, or another cleaner.

As your group investigates one kind of product, answer these questions:

- Look at the labels. What kinds of oils and other ingredients are listed?
- What do the makers claim these ingredients do? What language do they use to make these claims?
- How many kinds of surfaces can you clean with this product?

Next, collect several brands. Design an experiment to help you decide which brand works best.

- Decide what you will test for, such as how well the brand cleans grease.
- Develop a grading scale for rating the products.
- Before you begin, predict what your results will be.
- Keep all variables the same except for the brand.
- Perform the tests, collect data, and take careful notes.

Decide how to present your results to the class. You might include photographs of the test results, create a graph, or write a report describing and summarizing the results.

Chapter 9

Motion

Chapter Preview

1. **Describing and Measuring Motion**
   Discover *How Fast and How Far?*
   At-Home Activity *Roomy Size*
2. **Speed and Velocity**
   Discover *How Slow Can It Flow?*
   Active Art *Graphing Motion*
   Skills Lab *Inclined to Roll*
3. **Acceleration**
   Discover *Will You Hurry Up?*
   Skills Lab *Stopping on a Dime*

Interactive Textbook

The wild horses running across this meadow are in motion.

Discovery CHANNEL SCHOOL

Motion

▶ Video Preview
Video Field Trip
Video Assessment

Lab zone™ Chapter **Project**

Show Some Motion

Your Goal To identify the motion of several common objects and calculate how fast each one moves

To complete this project, you must

- measure distance and time carefully
- calculate the speed of each object using your data
- prepare display cards of your data, diagrams, and calculations
- follow the safety guidelines in Appendix A

Plan It! With your classmates, brainstorm several examples of objects in motion, such as a feather falling, your friend riding a bicycle, or the minute hand moving on a clock. Choose your examples and have your teacher approve them. Create a data table for each example and record your measurements. For accuracy, repeat your measurements. Then calculate the speed of each object. Make display cards for each example that show data, diagrams, and calculations.

Section 1

Describing and Measuring Motion

Reading Preview

Key Concepts

- When is an object in motion?
- How do scientists measure distance?

Key Terms

- motion
- reference point
- International System of Units
- meter

Target Reading Skill

Using Prior Knowledge Before you read, write what you know about motion in a graphic organizer like the one below. As you read, write what you learn.

What You Know
1. A moving object changes position.
2.

What You Learned
1.
2.

Lab zone Discover Activity

How Fast and How Far?

1. Using a stopwatch, find out how long it takes you to walk 5 meters at a normal pace. Record your time.
2. Now find out how far you can walk in 5 seconds if you walk at a normal pace. Record your distance.
3. Repeat Steps 1 and 2, walking slower than your normal pace. Then repeat Steps 1 and 2 walking faster than your normal pace.

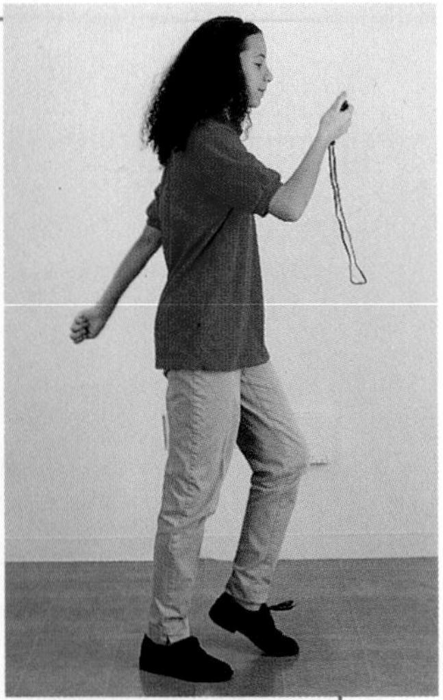

Think It Over

Inferring What is the relationship between the distance you walk, the time it takes you to walk, and your walking speed?

How do you know if you are moving? If you've ever traveled on a train, you know you cannot always tell if you are in motion. Looking at a building outside the window helps you decide. Although the building seems to move past the train, it's you and the train that are moving.

However, sometimes you may see another train that appears to be moving. Is the other train really moving, or is your train moving? How do you tell?

Describing Motion

Deciding if an object is moving isn't as easy as you might think. For example, you are probably sitting in a chair as you read this book. Are you moving? Well, parts of you may be. Your eyes blink and your chest moves up and down. But you would probably say that you are not moving. An object is in **motion** if its distance from another object is changing. Because your distance from your chair is not changing, you are not in motion.

Reference Points To decide if you are moving, you use your chair as a reference point. A **reference point** is a place or object used for comparison to determine if something is in motion. **An object is in motion if it changes position relative to a reference point.**

Objects that we call stationary—such as a tree, a sign, or a building—make good reference points. From the point of view of the train passenger in Figure 1, such objects are not in motion. If the passenger is moving relative to a tree, he can conclude that the train is in motion.

You probably know what happens if your reference point is moving. Have you ever been in a school bus parked next to another bus? Suddenly, you think your bus is moving backward. But, when you look out a window on the other side, you find that your bus isn't moving at all—the other bus is moving forward! Your bus seems to move backward because you used the other bus as a reference point.

Reading Checkpoint **What is a reference point?**

FIGURE 1
Reference Points
The passenger can use a tree as a reference point to decide if the train is moving. A tree makes a good reference point because it is stationary from the passenger's point of view.
Applying Concepts *Why is it important to choose a stationary object as a reference point?*

Relative Motion Are you moving as you read this book? The answer to that question depends on your reference point. When your chair is your reference point, you are not moving. But if you choose another reference point, you may be moving.

Suppose you choose the sun as a reference point instead of your chair. If you compare yourself to the sun, you are moving quite rapidly. This is because you and your chair are on Earth, which moves around the sun. Earth moves about 30 kilometers every second. So you, your chair, this book, and everything else on Earth move that quickly as well. Going that fast, you could travel from New York City to Los Angeles in about 2 minutes! Relative to the sun, both you and your chair are in motion. But because you are moving with Earth, you do not seem to be moving.

Measuring Distance

You can use units of measurement to describe motion precisely. You measure in units, or standard quantities of measurement, all the time. For example, you might measure 1 cup of milk for a recipe, run 2 miles after school, or buy 3 pounds of fruit at the store. Cups, miles, and pounds are all units of measurement.

Scientists all over the world use the same system of measurement so that they can communicate clearly. This system of measurement is called the **International System of Units** or, in French, *Système International* (SI).

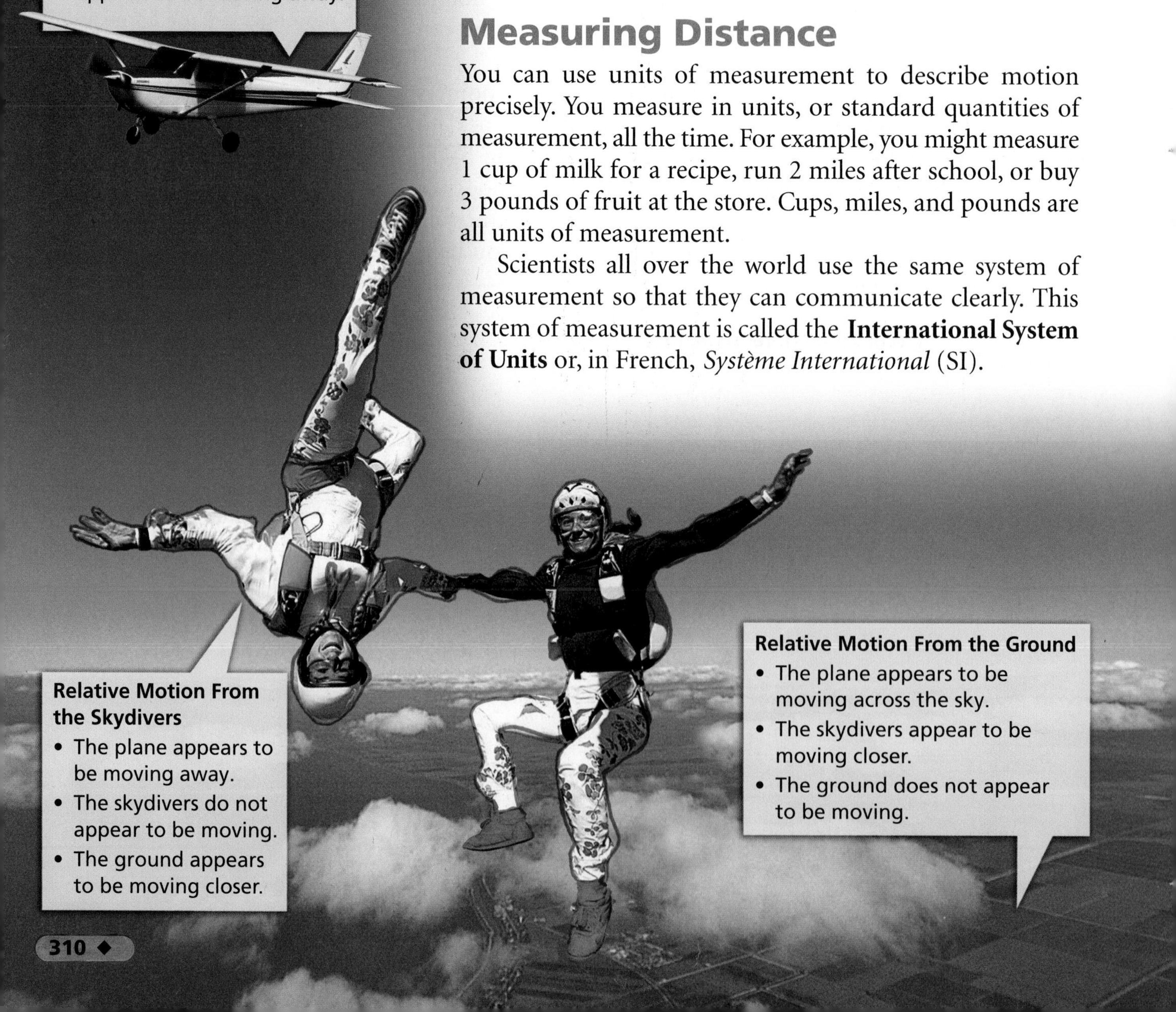

Relative Motion From the Plane
• The plane does not appear to be moving.
• The skydivers appear to be moving away.
• A point on the ground appears to be moving away.
Relative Motion From the Skydivers
• The plane appears to be moving away.
• The skydivers do not appear to be moving.
• The ground appears to be moving closer.
Relative Motion From the Ground
• The plane appears to be moving across the sky.
• The skydivers appear to be moving closer.
• The ground does not appear to be moving.

FIGURE 2 Relative Motion
Whether or not an object is in motion depends on the reference point.
Comparing and Contrasting *Are the skydivers moving relative to the airplane from which they jumped? Are they moving relative to the ground?*

Scientists use SI units to describe the distance an object moves. When you measure distance, you measure length. The SI unit of length is the meter (m). A meter is a little longer than a yard. An Olympic-size swimming pool is 50 meters long. A football field is about 91 meters long.

The length of an object smaller than a meter often is measured in a unit called the centimeter (cm). The prefix *centi-* means "one hundredth." A centimeter is one hundredth of a meter, so there are 100 centimeters in a meter. The wingspan of the butterfly shown in Figure 3 can be measured in centimeters. For lengths smaller than a centimeter, the millimeter (mm) is used. The prefix *milli-* means "one thousandth," so there are 1,000 millimeters in a meter. Distances too long to be measured in meters often are measured in kilometers (km). The prefix *kilo-* means "one thousand." There are 1,000 meters in a kilometer.

Scientists also use SI units to describe quantities other than length. You can find more information about SI units in the Skills Handbook at the end of this book.

Reading Checkpoint **What system of measurement do scientists use?**

FIGURE 3
Measuring Distance
You can measure distances shorter than 1 meter in centimeters. The wingspan of the butterfly is 7 cm.

Section 1 Assessment

Target Reading Skill

Using Prior Knowledge Review your graphic organizer and revise it based on what you just learned about motion.

Reviewing Key Concepts

1. a. **Reviewing** How do you know if an object is moving?
   b. **Explaining** Why is it important to know if your reference point is moving?
   c. **Applying Concepts** Suppose you are riding in a car. Describe your motion relative to the car, the road, and the sun.
2. a. **Identifying** What is the SI unit for length?
   b. **Defining** How many centimeters are there in a meter? How many meters are there in a kilometer?
   c. **Calculating** This week at swim practice, Jamie swam a total of 1,500 m, while Ellie swam 1.6 km. Convert Ellie's distance to meters. Which swimmer swam the greater distance?

Lab zone At-Home Activity

Roomy Size With the help of a family member, use a ruler to measure the length and width of a room at home to the nearest centimeter. Convert these measurements into meters and then into millimeters.

Section 2

Speed and Velocity

Reading Preview

Key Concepts

- How do you know an object's speed and velocity?
- How can you graph motion?

Key Terms

- speed • average speed
- instantaneous speed
- velocity • slope

Target Reading Skill

Previewing Visuals Before you read, preview Figure 5. Then write two questions that you have about the diagram in a graphic organizer like the one below. As you read, answer your questions.

Graphing Motion

Q.	How can you determine the slope of a graph?
A.	
Q.	

Lab zone Discover Activity

How Slow Can It Flow?

1. Put a spoonful of honey on a plate.
2. Place a piece of tape 4 cm from the bottom edge of the honey.
3. Lift one side of the plate just high enough that the honey starts to flow.
4. Reduce the plate's angle until the honey barely moves. Prop up the plate at this angle.
5. Time how long the honey takes to reach the tape. Calculate the speed of the honey.

Think It Over

Forming Operational Definitions When an object doesn't appear to be moving at first glance, how can you tell if it is?

A measurement of distance can tell you how far an object travels. A cyclist, for example, might travel 30 kilometers. An ant might travel 2 centimeters. **If you know the distance an object travels in a certain amount of time, you can calculate the speed of the object.** Speed is a type of rate. A rate tells you the amount of something that occurs or changes in one unit of time. The **speed** of an object is the distance the object travels per unit of time.

Calculating Speed

To calculate the speed of an object, divide the distance the object travels by the amount of time it takes to travel that distance. This relationship can be written as an equation.

$$\text{Speed} = \frac{\text{Distance}}{\text{Time}}$$

The speed equation consists of a unit of distance divided by a unit of time. If you measure distance in meters and time in seconds, you express speed in meters per second, or m/s. (The slash is read as "per.") If you measure distance in kilometers and time in hours, you express speed in kilometers per hour, or km/h. For example, a cyclist who travels 30 kilometers in 1 hour has a speed of 30 km/h. An ant that moves 2 centimeters in 1 second is moving at a speed of 2 centimeters per second, or 2 cm/s.

Average Speed The speed of most moving objects is not constant. The cyclists shown in Figure 4, for example, change their speeds many times during the race. They might ride at a constant speed along flat ground but move more slowly as they climb hills. Then they might move more quickly as they come down hills. Occasionally, they may stop to fix their bikes.

Although a cyclist does not have a constant speed, the cyclist does have an average speed throughout a race. To calculate **average speed**, divide the total distance traveled by the total time. For example, suppose a cyclist travels 32 kilometers during the first 2 hours. Then the cyclist travels 13 kilometers during the next hour. The average speed of the cyclist is the total distance divided by the total time.

$$\text{Total distance} = 32\text{ km} + 13\text{ km} = 45\text{ km}$$

$$\text{Total time} = 2\text{ h} + 1\text{ h} = 3\text{ h}$$

$$\text{Average speed} = \frac{45\text{ km}}{3\text{ h}} = 15\text{ km/h}$$

The cyclist's average speed is 15 kilometers per hour.

Instantaneous Speed Calculating the average speed of a cyclist during a race is important. However, it is also useful to know the cyclist's instantaneous speed. **Instantaneous speed** is the rate at which an object is moving at a given instant in time.

Reading Checkpoint How do you calculate average speed?

FIGURE 4
Measuring Speed
Cyclists use an electronic device known as a cyclometer to track the distance and time that they travel. A cyclometer can calculate both average and instantaneous speed.
Comparing and Contrasting *Explain why the instantaneous speed and the average speed shown below are different.*

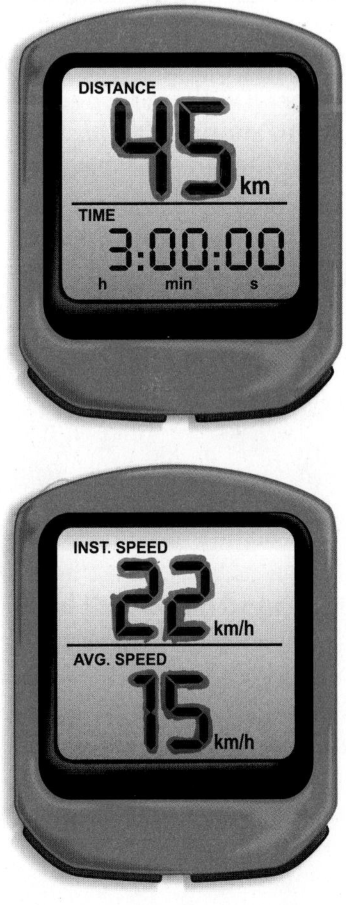

Discovery Channel School

Motion

Video Preview
▶ Video Field Trip
Video Assessment

Describing Velocity

Knowing the speed at which something travels does not tell you everything about its motion. To describe an object's motion completely, you need to know the direction of its motion. For example, suppose you hear that a thunderstorm is traveling at a speed of 25 km/h. Should you prepare for the storm? That depends on the direction of the storm's motion. Because storms usually travel from west to east in the United States, you need not worry if you live to the west of the storm. But if you live to the east of the storm, take cover.

When you know both the speed and direction of an object's motion, you know the velocity of the object. Speed in a given direction is called **velocity.** You know the velocity of the storm when you know that it is moving 25 km/h eastward.

• Tech & Design in History •

The Speed of Transportation

The speed with which people can travel from one place to another has increased over the years.

1818
National Road Constructed
The speed of transportation has been limited largely by the quality of roadways. The U.S. government paid for the construction of a highway named the Cumberland Road. It ran from Cumberland, Maryland, to Wheeling, in present-day West Virginia. Travel by horse and carriage on the roadway was at a speed of about 11 km/h.

1885
Benz Tricycle Car Introduced
This odd-looking vehicle was the first internal combustion (gasoline-powered) automobile sold to the public. Although it is an ancestor of the modern automobile, its top speed was only about 15 km/h—not much faster than a horse-drawn carriage.

1908
Ford Model T Mass-Produced
Between 1908 and 1927, over 15 million of these automobiles were sold. The Model T had a top speed of 65 km/h.

1800 1850 1900

At times, describing the velocity of moving objects can be very important. For example, air traffic controllers must keep close track of the velocities of the aircraft under their control. These velocities continually change as airplanes move overhead and on the runways. An error in determining a velocity, either in speed or in direction, could lead to a collision.

Velocity is also important to airplane pilots. For example, stunt pilots make spectacular use of their control over the velocity of their aircrafts. To avoid colliding with other aircraft, these skilled pilots must have precise control of both their speed and direction. Stunt pilots use this control to stay in close formation while flying graceful maneuvers at high speed.

Reading Checkpoint **What is velocity?**

Writing in Science

Research and Write What styles of automobile were most popular during the 1950s, 1960s, and 1970s? Were sedans, convertibles, station wagons, or sports cars the bestsellers? Choose an era and research automobiles of that time. Then write an advertisement for one particular style of car. Be sure to include information from your research.

1934 Zephyr Introduced

The first diesel passenger train in the United States was the *Zephyr*. The *Zephyr* set a long-distance record, traveling from Denver to Chicago at an average speed of 125 km/h for more than 1,600 km.

1956 Interstate Highway System Established

The passage of the Federal-Aid Highway Act established the Highway Trust Fund. This act allowed the construction of the Interstate and Defense Highways. Nonstop transcontinental auto travel became possible. Speed limits in many parts of the system were more than 100 km/h.

2003 Maglev in Motion

The first commercial application of high-speed maglev (magnetic levitation) was unveiled in Shanghai, China. During the 30-km trip from Pudong International Airport to Shanghai's financial district, the train operates at a top speed of 430 km/h, reducing commuting time from 45 minutes to just 8 minutes.

1950 2000 2050

Go Online
active art
For: Graphing Motion activity
Visit: PHSchool.com
Web Code: cgp-3011

FIGURE 5
Graphing Motion
Distance-versus-time graphs can be used to analyze motion. On the jogger's first day of training, her speed is the same at every point. On the second day of training, her speed varies. **Reading Graphs** *On the first day, how far does the jogger run in 5 minutes?*

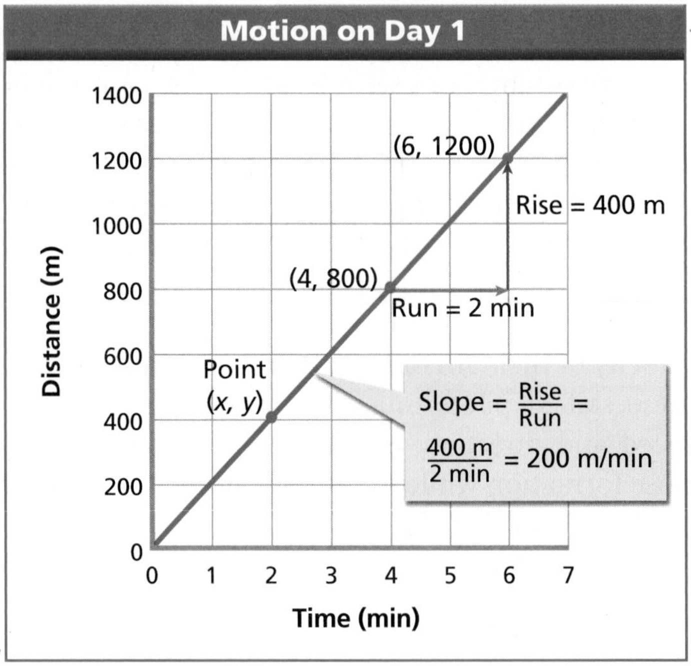

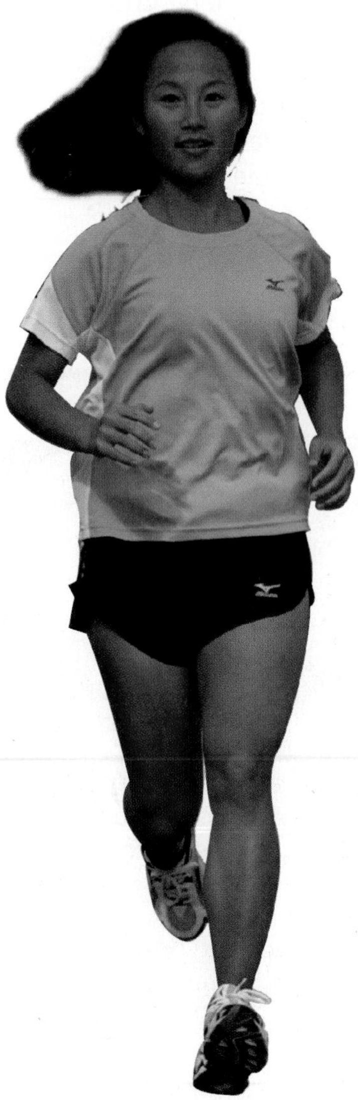

Graphing Motion

You can show the motion of an object on a line graph in which you plot distance versus time. The graphs you see in Figure 5 are distance-versus-time motion graphs. Time is shown on the horizontal axis, or *x*-axis. Distance is shown on the vertical axis, or *y*-axis. A point on the line represents the distance an object has traveled at a particular time. The *x* value of the point is time, and the *y* value is distance.

The steepness of a line on a graph is called **slope.** The slope tells you how fast one variable changes in relation to the other variable in the graph. In other words, slope tells you the rate of change. Since speed is the rate that distance changes in relation to time, the slope of a distance-versus-time graph represents speed. The steeper the slope is, the greater the speed. A constant slope represents motion at constant speed.

Calculating Slope You can calculate the slope of a line by dividing the rise by the run. The rise is the vertical difference between any two points on the line. The run is the horizontal difference between the same two points.

$$\text{Slope} = \frac{\text{Rise}}{\text{Run}}$$

In Figure 5, using the points shown, the rise is 400 meters and the run is 2 minutes. To find the slope, you divide 400 meters by 2 minutes. The slope is 200 meters per minute.

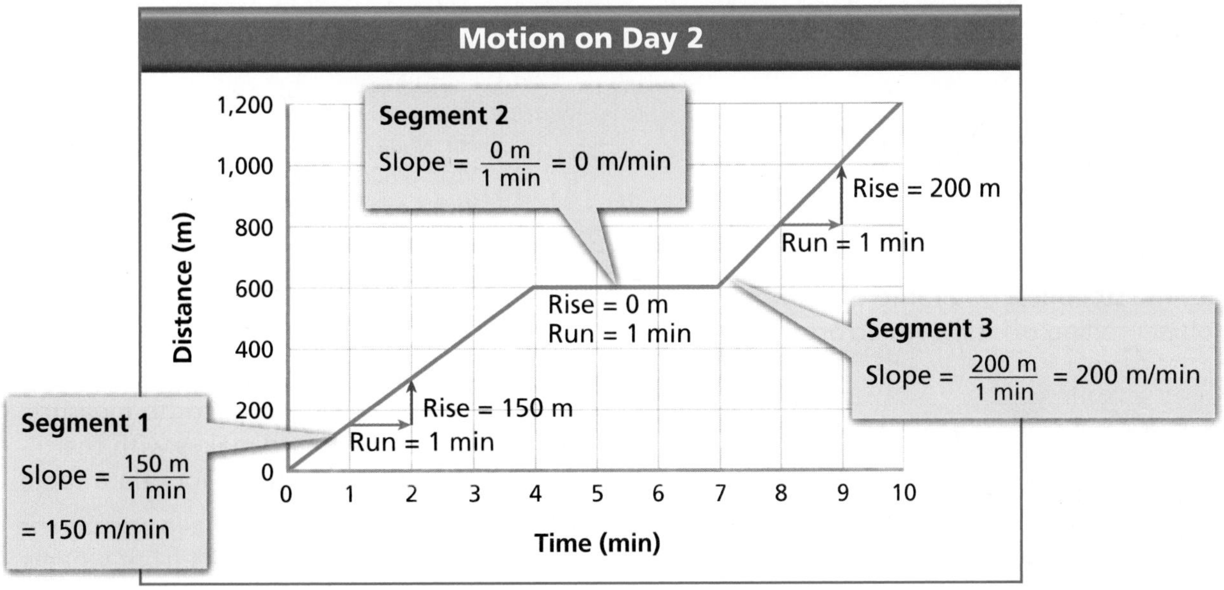

Different Slopes Most moving objects do not travel at a constant speed. The graph above shows a jogger's motion on her second day. The line is divided into three segments. The slope of each segment is different. From the steepness of the slopes you can tell that the jogger ran the fastest during the third segment. The horizontal line in the second segment shows that the jogger's distance did not change at all.

Reading Checkpoint **What is the slope of a graph?**

Section 2 Assessment

Target Reading Skill **Previewing Visuals** Refer to your questions and answers about Figure 5 to help you answer Question 2 below.

Reviewing Key Concepts

1. a. **Defining** What is speed?
   b. **Describing** What do you know about the motion of an object that has an average speed of 1 m/s?
   c. **Comparing and Contrasting** What is the difference between speed and velocity?
2. a. **Identifying** What does the slope of a distance-versus-time graph show you about the motion of an object?
   b. **Calculating** The rise of a line on a distance-versus-time graph is 600 m and the run is 3 minutes. What is the slope of the line?

Writing in Science

Explanation Think about a recent trip that you have taken. What was the approximate total distance that you traveled and the total time it took? Calculate your average speed from this information. Then explain how your instantaneous speed varied over the course of the trip.

Lab zone **Skills Lab**

Inclined to Roll

Go Online
PHSchool.com

For: Data sharing
Visit: PHSchool.com
Web Code: cgd-3012

Problem

How does the steepness of a ramp affect how fast an object rolling off it moves across the floor?

Skills Focus

measuring, calculating, graphing

Materials

- skateboard
- meter stick
- protractor
- masking tape
- flat board, about 1.5 m long
- small piece of sturdy cardboard
- supports to prop up the board (books, boxes)
- two stopwatches

Procedure

1. In your notebook, make a data table like the one below. Include space for five angles.
2. Lay the board flat on the floor. Using masking tape, mark a starting line in the middle of the board. Mark a finish line on the floor 1.5 m beyond one end of the board. Place a barrier after the finish line.
3. Prop up the other end of the board to make a slight incline. Use a protractor to measure the angle that the board makes with the ground. Record the angle in your data table.
4. Working in groups of three, have one person hold the skateboard so that its front wheels are even with the starting line. As the holder releases the skateboard, the other two students should start their stopwatches.
5. One timer should stop his or her stopwatch when the front wheels of the skateboard reach the end of the incline.
6. The second timer should stop his or her stopwatch when the front wheels reach the finish line. Record the times in your data table in the columns labeled Time 1 and Time 2.
7. Repeat Steps 4–6 two more times. If your results for the three times aren't within 0.2 second of one another, carry out more trials.

Data Table

Angle (degrees)	Trial Number	Time 1 (to bottom) (s)	Time 2 (to finish) (s)	Avg Time 1 (s)	Avg Time 2 (s)	Avg Time 2 – Avg Time 1 (s)	Avg Speed (m/s)
	1						
	2						
	3						
	1						
	2						
	3						
	1						
	2						

8. Repeat Steps 3–7 four more times, making the ramp gradually steeper each time.
9. For each angle of the incline, complete the following calculations and record them in your data table.
   a. Find the average time the skateboard takes to get to the bottom of the ramp (Time 1).
   b. Find the average time the skateboard takes to get to the finish line (Time 2).
   c. Subtract the average of Time 1 from the average of Time 2.

Analyze and Conclude

1. Calculating How can you find the average speed of the skateboard across the floor for each angle of the incline? Determine the average speed for each angle and record it in your data table.
2. Classifying Which is your manipulated variable and which is your responding variable in this experiment? Explain. (For a discussion of manipulated and responding variables, see the Skills Handbook.)
3. Graphing On a graph, plot the average speed of the skateboard (on the *y*-axis) against the angle of the ramp (on the *x*-axis).
4. Drawing Conclusions What does your graph show about the relationship between the skateboard's speed and the angle of the ramp?
5. Measuring If your measurements for distance, time, or angle were inaccurate, how would your results have been affected?
6. Communicating Do you think your method of timing was accurate? Did the timers start and stop their stopwatches exactly at the appropriate points? How could the accuracy of the timing be improved? Write a brief procedure for your method.

Design an Experiment

A truck driver transporting new cars needs to roll the cars off the truck. You offer to design a ramp to help with the task. What measurements would you make that might be useful? Design an experiment to test your ideas. *Obtain your teacher's permission before carrying out your investigation.*

Section 3

Integrating Mathematics

Acceleration

Reading Preview

Key Concepts

- What kind of motion does acceleration refer to?
- How is acceleration calculated?
- What graphs can be used to analyze the motion of an accelerating object?

Key Term

- acceleration

Target Reading Skill

Identifying Main Ideas As you read the What Is Acceleration? section, write the main idea in a graphic organizer like the one below. Then write three supporting details that give examples of the main idea.

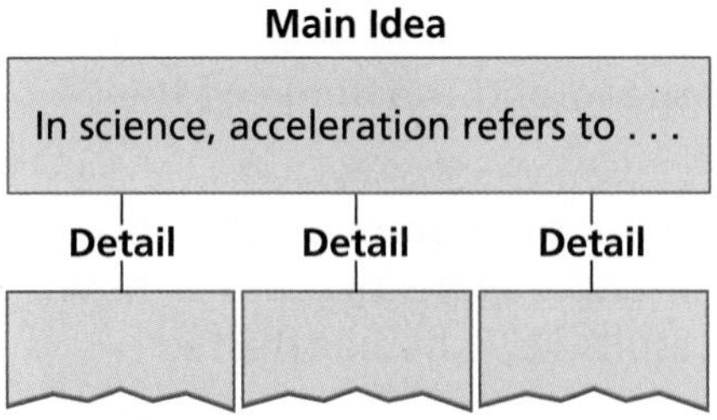

Lab zone Discover Activity

Will You Hurry Up?

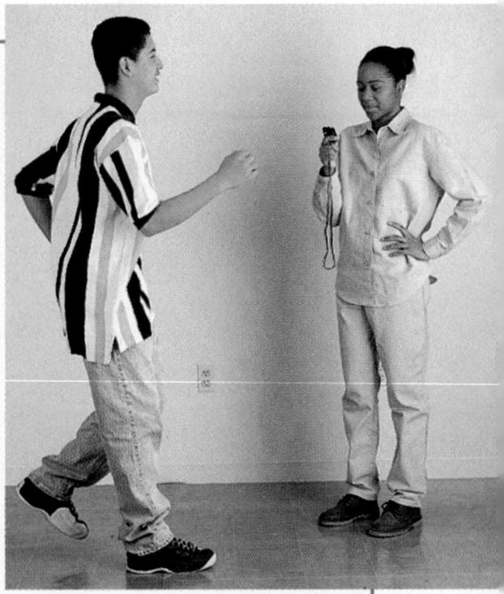

1. Measure 10 meters in an open area. Mark the distance with masking tape.
2. Walk the 10 meters in such a way that you keep moving faster throughout the entire distance. Have a partner time you.
3. Repeat Step 2, walking the 10 meters in less time than you did before. Then try it again, this time walking the distance in twice the time as the first. Remember to keep speeding up throughout the entire 10 meters.

Think It Over

Inferring How is the change in your speed related to the time in which you walk the 10-meter course?

The pitcher throws. The ball speeds toward the batter. Off the bat it goes. It's going, going, gone! A home run!

Before landing, the ball went through several changes in motion. It sped up in the pitcher's hand, and lost speed as it traveled toward the batter. The ball stopped when it hit the bat, changed direction, sped up again, and eventually slowed down. Most examples of motion involve similar changes. In fact, rarely does any object's motion stay the same for very long.

What Is Acceleration?

Suppose you are a passenger in a car stopped at a red light. When the light changes to green, the driver steps on the accelerator. As a result, the car speeds up, or accelerates. In everyday language, *acceleration* means "the process of speeding up."

Acceleration has a more precise definition in science. Scientists define **acceleration** as the rate at which velocity changes. Recall that velocity describes both the speed and direction of an object. A change in velocity can involve a change in either speed or direction—or both. **In science, acceleration refers to increasing speed, decreasing speed, or changing direction.**

A softball accelerates when it is thrown.
A softball changes direction when it is hit.
A softball decelerates when it is caught.

FIGURE 6
Acceleration
A softball experiences acceleration when it is thrown, caught, and hit. **Classifying** *What change in motion occurs in each example?*

Increasing Speed Whenever an object's speed increases, the object accelerates. A softball accelerates when the pitcher throws it, and again when a bat hits it. A car that begins to move from a stopped position or speeds up to pass another car is accelerating. People can accelerate too. For example, you accelerate when you coast down a hill on your bike.

Decreasing Speed Just as objects can speed up, they can also slow down. This change in speed is sometimes called deceleration, or negative acceleration. For example, a softball decelerates when it lands in a fielder's mitt. A car decelerates when it stops at a red light. A water skier decelerates when the boat stops pulling.

Changing Direction Even an object that is traveling at a constant speed can be accelerating. Recall that acceleration can be a change in direction as well as a change in speed. Therefore, a car accelerates as it follows a gentle curve in the road or changes lanes. Runners accelerate as they round the curve in a track. A softball accelerates when it changes direction as it is hit.

Many objects continuously change direction without changing speed. The simplest example of this type of motion is circular motion, or motion along a circular path. For example, the seats on a Ferris wheel accelerate because they move in a circle.

Reading Checkpoint **How can a car be accelerating if its speed is constant at 65 km/h?**

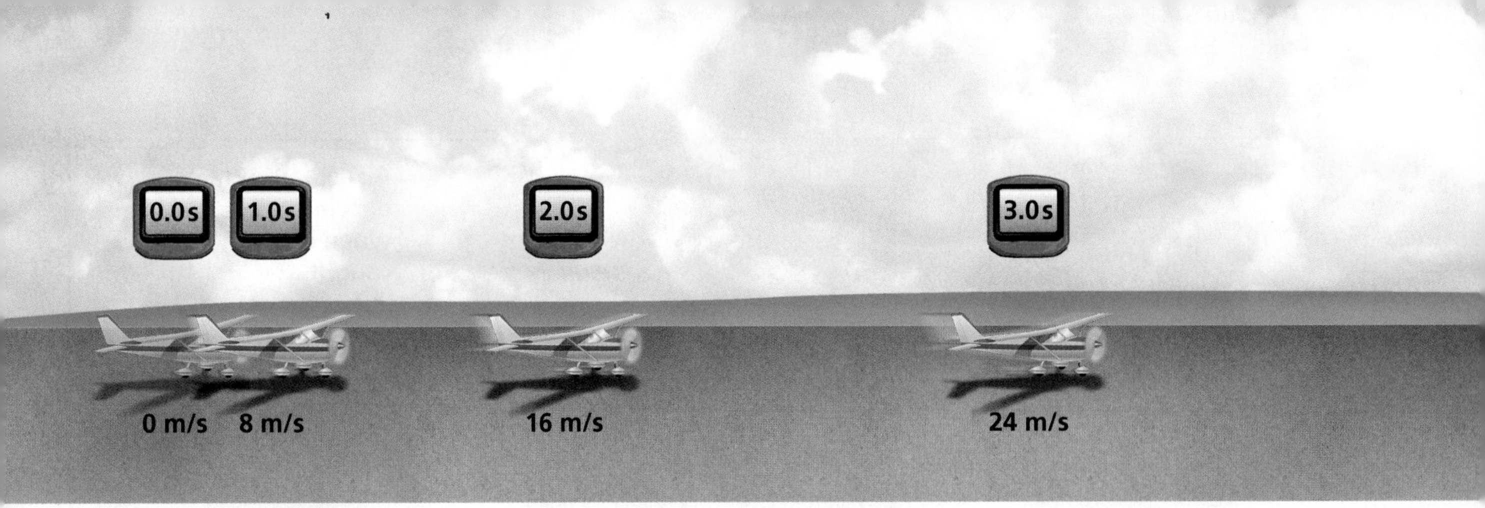

FIGURE 7
Analyzing Acceleration
The speed of the airplane above increases by the same amount each second. **Interpreting Diagrams** *How does the distance change in each second?*

Calculating Acceleration

Acceleration describes the rate at which velocity changes. If an object is not changing direction, you can describe its acceleration as the rate at which its speed changes. **To determine the acceleration of an object moving in a straight line, you must calculate the change in speed per unit of time.** This is summarized by the following formula.

$$\text{Acceleration} = \frac{\text{Final speed} - \text{Initial speed}}{\text{Time}}$$

If speed is measured in meters per second (m/s) and time is measured in seconds, the SI unit of acceleration is meters per second per second, or m/s^2. Suppose speed is measured in kilometers per hour and time is measured in hours. Then the unit for acceleration is kilometers per hour per hour, or km/h^2.

To understand acceleration, imagine a small airplane moving down a runway. Figure 7 shows the airplane's motion after each of the first five seconds of its acceleration. To calculate the average acceleration of the airplane, you must first subtract the initial speed of 0 m/s from the final speed of 40 m/s. Then divide the change in speed by the time, 5 seconds.

$$\text{Acceleration} = \frac{40\text{ m/s} - 0\text{ m/s}}{5\text{ s}}$$

$$\text{Acceleration} = 8\text{ m/s}^2$$

The airplane accelerates at a rate of 8 m/s^2. This means that the airplane's speed increases by 8 m/s every second. Notice in Figure 7 that, after each second of travel, the airplane's speed is 8 m/s greater than it was the previous second.

Reading Checkpoint **What must you know about an object that is moving in a straight line to calculate its acceleration?**

Go Online
SCINKS NSTA
For: Links on acceleration
Visit: www.SciLinks.org
Web Code: scn-1313

Math Sample Problem

Calculating Acceleration

As a roller coaster car starts down a slope, its speed is 4 m/s. But 3 seconds later, at the bottom, its speed is 22 m/s. What is its average acceleration?

1 Read and Understand

What information are you given?

Initial speed = 4 m/s

Final speed = 22 m/s

Time = 3 s

2 Plan and Solve

What quantity are you trying to calculate?

The average acceleration of the roller coaster car = ■

What formula contains the given quantities and the unknown quantity?

$$\text{Acceleration} = \frac{\text{Final speed} - \text{Initial speed}}{\text{Time}}$$

Perform the calculation.

$$\text{Acceleration} = \frac{22 \text{ m/s} - 4 \text{ m/s}}{3 \text{ s}}$$

$$\text{Acceleration} = \frac{18 \text{ m/s}}{3 \text{ s}}$$

$$\text{Acceleration} = 6 \text{ m/s}^2$$

The roller coaster car's average acceleration is 6 m/s^2.

3 Look Back and Check

Does your answer make sense?

The answer is reasonable. If the car's speed increases by 6 m/s each second, its speed will be 10 m/s after 1 second, 16 m/s after 2 seconds, and 22 m/s after 3 seconds.

Math Practice

1. **Calculating Acceleration** A falling raindrop accelerates from 10 m/s to 30 m/s in 2 seconds. What is the raindrop's average acceleration?
2. **Calculating Acceleration** A certain car can accelerate from rest to 27 m/s in 9 seconds. Find the car's average acceleration.

pineapples

A

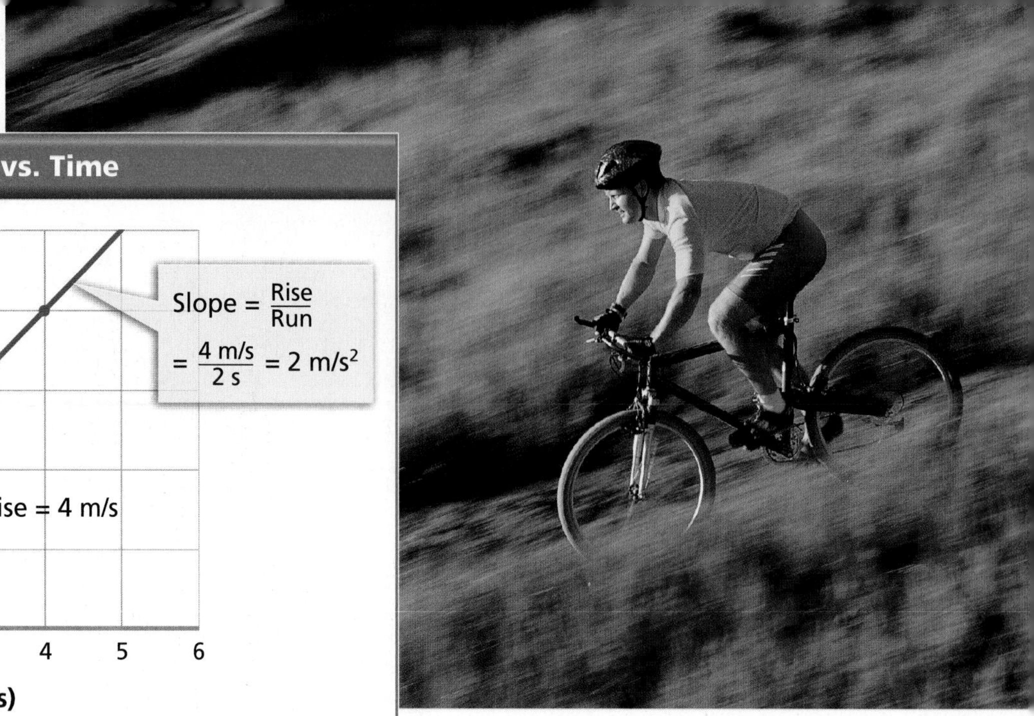

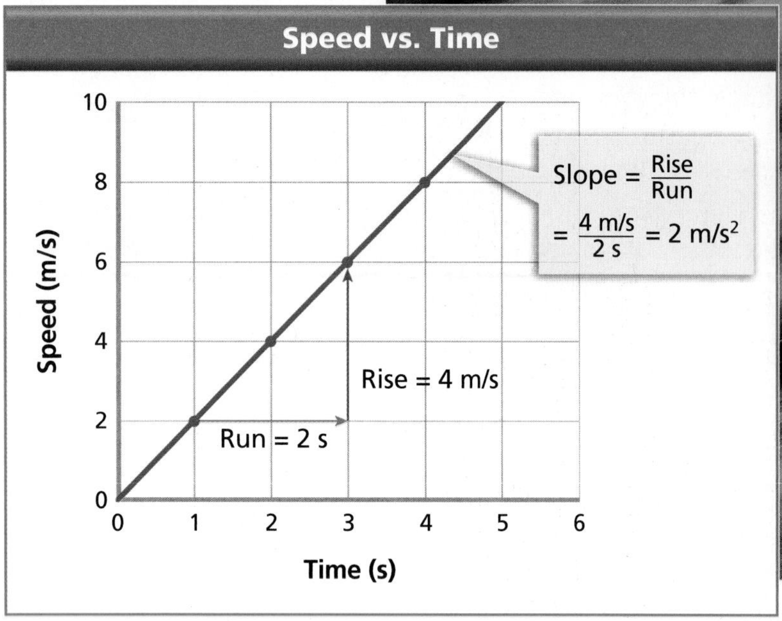

FIGURE 8
Speed-Versus-Time Graph
The slanted, straight line on this speed-versus-time graph tells you that the cyclist is accelerating at a constant rate. The slope of a speed-versus-time graph tells you the object's acceleration.
Predicting *How would the slope of the graph change if the cyclist were accelerating at a greater rate? At a lesser rate?*

Graphing Acceleration

Suppose you ride your bicycle down a long, steep hill. At the top of the hill your speed is 0 m/s. As you start down the hill, your speed increases. Each second, you move at a greater speed and travel a greater distance than the second before. During the five seconds it takes you to reach the bottom of the hill, you are an accelerating object. **You can use both a speed-versus-time graph and a distance-versus-time graph to analyze the motion of an accelerating object.**

Speed-Versus-Time Graph Figure 8 shows a speed-versus-time graph for your bicycle ride down the hill. What can you learn about your motion by analyzing this graph? First, since the line slants upward, the graph shows you that your speed was increasing. Next, since the line is straight, you can tell that your acceleration was constant. A slanted, straight line on a speed-versus-time graph means that the object is accelerating at a constant rate. You can find your acceleration by calculating the slope of the line. To calculate the slope, choose any two points on the line. Then, divide the rise by the run.

$$\text{Slope} = \frac{\text{Rise}}{\text{Run}} = \frac{8\text{ m/s} - 4\text{ m/s}}{4\text{ s} - 2\text{ s}} = \frac{4\text{ m/s}}{2\text{ s}}$$

$$\text{Slope} = 2\text{ m/s}^2$$

During your bike ride, you accelerated down the hill at a constant rate of 2 m/s^2.

Distance-Versus-Time Graph You can represent the motion of an accelerating object with a distance-versus-time graph. Figure 9 shows a distance-versus-time graph for your bike ride. On this type of graph, a curved line means that the object is accelerating. The curved line in Figure 9 tells you that during each second, you traveled a greater distance than the second before. For example, you traveled a greater distance during the third second than you did during the first second.

The curved line in Figure 9 also tells you that during each second your speed is greater than the second before. Recall that the slope of a distance-versus-time graph is the speed of an object. From second to second, the slope of the line in Figure 9 gets steeper and steeper. Since the slope is increasing, you can conclude that the speed is also increasing. You are accelerating.

Reading Checkpoint **What does a curved line on a distance-versus-time graph tell you?**

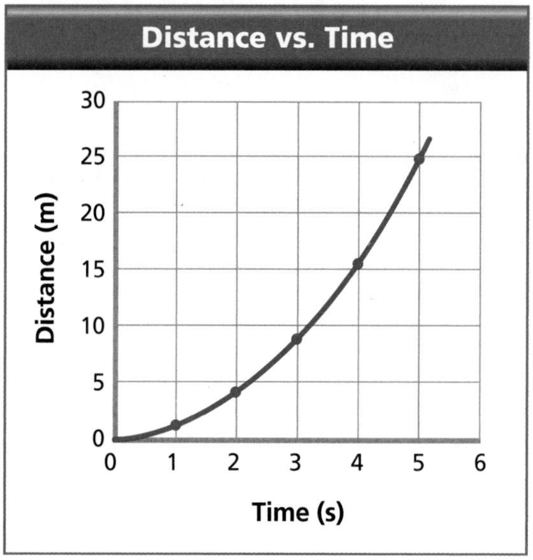

FIGURE 9
Distance-Versus-Time Graph
The curved line on this distance-versus-time graph tells you that the cyclist is accelerating.

Section 3 Assessment

Target Reading Skill Identifying Main Ideas Use information in your graphic organizer to answer Question 1 below.

Reviewing Key Concepts

1. a. Describing What are the three ways that an object can accelerate?
   b. Summarizing Describe how a baseball player accelerates as he runs around the bases after hitting a home run.
   c. Applying Concepts An ice skater glides around a rink at a constant speed of 2 m/s. Is the skater accelerating? Explain your answer.
2. a. Identifying What is the formula used to calculate the acceleration of an object moving in a straight line?
   b. Calculating A cyclist's speed changes from 0 m/s to 15 m/s in 10 seconds. What is the cyclist's average acceleration?
3. a. Naming What types of graphs can you use to analyze the acceleration of an object?
   b. Explaining How is an object moving if a slanted, straight line on a speed-versus-time graph represents its motion?
   c. Predicting What would a distance-versus-time graph look like for the moving object in part (b)?

Math Practice

4. Calculating Acceleration A downhill skier reaches the steepest part of a trail. Her speed increases from 9 m/s to 18 m/s in 3 seconds. What is her average acceleration?
5. Calculating Acceleration What is a race car's average acceleration if its speed changes from 0 m/s to 40 m/s in 4 seconds?

Lab zone **Skills Lab**

Stopping on a Dime

Problem

The school will put in a new basketball court in a small area between two buildings. Safety is an important consideration in the design of the court. What is the distance needed between an out-of-bounds line and a wall so that a player can stop before hitting the wall?

Skills Focus

calculating, interpreting data

Materials

- wooden meter stick
- tape measure
- 2 stopwatches or watches with second hands

Procedure

PART 1 Reaction Time

1. Have your partner suspend a wooden meter stick, zero end down, between your thumb and index finger, as shown. Your thumb and index finger should be about 3 cm apart.
2. Your partner will drop the meter stick without giving you any warning. Try to grab it with your thumb and index finger.

Reaction Time

Distance (cm)	Time (s)	Distance (cm)	Time (s)
15	0.175	25	0.226
16	0.181	26	0.230
17	0.186	27	0.235
18	0.192	28	0.239
19	0.197	29	0.243
20	0.202	30	0.247
21	0.207	31	0.252
22	0.212	32	0.256
23	0.217	33	0.260
24	0.221	34	0.263

3. Note the level at which you grabbed the meter stick and use the chart shown to determine your reaction time. Record the time in the class data table.
4. Reverse roles with your partner and repeat Steps 1–3.

PART 2 Stopping Distance

5. On the school field or in the gymnasium, mark off a distance of 25 m. **CAUTION:** *Be sure to remove any obstacles from the course.*
6. Have your partner time how long it takes you to run the course at full speed. After you pass the 25-m mark, come to a stop as quickly as possible and remain standing. You must not slow down before the mark.
7. Have your partner measure the distance from the 25-m mark to your final position. This is the distance you need to come to a complete stop. Enter your time and distance into the class data table.
8. Reverse roles with your partner. Enter your partner's time and distance into the class data table.

Class Data Table			
Student Name	Reaction Time (s)	Running Time (s)	Stopping Distance (m)

Analyze and Conclude

1. **Calculating** Calculate the average speed of the student who ran the 25-m course the fastest.
2. **Interpreting Data** Multiply the speed of the fastest student (calculated in Question 1) by the slowest reaction time listed in the class data table. Why would you be interested in this product?
3. **Interpreting Data** Add the distance calculated in Question 2 to the longest stopping distance in the class data table. What does this total distance represent?
4. **Drawing Conclusions** Explain why it is important to use the fastest speed, the slowest reaction time, and the longest stopping distance in your calculations.
5. **Controlling Variables** What other factors should you take into account to get results that apply to a real basketball court?
6. **Communicating** Suppose you calculate that the distance from the out-of-bounds line to the wall of the basketball court is too short for safety. Write a proposal to the school that describes the problem. In your proposal, suggest a strategy for making the court safer.

More to Explore

Visit a local playground and examine it from the viewpoint of safety. Use what you learned about stopping distance as one of your guidelines, but also try to identify other potentially unsafe conditions. Write a letter to the Department of Parks or to the officials of your town informing them of your findings.

Chapter 9 Study Guide

1 Describing and Measuring Motion

Key Concepts

- An object is in motion if it changes position relative to a reference point.
- Scientists use SI units to describe the distance an object moves.

Key Terms

motion
reference point
International System of Units
meter

2 Speed and Velocity

Key Concepts

- If you know the distance an object travels in a certain amount of time, you can calculate the speed of the object.
- $\text{Speed} = \dfrac{\text{Distance}}{\text{Time}}$
- When you know both the speed and direction of an object's motion, you know the velocity of the object.
- You can show the motion of an object on a line graph in which you plot distance versus time.
- $\text{Slope} = \dfrac{\text{Rise}}{\text{Run}}$

Key Terms

speed
average speed
instantaneous speed
velocity
slope

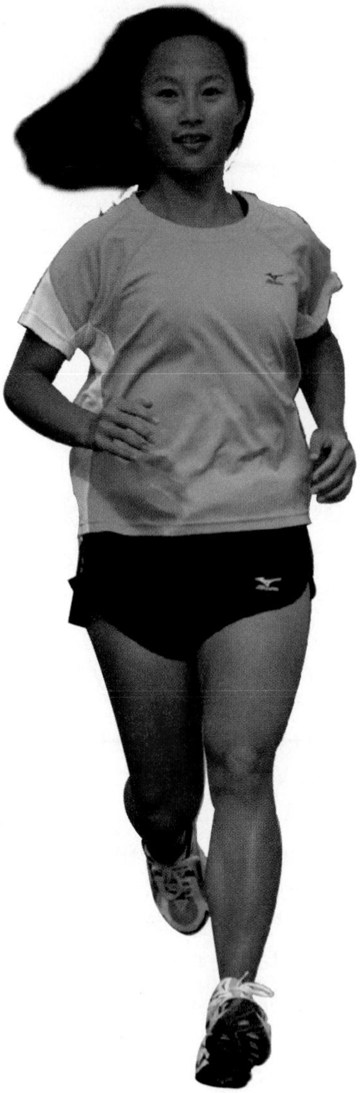

3 Acceleration

Key Concepts

- In science, acceleration refers to increasing speed, decreasing speed, or changing direction.
- To determine the acceleration of an object moving in a straight line, you must calculate the change in speed per unit of time.
- $\text{Acceleration} = \dfrac{\text{Final speed} - \text{Initial speed}}{\text{Time}}$
- You can use both a speed-versus-time graph and a distance-versus-time graph to analyze the motion of an accelerating object.

Key Term

acceleration

Review and Assessment

Go Online PHSchool.com
For: Self-Assessment
Visit: PHSchool.com
Web Code: cka-2090

Organizing Information

Concept Mapping Copy the concept map about motion onto a separate sheet of paper. Then complete it and add a title. (For more information on Concept Mapping, see the Skills Handbook.)

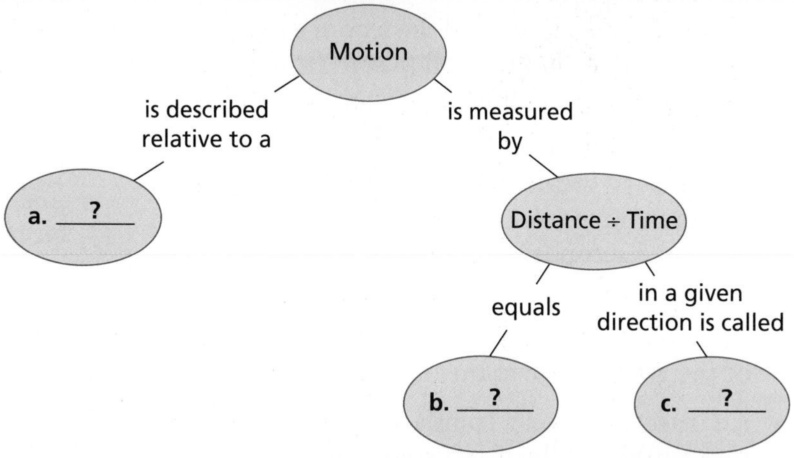

Reviewing Key Terms

Choose the letter of the best answer.

1. A change in position with respect to a reference point is
   a. acceleration.
   b. velocity.
   c. direction.
   d. motion.
2. You do not know an object's velocity until you know its
   a. speed and distance.
   b. reference point.
   c. speed and direction.
   d. acceleration.
3. If you know a car travels 30 km in 20 minutes, you can find its
   a. acceleration.
   b. average speed.
   c. direction.
   d. instantaneous speed.
4. Acceleration is a change in speed or
   a. time.
   b. slope.
   c. direction.
   d. distance.
5. The rate at which velocity changes is called
   a. acceleration. **b.** constant speed.
   c. average speed. **d.** velocity.

If the statement is true, write *true*. If it is false, change the underlined word or words to make the statement true.

6. The distance an object travels per unit of time is called acceleration.
7. The basic SI unit of length is the meter.
8. The SI unit of velocity is m/s^2.
9. The slope of a speed-versus-time graph represents acceleration.
10. Both speed and acceleration include the direction of an object's motion.

Writing in Science

News Report Two trucks have competed in a race. Write an article describing the race and who won. Explain the role the average speed of the trucks played. Tell how average speed can be calculated.

Discovery Channel School

Motion
Video Preview
Video Field Trip
▶ Video Assessment

Review and Assessment

Checking Concepts

11. A passenger walks toward the rear of a moving train. Describe her motion as seen from a reference point on the train. Then describe it from a reference point on the ground.

12. Which has a greater speed, a heron that travels 600 m in 60 seconds or a duck that travels 60 m in 5 seconds? Explain.

13. You have a motion graph for an object that shows distance and time. How does the slope of the graph relate to the object's speed?

14. An insect lands on a compact disc that is put into a player. If the insect spins with the disc, is the insect accelerating? Why or why not?

Thinking Critically

15. Interpreting Graphs The graph below shows the motion of a remote-control car. During which segment is the car moving the fastest? The slowest? How do you know?

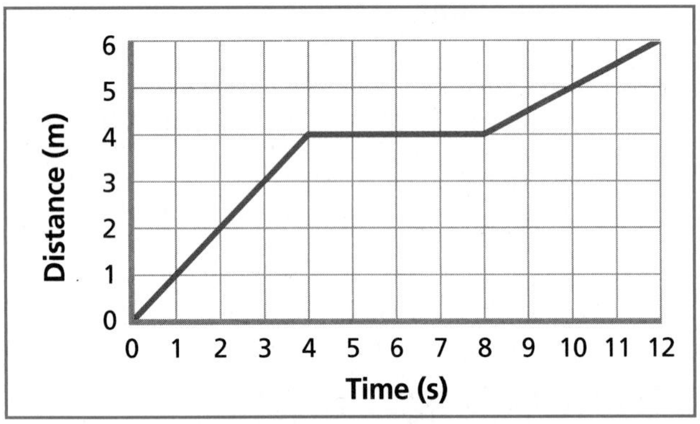

16. Inferring How can you tell if an object is moving when its motion is too slow to see?

17. Problem Solving Two drivers make a 100-km trip. Driver 1 completes the trip in 2 hours. Driver 2 takes 3 hours but stops for an hour halfway. Which driver had a greater average speed? Explain.

18. Applying Concepts A family takes a car trip. They travel for an hour at 80 km/h and then for 2 hours at 40 km/h. Find their average speed during the trip.

Math Practice

19. Converting Units Convert 119 cm to meters.

20. Converting Units Convert 22.4 km to meters.

21. Calculating Acceleration During a slap shot, a hockey puck takes 0.5 second to reach the goal. It started from rest and reached a final speed of 35 m/s. What is the puck's average acceleration?

Applying Skills

Use the illustration of the motion of a ladybug to answer Questions 22–24.

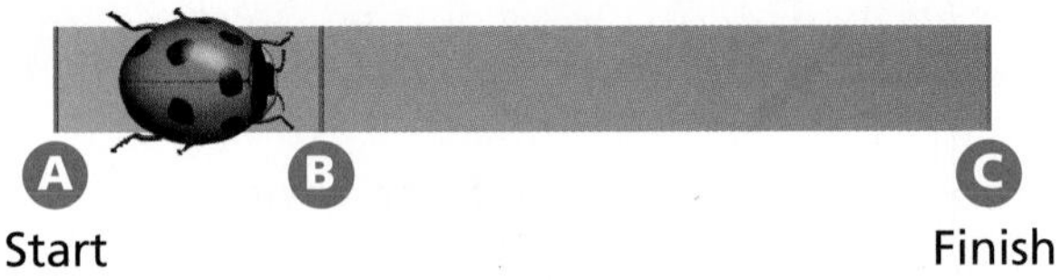

22. Measuring Measure the distance from the starting line to line B, and from line B to the finish line. Measure to the nearest tenth of a centimeter.

23. Calculating Starting at rest, the ladybug accelerated to line B and then moved at a constant speed until it reached the finish line. If the ladybug took 2.5 seconds to move from line B to the finish line, calculate its constant speed during that time.

24. Interpreting Data The speed you calculated in Question 21 is also the speed the ladybug had at the end of its acceleration at line B. If it took 2 seconds for the ladybug to accelerate from the start line to line B, what is its average acceleration during that time?

Lab zone Chapter Project

Performance Assessment Organize your display cards so that they are easy to follow. Remember to put a title on each card stating the speed that you measured. Place the cards in order from the slowest speed to the fastest. Then display them to your class. Compare your results with those of other students.

Standardized Test Prep

Test-Taking Tip

Converting Units

A test question may ask you to change one unit of measurement to another. You do this by using a conversion factor, a fraction that represents the relationship between the units. For example, to convert meters to centimeters, you need to remember that 1 meter equals 100 centimeters: 1 m = 100 cm. To figure out the answer, you would multiply by the conversion factor $\frac{100 \text{ cm}}{1 \text{ m}}$.

Sample Question

A garden measures 3.12 meters wide. How many centimeters wide is the garden?

A 0.312 cm
B 31.2 cm
C 312 cm
D 3,120 cm

Answer

The correct answer is **C.** When you multiply 3.12 m by 100 cm, you get 312 cm.

Choose the letter of the best answer.

1. Members of the Fairview Track Club are running a 1.5-km race. What is the distance of the race in meters?

A 0.15 m
B 15 m
C 150 m
D 1,500 m

2. Your father is driving to the beach. He drives at one speed for two hours. He drives at a different speed for another two hours and a third speed for the final hour. How would you find his average speed for all five hours?

F Divide the total driving time by the total distance.
G Multiply the total driving time by the total distance.
H Divide the total distance by the total driving time.
J Subtract the total driving time from the total distance.

3. Two objects traveling at the same speed have different velocities if they

A start at different times.
B travel different distances.
C have different masses.
D move in different directions.

4. The graph below shows the distance versus time for a runner moving at a constant 200 m/min. What could the runner do to make the slope of the line rise?

Distance vs. Time for a Runner

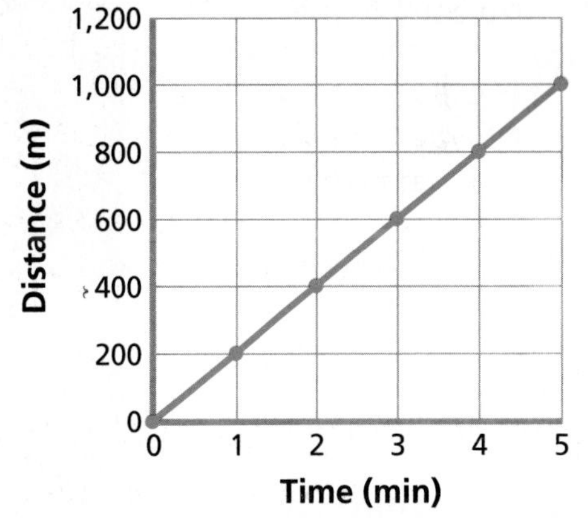

F stop running
G decrease speed
H maintain the same speed
J increase speed

5. An object used as a reference point to determine motion should be

A accelerating.
B stationary.
C decelerating.
D changing direction.

Constructed Response

6. Explain how speed, velocity, and acceleration are related.

Chapter 10

Forces

Chapter Preview

1. **The Nature of Force**
   Discover *Is the Force With You?*
   At-Home Activity *House of Cards*
   Consumer Lab *Sticky Sneakers*
2. **Friction and Gravity**
   Discover *Which Lands First?*
   Try This *Spinning Plates*
   Skills Activity *Calculating*
   Analyzing Data *Free Fall*
3. **Newton's First and Second Laws**
   Discover *What Changes Motion?*
   Try This *Around and Around*
4. **Newton's Third Law**
   Discover *How Pushy Is a Straw?*
   Try This *Colliding Cars*
   Active Art *Momentum*
   Skills Lab *Forced to Accelerate*
5. **Rockets and Satellites**
   Discover *What Makes an Object Move in a Circle?*
   At-Home Activity *Swing the Bucket*

Interactive Textbook

A golfer exerts a force on the golf ball. ▶

Discovery Channel School

Forces

- ▶ Video Preview
- Video Field Trip
- Video Assessment

Lab zone™ Chapter **Project**

Newton Scooters

Newton's laws of motion describe the relationship between forces and motion. In this Chapter Project, you will use Newton's third law to design a vehicle that moves without the use of gravity or a power source such as electricity. How can you make an object move without pushing or pulling it?

Your Goal To design and build a vehicle that moves without an outside force acting on it

Your vehicle must

- move forward by pushing back on something
- not be powered by any form of electricity or use gravity in order to move
- travel a minimum distance of 1.5 meters
- be built following the safety guidelines in Appendix A

Plan It! Preview the chapter to find out about Newton's laws of motion. Determine factors that will affect the acceleration of your vehicle. Brainstorm possible designs for your vehicle, but be careful not to lock yourself into a single idea. Remember that a car with wheels is only one type of vehicle.

Think of ways to use household materials to build your vehicle. Draw a diagram of your proposed design and identify the force that will propel your vehicle. Have your teacher approve your design. Then build your vehicle and see if it works!

Section 1

The Nature of Force

Reading Preview

Key Concepts

- How is a force described?
- How are unbalanced and balanced forces related to an object's motion?

Key Terms

- force
- newton
- net force
- unbalanced forces
- balanced forces

Target Reading Skill

Asking Questions Before you read, preview the red headings. In a graphic organizer like the one below, ask a *what* or *how* question for each heading. As you read, write the answers to your questions.

The Nature of Force

Question	Answer
What is a force?	A force is . . .

Lab zone Discover Activity

Is the Force With You?

1. Attach a spring scale to each end of a skateboard.
2. Gently pull on one spring scale with a force of 4 N, while your partner pulls on the other with the same force. Observe the motion of the skateboard.
3. Now try to keep your partner's spring scale reading at 2 N while you pull with a force of 4 N. Observe the motion of the skateboard.

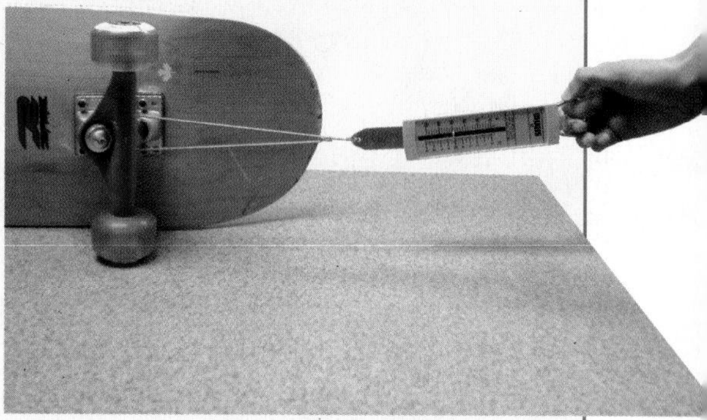

Think It Over

Observing Describe the motion of the skateboard when you and your partner pulled with the same force. How was the motion of the skateboard affected when you pulled with more force than your partner?

A hard kick sends a soccer ball shooting down the field toward the goal. Just in time, the goalie leaps forward, stops the ball, and quickly kicks it in the opposite direction. In a soccer game, the ball is rarely still. Its motion is constantly changing. Why? What causes an object to start moving, stop moving, or change direction? The answer is force.

What Is a Force?

In science, the word *force* has a simple and specific meaning. A **force** is a push or a pull. When one object pushes or pulls another object, you say that the first object exerts a force on the second object. You exert a force on a computer key when you push it and on a chair when you pull it away from a table.

Like velocity and acceleration, a force is described by its strength and by the direction in which it acts. If you push on a door, you exert a force in a different direction than if you pull on the door.

FIGURE 1
Force and Motion
The force of the kick changes the direction of the soccer ball.

The strength of a force is measured in the SI unit called the **newton** (N). This unit is named after the English scientist and mathematician Isaac Newton. You exert about one newton of force when you lift a small lemon.

The direction and strength of a force can be represented by an arrow. The arrow points in the direction of a force. The length of the arrow tells you the strength of a force—the longer the arrow, the greater the force.

Reading Checkpoint **What SI unit is used to measure the strength of a force?**

Combining Forces

Often, more than a single force acts on an object at one time. The combination of all forces acting on an object is called the **net force.** The net force determines whether an object moves and also in which direction it moves.

When forces act in the same direction, the net force can be found by adding the strengths of the individual forces. In Figure 2, the lengths of the two arrows, which represent two forces, are added together to find the net force.

When forces act in opposite directions, they also combine to produce a net force. However, you must pay attention to the direction of each force. Adding a force acting in one direction to a force acting in the opposite direction is the same as adding a positive number to a negative number. So when two forces act in opposite directions, they combine by subtraction. The net force always acts in the direction of the greater force. If the opposing forces are of equal strength, there is no net force. There is no change in the object's motion.

FIGURE 2
Combining Forces
The strength and direction of the individual forces determine the net force. **Calculating** *How do you find the net force when two forces act in opposite directions?*

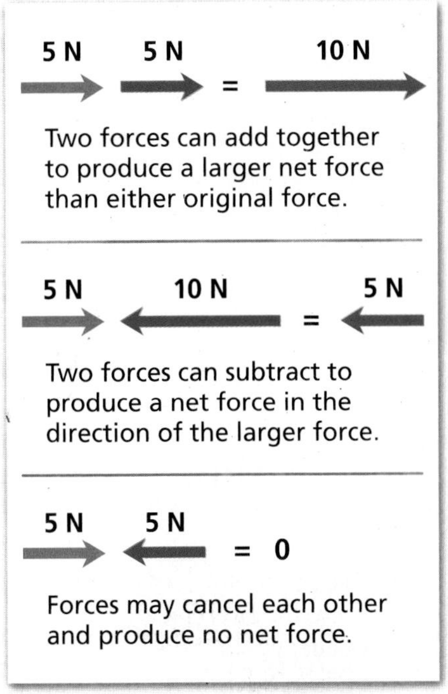

5 N
5 N
=
10 N
Two forces can add together to produce a larger net force than either original force.
5 N
10 N
=
5 N
Two forces can subtract to produce a net force in the direction of the larger force.
5 N
5 N
= 0
Forces may cancel each other and produce no net force.

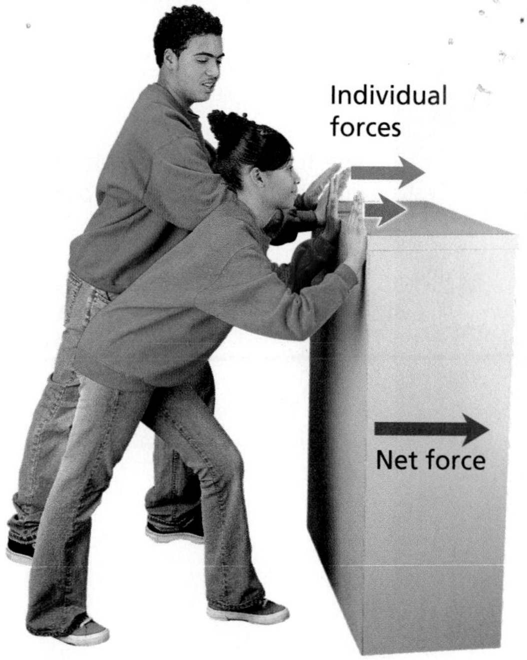

Unbalanced Forces in the Same Direction
When two forces act in the same direction, the net force is the sum of the two individual forces. The box moves to the right.

Unbalanced Forces in the Opposite Direction
When two forces act in opposite directions, the net force is the difference between the two individual forces. The box moves to the right.

Unbalanced Forces Whenever there is a net force acting on an object, the forces are unbalanced. **Unbalanced forces** can cause an object to start moving, stop moving, or change direction. **Unbalanced forces acting on an object result in a net force and cause a change in the object's motion.**

Figure 3 shows two people exerting forces on a box. When they both push a box to the right, their individual forces add together to produce a net force in that direction. Since a net, or unbalanced, force acts on the box, the box moves to the right.

When the two people push the box in opposite directions, the net force on the box is the difference between their individual forces. Because the boy pushes with a greater force than the girl, their forces are unbalanced and a net force acts on the box to the right. As a result, the box moves to the right.

Reading Checkpoint **What is the result of unbalanced forces acting on an object?**

Balanced Forces When forces are exerted on an object, the object's motion does not always change. In an arm wrestling contest, each person exerts a force on the other's arm, but the two forces are exerted in opposite directions. Even though both people push hard, their arm positions may not change.

Equal forces acting on one object in opposite directions are called **balanced forces.** Each force is balanced by the other.

Go Online SCI LINKS NSTA

For: Links on force
Visit: www.SciLinks.org
Web Code: scn-1321

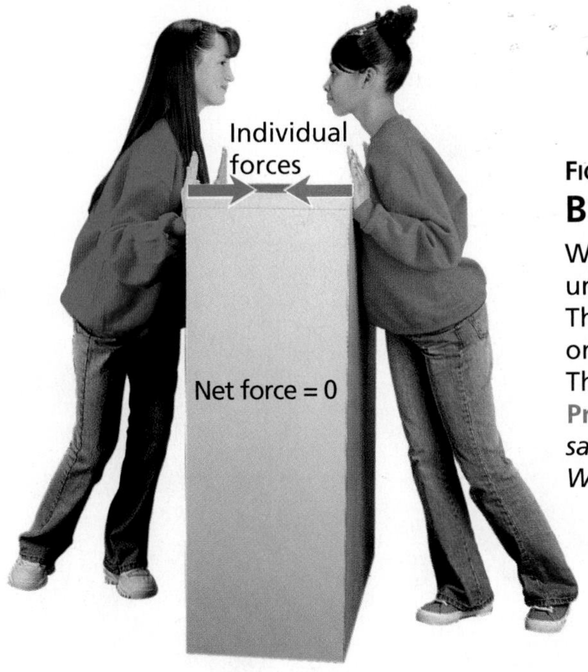

Balanced Forces in Opposite Directions
When two equal forces act in opposite directions, they cancel each other out. The box doesn't move.

FIGURE 3
Balanced and Unbalanced Forces

When the forces acting on an object are unbalanced, a net force acts on the object. The object will move. When balanced forces act on an object, no net force acts on the object. The object's motion remains unchanged.
Predicting *If both girls pushed the box on the same side, would the motion of the box change? Why or why not?*

Balanced forces acting on an object do not change the object's motion. When equal forces are exerted in opposite directions, the net force is zero. In Figure 3, when two people push on the box with equal force in opposite directions, the forces cancel out. The box does not move.

Section 1 Assessment

Target Reading Skill **Asking Questions** Use the answers to the questions you wrote about the headings to help you answer the questions below.

Reviewing Key Concepts

1. a. **Defining** What is a force?
   b. **Explaining** How is a force described?
   c. **Interpreting Diagrams** In a diagram, one force arrow is longer than the other arrow. What can you tell about the forces?
2. a. **Reviewing** How can you find the net force if two forces act in opposite directions?
   b. **Comparing and Contrasting** How do balanced forces acting on an object affect its motion? How do unbalanced forces acting on an object affect its motion?
   c. **Calculating** You exert a force of 120 N on a desk. Your friend exerts a force of 150 N in the same direction. What net force do you and your friend exert on the desk?

Lab zone **At-Home Activity**

House of Cards Carefully set two playing cards upright on a flat surface so that their top edges lean on each other. The cards should be able to stand by themselves. In terms of balanced forces, explain to a family member why the cards don't move. Then exert a force on one of the cards. Explain to a family member the role of unbalanced forces in what happens.

Lab zone **Consumer Lab**

Sticky Sneakers

Problem

Friction is a force that acts in the opposite direction to motion. How does the amount of friction between a sneaker and a surface compare for different brands of sneakers?

Skills Focus

controlling variables, interpreting data

Materials

- three or more different brands of sneakers
- 2 spring scales, 5-N and 20-N, or force sensors
- mass set(s)
- tape
- 3 large paper clips
- balance

Procedure

1. Sneakers are designed to deal with various friction forces, including these:
   - starting friction, which is involved when you start from a stopped position
   - forward-stopping friction, which is involved when you come to a forward stop
   - sideways-stopping friction, which is involved when you come to a sideways stop
2. Prepare a data table in which you can record each type of friction for each sneaker.
3. Place each sneaker on a balance. Then put masses in each sneaker so that the total mass of the sneaker plus the masses is 1,000 g. Spread the masses out evenly inside the sneaker.
4. You will need to tape a paper clip to each sneaker and then attach a spring scale to the paper clip. (If you are using force sensors, see your teacher for instructions.) To measure
   - starting friction, attach the paper clip to the back of the sneaker
   - forward-stopping friction, attach the paper clip to the front of the sneaker
   - sideways-stopping friction, attach the paper clip to the side of the sneaker

Data Table

Sneaker	Starting Friction (N)	Sideways-Stopping Friction (N)	Forward-Stopping Friction (N)
A			
B			

5. To measure starting friction, pull the sneaker backward until it starts to move. Use the 20-N spring scale first. If the reading is less than 5 N, use a 5-N scale. The force necessary to make the sneaker start moving is equal to the friction force. Record the starting friction force in your data table.
6. To measure either type of stopping friction, use the spring scale to pull each sneaker at a slow, constant speed. Record the stopping friction force in your data table.
7. Repeat Steps 4–6 for the remaining sneakers.

Analyze and Conclude

1. Controlling Variables What are the manipulated and responding variables in this experiment? Explain. (See the Skills Handbook to read about experimental variables.)
2. Observing Why is the reading on the spring scale equal to the friction force in each case?
3. Interpreting Data Which sneaker had the most starting friction? Which had the most forward-stopping friction? Which had the most sideways-stopping friction?
4. Drawing Conclusions Do you think that using a sneaker with a small amount of mass in it is a fair test of the friction of the sneakers? Why or why not? (*Hint*: Consider that sneakers are used with people's feet inside them.)
5. Inferring Why did you pull the sneaker at a slow speed to test for stopping friction? Why did you pull a sneaker that wasn't moving to test starting friction?
6. Developing Hypotheses Can you identify a relationship between the brand of sneaker and the amount of friction you observed? If so, describe the relationship. What do you observe that might cause one sneaker to grip the floor better than another?
7. Communicating Draw a diagram for an advertising brochure that shows the forces acting on the sneaker for each type of motion.

Design an Experiment

Wear a pair of your own sneakers. Start running and notice how you press against the floor with your sneaker. How do you think this affects the friction between the sneaker and the floor? Design an experiment that will test for this variable. *Obtain your teacher's permission before carrying out your investigation.*

Section 2

Friction and Gravity

Reading Preview

Key Concepts

- What factors determine the strength of the friction force between two surfaces?
- What factors affect the gravitational force between two objects?
- Why do objects accelerate during free fall?

Key Terms

- friction • static friction
- sliding friction
- rolling friction • fluid friction
- gravity • mass • weight
- free fall • air resistance
- terminal velocity • projectile

Target Reading Skill

Comparing and Contrasting As you read, compare and contrast friction and gravity by completing a table like the one below.

	Friction	Gravity
Effect on motion	Opposes motion	
Depends on		
Measured in		

Lab zone Discover Activity

Which Lands First?

1. Stack three quarters. Place tape between the quarters to hold them tightly together. Place the stack of quarters next to a single quarter near the edge of a desk.
2. Put a ruler flat on the desk behind the coins. Line it up parallel to the edge of the desk and just touching the coins.
3. Keeping the ruler parallel to the edge of the desk, push the coins over the edge at the same time. Observe how long the coins take to land.

Think It Over

Predicting Did you see a difference in the time the coins took to fall? Use what you observed to predict whether a soccer ball will fall more quickly than a marble. Will a pencil fall more quickly than a book? How can you test your predictions?

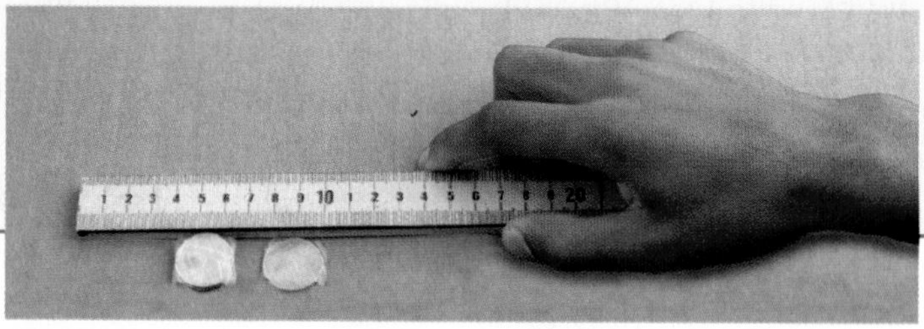

What happens when you jump on a sled on the side of a snow-covered hill? Without actually doing this, you can predict that the sled will slide down the hill. Now think about what happens at the bottom of the hill. Does the sled keep sliding? Again, without actually riding the sled, you can predict that the sled will slow down and stop.

Why does the sled's motion change on the side of the hill and then again at the bottom? In each case, unbalanced forces act on the sled. The force of gravity causes the sled to accelerate down the hill. The force of friction eventually causes the sled to stop. These two forces affect many motions on Earth.

Friction and gravity both act on the sled.

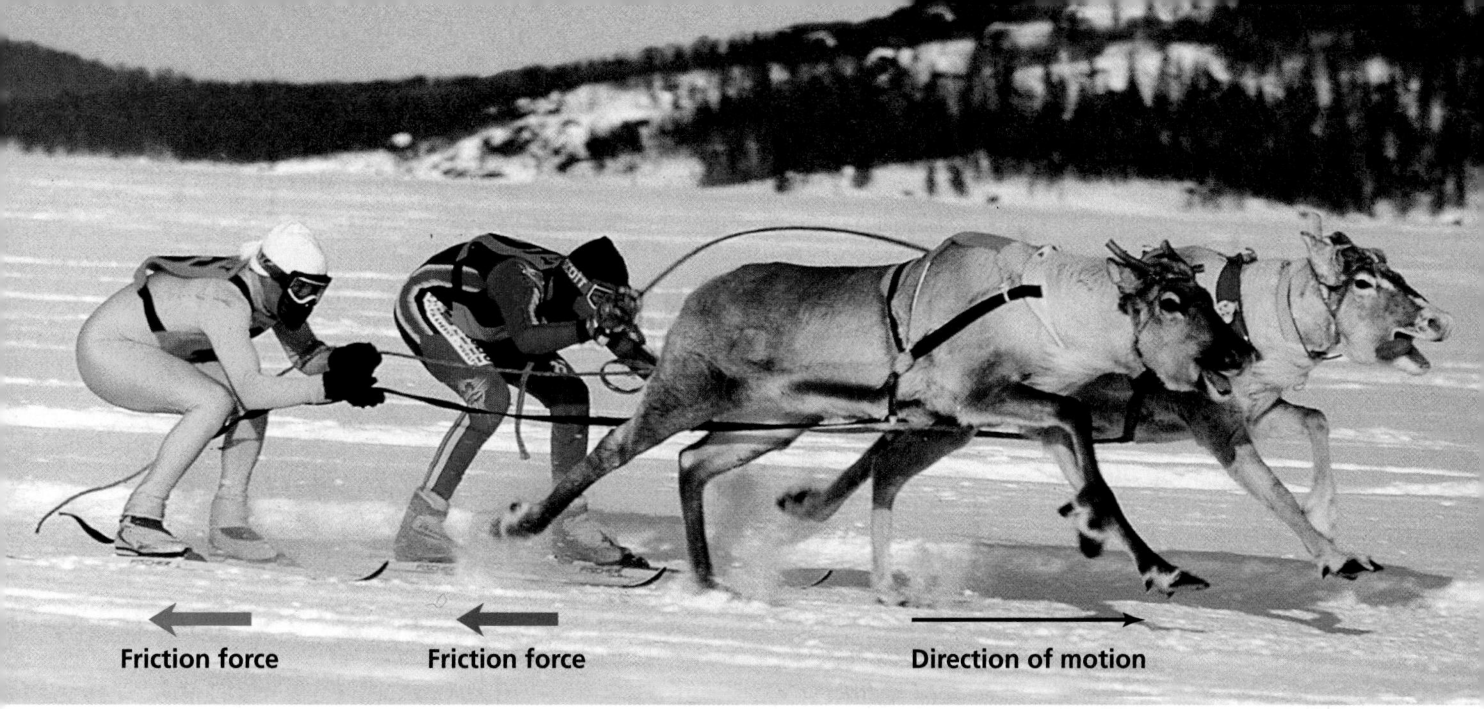

FIGURE 4
Friction and Smooth Surfaces The smooth surfaces of the skis make for a fast ride for these Finnish skiers.
Relating Diagrams and Photos *How does the direction of friction compare to the direction of motion?*

Friction

When a sled moves across snow, the bottom of the sled rubs against the surface of the snow. In the same way, the skin of a firefighter's hands rubs against the polished metal pole during the slide down the pole. The force that two surfaces exert on each other when they rub against each other is called **friction.**

The Causes of Friction In general, smooth surfaces produce less friction than rough surfaces. **The strength of the force of friction depends on two factors: how hard the surfaces push together and the types of surfaces involved.** The skiers in Figure 4 get a fast ride because there is very little friction between their skis and the snow. The reindeer would not be able to pull them easily over a rough surface such as sand. Friction also increases if surfaces push hard against each other. If you rub your hands together forcefully, there is more friction than if you rub your hands together lightly.

A snow-packed surface or a metal firehouse pole may seem quite smooth. But, as you can see in Figure 5, even the smoothest objects have irregular, bumpy surfaces. When the irregularities of one surface come into contact with those of another surface, friction occurs. Friction acts in a direction opposite to the direction of the object's motion. Without friction, a moving object might not stop until it strikes another object.

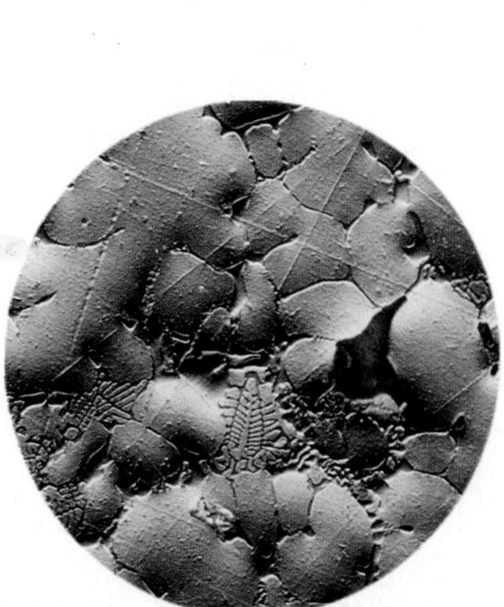

FIGURE 5
A Smooth Surface?
If you look at the polished surface of an aluminum alloy under a powerful microscope, you'll find that it is actually quite rough.

Lab zone Try This **Activity**

Spinning Plates

You can compare rolling friction to sliding friction.

1. Stack two identical pie plates together. Try to spin the top plate.
2. Now separate the plates and fill the bottom of one pie plate loosely with marbles.

3. Place the second plate in the plate with marbles.
4. Try to spin the top plate again. Observe the results.

Drawing Conclusions What applications can you think of for the rolling friction modeled in this activity?

Static Friction Four types of friction are shown in Figure 6. The friction that acts on objects that are not moving is called **static friction.** Because of static friction, you must use extra force to start the motion of stationary objects. For example, think about what happens when you try to push a heavy desk across a floor. If you push on the desk with a force less than the force of static friction between the desk and the floor, the desk will not move. To make the desk move, you must exert a force greater than the force of static friction. Once the desk is moving, there is no longer any static friction. However, there is another type of friction—sliding friction.

Sliding Friction **Sliding friction** occurs when two solid surfaces slide over each other. Sliding friction can be useful. For example, you can spread sand on an icy path to improve your footing. Ballet dancers apply a sticky powder to the soles of their ballet slippers so they won't slip on the dance floor. And when you stop a bicycle with hand brakes, rubber pads slide against the tire surfaces, causing the wheels to slow and eventually stop. On the other hand, sliding friction is a problem if you fall off your bike and skin your knee!

Rolling Friction When an object rolls across a surface, **rolling friction** occurs. Rolling friction is easier to overcome than sliding friction for similar materials. This type of friction is important to engineers who design certain products. For example, skates, skateboards, and bicycles need wheels that move freely. So engineers use ball bearings to reduce the friction between the wheels and the rest of the product. These ball bearings are small, smooth steel balls that reduce friction by rolling between moving parts.

Fluid Friction Fluids, such as water, oil, or air, are materials that flow easily. **Fluid friction** occurs when a solid object moves through a fluid. Like rolling friction, fluid friction is easier to overcome than sliding friction. This is why the parts of machines that must slide over each other are often bathed in oil. In this way, the solid parts move through the fluid instead of sliding against each other. When you ride a bike, fluid friction occurs between you and the air. Cyclists often wear streamlined helmets and specially designed clothing to reduce fluid friction.

Reading Checkpoint **What are two ways in which friction can be useful?**

Go Online
SCI LINKS NSTA

For: Links on friction
Visit: www.SciLinks.org
Web Code: scn-1322

FIGURE 6

Types of Friction

Types of friction include static, sliding, rolling, and fluid friction. **Making Generalizations** *In what direction does friction act compared to an object's motion?*

Static Friction ▼
To make the sled move, the athlete first has to overcome the force of static friction. Static friction acts in the opposite direction to the intended motion.

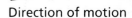

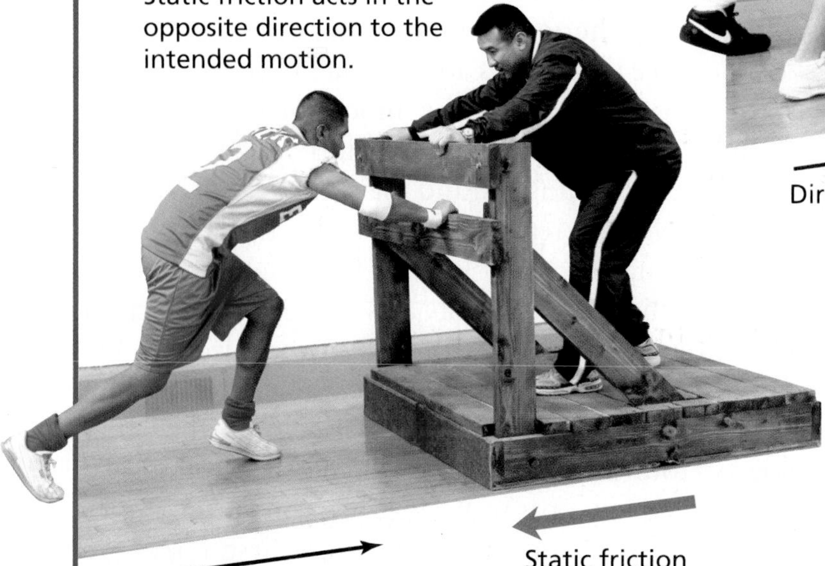

Sliding Friction ▲
Once the sled is moving, it slides over the floor. Sliding friction acts between the sled and the floor in the opposite direction to the sled's motion.

Rolling Friction ▼
Rolling friction occurs when an object rolls over a surface. For the skateboarder, rolling friction acts in the direction opposite to the skateboard's motion.

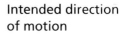

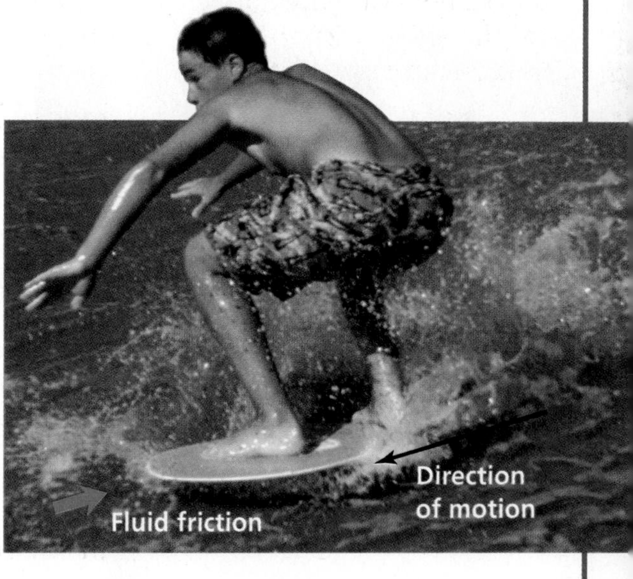

Fluid Friction ▲
When an object pushes fluid aside, friction occurs. The surfer must overcome the fluid friction of the water.

FIGURE 7
Gravity and Acceleration
Divers begin accelerating as soon as they leap from the platform.

Gravity

Would you be surprised if you let go of a pen you were holding and it did not fall? You are so used to objects falling that you may not have thought about why they fall. One person who thought about it was Isaac Newton. He concluded that a force acts to pull objects straight down toward the center of Earth. **Gravity** is a force that pulls objects toward each other.

Universal Gravitation Newton realized that gravity acts everywhere in the universe, not just on Earth. It is the force that makes an apple fall to the ground. It is the force that keeps the moon orbiting around Earth. It is the force that keeps all the planets in our solar system orbiting around the sun.

What Newton realized is now called the law of universal gravitation. The law of universal gravitation states that the force of gravity acts between all objects in the universe. This means that any two objects in the universe, without exception, attract each other. You are attracted not only to Earth but also to all the other objects around you. Earth and the objects around you are attracted to you as well. However, you do not notice the attraction among objects because these forces are small compared to the force of Earth's attraction.

Factors Affecting Gravity **Two factors affect the gravitational attraction between objects: mass and distance.** **Mass** is a measure of the amount of matter in an object. The SI unit of mass is the kilogram. One kilogram is the mass of about 400 modern pennies. Everything that has mass is made up of matter.

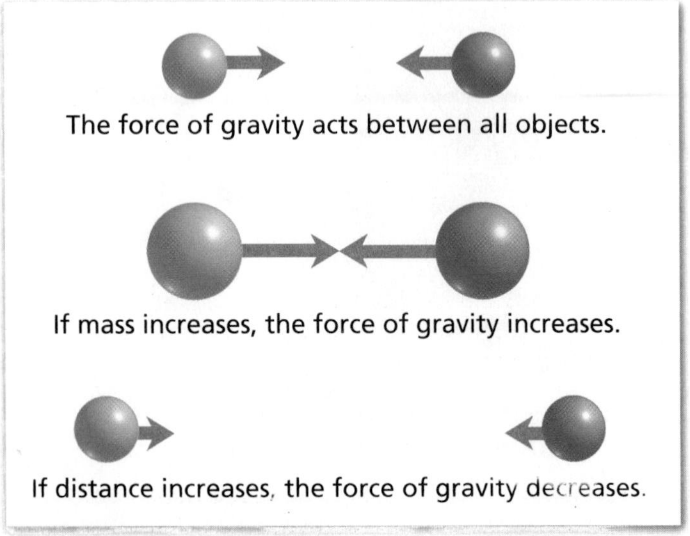

The force of gravity acts between all objects.
If mass increases, the force of gravity increases.
If distance increases, the force of gravity decreases.

FIGURE 8
Gravitational Attraction
Gravity increases with mass and decreases with distance. **Inferring** *What happens to the force of gravity between two objects if the distance between them decreases?*

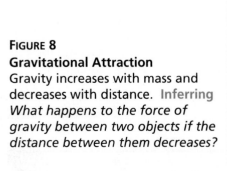

The more mass an object has, the greater its gravitational force. Because the sun's mass is so great, it exerts a large gravitational force on the planets. That's one reason why the planets orbit the sun.

In addition to mass, gravitational force depends on the distance between the objects. The farther apart two objects are, the lesser the gravitational force between them. For a spacecraft traveling toward Mars, Earth's gravitational pull decreases as the spacecraft's distance from Earth increases. Eventually the gravitational pull of Mars becomes greater than Earth's, and the spacecraft is more attracted toward Mars.

Weight and Mass Mass is sometimes confused with weight. Mass is a measure of the amount of matter in an object; weight is a measure of the gravitational force exerted on an object. The force of gravity on a person or object at the surface of a planet is known as **weight.** So, when you step on a bathroom scale, you are determining the gravitational force Earth is exerting on you.

Weight varies with the strength of the gravitational force but mass does not. Suppose you weighed yourself on Earth to be 450 newtons. Then you traveled to the moon and weighed yourself again. You might be surprised to find out that you weigh only about 75 newtons—the weight of about 8 kilograms on Earth! You weigh less on the moon because the moon's mass is only a fraction of Earth's.

Reading Checkpoint **What is the difference between weight and mass?**

Lab zone Skills Activity

Calculating

You can determine the weight of an object if you measure its mass.

1. Estimate the weight of four objects. (*Hint:* A small lemon weighs about 1 N.)
2. Use a balance to find the mass of each object. If the measurements are not in kilograms, convert them to kilograms.
3. Multiply each mass by 9.8 m/s^2 to find the weight in newtons.

How close to actual values were your estimates?

FIGURE 9
Mass and Weight This astronaut jumps easily on the moon. **Comparing and Contrasting** *How do his mass and weight on the moon compare to his mass and weight on Earth?*

Astronaut in Spacesuit

Weight on Moon	=	270 N
Weight on Earth	=	1,617 N
Mass on Moon	=	165 kg
Mass on Earth	=	165 kg

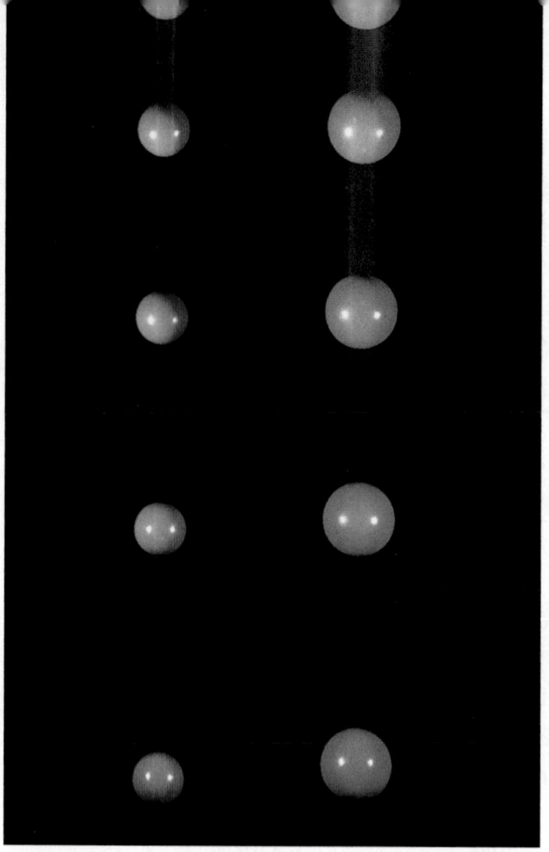

FIGURE 10
Free Fall
In the absence of air, two objects with different masses fall at exactly the same rate.

Gravity and Motion

On Earth, gravity is a downward force that affects all objects. When you hold a book, you exert a force that balances the force of gravity. When you let go of the book, gravity becomes an unbalanced force and the book falls.

Free Fall When the only force acting on an object is gravity, the object is said to be in **free fall.** An object in free fall is accelerating. Do you know why? **In free fall, the force of gravity is an unbalanced force, which causes an object to accelerate.**

How much do objects accelerate as they fall? Near the surface of Earth, the acceleration due to gravity is 9.8 m/s^2. This means that for every second an object is falling, its velocity increases by 9.8 m/s. For example, suppose an object is dropped from the top of a building. Its starting velocity is 0 m/s. After one second, its velocity has increased to 9.8 m/s. After two seconds, its velocity is 19.6 m/s (9.8 m/s + 9.8 m/s). The velocity continues to increase as the object falls.

While it may seem hard to believe at first, all objects in free fall accelerate at the same rate regardless of their masses. The two falling objects in Figure 10 demonstrate this principle.

Math Analyzing Data

Free Fall

Use the graph to answer the following questions.

1. **Interpreting Graphs** What variable is on the horizontal axis? The vertical axis?
2. **Calculating** Calculate the slope of the graph. What does the slope tell you about the object's motion?
3. **Predicting** What will be the speed of the object at 6 seconds?
4. **Drawing Conclusions** Suppose another object of the same size but with a greater mass was dropped instead. How would the speed values change?

Motion of an Object in Free Fall

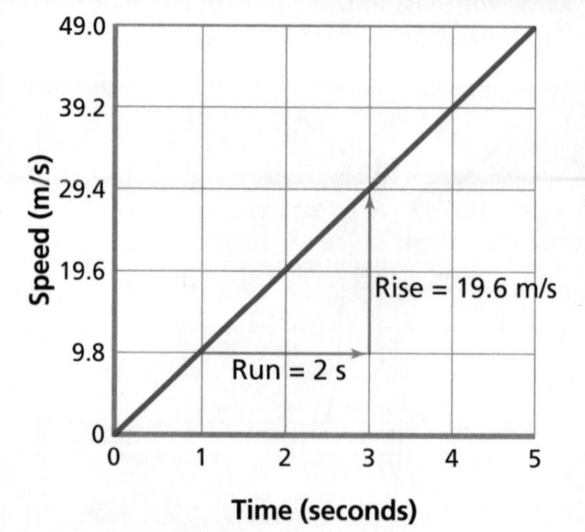

FIGURE 11
Air Resistance
Falling objects with a greater surface area experience more air resistance. If the leaf and the acorn fall from the tree at the same time, the acorn will hit first.
Comparing and Contrasting *If the objects fall in a vacuum, which one will hit first? Why?*

Air Resistance Despite the fact that all objects are supposed to fall at the same rate, you know that this is not always the case. For example, an oak leaf flutters slowly to the ground, while an acorn drops straight down. Objects falling through air experience a type of fluid friction called **air resistance.** Remember that friction is in the direction opposite to motion, so air resistance is an upward force exerted on falling objects. Air resistance is not the same for all objects. Falling objects with a greater surface area experience more air resistance. That is why a leaf falls more slowly than an acorn. In a vacuum, where there is no air, all objects fall with exactly the same rate of acceleration.

You can see the effect of air resistance if you drop a flat piece of paper and a crumpled piece of paper at the same time. Since the flat paper has a greater surface area, it experiences greater air resistance and falls more slowly. In a vacuum, both pieces of paper would fall at the same rate.

Air resistance increases with velocity. As a falling object speeds up, the force of air resistance becomes greater and greater. Eventually, a falling object will fall fast enough that the upward force of air resistance becomes equal to the downward force of gravity acting on the object. At this point the forces on the object are balanced. Remember that when forces are balanced, there is no acceleration. The object continues to fall, but its velocity remains constant. The greatest velocity a falling object reaches is called its **terminal velocity.** Terminal velocity is reached when the force of air resistance equals the weight of the object.

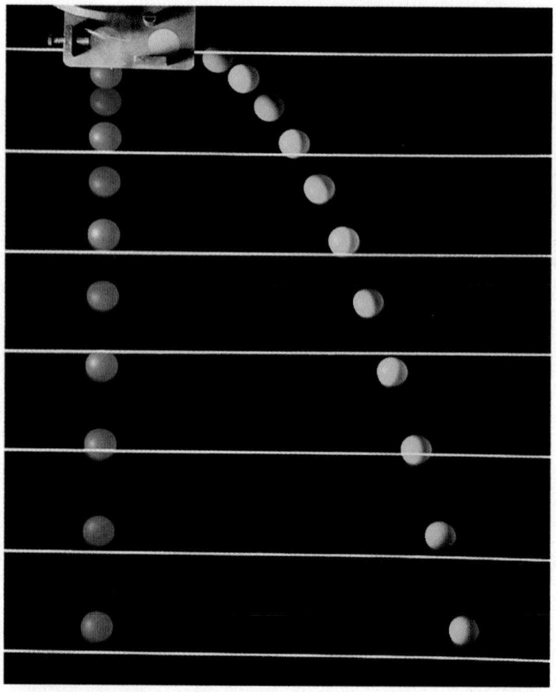

FIGURE 12
Projectile Motion
One ball is dropped vertically and a second ball is thrown horizontally at the same time.
Making Generalizations *Does the horizontal velocity of the ball affect how fast it falls?*

Projectile Motion Rather than dropping a ball straight down, what happens if you throw it horizontally? An object that is thrown is called a **projectile** (pruh JEK tul). Will a projectile that is thrown horizontally land on the ground at the same time as an object that is dropped?

Look at Figure 12. The yellow ball was given a horizontal push at the same time as the red ball was dropped. Even though the yellow ball moves horizontally, the force of gravity continues to act on it in the same way it acts on the red ball. The yellow ball falls at the same rate as the red ball. Thus, both balls will hit the ground at exactly the same time.

In a similar way, an arrow flying toward a target is a projectile. Because of the force of gravity, the arrow will fall as it flies toward the target. So if you try to hit the bull's-eye, you must aim above it to account for gravity's pull. When you throw a projectile at an upward angle, the force of gravity reduces its vertical velocity. Eventually, the upward motion of the projectile will stop, and gravity will pull it back toward the ground. From this point, the projectile will fall at the same rate as any dropped object.

Reading Checkpoint **How does gravity affect objects that are moving horizontally?**

Section 2 Assessment

Target Reading Skill

Comparing and Contrasting Use the information in your table about friction and gravity to help you answer the questions below.

Reviewing Key Concepts

1. a. **Listing** What are the four types of friction?
   b. **Summarizing** What factors affect the friction force between two surfaces?
   c. **Classifying** What types of friction occur when you ride a bike through a puddle?
2. a. **Identifying** What is the law of universal gravitation?
   b. **Explaining** How do mass and distance affect the gravitational attraction between objects?
   c. **Predicting** How would your weight change on the surface of an Earth-sized planet whose mass was greater than Earth's? Why?
3. a. **Reviewing** Why does an object accelerate when it falls toward Earth's surface?
   b. **Describing** How does the mass of an object affect its acceleration during free fall?
   c. **Applying Concepts** What force changes when a sky diver's parachute opens? What force stays the same?

Writing in Science

Cause-and-Effect Paragraph Suppose Earth's gravitational force were decreased by half. How would this change affect a game of basketball? Write a paragraph explaining how the motion of the players and the ball would be different.

Section 3

Newton's First and Second Laws

Reading Preview

Key Concepts

- What is Newton's first law of motion?
- What is Newton's second law of motion?

Key Term

- inertia

Target Reading Skill

Outlining As you read, make an outline about Newton's first and second laws. Use the red headings for the main topics and the blue headings for the subtopics.

Newton's First and Second Laws
I. The first law of motion
A. Inertia
B.
II. The second law of motion
A.

Isaac Newton ▼

Lab zone Discover Activity

What Changes Motion?

1. Stack several metal washers on top of a toy car.
2. Place a heavy book on the floor near the car.
3. Predict what will happen to both the car and the washers if you roll the car into the book. Test your prediction.

Think It Over

Observing What happened to the car when it hit the book? What happened to the washers? What might be the reason for any difference between the motions of the car and the washers?

How and why objects move as they do has fascinated scientists for thousands of years. In the early 1600s, the Italian astronomer Galileo Galilei suggested that, once an object is in motion, no force is needed to keep it moving. Force is needed only to change the motion of an object. Galileo's ideas paved the way for Isaac Newton. Newton proposed the three basic laws of motion in the late 1600s.

The First Law of Motion

Newton's first law restates Galileo's ideas about force and motion. **Newton's first law of motion states that an object at rest will remain at rest, and an object moving at a constant velocity will continue moving at a constant velocity, unless it is acted upon by an unbalanced force.**

If an object is not moving, it will not move until a force acts on it. Clothes on the floor of your room, for example, will stay there unless you pick them up. If an object is already moving, it will continue to move at a constant velocity until a force acts to change either its speed or direction. For example, a tennis ball flies through the air once you hit it with a racket. If your friend doesn't hit the ball back, the forces of gravity and friction will eventually stop the ball. On Earth, gravity and friction are unbalanced forces that often change an object's motion.

FIGURE 13
Inertia The inertia of the objects on the table keeps them from moving.
Inferring *Why should the girl use a slippery tablecloth?*

Inertia Whether an object is moving or not, it resists any change to its motion. Galileo's concept of the resistance to a change in motion is called inertia. **Inertia** (in UR shuh) is the tendency of an object to resist a change in motion. Newton's first law of motion is also called the law of inertia.

Inertia explains many common events, such as why you move forward in your seat when a car stops suddenly. When the car stops, inertia keeps you moving forward. A force, such as the pull of a seat belt, is required to change your motion.

Inertia Depends on Mass Some objects have more inertia than other objects. For example, suppose you needed to move an empty aquarium and an aquarium full of water. Obviously, the full aquarium is harder to move than the empty one, because it has more mass. The greater the mass of an object is, the greater its inertia, and the greater the force required to change its motion. The full aquarium is more difficult to move because it has more inertia than the empty aquarium.

Reading Checkpoint **How is mass related to inertia?**

Lab zone **Try This Activity**

Around and Around

An object moving in a circle has inertia.

1. Tape one end of a length of thread (about 1 m) to a table tennis ball.
2. Suspend the ball in front of you and swing it in a horizontal circle, keeping it 2–3 cm above the floor.
3. Let go of the thread and observe the direction in which the ball rolls.
4. Repeat this several times, letting go of the thread at different points.

Inferring At what point do you need to let go of the thread if you want the ball to roll directly away from you? Toward you? Draw a diagram as part of your answer.

The Second Law of Motion

Suppose you are baby-sitting two children who love wagon rides. Their favorite part is when you accelerate quickly. When you get tired and sit in the wagon, one of the children pulls you. He soon finds he cannot accelerate the wagon nearly as fast as you can. How is the wagon's acceleration related to the force pulling it? How is the acceleration related to the wagon's mass?

Determining Acceleration **According to Newton's second law of motion, acceleration depends on the object's mass and on the net force acting on the object.** This relationship can be written as an equation.

$$\text{Acceleration} = \frac{\text{Net force}}{\text{Mass}}$$

Acceleration is measured in meters per second per second (m/s^2), and mass is measured in kilograms (kg). According to Newton's second law, then, force is measured in kilograms times meters per second per second ($kg \cdot m/s^2$). The short form for this unit of force is the newton (N). Recall that a newton is the SI unit of force. You can think of 1 newton as the force required to give a 1-kg mass an acceleration of 1 m/s^2.

Go Online PHSchool.com

For: More on Newton's laws
Visit: PHSchool.com
Web Code: cgd-3023

Math Sample Problem

Calculating Force

A speedboat pulls a 55-kg water-skier. The force causes the skier to accelerate at 2.0 m/s^2. Calculate the net force that causes this acceleration.

1 Read and Understand

What information are you given?

Mass of the water-skier (m) = 55 kg

Acceleration of the water-skier (a) = 2.0 m/s^2

2 Plan and Solve

What quantity are you trying to calculate?

The net force (F_{net}) = ■

What formula contains the given quantities and the unknown quantity?

$$a = \frac{F_{net}}{m} \quad \text{or} \quad F_{net} = m \times a$$

Perform the calculation.

$$F_{net} = m \times a = 55\ kg \times 2.0\ m/s^2$$
$$F = 110\ kg \cdot m/s^2$$
$$F = 110\ N$$

3 Look Back and Check

Does your answer make sense?

A net force of 110 N is required to accelerate the water-skier. This may not seem like enough force, but it does not include the force of the speedboat's pull that overcomes friction.

Math Practice

1. **Calculating Force** What is the net force on a 1,000-kg object accelerating at 3 m/s^2?
2. **Calculating Force** What net force is needed to accelerate a 25-kg cart at 14 m/s^2?

FIGURE 14
Force and Mass
The force of the boy's pull and the mass of the wagon determine the wagon's acceleration.

Changes in Force and Mass How can you increase the acceleration of the wagon? Look again at the equation. One way to increase acceleration is by changing the force. If the mass is constant, acceleration and force change in the same way. So to increase the acceleration of the wagon, you can increase the force used to pull it.

Another way to increase acceleration is to change the mass. According to the equation, acceleration and mass change in opposite ways. If the force is constant, an increase in mass causes a decrease in acceleration. The opposite is also true: A decrease in mass causes an increase in acceleration with a constant force. To increase the acceleration of the wagon, you can decrease its mass. So, instead of you, the children should ride in the wagon.

Reading Checkpoint **What are two ways to increase the acceleration of an object?**

Section 3 Assessment

Target Reading Skill **Outlining** Use the information in your outline about Newton's first and second laws of motion to help you answer the questions below.

Reviewing Key Concepts

1. a. **Reviewing** What does Newton's first law of motion state?
   b. **Explaining** Why is Newton's first law of motion sometimes called the law of inertia?
   c. **Inferring** Use what you know about inertia to explain why you feel pressed back into the seat of a car when it accelerates.
2. a. **Defining** State Newton's second law of motion in your own words.
   b. **Problem Solving** How could you keep an object's acceleration the same if the force acting on the object were doubled?
   c. **Applying Concepts** Using what you know about Newton's second law, explain why a car with a large mass might use more fuel than a car with a smaller mass. Assume both cars drive the same distance.

Math Practice

3. **Calculating Force** Find the force it would take to accelerate an 800-kg car at a rate of 5 m/s^2.
4. **Calculating Force** What is the net force acting on a 0.15-kg hockey puck accelerating at a rate of 12 m/s^2?

Section 4

Newton's Third Law

Reading Preview

Key Concepts

- What is Newton's third law of motion?
- How can you determine the momentum of an object?
- What is the law of conservation of momentum?

Key Terms

- momentum
- law of conservation of momentum

Target Reading Skill

Previewing Visuals Before you read, preview Figure 18. Then write two questions that you have about the diagram in a graphic organizer like the one below. As you read, answer your questions.

Conservation of Momentum

Q.	What happens when two moving objects collide?
A.	
Q.	

Lab zone Discover Activity

How Pushy Is a Straw?

1. Stretch a rubber band around the middle of the cover of a medium-size hardcover book.
2. Place four marbles in a small square on a table. Place the book on the marbles so that the cover with the rubber band is on top.
3. Hold the book steady by placing one index finger on the binding. Then, as shown, push a straw against the rubber band with your other index finger.
4. Push the straw until the rubber band stretches about 10 cm. Then let go of both the book and the straw at the same time.

Think It Over

Developing Hypotheses What did you observe about the motion of the book and the straw? Write a hypothesis to explain what happened in terms of the forces on the book and the straw.

Have you ever tried to teach a friend how to roller-skate? It's hard if you are both wearing skates. When your friend pushes against you to get started, you move too. And when your friend runs into you to stop, you both end up moving! To understand these movements you need to know Newton's third law of motion and the law of conservation of momentum.

Newton's Third Law of Motion

Newton proposed that whenever one object exerts a force on a second object, the second object exerts a force back on the first object. The force exerted by the second object is equal in strength and opposite in direction to the first force. Think of one force as the "action" and the other force as the "reaction." **Newton's third law of motion states that if one object exerts a force on another object, then the second object exerts a force of equal strength in the opposite direction on the first object.** Another way to state Newton's third law is that for every action there is an equal but opposite reaction.

Action force
Reaction force
When the gymnast does a flip, he pushes down on the vaulting horse. The reaction force of the vaulting horse pushes him up to complete the flip.

Action force
Reaction force
The kayaker's paddle pulls on the water. The reaction force of the water pushes back on the paddle, causing the kayak to move.

Action force
Reaction force
When the dog leaps, it pushes down on the ground. The reaction force of the ground pushes the dog into the air.

FIGURE 15
Action-Reaction Pairs
Action-reaction pairs explain how a gymnast can flip over a vaulting horse, how a kayaker can move through the water, and how a dog can leap off the ground. **Observing** *Name some other action-reaction pairs that you have observed.*

Action-Reaction Pairs You're probably familiar with many examples of Newton's third law. Pairs of action and reaction forces are all around you. When you jump, you push on the ground with your feet. This is an action force. The ground pushes back on your feet with an equal and opposite force. This is the reaction force. You move upward when you jump because the ground is pushing you! In a similar way, a kayaker moves forward by exerting an action force on the water with a paddle. The water pushes back on the paddle with an equal reaction force that propels the kayak forward.

Now you can understand what happens when you teach your friend to roller-skate. Your friend exerts an action force when he pushes against you to start. You exert a reaction force in the opposite direction. As a result, both of you move in opposite directions.

Detecting Motion Can you always detect motion when paired forces are in action? The answer is no. For example, when Earth's gravity pulls on an object, you cannot detect Earth's equal and opposite reaction. Suppose you drop your pencil. Gravity pulls the pencil downward. At the same time, the pencil pulls Earth upward with an equal and opposite reaction force. You don't see Earth accelerate toward the pencil because Earth's inertia is so great that its acceleration is too small to notice.

Do Action-Reaction Forces Cancel? Earlier you learned that if two equal forces act in opposite directions on an object, the forces are balanced. Because the two forces add up to zero, they cancel each other out and produce no change in motion. Why then don't the action and reaction forces in Newton's third law of motion cancel out as well? After all, they are equal and opposite.

The action and reaction forces do not cancel out because they are acting on different objects. Look at the volleyball player on the left in Figure 16. She exerts an upward action force on the ball. In return, the ball exerts an equal but opposite downward reaction force back on her wrists. The action and reaction forces act on different objects.

On the other hand, the volleyball players on the right are both exerting a force on the *same* object—the volleyball. When they hit the ball from opposite directions, each of their hands exerts a force on the ball equal in strength but opposite in direction. The forces on the volleyball are balanced and the ball does not move either to the left or to the right.

Reading Checkpoint **Why don't action and reaction forces cancel each other?**

Discovery Channel School

Forces

Video Preview
▶Video Field Trip
Video Assessment

FIGURE 16
Action-Reaction Forces
In the photo on the left, the player's wrists exert the action force. In the photo below, the ball exerts reaction forces on both players.
Interpreting Diagrams *In the photo below, which forces cancel each other out? What force is not cancelled? What will happen to the ball?*

Momentum

All moving objects have what Newton called a "quantity of motion." What is this quantity of motion? Today we call it momentum. **Momentum** (moh MEN tum) is a characteristic of a moving object that is related to the mass and the velocity of the object. **The momentum of a moving object can be determined by multiplying the object's mass and velocity.**

Momentum = Mass × Velocity

Since mass is measured in kilograms and velocity is measured in meters per second, the unit for momentum is kilogram-meters per second (kg·m/s). Like velocity, acceleration, and force, momentum is described by its direction as well as its quantity. The momentum of an object is in the same direction as its velocity.

Math Sample Problem

Calculating Momentum

Which has more momentum: a 3.0-kg sledgehammer swung at 1.5 m/s, or a 4.0-kg sledgehammer swung at 0.9 m/s?

1 Read and Understand

What information are you given?

Mass of smaller sledgehammer = 3.0 kg

Velocity of smaller sledgehammer = 1.5 m/s

Mass of larger sledgehammer = 4.0 kg

Velocity of larger sledgehammer = 0.9 m/s

2 Plan and Solve

What quantities are you trying to calculate?

The momentum of each sledgehammer = ■

What formula contains the given quantities and the unknown quantity?

Momentum = Mass × Velocity

Perform the calculations.

Smaller sledgehammer: 3.0 kg × 1.5 m/s = 4.5 kg·m/s

Larger sledgehammer: 4.0 kg × 0.9 m/s = 3.6 kg·m/s

3 Look Back and Check

Does your answer make sense?

The 3.0-kg hammer has more momentum than the 4.0-kg one. This answer makes sense because it is swung at a greater velocity.

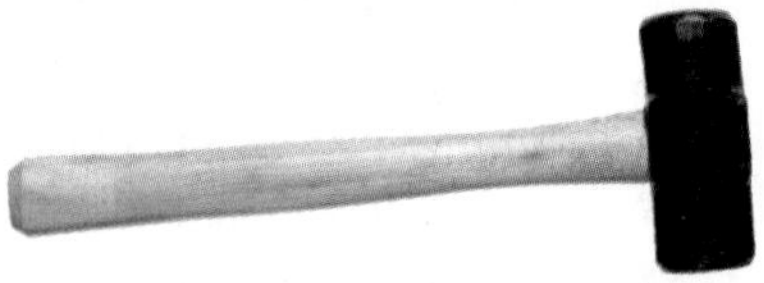

Math Practice

1. **Calculating Momentum** A golf ball travels at 16 m/s, while a baseball moves at 7 m/s. The mass of the golf ball is 0.045 kg and the mass of the baseball is 0.14 kg. Which has greater momentum?
2. **Calculating Momentum** What is the momentum of a bird with a mass of 0.018 kg flying at 15 m/s?

FIGURE 17
Momentum
An object's momentum depends on velocity and mass.
Problem Solving *If both dogs have the same velocity, which one has the greater momentum?*

The more momentum a moving object has, the harder it is to stop. The mass of an object affects the amount of momentum the object has. For example, you can catch a baseball moving at 20 m/s, but you cannot stop a car moving at the same speed. The car has more momentum because it has a greater mass. The velocity of an object also affects the amount of momentum an object has. For example, an arrow shot from a bow has a large momentum because, although it has a small mass, it travels at a high velocity.

Reading Checkpoint **What must you know to determine an object's momentum?**

Conservation of Momentum

The word *conservation* has a special meaning in physical science. In everyday language, conservation means saving resources. You might conserve water or fossil fuels, for example. In physical science, conservation refers to the conditions before and after some event. An amount that is conserved is the same amount after an event as it was before.

The amount of momentum objects have is conserved when they collide. Momentum may be transferred from one object to another, but none is lost. This fact is called the law of conservation of momentum.

The **law of conservation of momentum** states that, in the absence of outside forces, the total momentum of objects that interact does not change. The amount of momentum is the same before and after they interact. **The total momentum of any group of objects remains the same, or is conserved, unless outside forces act on the objects.** Friction is an example of an outside force.

Lab zone **Try This Activity**

Colliding Cars

Momentum is always conserved—even by toys!

1. Find two nearly identical toy cars that roll easily.
2. Make two loops out of masking tape (sticky side out). Put one loop on the front of one of the cars and the other loop on the back of the other car.
3. Place on the floor the car that has tape on the back. Then gently roll the other car into the back of the stationary car. Was momentum conserved? How do you know?

Predicting What will happen if you put masking tape on the fronts of both cars and roll them at each other with equal speeds? Will momentum be conserved in this case? Test your prediction.

Go Online active art

For: Momentum activity
Visit: PHSchool.com
Web Code: cgp-3024

FIGURE 18
Conservation of Momentum
In the absence of friction, momentum is conserved when two train cars collide. **Interpreting Diagrams** *In which diagram is all of the momentum transferred from the blue car to the green car?*

A Two Moving Objects

Before

(2 kg × 4 m/s) + (2 kg × 2 m/s) = 12 kg·m/s

After

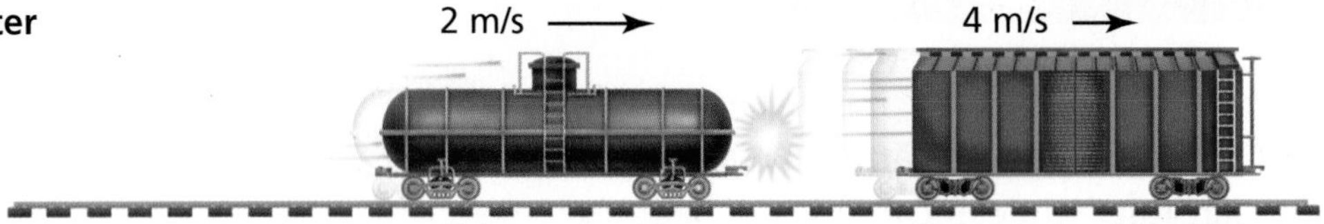

(2 kg × 2 m/s) + (2 kg × 4 m/s) = 12 kg·m/s

Before the collision, the blue car moves faster than the green car. Afterward, the green car moves faster. The total momentum stays the same.

B One Moving Object

When the green car is at rest before the collision, all of the blue car's momentum is transferred to it. Momentum is conserved.

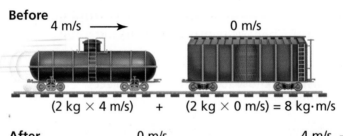

Before

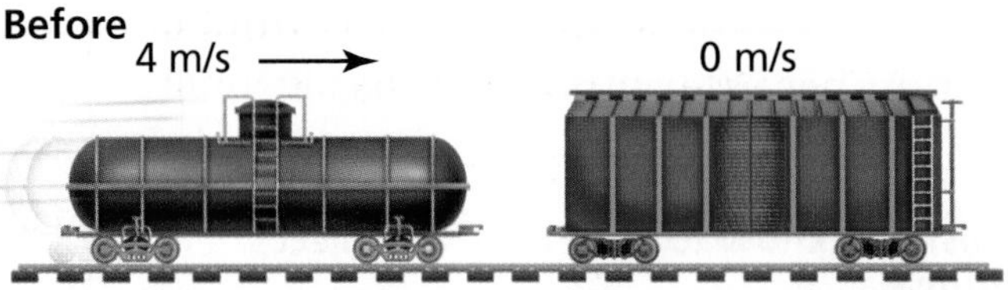

(2 kg × 4 m/s) + (2 kg × 0 m/s) = 8 kg·m/s

After

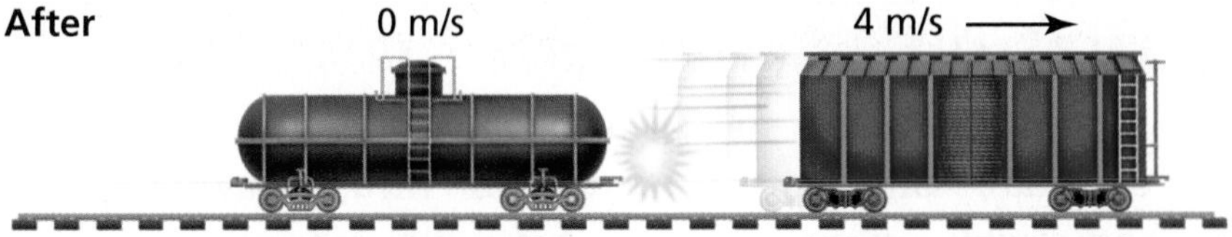

(2 kg × 0 m/s) + (2 kg × 4 m/s) = 8 kg·m/s

C Two Connected Objects

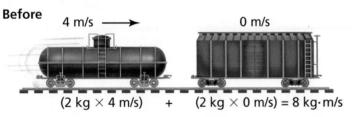

Before

(2 kg × 4 m/s) + (2 kg × 0 m/s) = 8 kg·m/s

If the two cars couple together, momentum is still conserved. Together, the cars move slower than the blue car did before the collision.

After

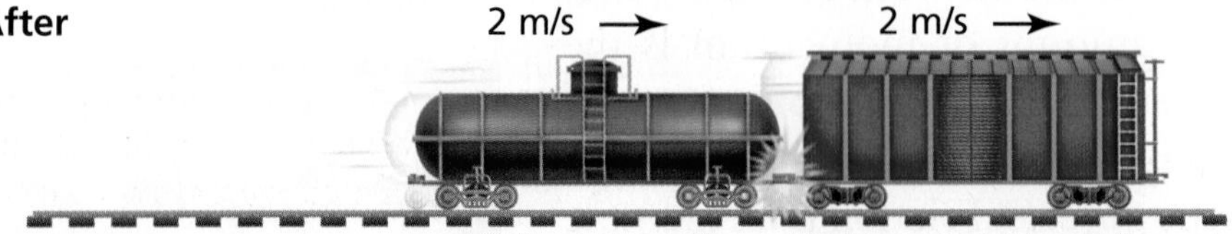

(2 kg × 2 m/s) + (2 kg × 2 m/s) = 8 kg·m/s

Collisions With Two Moving Objects In Figure 18A, a train car travels at 4 m/s down the same track as another train car traveling at only 2 m/s. The two train cars have equal masses. The blue car catches up with the green car and bumps into it. During the collision, the speed of each car changes. The blue car slows down to 2 m/s, and the green car speeds up to 4 m/s. Momentum is conserved—the momentum of one train car decreases while the momentum of the other increases.

Collisions With One Moving Object In Figure 18B, the blue car travels at 4 m/s but the green car is not moving. Eventually the blue car hits the green car. After the collision, the blue car is no longer moving, but the green car travels at 4 m/s. Even though the situation has changed, momentum is conserved. All of the momentum has been transferred from the blue car to the green car.

Collisions With Connected Objects Suppose that, instead of bouncing off each other, the two train cars couple together when they hit. Is momentum still conserved in Figure 18C? After the collision, the coupled train cars make one object with twice the mass. The velocity of the coupled trains is 2 m/s—half the initial velocity of the blue car. Since the mass is doubled and the velocity is divided in half, the total momentum remains the same.

Reading Checkpoint **What happens to the momentum of two objects after they collide?**

Section 4 Assessment

Target Reading Skill Previewing Visuals Refer to your questions and answers about Figure 18 to help you answer Question 3 below.

Reviewing Key Concepts

1. a. Reviewing State Newton's third law of motion.
   b. Summarizing According to Newton's third law of motion, how are action and reaction forces related?
   c. Applying Concepts What would happen if you tried to catch a ball when you were standing on roller skates?
2. a. Defining What is momentum?
   b. Predicting What is the momentum of a parked car?
   c. Relating Cause and Effect Why is it important for drivers to allow more distance between their cars when they travel at faster speeds?
3. a. Identifying What is conservation of momentum?
   b. Inferring The total momentum of two marbles before a collision is 0.06 kg·m/s. No outside forces act on the marbles. What is the total momentum of the marbles after the collision?

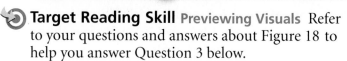

Math Practice

4. Calculating Momentum What is the momentum of a 920-kg car moving at a speed of 25 m/s?
5. Calculating Momentum Which has more momentum: a 250-kg dolphin swimming at 4 m/s, or a 350-kg manatee swimming at 2 m/s?

Lab zone **Skills Lab**

Forced to Accelerate

Problem

How is the acceleration of a skateboard related to the force that is pulling it?

Skills Focus

calculating, graphing, interpreting data

Materials

- skateboard
- meter stick
- string
- stopwatch
- masking tape
- spring scale, 5-N
- several bricks or other large mass(es)

Procedure

1. Attach a loop of string to a skateboard. Place the bricks on the skateboard.
2. Using masking tape, mark off a one-meter distance on a level floor. Label one end "Start" and the other "Finish."
3. Attach a spring scale to the loop of string. Pull it so that you maintain a force of 2.0 N. Be sure to pull with the scale straight out in front. Practice applying a steady force to the skateboard as it moves.
4. Copy the data table into your notebook.
5. Find the smallest force needed to pull the skateboard at a slow, constant speed. Do not accelerate the skateboard. Record this force on the first line of the table.
6. Add 0.5 N to the force in Step 5. This will be enough to accelerate the skateboard. Record this force on the second line of the table.
7. Have one of your partners hold the front edge of the skateboard at the starting line. Then pull on the spring scale with the force you found in Step 6.
8. When your partner says "Go" and releases the skateboard, maintain a constant force until the skateboard reaches the finish line. A third partner should time how long it takes the skateboard to go from start to finish. Record the time in the column labeled Trial 1.
9. Repeat Steps 7 and 8 twice more. Record your results in the columns labeled Trial 2 and Trial 3.
10. Repeat Steps 7, 8, and 9 using a force 1.0 N greater than the force you found in Step 5.
11. Repeat Steps 7, 8, and 9 twice more. Use forces that are 1.5 N and 2.0 N greater than the force you found in Step 5.

Data Table

Force (N)	Trial 1 Time (s)	Trial 2 Time (s)	Trial 3 Time (s)	Average Time (s)	Average Speed (m/s)	Final Speed (m/s)	Acceleration (m/s^2)

Analyze and Conclude

1. Calculating For each force, find the average of the three times that you measured. Record the average time in your data table.
2. Calculating For each force, find the average speed of the skateboard. Use this formula:

   Average speed = 1 m ÷ Average time

   Record this value for each force.
3. Calculating To obtain the final speed of the skateboard, multiply each average speed by 2. Record the result in your data table.
4. Calculating To obtain the acceleration, divide each final speed you found by the average time. Record the acceleration in your data table.
5. Graphing Make a line graph. Show the acceleration on the *y*-axis and the force on the *x*-axis. The *y*-axis scale should go from 0 m/s^2 to about 1 m/s^2. The *x*-axis should go from 0 N to 3.0 N. If your data points seem to form a straight line, draw a line through them.
6. Interpreting Data Your first data point is the force required for an acceleration of zero. How do you know the force for an acceleration of zero?
7. Interpreting Data According to your graph, how is the acceleration of the skateboard related to the pulling force?
8. Communicating Write a paragraph in which you identify the manipulated variable and the responding variable in this experiment. Describe other variables that might have affected the outcome of this experiment. (See the Skills Handbook to read about experimental variables.)

Design an Experiment

Design an experiment to test how the acceleration of the loaded skateboard depends on its mass. Think about how you would vary the mass of the skateboard. What quantity would you need to measure that you did not measure in this experiment? Do you have the equipment to make that measurement? If not, what other equipment would you need? *Obtain your teacher's permission before carrying out your investigation.*

Rockets and Satellites

Reading Preview

Key Concepts

- How does a rocket lift off the ground?
- What keeps a satellite in orbit?

Key Terms

- satellite
- centripetal force

Target Reading Skill

Identifying Main Ideas As you read the What Is a Satellite? section, write the main idea in a graphic organizer like the one below. Then write three supporting details that further explain the main idea.

Main Idea

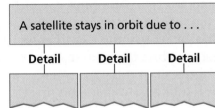

A satellite stays in orbit due to . . .

Detail | Detail | Detail

Lab zone Discover **Activity**

What Makes an Object Move in a Circle?

1. Tie a small mass, such as an empty thread spool, to the end of a string no more than one meter long.
2. Swing the object rapidly around in a circle that is perpendicular to the floor. Make sure no one is near the swinging object, and don't let it go!
3. Predict what will happen if you decrease the speed of the object. Test your prediction.
4. Predict how the length of the string affects the object's motion. Test your prediction.

Think It Over

Forming Operational Definitions Describe the object's motion. How do you know that the string exerts a force?

In October 1957, 14-year-old Homer Hickam looked upward and saw a speck of light move across the sky. It was the Russian satellite *Sputnik*, the first artificial satellite. It was propelled into space by a powerful rocket. This sight inspired Homer and his friends. They spent the next three years designing, building, and launching rockets in their hometown of Coalwood, West Virginia. Many of their first attempts failed, but they did not give up. Eventually, they built a rocket that soared to a height of almost ten kilometers. Their hard work paid off. In 1960, they won first place in the National Science Fair. Since then, rocket launches have become more familiar, but they are still an awesome sight.

◀ **Homer Hickam holds a rocket that he and his friends designed.**

How Do Rockets Lift Off?

A space shuttle like the one in Figure 19 has a mass of more than 2 million kilograms when loaded with fuel. To push the shuttle away from the pull of Earth's gravity and into space requires an incredible amount of force. How is this force generated? Rockets and space shuttles lift into space using Newton's third law of motion. As they lift off, they burn fuel and push the exhaust gases downward at a high velocity. In turn, the gases push upward on the rocket with an equal but opposite force. **A rocket can rise into the air because the gases it expels with a downward action force exert an equal but opposite reaction force on the rocket.** As long as this upward pushing force, called thrust, is greater than the downward pull of gravity, there is a net force in the upward direction. As a result, the rocket accelerates upward into space.

What Is a Satellite?

Rockets are often used to carry satellites into space. A **satellite** is any object that orbits another object in space. An artificial satellite is a device that is launched into orbit. Artificial satellites are designed for many purposes, such as communications, military intelligence, weather analysis, and geographical surveys. The International Space Station is an example of an artificial satellite. It was designed for scientific research.

Circular Motion Artificial satellites travel around Earth in an almost circular path. Recall that an object traveling in a circle is accelerating because it constantly changes direction. If an object is accelerating, a force must be acting on it. Any force that causes an object to move in a circular path is a **centripetal force** (sen TRIP ih tul). The word *centripetal* means "center-seeking."

In the Discovery Activity, the string supplies the centripetal force. The string acts to pull the object toward the center, and thereby keeps it moving in a circular path. For a satellite, the centripetal force is the gravitational force that pulls the satellite toward the center of Earth.

Reading Checkpoint **What type of force causes an object to move in a circular path?**

FIGURE 19
A Rocket Launch
The action force pushes the rocket's exhaust gases downward. The reaction force of the gases sends the rocket into space. **Predicting** *As the rocket ascends, how will its mass change?*

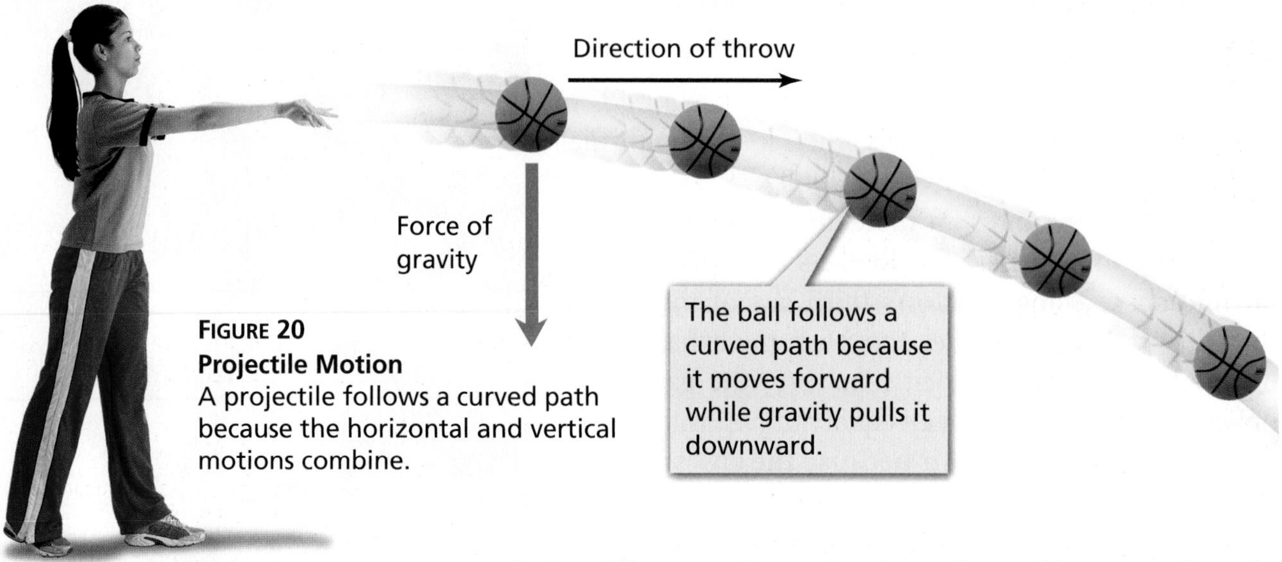
Direction of throw
Force of gravity
The ball follows a curved path because it moves forward while gravity pulls it downward.

FIGURE 20
Projectile Motion
A projectile follows a curved path because the horizontal and vertical motions combine.

Satellite Motion Gravity pulls satellites toward Earth. So why don't satellites fall, as a ball thrown into the air would? The answer is that satellites do not travel straight up into the air. Instead they move around Earth.

If you throw a ball horizontally, as shown in Figure 20, the ball will move away from you at the same time that it is pulled to the ground because of gravity. The horizontal and vertical motions combine, and the ball follows a curved path toward the ground. If you throw the ball faster, it will land even farther in front of you. The faster you throw a projectile, the farther it travels before it lands.

Now suppose, as Isaac Newton did, what would happen if you were on a high mountain and could throw a ball as fast as you wanted. The faster you threw it, the farther away it would land. But, at a certain speed, the path of the ball would match the curve of Earth. Although the ball would keep falling due to gravity, Earth's surface would curve away from the ball at the same rate. Thus the ball would circle Earth, as shown in Figure 21.

Satellites in orbit around Earth continuously fall toward Earth, but because Earth is curved they travel around it. In other words, a satellite is a falling projectile that keeps missing the ground! It falls around Earth rather than into it. A satellite does not need fuel because it continues to move ahead due to its inertia. At the same time, gravity continuously changes the satellite's direction. The speed with which an object must be thrown in order to orbit Earth turns out to be about 7,900 m/s! This speed is about 200 times faster than a pitcher can throw a baseball.

FIGURE 21
Satellite Motion
The faster a projectile is thrown, the farther it travels before it hits the ground. A projectile with enough velocity moves in a circular orbit. **Interpreting Diagrams** *How does the direction of gravity compare to the direction of the orbiting projectile's motion at any point?*

Satellite Location Some satellites, such as mapping and observation satellites, are put into low orbits of less than 1,000 kilometers. In a low orbit, satellites complete a trip around Earth in less than two hours. Other satellites are sent into higher orbits. At those distances, a satellite travels more slowly, taking longer to circle Earth. For example, communications satellites travel about 36,000 kilometers above Earth's surface. At that height, they circle Earth once every 24 hours. Because Earth rotates once every 24 hours, a satellite above the equator always stays at the same point above Earth as it orbits.

Reading Checkpoint **How does gravity help keep satellites in orbit?**

FIGURE 22
Satellite Locations
Depending on their uses, artificial satellites orbit at different heights.

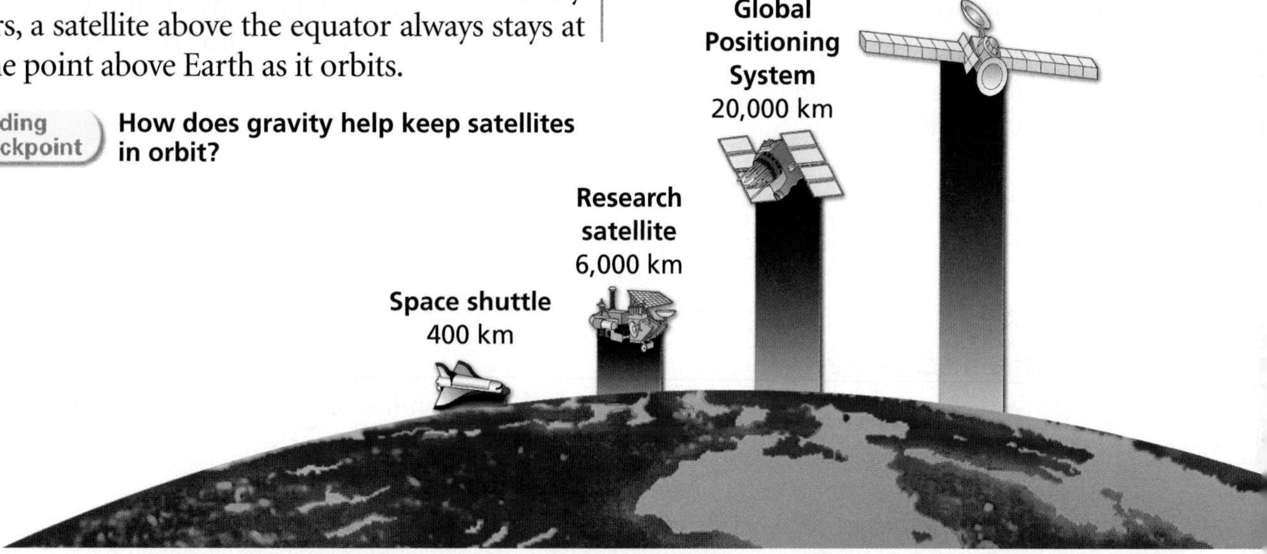

Section 5 Assessment

Target Reading Skill **Identifying Main Ideas** Use your graphic organizer to help you answer Question 2 below.

Reviewing Key Concepts

1. a. **Identifying** Which of Newton's three laws of motion explains how a rocket lifts off?
   b. **Explaining** How do action-reaction pairs explain how a rocket lifts off?
   c. **Applying Concepts** As a rocket travels upward from Earth, air resistance decreases along with the force of gravity. The rocket's mass also decreases as its fuel is used up. If thrust remains the same, how do these factors affect the rocket's acceleration?
2. a. **Defining** What is a satellite?
   b. **Relating Cause and Effect** What causes satellites to stay in orbit rather than falling toward Earth?
   c. **Inferring** In Figure 21, a projectile is thrown with enough velocity to orbit Earth. What would happen if the projectile were thrown with a greater velocity?

Lab zone At-Home Activity

Swing the Bucket Fill a small plastic bucket halfway with water and take it outdoors. Challenge a family member to swing the bucket in a vertical circle. Explain that the water won't fall out at the top if the bucket is moving fast enough. Tell your family member that if the bucket falls as fast as the water, the water will stay in the bucket. Relate this activity to a satellite that also falls due to gravity, yet remains in orbit.

Chapter 10 Study Guide

1 The Nature of Force

Key Concepts

- Like velocity and acceleration, a force is described by its strength and by the direction in which it acts.
- Unbalanced forces acting on an object result in a net force and cause a change in the object's motion.
- Balanced forces acting on an object do not change the object's motion.

Key Terms

force
newton
net force
unbalanced forces
balanced forces

2 Friction and Gravity

Key Concepts

- The strength of the force of friction depends on two factors: how hard the surfaces push together and the types of surfaces involved.
- Two factors affect the gravitational attraction between objects: mass and distance.
- In free fall, the force of gravity is an unbalanced force, which causes an object to accelerate.

Key Terms

friction
static friction
sliding friction
rolling friction
fluid friction
gravity
mass
weight
free fall
air resistance
terminal velocity
projectile

3 Newton's First and Second Laws

Key Concepts

- An object at rest will remain at rest, and an object moving at a constant velocity will continue moving at a constant velocity, unless it is acted upon by an unbalanced force.
- Acceleration depends on the object's mass and on the net force acting on the object.
- $\text{Acceleration} = \dfrac{\text{Net force}}{\text{Mass}}$

Key Term

inertia

4 Newton's Third Law

Key Concepts

- If one object exerts a force on another object, then the second object exerts a force of equal strength in the opposite direction on the first object.
- The momentum of a moving object is equal to its mass times its velocity.

$$\text{Momentum} = \text{Mass} \times \text{Velocity}$$

- The total momentum of any group of objects remains the same, or is conserved, unless outside forces act on the objects.

Key Terms

momentum
law of conservation of momentum

5 Rockets and Satellites

Key Concepts

- A rocket can rise into the air because the gases it expels with a downward action force exert an equal but opposite reaction force on the rocket.
- Satellites in orbit around Earth continuously fall toward Earth, but because Earth is curved they travel around it.

Key Terms

satellite
centripetal force

Review and Assessment

Go Online
PHSchool.com
For: Self-Assessment
Visit: PHSchool.com
Web Code: cga-3020

Organizing Information

Contrasting Copy the table about the different types of friction onto a sheet of paper. Then complete it and add a title. (For more on Comparing and Contrasting, see the Skills Handbook.)

Type of Friction	Occurs When	Example
Static	An object is not moving	a. ?
Sliding	b. ?	c. ?
Rolling	d. ?	e. ?
Fluid	f. ?	g. ?

Reviewing Key Terms

Choose the letter of the best answer.

1. When an unbalanced force acts on an object, the force
   a. changes the motion of the object.
   b. is canceled by another force.
   c. does not change the motion of the object.
   d. is equal to the weight of the object.
2. Air resistance is a type of
   a. rolling friction.
   b. sliding friction.
   c. centripetal force.
   d. fluid friction.
3. Which of the following is not a projectile?
   a. a satellite
   b. a thrown ball
   c. a ball on the ground
   d. a soaring arrow
4. The resistance of an object to any change in its motion is called
   a. inertia.
   b. friction.
   c. gravity.
   d. weight.
5. The product of an object's mass and its velocity is called the object's
   a. net force.
   b. weight.
   c. momentum.
   d. gravitation.

If the statement is true, write *true*. If it is false, change the underlined word or words to make the statement true.

6. Balanced forces are equal forces acting on an object in opposite directions.
7. Rolling friction occurs when two solid surfaces slide over each other.
8. The greatest velocity a falling object reaches is called its momentum.
9. The law of universal gravitation states that the total momentum of objects that interact does not change.
10. The type of force that causes a satellite to orbit Earth is a centripetal force.

Writing in Science

Descriptive Paragraph Suppose you have been asked to design a new amusement park ride. Write a description of how you will design it. Explain the role that friction and gravity will play in the ride's design.

Discovery Channel School

Forces
Video Preview
Video Field Trip
▶ Video Assessment

Review and Assessment

Checking Concepts

11. Four children pull on the same toy at the same time, yet there is no net force on the toy. How is that possible?

12. Why do slippery fluids such as oil reduce sliding friction?

13. Will a flat sheet of paper dropped from a height of 2 m accelerate at the same rate as a piece of paper crumpled into a ball? Why or why not?

14. Explain how force, mass, and acceleration are related by Newton's second law of motion.

15. Suppose you are an astronaut making a space walk outside your space station when your jet pack runs out of fuel. How can you use your empty jet pack to get you back to the station?

16. Draw a diagram showing the motion of a satellite around Earth. Label the forces acting on the satellite. Is the satellite accelerating?

Thinking Critically

17. Classifying What kind of friction allows you to walk without slipping?

18. Applying Concepts You are moving fast on a skateboard when your wheel gets stuck in a crack on the sidewalk. Using the term *inertia*, explain what happens.

19. Problem Solving Look at the diagram below of two students pulling a bag of volleyball equipment. The friction force between the bag and the floor is 15 N. What is the net force acting on the bag? What is the acceleration of the bag?

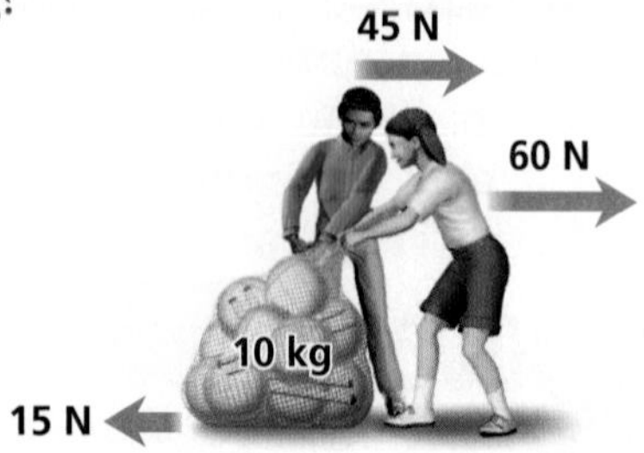

20. Relating Cause and Effect When you drop a golf ball to the pavement, it bounces up. Is a force needed to make it bounce up? If so, what exerts the force?

Math Practice

21. Calculating Force A 7.3-kg bowling ball accelerates at a rate of 3.7 m/s^2. What force acts on the bowling ball?

22. Calculating Momentum A 240-kg snowmobile travels at 16 m/s. The mass of the driver is 75 kg. What is the momentum of the snowmobile and driver?

Applying Skills

Use the illustration showing a collision between two balls to answer Questions 23–25.

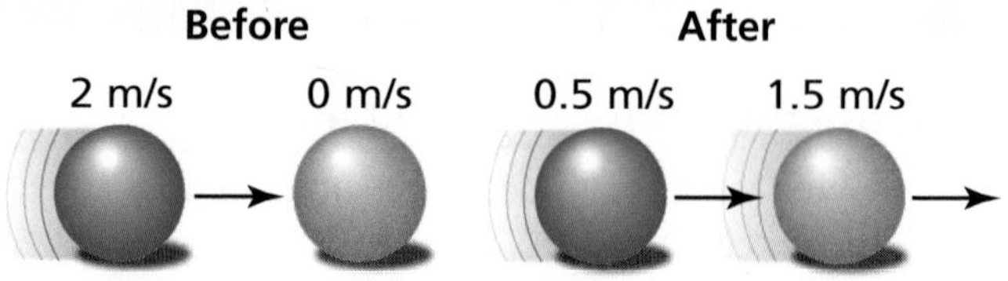

23. Calculating Use the formula for momentum to find the momentum of each ball before and after the collision. Assume the mass of each ball is 0.4 kg.

24. Inferring Find the total momentum before and after collision. Is the law of conservation of momentum satisfied in this collision? Explain.

25. Designing Experiments Design an experiment in which you could show that momentum is not conserved between the balls when friction is strong.

Lab zone Chapter Project

Performance Assessment Test your vehicle to make sure it will work on the type of floor in your classroom. Will the vehicle stay within the bounds set by your teacher? Identify all the forces acting on the vehicle. What was the most significant source of friction for your vehicle? List at least three features you included in the design of the vehicle that led to an improvement in its performance. For example, did you give it a smooth shape for low air resistance?

Standardized Test Prep

Test-Taking Tip

Interpreting Diagrams

On some tests, you may be asked questions about a diagram. Understanding the information in the diagram is the key to answering the question correctly. When you are shown a diagram, examine it carefully. Look at the objects and symbols in the diagram and read the labels.

Sample Question

What conclusion can you draw by looking at the diagram?

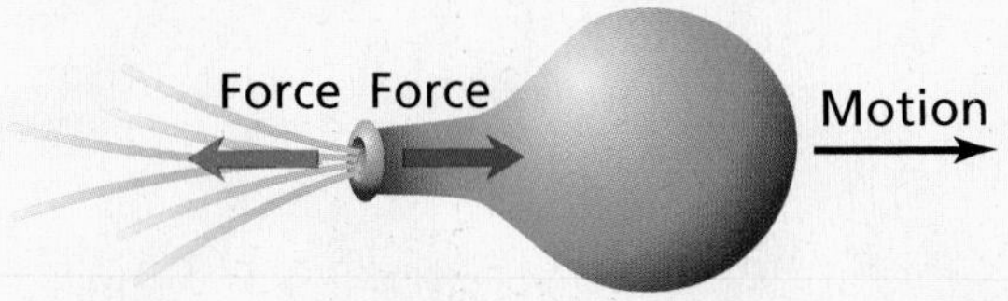

A Air resistance in front of the balloon pushes it backward.
B Gravity forces air out of the balloon's open end.
C The force of the air leaving the balloon propels it forward.
D Friction causes the balloon's acceleration to decrease.

Answer

The diagram shows a pair of action-reaction forces. The action force is caused by the balloon pushing out air. According to Newton's third law of motion, the reaction force of the air pushes on the balloon, propelling it forward. The answer is **C**.

Choose the letter of the best answer.

1. In the balloon diagram above, why don't the two forces cancel each other out?
A They are not equal.
B They both act on the air.
C They both act on the balloon.
D They act on different objects.

2. What force makes it less likely for a person to slip on a dry sidewalk as opposed to an icy sidewalk?
F air resistance
G friction
H inertia
J momentum

3. Which of the following is determined by the force of gravity?
A weight
B momentum
C mass
D distance

4. The table below shows the mass and velocity of four animals. Which animal has the greatest momentum?

Mass and Velocity of Animals

Animal	Mass (kg)	Velocity (m/s)
Cheetah	45	20
Grizzly bear	200	13
Hyena	70	18
Wild turkey	11	7

F cheetah
G grizzly bear
H hyena
J wild turkey

5. A 50-car freight train and an 8-car passenger train are stopped on parallel tracks. It is more difficult to move the freight train than the passenger train. What accounts for this fact?
A terminal velocity
B inertia
C centripetal force
D speed

Constructed Response

6. Write a short paragraph explaining how a parachute works in terms of forces.

Chapter

11 Forces in Fluids

Chapter Preview

1. **Pressure**
   Discover *Can You Blow Up a Balloon in a Bottle?*
   Math Skills *Area*
   Try This *Card Trick*
   Design Your Own Lab *Spinning Sprinklers*

2. **Floating and Sinking**
   Discover *What Can You Measure With a Straw?*
   Try This *Cartesian Diver*
   At-Home Activity *Changing Balloon Density*
   Skills Lab *Sink and Spill*

3. **Pascal's Principle**
   Discover *How Does Pressure Change?*
   Active Art *Hydraulic Systems*
   Analyzing Data *Comparing Hydraulic Lifts*

4. **Bernoulli's Principle**
   Discover *Does the Movement of Air Affect Pressure?*
   Try This *Faucet Force*
   At-Home Activity *Paper Chimney*

Interactive Textbook

The force of air pushing on a hang glider's wing helps to keep the glider aloft. ▶

Discovery Channel School

Forces in Fluids

▶ Video Preview
Video Field Trip
Video Assessment

Lab zone™ Chapter **Project**

Staying Afloat

Whether an object sinks or floats depends on more than just its weight. In this Chapter Project, you will design and build a boat that can float in water and carry cargo. You will find out what forces in fluids make an object sink or float.

Your Goal To construct a boat that can float in water and carry cargo

Your boat must

- be made of metal only
- support a cargo of 50 pennies without allowing any water to enter for at least 10 seconds
- travel at least 1.5 meters
- be built following the safety guidelines in Appendix A

Plan It! Before you design your boat, think about the shape of real ships. Preview the chapter to find out what makes an object float. Then look for simple metal objects that you can form into a boat. Compare different materials and designs to build the most efficient boat you can. After your teacher approves your design, build your boat and test it.

Section 1

Pressure

Reading Preview

Key Concepts

- What does pressure depend on?
- How do fluids exert pressure?
- How does fluid pressure change with elevation and depth?

Key Terms

- pressure
- pascal
- fluid
- barometer

Target Reading Skill

Previewing Visuals Before you read, preview Figure 5. Then write two questions that you have about the diagram in a graphic organizer like the one below. As you read, answer your questions.

Pressure Variations

Q. Why does pressure change with elevation and depth?
A.
Q.

Lab zone Discover Activity

Can You Blow Up a Balloon in a Bottle?

1. Insert a balloon into the neck of an empty bottle. Try to blow up the balloon.
2. Now insert a straw into the bottle, next to the balloon. Keep one end of the straw sticking out of the bottle. Try again to blow up the balloon.

Think It Over

Developing Hypotheses Did using the straw make a difference? If it did, develop a hypothesis to explain why.

Outside, deep snow covers the ground. You put on your sneakers and head out, shovel in hand. When you step outside, your foot sinks deep into the snow. It's nearly up to your knees! Nearby, a sparrow hops across the surface of the snow. Unlike you, the bird does not sink. In fact, it barely leaves a mark! Why do you sink into the snow while the sparrow rests on the surface?

What Is Pressure?

The word *pressure* is related to the word *press*. It refers to a force exerted over an area on the surface of an object. You may recall that Earth's gravity pulls you downward with a force equal to your weight. Due to gravity, your feet exert a force on the surface of Earth over an area the size of your feet. In other words, your feet exert pressure on the ground.

Exerting pressure on snow ▶

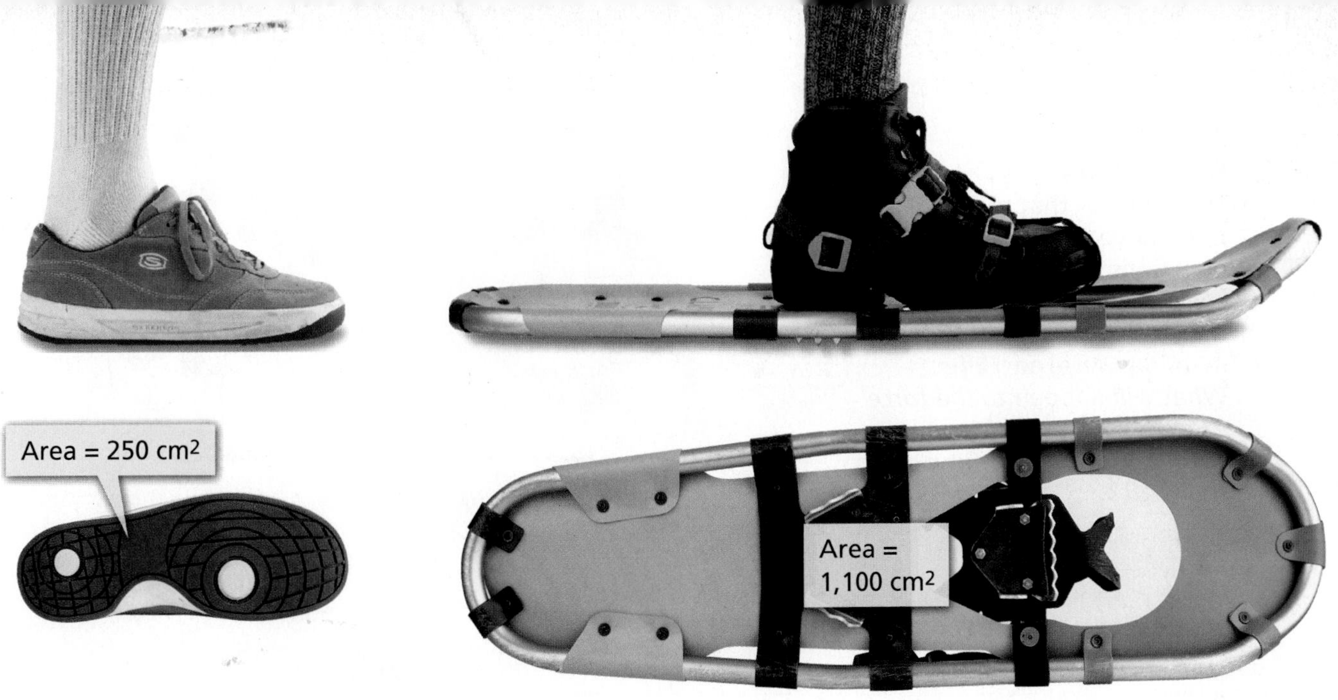

FIGURE 1
Pressure and Area
Pressure depends on the area over which a force is distributed.
Inferring *Which type of shoe would you use to keep from sinking into deep snow?*

Pressure and Area Force and pressure are closely related, but they are not the same thing. **Pressure decreases as the area over which a force is distributed increases.** The larger the area over which the force is distributed, the less pressure is exerted. In order to stand on snow without sinking, you can't make yourself weigh the same as a bird. However, you can change the area over which you exert the force of your weight.

If you wear sneakers, like those shown in Figure 1, your weight is distributed over the soles of both shoes. You'll exert pressure over an area of about 500 cm^2 and sink into the snow. But if you wear snowshoes, you'll exert pressure over a much greater area—about 2,200 cm^2. Because the force of your weight is distributed over a greater area, the overall pressure exerted on the snow is much less. Like a sparrow, you can stand on the snow without sinking!

Calculating Pressure The relationship of force, area, and pressure is summarized by a formula.

$$\text{Pressure} = \frac{\text{Force}}{\text{Area}}$$

Pressure is equal to the force exerted on a surface divided by the total area over which the force is exerted. Force is measured in newtons (N). Area is measured in square meters (m^2). Since force is divided by area, the SI unit of pressure is the newton per square meter (N/m^2). This unit of pressure is also called the **pascal** (Pa): 1 N/m^2 = 1 Pa.

Reading Checkpoint **What is the SI unit of pressure called?**

Math Skills

Area

The area of a surface is the number of square units that it covers. To find the area of a rectangle, multiply its length by its width. The area of the rectangle below is 2 cm × 3 cm, or 6 cm^2.

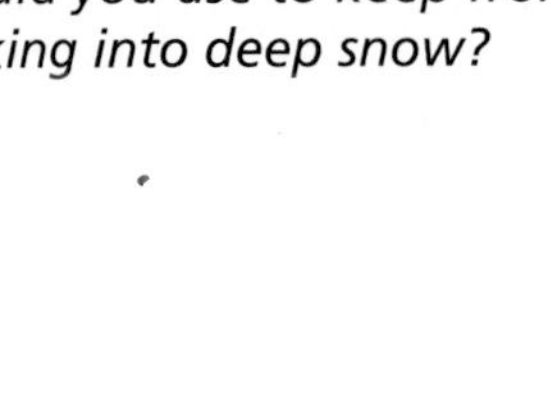

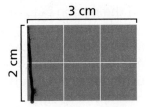

Practice Problem Which has a greater area: a rectangle that is 4 cm × 20 cm, or a square that is 10 cm × 10 cm?

FIGURE 2
Fluid Particles
The particles that make up a fluid move constantly in all directions. When a particle collides with a surface, it exerts a force on the surface.
Relating Cause and Effect *What will happen to the force exerted by the particles in the chair when you add more air to the chair?*

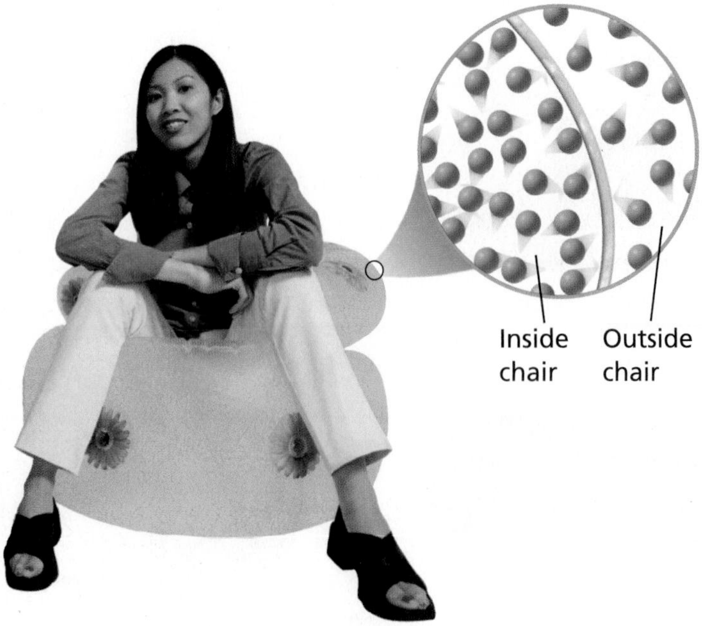

Fluid Pressure

Solids such as sneakers are not the only materials that exert pressure. Fluids also exert pressure. A **fluid** is a material that can easily flow. As a result, a fluid can change shape. Liquids such as water and oil and gases such as air and helium are examples of fluids.

What Causes Fluid Pressure? To understand how fluids exert forces that can result in pressure, think about the tiny particles that make up the fluid. Particles in a fluid constantly move in all directions, as shown in Figure 2. As they move, the particles collide with each other and with any surface that they meet.

As each particle in a fluid collides with a surface, it exerts a force on the surface. **All of the forces exerted by the individual particles in a fluid combine to make up the pressure exerted by the fluid.** Because the number of particles is large, you can consider the fluid as a whole. So, the fluid pressure is the total force exerted by the fluid divided by the area over which the force is exerted.

Air Pressure Did you know that you live at the bottom of 100 kilometers of fluid that surrounds Earth? This fluid, called air, is the mixture of gases that makes up Earth's atmosphere. These gases press down on everything on Earth's surface, all the time. Air exerts pressure because it has mass. You may forget that air has mass, but each cubic meter of air around you has a mass of about 1 kilogram. Because the force of gravity pulls down on this mass of air, the air has weight. The weight of the air is the force that produces air pressure, or atmospheric pressure.

Lab zone Try This Activity

Card Trick

1. Fill a small plastic cup to the brim with water. Gently place an index card over the top of the cup.
2. Hold the card in place and slowly turn the cup upside down. Let go of the card. What happens? Without touching the card, turn the container on its side.

Inferring Why does the water stay in the cup when you turn the cup upside down?

Balanced Pressure Hold out your hand, palm up. You are holding up air. At sea level, atmospheric pressure is about 10.13 N/cm^2. The surface area of your hand is about 100 cm^2. So, the weight supported by the surface area of your hand is about 1,000 newtons, or about the same weight as that of a large washing machine!

How could your hand possibly support that weight and not feel it? In a stationary fluid, pressure at a given point is exerted equally in all directions. The weight of the atmosphere does not just press down on your hand. It presses on your hand from every direction. The pressures balance each other.

Balanced pressures also explain why the tremendous air pressure pushing on you from all sides does not crush you. Your body contains fluids that exert outward pressure. For example, your lungs and sinus cavities contain air. Your cells and blood vessels contain liquids. So pressure from fluids inside your body balances the air pressure outside your body.

What happens when air pressure becomes unbalanced? Look at Figure 4. When the can is full of air, the air pressure inside the can balances the atmospheric pressure outside the can. When air is removed from the can, the unbalanced force of the outside air pressure crushes the can.

FIGURE 3
Atmospheric Pressure
The pressure of Earth's atmosphere is exerted over the entire surface of your hand.

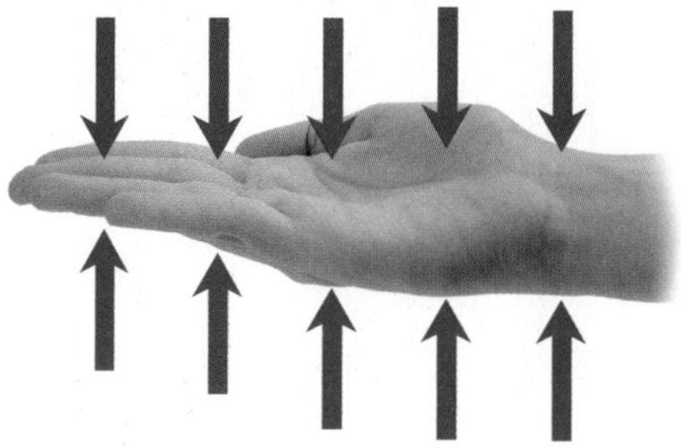

Reading Checkpoint **How is the pressure on your hand balanced?**

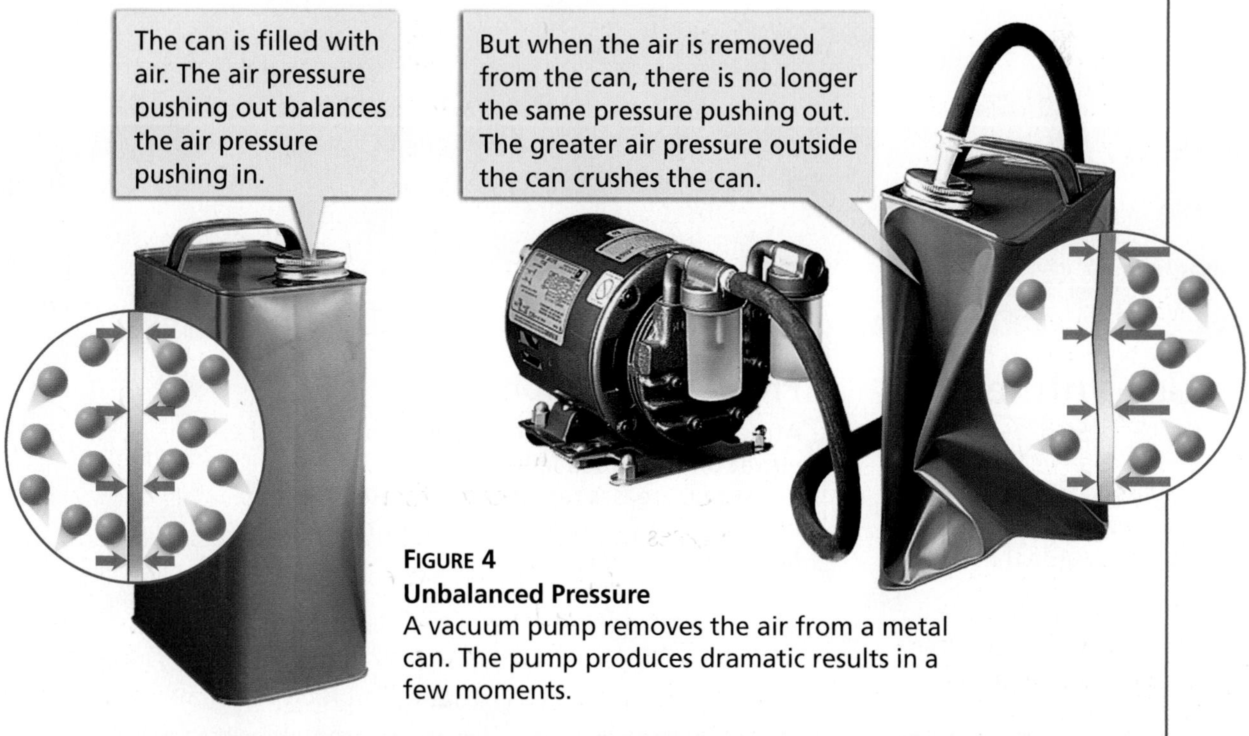

The can is filled with air. The air pressure pushing out balances the air pressure pushing in.
But when the air is removed from the can, there is no longer the same pressure pushing out. The greater air pressure outside the can crushes the can.

FIGURE 4
Unbalanced Pressure
A vacuum pump removes the air from a metal can. The pump produces dramatic results in a few moments.

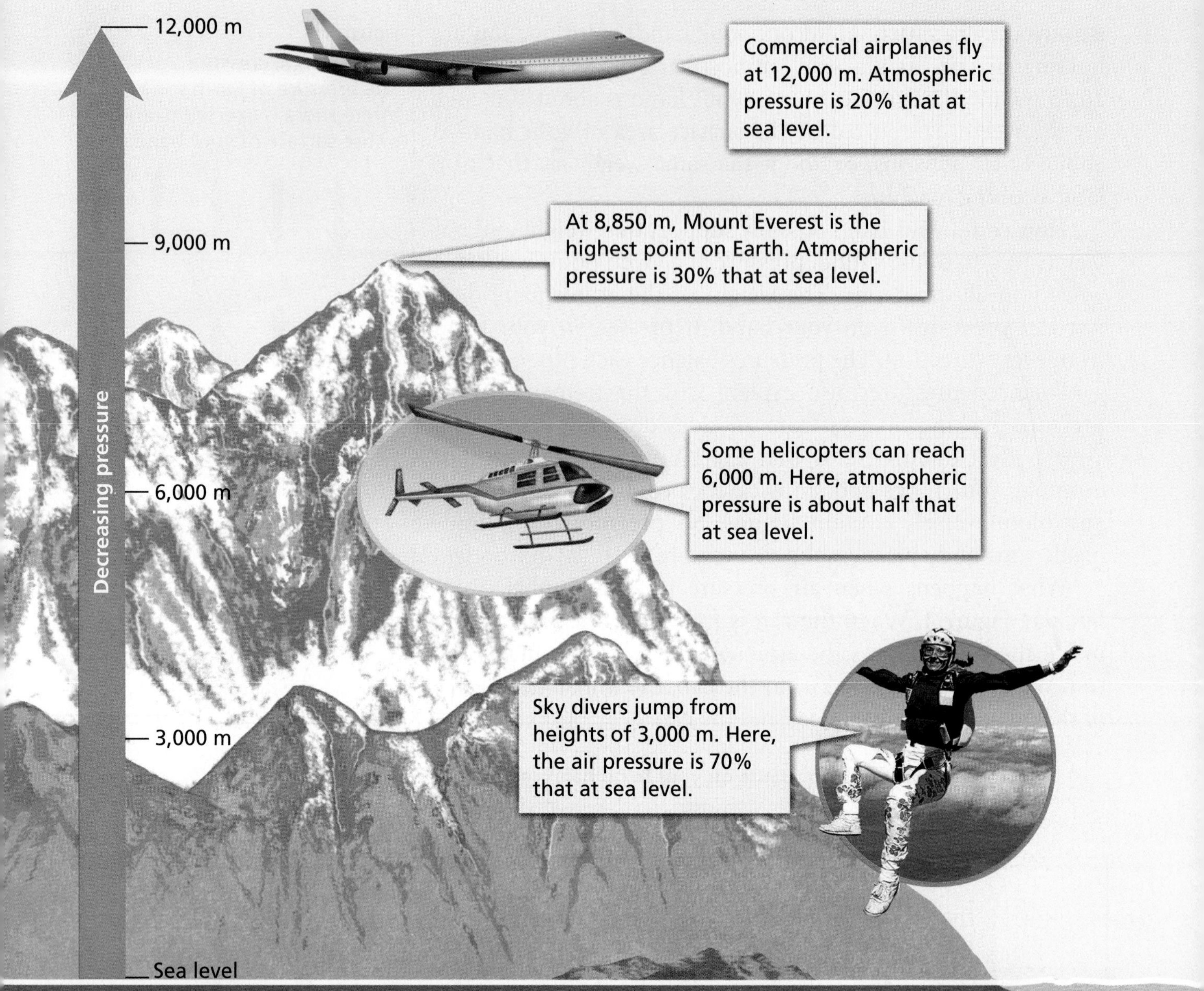

12,000 m
Commercial airplanes fly at 12,000 m. Atmospheric pressure is 20% that at sea level.
9,000 m
At 8,850 m, Mount Everest is the highest point on Earth. Atmospheric pressure is 30% that at sea level.
Decreasing pressure
6,000 m
Some helicopters can reach 6,000 m. Here, atmospheric pressure is about half that at sea level.
3,000 m
Sky divers jump from heights of 3,000 m. Here, the air pressure is 70% that at sea level.
Sea level

Go Online
SCI LINKS NSTA
For: Links on fluids and pressure
Visit: www.SciLinks.org
Web Code: scn-1331

FIGURE 5
Pressure Variations
Atmospheric pressure decreases gradually as the elevation above sea level increases. Water pressure increases rapidly as the water depth increases. **Applying Concepts** *Why do airplanes have pressurized cabins?*

Variations in Fluid Pressure

Does the pressure of a fluid ever change? What happens to pressure as you climb to a higher elevation or sink to a lower depth within a fluid? Figure 5 shows how pressure changes depending on where you are.

Atmospheric Pressure and Elevation Have you ever felt your ears "pop" as you rode up in an elevator? The "popping" has to do with changing air pressure. At higher elevations, there is less air above you and therefore less air pressure. **As your elevation increases, atmospheric pressure decreases.**

The fact that air pressure decreases as you move up in elevation explains why your ears pop. When the air pressure outside your body changes, the air pressure inside adjusts, but more slowly. So, for a moment, the air pressure behind your eardrums is greater than it is in the air outside. Your body releases this pressure with a "pop," balancing the pressures.

Water Pressure and Depth Fluid pressure depends on depth. The pressure at one meter below the surface of a swimming pool is the same as the pressure one meter below the surface of a lake. But if you dive deeper into either body of water, pressure becomes greater as you descend. The deeper you swim, the greater the pressure you feel. **Water pressure increases as depth increases.**

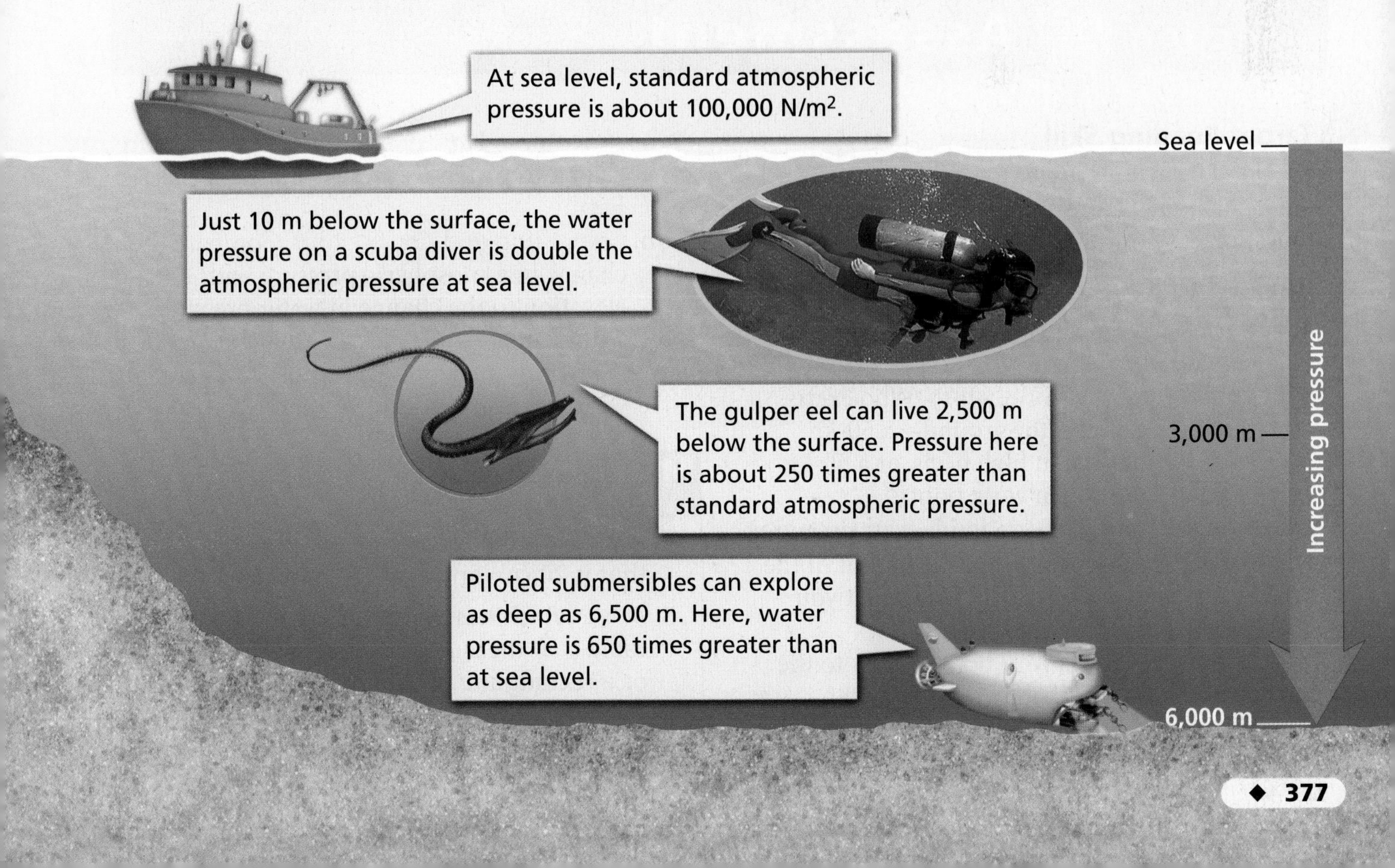

At sea level, standard atmospheric pressure is about 100,000 N/m².
Sea level
Just 10 m below the surface, the water pressure on a scuba diver is double the atmospheric pressure at sea level.
The gulper eel can live 2,500 m below the surface. Pressure here is about 250 times greater than standard atmospheric pressure.
3,000 m
Increasing pressure
Piloted submersibles can explore as deep as 6,500 m. Here, water pressure is 650 times greater than at sea level.
6,000 m

FIGURE 6
Aneroid Barometer
An aneroid barometer measures atmospheric pressure.
Interpreting Photographs *What type of weather might be coming when atmospheric pressure decreases?*

As with air, you can think of water pressure as being due to the weight of the water above a particular point. At greater depths, there is more water above that point and therefore more weight to support. In addition, air in the atmosphere pushes down on the water. Therefore, the total pressure at a given point beneath the water results from the weight of the water plus the weight of the air above it. In the deepest parts of the ocean, the pressure is more than 1,000 times the air pressure you experience every day.

Measuring Pressure You can measure atmospheric pressure with an instrument called a **barometer.** There are two types of barometers: a mercury barometer and an aneroid barometer. The aneroid barometer is the barometer you usually see hanging on a wall. Weather forecasters use the pressure reading from a barometer to help forecast the weather. Rapidly decreasing atmospheric pressure usually means a storm is on its way. Increasing pressure is often a sign of fair weather. You may hear barometric pressure readings expressed in millimeters, inches, or another unit called a millibar. For example, the standard barometric pressure at sea level may be reported as 760 millimeters, 29.92 inches, or 1,013.2 millibars.

Reading Checkpoint **What instrument measures atmospheric pressure?**

Section 1 Assessment

Target Reading Skill

Previewing Visuals Refer to your questions and answers about Figure 5 to help you answer Question 3 below.

Reviewing Key Concepts

1. a. **Reviewing** What two factors does pressure depend on?
   b. **Comparing and Contrasting** Who exerts more pressure on the ground—a 50-kg woman standing in high heels, or a 50-kg woman standing in work boots?
2. a. **Summarizing** How do fluids exert pressure?
   b. **Explaining** Since most of the weight of the atmosphere is above you, why aren't you crushed by it?
   c. **Inferring** How is your body similar to the can containing air shown in Figure 4?
3. a. **Describing** How does atmospheric pressure change as you move away from the surface of Earth?
   b. **Comparing and Contrasting** Compare the change in atmospheric pressure with elevation to the change in water pressure with depth.
   c. **Applying Concepts** Why must an astronaut wear a pressurized suit in space?

Math Practice

4. **Area** Find the area of a rectangular photo that is 20 cm long and 15 cm wide.
5. **Area** Which has a greater area: a square table that measures 120 cm × 120 cm, or a rectangular table that measures 200 cm × 90 cm?

Lab zone **Design Your Own Lab**

Spinning Sprinklers

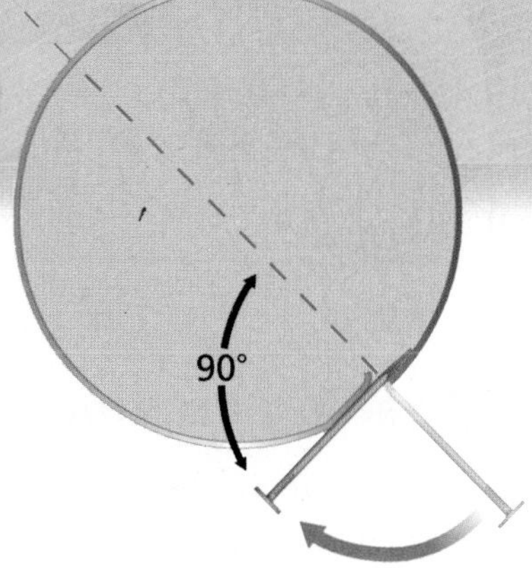

Problem

What factors affect the speed of rotation of a lawn sprinkler?

Skills Focus

designing experiments, controlling variables

Materials

- empty soda can
- fishing line, 30 cm
- waterproof marker
- wide-mouth jar or beaker
- stopwatch
- nails of various sizes
- large basin

Procedure

PART 1 Making a Sprinkler

1. Fill the jar with enough water to completely cover a soda can. Place the jar in the basin.
2. Bend up the tab of a can and tie the end of a length of fishing line to it. **CAUTION:** *The edge of the can opening can be sharp.*
3. Place a mark on the can to help you keep track of how many times the can spins.
4. Using the small nail, make a hole in the side of the can about 1 cm up from the bottom. Poke the nail straight in. Then twist the nail until it makes a right angle with the radius of the can as shown in the figure above. **CAUTION:** *Nails are sharp and should be used only to puncture the cans.*
5. Submerge the can in the jar and fill the can to the top with water.
6. Quickly lift the can with the fishing line so that it is 1–2 cm above the water level in the jar. Practice counting how many spins the can completes in 15 seconds.

PART 2 What Factors Affect Spin?

7. How does the size of the hole affect the number of spins made by the can? Propose a hypothesis and then design an experiment to test the hypothesis. Obtain your teacher's approval before carrying out your experiment. Record all your data.
8. How does the number of holes affect the number of spins made by the can? Propose a hypothesis and then design an experiment to test the hypothesis. Obtain your teacher's approval before carrying out your experiment. Record all your data.

Analyze and Conclude

1. **Designing Experiments** How does the size of the hole affect the rate of spin of the can? How does the number of holes affect the rate of spin of the can?
2. **Controlling Variables** What other variables might affect the number of spins made by the can?
3. **Interpreting Data** Explain the motion of the can in terms of water pressure.
4. **Classifying** Which of Newton's three laws of motion could you use to explain the motion of the can? Explain.
5. **Communicating** Use the results of your experiment to write a paragraph that explains why a spinning lawn sprinkler spins.

More to Explore

Some sprinkler systems use water pressure to spin. Examine one of these sprinklers to see the size, direction of spin, and number of holes. What would happen if you connected a second sprinkler to the first with another length of hose? If possible, try it.

Section 2

Floating and Sinking

Reading Preview

Key Concepts

- What is the effect of the buoyant force?
- How can you use density to determine whether an object will float or sink in a fluid?

Key Terms

- buoyant force
- Archimedes' principle
- density

Target Reading Skill

Relating Cause and Effect

As you read, identify the reasons why an object sinks. Write the information in a graphic organizer like the one below.

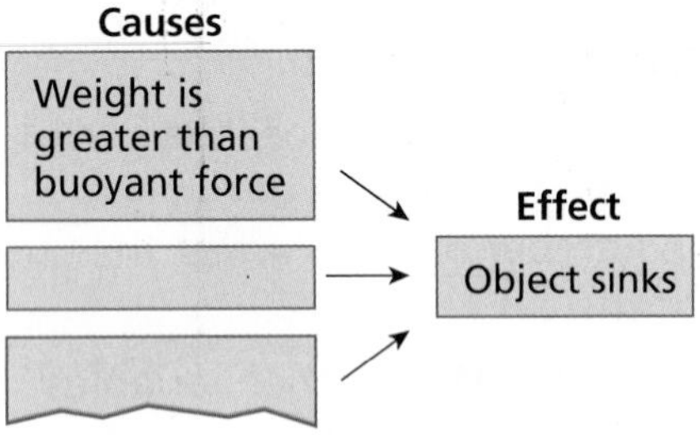

Lab zone Discover **Activity**

What Can You Measure With a Straw?

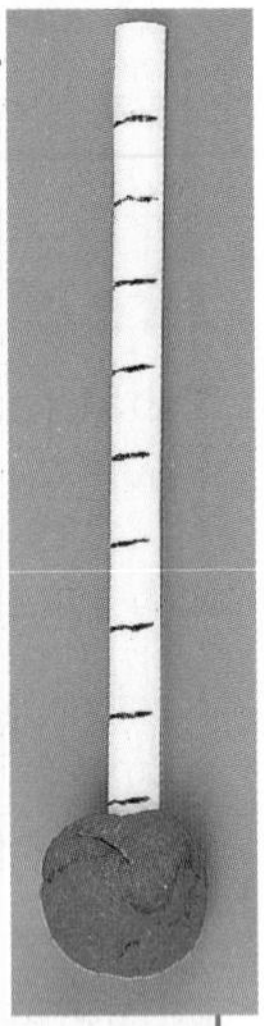

1. Cut a plastic straw to a 10-cm length.
2. Use a waterproof marker to make marks on the straw that are 1 cm apart.
3. Roll some modeling clay into a ball about 1.5 cm in diameter. Stick one end of the straw in the clay. You have built a device known as a hydrometer.
4. Place the hydrometer in a glass of water. About half of the straw should remain above water. If it sinks, remove some of the clay. Make sure no water gets into the straw.
5. Dissolve 10 spoonfuls of sugar in a glass of water. Try out your hydrometer in this liquid.

Think It Over

Predicting Compare your observations in Steps 4 and 5. Then predict what will happen if you use 20 spoonfuls of sugar in a glass of water. Test your prediction.

In April 1912, the *Titanic* departed from England on its first and only voyage. At the time, it was the largest ship afloat—nearly three football fields long. The *Titanic* was also the most technologically advanced ship in existence. Its hull was divided into compartments, and it was considered to be unsinkable.

Yet a few days into the voyage, the *Titanic* struck an iceberg. One compartment after another filled with water. Less than three hours later, the bow of the great ship slipped under the waves. As the stern rose high into the air, the ship broke in two. Both pieces sank to the bottom of the Atlantic Ocean. More than a thousand people died.

◀ **The bow section of the *Titanic* resting on the ocean floor**

Buoyancy

Ships are designed to have buoyancy—the ability to float. How is it possible that a huge ship can float easily on the surface of water under certain conditions, and then in a few hours become a sunken wreck? To answer this question, you need to understand the buoyant force.

Gravity and the Buoyant Force You have probably experienced the buoyant force. If you have ever picked up an object under water, you know that it seems much lighter in water than in air. Water and other fluids exert an upward force called the **buoyant force** that acts on a submerged object. **The buoyant force acts in the direction opposite to the force of gravity, so it makes an object feel lighter.**

As you can see in Figure 7, a fluid exerts pressure on all surfaces of a submerged object. Since the pressure in a fluid increases with depth, the upward pressure on the bottom of the object is greater than the downward pressure on the top. The result is a net force acting upward on the submerged object. This is the buoyant force.

Remember that the weight of a submerged object is a downward force. An object sinks if its weight is greater than the buoyant force because a net force acts downward on the object. If the weight of a submerged object is equal to the buoyant force, no net force acts on the object. The object floats on the surface while partly submerged or floats at a constant level while totally submerged, depending on its weight. For example, both the jellyfish and the turtle shown in Figure 8 have balanced forces acting on them.

FIGURE 7
Buoyant Force
The pressure on the bottom of a submerged object is greater than the pressure on the top. The result is a net force in the upward direction.

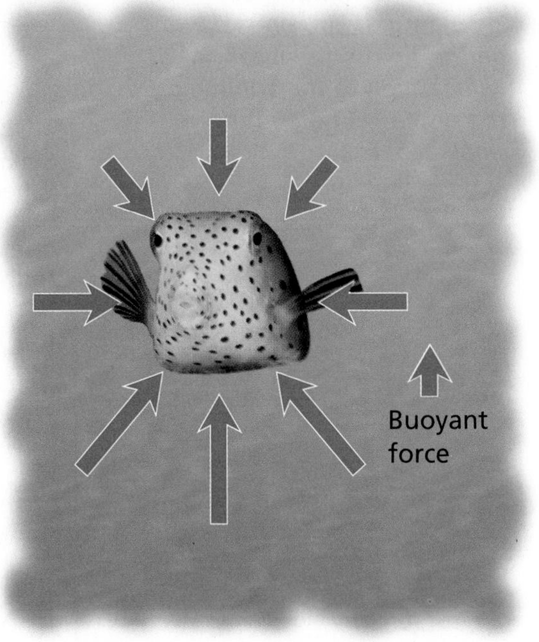

FIGURE 8
Buoyant Force and Weight
The weight of an object is a force that works opposite the buoyant force on the object. **Comparing and Contrasting** *Why don't all three creatures float?*

FIGURE 9
Archimedes' Principle
Archimedes' principle applies to sinking and floating objects.
Predicting *If you press down on the floating film can, what will happen to the volume of the displaced fluid in the small beaker?*

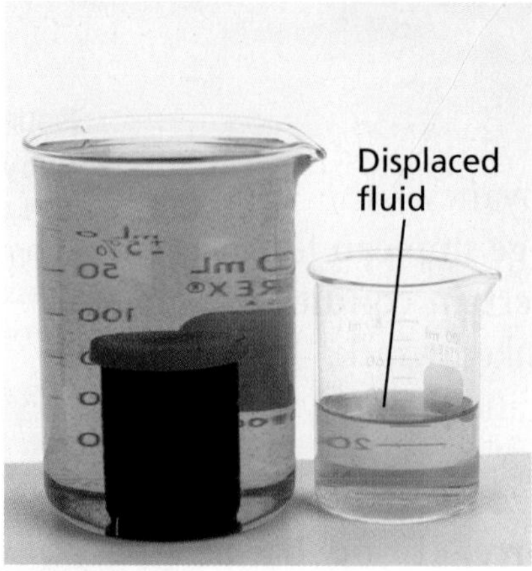

Sinking
When the film can has film in it, it sinks. The volume of fluid displaced by the can is equal to the volume of the can.

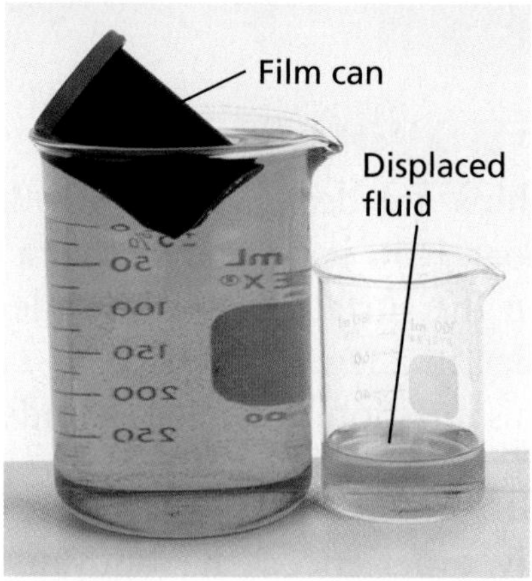

Floating
When the film can is empty, it floats. The volume of displaced fluid is equal to the volume of the submerged portion of the can.

Archimedes' Principle You know that all objects take up space. A submerged object displaces, or takes the place of, a volume of fluid equal to its own volume. A partly submerged object, however, displaces a volume of fluid equal to the volume of its submerged portion only. You can see this in Figure 9.

Archimedes, a mathematician of ancient Greece, discovered a connection between the weight of a fluid displaced by an object and the buoyant force acting on it. This connection is known as Archimedes' principle. **Archimedes' principle** states that the buoyant force acting on a submerged object is equal to the weight of the fluid the object displaces. To understand what this means, think about swimming in a pool. Suppose your body displaces 50 liters of water. The buoyant force exerted on you will be equal to the weight of 50 liters of water, or about 500 N.

You can use Archimedes' principle to explain why a ship floats on the surface. Since the buoyant force equals the weight of the displaced fluid, the buoyant force will increase if more fluid is displaced. A large object displaces more fluid than a small object. A greater buoyant force acts on the larger object even if the large object has the same weight as the small object.

Look at Figure 10. The shape of a ship's hull causes the ship to displace a greater volume of water than a solid piece of steel with the same mass. A ship displaces a volume of water equal in weight to the submerged portion of the ship. According to Archimedes' principle, the weight of the displaced water is equal to the buoyant force. Since a ship displaces more water than a block of steel, a greater buoyant force acts on the ship. A ship floats on the surface as long as the buoyant force acting on it is equal to its weight.

Discovery Channel School

Forces in Fluids

Video Preview
▶ Video Field Trip
Video Assessment

Reading Checkpoint **Does a greater buoyant force act on a large object or a small object?**

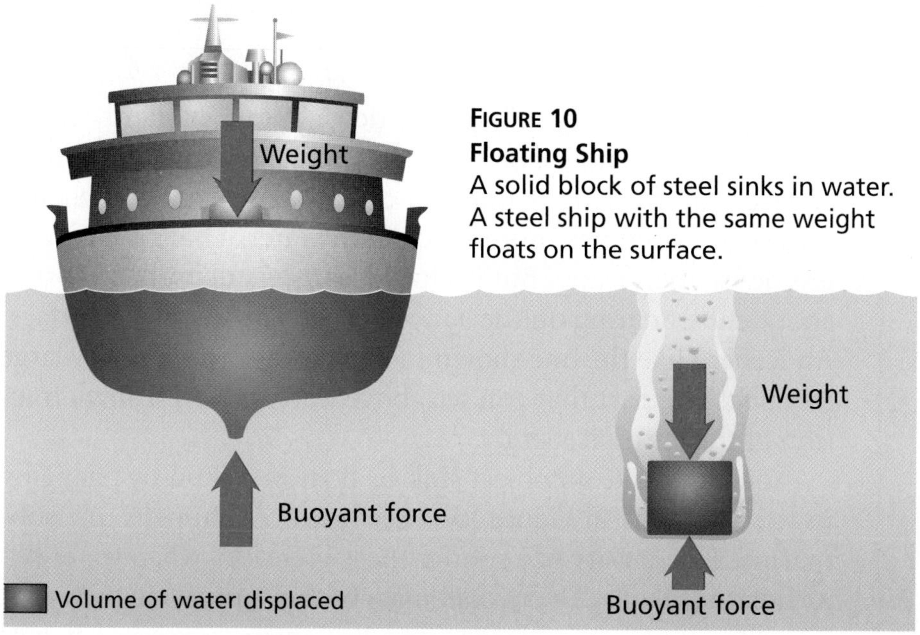

FIGURE 10
Floating Ship
A solid block of steel sinks in water. A steel ship with the same weight floats on the surface.

Density

Exactly why do some objects float and others sink? To find the answer, you must relate an object's mass to its volume. In other words, you need to know the object's density.

What Is Density? The **density** of a substance is its mass per unit volume.

$$\text{Density} = \frac{\text{Mass}}{\text{Volume}}$$

For example, one cubic centimeter (cm^3) of lead has a mass of 11.3 grams, so its density is 11.3 g/cm^3. In contrast, one cubic centimeter of cork has a mass of only about 0.25 gram. So the density of cork is about 0.25 g/cm^3. Lead is more dense than cork. The density of water is 1.0 g/cm^3. So water is less dense than lead but more dense than cork.

Comparing Densities of Substances In Figure 11, several liquids and other materials are shown along with their densities. Notice that liquids can float on top of other liquids. (You may have seen salad oil floating on top of vinegar.) The liquids and materials with the greatest densities are near the bottom of the cylinder.

By comparing densities, you can predict whether an object will float or sink in a fluid. An object that is more dense than the fluid in which it is immersed sinks. An object that is less dense than the fluid in which it is immersed floats to the surface. And if the density of an object is equal to the density of the fluid in which it is immersed, the object neither rises nor sinks in the fluid. Instead, it floats at a constant depth.

FIGURE 11
Densities of Substances
You can use density to predict whether an object will sink or float when placed in a liquid. **Interpreting Data** *Will a rubber washer sink or float in corn oil?*

Substance	Density (g/cm^3)
Wood	0.7
Corn oil	0.925
Plastic	0.93
Water	1.00
Tar ball	1.02
Glycerin	1.26
Rubber washer	1.34
Corn syrup	1.38
Copper wire	8.8
Mercury	13.6

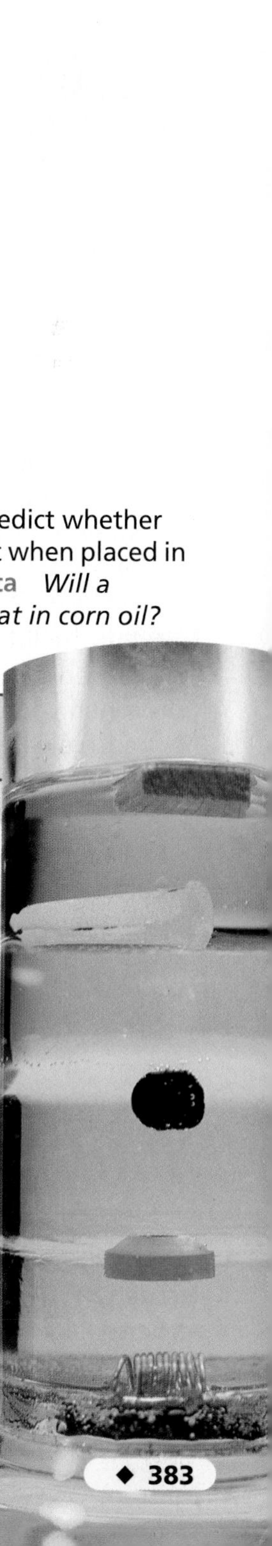

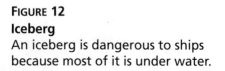

Lab zone **Try This Activity**

Cartesian Diver

1. Fill a plastic jar or bottle almost completely with water.

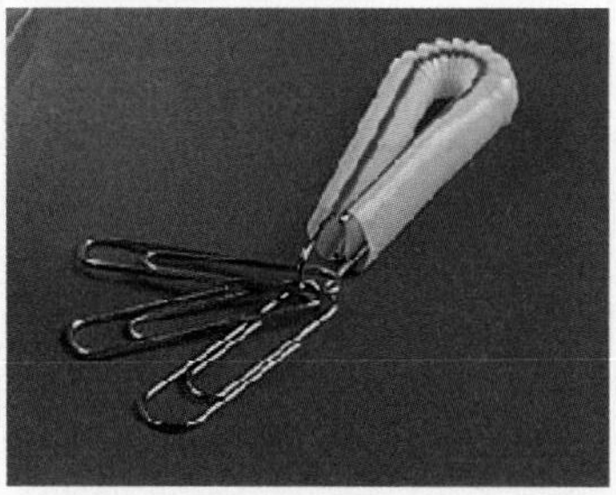

2. Bend a plastic straw into a U shape and cut the ends so that each side is 4 cm long. Attach the ends with a paper clip. Drop the straw in the jar, paper clip first.
3. Attach more paper clips to the first one until the straw floats with its top about 0.5 cm above the surface. This is the diver.
4. Put the lid on the jar. Observe what happens when you slowly squeeze and release the jar several times.

Drawing Conclusions
Explain the behavior of the Cartesian diver.

Changing Density Changing density can explain why an object floats or sinks. For example, you can change the density of water by freezing it into ice. Since water expands when it freezes, ice occupies more space than water. That's why ice is less dense than water. But it's just a little less dense! So most of an ice cube floating on the surface is below the water's surface. An iceberg like the one shown in Figure 12 is really a very large ice cube. The part that you see above water is only a small fraction of the entire iceberg.

You can make an object sink or float in a fluid by changing its density. Look at Figure 13 to see how this happens to a submarine. The density of a submarine is increased when water fills its flotation tanks. The overall mass of the submarine increases. Since its volume remains the same, its density increases when its mass increases. So the submarine will dive. To make the submarine float to the surface, water is pumped out of it, decreasing its mass. Its density decreases, and it rises toward the surface.

You can also explain why a submarine dives and floats by means of the buoyant force. Since the buoyant force is equal to the weight of the displaced fluid, the buoyant force on the submerged submarine stays the same. Changing the water level in the flotation tanks changes the weight of the submarine. The submarine dives when its weight is greater than the buoyant force. It rises to the surface when its weight is less than the buoyant force.

Don't forget that air is also a fluid. If you decrease the density of an object, such as a balloon, the object will float and not sink in air. Instead of air, you can fill a balloon with helium gas. A helium balloon rises because helium is less dense than air. A balloon filled with air, however, is denser than the surrounding air because the air inside it is under pressure. The denser air inside, along with the weight of the balloon, make it fall to the ground.

Reading Checkpoint **Why does a helium balloon float in air?**

FIGURE 12
Iceberg
An iceberg is dangerous to ships because most of it is under water.

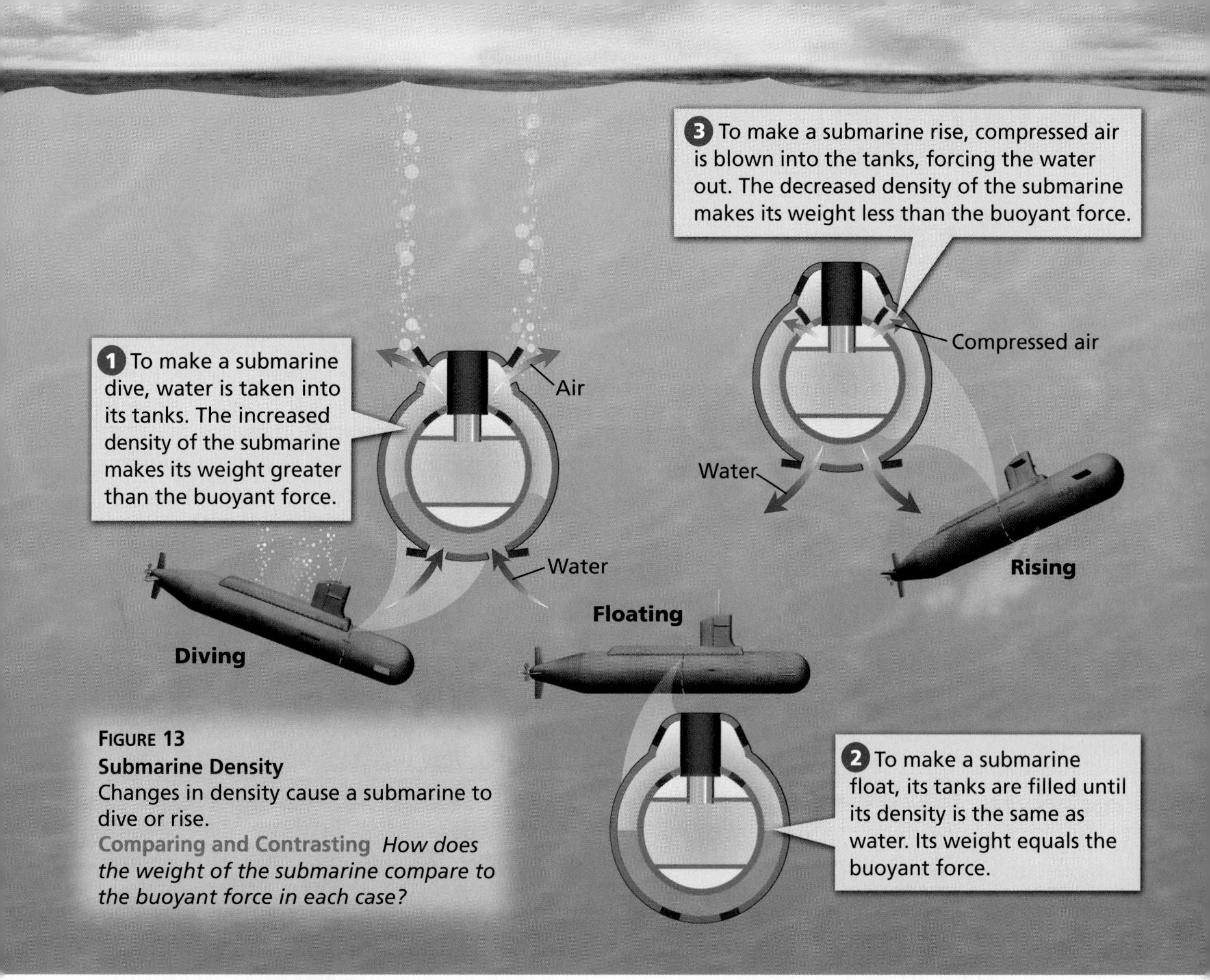

1 To make a submarine dive, water is taken into its tanks. The increased density of the submarine makes its weight greater than the buoyant force.
Air
Water
Diving
Floating
2 To make a submarine float, its tanks are filled until its density is the same as water. Its weight equals the buoyant force.
3 To make a submarine rise, compressed air is blown into the tanks, forcing the water out. The decreased density of the submarine makes its weight less than the buoyant force.
Compressed air
Water
Rising

FIGURE 13
Submarine Density
Changes in density cause a submarine to dive or rise.
Comparing and Contrasting *How does the weight of the submarine compare to the buoyant force in each case?*

Section 2 Assessment

Target Reading Skill

Relating Cause and Effect Refer to your graphic organizer to help you answer the questions below.

Reviewing Key Concepts

1. a. Explaining How does the buoyant force affect a submerged object?

b. Summarizing How does Archimedes' principle relate the buoyant force acting on an object to the fluid displaced by the object?

c. Calculating An object that weighs 340 N floats on a lake. What is the weight of the displaced water? What is the buoyant force?

2. a. Defining What is density?

b. Explaining How can you use the density of an object to predict whether it will float or sink in water?

c. Applying Concepts Some canoes have compartments on either end that are hollow and watertight. These canoes won't sink, even when they capsize. Explain why.

Lab zone At-Home Activity

Changing Balloon Density Attach paper clips to the string of a helium balloon. Ask a family member to predict how many paper clips you will need to attach to make the balloon sink to the floor. How many paper clips can you attach and still keep the helium balloon suspended in the air? Explain how adding paper clips changes the overall density of the balloon.

Lab zone Skills Lab

Sink and Spill

Problem

How is the buoyant force acting on a floating object related to the weight of the water it displaces?

Skills Focus

controlling variables, interpreting data, drawing conclusions

Materials

- paper towels
- pie pan
- triple-beam balance
- beaker, 600-mL
- jar with watertight lid, about 30-mL
- table salt

Procedure

1. Preview the procedure and copy the data table into your notebook.
2. Find the mass, in grams, of a dry paper towel and the pie pan together. Multiply the mass by 0.01. This gives you the weight in newtons. Record it in your data table.
3. Place the 600-mL beaker, with the dry paper towel under it, in the middle of the pie pan. Fill the beaker to the very top with water.
4. Fill the jar about halfway with salt. (The jar and salt must be able to float in water.) Then find the mass of the salt and the dry jar (with its cover on) in grams. Multiply the mass by 0.01. Record this weight in your data table.
5. Gently lower the jar into the 600-mL beaker. (If the jar sinks, take it out and remove some salt. Repeat Steps 2, 3, and 4.) Estimate the fraction of the jar that is underwater, and record it.
6. Once all of the displaced water has been spilled, find the total mass of the paper towel and pie pan containing the water. Multiply the mass by 0.01 and record the result in your data table.
7. Empty the pie pan. Dry off the pan and the jar.
8. Repeat Steps 3 through 7 several more times. Each time fill the jar with a different amount of salt, but make sure the jar still floats.
9. Calculate the buoyant force for each trial and record it in your data table. (*Hint*: When an object floats, the buoyant force is equal to the weight of the object.)
10. Calculate the weight of the displaced water in each case. Record it in your data table.

Data Table

Jar	Weight of Empty Pie Pan and Dry Paper Towel (N)	Weight of Jar, Salt, and Cover (N)	Weight of Pie Pan With Displaced Water and Paper Towel (N)	Fraction of Jar Submerged in Water	Buoyant Force (N)	Weight of Displaced Water (N)
1						
2						
3						

Analyze and Conclude

1. **Controlling Variables** In each trial, the jar had a different weight. How did this affect the way that the jar floated?
2. **Interpreting Data** The jar had the same volume in every trial. Why did the volume of displaced water vary?
3. **Drawing Conclusions** What can you conclude about the relationship between the buoyant force and the weight of the displaced water?
4. **Drawing Conclusions** If you put too much salt in the jar, it will sink. What can you conclude about the buoyant force in this case? How can you determine the buoyant force for an object that sinks?
5. **Communicating** Write a paragraph suggesting places where errors may have been introduced into the experiment. Propose some ways to control the errors.

Design an Experiment

How do you think your results would change if you used a liquid that is more dense or less dense than water? Design an experiment to test your hypothesis. What liquid or liquids will you use? Will you need equipment other than what you used for this experiment? If so, what will you need? *Obtain your teacher's permission before carrying out your investigation.*

Section 3

Pascal's Principle

Reading Preview

Key Concepts

- What does Pascal's principle say about change in fluid pressure?
- How does a hydraulic system work?

Key Terms

- Pascal's principle
- hydraulic system

Target Reading Skill

Asking Questions Before you read, preview the red headings. In a graphic organizer like the one below, ask a *what* or *how* question for each heading. As you read, write the answers to your questions.

Pascal's Principle

Question	Answer
How is pressure transmitted in a fluid?	Pressure is transmitted . . .

Lab zone Discover Activity

How Does Pressure Change?

1. Fill an empty 2-liter plastic bottle with water. Then screw on the cap. There should be no bubbles in the bottle (or only very small bubbles).
2. Lay the bottle on its side. At one spot, push in the bottle with your left thumb.
3. With your right thumb, push in fairly hard on a spot at the other end, as shown. What does your left thumb feel?
4. Pick another spot on the bottle for your left thumb and repeat Step 3.

Think It Over

Observing When you push in with your right thumb, does the water pressure in the bottle increase, decrease, or remain the same? How do you know?

At first, you hesitate, but then you hold out your hand. The aquarium attendant places the sea star in your palm. You can feel motion on your skin. The many tiny "feet" on the animal's underside look something like suction cups, and they tickle just a bit! The attendant explains that the sea star has a system of tubes containing water in its body. As the water moves around in the tubes, it creates fluid pressure that allows the sea star to move. The sea star also uses this system to obtain its food.

A sea star uses fluid pressure to move. ▶

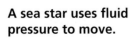

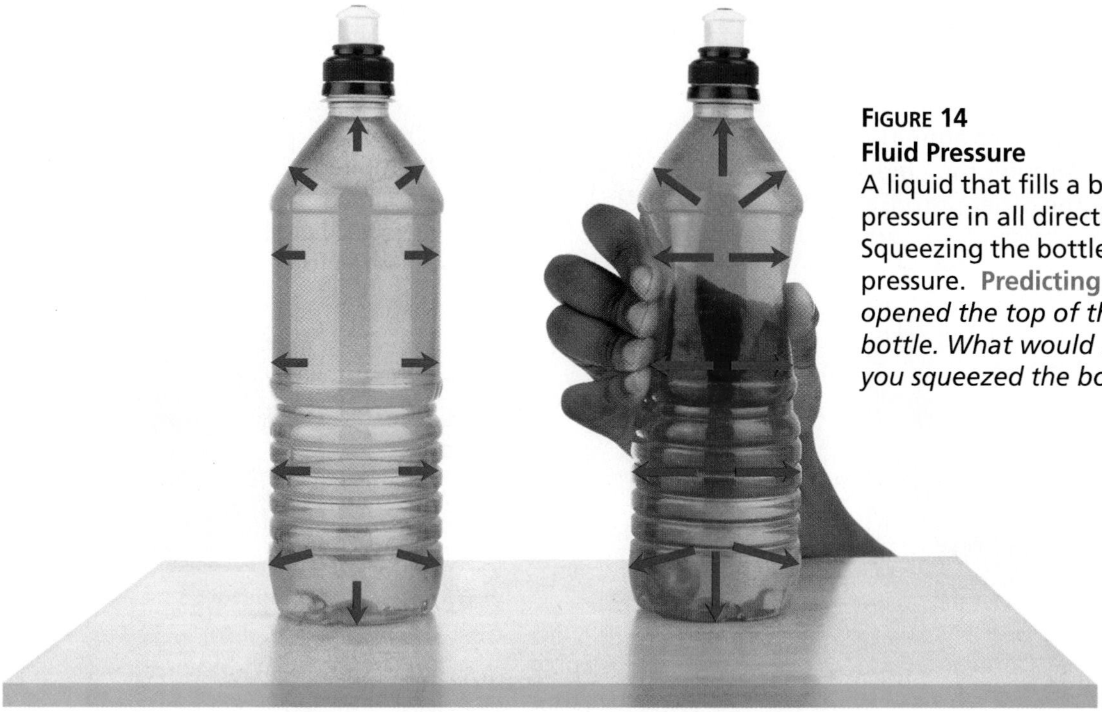

FIGURE 14
Fluid Pressure
A liquid that fills a bottle exerts pressure in all directions. Squeezing the bottle increases the pressure. **Predicting** *Suppose you opened the top of the water bottle. What would happen when you squeezed the bottle? Why?*

Transmitting Pressure in a Fluid

If you did the Discover Activity, you may be surprised to learn that a sea star's water-filled tube system is like the closed bottle you pushed your thumb against. Recall that the fluid pressure in the closed container increased when you pushed against its side. By changing the fluid pressure at any spot in the closed container, you transmitted pressure throughout the container. In the 1600s, a French mathematician named Blaise Pascal developed a principle to explain how pressure is transmitted in a fluid. Pascal's name is used for the unit of pressure.

What Is Pascal's Principle? As you may recall, fluid exerts pressure on any surface it touches. For example, the water in each bottle shown in Figure 14 exerts pressure on the entire surface of the bottle—up, down, and sideways.

What happens if you squeeze the bottle when its top is closed? The water has nowhere to go, so it presses harder on the inside surface of the bottle. The water pressure increases everywhere in the bottle. This is shown by the increased length of the arrows on the right in Figure 14.

Pascal discovered that pressure increases by the same amount throughout an enclosed or confined fluid. **When force is applied to a confined fluid, the change in pressure is transmitted equally to all parts of the fluid.** This relationship is known as **Pascal's principle.**

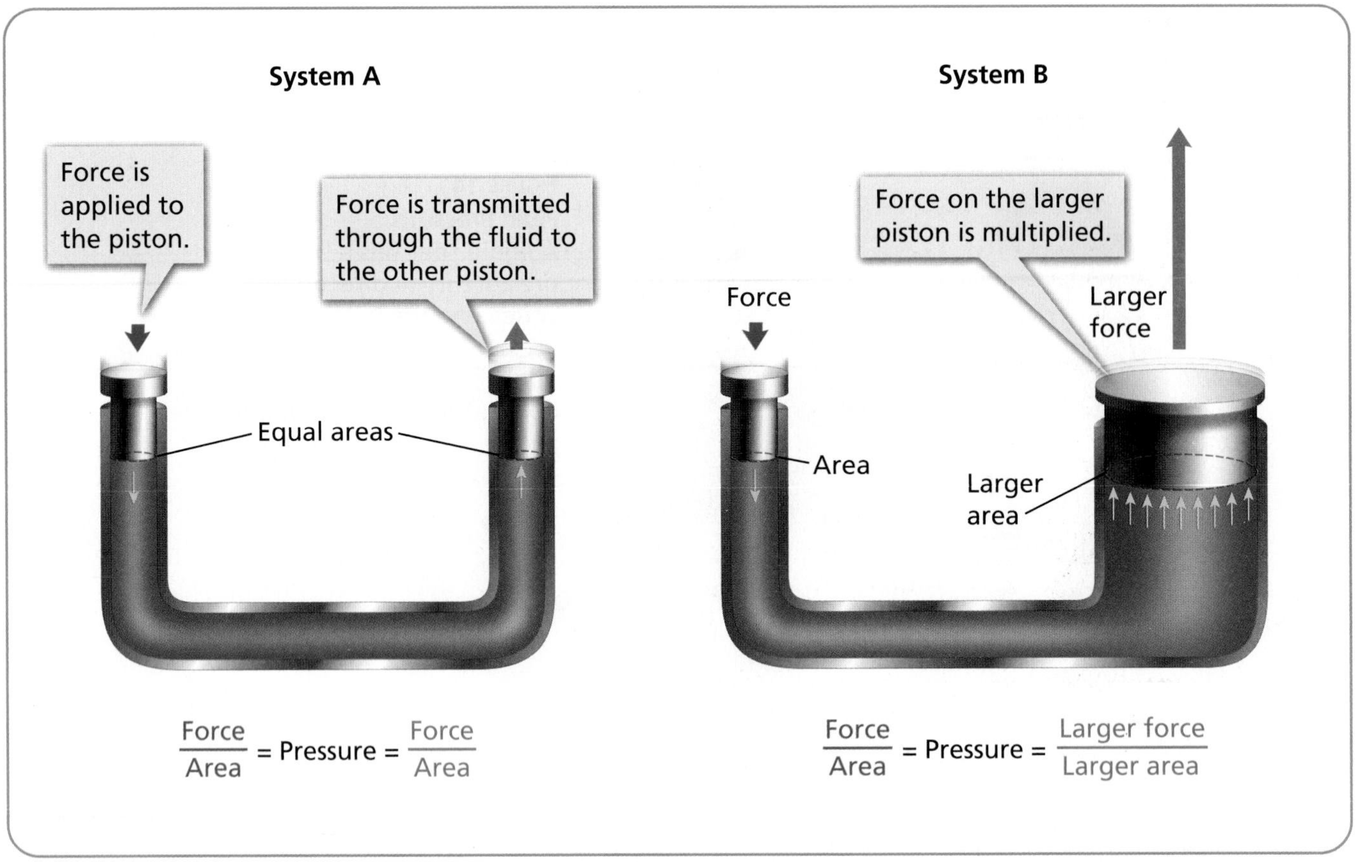
System A
Force is applied to the piston.
Force is transmitted through the fluid to the other piston.
Equal areas
Force / Area = Pressure = Force / Area
System B
Force on the larger piston is multiplied.
Force
Larger force
Area
Larger area
Force / Area = Pressure = Larger force / Larger area

FIGURE 15
Hydraulic Devices
In a hydraulic device, a force applied to one piston increases the fluid pressure equally throughout the fluid. By changing the size of the pistons, the force can be multiplied.
Problem Solving *To multiply the force applied to the left piston four times, how large must the right piston be?*

Go Online
active art

For: Hydraulic Systems activity
Visit: PHSchool.com
Web Code: cgp-3033

Using Pascal's Principle You can see Pascal's principle at work in Figure 15, which shows a model of a hydraulic device. A hydraulic device is operated by the movement and force of a fluid. The device consists of two pistons, one at each end of a U-shaped tube. A piston is like a stopper that slides up and down in a tube.

Suppose you fill System A with water and then push down on the left piston. The increase in fluid pressure will be transmitted to the right piston. According to Pascal's principle, both pistons experience the same fluid pressure. So, because both pistons have the same surface area, they will experience the same force.

Now look at System B. The right piston has a greater surface area than the left piston. Suppose the area of the small piston is 1 square centimeter and the area of the large piston is 9 square centimeters. Then the right piston has an area nine times greater than the area of the left piston. If you push down on the left piston, pressure is transmitted equally to the right piston. But, because the area of the right piston is nine times greater, the force you exert on the left piston is multiplied nine times on the right piston. By changing the size of the pistons, you can multiply force by almost any amount you wish.

Reading Checkpoint **How is force multiplied in System B?**

Hydraulic Systems

Hydraulic systems make use of hydraulic devices to perform a variety of functions. A **hydraulic system** uses liquids to transmit pressure in a confined fluid. **A hydraulic system multiplies force by applying the force to a small surface area. The increase in pressure is then transmitted to another part of the confined fluid, which pushes on a larger surface area.** You have probably seen a number of hydraulic systems at work, including lift systems and the brakes of a car. Because they use fluids to transmit pressure, hydraulic systems have few moving parts that can jam, break, or wear down.

Hydraulic Lifts Hydraulic lift systems are used to raise cars off the ground so mechanics can repair them with ease. You may be surprised to learn that hydraulic systems are also used to lift the heavy ladder on a fire truck to reach the upper windows of a burning building. In addition, hydraulic lifts are used to operate many pieces of heavy construction equipment such as dump trucks, backhoes, snowplows, and cranes. Next time you see a construction vehicle at work, see if you can spot the hydraulic pistons in action.

Reading Checkpoint What are some uses of hydraulic systems?

Math Analyzing Data

Comparing Hydraulic Lifts

In the hydraulic device in Figure 15, a force applied to the piston on the left produces a lifting force in the piston on the right. The graph shows the relationship between the applied force and the lifting force for two hydraulic lifts.

Hydraulic Lifts

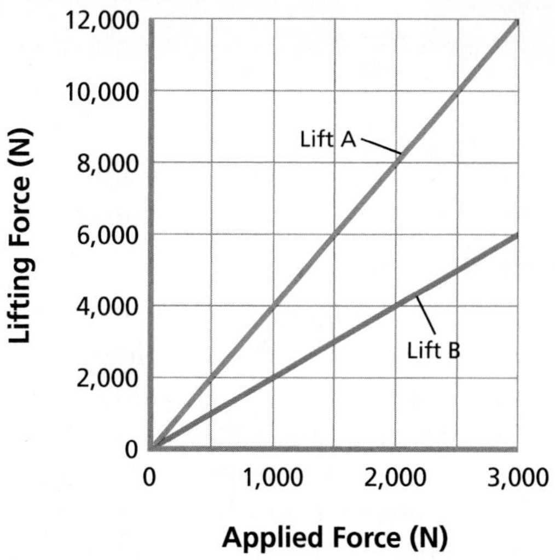

1. Reading Graphs Suppose a force of 1,000 N is applied to both lifts. Use the graph to determine the lifting force of each lift.
2. Reading Graphs For Lift A, how much force must be applied to lift a 12,000-N object?
3. Interpreting Data By how much is the applied force multiplied for each lift?
4. Interpreting Data What can you learn from the slope of the line for each lift?
5. Drawing Conclusions Which lift would you choose if you wanted to produce the greater lifting force?

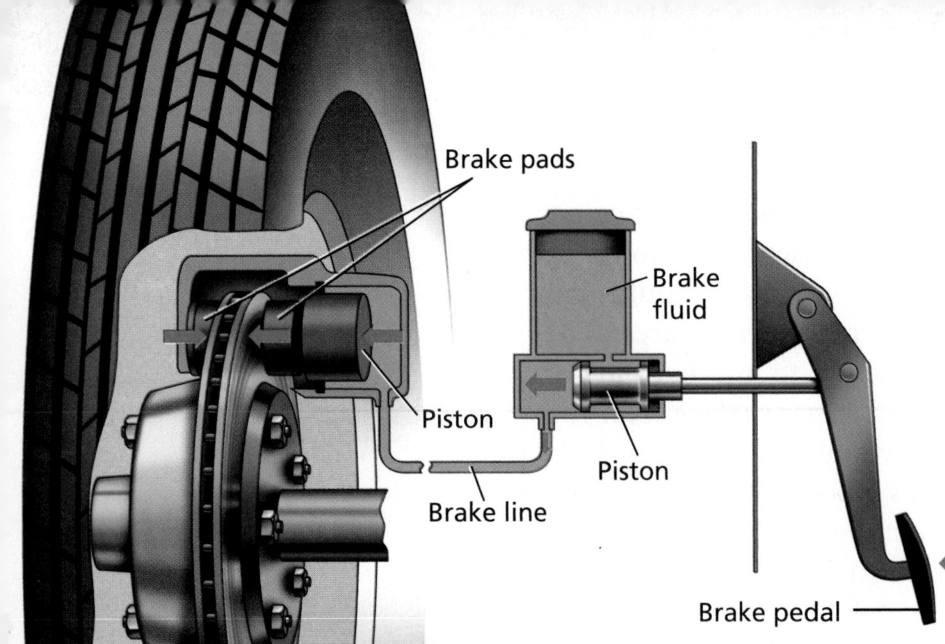

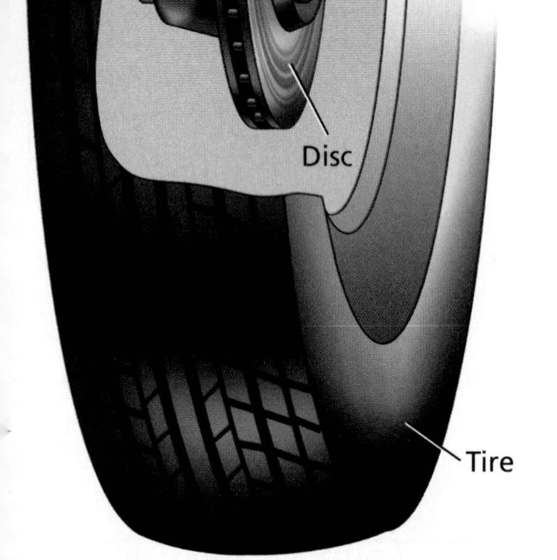

FIGURE 16
Hydraulic Brakes
The hydraulic brake system of a car multiplies the force exerted on the brake pedal.
Comparing and Contrasting *How does the size of the brake pedal piston compare with the size of a brake pad piston?*

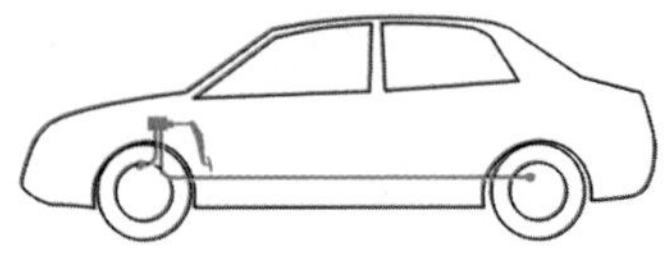

Hydraulic Brakes You rely on Pascal's principle when you ride in a car. The brake system of a car is a hydraulic system. Figure 16 shows a simplified brake system with disc brakes. When a driver pushes down on the brake pedal, he or she pushes a small piston. The piston exerts pressure on the brake fluid. The increased pressure is transmitted through the fluid in the brake lines to larger pistons within the wheels of the car. Each of these pistons pushes on a brake pad. The brake pads rub against the brake disc, and the wheel's motion is slowed down by the force of friction. Because the brake system multiplies force, a person can stop a large car with only a light push on the brake pedal.

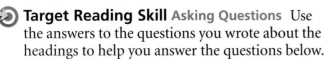

Section 3 Assessment

Target Reading Skill **Asking Questions** Use the answers to the questions you wrote about the headings to help you answer the questions below.

Reviewing Key Concepts

1. a. **Reviewing** According to Pascal's principle, how is pressure transmitted in a fluid?
   b. **Relating Cause and Effect** How does a hydraulic device multiply force?
   c. **Calculating** Suppose you apply a 10-N force to a 10-cm^2 piston in a hydraulic device. If the force is transmitted to another piston with an area of 100 cm^2, by how much will the force be multiplied?
2. a. **Defining** What is a hydraulic system?
   b. **Explaining** How does a hydraulic system work?
   c. **Sequencing** Describe what happens in the brake system of a car from the time a driver steps on the brake pedal to the time the car stops.

Writing in Science

Cause-and-Effect Letter You are a mechanic who fixes hydraulic brakes. A customer asks you why his brakes do not work. When you examine the car, you notice a leak in the brake line and repair it. Write a letter to the customer explaining why a leak in the brake line caused his brakes to fail.

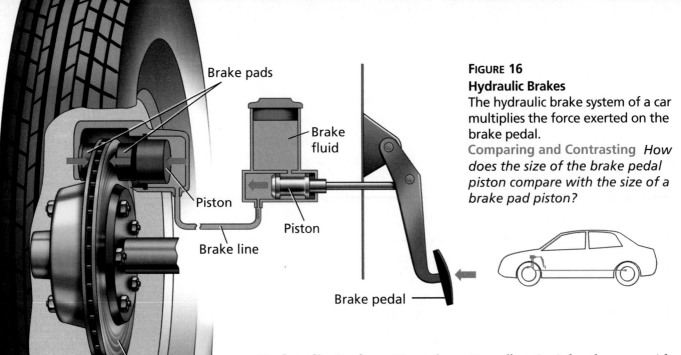

Section 4 · Tech & Design ·

Bernoulli's Principle

Reading Preview

Key Concepts

- According to Bernoulli's principle, how is fluid pressure related to the motion of a fluid?
- What are some applications of Bernoulli's principle?

Key Terms

- Bernoulli's principle
- lift

Target Reading Skill

Identifying Main Ideas As you read the Applying Bernoulli's Principle section, write the main idea in a graphic organizer like the one below. Then write three supporting details that give examples of the main idea.

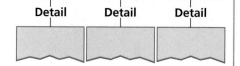

Main Idea

Bernoulli's principle is a factor that helps explain . . .

Detail | **Detail** | **Detail**

Lab zone Discover Activity

Does the Movement of Air Affect Pressure?

1. Use your thumb and forefinger to hold a sheet of paper by the corners.
2. Hold the paper just below your mouth, so that its edge is horizontal and the paper hangs down.
3. Blow across the top of the paper.
4. Repeat this several times, blowing harder each time.

Think It Over

Inferring On what side of the paper is the pressure lower? How do you know?

In December 1903, Wilbur and Orville Wright brought an odd-looking vehicle to a deserted beach in Kitty Hawk, North Carolina. People had flown in balloons for more than a hundred years, but the Wright brothers' goal was something no one had ever done before. They flew a plane that was heavier (denser) than air! They had spent years experimenting with different wing shapes and surfaces, and they had carefully studied the flight of birds. Their first flight at Kitty Hawk lasted just 12 seconds. The plane flew more than 36 meters and made history.

What did the Wright brothers know about flying that allowed them to construct the first airplane? And how can the principles they used explain how a jet can fly across the country? The answer has to do with fluid pressure and what happens when a fluid moves.

◄ **On December 17, 1903, the Wright brothers' plane *Flyer* flew for the first time.**

Lab zone Try This **Activity**

Faucet Force

1. Hold a plastic spoon loosely by the edges of its handle so it swings freely between your fingers.
2. Turn on a faucet to produce a steady stream of water. Predict what will happen if you touch the bottom of the spoon to the stream of water.
3. Test your prediction. Repeat the test several times.

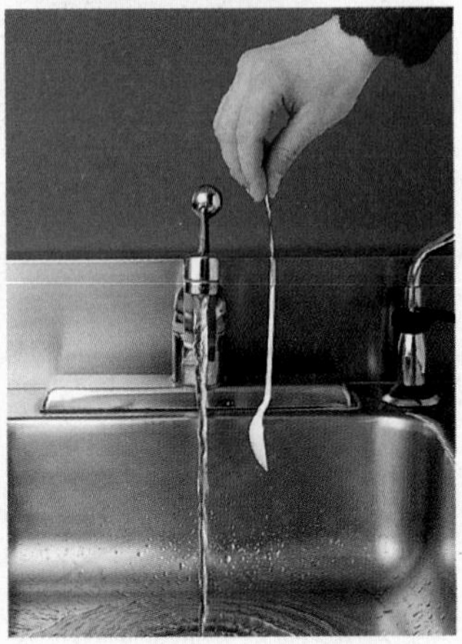

Developing Hypotheses Use your observations to develop a hypothesis explaining why the spoon moved as it did.

Pressure and Moving Fluids

So far in this chapter, you have learned about fluids that are not moving. What makes a fluid flow? And what happens to fluid pressure when a fluid moves?

Fluid Motion A fluid naturally flows from an area of high pressure to an area of low pressure. This happens, for example, when you sip a drink from a straw. When you start to sip, you remove the air from the straw. This creates an area of low pressure in the straw. The higher air pressure pushing down on the surface of your drink forces the drink up into the straw.

What Is Bernoulli's Principle? In the 1700s, Swiss scientist Daniel Bernoulli (bur NOO lee) discovered that the pressure of a moving fluid is different than the pressure of a fluid at rest. **Bernoulli's principle** states that the faster a fluid moves, the less pressure the fluid exerts.

If you did the Discover Activity, you saw that air moving over the paper caused the paper to rise. Bernoulli's principle explains the behavior of the paper. **Bernoulli's principle states that as the speed of a moving fluid increases, the pressure within the fluid decreases.** The air above the paper moves, but the air below the paper does not. The moving air exerts less pressure than the still air. As a result, the still air exerts greater pressure on the bottom of the paper, pushing the paper up.

Reading Checkpoint **What is Bernoulli's principle?**

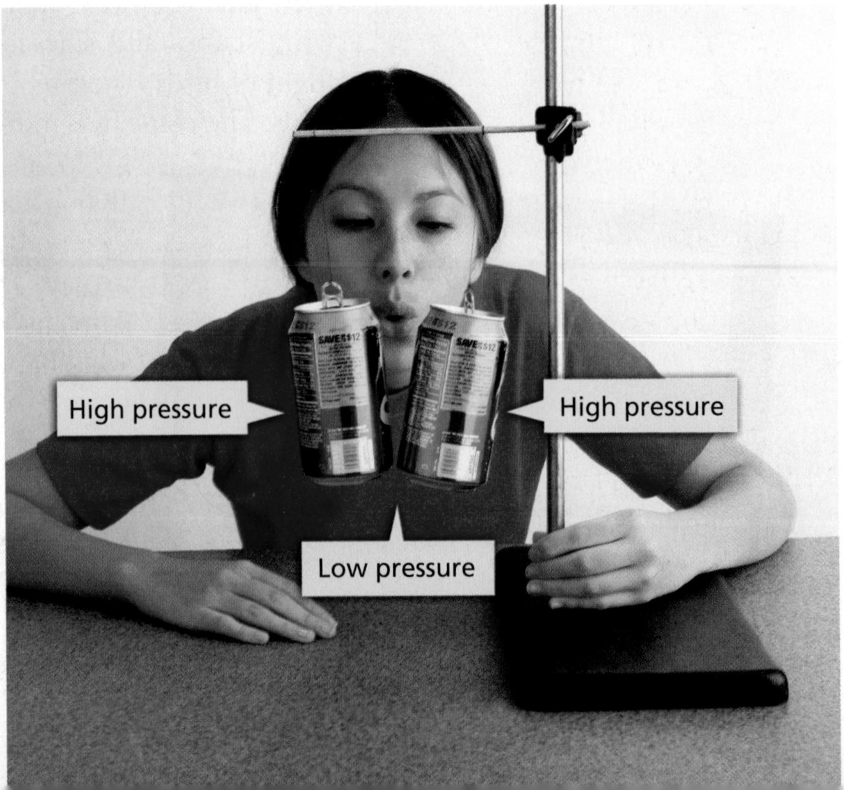

FIGURE 17
Making Air Move
Blowing air quickly between two cans lowers the air pressure between them. Higher pressure exerted by the still air to either side pushes the cans toward each other.
Relating Cause and Effect *How does the flowing air affect the air pressure around the two cans?*

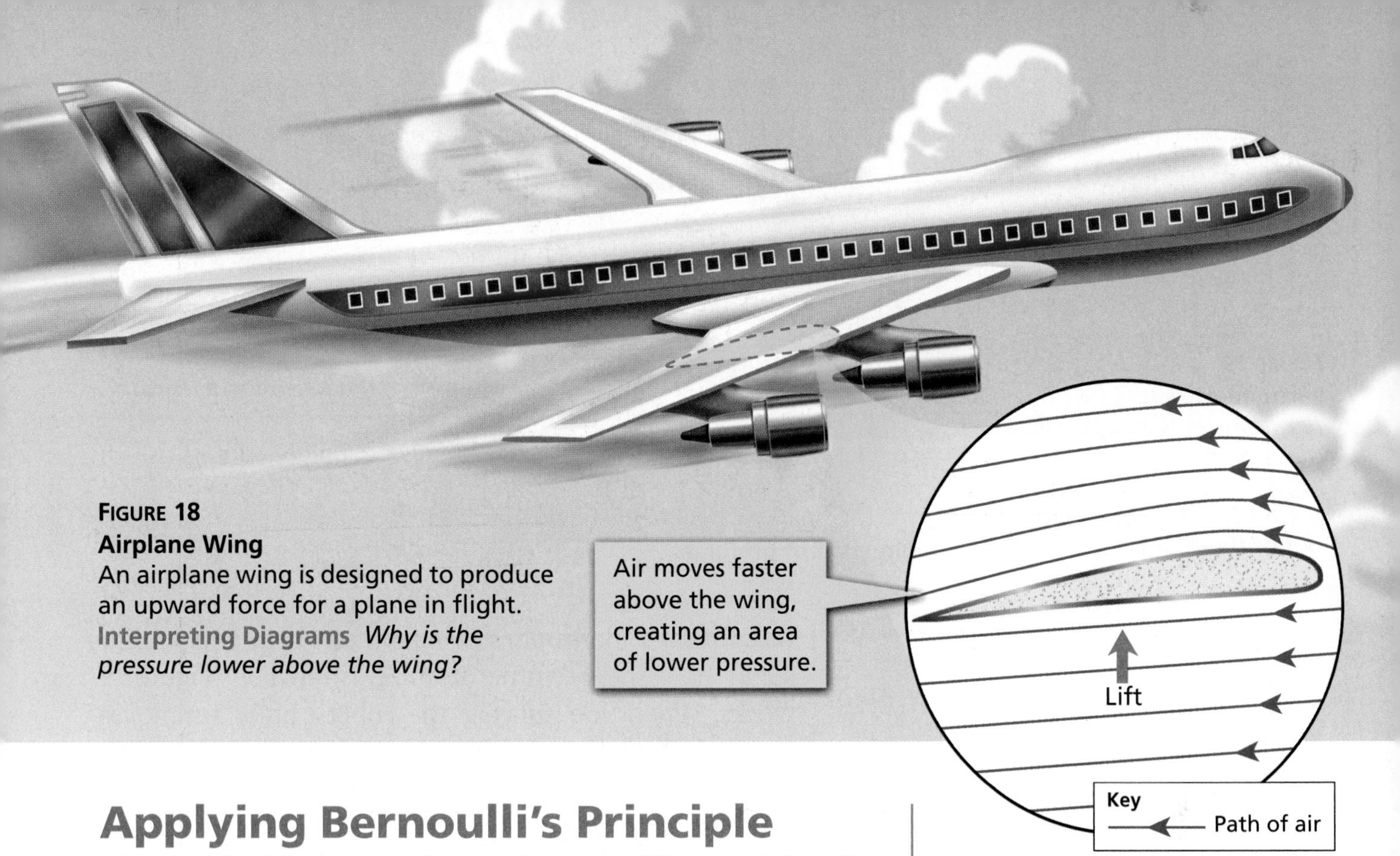
Air moves faster above the wing, creating an area of lower pressure.
Lift
Key
Path of air

FIGURE 18
Airplane Wing
An airplane wing is designed to produce an upward force for a plane in flight.
Interpreting Diagrams *Why is the pressure lower above the wing?*

Applying Bernoulli's Principle

The Wright brothers understood Bernoulli's principle. They used it when they designed and built their plane. **Bernoulli's principle helps explain how planes fly. It also helps explain why smoke rises up a chimney, how an atomizer works, and how a flying disk glides through the air.**

Objects in Flight Bernoulli's principle is one factor that helps explain flight—from a small kite to a huge airplane. Objects can be designed so that their shapes cause air to move at different speeds above and below them. If the air moves faster above the object, fluid pressure pushes the object upward. If the air moves faster below the object, fluid pressure pushes it downward.

The wing of an airplane is designed to produce **lift,** or an upward force. Look at Figure 18 to see the design of a wing. Both the slant and the shape of the wing are sources of lift. Because the wing is slanted, the air that hits it is forced downward as the plane moves. The air exerts an equal and opposite force on the wing and pushes it upward. This upward force helps an airplane to take off.

The curved shape of a wing also gives an airplane lift. Because the top of the wing is curved, air moving over the top has a greater speed than air moving under the bottom. As a result, the air moving over the top exerts less pressure than the air below. The difference in air pressure above and below the wing creates lift.

Go Online
SCI LINKS NSTA
For: Links on Bernoulli's principle
Visit: www.SciLinks.org
Web Code: scn-1334

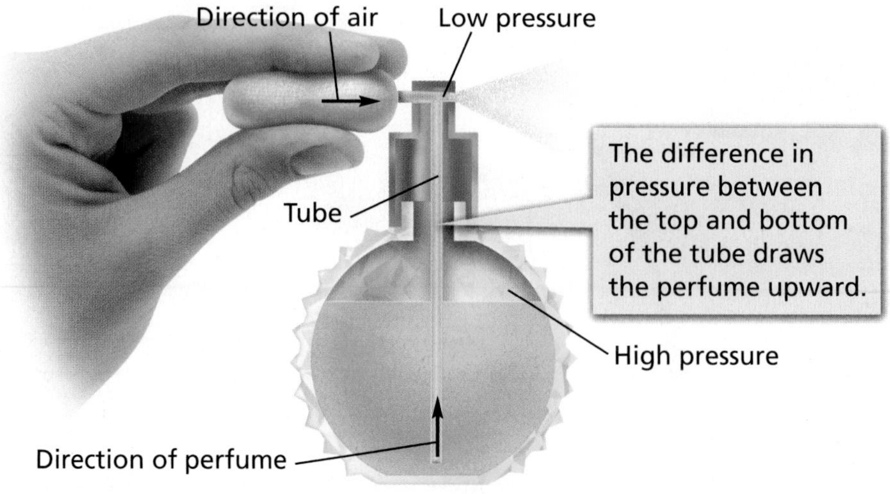

FIGURE 19
Perfume Atomizer
An atomizer is an application of Bernoulli's principle.
Applying Concepts *Why is the perfume pushed up and out of the flask?*

Atomizers Bernoulli's principle can help you understand how the perfume atomizer shown in Figure 19 works. When you squeeze the rubber bulb, air moves quickly past the top of the tube. The moving air lowers the pressure at the top of the tube. The greater pressure in the flask pushes the liquid up into the tube. The air stream breaks the liquid into small drops, and the liquid comes out as a fine mist. In a similar way, pressure differences in the carburetors of older gasoline engines push gasoline up a tube. There, the gasoline combines with air to create the mixture of air and fuel that runs the engine.

Chimneys You can sit next to a fireplace enjoying a cozy fire thanks in part to Bernoulli's principle. Smoke rises up the chimney partly because hot air rises, and partly because it is pushed. Wind blowing across the top of a chimney lowers the air pressure there. The higher pressure at the bottom pushes air and smoke up the chimney. Smoke will rise faster in a chimney on a windy day than on a calm day.

Reading Checkpoint **How does an atomizer work?**

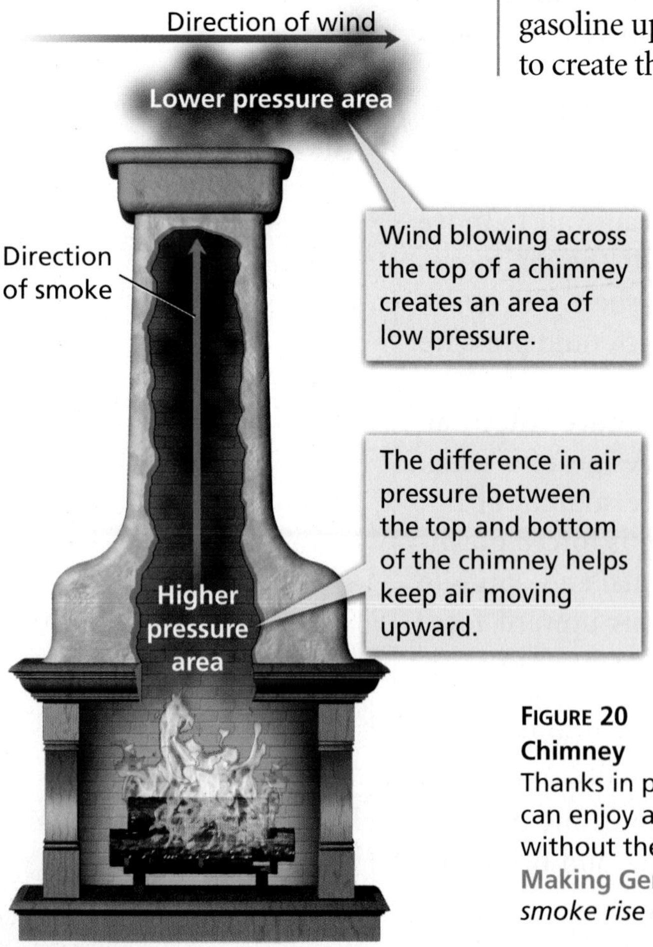

Direction of wind
Lower pressure area
Direction of smoke
Wind blowing across the top of a chimney creates an area of low pressure.
The difference in air pressure between the top and bottom of the chimney helps keep air moving upward.
Higher pressure area

FIGURE 20
Chimney
Thanks in part to Bernoulli's principle, you can enjoy an evening by a warm fireplace without the room filling up with smoke.
Making Generalizations *Why does the smoke rise up the chimney?*

FIGURE 21
Flying Disk
Like an airplane wing, a flying disk uses a curved upper surface to create lift. **Comparing and Contrasting** *How does a flying disk differ from an airplane wing?*

Flying Disks Did you ever wonder what allows a flying disk to glide through the air? The upper surface of a flying disk is curved like an airplane wing. Bernoulli's principle explains that the faster-moving air following the disk's curved upper surface exerts less pressure than the slower-moving air beneath it. A net force acts upward on the flying disk, creating lift. Tilting the disk slightly toward you as you throw it also helps to keep it in the air. A tilted disk pushes air down. The air exerts an equal and opposite force on the disk, pushing it up. The spinning motion of a flying disk keeps it stable as it flies.

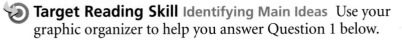

Section 4 Assessment

Target Reading Skill **Identifying Main Ideas** Use your graphic organizer to help you answer Question 1 below.

Reviewing Key Concepts

1. a. **Reviewing** What makes fluids flow?
   b. **Summarizing** What does Bernoulli's principle say about the pressure exerted by a moving fluid?
   c. **Applying Concepts** You are riding in a car on a highway when a large truck speeds by you. Explain why your car is pushed toward the truck.
2. a. **Listing** List four applications of Bernoulli's principle.
   b. **Explaining** Why does the air pressure above an airplane wing differ from the pressure below it? How is this pressure difference involved in flight?
   c. **Relating Cause and Effect** How could strong winds from a hurricane blow the roof off a house?

Lab zone At-Home Activity

Paper Chimney With a family member, see how a chimney works by using a paper cup and a hair dryer. Cut up several small pieces of tissue and place them in the bottom of a paper cup. Hold on to the paper cup with one hand. With your other hand, use the hair dryer to blow cool air across the top of the cup. Explain to your family member how Bernoulli's principle explains how the chimney works.

Technology and Society

• Tech & Design •

Helicopters

Most aircraft are like eagles—they take off majestically, glide among the clouds, and land with ease. But helicopters are the hummingbirds of aircraft. They can fly forward, backward, sideways, and up and down. They can stop abruptly and hover in midair. In fact, helicopters can fly circles around other types of aircraft.

Science in Action

On the top of a helicopter are large blades that turn rapidly. These blades are curved on top like the wings of an airplane. Air flowing over the curved blades helps cause lift—the upward force for the helicopter—just as air flowing over wings helps cause lift for most airplanes. Action and reaction forces as described by Newton's third law of motion also play a role in causing lift. As the tilted blades push down on the air, the air pushes up on the blade.

Main Rotor
The main rotor turns the blades and controls their angle.
Blades
Air flows over the curved, rotating blades. Along with action and reaction forces, this helps to give the helicopter lift.
As the main rotor spins, the reaction force pushes the helicopter's body in the opposite direction. If not for the tail rotor, the body would spin too.
Hand Controls and Foot Pedals
These controls are connected to the main rotor. The collective control guides the helicopter up or down. The cyclic control guides the helicopter forward, backward, or sideways. The foot pedals allow the helicopter to rotate in tight circles.

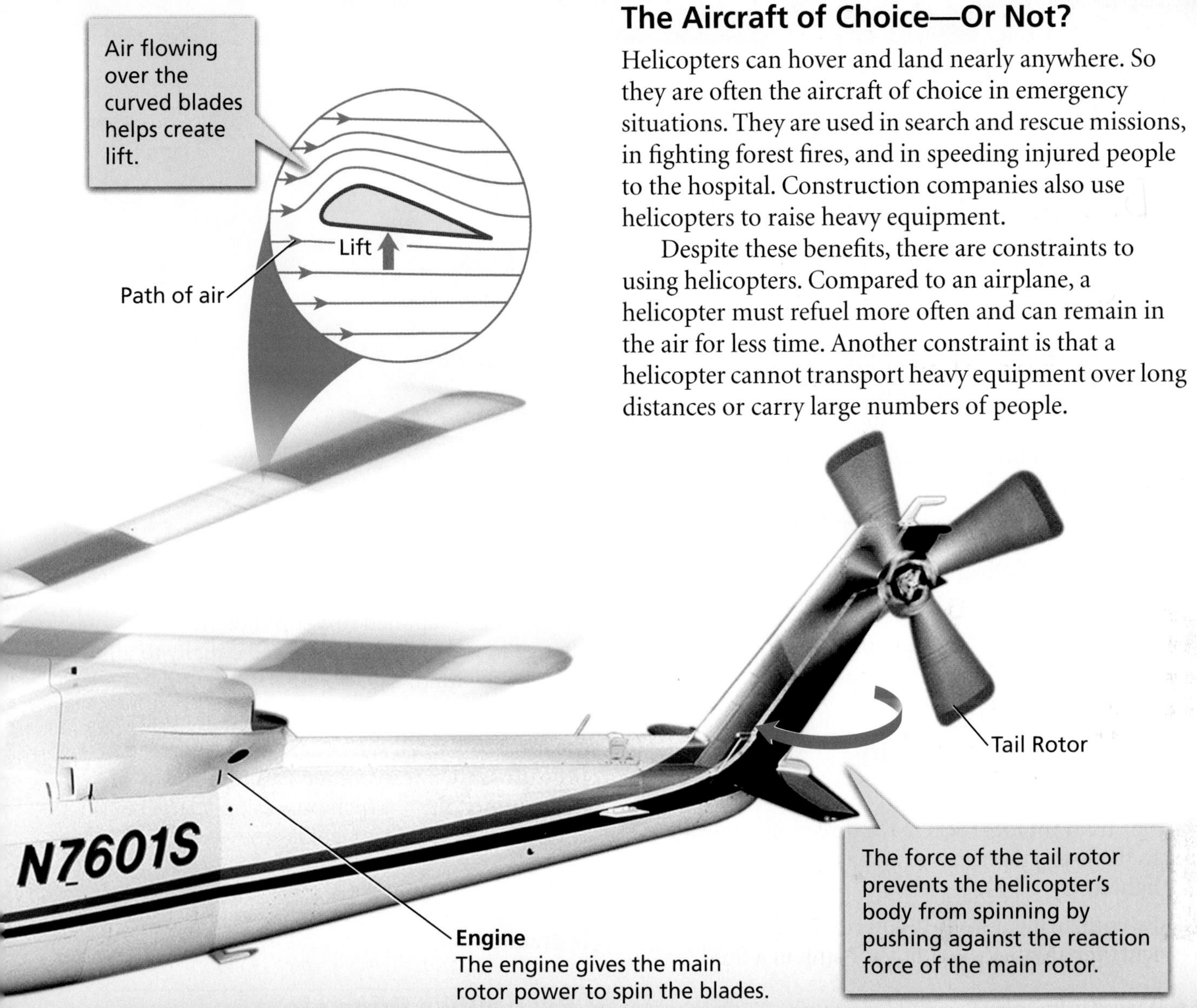

Air flowing over the curved blades helps create lift.
Lift
Path of air
N7601S
Engine
The engine gives the main rotor power to spin the blades.
Tail Rotor
The force of the tail rotor prevents the helicopter's body from spinning by pushing against the reaction force of the main rotor.

The Aircraft of Choice—Or Not?

Helicopters can hover and land nearly anywhere. So they are often the aircraft of choice in emergency situations. They are used in search and rescue missions, in fighting forest fires, and in speeding injured people to the hospital. Construction companies also use helicopters to raise heavy equipment.

Despite these benefits, there are constraints to using helicopters. Compared to an airplane, a helicopter must refuel more often and can remain in the air for less time. Another constraint is that a helicopter cannot transport heavy equipment over long distances or carry large numbers of people.

Weigh the Impact

1. Identify the Need
What advantages do helicopters have over airplanes?

2. Research
Using the Internet, research how helicopters are used in national parks, such as Yellowstone National Park. Choose one helicopter mission. Make notes on the mission's difficulty level, purpose, location, procedures, and outcome.

3. Write
Suppose you are a park ranger. Use your notes to write a report to your supervisor explaining why a helicopter was or was not the best technology to use for this mission.

Go Online
PHSchool.com

For: More on helicopters
Visit: PHSchool.com
Web Code: cgh-3030

Chapter 11

Study Guide

1 Pressure

Key Concepts

- Pressure decreases as the area over which a force is distributed increases.
- $\text{Pressure} = \dfrac{\text{Force}}{\text{Area}}$
- All of the forces exerted by the individual particles in a fluid combine to make up the pressure exerted by the fluid.
- As elevation increases, atmospheric pressure decreases.
- Water pressure increases as depth increases.

Key Terms

pressure
pascal
fluid
barometer

2 Floating and Sinking

Key Concepts

- The buoyant force acts in the direction opposite to the force of gravity, so it makes an object feel lighter.
- By comparing densities, you can predict whether an object will float or sink in a fluid.
- $\text{Density} = \dfrac{\text{Mass}}{\text{Volume}}$

Key Terms

buoyant force
Archimedes' principle
density

3 Pascal's Principle

Key Concepts

- When force is applied to a confined fluid, the change in pressure is transmitted equally to all parts of the fluid.
- A hydraulic system multiplies force by applying the force to a small surface area. The increase in pressure is then transmitted to another part of the confined fluid, which pushes on a larger surface area.

Key Terms

Pascal's principle
hydraulic system

4 Bernoulli's Principle

Key Concepts

- Bernoulli's principle states that as the speed of a moving fluid increases, the pressure within the fluid decreases.
- Bernoulli's principle helps explain how planes fly. It also helps explain why smoke rises up a chimney, how an atomizer works, and how a flying disk glides through the air.

Key Terms

Bernoulli's principle
lift

Review and Assessment

Go Online
PHSchool.com
For: Self-Assessment
Visit: PHSchool.com
Web Code: cga-3030

Organizing Information

Sequencing Create a flowchart that shows how a hydraulic device multiplies force. (For more on Sequencing, see the Skills Handbook.)

How a Hydraulic Device Works

Force applied to small piston
↓
a. ___?___
↓
b. ___?___
↓
c. ___?___
↓
d. ___?___

Reviewing Key Terms

Choose the letter of the best answer.

1. If you divide the force exerted on a surface by the total area of the surface, you will know
   a. density. **b.** pressure.
   c. lift. **d.** buoyant force.
2. If you know the weight of an object that floats, you know the
   a. object's density.
   b. object's mass.
   c. object's volume.
   d. buoyant force.
3. If you divide the mass of an object by its volume, you know the object's
   a. mass. **b.** weight.
   c. density. **d.** pressure.
4. The concept that an increase in pressure on a confined fluid is transmitted equally to all parts of the fluid is known as
   a. Pascal's principle.
   b. Bernoulli's principle.
   c. Archimedes' principle.
   d. Newton's third law.
5. The concept that the pressure in a fluid decreases as the speed of the fluid increases is known as
   a. Pascal's principle.
   b. Bernoulli's principle.
   c. Archimedes' principle.
   d. Newton's first law.

If the statement is true, write *true*. If it is false, change the underlined word or words to make the statement true.

6. Pressure is force per unit of <u>mass</u>. false-area
7. A <u>fluid</u> is a material that can easily flow. true
8. A factor that helps explain flight is <u>Archimedes' principle</u>. false - Bernoulli's
9. A hydraulic system is designed to take advantage of <u>Pascal's principle</u>.
10. <u>Lift</u> is an upward force.

Writing in Science

News Report Suppose that you are a newspaper journalist on the day after the *Titanic* sank. Write a news report that tells what happened. Explain how the buoyancy of a ship is affected when it fills with water. Include information about the various fluid forces involved.

Discovery Channel School

Forces in Fluids
Video Preview
Video Field Trip
▶ Video Assessment

Review and Assessment

Checking Concepts

11. How does the amount of pressure you exert on the floor when you are lying down compare with the amount of pressure you exert when you are standing up?

12. Why aren't deep-sea fish crushed by the tremendous pressure they experience?

13. Why do you seem to weigh more in air than you do in water?

14. In a hydraulic system, why is the force exerted on a small piston multiplied when it acts on a larger piston?

15. Name two hydraulic systems that an auto mechanic would know well.

16. Why is air pressure at the top of a chimney less than air pressure at the bottom?

Thinking Critically

17. **Making Generalizations** How does the water pressure change at each level in the jug below? How can you tell?

18. **Developing Hypotheses** A sphere made of steel is put in water and, surprisingly, it floats. Develop a possible explanation for this observation.

19. **Applying Concepts** One method of raising a sunken ship to the surface is to inflate large bags or balloons inside its hull. Explain why this procedure could work.

20. **Problem Solving** You have two fluids of unknown density. Suggest a method to determine which is denser, without mixing the two fluids.

Math Practice

21. **Area** The cover of your textbook measures about 28 cm × 22 cm. Find its area.

22. **Area** A dollar bill measures about 15.9 cm × 6.7 cm. The Chinese yuan note measures 14.5 cm × 7.0 cm. Which currency uses a larger bill?

Applying Skills

The illustration shows an object supported by a spring scale, both in and out of water. Use the illustration to answer Questions 23–25.

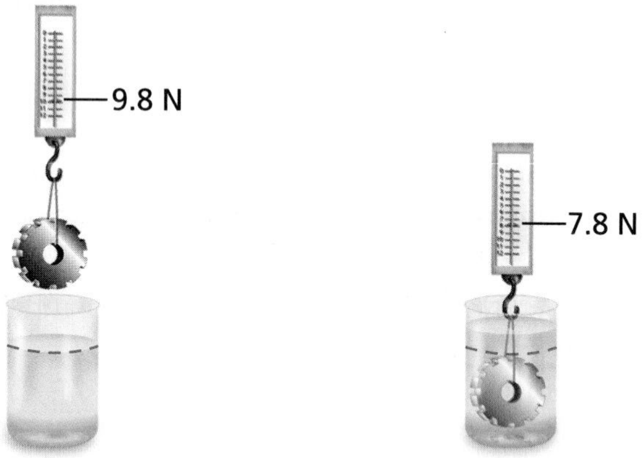

23. **Inferring** Why is there a difference between the weight of the object in air and its measured weight in water?

24. **Calculating** What is the buoyant force acting on the object?

25. **Drawing Conclusions** What can you conclude about the water above the dotted line?

Lab zone Chapter Project

Performance Assessment Test your boat to make sure it does not leak. Display the diagrams of different designs you tried and the observations and data you recorded for each design. Then demonstrate for the class how the boat floats. Point out to your classmates the features you used in your final design.

Standardized Test Prep

Test-Taking Tip

Anticipating the Answer

You can sometimes figure out an answer before you look at the answer choices. After you provide your own answer, compare it with the answer choices. Select the answer that most closely matches your own answer. This strategy can be especially useful for questions that test vocabulary. Try to answer the question below before you look at the answer choices.

Sample Question

Any material that can easily flow is considered a

A liquid.
B fluid.
C gas.
D metal.

Answer

Gases and liquids can easily flow. However, they are both fluids. The definition of a fluid is "a material that can easily flow." The correct answer is **B**.

Choose the letter of the best answer.

1. The upward force that acts on an airplane's wing is called
A density.
B inertia.
C lift.
D pressure.

2. Which of the following is an example of a hydraulic system?
F a car's brakes
G a barometer
H an airplane's wing
J a submarine's flotation tanks

3. A boat that weighs 28,800 N is loaded with 7,200 N of cargo. After it is loaded, what is the buoyant force acting on the boat?
A 400 N
B 22,000 N
C 36,000 N
D 360,000 N

4. Why doesn't air pressure crush human beings standing at sea level?
F Air pressure at sea level is very low.
G Clothing on our bodies shields us from air pressure.
H Air is not as heavy as human beings.
J Pressure from the fluids inside our bodies balances the air pressure outside.

5. You observe that a chunk of tar sinks in puddles of rainwater but floats on the ocean. An experiment to explain the behavior of the tar should measure
A the difference between atmospheric pressure and water pressure.
B the densities of fresh water, salt water, and tar.
C the height from which the chunk of tar is dropped.
D the depth of each type of water.

Constructed Response

Use the diagram below and your knowledge of science to help you answer Question 6.

6. Use Bernoulli's principle to explain why the fabric of a domed tent bulges outward on a windy day.

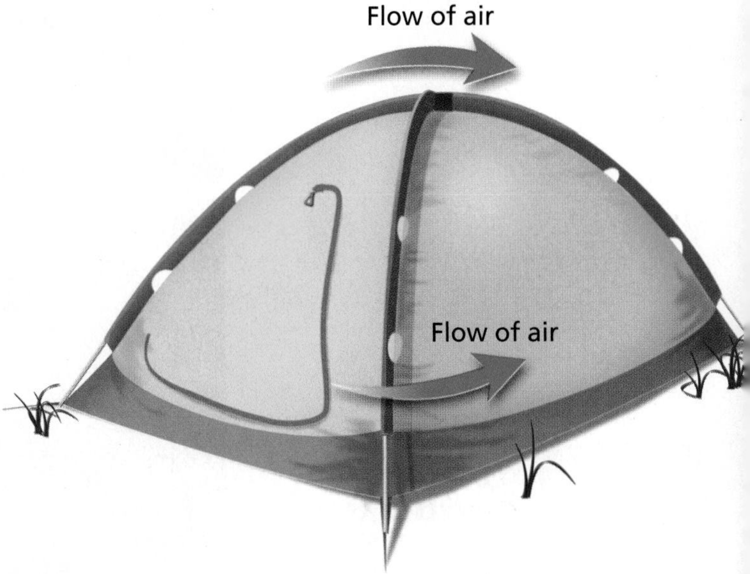

Chapter 12 Work and Machines

Chapter Preview

1 What Is Work?
Discover *What Happens When You Pull at an Angle?*
Try This *Is Work Always the Same?*

2 How Machines Do Work
Discover *Is It a Machine?*
Try This *Going Up*
Analyzing Data *Mechanical Advantage*
Skills Lab *Seesaw Science*

3 Simple Machines
Discover *How Can You Increase Force?*
Try This *A Paper Screw*
Skills Activity *Communicating*
Active Art *Types of Pulleys*
At-Home Activity *Machines in the Kitchen*
Skills Lab *Angling for Access*

Interactive Textbook

A Maori woodcarver in New Zealand creates a traditional carving. ▶

Discovery Channel School

Work and Machines

- ▶ Video Preview
- Video Field Trip
- Video Assessment

Lab zone™ Chapter **Project**

The Nifty Lifting Machine

In this Chapter Project, you will design and build a lifting machine and then demonstrate it to the class.

Your Goal To design, build, and test a complex machine that can lift a 600-gram soup can 5 centimeters

Your machine must

- be made of materials that are approved by your teacher
- consist of at least two simple machines working in combination
- be able to lift the soup can to a height of at least 5 centimeters
- be built following the safety guidelines in Appendix A

Plan It! Preview the chapter to find out what simple machines you can use and how to use them. Determine the amount of work your machine must do. Brainstorm different machine designs and materials with your classmates. Analyze factors affecting efficiency and mechanical advantage, and then construct your machine. When your teacher has approved your design, build and test your machine.

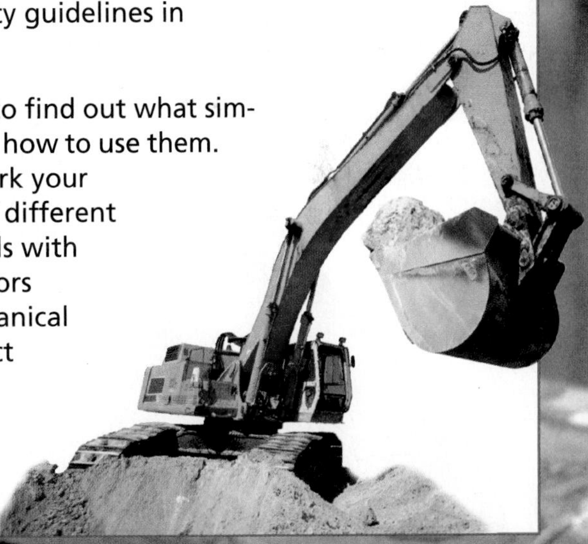

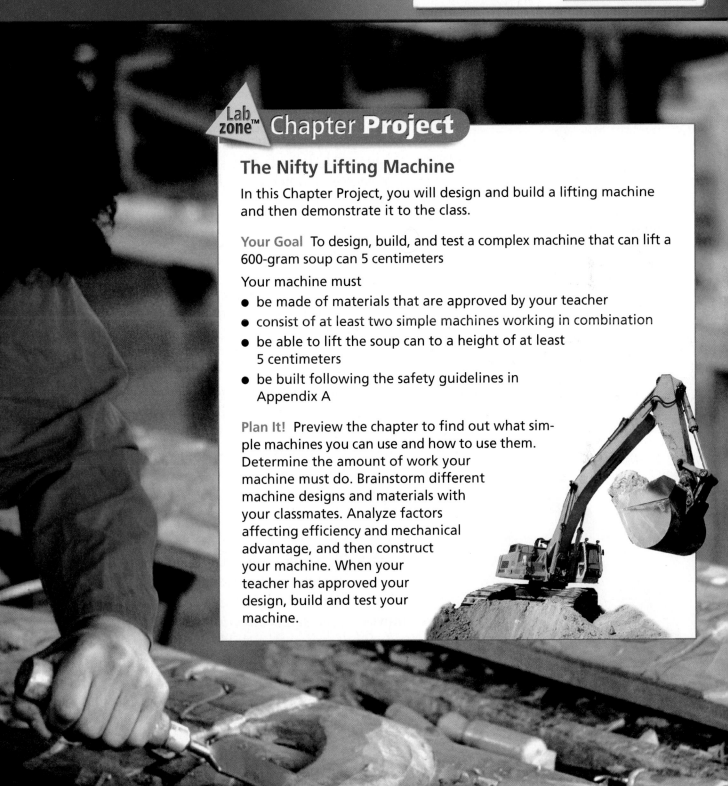

Section 1 What Is Work?

Reading Preview

Key Concepts

- When is work done on an object?
- How do you determine the work done on an object?
- What is power?

Key Terms

- work • joule • power

Target Reading Skill

Asking Questions Before you read, preview the red headings. In a graphic organizer like the one below, ask a *what* or *how* question for each heading. As you read, write the answers to your questions.

Question	Answer
What is work?	Work is . . .

Lab zone Discover Activity

What Happens When You Pull at an Angle?

1. Fill a mug half full with water.
2. Cut a medium-weight rubber band to make a strand of elastic. Thread the elastic through a mug handle. By pulling on the elastic, you can move the mug across a table.
3. You can hold the two halves of elastic parallel to each other or at an angle to each other, as shown. Predict which way will be more effective in moving the mug.
4. Pull on the elastic both ways. Describe any differences you observe.

Think It Over

Developing Hypotheses Which of the two pulls was more effective in moving the mug? Explain why.

This morning you probably woke up and went to school with your backpack of books. You lifted the backpack and then carried it with you. If you had a lot of books to bring home, carrying your backpack might have felt like a lot of work. But in the scientific definition of work, after you lifted the backpack, you did no work to carry it at all!

The Meaning of Work

In scientific terms, you do **work** when you exert a force on an object that causes the object to move some distance. **Work is done on an object when the object moves in the same direction in which the force is exerted.** If you push a child on a swing, for example, you are doing work on the child. If you pull your books out of your backpack, you do work on the books. If you lift a bag of groceries out of a shopping cart, you do work on the bag of groceries.

FIGURE 1
Doing Work
Lifting books out of a backpack is work, but carrying them to class is not.

No Work Without Motion To do work on an object, the object must move some distance as a result of your force. If the object does not move, no work is done, no matter how much force is exerted.

There are many situations in which you exert a force but don't do any work. Suppose, for example, you are pushing a car that is stuck in the snow. You certainly exert a force on the car, so it might seem as if you do work. But if the force you exert does not make the car move, you are not doing any work on it.

Force in the Same Direction So why didn't you do any work when you carried your books to school? To do work on an object, the force you exert must be in the same direction as the object's motion. When you carry an object at constant velocity, you exert an upward force to hold the object so that it doesn't fall to the ground. The motion of the object, however, is in the horizontal direction. Since the force is vertical and the motion is horizontal, you don't do any work on the object as you carry it.

How much work do you do when you pull a suitcase with wheels? When you pull a suitcase, you pull on the handle at an angle to the ground. As you can see in Figure 2, your force has both a horizontal part and a vertical part. When you pull this way, only part of your force does work—the part in the same direction as the motion of the suitcase. The rest of your force does not help pull the suitcase forward.

Reading Checkpoint **If you pull an object horizontally, what part of your force does work?**

FIGURE 2
Force, Motion, and Work
Whether the girl does work on the suitcase depends on the direction of her force and the suitcase's motion. **Drawing Conclusions** *Why doesn't the girl do work when she carries her suitcase rather than pulling it?*

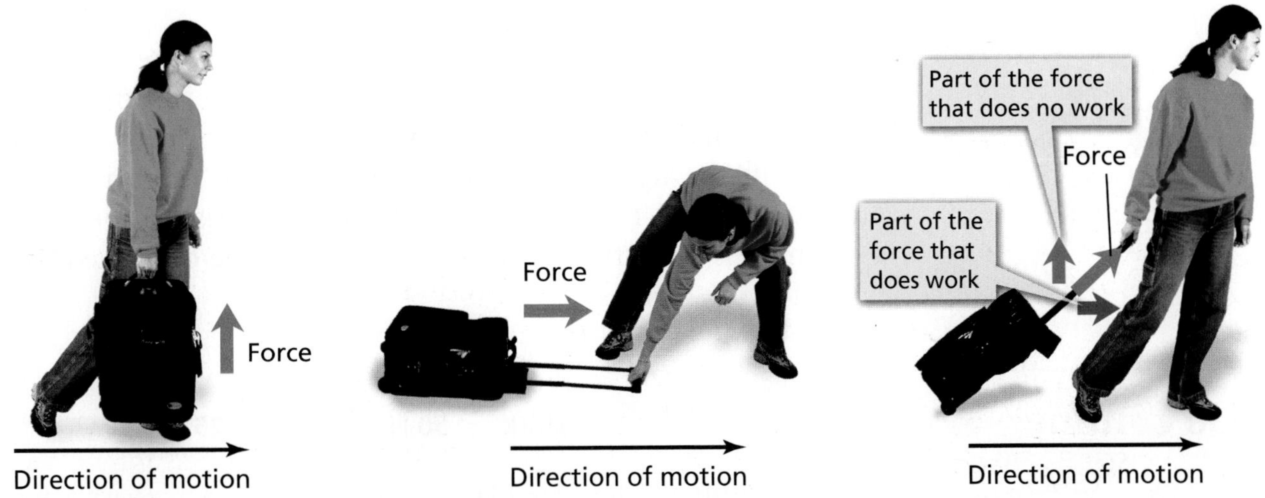

A The lifting force is not in the direction of the suitcase's motion, so no work is done.

B The force acts in the same direction as the suitcase's motion, so the maximum work is done.

C Only the horizontal part of the force does work to move the suitcase.

FIGURE 3
Amount of Work
When you lift a plant, you do work. You do more work when you lift a heavier plant the same distance.
Relating Cause and Effect
Why does it take more work to lift the heavier plant?

Calculating Work

Which do you think involves more work: lifting a 50-newton potted plant 0.5 meter off the ground onto a table, or lifting a 100-newton plant onto the same table? Your common sense may suggest that lifting a heavier object requires more work than lifting a lighter object. This is true. Is it more work to lift a plant onto a table or up to the top story of a building? As you might guess, moving an object a greater distance requires more work than moving the same object a shorter distance.

The amount of work you do depends on both the amount of force you exert and the distance the object moves. **The amount of work done on an object can be determined by multiplying force times distance.**

$$\text{Work} = \text{Force} \times \text{Distance}$$

You can use the work formula to calculate the amount of work you do to lift a plant. When you lift an object, the upward force you exert must be at least equal to the object's weight. So, to lift the lighter plant, you would have to exert a force of 50 newtons. The distance you lift the plant is 0.5 meter. The amount of work you do on the plant can be calculated using the work formula.

$$\text{Work} = \text{Force} \times \text{Distance}$$
$$\text{Work} = 50\ \text{N} \times 0.5\ \text{m} = 25\ \text{N}\cdot\text{m}$$

To lift the heavier plant, you would have to exert a force of 100 newtons. So the amount of work you do would be 100 newtons × 0.5 meter, or 50 N·m. As you can see, you do more work to lift the heavier object.

Go Online
SCI LINKS NSTA
For: Links on work
Visit: www.SciLinks.org
Web Code: scn-1341

When force is measured in newtons and distance in meters, the SI unit of work is the newton × meter (N•m). This unit is also called a joule (JOOL) in honor of James Prescott Joule, a physicist who studied work in the mid-1800s. One **joule** (J) is the amount of work you do when you exert a force of 1 newton to move an object a distance of 1 meter. You would have to exert 25 joules of work to lift the lighter plant and 50 joules of work to lift the heavier plant.

Reading Checkpoint **What is the SI unit for work?**

Power

The amount of work you do on an object is not affected by the time it takes to do the work. For example, if you carry a backpack up a flight of stairs, the work you do is the weight of the backpack times the height of the stairs. Whether you walk or run up the stairs, you do the same amount of work because time is not part of the definition of work.

But time is important when you talk about power. **Power** is the rate at which work is done. **Power equals the amount of work done on an object in a unit of time.** You need more power to run up the stairs with your backpack than to walk because it takes you less time to do the same work.

You can think of power in another way. A device that has more power than another device does more work in the same time. It can also mean doing the same amount of work in less time.

For example, a car's engine does work to accelerate the car from its rest position. The greater a car engine's power, the faster the engine can accelerate the car.

Lab zone **Try This Activity**

Is Work Always the Same?

1. Obtain a pinwheel along with a hair dryer that has at least two power settings.
2. Set the dryer on its lowest setting. Use it to blow the pinwheel. Observe the pinwheel's motion.
3. Set the dryer on its highest setting. Again, blow the pinwheel and observe its motion.

Inferring Explain why work is done on the pinwheel. How are the two situations different? Is the amount of work done greater for the high or low setting? Why?

FIGURE 4
Work and Power
Whether you use a rake or a blower, the same amount of work is done to gather leaves. However, the blower has more power.
Inferring *Will the blower or the rake do the same amount of work in less time?*

Calculating Power Whenever you know how fast work is done, you can calculate power. Power is calculated by dividing the amount of work done by the amount of time it takes to do the work. This can be written as the following formula.

$$\text{Power} = \frac{\text{Work}}{\text{Time}}$$

Since work is equal to force times distance, you can rewrite the equation for power as follows.

$$\text{Power} = \frac{\text{Force} \times \text{Distance}}{\text{Time}}$$

Math Sample Problem

Calculating Power

A tow truck exerts a force of 11,000 N to pull a car out of a ditch. It moves the car a distance of 5 m in 25 seconds. What is the power of the tow truck?

1 Read and Understand

What information are you given?

Force of the tow truck (F) = 11,000 N

Distance (d) = 5.0 m

Time (t) = 25 s

2 Plan and Solve

What quantity are you trying to calculate?

The power (***P***) of the tow truck = ■

What formula contains the given quantities and the unknown quantity?

$$\text{Power} = \frac{\text{Force} \times \text{Distance}}{\text{Time}}$$

Perform the calculation.

$$\text{Power} = \frac{11{,}000 \text{ N} \times 5.0 \text{ m}}{25 \text{ s}}$$

$$\text{Power} = \frac{55{,}000 \text{ N·m}}{25 \text{ s}} \text{ or } \frac{55{,}000 \text{ J}}{25 \text{ s}}$$

$$\text{Power} = 2{,}200 \text{ J/s} = 2{,}200 \text{ W}$$

3 Look Back and Check

Does your answer make sense?

The answer tells you that the tow truck pulls the car with a power of 2,200 W. This value is about the same as the power of three horses, so the answer is reasonable.

Math Practice

1. **Calculating Power** A motor exerts a force of 12,000 N to lift an elevator 8.0 m in 6.0 seconds. What is the power of the motor?
2. **Calculating Power** A crane lifts an 8,000-N beam 75 m to the top of a building in 30 seconds. What is the crane's power?

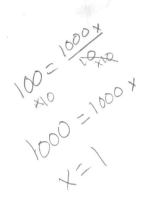

Power Units When work is measured in joules and time in seconds, the SI unit of power is the joule per second (J/s). This unit is also known as the watt (W), in honor of James Watt, who made great improvements to the steam engine. One joule of work done in one second is one watt of power. In other words, 1 J/s = 1 W.

A watt is a relatively small unit of power. Because a watt is so small, power is often measured in larger units. One kilowatt (kW) equals 1,000 watts.

When people talk about engines for vehicles, they use another power unit instead of the watt. This unit is the horsepower. One horsepower equals 746 watts. (The horsepower is not an SI unit.)

FIGURE 5
Horsepower
James Watt used the word *horsepower* to advertise the advantages of his improved steam engine (next to the chimney) of 1769.

Reading Checkpoint **What is a kilowatt?**

Section 1 Assessment

Target Reading Skill **Asking Questions** Use the answers to the questions you wrote about the headings to help you answer the questions below.

Reviewing Key Concepts

1. a. Reviewing What is work?

b. Describing In order for work to be done on an object, what must happen to the object?

c. Applying Concepts In which of the following situations is work being done: rolling a bowling ball, pushing on a tree for ten minutes, kicking a football?

2. a. Identifying What is a joule?

b. Explaining How can you determine the amount of work done on an object?

c. Problem Solving Is more work done when a force of 2 N moves an object 3 m or when a force of 3 N moves an object 2 m? Explain.

3. a. Defining What is power?

b. Summarizing How are power and work related?

Math Practice

4. Calculating Power Your laundry basket weighs 22 N and your room is 3.0 m above you on the second floor. It takes you 6.0 seconds to carry the laundry basket up. What is your power?

5. Calculating Power If you take only 4.4 seconds to carry the basket upstairs, what is your power?

Section 2

Integrating Mathematics

How Machines Do Work

Reading Preview

Key Concepts

- How do machines make work easier?
- What is a machine's mechanical advantage?
- How can you calculate the efficiency of a machine?

Key Terms

- machine • input force
- output force • input work
- output work
- mechanical advantage
- efficiency

Target Reading Skill

Identifying Main Ideas As you read the What Is a Machine? section, write the main idea in a graphic organizer like the one below. Then write three supporting details.

Main Idea

The mechanical advantage of a machine helps by . . .

Detail | Detail | Detail

Lab zone Discover Activity

Is It a Machine?

1. Examine the objects that your teacher gives you.
2. Sort the objects into those that are machines and those that are not machines.
3. Determine how each object that you classified as a machine functions. Explain each object to another student.

Think It Over

Forming Operational Definitions Why did you decide certain objects were machines while other objects were not?

A load of soil for your school garden has been dumped 10 meters from the garden. How can you move the soil easily and quickly? You could move the soil by handfuls, but that would take a long time. Using a shovel would make the job easier. If you had a wheelbarrow, that would make the job easier still! But be careful what you think. Using a machine may make work go faster, but it doesn't mean you do less work.

FIGURE 6
Using Machines
Shovels and rakes make the work of these students easier.

What Is a Machine?

Shovels and wheelbarrows are two examples of machines. A **machine** is a device that allows you to do work in a way that is easier or more effective. You may think of machines as complex gadgets with motors, but a machine can be quite simple. For example, think about using a shovel. A shovel makes the work of moving soil easier, so a shovel is a machine.

Moving a pile of soil will involve the same amount of work whether you use your hands or a shovel. What a shovel or any other machine does is change the way in which work is done. **A machine makes work easier by changing at least one of three factors. A machine may change the amount of force you exert, the distance over which you exert your force, or the direction in which you exert your force.** In other words, a machine makes work easier by changing either force, distance, or direction.

Input and Output Forces When you use a machine to do work, you exert a force over some distance. For example, you exert a force on the shovel when you use it to lift soil. The force you exert on the machine is called the **input force.** The input force moves the machine a certain distance, called the input distance. The machine does work by exerting a force over another distance, called the output distance. The force the machine exerts on an object is called the **output force.**

Input and Output Work The input force times the input distance is called the **input work.** The output force times the output distance is called the **output work.** When you use a machine, the amount of input work equals the amount of output work.

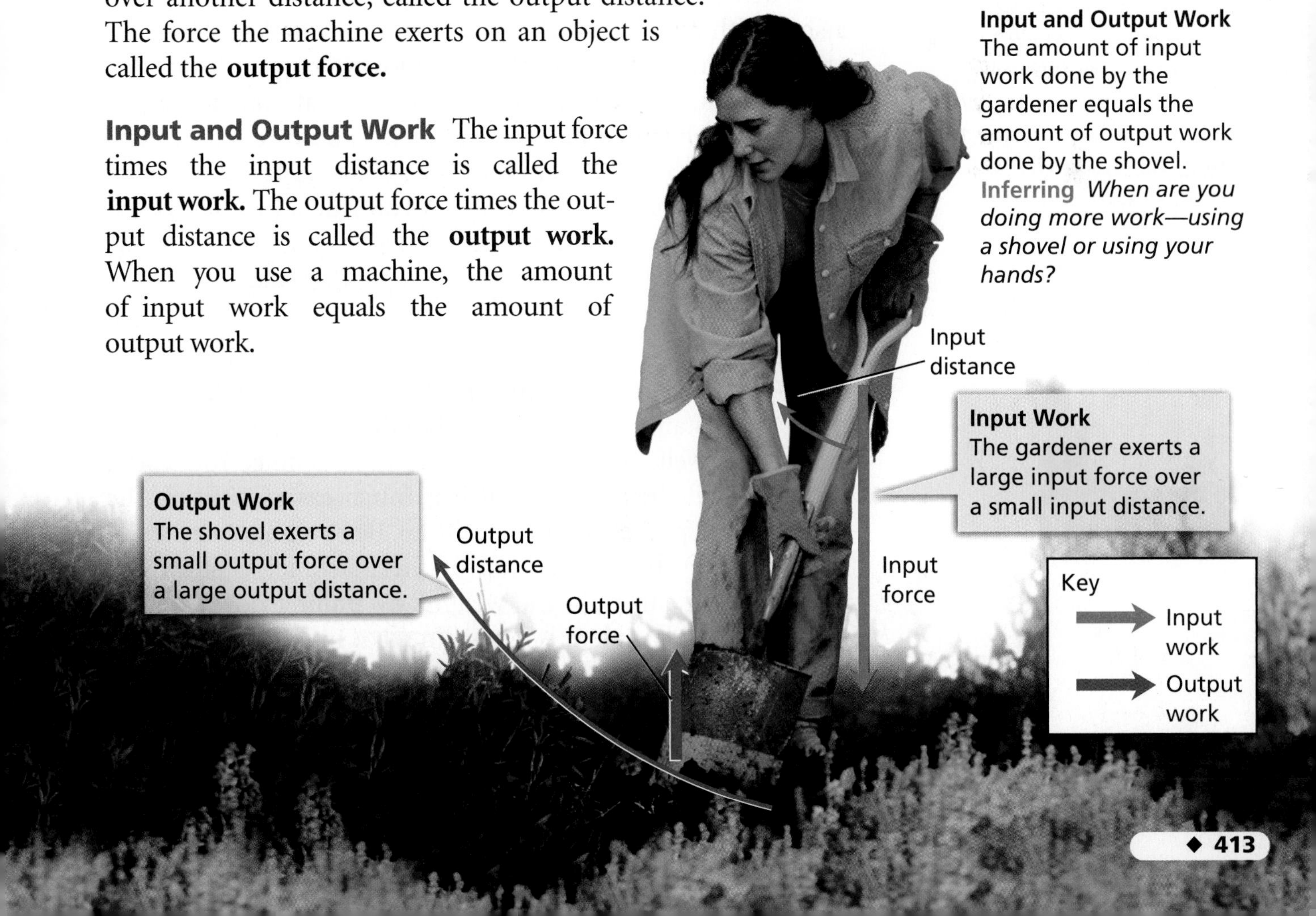

Input distance
Input Work
The gardener exerts a large input force over a small input distance.
Output Work
The shovel exerts a small output force over a large output distance.
Output distance
Output force
Input force
Key
Input work
Output work

FIGURE 7
Input and Output Work
The amount of input work done by the gardener equals the amount of output work done by the shovel.
Inferring *When are you doing more work—using a shovel or using your hands?*

Lab zone Try This **Activity**

Going Up

Does a rope simply turn your force upside down? Find out!

1. Tie a piece of string about 50 cm long to an object, such as an empty cooking pot. Make a small loop on the other end of the string.
2. Using a spring scale, slowly lift the pot 20 cm. Note the reading on the scale.
3. Now loop the string over a pencil and pull down on the spring scale to lift the pot 20 cm. Note the reading on the scale.

Developing Hypotheses
How did the readings on the spring scale compare? If the readings were different, suggest a reason why. What might be an advantage to using this system?

Changing Force In some machines, the output force is greater than the input force. How can this happen? Recall the formula for work: Work = Force × Distance. If the amount of work stays the same, a decrease in force must mean an increase in distance. So if a machine allows you to use less input force to do the same amount of work, you must apply that input force over a greater distance.

What kind of machine allows you to exert a smaller input force? Think about a ramp. Suppose you have to lift a heavy box onto a stage. Instead of lifting the box, you could push it up a ramp. Because the length of the ramp is greater than the height of the stage, you exert your input force over a greater distance. However, when you use the ramp, the work is easier because you can exert a smaller input force. The faucet knob in Figure 8 changes force in the same way.

Changing Distance In some machines, the output force is less than the input force. Why would you want to use a machine like this? This kind of machine allows you to exert your input force over a shorter distance. In order to apply a force over a shorter distance, you need to apply a greater input force.

When do you use this kind of machine? Think about taking a shot with a hockey stick. You move your hands a short distance, but the other end of the stick moves a greater distance to hit the puck. When you use chopsticks to eat your food, you move the hand holding the chopsticks a short distance. The other end of the chopsticks moves a greater distance, allowing you to pick up and eat food. When you ride a bicycle in high gear, you apply a force to the pedals over a short distance. The bicycle, meanwhile, travels a much longer distance.

Changing Direction Some machines don't change either force or distance. What could be the advantage of these machines? Well, think about a weight machine. You could stand and lift the weights. But it is much easier to sit on the machine and pull down than to lift up. By running a steel cable over a small wheel at the top of the machine, as shown in Figure 8, you can raise the weights by pulling down on the cable. This cable system is a machine that makes your job easier by changing the direction in which you exert your force.

Reading Checkpoint **How does the cable system on a weight machine make raising the weights easier?**

FIGURE 8
Making Work Easier

A machine can make work easier in one of three ways.

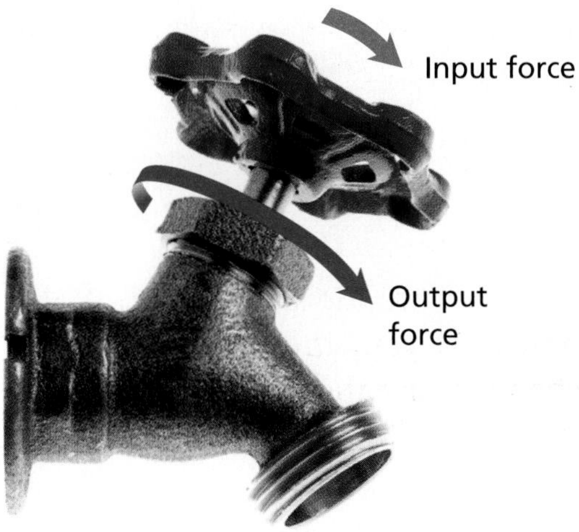

When a machine increases force, you must exert the input force over a greater distance.

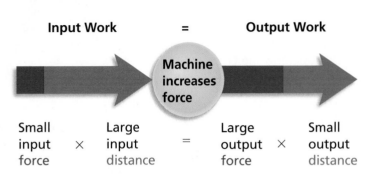

Input Work = **Output Work**

Small input force × Large input distance = Large output force × Small output distance

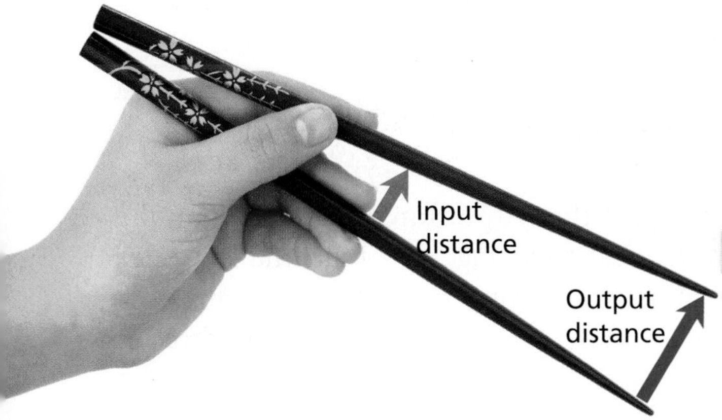

When a machine increases distance, you must apply a greater input force.

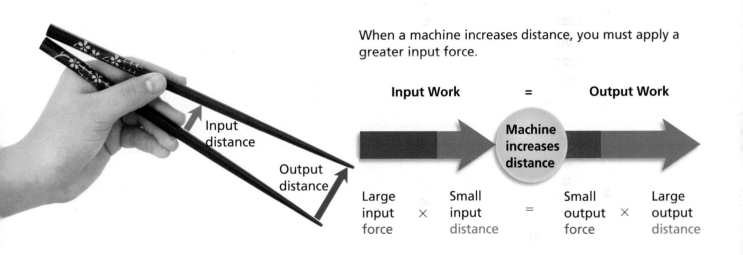

Input Work = **Output Work**

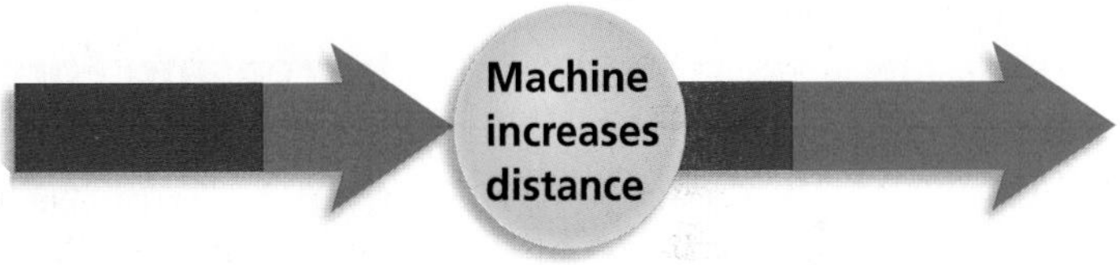

Large input force × Small input distance = Small output force × Large output distance

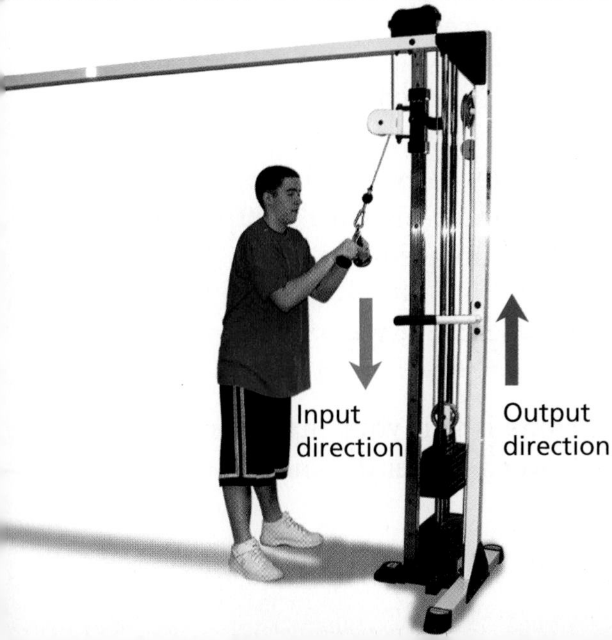

When a machine changes the direction of the input force, the amount of force and the distance remain the same.

Input Work = **Output Work**

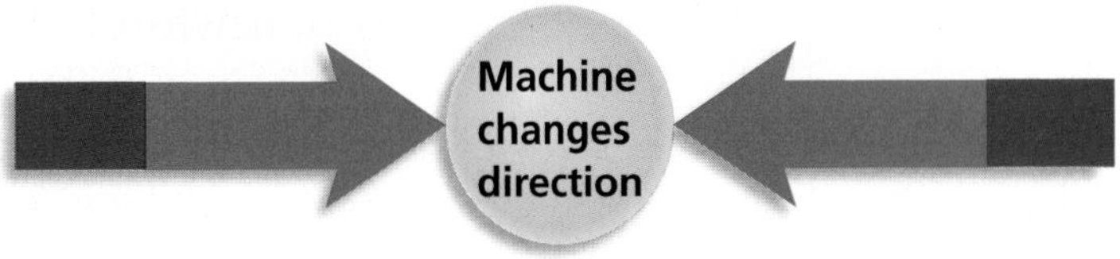

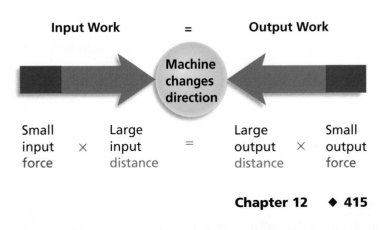

Small input force × Large input distance = Large output distance × Small output force

FIGURE 9
Mechanical Advantage
Without the mechanical advantage of the can opener, opening the can would be very difficult.

Mechanical Advantage

If you compare the input force to the output force, you can find the advantage of using a machine. **A machine's mechanical advantage is the number of times a machine increases a force exerted on it.** Finding the ratio of output force to input force gives you the **mechanical advantage** of a machine.

$$\text{Mechanical advantage} = \frac{\text{Output force}}{\text{Input force}}$$

Increasing Force When the output force is greater than the input force, the mechanical advantage of a machine is greater than 1. Suppose you exert an input force of 10 newtons on a hand-held can opener, and the opener exerts an output force of 30 newtons on a can. The mechanical advantage of the can opener is

$$\frac{\text{Output force}}{\text{Input force}} = \frac{30\text{ N}}{10\text{ N}} = 3$$

The can opener triples your input force!

Increasing Distance For a machine that increases distance, the output force is less than the input force. So in this case, the mechanical advantage is less than 1. For example, suppose your input force is 20 newtons and the machine's output force is 10 newtons. The mechanical advantage is

$$\frac{\text{Output force}}{\text{Input force}} = \frac{10\text{ N}}{20\text{ N}} = 0.5$$

The output force of the machine is half your input force, but the machine exerts that force over a longer distance.

Math Analyzing Data

Mechanical Advantage

The input force and output force for three different ramps are shown in the graph.

1. **Reading Graphs** What variable is plotted on the horizontal axis?
2. **Interpreting Data** If an 80-N input force is exerted on Ramp 2, what is the output force?
3. **Interpreting Data** Find the slope of the line for each ramp.
4. **Drawing Conclusions** Why does the slope represent each ramp's mechanical advantage? Which ramp has the greatest mechanical advantage?

Mechanical Advantages of Ramps

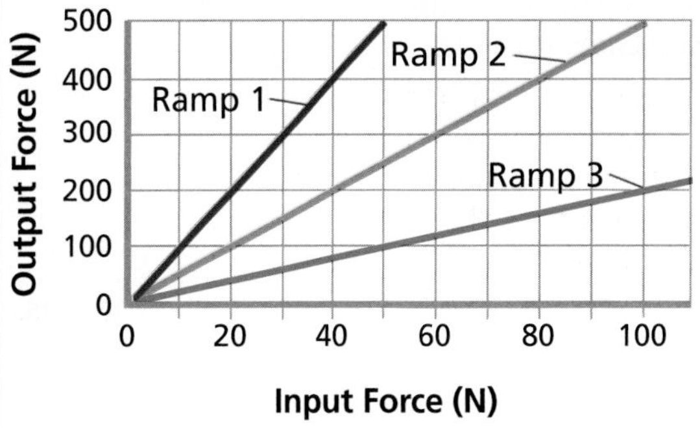

Changing Direction What can you predict about the mechanical advantage of a machine that changes the direction of the force? If only the direction changes, the input force will be the same as the output force. The mechanical advantage will always be 1.

Efficiency of Machines

So far, you have learned that the work you put into a machine is exactly equal to the work done by the machine. In an ideal situation, this equation is true. In real situations, however, the output work is always less than the input work.

Friction and Efficiency If you have ever tried to cut something with scissors that barely open and close, you know that a large part of your work is wasted overcoming the tightness, or friction, between the parts of the scissors.

In every machine, some work is wasted overcoming the force of friction. The less friction there is, the closer the output work is to the input work. The **efficiency** of a machine compares the output work to the input work. Efficiency is expressed as a percent. The higher the percent, the more efficient the machine is. If you know the input work and output work for a machine, you can calculate a machine's efficiency.

Reading Checkpoint **Why is output work always less than input work in real situations?**

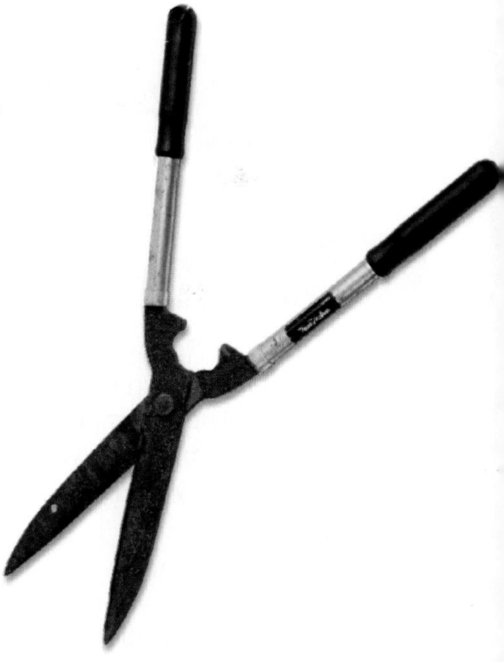

FIGURE 10
Efficiency
A rusty pair of shears is less efficient than a new pair of shears.
Applying Concepts *What force reduces the efficiency of the shears?*

Go Online
SCI LINKS NSTA

For: Links on mechanical efficiency
Visit: www.SciLinks.org
Web Code: scn-1342

Calculating Efficiency **To calculate the efficiency of a machine, divide the output work by the input work and multiply the result by 100 percent.** This is summarized by the following formula.

$$\textbf{Efficiency} = \frac{\textbf{Output work}}{\textbf{Input work}} \times \textbf{100\%}$$

If the tight scissors described above have an efficiency of 60%, only a little more than half of the work you do goes into cutting the paper. The rest is wasted overcoming the friction in the scissors.

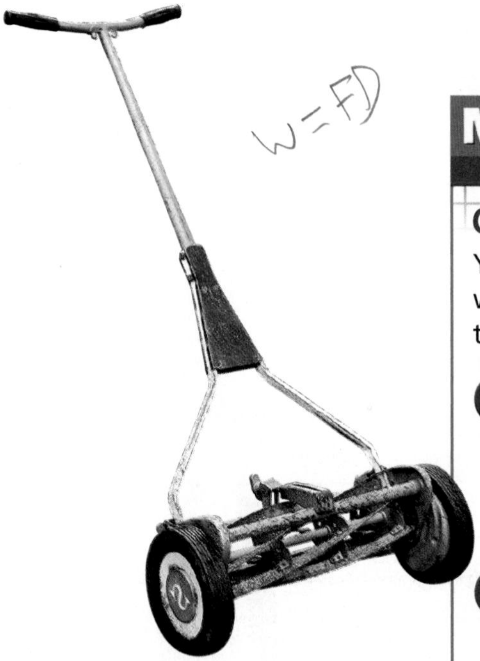

Math Sample Problem

Calculating Efficiency

You do 250,000 J of work to cut a lawn with a hand mower. If the work done by the mower is 200,000 J, what is the efficiency of the lawn mower?

1 Read and Understand.

What information are you given?

Input work (W_{input}) = 250,000 J

Output work (W_{output}) = 200,000 J

2 Plan and Solve

What quantity are you trying to calculate?

The efficiency of the lawn mower = ■

What formula contains the given quantities and the unknown quantity?

$$\text{Efficiency} = \frac{\text{Output work}}{\text{Input work}} \times 100\%$$

Perform the calculation.

$$\text{Efficiency} = \frac{200{,}000 \text{ J}}{250{,}000 \text{ J}} \times 100\%$$

$$\text{Efficiency} = 0.8 \times 100\% = 80\%$$

The efficiency of the lawn mower is 80%.

3 Look Back and Check

Does your answer make sense?

An efficiency of 80% means that 80 out of every 100 J of work went into cutting the lawn. This answer makes sense because most of the input work is converted to output work.

Math Practice

1. **Calculating Efficiency** You do 20 J of work while using a hammer. The hammer does 18 J of work on a nail. What is the efficiency of the hammer?
2. **Calculating Efficiency** Suppose you left your lawn mower outdoors all winter. Now it's rusty. Of your 250,000 J of work, only 100,000 J go to cutting the lawn. What is the efficiency of the lawn mower now?

FIGURE 11
An Ideal Machine?
M. C. Escher's print *Waterfall* illustrates an ideal machine. **Inferring** *Why won't Escher's waterfall machine work in real life?*

Real and Ideal Machines If you could find a machine with an efficiency of 100%, it would be an ideal machine. Unfortunately, an ideal machine, such as the one shown in Figure 11, does not exist. In all machines, some work is wasted due to friction. So all machines have an efficiency of less than 100%. The machines you use every day, such as scissors, screwdrivers, and rakes, lose some work due to friction.

A machine's ideal mechanical advantage is its mechanical advantage with 100% efficiency. However, if you measure a machine's input force and output force, you will find the efficiency is always less than 100%. A machine's measured mechanical advantage is called actual mechanical advantage.

Reading Checkpoint **What is a machine's ideal mechanical advantage?**

Section 2 Assessment

Target Reading Skill

Identifying Main Ideas Use your graphic organizer to help you answer Question 1 below.

Reviewing Key Concepts

1. a. **Defining** What is a machine?
   b. **Describing** In what three ways can machines make work easier?
   c. **Applying Concepts** How does a screwdriver make work easier?
2. a. **Reviewing** What is the mechanical advantage of a machine?
   b. **Making Generalizations** What is the mechanical advantage of a machine that changes only the direction of the applied force?
   c. **Calculating** If a machine has an input force of 40 N and an output force of 80 N, what is its mechanical advantage?
3. a. **Reviewing** What must you know in order to calculate a machine's efficiency?
   b. **Explaining** What is an ideal machine?
   c. **Comparing and Contrasting** How is a real machine like an ideal machine, and how is it different?

Math Practice

4. **Calculating Efficiency** The input work you do on a can opener is 12 J. The output work the can opener does is 6 J. What is the efficiency of the can opener?
5. **Calculating Efficiency** Suppose the efficiency of a manual pencil sharpener is 58%. If the output work needed to sharpen a pencil is 4.8 J, how much input work must you do to sharpen the pencil?

Seesaw Science

Problem

What is the relationship between distance and weight for a balanced seesaw?

Skills Focus

controlling variables, interpreting data

Materials

- meter stick • masking tape
- 28 pennies, minted after 1982
- small object with a mass of about 50 g
- dowel or other cylindrical object for pivot point, about 10 cm long and 3 cm in diameter

Procedure

1. Begin by using the dowel and meter stick to build a seesaw. Tape the dowel firmly to the table so that it does not roll.
2. Choose the meter stick mark that will rest on the dowel from the following: 55 cm or 65 cm. Record your choice. Position your meter stick so that it is on your chosen pivot point with the 100-cm mark on your right.
3. Slide the 50-g mass along the shorter end of the meter stick until the meter stick is balanced, with both sides in the air. (This is called "zeroing" your meter stick.)
4. Copy the data table into your notebook.
5. Place a stack of 8 pennies exactly over the 80-cm mark. Determine the distance, in centimeters, from the pivot point to the pennies. Record this distance in the "Distance to Pivot" column for the right side of the seesaw.
6. Predict where you must place a stack of 5 pennies in order to balance the meter stick. Test your prediction and record the actual position in the "Position of Pennies" column for the left side of the seesaw.

Data Table					
Your group's pivot point position: ______ cm					
Trial Number	Side of Seesaw	Number of Pennies or Weight of Pennies (pw)	Position of Pennies (cm)	Distance to Pivot (cm)	Weight of Pennies × Distance
1	Right				
	Left				
2	Right				
	Left				
3	Right				

7. Determine the distance, in centimeters, from the pivot point to the left stack of pennies. Record this distance in the "Distance to Pivot" column for the left side of the seesaw.
8. If you use an imaginary unit of weight, the pennyweight (pw), then one penny weighs 1 pw. Multiply the weight of each stack of pennies by the distance to the pivot point. Record the result in the last column of the data table.
9. Predict how the position of the pennies in Step 6 would change if you used 7, 12, 16, and 20 pennies instead of 5 pennies. Test your predictions.

Analyze and Conclude

1. Controlling Variables In this experiment, what is the manipulated variable? The responding variable? How do you know which is which?
2. Interpreting Data As you increase the number of pennies on the left, what happens to the distance at which you must place the stack in order to balance the meter stick?
3. Drawing Conclusions What conclusion can you draw about the relationship between distances and weights needed to balance a seesaw?
4. Controlling Variables Why was it important to zero the meter stick with the 50-g mass?
5. Interpreting Data Compare your results with those of the other groups. How do different pivot point positions affect the results?
6. Communicating Write a dialogue that occurs when two friends try to balance themselves on opposite sides of a seesaw. One friend has a mass of 54 kg and the other friend has a mass of 42 kg.

Design an Experiment

Suppose you have a seesaw with a movable pivot. You want to use it with a younger friend who weighs half what you weigh. If you and your friend sit on the ends of the seesaw, where should you position the pivot point? Develop a hypothesis and then design an experiment to test it. *Obtain your teacher's permission before carrying out your investigation.*

Section

3 Simple Machines

Reading Preview

Key Concepts

- What are the six kinds of simple machines, and how are they used?
- What is the ideal mechanical advantage of each simple machine?
- What is a compound machine?

Key Terms

- inclined plane
- wedge
- screw
- lever
- fulcrum
- wheel and axle
- pulley
- compound machine

Target Reading Skill

Previewing Visuals Before you read, preview Figure 17. Then write two questions that you have about the diagram in a graphic organizer like the one below. As you read, answer your questions.

Three Classes of Levers

Q. What are the three classes of levers?
A.
Q.

Lab zone Discover Activity

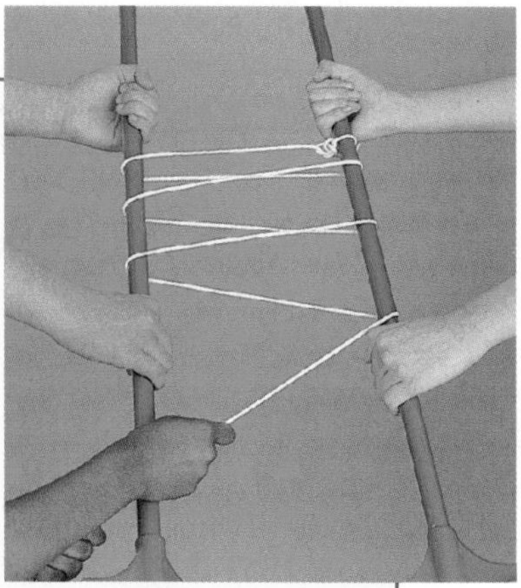

How Can You Increase Force?

1. Working with two partners, wrap a rope around two broomsticks as shown.
2. Your two partners should try to hold the brooms apart with the same amount of force throughout the activity. For safety, they should hold firmly, but not with all their strength.
3. Try to pull the two students together by pulling on the broomsticks. Can you do it?
4. Can you pull them together by pulling on the rope?

Think It Over

Predicting What do you think will be the effect of wrapping the rope around the broomsticks several more times?

Look at the objects shown on these pages. Which of them would you call machines? Would it surprise you to find out that each is made up of one or more simple machines? As you learned in the last section, a machine helps you do work by changing the amount or direction of the force you apply.

There are six basic kinds of simple machines: the inclined plane, the wedge, the screw, the lever, the wheel and axle, and the pulley. In this section, you will learn how the different types of simple machines help you do work.

◀ **An eggbeater, a bolt, and a fishing pole all make use of simple machines.**

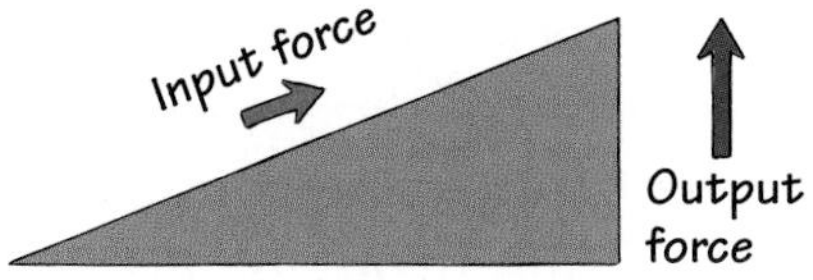

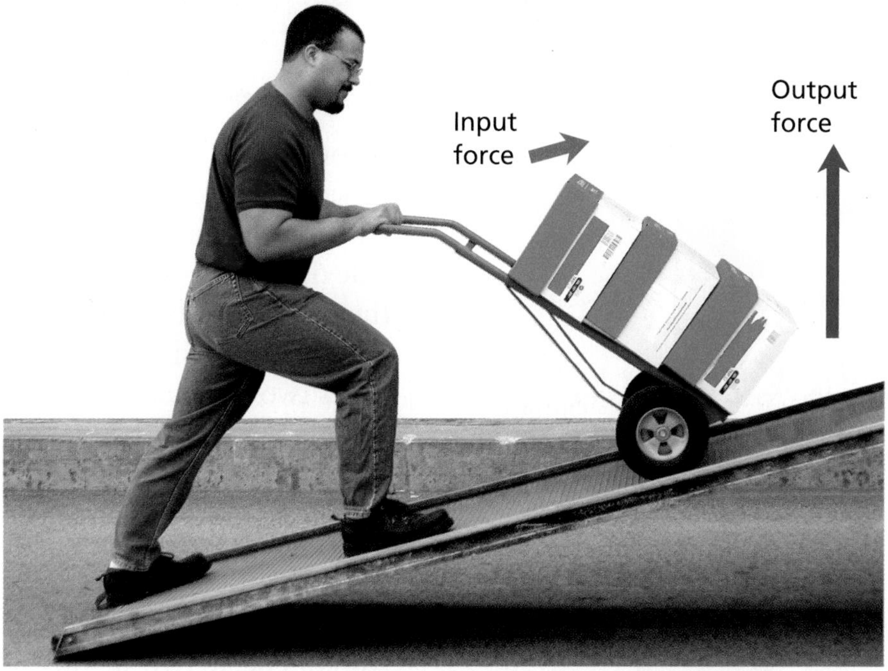

FIGURE 12
Inclined Plane
Although the amount of work is the same whether you lift the boxes or push them up the ramp to the truck, you need less force when you use an inclined plane.
Relating Cause and Effect *When you use a ramp, what happens to the distance over which you exert your force?*

Inclined Plane

Have you ever had to lift something from a lower level to a higher level? The job is much easier if you have a ramp. For example, a ramp makes it much easier to push a grocery cart over a curb. A ramp is an example of a simple machine called an inclined plane. An **inclined plane** is a flat, sloped surface.

How It Works An inclined plane allows you to exert your input force over a longer distance. As a result, the input force needed is less than the output force. The input force that you use on an inclined plane is the force with which you push or pull an object. The output force is the force that you would need to lift the object without the inclined plane. Recall that this force is equal to the weight of the object.

Mechanical Advantage You can determine the ideal mechanical advantage of an inclined plane by dividing the length of the incline by its height.

$$\textbf{Ideal mechanical advantage} = \frac{\textbf{Length of incline}}{\textbf{Height of incline}}$$

For example, if you are loading a truck that is 1 meter high using a ramp that is 3 meters long, the ideal mechanical advantage of the ramp is 3 meters ÷ 1 meter, or 3. The inclined plane increases the force you exerted three times. If the height of the incline does not change, increasing the length of the incline will increase the mechanical advantage. The longer the incline, the less input force you need to push or pull an object.

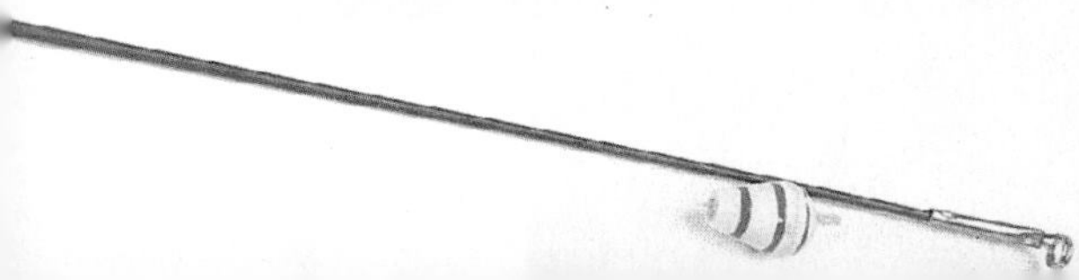

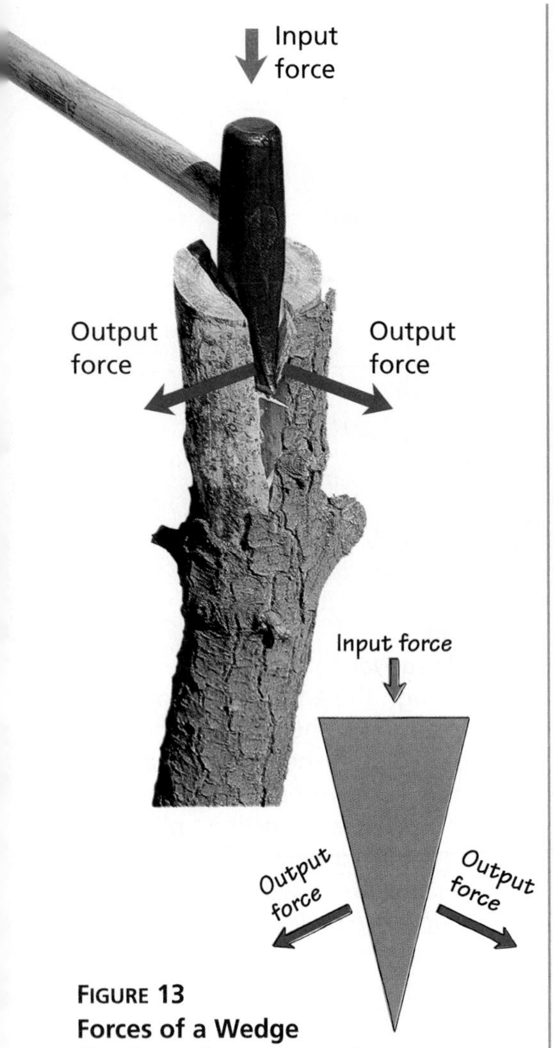

FIGURE 13
Forces of a Wedge
The input force exerted on a wedge results in output forces that can split the log.

Wedge

If you've ever sliced an apple with a knife, pulled up a zipper, or seen someone chop wood with an ax, you are familiar with another simple machine known as a wedge. A **wedge** is a device that is thick at one end and tapers to a thin edge at the other end. It might be helpful to think of a wedge, like the one shown in Figure 13, as an inclined plane (or sometimes two inclined planes back to back) that can move.

How It Works When you use a wedge, instead of moving an object along the inclined plane, you move the inclined plane itself. For example, when an ax is used to split wood, the ax handle exerts a force on the blade of the ax, which is the wedge. That force pushes the wedge down into the wood. The wedge in turn exerts an output force at a 90° angle to its slope, splitting the wood in two.

Wedges are a part of your everyday life. For example, a zipper depends on wedges to close and open. A pencil sharpener, a cheese grater, and a shovel all make use of wedges.

Mechanical Advantage The mechanical advantage of the wedge and the inclined plane are similar. **The ideal mechanical advantage of a wedge is determined by dividing the length of the wedge by its width.** The longer and thinner a wedge is, the greater its mechanical advantage. For example, the cutting edge of a steel carving knife is a wedge. When you sharpen a knife, you make the wedge thinner and increase its mechanical advantage. That is why sharp knives cut better than dull knives.

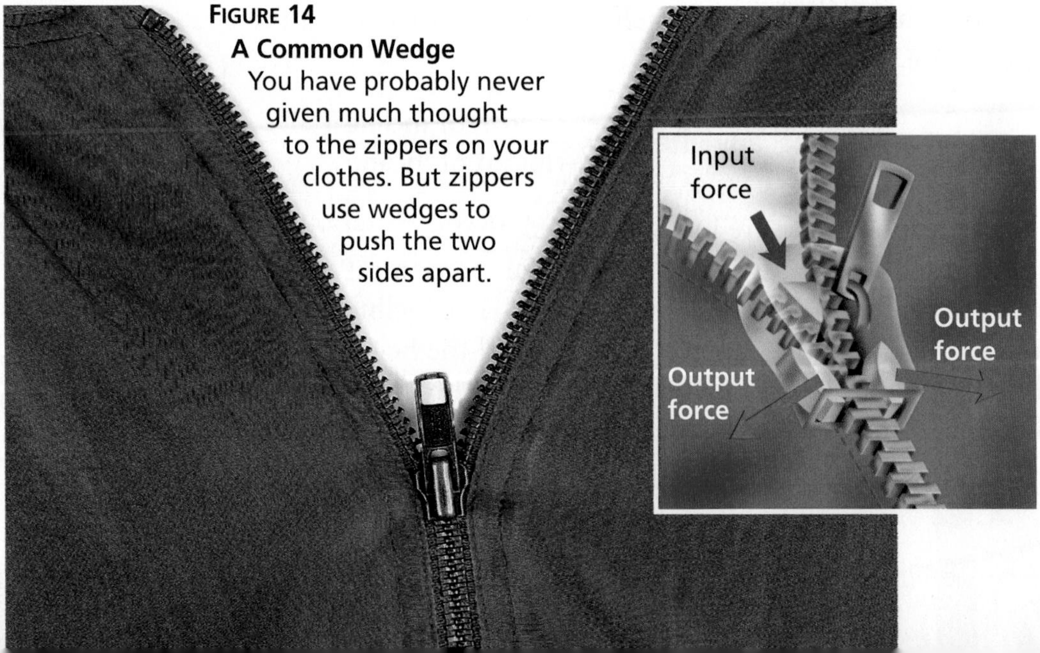

FIGURE 14
A Common Wedge
You have probably never given much thought to the zippers on your clothes. But zippers use wedges to push the two sides apart.

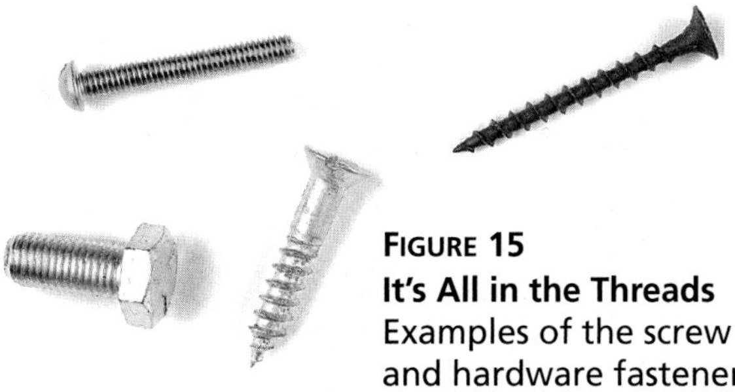

FIGURE 15
It's All in the Threads
Examples of the screw are found in jars and hardware fasteners.
Relating Cause and Effect *How does the distance between the threads of a screw affect its mechanical advantage?*

Screws

Like a wedge, a screw is a simple machine that is related to the inclined plane. A **screw** can be thought of as an inclined plane wrapped around a cylinder. This spiral inclined plane forms the threads of the screw.

How It Works When you twist a screw into a piece of wood, you exert an input force on the screw. The threads of a screw act like an inclined plane to increase the distance over which you exert the input force. As the threads of the screw turn, they exert an output force on the wood, pulling the screw into the wood. Friction between the screw and the wood holds the screw in place.

Many devices act like screws. Examples include bolts, light bulbs, and jar lids. Look at the jar lid in Figure 15. When you turn the lid, your small input force is greatly increased because of the screw threads on the lid. The threads on the lid are pulled against the matching threads on the jar with a strong enough force to make a tight seal.

Mechanical Advantage The closer together the threads of a screw are, the greater the mechanical advantage. This is because the closer the threads are, the more times you must turn the screw to fasten it into a piece of wood. Your input force is applied over a longer distance. The longer input distance results in an increased output force. Think of the length around the threads as the length of the inclined plane, and the length of the screw as the height of the inclined plane. **The ideal mechanical advantage of a screw is the length around the threads divided by the length of the screw.**

Reading Checkpoint **How is a screw like an inclined plane?**

Lab zone **Try This Activity**

A Paper Screw

1. To make a paper model of a screw, cut out a triangle from a piece of paper.
2. Tape the wide end of the triangle to a pencil. Then wind the paper around the pencil.

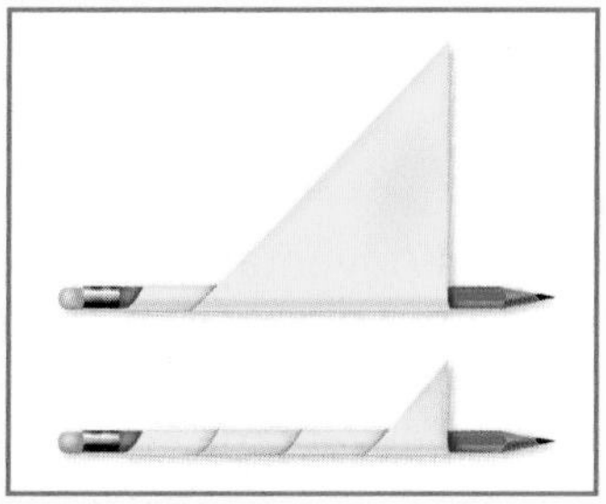

Making Models How does this model represent a real screw? Can you think of a way to calculate the ideal mechanical advantage of your model screw?

Levers

Have you ever ridden on a seesaw or pried open a paint can with an opener? If so, then you are already familiar with another simple machine called a lever. A **lever** is a rigid bar that is free to pivot, or rotate, on a fixed point. The fixed point that a lever pivots around is called the **fulcrum.**

How It Works To understand how levers work, think about using a paint-can opener. The opener rests against the edge of the can, which acts as the fulcrum. The tip of the opener is under the lid of the can. When you push down, you exert an input force on the handle, and the opener pivots on the fulcrum. As a result, the tip of the opener pushes up, thereby exerting an output force on the lid.

Mechanical Advantage A lever like the paint-can opener helps you in two ways. It increases your input force and it changes the direction of your input force. When you use the paint-can opener, you push the handle a long distance down in order to move the lid a short distance up. However, you are able to apply a smaller force than you would have without the opener.

The ideal mechanical advantage of a lever is determined by dividing the distance from the fulcrum to the input force by the distance from the fulcrum to the output force.

$$\text{Ideal mechanical advantage} = \frac{\text{Distance from fulcrum to input force}}{\text{Distance from fulcrum to output force}}$$

In the case of the paint-can opener, the distance from the fulcrum to the input force is greater than the distance from the fulcrum to the output force. This means that the mechanical advantage is greater than 1.

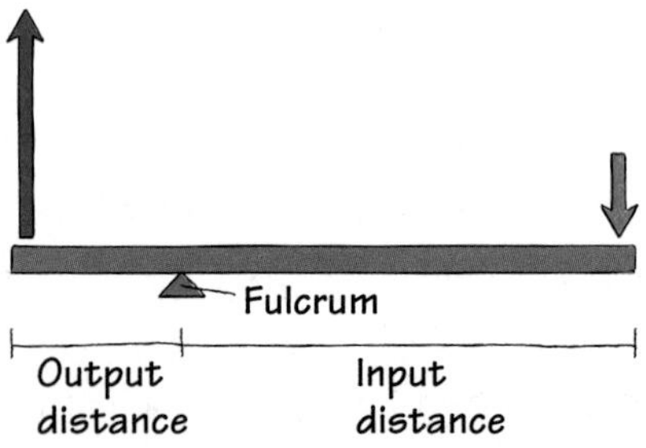

FIGURE 16
Mechanical Advantage of a Lever
A lever's input distance and output distance determine its ideal mechanical advantage.

Different Types of Levers When a paint-can opener is used as a lever, the fulcrum is located between the input and output forces. But this is not always the case. As shown in Figure 17, there are three different types of levers. Levers are classified according to the location of the fulcrum relative to the input and output forces.

Reading Checkpoint What point on a lever does not move?

FIGURE 17
Three Classes of Levers

The three classes of levers differ in the positions of the fulcrum, input force, and output force. **Applying Concepts** *Which type of lever always has an ideal mechanical advantage less than 1?*

First-Class Levers

First-class levers always change the direction of the input force. If the fulcrum is closer to the output force, these levers also increase force. If the fulcrum is closer to the input force, these levers also increase distance. Other examples include scissors, pliers, and seesaws.

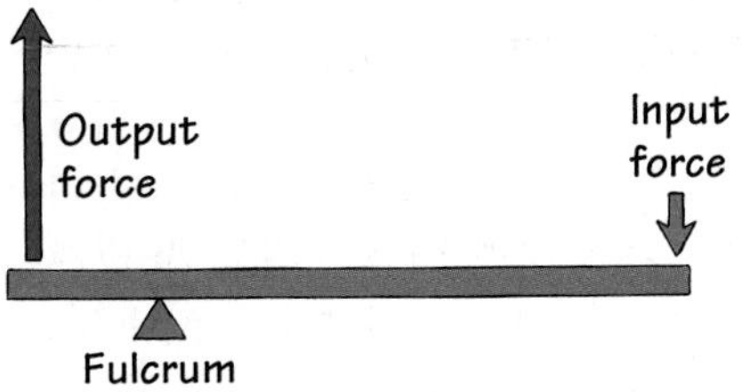

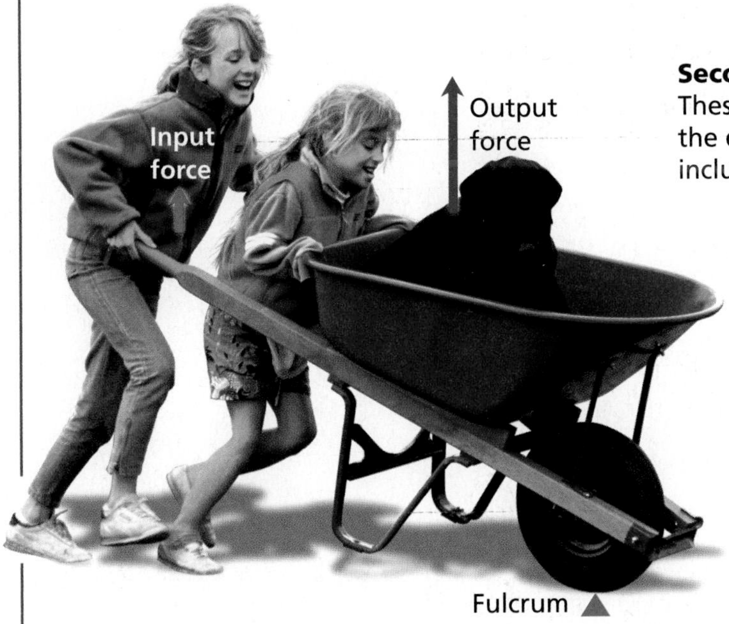

Second-Class Levers

These levers increase force, but do not change the direction of the input force. Other examples include doors, nutcrackers, and bottle openers.

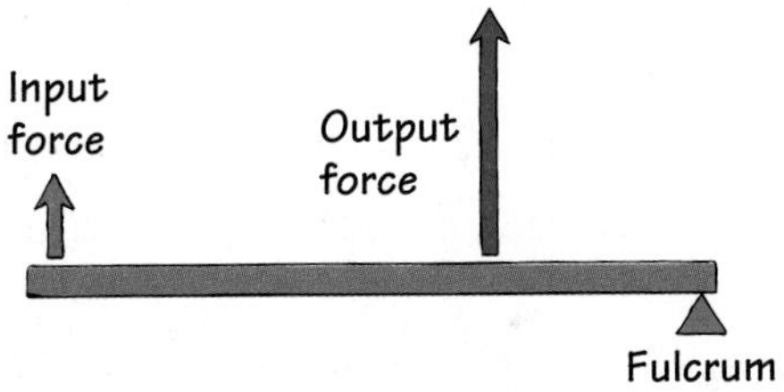

Third-Class Levers

These levers increase distance, but do not change the direction of the input force. Other examples include fishing poles, shovels, and baseball bats.

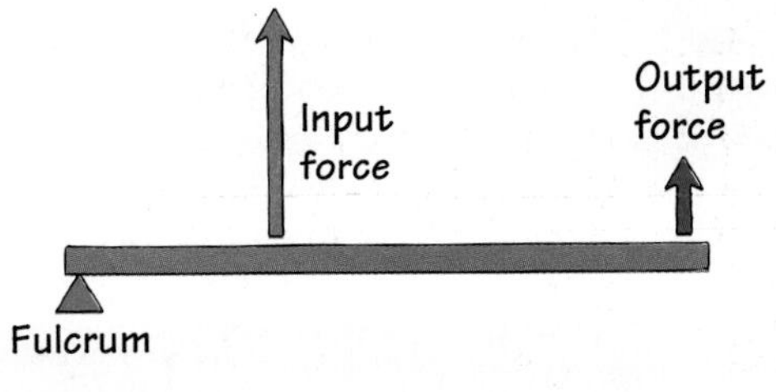

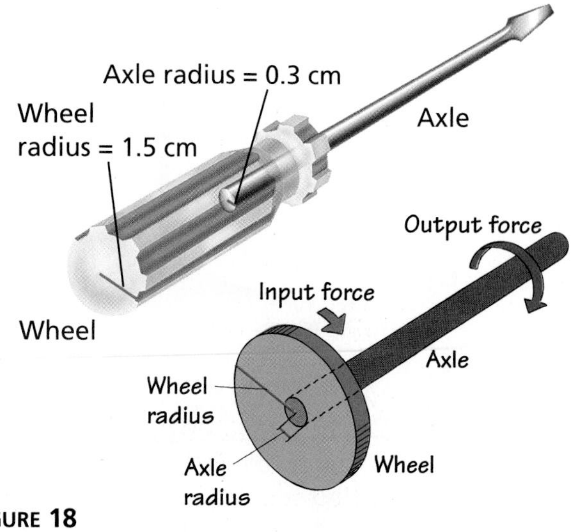

FIGURE 18
Wheel and Axle
A screwdriver increases force by exerting the output force over a shorter distance.
Observing *Which has a larger radius, the wheel or the axle?*

Wheel and Axle

It's almost impossible to insert a screw into a piece of wood with your fingers. But with a screwdriver, you can turn the screw easily. A screwdriver makes use of a simple machine known as the **wheel and axle.** A wheel and axle is a simple machine made of two circular or cylindrical objects fastened together that rotate about a common axis. The object with the larger radius is called the wheel and the object with the smaller radius is called the axle. In a screwdriver, the handle is the wheel and the shaft is the axle. A doorknob and a car's steering wheel are also examples of a wheel and axle.

Science and **History**

Engineering Marvels

Simple machines have been used to create some of the most beautiful and useful structures in the world.

2550 B.C.
Great Pyramid, Giza, Egypt
Workers used wedges to cut 2.3 million blocks of stone to build the pyramid. At the quarry, the wedges were driven into cracks in the rock. The rock split into pieces. Workers hauled the massive blocks up inclined planes to the tops of pyramid walls.

500 B.C.
Theater at Epidaurus, Greece
Instead of ramps, the Greeks relied on a crane powered by pulleys to lift the stone blocks to build this theater. The crane was also used to lower actors to the stage during performances.

3000 B.C. **2000 B.C.** **1000 B.C.**

How It Works How does a screwdriver make use of a wheel and axle to do work? Look at Figure 18. When you use a screwdriver, you apply an input force to turn the handle, or wheel. Because the wheel is larger than the shaft, or axle, the axle rotates and exerts a large output force. The wheel and axle increases your force, but you must exert your force over a long distance.

What would happen if the input force were applied to the axle rather than the wheel? For the riverboat in Figure 19 on the next page, the force of the engine is applied to the axle of the large paddle wheel. The large paddle wheel in turn pushes against the water. In this case, the input force is exerted over a short distance. So when the input force is applied to the axle, a wheel and axle mulitplies distance.

Writing in Science

Research and Write
Suppose that you are the person who first thought of using a simple machine at one of the construction sites in the timeline. Write out your proposal. You'll need to research the time and place. Explain to the people in charge why the simple machine you suggest will give workers a mechanical advantage.

A.D. 1000 Brihadeshwara Temple, India
The temple's tower at Thanjavur is more than 60 meters high. Workers dragged the dome-shaped capstone, a mass of 70,000 kilograms, to the top of the structure along an inclined plane several kilometers long.

A.D. 1056 Yingxian Pagoda, China
Slanted wooden beams called *ang* act as first-class levers to hold up the roof of this pagoda. The weight of the center of the roof presses down on one end of the beam. The other end of the beam swings up to support the outer edge of the roof.

A.D. 1994 The Chunnel, United Kingdom to France
Special drilling equipment was built to tunnel under the English Channel. Opened in May of 1994, the tunnel is 50 kilometers long. It carries only railway traffic.

0 | A.D. 1000 | A.D. 2000

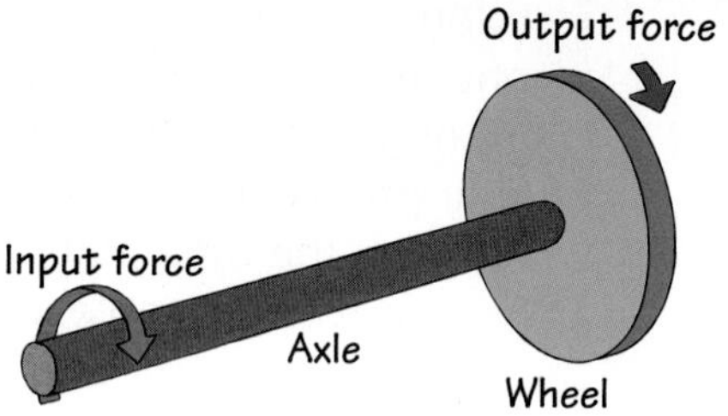

FIGURE 19
Increasing Distance
In a riverboat paddle wheel, the axle turns the wheel. The output force is less than the input force, but it is exerted over a longer distance.

Mechanical Advantage **You can find the ideal mechanical advantage of a wheel and axle by dividing the radius of the wheel by the radius of the axle.** (A radius is the distance from the outer edge of a circle to the circle's center.) The greater the ratio between the radius of the wheel and the radius of the axle, the greater the mechanical advantage.

$$\text{Mechanical advantage} = \frac{\text{Radius of wheel}}{\text{Radius of axle}}$$

Suppose the radius of a screwdriver's wheel is 1.5 cm and its axle radius is 0.3 cm. The screwdriver's ideal mechanical advantage would be 1.5 centimeters ÷ 0.3 centimeter, or 5.

Reading Checkpoint **What is a radius?**

Pulley

When you raise a flag on a flagpole or when you open and close window blinds, you are using a pulley. A **pulley** is a simple machine made of a grooved wheel with a rope or cable wrapped around it.

How It Works You use a pulley by pulling on one end of the rope. This is the input force. At the other end of the rope, the output force pulls up on the object you want to move. To move a heavy object over a distance, a pulley can make work easier in two ways. First, it can decrease the amount of input force needed to lift the object. Second, the pulley can change the direction of your input force. For example, you pull down on the flagpole rope, and the flag moves up.

Types of Pulleys There are two basic types of pulleys. A pulley that you attach to a structure is called a fixed pulley. Fixed pulleys are used at the tops of flagpoles. If you attach a pulley to the object you wish to move, you use a movable pulley. Construction cranes often use movable pulleys. By combining fixed and movable pulleys, you can make a pulley system called a block and tackle. **The ideal mechanical advantage of a pulley is equal to the number of sections of rope that support the object.**

Reading Checkpoint **A pulley is attached to the object that is being moved. What kind of pulley is it?**

Lab zone Skills Activity

Communicating

Write a packaging label for a machine that uses a wheel and axle. On your label, describe the advantages of using this simple machine. Include a drawing of the forces that act on the machine.

FIGURE 20

Types of Pulleys

A fixed pulley and a movable pulley are the two basic types of pulleys. A block and tackle combines a fixed and movable pulley. **Comparing and Contrasting** *Which type of pulley has the greatest mechanical advantage?*

Go Online active art

For: Types of Pulleys activity
Visit: PHSchool.com
Web Code: cgp-3043

Fixed Pulley

A fixed pulley does not change the amount of force applied. It does change the direction of the force.

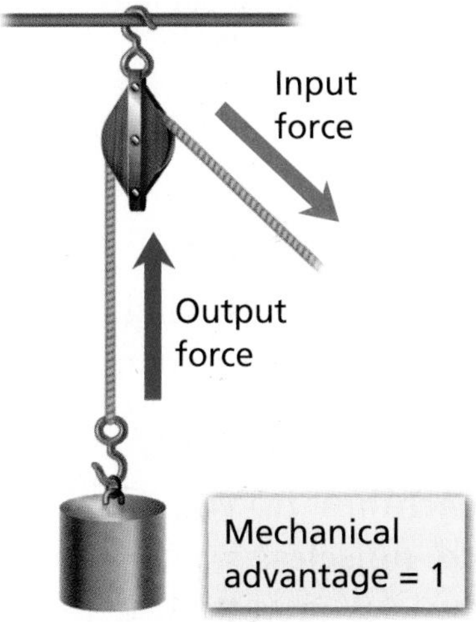

Movable Pulley

A movable pulley decreases the amount of input force needed. It does not change the direction of the force.

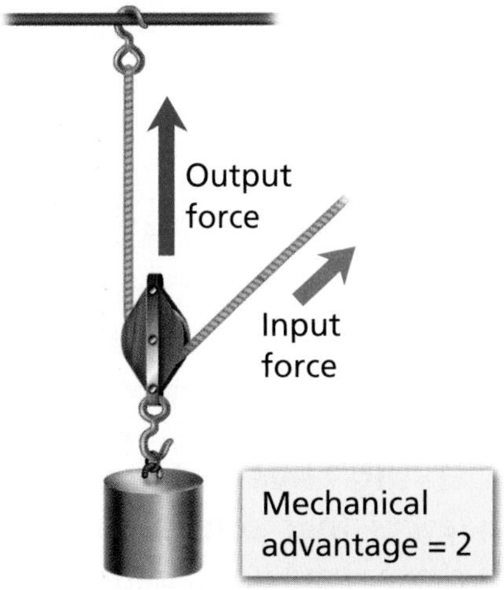

Block and Tackle

A block and tackle is a pulley system made up of fixed and movable pulleys.

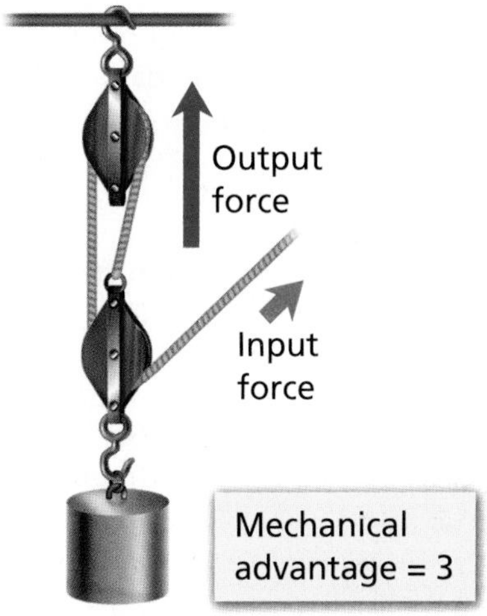

Cranes use block-and-tackle systems to lift heavy loads.

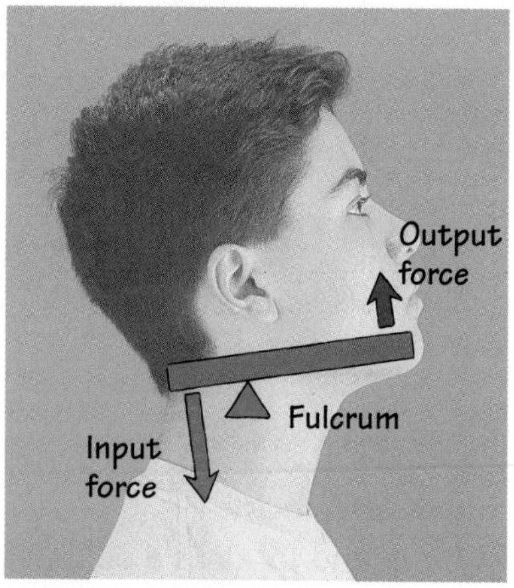

First-Class Lever The joint at the top of your neck is the fulcrum of a first-class lever. The muscles in the back of your neck provide the input force. The output force is used to tilt your head back.

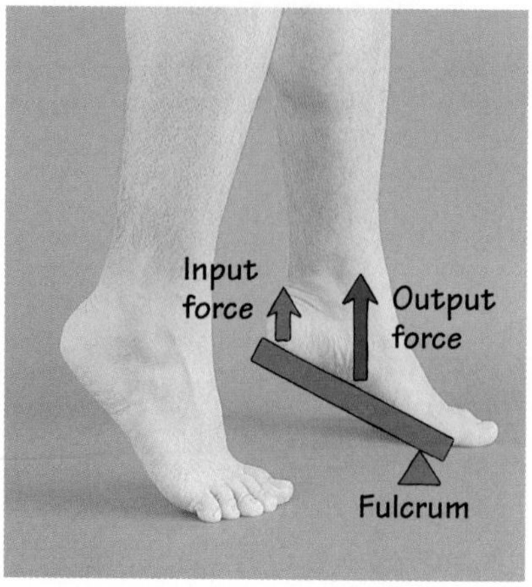

Second-Class Lever The ball of your foot is the fulcrum of a second-class lever. The muscle in the calf of your leg provides the input force. The output force is used to raise your body.

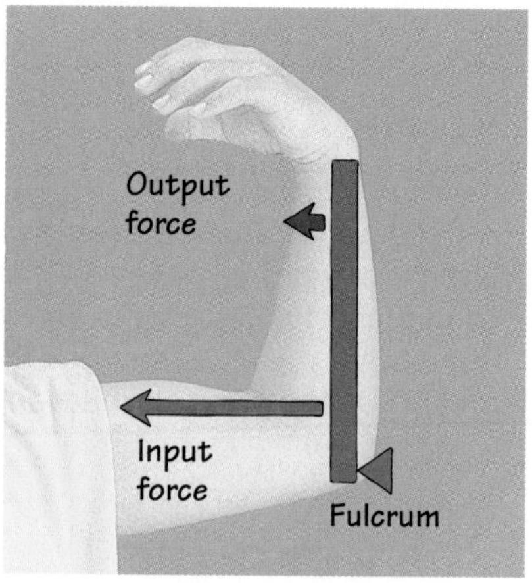

Third-Class Lever Your elbow is the fulcrum of a third-class lever. Your biceps muscle provides the input force. The output force is used to lift your arm.

FIGURE 21
Levers in the Body
You don't need to look further than your own body to find simple machines. Three different types of levers are responsible for many of your movements.

Simple Machines in the Body

You probably don't think of the human body as being made up of machines. Believe it or not, machines are involved in much of the work that your body does.

Living Levers Most of the machines in your body are levers that consist of bones and muscles. Every time you move, you use a muscle. Your muscles are attached to your bones by connecting structures called tendons. Tendons and muscles pull on bones, making them work as levers. The joint, near where the tendon is attached to the bone, acts as the fulcrum. The muscles produce the input force. The output force is used for doing work, such as lifting your hand.

Working Wedges When you bite into an apple, you use your sharp front teeth, called incisors. Your incisors are shaped like wedges to enable you to bite off pieces of food. When you bite down on something, the wedge shape of your front teeth produces enough force to break it into pieces, just as an ax splits a log. The next time you take a bite of a crunchy apple, think about the machines in your mouth!

Reading Checkpoint **What type of simple machine do your front teeth resemble?**

FIGURE 22
Wedges to Help You Eat
Your front teeth, known as incisors, are shaped like wedges.

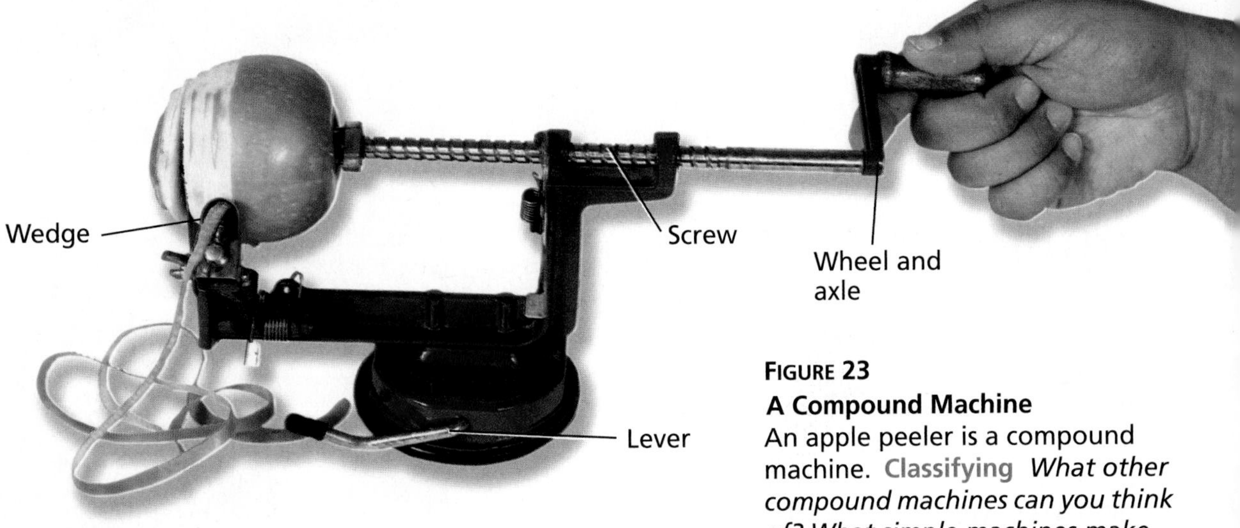

FIGURE 23
A Compound Machine
An apple peeler is a compound machine. Classifying *What other compound machines can you think of? What simple machines make them up?*

Compound Machines

Many machines do not resemble the six simple machines you just read about. That's because many machines consist of combinations of simple machines.

A **compound machine** is a machine that utilizes two or more simple machines. **The ideal mechanical advantage of a compound machine is the product of the individual ideal mechanical advantages of the simple machines that make it up.**

An apple peeler like the one shown in Figure 23 is a compound machine. Four different simple machines make it up. The handle is a wheel and axle. The axle is also a screw that turns the apple. A wedge peels the apple's skin. To hold the machine in place, a lever can be switched to engage a suction cup.

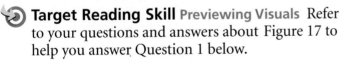

Section 3 Assessment

Target Reading Skill Previewing Visuals Refer to your questions and answers about Figure 17 to help you answer Question 1 below.

Reviewing Key Concepts

1. a. Listing List the six kinds of simple machines.
   b. Classifying What type of simple machine is a door stopper? A rake? A windmill? A slide?
   c. Developing Hypotheses Can you consider your thumb to be a lever? Why or why not?
2. a. Identifying What is the ideal mechanical advantage of each type of simple machine?
   b. Inferring How can you increase a pulley's mechanical advantage?
   c. Drawing Conclusions How is calculating the ideal mechanical advantage of an inclined plane similar to calculating that of a screw?
3. a. Reviewing How many simple machines are needed to make a compound machine?
   b. Describing How do you find the mechanical advantage of a compound machine?

Lab zone At-Home Activity

Machines in the Kitchen Look around your kitchen with a family member. Identify at least five machines. Classify each as a simple machine or a compound machine. Explain to your family member how each machine makes work easier.

Lab zone **Skills Lab**

Angling for Access

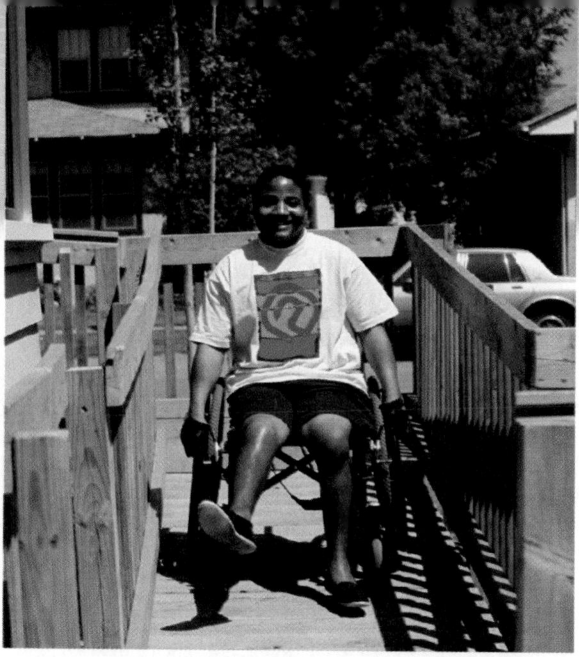

Problem

How does the steepness of a wheelchair-access ramp affect its usefulness?

Skills Focus

making models, calculating

Materials

- 4 books, about 2 cm thick
- metric ruler
- wooden block with eye-hook
- marker
- board, at least 10 cm wide and 50 cm long
- spring scale, 0–10 N, or force sensor

Procedure

1. Preview the following steps that describe how you can construct and use a ramp. Then copy the data table into your notebook.
2. The output force with an inclined plane is equal to the weight of the object. Lift the block with the spring scale to measure its weight. Record this value in the data table. If you are using a force sensor, see your teacher for instructions.
3. Make a mark on the side of the board about 3 cm from one end. Measure the length from the other end of the board to the mark and record it in the data table.
4. Place one end of the board on top of a book. The mark you made on the board should be even with the edge of the book.
5. Measure the vertical distance in centimeters from the top of the table to where the underside of the incline touches the book. Record this value in the data table as "Height of Incline."
6. Lay the block on its largest side and use the spring scale to pull the block straight up the incline at a slow, steady speed. Be sure to hold the spring scale parallel to the incline, as shown in the photograph. Measure the force needed and record it in the data table.
7. Predict how your results will change if you repeat the investigation using two, three, and four books. Test your predictions.
8. For each trial, determine the ideal mechanical advantage and the actual mechanical advantage. Record the calculations in your data table.

Data Table

Number of Books	Output Force (N)	Length of Incline (cm)	Height of Incline (cm)	Input Force (N)	Ideal Mechanical Advantage	Actual Mechanical Advantage
1						
2						
3						
4						

Analyze and Conclude

1. Interpreting Data How did the ideal mechanical advantage and the actual mechanical advantage compare each time you repeated the experiment? Explain your answer.
2. Making Models How did the model help you in determining the ramp's usefulness? What kind of limitations does your model have?
3. Making Models What happens to the actual mechanical advantage as the inclined plane gets steeper? On the basis of this fact alone, which of the four inclined planes models the best steepness for a wheelchair-access ramp? Explain your answer.
4. Drawing Conclusions What other factors, besides mechanical advantage, should you consider when deciding on the steepness of the ramp?
5. Calculating Suppose the door of the local public library is 2.0 m above the ground and the distance from the door to the parking lot is 15 m. What is the ideal mechanical advantage of a ramp built from the door to the parking lot?
6. Communicating Write a letter to a local business explaining how a ramp could help the employees and customers. Give some examples of work that could be made easier using a ramp. Explain how the steepness of a ramp affects its mechanical advantage.

More to Explore

Find actual ramps that provide access for people with disabilities. Measure the heights and lengths of these ramps and calculate their ideal mechanical advantages. Find out what the requirements are for access ramps in your area. Should your ramp be made of a particular material? Should it level off before it reaches the door? How wide should it be? How does it provide water drainage?

Chapter 12 Study Guide

1 What Is Work?

Key Concepts

- Work is done on an object when the object moves in the same direction in which the force is exerted.
- The amount of work done on an object can be determined by multiplying force times distance.

$$\text{Work} = \text{Force} \times \text{Distance}$$

- Power equals the amount of work done on an object in a unit of time.

$$\text{Power} = \frac{\text{Work}}{\text{Time}}$$

Key Terms

work
joule
power

2 How Machines Do Work

Key Concepts

- A machine makes work easier by changing at least one of three factors. A machine may change the amount of force you exert, the distance over which you exert your force, or the direction in which you exert your force.
- A machine's mechanical advantage is the number of times a machine increases a force exerted on it.
- $\text{Mechanical advantage} = \dfrac{\text{Output force}}{\text{Input force}}$
- To calculate the efficiency of a machine, divide the output work by the input work and multiply the result by 100 percent.

$$\text{Efficiency} = \frac{\text{Output work}}{\text{Input work}} \times 100\%$$

Key Terms

machine
input force
output force
input work
output work
mechanical advantage
efficiency

3 Simple Machines

Key Concepts

- There are six basic kinds of simple machines: the inclined plane, the wedge, the screw, the lever, the wheel and axle, and the pulley.
- You can determine the ideal mechanical advantage of an inclined plane by dividing the length of the incline by its height.
- The ideal mechanical advantage of a wedge is determined by dividing the length of the wedge by its width.
- The ideal mechanical advantage of a screw is the length around the threads divided by the length of the screw.
- The ideal mechanical advantage of a lever is determined by dividing the distance from the fulcrum to the input force by the distance from the fulcrum to the output force.
- You can find the ideal mechanical advantage of a wheel and axle by dividing the radius of the wheel by the radius of the axle.
- The ideal mechanical advantage of a pulley is equal to the number of sections of rope that support the object.
- Most of the machines in your body are levers that consist of bones and muscles.
- The ideal mechanical advantage of a compound machine is the product of the individual ideal mechanical advantages of the simple machines that make it up.

Key Terms

inclined plane
wedge
screw
lever
fulcrum
wheel and axle
pulley
compound machine

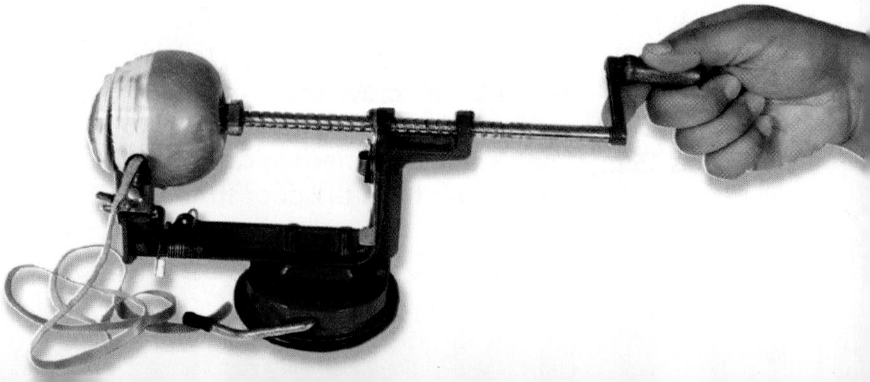

Review and Assessment

Go Online
PHSchool.com
For: Self-Assessment
Visit: PHSchool.com
Web Code: cga-3040

Organizing Information

Comparing and Contrasting Copy the compare/contrast table about simple machines onto a separate sheet of paper. Then complete it for each type of simple machine and add a title. (For more on Comparing and Contrasting, see the Skills Handbook.)

Simple Machine	Ideal Mechanical Advantage	Example
Inclined plane	Length of incline ÷ Height of incline	Ramp
a. ?	b. ?	c. ?

Reviewing Key Terms

Choose the letter of the best answer.

1. The amount of work done on an object is obtained by multiplying
   a. input force and output force.
   b. force and distance.
   c. time and force.
   d. efficiency and work.
2. The rate at which work is done is called
   a. output force.
   b. efficiency.
   c. power.
   d. mechanical advantage.
3. One way a machine can make work easier for you is by
   a. decreasing the amount of work you do.
   b. changing the direction of your force.
   c. increasing the amount of work required for a task.
   d. decreasing the friction you encounter.
4. The output force is greater than the input force for a
   a. pizza cutter.
   b. hockey stick.
   c. single fixed pulley.
   d. screw.
5. An example of a second-class lever is a
   a. seesaw.
   b. shovel.
   c. paddle.
   d. wheelbarrow.

If the statement is true, write *true*. If it is false, change the underlined word or words to make the statement true.

6. The SI unit of work is the newton.
7. The work you do on a machine is called the input work.
8. The ratio of output work to input work is mechanical advantage.
9. An inclined plane is a flat, sloped surface.
10. A pulley can be thought of as an inclined plane wrapped around a cylinder.

Writing in Science

Proposed Solution A community of people in Pennsylvania known as the Old Order Amish can build a wooden barn in a single day—without using electricity. Suppose you were faced with this task. Propose how you would use simple machines to help with the construction.

Discovery Channel School

Work and Machines

Video Preview
Video Field Trip
▶ Video Assessment

Review and Assessment

Checking Concepts

11. The mythical god Atlas was believed to hold the weight of the sky on his shoulders. Was Atlas performing any work? Explain.

12. The mechanical advantage of a machine is 3. If you exert an input force of 5 N, what output force is exerted by the machine?

13. Which has a greater mechanical advantage, a wedge that is 6 cm long and 3 cm wide, or a wedge that is 12 cm long and 4 cm wide? Explain your answer.

14. Why will decreasing the radius of the axle improve the mechanical advantage of a wheel and axle?

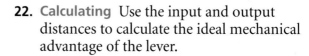

15. Describe a lever in your body. Locate the input force, output force, and fulcrum.

Thinking Critically

16. Relating Cause and Effect Describe the relationship between friction and the efficiency of a machine.

17. Classifying What type of simple machine would be used to lower an empty bucket into a well and then lift the bucket full of water?

18. Applying Concepts To open a door, you push on the part of the door that is farthest from the hinges. Why would it be harder to open the door if you pushed on the center of it?

19. Interpreting Diagrams Which ramp has the greater ideal mechanical advantage?

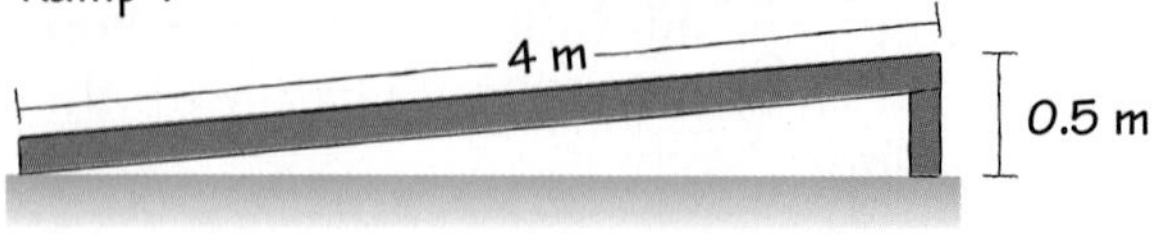

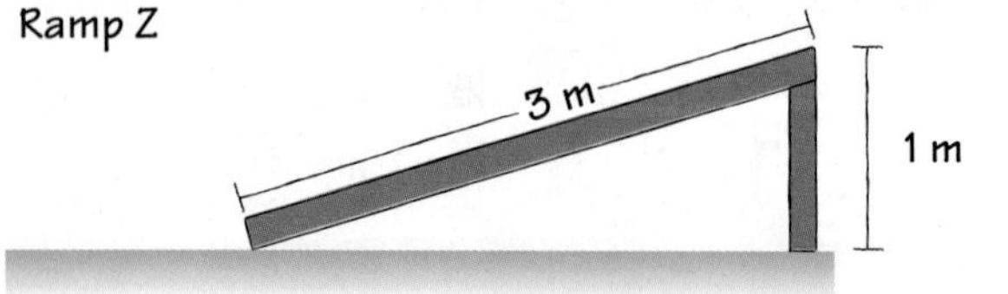

Math Practice

20. Calculating Power A bulldozer does 72,000 J of work in 48 seconds. How much power does the bulldozer use?

21. Calculating Efficiency A machine with 75% efficiency does 3,300 J of work. Using the machine, how much work did you do?

Applying Skills

Use the illustration to answer Questions 22–25.

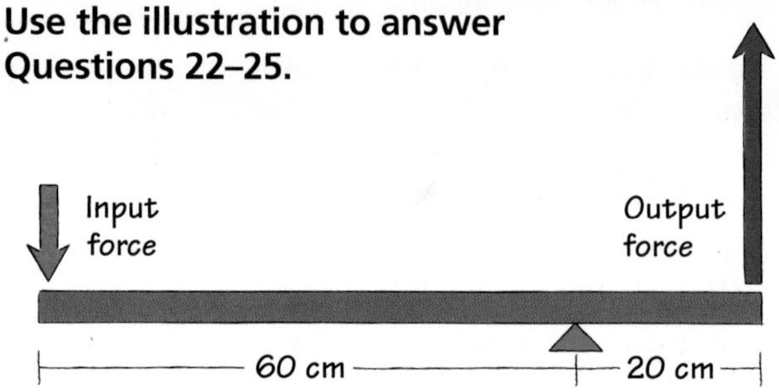

22. Calculating Use the input and output distances to calculate the ideal mechanical advantage of the lever.

23. Predicting What would the ideal mechanical advantage be if the distance from the fulcrum to the input force were 20 cm? 40 cm? 80 cm?

24. Graphing Use your answers to Questions 22 and 23 to graph the distance from the fulcrum to the input force on the *x*-axis and the ideal mechanical advantage on the *y*-axis.

25. Interpreting Data What does your graph show you about the relationship between the ideal mechanical advantage of a first-class lever and the distance between the fulcrum and the input force?

Lab zone Chapter **Project**

Performance Assessment Finalize your design and build your machine. Consider how you can improve the machine's efficiency. Check all measurements and calculations. Does it lift the soup can at least 5 cm? Is it made of two or more simple machines? When you show your machine to the class, explain why you built it as you did.

Standardized Test Prep

Test-Taking Tip

Reading All the Answer Choices

For multiple-choice questions, read every answer choice before you give your answer. Some choices may contain part of the answer but may not include all the information that the question asks for. Also look out for questions that may be answered by "all of the above." In this case, all of the answer choices may be correct in some way, but "all of the above" may be the only complete answer.

Sample Question

Why does it take more work to move a 2.3-kg bag of birdseed 100 m than it takes to move a 1.6-kg bag of cat food 50 m?

A The birdseed is packed in the store.
B The birdseed has to be moved farther.
C The cat food has less mass than the birdseed.
D The birdseed has greater mass and has to be moved farther.

Answer

The correct answer is **D.** Answer **A** is not related to the question. Answers **B** and **C** are both true, but provide only part of the correct answer. Only answer **D** is completely correct. It mentions both the mass of the object, which is needed to determine force, and the distance the object is to be moved. Both force and distance affect the amount of work.

Choose the letter of the best answer.

1. What simple machine is used in *all* of the following jobs: moving a flag to the top of a flagpole, lifting equipment with a construction crane, and using a block and tackle to move a crate?

A lever
B pulley
C wedge
D wheel and axle

2. The table below shows the input work and output work for four different pulleys. Which pulley has the highest efficiency?

Work of Different Pulleys

Pulley	Input Work	Output Work
Fixed pulley A	20,000 J	8,000 J
Fixed pulley B	20,000 J	10,000 J
Movable pulley	20,000 J	12,000 J
Block and tackle	20,000 J	16,000 J

F Fixed pulley A
G Fixed pulley B
H Movable pulley
J Block and tackle

3. Which is the *best* definition of a machine?

A A machine is a time-saving device that uses motors and gears.
B A machine changes the amount of input force.
C A machine makes work easier by changing force, distance, or direction.
D A machine can be either simple or compound.

4. Which of the following will increase the ideal mechanical advantage of a wheel and axle?

F increasing the wheel's radius
G decreasing the wheel's radius
H increasing the axle's radius
J increasing the wheel's radius and the axle's radius equally

5. Which activity describes work being done on an object?

A walking a dog on a leash
B lifting a bag of groceries
C holding up an umbrella
D pressing a stamp onto an envelope

Constructed Response

6. Explain why an engineer would design a road to wind around a mountain rather than go straight up the side. Show how this design would be better.

Chapter 13 Energy

Chapter Preview

1. **What Is Energy?**
   Discover *How High Does a Ball Bounce?*
   Math Skills *Exponents*

2. **Forms of Energy**
   Discover *What Makes a Flashlight Shine?*
   Analyzing Data *Calculating Mechanical Energy*
   Skills Lab *Can You Feel the Power?*

3. **Energy Transformations and Conservation**
   Discover *What Would Make a Card Jump?*
   Skills Activity *Classifying*
   Active Art *Energy Transformations*
   Try This *Pendulum Swing*
   At-Home Activity *Hot Wire*
   Skills Lab *Soaring Straws*

4. **Energy and Fossil Fuels**
   Discover *What Is a Fuel?*
   Skills Activity *Graphing*
   At-Home Activity *Burning Fossils*

interactive Textbook

Cars powered by the sun's energy race in Suzuka, Japan. ▶

Discovery Channel School

Energy

- ▶ Video Preview
- Video Field Trip
- Video Assessment

Lab zone™ Chapter **Project**

Design and Build a Roller Coaster

In this chapter, you will learn about energy, the forms it takes, and how it is transformed and conserved. You will use what you learn to design and construct your own roller coaster.

Your Goal To design and construct a roller coaster that uses kinetic and potential energy to move

Your roller coaster must

- be no wider than 2 meters and be easily disassembled and reassembled
- have a first hill with a height of 1 meter and have at least two additional hills
- have an object that moves along the entire track without stopping
- follow the safety guidelines in Appendix A

Plan It! Brainstorm the characteristics of a fun roller coaster. Consider how fast a roller coaster moves and how its speed changes throughout the ride. Then choose materials for your roller coaster and sketch a design. When your teacher has approved your design, build your roller coaster. Experiment with different hill heights and inclines. Add turns and loops to determine their effect.

Section 1

What Is Energy?

Reading Preview

Key Concepts

- How are energy, work, and power related?
- What are the two basic kinds of energy?

Key Terms

- energy • kinetic energy
- potential energy
- gravitational potential energy
- elastic potential energy

Target Reading Skill

Using Prior Knowledge Before you read, look at the section headings and visuals to see what this section is about. Then write what you know about energy in a graphic organizer like the one below. As you read, write what you learn.

What You Know

1. The joule is the unit of work.
2.

What You Learned

1.
2.

Lab zone Discover Activity

How High Does a Ball Bounce?

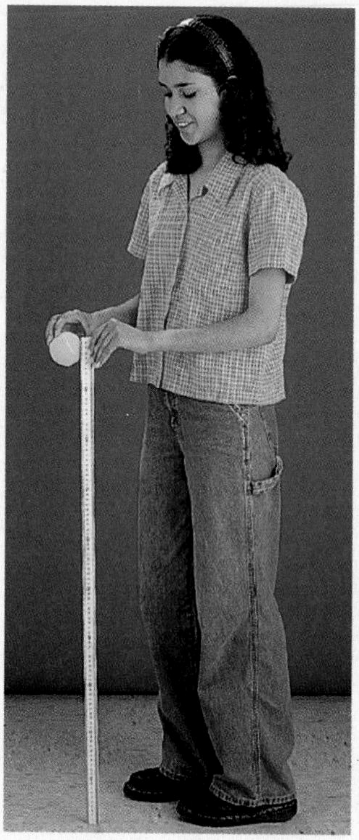

1. Hold a meter stick vertically, with the zero end on the ground.
2. Drop a tennis ball from the 50-cm mark and record the height to which it bounces.
3. Drop the tennis ball from the 100-cm mark and record the height to which it bounces.
4. Predict how high the ball will bounce if dropped from the 75-cm mark. Test your prediction.

Think It Over

Observing How does the height from which you drop the ball relate to the height to which the ball bounces?

Brilliant streaks of lightning flash across the night sky. The wind howls, and thunder cracks and rumbles. Then a sound like a runaway locomotive approaches, growing louder each second. Whirling winds rush through the town. Roofs are lifted off of buildings. Cars are thrown about like toys. Then, in minutes, the tornado is gone.

The next morning, a light breeze carries leaves past the debris. The wind that destroyed buildings hours before is now barely strong enough to move a leaf. Wind is just moving air, but it has energy.

When a breeze does work lifting leaves, it transfers energy to them. ▶

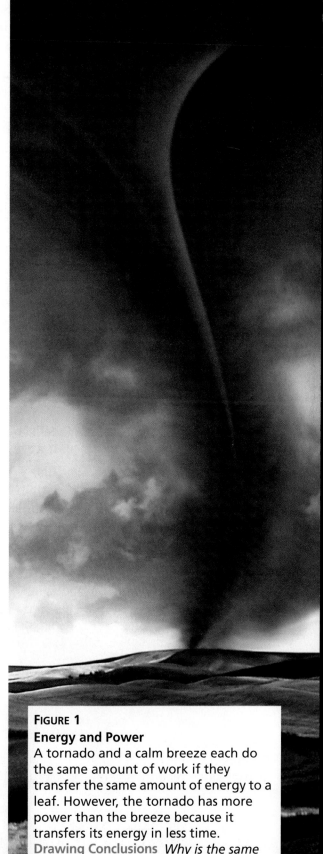

Energy, Work, and Power

When wind moves a house, or even a leaf, it causes a change. In this case, the change is in the position of the object. Recall that work is done when a force moves an object through a distance. The ability to do work or cause change is called **energy.** So the wind has energy.

Work and Energy When an object or living thing does work on another object, some of its energy is transferred to that object. You can think of work, then, as the transfer of energy. When energy is transferred, the object upon which the work is done gains energy. Energy is measured in joules—the same units as work.

Power and Energy You may recall that power is the rate at which work is done. **If the transfer of energy is work, then power is the rate at which energy is transferred, or the amount of energy transferred in a unit of time.**

$$\text{Power} = \frac{\text{Energy transferred}}{\text{Time}}$$

Power is involved whenever energy is being transferred. For example, a calm breeze has power when it transfers energy to lift a leaf a certain distance. The tornado in Figure 1 transfers the same amount of energy when it lifts the leaf the same distance. However, the tornado has more power than the breeze because it transfers energy to the leaf in less time.

Reading Checkpoint What is power in terms of energy?

Kinetic Energy

Two basic kinds of energy are kinetic energy and potential energy. Whether energy is kinetic or potential depends on whether an object is moving or not.

A moving object, such as the wind, can do work when it strikes another object and moves it some distance. Because the moving object does work, it has energy. The energy an object has due to its motion is called **kinetic energy.** The word *kinetic* comes from the Greek word *kinetos*, which means "moving."

FIGURE 1
Energy and Power
A tornado and a calm breeze each do the same amount of work if they transfer the same amount of energy to a leaf. However, the tornado has more power than the breeze because it transfers its energy in less time.
Drawing Conclusions *Why is the same amount of work done on the leaf?*

Math Skills

Exponents

An exponent tells how many times a number is used as a factor. For example, 3×3 can be written as 3^2. You read this number as "three squared." An exponent of 2 indicates that the number 3 is used as a factor two times. To find the value of a squared number, multiply the number by itself.

$$3^2 = 3 \times 3 = 9$$

Practice Problem What is the value of the number 8^2?

Factors Affecting Kinetic Energy The kinetic energy of an object depends on both its mass and its velocity. Kinetic energy increases as mass increases. For example, think about rolling a bowling ball and a golf ball down a bowling lane at the same velocity, as shown in Figure 2. The bowling ball has more mass than the golf ball. Therefore, you use more energy to roll the bowling ball than to roll the golf ball. The bowling ball is more likely to knock down the pins because it has more kinetic energy than the golf ball.

Kinetic energy also increases when velocity increases. For example, suppose you have two identical bowling balls and you roll one ball so it moves at a greater velocity than the other. You must throw the faster ball harder to give it the greater velocity. In other words, you transfer more energy to it. Therefore, the faster ball has more kinetic energy.

Calculating Kinetic Energy There is a mathematical relationship between kinetic energy, mass, and velocity.

$$\text{Kinetic energy} = \frac{1}{2} \times \text{Mass} \times \text{Velocity}^2$$

Do changes in velocity and mass have the same effect on kinetic energy? No—changing the velocity of an object will have a greater effect on its kinetic energy than changing its mass. This is because velocity is squared in the kinetic energy equation. For instance, doubling the mass of an object will double its kinetic energy. But doubling its velocity will quadruple its kinetic energy.

Reading Checkpoint **Which has a greater effect on an object's kinetic energy—its mass or its velocity?**

FIGURE 2
Kinetic Energy
Kinetic energy increases as mass and velocity increase.
Predicting *In each example, which object will transfer more energy to the pins? Why?*

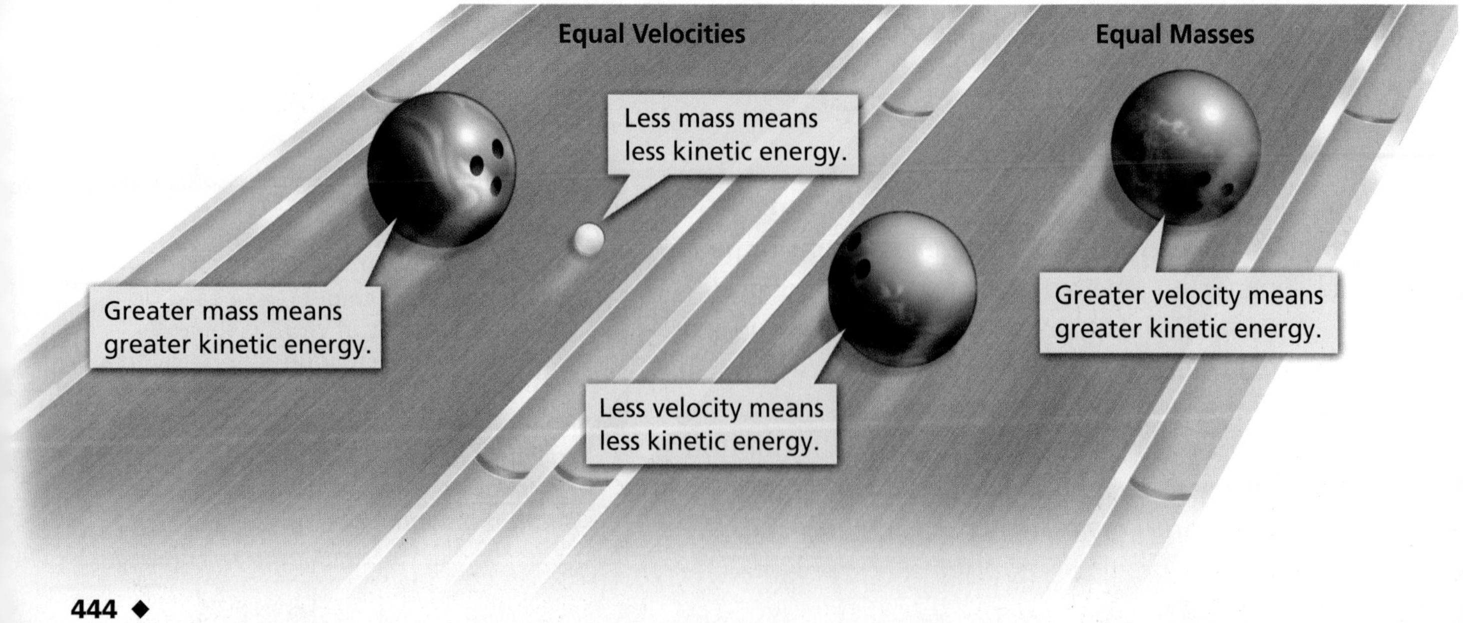
Equal Velocities
Equal Masses
Less mass means less kinetic energy.
Greater mass means greater kinetic energy.
Less velocity means less kinetic energy.
Greater velocity means greater kinetic energy.

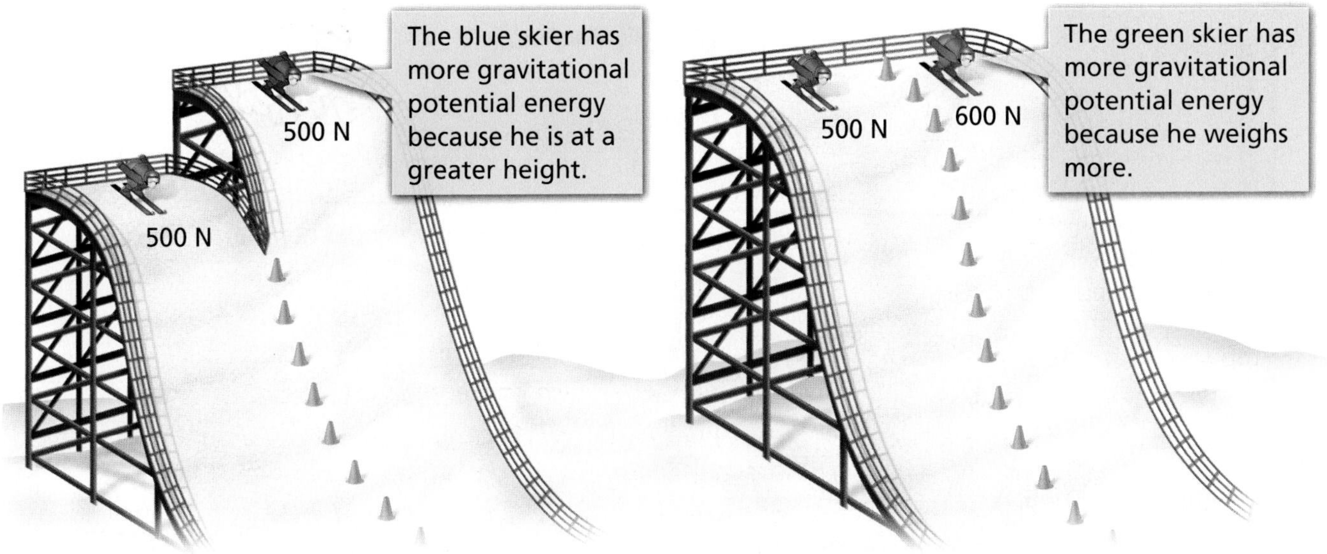
500 N
500 N
The blue skier has more gravitational potential energy because he is at a greater height.
500 N
600 N
The green skier has more gravitational potential energy because he weighs more.

Potential Energy

An object does not have to be moving to have energy. Some objects have stored energy as a result of their positions or shapes. When you lift a book up to your desk from the floor or compress a spring to wind a toy, you transfer energy to it. The energy you transfer is stored, or held in readiness. It might be used later when the book falls to the floor or the spring unwinds. Stored energy that results from the position or shape of an object is called **potential energy.** This type of energy has the potential to do work.

Gravitational Potential Energy Potential energy related to an object's height is called **gravitational potential energy.** The gravitational potential energy of an object is equal to the work done to lift it. Remember that Work = Force × Distance. The force you use to lift the object is equal to its weight. The distance you move the object is its height. You can calculate an object's gravitational potential energy using this formula.

Gravitational potential energy = Weight × Height

For example, the red skier on the left in Figure 3 weighs 500 newtons. If the ski jump is 40 meters high, then the skier has 500 newtons × 40 meters, or 20,000 J, of gravitational potential energy.

The more an object weighs, or the greater the object's height, the greater its gravitational potential energy. At the same height, a 600-newton skier has more gravitational potential energy than a 500-newton skier. Similarly, a 500-newton skier has more gravitational potential energy on a high ski jump than on a low one.

FIGURE 3
Gravitational Potential Energy
Gravitational potential energy increases as weight and height increase.
Interpreting Diagrams *Does the red skier have more gravitational potential energy on the higher ski jump or the lower one? Why?*

Go Online SciLinks NSTA
For: Links on energy
Visit: www.SciLinks.org
Web Code: scn-1351

The farther the string is pulled, the greater the bow's elastic potential energy.
Pulling the string changes the bow's shape and stores elastic potential energy.

FIGURE 4
Elastic Potential Energy
The energy stored in a stretched object, such as a bow, is elastic potential energy. **Interpreting Photographs** *When the energy stored in the bow is released, how is it used?*

Elastic Potential Energy An object gains a different type of potential energy when it is stretched. The potential energy associated with objects that can be stretched or compressed is called **elastic potential energy.** For example, when an archer pulls back an arrow, the bow changes shape. The bow now has potential energy. When the archer releases the string, the stored energy sends the arrow flying to its target.

Reading Checkpoint **What type of energy does a bow have when you pull back an arrow?**

Section 1 Assessment

Target Reading Skill

Using Prior Knowledge Review your graphic organizer and revise it based on what you just learned in the section.

Reviewing Key Concepts

1. a. **Defining** What is energy?
   b. **Describing** How are energy, work, and power related?
   c. **Applying Concepts** If a handsaw does the same amount of work on a log as a chainsaw does, which has a greater power? Why?
2. a. **Identifying** What is kinetic energy? What is potential energy?
   b. **Explaining** What factors affect an object's kinetic energy?
   c. **Problem Solving** At a given height above Earth, how would you determine the potential energy of a sky diver? The kinetic energy of a sky diver?

Math Practice

3. **Exponents** What is the value of the number 10^2?
4. **Exponents** What number when squared gives you the value 36?

Section 2

Forms of Energy

Reading Preview

Key Concepts

- How can you determine an object's mechanical energy?
- What are some forms of energy associated with the particles that make up objects?

Key Terms

- mechanical energy
- thermal energy
- electrical energy
- chemical energy
- nuclear energy
- electromagnetic energy

Target Reading Skill

Building Vocabulary After you read the section, reread the paragraphs that contain definitions of Key Terms. Use the information you have learned to write a definition of each Key Term in your own words.

Lab zone Discover Activity

What Makes a Flashlight Shine?

1. Remove the batteries from a flashlight and examine them. Think about what type of energy is stored in the batteries.
2. Replace the batteries and turn on the flashlight. What type of energy do you observe?
3. After a few minutes, place your hand near the bulb of the flashlight. What type of energy do you feel?

Think It Over

Inferring Describe how you think a flashlight works in terms of energy. Where does the energy come from? Where does the energy go?

You are on the edge of your seat as the quarterback drops back, steps forward, and then launches a deep pass. The ball soars down the field and drops into the receiver's hands. The electronic scoreboard flashes TOUCHDOWN. You jump to your feet and cheer!

As the crowd settles back down, you shiver. The sun is setting, and the afternoon is growing cool. A vendor hands you a hot dog, and its heat helps warm your hands. Suddenly, the stadium lights switch on. You can see the players more clearly as they line up for the next play.

The thrown football, the scoreboard, the sun, the hot dog, and the stadium lights all have energy. You have energy, too! Energy comes in many different forms.

Mechanical Energy

Think about the pass thrown by the quarterback. A football thrown by a quarterback has mechanical energy. So does a moving car or a trophy on a shelf. The form of energy associated with the position and motion of an object is called **mechanical energy.**

◀ **A quarterback transfers mechanical energy to the football.**

Go Online
SCI LINKS NSTA
For: Links on forms of energy
Visit: www.SciLinks.org
Web Code: scn-1352

An object's mechanical energy is a combination of its potential energy and kinetic energy. For example, a thrown football's mechanical energy is a combination of its position above the ground and its motion. Sometimes an object's mechanical energy is its kinetic energy or potential energy only. A car moving along a flat road possesses kinetic energy only. A trophy resting on a shelf has gravitational potential energy only. But both have mechanical energy.

You can find an object's mechanical energy by adding the object's kinetic energy and potential energy.

Mechanical Energy = Potential energy + Kinetic energy

You can use this formula to find the mechanical energy of the football in Figure 5. The football has 32 joules of potential energy due to its position above the ground. It also has 45 joules of kinetic energy due to its motion. The total mechanical energy of the football is 32 joules + 45 joules, or 77 joules.

An object with mechanical energy can do work on another object. In fact, you can think of mechanical energy as the ability to do work. The more mechanical energy an object has, the more work it can do.

Reading Checkpoint **What two forms of energy combine to make mechanical energy?**

FIGURE 5
Mechanical Energy
To find the football's mechanical energy, add its kinetic energy to its potential energy. **Observing** *Why does the football have potential energy?*

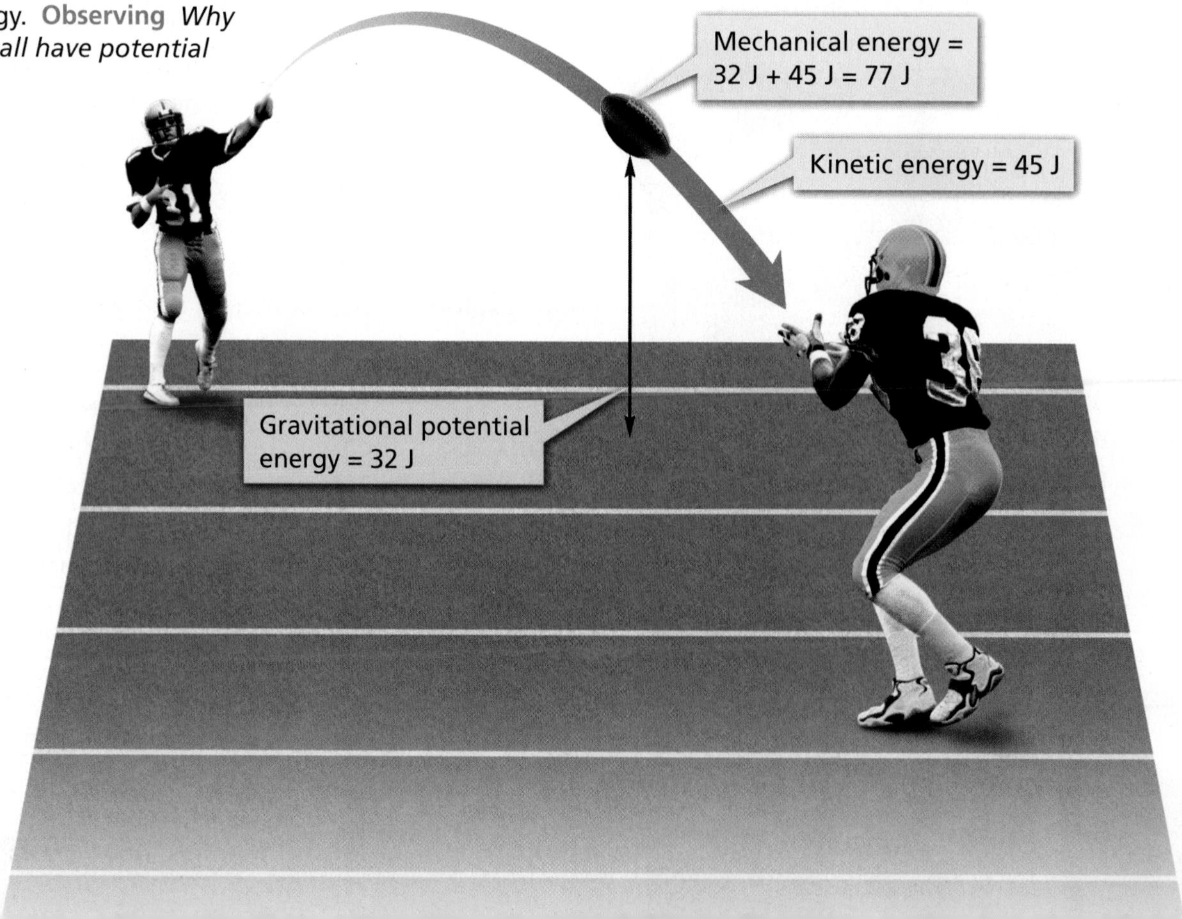

Math Analyzing Data

Calculating Mechanical Energy

The kinetic energy of a 500-N diver during a dive from a 10-m platform was measured. These data are shown in the graph.

1. **Reading Graphs** According to the graph, how much kinetic energy does the diver have at 8 m?
2. **Calculating** Using the graph, find the kinetic energy of the diver at 6 m. Then calculate the diver's potential energy at that point.
3. **Inferring** The mechanical energy of the diver is the same at every height. What is the mechanical energy of the diver?

Energy of a Diver

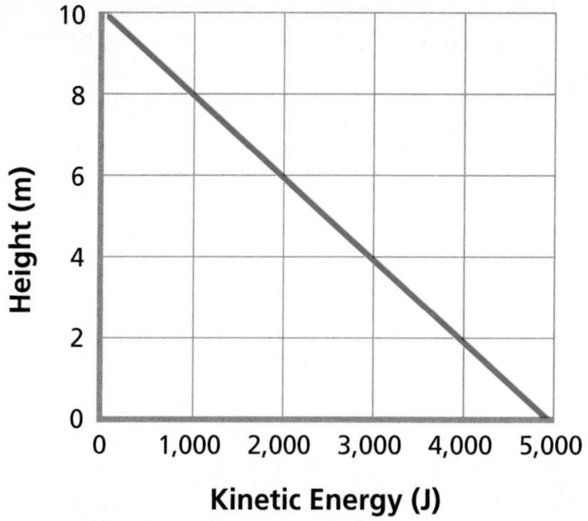

Other Forms of Energy

So far in this chapter, you have read about energy that involves the motion and position of an object. But an object can have other forms of kinetic and potential energy. Most of these other forms are associated with the particles that make up objects. These particles are far too small to see. **Forms of energy associated with the particles of objects include thermal energy, electrical energy, chemical energy, nuclear energy, and electromagnetic energy.**

Thermal Energy All objects are made up of particles called atoms and molecules. Because these particles are constantly in motion, they have kinetic energy. The faster the particles move, the more kinetic energy they have. These particles are arranged in specific ways in different objects. Therefore, they also have potential energy. The total potential and kinetic energy of the particles in an object is called **thermal energy.** Look at Figure 6. Even though the lava may be flowing slowly down the volcano, its particles are moving quickly. Because the particles have a large amount of kinetic energy, the lava has a large amount of thermal energy.

If you've ever eaten ice cream on a hot day, you've experienced thermal energy. Fast-moving particles in the warm air make the particles of ice cream move faster. As the kinetic energy of the particles increases, so does the thermal energy of the ice cream. Eventually, the ice cream melts.

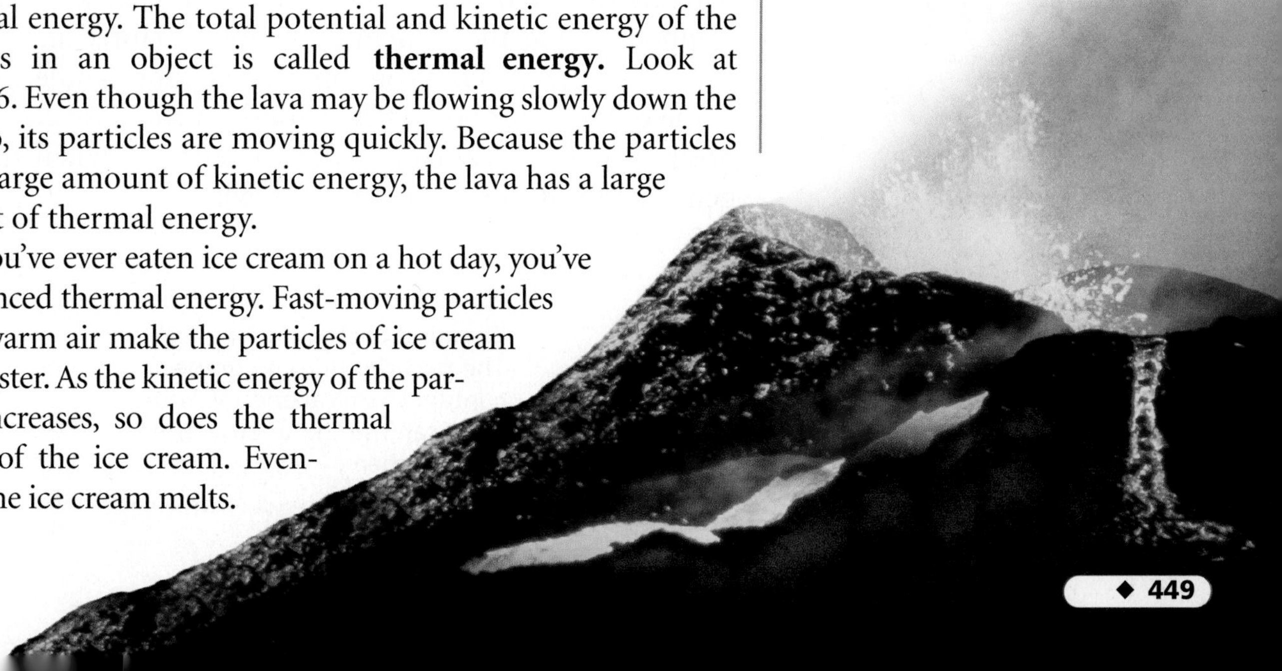

FIGURE 6
Thermal Energy
The lava flowing from this volcano has a large amount of thermal energy. **Predicting** *Will the thermal energy of the lava increase or decrease as it flows away from the volcano?*

FIGURE 7
Electrical Energy
Electric charges in lightning carry electrical energy.

Electrical Energy When you receive a shock from a metal doorknob, you are experiencing electrical energy. The energy of electric charges is **electrical energy.** Depending on whether the charges are moving or stored, electrical energy can be a form of kinetic or potential energy. The lightning in Figure 7 is a form of electrical energy. You rely on electrical energy from batteries or electrical lines to run devices such as flashlights, handheld games, and radios.

Chemical Energy Almost everything you see, touch, or taste is composed of chemical compounds. Chemical compounds are made up of atoms and molecules. Bonds between the atoms and molecules hold chemical compounds together. These bonds have chemical energy. **Chemical energy** is potential energy stored in the chemical bonds that hold chemical compounds together. Chemical energy is stored in the foods you eat, in the matches you can use to light a candle, and even in the cells of your body. When bonds in chemical compounds break, new chemical compounds may form. When this happens, chemical energy may be released.

FIGURE 8
Chemical Energy
The particles in these grapes contain chemical energy. Your body can use this energy after you eat them.

Nuclear Energy A type of potential energy called **nuclear energy** is stored in the nucleus of an atom. Nuclear energy is released during a nuclear reaction. One kind of nuclear reaction, known as nuclear fission, occurs when a nucleus splits. Nuclear power plants use fission reactions to produce electricity. Another kind of reaction, known as nuclear fusion, occurs when the nuclei of atoms fuse, or join together. Nuclear fusion reactions occur continuously in the sun, releasing tremendous amounts of energy.

Electromagnetic Energy The sunlight that you see each day is a form of **electromagnetic energy.** Electromagnetic energy travels in waves. These waves have some electrical properties and some magnetic properties.

The microwaves you use to cook your food and the X-rays doctors use to examine patients are types of electromagnetic energy. Other forms of electromagnetic energy include ultraviolet radiation, infrared radiation, and radio waves.

Reading Checkpoint **What form of energy are microwaves?**

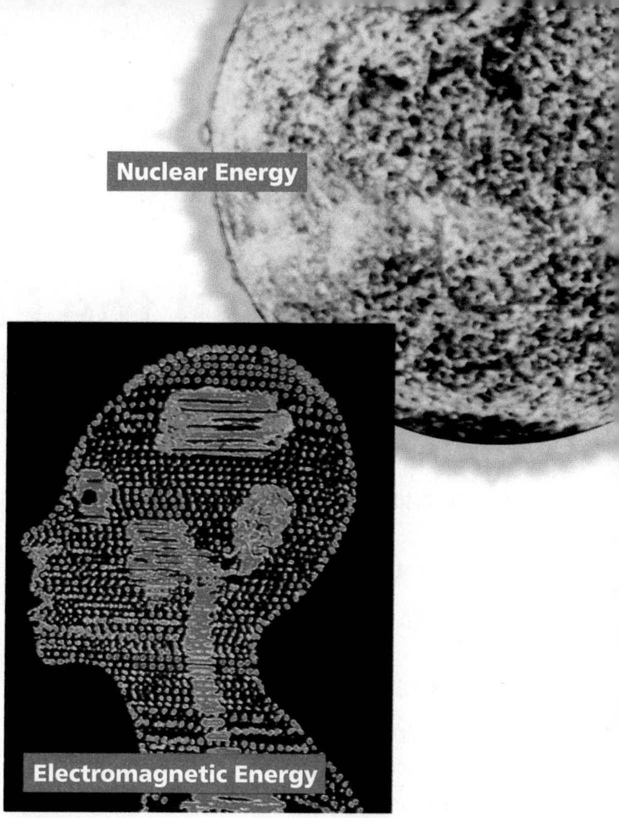

FIGURE 9
Nuclear and Electromagnetic Energy
The sun is a source of nuclear energy. Doctors use X-rays, a form of electromagnetic energy, when taking a CT scan to look for brain disorders. **Observing** *What other forms of energy from the sun can you observe?*

Section 2 Assessment

Target Reading Skill **Building Vocabulary** Use your definitions to help answer the questions.

Reviewing Key Concepts

1. a. **Defining** What is mechanical energy?
   b. **Drawing Conclusions** If an object's mechanical energy is equal to its potential energy, how much kinetic energy does the object have? How do you know?
   c. **Calculating** If the kinetic energy of a falling apple is 5.2 J and its potential energy is 3.5 J, what is its mechanical energy?
2. a. **Listing** List the five forms of energy associated with the particles that make up objects.
   b. **Explaining** Why do the particles of objects have both kinetic and potential energy?
   c. **Classifying** What kind of energy do you experience when you eat a peanut butter and jelly sandwich?

Writing in Science

Detailed Observation In terms of energy, think about what happens when you eat a hot meal. Describe all the different forms of energy that you experience. For example, if you are eating under a lamp, its electromagnetic energy helps you see the food. Explain the source of each form of energy.

Lab zone **Skills Lab**

Can You Feel the Power?

Problem

Can you change your power while exercising?

Skills Focus

calculating, interpreting data

Materials

- calculator
- meter stick
- stopwatch or clock with a second hand
- board, about 2.5 cm × 30 cm × 120 cm
- 18–20 books, each about 2 cm thick

Procedure

1. Construct a step by making two identical stacks of books. Each stack should be about 20 cm high. Place a board securely on top of the stacks of books so that the ends of the board are even with the outside edges of the books. **CAUTION:** *Be sure to have your partners hold the board steady and level throughout the procedure.*
2. Copy the data table into your notebook.
3. You gain gravitational potential energy every time you step up. Gaining energy requires work.
   Work = Weight × Height = Gravitational potential energy
   a. Assume your weight is 400 N and your partners' weights are 425 N and 450 N.
   b. Measure the vertical distance in centimeters from the floor to the top of the board. Convert to meters by dividing by 100 and record this height in the data table.
4. Calculate the work you do in stepping up onto the board once. Then calculate the work you do stepping up onto the board 20 times. Record both answers in your data table.
5. Step up onto the board with both feet and then step backwards off the board onto the floor. This up and down motion is one repetition. Make sure you are comfortable with the motion.
6. Have one partner time how long it takes you to do 20 repetitions performed at a constant speed. Count out loud to help the timer keep track of the number of repetitions. Record the time in your data table.
7. Calculate the power over 20 repetitions. (Power = Energy transferred ÷ Time.) Predict how your results will change if you step up and down at different speeds.
8. Repeat Steps 6 and 7, but climb the step more slowly than you did the first time. Record the new data in the Trial 2 row of your data table.
9. Switch roles with your partners and repeat Steps 3 through 8 with a different weight from Step 3(a).

Data Table

Trial	Weight (N)	Height of Board (m)	Time for 20 Repetitions (s)	Work for 1 Repetition (J)	Work for 20 Repetitions (J)	Power (W)
Student 1, Trial 1						
Student 1, Trial 2						

Analyze and Conclude

1. Calculating What is the gravitational potential energy gained from stepping up onto the board? How does this compare to the amount of work required to step up onto the board?
2. Interpreting Data Compare the amount of work you did during your first and second trials.
3. Interpreting Data Compare the power during your first and second trials.
4. Drawing Conclusions Did you and your partners all do the same amount of work? Did you all do work at the same rate? Explain your answers.
5. Communicating Often, a physical therapist will want to increase a patient's power. Write a letter to a physical therapist suggesting how he or she could use music to change a patient's power.

Design an Experiment

Design an experiment to test two other ways a physical therapist could change the power output of her patients. *Obtain your teacher's permission before carrying out your investigation.*

Section 3

Energy Transformations and Conservation

Reading Preview

Key Concepts

- How are different forms of energy related?
- What is a common energy transformation?
- What is the law of conservation of energy?

Key Terms

- energy transformation
- law of conservation of energy
- matter

Target Reading Skill

Asking Questions Before you read, preview the red headings and ask a *what* or *how* question for each heading. As you read, write the answers to your questions.

Energy Transformations

Question	Answer
What is an energy transformation?	An energy transformation is . . .

▼ **Niagara Falls is more than 50 meters high.**

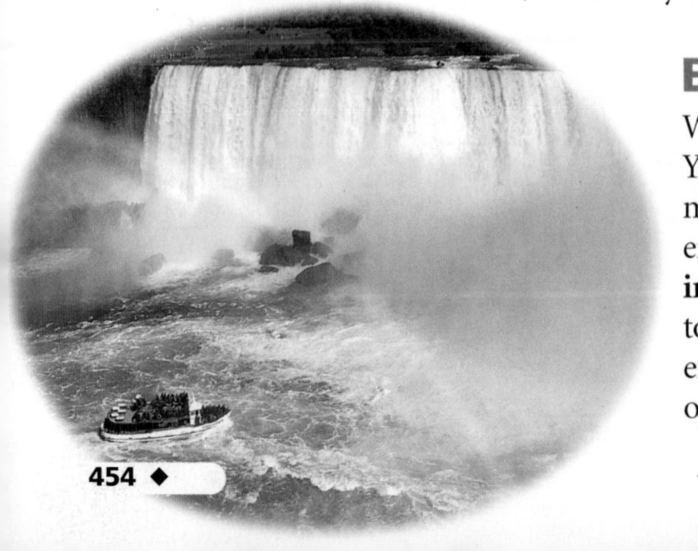

Lab zone Discover **Activity**

What Would Make a Card Jump?

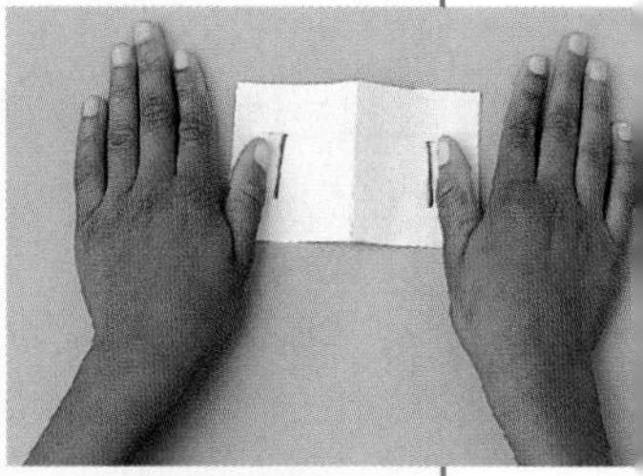

1. Fold an index card in half.
2. In the edge opposite the fold, cut two slits that are about 2 cm long and 2 cm apart.
3. Keep the card folded and loop a rubber band through the slits. With the fold toward you, gently open the card like a tent and flatten it against your desk.
4. Predict what will happen to the card if you let go. Then test your prediction.

Think It Over

Drawing Conclusions Describe what happened to the card. Based on your observations, what is the relationship between potential and kinetic energy?

The spray bounces off your raincoat as you look up at the millions of liters of water plunging toward you. The roar of the water is deafening. Are you doomed? Fortunately not—you are on a sightseeing boat at the foot of the mighty Niagara Falls. The waterfall carries the huge amount of water that drains from the upper Great Lakes. It lies on the border between Canada and the United States.

What many visitors don't know, however, is that Niagara Falls serves as much more than just a spectacular view. The Niagara Falls area is the center of a network of electrical power lines. Water that is diverted above the falls is used to generate electricity for much of the surrounding region.

Energy Transformations

What does flowing water have to do with electricity? You may already know that the mechanical energy of moving water can be transformed into electrical energy. **Most forms of energy can be transformed into other forms.** A change from one form of energy to another is called an **energy transformation.** Some energy changes involve single transformations, while others involve many transformations.

A cell phone transforms electrical energy to electromagnetic energy.
Your body transforms the chemical energy in food to mechanical energy.
A toaster transforms electrical energy to thermal energy.

FIGURE 10
Common Energy Transformations
Every day, energy transformations are all around you. Some of these transformations happen inside you! **Observing** *What other energy transformations do you observe every day?*

Single Transformations Sometimes, one form of energy needs to be transformed into another to get work done. You are already familiar with many such energy transformations. For example, a toaster transforms electrical energy to thermal energy to toast your bread. A cell phone transforms electrical energy to electromagnetic energy that travels to other phones.

Your body transforms the chemical energy in your food to mechanical energy you need to move your muscles. Chemical energy in food is also transformed to the thermal energy your body uses to maintain its temperature.

Multiple Transformations Often, a series of energy transformations is needed to do work. For example, the mechanical energy used to strike a match is transformed first to thermal energy. The thermal energy causes the particles in the match to release stored chemical energy, which is transformed to thermal energy and the electromagnetic energy you see as light.

In a car engine, another series of energy conversions occurs. Electrical energy produces a spark. The thermal energy of the spark releases chemical energy in the fuel. The fuel's chemical energy in turn becomes thermal energy. Thermal energy is converted to mechanical energy used to move the car, and to electrical energy to produce more sparks.

Reading Checkpoint **What is an example of a multiple transformation of energy?**

Lab zone **Skills Activity**

Classifying

Many common devices transform electrical energy into other forms. Think about the following devices in terms of energy transformations.

- steam iron
- ceiling fan
- digital clock
- dryer

For each device, describe which form or forms of energy the electrical energy becomes. Do these devices produce single or multiple transformations of energy?

FIGURE 11
Juggling The kinetic energy of an orange thrown into the air becomes gravitational potential energy. Its potential energy becomes kinetic energy as it falls.

Transformations Between Potential and Kinetic Energy

One of the most common energy transformations is the transformation between potential energy and kinetic energy. In waterfalls such as Niagara Falls, potential energy is transformed to kinetic energy. The water at the top of the falls has gravitational potential energy. As the water plunges, its velocity increases. Its potential energy becomes kinetic energy.

Energy Transformation in Juggling Any object that rises or falls experiences a change in its kinetic and gravitational potential energy. Look at the orange in Figure 11. When it moves, the orange has kinetic energy. As it rises, it slows down. Its potential energy increases as its kinetic energy decreases. At the highest point in its path, it stops moving. Since there is no motion, the orange no longer has kinetic energy. But it does have potential energy. As the orange falls, the energy transformation is reversed. Kinetic energy increases while potential energy decreases.

Energy Transformation in a Pendulum In a pendulum, a continuous transformation between kinetic and potential energy takes place. At the highest point in its swing, the pendulum in Figure 12 has no movement, so it only has gravitational potential energy. As it swings downward, it speeds up. Its potential energy is transformed to kinetic energy. The pendulum is at its greatest speed at the bottom of its swing. There, all its energy is kinetic energy.

Go Online
active art
For: Energy Transformations activity
Visit: PHSchool.com
Web Code: cgp-3053

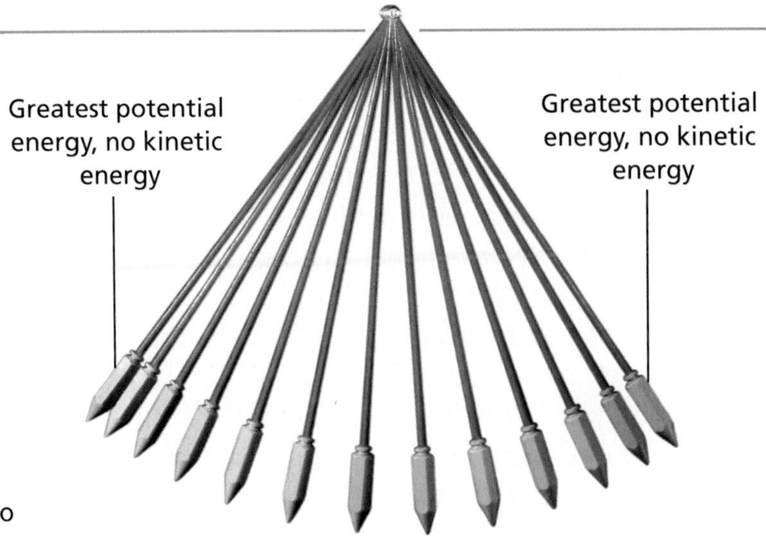

FIGURE 12
Pendulum
A pendulum continuously transforms energy from kinetic to potential energy and back.
Interpreting Diagrams *At what two points is the pendulum's potential energy greatest?*

Energy transformations enable this athlete to vault more than six meters into the air.

As the pendulum swings to the other side, its height increases. The pendulum regains gravitational potential energy and loses kinetic energy. At the top of its swing, it comes to a stop again. And so the pattern of energy transformation continues.

Energy Transformation in a Pole Vault A pole-vaulter transforms kinetic energy to elastic potential energy, which then becomes gravitational potential energy. The pole-vaulter you see in Figure 13 has kinetic energy as he runs forward. When the pole-vaulter plants the pole to jump, his velocity decreases and the pole bends. His kinetic energy is transformed to elastic potential energy in the pole. As the pole straightens out, the pole-vaulter is lifted high into the air. The elastic potential energy of the pole is transformed to the gravitational potential energy of the pole-vaulter. Once he is over the bar, the pole-vaulter's gravitational potential energy is transformed back into kinetic energy as he falls toward the safety cushion.

Reading Checkpoint **What kind of energy lifts a pole-vaulter over the bar?**

Discovery Channel School

Energy

Video Preview
▶ Video Field Trip
Video Assessment

Lab zone Try This **Activity**

Pendulum Swing

1. Set up a pendulum using washers or a rubber stopper, string, a ring stand, and a clamp.
2. Pull the pendulum back so that it makes a 45° angle with the vertical. Measure the height of the stopper. Release it and observe how high it swings.

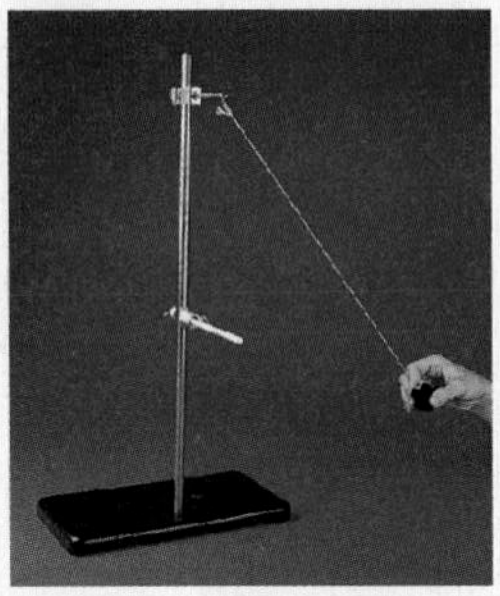

3. Use a second clamp to reduce the length of the pendulum as shown. The pendulum will run into the second clamp at the bottom of its swing.
4. Pull the pendulum back to the same height as you did the first time. Predict how high the pendulum will swing. Then set it in motion and observe.

Observing How high did the pendulum swing in each case? Explain your observations.

Conservation of Energy

If you set a spinning top in motion, will the top remain in motion forever? No, it will not. Then what happens to its energy? Is the energy destroyed? Again, the answer is no. The **law of conservation of energy** states that when one form of energy is transformed to another, no energy is destroyed in the process. **According to the law of conservation of energy, energy cannot be created or destroyed.** So the total amount of energy is the same before and after any transformation. If you add up all the new forms of energy after a transformation, all of the original energy will be accounted for.

Energy and Friction So what happens to the energy of the top in Figure 14? As the top spins, it encounters friction with the floor and friction from the air. Whenever a moving object experiences friction, some of its kinetic energy is transformed into thermal energy. So, the mechanical energy of the spinning top is transformed to thermal energy. The top slows and eventually falls on its side, but its energy is not destroyed—it is transformed.

The fact that friction transforms mechanical energy to thermal energy should not surprise you. After all, you take advantage of such thermal energy when you rub your cold hands together to warm them up. The fact that friction transforms mechanical energy to thermal energy explains why no machine is 100 percent efficient. You may recall that the output work of any real machine is always less than the input work. This reduced efficiency occurs because some mechanical energy is always transformed into thermal energy due to friction.

FIGURE 14
Conservation of Energy
A spinning top's kinetic energy is not lost. It is transformed into thermal energy through friction.
Applying Concepts *How much of the top's kinetic energy becomes thermal energy?*

Energy and Matter You might have heard of Albert Einstein's theory of relativity. His theory stated that energy *can* sometimes be created—by destroying matter! **Matter** is anything that has mass and takes up space. All objects are made up of matter.

Just as one form of energy can be transformed to other forms, Einstein discovered that matter can be transformed to energy. In fact, destroying just a small amount of matter releases a huge amount of energy.

Einstein's discovery meant that the law of conservation of energy had to be adjusted. In some situations, energy alone is not conserved. However, since matter can be transformed to energy, scientists say matter and energy together are always conserved.

Reading Checkpoint — **How can energy be created?**

FIGURE 15
Albert Einstein
Einstein published his theory of special relativity in 1905.

Section 3 Assessment

Target Reading Skill Asking Questions Use the answers to the questions you wrote about the headings to help you answer the questions below.

Reviewing Key Concepts

1. a. Reviewing What is the relationship between different forms of energy?

b. Relating Cause and Effect When you turn a toaster on, what happens to the electrical energy?

c. Sequencing Describe the energy transformations that happen when you strike a match. List them in the order in which they occur.

2. a. Identifying What common energy transformation allows you to send a rubber band flying across the room?

b. Describing Describe the energy transformations that occur when you bounce a ball.

c. Interpreting Diagrams Describe the energy transformations that occur in the pendulum in Figure 12.

3. a. Summarizing State the law of conservation of energy in your own words.

b. Explaining Thermal energy is produced when a firefighter slides down a pole. Where does it come from?

c. Making Generalizations Based on the theory of relativity, what must always be conserved?

Lab zone At-Home Activity

Hot Wire Straighten a wire hanger. Have a family member feel the wire and observe whether it feels cool or warm. Then hold the ends of the wire and bend it back and forth several times. **CAUTION:** *If the wire breaks, it can be sharp.* Do not bend it more than a few times. After bending the wire, have your family member feel it again. Explain how energy transformations can produce a change in temperature.

Lab zone **Skills Lab**

Soaring Straws

Problem

How does the gravitational potential energy of a straw rocket depend on the elastic potential energy of a rubber band launcher?

Skills Focus

controlling variables, graphing

Materials

- scissors
- rubber band
- 3 plastic straws
- meter stick
- marker
- metric ruler
- balance
- masking tape
- empty toilet paper tube

Procedure

1. Construct the rocket and launcher following the instructions in the box above. Use a balance to find the mass of the rocket in grams. Record the mass.
2. Hold the launcher in one hand with your fingers over the ends of the rubber band. Load the launcher by placing the straw rocket on the rubber band and pulling down from the other end as shown in the photograph. Let go and launch the rocket straight up. **CAUTION:** *Be sure to aim the straw rocket into the air, not at classmates.*
3. In your notebook, make a data table similar to the one on the next page.
4. Have your partner hold a meter stick, or tape it to the wall, so that its zero end is even with the top of the rocket launcher. Measure the height, in meters, to which the rocket rises. If the rocket goes higher than a single meter stick, use two meter sticks.

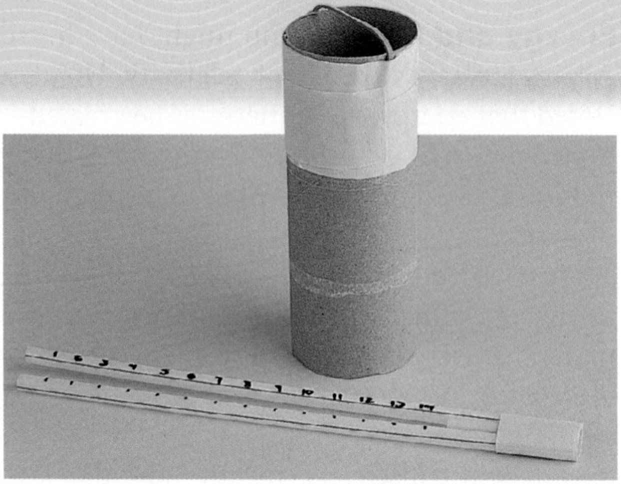

Making A Rocket and Launcher

A Cut a rubber band and tape it across the open end of a hollow cylinder, such as a toilet paper tube. The rubber band should be taut, but stretched only a tiny amount. This is the launcher.

B Cut about 3 cm off a plastic straw.

C Lay 2 full-length straws side by side on a flat surface with the 3-cm piece of straw between them. Arrange the straws so that their ends are even.

D Tape the straws together side by side. Starting from the untaped end, make marks every centimeter on one of the long straws. This is the rocket.

5. You can measure the amount of stretch of the rubber band by noting where the markings on the rocket line up with the bottom of the launching cylinder. Launch the rocket using five different amounts of stretch. Record your measurements.
6. For each amount of stretch, find the average height to which the rocket rises. Record the height in your data table.
7. Find the gravitational potential energy for each amount of stretch:

   Gravitational potential energy =
   Mass × Gravitational acceleration × Height

   You have measured the mass in grams. So the unit of energy is the millijoule (mJ), which is one thousandth of a joule. Record the results in your data table.

Data Table					
Amount of Stretch (cm)	Height Trial 1 (m)	Height Trial 2 (m)	Height Trial 3 (m)	Average Height (m)	Gravitational Potential Energy (mJ)

Analyze and Conclude

1. **Controlling Variables** Which variable in your data table is the manipulated variable? The responding variable? How do you know?
2. **Graphing** Graph your results. Show gravitational potential energy on the vertical axis and amount of stretch on the horizontal axis.
3. **Measuring** In this experiment, what measurement is related to elastic potential energy?
4. **Drawing Conclusions** Look at the shape of the graph. What conclusions can you reach about the relationship between the gravitational potential energy of the rocket and the elastic potential energy of the rubber band?
5. **Inferring** When you release the rocket, what kind of energy does the rocket have just after takeoff? What are the elastic potential energy and the gravitational potential energy at this point?
6. **Developing Hypotheses** Make an additional column on the right side of your data table labeled Kinetic Energy (mJ). For each row, write down what you think the rocket's kinetic energy is right after takeoff.
7. **Communicating** Write an advertisement for your rocket launcher. Include a diagram explaining how the rocket gains potential energy, how its potential energy is transformed to kinetic energy, and how its kinetic energy is transformed back into potential energy.

Design an Experiment

How would the height and distance the rocket travels be affected by the angle of launch? Design an experiment to measure the height and distance resulting from different launch angles. Keep the amount of stretch constant. *Obtain your teacher's permission before carrying out your investigation.*

Section 4

Integrating Earth Science

Energy and Fossil Fuels

Reading Preview

Key Concepts

- What is the source of the energy stored in fossil fuels?
- How is energy transformed when fossil fuels are used?

Key Terms

- fossil fuel
- combustion

Target Reading Skill

Previewing Visuals When you preview, you look ahead at the material to be read. Preview Figure 18. Then write two questions that you have about the diagram in a graphic organizer like the one below. As you read, answer your questions.

Using Fossil Fuel Energy

Q. What energy transformation occurs in the sun?
A.
Q.

Lab zone Discover Activity

What Is a Fuel?

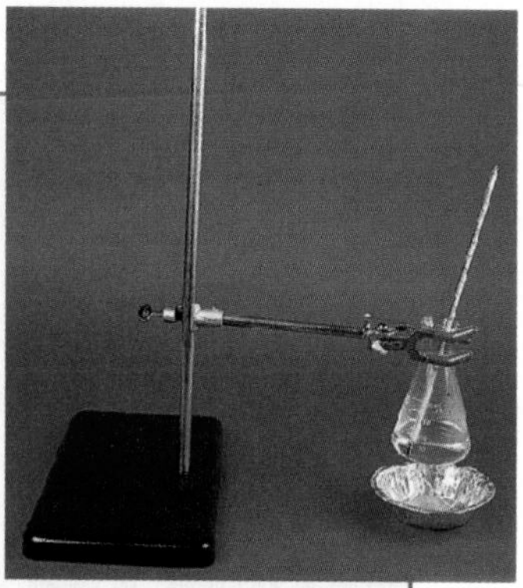

1. Put on your goggles. Attach a flask to a ring stand with a clamp. Then place a thermometer in the flask.
2. Add enough water to the flask to cover the thermometer bulb. Record the temperature of the water. Remove the thermometer.
3. Fold a wooden coffee stirrer in three places to look like a W. Stand it in a small aluminum pan so that the W is upright. Position the pan 4–5 cm directly below the flask.
4. Ignite the coffee stirrer at its center. **CAUTION:** *Be careful when using matches.*
5. When the coffee stirrer has stopped burning, read the temperature of the water again. Allow the flask to cool before cleaning up.

Think It Over

Forming Operational Definitions Gasoline in a car, kerosene in a lantern, and a piece of wood are all fuels. Based on your observations, what is a fuel?

Imagine a lush, green, swampy forest. Ferns as tall as trees block the view. Enormous dragonflies buzz through the warm, moist air. Huge cockroaches, some longer than your finger, crawl across the ground. Where is this place? Actually, a better question to ask would be, *when* is it? The time is more than 400 million years ago. That's even before the dinosaurs lived! But what does this ancient forest have to do with you?

Formation of Fossil Fuels

The plants of vast forests that once covered Earth provide the energy stored in fuels. A fuel is a material that contains stored potential energy. The gasoline used in vehicles and the propane used in a gas grill are examples of fuels. Some of the fuels used today were made from materials that formed hundreds of millions of years ago. These fuels, which include coal, petroleum, and natural gas, are known as **fossil fuels.**

Go Online SciLinks NSTA

For: Links on energy transformations
Visit: www.SciLinks.org
Web Code: scn-1354

The vast, ancient forests were the source of coal. When plants and animals died, their remains piled up in thick layers in swamps and marshes. Clay and sand sediments covered their remains. The resulting pressure and high temperature turned the remains into coal.

Energy From the Sun Remember that energy is conserved. That means that fuels do not create energy. So if fossil fuels store energy, they must have gotten energy from somewhere else. But where did it come from? **Fossil fuels contain energy that came from the sun.** In fact, the sun is the source of energy for most of Earth's processes. Within the dense core of the sun, during the process of nuclear fusion, nuclear energy is transformed to electromagnetic energy as well as other forms. Some of this electromagnetic energy reaches Earth in the form of light.

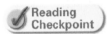

Reading Checkpoint **What is the source of the energy stored in fossil fuels?**

FIGURE 16
Fossil Fuels
Offshore oil rigs drill for the fossil fuel petroleum under the ocean floor.

FIGURE 17
Mining for Coal
Miners use heavy machinery to dig for coal. **Developing Hypotheses** *Why is coal usually found underground?*

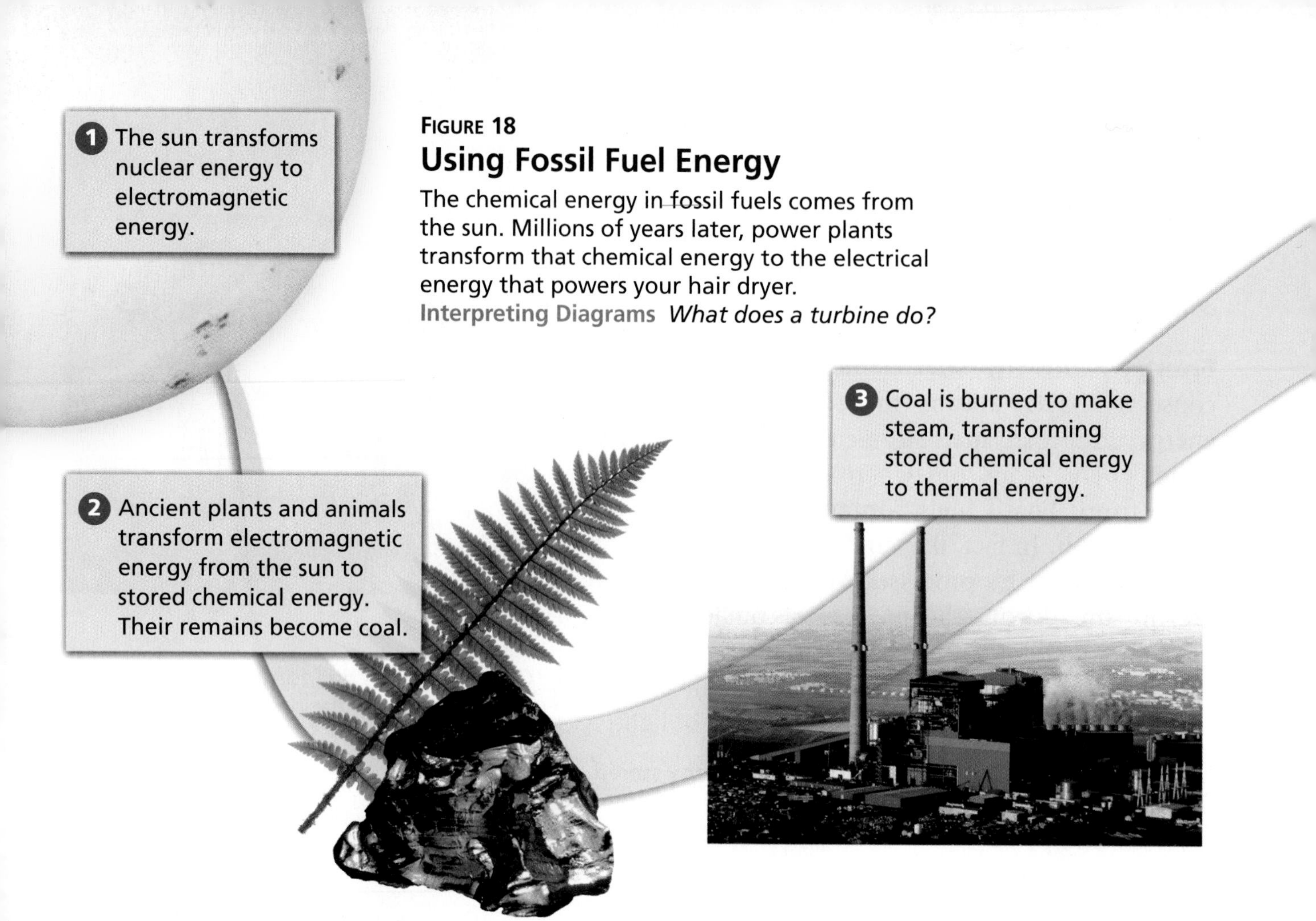

1 The sun transforms nuclear energy to electromagnetic energy.
2 Ancient plants and animals transform electromagnetic energy from the sun to stored chemical energy. Their remains become coal.
3 Coal is burned to make steam, transforming stored chemical energy to thermal energy.

FIGURE 18
Using Fossil Fuel Energy
The chemical energy in fossil fuels comes from the sun. Millions of years later, power plants transform that chemical energy to the electrical energy that powers your hair dryer.
Interpreting Diagrams *What does a turbine do?*

Lab zone Skills Activity

Graphing

The following list shows what percent of power used in the United States in a recent year came from each energy source: coal, 23%; nuclear, 8%; oil, 39%; natural gas, 24%; water, 3%; and biofuels, 3%. Prepare a circle graph that presents these data. (See the Skills Handbook for more on circle graphs.)

What power source does the United States rely on most? What percent of the country's total energy needs is met by coal, oil, and natural gas combined?

The Sun's Energy on Earth When the sun's energy reaches Earth, certain living things—plants, algae, and certain bacteria—transform some of it to chemical energy. Some of the energy in the chemical compounds they make is used for their daily energy needs. The rest is stored. Animals that eat plants store some of the plant's chemical energy in their own cells. When ancient animals and plants died, the chemical energy they had stored was trapped within them. This trapped energy is the chemical energy found in coal.

Use of Fossil Fuels

Fossil fuels can be burned to release the chemical energy stored millions of years ago. The process of burning fuels is known as **combustion.** During combustion, the fuel's chemical energy is transformed to thermal energy. This thermal energy can be used to heat water until the water boils and produces steam. In modern, coal-fired power plants, the steam is raised to a very high temperature in a boiler. When it leaves the boiler it has enough pressure to turn a turbine.

5 The turbines spin electric generators, transforming mechanical energy to electrical energy.

4 The steam turns turbines, transforming thermal energy to mechanical energy.

A turbine is like a fan, with blades attached to an axle. The pressure of the steam on the blades causes the turbine to spin very fast. In this process, the thermal energy of the steam is transformed to the mechanical energy of the moving turbine.

The turbines are connected to generators. When turbines spin them, generators produce electricity. As you can see in Figure 18, a power plant transforms chemical energy to thermal energy to mechanical energy to electrical energy. This electrical energy is then used to light your home and run other devices, such as a hair dryer.

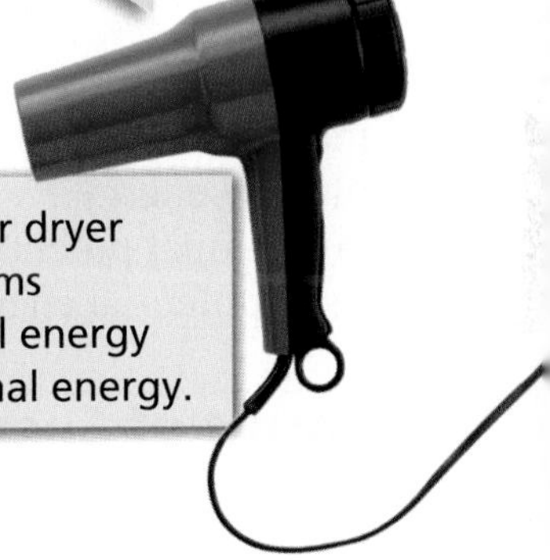

6 Your hair dryer transforms electrical energy to thermal energy.

Reading Checkpoint **What energy transformations take place in a power plant?**

Section 4 Assessment

Target Reading Skill Previewing Visuals Refer to your questions and answers about Figure 18 to help you answer Question 2 below.

Reviewing Key Concepts

1. a. Defining What are fossil fuels?

b. Explaining What role did the sun play in making fossil fuels?

c. Drawing Conclusions How did ancient animals receive stored energy from the sun?

2. a. Reviewing How is the chemical energy stored in coal released?

b. Sequencing Describe the steps in which a power plant transforms the energy in fossil fuels to electrical energy.

c. Inferring Which steps in the power plant process rely on potential energy? Which steps rely on kinetic energy? Why?

Lab zone At-Home Activity

Burning Fossils Some appliances in your home, such as ovens, grills, and water heaters, may use fossil fuels as an energy source. With a family member, search your home for appliances that use fossil fuels such as petroleum, coal, or natural gas as a source of energy. Explain to your family member what fossil fuels are and how they form.

Chapter 13 Study Guide

1 What Is Energy?

Key Concepts

- If the transfer of energy is work, then power is the rate at which energy is transferred, or the amount of energy transferred in a unit of time.
- $\text{Power} = \frac{\text{Energy transferred}}{\text{Time}}$
- Two basic kinds of energy are kinetic energy and potential energy.
- $\text{Kinetic energy} = \frac{1}{2} \times \text{Mass} \times \text{Velocity}^2$
- $\text{Gravitational potential energy} = \text{Weight} \times \text{Height}$

Key Terms

energy
kinetic energy
potential energy
gravitational potential energy
elastic potential energy

2 Forms of Energy

Key Concepts

- You can find an object's mechanical energy by adding the object's kinetic energy and potential energy.

  $\text{Mechanical energy} = \text{Kinetic energy} + \text{Potential energy}$

- Forms of energy associated with the particles of objects include thermal energy, electrical energy, chemical energy, nuclear energy, and electromagnetic energy.

Key Terms

mechanical energy
thermal energy
electrical energy
chemical energy
nuclear energy
electromagnetic energy

3 Energy Transformations and Conservation

Key Concepts

- Most forms of energy can be transformed into other forms.
- One of the most common energy transformations is the transformation between potential energy and kinetic energy.
- According to the law of conservation of energy, energy cannot be created or destroyed.

Key Terms

energy transformation
law of conservation of energy
matter

4 Energy and Fossil Fuels

Key Concepts

- Fossil fuels contain energy that came from the sun.
- Fossil fuels can be burned to release the chemical energy stored millions of years ago.

Key Terms

fossil fuel
combustion

Review and Assessment

Go Online PHSchool.com
For: Self-Assessment
Visit: PHSchool.com
Web Code: cga-3050

Organizing Information

Concept Mapping Copy the concept map about energy onto a separate sheet of paper. Then complete it and add a title. (For more on Concept Mapping, see the Skills Handbook.)

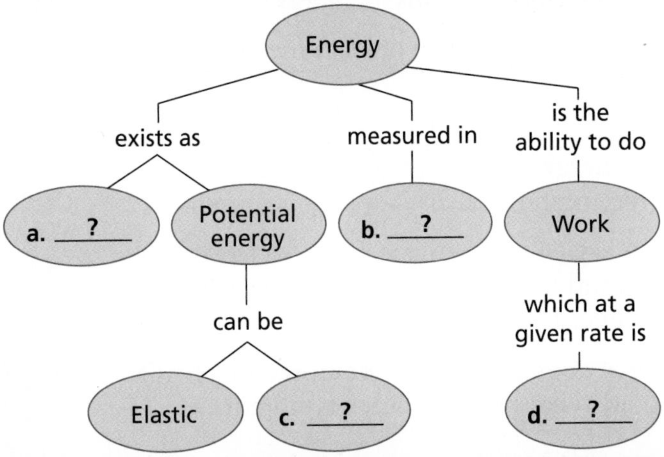

Reviewing Key Terms

Choose the letter of the best answer.

1. Energy of motion is called
   a. kinetic energy.
   b. elastic potential energy.
   c. gravitational potential energy.
   d. chemical energy.
2. When you stretch a rubber band, you give it
   a. kinetic energy.
   b. elastic potential energy.
   c. gravitational potential energy.
   d. electrical energy.
3. The energy associated with the position and motion of an object is called
   a. potential energy.
   b. nuclear energy.
   c. mechanical energy.
   d. thermal energy.
4. The energy stored in the nucleus of an atom is called
   a. electromagnetic energy.
   b. electrical energy.
   c. chemical energy.
   d. nuclear energy.
5. Fossil fuels store energy from the sun as
   a. chemical energy.
   b. thermal energy.
   c. electromagnetic energy.
   d. electrical energy.

If the statement is true, write *true*. If it is false, change the underlined word or words to make the statement true.

6. Kinetic energy is related to an object's height.
7. Electrical energy is the total kinetic and potential energy of the particles in an object.
8. The law of conservation of energy states that when one form of energy is transformed to another, no energy is destroyed.
9. Energy is anything that has mass and takes up space.
10. Combustion is the process of burning fuels.

Writing in Science

Interview You are preparing to interview an Olympic skier for a children's science magazine. Prepare a list of questions that you would ask the skier about the energy transformations that occur while skiing.

Discovery Channel School

Energy
Video Preview
Video Field Trip
▶ Video Assessment

Review and Assessment

Checking Concepts

11. Define work in terms of energy.

12. How do you find an object's mechanical energy?

13. For each of the following, decide which forms of energy are present: a walnut falls from a tree; a candle burns; a spring is stretched.

14. An eagle flies from its perch in a tree to the ground to capture and eat its prey. Describe its energy transformations.

15. How does energy become stored in a fossil fuel? What kind of energy is stored?

Thinking Critically

16. **Calculating** Find the power of a machine that transfers 450 J of energy in 9 s.

17. **Calculating** A 1,350-kg car travels at 12 m/s. What is its kinetic energy?

18. **Comparing and Contrasting** In the illustration below, which vehicle has the least kinetic energy? The greatest kinetic energy? Explain your answers.

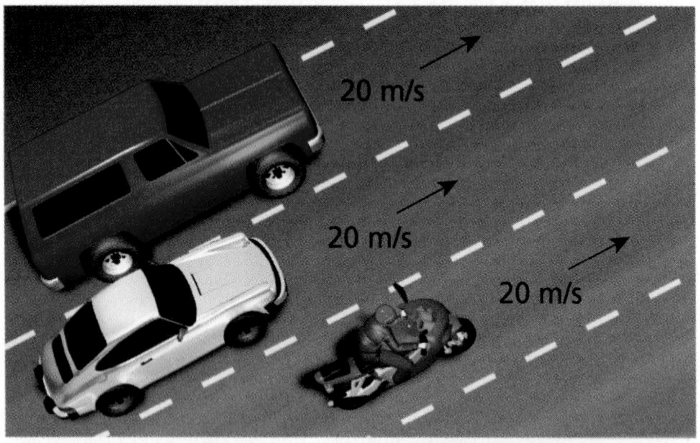

19. **Problem Solving** A 380-N girl walks down a flight of stairs so that she is 2.5 m below her starting level. What is the change in the girl's gravitational potential energy?

20. **Applying Concepts** One chef places a pie in the oven at a low setting so that it is baked in one hour. Another chef places a pie in the oven at a high setting so that the pie bakes in 30 minutes. Is the amount of energy the same in each case? Is the power the same?

Math Practice

21. **Exponents** What is the value of 12^2?

22. **Exponents** What is the value of $2^2 \times 3^2$?

Applying Skills

Use the photo to answer Questions 23–25.

The golfer in the photo is taking a swing. The golf club starts at Point A and ends at Point E.

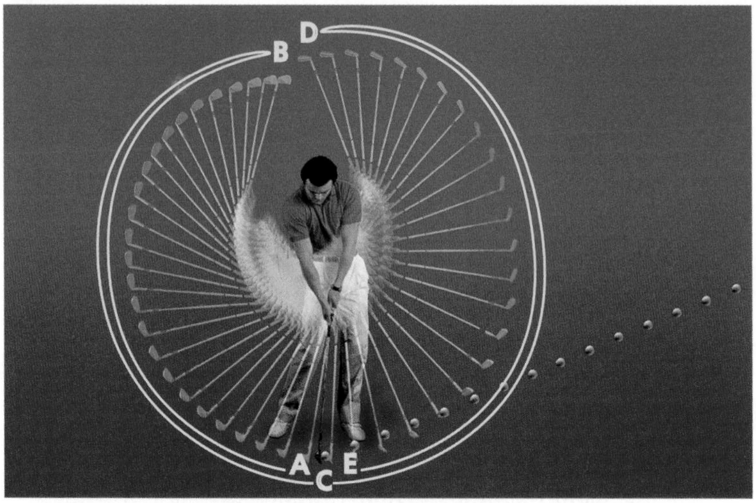

23. **Inferring** At which point(s) does the golf club have the greatest potential energy? At which point(s) does it have the greatest kinetic energy?

24. **Interpreting Diagrams** Describe the energy transformations from Point A to Point E.

25. **Drawing Conclusions** The kinetic energy of the club at Point C is more than the potential energy of the club at Point B. Does this mean that the law of conservation of energy is violated? Why or why not?

Lab zone Chapter Project

Performance Assessment Present your roller coaster to the class. Explain how you selected your materials, as well as the effect of hill height, incline, turns, and loops on the motion of the roller coaster. You should also explain how energy is transformed as the roller coaster moves along the tracks.

Standardized Test Prep

Test-Taking Tip

Watching for Qualifiers

Qualifiers are words like *most, least, greatest,* and *best*. When you answer a question with a qualifier, be sure to check and compare *all* the answer choices. Look for the answer that provides the information specified by the qualifier.

Sample Question

The table below gives the kinetic and potential energy of a 6-kg cat doing various activities.

Kinetic and Potential Energy of a Cat

Activity	Kinetic Energy (J)	Potential Energy (J)
Running	200	0
Leaping	150	100
Climbing a tree	3	300
Sleeping on a chair	0	30

The cat has the *greatest* mechanical energy when

A it is running.
B it is leaping.
C it is climbing a tree.
D it is sleeping on a chair.

Answer

The question asked for the cat's greatest mechanical energy. You can find the cat's mechanical energy for each activity by adding its kinetic and potential energy together. The values for climbing a tree (300 J + 3 J) give you the greatest sum (303 J). The answer is C.

Choose the letter of the best answer.

1. Wind has energy because
A it can change direction.
B it can do work.
C it has mass.
D it is electrically charged.

Use the table below and your knowledge of science to answer Questions 2 and 3.

Summer Classic Diving Competition

Name	Weight (N)	Height of Dive (m)
Clark	620	3
Simmons	640	3
Delgado	610	10
Chen	590	10

2. When standing on the diving board, which diver has the least gravitational potential energy?
F Clark
G Simmons
H Delgado
J Chen

3. In SI, which unit is used to express the divers' gravitational potential energy?
A newton
B kilowatt
C horsepower
D joule

4. A pendulum will eventually slow and stop because of
F friction.
G weight.
H kinetic energy.
J potential energy.

5. What energy transformation takes place when wood is burned?
A nuclear energy to thermal energy
B thermal energy to electrical energy
C chemical energy to thermal energy
D mechanical energy to thermal energy

Constructed Response

6. Explain the energy transformations involved in how fossil fuels formed and how they are used.

Chapter 14

Thermal Energy and Heat

Chapter Preview

Interactive Textbook

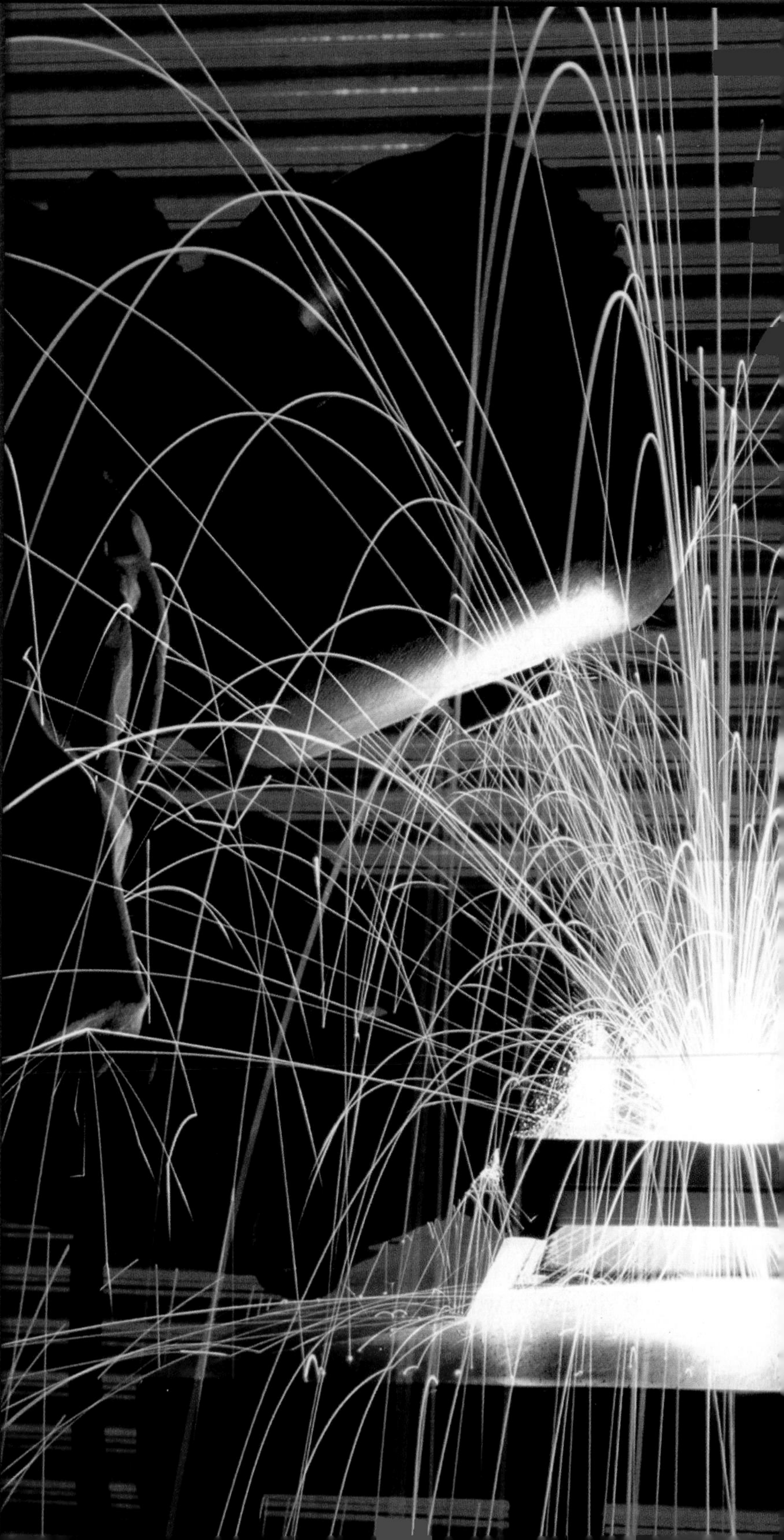

Sparks fly as a welder melts metal with intense heat. ▶

Discovery Channel School

Thermal Energy and Heat

▶ Video Preview
Video Field Trip
Video Assessment

Lab zone™ Chapter **Project**

In Hot Water

In this chapter, you will find out what heat is and how it relates to thermal energy and temperature. As you read the chapter, you will use what you learn to construct a device that will insulate a container of hot water.

Your Goal To build a container for a 355-mL aluminum can that keeps water hot

Your container must

- minimize the loss of thermal energy from the hot water
- be built from materials approved by your teacher
- have insulation no thicker than 3 cm
- not use electricity or heating chemicals
- follow the safety guidelines in Appendix A

Plan It! With a group of classmates, brainstorm different materials that prevent heat loss. Write a plan for how you will test these materials. Include a list of the variables you will control when doing your tests. Perform your tests to determine the best insulating materials. Keep a log of your results. Then build and test the device.

Section 1

Temperature, Thermal Energy, and Heat

Reading Preview

Key Concepts

- What are the three common temperature scales?
- How is thermal energy related to temperature and heat?
- What does having a high specific heat mean?

Key Terms

- temperature
- Fahrenheit scale
- Celsius scale
- Kelvin scale
- absolute zero
- heat
- specific heat

Target Reading Skill

Comparing and Contrasting

As you read, compare and contrast temperature, thermal energy, and heat by completing a table like the one below.

	Energy Measured	Units
Temp.	Average kinetic energy of particles	
Thermal energy		
Heat		

Lab zone Discover Activity

How Cold Is the Water?

1. Fill a plastic bowl with cold water, another with warm water, and a third with water at room temperature. Label each bowl and line them up.
2. Place your right hand in the cold water and your left hand in the warm water.
3. After about a minute, place both your hands in the third bowl at the same time.

Think It Over

Observing How did the water in the third bowl feel when you touched it? Did the water feel the same on both hands? If not, explain why.

The radio weather report says that today's high temperature will be 25 degrees. What should you wear? Do you need a coat to keep warm, or only shorts and a T-shirt? What you decide depends on what "25 degrees" means.

Temperature

You don't need a science book to tell you that the word *hot* means higher temperatures or the word *cold* means lower temperatures. When scientists think about high and low temperatures, however, they do not think about "hot" and "cold." Instead, they think about particles of matter in motion.

Recall that all matter is made up of tiny particles. These particles are always moving even if the matter they make up is stationary. Recall that the energy of motion is called kinetic energy. So all particles of matter have kinetic energy. The faster particles move, the more kinetic energy they have. **Temperature** is a measure of the average kinetic energy of the individual particles in matter.

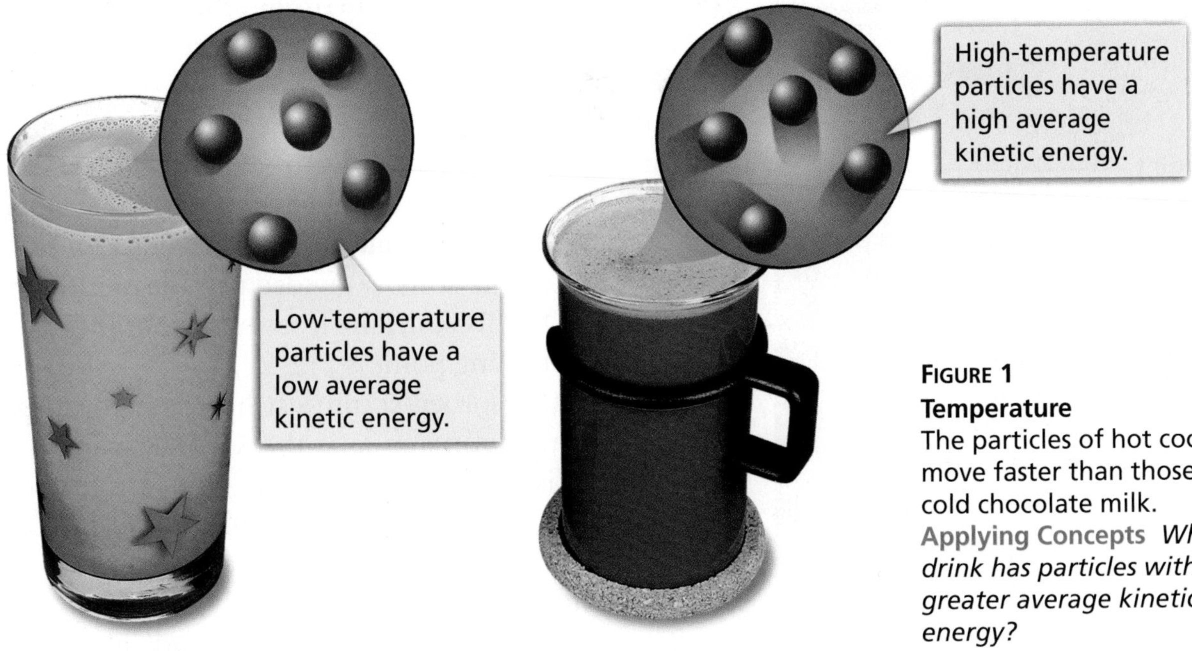

High-temperature particles have a high average kinetic energy.
Low-temperature particles have a low average kinetic energy.

FIGURE 1
Temperature
The particles of hot cocoa move faster than those of cold chocolate milk.
Applying Concepts *Which drink has particles with greater average kinetic energy?*

In Figure 1, the hot cocoa has a higher temperature than the cold chocolate milk. The cocoa's particles are moving faster, so they have greater average kinetic energy. If the milk is heated, its particles will move faster, so their kinetic energy will increase. The temperature of the milk will rise.

Measuring Temperature To measure the temperature of the heated milk, you would probably use a thermometer like the one shown in Figure 2. A thermometer usually consists of a liquid such as mercury or alcohol sealed inside a narrow glass tube. When the tube is heated, the particles of the liquid speed up and spread out so the particles take up more space, or volume. You see the level of the liquid move up the tube. The reverse happens when the tube is cooled. The particles of the liquid slow down and move closer, taking up less volume. You see the level of the liquid move down in the tube.

A thermometer has numbers and units, or a scale, on it. When you read the scale on a thermometer, you read the temperature of the surrounding matter. Thermometers can have different scales. The temperature reading you see depends on the thermometer's scale.

Reading Checkpoint **What happens to the liquid particles inside a thermometer when it is heated?**

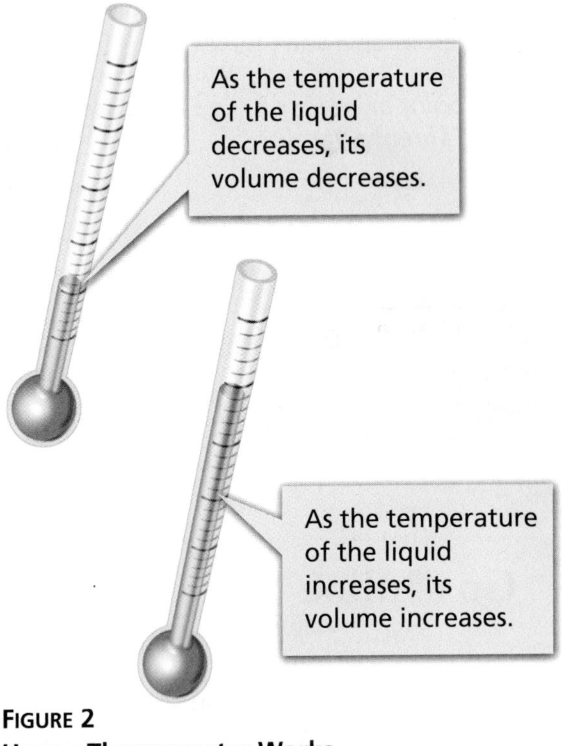

FIGURE 2
How a Thermometer Works
Temperature changes cause the level of the liquid inside a thermometer to rise and fall.

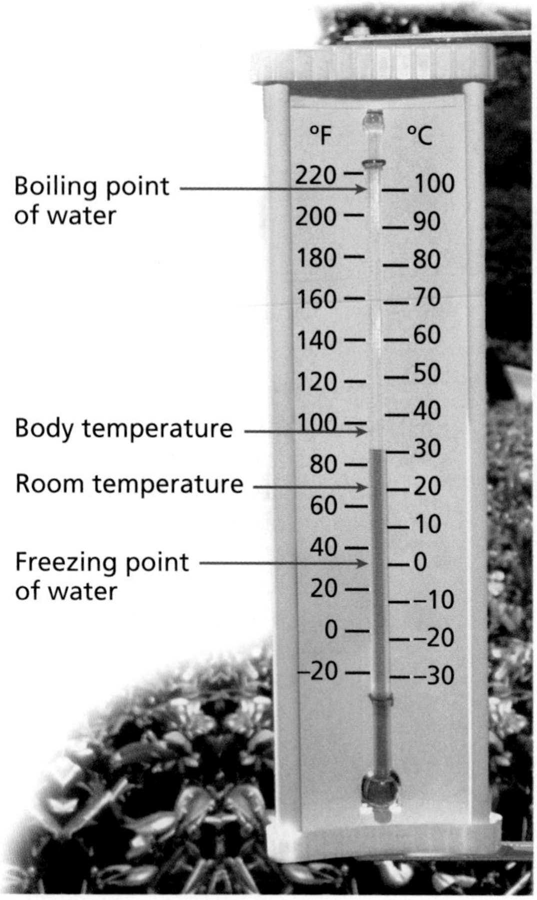

FIGURE 3
Temperature Scales
Many thermometers have both Celsius and Fahrenheit temperature scales.
Interpreting Photographs *What is the boiling point of water on the Celsius scale? On the Fahrenheit scale?*

Temperature Scales **The three common scales for measuring temperature are the Fahrenheit, Celsius, and Kelvin scales.** Each of these scales is divided into regular intervals.

The temperature scale you are probably most familiar with is the Fahrenheit scale. In the United States, the **Fahrenheit scale** is the most common temperature scale. The scale is divided into degrees Fahrenheit (°F). On this scale, the freezing point of water is 32°F and the boiling point is 212°F.

In nearly all other countries, however, the most common temperature scale is the **Celsius scale.** The Celsius scale is divided into degrees Celsius (°C), which are larger units than degrees Fahrenheit. On the Celsius scale, the freezing point of water is 0°C and the boiling point is 100°C.

The temperature scale commonly used in physical science is the **Kelvin scale.** Units on the Kelvin scale, called kelvins (K), are the same size as degrees on the Celsius scale. So, an increase of 1 K equals an increase of 1°C. The freezing point of water on the Kelvin scale is 273 K, and the boiling point is 373 K. The number 273 is special. Scientists have concluded from experiments that –273°C is the lowest temperature possible. No more thermal energy can be removed from matter at –273°C. Zero on the Kelvin scale represents –273°C and is called **absolute zero.**

Thermal Energy and Heat

Different objects at the same temperature can have different energies. To understand this, you need to know about thermal energy and about heat. You may be used to thinking about thermal energy as heat, but they are not the same thing. Temperature, thermal energy, and heat are closely related, but they are all different.

Thermal Energy You may recall that the total energy of all of the particles in an object is called thermal energy, or sometimes internal energy. The thermal energy of an object depends on the number of particles in the object, the temperature of the object, and the arrangement of the object's particles. You will learn about how the arrangement of particles affects thermal energy in Section 3.

Go Online
SciLinks NSTA
For: Links on temperature and heat
Visit: www.SciLinks.org
Web Code: scn-1361

The more particles an object has at a given temperature, the more thermal energy it has. For example, a 1-liter pot of hot cocoa at 75°C has more thermal energy than a 0.2-liter mug of hot cocoa at 75°C because the pot contains more cocoa particles. On the other hand, the higher the temperature of an object, the more thermal energy the object has. Therefore, if two 1-liter pots of hot cocoa have different temperatures, the pot with the higher temperature has more thermal energy. In Section 3, you will learn about how thermal energies differ for solids, liquids, and gases.

Heat Thermal energy that is transferred from matter at a higher temperature to matter at a lower temperature is called **heat.** The scientific definition of heat is different from its everyday use. In a conversation, you might say that an object contains heat. However, objects contain thermal energy, not heat. Only when thermal energy is transferred is it called heat. **Heat is thermal energy moving from a warmer object to a cooler object.** For example, when you hold an ice cube in your hand, as shown in Figure 4, the ice cube melts because thermal energy is transferred from your hand to the ice cube.

Recall that work also involves the transfer of energy. Since work and heat are both energy transfers, they are both measured in the same unit—joules.

Reading Checkpoint **Why does an ice cube melt in your hand?**

Math Skills

Converting Units

To convert a Fahrenheit temperature to a Celsius temperature, use the following formula.

$$°C = \frac{5}{9}(°F - 32)$$

For example, if the temperature in your classroom is 68°F, what is the temperature in degrees Celsius?

$$°C = \frac{5}{9}(68 - 32)$$

$$°C = \frac{5}{9} \times 36$$

$$°C = 20$$

The temperature of your classroom is 20°C.

Practice Problem While at the beach, you measure the ocean temperature as 77°F. What is the temperature of the ocean in degrees Celsius?

FIGURE 4
Heat Your hand transfers thermal energy to the ice cube. Even though your hand is cold, this transfer is called heat. Your hand feels cold because it is losing thermal energy.

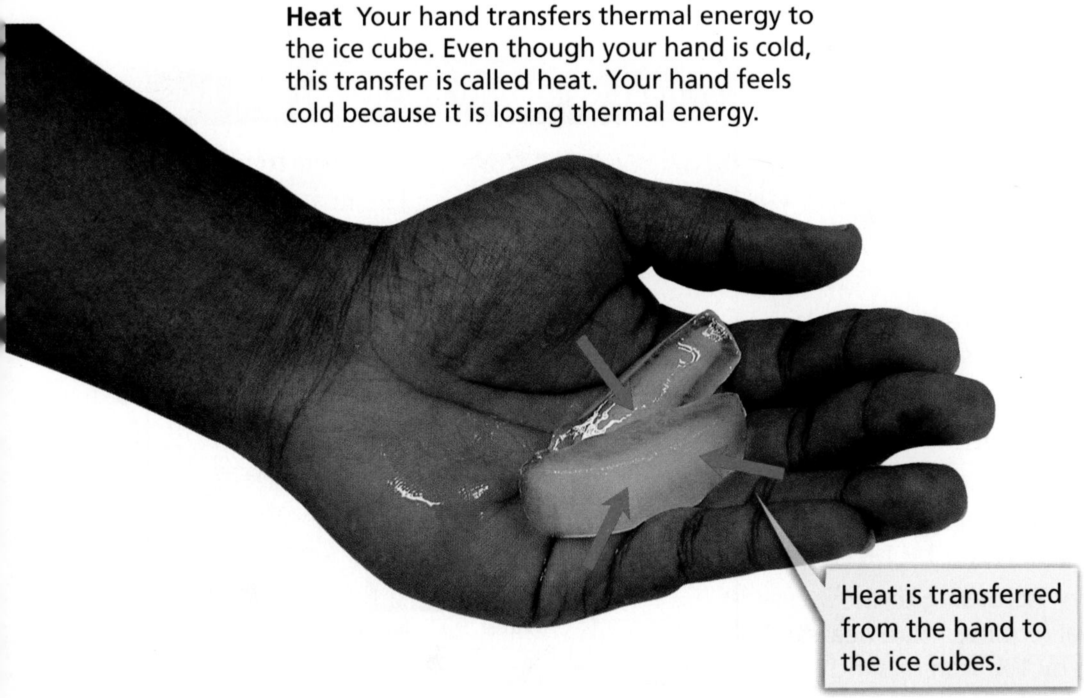
Heat is transferred from the hand to the ice cubes.

FIGURE 5
Specific Heat of Sand and Water
The specific heat of water is greater than the specific heat of sand. On a sunny day the water feels cooler than the sand.

Specific Heat

Imagine running across hot sand toward the ocean. You run to the water's edge, but you don't go any farther—the water is too cold. How can the sand be so hot and the water so cold? After all, the sun heats both of them. The answer is that water requires more heat to raise its temperature than sand does.

When an object is heated, its temperature rises. But the temperature does not rise at the same rate for all objects. The amount of heat required to raise the temperature of an object depends on the object's chemical makeup. To change the temperature of different objects by the same amount, different amounts of heat are required.

Scientists have defined a quantity to measure the relationship between heat and temperature change. The amount of energy required to raise the temperature of 1 kilogram of a material by 1 kelvin is called its **specific heat.** The unit of measure for specific heat is joules per kilogram-kelvin, or J/(kg·K).

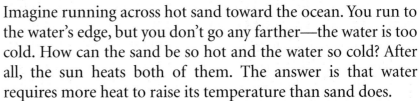

Math Analyzing Data

Specific Heat

The specific heat of three different materials was measured. These data are shown in the graph.

1. **Reading Graphs** What three materials are compared in the graph?
2. **Interpreting Data** About how much heat is required to raise 1 kg of water by 1 K?
3. **Drawing Conclusions** According to the graph, which material requires more heat to raise its temperature by 1 K, iron or sand?

Heat Needed to Raise 1 Kg by 1 K

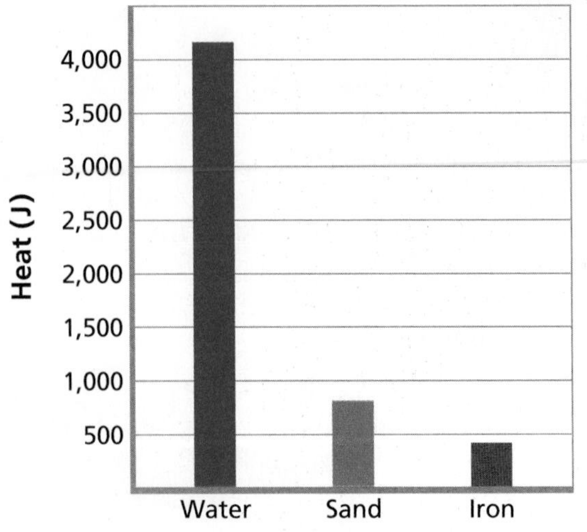

Look at the specific heats of the materials listed in Figure 6. Notice that the specific heat of water is quite high. One kilogram of water requires 4,180 joules of energy to raise its temperature 1 kelvin.

A material with a high specific heat can absorb a great deal of thermal energy without a great change in temperature. On the other hand, a material with a low specific heat would have a large temperature change after absorbing the same amount of thermal energy.

The energy gained or lost by a material is related to its mass, change in temperature, and specific heat. You can calculate thermal energy changes with the following formula.

Change in energy =
Mass × Specific heat × Change in temperature

How much heat is required to raise the temperature of 5 kilograms of water by 10 kelvins?

$$\text{Change in energy} = 5\text{ kg} \times 4{,}180\text{ J/(kg}\cdot\text{K)} \times 10\text{ K}$$
$$= 209{,}000\text{ J}$$

You need to transfer 209,000 joules to the water to increase its temperature by 10 kelvins.

Reading Checkpoint **What formula allows you to determine an object's change in thermal energy?**

Specific Heat of Common Materials	
Material	**Specific Heat (J/(kg·K))**
Aluminum	903
Copper	385
Glass	837
Ice	2,060
Iron	450
Sand	800
Silver	235
Water	4,180

FIGURE 6
This table lists the specific heats of several common materials.
Interpreting Tables *How much more energy is required to raise the temperature of 1 kg of iron by 1 K than to raise the temperature of 1 kg of copper by 1 K?*

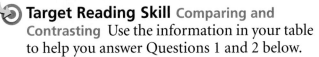

Section 1 Assessment

Target Reading Skill **Comparing and Contrasting** Use the information in your table to help you answer Questions 1 and 2 below.

Reviewing Key Concepts

1. a. **Identifying** What is temperature?
   b. **Describing** How do thermometers measure temperature?
   c. **Comparing and Contrasting** How are the three temperature scales alike? How are they different?
2. a. **Defining** What is heat?
   b. **Explaining** What is the relationship between thermal energy and temperature? Between thermal energy and heat?
   c. **Relating Cause and Effect** What happens to the motion of an object's particles as the object's thermal energy increases? What happens to the temperature of the object?
3. a. **Reviewing** Why do some materials get hot more quickly than others?
   b. **Calculating** You stir your hot cocoa with a silver spoon that has a mass of 0.032 kg. The spoon's temperature increases from 20 K to 60 K. What is the change in the spoon's thermal energy? (*Hint:* Use the table in Figure 6 to find the specific heat of silver.)

Math Practice

4. **Converting Units** Convert 5.0°F to degrees Celsius.
5. **Converting Units** The surface temperature on the planet Venus can reach 860°F. Convert this temperature to degrees Celsius.

Lab zone **Technology Lab**

• Tech & Design •

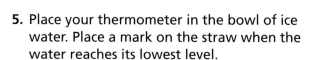

Build Your Own Thermometer

Problem

Can you build a thermometer out of simple materials?

Design Skills

evaluating the design, measuring, making models

Materials

- bowl of hot water • bowl of ice water
- water of unknown temperature
- tap water • 500-mL beaker
- clear glass juice or soda bottle, 20–25 cm
- clear plastic straw, 18–20 cm • food coloring
- plastic dropper • cooking oil
- modeling clay
- metric ruler
- fine-point marker

Procedure

1. You can use simple materials to build a model of an alcohol thermometer. First, mix food coloring into a beaker of tap water. Then fill a glass bottle with the colored water.
2. Place a straw in the bottle. Use modeling clay to position the straw so that it extends at least 10 cm above the bottle mouth. Do not let the straw touch the bottom. The clay should completely seal off the bottle mouth. Make sure there is no air in the bottle.
3. Using a dropper, add colored water into the straw to a level 5 cm above the bottle. Place a drop of cooking oil in the straw to prevent evaporation.
4. Place your thermometer into a bowl of hot water. When the colored water reaches its highest level, place a mark on the straw.
5. Place your thermometer in the bowl of ice water. Place a mark on the straw when the water reaches its lowest level.
6. Create a scale for your model thermometer. Divide the distance between the two marks into 5-mm intervals. Starting with the lowest point, label the intervals on the straw 0, 1, 2, 3, and so on.
7. Measure the temperature of two unknown samples with your thermometer. Record both temperatures.

Analyze and Conclude

1. **Evaluating the Design** Do you think your model accurately represents an alcohol thermometer? How is it like a real thermometer? How is it different?
2. **Inferring** How can you use the concepts of matter and the kinetic energy of particles to explain the way your model works?
3. **Measuring** Approximately what Celsius temperatures do you think your model measures? Explain your estimate.
4. **Making Models** Examine the structure and materials used in your model. Propose a change that would improve the model. Explain your choice.

Communicate

Create a poster to show how an alcohol thermometer works. Explain how the Celsius and Fahrenheit scales compare. For example, does 0° have the same meaning on both scales? Use a diagram with labels and captions to communicate your ideas.

Section 2

The Transfer of Heat

Reading Preview

Key Concepts

- What are the three forms of heat transfer?
- In what direction does heat move?
- How are conductors and insulators different?

Key Terms

- conduction • convection
- convection current • radiation
- conductor • insulator

Target Reading Skill

Identifying Main Ideas As you read the How Is Heat Transferred? section, write the main idea in a graphic organizer like the one below. Then write three supporting details that give examples of the main idea.

Main Idea

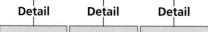

Heat can be transferred in three ways . . .		
Detail	Detail	Detail

Lab zone Discover Activity

What Does It Mean to Heat Up?

1. Obtain several utensils made of different materials, such as silver, stainless steel, plastic, and wood.
2. Stand the utensils in a beaker so that they do not touch each other.
3. Press a small gob of frozen butter on the handle of each utensil. Make sure that when the utensils stand on end, the butter is at the same height on each one.
4. Pour hot water into the beaker until it is about 6 cm below the butter. Watch the butter on the utensils for several minutes. What happens?
5. Wash the utensils in soapy water when you finish.

Think It Over

Observing What happened to the butter? Did the same thing happen on every utensil? How can you account for your observations?

Blacksmithing is hot work. A piece of iron held in the fire of the forge becomes warmer and begins to glow. At the same time, the blacksmith feels hot air rising from the forge, and his face and arms begin to feel warmer. Each of these movements of energy is a transfer of heat.

A blacksmith at work ▶

Go Online
SCI LINKS NSTA

For: Links on heat transfer
Visit: www.SciLinks.org
Web Code: scn-1362

Lab zone **Try This Activity**

Feel the Warmth

How is heat transferred from a light bulb?

1. Turn on a lamp without the shade. Wait about a minute.
2. Hold the palm of your hand about 10 cm from the side of the bulb for about 15 seconds. Remove it sooner if it gets too warm.
3. Now hold the palm of your hand about 10 cm above the top of the bulb for about 15 seconds.

Drawing Conclusions
In which location did your hand feel warmer? Explain your observations in terms of heat transfer.

How Is Heat Transferred?

There are three ways that heat can move. **Heat is transferred by conduction, convection, and radiation.** The blacksmith experiences all three.

Conduction In the process of **conduction,** heat is transferred from one particle of matter to another without the movement of the matter. Think of a metal spoon in a pot of water on an electric stove. The fast-moving particles in the hot electric coil collide with the slow-moving particles in the cool pot. The transfer of heat causes the pot's particles to move faster. Then the pot's particles collide with the water's particles, which in turn collide with the particles in the spoon. As the particles move faster, the metal spoon becomes hotter.

If you were to touch the spoon, heat would be transferred to your fingers. Too much heat transferred this way can cause a burn!

In Figure 7, heat from the fire is transferred to the stone beneath it. Then it is transferred from the stone to the metal tools. This transfer of heat from the fire to the tools is due to conduction.

Convection If you watch a pot of hot water on a stove, you will see the water moving. This movement transfers heat within the water. In **convection,** heat is transferred by the movement of currents within a fluid.

When the water at the bottom of the pot is heated, its particles move faster. The particles also move farther apart. As a result, the heated water becomes less dense. You may remember that a less dense fluid will float on top of a denser one. So the heated water rises. The surrounding, cooler water flows into its place. This flow creates a circular motion known as a **convection current.**

Convection currents can transfer heated air. As the air above the fire in Figure 7 is heated, it becomes less dense and rises up the chimney. When the warm air rises, cool air flows into its place.

Radiation **Radiation** is the transfer of energy by electromagnetic waves. You can feel the radiation from a fire in a fireplace all the way across the room. Unlike conduction and convection, radiation does not require matter to transfer thermal energy. All of the sun's energy that reaches Earth travels through millions of kilometers of empty space.

Reading Checkpoint **How does radiation transfer thermal energy?**

Convection
When the air around the fire is heated, it becomes less dense than the cooler air nearby. The warm air rises up the chimney, and cool air flows in to take its place.
Radiation
The fire transforms chemical energy in the wood to electro-magnetic energy, which radiates heat across the room.
Conduction
Fast-moving particles in the fire transfer heat as they collide with slow-moving particles in the stone hearth. Eventually the heat conducts through the stones to the metal tools.

FIGURE 7
Methods of Heat Transfer
Heat can be transferred by conduction, convection, or radiation. Heat from a fire is transferred by all three methods. **Interpreting Diagrams** *Which of these methods requires the movement of currents with a fluid?*

FIGURE 8
Heat Transfer From Food
The soup's heat is transferred to the bowl, the spoon, and the air.
Predicting *If the soup is not eaten, what will happen to its temperature?*

Heat Moves One Way

If two objects have different temperatures, heat will flow from the warmer object to the colder one. When heat flows into matter, the thermal energy of the matter increases. As the thermal energy increases, the temperature increases. At the same time, the temperature of the matter losing the heat decreases. Heat will flow from one object to the other until the two objects have the same temperature. You have probably seen this happen to your food. The bowl of hot soup shown in Figure 8, for example, cools to room temperature if you don't eat it quickly.

What happens when something becomes cold, such as when ice cream is made? The ingredients used to make it, such as milk and sugar, are not nearly as cold as the finished ice cream. In an ice cream maker, the ingredients are put into a metal can that is packed in ice. You might think that the ice transfers cold to the ingredients in the can. But this is not the case. There is no such thing as "coldness." Instead, the ingredients grow colder as thermal energy flows from them to the ice. Heat transfer occurs in only one direction.

Reading Checkpoint **Can heat flow from one object to a warmer object? Why or why not?**

Lab zone Skills Activity

Inferring

You pull some clothes out of the dryer as soon as they are dry. You grab your shirt without a problem, but when you pull out your jeans, you quickly drop them. The metal zipper is too hot to touch! What can you infer about which material in your jeans conducts thermal energy better? Explain.

Conductors and Insulators

Have you ever stepped from a rug to a tile floor on a cold morning? The tile floor feels colder than the rug. Yet if you measured their temperatures, they would be the same—room temperature. The difference between them has to do with how materials conduct heat. A material can be either a conductor or an insulator. **A conductor transfers thermal energy well. An insulator does not transfer thermal energy well.**

Conductors A material that conducts heat well is called a **conductor.** Metals such as silver and stainless steel are good conductors. A metal spoon conducts heat better than a wooden spoon. Some materials are good conductors because of the particles they contain and how those particles are arranged. A good conductor, such as a tile floor, feels cool to the touch because it easily transfers heat away from your skin.

Insulators A material that does not conduct heat well is called an **insulator.** Wood, wool, straw, and paper are good insulators. So are the gases in air. Clothes and blankets are insulators that slow the transfer of heat out of your body.

A well-insulated building is comfortable inside whether it is hot or cold outdoors. Insulation prevents heat from entering the building in hot weather and from escaping in cold weather. Much of the heat transfer in a building occurs through the windows. For this reason, insulating windows have two panes of glass with a thin space of air between them. The trapped air does not transfer heat well.

FIGURE 9
Insulating Windows
Air between the panes of this window acts as an insulator to slow the transfer of heat.

Reading Checkpoint Is air better as an insulator or as a conductor?

Section 2 Assessment

Target Reading Skill

Identifying Main Ideas Use your graphic organizer to help you answer Question 1 below.

Reviewing Key Concepts

1. a. **Describing** What are conduction, convection, and radiation?
   b. **Classifying** Identify each example of heat transfer as conduction, convection, or radiation: opening the windows in a hot room; a lizard basking in the sun; putting ice on a sprained ankle.
   c. **Inferring** How can heat be transferred across empty space?
2. a. **Reviewing** In what direction will heat flow between two objects with different temperatures?
   b. **Applying Concepts** How does a glass of lemonade become cold when you put ice in it?
3. a. **Identifying** What kind of substance conducts thermal energy well?
   b. **Making Judgments** Would a copper pipe work better as a conductor or an insulator? Why do you think so?
   c. **Interpreting Diagrams** Why are two panes of glass used in the window in Figure 9?

Writing in Science

Explanation Suppose you are camping on a mountain, and the air temperature is very cold. How would you keep warm? Would you build a fire or set up a tent? Write an explanation for each action you would take. Tell whether conduction, convection, or radiation is involved with each heat transfer.

Lab zone **Skills Lab**

Just Add Water

Problem

Can you build a calorimeter—a device that measures changes in thermal energy—and use it to determine how much thermal energy is transferred from hot water to cold water?

Skills Focus

observing, calculating, interpreting data

Materials

- hot tap water • balance • scissors
- pencil • 4 plastic foam cups
- 2 thermometers or temperature probes
- beaker of water kept in an ice bath

Procedure

1. Predict how the amount of thermal energy lost by hot water will be related to the amount of thermal energy gained by cold water.
2. Copy the data table into your notebook.
3. Follow the instructions in the box to make two calorimeters. Find the mass of each empty calorimeter (including the cover) on a balance and record each mass in your data table.
4. From a beaker of water that has been sitting in an ice bath, add water (no ice cubes) to the cold-water calorimeter. Fill it about one-third full. Put the cover on, find the total mass, and record the mass in your data table.
5. Add hot tap water to the hot-water calorimeter. **CAUTION:** *Hot tap water can cause burns.* Fill the calorimeter about one-third full. Put the cover on, find the total mass, and record the mass in your data table.
6. Calculate the mass of the water in each calorimeter. Record the results in your data table.
7. Put thermometers through the holes in the covers of both calorimeters. Wait a minute or two and then record the temperatures. If you are using temperature probes, see your teacher for instructions.

Making a Calorimeter

A Label a plastic foam cup with the letter C, which stands for cold water.

B Cut 2 to 3 cm from the top of a second plastic foam cup. Invert the second cup inside the first. Label the cover with a *C* also. The cup and cover are your cold-water calorimeter.

C Using a pencil, poke a hole in the cover large enough for a thermometer to fit into snugly.

D Repeat Steps A, B, and C with two other plastic foam cups. This time, label both cup and cover with an *H*. This is your hot-water calorimeter.

Data Table

Calorimeter	Mass of Empty Cup (g)	Mass of Cup and Water (g)	Mass of Water (g)	Starting Temp. (°C)	Final Temp. (°C)	Change in Temp. (°C)
Cold Water						
Hot Water						

8. Remove both thermometers and covers. Pour the water from the cold-water calorimeter into the hot-water calorimeter. Put the cover back on the hot-water calorimeter, and insert a thermometer. Record the final temperature as the final temperature for both calorimeters.

Analyze and Conclude

1. **Observing** What is the temperature change of the cold water? Record your answer in the data table.
2. **Observing** What is the temperature change of the hot water? Record your answer in the data table.
3. **Calculating** Calculate the amount of thermal energy that enters the cold water by using the formula for the transfer of thermal energy. The specific heat of water is 4.18 J/(g·K).
   Thermal energy transferred =
   4.18 J/(g·K) × Mass of cold water ×
   Temperature change of cold water
   Remember that a change of 1°C is equal to a change of 1 K.
4. **Calculating** Now use the same formula to calculate the amount of thermal energy leaving the hot water.
5. **Calculating** What unit should you use for your results for Questions 3 and 4?
6. **Interpreting Data** Was your prediction from Step 1 confirmed? How do you know?
7. **Communicating** What sources of error might have affected your results? Write a paragraph explaining how the lab could be redesigned in order to reduce the errors.

Design an Experiment

How would your results be affected if you started with much more hot water than cold? If you used more cold water than hot? Make a prediction. Then design a procedure to test your prediction. *Obtain your teacher's permission before carrying out your investigation.*

Section 3

Integrating Chemistry

Thermal Energy and States of Matter

Reading Preview

Key Concepts

- What are three states of matter?
- What causes matter to change state?
- What happens to a substance as its thermal energy increases?

Key Terms

- state
- change of state
- melting
- freezing
- evaporation
- boiling
- condensation
- thermal expansion

Target Reading Skill

Building Vocabulary Using a word in a sentence helps you think about how best to explain the word. After you read the section, reread the paragraphs that contain definitions of Key Terms. Use all the information you have learned to write a meaningful sentence for each Key Term.

Lab zone Discover Activity

What Happens to Heated Metal?

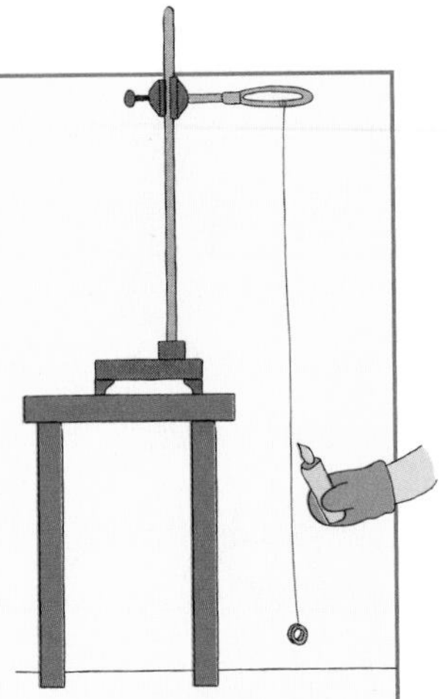

1. Wrap one end of a one-meter-long metal wire around a clamp on a ring stand.
2. Tie the other end through several washers. Adjust the clamp so that the washers swing freely, but nearly touch the floor.
3. Light a candle. Hold the candle with an oven mitt, and heat the wire. **CAUTION:** *Be careful near the flame, and avoid dripping hot wax on yourself.* Predict how heat from the candle will affect the wire.
4. With your hand in the oven mitt, swing the wire. Observe any changes in the motion of the washers.
5. Blow out the candle and allow the wire to cool. After several minutes, swing the wire again and observe its motion.

Think It Over

Inferring Based on your observations, what can you conclude about the effect of heating a solid?

Throughout the day, the temperature at an orange grove drops steadily. The anxious farmer awaits the updated weather forecast. The news is not good. The temperature is expected to fall even further during the night. Low temperatures could wipe out the entire crop. He considers picking the crop early, but the oranges are not yet ripe.

Instead, the farmer tells his workers to haul in hoses and spray the orange trees with water. As the temperature drops, the water begins to freeze. The ice keeps the oranges warm!

How can ice possibly keep anything warm? The answer has to do with how thermal energy is transferred as water becomes ice.

◄ Oranges at 0°C sprayed with water

States of Matter

What happens when you hold an ice cube in your hand? It melts. The solid and the liquid are both the same material—water. Water can exist in three different **states,** or forms. **In fact, most matter on Earth can exist in three states—solid, liquid, and gas.** Although the chemical composition of matter remains the same, the arrangement of the particles that make up the matter differs from one state to another.

Solids The particles that make up a solid are packed together in relatively fixed positions. Particles of a solid cannot move out of their positions. They can only vibrate back and forth. This is why solids retain a fixed shape and volume. Because the shape and volume of the plastic helmets shown in Figure 10 do not change, the plastic is a solid.

Liquids The particles that make up a liquid are close together, but they are not held together as tightly as those of a solid. Because liquid particles can move around, liquids don't have a definite shape. But liquids do have a definite volume. In Figure 10, notice how the river water changes shape.

Gases In gases, the particles are moving so fast that they don't even stay close together. Gases expand to fill all the space available. They don't have a fixed shape or volume. Because air is a gas, it can expand to fill the raft in Figure 10 and also take the raft's shape.

Go Online SCI LINKS NSTA

For: Links on changes of state
Visit: www.SciLinks.org
Web Code: scn-1363

FIGURE 10
Three States of Matter
The plastic helmets, the water in the river, and the air that fills the raft are examples of three states of matter—solid, liquid, and gas. Classifying *Which state of matter is represented by the plastic oars?*

FIGURE 11
Melted Chocolate
Though normally a solid at room temperature, this chocolate has absorbed enough thermal energy to become a liquid.

Changes of State

The physical change from one state of matter to another is called a **change of state.** The state of matter depends on the amount of thermal energy it has. The more thermal energy matter has, the faster its particles move. Since a gas has more thermal energy than a liquid, the particles of a gas move faster than the particles of the same matter in the liquid state.

Matter can change from one state to another when thermal energy is absorbed or released. The graph in Figure 12 shows that as thermal energy increases, matter changes from a solid to a liquid and then to a gas. A gas changes to a liquid and then to a solid as thermal energy is removed from it.

The flat regions of the graph show conditions under which thermal energy is changing but temperature remains the same. Under these conditions, matter is changing from one state to another. During a change of state, the addition or loss of thermal energy changes the arrangement of the particles. However, the average kinetic energy of those particles does not change. Since temperature is a measure of average kinetic energy, temperature does not change as the state of matter changes.

Solid–Liquid Changes of State The change of state from a solid to a liquid is called **melting.** Melting occurs when a solid absorbs thermal energy. As the thermal energy of the solid increases, the structure of its particles breaks down. The particles become freer to move around. The temperature at which a solid changes to a liquid is called the melting point.

The change of state from a liquid to a solid is called **freezing.** Freezing occurs when matter releases thermal energy. The temperature at which matter changes from a liquid to a solid is called its freezing point.

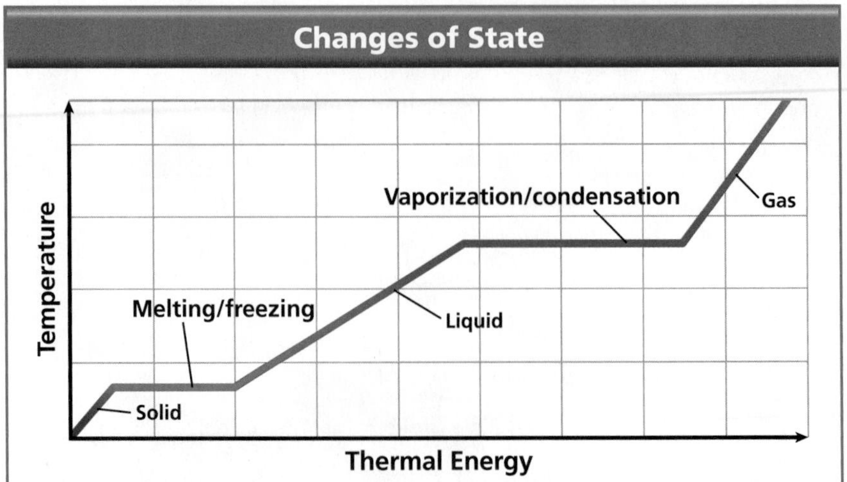

FIGURE 12
During a change in state, the thermal energy of matter increases while its temperature remains the same.

For a given type of matter, the freezing point and melting point are the same. The difference between the two is whether the matter is gaining or releasing thermal energy. The farmer had his workers spray the orange trees with water because the freezing water releases thermal energy into the oranges.

Liquid–Gas Changes of State The process by which matter changes from the liquid to the gas state is called vaporization. During this process, particles in a liquid absorb thermal energy and move faster. Eventually they move fast enough to escape the liquid as gas particles. If vaporization takes place at the surface of a liquid, it is called **evaporation.** At higher temperatures, vaporization can occur below the surface of a liquid as well. This process is called **boiling.** When a liquid boils, gas bubbles that form within the liquid rise to the surface. The temperature at which a liquid boils is called its boiling point.

When a gas loses a certain amount of thermal energy, it will change into a liquid. A change from the gas state to the liquid state is called **condensation.** You have probably seen beads of water appear on the outside of a cold drinking glass. This occurs because water vapor that is present in the air loses thermal energy when it comes in contact with the cold glass.

Reading Checkpoint **What change of state occurs in evaporation?**

Lab zone Skills Activity

Observing

Put a teakettle on a stove or a lab burner and bring the water to a boil. Look carefully at the white vapor coming out of the spout. **CAUTION:** *Steam and boiling water can cause serious burns.* In what state of matter is the white vapor that you see? What is present, but not visible, in the small space between the white vapor and the spout?

FIGURE 13
Condensation
Under certain weather conditions, water vapor in the air can condense into fog.
Applying Concepts *As it condenses, does water absorb or release thermal energy?*

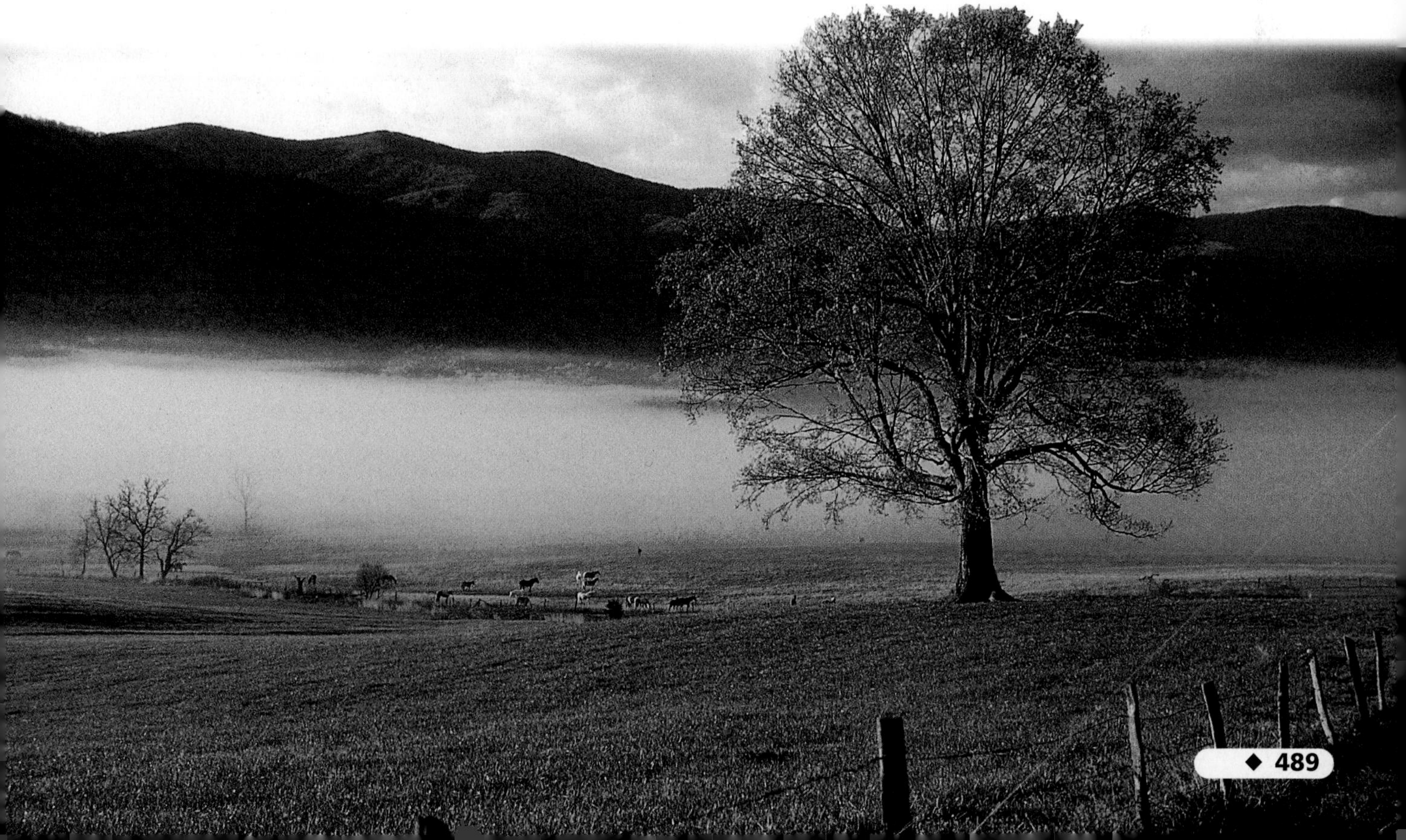

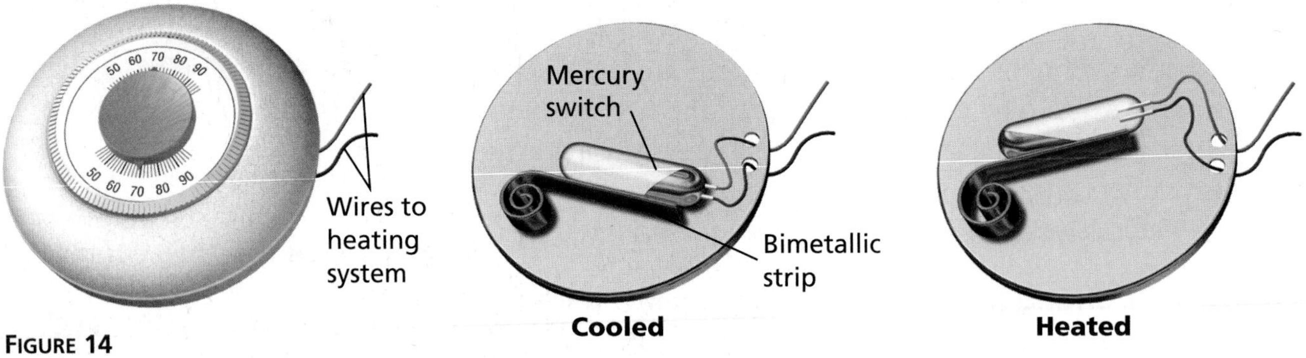

FIGURE 14
Thermostat
A bimetallic strip controls many thermostats. When it cools, the strip curls up and lowers the switch, allowing mercury to flow over the wires. When the strip warms up, it uncurls and raises the switch.

Discovery Channel School

Thermal Energy and Heat

Video Preview
▶ Video Field Trip
Video Assessment

Thermal Expansion

Have you ever loosened a tight jar lid by holding it under a stream of hot water? This works because the metal lid expands a little. Do you know why? **As the thermal energy of matter increases, its particles spread out and the substance expands.** With a few exceptions, this is true for all matter, even when the matter is not changing state. The expanding of matter when it is heated is known as **thermal expansion.**

When matter is cooled, thermal energy is released. The motion of the particles slows down and the particles move closer together. In nearly all cases, as matter is cooled, it contracts, or decreases in volume.

Heat-regulating devices called thermostats use thermal expansion to work. Many thermostats contain bimetallic strips, which are strips of two different metals joined together. Different metals expand at different rates. When the bimetallic strip is heated, one side expands more than the other. This causes the strip to uncurl. The movement of the strip operates a switch, which can turn a heating system on or off.

Section 3 Assessment

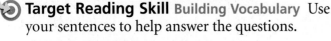

Target Reading Skill Building Vocabulary Use your sentences to help answer the questions.

Reviewing Key Concepts

1. **a.** Identifying Name three states of matter.
   b. Comparing and Contrasting How are the three states of matter different from each other? How are they the same?
2. **a.** Reviewing What causes a change in state?
   b. Describing Why does the temperature of matter remain the same while the matter changes state?
   c. Relating Cause and Effect What causes a solid to melt?
3. **a.** Defining How can a liquid expand without changing state?
   b. Applying Concepts Why should you poke holes in a potato before baking it?
   c. Interpreting Diagrams How does a thermostat make use of thermal expansion?

Lab zone At-Home Activity

Frosty Balloons Blow up two balloons so that they are the same size. Have a family member use a measuring tape to measure the circumference of the balloons. Place one of the balloons in the freezer for 15 to 20 minutes. Then measure both balloons again. Explain how changes in thermal energy cause the change in size.

Section 4

Uses of Heat

Reading Preview

Key Concepts

- How do heat engines use thermal energy?
- How do refrigerators keep things cold?

Key Terms

- heat engine
- external combustion engine
- internal combustion engine
- refrigerant

Target Reading Skill

Sequencing A sequence is the order in which the steps in a process occur. As you read, make a cycle diagram that shows how refrigerators work. Write each phase of the cooling system's cycle in a separate circle.

How Refrigerators Work

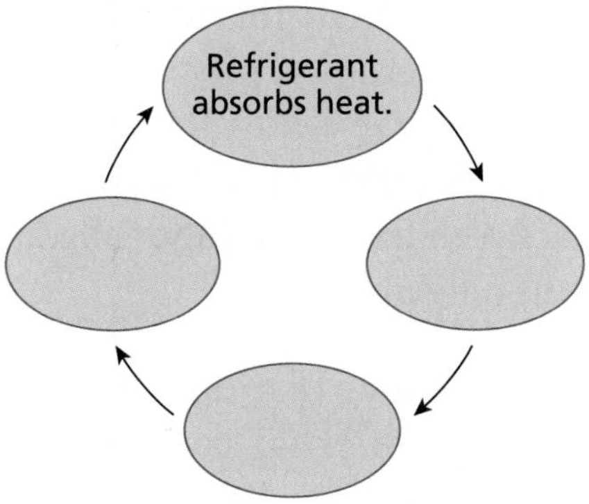

Refrigerant absorbs heat.

Lab zone Discover Activity

What Happens at the Pump?

1. Obtain a bicycle pump and a deflated basketball or soccer ball.
2. Feel the pump with your hand. Note whether it feels cool or warm to the touch.
3. Use the pump to inflate the ball to the recommended pressure.
4. As soon as you stop pumping, feel the pump again. Observe any changes in temperature.

Think It Over

Developing Hypotheses Propose an explanation for any changes that you observed.

For more than 100 years, the steam locomotive was a symbol of power and speed. It first came into use in the 1830s, and was soon hauling hundreds of tons of freight faster than a horse could gallop. Today, many trains are pulled by diesel locomotives that are far more efficient than steam locomotives.

Heat Engines

To power a coal-burning steam locomotive, coal is shoveled into a roaring fire. Heat is then transferred from the fire to water in the boiler. But how can heat move a train?

The thermal energy of the coal fire must be transformed to the mechanical energy, or energy of motion, of the moving train. You already know about the reverse process, the transformation of mechanical energy to thermal energy. It happens when you rub your hands together to make them warm.

The transformation of thermal energy to mechanical energy requires a device called a **heat engine.** Heat engines usually make use of combustion. You may recall that combustion is the process of burning a fuel, such as coal or gasoline. During combustion, chemical energy that is stored in fuel is transformed to thermal energy. **Heat engines transform thermal energy to mechanical energy.** Heat engines are classified according to whether combustion takes place outside the engine or inside the engine.

FIGURE 15
External Combustion Engine

In a steam-powered external combustion engine, expanding steam pushes a piston back and forth inside a cylinder. The steam's thermal energy is transformed to mechanical energy.

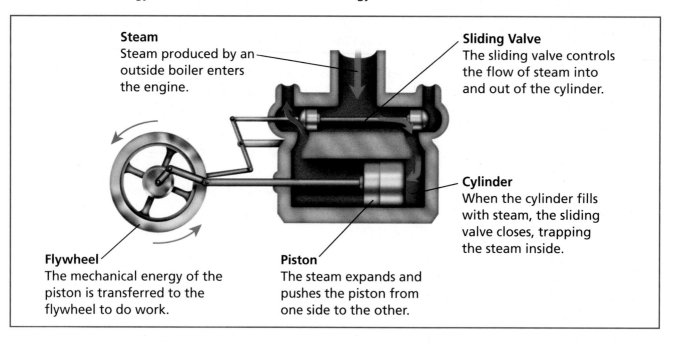

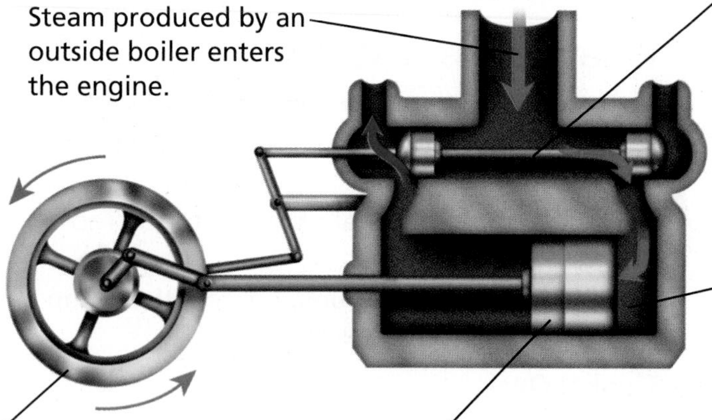

Steam
Steam produced by an outside boiler enters the engine.
Sliding Valve
The sliding valve controls the flow of steam into and out of the cylinder.
Cylinder
When the cylinder fills with steam, the sliding valve closes, trapping the steam inside.
Flywheel
The mechanical energy of the piston is transferred to the flywheel to do work.
Piston
The steam expands and pushes the piston from one side to the other.

External Combustion Engines Engines that burn fuel outside the engine in a boiler are called **external combustion engines.** A steam engine, like the one shown in Figure 15, is an example of an external combustion engine. The combustion of wood, coal, or oil heats water in a boiler. As its thermal energy increases, the liquid water turns to water vapor, or steam. The steam is then passed through a sliding valve into the engine, where it pushes against a metal plunger called a piston. Work is done on the piston as it moves back and forth in a tube called a cylinder. The piston's motion turns a flywheel.

Lab zone Try This Activity

Shake It Up

How does work relate to temperature?

1. Place a handful of dry sand in a metal container that has a cover.
2. Measure the temperature of the sand with a thermometer.
3. Cover the can and shake it vigorously for a minute or two.
4. Predict any change in the temperature of the sand. Was your prediction correct?

Classifying Identify any energy transformations and use them to explain your observations.

Internal Combustion Engines Engines that burn fuel in cylinders inside the engine are called **internal combustion engines.** Diesel and gasoline engines, which power most automobiles, are internal combustion engines. A piston inside a cylinder moves up and down, turning a crankshaft. The motion of the crankshaft is transferred to the wheels of the car.

Each up or down movement by a piston is called a stroke. Most diesel and gasoline engines are four-stroke engines, as shown in Figure 16. Automobile engines usually have four, six, or eight cylinders. The four-stroke process occurs in each cylinder, and is repeated many times each second.

Reading Checkpoint **How many cylinders do automobiles usually have?**

FIGURE 16
Four-Stroke Engine

Most automobiles use four-stroke engines. These four strokes occur repeatedly in each of the engine's cylinders.

Interpreting Diagrams *During which stroke is thermal energy transformed to mechanical energy?*

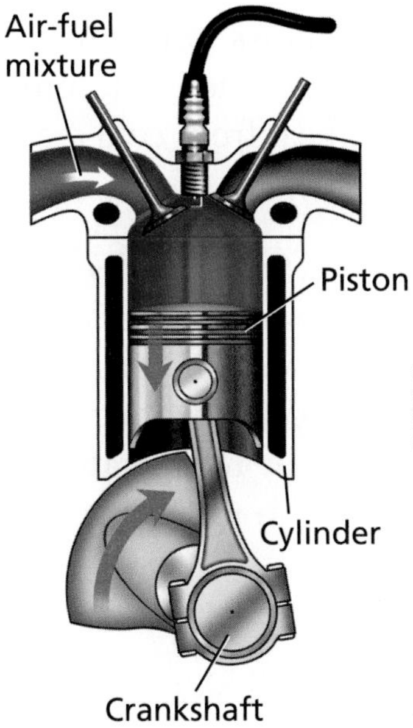

1 Intake Stroke
A mixture of fuel and air is drawn into the cylinder as the piston moves down.

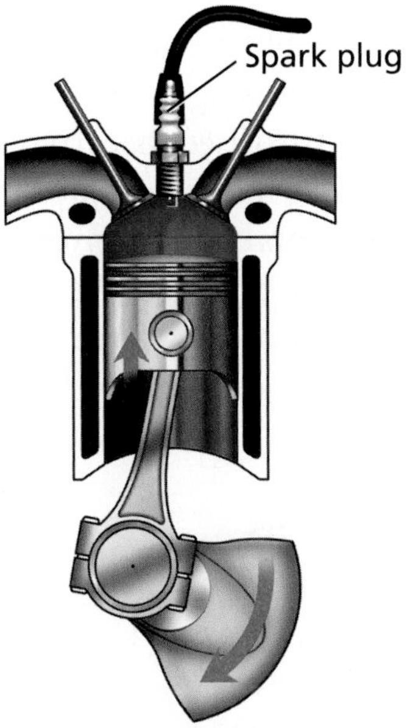

2 Compression Stroke
The mixture is compressed into a smaller space as the piston moves back up.

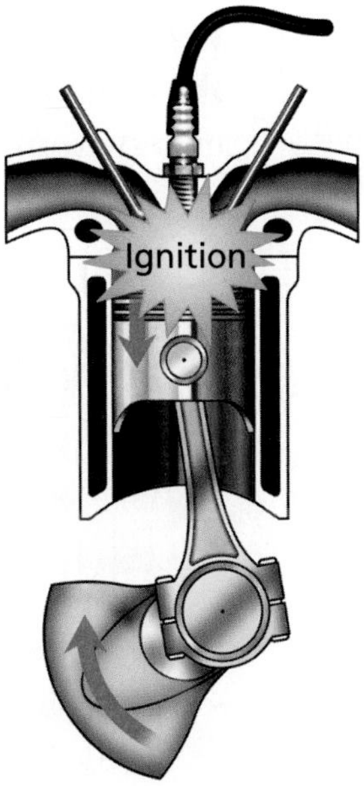

3 Power Stroke
A spark plug ignites the mixture. The heated gas expands and pushes the piston down. The piston moves the crankshaft.

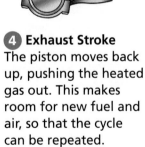

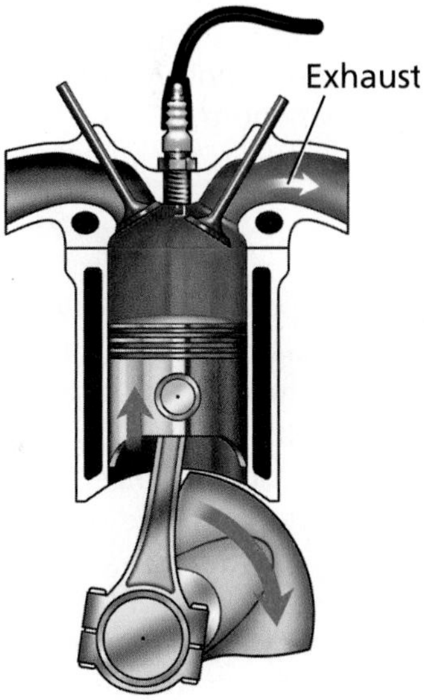

4 Exhaust Stroke
The piston moves back up, pushing the heated gas out. This makes room for new fuel and air, so that the cycle can be repeated.

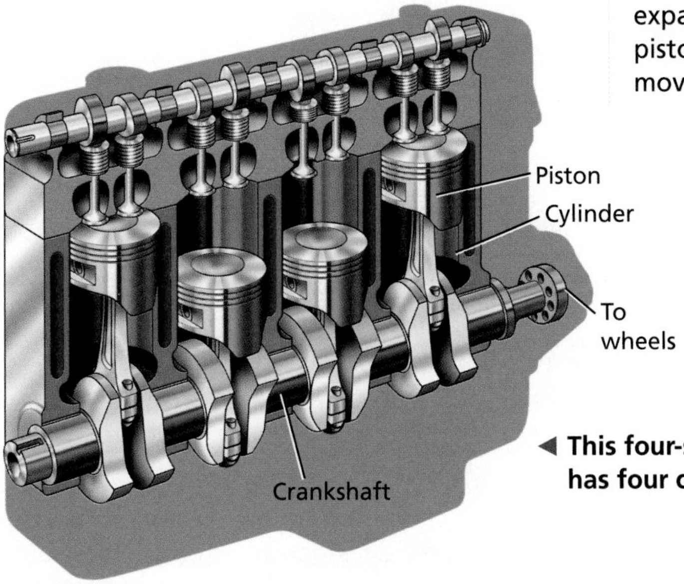

◀ **This four-stroke engine has four cylinders.**

Go Online
active art

For: Four-Stroke Engine activity
Visit: PHSchool.com
Web Code: cgp-3064

Cooling Systems

The transfer of heat can sometimes be used to keep things cool. Are you surprised? After all, heat naturally flows from a warm area to a cold area—not the other way around. But some devices, such as refrigerators, can transfer heat from cold areas to warm areas.

Refrigerators A refrigerator is cold inside. So where does the heat in the warm air rising from the back of a refrigerator come from? You may be surprised to learn that part of the heat actually comes from food in the refrigerator! **A refrigerator is a device that transfers thermal energy from inside the refrigerator to the room outside.** In doing so, the refrigerator transfers thermal energy from a cool area to a warm area.

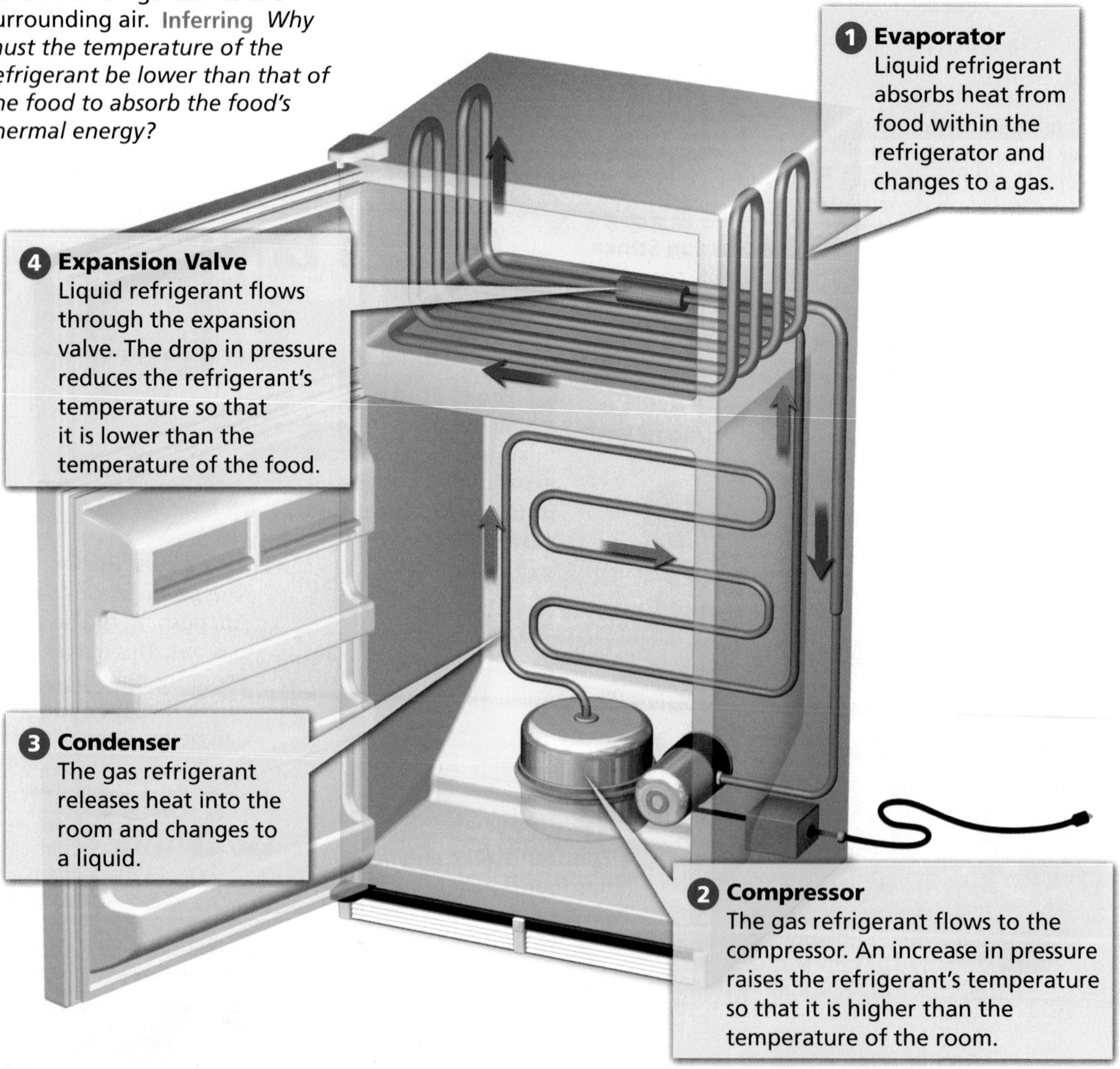

1 Evaporator
Liquid refrigerant absorbs heat from food within the refrigerator and changes to a gas.
4 Expansion Valve
Liquid refrigerant flows through the expansion valve. The drop in pressure reduces the refrigerant's temperature so that it is lower than the temperature of the food.
3 Condenser
The gas refrigerant releases heat into the room and changes to a liquid.
2 Compressor
The gas refrigerant flows to the compressor. An increase in pressure raises the refrigerant's temperature so that it is higher than the temperature of the room.

FIGURE 17
Refrigerator
Inside a refrigerator, refrigerant moves through a system of pipes, transferring thermal energy from inside the refrigerator to the surrounding air. **Inferring** *Why must the temperature of the refrigerant be lower than that of the food to absorb the food's thermal energy?*

A substance called a **refrigerant** absorbs and releases heat in a refrigerator. As shown in Figure 17, the refrigerant moves through a closed system of pipes. These pipes run along the back of the refrigerator and inside where food is stored. The coiled pipes inside make up the evaporator. As the refrigerant enters the evaporator, it is a liquid. Because it is colder than the food, it absorbs the thermal energy of the food. The food's thermal energy raises the refrigerant's temperature, causing it to evaporate. Then, the gas refrigerant enters an electric pump called a compressor. The compressor increases the refrigerant's pressure, further raising its temperature.

From the compressor, the gas refrigerant flows to the coiled pipes at the back of the refrigerator that make up the condenser. When it enters the condenser, the refrigerant is warmer than the air in the room. It releases heat into the air and its temperature drops, causing the refrigerant to condense. The pressure of the liquid refrigerant is decreased as it flows into a narrow opening called an expansion valve. The decreased pressure lowers the refrigerant's temperature further. The refrigerant recycles as it flows back to the evaporator.

Air Conditioners The air conditioners used in homes, schools, and cars cool air in the same way that a refrigerator cools food. Refrigerant in a system of pipes changes from a liquid to a gas and back again to transfer heat. Unlike a refrigerator, however, an air conditioner absorbs heat from the air inside a room or car and transfers it to the outdoors.

Reading Checkpoint **How are air conditioners and refrigerators similar?**

Section 4 Assessment

Target Reading Skill Sequencing Refer to your cycle diagram about cooling systems as you answer Question 2.

Reviewing Key Concepts

1. a. Describing What does a heat engine do?
   b. Comparing and Contrasting How are internal combustion engines different from external combustion engines? How are they similar?
   c. Making Generalizations Why do you think modern cars use internal rather than external combustion engines?
2. a. Identifying What changes of state occur in the refrigerant of a refrigerator?
   b. Explaining Where do the changes of state occur?
   c. Predicting If the compressor in a refrigerator stopped working, how would its failure affect the heat transfer cycle?

Writing in Science

Cause-and-Effect Paragraph The invention of the heat engine and refrigerator both had a great impact on society. Write about how daily life might be different if either system had not been invented.

Chapter 14 Study Guide

1 Temperature, Thermal Energy, and Heat

Key Concepts

- The three common scales for measuring temperature are the Fahrenheit, Celsius, and Kelvin scales.
- Heat is thermal energy moving from a warmer object to a cooler object.
- A material with a high specific heat can absorb a great deal of thermal energy without a great change in temperature.
- Change in energy =
  Mass × Specific heat × Change in temperature

Key Terms

temperature
Fahrenheit scale
Celsius scale
Kelvin scale
absolute zero
heat
specific heat

2 The Transfer of Heat

Key Concepts

- Heat is transferred by conduction, convection, and radiation.
- If two objects have different temperatures, heat will flow from the warmer object to the colder one.
- A conductor transfers thermal energy well. An insulator does not transfer thermal energy well.

Key Terms

conduction
convection
convection current
radiation
conductor
insulator

3 Thermal Energy and States of Matter

Key Concepts

- Most matter on Earth can exist in three states—solid, liquid, and gas.
- Matter can change from one state to another when thermal energy is absorbed or released.
- As the thermal energy of matter increases, its particles spread out and the substance expands.

Key Terms

state
change of state
melting
freezing
evaporation
boiling
condensation
thermal expansion

4 Uses of Heat

Key Concepts

- Heat engines transform thermal energy to mechanical energy.
- A refrigerator is a device that transfers thermal energy from inside the refrigerator to the room outside.

Key Terms

heat engine
external combustion engine
internal combustion engine
refrigerant

Review and Assessment

Go Online
PHSchool.com
For: Self-Assessment
Visit: PHSchool.com
Web Code: cga-3060

Organizing Information

Concept Mapping Copy the concept map about heat onto a separate sheet of paper. Then complete it and add a title. (For more on Concept Mapping, see the Skills Handbook.)

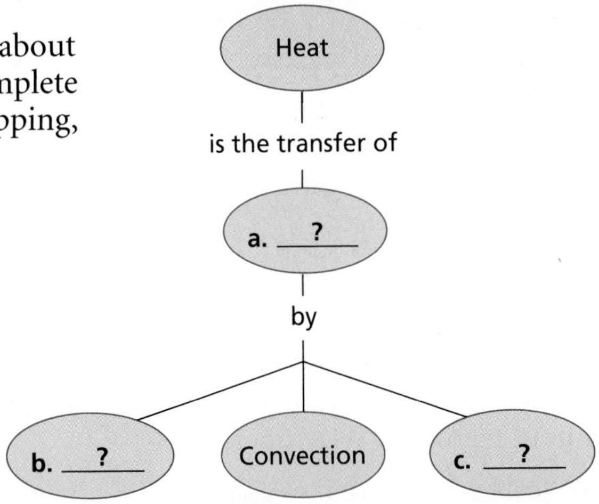

Reviewing Key Terms

Choose the letter of the best answer.

1. A measure of the average kinetic energy of the particles of an object is its
   a. heat.
   b. temperature.
   c. specific heat.
   d. thermal energy.
2. If you want to know the amount of heat needed to raise the temperature of 2 kg of steel by 10°C, you need to know steel's
   a. temperature. **b.** thermal energy.
   c. state. **d.** specific heat.
3. The process by which heat moves from one particle of matter to another without the movement of matter itself is called
   a. convection.
   b. conduction.
   c. radiation.
   d. thermal expansion.
4. Vaporization that occurs below the surface of a liquid is called
   a. evaporation. **b.** melting.
   c. boiling. **d.** freezing.
5. The process of burning a fuel is called
   a. combustion.
   b. thermal expansion.
   c. radiation.
   d. boiling.

If the statement is true, write *true*. If it is false, change the underlined word or words to make the statement true.

6. A temperature reading of zero on the <u>Celsius scale</u> is equal to absolute zero.
7. A <u>convection current</u> is the circular motion of a fluid caused by the rising of heated fluid.
8. An <u>insulator</u> conducts heat well.
9. When a substance is <u>freezing</u>, the thermal energy of the substance decreases.
10. In an <u>external combustion engine</u>, the fuel is burned inside the engine.

Writing in Science

Proposed Solution You have been asked to design a bridge for an area that is quite hot in the summer and cold in the winter. Propose a design plan for the bridge. Include in your plan how expansion joints will help the bridge react in hot and cold temperatures.

Discovery Channel School™

Thermal Energy and Heat
Video Preview
Video Field Trip
▶ Video Assessment

Review and Assessment

Checking Concepts

11. What happens to the particles of a solid as the thermal energy of the solid increases?
12. During a summer night, the air temperature drops by 10°C. Will the temperature of the water in a nearby lake change by the same amount? Explain why or why not.
13. When you heat a pot of water on the stove, a convection current is formed. Explain how this happens.
14. How can you add thermal energy to a substance without increasing its temperature?
15. When molten steel becomes solid, is energy absorbed or released by the steel? Explain.
16. Describe how a thermostat controls the temperature in a building.

Thinking Critically

17. **Relating Cause and Effect** Why is the air pressure in a car's tires different before and after the car has been driven for an hour?
18. **Applying Concepts** When they are hung, telephone lines are allowed to sag. Can you think of a reason why?
19. **Interpreting Diagrams** The three illustrations below represent the molecules in three different materials. Which is a solid? A liquid? A gas?

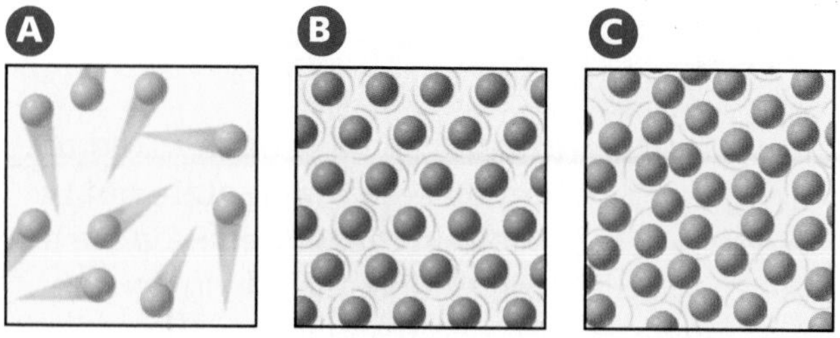

20. **Developing Hypotheses** A refrigerator is running in a small room. The refrigerator door is open, but the room does not grow any cooler. Use the law of conservation of energy to explain why the temperature does not drop.

Math Practice

21. **Converting Units** A recipe says to preheat your oven to 275°F. What is this temperature in degrees Celsius?
22. **Converting Units** The temperature in a greenhouse is 86°F. Convert this temperature to degrees Celsius.

Applying Skills

Use the illustration of three containers of water to answer Questions 23–25.

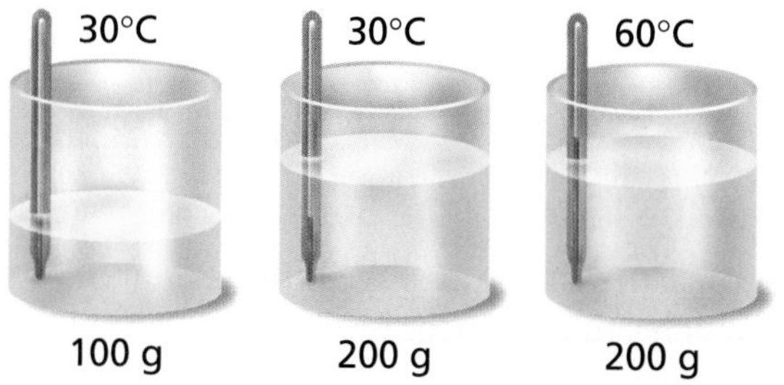

23. **Interpreting Data** Compare the average motion of the molecules in the three containers. Explain your answer.
24. **Drawing Conclusions** Compare the total amount of thermal energy in the three containers. Explain your answer.
25. **Calculating** Which container would need the least amount of thermal energy to raise its temperature by 1 K? The specific heat of water is 4,180 J/(kg·K).

Lab zone Chapter Project

Performance Assessment Talk with your classmates about their container designs. When you've had a chance to look them over, predict the final water temperature for each container. Record the starting temperature for each one, including your own. Record the final temperatures at the end of each demonstration. Which insulating materials seemed to work the best? Describe how you could improve your container, based on what you learned.

Standardized Test Prep

Test-Taking Tip

Using Formulas

For some questions, you will need to use a formula to find the correct answer. It is important to know which formula to use. Look for key words in the question to help you decide which formula will help you answer the question. Then substitute the values provided to make your calculations.

Sample Question

The specific heat of iron is 450 J/(kg·K). How much heat must be transferred to 15 kg of iron to raise its temperature by 4.0 K?

A 450 J
B 2,700 J
C 5,400 J
D 27,000 J

Answer

The question deals with the amount of heat needed to change the temperature of a material. The specific heat of that material, iron, is provided. You need to use the formula for calculating thermal energy changes.

Change in energy =
Mass × Specific heat × Change in temperature

Change in energy = 15 kg × 450 J/(kg·K) × 4.0 K
Change in energy = 27,000 J

The correct answer is **D**.

Choose the letter of the best answer.

1. When cold, dry air passes over a much warmer body of water, a type of fog called sea smoke is produced. Which process explains why this occurs?
A melting
B condensation
C boiling
D freezing

2. The table below shows the specific heat of four metals. If 1,540 J of heat is transferred to 4 kg of each metal, which metal will increase in temperature by 1 K?

Specific Heat of Metals

Metal	Specific Heat (J/(kg·K))
Silver	235
Iron	450
Copper	385
Aluminum	903

F Silver
G Copper
H Iron
J Aluminum

3. A student wants to measure the temperature at which several different liquids freeze. In the student's experiment, temperature is the
A hypothesis.
B responding variable.
C manipulated variable.
D operational definition.

4. Two solid metal blocks are placed in a container. If there is a transfer of heat between the blocks, then they must have different
F boiling points.
G melting points.
H specific heats.
J temperatures.

5. A thermometer measures
A temperature.
B thermal energy.
C heat.
D specific heat.

Constructed Response

Explain how heat is transferred by conduction, convection, and radiation. Give an example of each.

Interdisciplinary
Exploration

Bridges—From Vines to Steel

Have you ever

- balanced on a branch or log to cross a brook?
- jumped from rock to rock in a streambed?
- swung on a vine or rope over a river?

Vine Footbridge
A girl crosses over the Hunza River in northern Pakistan.

Then you have used the same ways that early people used to get over obstacles. Fallen trees, twisted vines, and natural stones formed the first bridges.

Bridges provide easy ways of getting over difficult obstacles. For thousands of years, bridges have also served as forts for defense, scenes of great battles, and homes for shops and churches. They have also been sites of mystery, love, and intrigue. They span history—linking cities, nations, and empires and encouraging trade and travel.

But bridges have not always been as elaborate as they are today. The earliest ones were made of materials that were free and plentiful. In deep forests, people used beams made from small trees. In tropical regions where vegetation was thick, people wove together vines and grasses, then hung them to make walkways over rivers and gorges.

No matter what the structures or materials, bridges reflect the people who built them. The ancient civilizations of China, Egypt, Greece, and Rome all designed strong, graceful bridges to connect and control their empires.

Roman Arch Bridge
Ponte Sant'Angelo is in Rome.

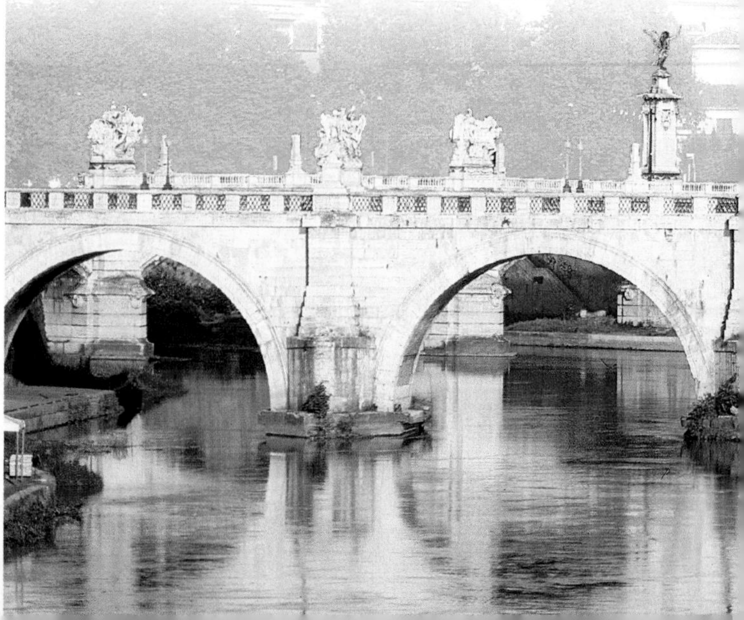

The Balance of Forces

What keeps a bridge from falling down? How does it support its own weight and the weight of people and traffic on it? Builders found the answers by considering the various forces that act on a bridge.

The weight of the bridge and the traffic on it are called the *load.* When a heavy truck crosses a beam bridge, the weight of the load forces the beam to curve downward. This creates tension forces that stretch the bottom of the beam. At the same time, the load also creates compression forces at the top of the beam.

Since the bridge doesn't collapse under the load, there must be upward forces to balance the downward forces. In simple beam bridges, builders anchor the beam to the ground or to end supports called abutments. To cross longer spans or distances, they construct piers under the middle span. Piers and abutments are structures that act as upward forces—reaction forces.

Another type of bridge, the arch bridge, supports its load by compression. A heavy load on a stone arch bridge squeezes or pushes the stones together, creating compression throughout the structure. Weight on the arch bridge pushes down to the ends of the arch. The side walls and abutments act as reaction forces.

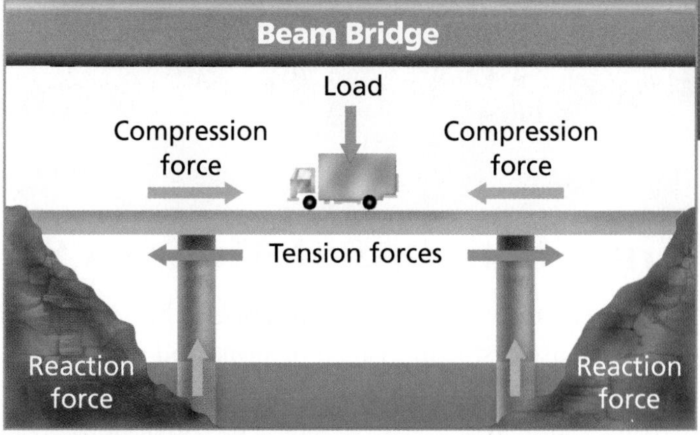

Beam Bridge
A beam bridge spans the Rhone River in France (top).

Early engineers discovered that arch bridges made of stone could span wider distances than simple beam bridges. Arch bridges are also stronger and more durable. Although the Romans were not the first to build arch bridges, they perfected the form in their massive, elegant structures. Early Roman arch bridges were built without mortar, or "glue." The arch held together because the stones were skillfully shaped to work in compression. After nearly 2,000 years, some of these Roman arch bridges are still standing.

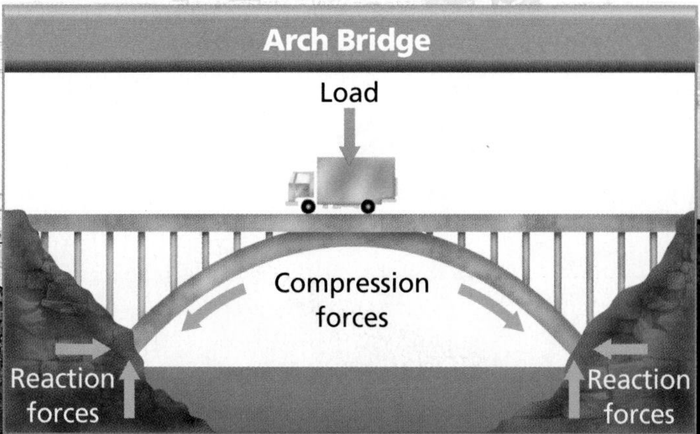

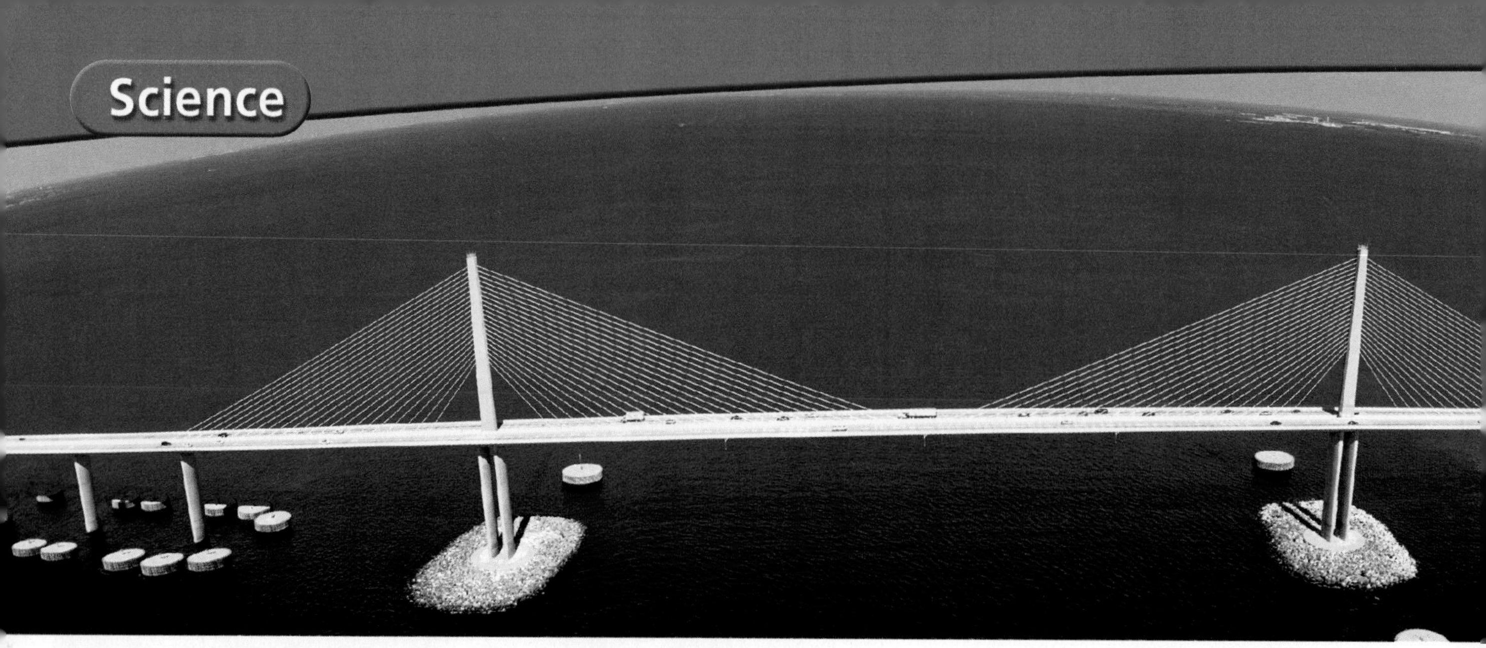

The Structure of Modern Bridges

By the 1800s in the United States, bridge builders began to use cast iron instead of stone and wood. By the late 1800s, they were using steel, which was strong and relatively lightweight. The use of new building materials was not the only change. Engineers began designing different types of bridges as well. They found that they could build longer, larger bridges by using a suspension structure.

Suspension bridges are modern versions of long, narrow, woven bridges found in tropical regions. These simple, woven suspension bridges can span long distances. Crossing one of these natural structures is like walking a tightrope. The weight of people and animals traveling over the bridge pushes down on the ropes, stretching them and creating tension forces.

Modern suspension bridges follow the same principles of tension as do woven bridges. A suspension bridge is strong in tension. In suspension bridges, parallel cables are stretched the entire length of the bridge—over giant towers. The cables are anchored at each end of the bridge. The roadway hangs from the cables, attached by wire suspenders. The weight of the bridge and the load on it act to pull apart or stretch the cables. This pulling apart creates tension forces.

The towers of a suspension bridge act as supports for the bridge cables. The abutments that anchor the cables exert reaction forces as well. So forces in balance keep a suspension bridge from collapsing.

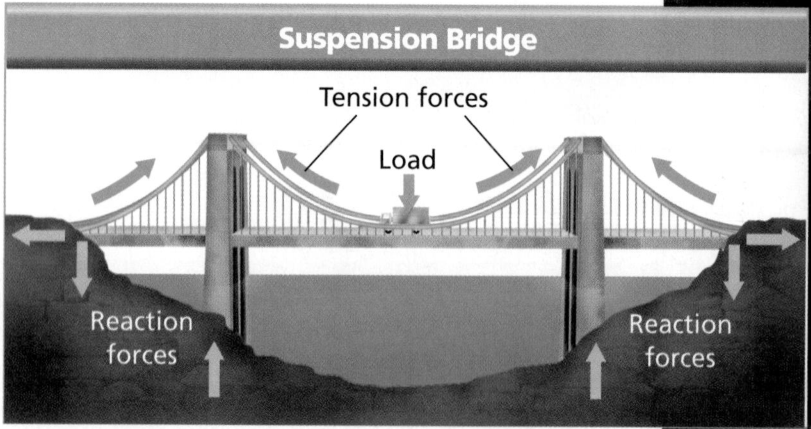

Suspension Bridge
The sun rises over the Golden Gate Bridge in California.

Cable-Stayed Bridge
The Sunshine Skyway Bridge spans a broad section of Tampa Bay in Florida. The cables, attached to the center of the roadway, enable travelers to have a clear view.

Science Activity

Work in groups to make a suspension bridge, using two chairs, a wooden plank, rope, and some books.

- Place two chairs back-to-back and stretch 2 ropes over the backs of the chairs. Hold the ropes at both ends.
- Tie three pieces of rope to the longer ropes. Place the plank through the loops.
- With a partner, hold the ropes tightly at each end. Load books on top of the plank to see how much it will hold.

Why is it important to anchor the ropes tightly at each end?

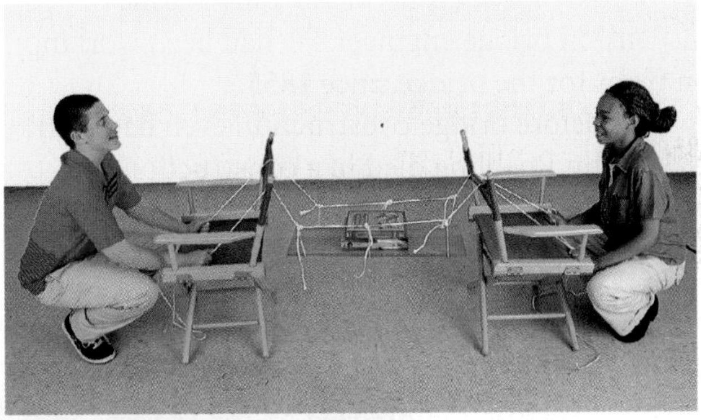

When the Brooklyn Bridge opened in New York City in 1883, it was the longest suspension bridge in the world. The Golden Gate Bridge in San Francisco, which was opened in 1937, was another great engineering feat.

Recently, engineers have developed a new bridge design called the cable-stayed bridge. It looks similar to a suspension bridge because both are built with towers and cables. But the two bridges are quite different. The cables on the cable-stayed bridge attach to the towers, so the towers bear the weight of the bridge and the load on it. In contrast, the cables on a suspension bridge ride over the towers and anchor at the abutments. So on a suspension bridge, both the towers and abutments bear the load.

Brooklyn Bridge
This bridge connects Brooklyn and Manhattan (above).
It took 14 years for workers to complete the bridge (left).

Against All Odds

When John Roebling was hired in 1868 to build the Brooklyn Bridge, he was already a skilled suspension bridge engineer. He had been working on plans for the bridge since 1855.

But before bridge construction even began in 1869, John Roebling died in a construction accident. Fortunately, he had worked out his bridge design to the last detail. His son, Colonel Washington Roebling, who was also a skilled engineer, dedicated himself to carrying out his father's plans.

The construction dragged on for 14 years and cost nearly 30 lives. Colonel Roebling himself became so disabled that he was forced to direct construction from his home. Using a telescope, Colonel Roebling followed every detail. His remarkable, energetic wife, Emily Warren Roebling, learned enough engineering principles to deliver and explain his orders to the workers.

As soon as the giant towers were up, workers unrolled the steel wire back and forth across the towers to weave the cables. The next step was to twist the wires together. But the workmen were terrified of hanging so high on the bridge and refused to work.

Finally, Frank Farrington, the chief mechanic, crossed the river on a small chair dangling from a wheel that ran across an overhead line. Farrington completed his journey to the roar of the crowd. Somewhat reassured, the builders returned to work. But it took two more years to string the cables. The bridge was one of the greatest engineering achievements of its time.

In the end, the Brooklyn Bridge project succeeded only because of the determination and sacrifices of the Roebling family. It became the model for hundreds of other suspension bridges.

Social Studies Activity

How do you think the Brooklyn Bridge changed the lives of New Yorkers? In groups, research the history of another famous bridge. Present your findings to your class along with drawings and photos. Find out

- when and why the bridge was built
- what type of bridge it is
- what effects the bridge has on people's lives—on trade, travel, and population
- how landforms affected the bridge building
- about events connected to the bridge

Two Great Cities United

May 25, 1883—The Brooklyn Bridge was successfully opened yesterday. The pleasant weather brought visitors by the thousands from all around. Spectators were packed in masses through which it was almost impossible to pass, and those who had tickets to attend the ceremonies had hard work to reach the bridge. Every available house-top and window was filled, and an adventurous party occupied a tall telegraph pole. It required the utmost efforts of the police to keep clear the necessary space.

After the exercises at the bridge were completed the Brooklyn procession was immediately re-formed and the march was taken up to Col. Roebling's residence. From the back study on the second floor of his house Col. Roebling had watched through his telescope the procession as it proceeded along from the New York side until the Brooklyn tower was reached. Mrs. Roebling received at her husband's side and accepted her share of the honors of the bridge.

For blocks and blocks on either side of the bridge there was scarcely a foot of room to spare. Many persons crossed and re-crossed the river on the ferry boats, and in that way watched the display. Almost every ship along the river front was converted into a grand stand.

The final ceremonies of the opening of the great bridge began at eight o'clock, when the first rocket was sent from the center of the great structure, and ended at nine o'clock, when a flight of 500 rockets illuminated the sky. The river-front was one blaze of light, and on the yachts and smaller vessels blue fires were burning and illuminating dark waters around them.

———Excerpted with permission from *The New York Times*

Brooklyn Bridge
This historic painting shows fireworks at the opening of the bridge in 1883.

Language Arts Activity

A reporter's goal is to inform and entertain the reader. Using a catchy opening line draws interest. Then the reader wants to know the facts—who, what, where, when, why, and how (5 W's and H).

You are a school reporter. Write about the opening of a bridge in your area. It could be a highway overpass or a bridge over water, a valley, or railroad tracks.

- Include some of the 5 W's and H.
- Add interesting details and descriptions.

Bridge Geometry

As railroad traffic increased in the late 1800s, truss bridges became popular. Designed with thin vertical and diagonal supports to add strength, truss bridges were actually reinforced beam bridge structures. Many of the early wood truss bridges couldn't support the trains that rumbled over them. Cast iron and steel trusses soon replaced wood trusses.

Using basic triangular structures, engineers went to work on more scientific truss bridge designs. The accuracy of the design is crucial to handling the stress from heavy train loads and constant vibrations. As in all bridge structures, each steel piece has to be measured and fitted accurately—including widths, lengths, angles, and points of intersection and attachment.

Geometric Angles and Figures
Engineers use various geometric figures in drawing bridge plans. Figures that have right angles are squares, rectangles, and right triangles. Figures that have acute angles and obtuse angles can be triangles and parallelograms.

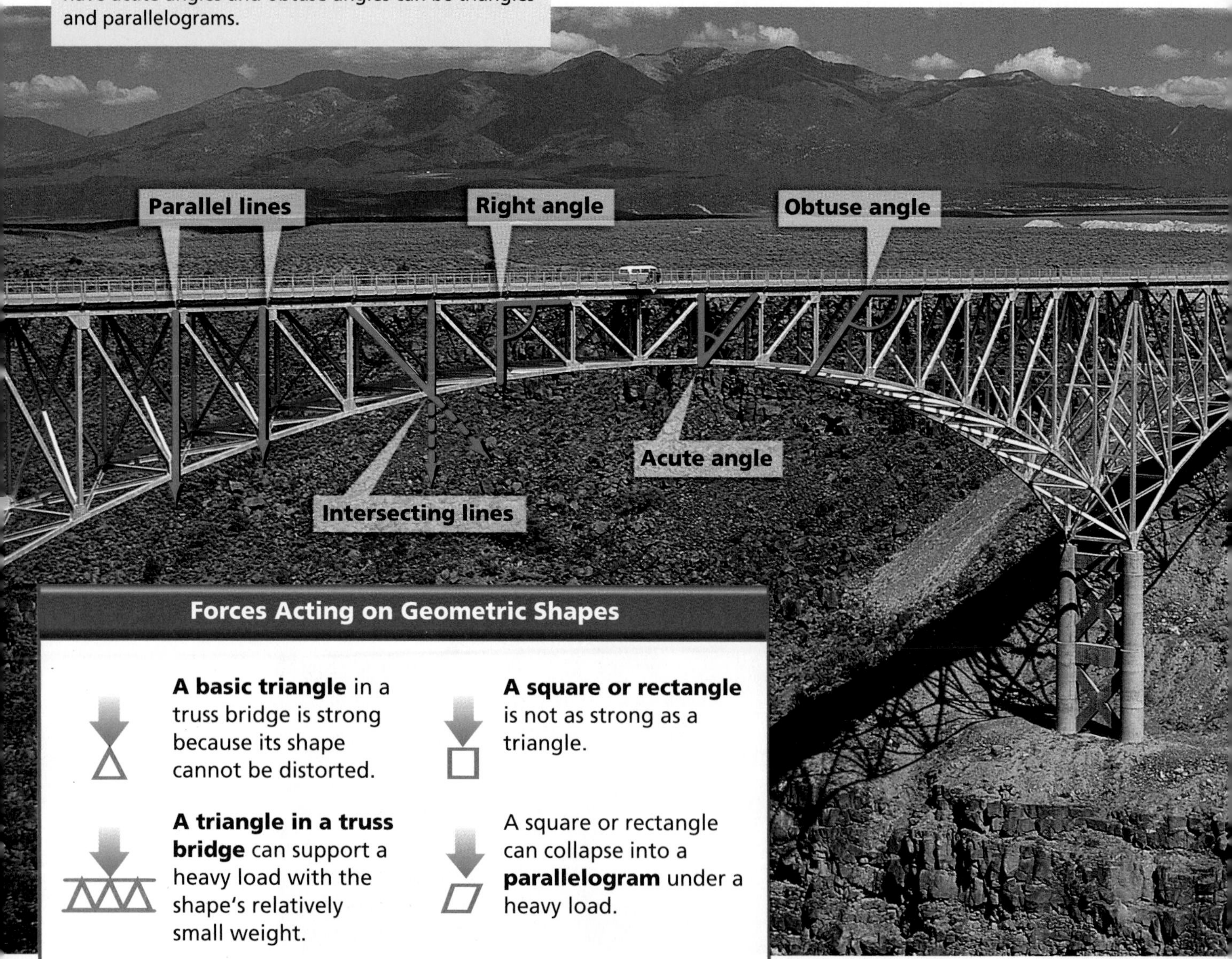

Forces Acting on Geometric Shapes

A basic triangle in a truss bridge is strong because its shape cannot be distorted.

A square or rectangle is not as strong as a triangle.

A triangle in a truss bridge can support a heavy load with the shape's relatively small weight.

A square or rectangle can collapse into a **parallelogram** under a heavy load.

Math Activity

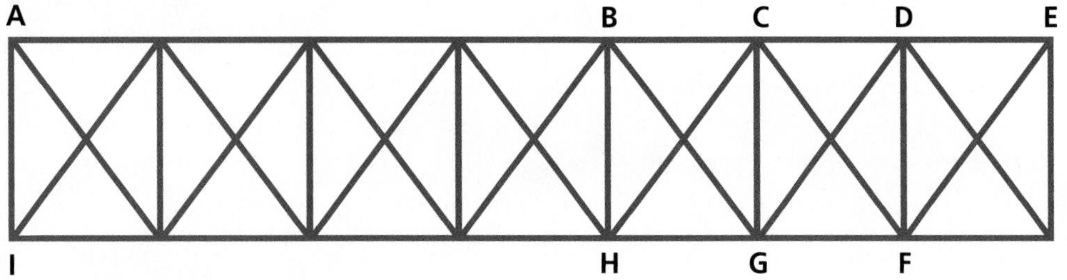

The chief building engineer has asked you to draw up exact plans for a new truss bridge. How well will you do as an assistant? Review the captions and labels on the previous page. Then answer these questions:

1. Which lines are parallel?
2. Which lines intersect?
3. What kind of figure is formed by *ABHI*?
4. What kind of figure is formed by *HCF*?
5. What kind of angle is *BGF*—obtuse or right?
6. What kind of angle is *CHG*?
7. What kind of triangle is *BHG*? What makes it this kind of triangle?
8. Why is a triangle stronger than a square?

▲ **Truss bridge over Rio Grande Gorge in New Mexico**

Tie It Together

Work in small groups to build a model of a bridge out of a box of spaghetti and a roll of masking tape. Meet as a group to choose the type of bridge you will build. Each bridge should be strong enough to hold a brick. You can build

- a beam bridge
- a truss bridge
- an arch bridge
- a suspension bridge (This one is challenging.)

After drawing a sketch of the bridge design, assign jobs for each team member. Then

- decide how long the bridge span will be
- measure and cut the materials
- build the roadway first for beam, truss, and suspension bridges
- build the arch first in an arch bridge

When your bridge is complete, display it in the classroom. Test the strength of each bridge by placing a brick on the roadway. Discuss the difference in bridge structures. Determine which bridge design is the strongest.

Chapter

15

Characteristics of Waves

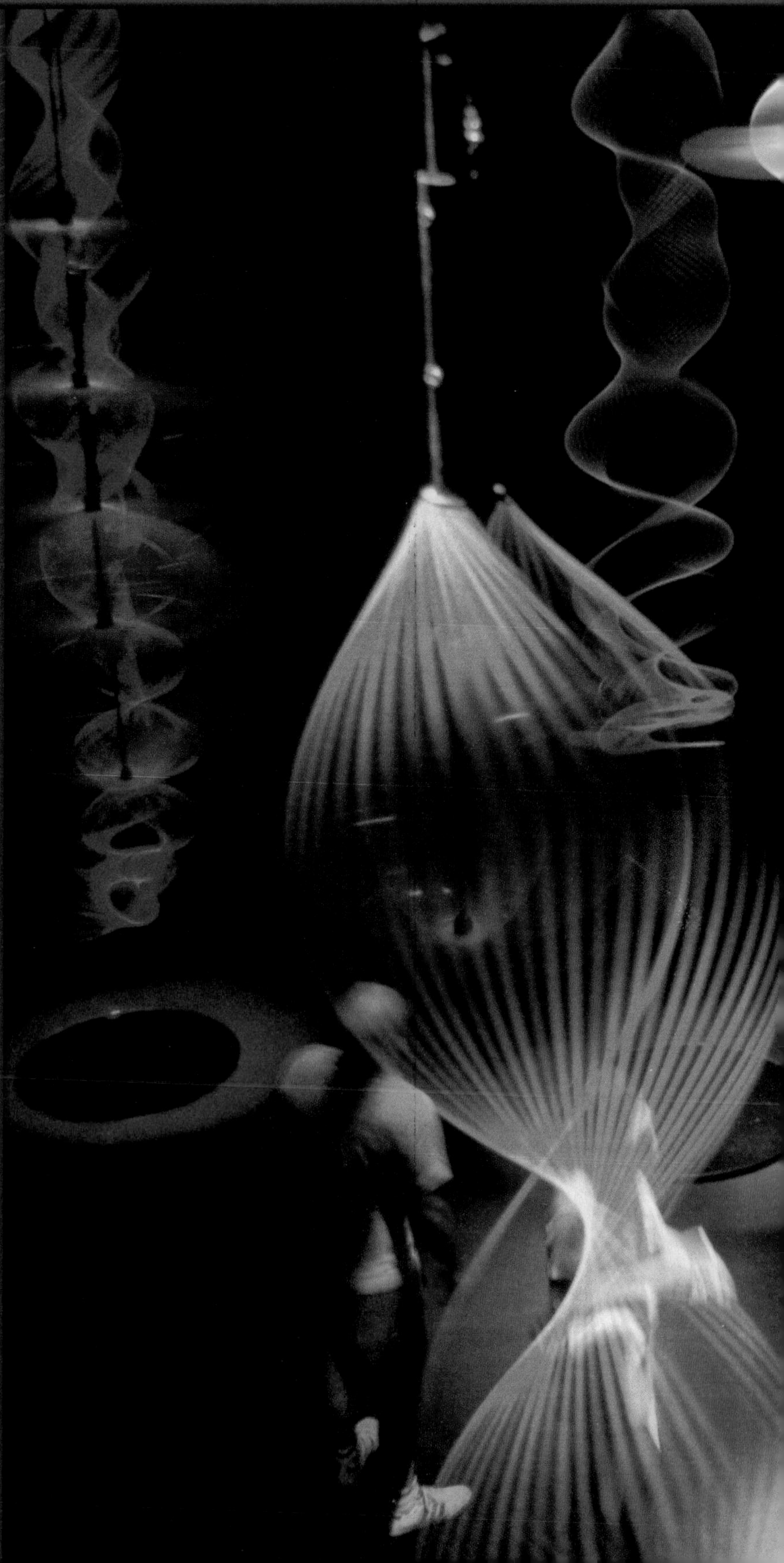

Chapter Preview

1 What Are Waves?
Discover *How Do Waves Travel?*
Math Skills *Angles*

2 Properties of Waves
Discover *Can You Change a Wave?*
Skills Activity *Calculating*
Skills Lab *Wavy Motions*

3 Interactions of Waves
Discover *How Does a Ball Bounce?*
Skills Activity *Observing*
Active Art *Wave Interference*
Try This *Interfering Waves*
At-Home Activity *Waves in a Sink*
Skills Lab *Making Waves*

4 Seismic Waves
Discover *Can You Find the Sand?*
Analyzing Data *Motion of a Tsunami*
At-Home Activity *Sounds Solid*

interactive Textbook

In this art, colored lights shine on waves moving along spinning ropes. ▶

Characteristics of Waves

▶ Video Preview
Video Field Trip
Video Assessment

Lab zone™ Chapter Project

Over and Over and Over Again

Some waves involve repeating patterns, or cycles. Any motion that repeats itself at regular intervals is called periodic motion. The hands moving on a clock, a child swinging on a swing, and a Ferris wheel going round and round are examples of periodic motion.

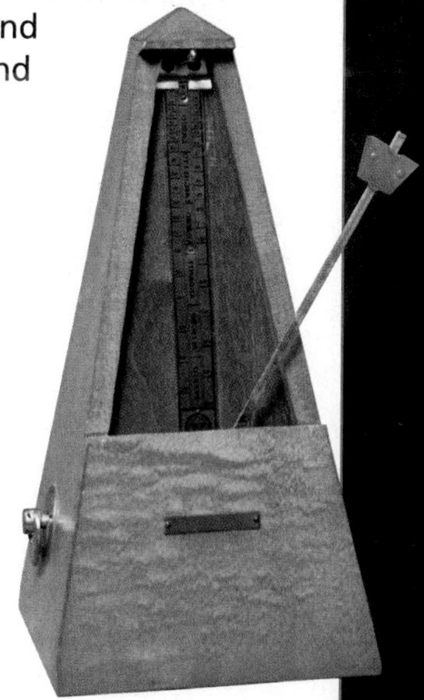

Your Goal To find examples of periodic motion and describe them

To complete this project you must

- identify examples of periodic motion or events that have periodic characteristics
- collect and organize data on the frequency and duration of each event
- present your findings as a poster, a display, or a demonstration

Plan It! With your group, brainstorm examples of objects or events that go back and forth or alternate from high to low, dark to light, loud to quiet, or crowded to uncrowded. Select at least two objects or events to observe. Record data such as how long it takes for the event to finish and start again or the highest and lowest point of the object's motion. Finally, organize your findings to present to your class.

Section 1

What Are Waves?

Reading Preview

Key Concepts

- What causes mechanical waves?
- What are two types of waves and how are they classified?

Key Terms

- wave • energy • medium
- mechanical wave • vibration
- transverse wave • crest
- trough • longitudinal wave
- compression • rarefaction

Target Reading Skill

Using Prior Knowledge Before you read, look at the section headings and visuals to see what this section is about. Then write what you know about waves and energy in a graphic organizer like the one below. As you read, continue to write in what you learn.

What You Know
1. Waves are high and low. 2.

What You Learned
1. 2.

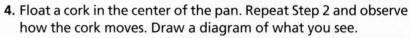

Lab zone Discover Activity

How Do Waves Travel?

1. Fill a shallow pan with about 3 cm of water.
2. With a pencil, touch the surface of the water at one end of the pan twice each second for about a minute.
3. Describe the pattern the waves make. Sketch a rough diagram of what you see.
4. Float a cork in the center of the pan. Repeat Step 2 and observe how the cork moves. Draw a diagram of what you see.

Think It Over

Observing How did the cork move in Step 4? How is its movement similar to the wave's movement? How is it different?

It was a long swim, but now you're resting on the swimming raft in the lake. You hear the water lapping gently against the raft as the sun warms your skin. Suddenly a motorboat zooms by. A few seconds later you're bobbing wildly up and down as the boat's waves hit the raft. Although the speedboat didn't touch the raft, its energy caused waves in the water. Then the waves moved the raft—and you!

You can see and feel the water waves when you're on a swimming raft. But did you know that many kinds of waves affect you every day? Sound is a wave. Sunlight is a different kind of wave. Light, sound, and water waves may seem very different, but they all are waves. What is a wave?

▼ A motorboat making waves

Waves and Energy

A **wave** is a disturbance that transfers energy from place to place. In science, **energy** is defined as the ability to do work. To understand waves, think about the swimming raft. A wave that disturbs the surface of the water also will disturb the raft. The wave's energy lifts the heavy raft as the wave passes under it. But the disturbance caused by the wave is temporary. After the wave passes, the water is calm again and the raft stops bobbing.

FIGURE 1
Motion of a Medium
Waves travel through water, but they do not carry the water (or the duck) with them. **Predicting** *If you add a sixth stage to the diagram, which earlier stage should it most resemble?*

What Carries Waves? Most kinds of waves need something to travel through. Sound waves travel through air. Water waves travel along the surface of the water. A wave can even travel along a rope. The material through which a wave travels is called a **medium.** Gases (such as air), liquids (such as water), and solids (such as rope) all act as mediums. Waves that require a medium through which to travel are called **mechanical waves.**

But not all waves require a medium to travel through. Light from the sun, for example, can carry energy through empty space. If light could not travel through empty space, you could not even see the sun! Waves that can travel without a medium are called electromagnetic waves. You will learn more about electromagnetic waves in a later chapter.

How Do Waves Transfer Energy? Although mechanical waves travel through a medium, they do not carry the medium with them. Look at the duck in Figure 1. When a wave travels under the duck, the duck moves up and down. But the duck does not travel with the wave. After the wave passes, the duck and the water return to where they started.

Why doesn't the medium travel along with the wave? All mediums are made of tiny particles. When a wave enters a medium, it transfers energy to the medium's particles. The particles bump into each other, passing the wave's energy along. To understand this, think about how food is passed at a table. You hand the food to the next person, who passes it to the next person, and so on. The food is transferred, but the people don't move. The food is like the wave's energy, and the people are like particles in a medium.

Math Skills

Angles

An angle is formed when two lines meet at a point. Angles are measured in degrees, indicated by the symbol °. A circle has 360 degrees. A right angle is an angle that contains 90 degrees. Two lines that meet at a point to form a 90° angle are said to be perpendicular to each other.

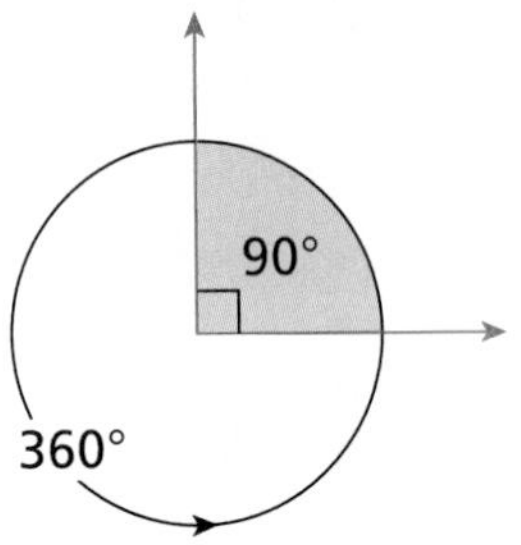

Practice Problems

1. Draw a circle on a piece of paper. How many right angles can you fit in the circle?
2. How many degrees do two right angles contain?

What Causes Waves? Energy always is required to make a wave. **Mechanical waves are produced when a source of energy causes a medium to vibrate.** A **vibration** is a repeated back-and-forth or up-and-down motion. When a vibration moves through a medium, a wave results.

Moving objects have energy. A moving object can transfer energy to a medium, producing waves. For example, you can make waves by dipping your finger in water. Your finger has energy because it is moving. When your finger touches the water, it transfers energy to the water and makes waves. In the same way, a motorboat slicing through calm water transfers energy to the water and makes waves.

Reading Checkpoint What is a vibration?

Types of Waves

Waves move through mediums in different ways. **Mechanical waves are classified by how they move. There are two types of mechanical waves: transverse waves and longitudinal waves.**

Transverse Waves When you make a wave on a rope, the wave moves from one end of the rope to the other. But the rope itself moves up and down or from side to side, at right angles to the direction in which the wave travels. Waves that move the medium at right angles to the direction in which the waves travel are called **transverse waves.** Transverse means "across." As a transverse wave moves, the particles of the medium move across, or at a right angle to, the direction of the wave.

In Figure 2, you can see that the red ribbon on the rope is first at a low point of the wave. Then it is at a high point. The high part of a transverse wave is called a **crest,** and the low part is called a **trough** (trawf).

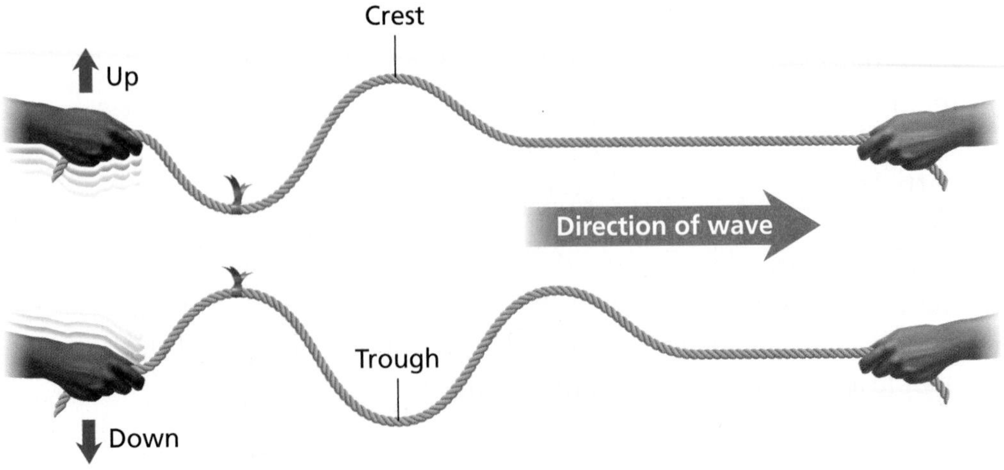

FIGURE 2
Transverse Waves
A transverse wave moves the rope up and down in a direction perpendicular to the direction in which the wave travels.

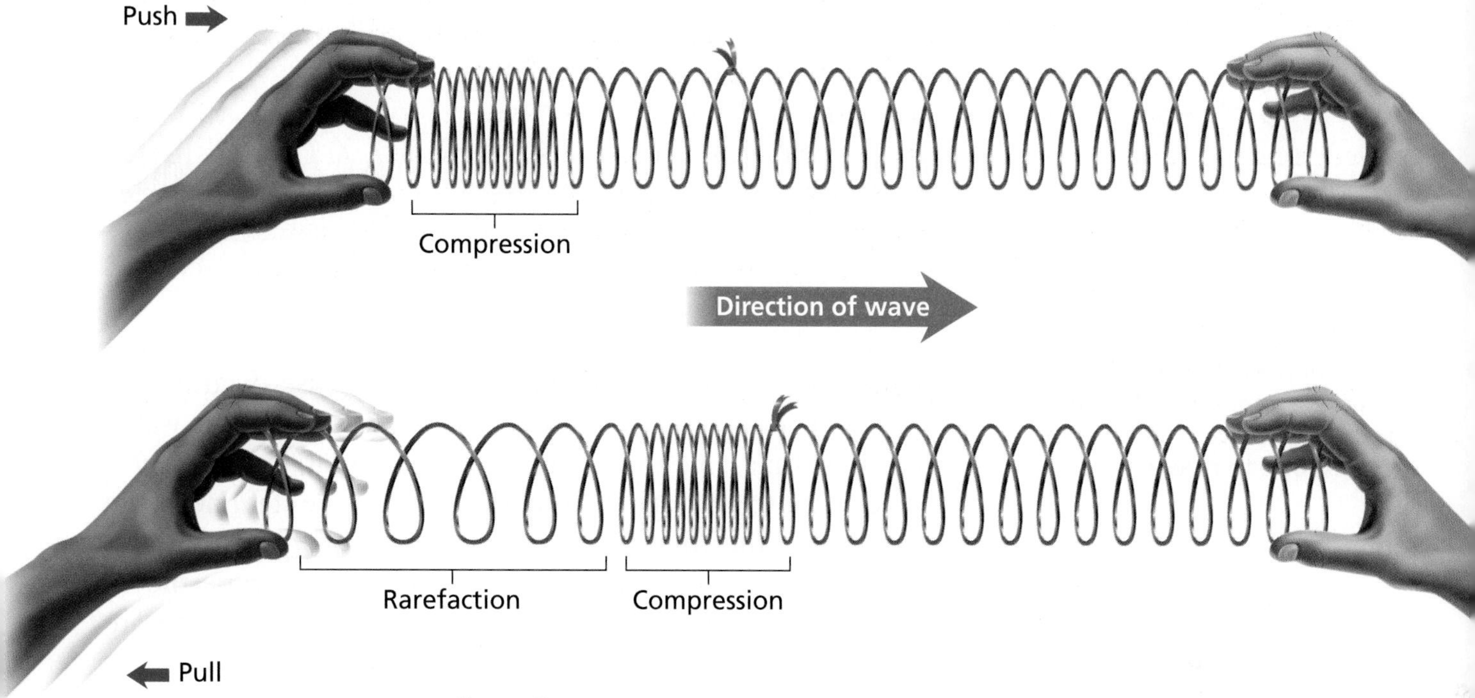

FIGURE 3
Longitudinal Waves
A longitudinal wave moves the coils of a spring toy back and forth in a direction parallel to the direction the wave travels. **Comparing and Contrasting** *How do the coils in a compression compare to the coils in a rarefaction?*

Longitudinal Waves Figure 3 shows a different kind of wave. If you stretch out a spring toy and push and pull one end, you can produce a longitudinal wave. **Longitudinal waves** (lawn juh TOO duh nul) move the medium parallel to the direction in which the waves travel. The coils in the spring move back and forth parallel to the wave motion.

Notice in Figure 3 that in some parts of the spring, the coils are close together. In other parts of the spring, the coils are more spread out. The parts where the coils are close together are called **compressions** (kum PRESH unz). The parts where the coils are spread out, or rarified, are called **rarefactions** (rair uh FAK shunz).

As compressions and rarefactions travel along the spring toy, each coil moves forward and then back. The energy travels from one end of the spring to the other, creating a wave. After the wave passes, each coil returns to the position where it started.

Sound is also a longitudinal wave. In air, sound waves cause air particles to move back and forth. In areas where the particles are pushed together, compressions form. In between the compressions, particles are spread out. These are rarefactions.

Go Online SCiLINKS NSTA

For: Links on waves
Visit: www.SciLinks.org
Web Code: scn-1511

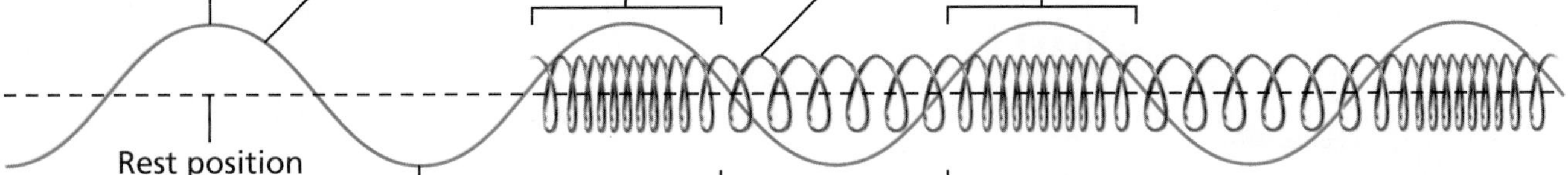

FIGURE 4
Representing Waves
The compressions of a longitudinal wave correspond to the crests of a transverse wave. The troughs correspond to rarefactions.

Representing Types of Waves You can use diagrams to represent transverse and longitudinal waves. Transverse waves like those on a rope are easy to draw. You can draw a transverse wave as shown in Figure 4. Think of the horizontal line as the position of the rope before it is disturbed. This position is called the rest position. As the wave passes, the rope moves above or below the rest position. Remember that the crests are the highest points of the wave and the troughs are the lowest points of the wave.

To draw longitudinal waves, think of the compressions in the spring toy as being similar to the crests of a transverse wave. The rarefactions in the spring toy are like the troughs of a transverse wave. By treating compressions as crests and rarefactions as troughs, you can draw longitudinal waves in the same way as transverse waves.

Reading Checkpoint **How do you draw the rest position of a transverse wave?**

Section 1 Assessment

Target Reading Skill **Using Prior Knowledge** Revise your graphic organizer about waves based on what you just learned in the section.

Reviewing Key Concepts

1. a. **Defining** What is a mechanical wave?
   b. **Explaining** How are mechanical waves produced?
   c. **Inferring** A wave moves a floating dock up and down several times, but then the dock stops moving. What happened to the wave?
2. a. **Identifying** What are the two types of mechanical waves?
   b. **Describing** Use a wave diagram to represent the crests and troughs of a wave. Then describe a crest and trough in your own words.
   c. **Comparing and Contrasting** How does a transverse wave move a medium? How does a longitudinal wave move a medium?

Writing in Science

Firsthand Account Suppose you are a particle of water in a lake. Describe what happens to you when a motorboat passes by. Be sure to use words like *vibration* and *crest* in your description.

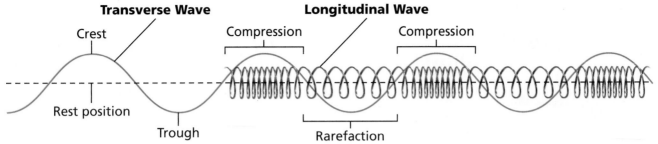

Section 2

Properties of Waves

Reading Preview

Key Concepts

- What are the basic properties of waves?
- How is a wave's speed related to its wavelength and frequency?

Key Terms

- amplitude
- wavelength
- frequency
- hertz (Hz)

Target Reading Skill

Outlining An outline shows the relationship between main ideas and supporting ideas. As you read, make an outline about the properties of waves that you can use for review. Use the red headings for the main ideas and the blue headings for the supporting ideas.

Properties of Waves
I. Amplitude
A. Amplitude of transverse waves
B.
II. Wavelength
III.

Lab zone Discover Activity

Can You Change a Wave?

1. Lay a 3-meter-long rope on the floor. Hold one end of the rope. Have a partner hold the other end.
2. Flick your end left and right about once per second. Observe the waves.
3. Now flick your end about twice per second. Observe the waves.
4. Switch roles with your partner and repeat Steps 2 and 3.

Think It Over

Predicting What happened to the waves when you flicked the rope more often? Predict how the wave will change if you flick the rope less often than once per second. Try it.

One of the most elegant and graceful Olympic sports is rhythmic gymnastics. A ribbon dancer flicks a stick attached to a ribbon, making waves that travel down the ribbon. Some of the waves are longer, while others are shorter. The rate at which the gymnast flicks her hands affects both the length and shape of the waves in the ribbon.

This is just one of many different kinds of waves. Waves can carry a little energy or a lot. They can be short or long. They can be rare or frequent. They can travel fast or slow. All waves, however, share certain properties. **The basic properties of waves are amplitude, wavelength, frequency, and speed.**

A rhythmic gymnast ▲

Amplitude

Some crests are very high, while others are very low. The distance the medium rises depends on the amplitude of the wave. **Amplitude** is the maximum distance that the particles of the medium carrying the wave move away from their rest positions. For example, the amplitude of a water wave is the maximum distance a water particle moves above or below the surface level of calm water. You can increase the amplitude of a wave in a rope by moving your hand up and down a greater distance. To do this, you have to use more energy. This energy is transferred to the rope. Thus, the more energy a wave has, the greater its amplitude.

Amplitude of Transverse Waves As shown in Figure 5, the amplitude of a transverse wave is the maximum distance the medium moves up or down from its rest position. You can find the amplitude of a transverse wave by measuring the distance from the rest position to a crest or to a trough.

Amplitude of Longitudinal Waves The amplitude of a longitudinal wave is a measure of how compressed or rarefied the medium becomes. A high-energy wave causes more compression and rarefaction than a low-energy wave. When the compressions are dense, it means that the wave's amplitude is large.

FIGURE 5

Amplitude, Wavelength, and Frequency

The basic properties of all waves include amplitude, wavelength, and frequency.

Developing Hypotheses *How could you increase the amplitude of a wave in a rope? How could you increase the frequency?*

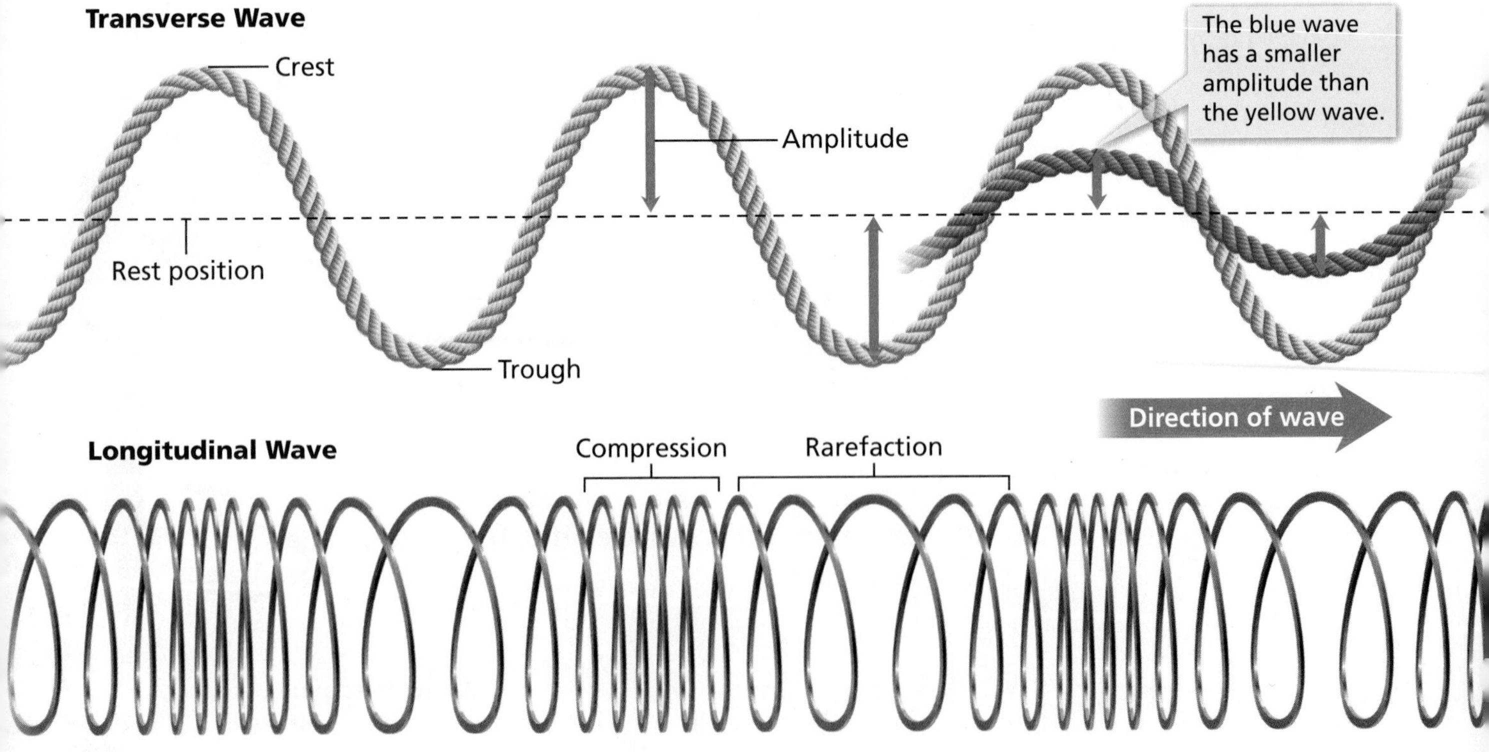

Wavelength

A wave travels a certain distance before it starts to repeat. The distance between two corresponding parts of a wave is its **wavelength.** You can find the wavelength of a transverse wave by measuring the distance from crest to crest, as shown in Figure 5. Or you could measure from trough to trough. The wavelength of a longitudinal wave is the distance between compressions.

Frequency

Wave **frequency** is the number of complete waves that pass a given point in a certain amount of time. For example, if you make waves on a rope so that one wave passes by every second, the frequency is 1 wave per second. How can you increase the frequency? Simply move your hand up and down more quickly, perhaps two or three times per second. To decrease the frequency, move your hand up and down more slowly.

Frequency is measured in units called **hertz** (Hz). A wave that occurs every second has a frequency of 1 Hz. If two waves pass you every second, then the frequency of the wave is 2 per second, or 2 hertz. The hertz was named after Heinrich Hertz, the German scientist who discovered radio waves.

Reading Checkpoint **In what unit is the frequency of a wave measured?**

Lab zone Skills Activity

Calculating

Tie a metal washer to one end of a 25-cm long string. Tape the other end of the string to the edge of a table. Let the washer hang and then pull it about 10 cm to the side and release it. Measure the time it takes the washer to swing through 10 complete cycles. (In 1 cycle, the washer swings forward and back, returning to its starting point.) Calculate the frequency by dividing 10 cycles by the time interval.

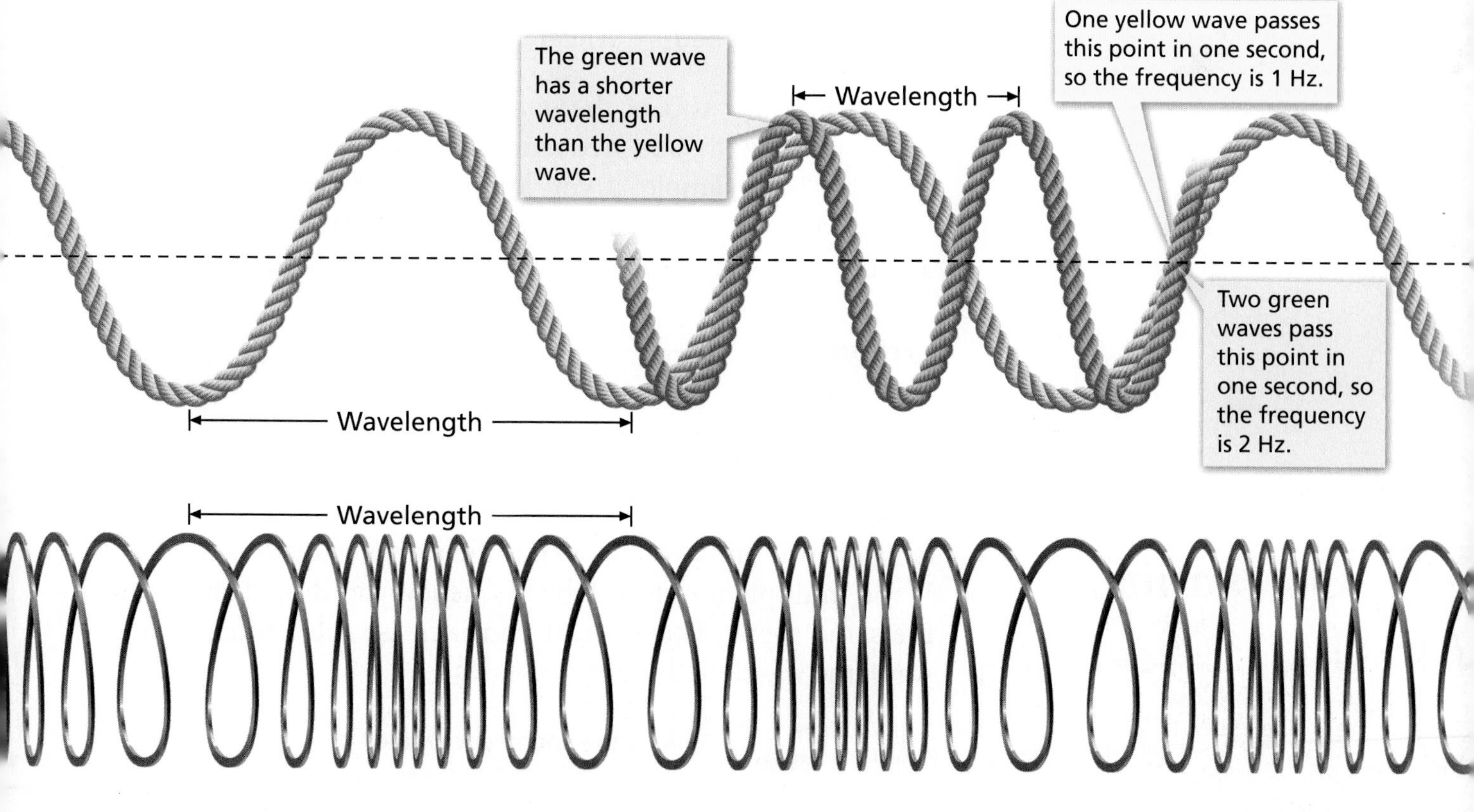
The green wave has a shorter wavelength than the yellow wave.
Wavelength
One yellow wave passes this point in one second, so the frequency is 1 Hz.
Two green waves pass this point in one second, so the frequency is 2 Hz.
Wavelength
Wavelength

FIGURE 6
Speed of Waves
Light waves travel much faster than sound waves.
Problem Solving *Why do you see lightning before hearing thunder?*

Speed

Imagine watching a distant thunderstorm approach on a hot summer day. First you see a flash of lightning. A few seconds later you hear the thunder rumble. Even though the thunder occurs the instant the lightning flashes, the light and sound reach you seconds apart. This happens because light waves travel much faster than sound waves. In fact, light waves travel about a million times faster than sound waves!

Different waves travel at different speeds. The speed of a wave is how far the wave travels in a given length of time, or its distance divided by the time it took to travel that distance. **The speed, wavelength, and frequency of a wave are related to one another by a mathematical formula:**

$$\text{Speed} = \text{Wavelength} \times \text{Frequency}$$

If you know two of the quantities in the speed formula—speed, wavelength, and frequency—you can calculate the third quantity. For example, if you know a wave's speed and wavelength, you can calculate the frequency. If you know the speed and the frequency, you can calculate the wavelength.

$$\text{Frequency} = \frac{\text{Speed}}{\text{Wavelength}} \qquad \text{Wavelength} = \frac{\text{Speed}}{\text{Frequency}}$$

If a medium does not change, the speed of a wave is constant. For example, in air at a given temperature and pressure, all sound waves travel at the same speed. If speed is constant, what do you think will happen if the wave's frequency changes? If you multiply wavelength by frequency, you should always get the same speed. Therefore, if you increase the frequency of a wave, the wavelength must decrease.

Reading Checkpoint What is the speed of a wave?

Go Online PHSchool.com
For: More on wave properties
Visit: PHSchool.com
Web Code: cgd-5012

Math Sample Problem

Calculating Frequency

The speed of a wave on a rope is 50 cm/s and its wavelength is 10 cm. What is the wave's frequency?

1 Read and Understand

What information are you given?

Speed = 50 cm/s

Wavelength = 10 cm

2 Plan and Solve

What quantity are you trying to calculate?

The frequency of a wave = ■Hz

What formula contains the given quantities and the unknown quantity?

$$\text{Frequency} = \frac{\text{Speed}}{\text{Wavelength}}$$

Perform the calculation.

$$\text{Frequency} = \frac{\text{Speed}}{\text{Wavelength}} = \frac{50\text{ cm/s}}{10\text{ cm}}$$

$$\text{Frequency} = \frac{5}{\text{s}} = 5\text{ Hz}$$

3 Look Back and Check

Does your answer make sense?

The wave speed is 50 cm per second. Because the distance from crest to crest is 10 cm, 5 crests will pass a point every second.

Math Practice

1. A wave has a wavelength of 2 mm and a frequency of 3 Hz. At what speed does the wave travel?
2. The speed of a wave on a guitar string is 142 m/s and the frequency is 110 Hz. What is the wavelength of the wave?

Section 2 Assessment

Target Reading Skill Outlining Use the information in your outline to help you answer the questions below.

Reviewing Key Concepts

1. a. Listing What are four basic properties of waves?
   b. Explaining Which wave property is directly related to energy?
   c. Comparing and Contrasting Which wave properties are distances? Which are measured relative to time?
2. a. Identifying What formula relates speed, wavelength, and frequency?
   b. Inferring Two waves have the same wavelength and frequency. How do their speeds compare?
   c. Calculating A wave's frequency is 2 Hz and its wavelength is 4 m. What is the wave's speed?

Math Practice

3. Calculating Frequency A wave travels at 3 m/s along a spring toy. If the wavelength is 0.2 m, what is the wave's frequency?

Lab zone **Skills Lab**

Wavy Motions

Problem
How do waves travel in a spring toy?

Skills Focus
comparing and contrasting, classifying

Materials
- spring toy
- meter stick

Procedure
1. On a smooth floor, stretch the spring to about 3 meters. Hold one end while your partner holds the other end. Do not over-stretch the spring toy.
2. Pull a few coils of the spring toy to one side near one end of the spring.
3. Release the coils and observe the motion of the spring. What happens when the disturbance reaches your partner? Draw what you observe.
4. Have your partner move one end of the spring toy to the left and then to the right on the floor. Be certain that both ends of the spring are held securely. Draw a diagram of the wave you observe.
5. Repeat Step 4, increasing the rate at which you move the spring toy left and right. Record your observations.
6. Squeeze together several coils of the spring toy, making a compression.
7. Release the compressed section of the spring toy and observe the disturbance as it moves down the spring. Record your observations. Draw and label what you see.

Analyze and Conclude
1. **Comparing and Contrasting** Compare the waves generated in Steps 1–5 with the waves generated in Steps 6–7.
2. **Classifying** Were the waves generated in Steps 1–5 transverse or longitudinal? Explain your answer.
3. **Comparing and Contrasting** In Step 3 of the procedure, compare the original wave to the wave that came back.
4. **Classifying** Were the waves generated in Steps 6 and 7 transverse or longitudinal? Explain your answer.
5. **Interpreting Data** What happened to the wavelength and frequency when you increased the rate at which the spring toy moved left and right?
6. **Developing Hypotheses** How might you change the amplitude of the longitudinal waves you made?
7. **Communicating** Use your drawings to make a poster that explains your observations.

Design an Experiment
Obtain some different spring toys. Look for different sizes and materials, such as metal and plastic. Design an experiment to test whether the differences of the spring toys result in differences in the waves the springs make. Have your teacher approve your procedure before you carry out the experiment.

Section 3

Interactions of Waves

Reading Preview

Key Concepts

- How do reflection, refraction, and diffraction change a wave's direction?
- What are the different types of interference?
- How do standing waves form?

Key Terms

- reflection • law of reflection
- refraction • diffraction
- interference
- constructive interference
- destructive interference
- standing wave • node
- antinode • resonance

Target Reading Skill

Asking Questions Before you read, preview the red headings. In a graphic organizer like the one below, ask a *what, how, when,* or *where* question for each heading. As you read, write the answers to your questions.

Interactions of Waves

Question	Answer
How are waves reflected?	Waves are reflected . . .

Lab zone **Discover Activity**

How Does a Ball Bounce?

1. Choose a spot at the base of a wall. From a distance of 1 m, roll a wet ball along the floor straight at the spot you chose. Watch the angle at which the ball bounces by looking at the path of moisture on the floor.
2. Wet the ball again. From a different position, roll the ball at the same spot, but at an angle to the wall. Again, observe the angle at which the ball bounces back.

Think It Over

Developing Hypotheses How do you think the angle at which the ball hits the wall is related to the angle at which the ball bounces back? Test your hypothesis.

You slip into the water in your snorkel gear. With your mask on, you can see clearly across the pool. As you start to swim, your flippers disturb the water, sending ripples moving outward in all directions. As each ripple hits the wall, it bounces off the wall and travels back toward you.

When water waves hit the side of a swimming pool, they bounce back because they cannot pass through the solid wall. Other kinds of waves may interact in a similar way when they hit the surface of a new medium. This type of interaction is called reflection.

Making waves in a pool ▶

Reflection

When an object or a wave hits a surface through which it cannot pass, it bounces back. This interaction with a surface is called **reflection.** There are many examples of reflection in your everyday life. When you did the Discover Activity, you saw that the ball hit the wall and bounced back, or was reflected. When you looked in your mirror this morning, you used light that was reflected to see yourself. If you have ever shouted in an empty gym, the echo you heard was caused by sound waves that reflected off the gym walls.

All waves obey the law of reflection. To help you understand this law, look at Figure 7. In the photo, you see light reflected off the surface of the sunglasses. The diagram shows how the light waves travel to make the reflection. The arrow labeled *Incoming wave* represents a wave moving toward the surface at an angle. The arrow labeled *Reflected wave* represents the wave that bounces off the surface at an angle. The dashed line labeled *Normal* is drawn perpendicular to the surface at the point where the incoming wave strikes the surface. The angle of incidence is the angle between the incoming wave and the normal. The angle of reflection is the angle between the reflected wave and the normal line. The **law of reflection** states that the angle of incidence equals the angle of reflection.

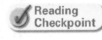

Reading Checkpoint **What is reflection?**

FIGURE 7
Law of Reflection
The angle of incidence equals the angle of reflection. All waves obey this law, including the light waves reflected from these sunglasses.
Predicting *What happens to the angle of reflection if the angle of incidence increases?*

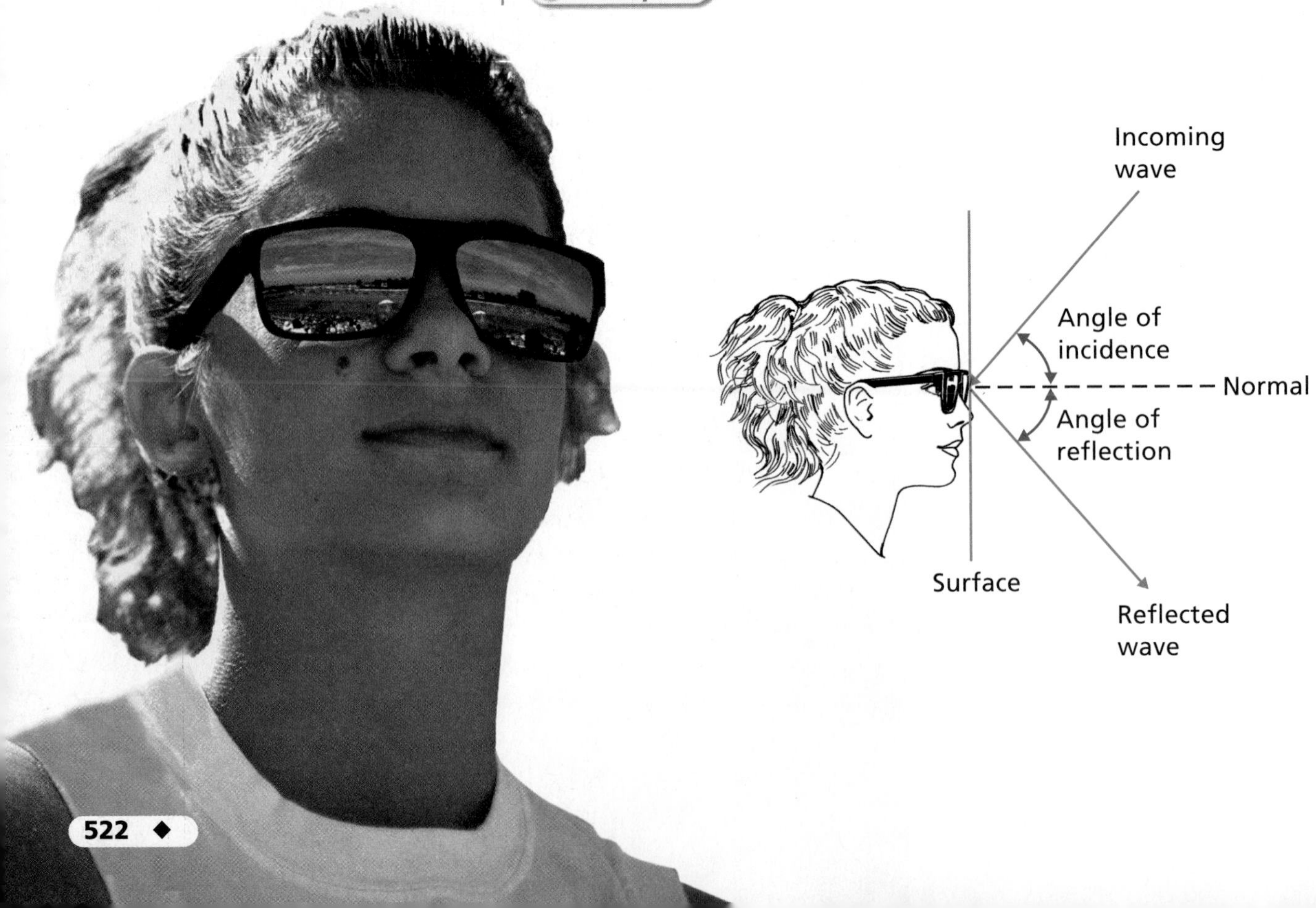

FIGURE 8
Refraction of Light Waves
Light bends when it enters water at an angle because one side of each wave slows down before the other side does.

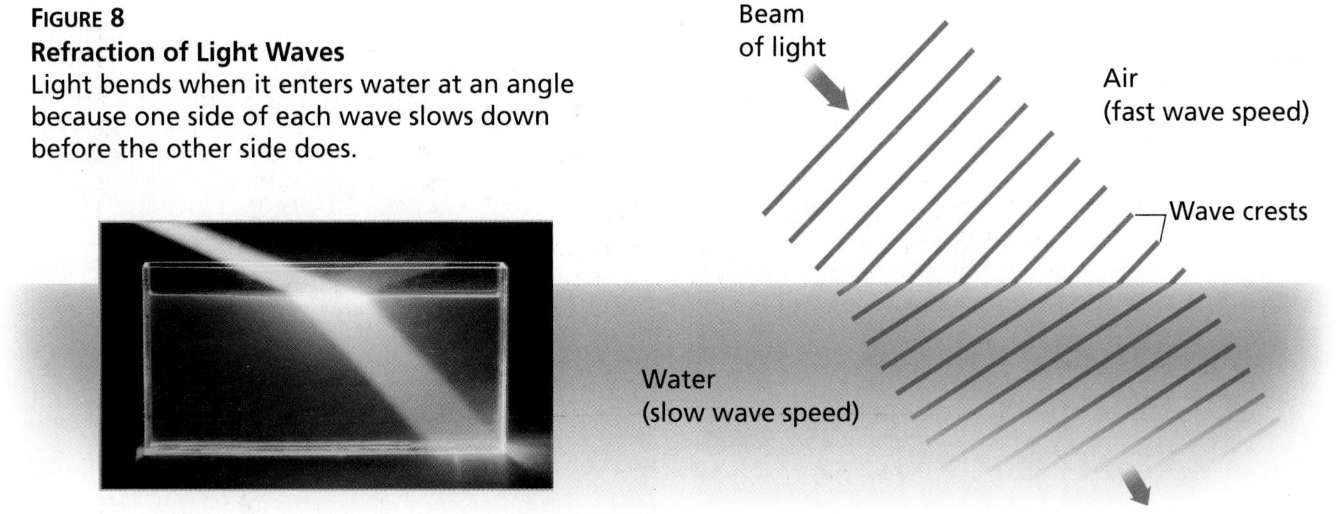

Refraction

Have you ever been riding a skateboard and gone off the sidewalk onto grass? If so, you know it's hard to keep moving in a straight line. The front wheel on the side moving onto the grass slows down. The front wheel still on the sidewalk continues to move fast. The difference in the speeds of the two front wheels causes the skateboard to change direction.

What Causes Refraction? Like the skateboard that changes direction, changes in speed can cause waves to change direction, as shown in Figure 8. **When a wave enters a new medium at an angle, one side of the wave changes speed before the other side, causing the wave to bend.** The bending of waves due to a change in speed is called **refraction.**

When Does Refraction Occur? A wave does not always bend when it enters a new medium. Bending occurs only when the wave enters the new medium at an angle. Then one side of the wave enters the medium first. This side changes speed, but the other side still travels at its original speed. Bending occurs because the two sides of the wave travel at different speeds.

Even if you don't skateboard, you have probably seen refraction in daily life. Have you ever had trouble grabbing something underwater? Have you ever seen a rainbow? Light can bend when it passes from water into air, making an underwater object appear closer than it really is. When you reach for the object, you miss it. When white light enters water, different colors in the light bend by different amounts. The white light separates into the colors you see in a rainbow.

Reading Checkpoint **When does refraction occur?**

Lab zone **Skills Activity**

Observing

You can simulate what happens as waves move from one medium to another.

1. Roll a drinking straw from a smooth tabletop straight onto a thin piece of terry cloth or a paper towel. Describe how the straw's motion changes as it leaves the smooth surface.
2. Repeat Step 1, but roll the straw at an angle to the cloth or paper.

Describe what happens as each side of the straw hits the cloth or paper. How are your results similar to what happens when waves are refracted?

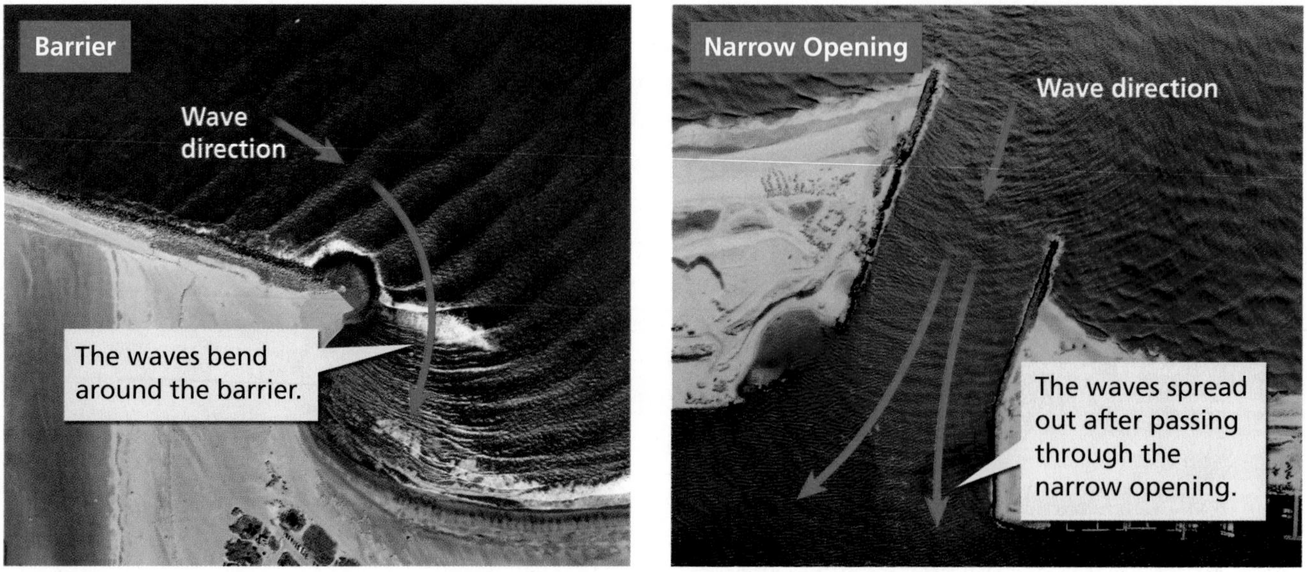
Barrier
Wave direction
The waves bend around the barrier.
Narrow Opening
Wave direction
The waves spread out after passing through the narrow opening.

FIGURE 9
Diffraction of Water Waves
Waves diffract when they move around a barrier or pass through an opening. As a wave passes a barrier, it bends around the barrier. After a wave goes through a narrow opening, it spreads out.

Diffraction

Sometimes waves bend around a barrier or pass through a hole. **When a wave moves around a barrier or through an opening in a barrier, it bends and spreads out.** These wave interactions are called **diffraction.** Figure 9 shows how waves bend and spread by diffraction.

Interference

Have you ever seen soccer balls collide in a practice drill? The balls bounce off each other because they cannot be in the same place at the same time. Surprisingly, this is not true of waves. Unlike two balls, two waves can overlap when they meet. **Interference** is the interaction between waves that meet. **There are two types of interference: constructive and destructive.**

Constructive Interference The interference that occurs when waves combine to make a wave with a larger amplitude is called **constructive interference.** You can think of constructive interference as waves "helping each other," or adding their energies. When the crests of two waves overlap, they make a higher crest. When the troughs of two waves overlap, they make a deeper trough. In both cases, the amplitude increases.

Figure 10 shows how constructive interference can occur when two waves travel toward each other. When the crests from each wave meet, constructive interference makes a higher crest in the area of overlap. The amplitude of this crest is the sum of the amplitudes of the two original crests. After the waves pass through each other, they continue on as if they had never met.

Reading Checkpoint **What is constructive interference?**

Destructive Interference The interference that occurs when two waves combine to make a wave with a smaller amplitude is called **destructive interference.** You can think of destructive interference as waves subtracting their energies.

Destructive interference occurs when the crest of one wave overlaps the trough of another wave. If the crest has a larger amplitude than the trough, the crest "wins" and part of it remains. If the original trough had a larger amplitude, the result is a trough. If the original waves had equal amplitudes, then the crest and trough can completely cancel as shown in Figure 10.

Go Online *active art*

For: Wave Interference activity
Visit: PHSchool.com
Web Code: cgp-5013

FIGURE 10
Wave Interference
Interference can be constructive or destructive.
Interpreting Diagrams *What does the black dotted line represent in the diagram below?*

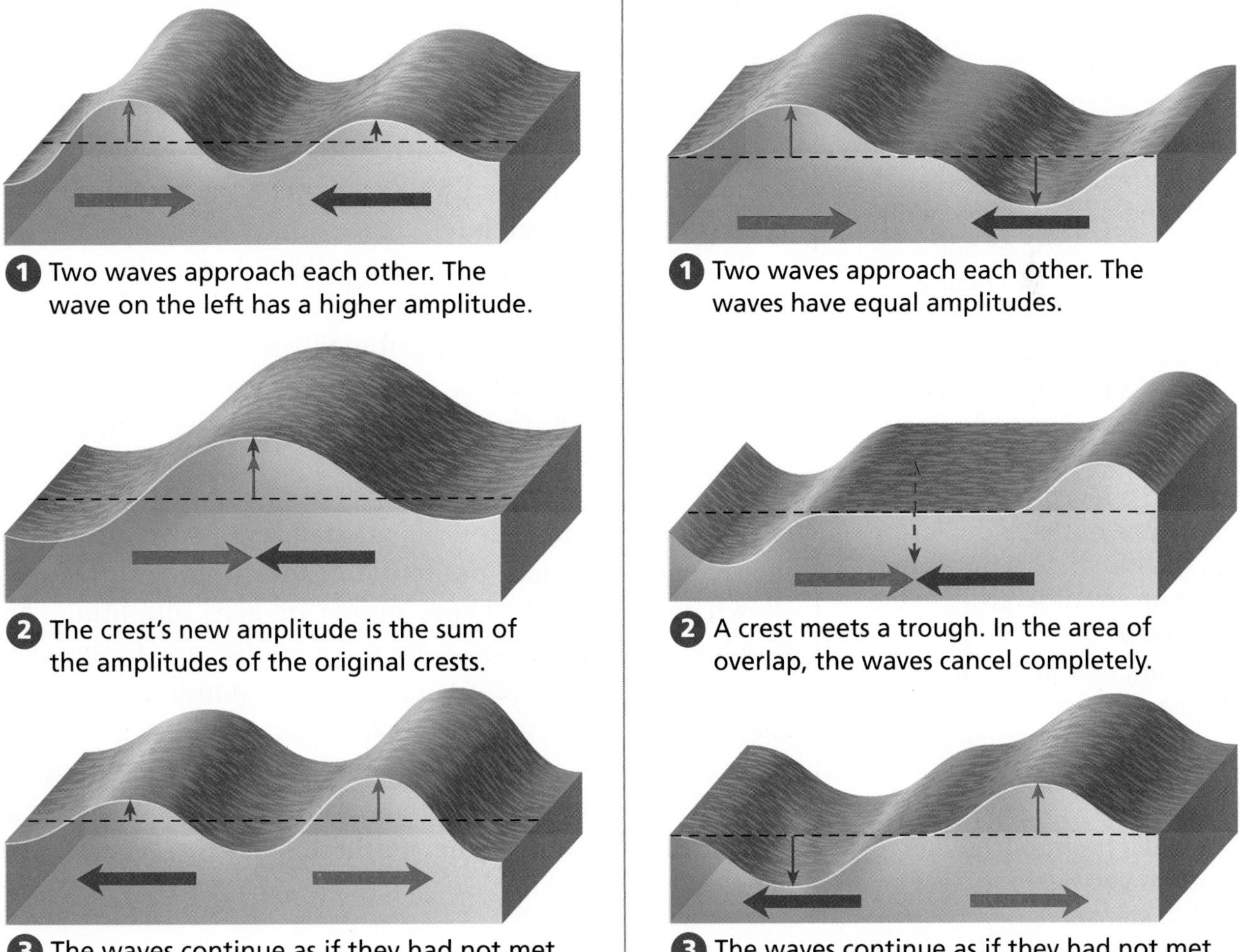

Constructive Interference

1. Two waves approach each other. The wave on the left has a higher amplitude.
2. The crest's new amplitude is the sum of the amplitudes of the original crests.
3. The waves continue as if they had not met.

Destructive Interference

1. Two waves approach each other. The waves have equal amplitudes.
2. A crest meets a trough. In the area of overlap, the waves cancel completely.
3. The waves continue as if they had not met.

FIGURE 11
Standing Waves
These photos show standing waves in vibrating elastic strings. The photographer used a bright flashing light called a strobe to "stop" the motion.

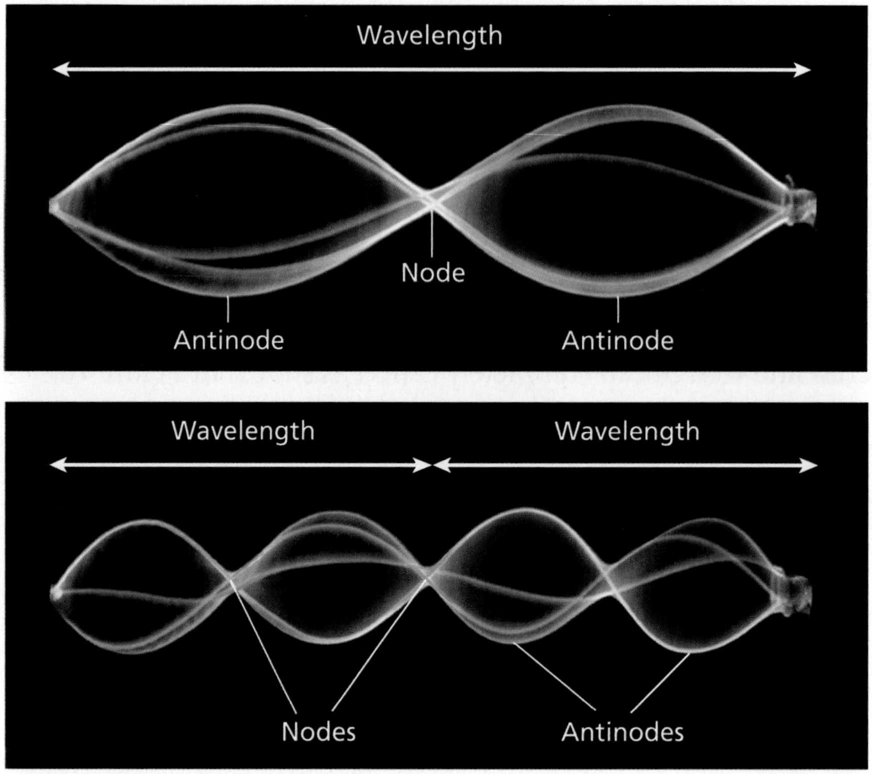

Lab zone Try This Activity

Interfering Waves

1. Place two identical empty bottles near each other. Using a straw, blow gently across the top of one bottle until you hear a sound. Describe the sound.
2. Using two straws, blow across the tops of both bottles at the same time. Describe what you hear.
3. Add a few drops of water to one bottle. Blow across the top of each bottle and note any differences in the sound.
4. Using two straws, blow across the tops of both bottles at the same time.

Observing Describe the sound you heard in Step 4. How did it differ from the sounds you heard in the other steps?

Standing Waves

If you tie a rope to a doorknob and continuously shake the free end, waves will travel down the rope, reflect at the end, and come back. The reflected waves will meet the incoming waves. When the waves meet, interference occurs.

If the incoming wave and a reflected wave have just the right frequency, they produce a combined wave that appears to be standing still. This combined wave is called a standing wave. A **standing wave** is a wave that appears to stand in one place, even though it is really two waves interfering as they pass through each other.

Nodes and Antinodes In a standing wave, destructive interference produces points with an amplitude of zero, as shown in Figure 11. These points of zero amplitude on a standing wave are called **nodes.** The nodes are always evenly spaced along the wave. At points in the standing wave where constructive interference occurs, the amplitude is greater than zero. The points of maximum amplitude on a standing wave are called **antinodes.** These are also the points of maximum energy on the wave. The antinodes always occur halfway between two nodes.

Resonance Have you ever pushed a child on a swing? At first, it is difficult to push the swing. But once you get it going, you need only push gently to keep it going. This is because the swing has a natural frequency. Even small pushes that are in rhythm with the swing's natural frequency produce large increases in the swing's amplitude.

Most objects have at least one natural frequency of vibration. Standing waves occur in an object when it vibrates at a natural frequency. If a nearby object vibrates at the same frequency, it can cause resonance. **Resonance** is an increase in the amplitude of a vibration that occurs when external vibrations match an object's natural frequency.

Resonance can be useful. For example, musical instruments use resonance to produce stronger, clearer sounds. But sometimes resonance can be harmful. Figure 12 shows Mexico City after an earthquake in 1985. Mexico City is built on a layer of clay. The frequency of the earthquake waves matched the natural frequency of the clay layer, so resonance occurred. City buildings 8 to 18 stories high had the same natural frequency. Due to resonance, these buildings had the most damage. Both shorter and taller buildings were left standing because their natural frequencies did not match the natural frequency of the clay layer.

Reading Checkpoint How can resonance be useful?

FIGURE 12
Destructive Power of Resonance
In the 1985 earthquake in Mexico City, resonance caused the greatest damage to buildings between 8 and 18 stories tall.
Inferring *Why did taller buildings survive the earthquake?*

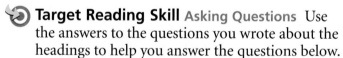

Section 3 Assessment

Target Reading Skill **Asking Questions** Use the answers to the questions you wrote about the headings to help you answer the questions below.

Reviewing Key Concepts

1. a. **Listing** What are three ways that waves change direction?
   b. **Summarizing** How does a wave change direction when it bounces off a surface?
   c. **Relating Cause and Effect** How does a change in speed cause a wave to change direction?
2. a. **Identifying** What are two types of interference?
   b. **Interpreting Diagrams** Look at Figure 10. What determines the amplitude of the wave produced by interference?
   c. **Predicting** Wave A has the same amplitude as wave B. What will happen when a crest of wave A meets a trough of wave B? Explain.
3. a. **Defining** What is a standing wave?
   b. **Explaining** How do nodes and antinodes form in a standing wave?

Lab zone At-Home Activity

Waves in a Sink With your parent's permission, fill the kitchen sink with water to a depth of about 10 cm. Dip your finger into the water repeatedly to make waves. Demonstrate reflection, diffraction, and interference for your family members.

Lab zone **Skills Lab**

Making Waves

Problem

How do water waves interact with each other and with solid objects in their paths?

Skills Focus

observing, making models

Materials

- water
- plastic dropper
- metric ruler
- paper towels
- modeling clay
- cork or other small floating object
- ripple tank (aluminum foil lasagna pan with mirror at the bottom)

Procedure

1. Fill the pan with water to a depth of 1.5 cm. Let the water come to rest. Make a data table like the one shown in your text.
2. Fill a plastic dropper with water. Then release a drop of water from a height of about 10 cm above the center of the ripple tank. Observe the reflection of the waves that form and record your observations.
3. Predict how placing a paper towel across one end of the ripple tank will affect the reflection of the waves. Record your prediction in your notebook.
4. Drape a paper towel across one end of the ripple tank so it hangs in the water. Repeat Step 2, and record your observations of the waves.
5. Remove the paper towel and place a stick of modeling clay in the water near the center of the ripple tank.

Data Table		
Type of Barrier	Observations Without Cork	Observations With Cork

6. From a height of about 10 cm, release a drop of water into the ripple tank halfway between the clay and one of the short walls. Record your observations.
7. Place the clay in a different position so that the waves strike it at an angle. Then repeat Step 6.
8. Place two sticks of clay end-to-end across the width of the tank. Adjust the clay so that there is a gap of about 2 cm between the ends of the two pieces. Repeat Step 6. Now change the angle of the barrier in the tank. Again repeat Step 6, and watch to see if the waves interact with the barrier any differently.

9. Cut the two pieces of clay in half. Use the pieces to make a barrier with three 2-cm gaps. Then repeat Step 6.
10. Remove all the clay and add a small floating object, such as a cork, to the water. Then repeat Steps 2–9 with the floating object. Observe and record what happens to the cork in each step.
11. Once you have finished all of the trials, clean and dry your work area.

Analyze and Conclude

1. **Observing** How are the waves affected by the paper towel hanging in the water?
2. **Observing** What happens when the waves strike a barrier head on? When they strike it at an angle?
3. **Observing** What happens when the waves strike a barrier with a gap in it? With three gaps in it?
4. **Making Models** What did the paper towel represent? What did the cork represent?
5. **Applying Concepts** How does the behavior of waves in your model compare to the behavior of waves in a harbor?
6. **Communicating** Evaluate your model. Write a paragraph about the ways your model represents a real situation. Then write a paragraph about your model's limitations.

More to Explore

Predict what would happen if you could send a steady train of uniform waves the length of the ripple tank for an extended time. Use a plastic bottle with a pinhole in the bottom to make a dropper that will help to test your prediction. Get permission from your teacher to try out your dropper device.

Section 4

Integrating Earth Science

Seismic Waves

Reading Preview

Key Concepts

- What are the types of seismic waves?
- How does a seismograph work?

Key Terms

- seismic wave
- P wave
- S wave
- surface wave
- tsunami
- seismograph

Target Reading Skill

Building Vocabulary Using a word in a sentence helps you think about how to best explain the word. As you read, carefully note the definition of each Key Term. Also note other details in the paragraph that contains the definition. Use all this information to write a sentence using the Key Term.

Lab zone Discover Activity

Can You Find the Sand?

1. Fill a plastic film canister with sand and replace the lid.
2. Place the canister on a table with four identical but empty canisters. Mix them around so that a classmate does not know which canister is which.
3. With your fist, pound on the table a few times. Ask your classmate which canister contains the sand.
4. Then stick each canister to the table with some modeling clay. Pound on the table again. Can your classmate tell which canister contains sand?

Think It Over

Inferring Pounding on a table makes waves. Why might the canister with sand respond differently from the empty canisters?

On May 22, 1960, a massive earthquake occurred under the Pacific Ocean about 120 km west of Chile. Traveling underground faster than the speed of sound, earthquake waves hit the coast in less than a minute. Buildings were demolished as the waves shook the ground. But the destruction wasn't finished. The earthquake sent water waves speeding toward the shore at almost 700 km/h. When the waves struck the shore, floods and mudslides killed many people who had survived the first wave of damage. For several more days, earthquakes occurred again and again. All told, thousands of people died and more than 2 million people in Chile were left homeless.

Earthquake damage in Chile in 1960 ▼

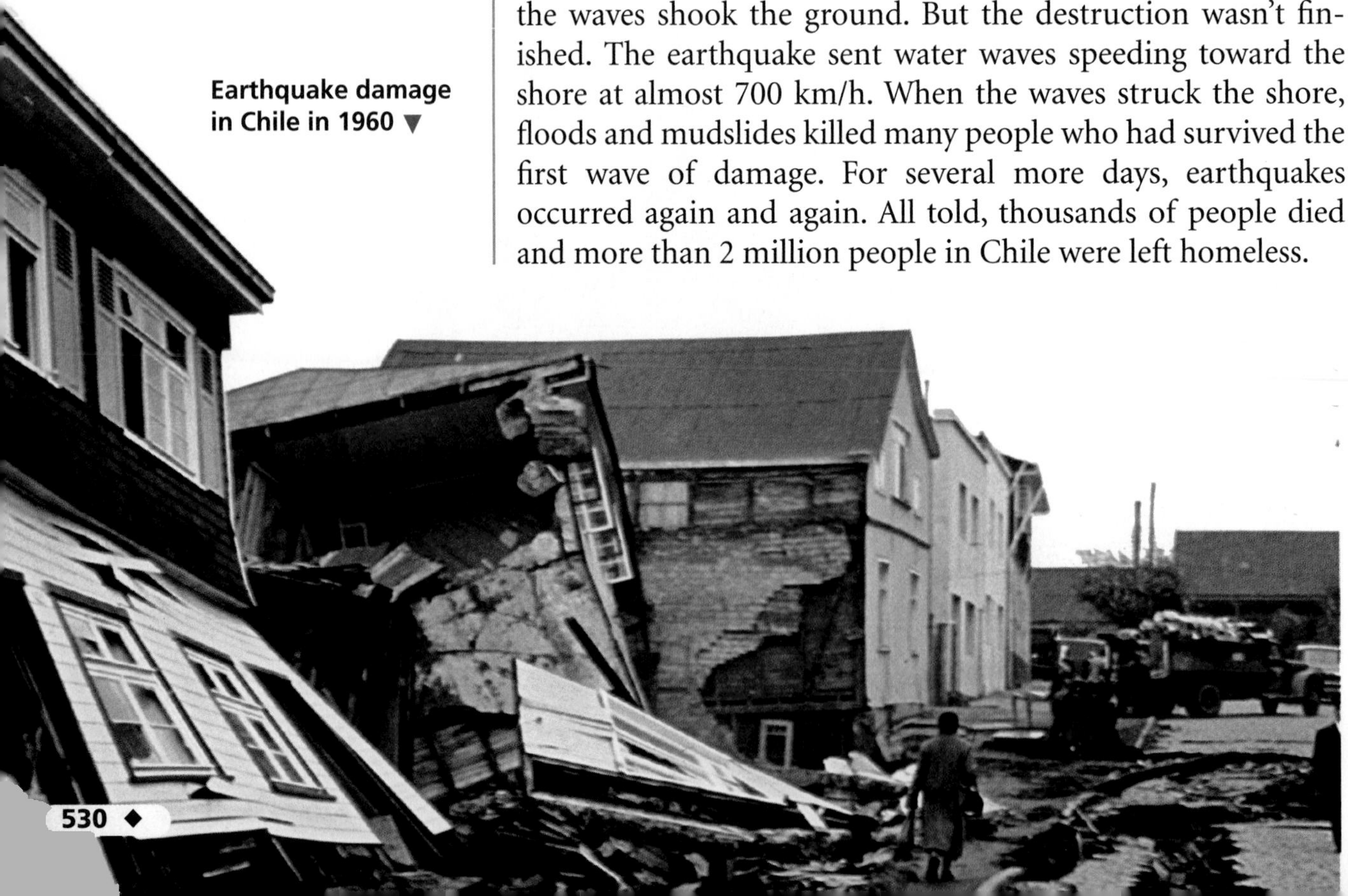

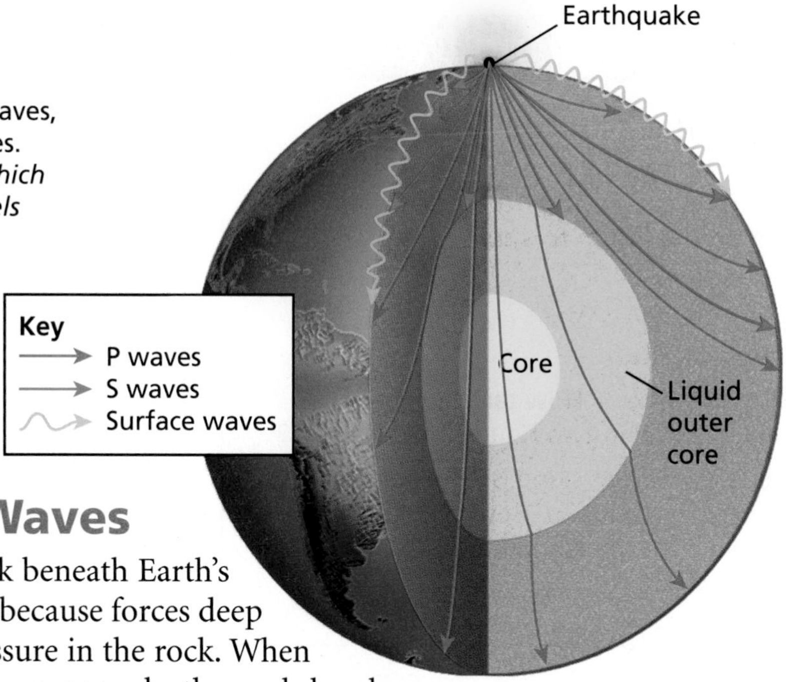

FIGURE 13
Seismic Waves
Seismic waves include P waves, S waves, and surface waves.
Interpreting Diagrams *Which kind of seismic wave travels through Earth's core?*

Types of Seismic Waves

An earthquake occurs when rock beneath Earth's surface moves. This rock moves because forces deep inside Earth create stress or pressure in the rock. When the pressure in the rock builds up enough, the rock breaks or changes shape, releasing energy in the form of waves. The waves produced by earthquakes are called **seismic waves.** (The word seismic comes from the Greek word *seismos*, which means "earthquake.")

Seismic waves ripple out in all directions from the point where the earthquake occurred. As the waves move, they carry energy through Earth. The waves can travel from one side of Earth to the other. **Seismic waves include P waves, S waves, and surface waves.** Figure 13 shows how each kind of wave travels through Earth.

P Waves Some seismic waves are longitudinal waves. Longitudinal seismic waves are known as **P waves,** or primary waves. They are called primary waves because they move faster than other seismic waves and so arrive at distant points before other seismic waves. P waves are made up of compressions and rarefactions of rock inside Earth. These waves compress and expand the ground like a spring toy as they move through it.

S Waves Other seismic waves are transverse waves with crests and troughs. Transverse seismic waves are known as **S waves,** or secondary waves. S waves shake the ground up and down and side to side as they move through it. They cannot travel through liquids. Because part of Earth's core is liquid, S waves do not travel directly through Earth like P waves. Therefore, S waves cannot be detected on the side of Earth opposite an earthquake. Scientists on the side of Earth opposite the earthquake detect mainly P waves.

Discovery Channel School

Characteristics of Waves
Video Preview
▶ Video Field Trip
Video Assessment

Go Online
SCILINKS NSTA
For: Links on seismic waves
Visit: www.SciLinks.org
Web Code: scn-1514

Math Analyzing Data

Motion of a Tsunami

This graph shows the rate at which a tsunami moves across the Pacific Ocean. Use the data plotted on the graph to answer the following questions.

1. **Reading Graphs** What two variables are plotted on the graph?
2. **Interpreting Data** How far does the tsunami travel in two hours? In four hours?
3. **Predicting** Easter Island is 3,700 kilometers from the earthquake. How many hours would it take the tsunami to reach Easter Island?

Speed of a Tsunami

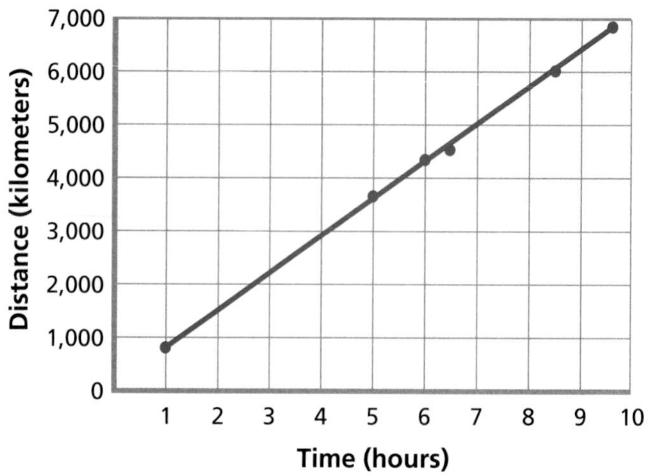

Surface Waves When P waves and S waves reach Earth's surface, they can create surface waves. A **surface wave** is a combination of a longitudinal wave and a transverse wave that travels along the surface of a medium. Surface waves produced by earthquakes move more slowly than P waves and S waves. However, they can cause the most severe ground movements. They combine up-and-down and side-to-side motions, making the ground roll like ocean waves.

Earthquakes that occur underwater, like the one off the coast of Chile in 1960, can produce huge surface waves on the ocean called **tsunamis** (tsoo NAH meez). Tsunamis come in all sizes, from 2 centimeters to 20 meters tall. They can travel thousands of kilometers across the ocean. In the deep ocean, the larger waves are only about 1 meter high. But as they near land, tsunamis slow down in the shallow water. The waves in the back catch up with those in the front and pile on top. Tsunamis caused by the 1960 earthquake in Chile traveled 10,000 kilometers across the Pacific Ocean to Hawaii. The waves that crashed over the coast in Hilo, Hawaii, were almost 11 meters high. The tsunamis killed 61 people and caused about $75 million in home and property damage.

FIGURE 14
This map shows the progress of the 1960 tsunami caused by an earthquake in Chile. **Classifying** *What type of wave interference—constructive or destructive—causes tsunamis?*

Tsunami Surface Waves

Reading Checkpoint **How are tsunamis produced?**

Detecting Seismic Waves

To detect and measure earthquake waves, scientists use instruments called **seismographs** (SYZ muh grafs). **A seismograph records the ground movements caused by seismic waves as they move through Earth.**

The frame of the seismograph is attached to the ground, so the frame shakes when seismic waves arrive. Seismographs used to have pens attached to the frame that made wiggly lines on a roll of paper as the ground shook. Now scientists use electronic seismographs to record data about Earth's motion.

Because P waves travel through Earth faster than S waves, P waves arrive at seismographs before S waves. By measuring the time between the arrival of the P waves and the arrival of the S waves, scientists can tell how far away the earthquake was. By comparing readings from at least three seismographs located at different places on Earth, scientists can tell where the earthquake occurred.

To find oil, water, and other valuable resources, geologists set off explosives at Earth's surface. Seismic waves from the explosions reflect from structures under the ground. Geologists then use seismograph data to locate the underground resources.

FIGURE 15
Seismologist Studying Data
A scientist studies the arrival time of seismic waves on the printout from a seismograph.

Section 4 Assessment

Target Reading Skill Building Vocabulary Use your sentences about seismic waves to help you answer the questions below.

Reviewing Key Concepts

1. **a.** Identifying What are three types of seismic waves?
   b. Classifying Which seismic waves are transverse waves? Which are longitudinal waves?
   c. Comparing and Contrasting Why do seismic waves that travel along Earth's surface cause more damage than other seismic waves?
2. **a.** Defining What is a seismograph?
   b. Explaining How does a seismograph work?
   c. Interpreting Data S waves arrive in Los Angeles 3 minutes after P waves. In Dallas, S waves arrive 1 minute after P waves. Which city is closer to the earthquake? Explain your answer.

Lab zone At-Home **Activity**

Sounds Solid Explore how waves travel through different solids. Have a family member or friend tap one end of a table with a spoon. Now put your ear to the table and listen again. What difference do you notice? Repeat the tapping on various surfaces around your home. What observations have you made?

Chapter 15 Study Guide

1 What Are Waves?

Key Concepts

- Mechanical waves are produced when a source of energy causes a medium to vibrate.
- Mechanical waves are classified by how they move. There are two types of mechanical waves: transverse waves and longitudinal waves.

Key Terms

wave
energy
medium
mechanical wave
vibration
transverse wave
crest
trough
longitudinal wave
compression
rarefaction

2 Properties of Waves

Key Concepts

- The basic properties of waves are amplitude, wavelength, frequency, and speed.
- The speed, wavelength, and frequency of a wave are related to one another by a mathematical formula:

$$\text{Speed} = \text{Wavelength} \times \text{Frequency}$$

Key Terms

amplitude
wavelength
frequency
hertz (Hz)

3 Interactions of Waves

Key Concepts

- When an object or a wave hits a surface through which it cannot pass, it bounces back.
- When a wave enters a new medium at an angle, one side of the wave changes speed before the other side, causing the wave to bend.
- When a wave moves around a barrier or through an opening in a barrier, it bends and spreads out.
- There are two types of interference: constructive and destructive.
- If the incoming wave and a reflected wave have just the right frequency, they produce a combined wave that appears to be standing still.

Key Terms

reflection
law of reflection
refraction
diffraction
interference
constructive interference
destructive interference
standing wave
node
antinode
resonance

4 Seismic Waves

Key Concepts

- Seismic waves include P waves, S waves, and surface waves.
- A seismograph records the ground movements caused by seismic waves as they move through Earth.

Key Terms

seismic wave
P wave
S wave
surface wave
tsunami
seismograph

Review and Assessment

Go Online
PHSchool.com
For: Self-Assessment
Visit: PHSchool.com
Web Code: cfa-5010

Organizing Information

Concept Mapping Copy the concept map about waves onto a sheet of paper. Then complete it and add a title. (For more on Concept Mapping, see the Skills Handbook.)

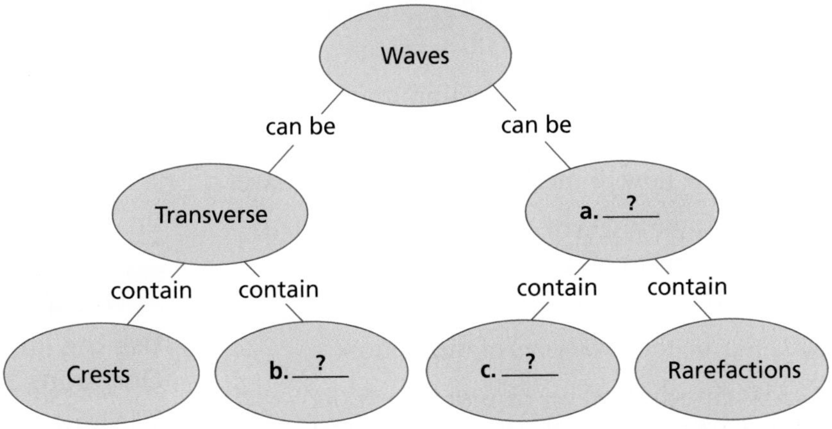

Reviewing Key Terms

Choose the letter of the best answer.

1. A wave transfers
   a. energy. **b.** particles.
   c. water. **d.** air.
2. A wave that moves the medium in the same direction that the wave travels is a
   a. transverse wave. **b.** longitudinal wave.
   c. standing wave. **d.** mechanical wave.
3. The distance between one crest and the next crest is the wave's
   a. amplitude. **b.** wavelength.
   c. frequency. **d.** speed.
4. The number of complete waves that pass a point in a certain amount of time is a wave's
   a. amplitude. **b.** frequency.
   c. wavelength. **d.** speed.
5. The bending of a wave due to a change in its speed is
   a. interference. **b.** reflection.
   c. diffraction. **d.** refraction.
6. The interaction between waves that meet is
   a. reflection. **b.** diffraction.
   c. refraction. **d.** interference.
7. A point of zero amplitude on a standing wave is called a
   a. crest. **b.** node.
   c. trough. **d.** antinode.
8. Seismic waves that do not travel through liquids are
   a. P waves. **b.** surface waves.
   c. S waves. **d.** tsunamis.

Writing in Science

Research Report Write an article for a boating magazine about tsunamis. Include details about what causes them and why they are dangerous. Explain what is being done to help reduce damage from tsunamis.

Discovery Channel School

Characteristics of Waves
Video Preview
Video Field Trip
▶ Video Assessment

Review and Assessment

Checking Concepts

9. Explain the difference between transverse and longitudinal waves. Use diagrams to illustrate your explanation.

10. How can you measure the amplitude of a transverse wave?

11. Describe how to measure the speed of a wave.

12. What is the angle of incidence if a reflected wave bounces off a mirror with an angle of reflection equal to 55°?

13. Describe the two types of diffraction.

14. Explain why S waves cannot be detected everywhere on Earth after an earthquake.

Math Practice

15. **Angles** Label a 90° angle on a transverse wave.

16. **Calculating Speed** A wave in a spring has a wavelength of 0.1 m and a frequency of 20 Hz. What is the wave's speed?

17. **Calculating Wavelength** A sound wave has a frequency of 660 Hz and its speed is 330 m/s. What is its wavelength?

Thinking Critically

18. **Applying Concepts** Suppose ripples move from one side of a lake to the other. Does the water move across the lake? Explain.

19. **Comparing and Contrasting** The waves shown below travel at the same speed.
a. Which wave has the higher frequency?
b. Which has the longer wavelength?
c. Which has the greater amplitude?

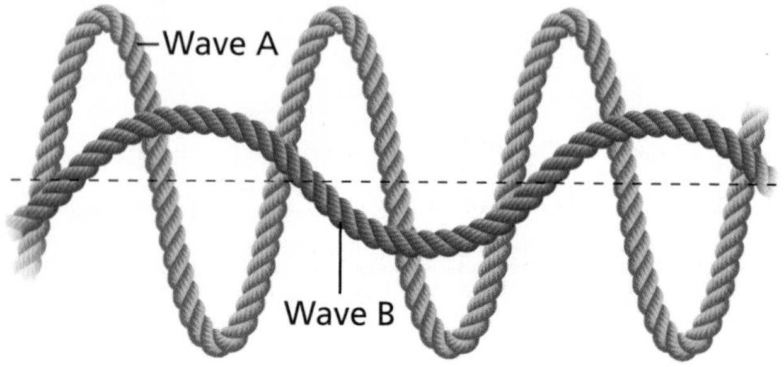

20. **Predicting** One wave has an amplitude of 2 m, and a second wave has an amplitude of 1 m. At a given time, crests from each wave meet. Draw a diagram and describe the result.

21. **Making Models** If you push a shopping cart that has a stiff or damaged wheel, it is difficult to steer the cart in a straight line. Explain how this is similar to refraction of a wave as it enters a new medium.

Applying Skills

Use the illustration below to answer Questions 22–25.

The wave in the illustration is a giant ocean wave produced by an underwater earthquake.

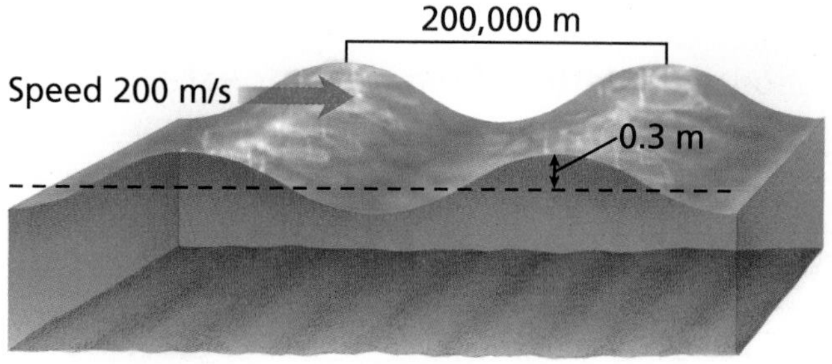

22. **Classifying** What kind of wave is shown in the diagram?

23. **Interpreting Diagrams** What is the amplitude of the wave? What is its speed?

24. **Calculating** Find the frequency of the wave.

25. **Calculating** How long would it take this wave to travel 5,000 km?

Lab zone Chapter Project

Performance Assessment Share your examples of periodic motion with your classmates. On your display, highlight the repeating patterns and the frequency of each example. Point out interesting connections. For example, track-and-field practice involves repetitions, as do other sports. Which examples involve waves moving through a medium?

Standardized Test Prep

Test-Taking Tip

Using Formulas

Some test questions require you to use a formula to answer the question. If you are given the formula, you may need to rearrange it to solve the problem. In the sample question below, you are asked to solve for frequency. Rearrange the formula by dividing both sides by wavelength:

$$\frac{\text{Speed}}{\text{Wavelength}} = \frac{\cancel{\text{Wavelength}} \times \text{Frequency}}{\cancel{\text{Wavelength}}}$$

$$\text{Frequency} = \frac{\text{Speed}}{\text{Wavelength}}$$

Then solve for frequency by substituting in the known values for speed and wavelength.

Sample Question

A sound wave has a wavelength of 2.0 m. The speed of the wave is 340 m/s. What is the frequency? (*Hint:* Speed = Wavelength × Frequency)

A 170 m/s
B 680 m/s
C 170 Hz
D 680 Hz

Answer

C is correct because 170 Hz equals 340 m/s divided by 2.0 m. You can eliminate **A** and **B** because the answers have a unit for speed. **D** was incorrectly calculated using multiplication.

Choose the letter of the best answer.

1. The speed of a wave in a spring is 3 m/s. If the wavelength is 0.1 m, what is the frequency?
A 30 Hz
B 0.3 Hz
C 30 m/s
D 0.3 m/s

2. A wave enters a new medium. The wave
F slows down and bends.
G speeds up and bends.
H may slow down or speed up.
J must always bend.

3. During a storm, a TV reporter says that the ocean waves are 3 meters high. This reported distance equals the distance
A from one crest to the next crest.
B from one trough to the next trough.
C from a crest to a trough.
D from a crest to the level of calm water.

4. Two waves move in opposite directions as shown in the diagram below. What will be the height of the crest produced when the crests from each wave meet?
F 20 cm
G 35 cm
H 15 cm
J 5 cm

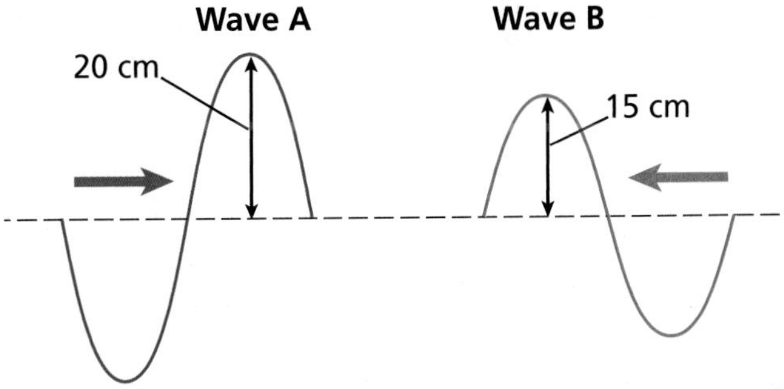

5. In an experiment, you and a friend stand at opposite ends of a football field. Your friend pops an inflated balloon while you observe. Which of the following is a testable hypothesis?
A If sound travels much faster than light, you will hear the balloon pop before you see it pop.
B If light travels much faster than sound, you will see the balloon pop before you hear it.
C If sound and light travel at the same speed, you will see and hear the balloon pop at the same time.
D all of the above

Constructed Response

6. A large rock is tossed into a pond to produce a water wave. Explain how you know that the wave transfers energy but not matter across the pond.

Chapter 16

Sound

Chapter Preview

1 The Nature of Sound
Discover *What Is Sound?*
Analyzing Data *Temperature and the Speed of Sound*
At-Home Activity *Ear to the Sound*

2 Properties of Sound
Discover *How Does Amplitude Affect Loudness?*
Skills Activity *Predicting*
Try This *Pipe Sounds*
At-Home Activity *Hum Stopper*

3 Music
Discover *How Can You Change Pitch?*
Active Art *Musical Instruments*
Design Your Own Lab *Changing Pitch*

4 How You Hear Sound
Discover *Where Is the Sound Coming From?*
Try This *Listen to This*
Technology Lab *Design and Build Hearing Protectors*
At-Home Activity *Sound Survey*
Science and Society *Keeping It Quiet*

5 Using Sound
Discover *How Can You Use Time to Measure Distance?*
Skills Activity *Designing Experiments*

In a recording studio, a microphone picks up sound waves from the singers. ▶

Lab zone™ Chapter Project

Music to Your Ears

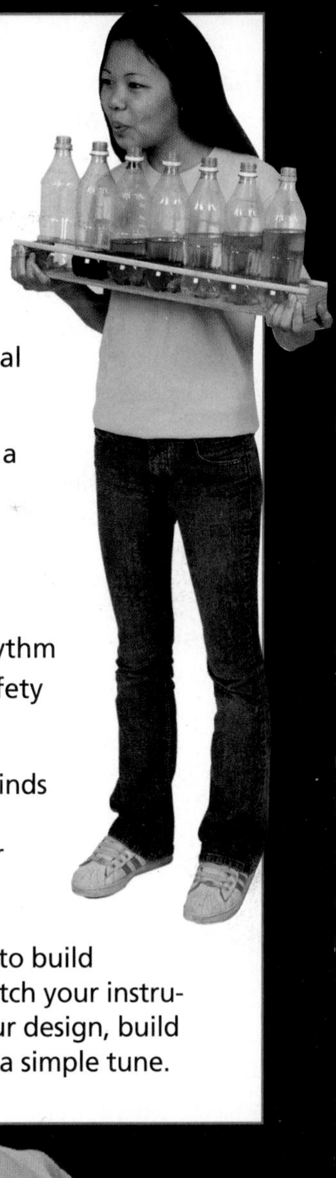

In this chapter you will investigate the properties of sound. You will learn how sound is produced by different objects, including musical instruments. As you work through the chapter, you will gather enough knowledge to create a musical instrument of your own.

Your Goal To design, build, and play a simple musical instrument

Your musical instrument must

- be made of materials that are approved by your teacher
- be able to play a simple tune or rhythm
- be built and used following the safety guidelines in Appendix A

Plan It! Begin by discussing different kinds of instruments with your classmates. What instruments are common in your favorite type of music? Which type of instrument would you like to build? Make a list of materials you could use to build your instrument. Then, design and sketch your instrument. After your teacher approves your design, build your instrument and test it by playing a simple tune.

Section 1

The Nature of Sound

Reading Preview

Key Concepts

- What is sound?
- How do sound waves interact?
- What factors affect the speed of sound?

Key Terms

- echo • elasticity • density

Target Reading Skill

Identifying Main Ideas As you read the Interactions of Sound Waves section, write the main idea—the biggest or most important idea—in a graphic organizer like the one below. Then write three supporting details that further explain the main idea.

Main Idea

Sound waves interact . . .

Detail | Detail | Detail

Lab zone Discover Activity

What Is Sound?

1. Fill a bowl with water.
2. Tap a tuning fork against the sole of your shoe. Place the tip of one of the prongs in the water. What do you see?
3. Tap the tuning fork again. Predict what will happen when you hold it near your ear. What do you hear?

Think It Over

Observing How are your observations related to the sound you hear? What might change if you use a different tuning fork?

Here is an old riddle: If a tree falls in a forest and no one hears it, does the tree make a sound? To answer the riddle, you must decide what the word "sound" means. If sound is something that a person must hear, then the tree makes no sound. If sound can happen whether a person hears it or not, then the tree makes a sound.

Sound Waves

To a scientist, a falling tree makes a sound whether someone hears it or not. When a tree crashes down, the energy with which it strikes the ground causes a disturbance. Particles in the ground and the air begin to vibrate, or move back and forth. The vibrations create a sound wave as the energy travels through the two mediums. **Sound is a disturbance that travels through a medium as a longitudinal wave.**

A falling tree ▶

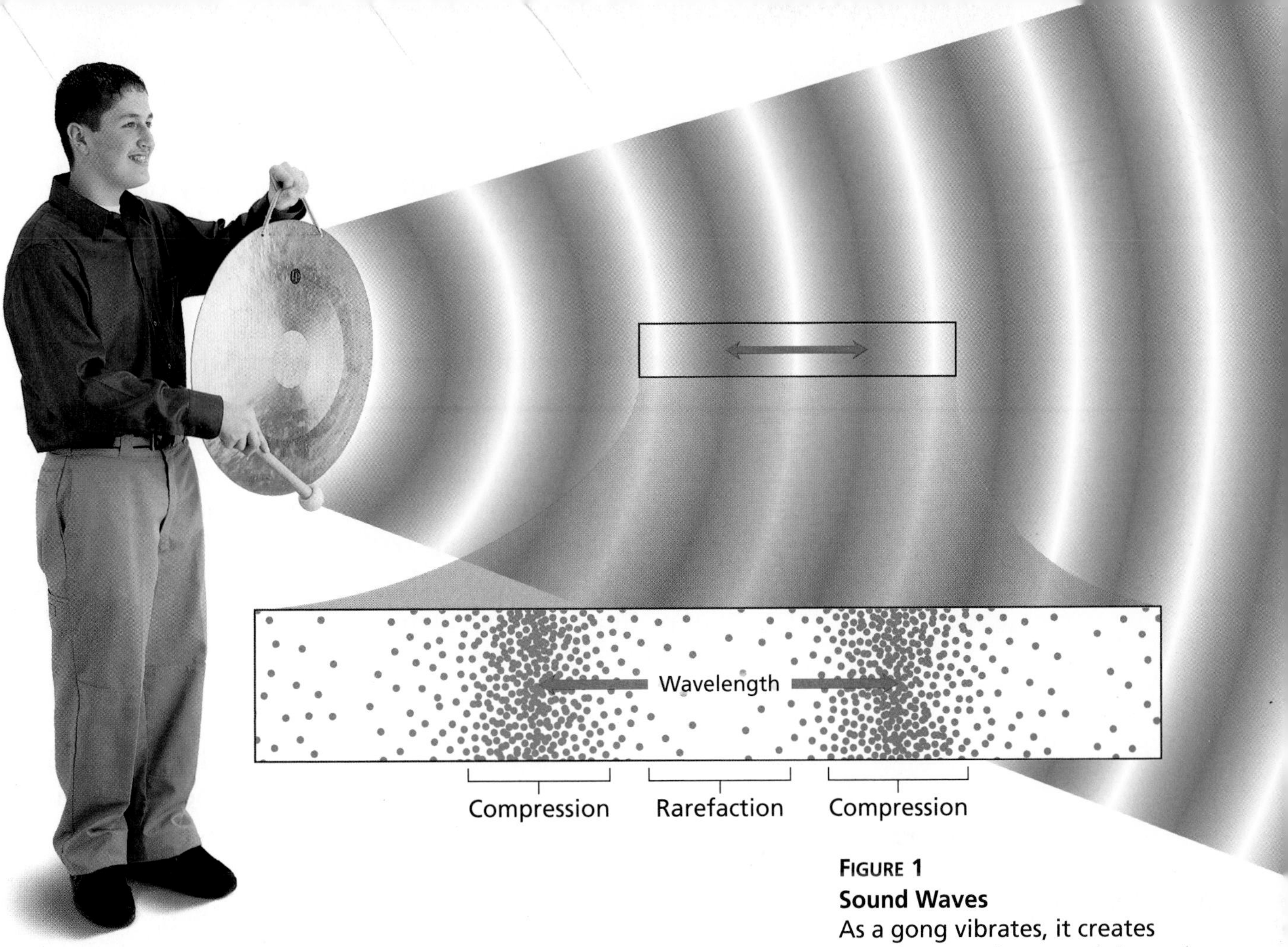

FIGURE 1
Sound Waves
As a gong vibrates, it creates sound waves that travel through the air. **Observing** *What do you observe about the spacing of particles in a compression?*

Making Sound Waves A sound wave begins with a vibration. Look at the metal gong shown in Figure 1. When the gong is struck, it vibrates rapidly. The vibrations disturb nearby air particles. Each time the gong moves to the right, it pushes air particles together, creating a compression. When the gong moves to the left, the air particles bounce back and spread out, creating a rarefaction. These compressions and rarefactions travel through the air as longitudinal waves.

How Sound Travels Like other mechanical waves, sound waves carry energy through a medium without moving the particles of the medium along. Each particle of the medium vibrates as the disturbance passes. When the disturbance reaches your ears, you hear the sound.

A common medium for sound is air. But sound can travel through solids and liquids, too. For example, when you knock on a solid wood door, the particles in the wood vibrate. The vibrations make sound waves that travel through the door. When the waves reach the other side of the door, they make sound waves in the air on the far side.

Reading Checkpoint **What are three types of mediums that sound can travel through?**

Go Online SCiLINKS NSTA
For: Links on sound
Visit: www.SciLinks.org
Web Code: scn-1521

FIGURE 2
Reflection of Sound
Clapping your hands in a gym produces an echo when sound waves reflect off the wall.
Drawing Conclusions *What kind of material is the wall made of?*

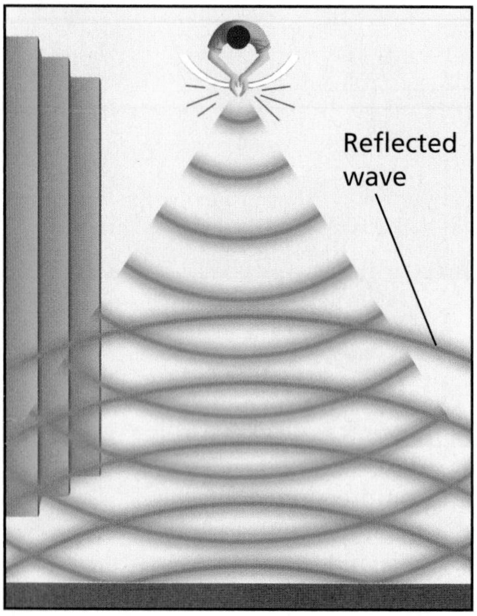
Reflected wave

Interactions of Sound Waves

Sound waves interact with the surfaces they contact and with each other. **Sound waves reflect off objects, diffract through narrow openings and around barriers, and interfere with each other.**

Reflection Sound waves may reflect when they hit a surface. A reflected sound wave is called an **echo.** In general, the harder and smoother the surface, the stronger the reflection. Look at Figure 2. When you clap your hands in a gym, you hear an echo because the hard surfaces—wood, brick, and metal—reflect sound directly back at you. But you don't always hear an echo in a room. In many rooms, there are soft materials that absorb most of the sound that strikes them.

Diffraction Have you ever wondered why you can hear your friends talking in a classroom before you walk through the doorway? You hear them because sound waves do not always travel in a straight line. Figure 3 shows how sound waves can diffract through openings such as doorways.

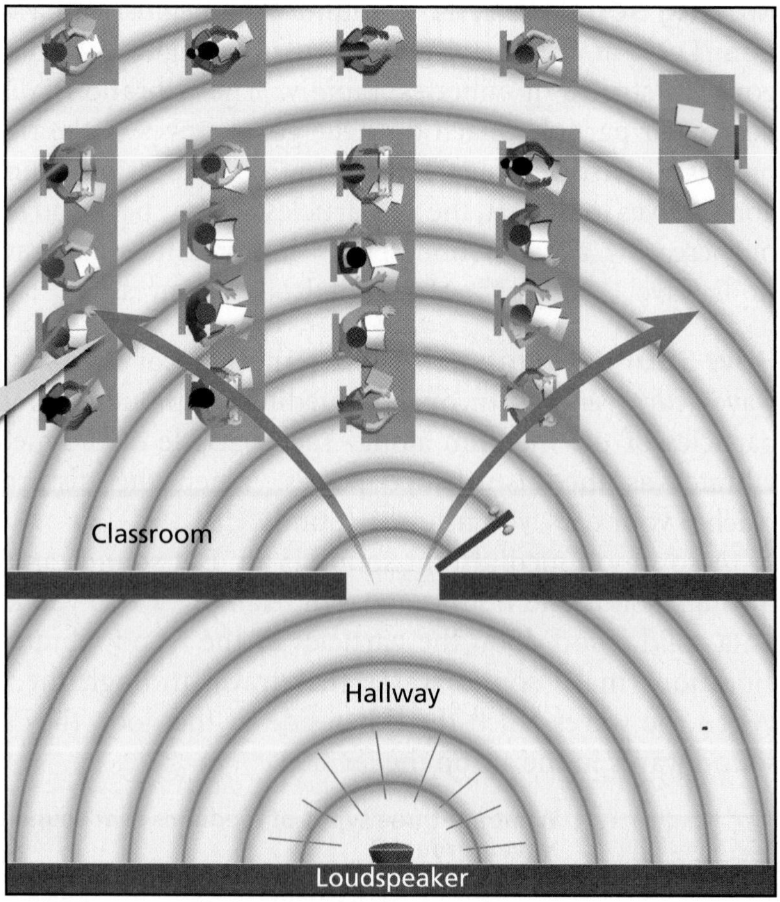
Sound waves spread out after passing through a doorway.
Classroom
Hallway
Loudspeaker

FIGURE 3
Diffraction of Sound
Sound waves can spread out after passing through a doorway, and can bend around a corner.

Sound waves can also diffract, or bend, around corners. This is why you can hear someone who is talking in the hallway before you come around the corner. The person's sound waves bend around the corner. Then they spread out so you can hear them even though you cannot see who is talking. Remember this the next time you want to tell a secret!

Interference Sound waves may meet and interact with each other. You may recall that this interaction is called interference. The interference that occurs when sound waves meet can be constructive or destructive. In Section 3, you will learn how interference affects the sound of musical instruments.

Reading Checkpoint **What are two ways that sound waves diffract?**

The Speed of Sound

Have you ever wondered why the different sounds from musicians and singers at a concert all reach your ears at the same time? It happens because the sounds travel through air at the same speed. At room temperature, about 20°C, sound travels through air at about 343 m/s. This speed is much faster than most jet planes travel through the air!

The speed of sound is not always 343 m/s. Sound waves travel at different speeds in different mediums. Figure 4 shows the speed of sound in different mediums. **The speed of sound depends on the elasticity, density, and temperature of the medium the sound travels through.**

Speed of Sound

Medium	Speed (m/s)
Gases	
Air (0°C)	331
Air (20°C)	343
Liquids (30°C)	
Fresh water	1,509
Salt water	1,546
Solids (25°C)	
Lead	1,210
Cast iron	4,480
Aluminum	5,000
Glass	5,170

FIGURE 4
The speed of sound depends on the medium it travels through.

Math Analyzing Data

Temperature and the Speed of Sound

The speed of sound in dry air changes as the temperature changes. The graph shows data for the speed of sound in air at temperatures from –20°C to 30°C.

1. **Reading Graphs** What is the speed of sound in air at –10°C?
2. **Interpreting Data** Does the speed of sound increase or decrease as temperature increases?
3. **Predicting** What might be the speed of sound at 30°C?

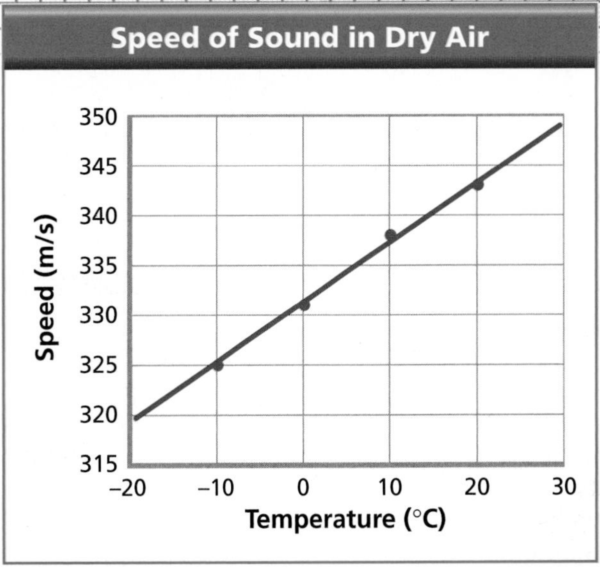

FIGURE 5
Modeling Elasticity
You can model elasticity by representing the particles in a medium as being held together by springs.

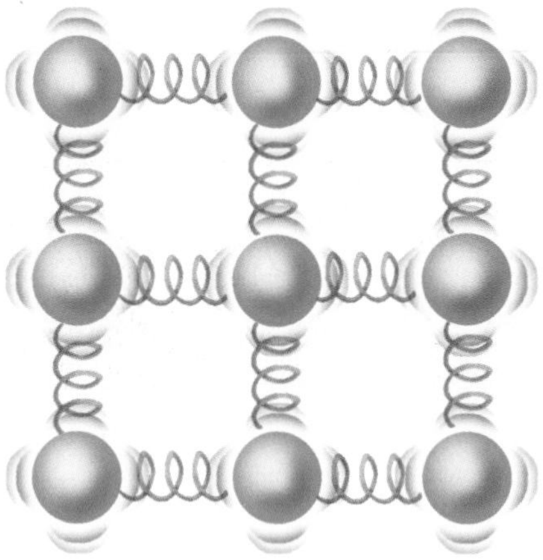

Elasticity If you stretch a rubber band and then let it go, it returns to its original shape. However, when you stretch modeling clay and then let it go, it stays stretched. Rubber bands are more elastic than modeling clay. **Elasticity** is the ability of a material to bounce back after being disturbed.

The elasticity of a medium depends on how well the medium's particles bounce back after being disturbed. To understand this idea, look at Figure 5. In this model, the particles of a medium are linked by springs. If one particle is disturbed, it is pulled back to its original position. In an elastic medium, such as a rubber band, the particles bounce back quickly. But in a less elastic medium, the particles bounce back slowly.

The more elastic a medium, the faster sound travels in it. Sounds can travel well in solids, which are usually more elastic than liquids or gases. The particles of a solid do not move very far, so they bounce back and forth quickly as the compressions and rarefactions of the sound waves pass by. Most liquids are not very elastic. Sound does not travel as well in liquids as it does in solids. Gases generally are not very elastic. Sound travels slowly in gases.

Density The speed of sound also depends on the density of a medium. **Density** is how much matter, or mass, there is in a given amount of space, or volume. The denser the medium, the more mass it has in a given volume. Figure 6 shows two cubes that have the same volume. The brass cube is denser because it has more mass in a given volume.

In materials in the same state of matter—solid, liquid, or gas—sound travels more slowly in denser mediums. The particles of a dense material do not move as quickly as those of a less dense material. Sound travels more slowly in dense metals, such as lead or silver, than in iron or steel.

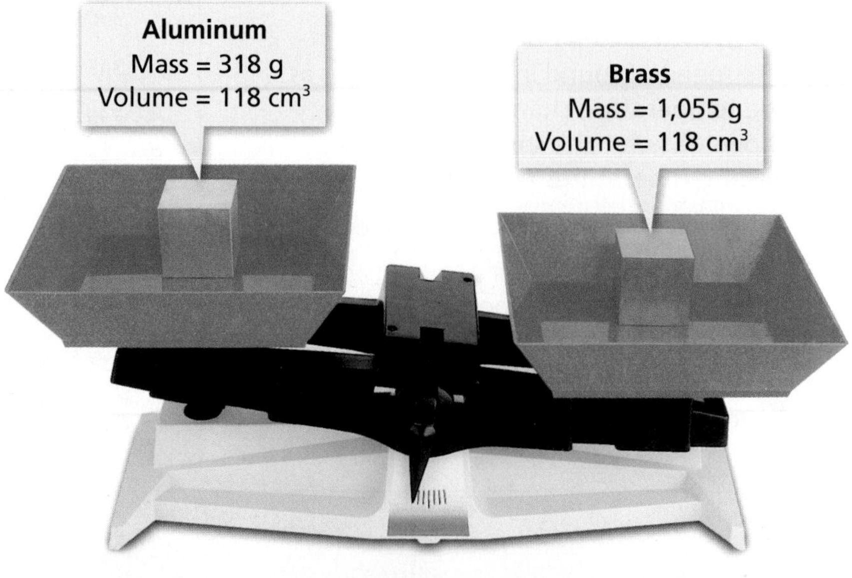

FIGURE 6
Comparing Density
The volumes of these cubes are the same, but the brass cube has more mass.
Interpreting Photographs *Which cube has a greater density: brass or aluminum?*

Temperature In a given medium, sound travels more slowly at lower temperatures than at higher temperatures. Why? At a low temperature, the particles of a medium move more slowly than at a high temperature. So, they are more difficult to move, and return to their original positions more slowly. For example, at 20°C, the speed of sound in air is about 343 m/s. But at 0°C, the speed of sound is about 330 m/s.

At higher altitudes, the air is colder than at lower altitudes, so sound travels more slowly at higher altitudes. On October 14, 1947, Captain Charles E. ("Chuck") Yeager of the United States Air Force used this knowledge to fly faster than the speed of sound.

To fly faster than the speed of sound, Captain Yeager flew his plane to an altitude of more than 12,000 meters. Here, the air temperature was −59°C. The speed of sound at this temperature is only about 293 m/s. At 12,000 meters, Captain Yeager accelerated his plane to a record-breaking 312 m/s. By doing this, he became the first person to "break the sound barrier."

FIGURE 7
Breaking the Sound Barrier
On October 14, 1947, Captain Chuck Yeager became the first person to fly a plane faster than the speed of sound.

Reading Checkpoint **How does temperature affect the speed of sound?**

Section 1 Assessment

Target Reading Skill Identifying Main Ideas
Use your graphic organizer to help you answer Question 2 below.

Reviewing Key Concepts

1. a. Reviewing What is sound?
   b. Explaining How is a sound wave produced?
   c. Sequencing Explain how a ringing telephone can be heard through a closed door.
2. a. Listing What are three ways that sound waves can interact?
   b. Applying Concepts Explain why you can hear a teacher through the closed door of a classroom.
   c. Inferring At a scenic overlook, you can hear an echo only if you shout in one particular direction. Explain why.
3. a. Identifying What property describes how a material bounces back after being disturbed?
   b. Summarizing What three properties of a medium affect the speed of sound?
   c. Developing Hypotheses Steel is denser than plastic, yet sound travels faster in steel than in plastic. Develop a hypothesis to explain why.

Lab zone At-Home Activity

Ear to the Sound Find a long metal fence or water pipe. **CAUTION:** *Beware of sharp edges and rust.* Put one ear to one end of the pipe while a family member taps on the other end. In which ear do you hear the sound first? Explain your answer to your family members. What accounts for the difference?

Section 2

Properties of Sound

Reading Preview

Key Concepts

- What factors affect the loudness of a sound?
- What does the pitch of a sound depend on?
- What causes the Doppler effect?

Key Terms

- loudness • intensity
- decibel (dB) • pitch
- ultrasound • infrasound
- larynx • Doppler effect

Target Reading Skill

Outlining An outline shows the relationship between main ideas and supporting ideas. As you read, make an outline about the properties of sound. Use the red headings for the main ideas and the blue headings for the supporting ideas.

Properties of Sound

I. Loudness
   A. Energy of a sound source
   B.
   C.
II. Pitch
   A.

Lab zone Discover Activity

How Does Amplitude Affect Loudness?

1. Your teacher will give you a wooden board with two nails in it. Attach a guitar string to the nails by wrapping each end tightly around a nail and tying a knot.
2. Hold the string near the middle. Pull it about 1 cm to one side. This distance is the amplitude of vibration. Let it go. How far does the string move to the other side? Describe the sound you hear.

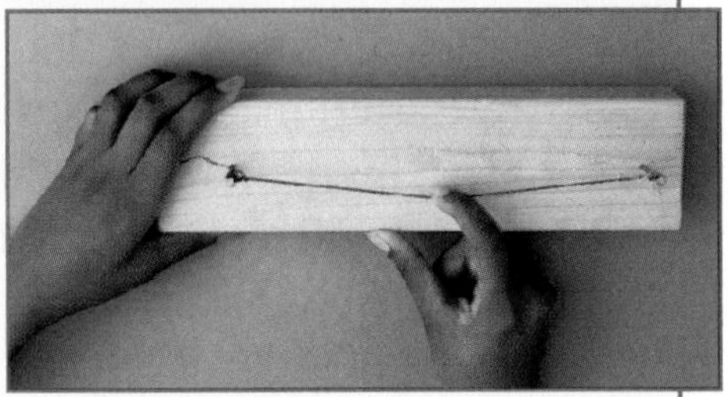

3. Repeat Step 2 four more times. Each time, pull the string back a greater distance. Describe how the sound changes each time.

Think It Over

Forming Operational Definitions How would you define the amplitude of the vibration? What effect did changing the amplitude have on the sound?

Suppose that you and a friend are talking on a sidewalk and a noisy truck pulls up next to you and stops, leaving its motor running. What would you do? You might talk louder, almost shout, so your friend can hear you. You might lean closer and speak into your friend's ear so you don't have to raise your voice. Or you might walk away from the noisy truck so it's not as loud.

Loudness

Loudness is an important property of sound. **Loudness** describes your perception of the energy of a sound. In other words, loudness describes what you hear. You probably already know a lot about loudness. For example, you know that your voice is much louder when you shout than when you speak softly. The closer you are to a sound, the louder it is. Also, a whisper in your ear can be just as loud as a shout from a block away. **The loudness of a sound depends on two factors: the amount of energy it takes to make the sound and the distance from the source of the sound.**

Energy of a Sound Source In general, the greater the energy used to make a sound, the louder the sound. If you did the Discover activity, you may have noticed this. The more energy you used to pull the guitar string back, the louder the sound when you let the string go. This happened because the more energy you used to pull the string, the greater the amplitude of the string's vibration. A string vibrating with a large amplitude produces a sound wave with a large amplitude. Recall that the greater the amplitude of a wave, the more energy the wave has. So, the larger the amplitude of the sound wave, the more energy it has and the louder it sounds.

Distance From a Sound Source If your friend is speaking in a normal voice and you lean in closer, your friend's voice sounds louder. Loudness increases the closer you are to a sound source. But why?

Imagine ripples spreading out in circles after you toss a pebble into a pond. In a similar way, a sound wave spreads out from its source. Close to the sound source, the sound wave covers a small area, as you can see in Figure 8. As the wave travels away from its source, it covers more area. The total energy of the wave, however, stays the same whether it is close to the source or far from it. Therefore, the closer the sound wave is to its source, the more energy it has in a given area. The amount of energy a sound wave carries per second through a unit area is its **intensity.** A sound wave of greater intensity sounds louder. As you move away from a sound source, loudness decreases because the intensity decreases.

Go Online PHSchool.com

For: More on the properties of sound
Visit: PHSchool.com
Web Code: cgd-5022

FIGURE 8
Intensity and Distance
Because sound waves spread out, intensity decreases with distance from the source.
Interpreting Diagrams *How does the intensity at 3 meters compare to the intensity at 2 meters?*

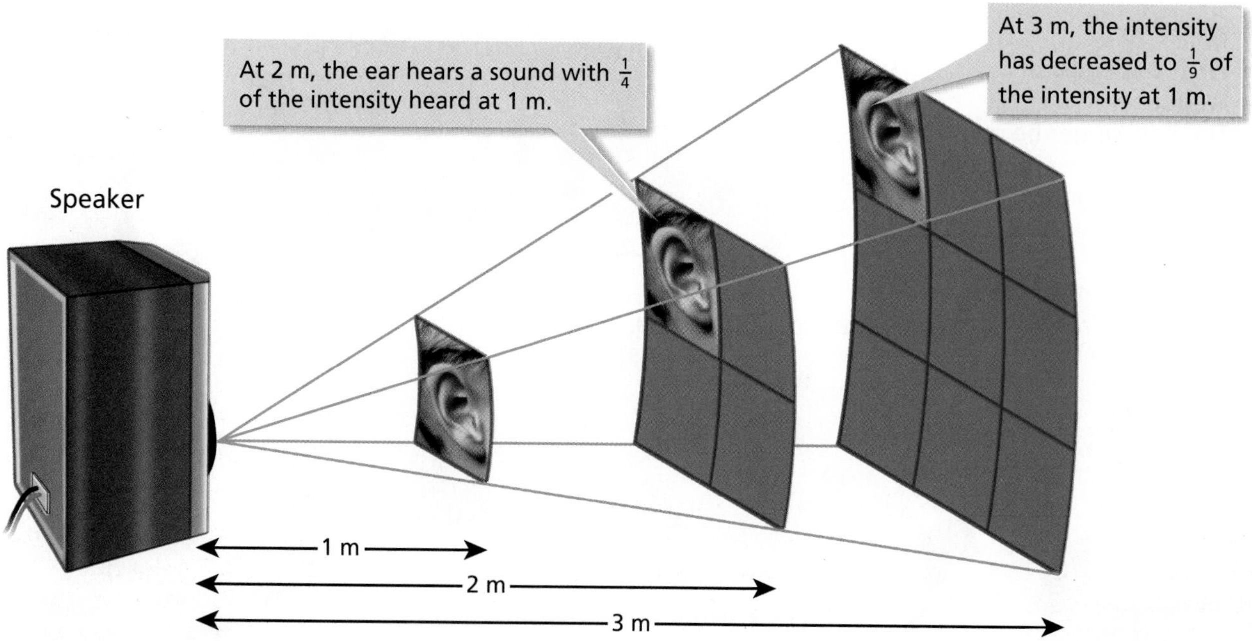

At 2 m, the ear hears a sound with $\frac{1}{4}$ of the intensity heard at 1 m.
At 3 m, the intensity has decreased to $\frac{1}{9}$ of the intensity at 1 m.
Speaker
1 m
2 m
3 m

Measuring Loudness	
Sound	**Loudness (dB)**
Rustling leaves	10
Whisper	15–20
Very soft music	20–30
Normal conversation	40–50
Heavy street traffic	60–70
Loud music	90–100
Rock concert	110–120
Jackhammer	120
Jet plane at takeoff	120–160

FIGURE 9
Some sounds are so soft that you can barely hear them. Others are so loud that they can damage your ears. **Interpreting Data** *Which sounds louder, a rock concert or a jet plane at takeoff?*

Measuring Loudness The loudness of different sounds is compared using a unit called the **decibel (dB).** Figure 9 shows the loudness of some familiar sounds. The loudness of a sound you can barely hear is about 0 dB. Each 10-dB increase in loudness represents a tenfold increase in the intensity of the sound. For example, soft music at 30 dB sounds ten times louder than a 20-dB whisper. The 30-dB music is 100 times louder than the 10-dB sound of rustling leaves. Sounds louder than 100 dB can cause damage to your ears, especially if you listen to those sounds for long periods of time.

Reading Checkpoint **What is a decibel?**

Pitch

Pitch is another property of sound you may already know a lot about. Have you ever described someone's voice as "high-pitched" or "low-pitched?" The **pitch** of a sound is a description of how high or low the sound seems to a person. **The pitch of a sound that you hear depends on the frequency of the sound wave.**

Pitch and Frequency Sound waves with a high frequency have a high pitch. Sound waves with a low frequency have a low pitch. Frequency is measured in hertz (Hz). For example, a frequency of 50 Hz means 50 vibrations per second. Look at Figure 10. A bass singer can produce frequencies lower than 80 Hz. A trained soprano voice can produce frequencies higher than 1,000 Hz.

FIGURE 10
Pitch Depends on Frequency
The bass singer below sings low notes, and the soprano singer on the right sings high notes.

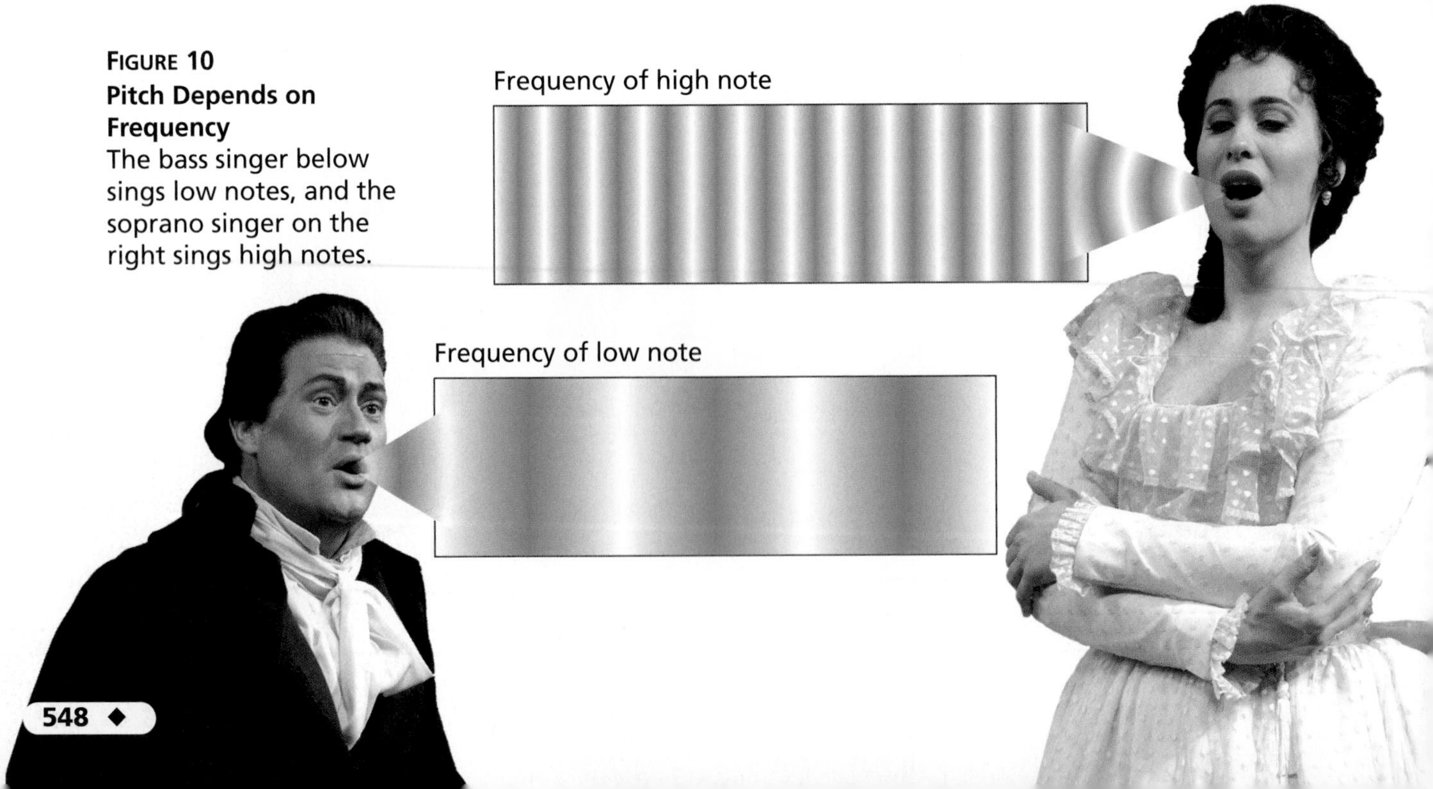

Most people can hear sounds with frequencies between 20 Hz and 20,000 Hz. Sound waves with frequencies above the normal human range of hearing are called **ultrasound.** The prefix *ultra-* means "beyond." Sounds with frequencies below the human range of hearing are called **infrasound.** The prefix *infra-* means "below." People cannot hear either ultrasound waves or infrasound waves.

Changing Pitch Pitch is an important property of music because music usually uses specific pitches called notes. To sing or play a musical instrument, you must change pitch often.

When you sing, you change pitch using your vocal cords. Your vocal cords are located in your voice box, or **larynx,** as shown in Figure 11. When you speak or sing, air from your lungs is forced up the trachea, or windpipe. Air then rushes past your vocal cords, making them vibrate. This produces sound waves. Your vocal cords are able to vibrate more than 1,000 times per second!

To sing different notes, you use muscles in your throat to stretch and relax your vocal cords. When your vocal cords stretch, they vibrate more quickly as the air rushes by them. This creates higher-frequency sound waves that have higher pitches. When your vocal cords relax, lower-frequency sound waves with lower pitches are produced.

With musical instruments, you change pitch in different ways depending on the instrument. For example, you can change the pitch of a guitar string by turning a knob to loosen or tighten the string. A tighter guitar string produces a higher frequency, which you hear as a note with higher pitch.

Reading Checkpoint **Where are your vocal cords located?**

Lab zone **Skills Activity**

Predicting

1. Flatten one end of a drinking straw and cut the end to form a point.
2. Blow through the straw. Describe what you hear.
3. Predict what changes you would hear if you shortened the straw by cutting off some of the straight end. Test your prediction by making two new straws of different lengths.

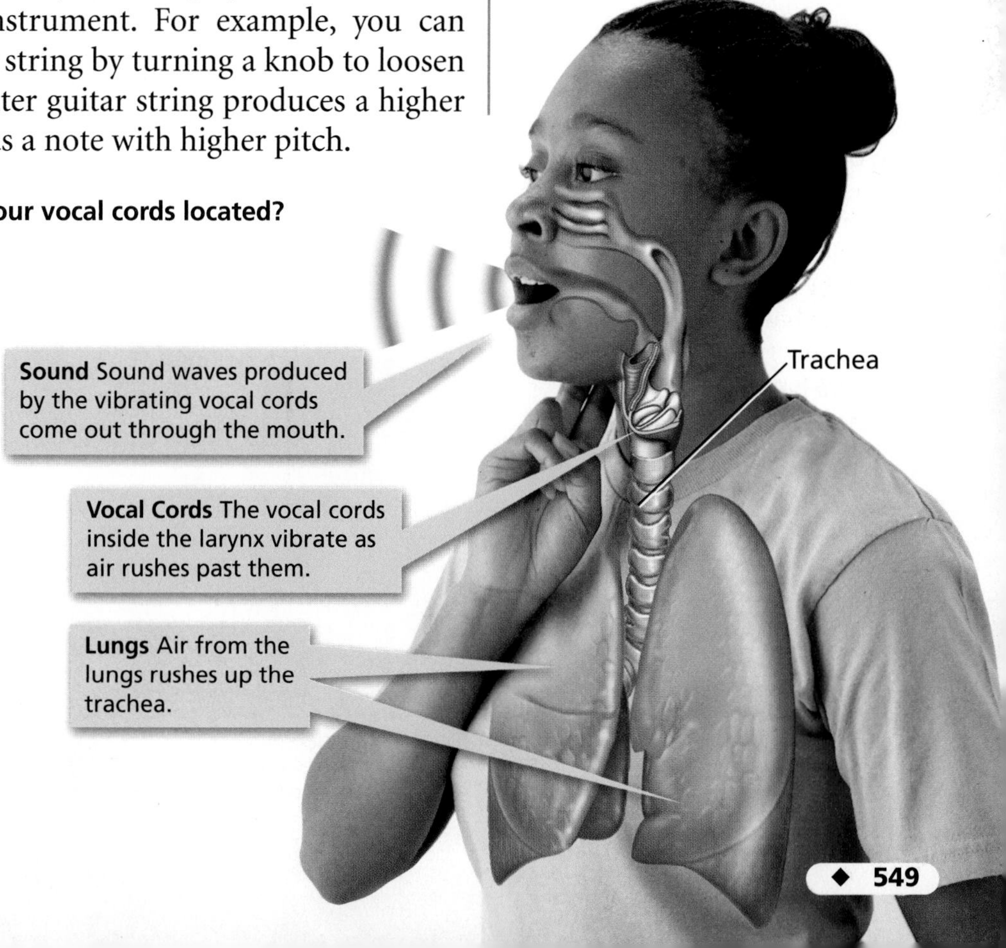
Sound Sound waves produced by the vibrating vocal cords come out through the mouth.
Vocal Cords The vocal cords inside the larynx vibrate as air rushes past them.
Lungs Air from the lungs rushes up the trachea.
Trachea

FIGURE 11
The Human Voice
When a person speaks or sings, the vocal cords vibrate. The vibrations produce sound waves in the air.

Lab zone
Try This **Activity**

Pipe Sounds

1. Find an open space without objects or people nearby.
2. Hold the end of a flexible plastic tube firmly (a vacuum cleaner hose works well). Swing the tube in a circle over your head to produce a sound.
3. Keeping the speed steady, listen to the sound. Have a partner stand at a safe distance and listen at the same time.

Observing Describe the sound you heard. How is it different from the sound your partner heard? Explain the difference.

The Doppler Effect

If you listen carefully to the siren of a firetruck on its way to a fire, you will notice something surprising. As the truck goes by you, the pitch of the siren drops. But the pitch of the siren stays constant for the firefighters in the truck. The siren's pitch changes only if it is moving toward or away from a listener.

The change in frequency of a wave as its source moves in relation to an observer is called the **Doppler effect.** If the waves are sound waves, the change in frequency is heard as a change in pitch. The Doppler effect is named after the Austrian scientist Christian Doppler (1803–1853).

What Causes the Doppler Effect? Figure 12 shows how sound waves from a moving source behave. When the source moves toward a listener, the frequency of the waves is higher than it would be if the source were stationary. **When a sound source moves, the frequency of the waves changes because the motion of the source adds to the motion of the waves.**

To understand why the frequency changes, imagine that you are standing still and throwing tennis balls at a wall in front of you. If you throw one ball each second the balls hit the wall at a rate of one per second. Now suppose you walk toward the wall while still throwing one ball per second. Because each ball has a shorter distance to travel than the one before, each takes less time to get there. The balls hit the wall more often than one per second, so the frequency is higher. On the other hand, if you throw balls at the wall as you back away, each ball has farther to travel and the frequency is lower.

FIGURE 12
The Doppler Effect
As the firetruck speeds by, the observers hear a change in the pitch of the siren.
Applying Concepts *How could you describe the pitch heard by the firefighter?*

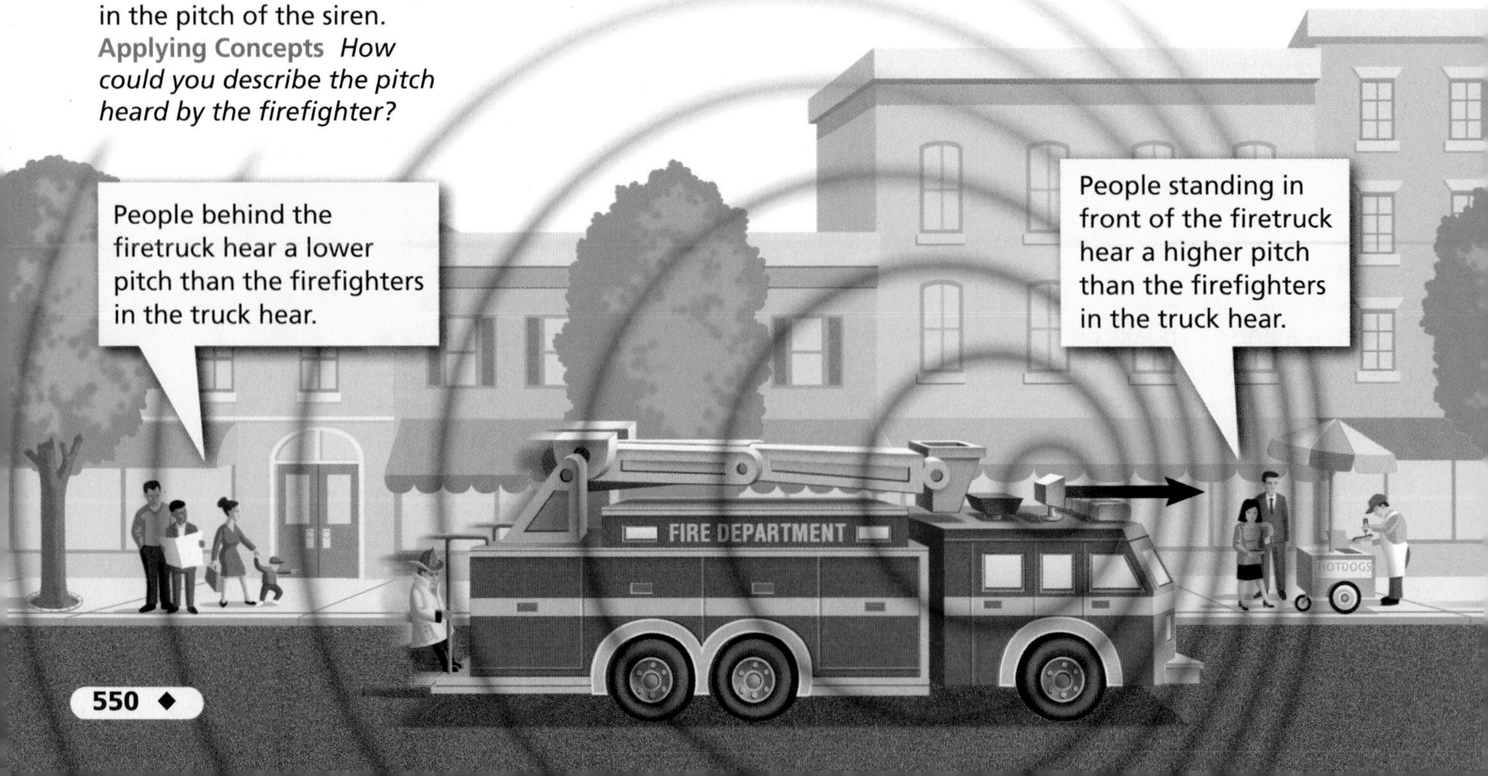
People behind the firetruck hear a lower pitch than the firefighters in the truck hear.
People standing in front of the firetruck hear a higher pitch than the firefighters in the truck hear.
FIRE DEPARTMENT
HOTDOGS

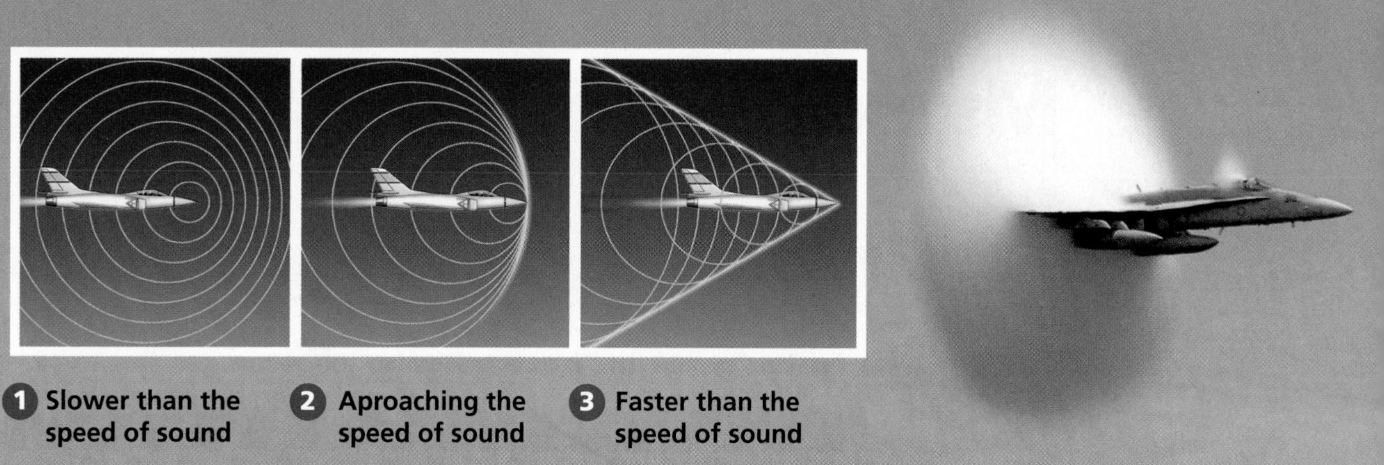

What Causes Shock Waves? At high speed, the Doppler effect can be spectacular. Look at Figure 13. When the plane travels almost as fast as the speed of sound, the sound waves pile up in front of the plane. This pile-up is the "sound barrier." As the plane flies faster than the speed of sound, it moves through the barrier. A shock wave forms as the sound waves overlap. The shock wave releases a huge amount of energy. People nearby hear a loud noise called a sonic boom when the shock wave passes by them.

FIGURE 13
Breaking the Sound Barrier
When a plane goes faster than the speed of sound, a shock wave is produced. The photo on the right shows how sudden changes in pressure at this speed can cause a small cloud to form.

Reading Checkpoint **What is a shock wave?**

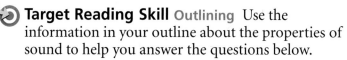

Section 2 Assessment

Target Reading Skill **Outlining** Use the information in your outline about the properties of sound to help you answer the questions below.

Reviewing Key Concepts

1. a. Identifying What two factors affect the loudness of a sound?
b. Applying Concepts Why does moving away from a radio affect the loudness you hear?
c. Calculating A band plays music at 60 dB and then changes to a rock song at 80 dB. How many times louder is the rock song?

2. a. Reviewing What determines the pitch of a sound?
b. Comparing and Contrasting How are high-pitch sounds different from low-pitch sounds?
c. Explaining How do your vocal cords produce different pitches?

3. a. Summarizing What is the Doppler effect?
b. Relating Cause and Effect What causes the Doppler effect?
c. Predicting Would you hear a change in pitch if you are on a moving train and the train's whistle blows? Explain.

Lab zone At-Home Activity

Hum Stopper When listening to a cat's heart, a veterinarian will cover the cat's nostrils to keep the cat from purring. At home, ask family members to hum with their lips closed. Then ask them to cover both of their nostrils while humming. Use Figure 11 to explain what happened.

Section 3 Music

Reading Preview

Key Concepts

- What determines the sound quality of a musical instrument?
- What are the basic groups of musical instruments?
- How is acoustics used in concert hall design?

Key Terms

- music
- fundamental tone
- overtone
- acoustics
- reverberation

Target Reading Skill

Previewing Visuals When you preview, you look ahead at the material to be read. Preview Figure 15. Then write two questions that you have about the diagrams in a graphic organizer like the one below. As you read, answer your questions.

Musical Instruments

Q.	How is pitch changed in each type of instrument?
A.	
Q.	

Lab zone Discover Activity

How Can You Change Pitch?

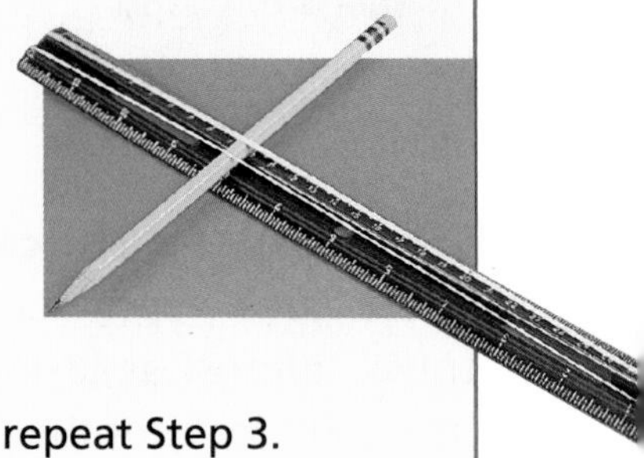

1. Wrap two rubber bands of different thickness lengthwise around a 30-cm plastic ruler. The bands should not touch each other.
2. Place a pencil under the bands at the 10-cm mark.
3. Pluck each band. How are the sounds different?
4. Move the pencil to the 15-cm mark and repeat Step 3.

Think It Over

Drawing Conclusions Why are the sounds you made in Step 4 different from the sounds in Step 3?

You are late. When you arrive at your orchestra rehearsal, your friends are already tuning up. With all the instruments playing different notes, it sounds like noise! You quickly pull out your instrument and take your seat. Then the music starts, and everything changes. What makes noise and music different? The answer is in the way sound waves combine.

Orchestra rehearsal ▶

Sound Quality

Most people agree on what is or is not music. **Music** is a set of notes that combine in patterns that are pleasing. Noise, on the other hand, has no pleasing patterns. When you describe a sound as pleasant or unpleasant, you are describing sound quality. The sound quality of music depends on the instruments making the music. **The sound quality of musical instruments results from blending a fundamental tone with its overtones. Resonance also plays a role in the sound quality.**

Fundamental Tones and Overtones You may recall that standing waves occur when waves with just the right frequency interfere as they reflect back and forth. Standing waves occur in musical instruments when they are played. In a guitar, for example, standing waves occur in a vibrating string. In a trumpet, standing waves occur in a column of vibrating air.

A standing wave can occur only at specific frequencies that are called natural frequencies. Every object has its own natural frequencies. The lowest natural frequency of an object is called the **fundamental tone.** The object's higher natural frequencies are called **overtones.** Overtones have frequencies that are two, three, or more times the frequency of the fundamental tone. Look at Figure 14 to see how the natural frequencies of a guitar string add together to produce a unique sound.

The fundamental tone determines what note you hear. For example, when a guitar and a trumpet play middle C, they both produce waves with a frequency of 262 Hz. But each instrument produces different overtones, so the blending of the fundamental tones and overtones produces different sound qualities.

Resonance Resonance affects the sound quality of a musical instrument by increasing the loudness of certain overtones. Recall that resonance occurs when one object causes a nearby object to vibrate at a natural frequency. A musical instrument is designed so that a part of it will resonate with the overtones it produces. In a guitar, for example, the vibrating strings cause the guitar's hollow body to resonate. The shape and material of the guitar determine which overtones are loudest.

Reading Checkpoint **What are overtones?**

FIGURE 14
Sound Quality
A guitar string can resonate at several frequencies that combine to produce a unique sound quality.
Interpreting Diagrams *What determines the resulting wave?*

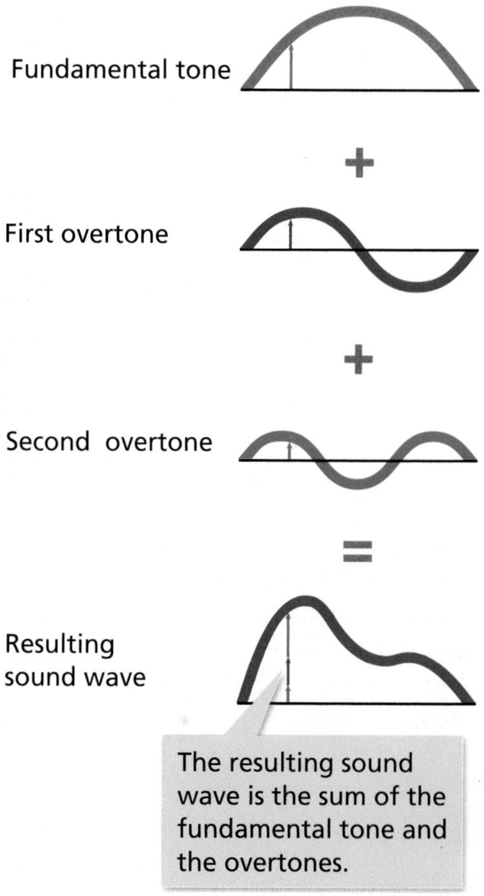
Fundamental tone
+
First overtone
+
Second overtone
=
Resulting sound wave
The resulting sound wave is the sum of the fundamental tone and the overtones.

Go Online
active art

For: Musical Instruments activity
Visit: PHSchool.com
Web Code: cgp-5023

FIGURE 15
Musical Instruments
A musician controls the vibrations of a musical instrument to change pitch and loudness. **Classifying** *How would you classify a tuba, a tambourine, and a banjo?*

Wind Instrument: Clarinet
Loudness is controlled by how hard the musician blows.

Stringed Instrument: Violin
Loudness is increased by the musician pressing the bow harder against the strings.

Pitch depends on the length and thickness of the strings, the material they are made of, and how tightly the strings are stretched. A short string produces a high pitch, and a longer string produces a lower pitch.

Groups of Musical Instruments

How does a musician control the sounds produced by a musical instrument? To control pitch, the musician changes the fundamental tones produced by the instrument. To control loudness, the musician changes the energy of the vibrations. The way that pitch and loudness are controlled varies among the groups of instruments, as shown in Figure 15. **There are three basic groups of musical instruments: stringed instruments, wind instruments, and percussion instruments.**

Stringed Instruments The guitar and the violin are stringed instruments. The strings of these instruments produce sound by vibrating when they are strummed or rubbed with a bow. Their loudness is increased by resonance when the instrument's hollow body vibrates as the strings vibrate. The pitch of each string depends on four factors: its length and thickness, the material it is made from, and how tightly it is stretched. An instrument with long strings, such as a cello, produces lower notes than an instrument with short strings, such as a violin.

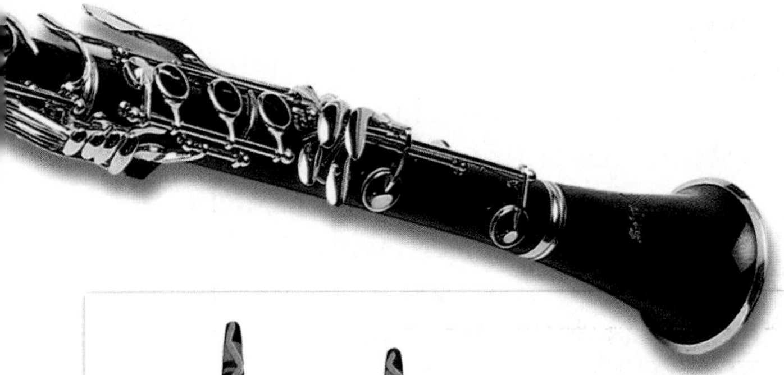

Pitch depends on the length of the air column, which can be changed by covering different holes. A short air column produces a high pitch, and a longer column produces a lower pitch.

Percussion Instrument: Drum

Loudness is controlled by how hard the musician strikes the drum.

Pitch depends on the size of the drum head, the material, and the tension in the drum head. A smaller drum produces a higher pitch.

Wind Instruments Wind instruments include brass instruments, such as trumpets, and woodwind instruments, such as clarinets. Brass instruments produce sound when a musician's lips vibrate against the mouthpiece, causing the air column in the instrument to vibrate. Woodwinds usually contain a thin, flexible strip of material called a reed. A woodwind produces sound when the reed vibrates, causing the instrument's air column to vibrate. In wind instruments, the length of the vibrating air column determines the note that you hear. A tuba, which has a long air column, produces lower notes than a flute, which has a short air column.

Percussion Instruments Percussion instruments include drums, bells, cymbals, and xylophones. These instruments vibrate when struck. The pitch of a drum depends on its size, the material it is made of, and the tension in the drumhead. A large drum produces lower pitches than a small drum.

Reading Checkpoint **What are four examples of percussion instruments?**

FIGURE 16
Concert Hall Acoustics
Surfaces in concert halls are designed with a variety of materials and shapes.
Inferring *What might be the purpose of the curved panels near the ceiling?*

Acoustics

Your surroundings affect the musical sounds that you hear at a concert. To understand this, compare the sound of your voice in different places—in class, outdoors, or in a gym. The differences you hear are due to the different ways that sounds interact. **Acoustics** is the study of how sounds interact with each other and the environment.

Sound waves can interfere with each other. Constructive interference may distort sound, while destructive interference can produce "dead spots" where loudness is reduced. Sound waves interact with the environment, also. For example, if you clap your hands in a gym, you hear echoes after you clap because sound waves reflect back and forth off the hard surfaces. This is **reverberation,** in which the echoes of a sound are heard after the sound source stops producing sound waves. The sound from a handclap can take more than a second to die out in a gym.

Acoustics is used in the design of concert halls to control reverberation and interference. Curved hard surfaces are used to direct sound waves to different parts of the concert hall. Soft surfaces absorb sound waves, reducing reverberation. But some reverberation is desirable. With too little reverberation, instruments would sound thin and distant. With too much reverberation, reflected waves interfere and individual notes become hard to pick out.

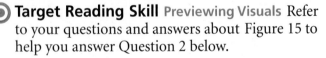

Section 3 Assessment

Target Reading Skill Previewing Visuals Refer to your questions and answers about Figure 15 to help you answer Question 2 below.

Reviewing Key Concepts

1. a. Describing How do overtones affect the sound quality of a musical instrument?
   b. Explaining How does resonance affect the sound quality of a musical instrument?
2. a. Listing What are the three groups of musical instruments?
   b. Summarizing How is pitch controlled in each group of musical instruments?
   c. Comparing and Contrasting How is loudness increased in a drum and in a guitar?
3. a. Defining What is acoustics?
   b. Relating Cause and Effect How is acoustics used in the design of concert halls?
   c. Making Judgments Why is some reverberation desirable in a concert hall?

Writing in Science

Explanation A friend e-mails you and asks how your new guitar produces music. Write an e-mail that answers your friend's question. Be sure to explain how you can change pitch, and why the guitar has a hollow body.

Changing Pitch

Problem

When you blow across the mouth of a bottle, you can play a "note." What determines the pitch you hear?

Skills Focus

controlling variables, designing experiments

Suggested Materials

- 1-L soda bottle • 2-L soda bottle
- 250-mL graduated cylinder • metric ruler
- straw • water

Design a Plan

1. Practice making a sound by using a straw to blow across the mouth of a 1-L bottle. Then blow across the mouth of a 2-L bottle in the same way. Compare the pitches. Record your observations in your notebook.
2. Add 250 mL of water to both the 1-L bottle and the 2-L bottle. Blow across the mouth of each bottle and compare the pitches. Record your observations in your notebook.
3. Analyze your observations from Steps 1 and 2 to predict what may have affected the pitches. For example, measure the height of the air column, and calculate the volume of air in each bottle. (*Hint:* Subtract the volume of water in the bottle from the total volume of the bottle.)
4. Develop a hypothesis about what determines the pitch of the sound produced by blowing across the mouth of a bottle. Record your hypothesis in your notebook.
5. Design an experiment to test your hypothesis. Create a data table to record information about the variables. Write your plan. (*Hint:* You can change the height of the air column in a bottle by changing the amount of water in the bottle.)
6. After receiving your teacher's approval of your plan, conduct your experiment and record the results in your notebook.

Analyze and Conclude

1. **Observing** Describe the pitch of the sound produced by each bottle in Steps 1 and 2.
2. **Designing Experiments** Did your experiment support your hypothesis? Explain.
3. **Controlling Variables** Identify the manipulated and responding variables in your experiment.
4. **Inferring** If you had a 1-L bottle that contained 250 mL of water, what would you do to produce a higher-pitched sound?
5. **Drawing Conclusions** What is the relationship between the height of the air column and the pitch of the sound produced by blowing across the mouth of a bottle?
6. **Communicating** Based on your results, describe how you could use a set of bottles as a musical instrument.

More to Explore

Use a set of tuning forks or a pitch pipe to "tune" five bottles to match the notes C, D, E, F, and G. What can you conclude about the pitches of the five notes from the height of the air column in each bottle? Use the bottles to play the following notes: E D C D E E E D D D E G G E D C D E E E E D D E D C.

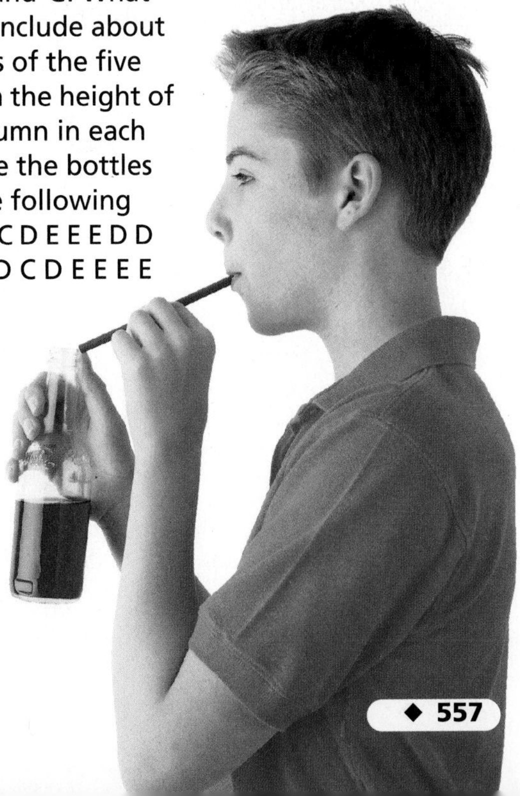

Section 4

Integrating Life Science

How You Hear Sound

Reading Preview

Key Concepts

- What is the function of each section of the ear?
- What causes hearing loss?

Key Terms

- ear canal
- eardrum
- cochlea

Target Reading Skill

Sequencing A sequence is the order in which the steps in a process occur. As you read, make a flowchart that shows how you hear sound. Put the steps of the process in separate boxes in the order in which they occur.

How You Hear Sound

The outer ear funnels sound waves into the ear canal.

↓

Sound waves make the eardrum vibrate.

↓

Lab zone Discover Activity

Where Is the Sound Coming From?

1. Ask your partner to sit on a chair, with eyes closed.
2. Clap your hands near your partner's left ear. Ask your partner what direction the sound came from. Record the answer.
3. Now clap near your partner's right ear. Again, ask your partner what direction the sound came from and record the answer. Continue clapping in different locations around your partner's head and face. How well did your partner identify the directions the sounds came from?
4. Switch places with your partner and repeat Steps 1–3.

Think It Over

Observing From which locations are claps easily identified? For which locations are claps impossible to identify? Is there a pattern? If so, suggest an explanation for the pattern.

The house is quiet. You are sound asleep. All of a sudden, your alarm clock goes off. Startled, you jump up out of bed. Your ears detected the sound waves produced by the alarm clock. But how exactly did your brain receive the information?

The Human Ear

The function of your ear is to gather sound waves and send, or transmit, information about sound to your brain. Your ear has three main sections: the outer ear, the middle ear, and the inner ear. Each section has a different function. **The outer ear funnels sound waves, the middle ear transmits the waves inward, and the inner ear converts sound waves into a form that travels to your brain.**

Outer Ear Look at Figure 17. The first section of your ear is the outer ear. The outermost part of your outer ear looks and acts like a funnel. It collects sound waves and directs them into a narrow region called the **ear canal.** Your ear canal is a few centimeters long and ends at the eardrum. The **eardrum** is a small, tightly stretched, drumlike membrane. The sound waves make your eardrum vibrate, just as a drum vibrates when you strike it.

FIGURE 17
The Human Ear

The ear is a complex structure that allows you to hear.
Interpreting Diagrams *What three bones make up the middle ear?*

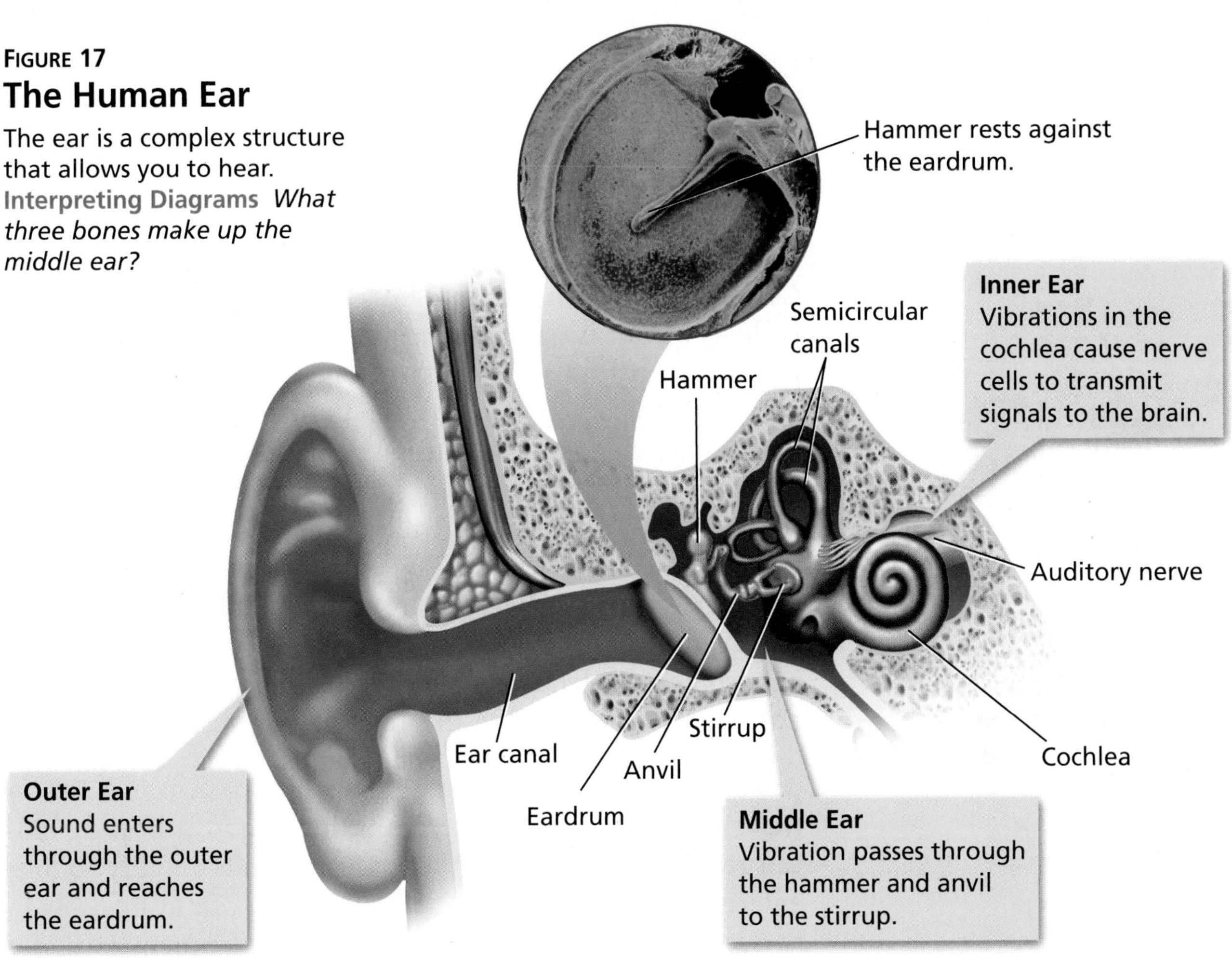

Hammer rests against the eardrum.
Inner Ear
Vibrations in the cochlea cause nerve cells to transmit signals to the brain.
Semicircular canals
Hammer
Auditory nerve
Stirrup
Cochlea
Ear canal
Anvil
Eardrum
Outer Ear
Sound enters through the outer ear and reaches the eardrum.
Middle Ear
Vibration passes through the hammer and anvil to the stirrup.

Middle Ear Behind the eardrum is the middle ear. The middle ear contains the three smallest bones in your body—the hammer, the anvil, and the stirrup. The hammer is attached to the eardrum, so when the eardrum vibrates, the hammer does too. The hammer then transmits vibrations first to the anvil and then to the stirrup.

Inner Ear A membrane separates the middle ear from the inner ear, the third section of the ear. When the stirrup vibrates against this membrane, the vibrations pass into the cochlea. The **cochlea** (KAHK lee uh) is a fluid-filled cavity shaped like a snail shell. The cochlea contains more than 10,000 tiny structures called hair cells. These hair cells have hairlike projections that float in the fluid of the cochlea. When vibrations move through the fluid, the hair cells move, causing messages to be sent to the brain through the auditory nerve. The brain processes these messages and tells you that you've heard sound.

Reading Checkpoint **What are the three main sections of the ear?**

Lab zone Try This Activity

Listen to This

1. Tie two strings to the handle of a metal spoon. Each string should be about 40 cm long.
2. Hold the loose end of each string in each hand. Bump the spoon against a desk or other hard solid object. Listen to the sound.
3. Now wrap the ends of the string around your fingers. Put your index fingers against your ears and bump the spoon again. How is the sound different?

Inferring What can you infer about how sound travels to your ears?

FIGURE 18
A Modern Hearing Aid
Some hearing aids are about the size of a dime. **Inferring** *What are some benefits and drawbacks of tiny hearing aids?*

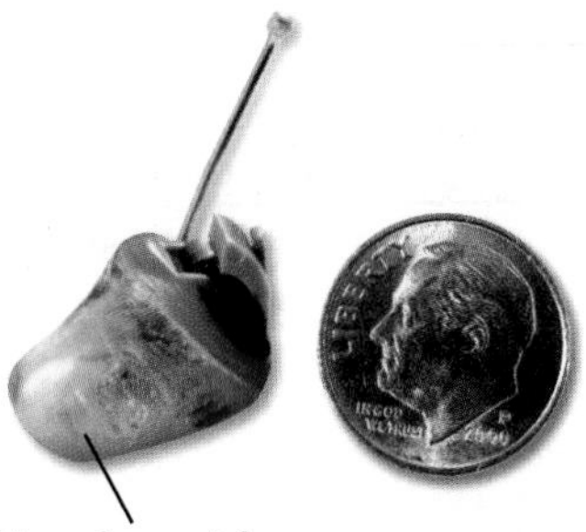

Hearing Loss

When hearing loss occurs, a person may have difficulty hearing soft sounds or high-pitched sounds. **There are many causes of hearing loss, including injury, infection, exposure to loud sounds, and aging.**

Causes of Hearing Loss Hearing loss can occur suddenly if the eardrum is damaged or punctured. (Imagine trying to play a torn drum!) For this reason, it is dangerous to put objects into your ear, even to clean it. Infections also can damage the delicate inner ear, causing permanent hearing loss.

Extended exposure to loud sounds can damage hair cells in the ear. The damaged cells will no longer send signals to the brain. You can prevent this type of hearing loss by wearing hearing protection when you are around loud sounds.

The most common type of hearing loss occurs gradually. As a person gets older, some hair cells in the cochlea die and are not replaced. People with this kind of hearing loss often have difficulty hearing high-frequency sounds.

Hearing Aids For some types of hearing loss, hearing aids can restore some ability to hear. Hearing aids amplify sounds entering the ear. Some are so tiny that they can fit invisibly in the ear canal. Others can amplify specific frequencies that a person has lost the ability to hear.

Reading Checkpoint **What happens when a hearing loss occurs?**

Section 4 Assessment

Target Reading Skill **Sequencing** Refer to your flowchart about hearing as you answer Question 1.

Reviewing Key Concepts

1. a. **Identifying** What is the function of each section of your ear?
   b. **Interpreting Diagrams** Look at Figure 17. What happens to a sound wave as it enters your ear canal?
   c. **Relating Cause and Effect** How are sound waves transmitted through the middle ear?
2. a. **Listing** What are four causes of hearing loss?
   b. **Explaining** How can loud sounds lead to hearing loss?
   c. **Making Judgments** Should people at a rock concert wear earplugs? Why or why not?

Lab zone **At-Home Activity**

Sound Survey Ask family members to survey the sounds they hear in a day. Ask them to rate the sounds as quiet, normal, loud, or painful. Then rate each sound as pleasant, neutral, or annoying. For each sound record the source, location, time of day, and time exposed to the sound. How are the ratings similar? How are they different?

Lab zone **Technology Lab**

• Tech & Design •

Design and Build Hearing Protectors

Problem

Can you design and build hearing protectors that block some sound from reaching your ears?

Design Skills

designing a solution, evaluating the design

Suggested Materials

- sound source (radio, tape player, or CD player)
- soundproofing materials
- tape measure
- scissors
- string
- pencil
- different types of headgear
- glue

Procedure

PART 1 Research and Investigate

1. Copy the data table on a separate sheet of paper.
2. Select a soundproofing material.
3. Stand quietly at the back of the room. Your teacher will adjust the loudness of a sound source until you are just able to hear it. Ask your partner to measure and record your distance from the sound source. Record the measurement in your data table.
4. Cover both ears with the soundproofing material. **CAUTION:** *Do not insert any material into your ears.* Move slowly forward until you can just hear the sound source again. Stop. Then have your partner measure your distance from the sound source. Record the measurement in your data table.
5. Repeat Steps 2–4 using three other materials.

Data Table

Soundproofing Material	Distance From Sound Source (m)
No material	
Material 1	
Material 2	
Material 3	
Material 4	

PART 2 Design and Build

6. Based on what you learned in Part 1, design and build hearing protectors. Your device should
   - keep you from hearing a pencil dropped on a table at a distance of 5 meters
   - fit comfortably on your head without needing to be held in place
   - be made of materials approved by your teacher
7. Sketch your design and list the materials you will use. After your teacher approves your design, build your hearing protectors.

Analyze and Conclude

1. **Designing a Solution** What did you learn about soundproofing materials in Part 1 that helped you design your device?
2. **Evaluating the Design** Test your hearing protectors. Did your device meet all of the goals stated in Step 6? Explain.
3. **Troubleshooting** As you designed, built, and tested your hearing protectors, what problems did you encounter? How did you solve them?

Communicate

A construction company is considering buying your hearing protectors. Write a summary of your test results to convince the company that the device meets the design goals stated in Step 6.

Keeping It Quiet...

A construction worker uses a jackhammer; a woman waits in a noisy airport; a spectator watches a car race. All three experience noise pollution. In the United States alone, 40 million people face danger to their health from noise pollution.

People start to feel pain at about 120 decibels. But noise that "doesn't hurt" can still damage your hearing. Exposure to 85 decibels (a kitchen blender) can slowly damage the hair cells in your cochlea. As many as 9 million Americans have hearing loss caused by noise. What can be done about noise pollution?

The Issues

What Can Individuals Do?

Some work conditions are noisier than others. Construction workers, airport employees, and truck drivers are all at risk. Workers in noisy environments can help themselves by using ear protectors, which can reduce noise levels by 35 decibels.

Many leisure activities also pose a risk. A listener at a rock concert or someone riding a motorbike can prevent damage by using ear protectors. People can also reduce noise at the source. They can buy quieter machines and avoid using lawnmowers or power tools at quiet times of the day. Simply turning down the volume on headphones for radios and CD players can help prevent hearing loss in young people.

What Can Communities Do?

Transportation—planes, trains, trucks, and cars—is the largest source of noise pollution. About 15 million Americans live near airports or under airplane flight paths. Careful planning to locate airports away from dense populations can reduce noise. Cities can also prohibit late-night flights.

Many communities have laws against noise that exceeds a certain decibel level, but these laws are hard to enforce. In some cities, "noise police" can give fines to people who use noisy equipment.

What Can the Government Do?

A National Office of Noise Abatement and Control was set up in the 1970s. It required labels on power tools to tell how much noise they made. But in 1982, this office lost its funding. In 1997, lawmakers proposed The Quiet Communities Act to bring the office back and set limits to many types of noise. But critics say that national laws have little effect. They want the federal government to encourage—and pay for—research into making quieter vehicles and machines.

You Decide

1. Identify the Problem
In your own words, describe the issues of noise pollution.

2. Analyze the Options
List as many methods as you can for dealing with noise. How would each method reduce noise or protect people from noise?

3. Find a Solution
Choose one method for reducing noise in your community. Make a poster to convince people to support your proposal.

Go Online
PHSchool.com

For: More on noise pollution
Visit: PHSchool.com
Web Code: cgh-5020

Section 5

Using Sound

Reading Preview

Key Concepts

- Why do some animals use echolocation?
- What are ultrasound technologies used for?

Key Terms

- echolocation
- sonar
- sonogram

Target Reading Skill

Comparing and Contrasting
As you read, compare and contrast echolocation and sonar by completing a table like the one below.

Using Sound

Feature	Echolocation	Sonar
Type of wave	Ultrasound	
Medium(s)		Water
Purposes		

Lab zone Discover Activity

How Can You Use Time to Measure Distance?

1. Measure a distance 3 meters from a wall and mark the spot with a piece of masking tape.
2. Roll a soft ball in a straight line from that spot toward the wall. What happens to the ball?
3. Roll the ball again. Try to roll the ball at the same speed each time. Have a classmate use a stopwatch to record the time it takes for the ball to leave your hand, reflect off the wall, and then return to you.
4. Now move 6 meters away from the wall. Mark the spot with tape. Repeat Steps 2 and 3.
5. Compare the time for both distances.

Think It Over
Inferring What does the difference in time tell you about the distance the ball has traveled?

A dog trainer stands quietly, watching the dog a short distance away. To get the dog's attention, the trainer blows into a small whistle. You don't hear a thing. But the dog stops, cocks an ear, and then comes running toward the trainer. Dogs can hear ultrasound frequencies up to about 45,000 Hz, well above the upper limit for humans. Other animals, such as cats and mice, can also hear ultrasound frequencies.

Some types of animals not only hear ultrasound, but also produce ultrasound waves. They use ultrasound waves to "see in the dark."

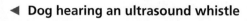

◀ **Dog hearing an ultrasound whistle**

Echolocation

Imagine trying to walk around in a totally dark room. You would probably bump into objects every few steps. Unlike you, bats find it easy to move around in dark places. This is because they use echolocation. **Echolocation** (ek oh loh KAY shun) is the use of reflected sound waves to determine distances or to locate objects. **Some animals, including bats and dolphins, use echolocation to navigate and to find food.**

Bats Bats use ultrasound waves with frequencies up to 100,000 Hz to move around and hunt. As a bat flies, it sends out short pulses of ultrasound waves—as many as 200 pulses per second! The waves reflect off objects and return to the bat's ears. The time it takes for the sound waves to return tells the bat how far it is from obstacles or prey. The bat uses the reflected sound waves to build up a "picture" of what lies ahead.

Dolphins, Porpoises, and Whales Dolphins, porpoises, and some whales must often hunt in darkness. Like bats, these animals use echolocation. For example, dolphins send out ultrasound waves with frequencies up to 150,000 Hz. The sound waves travel through the water and bounce off fish or other prey, as shown in Figure 19. Dolphins sense the reflected sound waves through their jawbones. They use echolocation to hunt at night or in murky or deep water.

Discovery Channel School

Sound

Video Preview
▶ Video Field Trip
Video Assessment

Reading Checkpoint **What animals use echolocation?**

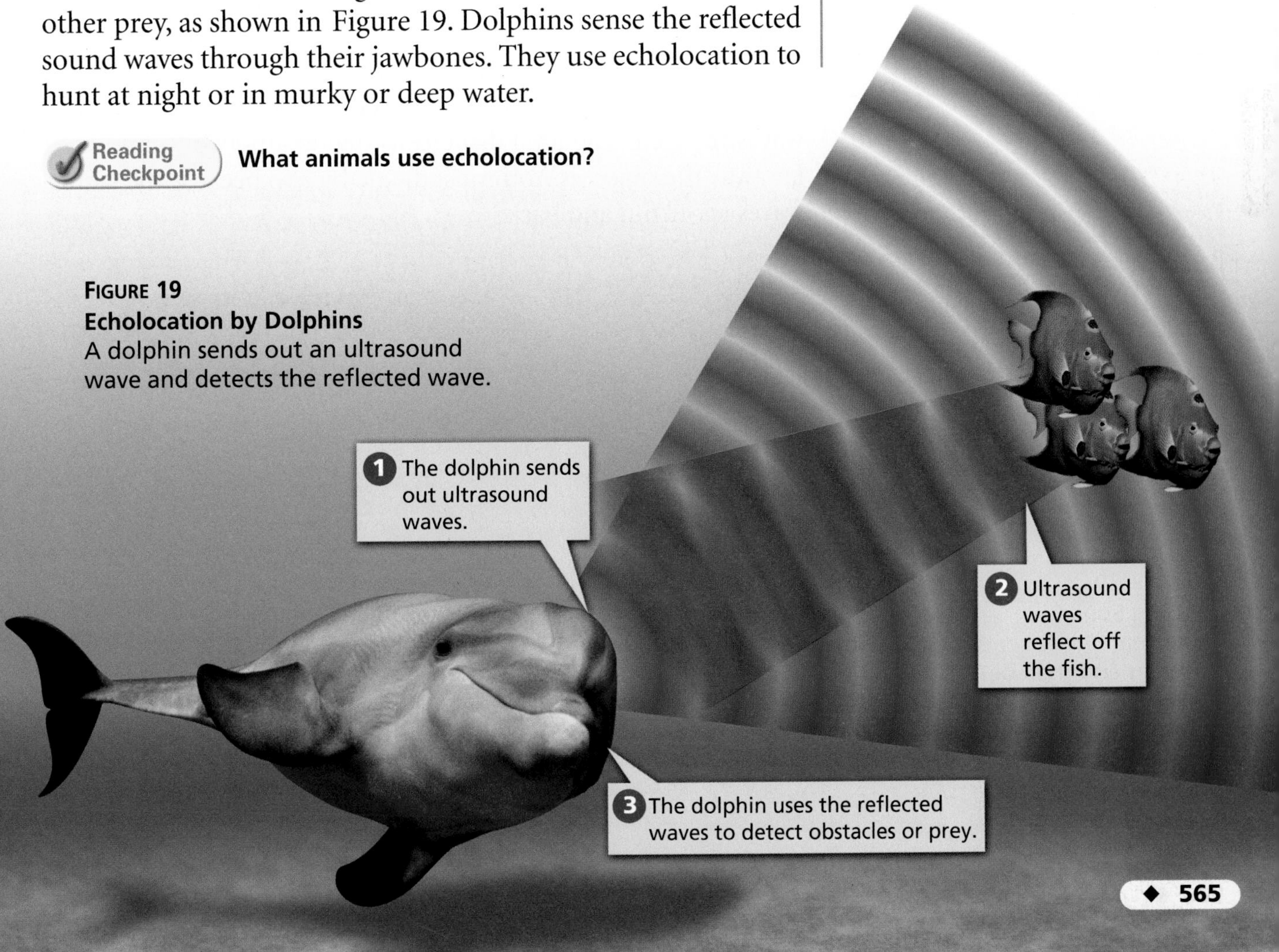

1 The dolphin sends out ultrasound waves.
2 Ultrasound waves reflect off the fish.
3 The dolphin uses the reflected waves to detect obstacles or prey.

FIGURE 19
Echolocation by Dolphins
A dolphin sends out an ultrasound wave and detects the reflected wave.

Lab zone **Skills Activity**

Designing Experiments

1. Stand a square piece of cardboard on a table. Prop it up with a book.
2. Lay two cardboard tubes flat on the table. The tubes should be angled to make a V shape, with the point of the V near the cardboard square. Leave a gap of about 6 cm between the cardboard square and the ends of the tubes.
3. Place a ticking watch in one tube. Put your ear near the open end of the second tube. Cover your free ear with your hand. What do you hear?
4. Design an experiment to determine how well sound reflects off different materials.

Go Online PHSchool.com

For: More on sonar
Visit: PHSchool.com
Web Code: cgd-5025

Ultrasound Technologies

People cannot send out pulses of ultrasound to help them move around in the dark. But people sometimes need to explore places they cannot easily reach, such as deep underwater or inside the human body. **Ultrasound technologies such as sonar and ultrasound imaging are used to observe things that cannot be seen directly.**

Sonar A system that uses reflected sound waves to detect and locate objects underwater is called **sonar**. The word *sonar* comes from the initial letters of **so**und **n**avigation **a**nd **r**anging. *Navigation* means finding your way around on the ocean (or in the air), and *ranging* means finding the distance between objects. Today, sonar is used to determine the depth of water, to map the ocean floor, and to locate sunken ships, schools of fish, and other objects in the ocean.

A sonar device sends a burst of ultrasound waves that travel through the water. When the sound waves strike an object or the ocean floor, they reflect as shown in Figure 20. The sonar device detects the reflected waves.

The farther a sound wave travels before bouncing off an object, the longer it takes to return to the sonar device. A computer in the sonar device measures the time it takes for the sound waves to go out and return. Then, it multiplies this time by the speed of sound in water. The result is the total distance the sound waves traveled. The total distance is divided by two to find how far away the object is. You must divide by two because the sound waves travel out and back.

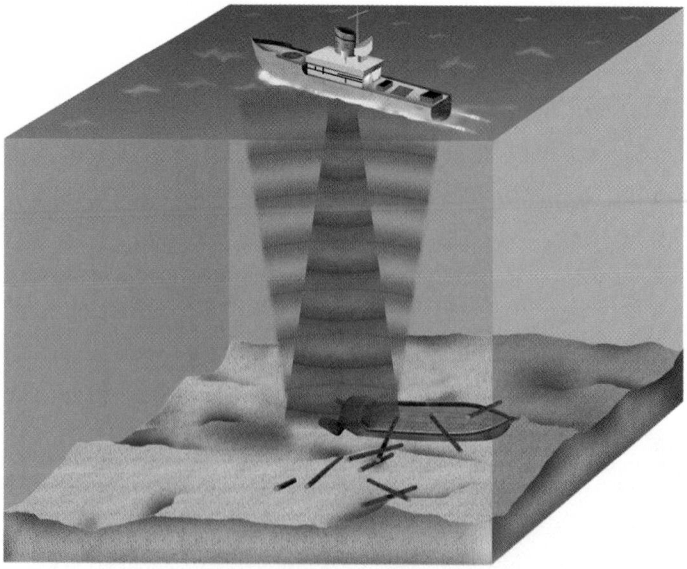

FIGURE 20
Using Sonar
A sonar device sends out ultrasound waves and then detects the reflected waves. **Interpreting Diagrams** *What happens to the reflected sound waves?*

Ultrasound Imaging Doctors use ultrasound imaging to look inside the human body. Ultrasound imaging devices send ultrasound waves into the body and detect the reflected sound waves. Different parts of the body, such as bones, muscles, the liver, or the heart, reflect sound differently. The device uses the reflected ultrasound waves to create a picture called a **sonogram**. A doctor can use sonograms to diagnose and treat many medical conditions.

Ultrasound imaging is used to examine developing babies before they are born. A technician or doctor holds a small probe on a pregnant woman's abdomen. The probe sends out very high frequency ultrasound waves (about 4 million Hz). By analyzing the reflected sound waves, the device builds up a sonogram. The sonogram can show the position of the baby. Sonograms can also show if more than one baby will be born. In addition to a still picture, ultrasound imaging can produce a video of a developing baby.

Reading Checkpoint What is a sonogram?

FIGURE 21
Ultrasound in Medicine
An ultrasound imaging device uses reflected ultrasound waves to build up a picture of a developing baby.

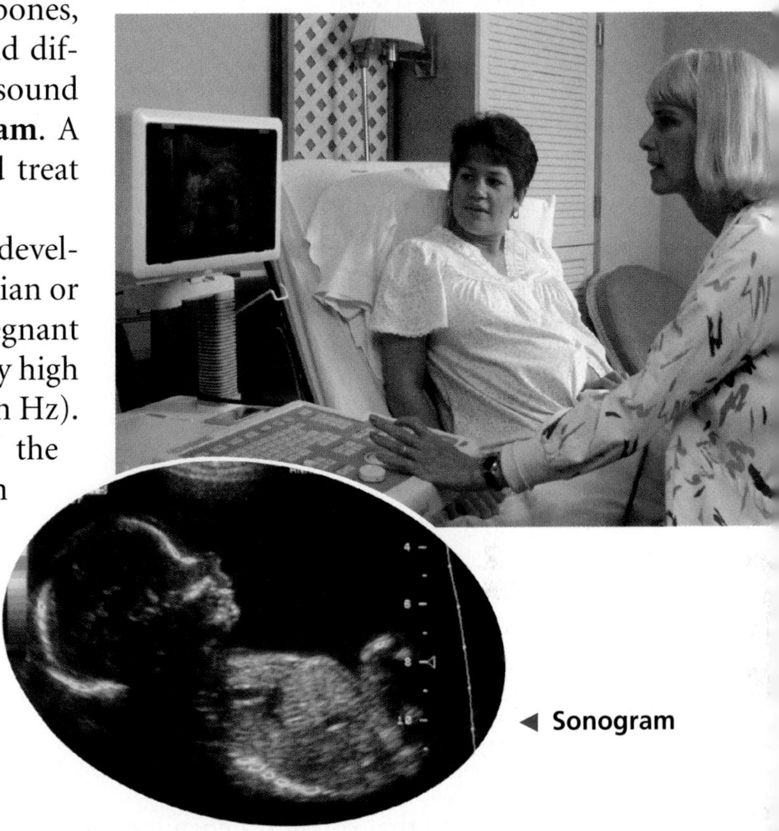

◄ **Sonogram**

Section 5 Assessment

Target Reading Skill

Comparing and Contrasting Use your table about echolocation and sonar to help you answer the questions below.

Reviewing Key Concepts

1. a. **Defining** What is echolocation?
   b. **Summarizing** Why do bats and dolphins use echolocation?
   c. **Interpreting Diagrams** Look at Figure 19. Why would a dolphin need to continue sending out sound waves as it nears its prey?
2. a. **Reviewing** Why do people use ultrasound technologies?
   b. **Drawing Conclusions** A sonar device can show the size of a fish but not the type of fish. Explain why.
   c. **Comparing and Contrasting** How is sonar similar to ultrasound imaging used in medicine? How is it different?

Writing in Science

Advertisement Write a short advertisement for a depth finder used on fishing boats. Describe how the depth finder can determine the depth and direction of fish in the area. Include a diagram to show how the depth finder works.

Chapter 16 Study Guide

1 The Nature of Sound

Key Concepts

- Sound is a disturbance that travels through a medium as a longitudinal wave.
- Sound waves reflect off objects, diffract through narrow openings and around barriers, and interfere with each other.
- The speed of sound depends on the elasticity, density, and temperature of the medium the sound travels through.

Key Terms

echo
elasticity
density

2 Properties of Sound

Key Concepts

- The loudness of a sound depends on two factors: the amount of energy it takes to make the sound and the distance from the source of the sound.
- The pitch of a sound that you hear depends on the frequency of the sound wave.
- When a sound source moves, the frequency of the waves changes because the motion of the source adds to the motion of the waves.

Key Terms

loudness
intensity
decibel (dB)
pitch
ultrasound
infrasound
larynx
Doppler effect

3 Music

Key Concepts

- Sound quality results from the blending of a fundamental tone with its overtones. Resonance also plays a role in sound quality.
- There are three basic groups of musical instruments: stringed instruments, wind instruments, and percussion instruments.
- Acoustics is used in the design of concert halls to control reverberation and interference.

Key Terms

music
fundamental tone
overtone
acoustics
reverberation

4 How You Hear Sound

Key Concepts

- The outer ear funnels sound waves, the middle ear transmits the waves inward, and the inner ear converts sound waves into a form that travels to your brain.
- There are many causes of hearing loss, including injury, infection, exposure to loud sounds, and aging.

Key Terms

ear canal
eardrum
cochlea

5 Using Sound

Key Concepts

- Some animals, including bats and dolphins, use echolocation to navigate and to find food.
- Ultrasound technologies such as sonar and ultrasound imaging are used to observe things that cannot be seen directly.

Key Terms

echolocation
sonar
sonogram

Review and Assessment

Go Online PHSchool.com
For: Self-Assessment
Visit: PHSchool.com
Web Code: cga-5020

Organizing Information

Concept Mapping Copy the concept map about sound onto a separate sheet of paper. Then complete it and add a title. (For more on Concept Mapping, see the Skills Handbook.)

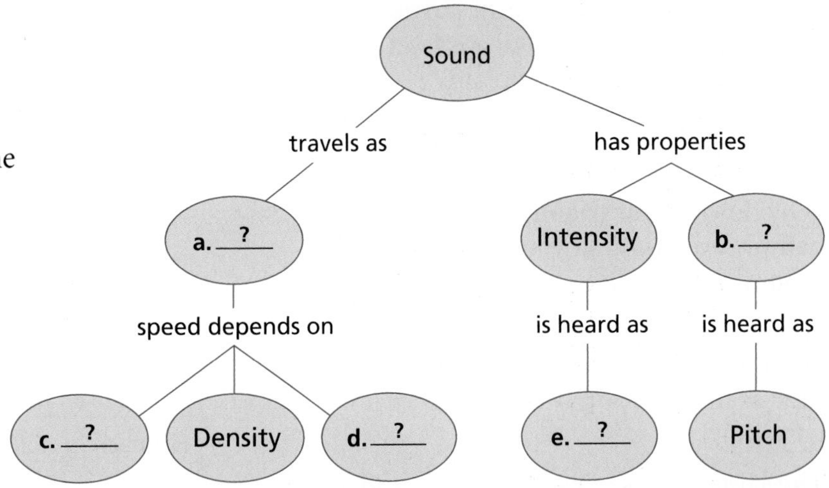

Reviewing Key Terms

Choose the letter of the best answer.

1. The ability of a medium to bounce back after being disturbed is called
   a. echolocation. **b.** elasticity.
   c. density. **d.** interference.
2. Which property of sound describes your perception of the energy of a sound?
   a. loudness
   b. intensity
   c. pitch
   d. wave speed
3. The lowest natural frequency of a sound is
   a. a standing wave.
   b. an overtone.
   c. an echo.
   d. the fundamental tone.
4. In the ear, a fluid-filled cavity that is shaped like a snail shell is the
   a. ear canal. **b.** eardrum.
   c. cochlea. **d.** larynx.
5. A system of using reflected sound waves to detect and locate objects underwater is called
   a. sonar. **b.** acoustics.
   c. echolocation. **d.** reverberation.

If the statement is true, write *true*. If it is false, change the underlined word or words to make the statement true.

6. Intensity is mass per unit volume.
7. Loudness is how the ear perceives frequency.
8. Music is a set of notes that are pleasing.
9. The ear canal is a small, drumlike membrane.
10. A sonogram is a picture made using reflected ultrasound waves.

Writing in Science

Firsthand Account Imagine that you are a dolphin researcher. Write a letter to a friend describing your latest research. Be sure to include information about how dolphins use their sonar.

Discovery Channel School

Sound
Video Preview
Video Field Trip
▶ Video Assessment

Review and Assessment

Checking Concepts

11. When a gong vibrates, the air particles next to the gong do not reach your ears, yet you hear the sound of the gong. Explain.

12. Explain when a whisper would sound louder than a shout.

13. Why do you hear friends talking in the hallway even though you cannot see them around a corner?

14. As a car drives past you, the driver keeps a hand pressing on the horn. Describe what you hear as the car approaches and after it has passed by.

15. The same note is played on a flute and a cello. Why is there a difference in the sound?

16. How can a sound continue to be heard after a sound source stops making the sound?

17. How can loud noises damage your hearing?

18. How are ultrasound waves used in medicine?

Thinking Critically

19. **Comparing and Contrasting** How do sound waves behave like waves in a spring toy? How are they different?

20. **Inferring** Thunder and lightning happen at the same time. Explain why you see the lightning before you hear the thunder.

21. **Predicting** Look at the table below. Which material would you use in hearing protectors to reduce the transmission of sound waves? Explain your answer.

Substance	Speed (m/s)
Rubber	60
Plastic	1,800
Gold	3,240
Brick	3,650
Steel	5,200

22. **Classifying** Classify the following instruments into three groups: a guitar, a tuba, a bell, a clarinet, a drum, and a harp.

Applying Skills

Use the data in the table below to answer Questions 23–25.

The table shows the range of frequencies produced and heard by various animals.

Animal	Highest Frequency Heard (Hz)	Highest Frequency Produced (Hz)
Human	20,000	1,100
Dog	50,000	1,800
Cat	65,000	1,500
Bat	120,000	120,000
Porpoise	150,000	120,000

23. **Interpreting Data** Can you hear the ultrasound waves that a bat uses for echolocation? Why or why not?

24. **Graphing** Draw a bar graph to compare the highest frequencies heard and the highest frequencies produced by the animals.

25. **Calculating** If the speed of sound in air is 343 m/s, what is the shortest wavelength of sound that humans can hear? (*Hint:* Wavelength = Speed ÷ Frequency)

Lab zone Chapter Project

Performance Assessment Present your musical instrument to your class. Explain how it was built and how you solved any design problems. Then demonstrate how you can change the pitch or loudness of your instrument. Brainstorm with the class methods for improving the design of the instrument. How is your instrument similar to or different from instruments your classmates built?

Standardized Test Prep

Test-Taking Tip

Interpreting Graphs

If you are asked to interpret a bar graph, look at the labels of the horizontal and vertical axes. The labels tell you what variables are being compared. A bar graph is used to show data in several categories that are not related. The graph on this page compares the loudness of four common sounds. In this graph, the sounds that are being compared are otherwise unrelated to each other. Study the graph and answer the sample question below.

Sample Question

Which sounds are likely to cause hearing damage?

A noise from a classroom
B noise from loud thunder or jet engines
C noise from street traffic or thunder
D none of the sounds shown on the graph

Answer

B is correct because both sounds are louder than 100 dB. You can eliminate **A** and **C** because they include a sound softer than 100 dB. **D** is incorrect because two sounds are louder than 100 dB.

Choose the letter of the best answer.

1. Bats and dolphins use echolocation to determine distances and find prey. What characteristic of sound waves is most important for echolocation?
   A Sound waves reflect when they hit a surface.
   B Sound waves spread out from a source.
   C Sound waves diffract around a corner.
   D Sound waves interfere when they overlap.

2. A scientist is doing research with 110-dB sound waves. What piece of safety equipment must she wear in the lab?
   F goggles
   G gloves
   H lab apron
   J hearing protectors

Comparing Loudness

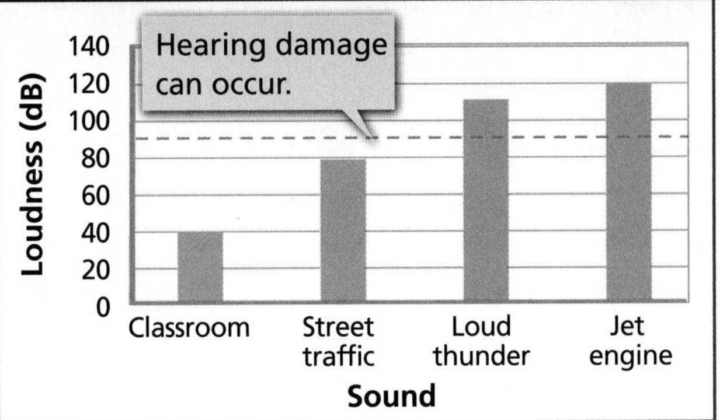

3. Use the graph above to determine how much more intense the sound of a jet engine is than the sound of loud thunder.
   A ten times more intense
   B two times more intense
   C four times more intense
   D Both sounds are about the same intensity.

4. An experiment was conducted in which two containers held solids *A* and *B* at the same temperature. The speed of a sound wave traveling through solid *A* was greater than its speed through solid *B*. What can you conclude from this experiment?
   F Solid *A* is denser than solid *B*.
   G Solid *A* is less dense than solid *B*.
   H Solid *A* is more elastic than solid *B*.
   J Solid *A* is less dense than solid *B* or solid *A* is more elastic than solid *B*.

5. After a new concert hall is built, it is found that the acoustics are poor because of reverberation. How can the acoustics be improved?
   A Add metal seats to the hall.
   B Remove the drapes covering the windows.
   C Cover the wooden floor with carpeting.
   D Install a wooden backdrop behind the stage.

Constructed Response

6. You drop a book onto the floor in the bedroom of your apartment. Your neighbor downstairs hears the sound. Describe how the sound travels to your neighbor's ears. What mediums do the sound waves have to travel through?

Chapter 17

The Electromagnetic Spectrum

Chapter Preview

interactive Textbook

Astronomers use these telescopes to map radio waves given off by objects in space. ▶

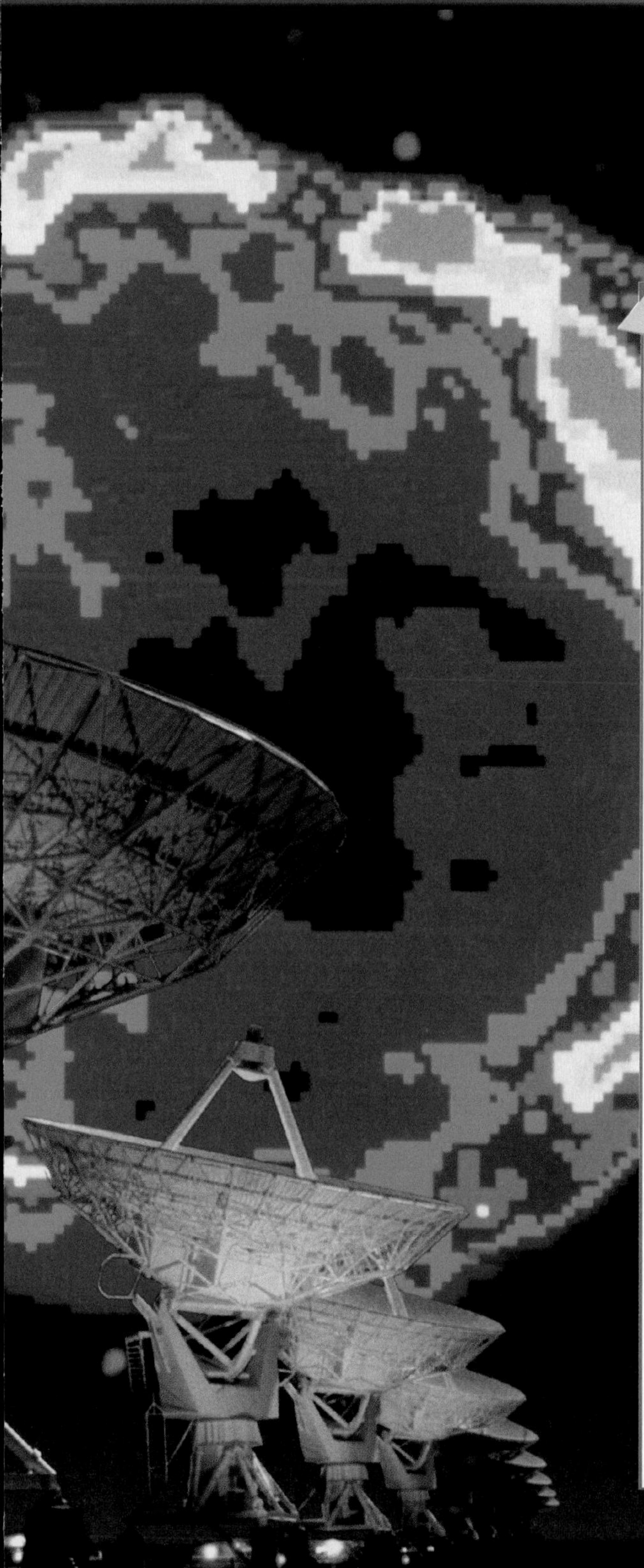

Lab zone™ Chapter **Project**

You're on the Air

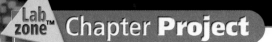

How do people communicate? Look around you! Radios, televisions, and cellular phones are part of everyday life. Wireless communication has made it convenient for people to communicate anytime and anywhere. In this Chapter Project, you will conduct a survey to find out how people use wireless communication devices.

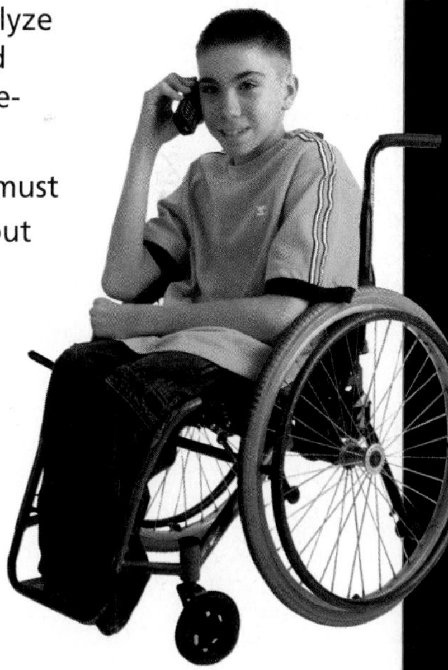

Your Goal To collect and analyze data about when, where, and why people use different wireless communication devices

To complete this project you must

- develop a survey sheet about communication devices
- distribute your survey sheet to other students, family members, and neighbors
- compile and analyze your data
- create tables and graphs to display your findings

Plan It! To get started, think about the format and content of your survey sheet. Brainstorm what kinds of questions you will ask. Develop a plan for involving students in other classes so you can gather more data.

Section 1

The Nature of Electromagnetic Waves

Reading Preview

Key Concepts

- What does an electromagnetic wave consist of?
- What models explain the behavior of electromagnetic waves?

Key Terms

- electromagnetic wave
- electromagnetic radiation
- polarized light
- photoelectric effect
- photon

Target Reading Skill

Outlining An outline shows the relationship between major ideas and supporting ideas. As you read, make an outline about electromagnetic waves. Use the red headings for the main topics and the blue headings for the subtopics.

The Nature of Electromagnetic Waves
I. What is an electromagnetic wave?
A. Producing electromagnetic waves
B.
C.
II. Models of electromagnetic waves
A.
B.

Lab zone Discover Activity

How Does a Beam of Light Travel?

1. Punch a hole (about 0.5 cm in diameter) through four large index cards.
2. Use binder clips or modeling clay to stand each card upright so that the long side of the index card is on the tabletop. Space the cards about 10 cm apart, as shown in the photo. To line the holes up in a straight line, run a piece of string through them and pull it tight.
3. Place a flashlight in front of the card nearest you. Shut off all light except the flashlight. What do you see on the wall?
4. Move one of the cards sideways about 3 cm and repeat Step 3. Now what do you see on the wall?

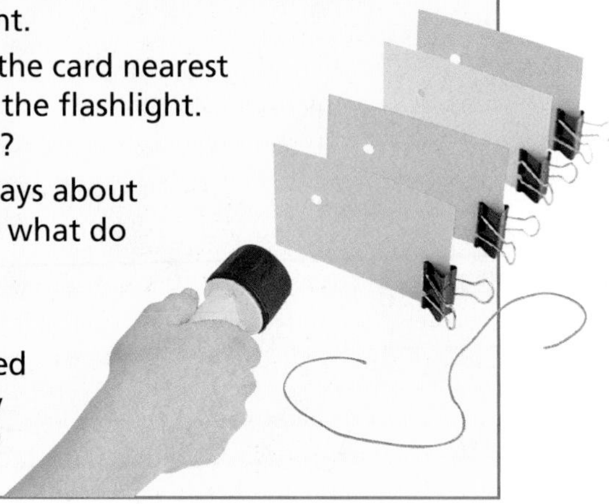

Think It Over

Inferring Explain what happened in Step 4. What does this activity tell you about the path of light?

Have you ever been caught in a rain shower? You run for cover until it passes, so you don't get wet. Believe it or not, you are being "showered" all the time, not by rain but by waves. You cannot see, feel, or hear most of these waves. But as you read this, you are surrounded by radio waves, infrared rays, visible light, ultraviolet rays, and maybe even tiny amounts of X-rays and gamma rays. They are all electromagnetic waves.

Electromagnetic waves ▶

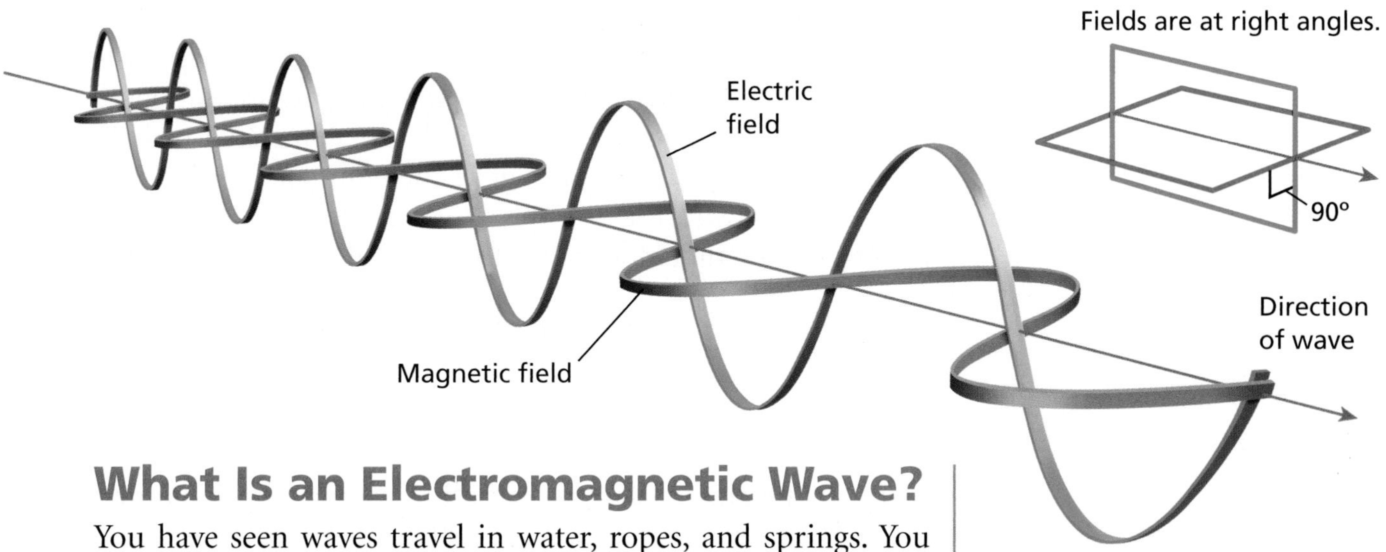

What Is an Electromagnetic Wave?

You have seen waves travel in water, ropes, and springs. You have heard sound waves that travel through air and water. All these waves have two things in common—they transfer energy and they also require a medium through which to travel. But electromagnetic waves can transfer energy without a medium. An **electromagnetic wave** is a transverse wave that transfers electrical and magnetic energy. **An electromagnetic wave consists of vibrating electric and magnetic fields that move through space at the speed of light.**

FIGURE 1
Electromagnetic Wave
In an electromagnetic wave, electric and magnetic fields vibrate at right angles to each other. Classifying *What type of wave is an electromagnetic wave?*

Producing Electromagnetic Waves Light and all other electromagnetic waves are produced by charged particles. Every charged particle has an electric field surrounding it. The electric field produces electric forces that can push or pull on other charged particles.

When a charged particle moves, it produces a magnetic field. A magnetic field exerts magnetic forces that can act on certain materials. If you place a paper clip near a magnet, for example, the paper clip moves toward the magnet because of the magnetic field surrounding the magnet.

When a charged particle changes its motion, its magnetic field changes. The changing magnetic field causes the electric field to change. When one field vibrates, so does the other. In this way, the two fields constantly cause each other to change. The result is an electromagnetic wave, as shown in Figure 1. Notice that the two fields vibrate at right angles to each other.

Energy The energy that is transfered through space by electromagnetic waves is called **electromagnetic radiation.** Electromagnetic waves do not require a medium, so they can transfer energy through a vacuum, or empty space. This is why you can see the sun and stars—their light reaches Earth through the vacuum of space.

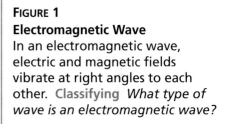

Go Online
SCI LINKS NSTA
For: Links on the nature of waves
Visit: www.SciLinks.org
Web Code: scn-1531

Speed All electromagnetic waves travel at the same speed in a vacuum—about 300,000 kilometers per second. This speed is called the speed of light. At this speed, light from the sun takes about 8 minutes to travel the 150 million kilometers to Earth. When light waves travel through a medium such as air, they travel more slowly. But the speed of light waves in air is still about a million times faster than the speed of sound waves in air.

Reading Checkpoint **What is the speed of light in a vacuum?**

Models of Electromagnetic Waves

Many properties of electromagnetic waves can be explained by a wave model. However, some properties are best explained by a particle model. As you have learned, light is an electromagnetic wave. Both a wave model and a particle model are needed to explain all of the properties of light.

Wave Model of Light The lenses of many sunglasses, like the ones shown in Figure 2, are polarizing filters. Light acts as a wave when it passes through a polarizing filter. Ordinary light has waves that vibrate in all directions—up and down, left and right, and at all other angles. A polarizing filter acts as though it has tiny slits that are aligned in one direction.

Only some light waves pass through a polarizing filter. The light that passes through vibrates in only one direction and is called **polarized light.** No light passes through two polarizing filters that are placed at right angles to each other.

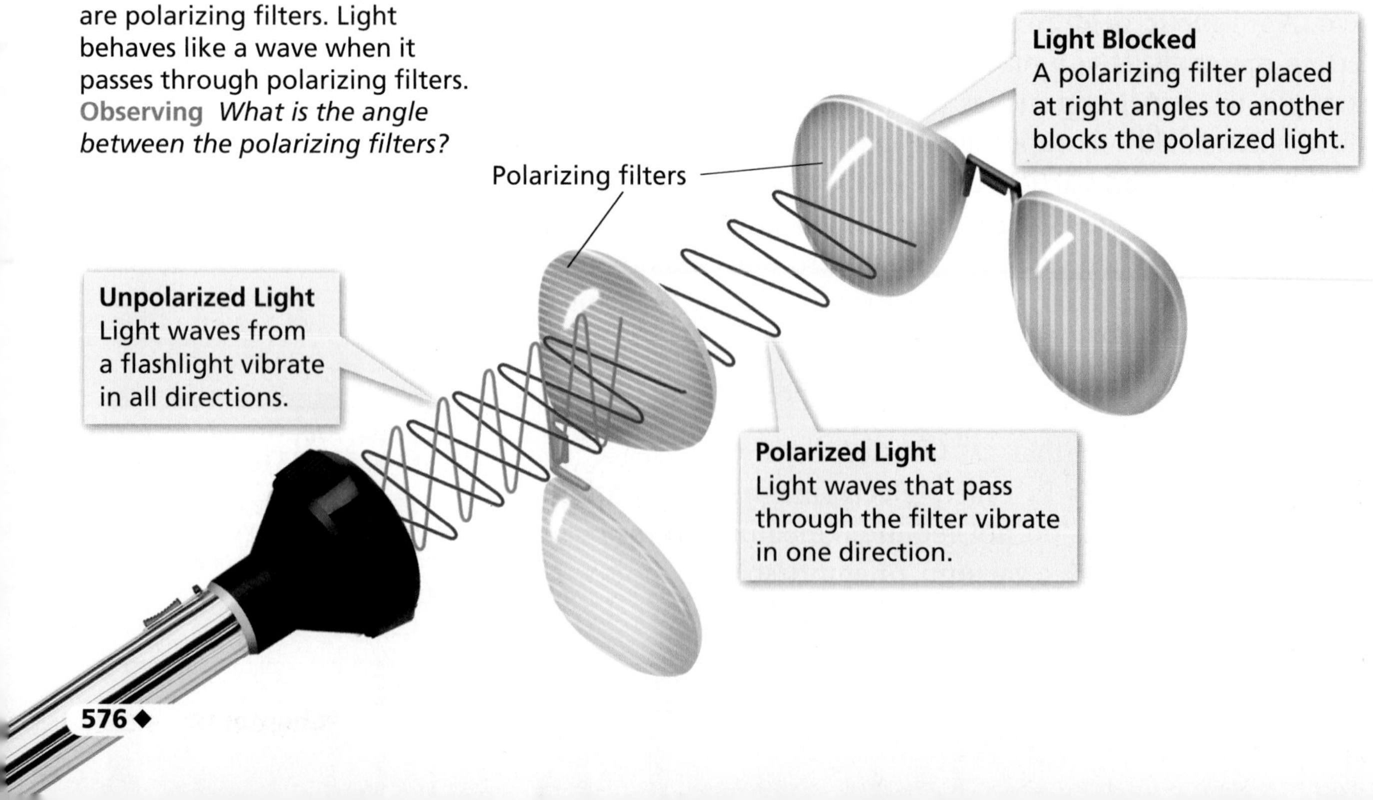

Light Blocked
A polarizing filter placed at right angles to another blocks the polarized light.
Polarizing filters
Unpolarized Light
Light waves from a flashlight vibrate in all directions.
Polarized Light
Light waves that pass through the filter vibrate in one direction.

FIGURE 2
Light as a Wave
The lenses of some sunglasses are polarizing filters. Light behaves like a wave when it passes through polarizing filters.
Observing *What is the angle between the polarizing filters?*

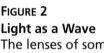

To help you understand the wave model of light, think of waves of light as being like transverse waves on a rope. If you shake a rope through a fence with vertical slats, only waves that vibrate up and down will pass through. If you shake the rope side to side, the waves will be blocked. A polarizing filter acts like the slats in a fence. It allows only waves that vibrate in one direction to pass through.

Particle Model of Light Sometimes light behaves like a stream of particles. When a beam of light shines on some substances, it causes tiny particles called electrons to move. The movement of electrons causes an electric current to flow. Sometimes light can even cause an electron to move so much that it is knocked out of the substance. This is called the **photoelectric effect.** The photoelectric effect can be explained only by thinking of light as a stream of tiny packets, or particles, of energy. Each packet of light energy is called a **photon.** Albert Einstein first explained the science behind the photoelectric effect in 1905.

It may be difficult for you to picture light as being particles and waves at the same time. But both models are necessary to explain all the properties of light.

Reading Checkpoint **What is a photon?**

Lab zone Try This Activity

Waves or Particles?

1. Fill two plastic cups with water. Slowly pour the water from both cups into a sink so the streams of water cross. How do the two streams interfere with each other?
2. Darken a room. Use a slide projector to project a slide on a wall. Shine a flashlight beam across the projector's beam. What is the effect on the projected picture?

Drawing Conclusions Compare the interference of light beams with the interference of water streams. Does this activity support a wave model or a particle model of light? Explain.

Section 1 Assessment

Target Reading Skill **Outlining** Use the information in your outline about electromagnetic waves to help you answer the questions below.

Reviewing Key Concepts

1. a. **Defining** What is an electromagnetic wave?
   b. **Explaining** How do electromagnetic waves travel?
   c. **Comparing and Contrasting** What is an electric field? What is a magnetic field?
2. a. **Reviewing** What two models explain the properties of electromagnetic waves?
   b. **Describing** Use one of the models of light to describe what happens when light passes through a polarizing filter.
   c. **Relating Cause and Effect** Use one of the models of light to explain what causes the photoelectric effect.

Lab zone At-Home Activity

Polarized Sunglasses On a sunny day, go outside with your family members and compare your sunglasses. Do any have polarizing lenses? If so, which ones? Try rotating sunglasses as you look through them at surfaces that create glare, such as water or glass. Which sunglasses are best designed to reduce glare? **CAUTION:** *Do not look directly at the sun.*

Section 2

Waves of the Electromagnetic Spectrum

Reading Preview

Key Concepts

- How are electromagnetic waves alike, and how are they different?
- What waves make up the electromagnetic spectrum?

Key Terms

- electromagnetic spectrum
- radio waves • microwaves
- radar • infrared rays
- thermogram • visible light
- ultraviolet rays • X-rays
- gamma rays

Target Reading Skill

Previewing Visuals Before you read, preview Figure 3. Then write two questions that you have about the diagram in a graphic organizer like the one below. As you read, answer your questions.

The Electromagnetic Spectrum

Q.	Which electromagnetic waves have the shortest wavelength?
A.	
Q.	

Lab zone Discover Activity

What Is White Light?

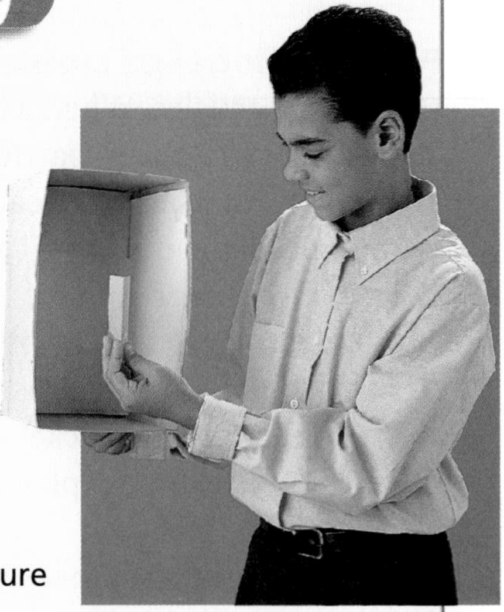

1. Line a cardboard box with white paper. Hold a small triangular prism up to direct sunlight. **CAUTION:** *Do not look directly at the sun.*
2. Rotate the prism until the light coming out of the prism appears on the inside of the box as a wide band of colors. Describe the colors and their order.
3. Using colored pencils, draw a picture of what you see inside the box.

Think It Over

Forming Operational Definitions The term *spectrum* describes a range. How is this term related to what you just observed?

Can you imagine trying to take a photo with a radio? How about trying to tune in a radio station on your flashlight or heat your food with X-rays? Light, radio waves, and X-rays are all electromagnetic waves. But each has properties that make it more useful for some purposes and less useful for others. What makes light different from radio waves and X-rays?

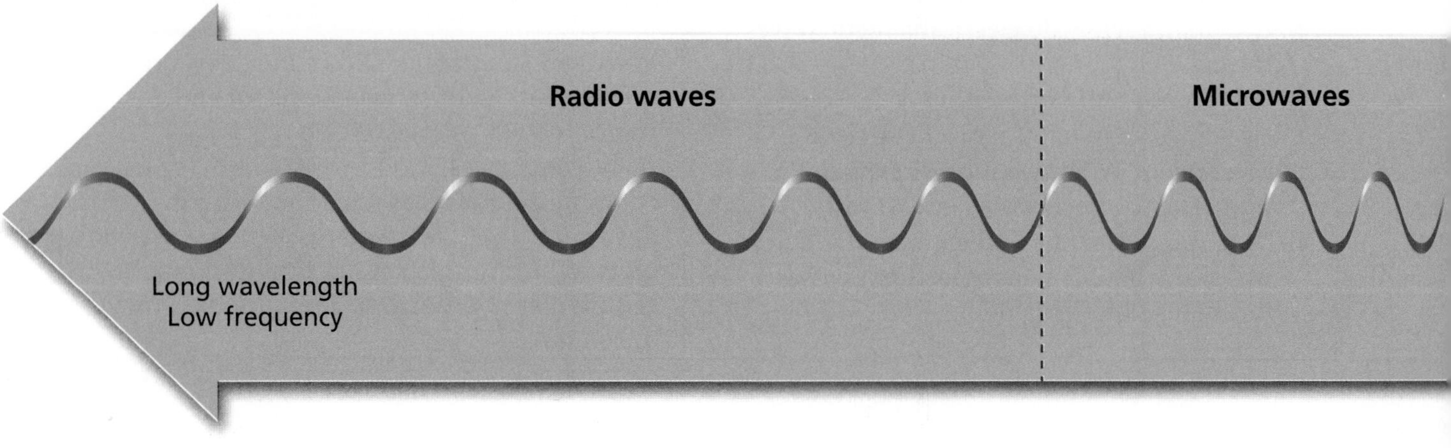

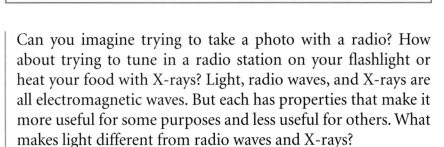

What Is the Electromagnetic Spectrum?

All electromagnetic waves travel at the same speed in a vacuum, but they have different wavelengths and different frequencies. Radiation in the wavelengths that your eyes can see is called visible light. But only a small portion of electromagnetic radiation is visible light. The rest of the wavelengths are invisible. Your radio detects radio waves, which have much longer wavelengths than visible light. X-rays, on the other hand, are waves with much shorter wavelengths than visible light.

Recall how speed, wavelength, and frequency are related:

Speed = Wavelength × Frequency

Because the speed of all electromagnetic waves is the same, as the wavelength decreases, the frequency increases. Waves with the longest wavelengths have the lowest frequencies. Waves with the shortest wavelengths have the highest frequencies. The amount of energy carried by an electromagnetic wave increases with frequency. The higher the frequency of a wave, the higher its energy.

The **electromagnetic spectrum** is the complete range of electromagnetic waves placed in order of increasing frequency. The full spectrum is shown in Figure 3. **The electromagnetic spectrum is made up of radio waves, infrared rays, visible light, ultraviolet rays, X-rays, and gamma rays.**

Reading Checkpoint: What is the electromagnetic spectrum?

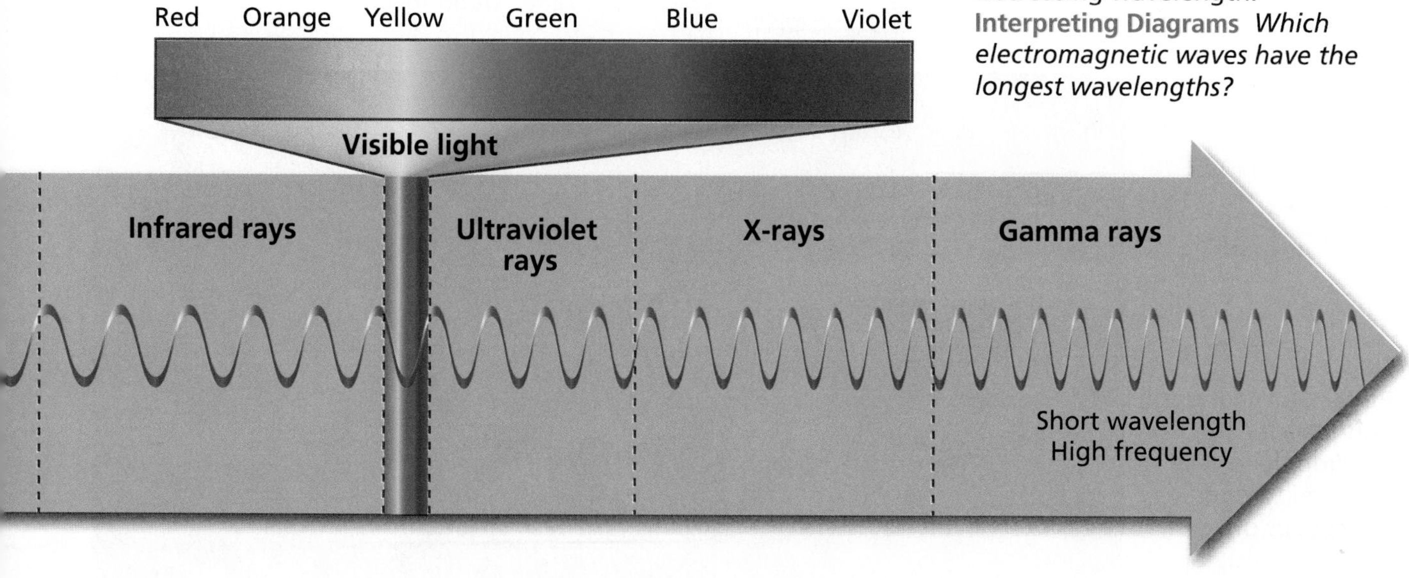

FIGURE 3
The Electromagnetic Spectrum

The electromagnetic spectrum shows the range of different electromagnetic waves in order of increasing frequency and decreasing wavelength.
Interpreting Diagrams *Which electromagnetic waves have the longest wavelengths?*

Lab zone Try This **Activity**

Microwave Test

In this activity, you will compare how water, corn oil, and sugar absorb microwaves.

1. Add 25 mL of water to a glass beaker. Record the temperature of the water.
2. Microwave the beaker for 10 seconds and record the water temperature again.
3. Repeat Steps 1 and 2 two more times, using 25 mL of corn oil and 25 mL of sugar.

Drawing Conclusions Compare the temperature change of the three materials. Which material absorbed the most energy from the microwaves?

Radio Waves

Radio waves are the electromagnetic waves with the longest wavelengths and lowest frequencies. They include broadcast waves (for radio and television) and microwaves.

Broadcast Waves Radio waves with longer wavelengths are used in broadcasting. They carry signals for both radio and television programs. A broadcast station sends out radio waves at certain frequencies. Your radio or TV antenna picks up the waves and converts the radio signal into an electrical signal. Inside your radio, the electrical signal is converted to sound. Inside your TV, the signal is converted to sound and pictures.

Microwaves The radio waves with the shortest wavelengths and the highest frequencies are **microwaves.** When you think of microwaves, you probably think of microwave ovens that cook and heat your food. But microwaves have many uses, including cellular phone communication and radar.

Radar stands for **ra**dio **d**etection **a**nd **r**anging. **Radar** is a system that uses reflected radio waves to detect objects and measure their distance and speed. To measure distance, a radar device sends out radio waves that reflect off an object. The time it takes for the reflected waves to return is used to calculate the object's distance. To measure speed, a radar device uses the Doppler effect, which you learned about in an earlier chapter. For example, a police radar gun like the one in Figure 4 sends out radio waves that reflect off a car. Because the car is moving, the frequency of the reflected waves is different from the frequency of the original waves. The difference in frequency is used to calculate the car's speed.

Reading Checkpoint What does *radar* stand for?

FIGURE 4
Radar Gun
Radio waves and the Doppler effect are used to find the speeds of moving vehicles.

FIGURE 5
Infrared Images
An infrared camera produced this image, called a thermogram. Regions of different temperatures appear in different colors.
Interpreting Photographs *Which areas of the house are warmest (color-coded white)? Which are coolest (color-coded blue)?*

Infrared Rays

If you turn on a burner on an electric stove, you can feel it warm up before the heating element starts to glow. The invisible heat you feel is infrared radiation, or infrared rays. **Infrared rays** are electromagnetic waves with wavelengths shorter than those of radio waves.

Heat Lamps Infrared rays have a higher frequency than radio waves, so they have more energy than radio waves. Because you can feel the energy of infrared rays as heat, these rays are often called heat rays. Heat lamps have bulbs that give off mostly infrared rays and very little visible light. These lamps are used to keep food warm at a cafeteria counter. Some people use heat lamps to warm up their bathrooms quickly.

Infrared Cameras Most objects give off some infrared rays. Warmer objects give off infrared waves with more energy and higher frequencies than cooler objects. An infrared camera takes pictures using infrared rays instead of light. These pictures are called thermograms. A **thermogram** is an image that shows regions of different temperatures in different colors. Figure 5 shows a thermogram of a house. You can use an infrared camera to see objects in the dark. Firefighters use infrared cameras to locate fire victims inside a dark or smoky building. Satellites in space use infrared cameras to study the growth of plants and the motions of clouds.

Reading Checkpoint **What does an infrared camera use to take pictures?**

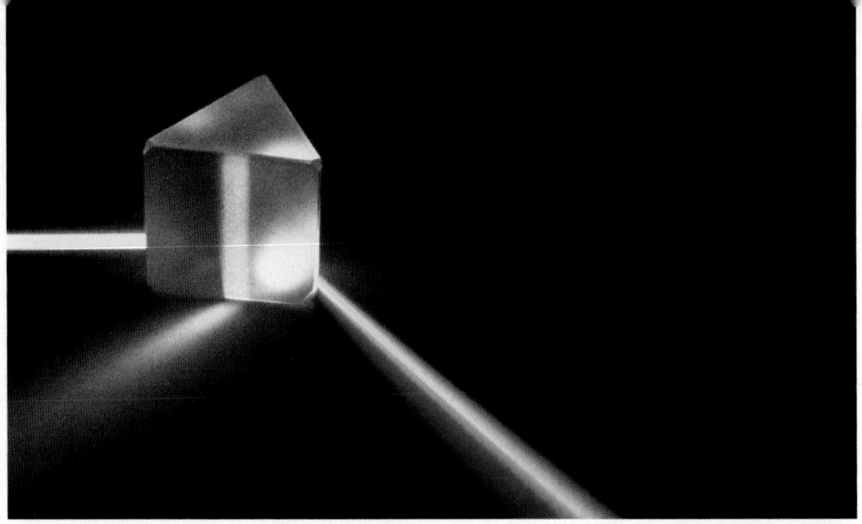

FIGURE 6
Refraction in a Prism
When white light passes through a prism, refraction causes the light to separate into its wavelengths.
Observing *Which color of light is refracted the least?*

Visible Light

Electromagnetic waves that you can see are called **visible light.** They make up only a small part of the electromagnetic spectrum. Visible light waves have shorter wavelengths and higher frequencies than infrared rays. Visible light waves with the longest wavelengths appear red in color. As the wavelengths decrease, you can see other colors of light. The shortest wavelengths of visible light appear violet in color.

Visible light that appears white is actually a mixture of many colors. White light from the sun can be separated by a prism into the colors of the visible spectrum—red, orange, yellow, green, blue, and violet. Recall that when waves enter a new medium, the waves bend, or refract. The prism refracts different wavelengths of visible light by different amounts and thereby separates the colors. Red light waves refract the least. Violet light waves refract the most.

Ultraviolet Rays

Electromagnetic waves with wavelengths just shorter than those of visible light are called **ultraviolet rays.** Ultraviolet rays have higher frequencies than visible light, so they carry more energy. The energy of ultraviolet rays is great enough to damage or kill living cells. In fact, ultraviolet lamps are often used to kill bacteria on hospital equipment.

Small doses of ultraviolet rays are useful. For example, ultraviolet rays cause skin cells to produce vitamin D, which is needed for healthy bones and teeth. However, too much exposure to ultraviolet rays is dangerous. Ultraviolet rays can burn your skin, cause skin cancer, and damage your eyes. If you apply sunblock and wear sunglasses that block ultraviolet rays, you can limit the damage caused by ultraviolet rays.

Reading Checkpoint **How can ultraviolet rays be useful?**

Math Skills

Scientific Notation

Frequencies of waves often are written in scientific notation. A number in scientific notation consists of a number between 1 and 10 that is multiplied by a power of 10. To write 150,000 Hz in scientific notation, move the decimal point left to make a number between 1 and 10:

1.50,000 Hz

In this case, the number is 1.5. The power of 10 is the number of spaces you moved the decimal point. In this case, it moved 5 places, so

$$150{,}000 \text{ Hz} = 1.5 \times 10^5 \text{ Hz}$$

Practice Problem A radio wave has a frequency of 5,000,000 Hz. Write this number in scientific notation.

X-Rays

X-rays are electromagnetic waves with wavelengths just shorter than those of ultraviolet rays. Their frequencies are just a little higher than ultraviolet rays. Because of their high frequencies, X-rays carry more energy than ultraviolet rays and can penetrate most matter. But dense matter, such as bone or lead, absorbs X-rays and does not allow them to pass through. Therefore, X-rays are used to make images of bones inside the body or of teeth, as shown in Figure 7. X-rays pass through skin and soft tissues, causing the photographic film in the X-ray machine to darken when it is developed. The bones, which absorb X-rays, appear as the lighter areas on the film.

Too much exposure to X-rays can cause cancer. If you've ever had a dental X-ray, you'll remember that the dentist gave you a lead apron to wear during the procedure. The lead absorbs X-rays and prevents them from reaching your body.

X-rays are sometimes used in industry and engineering. For example, to find out if a steel or concrete structure has tiny cracks, engineers can take an X-ray image of the structure. X-rays will pass through tiny cracks that are invisible to the human eye. Dark areas on the X-ray film show the cracks. This technology is often used to check the quality of joints in oil and gas pipelines.

Reading Checkpoint **What kind of matter blocks X-rays?**

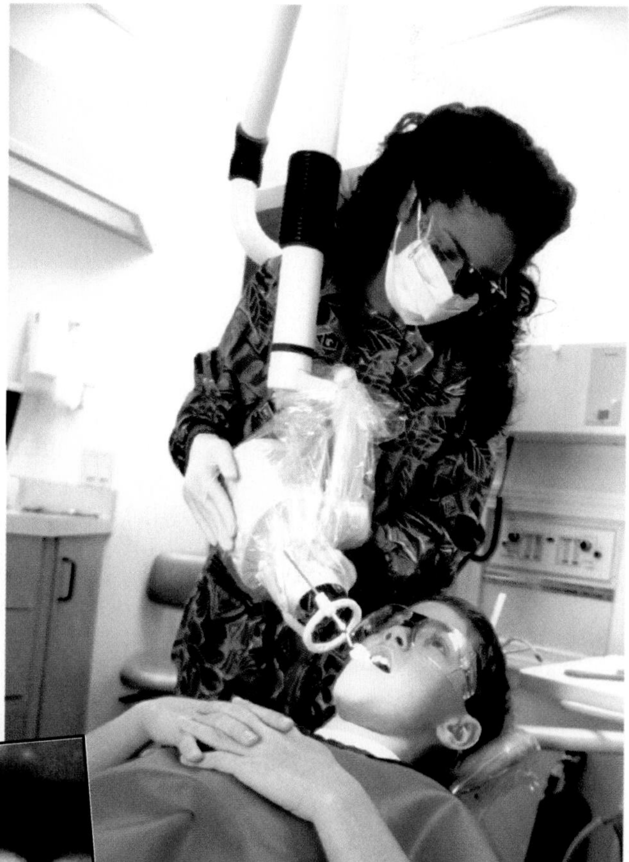

FIGURE 7
Dental X-Ray
X-rays pass through soft parts of the body but are absorbed by teeth. When the photographic plate is developed, the teeth and fillings show up as lighter areas.

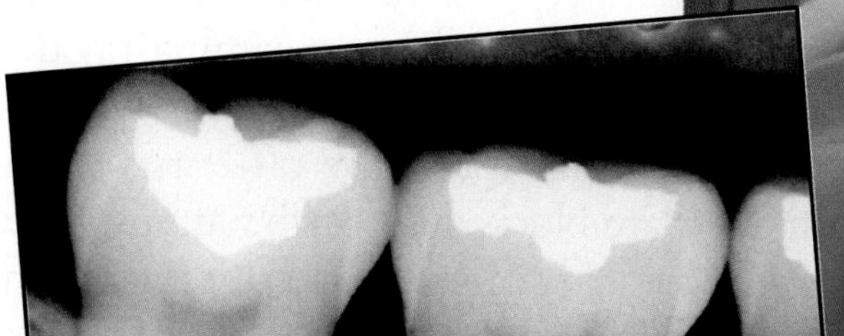

FIGURE 8
Electromagnetic Waves
Electromagnetic waves are all around you—in your home, your neighborhood, and your town.

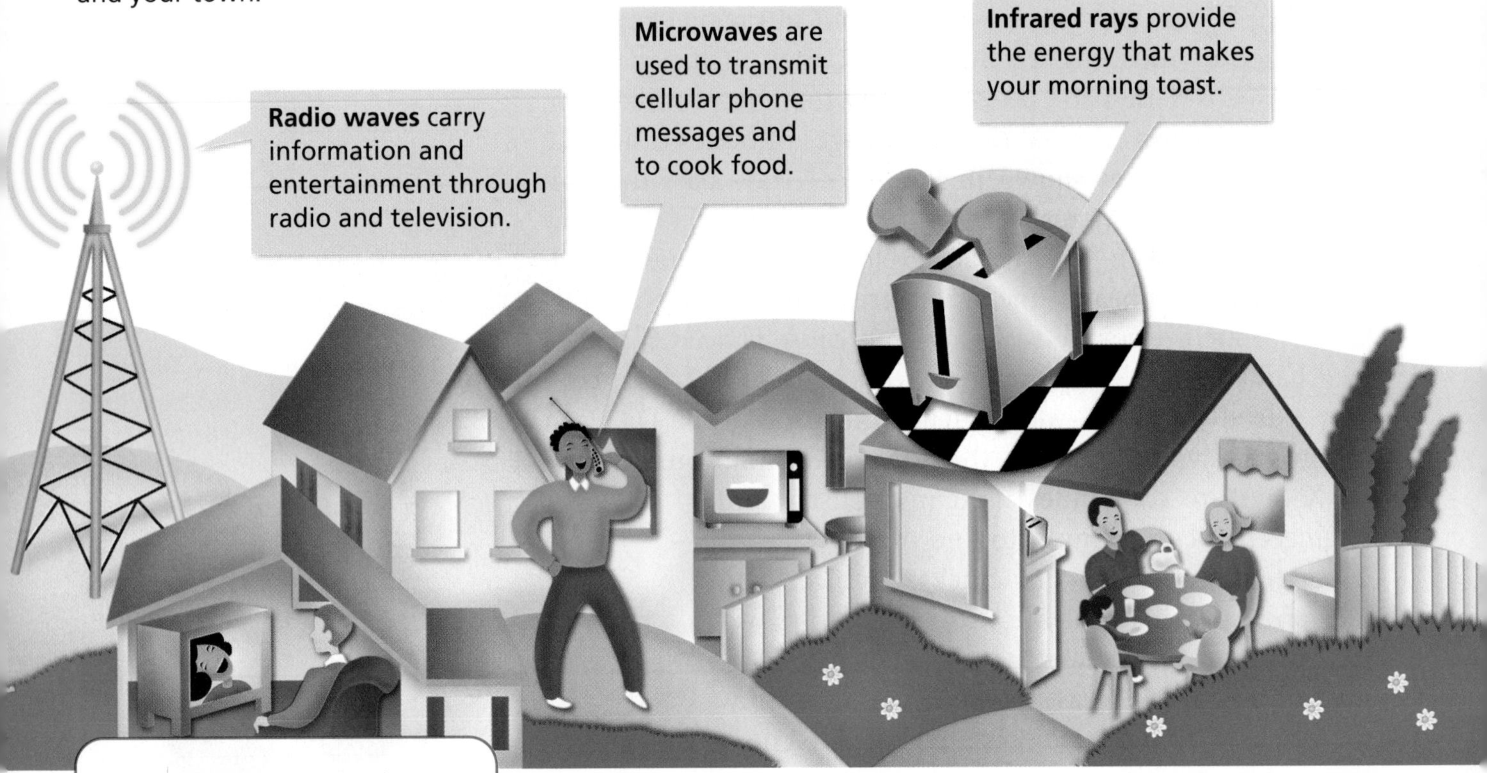
Radio waves carry information and entertainment through radio and television.
Microwaves are used to transmit cellular phone messages and to cook food.
Infrared rays provide the energy that makes your morning toast.

Go Online
active art
For: Electromagnetic Waves activity
Visit: PHSchool.com
Web Code: cgp-5032

Gamma Rays

Gamma rays are the electromagnetic waves with the shortest wavelengths and highest frequencies. Because they have the greatest amount of energy, gamma rays are the most penetrating of all the electromagnetic waves.

Some radioactive substances and certain nuclear reactions produce gamma rays. Because of their great penetrating ability, gamma rays have some medical uses. For example, gamma rays can be used to kill cancer cells inside the body. To examine the body's internal structures, a patient can be injected with a fluid that emits gamma rays. Then a gamma-ray detector can form an image of the inside of the body.

Some objects in space give off bursts of gamma rays. The gamma rays are blocked by Earth's atmosphere, so gamma-ray telescopes that detect them must orbit above Earth's atmosphere. Astronomers think that explosions of stars in distant galaxies are one way of producing these gamma rays.

Reading Checkpoint **How are gamma rays produced?**

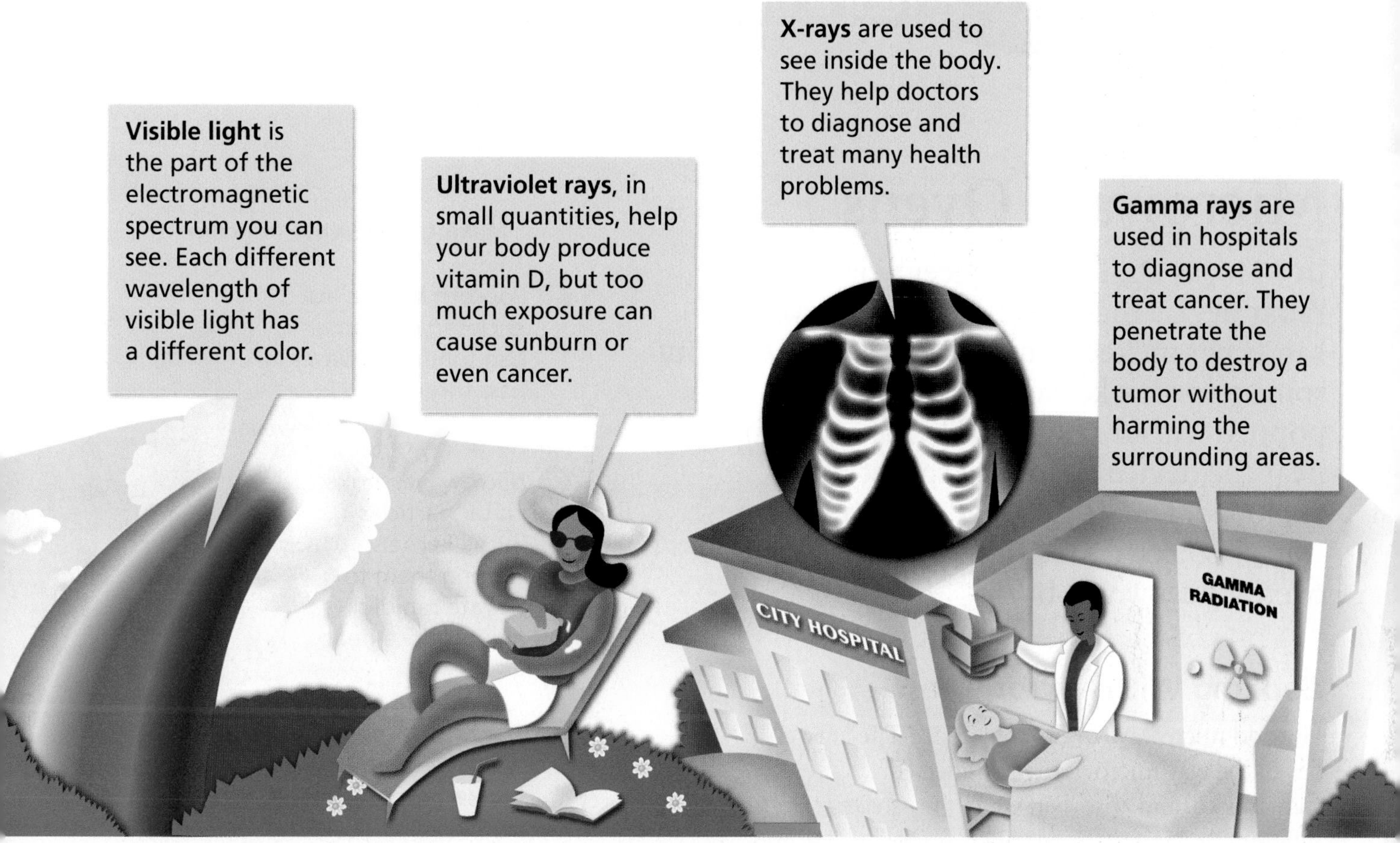
Visible light is the part of the electromagnetic spectrum you can see. Each different wavelength of visible light has a different color.
Ultraviolet rays, in small quantities, help your body produce vitamin D, but too much exposure can cause sunburn or even cancer.
X-rays are used to see inside the body. They help doctors to diagnose and treat many health problems.
Gamma rays are used in hospitals to diagnose and treat cancer. They penetrate the body to destroy a tumor without harming the surrounding areas.
CITY HOSPITAL
GAMMA RADIATION

Section 2 Assessment

Target Reading Skill Previewing Visuals
Refer to your questions and answers about Figure 3 to help you answer Question 2 below.

Reviewing Key Concepts

1. a. **Reviewing** What is the mathematical relationship among wavelength, frequency, and speed?
   b. **Summarizing** In what way are all electromagnetic waves the same? In what ways are they different?
   c. **Making Generalizations** As the wavelengths of electromagnetic waves decrease, what happens to their frequencies? To their energies?
2. a. **Listing** List the waves in the electromagnetic spectrum in order from lowest frequency to highest frequency.
   b. **Explaining** Why are some electromagnetic waves harmful to you but others are not?
   c. **Classifying** List one or more types of electromagnetic waves that are useful for each of these purposes: cooking food, communication, seeing inside the body, curing diseases, reading a book, warming your hands.

Math Practice

Scientific Notation

3. An FM radio station broadcasts at a frequency of 9×10^5 Hz. Write the frequency as a number without an exponent.
4. Red light has a frequency of 4×10^{14} Hz. Express the frequency without using an exponent.

Microwave Ovens

In 1946, as Dr. Percy Spencer worked on a radar device that produced microwaves, a candy bar melted in his pocket. Curious, he put some popcorn kernels near the device—they popped within minutes. Then, he put an egg near the device. It cooked so fast that it exploded. Dr. Spencer had discovered a new way of cooking food quickly. The microwave-oven industry was born.

Making Microwave Popcorn

1. Popcorn kernels are enclosed in a paper bag that microwaves pass through.
2. Microwaves strike water particles in the kernels, causing them to vibrate rapidly and produce heat.
3. The heat turns the water to steam, causing the kernels to explode.

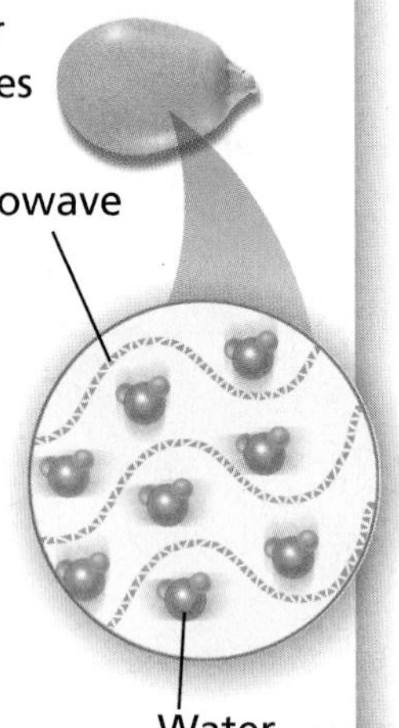

Cooking With Microwaves

How do microwave ovens cook food? The answer lies in the way microwaves are reflected, transmitted, and absorbed when they strike different types of materials, such as food, metal, and plastic. In a microwave oven, microwaves reflect off the inner metal walls, bouncing around in the cooking chamber. They mostly pass right through food-wrapping materials such as plastic, glass, and paper. But foods absorb microwaves. Within seconds, the energy from the absorbed microwaves causes water and fat particles in the foods to start vibrating rapidly. These vibrations produce the heat that cooks the food.

Faster Cooking, But Is It Safe?

Using microwave ovens has made preparing food faster and easier than using conventional ovens. But, using microwave ovens has drawbacks. Overheating liquids in a microwave oven can cause the liquids to boil over or can cause serious burns. Also, microwave ovens can cook foods unevenly. This can result in foods being undercooked. Health risks can result from not cooking some foods, such as meats and poultry, thoroughly.

How a Microwave Oven Works

A microwave oven produces microwaves and scatters them throughout the oven to reach the food to be cooked.

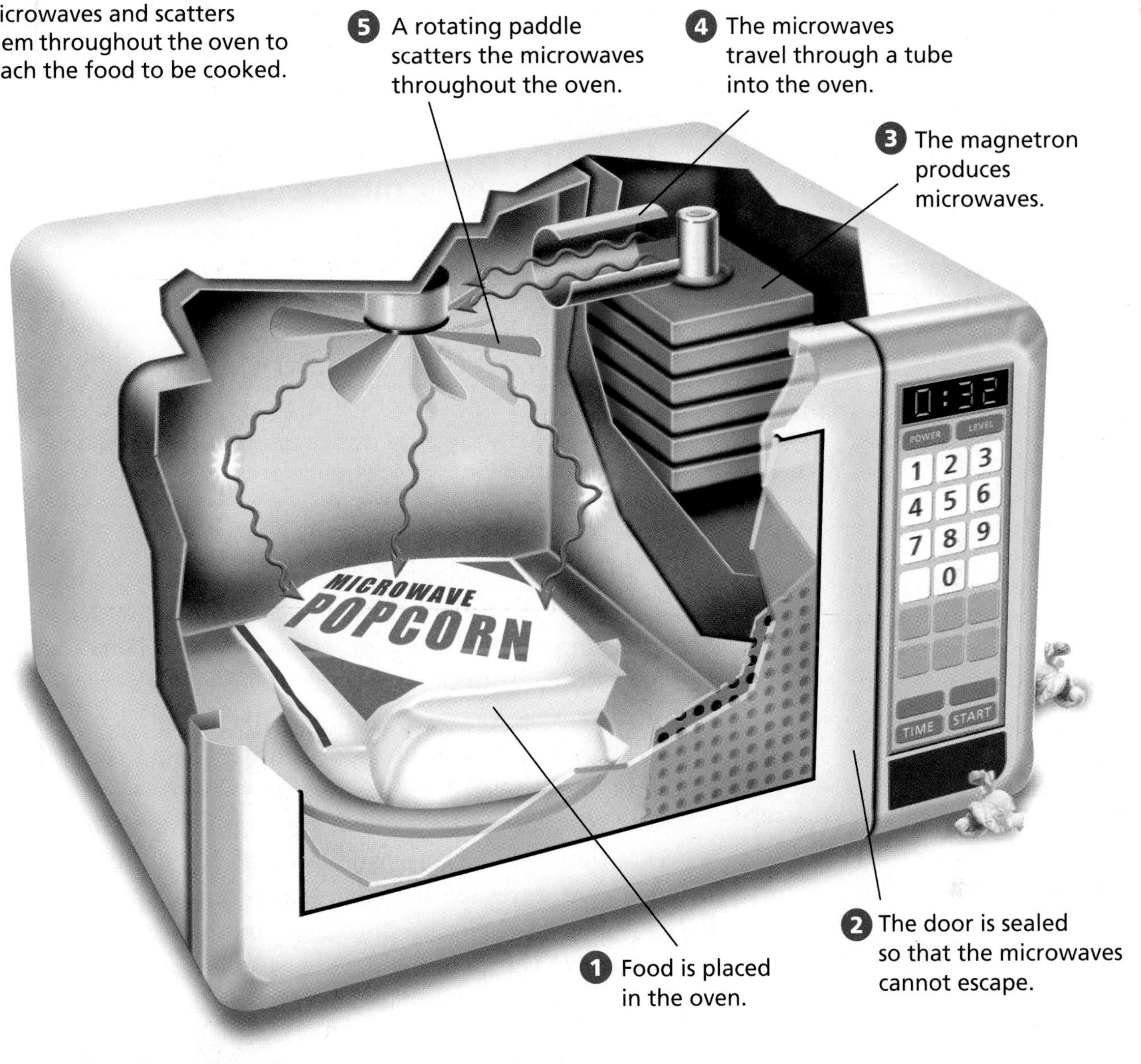
5 A rotating paddle scatters the microwaves throughout the oven.
4 The microwaves travel through a tube into the oven.
3 The magnetron produces microwaves.
MICROWAVE POPCORN
0:32
POWER
LEVEL
1 2 3
4 5 6
7 8 9
0
TIME
START
2 The door is sealed so that the microwaves cannot escape.
1 Food is placed in the oven.

Weigh the Impact

1. Identify the Need
What advantages do microwave ovens have over conventional ovens?

2. Research
The U.S. Food and Drug Administration (FDA) regulates safety issues for microwave ovens. Research microwave ovens on the Internet to find FDA guidelines about this technology. What safety measures does the FDA recommend?

3. Write
Based on your research, create a poster showing how to use microwave ovens safely. With your teacher's permission, display your poster in the school cafeteria.

Go Online
PHSchool.com

For: More on microwave ovens
Visit: PHSchool.com
Web Code: cgh-5030

Section 3

Producing Visible Light

Reading Preview

Key Concept

- What are the different types of light bulbs?

Key Terms

- illuminated
- luminous
- spectroscope
- incandescent light
- tungsten-halogen bulb
- fluorescent light
- vapor light
- neon light

Target Reading Skill

Comparing and Contrasting
Compare and contrast the five types of light bulbs by completing a table like the one below.

Light Bulbs

Feature	Ordinary Light Bulb	Tungsten-Halogen
Bulb material	Glass	
Hot/Cool		

Lab zone Discover Activity

How Do Light Bulbs Differ?

1. Your teacher will give you one incandescent and one fluorescent light bulb.
2. Examine the bulbs. Record your observations and describe any differences. Draw each type of bulb.
3. How do you think each bulb produces light?

Think It Over
Posing Questions Make a list of five questions you could ask to help you understand how each bulb works.

Look around you. Most of the objects you see are visible because they reflect light from some kind of light source. An object is **illuminated** if you see it by reflected light. The page you are reading, your desk, and the moon are examples of illuminated objects. An object is **luminous** if it gives off its own light. A light bulb, a burning log, and the sun all are examples of luminous objects.

Different types of light bulbs may be used to illuminate the spaces around you. **Common types of light bulbs include incandescent, tungsten-halogen, fluorescent, vapor, and neon lights.** Some light bulbs produce a continuous spectrum of all of the wavelengths of visible light. Others produce only a few wavelengths. You can use an instrument called a **spectroscope** to view the different colors of light produced by a light bulb.

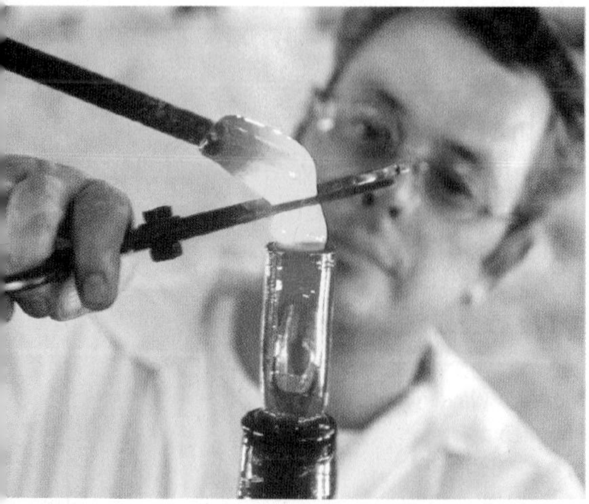

Incandescent Lights

Have you heard the phrase "red hot"? When a glassblower heats glass, it glows and gives off red light. At a higher temperature, it gives off white light and the glass is said to be "white hot." An **incandescent light** (in kun DES unt) is a light bulb that glows when a filament inside it gets white hot. Thomas Edison, the American inventor, patented the first practical incandescent light bulb in 1879.

◀ **Glassblower working with heated glass**

FIGURE 9

Incandescent Lights

A filament glows when electric current passes through it. **Comparing and Contrasting** *How are ordinary light bulbs like tungsten-halogen bulbs? How are they different?*

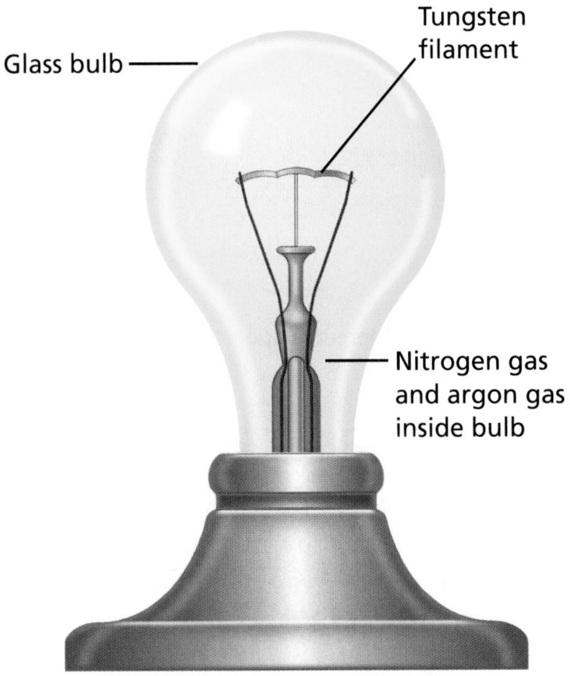

Ordinary Light Bulb

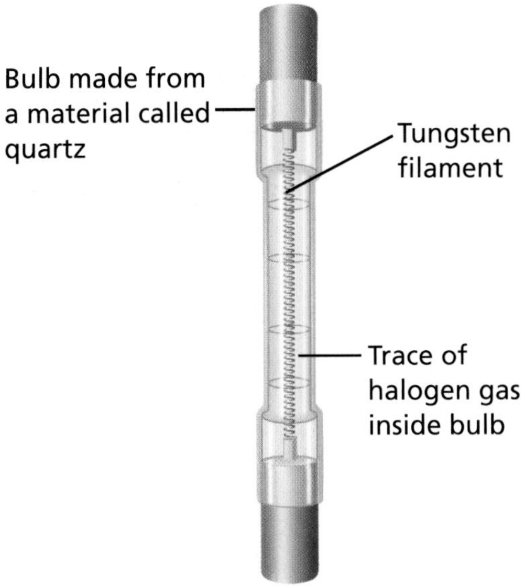

Tungsten-Halogen Bulb

Ordinary Light Bulbs Look closely at the ordinary light bulb shown in Figure 9. Notice the thin wire called the filament. It is made of a metal called tungsten. When an electric current passes through the filament, it quickly heats up and becomes hot, giving off white light. The filament is enclosed in an airtight glass bulb. Most ordinary light bulbs contain small amounts of nitrogen and argon gases.

Ordinary light bulbs are not efficient. Less than 10 percent of their energy is given off as light. Most of their energy is given off as infrared rays. That's why they get so hot.

Tungsten-Halogen Bulbs A bulb that has a tungsten filament and contains a halogen gas such as iodine or bromine is called a **tungsten-halogen bulb.** The filament of this bulb gets much hotter than in an ordinary light bulb, so the bulb looks whiter.

Tungsten-halogen bulbs are more efficient than ordinary bulbs because they give off more light and use less electrical energy. But they also give off more heat. Because tungsten-halogen bulbs get so hot, they must be kept away from materials that could catch fire.

Reading Checkpoint **What gases are used in tungsten-halogen bulbs?**

Lab zone **Skills Activity**

Observing

Use a spectroscope to view light from two sources. **CAUTION:** *Do not view the sun with the spectroscope.*

1. Look through the spectroscope at an ordinary light bulb. Use colored pencils to draw and label what you see.
2. Now, look at a fluorescent light through the spectroscope. Again, draw and label what you see.

How are the colors you see the same? How are they different?

FIGURE 10
Fluorescent Light
A fluorescent light is cool because very little energy is given off as infrared rays. **Inferring** *Why is a fluorescent light efficient?*

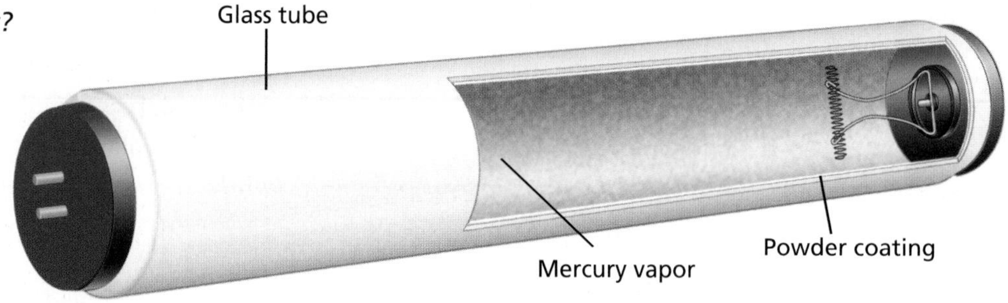

Other Light Sources

Incandescent light bulbs are not the only light bulbs you see around you. Some spaces are lit by fluorescent lights. Streets and parking lots may be lit with vapor lights. Neon lights are often used to attract attention to stores and theaters.

Fluorescent Lights Have you ever noticed long, narrow glass tubes that illuminate schools and stores? These are fluorescent light bulbs. A **fluorescent light** (floo RES unt) is a bulb that contains a gas and is coated on the inside with a powder. When an electric current passes through the bulb, it causes the gas inside to give off ultraviolet rays. When the ultraviolet rays hit the powder in the tube, the powder gives off visible light.

Fluorescent lights give off most of their energy as visible light and only a little energy as infrared rays. Therefore, fluorescent lights do not get as hot as incandescent light bulbs. They also usually last longer than incandescent lights and use less electrical energy for the same brightness. So, fluorescent lights are very efficient.

FIGURE 11
Sodium Vapor Lights
Sodium vapor lights give off a yellowish light.

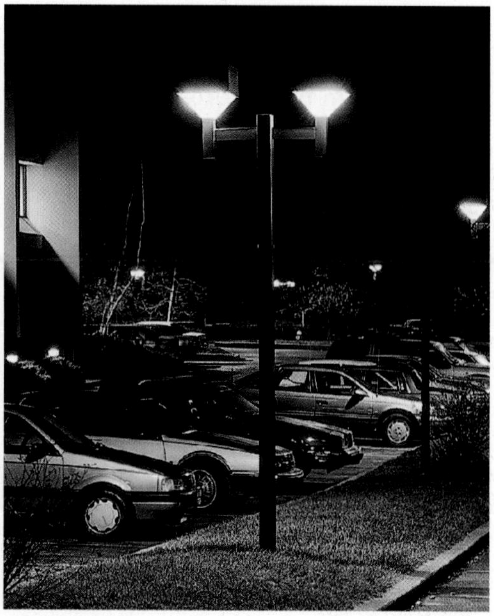

Vapor Lights A bulb that contains neon or argon gas and a small amount of solid sodium or mercury is a **vapor light.** When an electric current passes through the gas, the gas heats up. The hot gas then heats the sodium or mercury. The heating causes the sodium or mercury to change from a solid into a gas. In a sodium vapor light, the particles of sodium gas glow to give off a yellowish light. A mercury vapor light produces a bluish light.

Both sodium and mercury vapor lights are used for street lighting and parking lots. They require very little electrical energy to give off a great deal of light, so they are quite efficient.

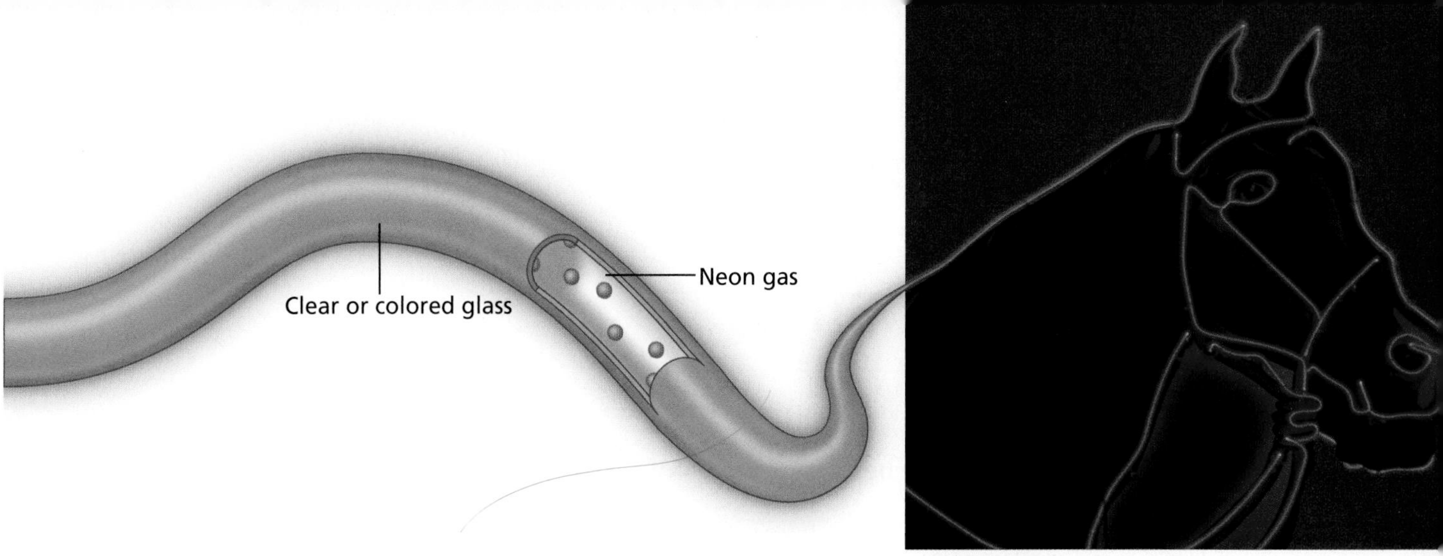

Neon Lights A **neon light** is a sealed glass tube that contains neon gas. When an electric current passes through the neon, particles of the gas absorb energy. However, the gas particles cannot hold the energy for very long. The energy is released in the form of light. This process is called electric discharge through gases.

A true neon light gives off red light, as shown in Figure 12. But often, lights that contain different gases or a mixture of gases are also called neon lights. Different gases produce different colors of light. For example, both argon gas and mercury vapor produce greenish-blue light. Helium gives pink light. Krypton gives a pale violet light. Sometimes colored glass tubes are used to produce other colors. Neon lights are commonly used for bright, flashy signs.

FIGURE 12
Neon Lights
The color of a neon light depends in part on which gas or gases are in the tube.

Reading Checkpoint **What color of light does a neon light give off?**

Section 3 Assessment

Target Reading Skill **Comparing and Contrasting** Use the information in your table about light bulbs to help you answer Question 1 below.

Reviewing Key Concepts

1. a. **Listing** What are five common types of light bulbs?
   b. **Explaining** How do incandescent light bulbs work?
   c. **Inferring** Lamps that use ordinary light bulbs often have cloth or paper shades. But tungsten-halogen lamps usually have metal shades. Explain.
   d. **Making Generalizations** What gives off light in incandescent light bulbs? What gives off light in other types of light bulbs?

Lab zone At-Home Activity

Buying Light Bulbs Invite family members to visit a hardware store. Ask a salesperson to describe the different kinds of light bulbs available. Read the information about each bulb on the packages. Look for the cost and the expected life of the bulbs. How does this information help you and your family to choose bulbs for different purposes?

Comparing Light Bulbs

Problem

Which types of light bulbs provide the best illumination?

Skills Focus

inferring, interpreting data, drawing conclusions

Materials

- a variety of incandescent light bulbs that can fit in the same lamp or socket
- medium-sized cardboard box
- light socket or lamp (without shade)
- meter stick
- wax paper
- scissors
- plain paper
- tape

Procedure

1. Following the instructions below, construct your own light box. The box allows you to test the illumination that is provided by each light bulb.
2. Make a data table like the one shown to record your data.
3. With a partner, examine the different bulbs. What is the power (watts), light output (lumens), and life (hours) for each bulb? Predict which light bulb will be the brightest. Explain your choice.
4. How will you test your prediction? What kinds of incandescent light bulbs will you use? What variables will you keep constant? What variables will you change?
5. Review your plan. Will your procedure help you find an answer to the problem?
6. Ask your teacher to check your procedure.
7. Before you repeat the steps for a second light bulb, look back at your procedure. How could you improve the accuracy of your results?
8. Test the illumination of the rest of your light bulbs.

How to Build and Use a Light Box

A Use a medium-sized cardboard box, such as the kind of box copy paper comes in. If the box has flaps, cut them off.

B Carefully cut a viewing hole (about 2 cm x 4 cm) in the bottom of the box. This will be on top when the box is used. This is hole A.

C Punch another hole (about 1 cm x 1 cm) on one side of the box. This is hole B. It will allow light from the bulb to enter the box.

D To decrease the amount of light that can enter, cover hole B with two layers of wax paper.

E Put one of your light bulbs in the lamp and place it at the side of the box, about 1 m from hole B.

F Have your partner write a secret letter on a piece of plain paper. Put the paper on the table. Place the light box over the paper with the viewing hole facing up.

G Now look through hole A. Turn the lamp on and move the light toward the box until you can read the secret letter. Measure the distance between the light bulb and hole B.

Data Table						
Bulb Number	Brand Name	Power (watts)	Light Output (lumens)	Life (h)	Cost (dollars)	Distance From Bulb to Light Box (cm)

Analyze and Conclude

1. **Observing** How does the distance between the bulb and hole B affect how easily you can read the secret letter?
2. **Inferring** Based on your observations, what can you infer about the illumination provided by each bulb? Which bulb gave the most illumination?
3. **Interpreting Data** How did your results compare with your prediction? What did you learn that you did not know when you made your prediction?
4. **Interpreting Data** What factors affect the illumination given by a light bulb?
5. **Drawing Conclusions** Based on your results, do you think that the most expensive bulb is the best?
6. **Communicating** Using what you have learned, write an advertisement for the best light bulb. Explain why it is the best.

Design an Experiment

A lighting company claims that one of their 11-watt fluorescent bulbs gives off as much light as a 75-watt ordinary light bulb. Design an experiment to test this claim. *Obtain your teacher's permission before carrying out your investigation.*

Go Online
PHSchool.com

For: Data sharing
Visit: PHSchool.com
Web Code: cgd-5033

Section 4

• Tech & Design •

Wireless Communication

Reading Preview

Key Concepts

- How do radio waves transmit information?
- How do cellular phones work?
- How do communications satellites relay information?

Key Terms

- amplitude modulation
- frequency modulation

Target Reading Skill

Using Prior Knowledge Your prior knowledge is what you know before you read about a topic. Before you read, write what you know about wireless communication in a graphic organizer. As you read, continue to write in what you learn.

Lab zone Discover Activity

How Can Radio Waves Change?

1. Trace the wave diagram onto a piece of tracing paper. Then transfer the tracing onto a flat piece of latex from a balloon or a glove.
2. Stretch the latex horizontally. How is the stretched wave different from the wave on the tracing paper?
3. Now stretch the latex vertically. How is this wave different from the wave on the tracing paper? How is it different from the wave in Step 2?

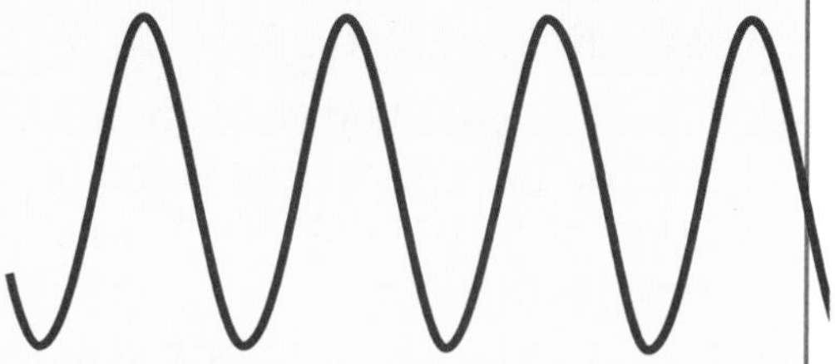

Think It Over

Making Models Which stretch changes the wave's amplitude? The wave's frequency?

You race home from school and switch on the TV to catch the final innings of your favorite team's big game. In an instant, you see and hear the game just as if you were sitting in the stands.

Today you can communicate with people far away in just seconds. You can watch a live television broadcast of a soccer game from Europe or listen to a radio report from Africa. How do these radio and television programs reach you?

FIGURE 13
Miniature Television
Radio waves transmit the signals for this small portable television.

Radio and Television

Radio waves carry, or transmit, signals for both radio and television programs. The radio waves are produced by charged particles moving back and forth inside transmission antennas. **Transmission antennas send out, or broadcast, radio waves in all directions. Radio waves carry information from the antenna of a broadcasting station to the receiving antenna of your radio or television.** There are two methods of transmitting the signals—amplitude modulation and frequency modulation. Radio stations broadcast using either method. Television stations use both methods—amplitude modulation for pictures and frequency modulation for sound.

Amplitude Modulation AM stands for amplitude modulation. **Amplitude modulation** is a method of transmitting signals by changing the amplitude of a wave. The information that will become sound, such as speech and music, is coded in changes, or modulations, of a wave's amplitude. The frequency of the wave remains constant, as shown in Figure 14. At a radio broadcasting station, sound is converted into electronic signals. The electronic signals are then converted into a pattern of changes in the amplitude of a radio wave. Your radio receives the wave and converts it back into sound.

AM radio waves have relatively long wavelengths and are easily reflected by Earth's ionosphere. The ionosphere is a region of charged particles high in the atmosphere. The reflected waves bounce back to Earth's surface. Therefore, AM radio stations can broadcast over long distances.

Frequency Modulation FM stands for frequency modulation. **Frequency modulation** is a method of transmitting signals by changing the frequency of a wave. FM signals travel as changes, or modulations, in the frequency of the wave. The amplitude of the wave remains constant.

FM waves have higher frequencies and more energy than AM waves. As shown in Figure 14, they pass through the ionosphere instead of being reflected back to Earth. Thus, FM waves do not travel as far as AM waves. So, if you go on a long car trip with an FM radio station tuned in, you may quickly lose reception of the station. But FM waves are usually received clearly and produce better sound quality than AM waves.

FIGURE 14
AM and FM Radio Waves
In AM transmissions, the amplitude of a radio wave is changed. In FM transmissions, the frequency is changed.
Interpreting Diagrams *What property is constant in the AM wave? In the FM wave?*

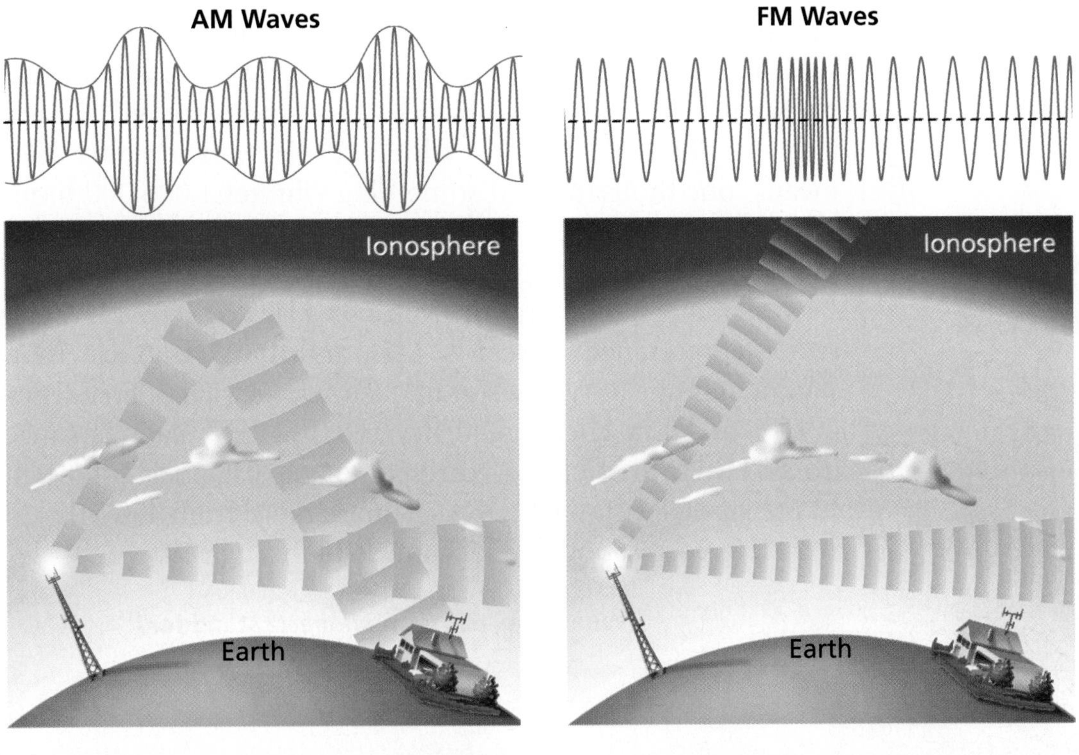

Math Analyzing Data

Comparing Frequencies

The table shows the ranges of radio broadcast frequencies used for AM radio, UHF television, FM radio, and VHF television.

1. **Interpreting Data** In the table, what units of measurement are used for frequency?
2. **Interpreting Data** Which type of broadcast shown in the table uses the highest-frequency radio waves? Which uses the lowest-frequency waves?
3. **Calculating** Which type of broadcast uses waves with the shortest wavelength?

Broadcast Frequencies

Type of Broadcast	Frequency Range
AM radio broadcast	535 kHz to 1,605 kHz
VHF television	54 MHz to 216 MHz
FM radio broadcast	88 MHz to 108 MHz
UHF television	470 MHz to 806 MHz

4. **Inferring** A broadcast uses a frequency of 100 MHz. Can you tell from this data if it is a television or a radio program? Explain.

The Radio Spectrum In addition to radio and television broadcasts, radio waves are used for many types of communication. For example, taxi drivers, firefighters, and police officers all use radio waves to do their jobs. The Federal Communications Commission, or FCC, assigns different radio frequencies for different uses. Radio stations are allowed to use one part of the radio spectrum. Television stations use other parts. Taxi and police radios are assigned separate sets of frequencies. Because the signals all have different assigned frequencies, they travel without interfering.

You probably have seen these assigned frequencies when you tune a radio. AM radio stations use frequencies measured in kilohertz (kHz), while FM radio stations use frequencies measured in megahertz (MHz). Recall that a hertz is one cycle per second. If something vibrates 1,000 times a second, it has a frequency of 1,000 Hz, or 1 kilohertz (kHz). (The prefix *kilo-* means "one thousand.") If something vibrates 1,000,000 times a second, it has a frequency of 1,000,000 Hz, or 1 megahertz (MHz). (The prefix *mega-* means "one million.")

AM radio stations range from 535 kHz to 1,605 kHz. FM radio stations range between 88 MHz and 108 MHz. A television station uses one of two sets of frequencies: Very High Frequency (VHF) or Ultra High Frequency (UHF). VHF stations range from 54 MHz to 216 MHz, corresponding to Channels 2 through 13 on your television set. UHF channels range from 470 MHz to 806 MHz, corresponding to Channels 14 through 69.

Reading Checkpoint **What does the term *kilohertz* stand for?**

Discovery Channel School™

The Electromagnetic Spectrum

Video Preview
▶ Video Field Trip
Video Assessment

Cellular Phones

Cellular telephones have become very common, but they only work if they are in or near a cellular system. The cellular system, which is shown in Figure 15, works by dividing regions into many small cells, or geographical areas. Each cell has one or more towers that relay signals to a central hub.

Cellular phones transmit and receive signals using high-frequency microwaves. When you place a call on a cellular phone, the phone sends out microwaves. The microwaves are tagged with a number unique to your phone. A tower picks up the microwaves and transfers the signal to a hub. In turn, the hub channels and transmits the signal to a receiver. The receiver may be another tower or another hub, depending on the distance between the two phones. That tower or hub transmits the signal to the receiving cellular phone. The receiving phone rings when it picks up the microwave signal from a tower or hub. The whole exchange seems to be instantaneous.

In addition to making phone calls, you can also use some cellular phones to page someone, to send text messages, or to get information from the Internet. Some modern cellular phones can even be used as digital cameras.

Reading Checkpoint **What are three ways to communicate with a cellular phone?**

FIGURE 15
Cellular Phone System
In the cellular phone system, cellular phones transmit and receive radio waves that travel to the nearest tower.
Predicting *What happens if a cellular phone is far away from a tower?*

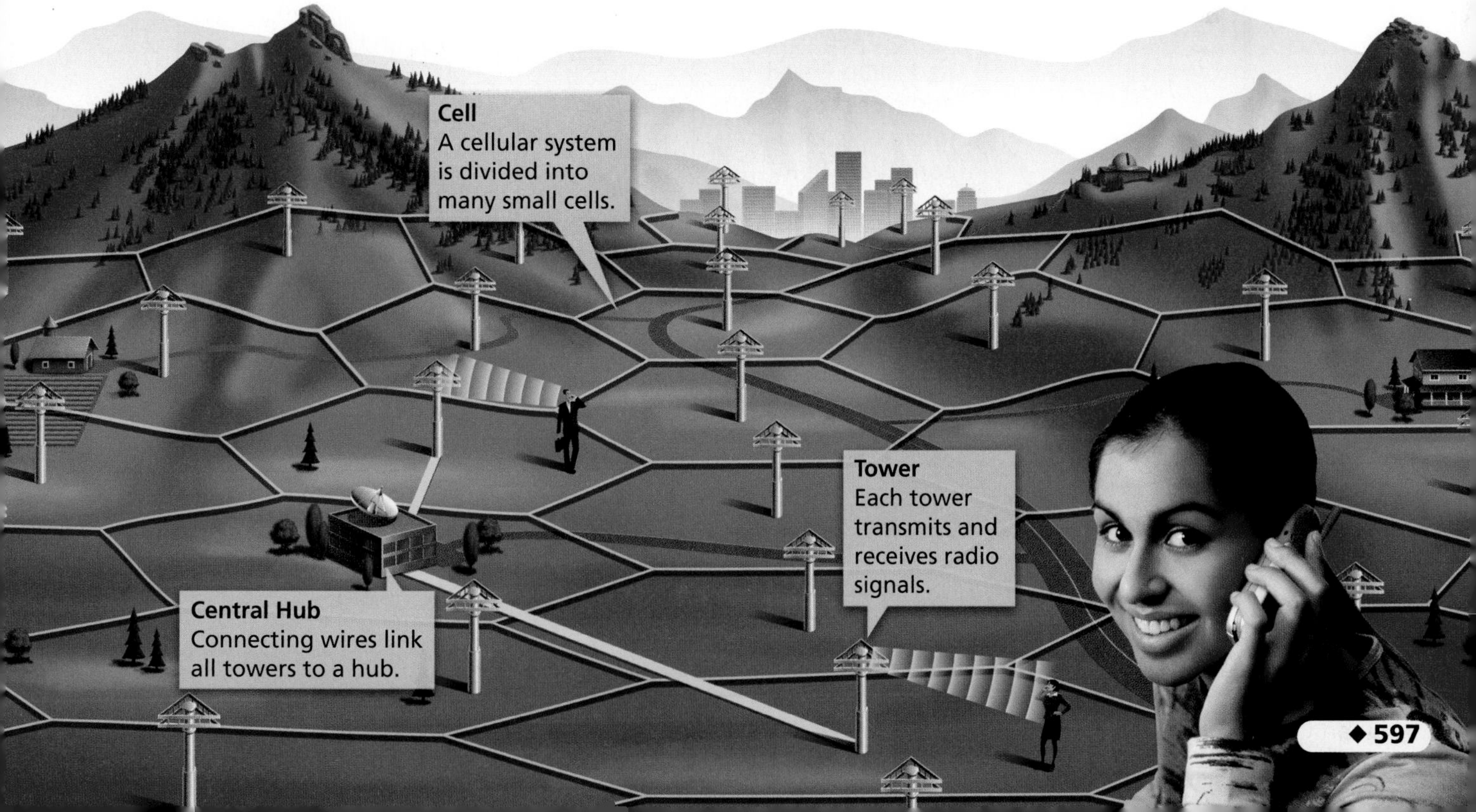

Cell
A cellular system is divided into many small cells.
Tower
Each tower transmits and receives radio signals.
Central Hub
Connecting wires link all towers to a hub.

Go Online
SCI LINKS NSTA
For: Links on using waves to communicate
Visit: www.SciLinks.org
Web Code: scn-1534

Communications Satellites

Satellites orbiting Earth are used to send information around the world. Communications satellites work like the receivers and transmitters of a cellular phone system. **Communications satellites receive radio, television, and telephone signals and relay the signals back to receivers on Earth.** Because a satellite can "see" only part of Earth at any given time, more than one satellite is needed for any given purpose.

Satellite Phone Systems Several companies have developed satellite phone systems. The radio waves from one phone are sent up to a communications satellite. The satellite transmits the waves back to the receiving phone on Earth. With this kind of phone, you can call anywhere in the world, but the cost is greater than using a cellular phone.

Science and **History**

Wireless Communication

Since the late 1800s, many developments in communication have turned our world into a global village.

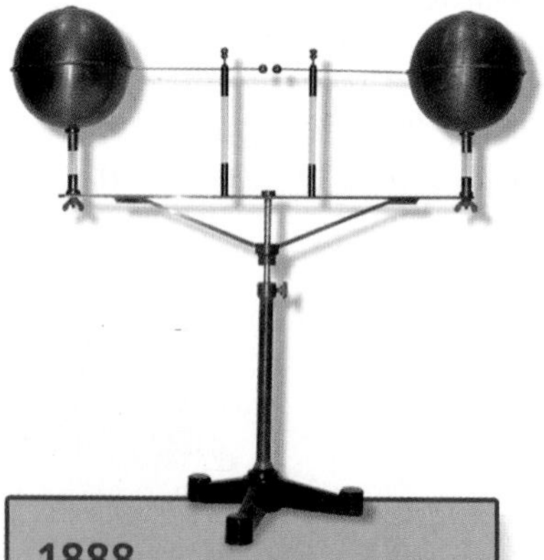

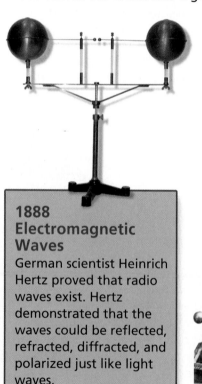

1888 Electromagnetic Waves
German scientist Heinrich Hertz proved that radio waves exist. Hertz demonstrated that the waves could be reflected, refracted, diffracted, and polarized just like light waves.

1895 First Wireless Transmission
Italian engineer and inventor Guglielmo Marconi successfully used radio waves to send a coded wireless signal a distance of more than 2 km.

1901 First Transatlantic Signals
On December 12, the first transatlantic radio signal was sent from Poldhu Cove, Cornwall, England, to Signal Hill, Newfoundland. The coded radio waves traveled more than 3,000 km through the air.

1923 Ship-to-Ship Communication
For the first time, people on one ship could talk to people on another. The signals were sent as electromagnetic waves, received by an antenna, and converted into sound.

1880 1900 1920

Television Satellites Both television networks and cable companies use communications satellites. First, the television signals are changed into AM and FM waves. These radio waves are sent up to satellites. Then the signals are relayed to local stations around the world.

Some people have their own antennas to receive signals for television programs directly from satellites. Many of the antennas are dish-shaped, so they are known as satellite dishes. Older satellite dishes were very large, more than 2 meters in diameter. But newer dishes are much smaller because the signals from satellites have become more powerful.

Television signals from satellites often are scrambled to make sure that only people who pay for the programs can use the signal. Customers need a decoding box to unscramble the signals.

Writing in Science

Research and Write Use library or Internet resources to find out more about Guglielmo Marconi. Imagine that you were hired as his assistant. Write a short letter to a friend that describes your new job.

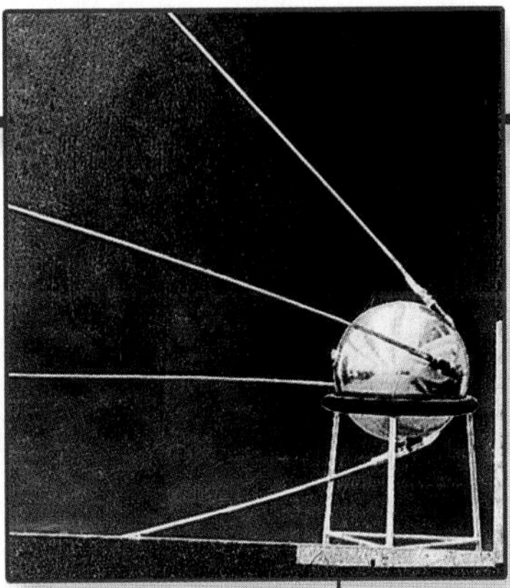

1957 *Sputnik I*
On October 4, the Soviet Union became the first country to successfully launch an artificial satellite into orbit. This development led to a new era in communications. Since then, more than 5,000 artificial satellites have been placed in orbit.

1963 Geosynchronous Orbit
Communications satellites are launched into orbits at altitudes of about 35,000 km. At this altitude, a satellite orbits Earth at the same rate as Earth rotates.

1979 Cellular Phone Network
In Japan, the world's first cellular phone network allowed people to make wireless phone calls. Today, cellular phone towers like the one above are common.

1960 1980 2000

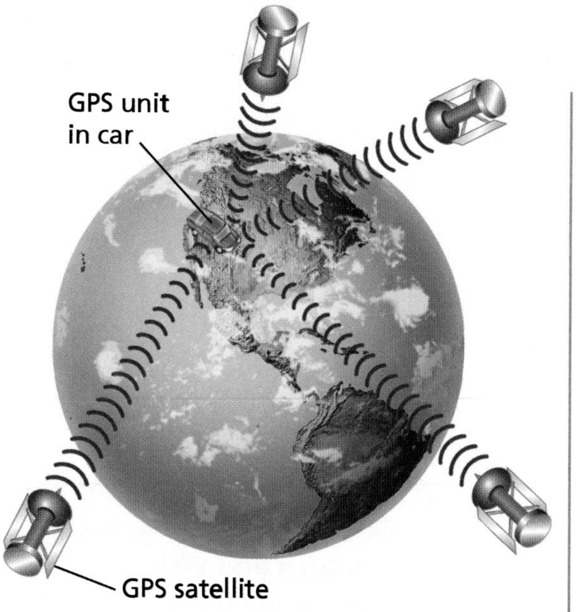

FIGURE 16
Global Positioning System
In the Global Positioning System (GPS), signals from four satellites are used to pinpoint a location on Earth.

Global Positioning System The Global Positioning System (GPS) is a system of navigation originally designed for the military. Now many other people use the system. GPS uses a network of satellites that broadcast radio signals to Earth. These signals carry information that tells you your exact location on Earth's surface, or even in the air. Anybody with a GPS receiver can pick up these signals.

Figure 16 shows how the signals from four GPS satellites are used to determine your position. The signals from three satellites tell you where you are on Earth's surface. The signal from the fourth satellite tells you how far above Earth's surface you are.

Today, GPS receivers are found in airplanes, boats, and cars. In a car, you can type your destination into a computer. The computer uses GPS data to map out your route. A computerized voice might even tell you when to turn right or left.

Reading Checkpoint **What does GPS stand for?**

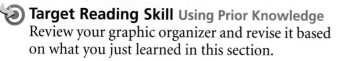

Section 4 Assessment

Target Reading Skill **Using Prior Knowledge** Review your graphic organizer and revise it based on what you just learned in this section.

Reviewing Key Concepts

1. a. **Identifying** What type of wave carries signals for radio and television programs?
   b. **Sequencing** Describe the events that bring an AM broadcast into your home.
   c. **Comparing and Contrasting** How are AM waves different from FM waves? How are they the same?
2. a. **Summarizing** How does a cellular telephone work?
   b. **Interpreting Diagrams** A cellular phone transmits a signal to a receiving tower in Figure 15. How is the signal passed on to another cellular phone user?
   c. **Relating Cause and Effect** Your cellular phone transmits a signal at a specific frequency. What will happen if a cellular phone next to you also uses this frequency?
3. a. **Listing** What are three kinds of communications satellites?
   b. **Reviewing** How do communications satellites work?
   c. **Predicting** If your GPS device received signals from only three satellites, what information about your location would you be missing?

Writing in Science

Cause and Effect Paragraph Just before going to sleep one night, you search for an AM station on your radio. To your surprise, you pick up a station coming from a city 1,000 kilometers away. Your older brother tells you it is because of Earth's ionosphere. Write a paragraph explaining your brother's statement. Be sure to describe how the ionosphere affects AM radio transmissions.

Build a Crystal Radio

Problem

Can you build a device that can collect and convert radio signals?

Skills Focus

observing, drawing conclusions, making models

Materials

- cardboard tube (paper towel roll)
- 3 pieces of enameled or insulated wire, 1 about 30 m long, and 2 about 30 cm long
- wirestrippers or sandpaper
- 2 alligator clips
- scissors
- aluminum foil
- 2 pieces of cardboard (sizes can range from 12.5 cm × 20 cm to 30 cm × 48 cm)
- masking tape
- crystal diode
- earphone
- 2 pieces of insulated copper antenna wire, 1 about 30 m long, and 1 about 0.5 m long

Procedure

PART 1 Wind the Radio Coil

(*Hint*: All ends of the insulated wires need to be stripped to bare metal. If the wire is enameled, you need to sandpaper the ends.)

1. Carefully punch two holes approximately 2.5 cm apart in each end of a cardboard tube. The holes should be just large enough to thread the insulated wire through.
2. Feed one end of the 30-m piece of insulated wire through one set of holes. Leave a 50-cm lead at that end. Attach alligator clip #1 to this lead. See Figure 1.

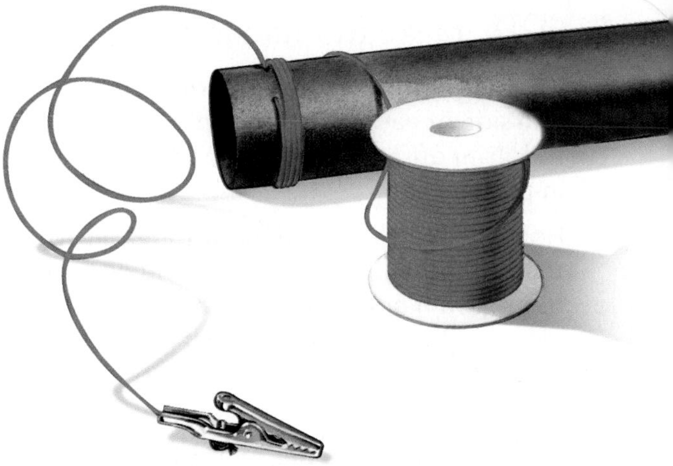

▲ **Figure 1** Winding the Coil

3. Wind the wire tightly around the cardboard tube. Make sure the coils are close together but do not overlap one another.
4. Wrap the wire until you come to the end of the tube. Feed the end of the wire through the other set of holes, leaving a 50-cm lead as before. Attach alligator clip #2 to this lead. See Figure 2.

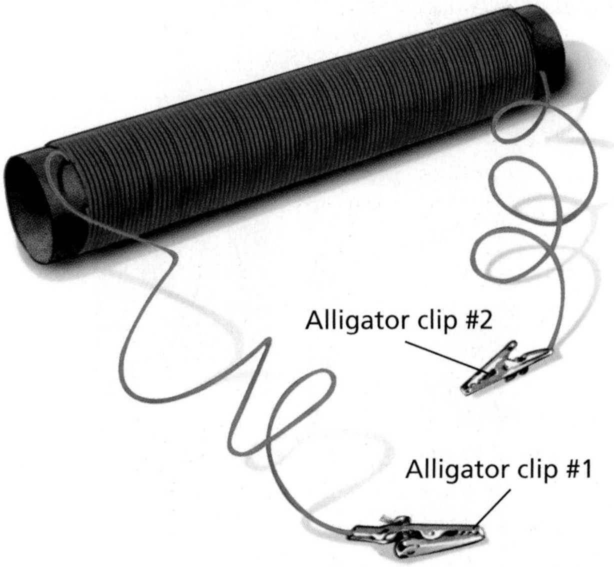

▲ **Figure 2** The Finished Coil

PART 2 Make the Tuning Plates

5. Without wrinkling the aluminum foil, cover one side of each piece of cardboard with the foil. Trim off any excess foil and tape the foil in place.
6. Hold the pieces of cardboard together with the foil facing inward. Tape along one edge to make a hinge. It is important for the foil pieces to be close together but not touching. See Figure 3.

▼ **Figure 3** Taping the Tuning Plates

7. Make a small hole through the cardboard and foil near a corner of one side. Feed one of the short pieces of insulated wire through the hole and tape it onto the foil as shown. Tape the other short piece of insulated wire to the corner of the other side. See Figure 4.

▼ **Figure 4** Connecting the Tuning Plates

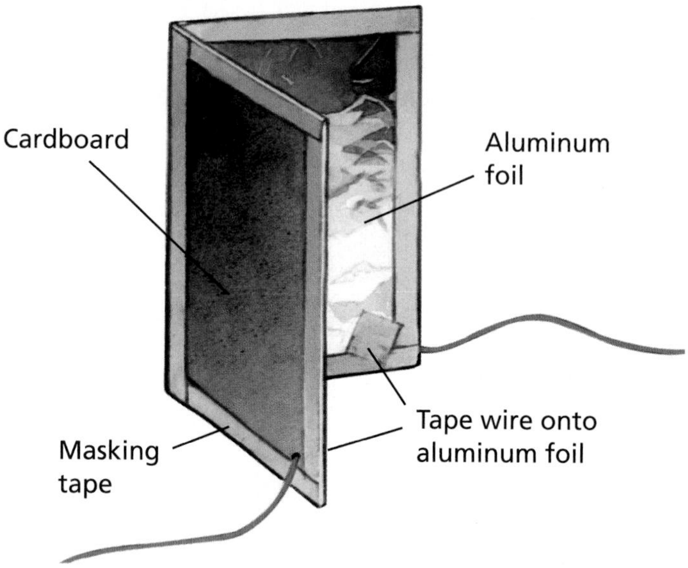

8. Connect one end of the wire from the foil to alligator clip #1. Connect the other wire from the foil to alligator clip #2.

PART 3 Prepare the Earphone

9. Handle the diode carefully. Connect one wire from the diode to alligator clip #1. The arrow on the diode should point to the earphone. Tape the other end of the diode wire to one of the earphone wires.
10. Connect the other wire from the earphone to alligator clip #2. See Figure 5.

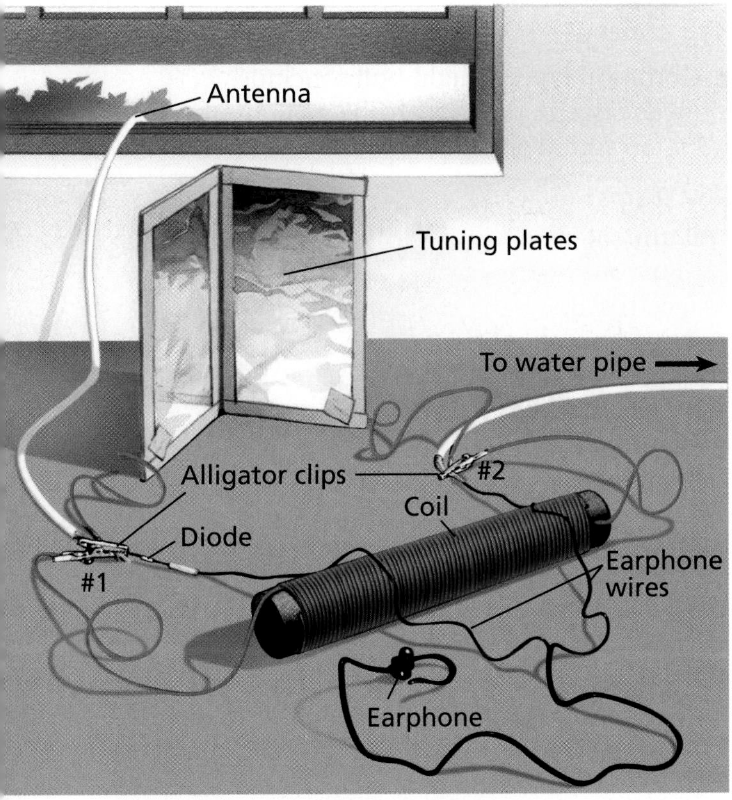

▲ **Figure 5 The Completed Radio**

PART 4 Hook Up the Antenna

11. String the long piece of antenna wire along the floor to an outside window. Connect the other end of the wire to alligator clip #1.
12. Connect one end of the shorter piece of antenna wire to a cold-water pipe or faucet. Connect the other end to alligator clip #2. See Figure 5.
13. Put on the earphone and try to locate a station by squeezing the tuning plates slowly until you hear a signal. Some stations will come in when the plates are close together. Other stations will come in when the plates are opened far apart.

Analyze and Conclude

1. **Observing** How many stations can you pick up? Where are these stations located, and which station has the strongest signal? Keep a log of the stations your receive.
2. **Forming Operational Definitions** In your own words, give a definition of "signal strength." How did you compare the signal strengths of different radio stations?
3. **Drawing Conclusions** How does adjusting the tuning plates affect reception of the radio signals?
4. **Making Models** You can improve reception by having a good antenna. How can you improve your antenna?
5. **Communicating** Write a paragraph describing the various parts of the radio and how they are linked together.

Design an Experiment

Use a radio to test signal reception at various times of the day. Do you receive more stations at night or in the morning? Does weather affect reception? *Obtain your teacher's permission before carrying out your investigation.*

Chapter 17 Study Guide

1 The Nature of Electromagnetic Waves

Key Concepts

- An electromagnetic wave consists of vibrating electric and magnetic fields that move through space at the speed of light.
- Many properties of electromagnetic waves can be explained by a wave model. However, some properties are best explained by a particle model.

Key Terms

electromagnetic wave
electromagnetic radiation
polarized light
photoelectric effect
photon

2 Waves of the Electromagnetic Spectrum

Key Concepts

- All electromagnetic waves travel at the same speed in a vacuum, but they have different wavelengths and different frequencies.
- The electromagnetic spectrum is made up of radio waves, infrared rays, visible light, ultraviolet rays, X-rays, and gamma rays.

Key Terms

electromagnetic spectrum
radio waves
microwaves
radar
infrared rays
thermogram
visible light
ultraviolet rays
X-rays
gamma rays

3 Producing Visible Light

Key Concept

- Common types of light bulbs include incandescent, tungsten-halogen, fluorescent, vapor, and neon lights.

Key Terms

illuminated
luminous
spectroscope
incandescent light
tungsten-halogen bulb
fluorescent light
vapor light
neon light

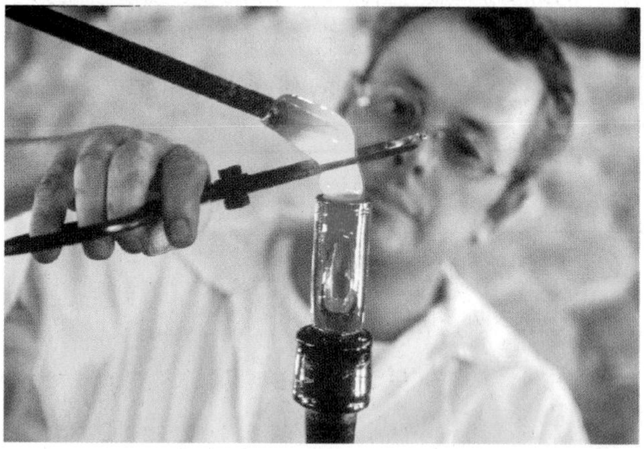

4 Wireless Communication

Key Concepts

- Transmission antennas send out, or broadcast, radio waves in all directions. Radio waves carry information from the antenna of a broadcasting station to the receiving antenna of your radio or television.
- Cellular phones transmit and receive signals using high-frequency microwaves.
- Communications satellites receive radio, television, and telephone signals, and relay the signals back to receivers on Earth.

Key Terms

amplitude modulation
frequency modulation

Review and Assessment

Go Online PHSchool.com
For: Self-Assessment
Visit: PHSchool.com
Web Code: cga-5030

Organizing Information

Concept Mapping Copy the concept map about electromagnetic waves onto a separate sheet of paper. Then complete it and add a title. (For more on Concept Mapping, see the Skills Handbook.)

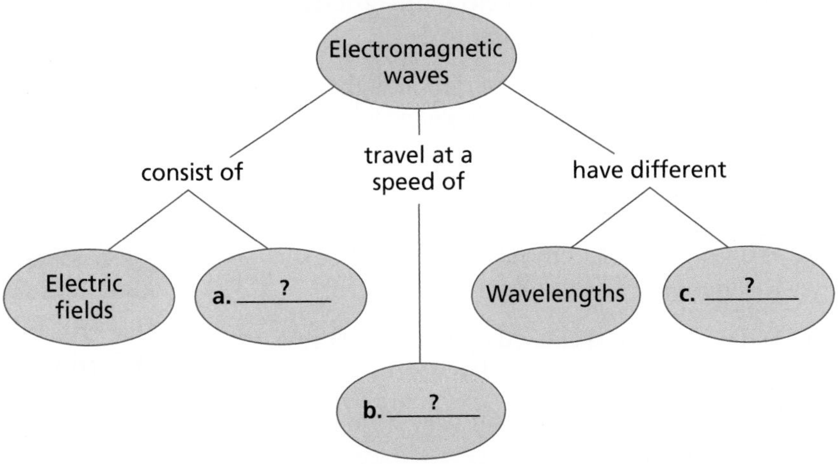

Reviewing Key Terms

Choose the letter of the best answer.

1. Electromagnetic waves are transverse waves that transfer
   - **a.** sound energy.
   - **b.** photons.
   - **c.** electrical and magnetic energy.
   - **d.** the particles of a medium.
2. Light that vibrates in only one direction is called
   - **a.** luminous.
   - **b.** illuminated.
   - **c.** visible light.
   - **d.** polarized light.
3. The electromagnetic waves with the longest wavelengths and lowest frequencies are
   - **a.** radio waves.
   - **b.** infrared rays.
   - **c.** X-rays.
   - **d.** gamma rays.
4. Radar is a system that uses reflected radio waves to
   - **a.** detect objects and measure their speed.
   - **b.** kill bacteria.
   - **c.** carry AM signals.
   - **d.** cook food.
5. A light bulb that glows when a filament inside it gets hot is a(n)
   - **a.** vapor light.
   - **b.** fluorescent light.
   - **c.** incandescent light.
   - **d.** neon light.

If the statement is true, write *true*. If it is false, change the underlined word or words to make the statement true.

6. In the photoelectric effect, light strikes a material and causes electrons to be ejected.
7. Electromagnetic waves that you can see are called infrared rays.
8. An illuminated object gives off its own light.
9. A(n) incandescent light contains a gas and is coated on the inside with a powder.
10. In frequency modulation, the amplitude of a wave is changed.

Writing in Science

Letter Write a letter to a friend about the rescue of a ship's crew at sea. Include details about the ship's emergency radio and the role of satellites.

Discovery Channel School

The Electromagnetic Spectrum
Video Preview
Video Field Trip
▶ Video Assessment

Review and Assessment

Checking Concepts

11. How do you know that electromagnetic waves can travel through a vacuum?

12. Two polarizing filters overlap at right angles. Why does the area of overlap look dark?

13. Explain why the energy of infrared rays is greater than the energy of radio waves.

14. Which color of light has the longest wavelength? The shortest wavelength?

15. What damage is caused by ultraviolet rays in sunlight? How can this damage be limited?

16. Which light bulbs give off very little energy as infrared rays?

17. Which of these is most efficient: an ordinary light bulb, a tungsten-halogen bulb, or a fluorescent light? Which is least efficient?

18. Which wave shown below is an AM wave? Which is an FM wave? Explain your answers.

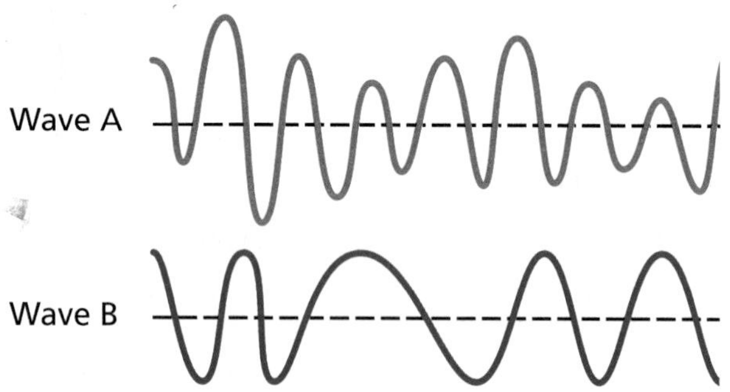

19. Explain how the Global Positioning System works.

Math Practice

20. Scientific Notation A cellular phone uses a frequency of 1.9×10^9 Hz. Write this frequency as a number without an exponent.

Thinking Critically

21. Relating Cause and Effect Gamma rays can cause more harm than X-rays. Explain why.

22. Classifying List examples of five luminous objects and five illuminated objects.

23. Problem Solving To build an incubator for young chicks, you need a source of heat. What type of light bulb could you use? Explain.

24. Comparing and Contrasting Make a table to compare the different types of wireless communication. Include headings such as type of information transmitted, frequencies, and one-way or two-way communication.

Applying Skills

Use the table below to answer Questions 25–27.

The table gives data about four radio stations.

Radio Station Frequencies

Station Name	Frequency
KLIZ	580 kHz
KMOM	103.7 MHz
WDAD	1030 kHz
WJFO	89.7 MHz

25. Interpreting Data Which radio station broadcasts at the longest wavelength? The shortest wavelength?

26. Classifying Which radio stations are AM? Which are FM?

27. Predicting You are going on a car trip across the United States. Which station would you expect to receive for the greater distance: KLIZ or KMOM?

Lab zone Chapter Project

Performance Assessment Decide how to present to your class the results of your survey about wireless communication. You might make a poster to display tables and graphs. Or you could make a computer presentation. Prepare summary statements for each table and graph. Then make your presentation to the class.

Standardized Test Prep

Test-Taking Tip

Interpreting Diagrams

When answering questions about diagrams, read all parts of the diagram carefully, including the title, captions, and labels. Make sure you understand the meanings of arrows and other symbols. Determine exactly what the question asks. Then eliminate those answer choices that are not supported by the diagram.

Sample Question

The electromagnetic waves in the diagram at right that have the shortest wavelength are

A radio waves.
B ultrasound waves.
C X-rays.
D gamma rays.

Answer

The correct answer is **D**, because gamma rays have the highest frequency and therefore the shortest wavelength. Answer **B** is wrong because ultrasound waves are not electromagnetic waves. Answers **A** and **C** are incorrect because these waves have longer wavelengths than gamma rays.

Choose the letter of the best answer.

1. The moon does not give off its own light. You can infer that the moon

A is luminous.
B has no atmosphere.
C is illuminated.
D is incandescent.

2. Ultraviolet rays from the sun are able to reach Earth's surface because

F they require air to travel through.
G they have more energy than infrared rays.
H they can travel through empty space.
J they can penetrate through clouds.

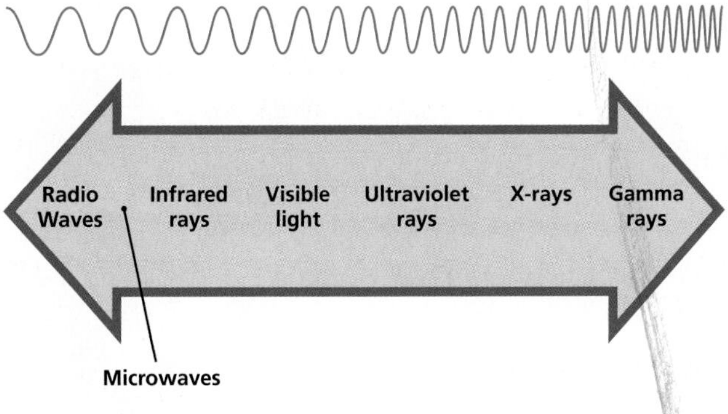

Use the diagram to answer Questions 3 and 4.

3. The amount of energy carried by an electromagnetic wave increases with frequency. Which of the following groups of waves is listed correctly in order of increasing energy?

A X-rays, visible light, radio waves
B radio waves, visible light, X-rays
C infrared rays, visible light, radio waves
D visible light, gamma rays, X-rays

4. Microwaves are a type of

F radio wave.
G X-ray.
H visible light.
J ultraviolet ray.

5. An experiment is set up to determine the efficiency of a 60-W light bulb. The light output is measured as 6 watts. The power used is assumed to be 60 watts. The experimenter calculates the efficiency using this equation:

$$\text{Efficiency} = \frac{\text{Measured light output (watts)}}{\text{Measured power used (watts)}}$$

Why is this experiment flawed?

A The efficiency cannot be measured.
B The efficiency of the light bulb can only be compared to a second light bulb.
C The light output needs to be measured more precisely.
D The actual power used was not measured.

Constructed Response

6. Explain how a spectrum is formed when white light passes through a prism. In your answer, explain what white light is composed of.

Chapter 18

Light

Chapter Preview

Interactive Textbook

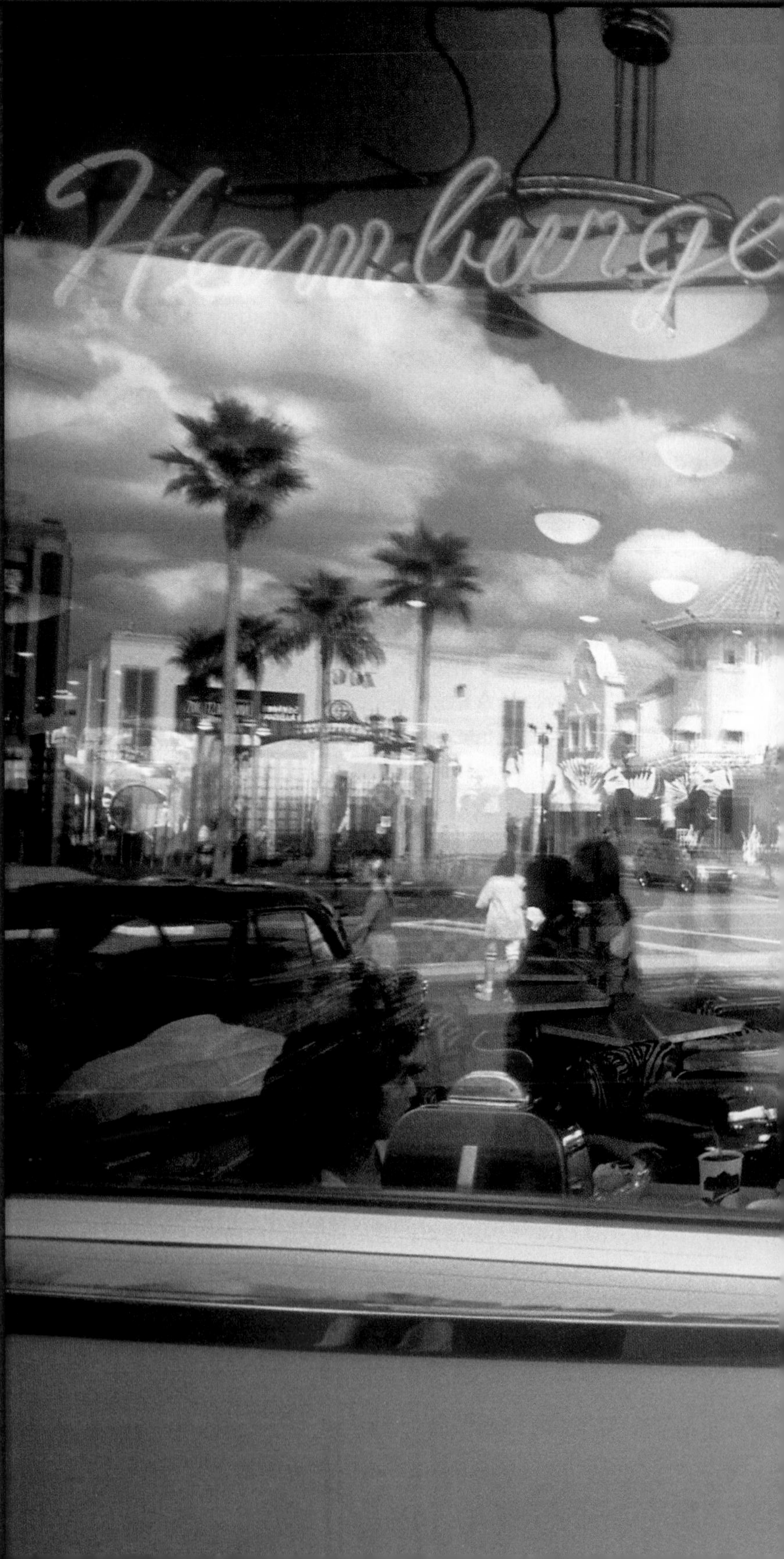

These windows reflect light, but they also let light pass straight through. ▶

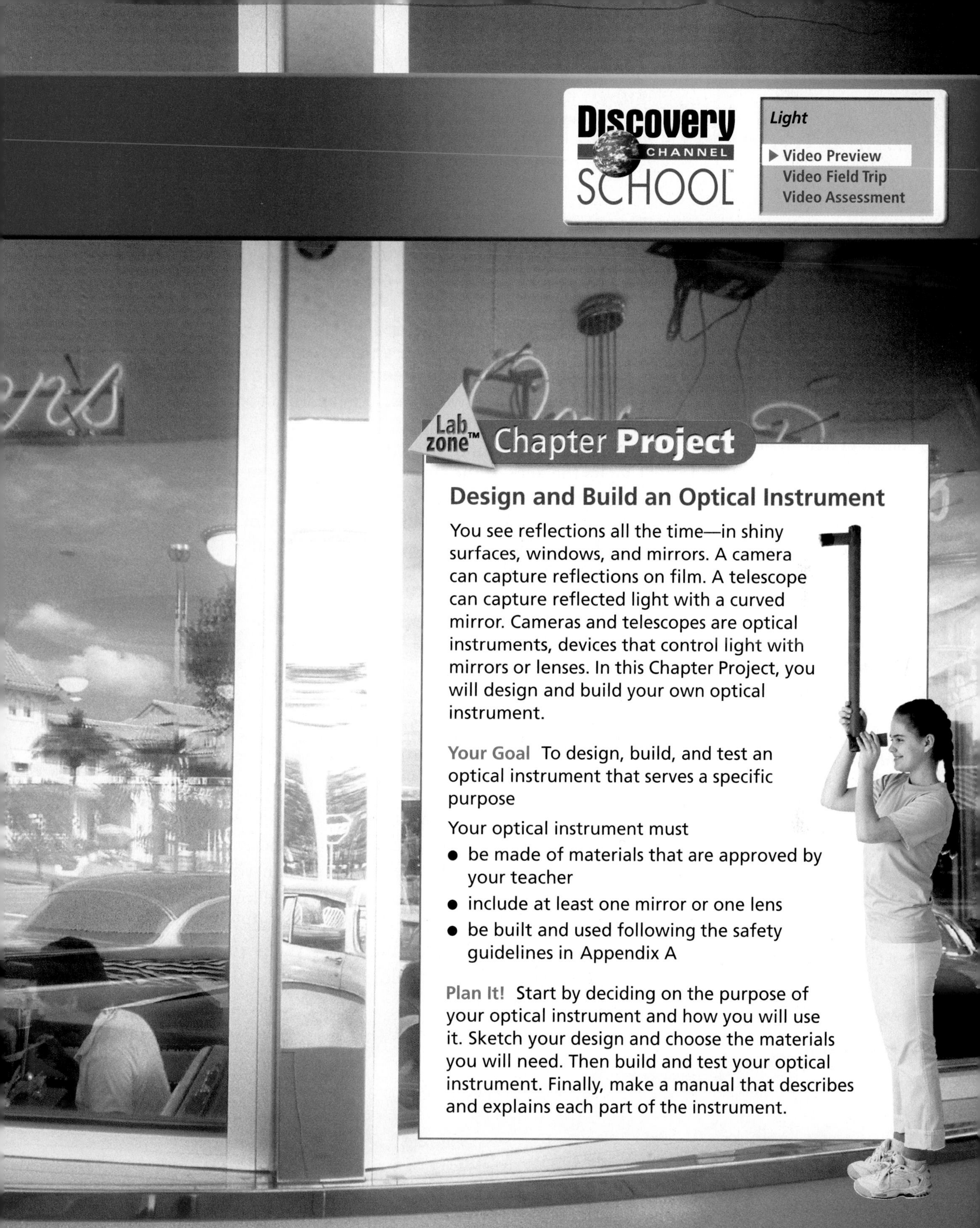

Discovery Channel School

Light

- ▶ Video Preview
- Video Field Trip
- Video Assessment

Lab zone™ Chapter **Project**

Design and Build an Optical Instrument

You see reflections all the time—in shiny surfaces, windows, and mirrors. A camera can capture reflections on film. A telescope can capture reflected light with a curved mirror. Cameras and telescopes are optical instruments, devices that control light with mirrors or lenses. In this Chapter Project, you will design and build your own optical instrument.

Your Goal To design, build, and test an optical instrument that serves a specific purpose

Your optical instrument must
- be made of materials that are approved by your teacher
- include at least one mirror or one lens
- be built and used following the safety guidelines in Appendix A

Plan It! Start by deciding on the purpose of your optical instrument and how you will use it. Sketch your design and choose the materials you will need. Then build and test your optical instrument. Finally, make a manual that describes and explains each part of the instrument.

Section 1 Light and Color

Reading Preview

Key Concepts

- What happens to the light that strikes an object?
- What determines the color of an opaque, transparent, or translucent object?
- How is mixing pigments different from mixing colors of light?

Key Terms

- transparent material
- translucent material
- opaque material
- primary colors
- secondary color
- complementary colors
- pigment

Target Reading Skill

Building Vocabulary Using a word in a sentence helps you think about how to best explain the word. As you read, carefully note the definition of each Key Term. Also note other details in the paragraph that contains the definition. Use all this information to write a sentence using the Key Term.

Lab zone Discover Activity

How Do Colors Mix?

1. Cut a disk with a diameter of 10 cm out of white cardboard. Divide the disk into three equal-sized segments. Color one segment red, the next green, and the third blue.
2. Carefully punch two holes, 2 cm apart, on opposite sides of the center of the disk.
3. Thread a 1-m long string through the holes. Tie the ends of the string together to make a loop that passes through both holes.
4. With equal lengths of string on each side of the disk, tape the string in place. Turn the disk to wind up the string. Predict what color(s) you will see if the disk spins fast.
5. Spin the disk by pulling the loops to unwind the string.

Think It Over

Observing What color do you see as the wheel spins fast? Was your prediction correct?

It was hard work, but you are finally finished. You stand back to admire your work. Color is everywhere! The bright green grass rolls right up to the flower garden you just weeded. In the bright sunlight, you see patches of yellow daffodils, purple hyacinths, and red tulips. The sun's light allows you to see each color. But sunlight is white light. What makes each flower appear to be a different color?

Flowers in sunlight ▼

When Light Strikes an Object

To understand why objects have different colors, you need to know how light can interact with an object. **When light strikes an object, the light can be reflected, transmitted, or absorbed.** Think about a pair of sunglasses. If you hold the sunglasses in your hand, you can see light that reflects off the lenses. If you put the sunglasses on, you see light that is transmitted by the lenses. The lenses also absorb some light. That is why objects appear darker when seen through the lenses.

Lenses, like all objects, are made of one or more materials. Most materials can be classified as transparent, translucent, or opaque based on what happens to light that strikes the material.

Transparent Materials A **transparent material** transmits most of the light that strikes it. The light passes right through without being scattered. This allows you to see clearly what is on the other side. Clear glass, water, and air all are transparent materials. In Figure 1, you can clearly see the straw through the glass on the left.

Translucent Materials A **translucent material** (trans LOO sunt) scatters light as it passes through. You can usually see something behind a translucent object, but the details are blurred. Wax paper and a frosted glass like the middle glass in Figure 1 are translucent materials.

Opaque Materials An **opaque material** (oh PAYK) reflects or absorbs all of the light that strikes it. You cannot see through opaque materials because light cannot pass through them. Wood, metal, and tightly woven fabric all are opaque materials. You cannot see the straw through the white glass in Figure 1 because the glass is opaque.

Reading Checkpoint **What happens when light strikes an opaque material?**

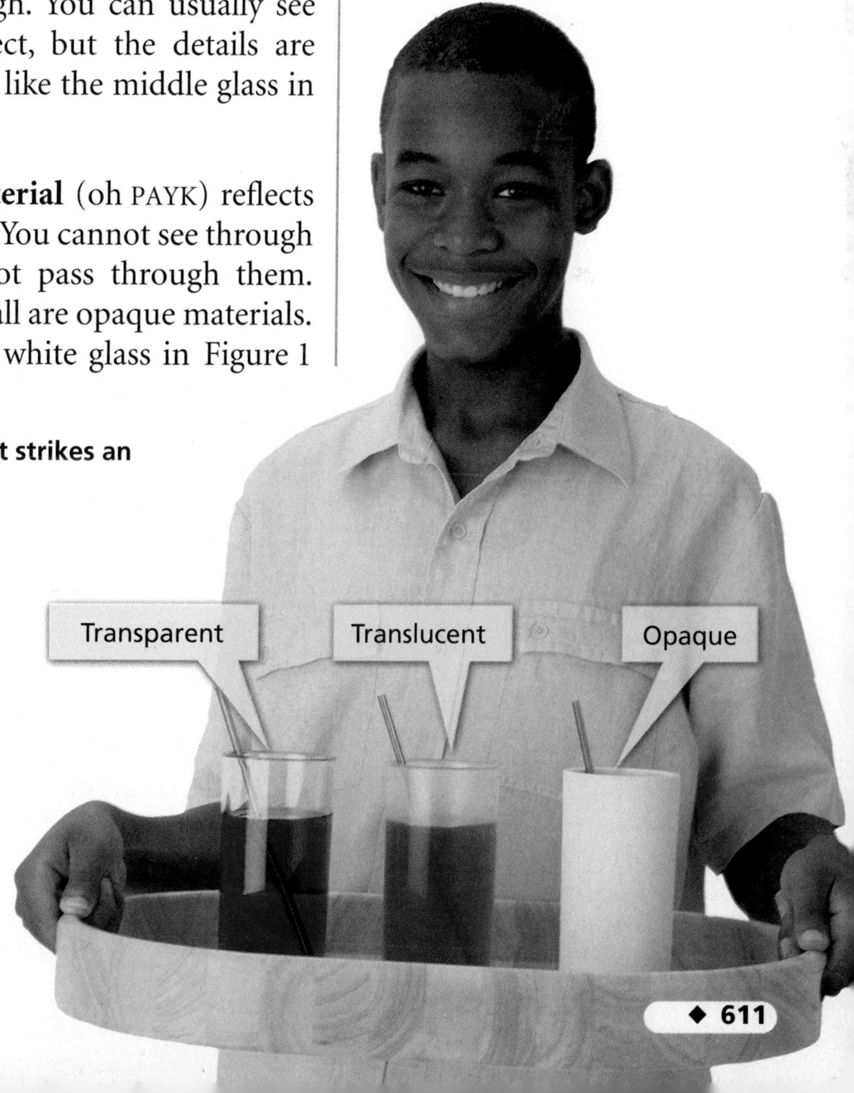

FIGURE 1
Types of Materials
Different types of materials reflect, transmit, and absorb different amounts of light.
Comparing and Contrasting
How does a straw seen through transparent glass compare with a straw seen through translucent glass?

FIGURE 2
Colored Light

The color an apple appears to be depends on the color of the light that strikes it.
Applying Concepts *What color of light is reflected by a red apple?*

In red light, the apple appears red because it reflects the red light. But the leaves look black.

In green light, the apple appears black because no red light strikes it. But the leaves look green.

In blue light, both the apple and the leaves appear black.

The Color of Objects

If you know how light interacts with objects, you can explain why objects such as flowers have different colors. The color of any object depends on the material the object is made of and the color of light striking the object.

Color of Opaque Objects The color of an opaque object depends on the wavelengths of light that the object reflects. Every opaque object absorbs some wavelengths of light and reflects others. **The color of an opaque object is the color of the light it reflects.** For example, look at the apple shown at the top of Figure 2. The apple appears red because it reflects red wavelengths of light. The apple absorbs the other colors of light. The leaf looks green because it reflects green light and absorbs the other colors.

Objects can appear to change color if you view them in a different color of light. In red light, the apple appears red because there is red light for it to reflect. But the leaf appears black because there is no green light to reflect. In green light, the leaf looks green but the apple looks black. And in blue light, both the apple and the leaf look black.

Go Online
SCI LINKS NSTA

For: Links on colors
Visit: www.SciLinks.org
Web Code: scn-1543

FIGURE 3

Color Filters

When you look at an apple through different filters, the color of the apple depends on the color of the filter.
Interpreting Photographs *Why do both the apple and the leaves appear black through the blue filter?*

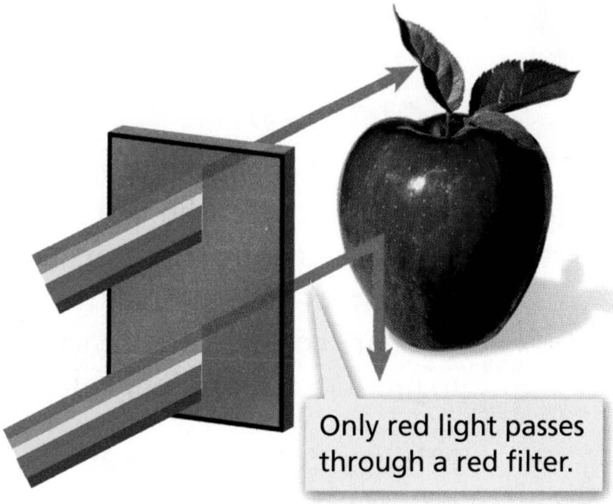

Only red light passes through a red filter.

The red filter transmits red light, so the apple looks red. But the leaf looks black.

The green filter transmits green light, so the leaf looks green. But the apple looks black.

The blue filter transmits blue light. Both the apple and the leaf look black.

Color of Transparent and Translucent Objects Materials that are transparent or translucent allow only certain colors of light to pass through them. They reflect or absorb the other colors. **The color of a transparent or translucent object is the color of the light it transmits.** For example, when white light shines through a transparent blue glass, the glass appears blue because it transmits blue light.

Transparent or translucent materials are used to make color filters. For example, a piece of glass or plastic that allows only red light to pass through is a red color filter. When you look at an object through a color filter, the color of the object may appear different than when you see the object in white light, as shown in Figure 3.

The lenses in sunglasses often are color filters. For example, lenses that are tinted yellow are yellow filters. Lenses that are tinted green are green filters. When you put on these tinted sunglasses, some objects appear to change color. The color you see depends on the color of the filter and on the color that the object appears in white light.

Reading Checkpoint What is a color filter?

Lab zone Skills Activity

Developing Hypotheses

1. Predict what colors you will see if you view a red, white, and blue flag through a red filter. Write a hypothesis of what the outcome will be. Write your hypothesis as an "If ... then ..." statement.
2. View an American flag using a red filter. What do you see? Is your hypothesis confirmed?
3. Repeat Steps 1 and 2 using a yellow filter.

Combining Colors

Color is used in painting, photography, theater lighting, and printing. People who work with color must learn how to produce a wide range of colors using just a few basic colors. Three colors that can combine to make any other color are called **primary colors.** Two primary colors combine in equal amounts to produce a **secondary color.**

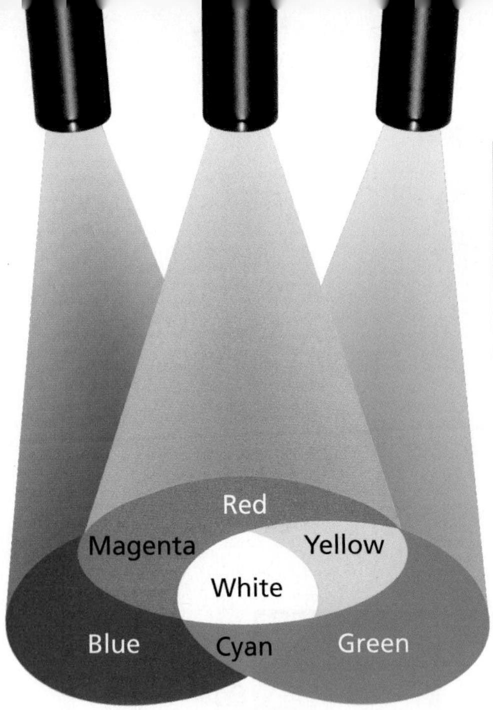

FIGURE 4
Primary Colors of Light
The primary colors of light combine in equal amounts to form white light.

Mixing Colors of Light The primary colors of light are red, green, and blue. **When combined in equal amounts, the three primary colors of light produce white light.** If they are combined in different amounts, the primary colors can produce other colors. For example, red and green combine to form yellow light. Yellow is a secondary color of light because two primary colors produce it. The secondary colors of light are yellow (red + green), cyan (green + blue), and magenta (red + blue). Figure 4 shows the primary and secondary colors of light.

A primary and a secondary color can combine to make white light. Any two colors that combine to form white light are called **complementary colors.** Yellow and blue are complementary colors, as are cyan and red, and magenta and green.

A color television produces many colors using only the primary colors of light—red, green, and blue. Figure 5 shows a magnified view of a color television screen. The picture in the screen is made up of little groups of red, green, and blue light. By varying the brightness of each colored bar, the television can produce thousands of different colors.

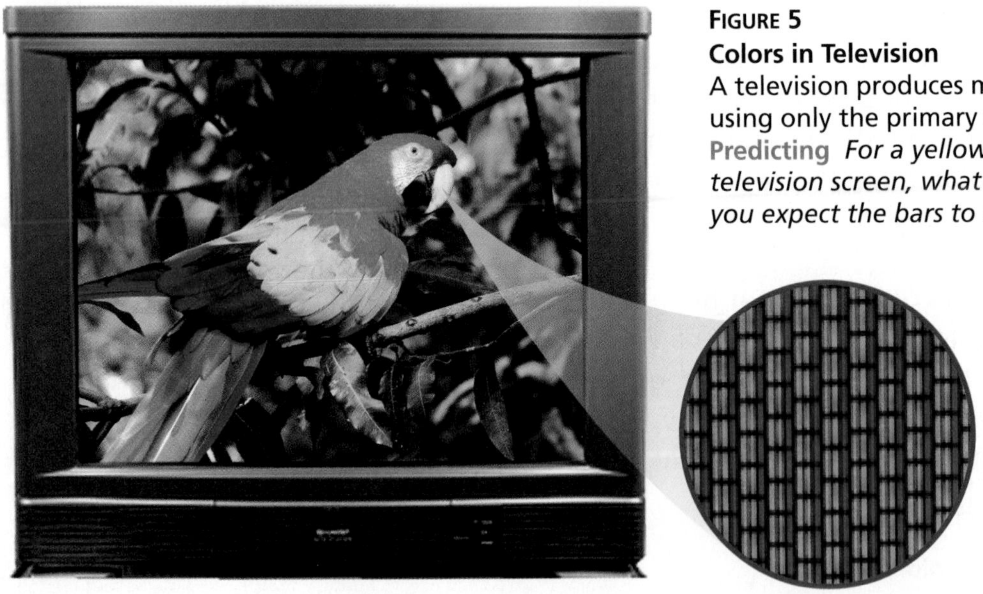

FIGURE 5
Colors in Television
A television produces many colors using only the primary colors of light.
Predicting *For a yellow area on a television screen, what color would you expect the bars to be?*

Equal amounts of red, green, and blue appear white from a distance.

Mixing Pigments How does a printer produce the many shades of colors you see in this textbook? Inks, paints, and dyes contain **pigments,** or colored substances that are used to color other materials. Pigments absorb some colors and reflect others. The color you see is the result of the colors that particular pigment reflects.

Mixing colors of pigments is different from mixing colors of light. **As pigments are added together, fewer colors of light are reflected and more are absorbed.** The more pigments that are combined, the darker the mixture looks.

Cyan, yellow, and magenta are the primary colors of pigments. These colors combine in equal amounts to produce black. By combining pigments in varying amounts, you can produce many other colors. If you combine two primary colors of pigments, you get a secondary color, as shown in Figure 6. The secondary colors of pigments are red, green, and blue.

Look at the pictures in this book with a magnifying glass. You can see tiny dots of different colors of ink. The colors used are cyan, yellow, and magenta. Black ink is also used, so the printing process is called four-color printing.

FIGURE 6
Primary Colors of Pigments
The primary colors of pigments combine in equal amounts to form black.

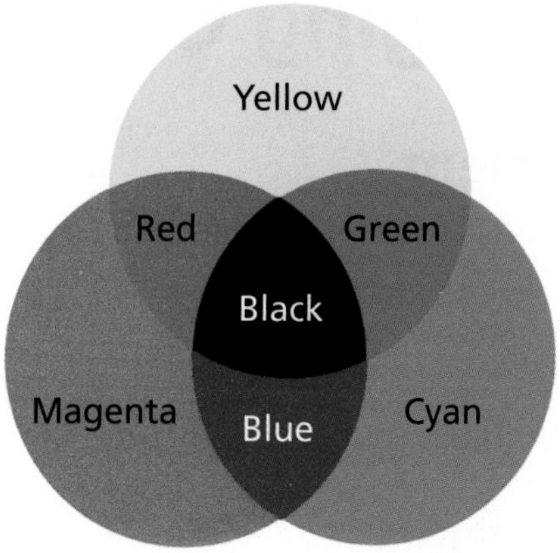

Reading Checkpoint What are pigments?

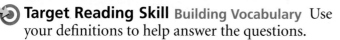

Section 1 Assessment

Target Reading Skill **Building Vocabulary** Use your definitions to help answer the questions.

Reviewing Key Concepts

1. a. **Identifying** What three things may happen to the light that strikes an object?
   b. **Applying Concepts** What happens to light that strikes the following materials: clear plastic, aluminum foil, and tissue paper?
   c. **Problem Solving** Room-darkening window shades are used to keep sunlight out of a theater. What type of material should the shades be made of? Explain.
2. a. **Reviewing** What determines the color of an opaque object? Of a transparent or translucent object?
   b. **Drawing Conclusions** An actor's red shirt and blue pants both appear black. What color is the stage light shining on the actor?
3. a. **Describing** What are the primary colors of light? The primary colors of pigments?
   b. **Comparing and Contrasting** How does the result of mixing the primary colors of pigments compare to the result of mixing the primary colors of light?
   c. **Interpreting Diagrams** In Figure 6, which pairs of colors combine to make black?

Lab zone **At-Home Activity**

Color Mix See how many different shades of green you can make by mixing blue and yellow paint in different proportions. On white paper, paint a "spectrum" from yellow to green to blue. Show the results to your family. Then explain how magazine photos reproduce thousands of colors.

Changing Colors

Problem

How do color filters affect the appearance of objects in white light?

Skills Focus

observing, inferring, predicting

Materials

- shoe box
- scissors
- flashlight
- removable tape
- red object (such as a ripe tomato)
- yellow object (such as a ripe lemon)
- blue object (such as blue construction paper)
- red, green, and blue cellophane, enough to cover the top of the shoe box

Procedure

1. Carefully cut a large rectangular hole in the lid of the shoe box.
2. Carefully cut a small, round hole in the center of one of the ends of the shoe box.
3. Tape the red cellophane under the lid of the shoe box, covering the hole in the lid.
4. Place the objects in the box and put the lid on.
5. In a darkened room, shine the flashlight into the shoe box through the side hole. Note the apparent color of each object in the box.
6. Repeat Steps 3–5 using the other colors of cellophane.

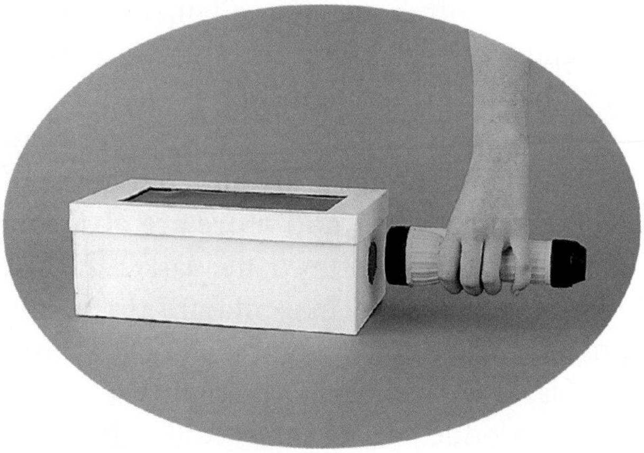

Analyze and Conclude

1. **Observing** What did you see when you looked through the red cellophane? Explain why each object appeared as it did.
2. **Observing** What did you see when you looked through the blue cellophane? Explain.
3. **Inferring** What color(s) of light does each piece of cellophane allow through?
4. **Predicting** Predict what you would see under each piece of cellophane if you put a white object in the box. Test your prediction.
5. **Predicting** What do you think would happen if you viewed a red object through yellow cellophane? Draw a diagram to support your prediction. Then test your prediction.
6. **Communicating** Summarize your conclusions by drawing diagrams to show how each color filter affects white light. Write captions to explain your diagrams.

Design an Experiment

Do color filters work like pigments or like colors of light? Design an experiment to find out what happens if you shine a light through both a red and a green filter. *Obtain your teacher's permission before carrying out your investigation.*

Section 2

Reflection and Mirrors

Reading Preview

Key Concepts

- What are the kinds of reflection?
- What types of images are produced by plane, concave, and convex mirrors?

Key Terms

- ray • regular reflection
- diffuse reflection
- plane mirror • image
- virtual image
- concave mirror • optical axis
- focal point • real image
- convex mirror

Target Reading Skill

Comparing and Contrasting

As you read, compare and contrast concave and convex mirrors in a Venn diagram like the one below. Write the similarities in the space where the circles overlap and the differences on the left and right sides.

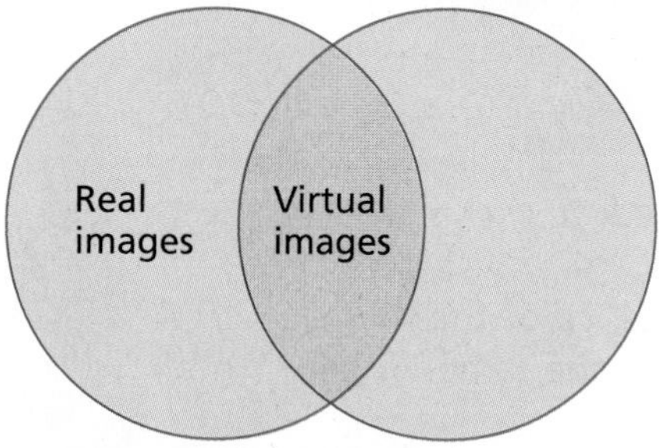

Lab zone Discover Activity

How Does Your Reflection Wink?

1. Look at your face in a mirror. Wink your right eye. Which eye does your reflection wink?
2. Tape two mirrors together so that they open and close like a book. Open them so they form a 90-degree angle with each other. **CAUTION:** *Be careful of any sharp edges.*
3. Looking into both mirrors at once, wink at your reflection again. Which eye does your reflection wink now?

Think It Over

Observing How does your reflection wink at you? How does the second reflection compare with the first reflection?

You laugh as you and a friend move toward the curved mirror. First your reflections look tall and skinny. Then they become short and wide. At one point, your reflections disappear even though you are still in front of the mirror. Imagine what it would be like if this happened every time you tried to comb your hair in front of a mirror!

Funhouse mirror ▶

Lab zone Skills Activity

Observing

In a dark room, hold a flashlight next to a table. **CAUTION:** *Do not look directly into the flashlight.* Point its beam straight up so no light shines on the tabletop. Then hold a metal can upright 5 cm above the flashlight. Tilt the can so its flat bottom reflects light onto the table. Try this again using a white paper cup. How does the light reflected by the can compare with the light reflected by the cup?

Reflection of Light Rays

The reflection you see in a mirror depends on how the surface reflects light. To show how light reflects, you can represent light waves as straight lines called **rays.** You may recall that light rays obey the law of reflection—the angle of reflection equals the angle of incidence.

Figure 7 shows two kinds of reflection. In the choppy water, you do not see a clear reflection of the person in the boat. But in the smooth water, you see a sharp reflection. **The two ways in which a surface can reflect light are regular reflection and diffuse reflection.**

Regular Reflection When parallel rays of light hit a smooth surface, **regular reflection** occurs. All of the light rays are reflected at the same angle because of the smooth surface. So, you see a sharp reflection.

Diffuse Reflection When parallel rays of light hit a bumpy or uneven surface, **diffuse reflection** occurs. Each light ray obeys the law of reflection but hits the surface at a different angle because the surface is uneven. Therefore, each ray reflects at a different angle, and you don't see a clear reflection.

Reading Checkpoint **What kind of surface results in diffuse reflection?**

FIGURE 7
Diffuse and Regular Reflection
The type of reflection that occurs at a surface depends on whether the surface is rough or smooth.

Diffuse Reflection
When parallel light rays strike a rough surface, the rays are reflected at different angles.
Regular Reflection
When parallel light rays strike a smooth surface, all of the rays are reflected at the same angle.

FIGURE 8
Image in a Plane Mirror
A plane mirror forms a virtual image. The reflected light rays appear to come from behind the mirror, where the image forms.
Observing *Is the raised hand in the image a left hand or a right hand?*

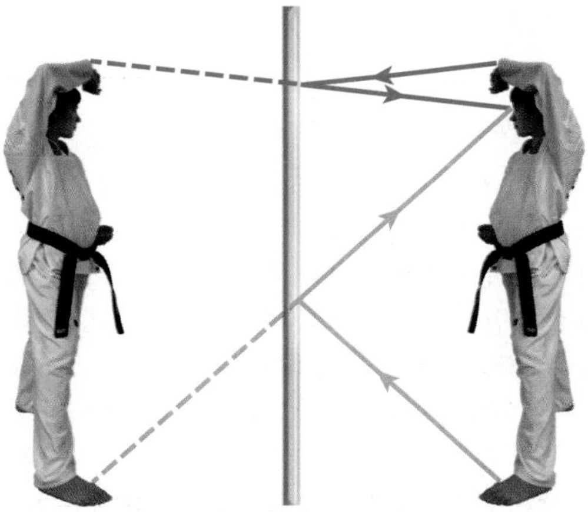

Plane Mirrors

Did you look into a mirror this morning to comb your hair or brush your teeth? If you did, you probably used a plane mirror. A **plane mirror** is a flat sheet of glass that has a smooth, silver-colored coating on one side. Often the coating is on the back of the mirror to protect it from damage. When light strikes a mirror, the coating reflects the light. Because the coating is smooth, regular reflection occurs and a clear image forms. An **image** is a copy of an object formed by reflected or refracted rays of light.

What Kind of Image Forms The image you see in a plane mirror is a **virtual image**—an upright image that forms where light seems to come from. "Virtual" describes something that does not really exist. Your image appears to be behind the mirror, but you can't reach behind the mirror and touch it.

A plane mirror produces a virtual image that is upright and the same size as the object. But the image is not quite the same as the object. The left and right of the image are reversed. For example, when you look in a mirror, your right hand appears to be a left hand in the image.

How Images Form Figure 8 shows how a plane mirror forms an image. Some light rays from the karate student strike the mirror and reflect toward his eye. Even though the rays are reflected, the student's brain treats them as if they had come from behind the mirror. The dashed lines show where the light rays appear to come from. Because the light appears to come from behind the mirror, this is where the student's image appears to be located.

Reading Checkpoint **Where does an image in a plane mirror appear to be located?**

FIGURE 9
Focal Point of a Concave Mirror
A concave mirror reflects rays of light parallel to the optical axis back through the focal point.

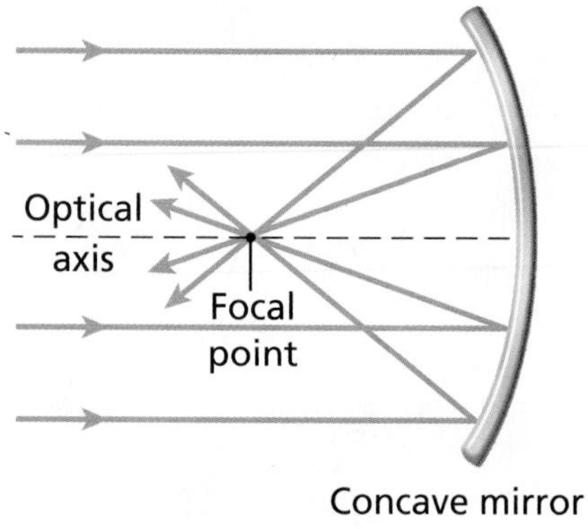

Concave Mirrors

A mirror with a surface that curves inward like the inside of a bowl is a **concave mirror.** Figure 9 shows how a concave mirror can reflect parallel rays of light so that they meet at a point. Notice that the rays of light shown are parallel to the optical axis. The **optical axis** is an imaginary line that divides a mirror in half, much like the Equator that divides Earth into northern and southern halves. The point at which rays parallel to the optical axis meet is called the **focal point.** The location of the focal point depends on the shape of the mirror. The more curved the mirror is, the closer the focal point is to the mirror.

Representing How Images Form Ray diagrams are used to show where a focused image forms in a concave mirror. A ray diagram shows rays of light coming from points on the object. Two rays coming from one point on the object meet or appear to meet at the corresponding point on the image. Figure 10 shows how a ray diagram is drawn.

FIGURE 10
Drawing a Ray Diagram

Ray diagrams show where an image forms and the size of the image. The steps below show how to draw a ray diagram.

1. Draw a red ray from a point on the object (point **A**) to the mirror. Make this ray parallel to the optical axis. Then draw the reflected ray, which passes through the focal point.
2. Draw the green ray from the same point on the object to the mirror. Draw this ray as if it comes from the focal point. Then draw the reflected ray, which is parallel to the optical axis.
3. Draw dashed lines behind the mirror to show where the reflected rays appear to come from. The corresponding point on the image is located where the dashed lines cross.

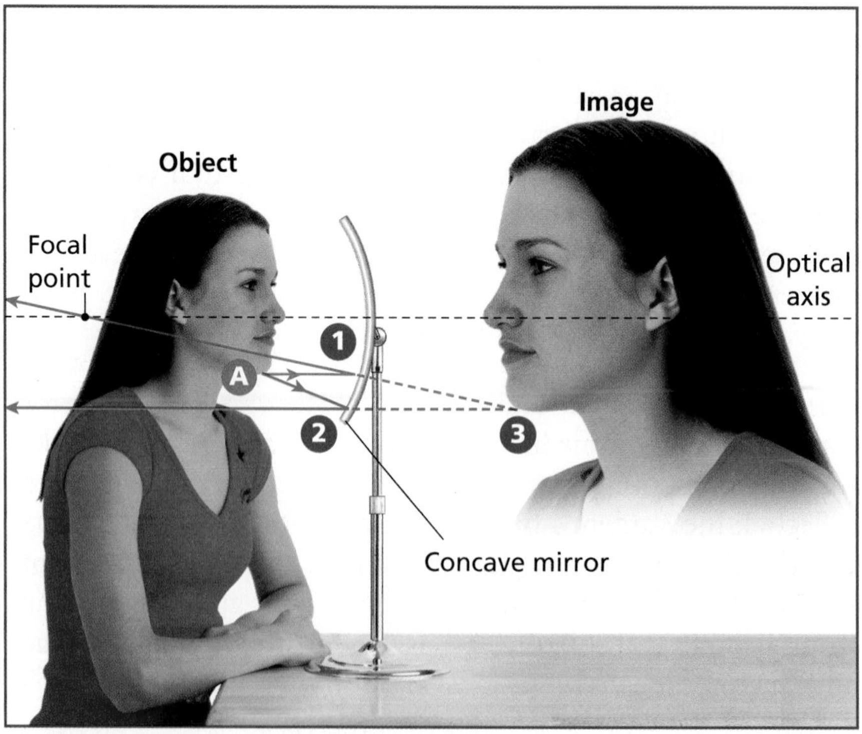

FIGURE 11
Images in Concave Mirrors
The type of image formed depends on the location of the object.
Interpreting Diagrams *When light rays actually meet, what kind of image is formed?*

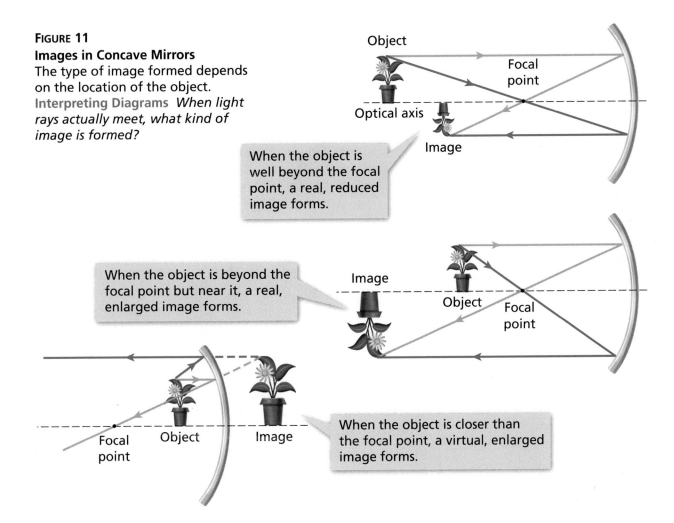

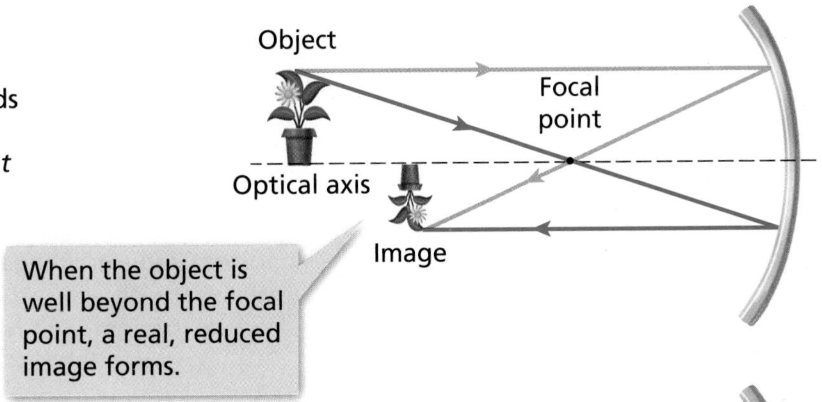
Object
Focal point
Optical axis
Image
When the object is well beyond the focal point, a real, reduced image forms.

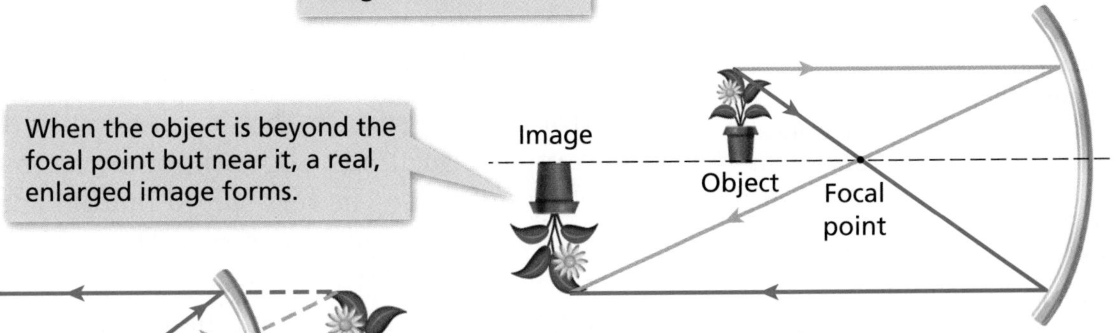
When the object is beyond the focal point but near it, a real, enlarged image forms.
Image
Object
Focal point

Focal point
Object
Image
When the object is closer than the focal point, a virtual, enlarged image forms.

Determining the Type of Image The type of image that is formed by a concave mirror depends on the location of the object. **Concave mirrors can form either virtual images or real images.** If the object is farther away from the mirror than the focal point, the reflected rays form a real image as shown in Figure 11. A **real image** forms when rays actually meet. Real images are upside down. A real image may be larger or smaller than the object.

If the object is between the mirror and the focal point, the reflected rays form a virtual image. The image appears to be behind the mirror and is upright. Virtual images formed by a concave mirror are always larger than the object. Concave mirrors produce the magnified images you see in a makeup mirror.

If an object is placed at the focal point, no image forms. But if a light source is placed at the focal point, the mirror can project parallel rays of light. A car headlight, for example, has a light bulb at the focal point of a concave mirror. Light hits the mirror, forming a beam of light that shines on the road ahead.

Go Online
active art
For: Mirrors activity
Visit: PHSchool.com
Web Code: cgp-5042

Reading Checkpoint **What is a real image?**

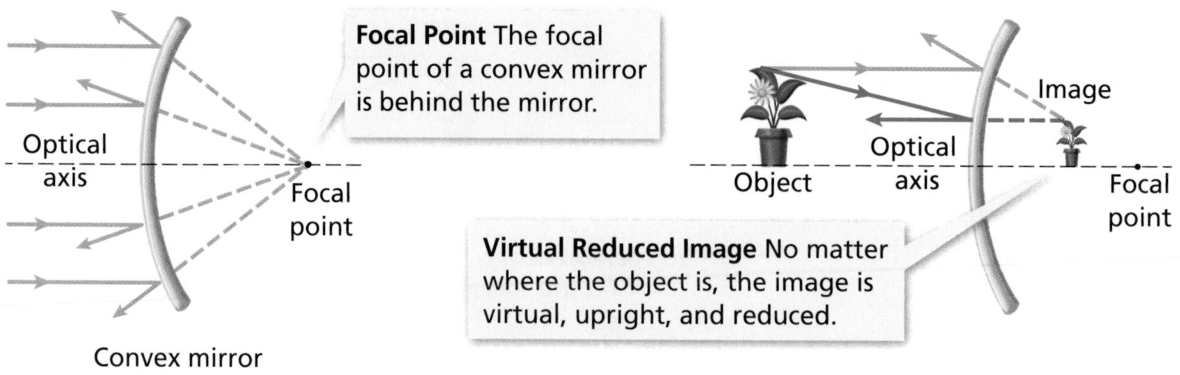

Optical axis
Focal point
Convex mirror
Focal Point The focal point of a convex mirror is behind the mirror.
Image
Object
Optical axis
Focal point
Virtual Reduced Image No matter where the object is, the image is virtual, upright, and reduced.

FIGURE 12
Convex Mirrors
Light rays parallel to the optical axis reflect as if they came from the focal point behind the mirror. The image formed by a convex mirror is always virtual.
Making Generalizations *Describe the directions of the parallel rays reflected by a convex mirror.*

Convex Mirrors

A mirror with a surface that curves outward is called a **convex mirror.** Figure 12 shows how convex mirrors reflect parallel rays of light. The rays spread out but appear to come from a focal point behind the mirror. The focal point of a convex mirror is the point from which the rays appear to come. **Because the rays never meet, images formed by convex mirrors are always virtual and smaller than the object.**

Perhaps you have seen this warning on a car mirror: "Objects in mirror are closer than they appear." Convex mirrors are used in cars as passenger-side mirrors. The advantage of a convex mirror is that it allows you to see a larger area than you can with a plane mirror. The disadvantage is that the image is reduced in size, so it appears to be farther away than it actually is.

Reading Checkpoint **Where are convex mirrors typically used?**

Section 2 Assessment

Target Reading Skill

Comparing and Contrasting Use your Venn diagram about mirrors to help you answer Question 2 below.

Reviewing Key Concepts

1. a. **Reviewing** What are two kinds of reflection?
   b. **Explaining** Explain how both kinds of reflection obey the law of reflection.
   c. **Inferring** Why is an image clear in a shiny spoon but fuzzy in a tarnished spoon?
2. a. **Defining** What is an image?
   b. **Classifying** Which mirrors can form real images? Which can form virtual images?
   c. **Comparing and Contrasting** How are images in concave mirrors like images in convex mirrors? How are they different?

Writing in Science

Dialogue At a funhouse mirror, your younger brother notices he can make his image disappear as he walks toward the mirror. He asks you to explain, but your answer leads to more questions. Write the dialogue that might take place between you and your brother.

Section 3 Refraction and Lenses

Reading Preview

Key Concepts

- Why do light rays bend when they enter a medium at an angle?
- What determines the types of images formed by convex and concave lenses?

Key Terms

- index of refraction
- mirage
- lens
- convex lens
- concave lens

Target Reading Skill

Asking Questions Before you read, preview the red headings. In a graphic organizer like the one below, ask a *what, when, where* or *how* question for each heading. As you read, write the answers to your questions.

Refraction and Lenses

Question	Answer
When does refraction occur?	Refraction occurs . . .

Lab zone Discover Activity

How Can You Make an Image Appear?

1. Stand about 2 meters from a window. Hold a hand lens up to your eye and look through it. What do you see? **CAUTION:** *Do not look at the sun.*
2. Move the lens farther away from your eye. What changes do you notice?
3. Now hold the lens between the window and a sheet of paper, but very close to the paper. Slowly move the lens away from the paper and toward the window. Keep watching the paper. What do you see? What happens as you move the lens?

Think It Over

Observing How is an image formed on a sheet of paper? Describe the image. Is it real or virtual? How do you know?

A fish tank can play tricks on you. If you look through the side of a fish tank, a fish seems closer than if you look over the top. If you look through the corner, you may see the same fish twice. You see one image of the fish through the front of the tank and another through the side. The two images appear in different places! How can this happen?

FIGURE 13
Optical Illusion in a Fish Tank
There is only one fish in this tank, but refraction makes it look as though there are two.

Math Analyzing Data

Bending Light

The index of refraction of a medium is a measure of how much light bends as it travels from air into the medium. The table shows the index of refraction of some common mediums.

1. **Interpreting Data** Which medium causes the greatest change in the direction of a light ray?
2. **Interpreting Data** According to the table, which tends to bend light more: solids or liquids?
3. **Predicting** Would you expect light to bend if it entered corn oil at an angle after traveling through glycerol? Explain.

Index of Refraction

Medium	Index of Refraction
Air (gas)	1.00
Water (liquid)	1.33
Ethyl alcohol (liquid)	1.36
Quartz (solid)	1.46
Corn oil (liquid)	1.47
Glycerol (liquid)	1.47
Glass, crown (solid)	1.52
Sodium chloride (solid)	1.54
Zircon (solid)	1.92
Diamond (solid)	2.42

Refraction of Light

Refraction can cause you to see something that may not actually be there. As you look at a fish in a tank, the light coming from the fish to your eye bends as it passes through three different mediums. The mediums are water, the glass of the tank, and air. As the light passes from one medium to the next, it refracts. **When light rays enter a medium at an angle, the change in speed causes the rays to bend, or change direction.**

Refraction in Different Mediums Some mediums cause light to bend more than others, as shown in Figure 14. When light passes from air into water, the light slows down. Light slows down even more when it passes from water into glass. When light passes from glass back into air, the light speeds up. Light travels fastest in air, a little slower in water, and slower still in glass. Notice that the ray that leaves the glass is traveling in the same direction as it was before it entered the water.

Glass causes light to bend more than either air or water. Another way to say this is that glass has a higher index of refraction than either air or water. A material's **index of refraction** is a measure of how much a ray of light bends when it enters that material. The higher the index of refraction of a medium, the more it bends light. The index of refraction of water is 1.33, and the index of refraction of glass is about 1.5. So light is bent more by glass than by water.

FIGURE 14
Refraction of Light
As light passes from a less dense medium into a more dense medium, it slows down and is refracted.

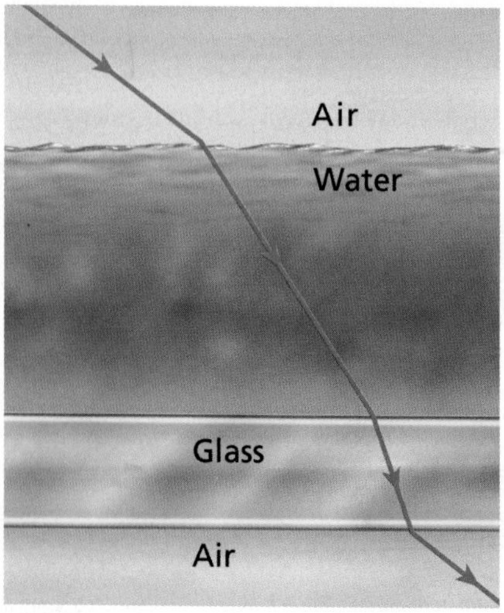

Prisms and Rainbows Recall that when white light enters a prism, each wavelength is refracted by a different amount. The longer the wavelength, the less the wave is bent by a prism. Red, with the longest wavelength, is refracted the least. Violet, with the shortest wavelength, is refracted the most. This difference in refraction causes white light to spread out into the colors of the spectrum—red, orange, yellow, green, blue, and violet.

The same process occurs in water droplets suspended in the air. When white light from the sun shines through the droplets, a rainbow may appear. The water droplets act like tiny prisms, refracting and reflecting the light and separating the colors.

FIGURE 15
Rainbows
A rainbow forms when sunlight is refracted and reflected by tiny water droplets. **Observing** *What is the order of colors in a rainbow?*

Mirages You're traveling in a car on a hot day, and you notice that the road ahead looks wet. Yet when you get there, the road is dry. Did the puddles dry up? No, the puddles were never there! You saw a **mirage** (mih RAHJ)—an image of a distant object caused by refraction of light. The puddles on the road are light rays from the sky that are refracted to your eyes.

Figure 16 shows a mirage. Notice the shiny white areas on the road behind the white car. The air just above the road is hotter than the air higher up. Light travels faster in hot air. So, light rays from the white car that travel toward the road are bent upward by the hot air. Your brain assumes that the rays traveled in a straight line. So the rays look as if they have reflected off a smooth surface. What you see is a mirage.

Reading Checkpoint **What causes a mirage?**

FIGURE 16
Mirages
The puddles and white reflections on the road are mirages. Light refracts as it goes from hot air to cool air. The refracted light appears to come from the ground.

FIGURE 17
Convex and Concave Lenses
A convex lens can focus parallel rays at a focal point. A concave lens causes parallel rays to spread apart.

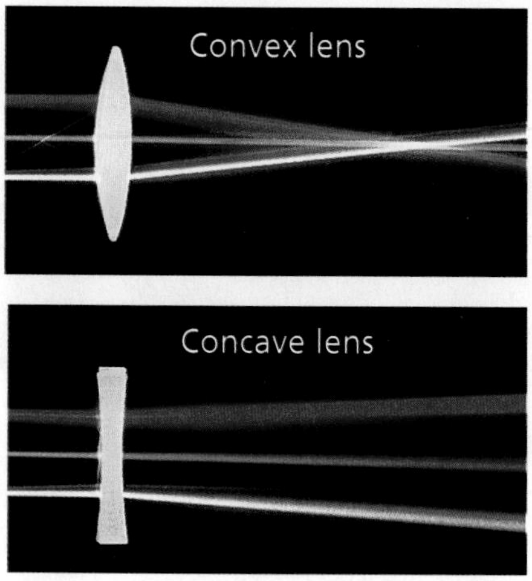

Lenses

Anytime you look through binoculars, a camera, or eyeglasses, you are using lenses to bend light. A **lens** is a curved piece of glass or other transparent material that is used to refract light. A lens forms an image by refracting light rays that pass through it. Like mirrors, lenses can have different shapes. The type of image formed by a lens depends on the shape of the lens and the position of the object.

Convex Lenses A **convex lens** is thicker in the center than at the edges. As light rays parallel to the optical axis pass through a convex lens, they are bent toward the center of the lens. The rays meet at the focal point of the lens and continue to travel beyond. The more curved the lens, the more it refracts light. A convex lens acts somewhat like a concave mirror, because it focuses rays of light.

An object's position relative to the focal point determines whether a convex lens forms a real image or a virtual image. Figure 18 shows that if the object is farther away than the focal point, the refracted rays form a real image on the other side of the lens. If the object is between the lens and the focal point, a virtual image forms on the same side of the lens as the object.

FIGURE 18
Images in Convex Lenses
The type of image formed by a convex lens depends on the object's position.

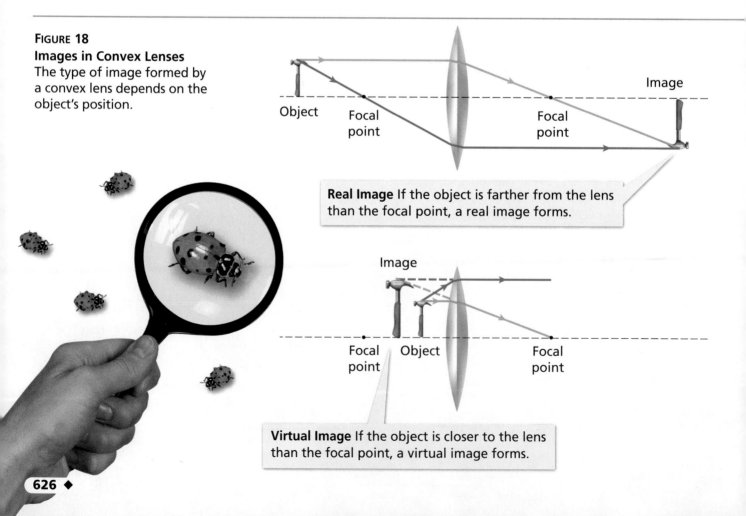

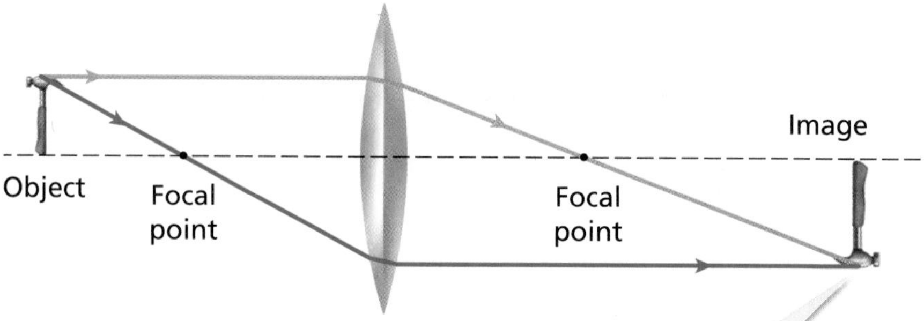

Real Image If the object is farther from the lens than the focal point, a real image forms.

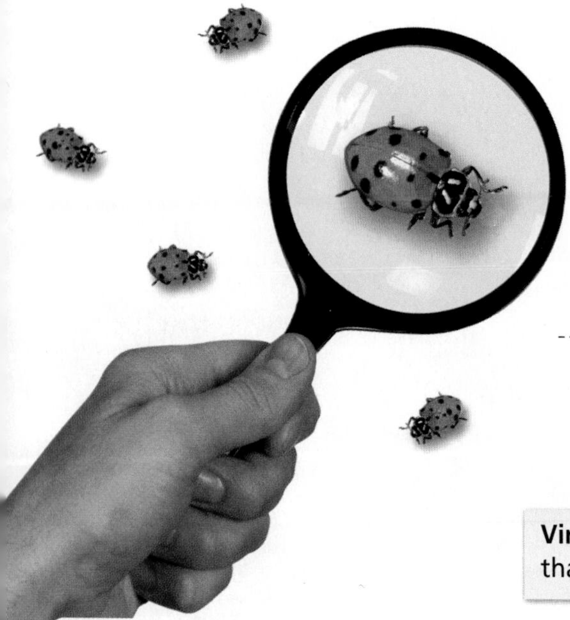

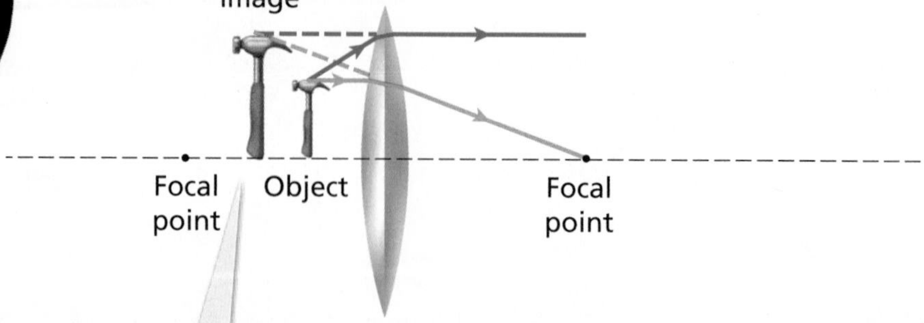

Virtual Image If the object is closer to the lens than the focal point, a virtual image forms.

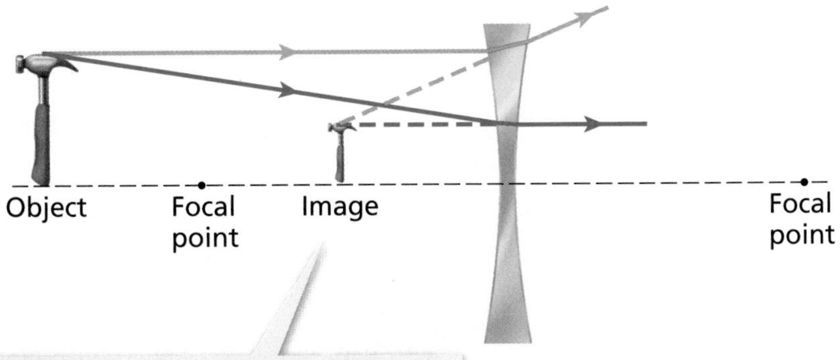

Virtual, Reduced Image Wherever the object is placed, a virtual image forms.

FIGURE 19
Images in Concave Lenses
A concave lens produces virtual images that are upright and smaller than the object.
Interpreting Diagrams *Why can a concave lens only form a virtual image?*

Go Online
active art

For: Lenses activity
Visit: PHSchool.com
Web Code: cgp-5042

Concave Lenses A **concave lens** is thinner in the center than at the edges. When light rays traveling parallel to the optical axis pass through a concave lens, they bend away from the optical axis and never meet. **A concave lens can produce only virtual images because parallel light rays passing through the lens never meet.**

Figure 19 shows how an image forms in a concave lens. The virtual image is located where the light rays appear to come from. The image is always upright and smaller than the object.

Reading Checkpoint What is the shape of a concave lens?

Section 3 Assessment

Target Reading Skill **Asking Questions** Use the answers to the questions you wrote about the headings to help you answer the questions below.

Reviewing Key Concepts

1. a. **Identifying** What is a material's index of refraction?
   b. **Relating Cause and Effect** What causes light rays to bend when they enter a new medium at an angle?
   c. **Predicting** If a glass prism were placed in a medium such as water, would it separate white light into different colors? Explain.
2. a. **Defining** What is a lens?
   b. **Comparing and Contrasting** Describe the shapes of a concave lens and a convex lens.
   c. **Interpreting Diagrams** Use Figure 18 to explain how you can tell whether a convex lens will form a real or virtual image.

Lab zone **At-Home Activity**

Bent Pencil Here's how you can bend a pencil without touching it. Put a pencil in a glass of water so that it is half in and half out of the water. Have your family members look at the pencil from the side. Using your understanding of refraction, explain to your family why the pencil appears as it does.

Looking at Images

Problem

How does the distance between an object and a convex lens affect the image formed?

Skills Focus

controlling variables, interpreting data

Materials

- tape
- convex lens
- cardboard stand
- blank sheet of paper
- light bulb and socket
- clay, for holding the lens
- battery and wires
- meter stick
- centimeter ruler

Procedure

1. Tape the paper onto the cardboard stand.
2. Place a lit bulb more than 2 m from the paper. Use the lens to focus light from the bulb onto the paper. Measure the distance from the lens to the paper. This is the approximate focal length of the lens you are using.
3. Copy the data table into your notebook.
4. Now place the bulb more than twice the focal length away from the lens. Adjust the cardboard until the image is focused. Record the size of the image on the paper and note the orientation of the image. Record the distance from the bulb to the lens and from the lens to the cardboard.
5. Now, move the bulb so that it is just over one focal length away from the lens. Record the position and size of the image.

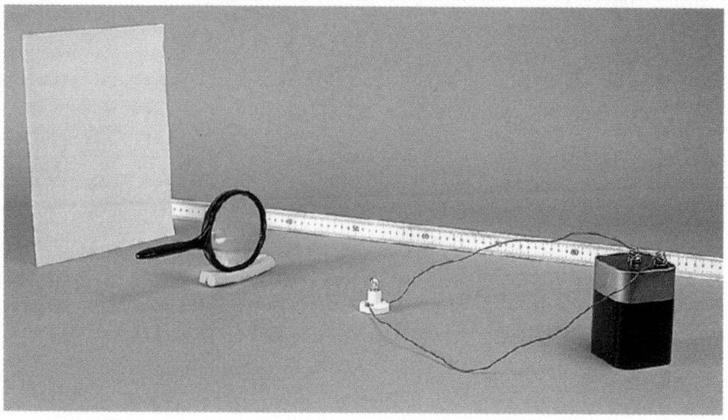

Analyze and Conclude

1. **Controlling Variables** Make a list of the variables in this experiment. Which variables did you keep constant? Which was the manipulated variable? Which were the responding variables?
2. **Observing** What happened to the position of the image as the bulb moved toward the lens?
3. **Interpreting Data** Was the image formed by the convex lens always enlarged? If not, under what conditions was the image reduced?
4. **Predicting** What would happen if you look through the lens at the bulb when it is closer to the lens than the focal point? Explain your prediction.
5. **Communicating** Write a paragraph explaining how the distance between an object and a convex lens affects the image formed. Use ray diagrams to help you summarize your results.

Design an Experiment

Design an experiment to study images formed by convex lenses with different thicknesses. How does the lens thickness affect the position and size of the images? *Obtain your teacher's permission before carrying out your investigation.*

Data Table			
Focal Length of Lens: ____ cm		Height of Bulb: ____ cm	
Distance From Bulb to Lens (cm)	Distance From Lens to Cardboard (cm)	Image Orientation (upright or upside down)	Image Size (height in cm)

Section 4

Integrating Life Science

Seeing Light

Reading Preview

Key Concepts

- How do you see objects?
- What types of lenses are used to correct vision problems?

Key Terms

- cornea • pupil • iris • retina
- rods • cones • optic nerve
- nearsighted • farsighted

Target Reading Skill

Sequencing A sequence is the order in which the steps in a process occur. As you read, make a flowchart that shows how you see objects. Put the steps of the process in separate boxes in the flowchart in the order in which they occur.

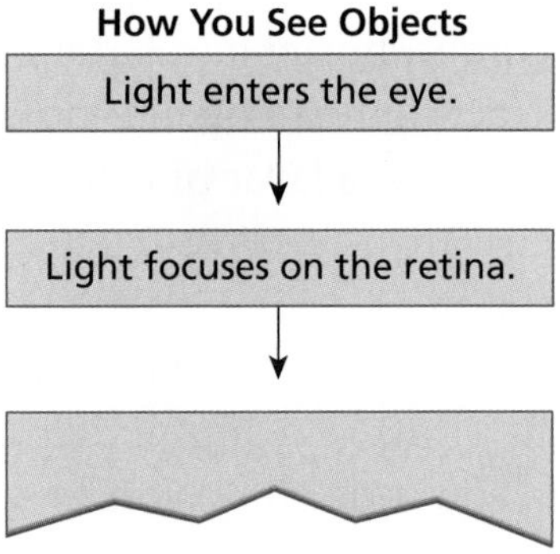
How You See Objects
Light enters the eye.
Light focuses on the retina.

Lab zone Discover Activity

Can You See Everything With One Eye?

1. Write an X and an O on a sheet of paper. The O should be about 5 cm to the right of the X.
2. Hold the sheet of paper at arm's length.
3. Close or cover your left eye. Stare at the X with your right eye.
4. Slowly move the paper toward your face while staring at the X. What do you notice?
5. Repeat the activity, keeping both eyes open. What difference do you notice?

Think It Over

Posing Questions Write two questions about vision that you could investigate using the X and the O.

The pitcher goes into her windup, keeping her eye on the strike zone. The batter watches the pitcher release the ball and then swings. Crack! She drops the bat and sprints toward first base. From your seat, you watch the ball travel toward the outfield. Will it be a base hit? The left fielder watches the ball speed toward her. It's over her head for a double!

Players and spectators alike followed the first rule of baseball: Keep your eye on the ball. As the ball moves near and far, your eyes must adjust continuously to keep it in focus. Fortunately, this change in focus happens automatically.

Keep your eye on the ball! ▶

Lab zone Try This Activity

True Colors

When you stare too long at a color, the cones in your eyes get tired.

1. Stare at the bottom right star of the flag for at least 60 seconds. Do not move your eyes or blink during that time.

2. Now stare at a sheet of blank white paper.

Observing What do you see when you look at the white paper? How are the colors you see related to the colors in the original flag?

The Human Eye

Your eyes allow you to sense light. The eye is a complex structure with many parts, as you can see in Figure 20. Each part plays a role in vision. **You see objects when a process occurs that involves both your eyes and your brain.**

Light Enters the Eye Light enters the eye through the transparent front surface called the **cornea** (KAWR nee uh). The cornea protects the eye. It also acts as a lens to help focus light rays.

After passing through the cornea, light enters the pupil, the part of the eye that looks black. The **pupil** is an opening through which light enters the inside of the eye. In dim light, the pupil becomes larger to allow in more light. In bright light, the pupil becomes smaller to allow in less light. The **iris** is a ring of muscle that contracts and expands to change the size of the pupil. The iris gives the eye its color. In most people the iris is brown; in others it is blue, green, or hazel.

An Image Forms After entering the pupil, the light passes through the lens. The lens is a convex lens that refracts light to form an image on the lining of your eyeball. Muscles, called ciliary muscles, hold the lens in place behind the pupil. When you focus on a distant object, the ciliary muscles relax, and the lens becomes longer and thinner. When you focus on a nearby object, the muscles contract, and the lens becomes shorter and fatter.

When the cornea and the lens refract light, an upside-down image is formed on the retina. The **retina** is a layer of cells that lines the inside of the eyeball. (Cells are the tiny structures that make up living things.)

The retina is made up of tiny, light-sensitive cells called rods and cones. **Rods** are cells that contain a pigment that responds to small amounts of light. The rods allow you to see in dim light. **Cones** are cells that respond to color. They may detect red light, green light, or blue light. Cones respond best in bright light. Both rods and cones help change images on the retina into signals that then travel to the brain.

A Signal Goes to the Brain The rods and cones send signals to the brain along a short, thick nerve called the **optic nerve.** The optic nerve begins at the blind spot, an area of the retina so called because it has no rods or cones. Your brain interprets the signals as an upright image. It also combines the images from each of your eyes into a single three-dimensional image.

Reading Checkpoint Where does an image form in the eye?

FIGURE 20
The Human Eye

The eye is a complex structure with many parts that allow you to see.
Relating Cause and Effect *What is the main function of each part of the eye?*

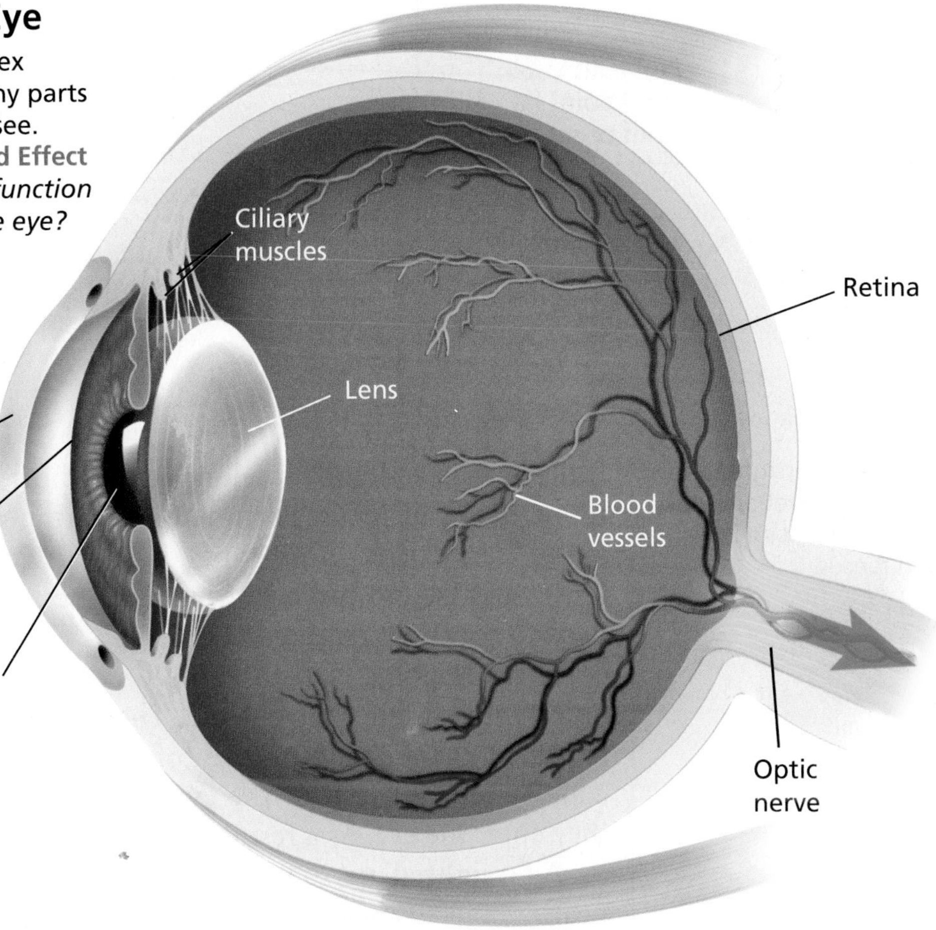

Pupil and Iris
The iris controls the size of the pupil, which determines how much light enters the eye.

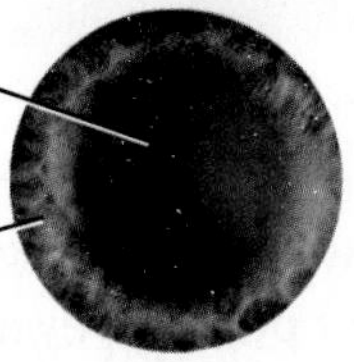

Dim Light The iris contracts, making the pupil large.

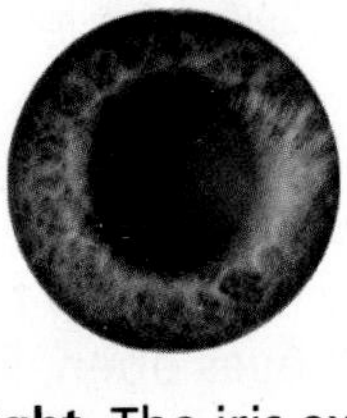

Bright Light The iris expands, making the pupil small.

Lens and Ciliary Muscles
The ciliary muscles change the shape of the lens.

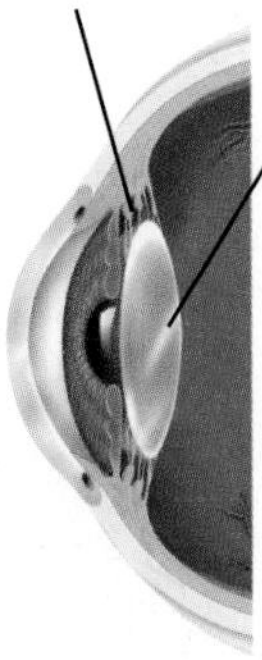

Seeing Far Away The ciliary muscles relax, making the lens thin.

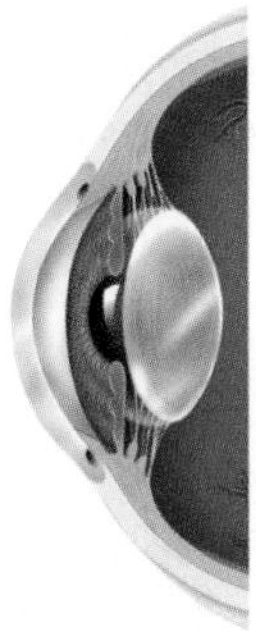

Seeing Close Up The ciliary muscles contract, making the lens thick.

Retina
The retina has two kinds of cells that detect light. The rods respond to dim light. The cones respond to red, green, and blue light.

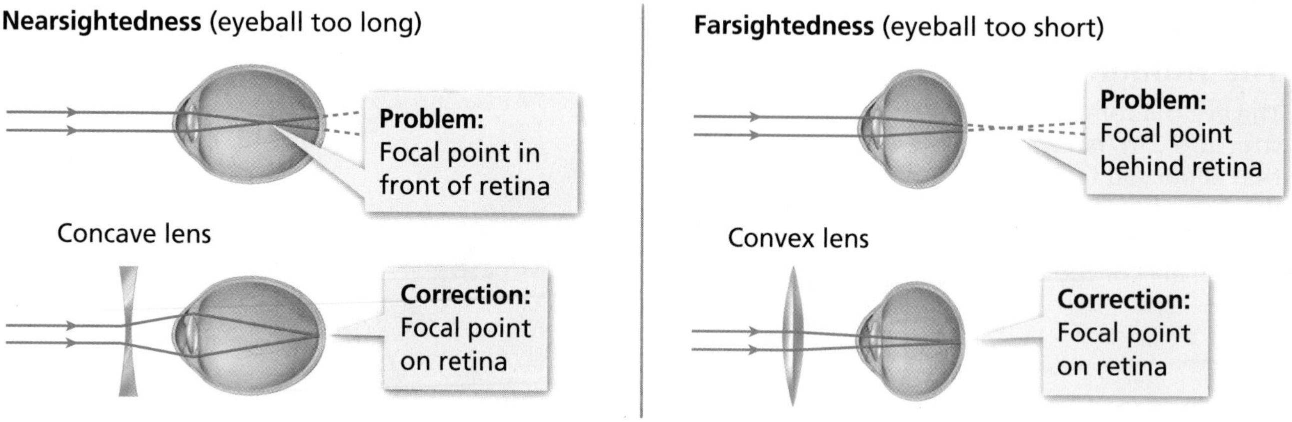

FIGURE 21
Vision Correction
Nearsightedness and farsightedness are caused when the eyeball is too long or too short. Both can be corrected with lenses.

Correcting Vision

If the eyeball is slightly too long or too short, the image on the retina is out of focus. Fortunately, wearing glasses or contact lenses can correct this type of vision problem. **Concave lenses are used to correct nearsightedness. Convex lenses are used to correct farsightedness.**

A **nearsighted** person can see nearby things clearly, but objects at a distance are blurred. The eyeball is too long, so the lens focuses the image in front of the retina. To correct this, a concave lens in front of the eye spreads out light rays before they enter the eye. As a result, the image forms on the retina.

A **farsighted** person can see distant objects clearly, but nearby objects appear blurry. The eyeball is too short, so the image that falls on the retina is out of focus. A convex lens corrects this by bending light rays toward each other before they enter the eye. An image then focuses on the retina.

Section 4 Assessment

Target Reading Skill **Sequencing** Refer to your flowchart about how you see as you answer Question 1.

Reviewing Key Concepts

1. a. **Identifying** Which parts of your body are involved in seeing objects?
   b. **Explaining** How is an image formed on the retina?
   c. **Sequencing** What happens to light after it strikes the retina?
2. a. **Reviewing** What types of lenses help correct vision problems?
   b. **Describing** Describe a nearsighted person's eye.
   c. **Comparing and Contrasting** With uncorrected vision, where does an image form in a nearsighted person's eye? In a farsighted person's eye?

Lab zone At-Home Activity

Optical Illusion Look through a cardboard tube with your right eye. Hold your left hand against the far end of the tube with the palm facing you. Keeping both eyes open, look at a distant object. Draw what you see. What do you think causes this illusion?

Section 5

Using Light

Reading Preview

Key Concepts

- How are lenses used in telescopes, microscopes, and cameras?
- What makes up laser light, and how is it used?
- Why can optical fibers carry laser beams a long distance?

Key Terms

- telescope
- refracting telescope
- objective
- eyepiece
- reflecting telescope
- microscope
- camera
- laser
- hologram
- optical fiber
- total internal reflection

Target Reading Skill

Building Vocabulary A definition states the meaning of a word or a phrase by telling about its most important feature or function. Carefully read the definition of each Key Term and also read the neighboring sentences. Then write a definition of each Key Term in your own words.

Lab zone Discover Activity

How Does a Pinhole Viewer Work?

1. Carefully use a pin to make a tiny hole in the center of the bottom of a paper cup.
2. Place a piece of wax paper over the open end of the cup. Hold the paper in place with a rubber band.
3. Turn off the room lights. Point the end of the cup with the hole in it at a bright window. **CAUTION:** *Do not look directly at the sun.*
4. Look at the image on the wax paper.

Think It Over

Classifying Describe the image you see. Is it upside down or right-side up? Is it smaller or larger than the actual object? What type of image is it?

Have you ever seen photos of the moons of Jupiter? Have you ever thought it would be exciting to fly close to the rings of Saturn? You know that traveling in space has been done for only a few decades. But you might be surprised to know that the moons of Jupiter and the rings of Saturn had not been seen before the year 1600. It was only about 1607 that a new invention, the telescope, made those objects visible to people.

Since the 1600s, astronomers have built more powerful telescopes that allow them to see objects in space that are very far from Earth. For example, the star-forming nebula, or cloud of gas and dust in space, shown below is located trillions of kilometers from Earth. It took about 3 million years for light from this nebula to travel to Earth.

Nebula image from the Hubble Space Telescope ▶

Figure 22
Refracting and Reflecting Telescopes
Both reflecting and refracting telescopes gather light from distant objects.

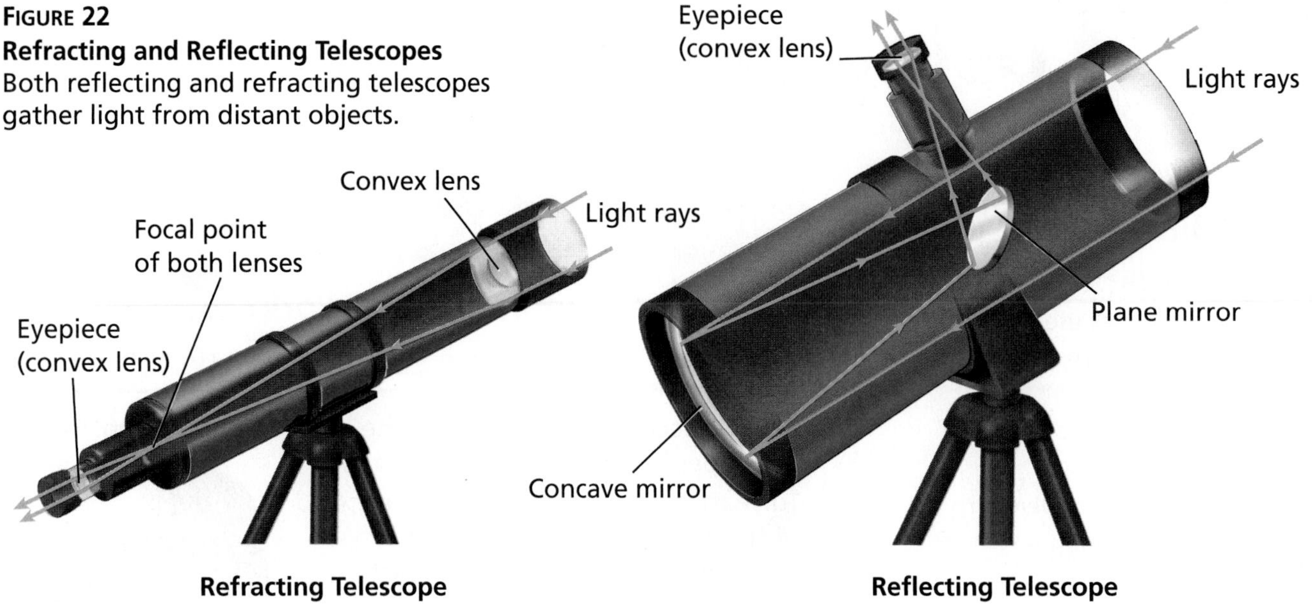

Optical Instruments

A telescope helps you see objects that are far away. But another type of optical instrument, a microscope, helps you see objects that are nearby. Three common types of optical instruments are telescopes, microscopes, and cameras.

Telescopes Distant objects are difficult to see because light from them has spread out by the time it reaches your eyes. Your eyes are too small to gather much light. A **telescope** forms enlarged images of distant objects. **Telescopes use lenses or mirrors to collect and focus light from distant objects.** The most common use of telescopes is to study objects in space.

Figure 22 shows the two main types of telescopes: refracting telescopes and reflecting telescopes. A **refracting telescope** consists of two convex lenses, one at each end of a tube. The larger lens is called the objective. The **objective** gathers the light coming from an object and focuses the rays to form a real image. The lens close to your eye is called the eyepiece. The **eyepiece** magnifies the image so you can see it clearly. The image seen through the refracting telescope in Figure 22 is upside down.

A **reflecting telescope** uses a large concave mirror to gather light. The mirror collects light from distant objects and focuses the rays to form a real image. A small mirror inside the telescope reflects the image to the eyepiece. The images you see through a reflecting telescope are upside down, just like the images seen through a refracting telescope.

Lab zone Try This Activity

What a View!

You can use two hand lenses of different strengths to form an image.

1. Hold the stronger lens close to your eye.
2. Hold the other lens at arm's length.
3. Use your lens combination to view a distant object. **CAUTION:** *Do not look at the sun.* Adjust the distance of the farther lens until the image is clear.

Classifying What type of image do you see? What type of telescope is similar to this lens combination?

Microscopes To look at small, nearby objects, you would use a microscope. A **microscope** is an optical instrument that forms enlarged images of tiny objects. **A microscope uses a combination of lenses to produce and magnify an image.** For example, the microscope shown in Figure 23 uses two convex lenses to magnify an object, or specimen. The specimen is placed near the objective. The objective forms a real, enlarged image of the specimen. Then the eyepiece enlarges the image even more.

Cameras A **camera** uses one or more lenses to focus light, and film to record an image. Figure 24 shows the structure of a camera. Light from an object travels to the camera and passes through the lens. **The lens of the camera focuses light to form a real, upside-down image on film in the back of the camera.** In many cameras, the lens automatically moves closer to or away from the film until the image is focused.

To take a photo, you press a button that briefly opens the shutter, a screen in front of the film. Opening the shutter allows light passing through the lens to hit the film. The diaphragm is a device with a hole that can be made smaller or larger. Changing the size of the hole controls how much light hits the film. This is similar to the way the pupil of your eye changes size.

Reading Checkpoint **What part of a camera controls the amount of light that enters the camera?**

FIGURE 23
Microscope
This microscope uses a combination of lenses to form enlarged images of tiny objects.

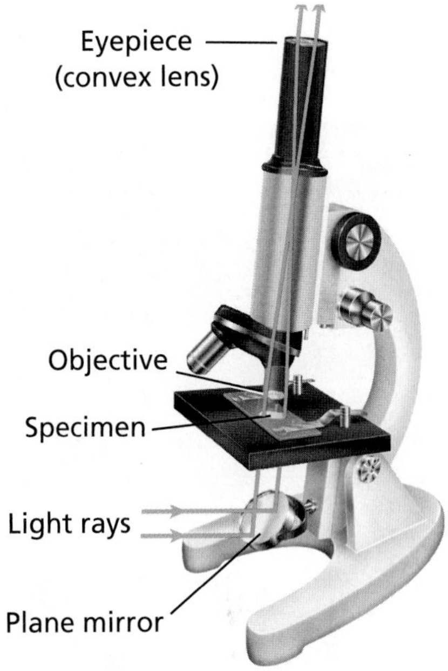

FIGURE 24
Camera
A camera uses a lens to project an image onto film. Interpreting Diagrams *What happens to each light ray as it passes through the lens?*

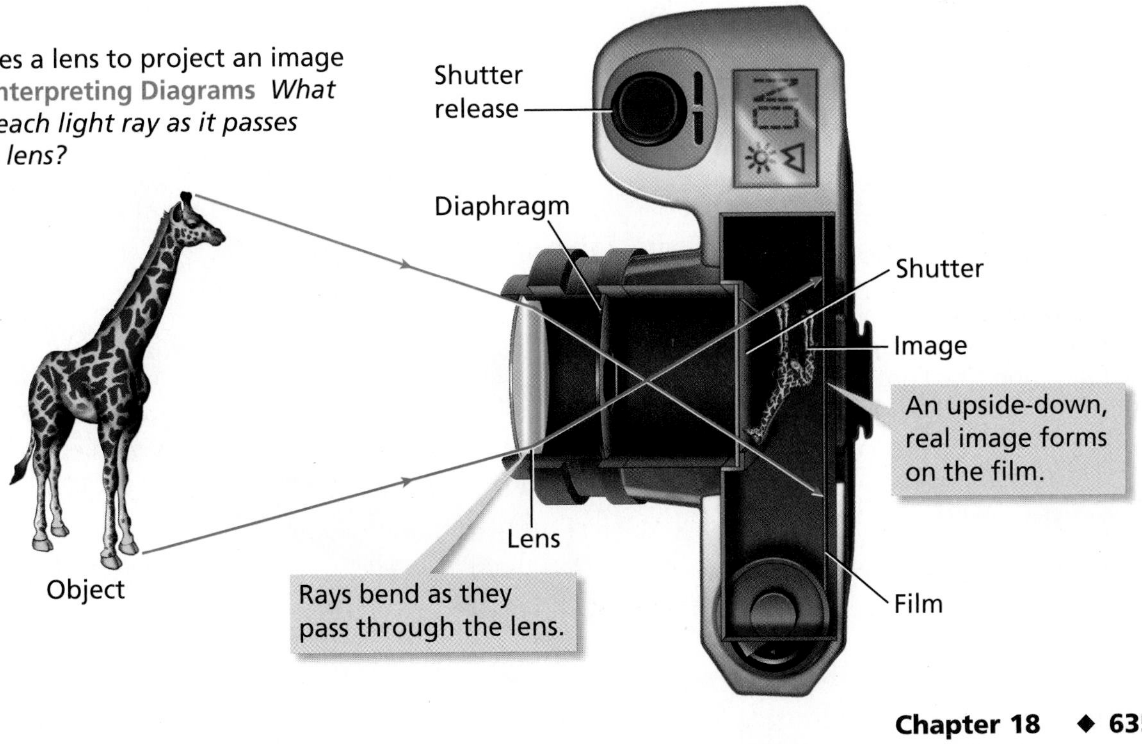

FIGURE 25
Coherent and Incoherent Light
White light is made up of many different wavelengths. Laser light waves all have the same wavelength. **Inferring** *What can you infer about the color of laser light?*

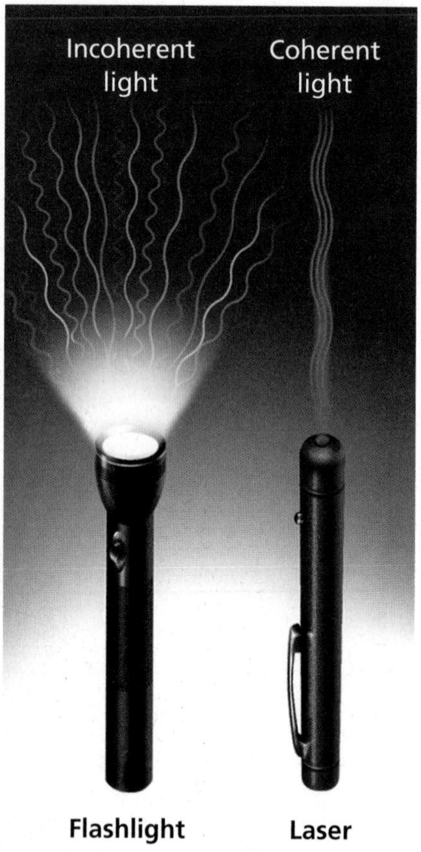
Incoherent light
Coherent light
Flashlight
Laser

Lasers

When you turn on a flashlight, the light spreads out as it travels. Ordinary light is made up of different colors and wavelengths. Laser light is different from ordinary light. **Laser light consists of light waves that all have the same wavelength, or color. The waves are coherent, or in step.** All of the crests of the waves align with one another, as shown in Figure 25.

What Is a Laser? A **laser** is a device that produces a narrow beam of coherent light. The word *laser* comes from a phrase that describes how it works: **l**ight **a**mplification by **s**timulated **e**mission of **r**adiation. *Light amplification* means that the light is strengthened. *Stimulated emission* means that the atoms emit light when exposed to electromagnetic radiation.

Producing Laser Light A helium-neon laser is shown in Figure 26. The laser tube contains a mixture of helium and neon gases. An electric current causes this gas mixture to emit photons. You may recall that a photon is a packet of light energy. The mirrors at both ends of the tube reflect the photons back and forth. As a photon travels back and forth, it may bump into a neon particle. This causes the neon particle to emit a photon with the same energy as the one that caused the collision. Then the two photons travel together in step with one another. This process continues until there is a stream of in-step photons traveling up and down the tube. Some of the light "leaks" through the partially reflecting mirror. This light is the laser beam.

Reading Checkpoint **What is a laser?**

FIGURE 26
Helium-Neon Laser
Photons travel in step up and down the laser tube. The light that comes out of the tube is laser light.

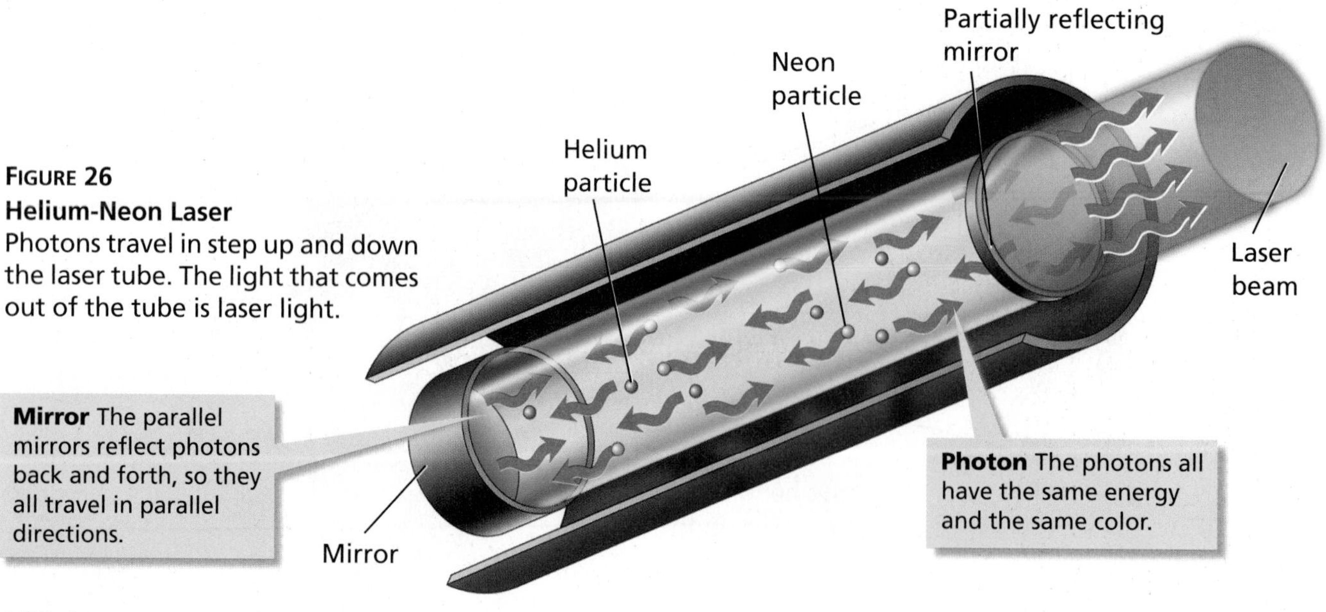
Partially reflecting mirror
Neon particle
Helium particle
Laser beam
Mirror
Mirror The parallel mirrors reflect photons back and forth, so they all travel in parallel directions.
Photon The photons all have the same energy and the same color.

Uses of Lasers

Lasers have many practical uses. Many stores use lasers to scan bar codes. The store's computer then displays the price of the item. Lasers are used in industry to cut through metal. Engineers use laser beams to make sure that surfaces are level and bridges or tunnels are properly aligned. **In addition to their use by stores, industry, and engineers, lasers are used to read information on compact discs, create holograms, and perform surgery.**

Go Online
SciLinks NSTA

For: Links on lasers
Visit: www.SciLinks.org
Web Code: scn-1545

FIGURE 27
Using Lasers

Lasers have become commonplace in everyday living. They are found at home, in stores, and in industry.

▲ Lasers are used for precision cutting in industry.

Scientists use laser scan microscopes to study cells.

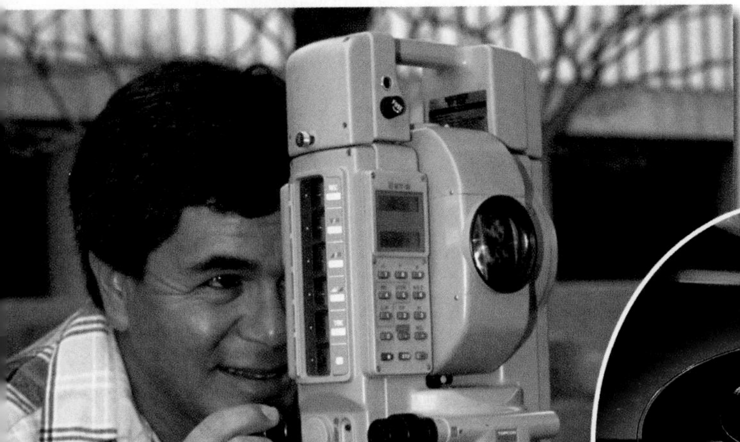

▲ Lasers are used in surveying.

Compact discs (CDs) are read by a laser.

▼ Bar codes are scanned with lasers.

Discovery Channel School

Light

Video Preview
▶ Video Field Trip
Video Assessment

Compact Discs Lasers can be used to store and read information. A compact disc is produced by converting data into electrical signals. The electrical signals are used to control a laser beam, which cuts a pattern of pits on a blank disc. When you play a compact disc or read one with a computer, a laser beam shines on the surface and is reflected. The reflection patterns vary because of the pits. The compact disc player or disc drive changes these patterns into electrical signals. The signals are then converted into sound or computer data.

Holography Check out your local video store or newsstand. Some videos and magazines have pictures that appear to move as you walk by. These pictures are called holograms. A **hologram** is a three-dimensional photograph created by using the light from a laser. The process of making these photographs is called holography.

• Tech & Design in History •

Instruments That Use Light

The development of technologies that use light has changed the way we look at the world and beyond. It has allowed major scientific discoveries.

1286 Spectacles
Italian craftsmen made small disks of glass that could be framed and worn in front of the eyes. Early spectacles consisted of convex lenses. They were used as reading glasses.

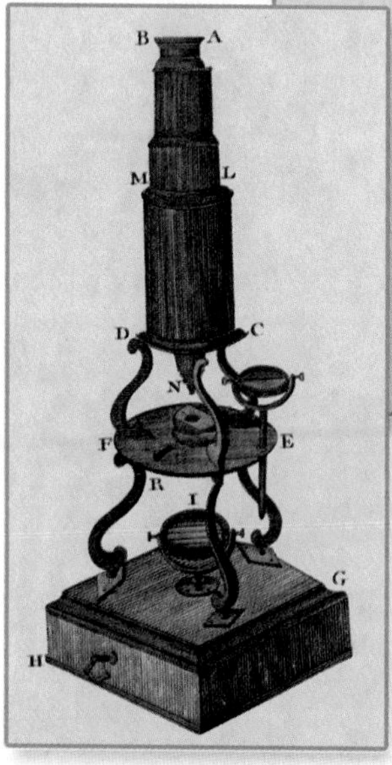

1595 Microscope
The first useful microscope is thought to have been constructed in the Netherlands by Zacharias Jansen or his father, Hans. The Jansen microscope could magnify images up to nine times the size of the object. By the mid-1600s, microscopes looked like the one shown here.

1608 Telescope
The first telescope was made of two convex lenses. From this simple invention the Italian scientist Galileo developed his more powerful telescopes shown here.

1300 | 1400 | 1500 | 1600

Laser Surgery A beam of laser light can be powerful enough to replace a sharp knife. For example, doctors may use lasers instead of scalpels to cut into a person's body. As the laser cuts, it seals the blood vessels. This reduces the amount of blood a patient loses. Wounds from laser surgery usually heal faster than wounds from surgery done with a scalpel.

A common use of laser surgery is to correct vision by reshaping the cornea of the eye. Doctors can also use lasers to repair detached retinas. If the retina falls away from the inside of the eye, the rods and cones can no longer send signals to the brain. This can lead to total or partial blindness. The doctor can use a laser to "weld" or burn the retina back onto the eyeball. Lasers can also be used to destroy or remove skin blemishes and cancerous growths.

Reading Checkpoint **What are three types of surgery done with lasers?**

Writing in Science

Research and Write Find out more about early photography. Then imagine you are a newspaper reporter in 1855 asked to interview a photographer. Write a newspaper article about the photographic processes and the possible uses it might have in the future.

1826 Camera
The earliest camera, the pinhole camera, was adapted to form and record permanent images by Joseph Nicéphore Niépce and Louis-Jacques-Mandé Daguerre of France. This is one of Niépce's earliest photographic images.

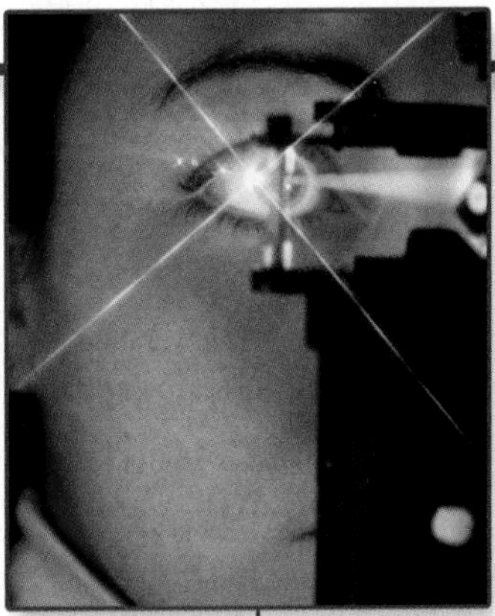

1960 Laser
The first laser, built by American Theodore Maiman, used a rod of ruby to produce light. Since then, lasers have been used in numerous ways, including in engineering, medicine, and communications.

1990 Hubble Space Telescope
This large reflecting telescope was launched by the crew of the space shuttle *Discovery*. It can detect infrared, visible, and ultraviolet rays in space and send pictures back to Earth.

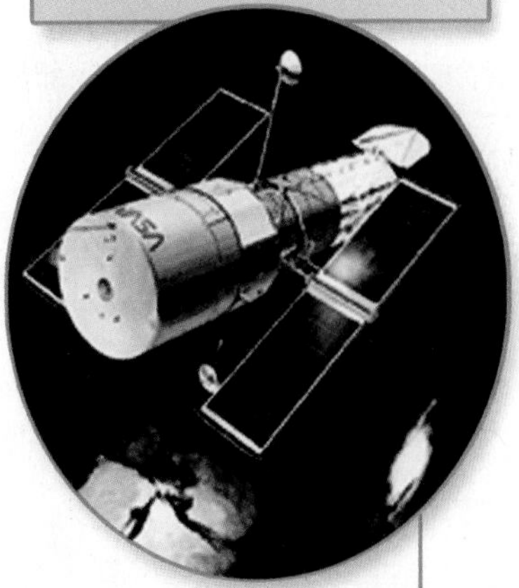

1700 1800 1900 2000

FIGURE 28
Total Internal Reflection
The floodlight in the swimming pool gives off light rays that travel to the surface. If the angle of incidence is great enough, a light ray is completely reflected back into the water.

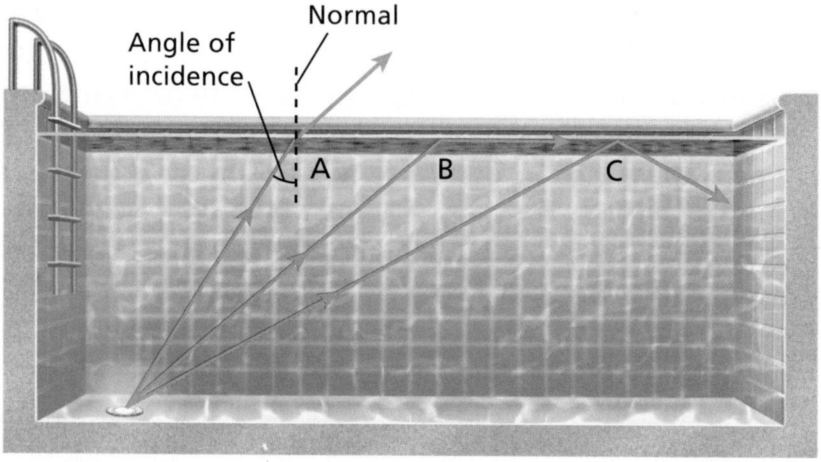

Optical Fibers

Laser beams, like radio waves, can carry signals from one place to another. But, laser beams are not usually sent through the air. Instead, they are sent through optical fibers. **Optical fibers** are long, thin strands of glass or plastic that can carry light for long distances without allowing the light to escape.

Optical fibers can carry a laser beam for long distances because the beam stays totally inside the fiber as it travels. Figure 28 shows how light rays can stay inside a medium and not pass through the surface to the outside. The angle of incidence determines whether or not light passes through the surface.

When ray A strikes the water's surface, some light is reflected, but most passes through and is bent. As the angle of incidence gets larger, the light is bent more and more. Ray B is bent so much that it travels parallel to the surface. If the angle of incidence is great enough, no light passes through the surface. Then all of the light is reflected back into the water, as shown by ray C. This complete reflection of light by the inside surface of a medium is called **total internal reflection.**

Figure 29 shows how total internal reflection allows light to travel a long distance in an optical fiber. Each time the light ray strikes the side of the optical fiber, the angle of incidence is large. Because the angle is large, the light ray is always completely reflected. So, no light can escape through the sides of the optical fiber.

Because the angle of incidence is large, all of the laser light reflects each time it strikes the side of the optical fiber.

FIGURE 29
Optical Fibers
Light travels long distances through optical fibers. **Drawing Conclusions** *Why doesn't light exit through the sides of the optical fiber?*

Medicine Optical fibers are commonly used in medical instruments. Doctors can insert a thin optical fiber inside various parts of the body, such as the heart or the stomach. The optical fiber can be attached to a microscope or a camera. In this way, doctors can examine internal organs without having to perform major surgery.

Doctors often use optical fibers to repair damage to joints. In knee surgery, for example, doctors make small cuts to insert optical fibers and tiny surgical tools. Because the surgery does less damage to the knee, the recovery is easier.

Communications To send signals through optical fibers, the electrical signals that start out over copper wires are changed into pulses of light by tiny lasers. Then the signals can travel over long distances in the optical fiber. Optical fibers have led to great improvements in telephone service, computer networks, and cable television systems. Signals sent over optical fibers are usually faster and clearer than those sent over copper wire. One tiny optical fiber can carry thousands of phone conversations at the same time. Optical fibers are so much thinner than copper wire that many more fibers can be bundled together in the same space.

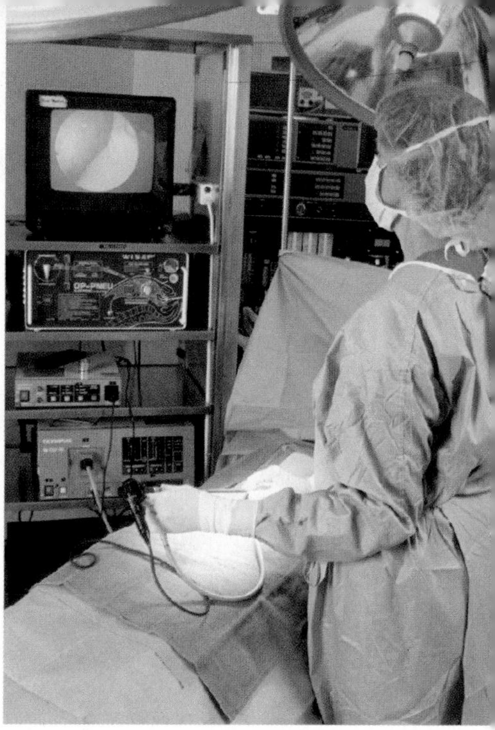

FIGURE 30
Optical-Fiber Surgery
Using optical fibers, surgeons can avoid damaging nearby healthy parts of the body.

Reading Checkpoint **How do optical fibers carry signals?**

Section 5 Assessment

Target Reading Skill Building Vocabulary
Use your definitions to help you answer the questions below.

Reviewing Key Concepts

1. a. Reviewing How are lenses used in telescopes, microscopes, and cameras?
   b. Comparing and Contrasting Compare and contrast how images form in a refracting telescope, a reflecting telescope, and a microscope.
   c. Classifying A pair of binoculars has two lenses in each tube. Which type of optical instrument are the binoculars most similar to?
2. a. Identifying What is laser light?
   b. Summarizing How can laser light be used?
   c. Sequencing How does a laser produce laser light?
3. a. Defining What are optical fibers?
   b. Describing What are three uses of optical fibers?
   c. Relating Cause and Effect Why can optical fibers carry laser beams long distances?

Writing in Science

Advertisement A company has asked you to write an advertisement for its new, easy-to-use camera. In the ad, the company wants you to describe the camera's features so that buyers will understand how the camera works. Be sure to mention the shutter, lens, and diaphragm.

Chapter 18 Study Guide

1 Light and Color

Key Concepts

- When light strikes an object, the light can be reflected, transmitted, or absorbed.
- An opaque object is the color of the light it reflects. A transparent or translucent object is the color of the light it transmits.
- When combined in equal amounts, the three primary colors of light produce white light. As pigments are added together, fewer colors of light are reflected and more are absorbed.

Key Terms

transparent material
translucent material
opaque material
primary colors
secondary color
complementary colors
pigment

2 Reflection and Mirrors

Key Concepts

- There are two types of reflection—regular reflection and diffuse reflection.
- A plane mirror produces a virtual image that is upright and the same size as the object.
- Concave mirrors form virtual or real images. Convex mirrors form only virtual images.

Key Terms

ray
regular reflection
diffuse reflection
plane mirror
image
virtual image
concave mirror
optical axis
focal point
real image
convex mirror

3 Refraction and Lenses

Key Concepts

- A convex lens can form virtual images or real images. A concave lens can produce only virtual images.

Key Terms

index of refraction
mirage
lens
convex lens
concave lens

4 Seeing Light

Key Concepts

- You see objects when a process occurs that involves both your eyes and your brain.
- Convex lenses are used to correct nearsightedness. Concave lenses are used to correct farsightedness.

Key Terms

cornea
pupil
iris
retina
rods
cones
optic nerve
nearsighted
farsighted

5 Using Light

Key Concepts

- Telescopes use lenses or mirrors to collect and focus light from distant objects. A microscope uses a combination of lenses to produce and magnify an image. The lens of a camera focuses light to form a real, upside-down image on film in the back of the camera.
- Laser light consists of light waves that all have the same wavelength, or color. The waves are coherent, or in step.
- In addition to their use by stores, industry, and engineers, lasers are used to read information on compact discs, create holograms, and perform surgery.
- Optical fibers can carry a laser beam for long distances because the beam stays totally inside the fiber as it travels.

Key Terms

telescope
refracting telescope
objective
eyepiece
reflecting telescope
microscope
camera
laser
hologram
optical fiber
total internal reflection

Review and Assessment

Go Online PHSchool.com
For: Self-Assessment
Visit: PHSchool.com
Web Code: cga-5040

Organizing Information

Comparing and Contrasting
Copy the graphic organizer about mirrors and lenses onto a separate sheet of paper. Then complete it and add a title. (For more on Comparing and Contrasting, see the Skills Handbook.)

Mirrors and Lenses

Type of Mirror	Effect on Light Rays	Type of Image
Plane	Regular reflection	a. ___?___
b. ___?___	c. ___?___	Real or virtual
Convex	Spread out	d. ___?___

Type of Lens	Effect on Light Rays	Type of Image
Convex	e. ___?___	f. ___?___
g. ___?___	h. ___?___	Virtual

Reviewing Key Terms

Choose the letter of the best answer.

1. A material that reflects or absorbs all of the light that strikes it is a(n)
   a. translucent material.
   b. opaque material.
   c. transparent material.
   d. polarizing filter.
2. When light bounces off an uneven surface, the result is called
   a. regular reflection.
   b. refraction.
   c. diffuse reflection.
   d. internal reflection.
3. A curved piece of glass or other transparent material that is used to refract light is a
   a. prism. b. lens.
   c. mirage. d. mirror.
4. A ring of muscle that changes the size of the eye's pupil is the
   a. retina.
   b. cornea.
   c. iris.
   d. ciliary muscle.
5. A device that produces coherent light is a(n)
   a. telescope.
   b. microscope.
   c. laser.
   d. optical fiber.

If the statement is true, write *true.* If it is false, change the underlined word or words to make the statement true.

6. Primary colors combine to make any color.
7. Lines that represent light waves are called rays.
8. An upright image that forms where light seems to come from is a virtual image.
9. For a nearsighted person, nearby objects appear blurry.
10. Holograms are long, thin strands of glass or plastic that can carry light for long distances.

Writing in Science

Persuasive Letter Write a short letter to your representative in Congress asking him or her to continue supporting telescopes in space. Include at least two advantages of space telescopes in your letter.

Discovery Channel School

Light
Video Preview
Video Field Trip
▶ Video Assessment

Review and Assessment

Checking Concepts

11. Describe transparent, translucent, and opaque materials. Give an example of each.

12. Why do you see the petals of a rose as red and the leaves as green?

13. What colors can be formed by combining complementary colors?

14. Sketch the optical axis and focal point(s) of a concave mirror and a convex mirror.

15. Describe real and virtual images. How can each type of image be formed by mirrors?

16. How is the index of refraction of a substance related to the speed of light in the substance?

17. Explain why you see a mirage on a hot road.

18. Which parts of the eye help to focus light? Which part carries a signal to the brain?

19. Explain how your eyes are able to clearly see both near and distant objects.

20. How does total internal reflection depend on the angle of incidence of light rays?

Thinking Critically

21. **Classifying** Do the colors shown below represent pigments or colors of light? Explain.

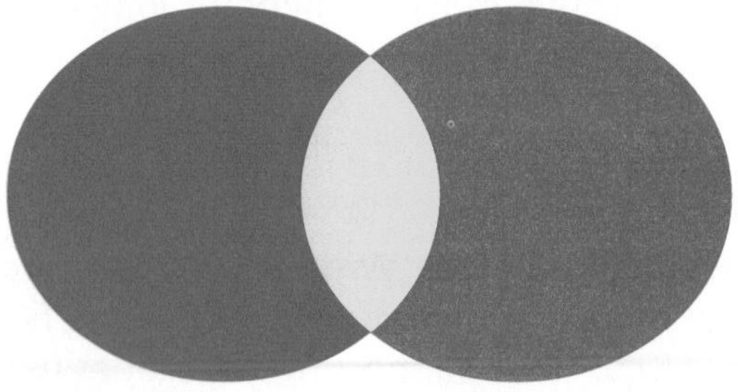

22. **Applying Concepts** Can a plane mirror produce a real image? Explain.

23. **Comparing and Contrasting** How are convex and concave mirrors alike? How are they different?

24. **Inferring** You shine a light through a convex lens so it forms a spot on an index card. Where should the lens and card be located to make the spot as small as possible?

25. **Relating Cause and Effect** Explain why your eyes can only see shades of gray in dim light.

26. **Problem Solving** A telescope produces an upside-down image. How could you modify the telescope so the image is upright?

27. **Comparing and Contrasting** How is a microscope similar to a convex lens used as a magnifying lens? How is it different?

28. **Making Generalizations** Why is laser light never white?

Applying Skills

Use the diagram to answer Questions 29–31.

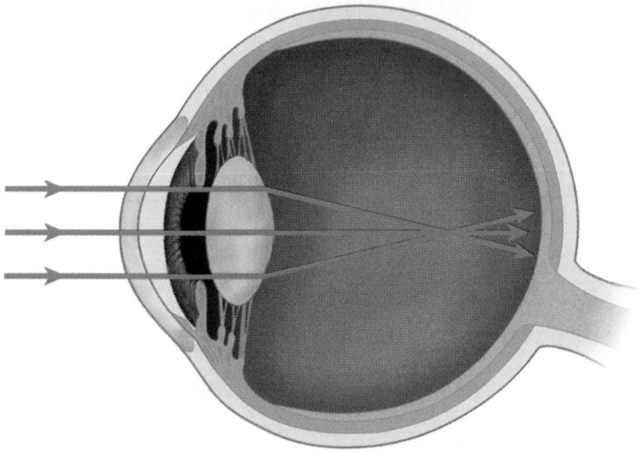

29. **Classifying** Which type of vision problem does this eye have?

30. **Problem Solving** What type of lens can correct this vision problem?

31. **Communicating** Copy the diagram above on a separate sheet of paper. Add a correcting lens to your diagram and show how the lens makes the three rays focus on the retina.

Lab zone Chapter Project

Performance Assessment Demonstrate your optical instrument to your class. Explain how your instrument works and how it can be used. Use diagrams that show how the mirrors or lenses in your instrument reflect or refract light.

Standardized Test Prep

Test-Taking Tip

Reading All the Answer Choices

It is important that you read all of the answer choices in a multiple-choice question before selecting the one you think is correct. More than one answer choice may be correct, but one choice may be clearly better than the others. "All of the above" may also be a choice and is usually listed last. If you don't read all of the choices, you may miss the best answer.

Sample Question

The compound microscope has at least two convex lenses: an objective and an eyepiece. The objective forms an enlarged real image of the specimen. The eyepiece enlarges the first image, producing the virtual image you see when you look through the microscope.

Compound microscopes

A have two or more convex lenses.
B produce a virtual image.
C have both an eyepiece and an objective.
D all of the above

Answer

The best answer is **D** because choices **A, B,** and **C** are all correct statements.

Choose the letter of the best answer.

1. The index of refraction for water is 1.33 and for glass is 1.5. When light moves from glass into water, the speed of light

A increases.
B decreases.
C remains the same.
D depends on the angle of incidence.

2. A convex lens can produce a real or a virtual image. Which type of mirror is most similar to a convex lens?

F plane mirror
G convex mirror
H concave mirror
J none of the above

Periscope

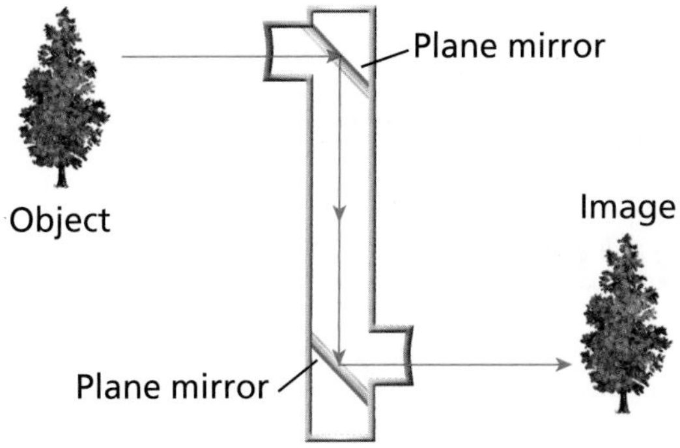

Use the diagram above and your knowledge of science to answer Question 3.

3. If you want to build a periscope, what measurement is most important?

A the angle between the two mirrors
B the distance between the mirrors
C the width of the mirrors
D the width of the tube

4. A friend hypothesizes that a periscope produces an upright image that reverses left and right. How could you test this hypothesis?

F Test A: Draw a ray diagram to determine the type of image that is produced.
G Test B: Look at your friend through the periscope to see if her image is upright.
H Test C: Look at your friend through the periscope and ask her to move her right hand. Observe which hand (left or right) is moving in the image.
J Conduct both Test B and Test C.

5. You view an American flag through sunglasses that are tinted green. What colors do you see?

A green
B black
C green and black
D red and blue

Constructed Response

6. How is a camera like a human eye? Give the function of each part of a camera and identify the part of the eye that has the same function. Use the following terms in your answer: *lens, diaphragm, film, cornea, pupil,* and *retina.*

Interdisciplinary Exploration

Edison—Genius of Invention

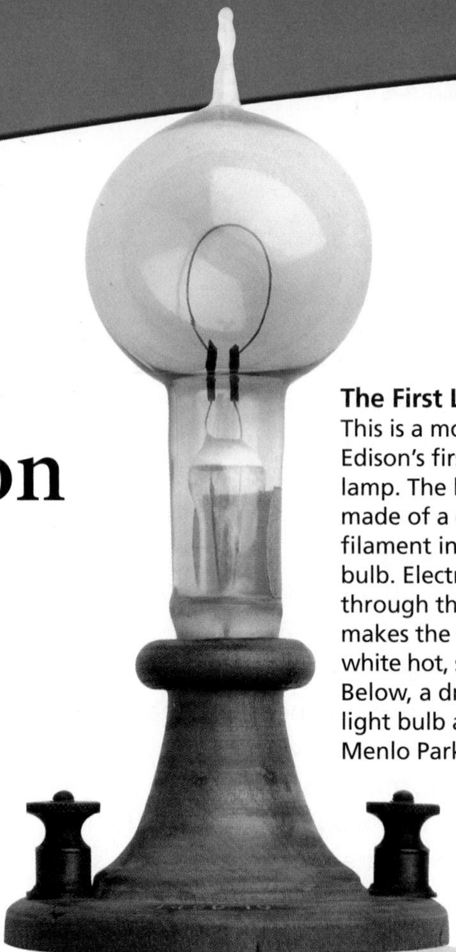

The First Light Bulb
This is a model of Edison's first successful lamp. The light bulb is made of a carbon filament inside a glass bulb. Electricity flowing through the filament makes the filament white hot, so that it glows. Below, a drawing of the light bulb appears in a Menlo Park notebook.

What inventor gave us

- sound recording?
- motion pictures?
- electric lighting?

In 1881, the electric light was a novelty. City streets and some homes were lit with gas. Most homes used oil lamps or candles. Thomas Edison was still developing his system of indoor electric lighting.

Electric lights brought with them a system of power distribution, which made other uses of electricity possible. Imagine living without any electrical appliances, and you'll understand the changes in everyday life that Edison started.

Thomas Edison (1847–1931) had almost no schooling. Yet his mind bubbled with ideas. At the time of his death, Edison held 1,093 patents. A patent is a government license protecting an inventor's right to make and sell a product. One of Edison's most important ideas was never patented. He created the first laboratory for industrial research.

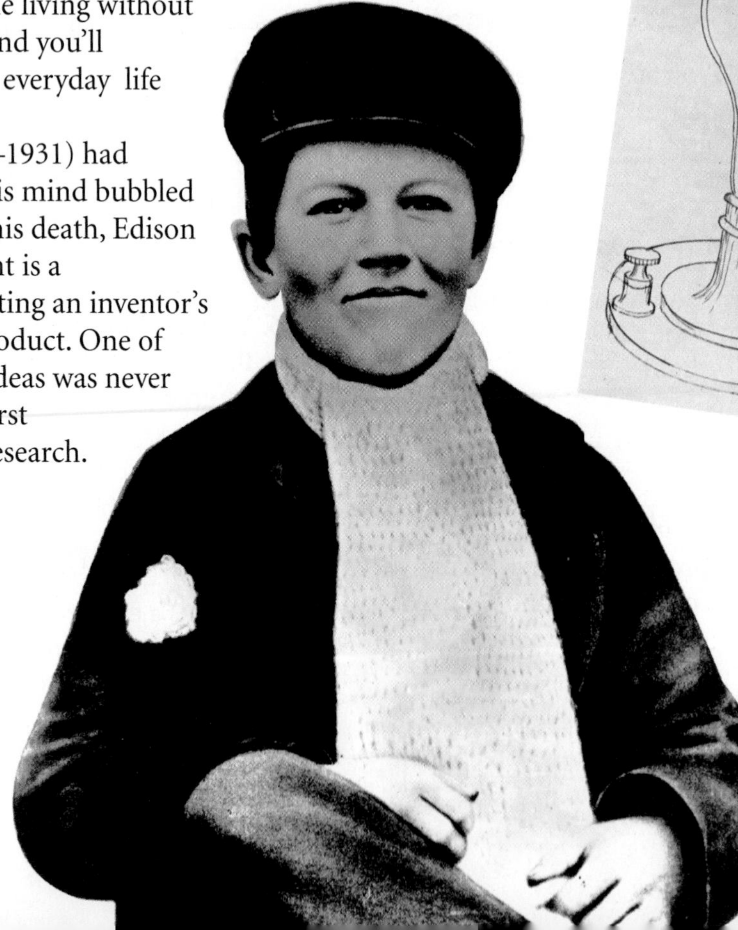

Thomas Edison at 14
Edison worked as a telegrapher for about six years.

The Wizard of Menlo Park

Before 1900, most inventors worked alone. Edison, in contrast, depended on a strong team of research co-workers to carry out his ideas. Edison had an unusual ability to inspire those who worked for him. Some of his original team stayed with him for years. A very hard worker himself, Edison demanded that everyone on his team also work long hours.

By 1876, Edison had enough money to set up an "invention factory." He chose the small town of Menlo Park, New Jersey. His Menlo Park laboratory became the world's first industrial research laboratory.

Edison's team often made improvements on other people's inventions. The light bulb is an example. Other scientists had invented electric lamps, but their light bulbs burned rapidly. The problem was to find a material for the filament that would not overheat or burn out quickly.

The Menlo Park team spent months testing hundreds of materials. First, they rolled each material into a long, thin strand. Then, they carbonized it, which meant baking it until it turned to charcoal. Finally, they tested it in a vacuum, or in the absence of air. Most materials failed in only a few minutes or a few hours. The breakthrough came in 1879. The first successful filament was a length of ordinary cotton thread, carefully carbonized. The newspapers carried the headlines "Success in a Cotton Thread" and "It Makes a Light, Without Gas or Flame."

Edison's Lab
Edison set up his research laboratory in Menlo Park.

Science Activity

Work together as a team to invent a new electrical device.

- What could a new electrical device help you do? How could it make your life easier?
- Brainstorm for possible products that would help you in some way. Write down all possible ideas.
- Evaluate each solution and agree on the best one.
- Plan your design and make a labeled drawing. List the supplies you will need. Note any new skills you should learn.
- Write down the steps you will use to build your device.

Language Arts

Lighting Manhattan

Edison recognized the value of publicity. Besides being a productive inventor, he knew how to promote himself. He made glowing predictions about his new electric system. Electricity would soon be so cheap, he said, that "only the rich would be able to afford candles."

When he built his first neighborhood generating station, Edison made a shrewd choice of location. The Pearl Street power station brought light and power to about 2.6 square kilometers of downtown Manhattan. It supplied businesses and factories, as well as private homes. The circuits could light 400 light bulbs. Some of those lights were in the offices of J. P. Morgan, the leading banker and financier of the time. Other lights were located in the offices of *The New York Times.* Here's what the *Times* reporter wrote on September 5, 1882.

New York City
This photo shows Broadway in the 1880s.

SEPTEMBER 5, 1882—Yesterday for the first time The Times Building was illuminated by electricity. Mr. Edison had at last perfected his incandescent light, had put his machinery in order, and had started up his engines, and last evening his company lighted up about one-third of the lower City district in which The Times Building stands.

It was not until about seven o'clock, when it began to grow dark, that the electric light really made itself known and showed how bright and steady it is. It was a light that a man could sit down under and write for hours without the consciousness of having any artificial light about him. There was a very slight amount of heat from each lamp, but not nearly as much as from a gas-burner—one-fifteenth as much as from gas, the inventor says. The light was soft, mellow, and grateful to the eye, and it seemed almost like writing by daylight to have a light without a particle of flicker and with scarcely any heat to make the head ache. The decision was unanimously in favor of the Edison electric lamp as against gas.

———Excerpted with permission from *The New York Times.*

Language Arts Activity

The reporter who wrote the newspaper story observed details carefully and used them to write about an event—the first lights in his office. Look back at the story. Now write about the event as Edison would have told it to convince people to buy light bulbs and install electrical power systems. You could make an advertisement. Inform your readers about the product and persuade them to buy it.

Solving Practical Problems

As he grew older, Edison worried that American students were not learning mathematics well enough. To motivate students, he suggested using problems that related to real-life situations. In 1925, when he was 78, he proposed these problems below as recorded in his notebooks. Note that light bulbs were called lamps. Tungsten is a metal used in light bulbs.

Edison Lamp
This advertisement promotes reading by Edison's Mazda lamp.

Problem 1

American electric plants now serve 9,500,000 homes. The estimated number of homes in the United States is 21,000,000. What percentage receives electrical energy?

Problem 2

It needs about 280,000,000 tungsten lamps [bulbs] each year to supply the market today. And yet the first lamp factory in the world—the Edison Lamp Works. . .—was not started until 1880, and I was told it would never pay. The output for our first year was about 25,000 globes [bulbs]. How many times that figure would be required for the present market?

Problem 3

A household using 21 lamps requires about 7 new lamps each year. What percentage is this?

Problem 4

If these lamps had been bought at the retail prices of the first year of the lamp factory, they would have cost $1.25 each. How much would the family save by the decreased prices of today?

Inventor Thomas Edison
Edison stands next to his original light bulb invention. In his hand, he holds a smaller model.

Math Activity

Solve the four math problems that Edison wrote. To solve Problem 4, use 1925 prices. That year, incandescent light bulbs (or lamps) cost $.30 each.

Daily Life Transformed

Edison's inventions in the late 1800s helped spark a technological and social revolution. Some of these inventions forever transformed the way people live, play, and work.

Edison's light bulb made indoor lighting practical. Along with the light bulb, he developed the idea of a central power system to distribute electricity to homes and businesses. That system included generators, underground cables, junction boxes, and meters. Other inventors improved on Edison's ideas for lights and electricity.

Other Edison inventions influenced ways that people entertain themselves. Edison created the phonograph, a rotating disk that could record and play back sounds. About that same time, Edison invented the first movie camera, a device that could store pictures. These inventions spurred the development of the recording and film industries.

Edison Movie
This poster advertises one of Edison's early movies.

Phonograph
In 1878, Edison demonstrated his phonograph, which recorded sound on a rotating cylinder. A needle attached to a thin metal disk played the sound.

Improved Phonograph
A later version of Edison's phonograph included a horn to project the sound.

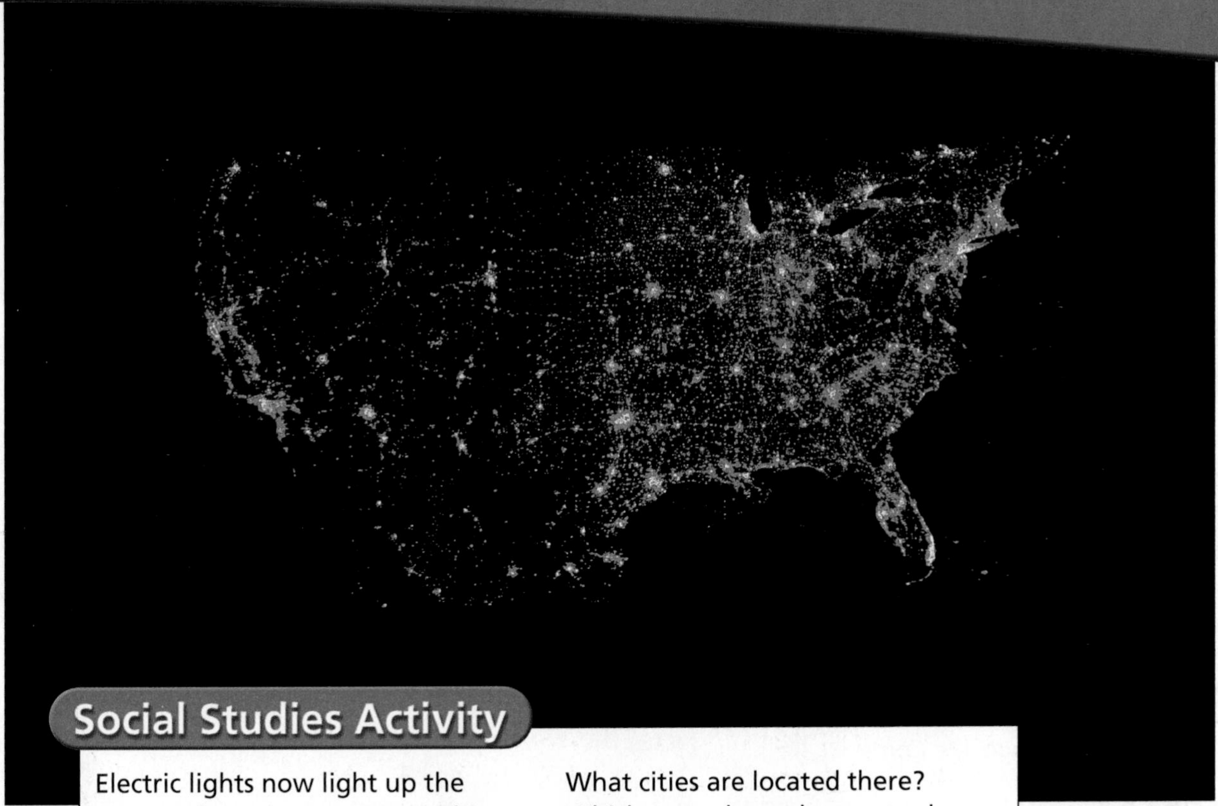

Social Studies Activity

Electric lights now light up the country from coast to coast. This map, based on population data, shows what the United States might look like from space at night. Using a map of the United States, identify the regions that are the brightest. What cities are located there? Which states have the most urban areas? Which have the least? Use an almanac to find out the population of five of the largest cities. Compare these data with the total United States population.

Tie It Together

Modern Times

Many of the inventions that came out of Menlo Park still affect things we do today. Work in pairs to research one of Edison's inventions. Or research another scientist's inventions. Find out how the device changed and improved in the 1900s. Write up your research and present it to the class. If the device is no longer used, explain what has replaced it. Here are a few inventions from which to choose. (Not all of them were Edison's.)

- stock ticker
- telegraph
- phonograph
- disk record
- voting machine
- electric pen and press
- radio transmitter
- linotype
- typewriter
- telephone
- automobile
- vacuum tube
- mechanical music

Cassette Player
Is this device related to Edison's invention?

Chapter 19 Magnetism

Chapter Preview

1 What Is Magnetism?
Discover *What Do All Magnets Have in Common?*
Skills Activity *Observing*
Active Art *Magnetic Field Lines*
At-Home Activity *Magnetic Helpers*
Skills Lab *Detecting Fake Coins*

2 Inside a Magnet
Discover *How Can Materials Become Magnetic?*
Technology Lab *Design and Build a Magnetic Paper Clip Holder*

3 Magnetic Earth
Discover *Can You Use a Needle to Make a Compass?*
Analyzing Data *Movement of Earth's Magnetic Poles*
Skills Activity *Measuring*
Try This *Spinning in Circles*
At-Home Activity *House Compass*

iNteractive Textbook

The aurora borealis glows above a cabin in Manitoba, Canada.

Discovery Channel School

Magnetism

▶ Video Preview
Video Field Trip
Video Assessment

Lab zone™ Chapter **Project**

Magnetic Art

Magnetism is often used to do work, but it can also be used to create art! In this chapter project you will create a sculpture using nothing but magnetism to hold it together.

Your Goal To create a magnetic sculpture.

To complete this project, your sculpture must

- be held together *only* by magnets and objects with magnetic properties
- be at least 20 cm tall
- keep its shape for at least two hours
- follow the safety guidelines in Appendix A

Plan It! Your teacher will suggest a variety of materials that you can use to make your sculpture. With your group, brainstorm ideas for your plan. Decide which materials can be magnetized. After obtaining your teacher's approval for your plan, make your sculpture.

Section 1

What Is Magnetism?

Reading Preview

Key Concepts

- What are the properties of a magnet?
- How do magnetic poles interact?
- What is the shape of a magnetic field?

Key Terms

- magnet • magnetic pole
- magnetic force
- magnetic field
- magnetic field lines

Target Reading Skill

Using Prior Knowledge Before you read, look at the headings and visuals to see what this section is about. Then write what you know about magnetism in a graphic organizer like the one below. As you read, write what you learn.

What You Know
1. Magnets stick to refrigerators. 2.

What You Learned
1. 2.

Lab zone Discover Activity

What Do All Magnets Have in Common?

1. Obtain a bar magnet and a horseshoe magnet.
2. See how many paper clips you can attract to different parts of each magnet.
3. Draw a diagram showing the number and location of paper clips on each magnet.

Think It Over

Observing Where does each magnet hold the greatest number of paper clips? What similarities do you observe between the two magnets?

Imagine zooming along in a train that glides without even touching the ground. You feel no vibration and hear no noise from the steel tracks below. You can just sit back and relax as you speed toward your destination at nearly 500 kilometers per hour.

Are you dreaming? No, you are not. You are floating a few centimeters in the air on a magnetically levitating train, or maglev train. Although you have probably not ridden on such a train, they do exist. What makes them float? Believe it or not, it is magnetism that makes them float.

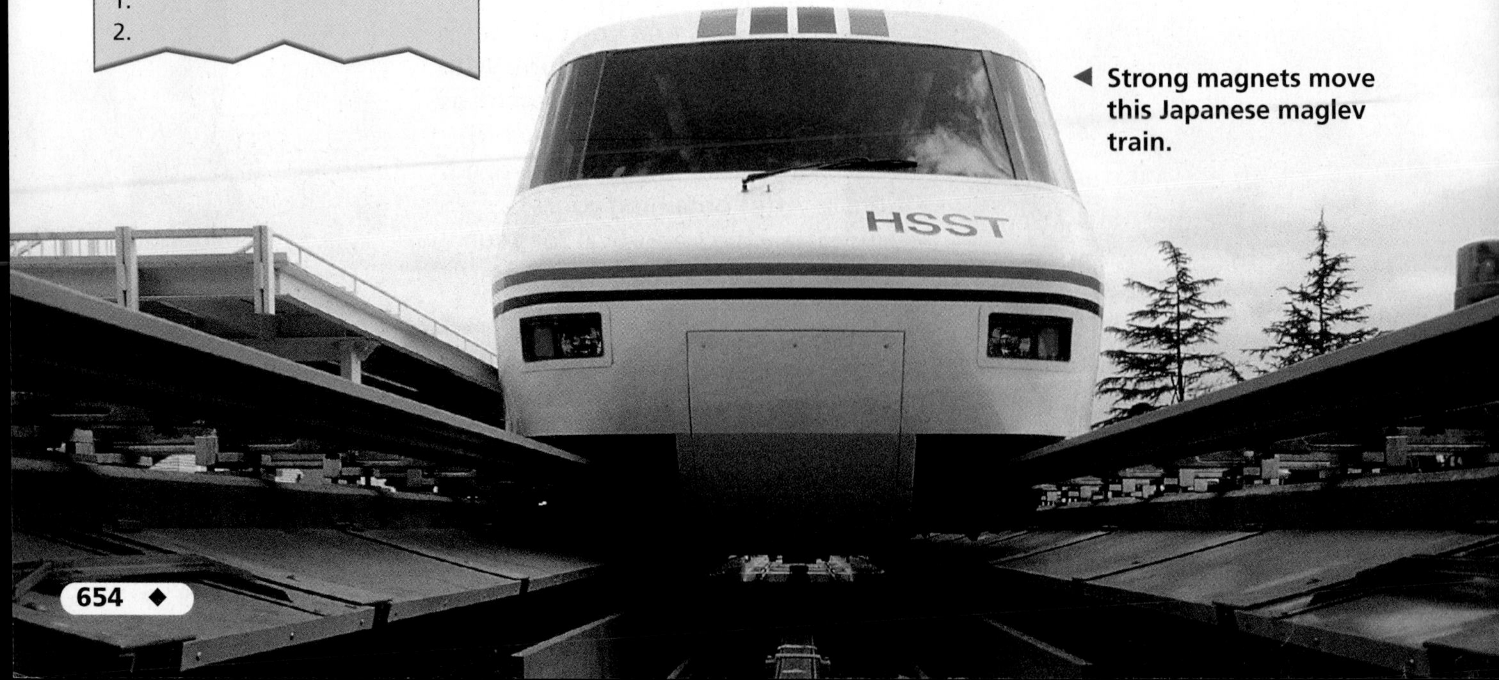

◀ **Strong magnets move this Japanese maglev train.**

Properties of Magnets

When you think of magnets, you might think about the objects that hold notes to your refrigerator. But magnets can also be found in many other everyday items such as wallets, kitchen cabinets, and security tags at a store. A **magnet** is any material that attracts iron and materials that contain iron.

Magnets have many modern uses, but they are not new. More than 2,000 years ago, people living in the ancient Greek city of Magnesia (in what is now Turkey) discovered an unusual kind of rock. This kind of rock contained a mineral called magnetite. Both the word *magnetite* and the word *magnet* come from the name Magnesia. Rocks containing magnetite attracted materials that contained iron. They also attracted or repelled other magnetic rocks. The attraction or repulsion of magnetic materials is called magnetism.

About a thousand years ago, people in other parts of the world discovered another property of magnetic rocks. If they allowed such a rock to swing freely from a string, one part of the rock would always point in the same direction. That direction was toward the North Star, Polaris. This star is also called the leading star, or lodestar. For this reason, magnetic rocks are known as lodestones.

Magnets have the same properties as magnetic rocks. **Magnets attract iron and materials that contain iron. Magnets attract or repel other magnets. In addition, one part of a magnet will always point north when allowed to swing freely.**

Reading Checkpoint **What mineral found in rocks can attract materials containing iron?**

FIGURE 1
A Natural Magnet
Some magnets are found in nature. This rock attracts iron nails because it contains the magnetic mineral called magnetite.

FIGURE 2
Modern Magnets
Magnets come in a variety of shapes and sizes, but they share certain characteristics.
Inferring *What substance might the scissors, paper clips, and spoon have in common?*

FIGURE 3
Attraction and Repulsion
Two bar magnets suspended by strings are brought near each other. Unlike poles attract each other; like poles repel each other.
Predicting *What would happen if two south poles were brought near one another?*

Magnetic Poles

The magnets in your everyday life have the same properties as magnetic rocks because they are made to have them. Recall that one end of a magnet always points north. Any magnet, no matter what its shape, has two ends, each one called a **magnetic pole.** The magnetic effect of a magnet is strongest at the poles. The pole of a magnet that points north is labeled the north pole. The other pole is labeled the south pole. A magnet always has a pair of poles, a north pole and a south pole.

Magnetic Interactions What happens if you bring two magnets together? The answer depends on how you hold the poles of the magnets. If you bring the north pole of one magnet near the south pole of another, the two unlike poles attract one another. However, if you bring two north poles together, the like poles move away from each other. The same is true if two south poles are brought together. **Magnetic poles that are unlike attract each other, and magnetic poles that are alike repel each other.** Figure 3 shows how two bar magnets interact.

Magnetic Force The attraction or repulsion between magnetic poles is **magnetic force.** A force is a push or a pull that can cause an object to move. A magnetic force is produced when magnetic poles interact. Any material that exerts a magnetic force is considered to be a magnet.

The maglev train you read about earlier depends on magnetic force to move. Magnets in the bottom of the train and in the guideway on the ground have like poles facing each other. Because like poles repel, the two magnets move away from each other. The result is that the train car is lifted up, or levitated. Other magnets make the train move forward.

Reading Checkpoint What does every magnet have in common?

Lab zone Skills Activity

Observing

1. Use a pencil to poke a hole in the bottom of a foam cup. Turn the cup upside down and stand the pencil in the hole.
2. Place two circular magnets on the pencil, so that their like sides are together, and observe them.
3. Remove the top magnet. Flip it over, replace it on the pencil, and observe it.

What happens to the magnets in each case? Explain your observations.

Magnetic Fields

A magnetic force is strongest at the poles of a magnet, but it is not limited to the poles. Magnetic forces are exerted all around a magnet. The area of magnetic force around a magnet is known as its **magnetic field.** Because of magnetic fields, magnets can interact without even touching.

Figure 4 shows the magnetic field of a bar magnet. Notice the red lines, called magnetic field lines, around the magnet. **Magnetic field lines** are invisible lines that map out the magnetic field around a magnet. **Magnetic field lines spread out from one pole, curve around the magnet, and return to the other pole.** The lines form complete loops from pole to pole and never cross. Arrows are used to indicate the direction of the magnetic field lines—always leaving the north pole and entering the south pole.

The distance between magnetic field lines indicates the strength of a magnetic field. The closer together the lines are, the stronger the field. A magnet's magnetic field lines are closest together at the poles.

Reading Checkpoint Where is the magnetic field strongest?

Go Online
active art

For: Magnetic Field Lines activity
Visit: PHSchool.com
Web Code: cgp-4011

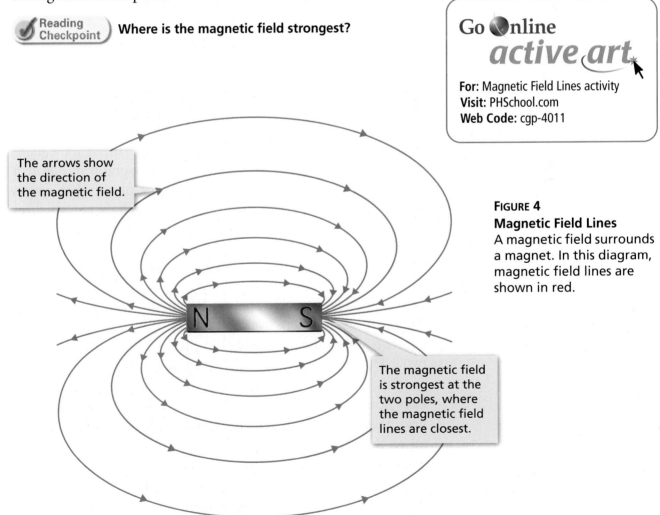

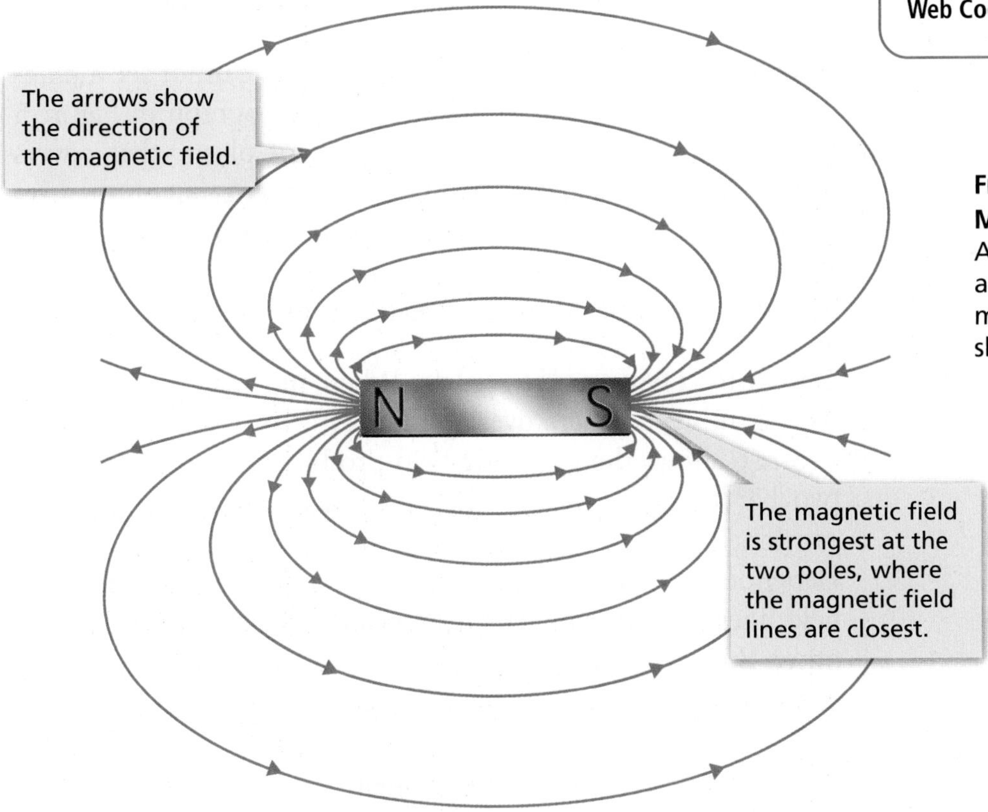

FIGURE 4
Magnetic Field Lines
A magnetic field surrounds a magnet. In this diagram, magnetic field lines are shown in red.

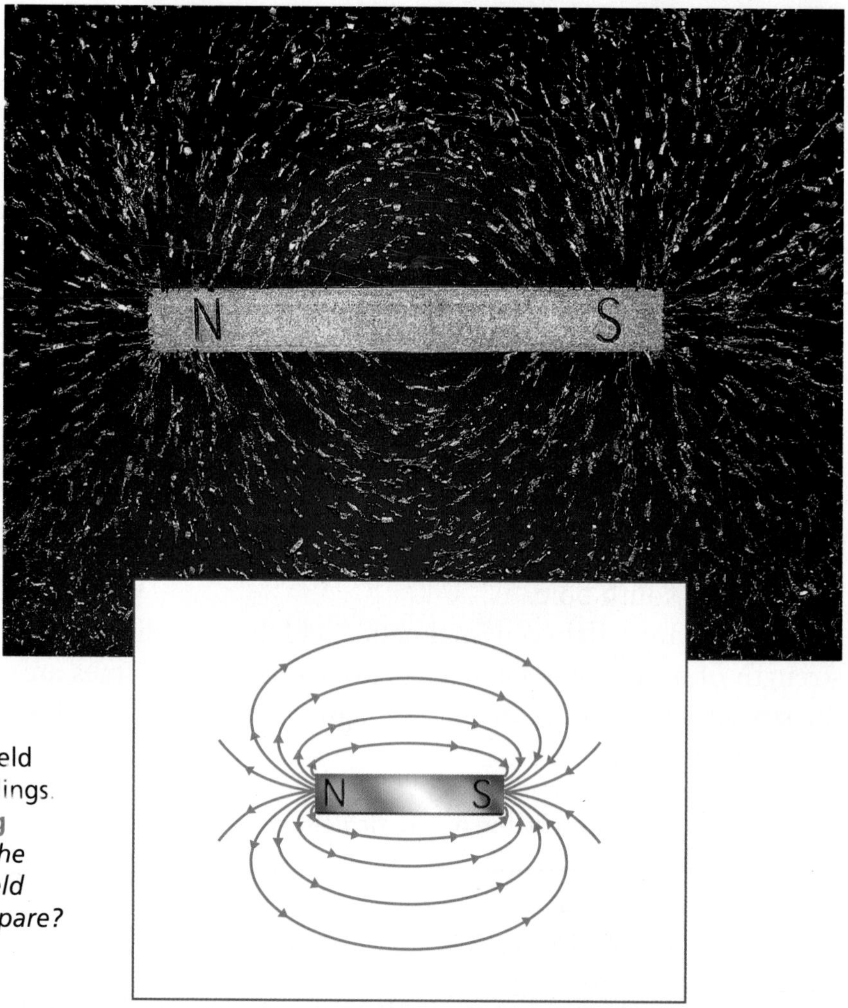

FIGURE 5
A Single Magnetic Field
A bar magnet's magnetic field is mapped out using iron filings.
Comparing and Contrasting
How do the iron filings in the photo and the magnetic field lines in the illustration compare?

A Single Magnetic Field Although you cannot see a magnetic field, you can see its effects. The photograph in Figure 5 shows iron filings sprinkled on a sheet of plastic that covers one magnet. The magnetic forces of the magnet act on the iron filings and align them along the invisible magnetic field lines. The result is that the iron filings form a pattern similar to the magnetic field lines shown in the diagram in Figure 5.

Combined Magnetic Fields When the magnetic fields of two or more magnets overlap, the result is a combined field. Figure 6 shows the magnetic field produced when the poles of two bar magnets are brought near each other. Compare the combined field of two like poles to that of two unlike poles. Depending on which poles are near each other, the magnetic field lines are different. The fields from the like poles repel each other. But the fields from unlike poles attract each other. They combine to form a strong field between the two poles.

Reading Checkpoint **What happens when the magnetic fields of two or more magnets overlap?**

FIGURE 6
Combined Magnetic Fields
The magnetic field of a single bar magnet is altered when another bar magnet is brought near it.

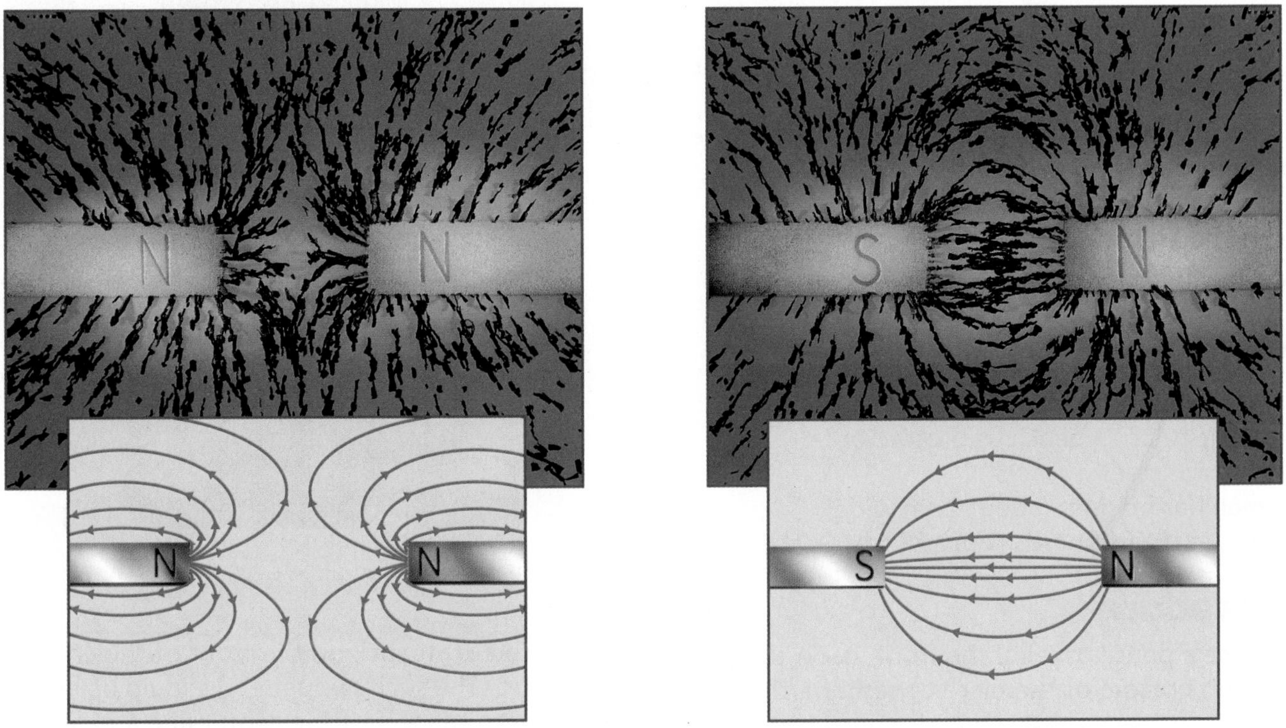

Section 1 Assessment

Target Reading Skill **Using Prior Knowledge** Review your graphic organizer and revise it based on what you just learned in the section.

Reviewing Key Concepts

1. a. **Reviewing** What is a magnet?
   b. **Summarizing** What are three properties of a magnet?
   c. **Predicting** What will happen to a bar magnet that is allowed to swing freely?
2. a. **Describing** What area of a magnet has the strongest magnetic effect?
   b. **Explaining** How does a magnet's north pole behave when brought near another north pole? Near a magnet's south pole?
   c. **Relating Cause and Effect** How can the behavior of two magnets show the presence of a magnetic force?
3. a. **Defining** What is a magnetic field?
   b. **Interpreting Diagrams** Look at Figure 4. What is the shape of the magnetic field?

Lab zone **At-Home Activity**

Magnetic Helpers Explain the properties of magnets to a member of your family. Then make a list of objects around your home that are most likely to contain or use one or more magnets. For example, magnets are used to hold some cabinet doors closed. Have your family member make a separate list. Compare the two lists and explain to your family member why each object is or is not likely to contain or use magnets.

Lab zone **Skills Lab**

Detecting Fake Coins

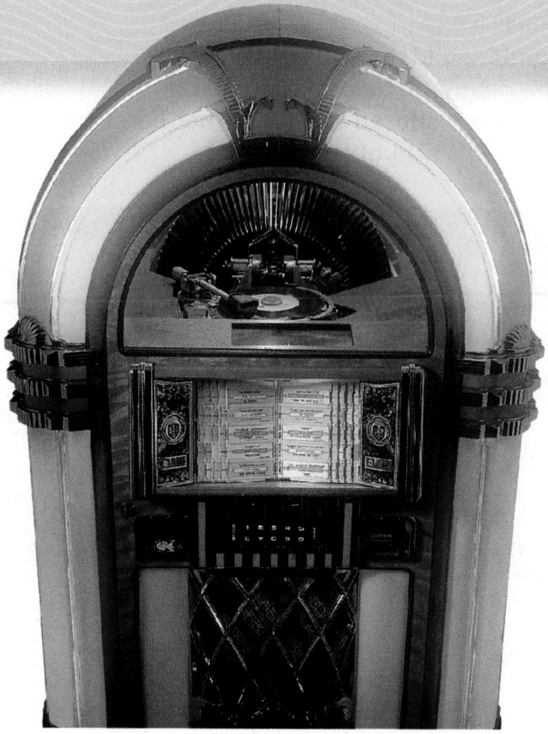

Problem

How can you use a magnet to tell the difference between real and fake coins?

Skills Focus

predicting, observing, developing hypotheses

Materials

- various coins • craft stick • tape
- metric ruler • pencil • protractor
- coin-size steel washers
- small bar magnet, about 2 cm wide
- thin, stiff cardboard, about 25 cm × 30 cm

Procedure

1. Use a pencil to label the front, back, top, and bottom of the piece of cardboard.
2. Draw a line lengthwise down the middle of both sides of the cardboard.
3. On the back of the cardboard, draw a line parallel to the first and about 2 cm to the right.
4. Place a magnet, aligned vertically, about a third of the way down the line you drew in Step 3. Tape the magnet in place.

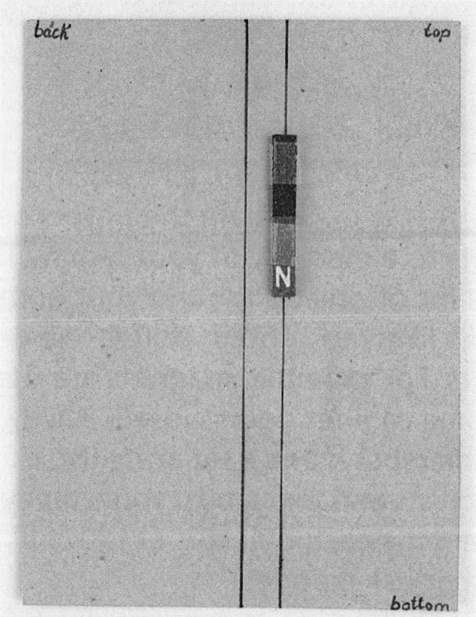

5. Place a craft stick on the front of the cardboard. The stick's upper end should be about 1 cm to the left of the center line and about 8 cm from the bottom of the cardboard.
6. Tape the stick at an angle, as shown in the photograph on the following page.
7. Prop the cardboard against something that will hold it at an angle of about 45°. Predict what will happen when you slide a coin down the front of the cardboard.
8. Place a coin on the center line and slide the coin down the front of the cardboard. (*Hint*: If the coin gets stuck, slowly increase the angle.)
9. Predict what will happen when you slide a steel washer.
10. Test your prediction by sliding a washer down the cardboard. Again, if the washer gets stuck, slowly increase the angle and try again.
11. Once you have reached an angle at which the objects slide easily, send down a randomly mixed group of coins and washers one at a time.

Analyze and Conclude

1. **Predicting** What was your prediction from Step 7? Explain your reasoning.
2. **Predicting** What was your prediction from Step 9? Explain your reasoning.
3. **Observing** Describe how observations made during the lab either supported or did not support your predictions.
4. **Developing Hypotheses** What is the role of the magnet in this lab?
5. **Developing Hypotheses** What is the role of the craft stick?
6. **Drawing Conclusions** What can you conclude about the metals from which the coins are made? About the metals in the washers?
7. **Controlling Variables** Why does the steepness of the cardboard affect how the coin-separating device works?
8. **Predicting** Some Canadian coins contain metals that are attracted to magnets. Would this device be useful in Canada to detect fake coins? Explain your answer.
9. **Communicating** Write a brochure that explains how the device could be used to separate real coins from fake coins and what advantages it might have for vending machine owners.

More to Explore

Go to a store that has vending machines. Find out who owns the vending machines. Ask the owners if they have a problem with counterfeit coins (sometimes called "slugs"). Ask how they or the makers of the vending machines solve the problem. How is their solution related to the device you built in this lab?

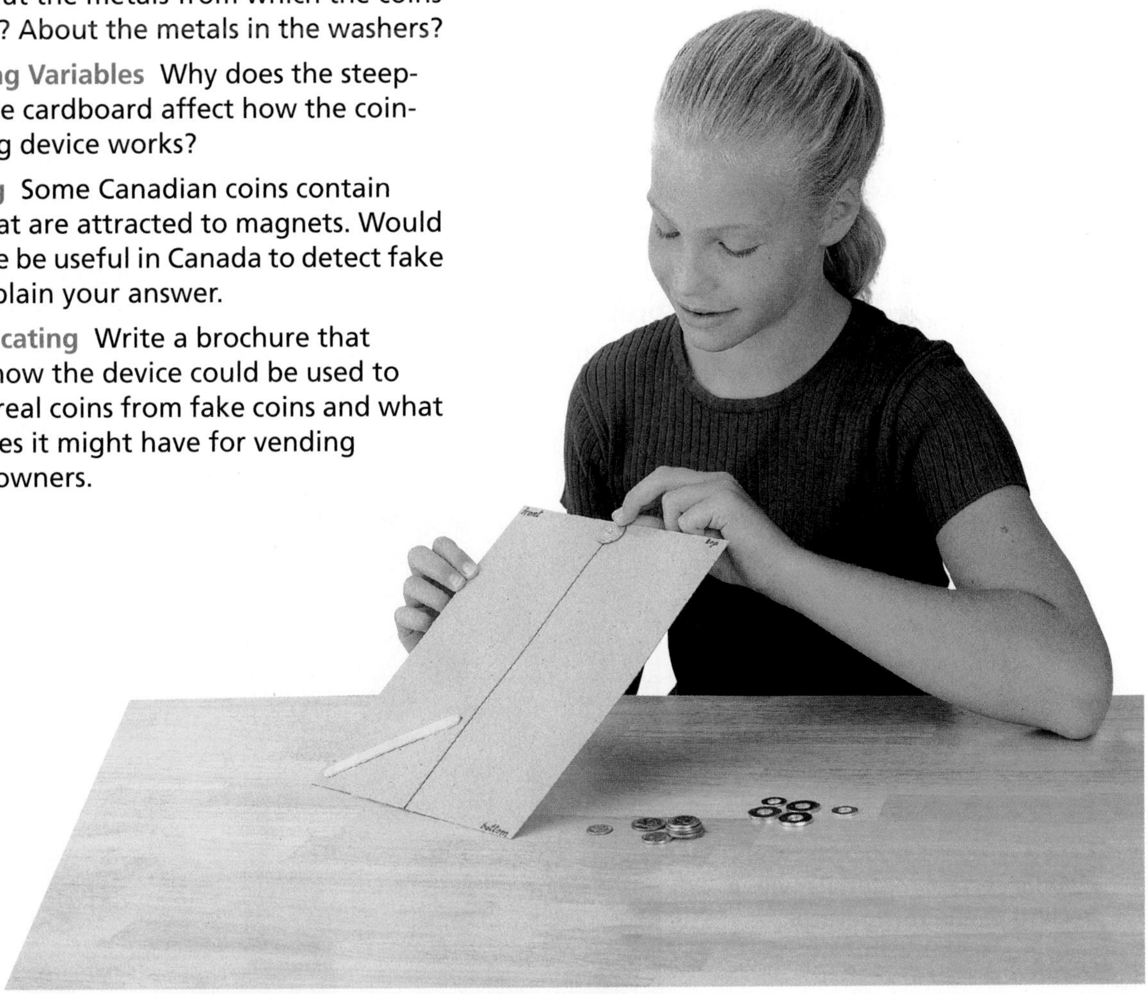

Section 2

Inside a Magnet

Reading Preview

Key Concepts

- How can an atom behave like a magnet?
- How are magnetic domains arranged in a magnetic material?
- How can magnets be changed?

Key Terms

- atom • element • nucleus
- proton • neutron • electron
- magnetic domain
- ferromagnetic material
- temporary magnet
- permanent magnet

Target Reading Skill

Asking Questions Before you read, preview the red headings. In a graphic organizer like the one below, ask a *what* or *how* question for each heading. As you read, write the answers to your questions.

Inside an Atom

Question	Answer
What are the three particles that make up an atom?	The three particles that make up an atom are . . .

Only certain materials will cling to the refrigerator using magnetism. ▶

Lab zone Discover Activity

How Can Materials Become Magnetic?

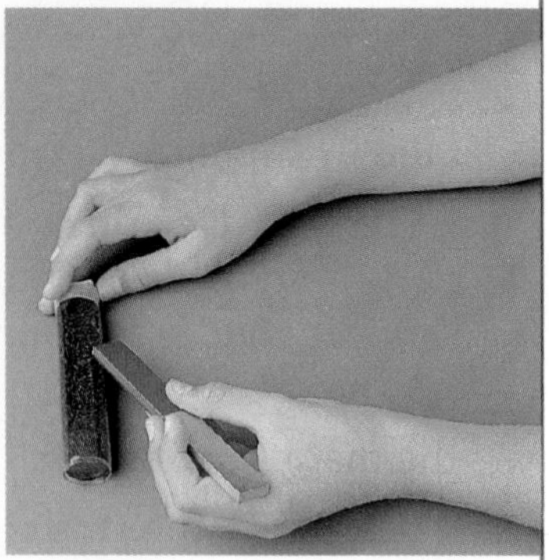

1. Fill a clear plastic tube about two-thirds full with iron filings.
2. Observe the arrangement of the filings.
3. Rub the tube lengthwise about 30 times in the same direction with one end of a strong magnet.
4. Again, observe the arrangement of the filings.

Think It Over

Drawing Conclusions What can you conclude from your observations?

You've probably noticed that if you bring a magnet near the door of your refrigerator, it clings. But what happens if you bring a piece of paper near the same refrigerator door? Nothing. You have to use a magnet to hold the paper against the door. Materials such as paper, plastic, rubber, and glass do not have magnetic properties. They will not cling to magnets and certain metals. Why are some materials magnetic while others are not?

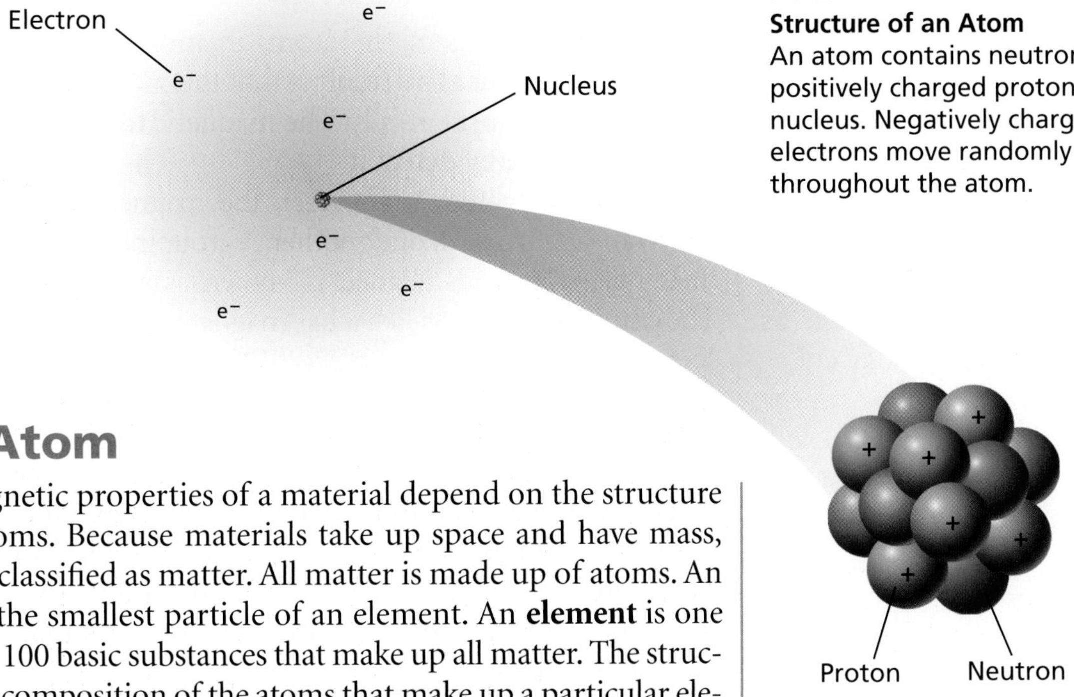

FIGURE 7
Structure of an Atom
An atom contains neutrons and positively charged protons in its nucleus. Negatively charged electrons move randomly throughout the atom.

The Atom

The magnetic properties of a material depend on the structure of its atoms. Because materials take up space and have mass, they are classified as matter. All matter is made up of atoms. An **atom** is the smallest particle of an element. An **element** is one of about 100 basic substances that make up all matter. The structure and composition of the atoms that make up a particular element make that element different from any other element.

Structure of an Atom Although atoms can differ, they have some characteristics in common. Every atom has a center region and an outer region. The center region of an atom is called a **nucleus.** Inside the nucleus two kinds of particles may be found: protons and neutrons. A **proton** is a particle that carries a positive charge. A **neutron** is a particle that does not carry a charge.

The outer region of an atom is mainly empty space. However, particles called electrons usually exist there. An **electron** is a particle that carries a negative charge. Electrons move randomly throughout the atom. They are much smaller than neutrons and protons. Look at Figure 7 to see the structure of an atom.

Electron Spin Each electron in an atom has a property called electron spin, so it behaves as if it were spinning. **A spinning electron produces a magnetic field that makes the electron behave like a tiny magnet in an atom.**

In most atoms, electrons form pairs that spin in opposite directions. Opposite spins produce opposite magnetic fields that cancel. Therefore, most atoms have weak magnetic properties. But some atoms contain electrons that are not paired. These atoms tend to have strong magnetic properties.

Reading Checkpoint **Why are most materials not magnetic?**

Magnetic Domains

The magnetic fields of the atoms in most materials point in random directions. The result is that the magnetic fields cancel one another almost entirely. The magnetic force is so weak that you cannot usually detect it.

In certain materials, however, the magnetic fields of many atoms are aligned with one another. A grouping of atoms that have their magnetic fields aligned is known as a **magnetic domain.** The entire domain acts like a bar magnet with a north pole and a south pole.

Alignment of Domains The direction in which the domains point determines if the material is magnetized or not magnetized. In a material that is not magnetized, the magnetic domains point in random directions, as shown in Figure 8. Therefore, the magnetic fields of some domains cancel the magnetic fields of other domains. The result is that the material is not a magnet.

Figure 8 has a diagram showing the arrangement of the domains in a magnetized material. You can see that most of the domains are pointing in the same direction. **In a magnetized material, all or most of the magnetic domains are arranged in the same direction.** In other words, the magnetic fields of the domains are aligned. If you did the Discover Activity at the beginning of this section you aligned the magnetic domains of the iron filings.

Reading Checkpoint **What is the arrangement of the magnetic domains in a material that is not magnetized?**

FIGURE 8
Magnetic Domains
The arrows represent the magnetic domains of a material. The arrows point toward the north pole of each magnetic domain.
Comparing and Contrasting *How does the arrangement of domains differ between magnetized iron and unmagnetized iron?*

Unmagnetized Iron

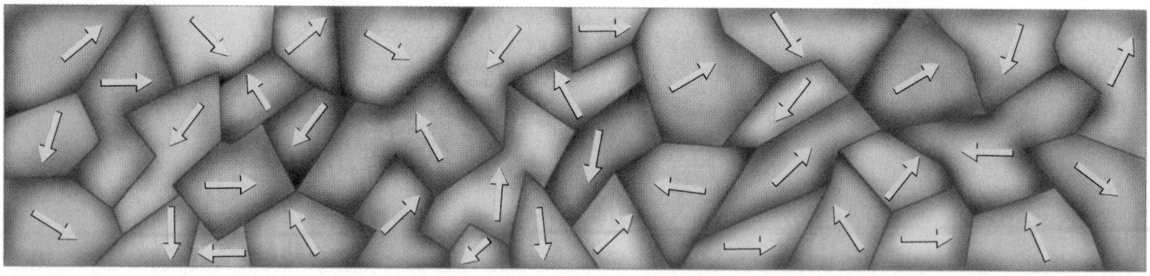

Magnetized Iron

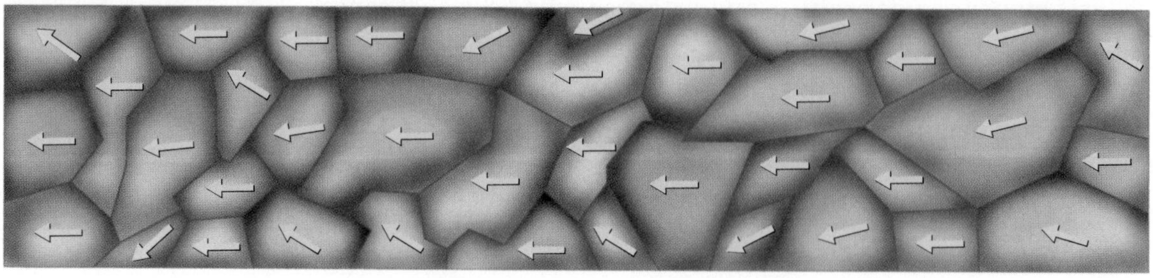

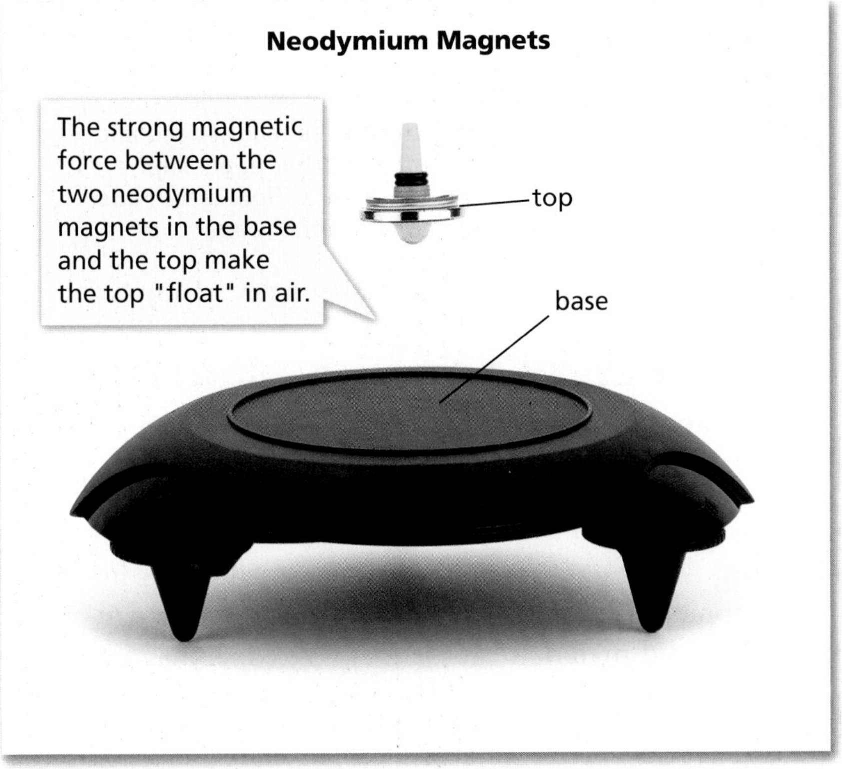

Neodymium Magnets
The strong magnetic force between the two neodymium magnets in the base and the top make the top "float" in air.
top
base

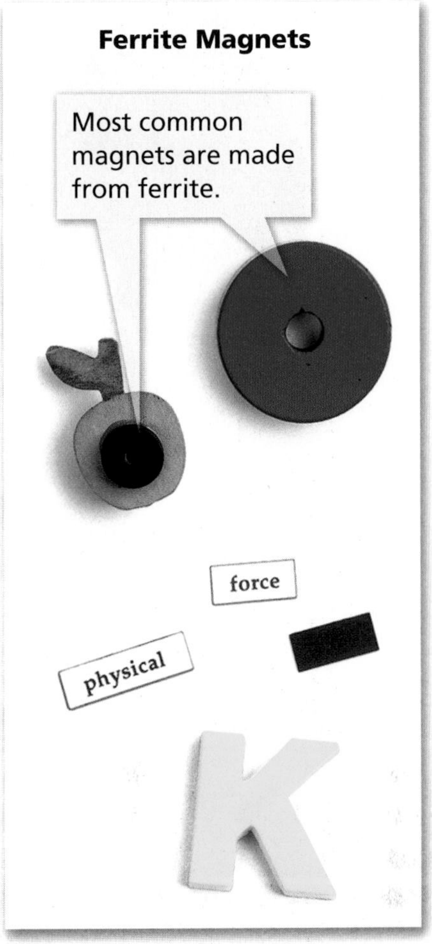

Ferrite Magnets
Most common magnets are made from ferrite.
force
physical

FIGURE 9
Magnets of Different Materials
Modern magnets come in a variety of shapes and are made from many different materials.

Magnetic Materials A material can be a strong magnet if its magnetic domains align. A material that shows strong magnetic properties is said to be a **ferromagnetic material**. The word *ferromagnetic* comes from the Latin *ferrum*, which means "iron." So a ferromagnetic material behaves like a piece of iron when it is placed in a magnetic field. In nature, iron, nickel, cobalt, and gadolinium are common ferromagnetic materials. Others include the rare elements samarium and neodymium, which can be made into extremely strong magnets as you can see in Figure 9.

Some magnets are made from several different metals. A combination of several metals is called an alloy. For example, the magnetic alloy alnico is made of aluminum, nickel, iron, and cobalt. Powerful magnets are also made of alloys of platinum and cobalt, and alloys of cobalt and neodymium.

Today, the most commonly used magnets are not made from alloys, but rather from a material called ferrite. Ferrite is a mixture of substances that contain ferromagnetic elements. Ferrite is a brittle material that chips easily, like some dishes. However, ferrite magnets are usually stronger and less expensive than metal magnets of similar size. Figure 9 shows some ferrite magnets.

Reading Checkpoint **What are some common ferromagnetic materials found in nature?**

Go Online SCILINKS NSTA

For: Links on magnetic materials
Visit: www.SciLinks.org
Web Code: scn-1412

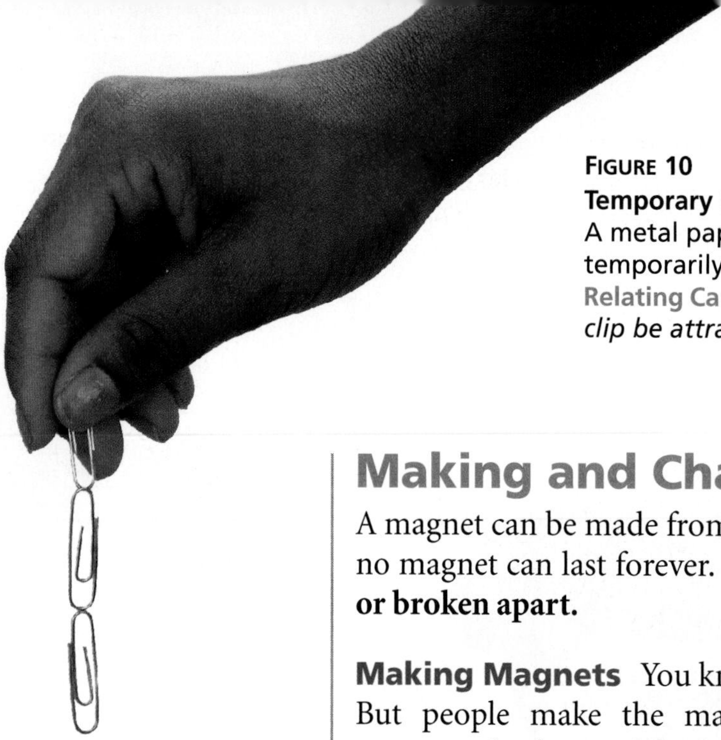

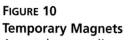

FIGURE 10
Temporary Magnets
A metal paper clip can be magnetized and temporarily attract another paper clip.
Relating Cause and Effect *How can a paper clip be attracted to another paper clip?*

Making and Changing Magnets

A magnet can be made from ferromagnetic material. However, no magnet can last forever. **Magnets can be made, destroyed, or broken apart.**

Making Magnets You know that magnetite exists in nature. But people make the magnets you use every day. Some unmagnetized materials can be magnetized. A magnet can be made by placing an unmagnetized ferromagnetic material in a strong magnetic field or by rubbing the material with one pole of a magnet.

Suppose, for example, that you want to magnetize a steel paper clip. Steel contains iron. So you can magnetize the paper clip by rubbing in one direction with one pole of a magnet. The magnetic field of the magnet causes some domains in the paper clip to line up in the same direction as the domains in the magnet. The more domains that line up, the more magnetized the paper clip becomes.

Some materials, such as the steel in a paper clip or pure iron, are easy to magnetize, but lose their magnetism quickly. A magnet made from a material that easily loses its magnetism is called a **temporary magnet**. Other materials, such as those in strong magnets, are hard to magnetize, but tend to stay magnetized. A magnet made from a material that keeps its magnetism for a long time is called a **permanent magnet**.

Destroying Magnets Like a temporary magnet, a permanent magnet can also become unmagnetized. One way for a magnet to become unmagnetized is to drop it or strike it hard. If a magnet is hit hard, its domains can be knocked out of alignment. Heating a magnet will also destroy its magnetism. When an object is heated, its particles vibrate faster and more randomly. These movements make it more difficult for all the domains to stay lined up. Above a certain temperature, every ferromagnetic material loses its magnetic properties. The temperature depends on the material.

Breaking Magnets What happens if you break a magnet in two? Do you have a north pole in one hand and a south pole in the other? The answer is no—you have two smaller magnets. Each smaller magnet has its own north pole and south pole. If you break those two halves again, you have four magnets.

Now that you know about domains, you can understand why breaking a magnet in half does not result in two pieces that are individual poles. Within the original magnet shown in Figure 11, many north and south poles are facing each other. Many of the magnet's domains are lined up in one direction. This produces a strong magnetic force at the magnet's north and south poles. If the magnet is cut in half, the domains in the two halves will still be lined up in the same way. So the shorter pieces will still have strong ends made up of many north or south poles.

Reading Checkpoint **What is a temporary magnet?**

FIGURE 11
Magnet Pieces
Each piece of a magnet retains its magnetic properties after it is cut in half.

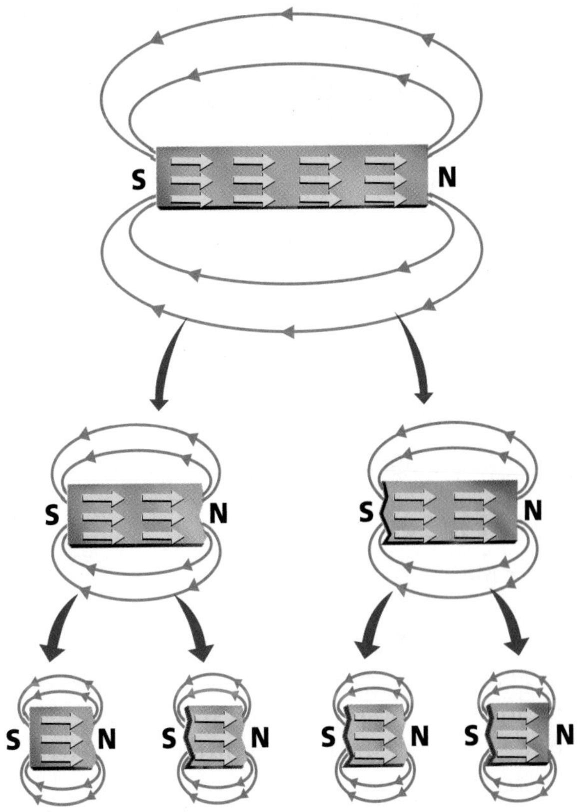

Section 2 Assessment

Target Reading Skill Asking Questions Work with a partner to check the answers in your graphic organizer.

Reviewing Key Concepts

1. a. Listing What particles are found in an atom?
   b. Identifying Which particle is responsible for a material's magnetic properties?
   c. Relating Cause and Effect How is a magnetic field produced in an atom?
2. a. Defining What is a magnetic domain?
   b. Explaining How are domains arranged in materials that are magnetized and in ones that are not?
   c. Applying Concepts What happens to the domains in iron filings that line up with the magnetic field of a bar magnet?
3. a. Reviewing How can magnets be changed?
   b. Comparing and Contrasting How are temporary and permanent magnets alike? How are they different?

Writing in Science

Writing Dialogue You are discussing magnets with another person. That person thinks that breaking a magnet will destroy the magnet's magnetic properties. Write a conversation you might have with the other person as you try to explain why the person's idea is incorrect.

Lab zone **Technology Lab**

• Tech & Design •

Design and Build a Magnetic Paper Clip Holder

Problem

Many objects that you use in your daily life contain magnets. Can you design and build a magnetic paper clip holder?

Skills Focus

designing the solution, evaluating the design, troubleshooting

Materials

- 2 bar magnets
- masking tape
- container of 150 regular size paper clips
- an assortment of types, shapes, and sizes of magnets, including two bar magnets
- modeling clay, string, and other materials approved by your teacher

Procedure

PART 1 Research and Investigate

1. Copy the data table into your notebook.
2. Place one pole of a bar magnet into a container of paper clips. Slowly lift the magnet and count how many paper clips are attached to it. Record the number of paper clips in your data table. Return the paper clips to the container.
3. Repeat Step 2 two more times.
4. Calculate the average number of paper clips you lifted in the three trials.

Data Table

Type of magnet	Number of paper clips

5. Use the other pole of the bar magnet and repeat Step 2.
6. Repeat Step 2 again using the poles of each of the other magnets to pick up the paper clips.
7. Repeat Step 2 using 3 or 4 different combinations of magnets. For example, you can tape two magnets together, as shown in the photo.

PART 2 Design and Build

8. Examine your data. Use it to design a magnetic paper clip holder that
   - holds at least 150 paper clips
   - allows easy access to the paper clips *(Hint:* The holder could sit on a desk or hang suspended from an object)
   - is made of materials approved by your teacher
   - is built following the Safety Guidelines in Appendix A
9. Draw a sketch of your paper clip holder and include a list of materials you'll need. Obtain your teacher's approval of your design. Then build your holder.

PART 3 Evaluate and Redesign

10. Test your holder. Does the device meet the criteria listed in Step 8? Compare the design and performance of your holder with the holders of some of your classmates.
11. Based on what you learned, redesign your holder. After you receive your teacher's approval, build and test your redesigned holder.

Analyze and Conclude

1. **Inferring** Why did you test each magnet three times in Part 1?
2. **Drawing Conclusions** What conclusions did you draw from the data you collected in Part 1?
3. **Designing a Solution** How did you use the data you collected to design your paper clip holder?
4. **Troubleshooting** Describe one problem you faced while designing or building your holder. How did you solve the problem?
5. **Working With Design Constraints** What limitations did the criteria of holding at least 150 paper clips place on your design? How did you solve those limitations?
6. **Evaluating the Impact on Society** Describe how a device that uses magnets affects your life on a daily basis.

Communicate

Write a letter to a friend that describes how you combined magnets to build a practical paper clip holder.

Go Online
PHSchool.com

For: Data sharing
Visit: PHSchool.com
Web Code: cgd-4034

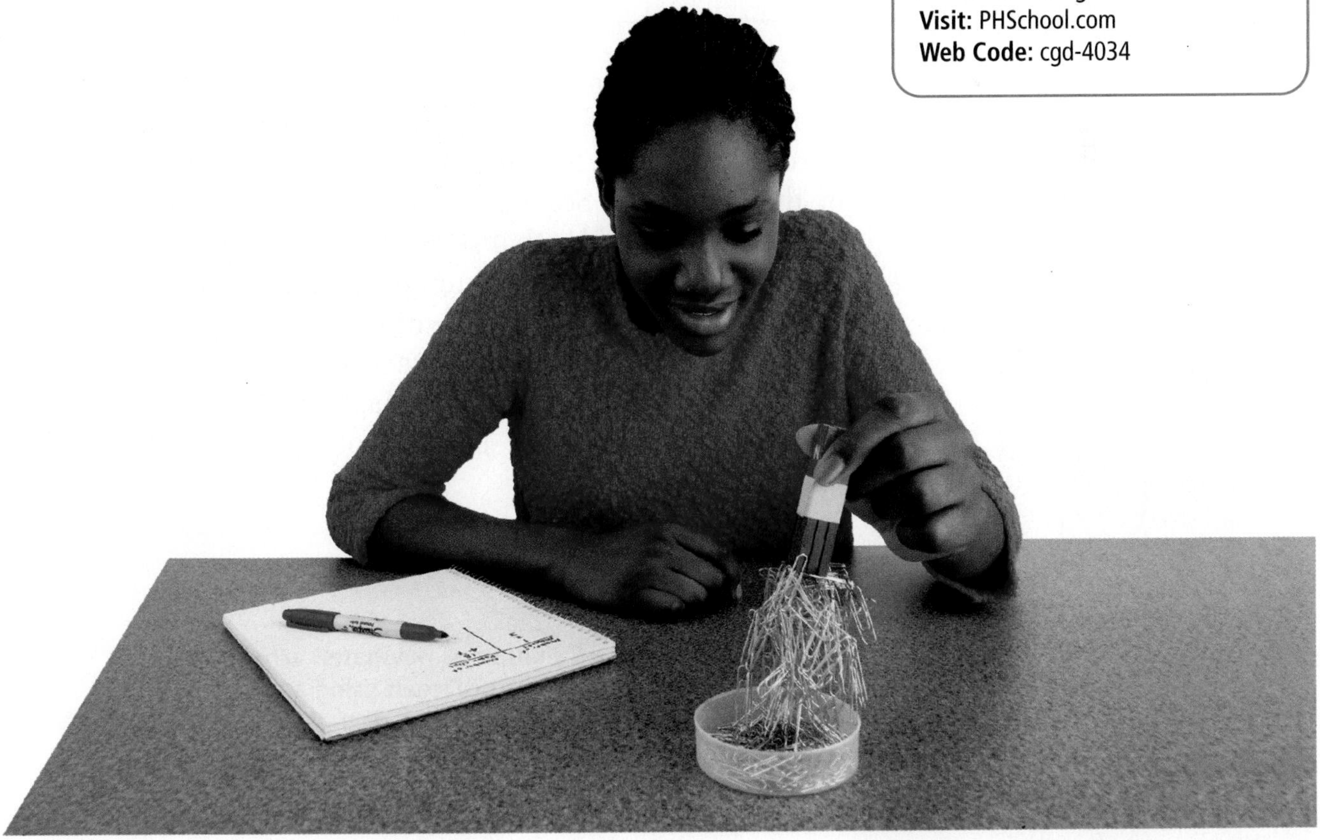

Section 3

Integrating Earth Science

Magnetic Earth

Reading Preview

Key Concepts

- How is Earth like a bar magnet?
- What are the effects of Earth's magnetic field?

Key Terms

- compass
- magnetic declination
- Van Allen belts
- solar wind
- magnetosphere
- aurora

Target Reading Skill

Building Vocabulary Using a word in a sentence helps you think about how best to explain the word. After you read the section, reread the paragraphs that contain definitions of Key Terms. Use all the information you have learned to write a meaningful sentence using the Key Term.

Lab zone **Discover Activity**

Can You Use a Needle to Make a Compass?

1. Magnetize a large needle by rubbing it several times in the same direction with one end of a strong bar magnet. Push the needle through a ball of foam or tape it to a small piece of cork.
2. Place a drop of dishwashing soap in a bowl of water. Then float the foam or cork in the water. Adjust the needle until it floats horizontally.
3. Allow the needle to stop moving. Note the direction it points.
4. Use a local map to determine the direction in which it points.

Think It Over

Observing In what direction did the needle point? If you repeat the activity, will it still point in the same direction? What does this tell you about Earth?

When Christopher Columbus sighted land in 1492, he didn't know what he had found. He was trying to find a shortcut from Europe to India. Where he landed, however, was on an island in the Caribbean Sea just south of the present-day United States. He had no idea that such an island even existed.

In spite of his error, Columbus had successfully followed a course west to the Americas without the help of an accurate map. Instead, Columbus used a compass for navigation. A **compass** is a device that has a magnetized needle that spins freely. A compass needle usually points north. As you read, you'll find out why.

◀ Columbus navigated across the Atlantic Ocean using a compass similar to one of these.

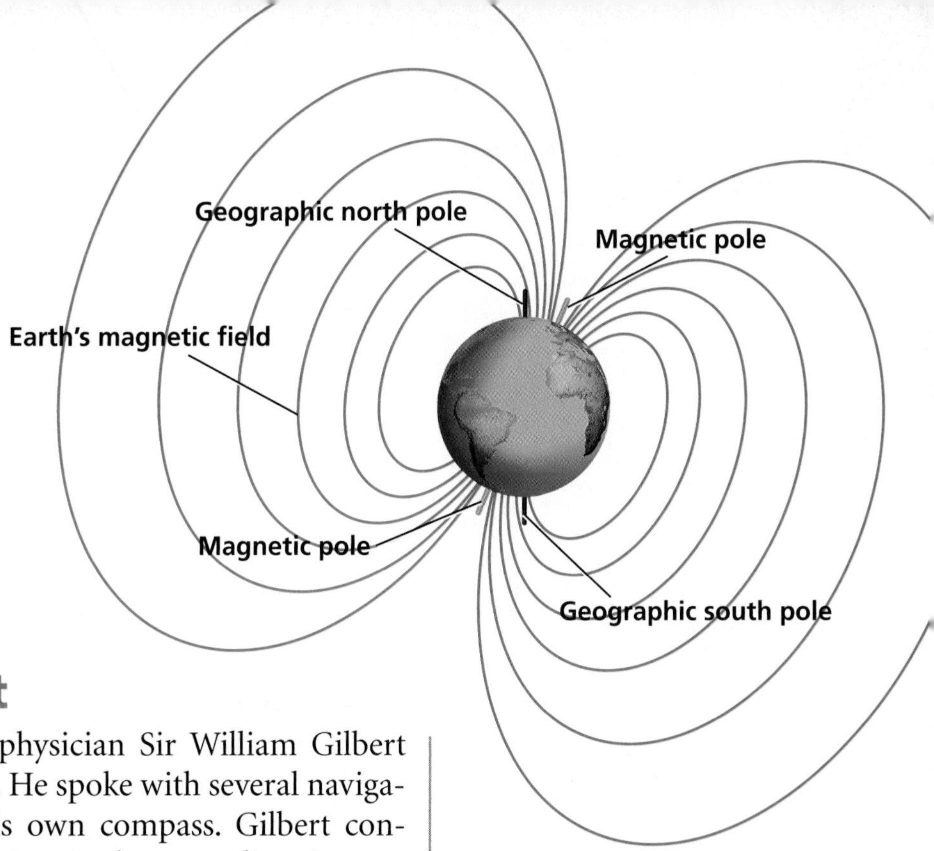

FIGURE 12
Earth's Magnetic Field
The magnetic field lines show the shape of Earth's magnetic field.
Observing *What magnetic properties does Earth have?*

Earth as a Magnet

In the late 1500s, the English physician Sir William Gilbert became interested in compasses. He spoke with several navigators and experimented with his own compass. Gilbert confirmed that a compass always points in the same direction, no matter where it is. But no one knew why.

Gilbert hypothesized that a compass behaves as it does because Earth acts as a giant magnet. Although many educated people of his time laughed at this idea, Gilbert turned out to be correct. **Just like a bar magnet, Earth has a magnetic field surrounding it and two magnetic poles.**

The fact that Earth has a magnetic field explains why a compass works as it does. The poles of the magnetized needle on the compass align themselves with Earth's magnetic field.

Earth's Core Gilbert thought that Earth's center, or core, contains magnetic rock. Scientists now think that this is not the case, since the material inside Earth's core is too hot to be solid. Also, the temperature is too high for the material to be magnetic. Earth's magnetism is still not completely understood. But scientists do know that the circulation of molten material in Earth's core is related to Earth's magnetism.

Earth's Magnetic Poles You know that Earth rotates on its axis, around the geographic poles. But Earth also has magnetic poles. These magnetic poles are located on Earth's surface where the magnetic force is strongest. As you can see in Figure 12, the magnetic poles are not in the same place as the geographic poles. For example, the magnetic pole in the Northern Hemisphere is located in northern Canada about 1,250 kilometers from the geographic North Pole.

Discovery Channel School

Magnetism

Video Preview
▶ Video Field Trip
Video Assessment

Magnetic Pole Movement

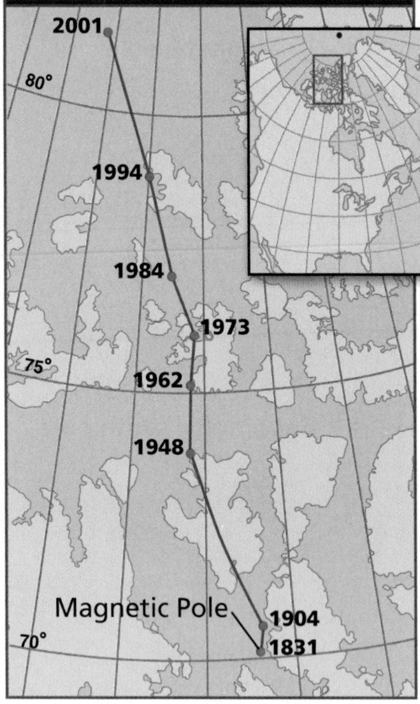

FIGURE 13
The location of Earth's magnetic poles does not stay the same.

Magnetic Declination If you use a compass, you have to account for the fact that Earth's geographic and magnetic poles are different. Suppose you could draw a line between you and the geographic North Pole. The direction of this line is geographic north. Then imagine a second line drawn between you and the magnetic pole in the Northern Hemisphere. The angle between these two lines is the angle between geographic north and the north to which a compass needle points. This angle is known as **magnetic declination**. So, magnetic declination differs depending on your location on Earth.

The magnetic declination of a location on Earth today is not the same as it was 10 years ago. The magnetic declination of a location changes. Earth's magnetic poles do not stay in one place as the geographic poles do. Figure 13 shows how the location of Earth's magnetic pole in the Northern Hemisphere has drifted over time.

Earth's Magnetic Field

You learned that a material such as iron can be made into a magnet by a strong magnetic field. **Since Earth produces a strong magnetic field, Earth itself can make magnets out of ferromagnetic materials.**

Earth as a Magnet Maker Suppose you leave an iron bar lying in a north-south direction for many years. Earth's magnetic field may attract the domains strongly enough to cause them to line up in the same direction. When the domains in the iron bar align, the bar becomes a magnet. This can happen to some everyday objects. So even though no one has tried to make metal objects such as file cabinets in your school into magnets, Earth might have done so anyway!

Math Analyzing Data

Movement of Earth's Magnetic Poles

Earth's magnetic poles move slowly over time. The data in the table show the position of Earth's magnetic north pole in specific years.

1. Interpreting Data What is the trend in the speed of the pole's movement?
2. Calculating What is the total distance the pole has traveled over the time shown?
3. Predicting Using this data, predict the average speed of the pole's movement between 2001 and 2010. Explain.

Magnetic North Pole Movement

Year of Reading	Distance Moved Since Previous Reading (km)	Average Speed (km/yr)
1948	420	9.5
1962	150	10.7
1973	120	10.9
1984	120	10.9
1994	180	18.0
2001	287	41.0

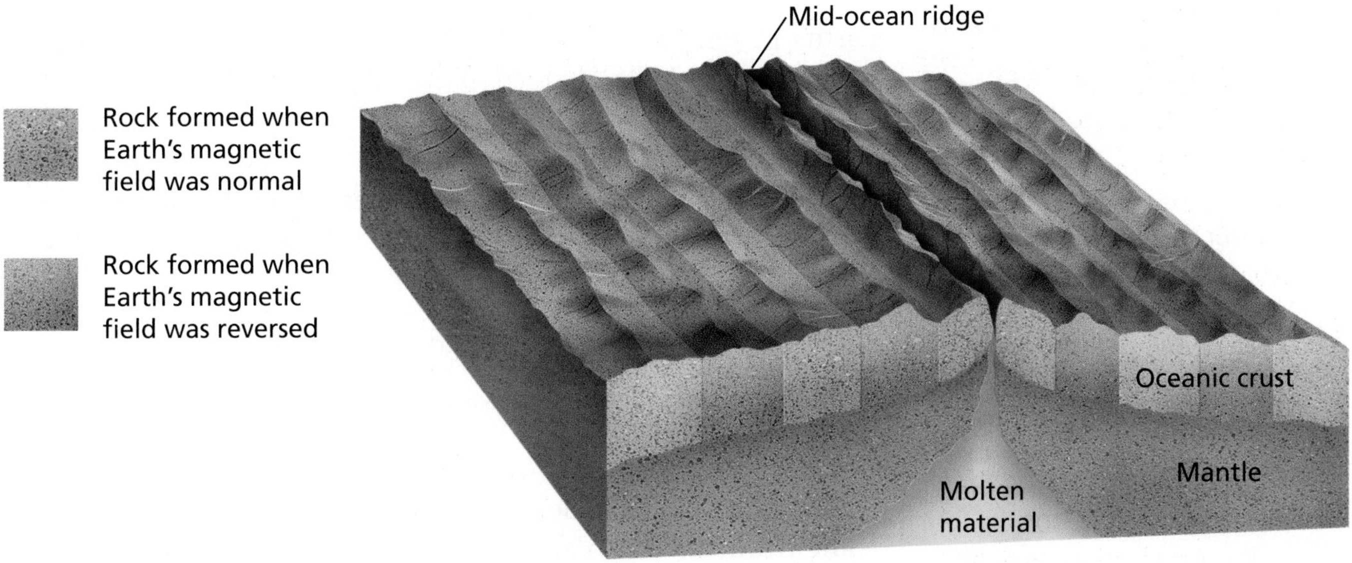

FIGURE 14
Earth's Magnetic Stripes
When molten material hardens into the rock of the ocean floor, the direction of Earth's magnetic field at that time is permanently recorded. **Applying Concepts** *How can scientists use this rock record to study changes in Earth's magnetic field?*

Earth Leaves a Record Earth's magnetic field also acts on rocks that contain magnetic material, such as rock on the ocean floor. Rock is produced on the ocean floor from molten material that seeps up through a long crack in the ocean floor known as a mid-ocean ridge. When the rock is molten, the iron it contains lines up in the direction of Earth's magnetic field. As the rock cools and hardens, the iron is locked in place. This creates a permanent record of the magnetic field.

As scientists studied such rock, they discovered that the direction and strength of Earth's magnetic field have changed over time. Earth's magnetic field has completely reversed direction every million years or so.

The different colored layers in Figure 14 indicate the directions of Earth's magnetic field over time. Notice that the patterns of bands on either side of the ridge are mirror images. This is because the sea floor spreads apart from the mid-ocean ridge. So rocks farther from the ridge are older than rocks near the ridge. Scientists can determine when the rock was formed by looking at the rock's magnetic record.

Why does Earth's magnetic field change direction? No one knows. Scientists hypothesize that changes in the motion of molten material in Earth's core may cause changes in Earth's magnetic field. But scientists cannot explain why changes in the molten material take place.

Reading Checkpoint **What evidence shows that Earth's magnetic field changes?**

Lab zone Skills Activity

Measuring

1. Use a local map to locate geographic north relative to your school. Mark the direction on the floor with tape or chalk.
2. Use a compass to find magnetic north. Again mark the direction.
3. Use a protractor to measure the number of degrees between the two marks.

Compare the directions of magnetic and geographic north. Is magnetic north to the east or west of geographic north?

Lab zone Try This **Activity**

Spinning in Circles

Which way will a compass point?

1. Place a bar magnet in the center of a sheet of paper.
2. Place a compass about 2 cm beyond the north pole of the magnet. Draw a small arrow showing the direction of the compass needle.
3. Repeat Step 2, placing the compass at 20 to 30 different positions around the magnet.
4. Remove the magnet and observe the pattern of arrows you drew.

Drawing Conclusions What does your pattern of arrows represent? Do compasses respond only to Earth's magnetic field?

The Magnetosphere

Earth's magnetic field extends into space. Space is not empty. It contains electrically charged particles. **Earth's magnetic field affects the movements of electrically charged particles in space.** Those charged particles also affect Earth's magnetic field.

Between 1,000 and 25,000 kilometers above Earth's surface are two doughnut-shaped regions called the **Van Allen belts.** They are named after their discoverer, J. A. Van Allen. These regions contain electrons and protons traveling at very high speeds. At one time it was feared that these particles would be dangerous for spacecraft passing through them, but this has not been the case.

Solar Wind Other electrically charged particles in space come from the sun. Earth and the other objects in our solar system experience a solar wind. The **solar wind** is a stream of electrically charged particles flowing at high speeds from the sun. The solar wind pushes against Earth's magnetic field and surrounds the field, as shown in Figure 15. The region of Earth's magnetic field shaped by the solar wind is called the **magnetosphere.** The solar wind constantly reshapes the magnetosphere as Earth rotates on its axis.

Although most particles in the solar wind cannot penetrate Earth's magnetic field, some particles do. They follow Earth's magnetic field lines to the magnetic poles. At the poles, the magnetic field lines dip down to Earth's surface.

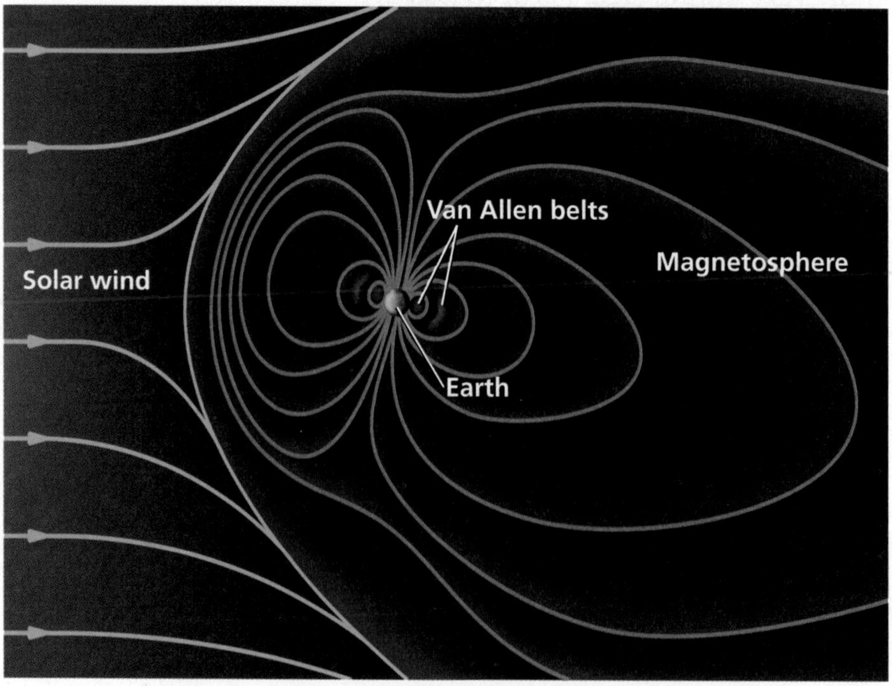

FIGURE 15
Earth's Magnetosphere
The solar wind causes Earth's magnetic field to stretch out on the side of Earth not facing the sun.
Relating Cause and Effect *What shapes the magnetosphere?*

FIGURE 16
Aurora
A band of colored light called an aurora occasionally appears in the night sky near the magnetic poles.

Auroras When high-speed, charged particles get close to Earth's surface, they interact with atoms in the atmosphere. This causes some of the atoms to give off light. The result is one of Earth's most spectacular displays—a curtain of shimmering bright light in the atmosphere. A glowing region in the atmosphere caused by charged particles from the sun is called an **aurora.** In the Northern Hemisphere, an aurora is called the Northern Lights, or aurora borealis. In the Southern Hemisphere, it is called the Southern Lights, or aurora australis.

Reading Checkpoint **What causes an aurora?**

Go Online PHSchool.com
For: More on Earth's magnetic field
Visit: PHSchool.com
Web Code: cgd-4013

Section 3 Assessment

Target Reading Skill **Building Vocabulary** Use your sentences to help answer the questions.

Reviewing Key Concepts

1. a. **Reviewing** How are Earth and a bar magnet similar?
   b. **Describing** How do Earth's magnetic properties explain how a compass works?
   c. **Interpreting Diagrams** Look at Figure 12. How do the positions of the geographic and magnetic poles compare?
2. a. **Identifying** What are two effects of Earth's magnetic field?
   b. **Explaining** How can scientists use rocks to learn about Earth's magnetic field?
   c. **Relating Cause and Effect** What causes the part of Earth's magnetic field called the magnetosphere to exist?

Lab zone **At-Home Activity**

House Compass With a family member, explore your home with a compass. Use the compass to discover magnetic fields in your house. Try metal objects that have been in the same position over a long period of time. Explain to your family member why the compass needle moves away from north near some objects.

Chapter 19

Study Guide

1 What Is Magnetism?

Key Concepts

- Magnets attract iron and similar materials that contain iron. They attract or repel other magnets. In addition, one part of a magnet will always point north when allowed to swing freely.
- Magnetic poles that are unlike attract each other and magnetic poles that are alike repel each other.
- Magnetic field lines spread out from one pole, curve around the magnet, and return to the other pole.

Key Terms

magnet
magnetic pole
magnetic force
magnetic field
magnetic field lines

2 Inside a Magnet

Key Concepts

- A spinning electron produces a magnetic field that makes the electron behave like a tiny magnet in an atom.
- In a magnetized material, all or most of the magnetic domains are arranged in the same direction.
- Magnets can be made, destroyed, or broken apart.

Key Terms

atom
element
nucleus
proton
neutron
electron
magnetic domain
ferromagnetic material
temporary magnet
permanent magnet

3 Magnetic Earth

Key Concepts

- Just like a bar magnet, Earth has a magnetic field surrounding it and two magnetic poles.
- Since Earth produces a strong magnetic field, Earth itself can make magnets out of ferromagnetic materials.
- Earth's magnetic field affects the movements of electrically charged particles in space.

Key Terms

compass
magnetic declination
Van Allen belts
solar wind
magnetosphere
aurora

Review and Assessment

Go Online
PHSchool.com
For: Self-Assessment
Visit: PHSchool.com
Web Code: cga-4010

Organizing Information

Concept Mapping Copy the concept map about magnetism onto a separate sheet of paper. Then complete it and add a title. (For more on concept maps, see the Skills Handbook.)

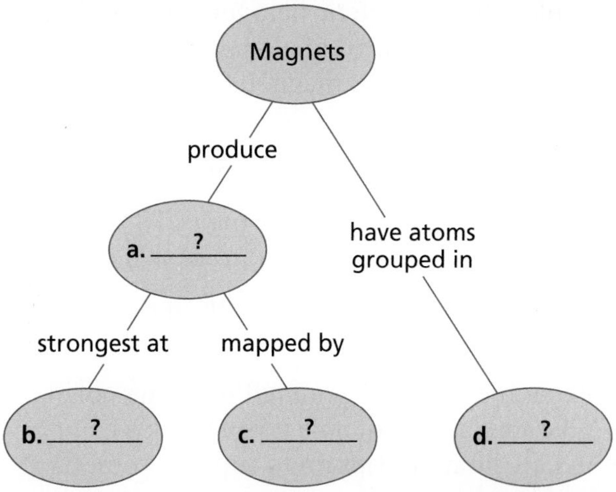

Reviewing Key Terms

Choose the letter of the best answer.

1. The area of a magnet where the magnetic force is strongest is a
   a. magnetic pole.
   b. magnetic field.
   c. magnetic field line.
   d. magnetosphere.
2. The negatively charged particles within atoms are
   a. electrons. **b.** nuclei.
   c. protons. **d.** orbits.
3. An example of a ferromagnetic material is
   a. plastic.
   b. copper.
   c. wood.
   d. iron.
4. A compass works because its magnetic needle
   a. contains atoms.
   b. contains charged particles.
   c. repels magnets.
   d. spins freely.
5. A stream of electrically charged particles flowing from the sun is called the
   a. Van Allen belt.
   b. magnetosphere.
   c. solar wind.
   d. magnetic field.

If the statement is true, write *true*. If it is false, change the underlined word or words to make the statement true.

6. Magnetic field lines map out the magnetic field around a magnet.
7. In an atom, the electrons and protons are located in the nucleus.
8. A ferromagnetic material is a material like iron that has strong magnetic properties.
9. A magnet that keeps its magnetism for a long time is called a temporary magnet.
10. The region of Earth's magnetic field shaped by the solar wind is called the aurora.

Writing in Science

Research Report You are a geologist reporting about Earth's magnetic field. In your report, explain what causes the field and give information on how scientists study it.

Discovery Channel School™

Magnetism
Video Preview
Video Field Trip
▶ Video Assessment

Review and Assessment

Checking Concepts

11. Explain how magnetic field lines are used to represent the field of a magnet. Draw a diagram that shows magnetic field lines around a magnet.

12. Describe the structure of an atom.

13. How do the atoms differ in materials that can be used as magnets and materials that cannot?

14. Describe the magnetic domains in a magnetized material.

15. Explain why you are not left with one north pole and one south pole if you break a magnet in half. Draw a diagram to support your answer.

16. How does a material become a magnet?

17. How does Earth act like a magnet?

18. What is an aurora? How is it produced?

Thinking Critically

19. **Applying Concepts** Examine the diagram below. Is the magnetic pole on the left a north or south pole? Are the two poles like or unlike?

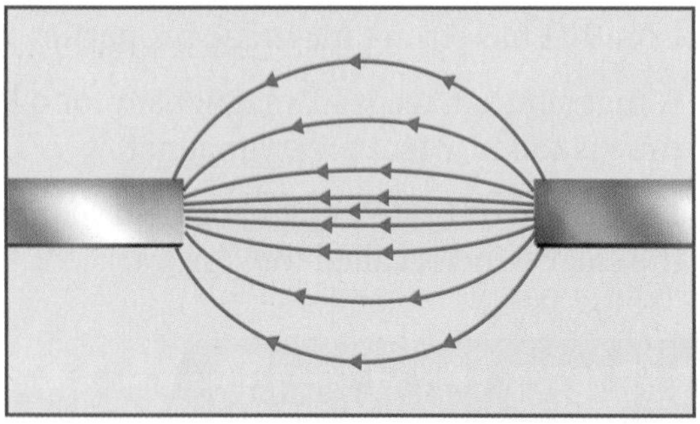

20. **Applying Concepts** The north pole of a bar magnet is held next to one end of an iron rod. Is the other end of the iron rod a north pole or a south pole? Why?

21. **Inferring** A compass points north until a bar magnet is brought next to it. The compass needle is then attracted or repelled by the magnet. What inference can you make about the strengths of the magnetic fields of Earth and the bar magnet?

22. **Problem Solving** Cassia borrowed her brother's magnet. When she returned it, it was barely magnetic. What might Cassia have done to the magnet?

23. **Drawing Conclusions** Why might an inexperienced explorer get lost using a compass?

24. **Relating Cause and Effect** What might happen to a metal pair of scissors if rubbed in one direction with the north pole of a magnet?

Applying Skills

Use the illustration to answer Questions 25–27.

The illustration shows two pairs of magnets.

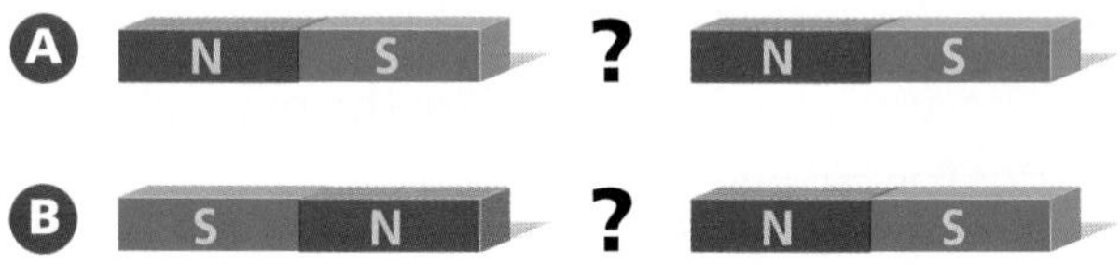

25. **Interpreting Diagrams** Which pair of magnets will have a force of attraction between them? Which pair will have a force of repulsion between them? Explain your choices.

26. **Predicting** Suppose the left-side magnet in pair A traded places with the left-side magnet in pair B. Use magnetic field lines to make a sketch to show how the new pairs would look. Predict if the pairs will attract or repel. Explain.

27. **Problem Solving** If the poles of the magents were not identified, how could you identify them without using a compass?

Lab zone Chapter Project

Performance Assessment Present your sculpture to the class. Use a diagram of your sculpture to show the materials you used to create it and to show how the materials are connected to each other. Explain how you included any materials that were not originally magnetic.

Standardized Test Prep

Test-Taking Tip

Interpreting a Diagram

Some questions ask you to interpret a diagram. Examine the diagram in detail, paying attention to labels, titles, and arrows. Study the diagram of the magnetic field of an iron bar for Question 3 and answer the sample question.

Sample Question

The distance between the magnetic field lines on the diagram indicates that the magnetic field is

A strongest where the lines are farthest apart.
B strongest where the lines are closest together.
C weakest where the lines are closest together.
D uniform.

Answer

The correct answer is **B.** The distance between the magnetic field lines on a magnetic field diagram indicate the strength of the magnetic field, which is strongest where the lines are closest together.

Choose the letter of the best answer.

1. Maglev trains use magnets to elevate trains so that they never touch the tracks. The poles of the magnets on the trains facing the poles of the magnets on the tracks must be

A the same, so they attract each other.
B the same, so they repel each other.
C opposites, so they repel each other.
D opposites, so they attract each other.

2. In lab, Claudio rubs the north pole of a bar magnet against a wooden coffee stirrer, iron nail, and plastic spoon. After rubbing each item for 2 minutes, Claudio tries to pick up one steel paper clip using each object. The variable tested in this experiment was

F the magnetic strength of the bar magnet.
G time.
H the magnetic properties of selected materials.
J the amount of rubbing.

Use the diagram below to answer Question 3.

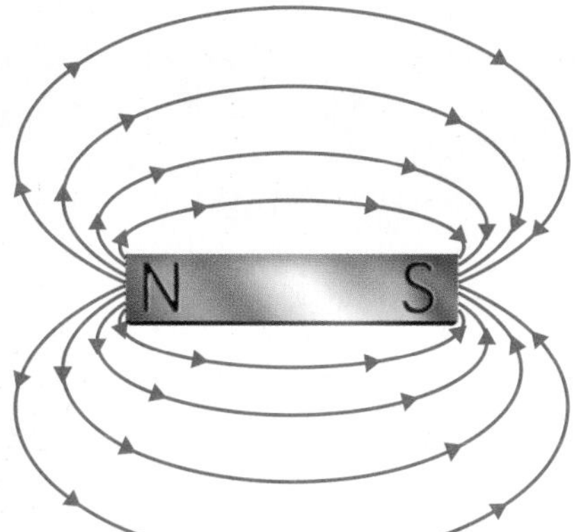

3. If the bar magnet in the above diagram were cut in half, which diagram below *best* represents the magnetic field of the two new pieces?

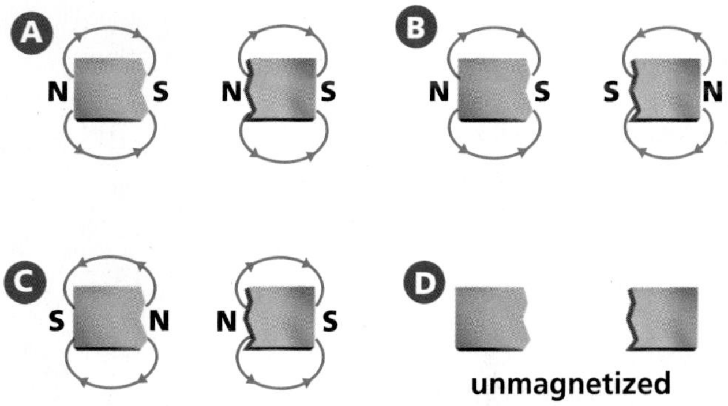

4. Which of the following statements *best* describes why compasses point north?

F Compasses, like all magnets, always point to the geographic North Pole.
G The magnetized compass needle aligns itself with Earth's magnetic field.
H Compass needles point toward the sun.
J The compass needle is repelled by Earth's geographic South Pole.

Constructed Response

5. A bar magnet picks up one paper clip. A second paper clip clings to the first paper clip but does not directly touch the magnet. Explain why the second paper clip clings to the first without touching the bar magnet.

Chapter

20 Electricity

Chapter Preview

1. **Electric Charge and Static Electricity**
   Discover *Can You Move a Can?*
   Try This *Sparks Are Flying*
   At-Home Activity *TV Attraction*
   Skills Lab *The Versorium*

2. **Electric Current**
   Discover *How Can Current Be Measured?*
   Try This *Down the Tubes*
   Skills Lab *Dimmer Switch*

3. **Batteries**
   Discover *Can You Make Electricity Using a Penny?*
   At-Home Activity *Reviving Old Cells*

4. **Electric Circuits and Power**
   Discover *Do the Lights Keep Shining?*
   Math Skills *Decimals*
   Active Art *Series and Parallel Circuits*
   Skills Activity *Predicting*

5. **Electrical Safety**
   Discover *How Can You Blow a Fuse?*
   Analyzing Data *Electrical Equipment and Fires*
   At-Home Activity *Checking Circuits*

Interactive Textbook

Electric lights sparkle in New York City at night. ▶

Discovery Channel School

Electricity

▶ Video Preview
Video Field Trip
Video Assessment

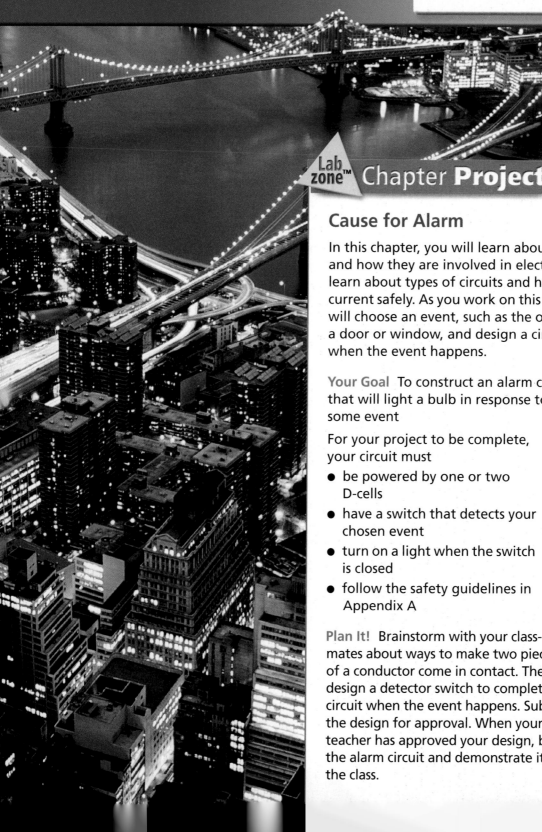

Lab zone™ Chapter **Project**

Cause for Alarm

In this chapter, you will learn about electric charges and how they are involved in electricity. You will also learn about types of circuits and how to use electric current safely. As you work on this chapter project, you will choose an event, such as the opening or closing of a door or window, and design a circuit that alerts you when the event happens.

Your Goal To construct an alarm circuit that will light a bulb in response to some event

For your project to be complete, your circuit must

- be powered by one or two D-cells
- have a switch that detects your chosen event
- turn on a light when the switch is closed
- follow the safety guidelines in Appendix A

Plan It! Brainstorm with your classmates about ways to make two pieces of a conductor come in contact. Then, design a detector switch to complete a circuit when the event happens. Submit the design for approval. When your teacher has approved your design, build the alarm circuit and demonstrate it to the class.

Section 1

Electric Charge and Static Electricity

Reading Preview

Key Concepts

- How do electric charges interact?
- What is an electric field?
- How does static electricity build up and transfer?

Key Terms

- electric force • electric field
- static electricity
- conservation of charge
- friction • conduction
- induction • static discharge

Target Reading Skill

Previewing Visuals Before you read, preview Figure 4. Then write two questions that you have about the diagram in a graphic organizer like the one below. As you read, answer your questions.

Transferring Static Electricity

Q. What are three ways static electricity can be transferred?
A.
Q.

Lab zone Discover Activity

Can You Move a Can Without Touching It?

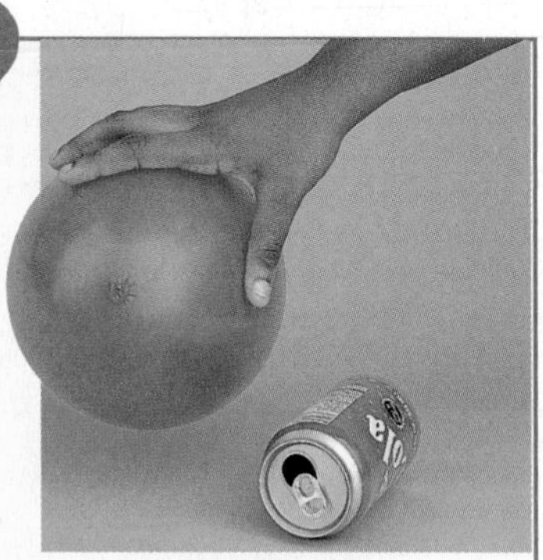

1. Place an empty aluminum can on its side on the floor.
2. Blow up a balloon. Then rub the balloon back and forth on your hair several times.
3. Hold the balloon about 2 to 3 centimeters away from the can.
4. Slowly move the balloon farther away from the can. Observe what happens.
5. Move the balloon to the other side of the can and observe what happens.

Think It Over

Inferring What happens to the can? What can you infer from your observation?

You're in a hurry to get dressed for school, but you can't find one of your socks. You quickly head for the pile of clean laundry. You've gone through everything, but where's your matching sock? The dryer couldn't have really destroyed it, could it? Oh no, there it is. It's sticking to the back of your blanket. What makes clothes and blankets stick together? The explanation has to do with tiny electric charges.

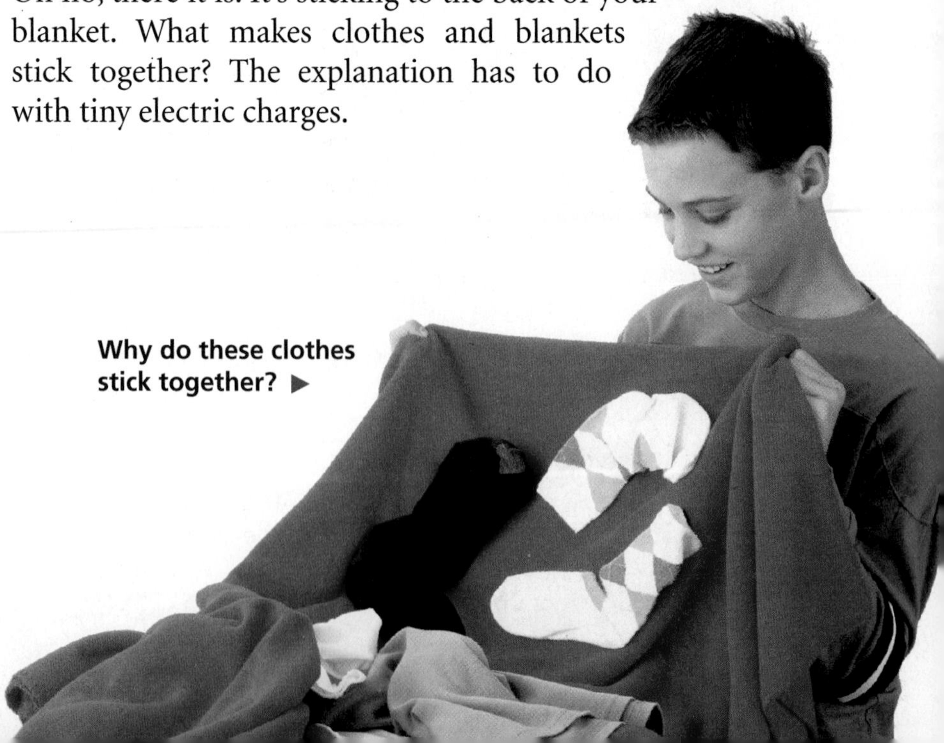

Why do these clothes stick together? ▶

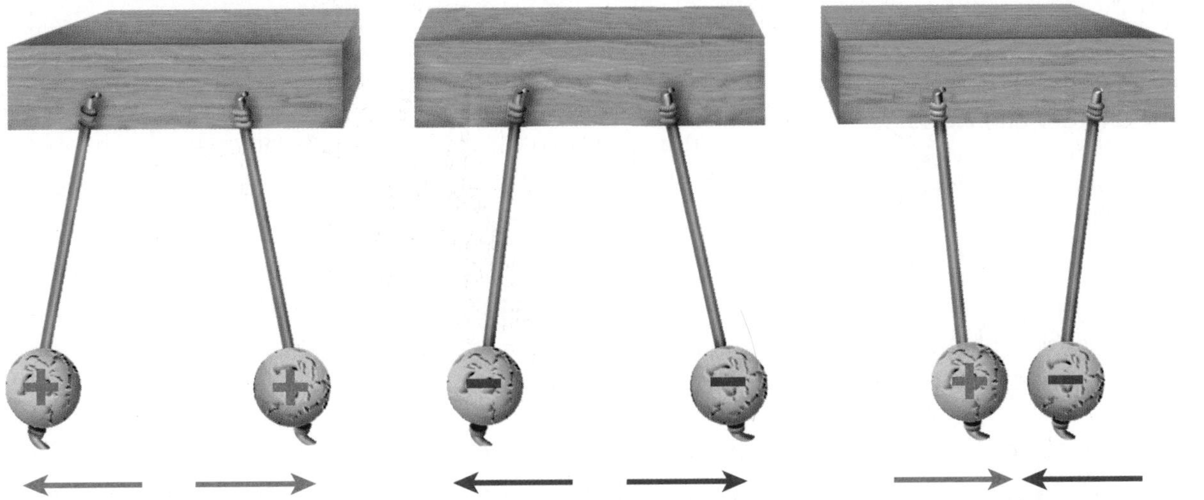
Positive charges repel each other
Negative charges repel each other
Positive and negative charges attract each other

FIGURE 1
Repel or Attract?
The two types of charge, positive and negative, react to one another in specific ways.
Interpreting Diagrams *Which combinations of charges repel each other?*

Electric Charge

Recall that the charged parts of atoms are electrons and protons. When two protons come close together, they push one another apart. In other words, the protons repel each other. But if a proton and an electron come close together, they attract one another.

Why do protons repel protons but attract electrons? The reason is that they have different types of electric charge. Electric charge is a property of electrons and protons. Protons and electrons have opposite charges. The charge on a proton is called positive (+), and the charge on a electron is called negative (–). The names *positive* and *negative* were given to charges by Benjamin Franklin in the 1700s.

The two types of electric charges interact in specific ways, as you see in Figure 1. **Charges that are the same repel each other. Charges that are different attract each other.** Does this sound familiar to you? This rule is the same as the rule for interactions between magnetic poles. Recall that magnetic poles that are alike repel each other, and magnetic poles that are different attract each other. This interaction between magnetic poles is called magnetism. The interaction between electric charges is called electricity.

There is one important difference between electric charges and magnetic poles. Recall that magnetic poles cannot exist alone. Whenever there is a south pole, there is always a north pole. In contrast, electric charges can exist alone. In other words, a negative charge can exist without a positive charge.

Reading Checkpoint **What is one important difference between magnetism and electricity?**

Lab zone Skills Activity

Drawing Conclusions

1. Tear tissue paper into small pieces, or use a hole punch to cut circles.
2. Run a plastic comb through your hair several times.
3. Place the comb close to, but not touching, the tissue paper pieces. What do you observe?

What can you conclude about the electric charges on the comb and the tissue paper?

FIGURE 2
Electric Charges and Fields
The lines in each diagram represent an electric field. The stronger the field, the closer together the lines are.

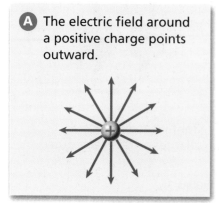

A The electric field around a positive charge points outward.

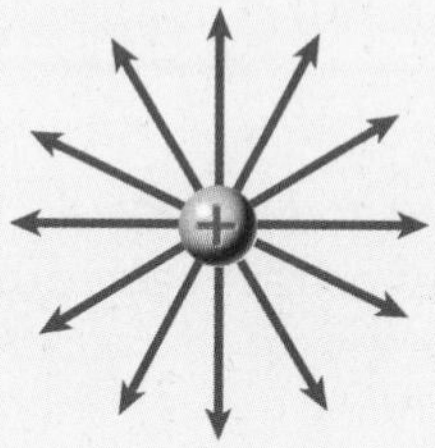

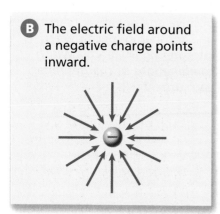

B The electric field around a negative charge points inward.

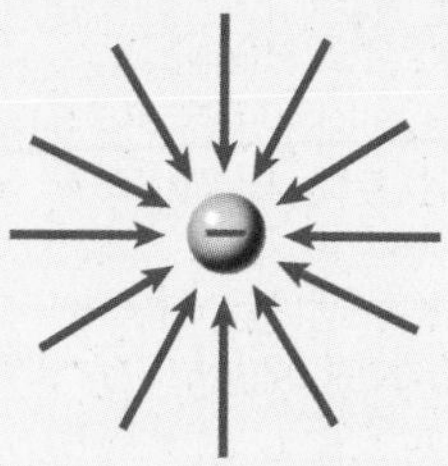

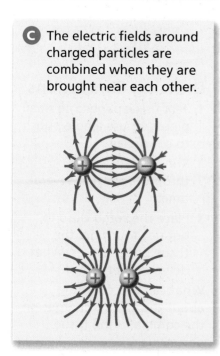

C The electric fields around charged particles are combined when they are brought near each other.

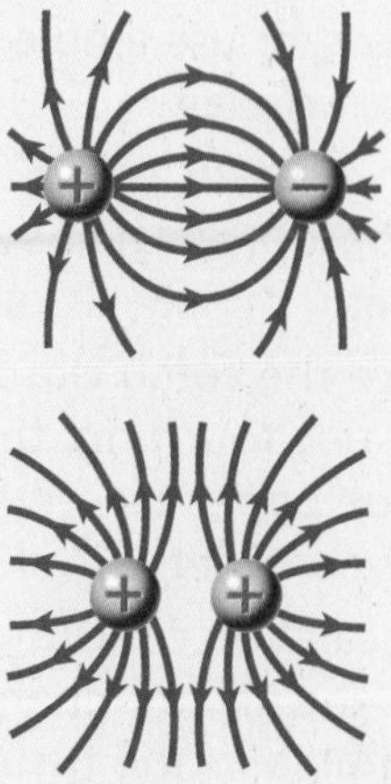

Electric Force

You may think of force as a push or pull on an object. For example, the force of gravity pulls objects toward the ground. You have learned that magnetic force is the attraction or repulsion between magnetic poles. In electricity, **electric force** is the attraction or repulsion between electric charges.

Electric Field Just as magnetic poles exert their forces over a distance, so do electric charges. Recall that a magnetic field extends around a magnet. Similarly, an **electric field** extends around a charged object. **An electric field is a region around a charged object where the object's electric force is exerted on other charged objects.**

When one charged object is placed in the electric field of another charged object, it is either pushed or pulled. It is pushed away if the two objects have the same charge. It is pulled toward the other charged object if their charges are different.

Electric Field Around a Single Charge An electric field is invisible, just like a magnetic field. You may recall using magnetic field lines to represent a magnetic field. In a similar way, you can use electric field lines to represent the electric field. Electric field lines are drawn with arrows to show the direction of the electric force. The electric force always points away from positive charges, as shown in Figure 2A. Notice in Figure 2B that the electric force always points toward negative charges.

The strength of an electric field is related to the distance from the charged object. The greater the distance, the weaker the electric field is. The strength of an electric field is represented by how close the electric field lines are to each other. The electric field is strongest where the lines are closest together. Since the strength of the electric field is greatest near the charged object, that's where the lines appear closest together. Farther from the charged object, the lines appear more spread out because the magnetic field is weaker.

Electric Field Around Multiple Charges When there are two or more charges, the shape of the electric field of each charge is altered. The electric fields of each individual charge combine by repelling or attracting. Figure 2C shows the interaction of the electric fields from two pairs of charges.

Reading Checkpoint **What is electric force?**

Static Electricity

Most objects normally have no overall charge, which means that they are neutral. Each atom has an equal number of protons and electrons. So each positive charge is balanced by a negative charge. As a result, there is no overall electric force on an atom.

Some objects, however, can become charged. Protons are bound tightly in the center of an atom, but electrons can sometimes leave their atoms. In materials such as silver, copper, gold, and aluminum, some electrons are held loosely by the atoms. These electrons can move to other atoms. As you see in Figure 3, an uncharged object becomes charged by gaining or losing electrons. If an object loses electrons, it is left with more protons than electrons. Therefore, the object has an overall positive charge. If an object gains electrons, it has more electrons than protons and has an overall negative charge.

The buildup of charges on an object is called **static electricity.** *Static* means "not moving or changing." **In static electricity, charges build up on an object, but they do not flow continuously.**

Go Online SCI LINKS NSTA
For: Links on static electricity
Visit: www.SciLinks.org
Web Code: scn-1421

FIGURE 3
Charging by Friction
Rubbing two objects together may produce a buildup of static electricity.
Relating Cause and Effect *In what two ways can an uncharged object become charged?*

An uncharged balloon does not attract the girl's hair.

Rubbing the balloon allows more electrons to move onto the balloon. The balloon gains a negative charge.

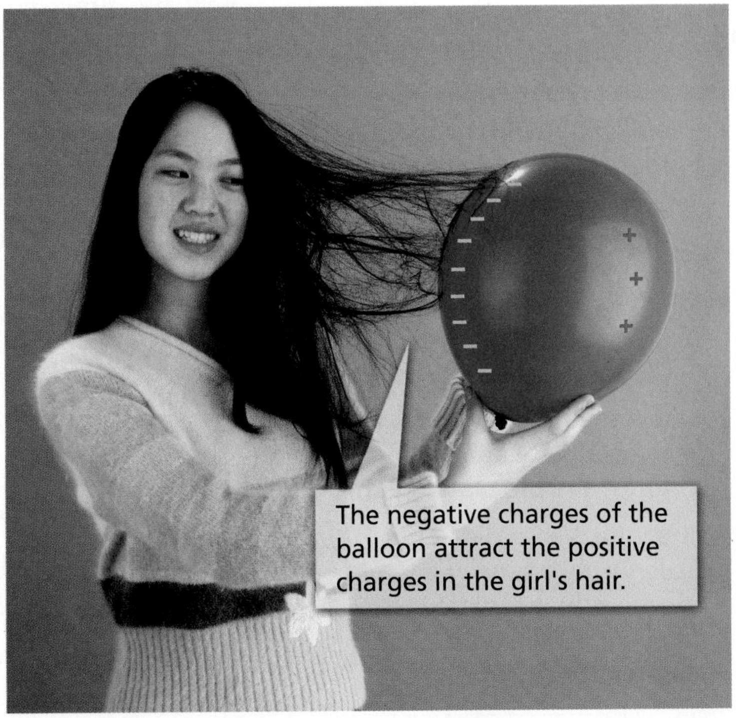

The negative charges of the balloon attract the positive charges in the girl's hair.

Transferring Charge

An object becomes charged only when electrons are transferred from one location to another. Charges are neither created nor destroyed. This is a rule known as the law of **conservation of charge.** If one object gives up electrons, another object gains those electrons. **There are three methods by which charges can be transferred to build up static electricity: charging by friction, by conduction, and by induction.**

Charging by Friction When two uncharged objects rub together, some electrons from one object can move onto the other object. The object that gains electrons becomes negatively charged, and the object that loses electrons becomes positively charged. Charging by **friction** is the transfer of electrons from one uncharged object to another by rubbing. In Figure 4, when the girl's socks rub the carpet, electrons move from the carpet onto her sock. This causes an overall negative charge on the sock. Clothing that sticks together when it is taken out of the dryer is another example of charging by friction.

Charging by Conduction When a charged object touches another object, electrons can be transferred between the objects. Electrons transfer from the object that has the more negative charge to the one that has the more positive charge. For example, a positively charged object will gain electrons when it touches an uncharged object. Charging by **conduction** is the transfer of electrons from a charged object to another object by direct contact. In Figure 4, charges are transferred from the girl's feet to the rest of her body because of charging by conduction.

Charging by Induction In charging by friction and by conduction, electrons are transferred when objects touch one another. In charging by induction, however, objects do not touch when the charges transfer. Charging by **induction** is the movement of electrons to one part of an object that is caused by the electric field of a second object. The electric field around the charged object attracts or repels electrons in the second object. In Figure 4, for example, the negative charges in the girl's fingertip produce an electric field that repels the electrons on the surface of the doorknob. The electrons on the doorknob move away from the finger. This movement produces an induced positive charge on the doorknob.

Reading Checkpoint **What is the difference between charging by induction and charging by conduction?**

Lab zone Try This **Activity**

Sparks Are Flying

Lightning is the result of static electricity. You can make your own lightning.

1. Cut a strip 3 cm wide from the middle of a foam plate. Fold the strip to form a W. Tape it to the center of an aluminum pie plate as a handle.

2. Rub a second foam plate on your hair. Place it upside down on a table.
3. Use the handle to pick up the pie plate. Hold the pie plate about 30 cm over the foam plate and drop it.
4. Now, very slowly, touch the tip of your finger to the pie plate. Be careful not to touch the foam plate. Then take your finger away.
5. Use the handle to pick up the pie plate again. Slowly touch the pie plate again.

Inferring What did you observe each time you touched the pie plate? How can you explain your observations?

FIGURE 4
Transferring Electrons

Static electricity involves the transfer of electrons from one object to another. Electrons can be transferred by friction, conduction, or induction.

Interpreting Photos *How can charges on the carpet induce a charge on the doorknob?*

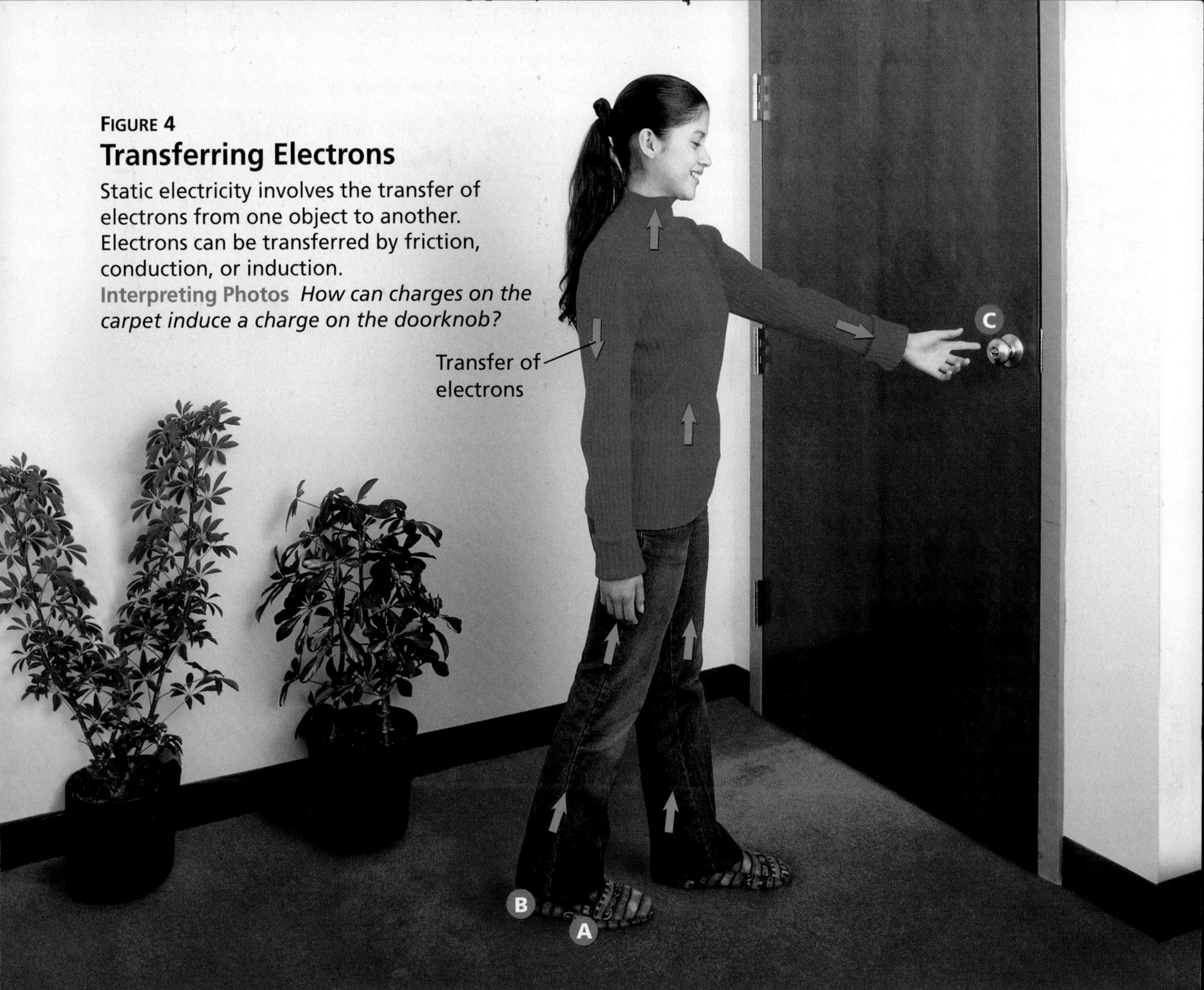

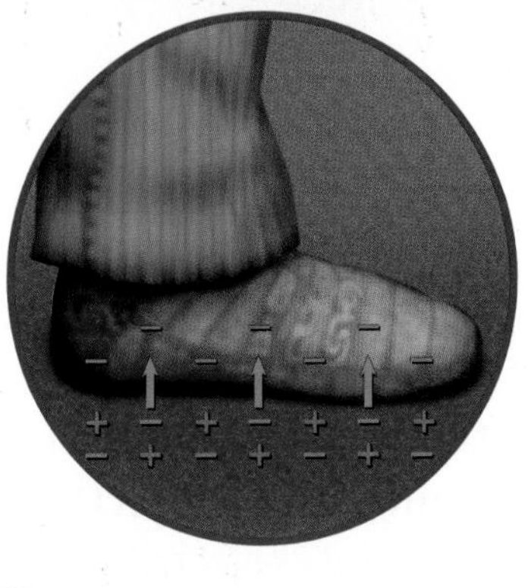

A Charging by Friction Electrons are rubbed from the carpet to the girl's sock. The charges are distributed evenly over the sock.

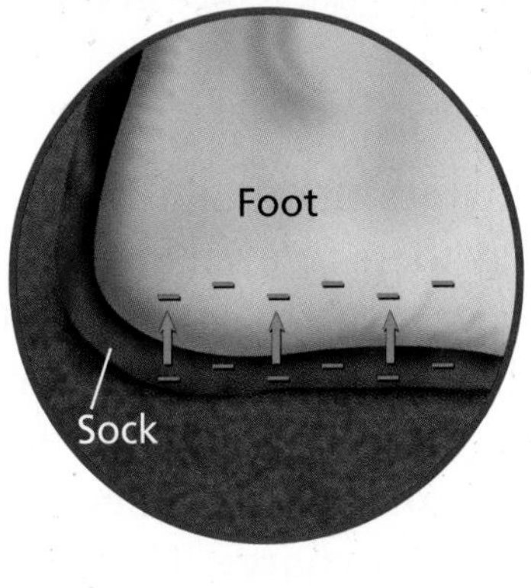

B Charging by Conduction When the negatively charged sock touches the skin, electrons are transferred by direct contact. Electrons are then distributed throughout the girl's body.

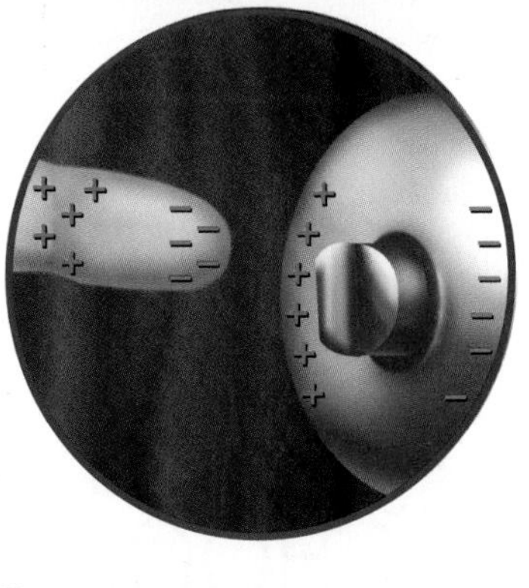

C Charging by Induction Electrons on the girl's finger-tip produce an electric field that repels negative charges and attracts positive charges on the doorknob. An overall positive charge is induced on the edge of the doorknob.

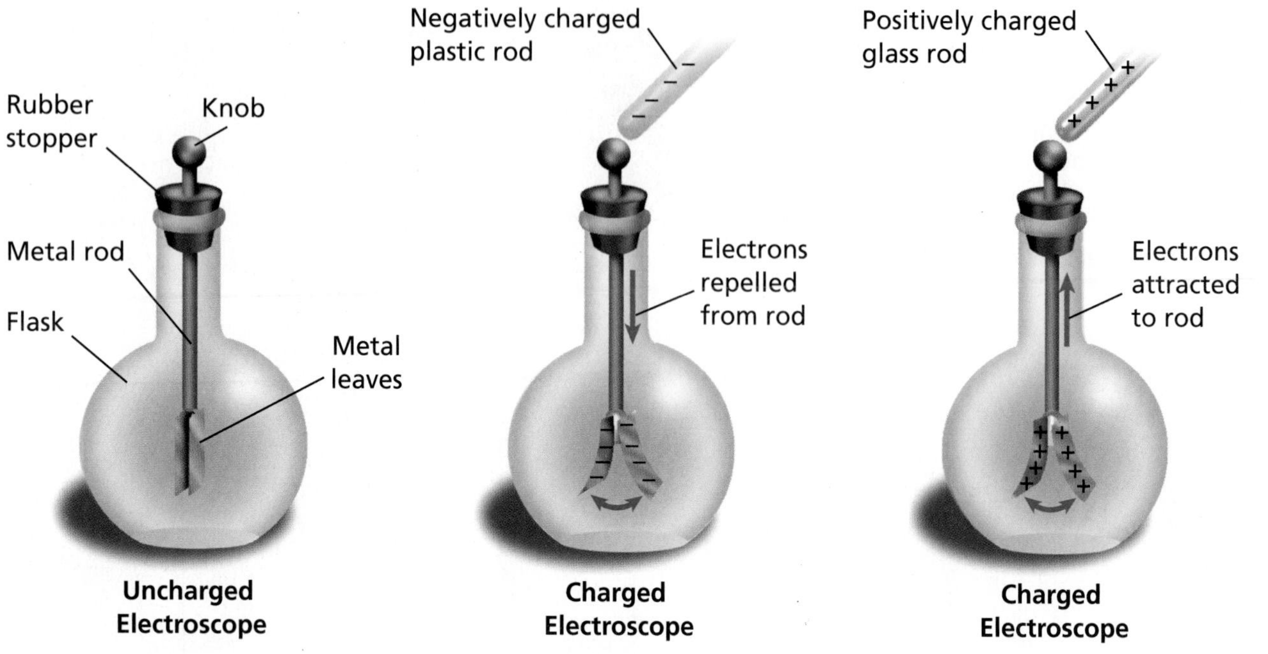

FIGURE 5
An Electroscope
An electroscope can be used to detect the presence of a charge, but it does not tell you whether the charge is positive or negative.
Relating Cause and Effect *Why do the leaves of the electroscope move apart when a charged object touches the knob?*

Detecting Charge Electric charge is invisible, but it can be detected by an instrument called an electroscope. A typical electroscope, shown in Figure 5, consists of a metal rod with a knob at the top and two thin metal leaves at the bottom. When the electroscope is uncharged, its metal leaves hang straight down. When a charged object touches the knob, electric charge travels by conduction into or out of the leaves. Since the charge on both leaves is the same, the leaves repel each other and spread apart. The leaves move apart in response to either negative charge or positive charge. Therefore, you cannot use an electroscope to determine the type of charge.

Static Discharge

Charges that build up as static electricity on an object don't stay there forever. Electrons tend to move, returning the object to its neutral condition. Consider what happens when two objects with opposite charges touch one another. **When a negatively charged object and a positively charged object are brought together, electrons transfer until both objects have the same charge.** The loss of static electricity as electric charges transfer from one object to another is called **static discharge**.

Often, a static discharge produces a spark. As electrons transfer between objects, they heat the air around the path they travel until it glows. The glowing air is the spark you see. The tiny spark you may have seen when you touch a doorknob or metal object is an example of static discharge.

Discovery Channel School

Electricity

Video Preview
▶ Video Field Trip
Video Assessment

Lightning is a dramatic example of static discharge. You can think of lightning as a huge spark. During thunderstorms, air swirls violently. Water droplets within the clouds become electrically charged. To restore a neutral condition in the clouds, electrons move from areas of negative charge to areas of positive charge and produce an intense spark. You see that spark as lightning.

Some lightning reaches Earth because negative charges at the bottom of storm clouds may cause the surface of Earth to become positively charged by induction. Electrons jump between the cloud and Earth's surface, producing a giant spark as they travel through the air. This is possible because of charging by conduction.

Reading Checkpoint **How is lightning formed?**

FIGURE 6
Static Discharge
Lightning is a spectacular discharge of static electricity. Lightning can occur within a cloud, between two clouds, or between a cloud and Earth.

Section 1 Assessment

Target Reading Skill **Previewing Visuals** Refer to your questions and answers about Figure 4 to help you answer Question 3 below.

Reviewing Key Concepts

1. a. **Identifying** What are the two types of electric charge?
   b. **Explaining** How do objects with the same charge interact? How do objects with opposite charges interact?
   c. **Comparing and Contrasting** How are electric charges similar to magnetic poles? How are they different?
2. a. **Defining** What is an electric field?
   b. **Interpreting Diagrams** What do the lines represent in an electric field diagram?
3. a. **Reviewing** What is static electricity?
   b. **Describing** How is static electricity transferred during charging by conduction?
   c. **Applying Concepts** What role does induction play when lightning strikes Earth?

Lab zone At-Home Activity

TV Attraction Rub a balloon against your hair and bring the balloon near one of your arms. Observe the hair on your arm; then put down the balloon. Then bring your other arm near the front of a television screen that is turned on. Ask a family member to explain why the hairs on your arms are attracted to the balloon and to the screen. Explain that this is evidence that there is static electricity present on both the balloon and the screen.

The Versorium

Problem

A versorium is a device that was first described in 1600 by Sir William Gilbert. Why does a versorium turn?

Skills Focus

observing, predicting, classifying

Materials

- foam cup
- plastic foam plate
- pencil
- aluminum foil
- wool fabric
- paper
- scissors

Procedure

PART 1 Aluminum Foil Versorium

1. Cut a piece of aluminum foil approximately 3 cm by 10 cm.
2. Make a tent out of the foil strip by gently folding it in half in both directions.
3. Push a pencil up through the bottom of an inverted cup. **CAUTION:** *Avoid pushing the sharpened pencil against your skin.* Balance the center point of the foil tent on the point of the pencil as shown.
4. Make a copy of the data table.
5. Predict what will happen if you bring a foam plate near the foil tent. Record your prediction in the data table.
6. Predict what will happen if you rub the foam plate with wool fabric and then bring the plate near the foil tent. Record your prediction.
7. Predict what will happen if you bring the rubbed wool near the foil tent. Again record your prediction.
8. Test each of your three predictions and record your observations in the data table.

PART 2 Paper Tent Versorium

9. What might happen if you used a paper tent versorium instead of aluminum foil? Record your prediction for each of the three tests.
10. Test your prediction and record your observations in the data table.

Data Table

	Unrubbed Foam Plate	Rubbed Foam Plate	Rubbed Wool Fabric
Aluminum Tent: Prediction			
Aluminum Tent: Observation			
Paper Tent: Prediction			
Paper Tent: Observation			

Analyze and Conclude

1. Inferring At the beginning of the lab, is the foil negatively charged, positively charged, or uncharged? Use your observations to explain your answer.
2. Predicting Refer to the predictions you recorded in Steps 5, 6, and 7. Explain the reasoning behind those predictions.
3. Observing Did the behavior of the foil match each of your predictions in Steps 5, 6, and 7? Refer to your observations to explain your answer.
4. Classifying Did the effect of the foam plate differ in Steps 5 and 6? If so, identify which process—charging by friction, by conduction, or by induction—produced that change.
5. Classifying In Step 7, which process—charging by friction, by conduction, or by induction—explains the behavior of the foil when you brought the rubbed wool near it? Explain.
6. Predicting Explain the reasoning for your prediction about the paper tent versorium in Part 2.
7. Observing Did the behavior of the paper tent match your prediction in Step 9? Refer to your observations to explain your answer.
8. Drawing Conclusions Were the procedures and results in Part 2 generally similar to those in Part 1? Explain your answer with reference to charging by friction, by conduction, or by induction.
9. Controlling Variables During this lab, why is it important to avoid touching the foam plate or the wool with other objects before testing them with the versorium?
10. Communicating Another student who did this lab says that the versorium can show whether an object has a positive or negative charge. Write an e-mail to that student giving your reasons for agreeing or disagreeing.

Design an Experiment

What other materials besides foam or wool might have an effect on the versorium? What other materials could you use to make the versorium tent? Design an experiment to test specific materials and see how they respond. *Obtain your teacher's permission before carrying out your investigation.*

Section 2

Electric Current

Reading Preview

Key Concepts

- How is an electric current produced?
- How are conductors different from insulators?
- What causes electric charges to flow in a circuit?
- How does resistance affect current?

Key Terms

- electric current
- electric circuit • conductor
- insulator • voltage
- voltage source • resistance

Target Reading Skill

Outlining As you read, make an outline about electric current. Use the red headings for the main ideas and the blue headings for the supporting ideas.

Lab zone Discover Activity

How Can Current Be Measured?

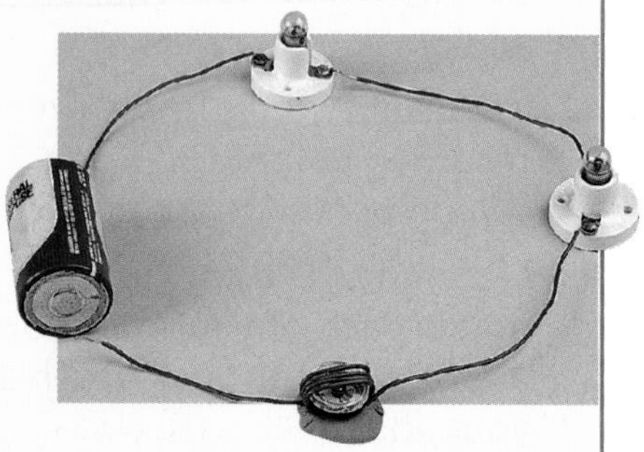

1. Obtain four pieces of wire with the insulation removed from both ends. Each piece should be about 25 cm long.
2. Wrap one of the wires four times around a compass as shown. You may use tape to keep the wire in place.
3. Build a circuit using the remaining wire, wrapped compass, two bulbs, and a D-cell as shown. Adjust the compass position so that the wire is aligned directly over the compass needle.
4. Make sure the compass is level. If it is not, place it on a piece of modeling clay so that the needle swings freely.
5. Observe the compass needle as you complete the circuit. Record the number of degrees the needle moves.
6. Repeat the activity using only one bulb, and again with no bulb. Record the number of degrees the needle moves.

Think It Over

Inferring Based on your observations of the compass, when did the compass needle move the most? How can you explain your observations?

Thousands of tomatoes ride along a conveyer belt through a giant machine. The conveyer belt carries the tomatoes through a cleaning station, a sorter, and into a lane to be packaged. You might be wondering what a huge conveyer belt of tomatoes could possibly have to do with electricity. Like the tomatoes, electric charges can be made to move in a confined path.

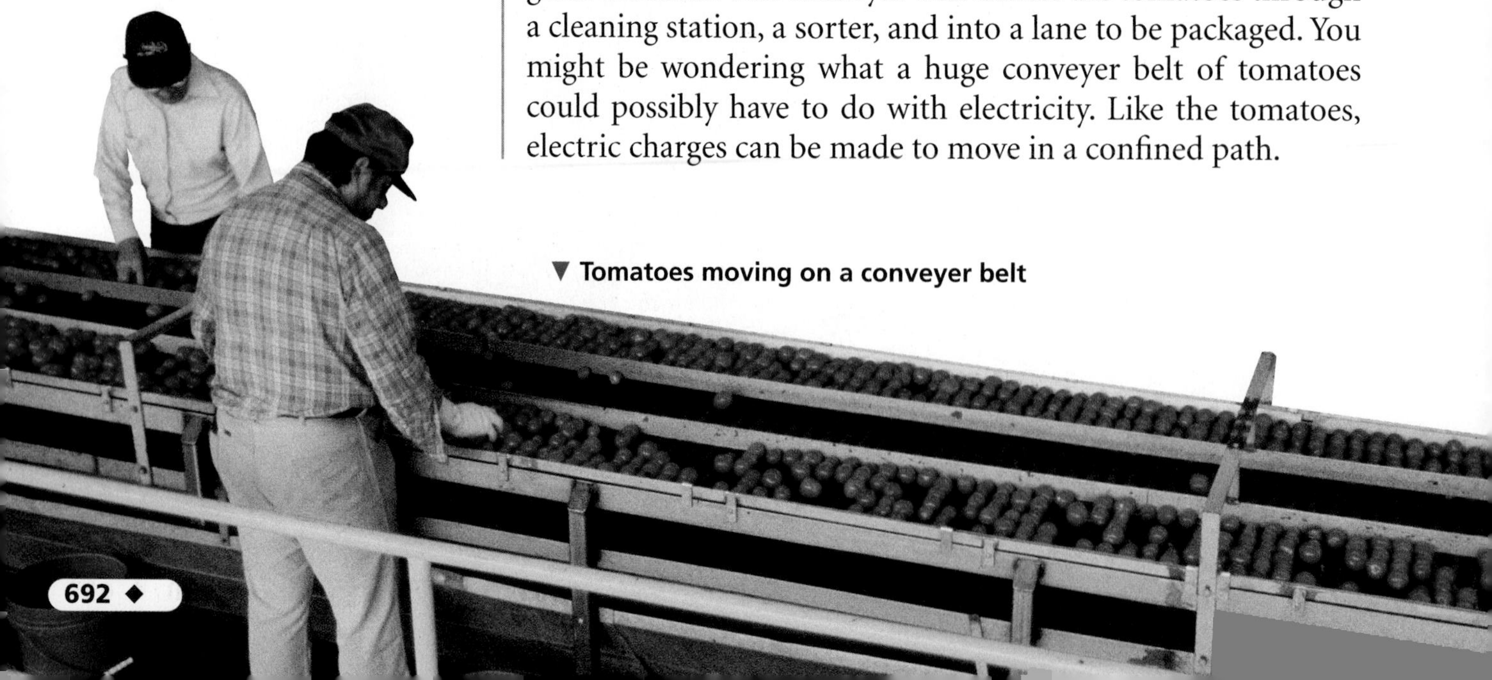

▼ **Tomatoes moving on a conveyer belt**

Flow of Electric Charges

Lightning releases a large amount of electrical energy. However, the electric charge from lightning can't be used to power your TV, clock radio, video game, or kitchen lights because it only lasts for an instant. These electric devices need electric charges that flow continuously. They require electric current.

What Is Electric Current? Recall that static electric charges do not flow continuously. However, when electric charges are made to flow through a wire or similar material, they produce an electric current. **Electric current** is the continuous flow of electric charges through a material. The amount of charge that passes through the wire in a unit of time is the rate of electric current. The unit for the rate of current is the ampere, named for André Marie Ampère, an early investigator of electricity. The name of the unit is often shortened to *amp* or *A*. The number of amps describes the amount of charge flowing past a given point each second.

FIGURE 7
Representing an Electric Current
Tomatoes moving on a conveyer belt are similar to charges moving in a wire, or electric current.
Interpreting Photos *Which characteristics of electric current are represented in the illustrations?*

Tomatoes on a conveyer belt are similar to electric current in a wire. Both the tomatoes and the current move in a confined path.

If the tomatoes move faster, more tomatoes pass the worker every second. Similarly, if current is increased in a wire, more charges pass by a point on the wire every second.

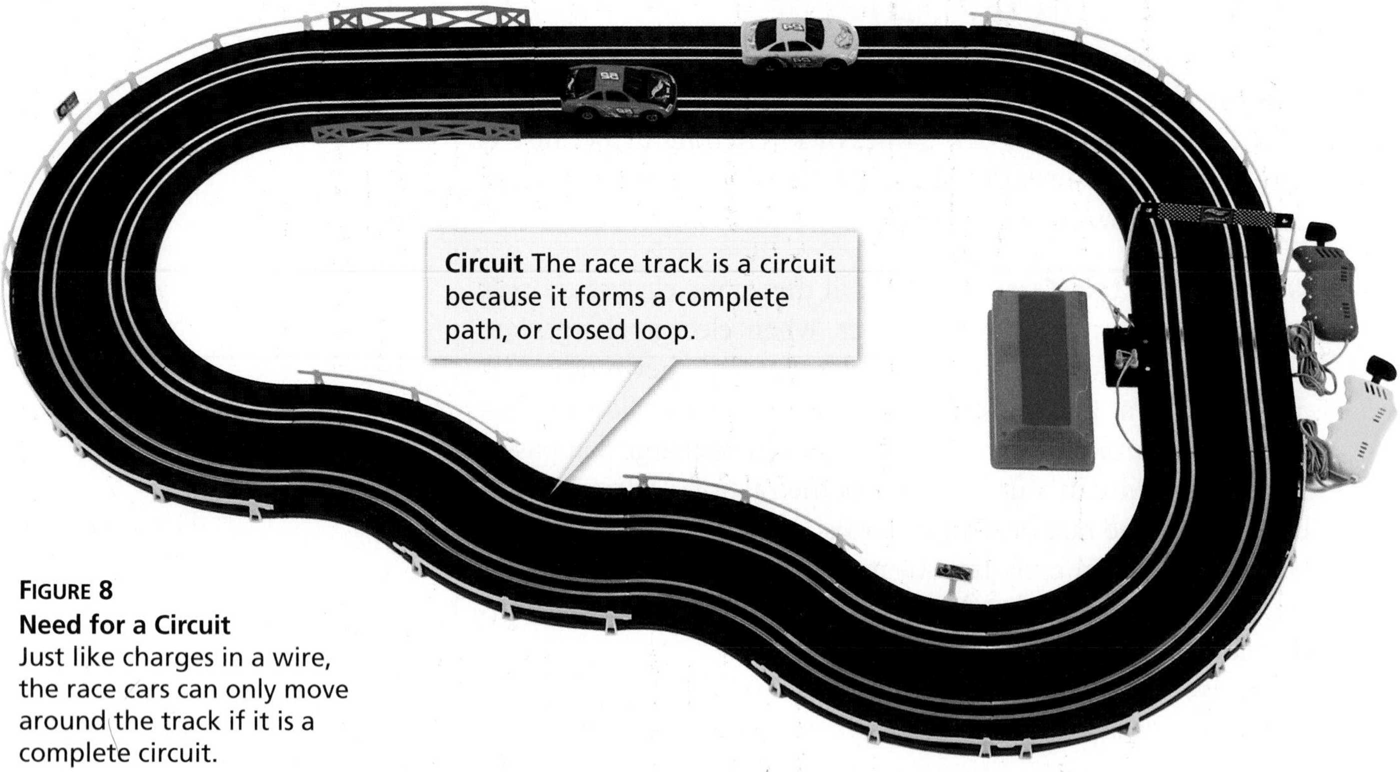

Circuit The race track is a circuit because it forms a complete path, or closed loop.

FIGURE 8
Need for a Circuit
Just like charges in a wire, the race cars can only move around the track if it is a complete circuit.

Current in a Circuit Electric current does not automatically exist in a material. Current requires a specific path to follow. **To produce electric current, charges must flow continuously from one place to another.** Current requires an electric circuit. An **electric circuit** is a complete, unbroken path through which electric charges can flow.

The cars on the racetrack in Figure 8 are like the charges in an electric circuit. If the racetrack forms a complete loop, the cars can move around the track continuously. However, if a piece of the racetrack is missing, the cars are unable to move around the loop. Similarly, if an electric circuit is complete, charges can flow continuously. If an electric circuit is broken, charges will not flow.

Electric circuits are all around you. All electrical devices, from toasters to radios to electric guitars and televisions, contain electric circuits. You will learn more about the characteristics of electric circuits in Section 4.

Reading Checkpoint **What is an electric circuit?**

Conductors and Insulators

Charges flow easily through a circuit made of metal wires. But would charges flow in wires made of plastic? The answer is no. Electric charges do not flow easily through every material. **A conductor transfers electric charge well. An insulator does not transfer electric charge well.** Figure 9 shows materials that are good conductors and materials that are insulators.

Conductors Metals, such as silver, copper, aluminum, and iron, are good conductors. A **conductor** is a material through which charge can flow easily. In a conductor, atoms contain electrons that are bound loosely. These electrons, called conduction electrons, are able to move throughout the conductor. As these electrons flow through a conductor, they form an electric current. Conductors are used to carry electric charge.

Did you ever wonder why a light goes on the instant you flip the switch? How do the electrons get to your lamp from the electric company so fast? The answer is that electrons are not sent to your house when you flip a switch. They are already present inside the conductors that make up the circuit. When you flip the switch, electrons at one end of the wire are pulled, while those at the other end are pushed. The result is a continuous flow of electrons through all parts of the circuit as soon as the circuit is completed.

Insulators A material through which charges cannot flow easily is called an **insulator**. The electrons in an insulator are bound tightly to their atoms and do not move easily. Rubber, glass, sand, plastic, and wood are good insulators. Insulators are used to stop the flow of charges.

The rubber coating on an appliance cord is an example of an insulator. A cord carries charges from an electrical outlet to an appliance. So why don't you get a shock when you touch a cord? The inner wire is the conductor for the current. The rubber coating around the wire is an insulator. The cord allows charge to continue to flow to the appliance, but stops it from flowing into your hand and shocking you.

Reading Checkpoint **Why don't you get a shock from touching an extension cord?**

Go Online PHSchool.com

For: More on electric current
Visit: PHSchool.com
Web Code: cgd-4022

Conductors

Insulators

FIGURE 9
Conductors and Insulators
Charges easily move through conductors. In contrast, charges do not move easily through insulators. Classifying *In which category do metals belong?*

Lab zone Try This Activity

Down the Tubes

Use water to model voltage.

1. Set up a funnel, tubing, beaker, and ring stand as shown.

2. Have a partner start a stopwatch as you pour 200 mL of water into the funnel.
3. Stop the stopwatch when all of the water has flowed into the beaker.
4. Repeat steps 2 and 3 setting the funnel at different heights.

Making Models How did your model represent voltage? How did changing the height affect the model's "voltage"?

Voltage

Imagine you are on a roller coaster at an amusement park. Strapped in your seat, you wait anxiously as your car climbs to the top of the hill. Then, whoosh! Your car speeds down the steel track. Believe it or not, electric charges flow in much the same way as your roller coaster car moves on the track.

Charges Need Energy to Flow The roller coaster cars need energy to give you an exciting ride, but they have no energy when you first climb aboard. A motor provides energy to move a chain attached to the cars. The moving chain pulls the cars to the top of the hill. As they climb, the cars gain potential energy. Potential energy is the energy an object has as a result of its position, or height. The higher up the hill the chain carries the cars, the more potential energy the cars gain. Then, after reaching the hilltop, the cars rush down the hill. As they do, they move from a place of high potential energy—the hilltop—to a place of low potential energy—the bottom of the hill. It is the difference in potential energy between the hilltop and the bottom of the hill that allows the cars to speed down the hill.

In a similar way, charges in an electric circuit flow because of a difference in electrical potential energy. Think of the charges that make up the electric current as being like the roller coaster cars. The circuit is like the steel track. An energy source, such as a battery, is like the roller coaster motor. The battery provides the potential energy difference for the circuit. However, its potential energy is not related to height, as in the roller coaster. Instead it is related to the charges inside the battery.

Voltage Just as the roller coaster creates a difference in potential energy between two places, so does an electric circuit. The difference in electrical potential energy between two places in a circuit is called **voltage,** or potential difference. The unit of measure of voltage is the volt (V). **Voltage causes a current in an electric circuit.** You can think of voltage as the amount of force pushing an electric current.

Voltage Sources At the amusement park, if there were no way of pulling the roller coaster cars to the top of the first hill, there would be no ride. Recall that the ride has a source of energy, a motor. The motor moves the chain that takes the cars to the top of the hill. Once the cars reach the top of any hill, they gain a high potential energy.

An electric circuit also requires a source of energy, such as a battery, to maintain a voltage. A **voltage source** is a device that creates a potential difference in an electric circuit. Batteries and generators are examples of voltage sources. A voltage source has two terminals. The voltage between the terminals causes charges to move around the circuit.

Reading Checkpoint **What does a voltage source do?**

FIGURE 10

Voltage

Voltage in a circuit is similar to the difference in potential energy on a roller coaster. **Interpreting Diagrams** *From where do the cars get their energy?*

The difference in potential energy between the top and bottom of the roller coaster's hill is like the voltage in an electric circuit.

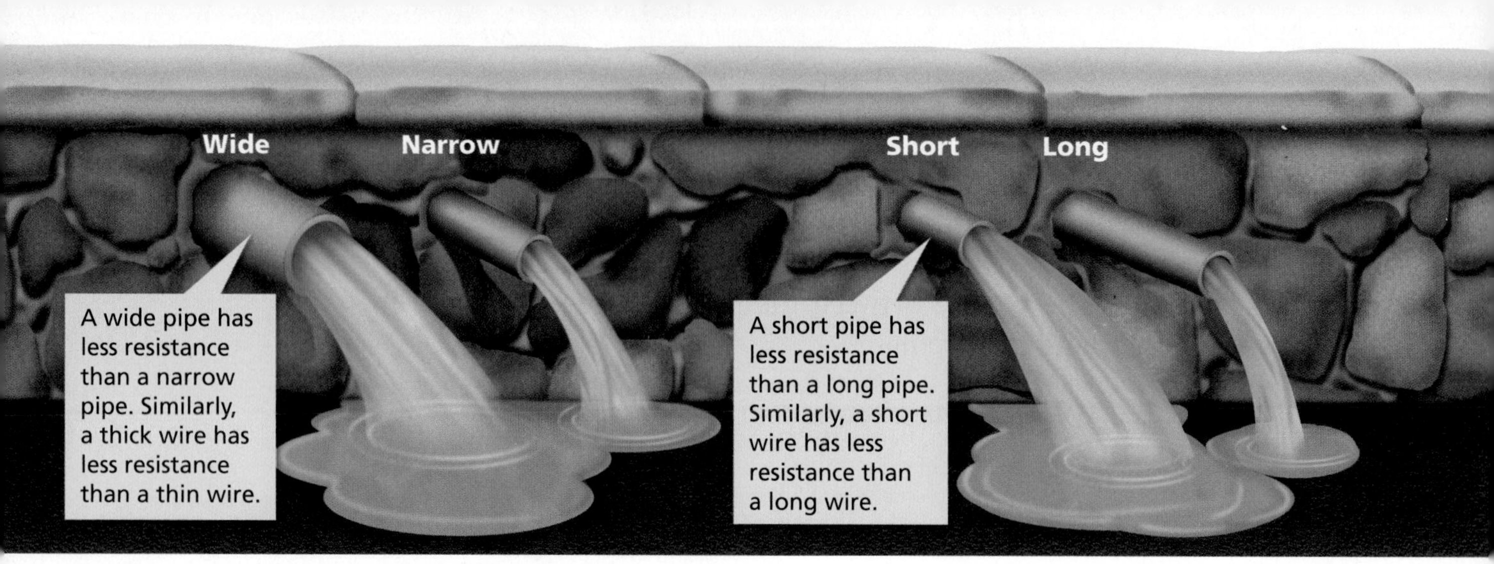

Wide
Narrow
Short
Long
A wide pipe has less resistance than a narrow pipe. Similarly, a thick wire has less resistance than a thin wire.
A short pipe has less resistance than a long pipe. Similarly, a short wire has less resistance than a long wire.

FIGURE 11
Resistance
Two factors that affect the resistance of water flowing in a pipe are diameter and length. The diameter and length of a wire also affect resistance in a circuit.
Inferring *If you reduce the resistance in a circuit, will there be more or less current?*

Resistance

In the example of the roller coaster, you only learned how the height difference, or "voltage," affected the cars' speed. But other factors affect how fast the cars move. For instance, if the roller coaster cars have rusty wheels, their speed will decrease because the wheels do not turn as well. Current in a circuit works in a similar way.

Current Depends on Resistance The amount of current that exists in a circuit depends on more than just the voltage. Current also depends on the resistance of the material. **Resistance** is the measure of how difficult it is for charges to flow through a material. **The greater the resistance, the less current there is for a given voltage.** The unit of measure of resistance is the ohm (Ω). The ohm is named for Georg Ohm, a German physicist who investigated resistance.

Factors That Determine Resistance There are four factors that determine the resistance of a wire, or any object. The first factor is the material from which the wire is made. Some materials, such as insulators, have electrons that are tightly held to their atoms. Insulators have a high resistance because it is difficult for charges to move. Other materials, such as conductors, have electrons that are loosely held to their atoms. Conductors have a low resistance because charges can move through them easily.

The second factor is length. Long wires have more resistance than short wires. The resistance of current in a wire can be compared to the resistance of water flowing through a pipe. Suppose water is being released from a reservoir held by a dam. As shown in Figure 11, less water flows from the reservoir through the long pipe than through the short pipe. The water in the long pipe slows down because it bumps into more of the pipe's inner wall.

Diameter is the third factor. In Figure 11, the pipe with the small diameter has less water flowing through it than the pipe with the large diameter. In the small-diameter pipe, there is less area through which the water can flow. Similarly, thin wires have more resistance than thick wires.

The fourth factor that determines the resistance of a wire is the temperature of the wire. The electrical resistance of most materials increases as temperature increases. As the temperature of most materials decreases, resistance decreases as well.

Path of Least Resistance Perhaps you have heard it said that someone is taking the "path of least resistance." This means that the person is doing something in the easiest way possible. In a similar way, if electric charge can flow through either of two paths, more of the charge will flow through the path with lower resistance.

Have you seen a bird perched on an uninsulated electric fence? The bird doesn't get hurt because charges flow through the path of least resistance. Since the bird's body offers more resistance than the wire, charges flow directly through the wire without harming the bird.

FIGURE 12
Which Path?
Charges flow through the wire, not the bird, because the wire offers less resistance.

Reading Checkpoint What is the "path of least resistance"?

Section 2 Assessment

Target Reading Skill Outlining Use your outline to help you answer the questions below.

Reviewing Key Concepts

1. a. **Reviewing** What happens when an electric current is produced?
   b. **Comparing and Contrasting** Contrast electric current and static electricity.
   c. **Relating Cause and Effect** Explain why electric current cannot exist if an electric circuit is broken.
2. a. **Defining** Define *conductor* and *insulator.*
   b. **Listing** List materials that make good conductors. List materials that are insulators.
   c. **Applying Concepts** If a copper wire in a working electric circuit is replaced by a piece of rubber tubing, will there be a current in the circuit? Explain.
3. a. **Listing** What are two examples of voltage sources?
   b. **Explaining** How does voltage cause electrons to flow in a circuit?
   c. **Predicting** The electrical potential energy at one point in a circuit is greater than the electrical potential energy at another point. Will there be a current between the two points? Explain.
4. a. **Reviewing** What is resistance?
   b. **Summarizing** What are four factors that determine resistance?

Writing in Science

Analogies An analogy can help people understand new information by comparing it to something familiar. Write a paragraph that compares an electric circuit to skiing down a slope and riding the chairlift to the top.

Lab zone **Skills Lab**

Constructing a Dimmer Switch

Problem

What materials can be used to make a dimmer switch?

Skills Focus

predicting, observing

Materials

- D-cell
- masking tape
- flashlight bulb in a socket
- thick lead from mechanical pencil
- uninsulated copper wire, the same length as the pencil lead
- rubber tubing, the same length as the pencil lead
- 1 wire, 10–15 cm long
- 2 wires, 20–30 cm long
- 2 alligator clips

Procedure

1. To make a device that can dim a light bulb, construct the circuit shown in the photo on the opposite page. To begin, attach wires to the ends of the D-cell.
2. Connect the other end of one of the wires to the bulb in a socket. Attach a wire with an alligator clip to the other side of the socket.
3. Attach an alligator clip to the other wire.
4. The pencil lead will serve as a resistor that can be varied—a variable resistor. Attach one alligator clip firmly to the tip of the pencil lead. Be sure the clip makes good contact with the lead. (*Note*: Pencil "lead" is actually graphite, a form of the element carbon.)
5. Predict how the brightness of the bulb will change as you slide the other alligator clip back and forth along the lead. Test your prediction.

6. What will happen to the brightness of the bulb if you replace the lead with a piece of uninsulated copper wire? Adapt your pencil-lead investigation to test the copper wire.
7. Predict what will happen to the brightness of the bulb if you replace the pencil lead with a piece of rubber tubing. Adapt your pencil-lead investigation to test the rubber tubing.

Analyze and Conclude

1. Controlling Variables What variable did you manipulate by sliding the alligator clip along the pencil lead in Step 5?
2. Observing What happened to the brightness of the bulb when you slid the alligator clip along the pencil lead?
3. Predicting Explain your reasoning in making predictions about the brightness of the bulb in Steps 6 and 7. Were your predictions supported by your observations?
4. Interpreting Data Do you think that pencil lead has more or less resistance than copper? Do you think it has more or less resistance than rubber? Use your observations to explain your answers.
5. Drawing Conclusions Which material tested in this lab would make the best dimmer switch? Explain your answer.
6. Communicating Suppose you want to sell your dimmer switch to the owner of a theater. Write a product information sheet that describes your device and explains how it works.

More to Explore

The volume controls on some car radios and television sets contain resistors that can be varied, called rheostats. The sliding volume controls on a sound mixing board are rheostats as well. Homes and theaters may use rheostats to adjust lighting. Where else in your house would rheostats be useful? (*Hint*: Look for applications where you want to adjust a device gradually rather than just turn it on or off.)

Batteries

Reading Preview

Key Concepts

- What was the first battery made of?
- How does an electrochemical cell work?

Key Terms

- chemical energy
- chemical reaction
- electrochemical cell
- electrode • electrolyte
- terminal • battery
- wet cell • dry cell

Target Reading Skill

Building Vocabulary After you read the section, reread the paragraphs that contain definitions of Key Terms. Use the information you have learned to write a definition of each Key Term in your own words.

Lab zone Discover Activity

Can You Make Electricity Using a Penny?

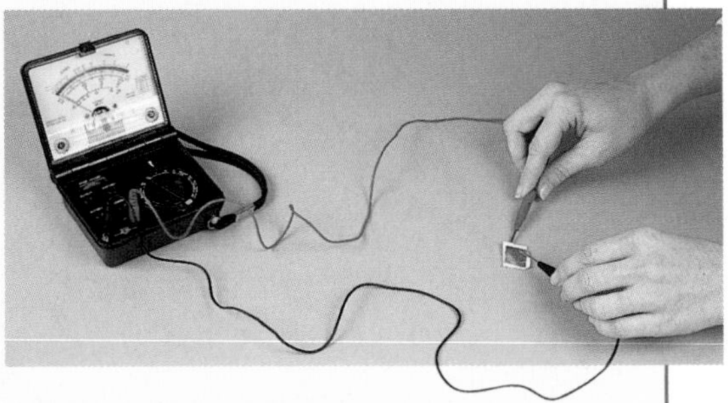

1. Clean a penny with vinegar. Wash your hands.
2. Cut a 2-cm × 2-cm square from a paper towel and a similar square from aluminum foil.
3. Stir salt into a glass of warm water until the salt begins to sink to the bottom. Then soak the paper square in the salt water.
4. Put the penny on your desktop. Place the wet paper square on top of it. Then place the piece of aluminum foil on top of the paper.
5. Set a voltmeter to read DC volts. Touch the red lead to the penny and the black lead to the foil. Observe the reading on the voltmeter.

Think It Over

Observing What happened to the voltmeter? What type of device did you construct?

Using a headlamp for light ▼

When you finally step into camp, barely enough light is left to see the trees in front of you. But you must still set up your tent. You need more light. There are no generators or electric lines nearby. Where can you find enough electrical energy to produce some light? Fortunately, your headlamp contains a battery that provides electrical energy to its bulb. In this section, you'll find out how a battery produces electrical energy.

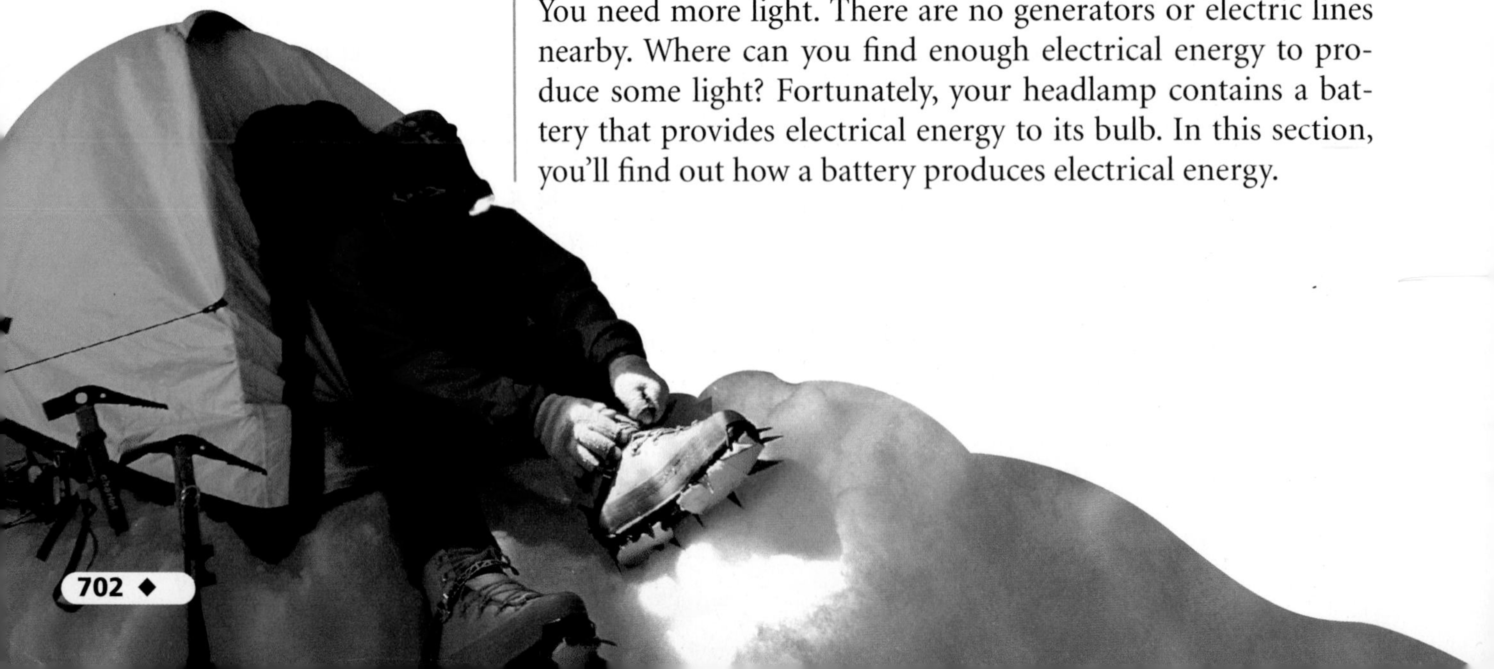

The First Battery

Energy can be transformed from one form into another. For example, batteries transform chemical energy into electrical energy. **Chemical energy** is energy stored in chemical compounds.

Luigi Galvani The research that led to the development of the battery came about by accident. In the 1780s, an Italian physician named Luigi Galvani was studying the anatomy, or body structure, of a frog. He was using a brass hook to hold a leg muscle in place. As he touched one end of the hook to an iron railing, he noticed that the frog's leg twitched. Galvani hypothesized that there was some kind of "animal electricity" present only in living tissue. This hypothesis was later proven to be incorrect. However, Galvani's observations and hypothesis led to further research.

Alessandro Volta An Italian scientist named Alessandro Volta developed a different hypothesis to account for Galvani's observations. Volta argued that the electrical effect Galvani observed was actually a result of a chemical reaction. A **chemical reaction** is a process in which substances change into new substances with different properties. In this case, Volta hypothesized that a chemical reaction occurred between the two different metals (the iron railing and the brass hook) and the salty fluids in the frog's leg muscle.

To confirm his hypothesis, Volta placed a piece of paper that had been soaked in salt water in between a piece of zinc and a piece of silver. Volta found that if he connected wires to the silver and zinc, current was produced. Then he repeated the layers: zinc, paper, silver, zinc, and so on. When he added more layers, a greater current was produced. If you did the Discover activity, you did something similar to what Volta did.

Volta built the first electric battery by layering zinc, paper soaked in salt water, and silver. In 1800, he made his discovery public. Although his battery was much weaker than those made today, it produced a current for a relatively long period of time. Volta's battery was the basis of more powerful modern batteries.

Reading Checkpoint **What is a chemical reaction?**

FIGURE 13
The First Battery
Alessandro Volta demonstrates the first battery. **Interpreting Diagrams** *What materials made up Volta's battery?*

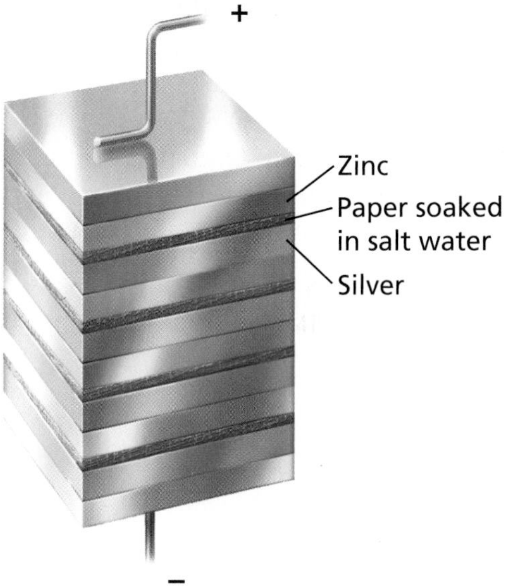

FIGURE 14
An Electrochemical Cell
An electrochemical cell can make a complete circuit. **Sequencing** *Start with the negative terminal and trace the path of the current from the terminal and back to it.*

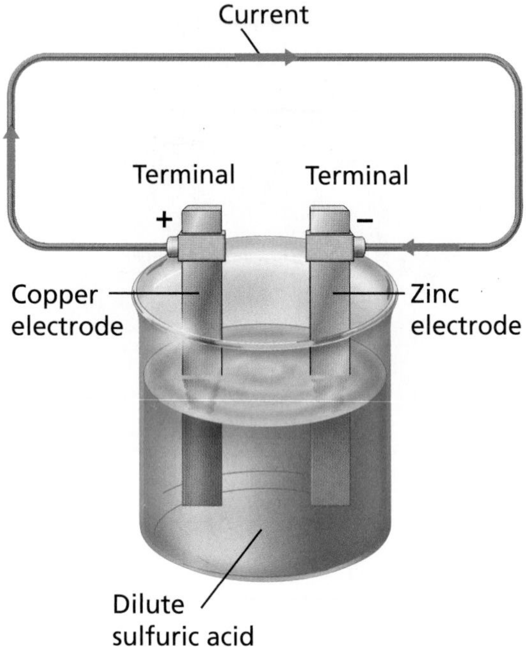

Electrochemical Cells

In Volta's setup, each pair of zinc and silver layers separated by paper soaked in salt water acted as an electrochemical cell. An **electrochemical cell** is a device that converts chemical energy into electrical energy. An electrochemical cell consists of two different metals called **electrodes,** which are immersed in a substance called an electrolyte. An **electrolyte** is a substance that conducts electric current. Volta used silver and zinc as electrodes and salt water as his electrolyte.

A Simple Cell In the cell in Figure 14, the electrolyte is dilute sulfuric acid. Dilute means that the sulfuric acid has been mixed with water. One of the electrodes in this cell is made of copper and the other is made of zinc. The part of an electrode above the surface of the electrolyte is called a **terminal.** The terminals are used to connect the cell to a circuit.

Chemical reactions occur between the electrolyte and the electrodes in an electrochemical cell. These reactions cause one electrode to become negatively charged and the other electrode to become positively charged. Because the electrodes have opposite charges, there is a voltage between them. Recall that voltage causes charges to flow. If the terminals are connected by a wire, charge will flow from one terminal to the other. In other words, the electrochemical cell produces an electric current in the wire. Charges flow back through the electrolyte to make a complete circuit.

Batteries Several electrochemical cells can be stacked together to form a battery. A **battery** is a combination of two or more electrochemical cells in a series. Today, single cells are often referred to as "batteries." So the "batteries" you use in your flashlight are technically cells rather than batteries.

In a battery, two or more electrochemical cells are connected in series. This means the positive terminal of one cell is connected to the negative terminal of the next. The voltage of the battery is the sum of the voltages of the cells. You connect two cells in this way inside a flashlight. The total voltage of a battery is found by adding the voltages of the individual cells.

Reading Checkpoint **What is a battery?**

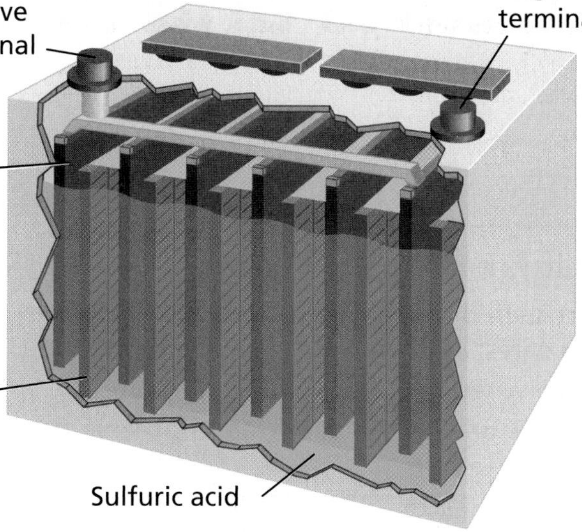

FIGURE 15
Wet and Dry Cells
The wet electrolyte in the car battery on the left is sulfuric acid. The diagram on the right shows the parts of a typical dry cell. The electrolyte is not really dry — it is a paste.

Wet Cells There are two kinds of electrochemical cells: wet cells and dry cells. An electrochemical cell in which the electrolyte is a liquid is a **wet cell.** Volta's battery consisted of wet cells because the electrolyte was salt water. The 12-volt automobile battery in Figure 15 consists of six wet cells. In this case, the electrolyte is sulfuric acid.

Dry Cells Flashlights and many other devices use dry cells. A **dry cell** is an electrochemical cell in which the electrolyte is a paste. Figure 15 shows the parts of a dry cell.

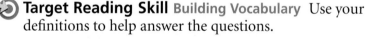

Section 3 Assessment

Target Reading Skill **Building Vocabulary** Use your definitions to help answer the questions.

Reviewing Key Concepts

1. a. **Describing** Describe the parts of Volta's battery and how they were arranged.
   b. **Explaining** What happened when Volta connected the parts of his cells in a circuit?
   c. **Relating Cause and Effect** What caused the event in Question b to happen?
   d. **Explaining** Explain how Volta used Galvani's observations to develop a relationship between chemical energy and electrical energy.
2. a. **Listing** What are the parts of an electrochemical cell?
   b. **Summarizing** Summarize how the parts of a cell interact to produce a current.
   c. **Predicting** Would a current be produced if both terminals had the same charge? Explain your answer.

Lab zone At-Home Activity

Reviving Old Cells Test a flashlight with two old D-cells and observe its brightness. Then ask a family member to remove the D-cells and place them in direct sunlight to warm up. After an hour or more, use the cells to test the flashlight. Compare the brightness of the bulb in the two tests. Explain what your observations indicate about the chemical reactions in the battery.

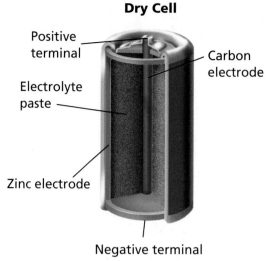

Section 4

Electric Circuits and Power

Reading Preview

Key Concepts

- What is Ohm's law?
- What are the basic features of an electric circuit?
- How many paths can currents take in series and parallel circuits?
- How do you calculate electric power and the energy used by an appliance?

Key Terms

- Ohm's law
- series circuit
- ammeter
- parallel circuit
- voltmeter
- power

Target Reading Skill

Comparing and Contrasting

As you read, compare and contrast series circuits and parallel circuits in a Venn diagram like the one below. Write the similarities in the space where the circles overlap and the differences on the left and right sides.

Lab zone Discover Activity

Do the Lights Keep Shining?

1. Construct both of the circuits shown using a battery, several insulated wires, and two light bulbs for each circuit.
2. Connect all wires and observe the light bulbs.
3. Now unscrew one bulb in each circuit. Observe the remaining bulbs.

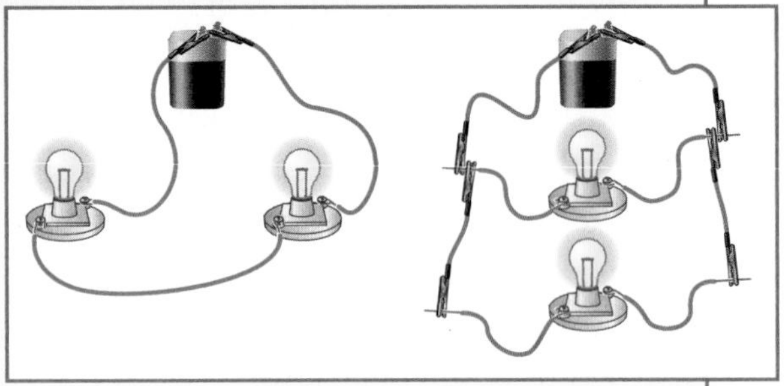

Think It Over

Observing What happened to the remaining light bulbs when you unscrewed one bulb? How can you account for your observations?

It's a cool, clear night as you stroll along the river with your family. The city is brightly lit, and the river water sparkles with reflected light. In addition to the lights at the top of the lampposts, a string of lights borders the river path. They make a striking view.

As you walk, you notice that a few of the lights in the string are burned out. The rest of the lights, however, burn brightly. If one bulb is burned out, how can the rest of the lights continue to shine? The answer depends on how the electric circuit is designed.

Although most lights in the string are shining, some lights are burned out. ▶

Ohm's Law

To understand electric circuits, you need to understand how current, voltage, and resistance are related to one another. In the 1800s, Georg Ohm performed experiments that demonstrated how those three factors are related. Ohm experimented with many substances while studying electrical resistance. He analyzed different types of wire in order to determine the characteristics that affect a wire's resistance.

Ohm's Results Ohm set up a circuit with a voltage between two points on a conductor. He measured the resistance of the conductor and the current between those points. Then he varied the voltage and took new measurements.

Ohm found that if the factors that affect resistance are held constant, the resistance of most conductors does not depend on the voltage across them. Changing the voltage in a circuit changes the current, but will not change the resistance. Ohm concluded that conductors and most other devices have a constant resistance regardless of the applied voltage.

Calculating With Ohm's Law The relationship between resistance, voltage, and current is summed up in **Ohm's law. Ohm's law says that the resistance is equal to the voltage divided by the current.**

This relationship can be represented by the equation below:

$$\text{Resistance} = \frac{\text{Voltage}}{\text{Current}}$$

The units are ohms (Ω) = volts (V) ÷ amps (A). You can rearrange Ohm's law as follows:

$$\text{Voltage} = \text{Current} \times \text{Resistance}$$

You can use the formula to see how changes in resistance, voltage, and current are related. For example, what happens to current if voltage is doubled without changing the resistance? For a constant resistance, if voltage is doubled, current is doubled as well.

Math Skills

Decimals

When calculating voltage, you often use decimals. When you multiply two decimals, the number of decimal places in the product is the sum of the number of decimal places in each decimal you multiply.

If a circuit has a resistance of 30.5 ohms and a current of 0.05 amps, what is its voltage?

$$30.5 \text{ ohms} \times \frac{0.05 \text{ amps}}{1.525 \text{ volts}}$$

Practice Problems Use Ohm's law to calculate the voltage of a circuit with a resistance of 15.2 ohms and a current of 0.10 amps.

FIGURE 16
Measuring Factors in a Circuit
You can use a meter to measure voltage, current, and resistance. Measuring *What units are used to measure current and voltage?*

Math Practice

1. In a circuit, there is a 0.5-A current in the bulb. The voltage across the bulb is 4.0 V. What is the bulb's resistance?
2. A waffle iron has a 12-A current. If the resistance of the coils is 10 Ω, what must the voltage be?

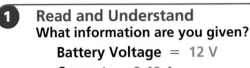

Math Sample Problem

Calculating Resistance

The brake light on an automobile is connected to a 12-volt battery. If the resulting current is 0.40 amps, what is the resistance of the brake light?

1 Read and Understand

What information are you given?

Battery Voltage = 12 V

Current = 0.40 A

2 Plan and Solve

What quantity are you trying to calculate?

The resistance of the brake light.

What formula contains the given quantities and the unknown quantity?

$$\text{Resistance} = \frac{\text{Voltage}}{\text{Current}}$$

Perform the calculation.

$$\text{Resistance} = \frac{12\ \text{V}}{0.40\ \text{A}} = 30\ \Omega$$

3 Look Back and Check

Does the answer make sense?

The answer makes sense because you are dividing the voltage by a decimal. The answer should be greater than either number in the fraction, which it is.

Features of a Circuit

All electric circuits have the same basic features. **First, circuits have devices that are run by electrical energy.** A radio, a computer, a light bulb, and a refrigerator are all devices that transform electrical energy into another form of energy. A light bulb, for example, transforms electrical energy into electromagnetic energy by giving off light. The light bulb also produces thermal energy by giving off heat. By making fan blades rotate, electric fans transform electrical energy to mechanical energy. Devices such as light bulbs and fans resist the flow of electric current. They are therefore represented as resistors in a circuit.

Second, a circuit has a source of electrical energy. Batteries, generators, and electric plants all supply energy to circuits. Recall that energy is the ability to do work. The source of electrical energy makes charges move around a circuit, allowing the device to do work.

Third, electric circuits are connected by conducting wires. The conducting wires complete the path of the current. They allow charges to flow from the energy source to the device that runs on electric current and back to the energy source. A switch is often included in a circuit to control the current in the circuit. Using a switch, you can turn a device on or off by closing or opening the circuit.

Notice that all the parts of a circuit are shown in Figure 17. Each part shown in the photograph is represented in the diagram by a simple symbol. Arrows indicate the direction of current from positive to negative. The + and – on the battery indicate the positive and negative terminals.

Reading Checkpoint **What is the function of conducting wires in a circuit?**

FIGURE 17
Diagraming a Circuit
Simple symbols make it easy to diagram a circuit. The resistor represents the device that is being run by the current. Resistors include light bulbs, appliances, and huge machines.
Interpreting Diagrams *Which symbol is used to represent a battery?*

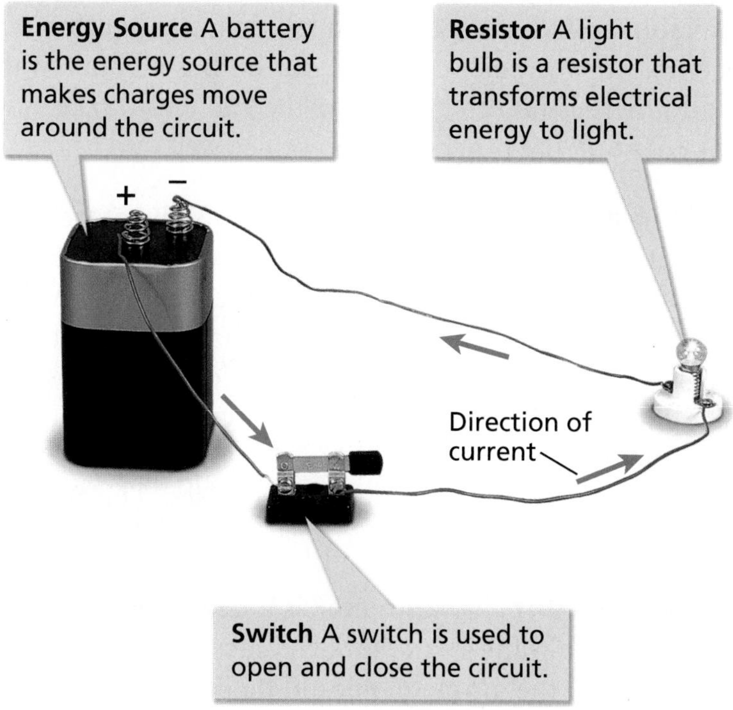
Energy Source A battery is the energy source that makes charges move around the circuit.
Resistor A light bulb is a resistor that transforms electrical energy to light.
+
–
Direction of current
Switch A switch is used to open and close the circuit.

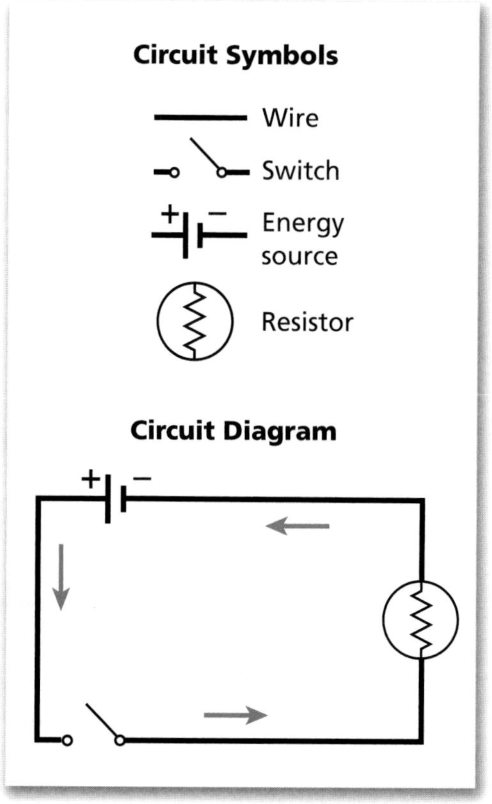
Circuit Symbols
Wire
Switch
Energy source
Resistor
Circuit Diagram
+
–

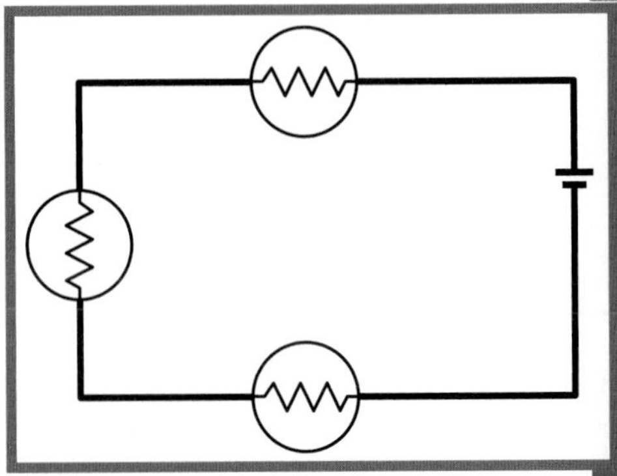

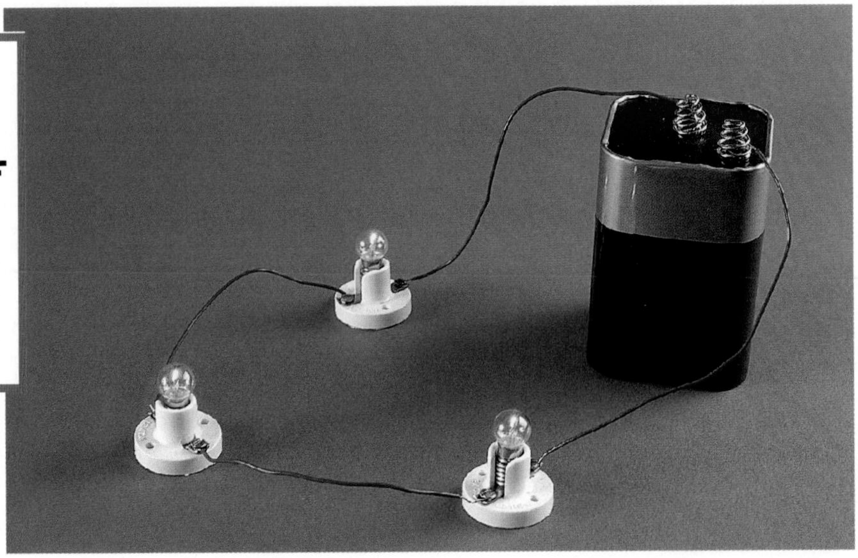

FIGURE 18
A Series Circuit
A series circuit provides only one path for the flow of electrons. **Predicting** *What will happen in a series circuit if one bulb burns out?*

Go Online
active art

For: Series and Parallel Circuits Activity
Visit: PHSchool.com
Web Code: cgp-4023

Series Circuits

If all the parts of an electric circuit are connected one after another along one path, the circuit is called a **series circuit**. Figure 18 illustrates a series circuit. **In a series circuit, there is only one path for the current to take.** For example, a switch and two light bulbs connected by a single wire are in series with each other.

One Path A series circuit is very simple to design and build, but it has some disadvantages. What happens if a light bulb in a series circuit burns out? A burned-out bulb is a break in the circuit, and there is no other path for the current to take. So if one light goes out, the other lights go out as well.

Resistors in a Series Circuit Another disadvantage of a series circuit is that the light bulbs in the circuit become dimmer as more bulbs are added. Why does that happen? A light bulb is a type of resistor. Think about what happens to the overall resistance of a series circuit as you add more bulbs. The resistance increases. Remember that for a constant voltage, if resistance increases, current decreases. So as light bulbs are added to a series circuit, the current decreases. The result is that the bulbs burn less brightly.

Measuring Current An **ammeter** is a device used to measure current. If you want to measure the current through some device in a circuit, the ammeter should be connected in series with that device.

Reading Checkpoint **How does resistance change as you add bulbs to a series circuit?**

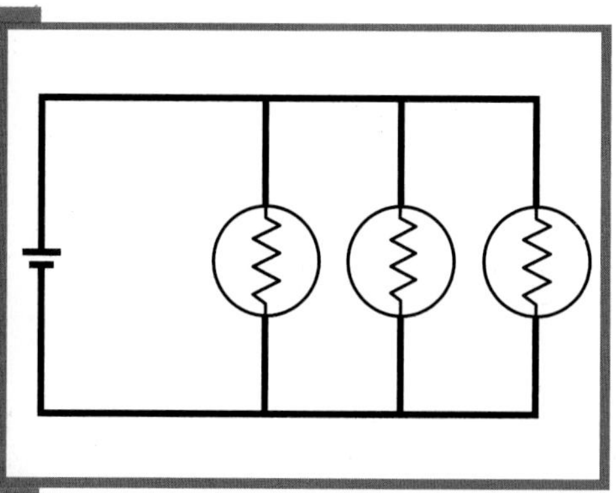

FIGURE 19
A Parallel Circuit
A parallel circuit provides several paths for the flow of electrons. **Predicting** *What will happen in a parallel circuit if one bulb burns out?*

Parallel Circuits

As you gaze at a string of lights, you observe that some bulbs burn brightly, but others are burned out. Your observation tells you that these bulbs are connected in a parallel circuit. In a **parallel circuit,** the different parts of the circuit are on separate branches. Figure 19 shows a parallel circuit. **In a parallel circuit, there are several paths for current to take.** Each bulb is connected by a separate path from the battery and back to the battery.

Several Paths What happens if a light burns out in a parallel circuit? If there is a break in one branch, charges can still move through the other branches. So if one bulb goes out, the others remain lit. Switches can be added to each branch to turn lights on and off without affecting the other branches.

Resistors in a Parallel Circuit What happens to the resistance of a parallel circuit when you add a branch? The overall resistance actually decreases. To understand why this happens, consider blowing through a single straw. The straw resists the flow of air so that only a certain amount of air comes out. However, if you use two straws, twice as much air can flow. The more straws you have, the more paths the air has to follow. The air encounters less resistance. As new branches are added to a parallel circuit, the electric current has more paths to follow, so the overall resistance decreases.

Remember that for a given voltage, if resistance decreases, current increases. The additional current travels along each new branch without affecting the original branches. So as you add branches to a parallel circuit, the brightness of the light bulbs does not change.

Lab zone Skills Activity

Predicting

1. Look at the circuit diagram below. Predict whether all three light bulbs will shine with the same brightness.

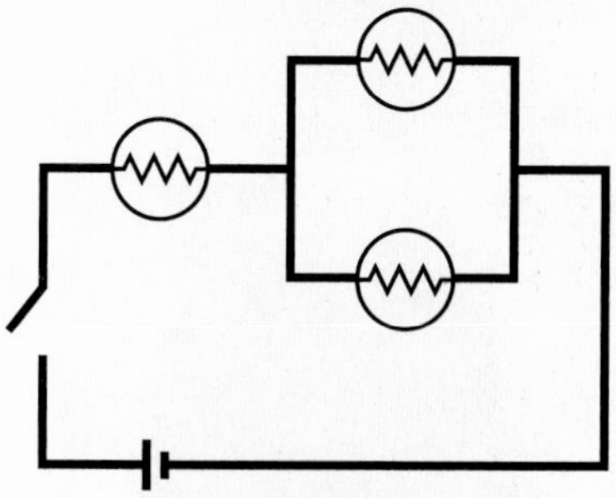

2. Construct the circuit using a battery and three identical light bulbs. Observe the brightness of the bulbs.

Does this circuit behave like a parallel circuit or a series circuit? Explain.

Measuring Voltage A **voltmeter** is a device used to measure voltage, or electrical potential energy difference. When you measure the voltage of a device, the voltmeter and the device should be wired as a parallel circuit.

Household Circuits Would you want the circuits in your home to be series circuits? Of course not. With a series circuit, all the electrical devices in your home would stop working every time a switch was turned off or a light bulb burned out. Instead, the circuits in your home are parallel circuits.

Electrical energy enters a home through heavy-duty wires. These heavy-duty wires have very low resistance. Parallel branches extend out from the heavy-duty wires to wall sockets, and then to appliances and lights in each room. Switches are installed to control one branch of the circuit at a time. The voltage in most household circuits is 120 volts.

Electric Power

An electrical appliance transforms electrical energy into another form. The energy transformation enables the appliance to work. Hair dryers transform electrical energy to thermal energy to dry your hair. A guitar amplifier transforms electrical energy into sound. A washing machine transforms electrical energy to mechanical energy to wash your clothes. The rate at which energy is transformed from one form to another is known as **power.** The unit of power is the watt (W).

Power Ratings You are already familiar with different amounts of electric power. The power rating of a bright light bulb, for example, might be 100 W. The power rating of a dimmer bulb might be 60 W. The bright bulb transforms (or uses) electrical energy at a faster rate than the dimmer bulb.

FIGURE 20
Power Ratings
Consumers can use power rating information in buying and using appliances. **Interpreting Diagrams** *Which of the appliances shown here use the most power?*

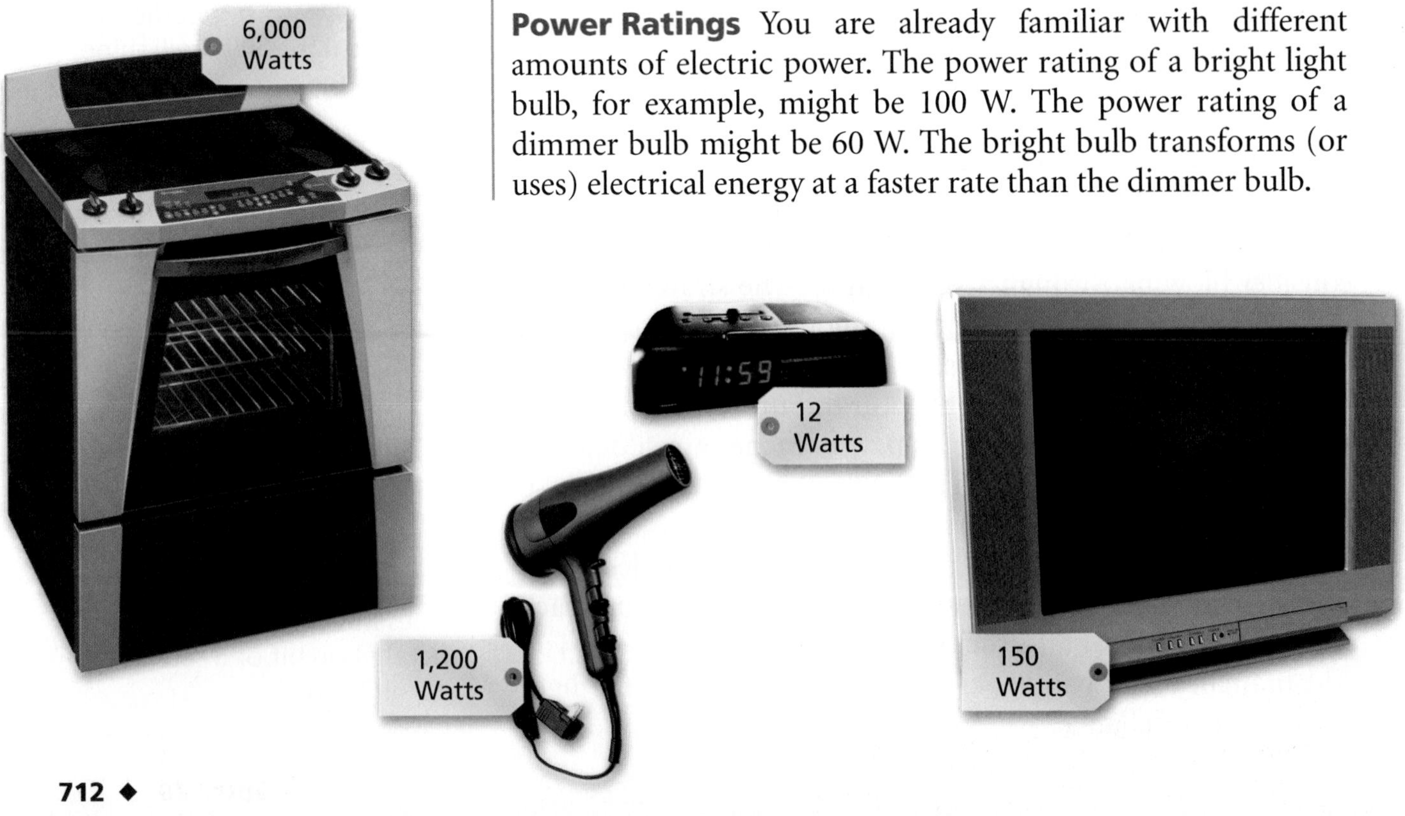

The appliances in your home vary greatly in their power ratings. New appliances are sold with labels that show the power rating for each product. Look at Figure 20 to see typical power ratings of some common household appliances.

Calculating Power The power of a light bulb or appliance depends on two factors: voltage and current. **You can calculate power by multiplying voltage by current.**

Power = Voltage × Current

The units are watts (W) = volts (V) × amperes (A). Using the symbols *P* for power, *V* for voltage, and *I* for current, this equation can be rewritten

$$P = VI$$

Reading Checkpoint **How can you calculate power if you know the voltage and current?**

Lab zone Skills Activity

Observing

Study the back or bottom of some electrical appliances around your home. Make a chart of their power ratings. Do you see any relationship between the power rating and whether or not the appliance produces heat?

Math Sample Problem

Calculating Power

A household light bulb has about 0.5 amps of current in it. Since the standard household voltage is 120 volts, what is the power rating for this bulb?

1 Read and Understand

What information are you given?

Current = 0.5 A

Voltage = 120 V

2 Plan and Solve

What quantity are you trying to calculate?

The power of the light bulb = ?

What formula contains the given quantities and the unknown quantity?

Power = Voltage × Current

Perform the calculation.

Power = 120 V × 0.5 A

Power = 60 W

3 Look Back and Check

Does your answer make sense?

The answer is reasonable, because 60 W is a common rating for household light bulbs.

Math Practice

1. A flashlight bulb uses two 1.5-V batteries in series to create a current of 0.5 A. What is the power rating of the bulb?
2. A hair dryer has a power rating of 1,200 W and uses a standard voltage of 120 V. What is the current through the hair dryer?

FIGURE 21
Paying for Electricity
Electric bills are based on the amount of time various appliances are used. For any appliance type, energy guides help consumers make the most efficient purchase.

Paying for Electrical Energy

The electric bill that comes to your home charges for energy use, not power. Energy use depends on both power and time. Different appliances transform electrical energy at different rates. And you use some appliances more than others. **The total amount of energy used by an appliance is equal to the power of the appliance multiplied by the amount of time the appliance is used.**

Energy = Power × Time

Electric power is usually measured in thousands of watts, or kilowatts (kW), and time is measured in hours. The unit of electrical energy is the kilowatt-hour (kWh).

Kilowatt-hours = Kilowatts × Hours

Ten 100-watt bulbs lit for one hour use 1,000 watt-hours, or 1 kilowatt-hour, of energy.

The amount of electrical energy used in your home is measured by a meter. The electric company uses the meter to keep track of the number of kilowatt-hours used. You pay a few cents for each kilowatt-hour.

Section 4 Assessment

Target Reading Skill

Comparing and Contrasting Use the information in your Venn diagram about series and parallel circuits to help you answer Question 3.

Reviewing Key Concepts

1. a. **Reviewing** What three related electrical factors did Georg Ohm investigate?
   b. **Explaining** What relationship did Ohm discover between these three factors?
   c. **Predicting** In a circuit with a constant resistance, what will happen to the current if the voltage is multiplied four times?
2. a. **Listing** List three basic features of an electric circuit.
   b. **Interpreting Diagrams** How is each feature represented in the circuit diagram in Figure 17.
3. a. **Comparing and Contrasting** Compare and contrast series and parallel circuits.
   b. **Relating Cause and Effect** If you remove one bulb from a string of lights, all the remaining lights will go out. Are the lights in a series circuit or parallel circuit? Explain.
4. a. **Defining** What is electric power?
   b. **Calculating** What formula can you use to calculate power?
   c. **Making Generalizations** Is it true that the bigger the electrical device, the more power it uses? Use Figure 20 to explain your answer.

Math Practice

5. **Calculating Resistance** The current through a resistor is 0.025 A when it is connected to a 10.0-V source. What is the resistance?
6. **Calculating Power** A refrigerator uses a standard voltage of 120 V and has a current of about 4.2 A. What is its power rating?

Section 5

Integrating Health

Electrical Safety

Reading Preview

Key Concepts

- What measures help protect people from electrical shocks and short circuits?

Key Terms

- short circuit
- grounded
- third prong
- fuse
- circuit breaker

Target Reading Skill

Using Prior Knowledge Before you read, write what you know about electrical safety in a graphic organizer like the one below. As you read, write what you learn.

What You Know
1. An electric shock can be dangerous. 2.

What You Learned
1. 2.

Lab zone Discover Activity

How Can You Blow a Fuse?

1. Begin by constructing the circuit shown using a D-cell, a light bulb, and two alligator clips.
2. Pull a steel fiber out of a piece of steel wool. Wrap the ends of the steel fiber around the alligator clips.
3. Complete the circuit and observe the steel fiber and the bulb.

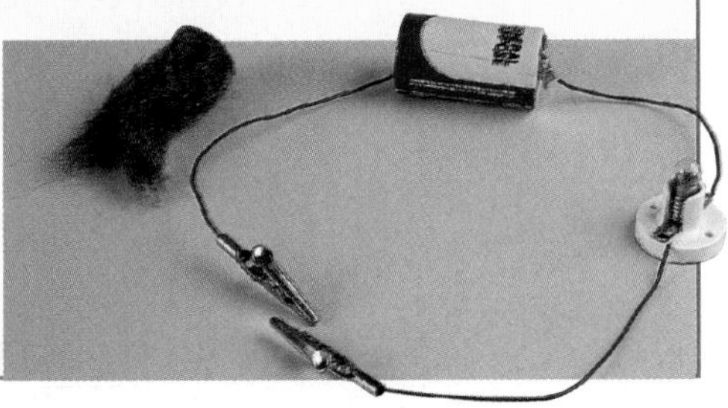

Think It Over

Developing Hypotheses Write a hypothesis to explain your observations.

The ice storm has ended, but it has left a great deal of destruction in its wake. Trees have been stripped of their branches, and a thick coating of ice covers the countryside. Perhaps the greatest danger is from the downed high-voltage electric wires. Residents are being warned to stay far away from them. What makes these high-voltage wires so dangerous?

Personal Safety

You may have noticed high-voltage wires hanging from poles beside the highway. These wires form a circuit to and from the electric plant. The wires carry electric current from the electric plant to the customer. If these wires are damaged, they can cause serious injury. Potential dangers include short circuits, electric shocks, and ungrounded wires.

Short Circuits If someone touches a downed electric wire, the person's body can form a short circuit between the wire and the ground. A short circuit can also occur in your home if you touch frayed wires. A **short circuit** is a connection that allows current to take the path of least resistance. For example, the electric charge can flow through the person rather than through the wire to the power plant. The unintended path usually has less resistance than the intended path. Therefore, the current can be very high. The shock that the person receives may be fatal.

Math Analyzing Data

Electrical Equipment and Fires

If electrical equipment is not properly used and maintained, it can cause fires. The circle graph shows the percentage of fires caused by different types of electrical equipment.

1. **Reading Graphs** What determines the size of each wedge in the graph?
2. **Reading Graphs** What percentage of fires are caused by appliances?
3. **Interpreting Data** Which category of equipment is responsible for most fires? Which category is responsible for the fewest fires?

Fires From Electrical Equipment

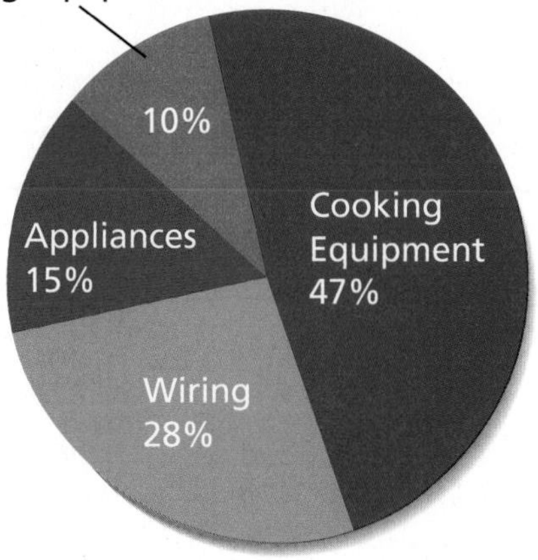

Electric Shocks Electrical signals in the human body control breathing, heartbeat, and muscle movement. If your body receives an electric current from an outside source, it can result in a shock that interferes with your body's electrical signals.

The shock you feel from static discharge after walking across a carpet is very different from the shock that could come from touching a fallen high-voltage wire. The severity of an electric shock depends on the current. A current of less than 0.01 A is almost unnoticeable. But a current greater than 0.2 A can be dangerous, causing burns or even stopping your heart.

Grounding Earth plays an important role in electrical safety. **One way to protect people from electric shock and other electrical danger is to provide an alternate path for electric current.** Most buildings have a wire that connects all the electric circuits to the ground, or Earth. A circuit is electrically **grounded** when charges are able to flow directly from the circuit into Earth in the event of a short circuit.

One method of grounding is to use a third prong on a plug. Two flat prongs of a plug connect an appliance to the household circuit. The **third prong,** which is round, connects any metal pieces of the appliance to the ground wire of the building. If a short circuit occurs in the appliance, the electric charge will flow directly into Earth. Any person who touches the device will be protected.

Reading Checkpoint **What is the function of a third prong?**

Go Online SCI LINKS NSTA

For: Links on electric safety
Visit: www.SciLinks.org
Web Code: scn-1426

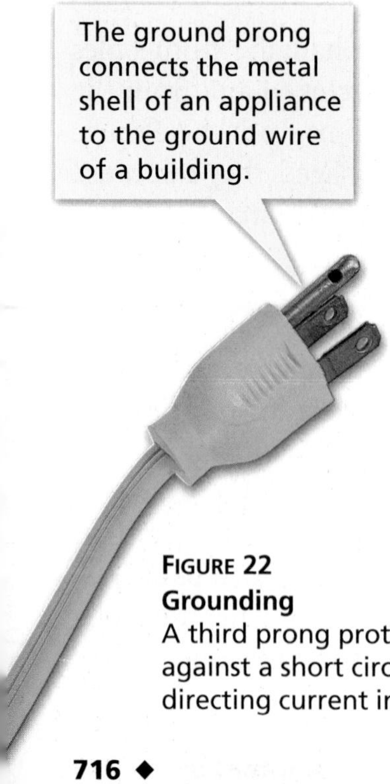

The ground prong connects the metal shell of an appliance to the ground wire of a building.

FIGURE 22
Grounding
A third prong protects against a short circuit by directing current into Earth.

Breaking a Circuit

If you use too many appliances at once, a circuit's current can become dangerously high and heat the wires that carry it. Overloading a circuit can result in a fire. **In order to prevent circuits from overheating, devices called fuses and circuit breakers are added to circuits.**

A **fuse** is a device that contains a thin strip of metal that will melt if there is too much current through it. When the strip of metal "blows," or melts, it breaks the circuit. The breaking of the circuit stops the current. Fuses are commonly found in cars and older buildings. Figure 23 shows how a fuse works.

A disadvantage of using a fuse is that once it burns out, it must be replaced. To avoid the task of replacing fuses, circuits in new buildings are protected by devices called circuit breakers. A **circuit breaker** is a reusable safety switch that breaks the circuit when the current gets too high. In some circuit breakers, a high current causes a small metal band to heat up. As the band heats up it bends away from wires in the circuit, disrupting the current.

It's easy to reset the circuit breaker. By pulling the switch back, you reconnect the metal band to the wires. However, the appliances that are causing the high current in the circuit need to be turned off first.

FIGURE 23
A Fuse
When a circuit becomes overloaded, a fuse stops the current. **Interpreting Diagrams** *How does a fuse work?*

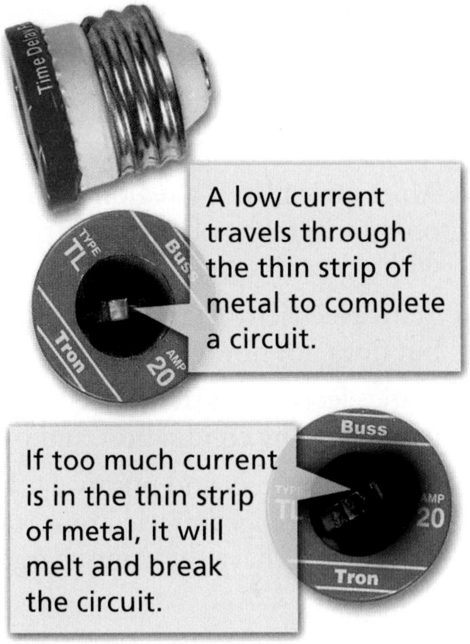
Time Delay
TYPE TL
Buss
Tron
AMP 20
A low current travels through the thin strip of metal to complete a circuit.
If too much current is in the thin strip of metal, it will melt and break the circuit.
Buss
AMP 20
Tron

Reading Checkpoint **What is the difference between a fuse and a circuit breaker?**

Section 5 Assessment

Target Reading Skill **Using Prior Knowledge** Review your graphic organizer about electrical safety and revise it based on what you have just learned in the section.

Reviewing Key Concepts

1. a. **Defining** What are grounded electric circuits? What are fuses and circuit breakers?
   b. **Explaining** Explain how grounding, fuses, and circuit breakers protect people from electrical shocks and short circuits.
   c. **Predicting** Without a fuse or circuit breaker, what might happen in a house with an overloaded electric circuit? Explain your answer.

Lab zone At-Home **Activity**

Checking Circuits Along with members of your family, find out whether the circuits in your home are protected by fuses or circuit breakers. **CAUTION:** *Be careful not to touch the wiring during your inspection.* How many circuits are there in your home? Make a diagram showing the outlets and appliances on each circuit. Explain the role of fuses and circuit breakers. Ask your family members if they are aware of these devices in other circuits, such as in a car.

Chapter 20 Study Guide

1 Electric Charge and Static Electricity

Key Ideas

- Charges that are the same repel each other. Charges that are different attract each other.
- An electric field is a region around a charged object where the object's electric force interacts with other charged objects.
- Static electricity charge builds up on an object but does not flow continuously.
- Static electricity is transferred through charging by friction, by conduction, and by induction.
- When negatively and positively charged objects are brought together, electrons transfer until both objects have the same charge.

Key Terms

• electric force • electric field • static electricity
• conservation of charge • friction
• conduction • induction • static discharge

2 Electric Current

Key Ideas

- To produce electric current, charges must flow continuously from one place to another.
- A conductor transfers electric charge well. An insulator does not transfer electric charge well.
- Voltage causes a current in an electric circuit.
- The greater the resistance, the less current there is for a given voltage.

Key Terms

• electric current • electric circuit • conductor
• insulator • voltage • voltage source
• resistance

3 Batteries

Key Ideas

- Volta built the first battery by layering zinc, paper soaked in salt water, and silver.
- Chemical reactions in an electrochemical cell cause one electrode to become negatively charged and the other electrode to become positively charged.

Key Terms

• chemical energy • chemical reaction
• electrochemical cell • electrode • electrolyte
• terminal • battery • wet cell • dry cell

4 Electric Circuits and Power

Key Ideas

- Ohm's law says that the resistance is equal to the voltage divided by the current.

$$\text{Resistance} = \text{Voltage} \div \text{Current}$$

- Circuits have a source of electrical energy and devices that are run by electrical energy. Circuits are connected by conducting wires.
- In a series circuit, there is only one path for the current to take. In a parallel circuit, there are several paths for the current to take.
- You can calculate power by multiplying voltage by current.

$$\text{Power} = \text{Voltage} \times \text{Current}$$

- The total amount of energy used by an appliance is equal to its power multiplied by the amount of time it is used.

$$\text{Energy} = \text{Power} \times \text{Time}$$

Key Terms

• Ohm's law • series circuit • ammeter
• parallel circuit • voltmeter • power

5 Electrical Safety

Key Ideas

- One way to protect people from electric shock and other electrical danger is to provide an alternate path for electric current.
- In order to prevent circuits from overheating, devices called fuses and circuit breakers are added to circuits.

Key Terms

• short circuit • grounded • third prong
• fuse • circuit breaker

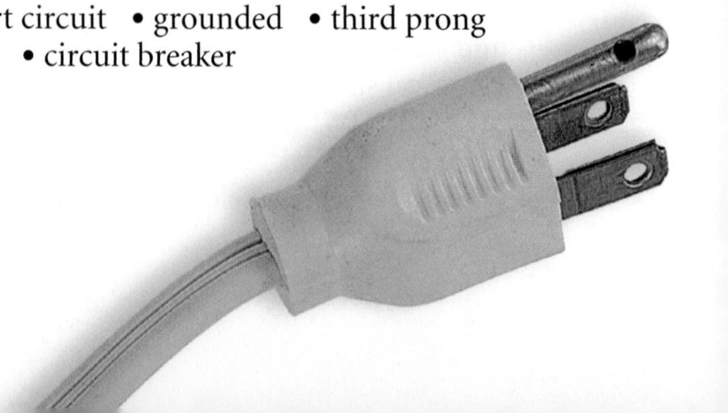

Review and Assessment

Go Online PHSchool.com
For: Self-Assessment
Visit: PHSchool.com
Web Code: cka-4200

Organizing Information

Concept Mapping Copy the concept map about devices that prevent circuits from overheating. Then complete the concept map. (For more information on concept maps, see the Skills Handbook.)

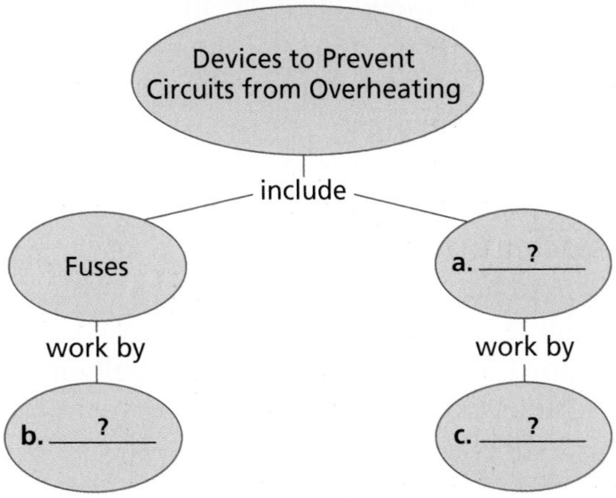

Reviewing Key Terms

Choose the letter of the best answer.

1. The attraction or repulsion between electric charges is called a(n)
   a. electric field.
   b. electric force.
   c. electron.
   d. static electricity.
2. The potential difference that causes charges to move in a circuit is called
   a. current.
   b. electric discharge.
   c. resistance.
   d. voltage.
3. A combination of two or more electrical cells in a series is called a(n)
   a. wet cell.
   b. dry cell.
   c. battery.
   d. electrode.
4. A device that measures electric current is a(n)
   a. ammeter.
   b. battery.
   c. resistor.
   d. voltmeter.
5. Connecting a circuit to Earth as a safety precaution is called
   a. a short circuit. **b.** an insulator.
   c. grounding. **d.** static discharge.

If the statement is true, write *true*. If it is false, change the underlined word or words to make the statement true.

6. Conduction is the process of charging an object without touching it.
7. Electrical resistance is low in a good conductor.
8. An electrolyte is an attachment point used to connect a cell or battery to a circuit.
9. In a series circuit, all parts of the circuit are connected in a single path.
10. Power is the rate at which energy is transformed from one form to another.

Writing in Science

Descriptive Paragraph Describe the journey of an electron in a lightning bolt. Begin at the thundercloud and follow the path of the electron until the lightning bolt strikes the ground.

Discovery Channel School

Electricity

Video Preview
Video Field Trip
▶ Video Assessment

Review and Assessment

Checking Concepts

11. Describe the three ways in which an object can become charged.

12. What units are used to measure voltage, current, and resistance?

13. Explain how the components of an electrochemical cell produce voltage.

14. What is Ohm's law?

15. What would happen if the circuits in your school building were series circuits? Explain.

16. Which glows more brightly—a 100-W bulb or a 75-W bulb? Explain your answer.

17. What is a short circuit?

Thinking Critically

18. **Classifying** Identify each of the following statements as characteristic of series circuits, parallel circuits, or both:

- **a.** Current = Voltage ÷ Resistance
- **b.** Total resistance increases as more light bulbs are added.
- **c.** Total resistance decreases as more branches are added.
- **d.** Current in each part of the circuit is the same.
- **e.** A break in any part of the circuit will cause current to stop.

19. **Interpreting Diagrams** Is the electroscope shown below charged or uncharged? Explain.

20. **Applying Concepts** Explain why the third prong of a plug should not be removed.

21. **Comparing and Contrasting** Compare and contrast wet cells and dry cells.

Math Practice

22. **Calculating Resistance** A toaster is plugged into a 120-volt socket. If it has a current of 0.25 amps in its coils, what is the resistance of the toaster? Show your work.

23. **Calculating Power** The voltage of a car battery is 12 volts. When the car is started, the battery produces a 40-amp current. How much power does it take to start the car?

Applying Skills

Use the diagram below for Questions 24–27.

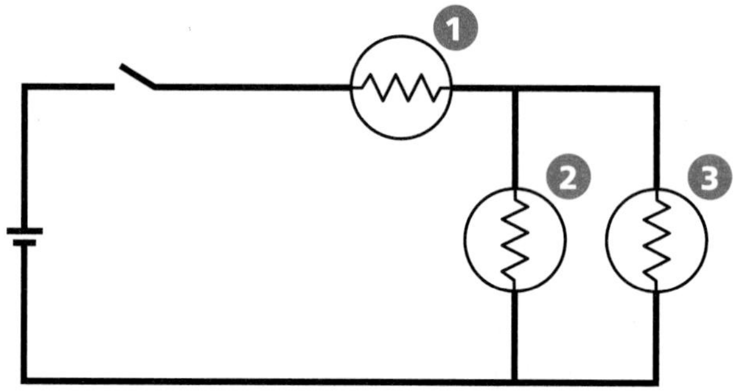

24. **Classifying** Is the circuit in the illustration a series or parallel circuit? Explain.

25. **Controlling Variables** Would the other bulbs continue to shine if you removed bulb 1? Would they shine if you removed bulb 2 instead? Explain your reasoning.

26. **Predicting** Will any of the bulbs be lit if you open the switch? Explain.

27. **Making Models** Redraw the circuit diagram to include a switch that controls only Bulb 3.

Lab zone Chapter Project

Performance Assessment Prepare a description and circuit diagram for your display. If any parts of your alarm circuit are not visible, draw a second diagram showing how all the parts are assembled. Then present your alarm to your class and explain how it could be used. Include a description of the reliability of your switch.

Standardized Test Prep

Test-Taking Tip

Using Formulas

Some test questions require you to use a formula. Find out what you are being asked to determine. Then recall formulas and other information necessary to answer the question. To solve for a specific quantity in the formula, substitute the known values for the variables.

Sample Question

Your alarm clock has a voltage of 120 V and a resistance of 1,200 Ω. What is the current?

A 0.10 A
B 10.0 A
C 12.0 A
D 100 A

Answer

The answer is A. To find the current, you use the formula for Ohm's law, which is Resistance = Voltage ÷ Current. The rearranged formula is Current = Voltage ÷ Resistance. Divide the voltage (120 V) by the resistance (1,200 Ω).

Choose the letter of the best answer.

1. Which of the following is a reusable device that protects a circuit from becoming overheated?

A a circuit breaker
B a third prong
C a fuse
D an electroscope

2. You want to build a device that can conduct current but that will be safe if touched by a person. Which of the following pairs of materials could you use?

F glass for the conductor and rubber for the insulator
G copper for the insulator and silver for the conductor
H sand for the conductor and plastic for the insulator
J plastic for the insulator and silver for the conductor

3. The graph shows the cost of using three household appliances. Which of the following is a valid interpretation of the graph?

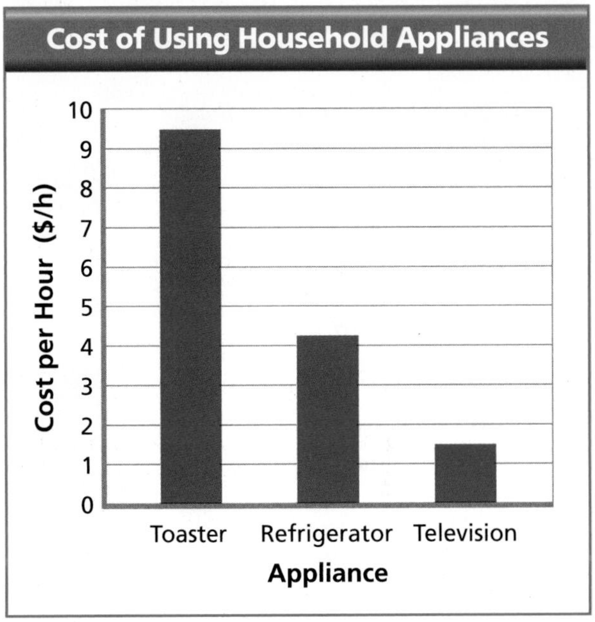

A A toaster has high voltage.
B It costs more per hour to run a refrigerator than a television.
C During a month, a family pays more to run a toaster than a refrigerator.
D A toaster uses more current than any other appliance.

4. An electrochemical cell has one copper nail and one zinc nail. When the nails are placed in vinegar, the light bulb lights up. What conclusion can be made?

F No chemical reaction occurred.
G Vinegar is an electrolyte.
H All electrochemical cells contain vinegar.
J The zinc nail reacted with the vinegar but the copper nail did not.

Constructed Response

5. Explain why people should never touch a high-voltage wire that has blown down in a storm. In your explanation, use the words *electric shock* and *short circuit.*

Chapter 21

Using Electricity and Magnetism

Chapter Preview

1. **What Is Electromagnetism?**
   Discover *Are Magnetic Fields Limited to Magnets?*
   Try This *On/Off*
2. **Electricity, Magnetism, and Motion**
   Discover *How Does a Magnet Move a Wire?*
   Try This *Making Motion*
   Skills Lab *Building an Electric Motor*
3. **Electricity From Magnetism**
   Discover *Can You Produce Current Without a Battery?*
   Science and History *Generating Electrical Energy*
   Active Art *How a Generator Works*
   At-Home Activity *Step-Up and Step-Down*

Interactive Textbook

To deliver the mail, this letter carrier rides a machine that uses electromagnetism. ▶

Using Electricity and Magnetism

▶ Video Preview
Video Field Trip
Video Assessment

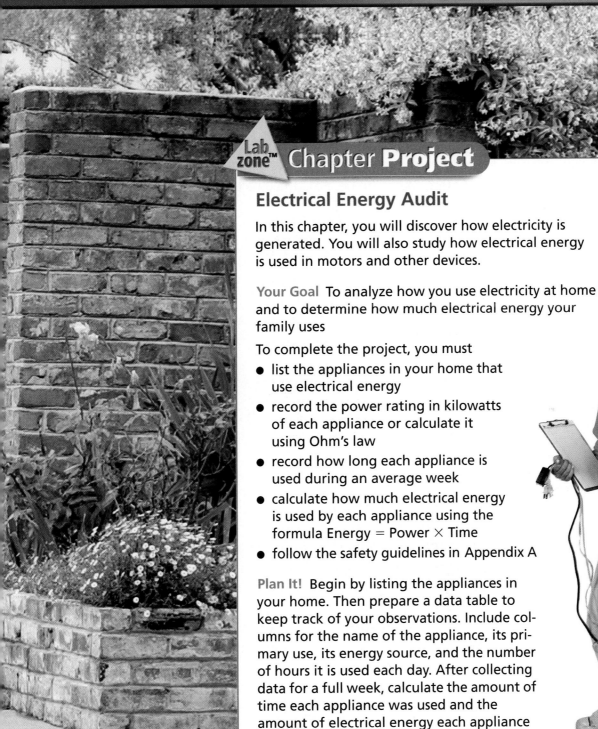

Lab zone™ Chapter **Project**

Electrical Energy Audit

In this chapter, you will discover how electricity is generated. You will also study how electrical energy is used in motors and other devices.

Your Goal To analyze how you use electricity at home and to determine how much electrical energy your family uses

To complete the project, you must

- list the appliances in your home that use electrical energy
- record the power rating in kilowatts of each appliance or calculate it using Ohm's law
- record how long each appliance is used during an average week
- calculate how much electrical energy is used by each appliance using the formula Energy = Power × Time
- follow the safety guidelines in Appendix A

Plan It! Begin by listing the appliances in your home. Then prepare a data table to keep track of your observations. Include columns for the name of the appliance, its primary use, its energy source, and the number of hours it is used each day. After collecting data for a full week, calculate the amount of time each appliance was used and the amount of electrical energy each appliance consumed.

Section 1 What Is Electromagnetism?

Reading Preview

Key Concepts

- How is an electric current related to a magnetic field?
- What are some characteristics of a magnetic field produced by a current?
- What are the characteristics of an electromagnet?

Key Terms

- electromagnetism
- solenoid
- electromagnet

Target Reading Skill

Identifying Main Ideas As you read the Solenoid section, write the main idea—the biggest or most important idea—in a graphic organizer like the one below. Then write three supporting details. The supporting details further explain the main idea.

Main Idea

A solenoid is useful because its magnetic field can be changed.

Detail	Detail	Detail

Go Online SCILINKS NSTA

For: Links on electromagnetism
Visit: www.SciLinks.org
Web Code: scn-1431

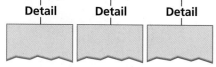

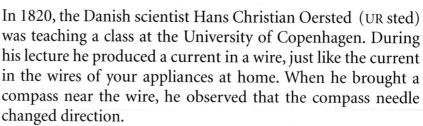

Lab zone Discover Activity

Are Magnetic Fields Limited to Magnets?

1. Obtain two wires with the insulation removed from both ends. Each wire should be 20 to 30 cm long.
2. Connect one end of each wire to a socket containing a small light bulb.
3. Connect the other end of one of those wires to a D-cell battery.
4. Place three compasses near the wire at different positions. Before you continue, note the direction in which each of the compasses is pointing.
5. Center the wire over the compasses. Make sure the compass needles are free to turn.
6. Touch the free end of the remaining wire to the battery. Observe the compasses as charges flow through the wire. Move the wire away from the battery, and then touch it to the battery again. Watch the compasses.

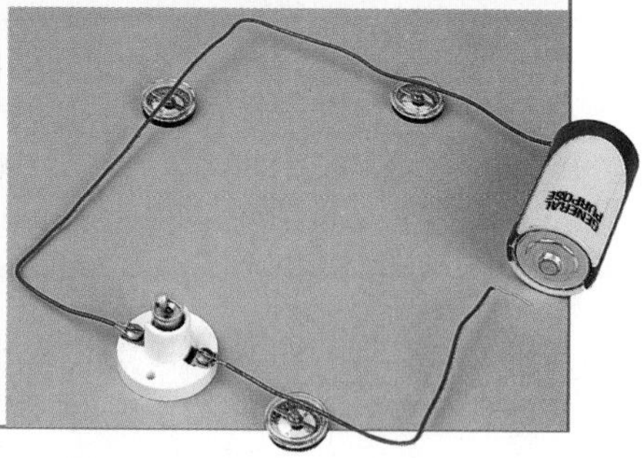

Think It Over

Inferring What happened to the compasses when charges flowed through the wire? What can you infer about electricity and magnetism?

In 1820, the Danish scientist Hans Christian Oersted (UR sted) was teaching a class at the University of Copenhagen. During his lecture he produced a current in a wire, just like the current in the wires of your appliances at home. When he brought a compass near the wire, he observed that the compass needle changed direction.

Oersted was surprised. He could have assumed that something was wrong with his equipment and ignored what he saw. Instead, he investigated further. He set up several compasses around a wire. Oersted discovered that whenever he produced a current in the wire, the compass needles lined up around the wire in the shape of a circle.

Oersted's discovery showed that magnetism and electricity are related. But just how are they related?

FIGURE 1
Currents and Magnetic Fields
Current in a wire affects nearby compasses.

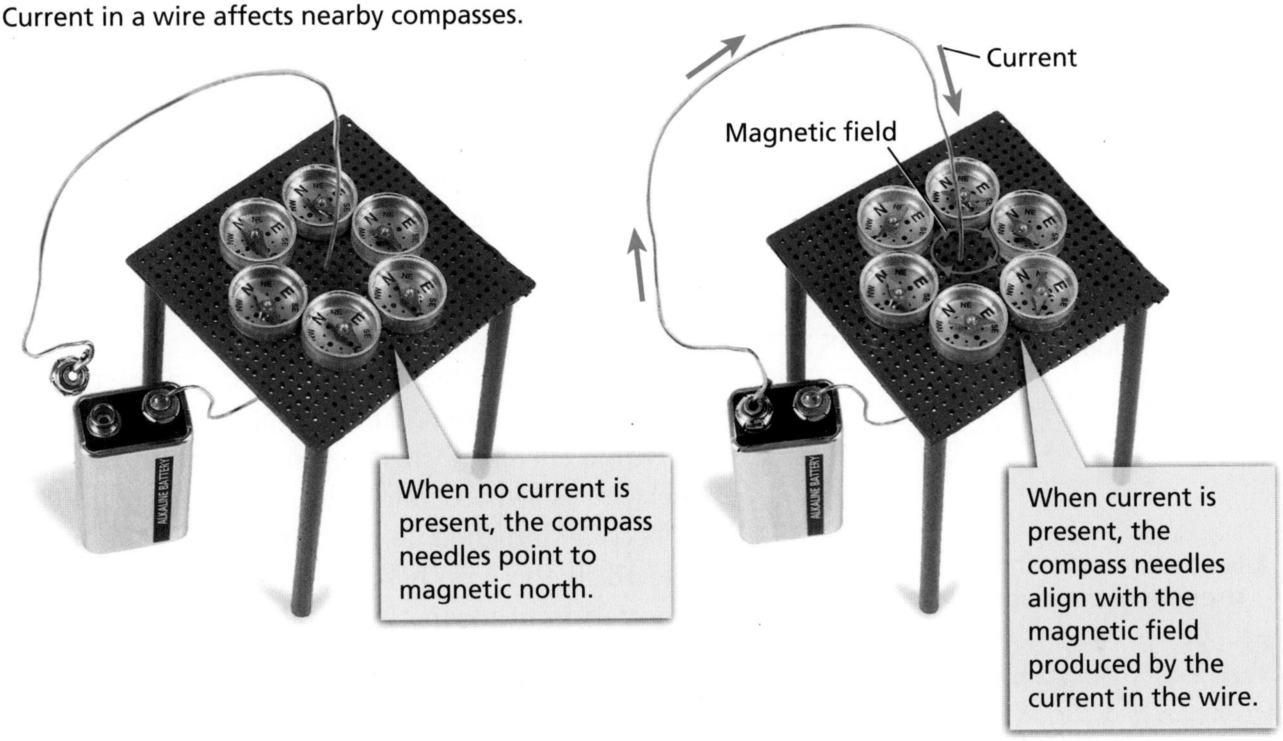
Current
Magnetic field
When no current is present, the compass needles point to magnetic north.
When current is present, the compass needles align with the magnetic field produced by the current in the wire.

Electric Current and Magnetism

Wherever there is electricity, there is magnetism. **An electric current produces a magnetic field.** This relationship between electricity and magnetism is called **electromagnetism.**

You can't see electromagnetism, but you can use a compass and an electric current to observe its effect on objects. A compass needle normally points north because it aligns itself with Earth's magnetic field. It will point in a different direction only if another magnetic field is present. For example, look at the compasses shown in the photo on the left in Figure 1. They surround a straight wire that has no current. Because there is no current, the wire has no magnetic field. Therefore, the compasses align with Earth's magnetic field and point north.

In the photo on the right in Figure 1, the wire has a current. Notice that in this case the compasses no longer point north. The needles of the compasses change direction because a magnetic field is produced around a wire that has a current. The needles of the compasses align with the magnetic field that the current produces.

In Figure 2, iron filings surround a wire that has a current. You can see that the filings form a pattern. They map out the magnetic field produced by the current in the wire.

Reading Checkpoint **What can produce a magnetic field?**

FIGURE 2
A Magnetic Field Map
Iron filings show the magnetic field lines around a wire with a current. Observing *What is the shape of the field lines?*

FIGURE 3
Controlling a Magnetic Field
Both the direction and strength of a magnetic field produced by a current can be controlled.

A Reversing the direction of the current reverses the direction of the magnetic field.

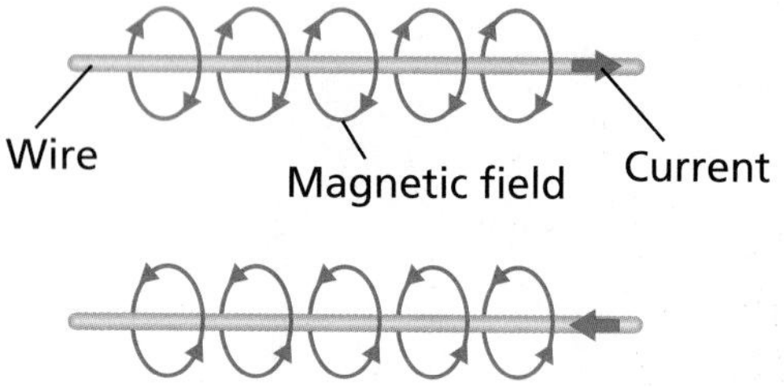

B Looping the wire increases the strength of the magnetic field.

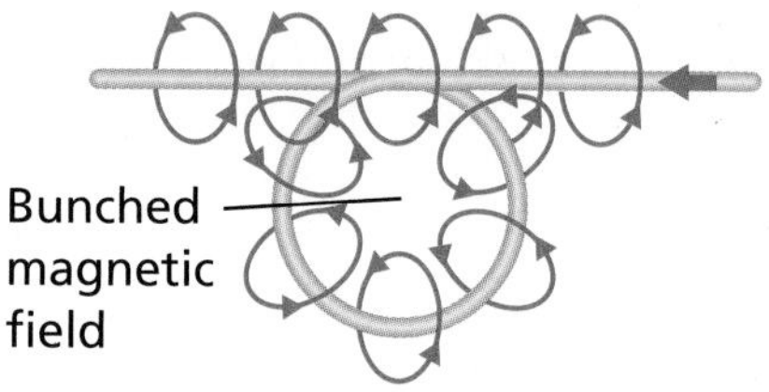

Solenoids

The magnetic field produced by a current has three distinct characteristics. The field can be turned on or off, have its direction reversed, or have its strength changed. Unlike Earth's magnetic field, you can turn a magnetic field produced by a current on or off. To do so you simply turn the current on or off. In addition, you can change the direction of the magnetic field by reversing the direction of the current. When the current reverses, the magnetic field reverses also, as shown in Figure 3A.

You can also change the strength of a magnetic field produced by a current. The magnetic field around a wire with a current forms a cylinder around the wire. If the wire is twisted into a loop, the magnetic field lines become bunched up inside the loop, as shown in Figure 3B. If the wire is bent into a second loop, the concentration of magnetic field lines within the loops is twice as great. So, the strength of the magnetic field increases as the number of loops, or coils, increases.

By winding a wire with a current into many loops you strengthen the magnetic field in the center of the coil. A coil of wire with a current is called a **solenoid.** The two ends of a solenoid act like magnetic poles. In Figure 4 you can see that the iron filings around a solenoid line up much as they would around a bar magnet. However, in a solenoid, the north and south poles change with the direction of the current.

Reading Checkpoint **What happens to the magnetic field lines in a twisted loop of wire?**

FIGURE 4
Magnetic Field Around a Solenoid
The magnetic field around a solenoid resembles that of a bar magnet.
Comparing and Contrasting *How is a solenoid different from a bar magnet?*

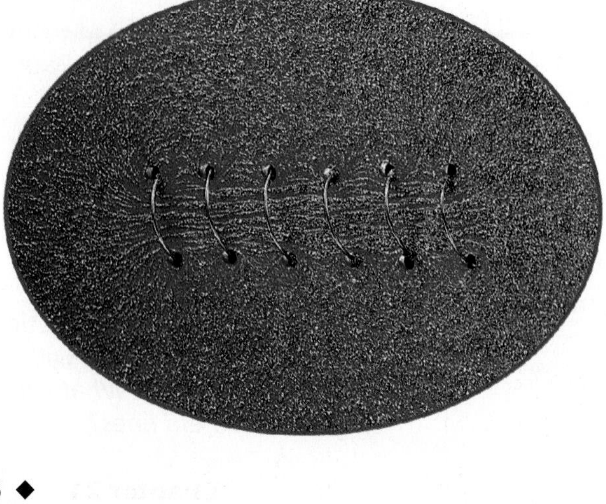

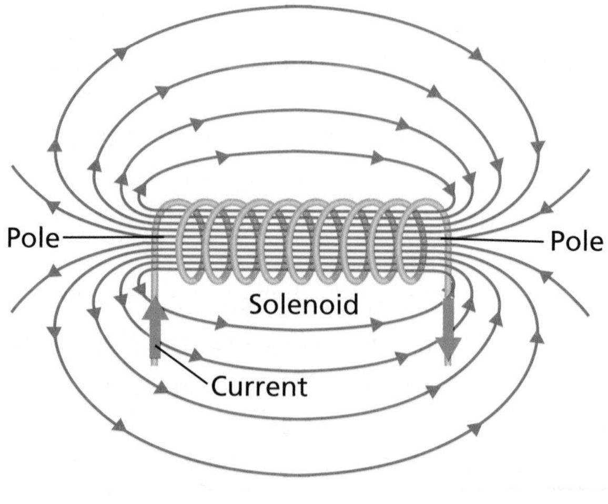

FIGURE 5
How a Doorbell Works
A doorbell rings as the magnetic field of an electromagnet changes.

Closed Circuit
Pressing the button closes the circuit of the doorbell. Closing the circuit turns on the electromagnet in the doorbell.

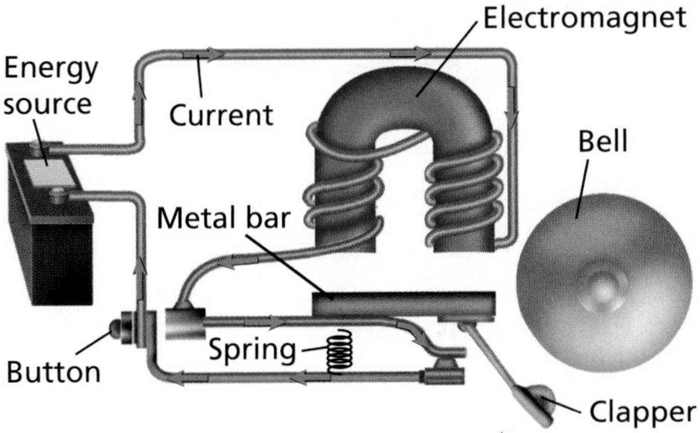

Open Circuit
The electromagnet attracts a metal bar, and the clapper strikes the bell. At the same time, the circuit opens, turning off the electromagnet. The spring returns the metal bar to its resting position.

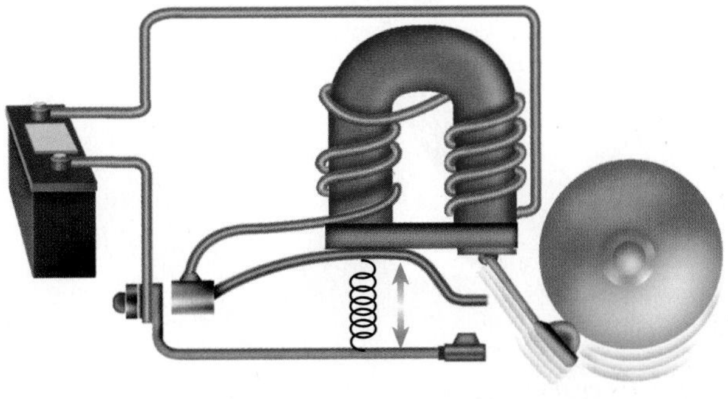

Electromagnets

If you place a ferromagnetic material such as iron inside a solenoid, the strength of the magnetic field increases. The increase in strength occurs because the ferromagnetic material becomes a magnet.

What Is an Electromagnet? A solenoid with a ferromagnetic core is called an **electromagnet.** The magnetic field of an electromagnet is produced by both the current in the wire and the magnetized core. The overall magnetic field of an electromagnet can be hundreds or thousands of times stronger than the magnetic field produced by the current alone. **An electromagnet is a strong magnet that can be turned on and off.**

You can increase the strength of an electromagnet in a number of ways. First, you can increase the current in the solenoid; second, you can add more loops of wire to the solenoid. Third, you can wind the coils of the solenoid closer together. Finally, you can increase the strength of an electromagnet by using a stronger ferromagnetic material for the core.

Common Electromagnets Electromagnets are very common. You probably use many every day. Electromagnets are used to record information onto audiotapes, videotapes, computer hard drives, and credit cards. In addition, many devices, such as the doorbell shown in Figure 5, use electromagnets.

Lab zone **Try This Activity**

On/Off

1. Your teacher will give you a piece of insulated copper wire. Tightly wrap it around a nail 10–12 times.
2. Tape one end of the wire to a battery terminal.
3. Touch the other end of the wire to the other battery terminal and dip the nail into a container of paper clips. Slowly lift the nail above the container.
4. Pull the wire away from the battery terminal and observe what happens.

Inferring Why did the paper clips drop when you pulled the wire away from the battery terminal?

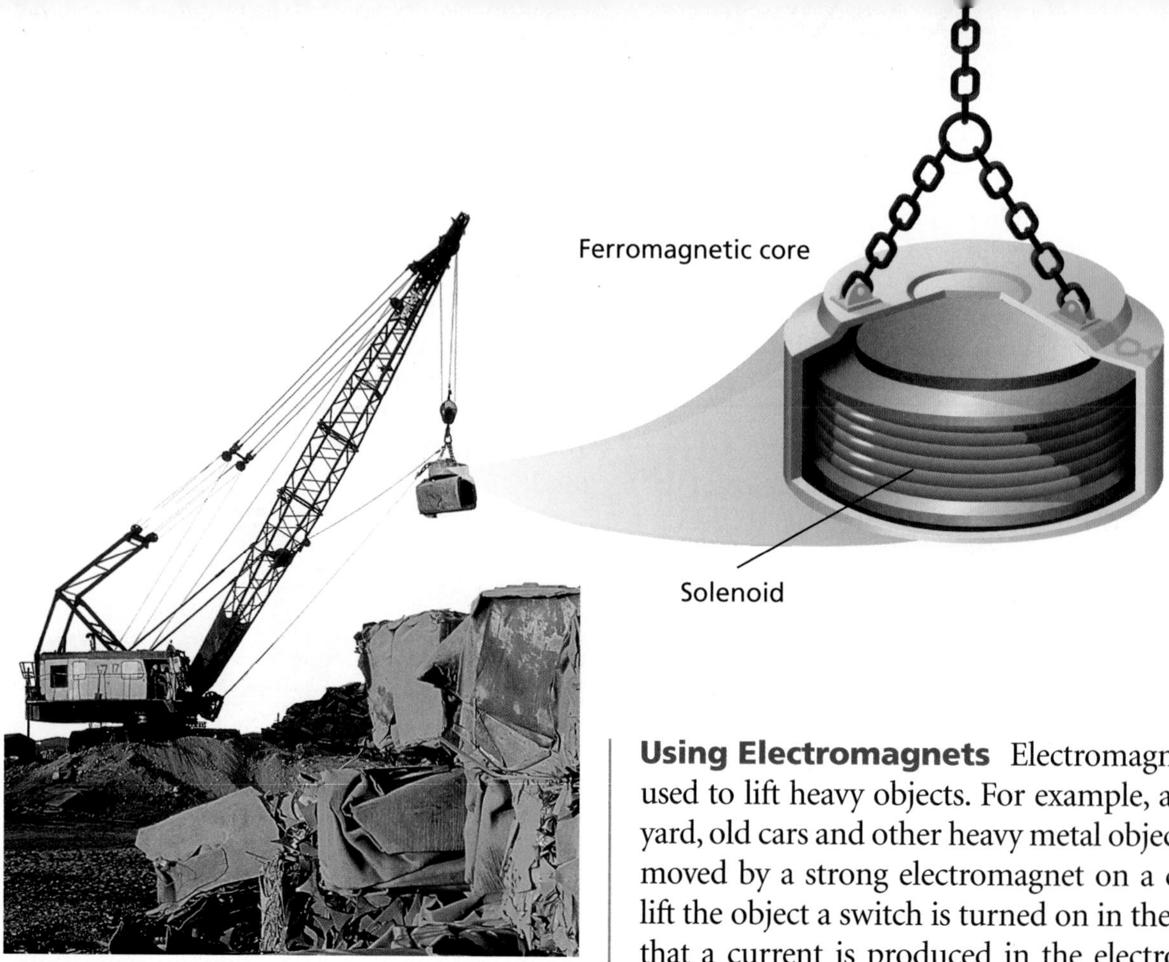

FIGURE 6
Electromagnets at Work
These heavy loads can be lifted easily because of powerful electromagnets.

Using Electromagnets Electromagnets are used to lift heavy objects. For example, at a junkyard, old cars and other heavy metal objects can be moved by a strong electromagnet on a crane. To lift the object a switch is turned on in the crane so that a current is produced in the electromagnet. The current forms a strong magnetic field that attracts metal objects. When the object needs to be dropped, the switch is turned off and the object falls from the magnet.

Section 1 Assessment

Target Reading Skill **Identifying Main Ideas** Use your graphic organizer to help you answer Question 2 below.

Reviewing Key Concepts

1. a. **Identifying** Who discovered that electricity and magnetism are related?
   b. **Explaining** What is the relationship between an electric current and a magnetic field?
   c. **Relating Cause and Effect** How can a magnetic field be produced around a wire?
2. a. **Defining** What is a solenoid?
   b. **Explaining** What are the three characteristics of a magnetic field produced by a current?
   c. **Applying Concepts** How could you increase the strength of a solenoid?
3. a. **Reviewing** What makes an electromagnet stronger than a solenoid?
   b. **Describing** What are four ways to make an electromagnet stronger?

Writing in Science

Product Description Suppose you are an inventor who just built a device that will lift heavy objects using an electromagnet. Write a description for your product brochure that explains how the magnet can move heavy objects.

Section 2 Electricity, Magnetism, and Motion

Reading Preview

Key Concepts

- How can electrical energy be transformed into mechanical energy?
- How does a galvanometer work?
- What does an electric motor do?

Key Terms

- energy • electrical energy
- mechanical energy
- galvanometer • electric motor

Target Reading Skill

Outlining As you read, make an outline about the section that you can use for review. Use the red headings for the main ideas and the blue headings for the supporting ideas.

Electricity, Magnetism, and Motion

I. Electrical Energy and Motion
  A. Types of Energy
  B.
II. Galvanometers
III. Electric Motors
  A.

Lab zone Discover Activity

How Does a Magnet Move a Wire?

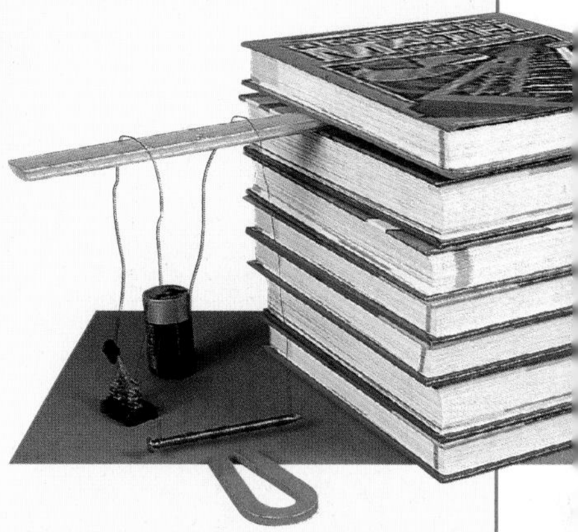

1. Make an electromagnet by winding insulated copper wire around a steel nail. Leave 30–40 cm of wire at each end of the electromagnet.
2. Pile up some books. Place a ruler between the top two books.
3. Hang the electromagnet over the ruler so that it hangs free.
4. Complete the circuit by connecting the electromagnet to a switch and a battery.
5. Place a horseshoe magnet near the electromagnet. Then close the switch briefly and observe what happens to the electromagnet.
6. Reverse the wires connected to the battery and repeat Step 5.

Think It Over

Inferring What happened to the electromagnet when you closed the switch? Was anything different when you reversed the wires? How can you use electricity to produce motion?

What do you think about when you hear the word *electricity?* You may think about the bright lights of a big city, the lightning during a thunderstorm, or the music from your stereo in the morning. You might think about how useful electricity is. For example, if you are familiar with electric motors like the one in a blender, then you already know about an important use of electricity. Electricity can produce motion.

Electricity makes the blades spin. ▶

FIGURE 7
Producing Motion
The magnetic field of a permanent magnet interacts with the magnetic field produced by a current.
Relating Cause and Effect *How does the direction of the current affect the motion of the wire?*

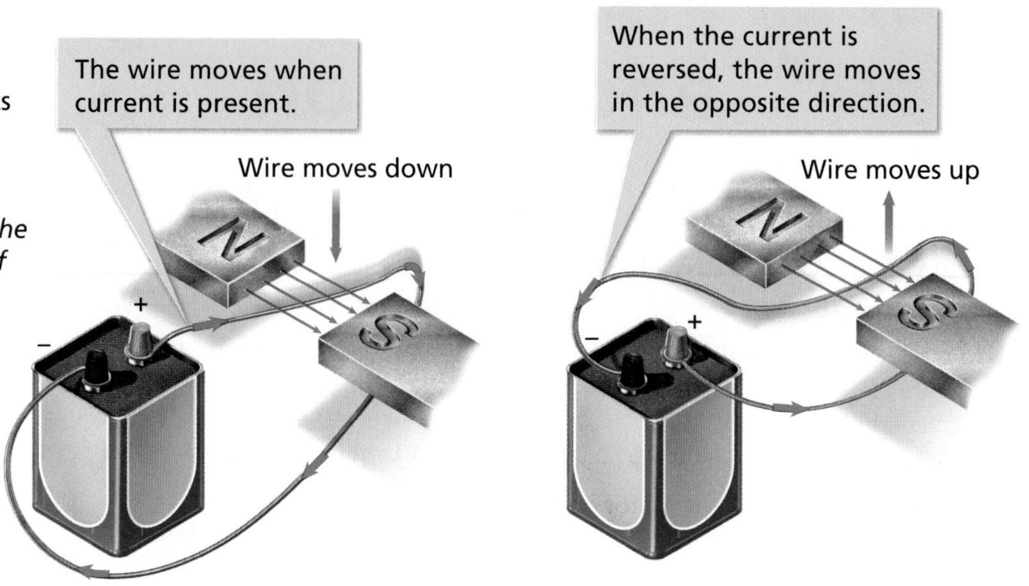
The wire moves when current is present.
Wire moves down
When the current is reversed, the wire moves in the opposite direction.
Wire moves up
N
S
+
–

Lab zone Try This Activity

Making Motion

1. Attach one end of the wire your teacher gives you to a terminal of a 6-volt battery. Let the wire hang over the edge of a table.
2. Slowly move the north pole of a bar magnet toward the wire and observe what happens. Switch poles and repeat.
3. Attach the other end of the wire to the other terminal. Let the loop of wire hang over the edge of the table.
4. Repeat Step 2. Then immediately disconnect the wire.

Drawing Conclusions What happened each time you moved the magnet near the wire? What can you conclude from your observations?

Electrical Energy and Motion

As you know, magnetic force can produce motion. Magnets can move together or move apart, depending on how their poles are arranged. You also know that an electric current in a wire produces a magnetic field similar to that of a permanent magnet. So a magnet can move a wire with a current, just as it would move another magnet.

In Figure 7 you can see how a wire placed in the magnetic field of two permanent magnets can move. With current in the wire, the magnetic field of the wire interacts with the magnetic field of the permanent magnets. The wire moves down. If the current is reversed, the wire moves up. The direction in which the wire moves depends on the direction of the current.

Types of Energy When electricity and magnetism interact, something can move—in this case, a wire moved. The ability to move an object over a distance is called **energy.** The energy associated with electric currents is called **electrical energy.** And the energy an object has due to its movement or position is called **mechanical energy.**

Energy Transformation Energy can be transformed from one form into another. **When a wire with a current is placed in a magnetic field, electrical energy is transformed into mechanical energy.** This happens when the magnetic field produced by the current causes the wire to move.

Reading Checkpoint **What is mechanical energy?**

Galvanometers

The wire shown in Figure 7 that moves in the magnetic field is straight. But what happens if you place a loop with a current in a magnetic field? Look at Figure 8. The current in one side of the loop is in the opposite direction than the current in the other side of the loop. Because the direction of the current determines the direction in which the wire moves, the two sides of the loop move in opposite directions. Once each side has moved as far up or down as it can go, it will stop moving. As a result, the loop can rotate a half turn.

The rotation of a wire loop in a magnetic field is the basis of a galvanometer. A **galvanometer** is a device that measures small currents. In a galvanometer, an electromagnet is suspended between opposite poles of two permanent magnets. The electromagnet's coil is attached to a pointer, as shown in Figure 9. When a current is in the electromagnet's coil, a magnetic field is produced. This field interacts with the permanent magnet's field, causing the loops of wire and the pointer to rotate. **An electric current is used to turn the pointer of a galvanometer.** The distance the loops and the pointer rotate depends on the amount of current in the wire.

A galvanometer has a scale that is marked to show how much the pointer turns for a known current. An unknown current can then be measured using the galvanometer. So galvanometers are very useful in everyday life. For example, electricians use them in their work and drivers of cars use them to know when to stop for fuel.

FIGURE 8
How a Galvanometer Works
Current is in different directions in each side of the wire loop, so one side of the loop moves down as the other side moves up. This causes the loop to rotate.

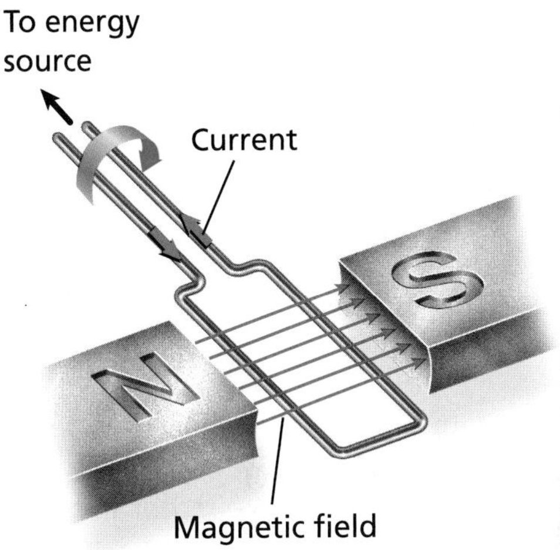

Reading Checkpoint **Where are galvanometers used?**

FIGURE 9
Inside a Galvanometer
An electromagnet turns the pointer to indicate the amount of current present. The amount of current can be read on the scale.

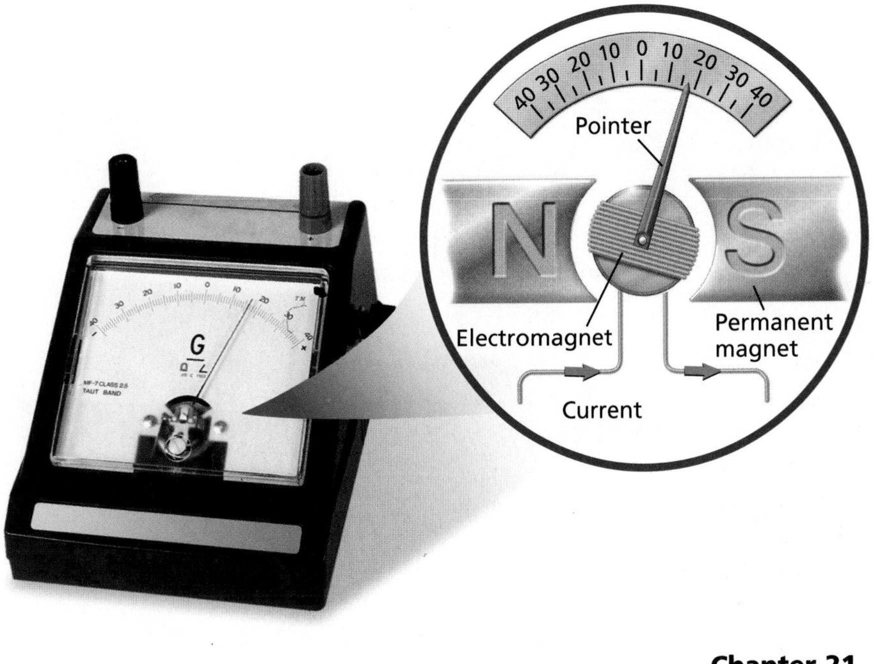

Go Online

SCI LINKS NSTA

For: Links on electric motors
Visit: www.SciLinks.org
Web Code: scn-1432

Electric Motors

The electromagnet in the magnetic field of a galvanometer cannot rotate more than half a turn. But suppose you could make it rotate continuously. Instead of moving a pointer, the electromagnet could turn a rod, or axle. The axle could then turn something else, such as the blades of a fan or a blender. Such a device would be what is called an electric motor. An **electric motor** is a device that uses an electric current to turn an axle. **An electric motor transforms electrical energy into mechanical energy.**

How a Motor Works How can you make a loop of wire continue to spin? Recall that the direction in which the loop moves in a magnetic field depends on the direction of the current in the loop. In a motor, current is reversed just as the loop, or armature, gets to the vertical position. This reverses the direction of the movement of both sides of the loop. The side of the loop that moved up on the left now moves down on the right. The side of the loop that moved down on the right now moves up on the left. The current reverses after each half turn so that the loop spins continuously in the same direction. You can see how a motor works in Figure 10.

FIGURE 10
An Electric Motor
A loop of wire in a motor spins continuously because the current reverses every half turn.
Observing *What part of an electric motor must be attached directly to the energy source?*

1 Brushes
The brushes that touch the commutator conduct current to the armature. The brushes do not move.

2 Armature
The current is in opposite directions on each side of the armature causing one side to move up while the other side moves down.

3 Commutator
The commutator rotates with the armature. The direction of current reverses with each half turn so the armature spins continuously.

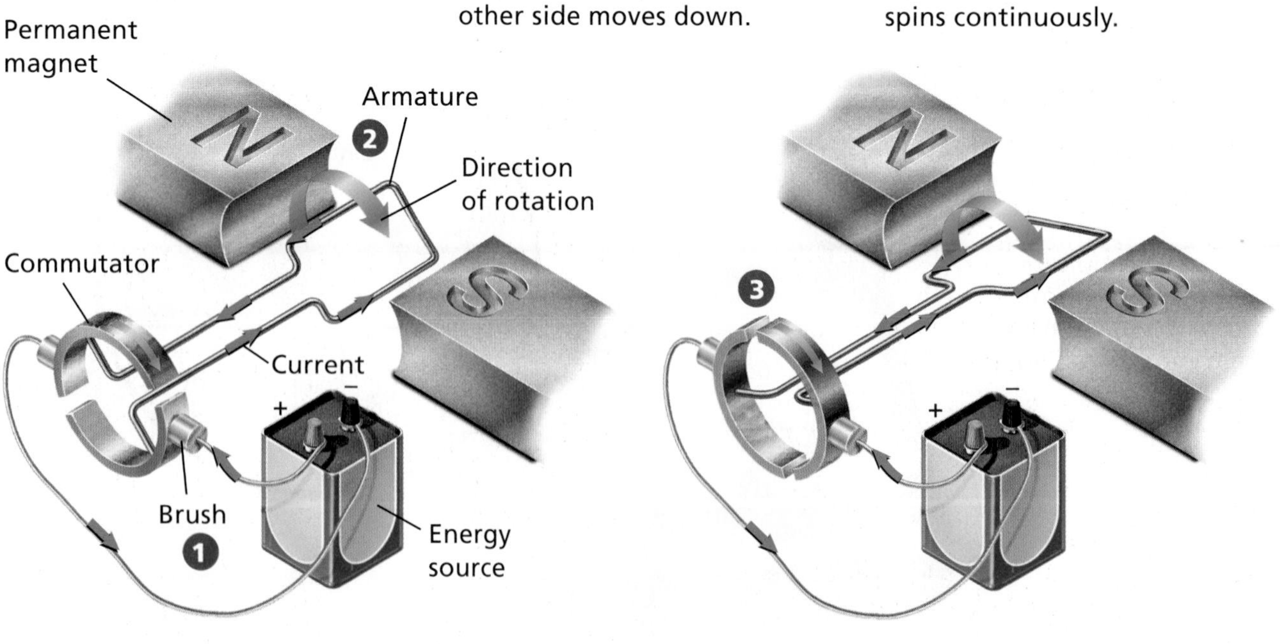

Parts of a Motor Notice that the armature in Figure 10 is only one loop of wire. However, practical armatures, like the one shown in Figure 11, have dozens or hundreds of wire loops wrapped around a ferromagnetic core. Using many loops increases the strength of the motor and allows it to rotate more smoothly. Large electric motors also use electromagnets instead of permanent magnets to increase the strength of the magnetic field.

FIGURE 11
Inside a Motor
The armature inside this motor contains hundreds of loops of copper wire wrapped around a ferromagnetic core.
Applying Concepts *How does a motor transform energy?*

A commutator repeatedly reverses the flow of current through the armature. A commutator is a ring split in half. Each half is attached to one end of the armature. When the armature rotates, the commutator rotates as well. As it moves, the commutator slides past two contact points called brushes. Each half of the commutator is connected to the current source by one of the brushes. As the armature rotates, each part of the commutator contacts one brush and then the other. Because the brushes conduct the current, changing brushes reverses the direction of the current in the armature. The reversing of the direction of the current causes the armature to spin continuously.

Reading Checkpoint How can the strength of a motor be increased?

Section 2 Assessment

Target Reading Skill Outlining Use the information in your outline about electricity, magnetism, and motion to help you answer the questions below.

Reviewing Key Concepts

1. a. **Identifying** What is energy?
   b. **Applying Concepts** What energy transformation occurs when a wire with a current is placed in a magnetic field?
   c. **Predicting** If a wire with a current moved upward in a magnetic field, how would it move when the direction of the current reversed?
2. a. **Reviewing** What does a galvanometer measure?
   b. **Describing** What energy transformation occurs in a galvanometer?
   c. **Relating Cause and Effect** What causes the pointer to move in a galvanometer?
3. a. **Defining** What is an electric motor?
   b. **Classifying** What type of energy transformation occurs in a motor?
   c. **Relating Cause and Effect** What does the commutator do in an electric motor?

Writing in Science

Make a List Make a list of at least ten motor-operated devices in your community. Beside each device, describe the motion produced by the motor.

Lab zone **Skills Lab**

Building an Electric Motor

Problem

Electric trolley cars, food blenders, garage door openers, and computer disk drives are only some of the everyday devices that have electric motors. How does an electric motor operate?

Skills Focus

classifying, inferring, drawing conclusions

Materials

- D-cell
- 2 large paper clips
- permanent disk magnet
- 3 balls of clay
- empty film canister
- pliers
- sandpaper
- 2 insulated wires, approximately 15 cm each
- enamel-coated wire, 22–24 gauge, approximately 1 meter

Procedure

1. Wrap about 1 meter of enamel-coated wire around a film canister to produce a wire coil. Leave approximately 5 cm free at each end.
2. Remove the film canister and wrap the two free ends three or four times around the wire coil to keep the coil from unwinding.
3. Use sandpaper to scrape off all the enamel from about 2 or 3 centimeters of one end of the wire coil.
4. Use sandpaper to scrape off one side of the enamel from about 2 or 3 centimeters of the other end of the wire. See the illustration below.
5. Bend two paper clips as shown in the photo on the next page.

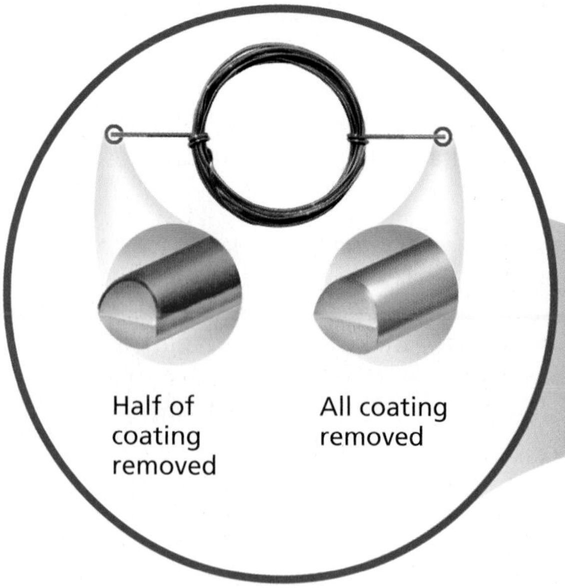

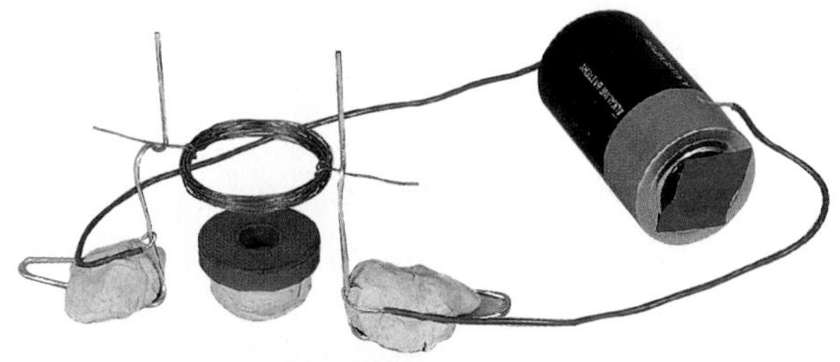

6. Place the free ends of the wire coil on the paper clips. Make sure the coil is perfectly balanced. Adjust the paper clips and wire so that the coil can rotate freely.
7. Use clay to hold a permanent magnet in place directly below the wire coil. The coil needs to be able to rotate without hitting the magnet.
8. Remove the insulation from the ends of two 15-cm insulated wires. Use these wires to connect the paper clips to a D-cell.
9. Give the coil a gentle push to start it turning. If it does not spin or stops spinning after a few seconds, check the following:
   - Are the paper clips in good contact with the D-cell?
   - Will the coil spin in the opposite direction?
   - Will the coil work on someone else's apparatus?

Analyze and Conclude

1. **Observing** Describe the movement of the wire coil when your setup was complete and working.
2. **Classifying** Which part of your setup contained a permanent magnet? Describe the location of the magnetic field produced by that magnet.
3. **Inferring** What was the effect of removing all the insulation from one end of the wire coil but only half from the other end?
4. **Inferring** Explain how a magnetic field is produced when the motor is connected to the D-cell.
5. **Drawing Conclusions** How do magnetism and electricity interact to cause the wire coil to rotate?
6. **Communicating** Your motor produced motion, but it does not yet do useful work. Think of an object your motor might cause to move. Consider how you could modify the motor to move that object. Write a procedure for changing your motor to carry out the task.

Design an Experiment

You have built a simple electric motor. List three factors that may affect the motion of the coil. Design an experiment to test one of those factors. *Obtain your teacher's permission before carrying out your investigation.*

Section 3 • Tech & Design •

Electricity From Magnetism

Reading Preview

Key Concepts

- How can an electric current be produced in a conductor?
- How does a generator work?
- What is the function of a transformer?

Key Terms

- electromagnetic induction
- direct current
- alternating current
- electric generator
- transformer
- step-up transformer
- step-down transformer

Target Reading Skill

Previewing Visuals When you preview, you look ahead at the material to be read. Preview Figure 13. Then write two questions that you have about the diagram in a graphic organizer like the one below. As you read, answer your questions.

Generators

Q.	What are the parts of a generator?
A.	
Q.	

Lab zone Discover Activity

Can You Produce Current Without a Battery?

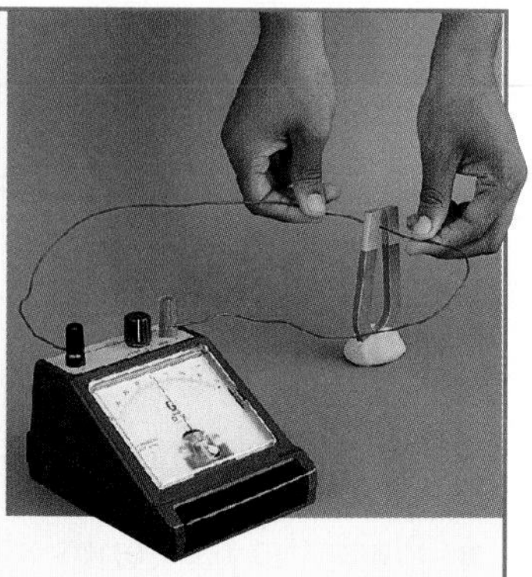

1. Obtain one meter of wire with the insulation removed from both ends.
2. Connect the wire to the terminals of a galvanometer or a sensitive multimeter.
3. Hold the wire between the poles of a strong horseshoe magnet. Observe the meter.
4. Move the wire up and down between the poles. Observe the meter.
5. Move the wire faster, and again observe the meter.

Think It Over

Developing Hypotheses In which steps does the meter indicate a current? Propose a hypothesis to explain why a current is present. Try using an "If . . . then . . ." statement.

An electric motor uses electrical energy to produce motion. Is the reverse true? Can motion produce electrical energy? In 1831, scientists found out that moving a wire in a magnetic field can cause an electric current. That discovery has allowed electrical energy to be supplied to homes, schools, and businesses all over the world.

Induction of Electric Current

Before you can understand how electrical energy is supplied by your electric company, you need to know how it is produced. A magnet and a conductor, such as a wire, can be used to induce a current in the conductor. The key is motion. **An electric current is induced in a conductor when the conductor moves through a magnetic field.** Generating an electric current from the motion of a conductor through a magnetic field is called **electromagnetic induction.** Current that is generated in this way is called induced current.

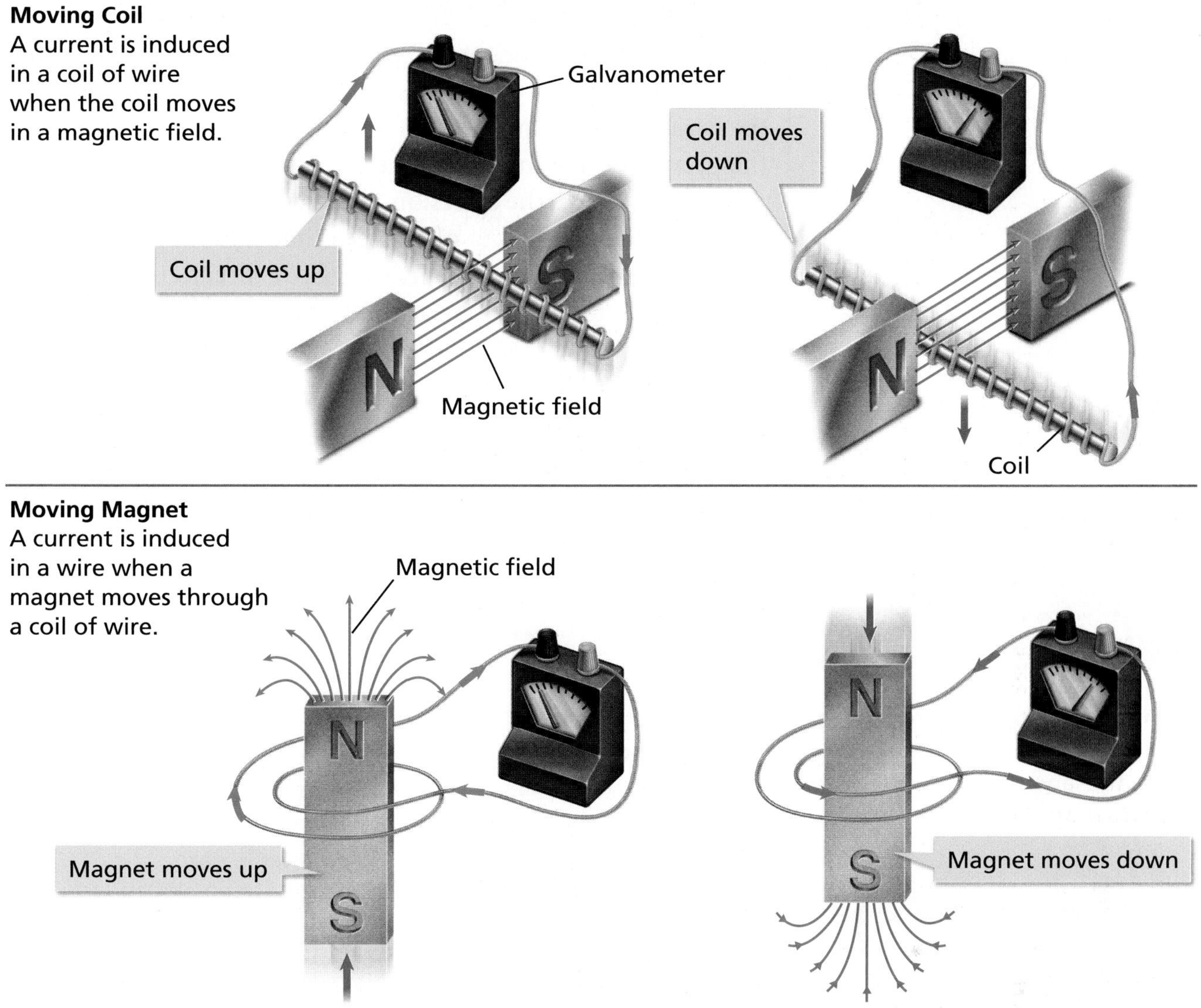
Moving Coil
A current is induced in a coil of wire when the coil moves in a magnetic field.
Galvanometer
Coil moves up
Magnetic field
Coil moves down
Coil
Moving Magnet
A current is induced in a wire when a magnet moves through a coil of wire.
Magnetic field
N
S
Magnet moves up
Magnet moves down

FIGURE 12
Inducing Current

When a coil of wire moves up or down in a magnetic field, a current is induced in the wire. If a magnet moves up or down through a coil of wire, a current is induced in the wire.
Interpreting Diagrams *How does the direction in which you move the wire and magnet affect the current?*

To induce a current in a conductor, either the conductor can move through the magnetic field or the magnet itself can move. In Figure 12, you can see what happens when a wire coil moves in a magnetic field. The coil of wire is connected to a galvanometer forming a closed circuit. If the wire coil is held still, the galvanometer will not register any current. But if the coil is moved up or down, the galvanometer shows an electric current is present. A current is induced without a battery or other voltage source by moving the coil! You saw this for yourself if you did the Discover Activity. In Figure 12, you can also see what happens when a magnet placed inside a wire coil is moved instead of the wire. The result is the same as moving the coil in the magnetic field. An electric current is induced in the coil.

Reading Checkpoint **What happens when a wire coil moves in a magnetic field?**

Direct Current In an induced current, charges may flow in one direction only, or they may alternate directions. The direction of an induced current depends on the direction in which the wire or magnet moves. You probably noticed in Figure 12 on the previous page that when the direction of the motion of the wire coil changed, the direction of the current reversed.

A current consisting of charges that flow in one direction only is called **direct current,** or DC. A direct current can be induced from a changing magnetic field or produced from an energy source such as a battery. When a battery is placed in a circuit, charges flow away from one end of the battery, around the circuit, and into the other end of the battery. Thomas Edison used direct current in his first electric generating plant.

Science and **History**

Generating Electrical Energy

Several scientists were responsible for bringing electricity from the laboratory into everyday use.

1820 Electromagnetism
Hans Christian Oersted discovers that an electric current creates a magnetic field. The relationship between electricity and magnetism is called electromagnetism.

1830–1831
Electric Induction
Michael Faraday and Joseph Henry each discover that an electric current can be induced by a changing magnetic field. Understanding induction makes possible the development of motors and generators.

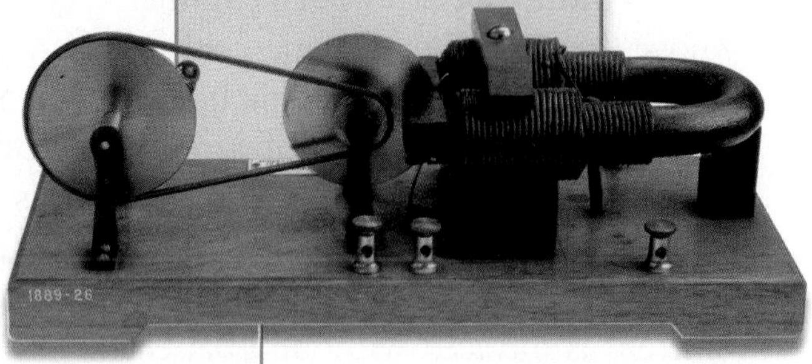

1800 1820 1840

Alternating Current What would happen if a wire in a magnetic field were moved up and down repeatedly? The induced current in the wire would reverse direction repeatedly as well. This kind of current is called **alternating current,** or AC. An alternating current consists of charges that move back and forth in a circuit. The electric current in the circuits in homes, schools, and other buildings is alternating current.

Alternating current has a major advantage over direct current. An AC voltage can be easily raised or lowered to a higher or lower voltage. This means that a high voltage can be used to send electrical energy over great distances. Then the voltage can be reduced to a safer level for everyday use.

Reading Checkpoint **What is the advantage of using alternating current?**

Writing in Science

Letter Find out more about the work of Michael Faraday, Joseph Henry, or Hans Christian Oersted. Write a letter to a friend in which you describe your work as a research assistant for the scientist you choose. Include descriptions of his experimental procedures and the equipment he uses. Tell how his work has led to surprising discoveries.

1882
Direct Current
Thomas Edison opens a generating plant in New York City. The Pearl Street Station consists of six DC generators, serving an area of about 2.6 square kilometers.

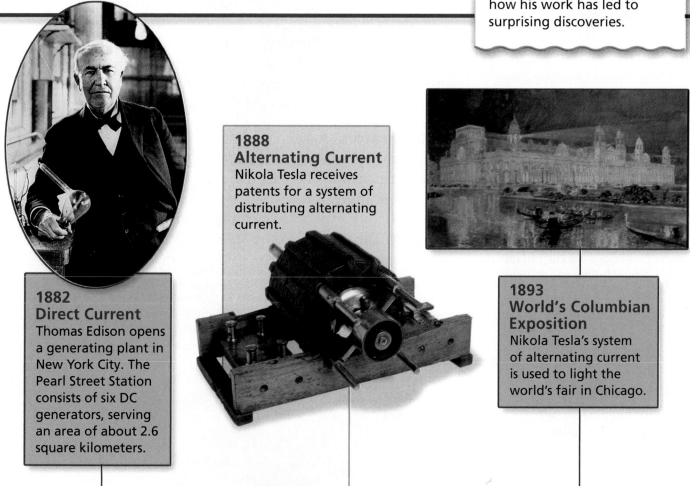

1888
Alternating Current
Nikola Tesla receives patents for a system of distributing alternating current.

1893
World's Columbian Exposition
Nikola Tesla's system of alternating current is used to light the world's fair in Chicago.

1860 1880 1900

Generators

An **electric generator** is a device that transforms mechanical energy into electrical energy. An electric generator is the opposite of an electric motor. An electric motor uses an electric current in a magnet field to produce motion. **A generator uses motion in a magnetic field to produce an electric current.**

AC Generators In Figure 13 you can see how a simple AC generator works. As the crank is turned, the armature rotates in the magnetic field. One side of the armature moves up, and the other side moves down. The up and down motion induces a current in the wire. The current is in opposite directions on the two sides of the armature.

After the armature turns halfway, each side of it reverses direction in the magnetic field. The side that moved up moves down, and vice versa. The current in the wire changes direction as well. The result is an alternating current is induced.

As the armature turns, slip rings turn with it. Slip rings may remind you of the commutator in a motor. They are attached to the ends of the armature. As they turn, they make contact with the brushes. The brushes can be connected to the rest of the circuit. In this way, a generator becomes an energy source.

DC Generators A DC generator is like an AC generator, except that it contains a commutator instead of slip rings. In fact, a DC generator and the motor you read about in Section 2 are the same thing. If you supply electrical energy to the motor, it will spin. But if you spin the motor, you will produce electrical energy. The motor becomes a DC generator.

Go Online
active art

For: Motors and Generators activity
Visit: PHSchool.com
Web Code: cgp-4033

FIGURE 13
How a Generator Works
In an AC generator, an armature is rotated in a magnetic field. This induces an electric current in the armature. Applying Concepts *How many times does the current reverse direction each time the armature rotates?*

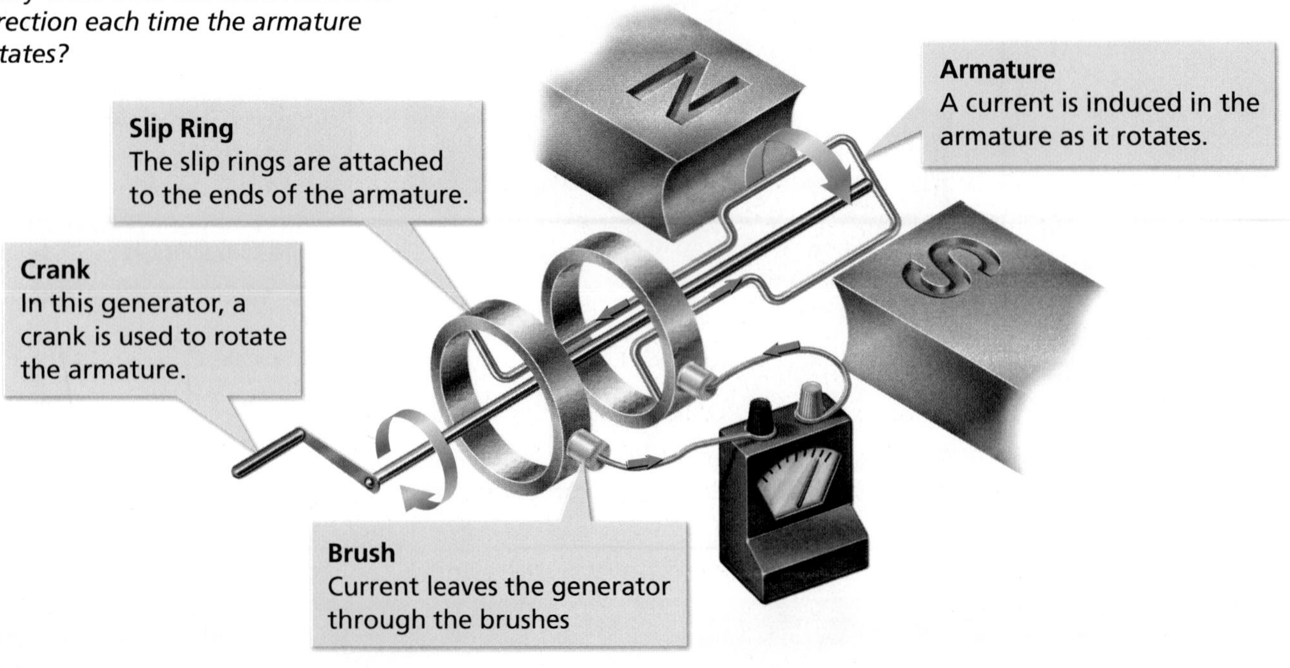

Armature
A current is induced in the armature as it rotates.
Slip Ring
The slip rings are attached to the ends of the armature.
Crank
In this generator, a crank is used to rotate the armature.
Brush
Current leaves the generator through the brushes
N
S

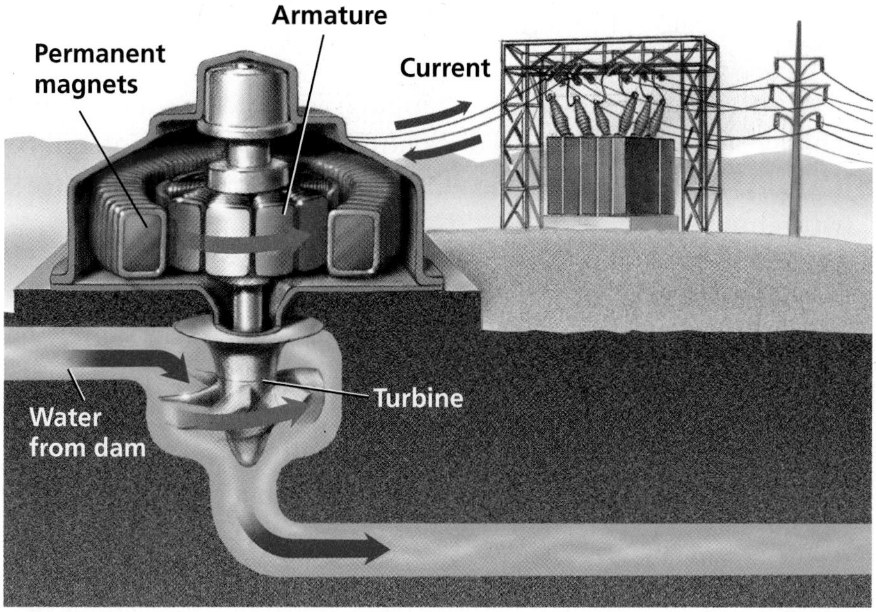

FIGURE 14
Turbines
In most generators, a source of mechanical energy turns huge turbines such as this one. The turbine is attached to the armature of a generator, which produces current.

Using Generators The electric company uses giant generators to produce most of the electrical energy you use in your home and school. But, instead of using a crank to supply the mechanical energy to turn the armature, a turbine is used. Turbines are large circular devices made up of many blades. Figure 14 shows how a turbine is attached to the armature in a generator. The turbine spins as the water flows by it. As a result, the armature spins and generates electric current.

Reading Checkpoint **What is a turbine?**

Transformers

The electrical energy generated by electric companies is transmitted over long distance at very high voltages. However in your home, electrical energy is used at much lower voltages. What changes the voltage of the electrical energy? The answer is transformers.

What is a Transformer? A transformer is a device that increases or decreases voltage. A **transformer** consists of two separate coils of insulated wire wrapped around an iron core. One coil, called the primary coil, is connected to a circuit with a voltage source and alternating current. The other coil, the secondary coil, is connected to a separate circuit that does not contain a voltage source.

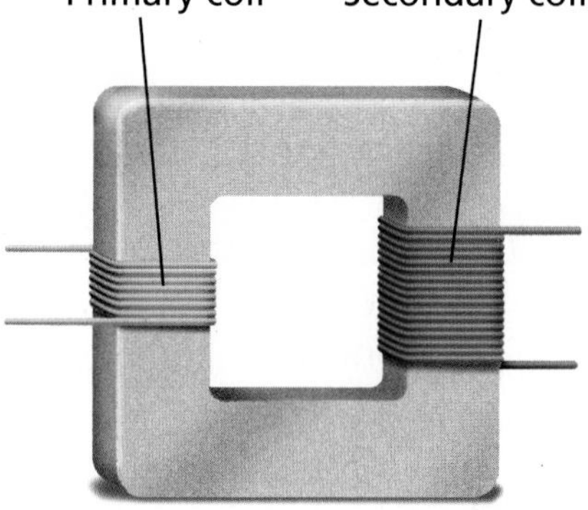

FIGURE 15
A Transformer
The primary coil of a transformer is connected to a voltage source. The secondary coil is not connected to a voltage source.

A Transformer at Work When a current is in the primary coil of the transformer, it produces a magnetic field. The magnetic field changes as the current alternates. This changing magnetic field is like a moving magnetic field. It induces a current in the secondary coil. A transformer works only if the current in the primary coil is changing. If the current does not change, the magnetic field does not change. No current will be induced in the secondary coil. So a transformer will not work with direct current.

Types of Transformers If the number of loops in the primary and secondary coils of a transformer is the same, the voltage of the induced current is the same as the original voltage. But if the secondary coil has more loops than the primary coil, the voltage in the secondary coil will be greater. A transformer that increases voltage is called a **step-up transformer.**

FIGURE 16
Changing Voltage
Transformers are involved in the transmission of electrical energy from an electric plant to a home. **Relating Cause and Effect** *How does the number of loops in the primary and secondary coils affect the voltage of the induced current?*

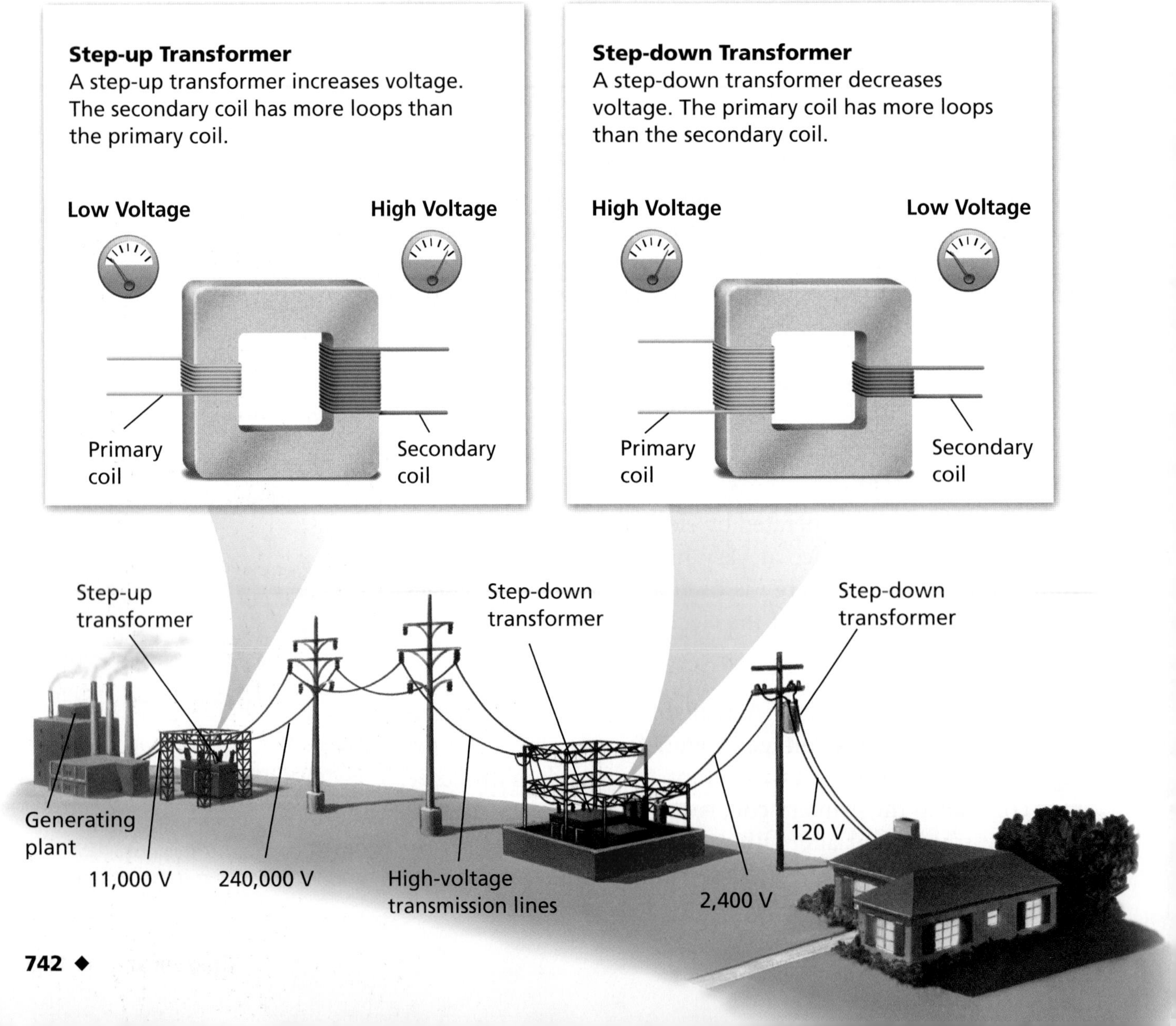

Suppose there are fewer loops in the secondary coil than in the primary coil. The voltage in the secondary coil will be less than in the primary coil. A transformer that decreases voltage is called a **step-down transformer.** Figure 16 shows both types of transformers.

Uses of Transformers An important use of transformers is in the transmission of electrical energy from generating plants. The most efficient way to transmit current over long distances is to maintain high voltages—about 11,000 volts to 765,000 volts. But the high voltage must be decreased to be used safely in your home. The use of step-up and step-down transformers allows safe transmission of electrical energy from generating plants to the consumer.

Transformers are also used in some electrical devices. Fluorescent lights, televisions, and X-ray machines require higher voltages than the current in your home, which is about 120 volts. These devices contain step-up transformers. Other devices, such as doorbells, electronic games, and portable CD players, require lower voltages, about 6 to 12 volts. They contain step-down transformers.

Discovery Channel School

Using Electricity and Magnetism

Video Preview
▶Video Field Trip
Video Assessment

Reading Checkpoint **What is the voltage in your house?**

Section 3 Assessment

Target Reading Skill Previewing Visuals
Refer to your questions and answers about Figure 13 to help you answer Question 2 below.

Reviewing Key Concepts

1. a. Defining What is electromagnetic induction?
   b. Describing What are two ways to induce an electric current?
   c. Relating Cause and Effect What determines whether an induced current is a direct current or an alternating current?
2. a. Reviewing How is energy transformed by a generator?
   b. Summarizing How does a generator produce an alternating current?
   c. Comparing and Contrasting How are an AC generator and a DC generator the same? How are they different?
3. a. Reviewing What does a transformer do?
   b. Interpreting Diagrams Look at Figure 16. What is the difference between a step-up transformer and a step-down transformer?
   c. Applying Concepts Why do some appliances have step-down transformers built into them?

Lab zone At-Home Activity

Step-Up and Step-Down Draw a diagram that shows how electric current gets to your home from the place it is generated. Include in your diagram the likely locations of step-up and step-down transformers. Explain your diagram to a family member. Then with your family member, try to locate the step-down transformer that provides your home's electricity.

Chapter 21 Study Guide

1 What Is Electromagnetism?

Key Concepts

- An electric current produces a magnetic field.
- The magnetic field produced by a current has three characteristics. The field can be turned on or off, have its direction reversed, or have its strength changed.
- An electromagnet is a strong magnet that can be turned on and off.

Key Terms

electromagnetism
solenoid
electromagnet

2 Electricity, Magnetism, and Motion

Key Concepts

- When a wire with a current is placed in a magnetic field, electrical energy is transformed into mechanical energy.
- Electric current is used to turn the pointer of a galvanometer.
- An electric motor transforms electrical energy into mechanical energy.

Key Terms

energy
electrical energy
mechanical energy
galvanometer
electric motor

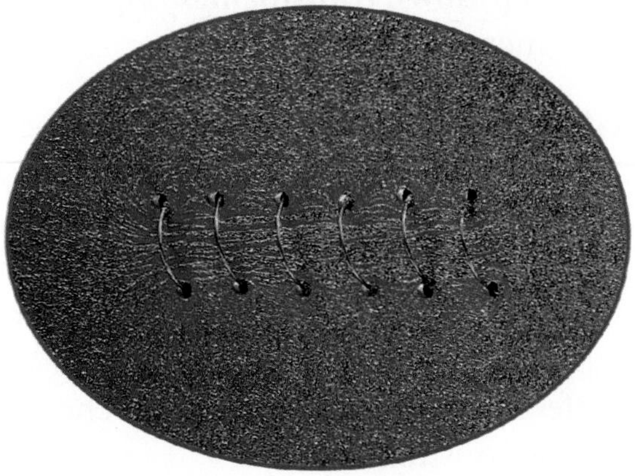

3 Electricity From Magnetism

Key Concepts

- An electric current is induced in a conductor when the conductor moves through a magnetic field.
- A generator uses motion in a magnetic field to produce an electric current.
- A transformer is a device that increases or decreases voltage.

Key Terms

electromagnetic induction
direct current
alternating current
electric generator
transformer
step-up transformer
step-down transformer

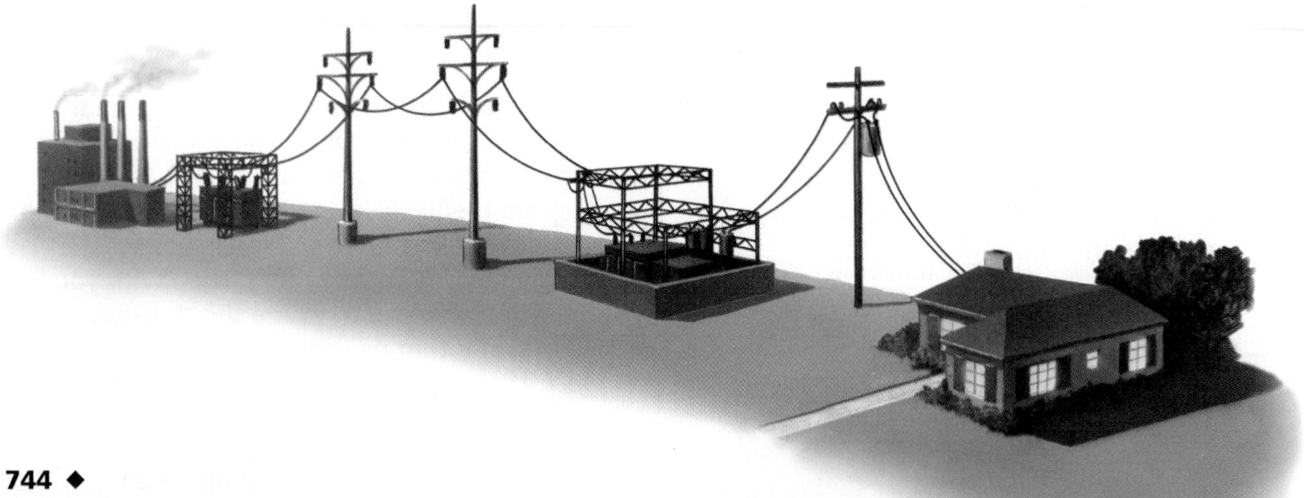

Review and Assessment

Go Online
PHSchool.com
For: Self-Assessment
Visit: PHSchool.com
Web Code: cga-4030

Organizing Information

Concept Mapping Copy the concept map about electromagnetism onto a separate sheet of paper. Then complete the concept map and add a title. (For more about concept maps, see the Skills Handbook.)

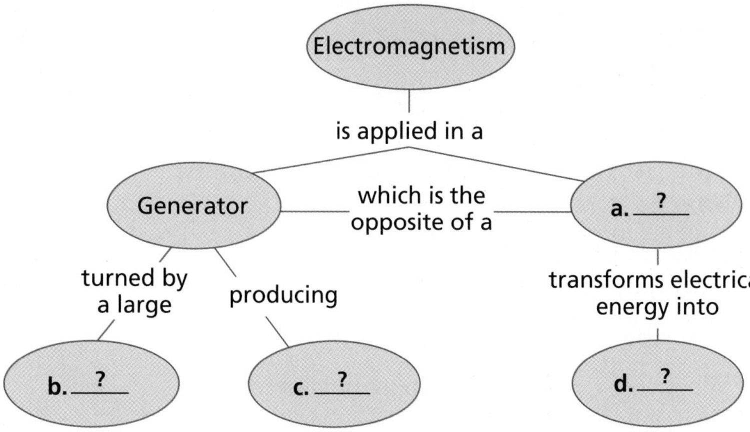

Reviewing Key Terms

Choose the letter of the best answer.

1. The relationship between electricity and magnetism is called
a. electrical energy.
b. an electromagnet.
c. electromagnetism.
d. induced current.

2. A coil of wire with a current is called a
a. generator.
b. motor.
c. solenoid.
d. transformer.

3. When a ferromagnetic material is placed within a solenoid, the resulting device is called a(n)
a. galvanometer. **b.** electromagnet.
c. motor. **d.** transformer.

4. Electrical energy is transformed into mechanical energy in a
a. motor. **b.** generator.
c. transformer. **d.** electromagnet.

5. A device that changes the voltage of alternating current is a
a. transformer. **b.** motor.
c. generator. **d.** galvanometer.

If the statement is true, write *true*. If it is false, change the underlined word or words to make the statement true.

6. The device that turns a needle in a galvanometer is called an electromagnet.

7. Several loops of wire wrapped around an iron core form the armature of a motor.

8. Generating a current by moving a conductor in a magnetic field is induction.

9. An electric motor transforms mechanical energy into electrical energy.

10. A solenoid increases or decreases voltage.

Writing in Science

News Report You are a television news reporter covering the opening of a new dam that generates electrical energy. Write a short news story describing how the dam transforms mechanical energy from the motion of the water into electrical energy.

Discovery Channel School
Using Electricity and Magnetism
Video Preview
Video Field Trip
▶ Video Assessment

Review and Assessment

Checking Concepts

11. How can the magnetic field produced by a current be changed?
12. How is a galvanometer similar to a motor? How is it different?
13. What are the roles of the commutator and the brushes in an electric motor?
14. How are alternating current and direct current the same? How are they different?
15. Describe how an AC generator operates.
16. What role does a turbine play in generating electricity?
17. Explain how transformers are used to efficiently transmit electrical energy from the electric company where it is produced to your home where it is used.

Thinking Critically

18. Relating Cause and Effect Why does a compass needle move when placed near a wire with an electric current? What do you think happens to the compass needle when the circuit is shut off?
19. Inferring How could you modify a solenoid to produce a stonger magnetic field?
20. Applying Concepts Make a diagram of a wire loop in a magnetic field. Show how the direction of a current in the wire is related to the direction of rotation of the loop.
21. Predicting Four electromagnets are illustrated in the diagram below. Will the electromagnet labeled **A** or **B** produce a stronger magnetic field? Will the electromagnet **B** or **C** produce a stronger field? Explain your choices.

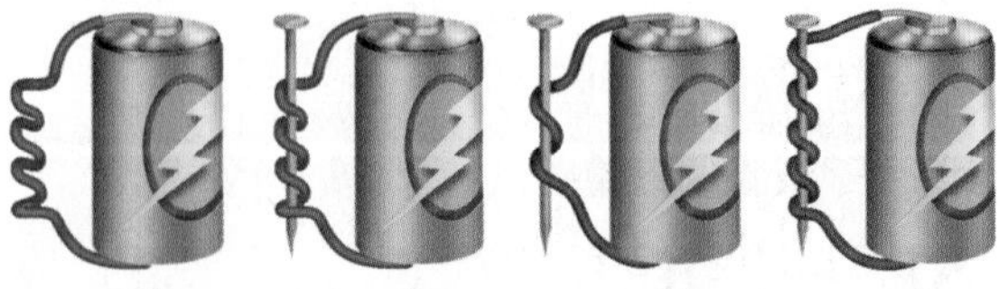

22. Comparing and Contrasting Compare a motor and a generator. Include information about the kind of energy conversion that takes place in each device.
23. Applying Concepts How are the uses of an electromagnet different from those of a permanent magnet?

Applying Skills

Use the illustration of a transformer to answer Questions 24–26.

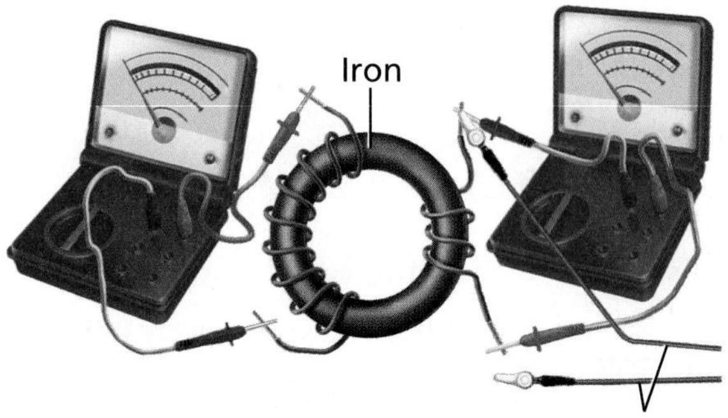

24. Classifying What type of transformer is shown in the illustration above? Explain how you know.
25. Inferring Which coil is the primary coil and which is the secondary coil?
26. Predicting What will the two voltmeters show when the circuit on the right side of the diagram is completed?

Lab zone Chapter Project

Performance Assessment Present the results of your energy audit to the class in a visual format. Make a bar, circle, or line graph showing the appliances and the energy they used. Identify the appliance that uses the most electrical energy in a week. Also discuss the way you calculated energy use. What problems did you have? What information couldn't you collect?

Standardized Test Prep

Test-Taking Tip

Interpreting a Graph

If you are asked to interpret a line graph, look at the labels of the horizontal and vertical axes. The labels inform you what relationship is plotted on the graph—in other words, what variables are being compared. Study the graph for Questions 4–5 and answer the sample question.

Sample Question

What variable is plotted on the *x*-axis?

A the number of solenoids
B the magnetic field strength
C the number of loops in the solenoid
D the length of solenoid

Answer

Choice **C** is correct. You can eliminate **A** and **D**, because neither axis mentions the number of solenoids or the length of the solenoid. **B** is incorrect because it is on the vertical axis, or *y*-axis.

Choose the letter of the best answer.

1. If a step-up transformer is to increase voltage, it needs

A a DC source connected to the primary coil.
B a DC source connected to the secondary coil.
C more turns in the primary coil than in the secondary coil.
D more turns in the secondary coil than in the primary coil.

2. To measure the current induced from moving a wire through a magnetic field, which piece of equipment would a scientist need?

F a galvanometer
G a flashlight bulb
H an insulated wire
J an LED

3. What happens when a magnet moves through a coil of wire?

A The magnet loses magnetism.
B A current is induced in the magnet.
C A current is induced in the wire.
D Electrical energy is transformed into mechanical energy.

A scientist measured the magnetic field strength of a solenoid after increasing the number of loops. Magnetic field strength is measured using a unit called a gauss. The graph below plots the results. Use the graph to answer Questions 4–5.

Magnetic Field Strength of a Solenoid

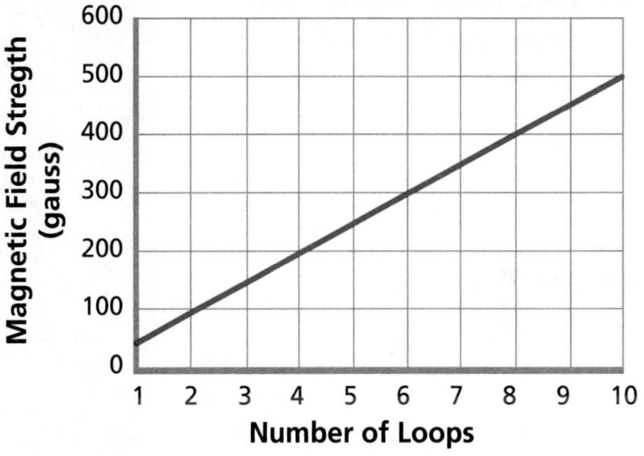

4. Which of the following statements expresses the relationship shown on the graph?

F As the number of loops decreases, the magnetic field strength increases.
G As the number of loops increases, the magnetic field strength decreases.
H As the number of loops increases, the magnetic field strength increases.
J The number of loops does not affect the magnetic field strength.

5. What would you expect the magnetic field strength of the solenoid with 12 loops to be?

A 300 gauss
B 600 gauss
C 700 gauss
D 1200 gauss

Constructed Response

6. Explain how a generator transforms mechanical energy into electrical energy.

Chapter 22

Electronics

Chapter Preview

1. **Electronic Signals and Semiconductors**
   Discover *Can You Send Information With a Flashlight?*
   Skills Activity *Communicating*
   Technology Lab *Design a Battery Sensor*

2. **Electronic Communication**
   Discover *Are You Seeing Spots?*
   Active Art *Modulating Waves*
   At-Home Activity *What's a Remote?*

3. **Computers**
   Discover *How Fast Are You?*
   Skills Activity *Calculating*
   Tech & Design in History *Development of Computers*
   Try This *What a Web You Weave*
   Skills Lab *Computer Programming*
   Science and Society *When Seeing ISN'T Believing*

Interactive Textbook

This circuit board is made up of thousands of tiny electronic devices. ▶

Discovery Channel School

Electronics

▶ **Video Preview**
Video Field Trip
Video Assessment

Lab zone™ Chapter **Project**

Bits and Bytes

In this chapter, you will learn about the devices that make computers possible, how computers work, and how they are used. As you complete the chapter, you will identify a new computer use, or application.

Your Goal To study an existing computer application and then propose and detail a new application

Your project must

- show what the existing computer application does and explain its benefits
- explain how data are received and transformed by the computer as you use the application
- describe each step that occurs as your new application runs

Plan It! Brainstorm with your classmates about existing computer applications. Make a list of devices that use programmed information, such as clock radios, automated bank teller machines, and grocery store bar code scanners. Choose a new application and make a plan for your teacher's approval. Then present the existing application and your new one to the class.

Section 1

Electronic Signals and Semiconductors

Reading Preview

Key Concepts

- What are two types of electronic signals?
- How are semiconductors used to make electronic components?

Key Terms

- electronics • electronic signal
- analog signal • digital signal
- semiconductor • diode
- transistor • integrated circuit

Target Reading Skill

Asking Questions Before you read, preview the red headings. In a graphic organizer like the one below, ask a *what* question for each heading. As you read, write the answers to your questions.

Electronic Signals and Devices

Question	Answer
What are analog and digital signals?	Analog signals are . . .

Lab zone Discover Activity

Can You Send Information With a Flashlight?

1. Write a short sentence on a sheet of paper.
2. Morse code is a language that uses dots and dashes to convey information. Convert your sentence to dots and dashes using the International Morse Code chart at the right.
3. Turn a flashlight on and off quickly to represent dots. Leave the flashlight on a little longer to represent dashes. Practice using the flashlight for different letters.
4. Use the flashlight to transmit your sentence to a partner. Ask your partner to translate your message and write down your sentence.

International Morse Code

A •–	B –•••	C –•–•	D –••
E •	F ••–•	G ––•	H ••••
I ••	J •–––	K –•–	L •–••
M ––	N –•	O –––	P •––•
Q ––•–	R •–•	S •••	T –
U ••–	V •••–	W •––	X –••–
Y –•––	Z ––••		

Think It Over

Inferring Were you able to transmit information using light? How does your light message differ from the same message read aloud?

Every day, you use devices that run on electric current. But not all these devices are the same. Light bulbs and toasters are examples of *electrical* devices. An electrical device relies on a continuous supply of electric current.

When you watch television or talk on a cell phone, you are using *electronic* devices. The difference between electronic and electrical devices is in the way that they use electric current.

Electronics is the use of electric current to control, communicate, and process information. How do electronic devices work? Electronics is based on electronic signals. Any information that can be measured or numbered, whether it is electrical or not, can be converted to a signal. An **electronic signal** is a varying electric current that represents information.

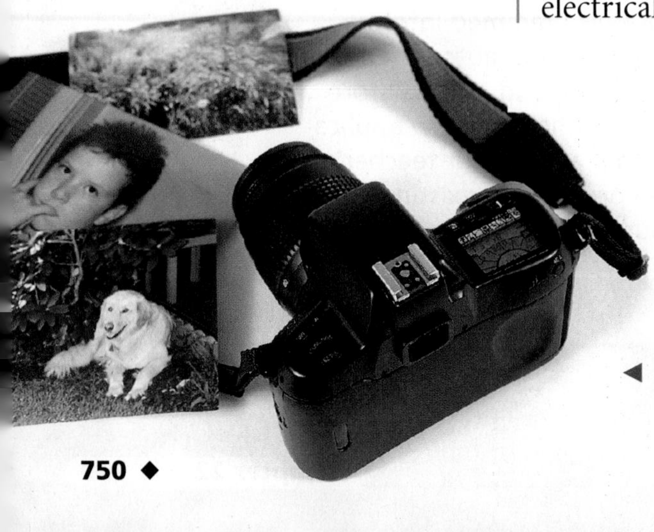

◀ Cameras can use electronic signals to take photographs.

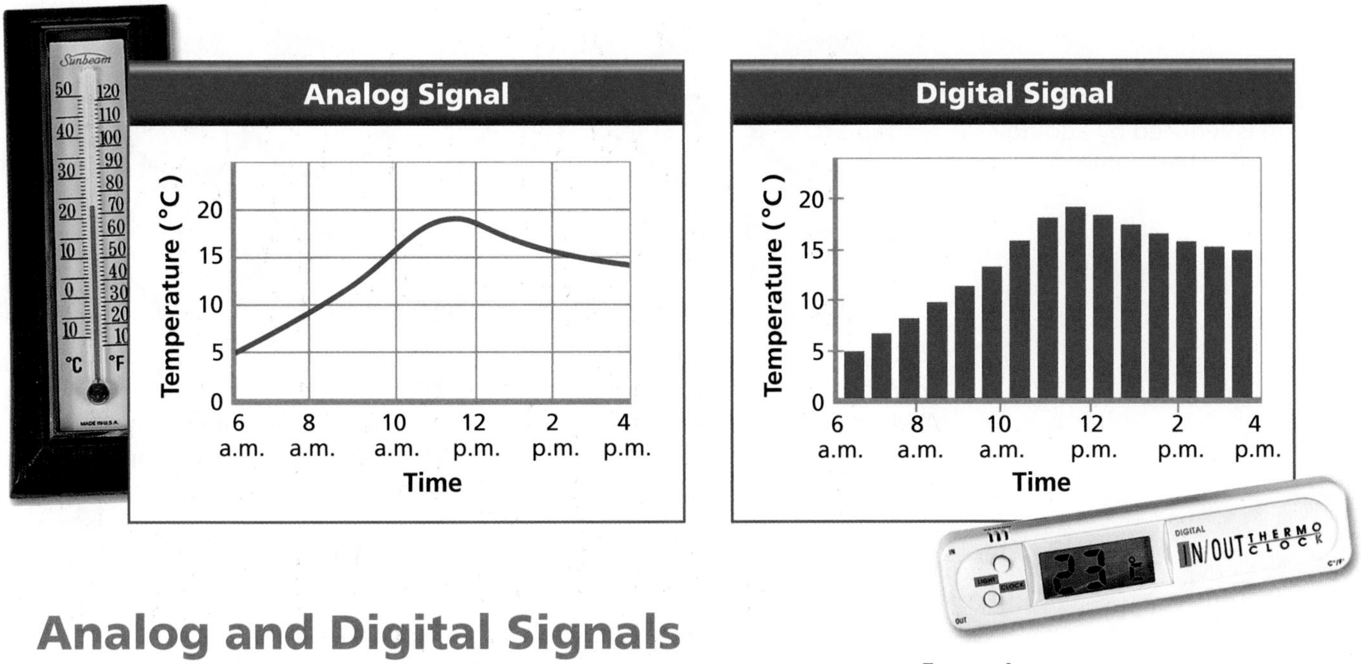

FIGURE 1
Analog and Digital
An analog signal varies smoothly. A digital signal varies in steps.
Predicting *How would the bar graph be different if it showed temperature measurements made every minute?*

Analog and Digital Signals

There are two basic kinds of electronic signals: analog signals and digital signals. The two types of signals represent information in different ways.

Analog Signals In **analog signals,** a current is varied smoothly to represent information. An analog signal varies in much the same way that temperature varies in a liquid-filled thermometer. This kind of thermometer shows temperature as the height of a liquid in a tube. The height of the liquid rises and falls smoothly with the temperature. The "analog signal" from the liquid-filled thermometer can be represented by a line graph like the one in Figure 1.

Digital Signals In **digital signals,** pulses of current are used to represent information. Rather than varying smoothly to represent information, a digital signal carries information in pulses, or steps. If you did the Discover activity, you used pulses of light to represent letters.

A digital signal varies much the same way the numbers on a digital thermometer vary. You have probably seen a digital thermometer in front of a bank. The number on the thermometer is constant for a while and then changes suddenly by a whole degree. Of course, the temperature doesn't really change so suddenly. But the thermometer can only show the temperature to the nearest degree, and so the temperature seems to jump. The digital signal from a digital thermometer can be represented by a bar graph, as shown in Figure 1.

Reading Checkpoint **How is the changing temperature on a liquid-filled thermometer like an analog signal?**

Go Online
SCILINKS NSTA
For: Links on electronic signals
Visit: www.SciLinks.org
Web Code: scn-1441

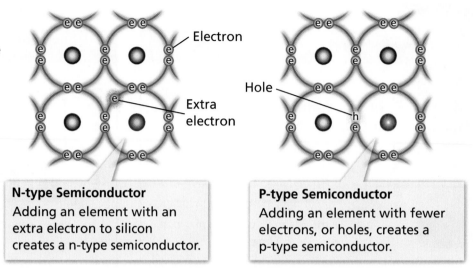

FIGURE 2
Semiconductors
The electrical resistance of pure silicon is reduced by adding atoms of other elements to it.

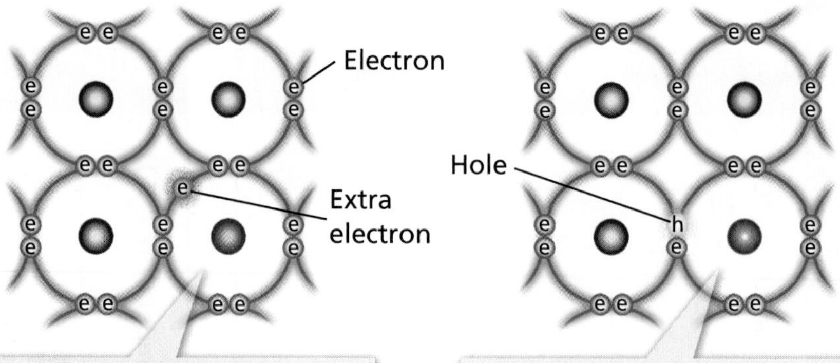

N-type Semiconductor
Adding an element with an extra electron to silicon creates a n-type semiconductor.

P-type Semiconductor
Adding an element with fewer electrons, or holes, creates a p-type semiconductor.

Semiconductor Devices

How can an electronic device transmit electronic signals? To transmit an electronic signal, an electronic device must be able to vary the current through a circuit. To vary current, electronic devices use semiconductors. A **semiconductor** is a material that conducts current better than insulators but not as well as conductors. A semiconductor conducts current only under certain conditions.

How Semiconductors Work How can a material conduct current only under certain conditions? Silicon and other semiconductors are elements that have extremely high resistance in their pure forms. However, if atoms of other elements are added to semiconductors, the resulting material can conduct current much more easily.

By controlling the number and type of atoms added, scientists produce two types of semiconductors. In Figure 2, you can see that adding atoms with extra electrons to silicon produces an n-type semiconductor. "N," for "negative," indicates that the material can release, or give off, electrons. Look again at Figure 2. Notice that adding atoms with fewer electrons, or holes, to silicon produces a p-type semiconductor. "P," for "positive," indicates that the material has room for and can receive an electron.

Scientists combine n-type and p-type semiconductors in layers. This layered structure allows for the delicate control of current needed for many electronic devices. **The two types of semiconductors can be combined in different ways to make diodes, transistors, and integrated circuits.** These components control current in electronic devices.

Lab zone Skills Activity

Communicating

How do you make someone understand how tiny a chip is or how fast an electronic signal travels? An analogy can help communicate what a measurement means. An analogy uses a similarity between two things that are otherwise unlike each other. For example, "a chip is as small as a baby's fingernail" is an analogy. So is "an electronic signal moves as fast as a bolt of lightning." Write your own analogies to describe how many diodes there are in one integrated circuit chip.

Diodes An electronic component that consists of an n-type and a p-type semiconductor joined together is a **diode.** A diode, shown in Figure 3, allows current in one direction only. If you connect a diode in a circuit in one direction, there will be a current. But if you turn the diode around, there will not be a current. Diodes can be used to change an alternating current to a direct current. Diodes can also be used as a switch.

Transistors When a layer of one type of semiconductor is sandwiched between two layers of the other type of semiconductor, a transistor is formed. Figure 3 shows the structure of a transistor. A **transistor** has two uses: it either amplifies an electronic signal or switches current on and off.

When electronic signals travel great distances, they gradually grow weak. When they are received, signals must be amplified, or made stronger, so that they can be used. Transistors revolutionized the electronics industry by making amplifiers much cheaper and more reliable.

When a transistor acts as a switch, it either allows a current or cuts it off. Millions of transistors that act as switches are what make computers work.

FIGURE 3
Diodes and Transistors
Diodes (top) allow current in only one direction. Transistors (bottom) can amplify electronic signals or act as switches. **Comparing and Contrasting** *How are diodes and transistors similar? How are they different?*

Diode A diode is a combination of an n-type and a p-type semiconductor.

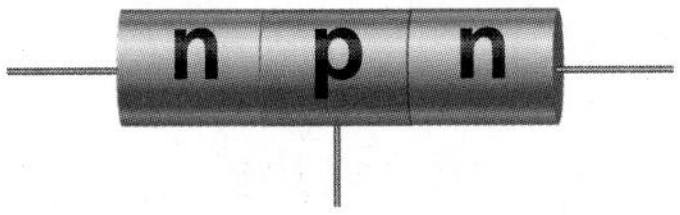

Transistor A transistor is a combination of three layers of semiconductors.

FIGURE 4
Combining Electronic Components
Diodes and transistors can be combined to carry out specific tasks within electronic devices. The singing fish uses electronics to move and make sounds when a person walks by.

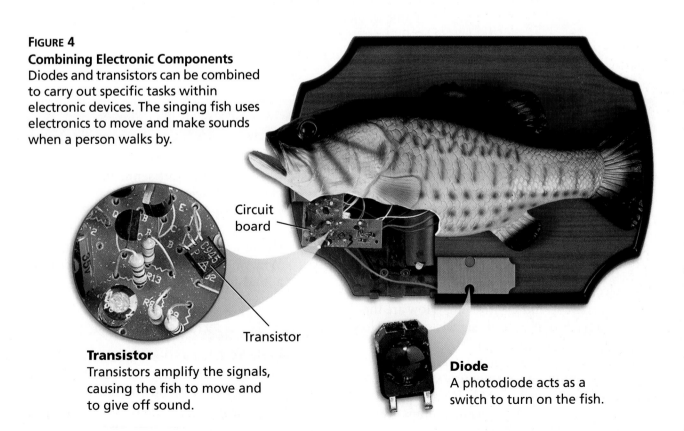

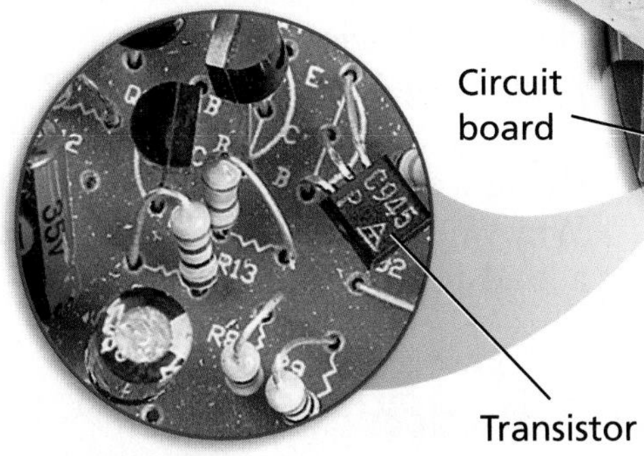

Transistor
Transistors amplify the signals, causing the fish to move and to give off sound.

Diode
A photodiode acts as a switch to turn on the fish.

FIGURE 5
Integrated Circuits
An integrated circuit chip is smaller than an ant. Yet the integrated circuit contains hundreds of thousands of diodes and transistors.

Integrated Circuits Individual electronic components can be combined into larger groups, called integrated circuits, to increase their usefulness. An **integrated circuit** is a thin slice of semiconductor that contains many diodes, transistors, and other electronic components. Integrated circuits are also called chips. Figure 5 shows a magnified view of a chip from a computer. A chip smaller than one millimeter on each side can contain hundreds of thousands of components. Electronic signals flow through integrated circuits at tremendous speeds because the various components are so close together. On some chips, the space between two components can be one hundredth as thick as a human hair. The high-speed signals of integrated circuits make possible devices from video games to spacecraft. The small size of integrated circuits has allowed the size of electronic devices such as computers to be greatly reduced.

Reading Checkpoint **What is a chip?**

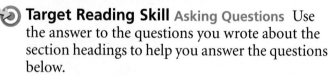

Section 1 Assessment

Target Reading Skill **Asking Questions** Use the answer to the questions you wrote about the section headings to help you answer the questions below.

Reviewing Key Concepts

1. a. **Listing** What are the two basic kinds of electronic signals?

b. **Comparing and Contrasting** How are the two types of electronic signals similar? How are they different?

c. **Classifying** A grandfather clock uses a pendulum that continuously swings to control the clock's hands. What type of signal does the swinging pendulum represent? Explain.

2. a. **Reviewing** How are semiconductors used in electronic devices?

b. Explaining What is a transistor?

c. **Relating Cause and Effect** A loudspeaker changes electronic signals into sounds. Why would transistors be useful parts of a loudspeaker?

Writing in Science

Directions Review the Morse code at the beginning of the section. Write directions a friend could use to send you messages using light or sound.

Design a Battery Sensor

Problem

How can an LED be used to tell if a battery is installed correctly?

Skills Focus

evaluating the design, redesigning, observing, drawing conclusions

Materials

- 2 D cells
- LED
- bicolor LED (optional)
- flashlight using 2 D-cells
- flashlight bulb and socket
- two insulated wires with alligator clips

Procedure

PART 1 LED Properties

1. Attach one wire to each terminal of the LED.
2. Tape the two cells together, positive terminal to negative terminal, to make a 3-volt battery.
3. Attach the other ends of the wires to the terminals of the battery and observe the LED.
4. Switch the wires connected to the battery terminals and observe the LED again.
5. Repeat Steps 1–4, but substitute a flashlight bulb in its socket for the LED.

PART 2 Sensor Design

6. Many electrical devices that run on batteries will not run if the batteries are installed backwards (positive where negative should be). Design a device that uses an LED to indicate if batteries are installed backwards.
7. Draw your design. Show how the LED, the device, and the battery are connected. (*Hint:* The LED can be connected either in series or in parallel with the battery and the device.)
8. Make a model of your sensor to see if it works with a flashlight.

Analyze and Conclude

1. **Observing** What did you observe in Part 1 when you connected the LED to the battery the first time? The second time?
2. **Drawing Conclusions** Based on your observations, is the LED a diode? How do you know?
3. **Evaluating the Design** How did your observations of the LED's properties affect your design in Part 2?
4. **Troubleshooting** Describe any problems you had while designing and building your sensor.
5. **Redesigning** In what ways could you improve your sensor?

Communicate

Write a product brochure for your battery sensor. Be sure to describe in detail how your sensor can be used to tell if batteries are installed correctly in electrical devices. Include other possible uses for your sensor. What practical application can you see for such an LED?

Section 2 Electronic Communication

Reading Preview

Key Concepts
- How is sound transmitted by telephone?
- What are two ways that sounds can be reproduced?
- How are electromagnetic waves involved in the transmission of radio and television signals?

Key Terms
- transmitter
- receiver

Target Reading Skill
Using Prior Knowledge Before you read, look at the section headings and visuals to see what this section is about. Then write what you know about electronic communication in a graphic organizer. As you read, write what you learn.

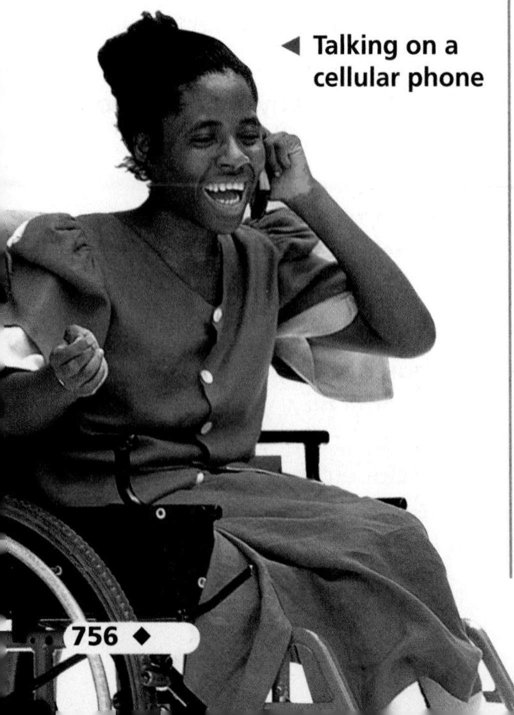

◄ Talking on a cellular phone

Lab zone Discover Activity

Are You Seeing Spots?

1. Turn on a color television. Hold a hand lens at arm's length up to the television screen.
2. Move the lens closer to and farther from the screen until you can see a clear image through it. What do you see within the image?

Think It Over

Classifying What three colors make up the images on the television screen? How do you think these colors make up the wide range of colors you see on television?

Have you ever thought about the amazing technology that enables you to see and hear an event as it happens halfway around the globe? Since the first telegraph message was sent in 1844, people have become accustomed to long distance communication by telephone, radio, and television. Compared with the past, communication today is fast, dependable, and cheap. This is because of advancements in the field of electronics.

Telephones

In a telephone, sound is transformed into an electronic signal that is transmitted and then transformed back into sound. The first telephone was invented by Alexander Graham Bell in 1876. Modern telephones have some of the same main parts as the telephone patented by Bell: a transmitter, a receiver, and a dialing mechanism.

Transmitter A **transmitter** is a device that transfers signals from one form to another. In a telephone, a transmitter transforms sound into an electronic signal. Transforming sound into an electronic signal is possible because sound travels as a wave. These waves cause a metal disk in the microphone to vibrate, transforming the sound into an electronic signal. The signal can travel through a series of switches and wires to the receiving telephone. Modern telephone equipment can also transform the electronic signals to a pattern of light that travels through optical fibers.

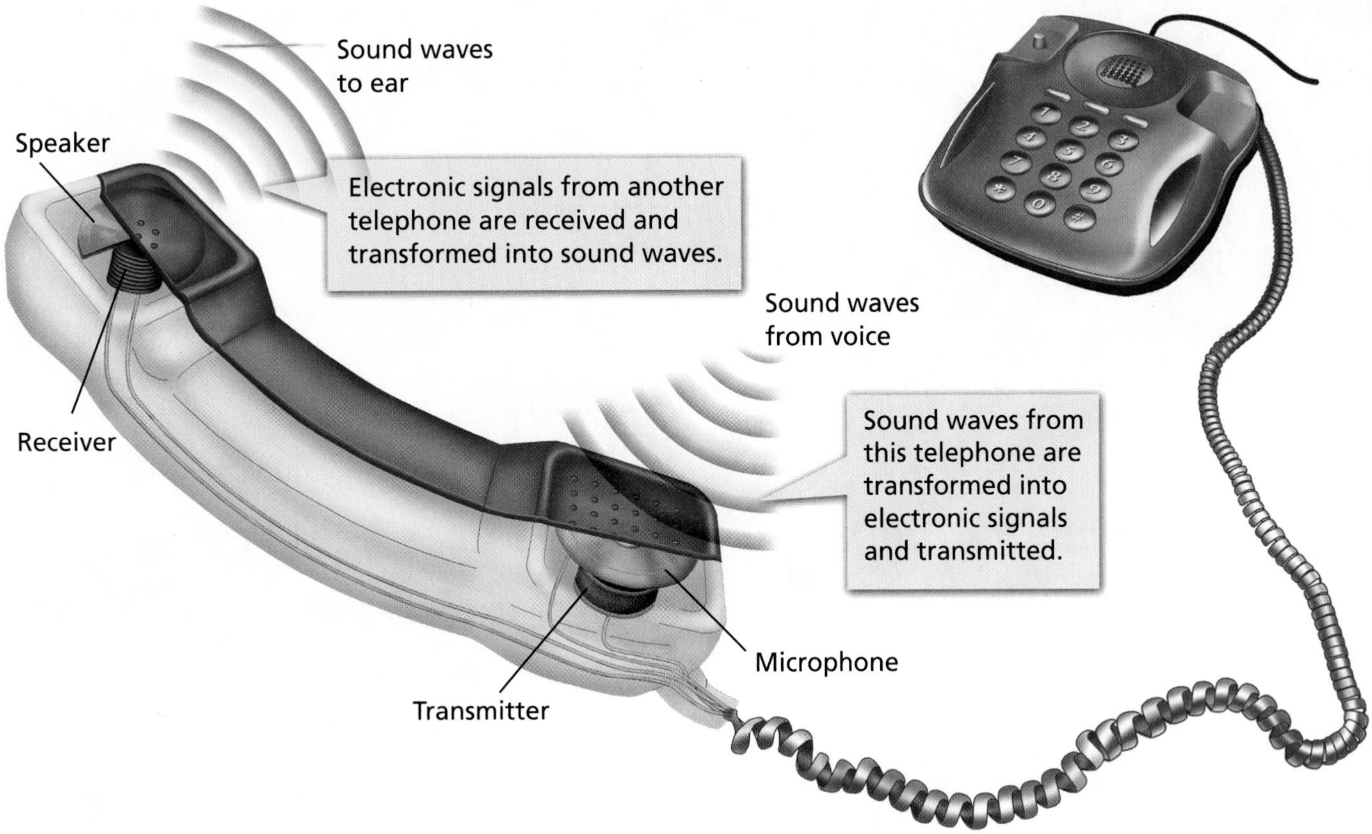
Sound waves to ear
Speaker
Electronic signals from another telephone are received and transformed into sound waves.
Sound waves from voice
Receiver
Sound waves from this telephone are transformed into electronic signals and transmitted.
Microphone
Transmitter

FIGURE 6
How a Telephone Works
When you speak into a telephone, your voice is transformed into electronic signals. The signals are transmitted to the listener's phone, where they are transformed back into sound.
Applying Concepts *How does the dialing mechanism work?*

Receiver The receiver is located in the earpiece of a telephone. A **receiver** is a device that uses a speaker to transform an electronic signal into sound. A speaker is made up of an electromagnet and a thin metal disk. During a conversation, the amount of electric current in the electromagnet varies with the signal strength. Therefore, the strength of the magnetic field around the electromagnet varies as well. This causes the disk to vibrate in a pattern that matches the electronic signal. These vibrations produce sound waves, which represent the voice on the other telephone. Many modern receivers now use semiconductors instead of electromagnets.

Dialing Mechanism Another part of the telephone is the dialing mechanism. When you dial a telephone number, you are telling the telephone company's switching system where you want the call to go. A dial telephone sends a series of pulses or clicks to the switching network. A push-button device sends different tones. The tones act as signals to the electronic circuits in the switching network. Today, push-button devices have become standard on almost all telephones.

Reading Checkpoint **What does a telephone transmitter do?**

▲ Magnified view of a stylus in a record groove

FIGURE 7

Analog Sound: Phonograph The needle of a record player moves along the groove of a record. **Interpreting Photos** *Why does the smooth shape tell you that the groove represents an analog signal?*

Sound Recordings

Sound recordings also communicate information using electronic signals. **Sound can be reproduced using an analog device such as a phonograph or a digital device such as a CD player.**

Analog Sound Recording When a deejay spins a record by moving it back and forth, the sound varies smoothly. The music the deejay in Figure 7 is playing is stored as analog signals on a plastic record. But how does sound come from a piece of plastic? When you play a record, a needle, or stylus, runs along a spiral groove in the plastic. The wavy pattern of the groove varies in the same way that the sound waves from the musicians did. The needle in the groove follows the groove's wavy pattern. The needle's movement, in turn, moves a tiny magnet that induces an electric current in a coil of wire. This current matches the pattern of the groove in the record.

The current produced by the needle is an analog signal representing the original sounds played by the musicians. The signal varies continuously as it copies the information stored on the record. The analog signal is fed into an amplifier and then into a speaker, which changes the signal back into sound.

Digital Sound Recording As you can see in Figure 8, a CD, or compact disc, is very different from a plastic record. It contains microscopic holes, called pits. The level areas between the pits are called flats. Like the groove on a record, these pits and flats are arranged in a spiral. They allow sound to be stored in steps. Although you can't tell from the photograph, the spiral on a compact disc is divided into pieces of equal time. The arrangement of pits and flats within each piece of the spiral is a code. Each piece of this code represents the sound at one instant.

When the CD spins, a beam of light scans the pits and flats. The light reflects from the flats but not from the pits. This causes the reflected light to form a pattern of tiny flashes of light. The flashes are then transformed into pulses of electric current, or a digital signal. The digital signal is fed into an amplifier and then a speaker, where it is changed back into sound.

Reading Checkpoint **How do the pits and flats on a CD make a digital signal?**

FIGURE 8
Digital Sound: CD Player
Each series of 3 pits or flats on this diagram of a CD represents the sound at one instant.

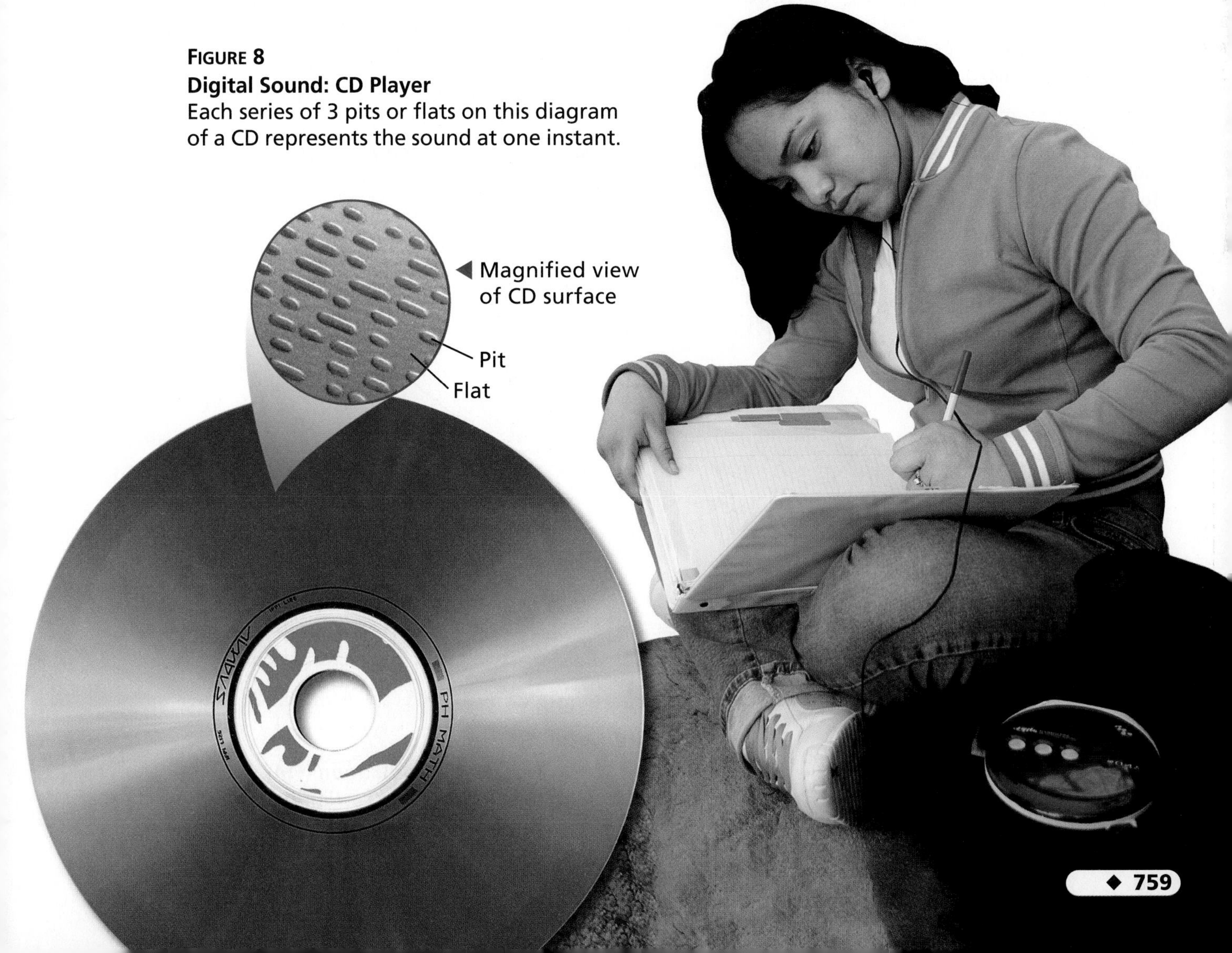

Radio

Voices or music on an AM or FM radio station are electronic signals carried by an electromagnetic wave. But where do the sounds you hear come from?

Transmission The process begins at a radio station where sounds are generated and transformed into an electronic signal. When a musician plays into a microphone at a radio station, the sound waves produce a varying electric current. This current is an analog signal that represents the sound waves. It is sometimes called an audio signal.

The audio signal is then sent to a transmitter. The transmitter amplifies the audio signal and combines it with a carrier wave. The combined electromagnetic wave is then sent to an antenna, which sends it out in all directions.

Recall that the carrier wave can be modulated to match the electronic signal in two different ways, as shown in Figure 9. One way is to change the amplitude of the carrier wave to match that of the signal. This process is known as amplitude modulation (AM). The other way is to change the frequency of the carrier wave to match the amplitude of the signal. Then the space between the waves varies with the strength of the signal. This process is known as frequency modulation (FM).

Go Online
active art

For: Modulating Electromagnetic Waves activity
Visit: PHSchool.com
Web Code: cgp-4042

Reading Checkpoint **What is an audio signal?**

FIGURE 9
Modulating Waves
A carrier wave's amplitude and frequency can be modulated to carry an electronic signal.
Interpreting Diagrams *How is a carrier wave modulated to transmit an AM radio signal?*

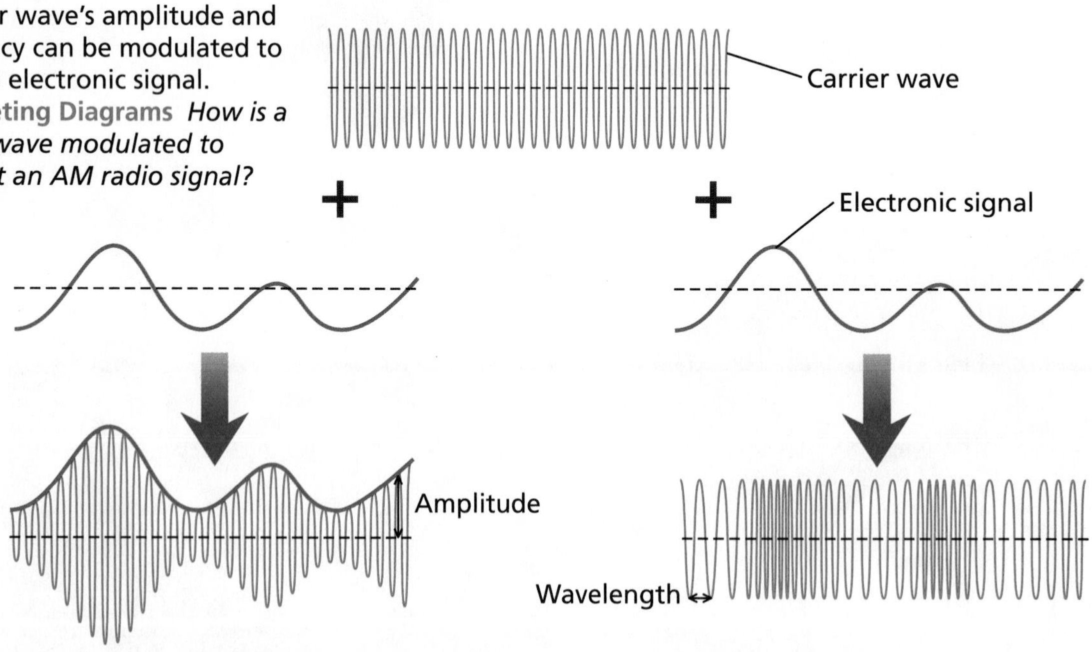

Amplitude Modulation (AM) The amplitude of the carrier wave varies with the strength of the electronic signal.

Frequency Modulation (FM) The frequency of the carrier wave varies with the strength of the electronic signal.

1 Signal Generated A person generates sound waves that are transformed into an audio signal.

2 Transmission The audio signal is sent to a transmitter and combined with a carrier wave that is broadcast at a specific frequency.

3 Reception A radio receives the wave at a specific frequency and separates the audio signal. Speakers transform the audio signal into sound.

FIGURE 10
How Radios Work
At the radio station, voices and music are transformed into electronic signals and then broadcast. Individual radios pick up the electronic signals and change them back to sound.
Interpreting Photos *What is the role of the transmitter?*

Reception Your radio has its own antenna that receives electromagnetic waves from the radio station. The carrier wave has a specific frequency. You tune in to the wave by selecting that frequency on your radio. Your radio amplifies the audio signal and separates it from the carrier wave. The signal is then sent to the radio's speaker, which is the reverse of a microphone. The speaker transforms the audio signal back into sound.

Television

Electromagnetic waves can be used to carry images as well as sound. The transmission of the images and sounds on television is very similar to that of radio sounds.

Transmission The audio and video signals that make up the image on your television screen are generated at a television station. Both signals are carried by electromagnetic waves. The signals are usually sent from transmitting antennas at the station. They may be transmitted directly to your home or to a communication satellite that relays them. Signals may be relayed to a central receiver at your local cable television network. Then they are sent through cables to your home.

Reception Each television contains a receiver that accepts video and audio signals. As in a radio, the carrier wave for each television station is at a specific frequency. You tune in the frequency by selecting a channel. Your television amplifies the signal and separates it from the carrier wave. The audio signal is transformed back into sound by the television's speakers.

Discovery Channel School

Electronics

Video Preview
▶ Video Field Trip
Video Assessment

FIGURE 11
Types of Televisions
Traditional televisions use bulky cathode-ray tubes to produce images. Newer technologies permit televisions to be thinner and lighter.

Cathode-ray tube television

Thin screen television

Television Screens How does a television set change a video signal into the picture on a television screen? Today there are several technologies that can do this.

Most televisions use cathode-ray tubes. A cathode-ray tube contains solid fluorescent materials that transform beams of electrons into tiny, colored dots of light. The dots are in the primary colors of light—red, blue, and green. Your eyes combine these three colors to form all of the colors in the images you see.

Newer televisions produce images in other ways. Video signals can be sent to a liquid crystal or to a mixture of gases called a plasma. Both of these technologies can be used to produce a thin screen television like the one shown in Figure 11. A liquid crystal display television produces images in the same way a laptop computer does. In a plasma television, the video signal heats tiny pockets of gases, causing them to glow in different colors.

Reading Checkpoint **How are television images produced?**

Section 2 Assessment

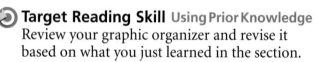

Target Reading Skill **Using Prior Knowledge** Review your graphic organizer and revise it based on what you just learned in the section.

Reviewing Key Concepts

1. a. **Identifying** What are the three main parts of a telephone?
   b. **Summarizing** How is sound transmitted and received during a telephone call?
   c. **Relating Cause and Effect** In telephones, what causes electric current to vary in the transmitter, producing an electronic signal?
2. a. **Naming** What are the two ways that sound can be reproduced?
   b. **Explaining** What is the purpose of the pits and flats on a CD?
   c. **Summarizing** How does a beam of light scan a CD to produce sound?
3. a. **Reviewing** How is information transmitted to radios and televisions?
   b. **Sequencing** What happens to an electronic signal when it reaches your television?

Lab zone **At-Home Activity**

What's a Remote? A remote control uses electromagnetic waves to operate an electronic device—for instance, a television, VCR, radio, or toy—from a distance. Find a device with a remote control. Ask your family members to help you locate the receiver for the remote control on the device. Find out how far away from the device you can stand and still operate it. Find out what objects the waves will travel through. Will they bounce off mirrors? Off walls? Off your hand?

Section 3 • Tech & Design •

Computers

Reading Preview

Key Concepts

- How is information stored and processed in a computer?
- What are the functions of computer hardware and software?
- What is the purpose of a computer network?

Key Terms

• computer • binary system
• hardware • central processing unit (CPU) • input device
• output device • software
• computer programmer
• computer network • Internet
• World Wide Web

Target Reading Skill

Outlining As you read, make an outline about computers. Use the red headings for main topics and the blue headings for subtopics.

Computers

I. What is a computer?
   A. The binary system
   B.
II. Computer hardware
   A.

Lab zone Discover Activity

How Fast Are You?

1. Write out ten math problems involving the addition or subtraction of two two-digit numbers.
2. Switch lists with a friend.
3. Take turns timing how long it takes each of you to solve the ten problems by hand.
4. Then time how long it takes each of you to solve the ten problems using a calculator. What is the time difference? Is there a difference in accuracy?

Think It Over

Inferring What are the advantages of using an electronic device to complete calculations?

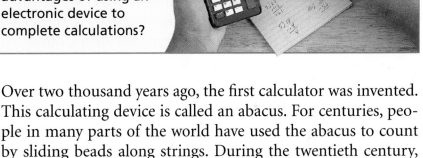

Over two thousand years ago, the first calculator was invented. This calculating device is called an abacus. For centuries, people in many parts of the world have used the abacus to count by sliding beads along strings. During the twentieth century, mechanical adding machines were developed. Then, in the 1960s, electronic calculators and computers began to be widely used. In just a few decades, these electronic devices changed the way people around the world perform calculations.

What Is a Computer?

A **computer** is an electronic device that stores, processes, and retrieves information. One of the reasons that computers can process and store so much information is that they do not store information in the same form that you see it—numbers, letters, and pictures. **Computer information is represented in the binary system.** The **binary system** uses combinations of just two digits, 0 and 1. Although computers can use analog signals, almost all modern computers are digital.

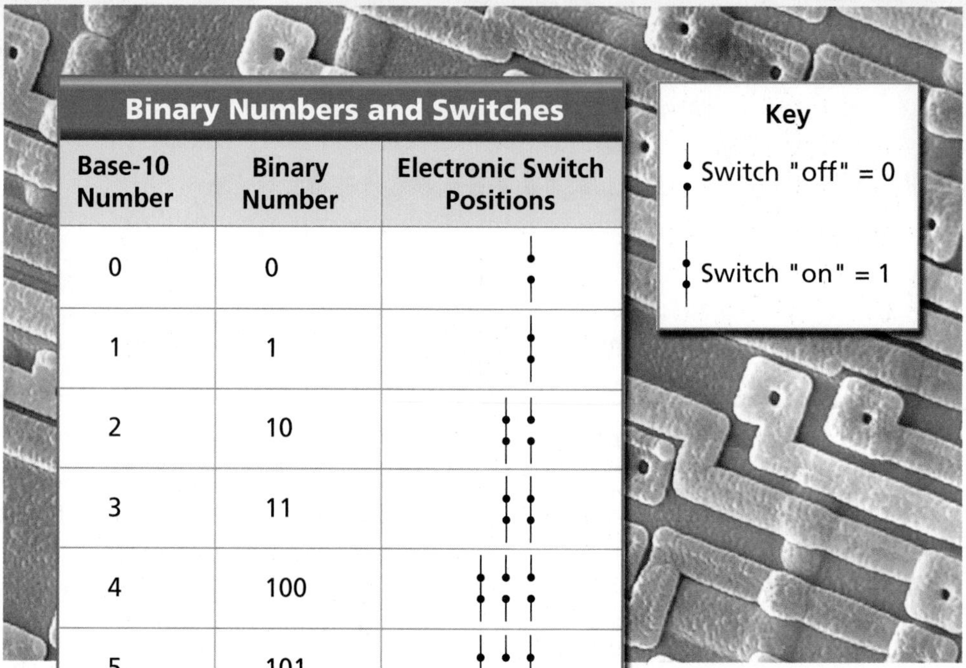

Figure 12
Binary Switches
To store information, a computer translates binary numbers into electronic switch positions. The background photo shows electronic switches in an enlarged view.
Interpreting Diagrams *What is the base-10 number 5 in the binary system?*

Binary Numbers and Switches

Base-10 Number	Binary Number	Electronic Switch Positions
0	0	
1	1	
2	10	
3	11	
4	100	
5	101	
10	1010	

Key
Switch "off" = 0
Switch "on" = 1

The Binary System How can large numbers be represented using only series of 1's and 0's? Begin by thinking about the numbers with which you are more familiar. You are used to using the base-10 number system. Each place value in a number represents the number 10 raised to some power. The digits 0 through 9 are then multiplied by the place value in each position. For example, the number 327 means 3 × 100 plus 2 × 10 plus 7 × 1.

Using the Binary System The binary system is similar to the base-10 number system, except that the base number is 2. A binary number's place value begins with 1, 2, 4, and 8 instead of 1, 10, 100, and 1,000. In the binary system, only 0 and 1 are multiplied by each place value.

Computers use the binary system because electronic signals can represent the 0's and 1's. Computer chips contain thousands of tiny circuits with transistors that act as switches. A switch in the off position represents a 0 and a switch in the on position represents a 1. Look at Figure 12 to see how switches can represent binary numbers.

Bits and Bytes Each 1 or 0 in the binary system is called a bit, short for binary digit. Arrangements of eight bits are called bytes. Computer memories are rated in kilobytes (one thousand bytes), megabytes (one million bytes), gigabytes (one billion bytes) or even terabytes (one trillion bytes).

Reading Checkpoint **What two digits are used in the binary system?**

Lab zone Skills Activity

Calculating

A set of encyclopedias contains 25 volumes with an average of 400 pages per book. Each page contains 1,200 words and the average word is 6 letters long. Suppose each letter requires 1 byte. Could the entire set fit on a single gigabyte chip?

Computer Hardware

The physical parts that allow a computer to receive, store, and present information make up the computer's **hardware.** Computer hardware refers to the permanent components of the computer. **Computer hardware includes a central processing unit, input devices, output devices, and memory storage devices.** You can identify the different devices in Figure 13.

Central Processing Unit The **central processing unit,** or CPU, serves as the brain of a computer. It directs the operation of the computer, performs logical operations and calculations, and directs the storage and retrieval of information.

Input and Output Devices Data are fed to the CPU by an **input device.** There are several different types of input devices. The one most familiar to you is probably the keyboard. A mouse, joystick, light pen, scanner, microphone, and touch-sensitive screen are also input devices.

Data from a computer are presented on an **output device.** A computer monitor is the most familiar output device. Other output devices are printers and speakers. Some devices, such as modems, may serve as both input and output devices. A modem allows a computer to exchange information with other computers.

Reading Checkpoint **What is a central processing unit?**

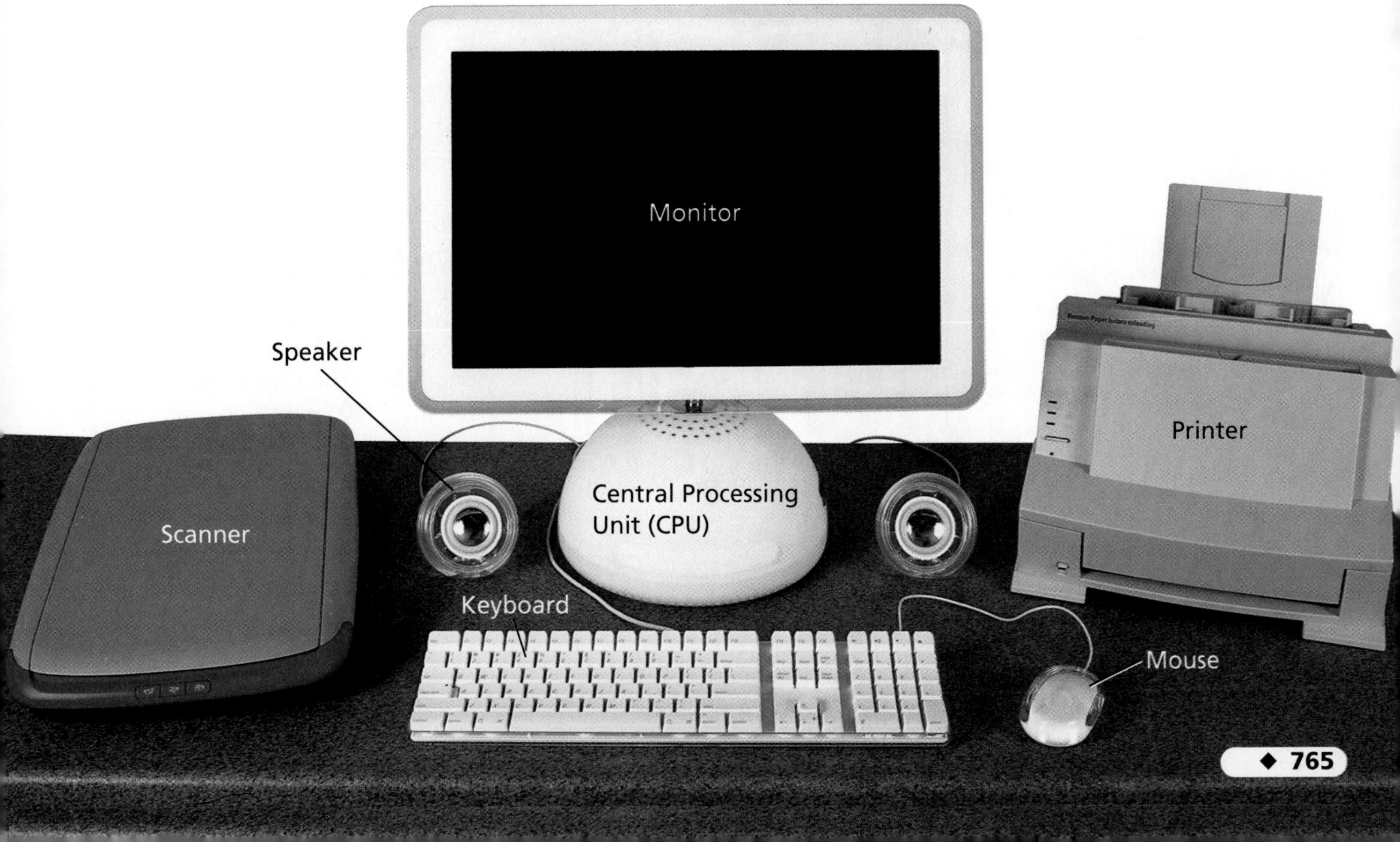

FIGURE 13
Computer Hardware
Here are a number of common computer components. The different devices that make up a computer are called hardware.

Go Online
SCI LINKS NSTA

For: Links on computers
Visit: www.SciLinks.org
Web Code: scn-1443

Memory Computers store information in their memory. The two types of computer memory are internal and external. The internal memory is in the CPU. Internal memory called Random Access Memory (RAM) is a temporary storage area for data while the computer is operating. Read Only Memory (ROM) is internal memory that contains information the computer needs to operate properly. The CPU can read these data but cannot change them. Information in ROM is permanently stored.

Neither RAM nor ROM allows you to save information when you turn your computer off. For that reason, devices outside the main CPU circuit are used to store information. They are called external memory. One form of external storage is the disk. Information is read from a disk or entered onto a disk by a disk drive. Information on a disk drive remains in the computer and can be accessed whenever you use the computer.

• Tech & Design in History •

Development of Computers

Although some modern computers can fit in the palm of your hand, this wasn't always the case. Computers have come a long way in a relatively short period of time.

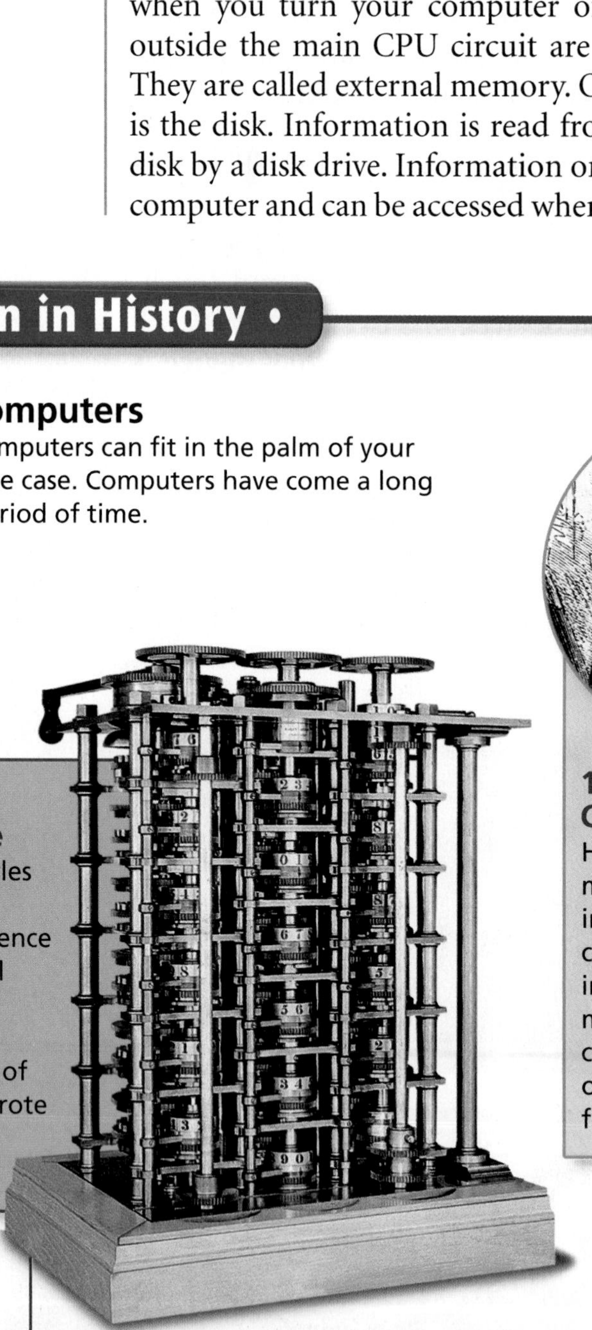

1823
The Difference Engine
British mathematician Charles Babbage designed the first computer, called the Difference Engine. It was a mechanical computing device that had more than 50,000 moving parts. For a later computer of Babbage's, Ada Lovelace wrote what is considered the first computer program.

1890
Census Counting Machine
Herman Hollerith constructed a machine that processed information by allowing electric current to pass through holes in punch cards. With Hollerith's machine, the United States census of 1890 was completed in one fourth the time needed for the 1880 census.

1800 1825 1850 1875

Computer Software

A computer needs **software,** or instructions, to tell it what to do. **Software is a set of instructions that directs the computer hardware to perform operations on stored information.** The software is also called a computer program. Whenever you use a word processor, or play a computer game, a computer program is instructing the computer to perform in a certain way.

Two Kinds of Software One kind of software is a computer's operating system. An operating system is a set of basic instructions that keep a computer running. Examples of operating systems include DOS and Unix.

A second type of software is usually called applications software. Applications are specific tasks that a computer may carry out, such as word processing, graphics, games, or simulations.

Writing in Science

Newspaper Article In 1953 there were only about 100 computers in the entire world. Today, there are hundreds of millions of computers in businesses, homes, government offices, schools, and stores. Select one of the early forms of the computer. Write a newspaper article introducing it and its applications to the public.

1946
ENIAC
The first American-built computer was developed by the United States Army. The Electronic Numerical Integrator and Calculator, or ENIAC, consisted of thousands of vacuum tubes and filled an entire warehouse. To change the program, programmers had to rewire the entire machine.

1974
Personal Computers
The first personal computer (PC) went on the market. Today's personal computer is 400 times faster than the ENIAC, 3,000 times lighter, and several million dollars cheaper.

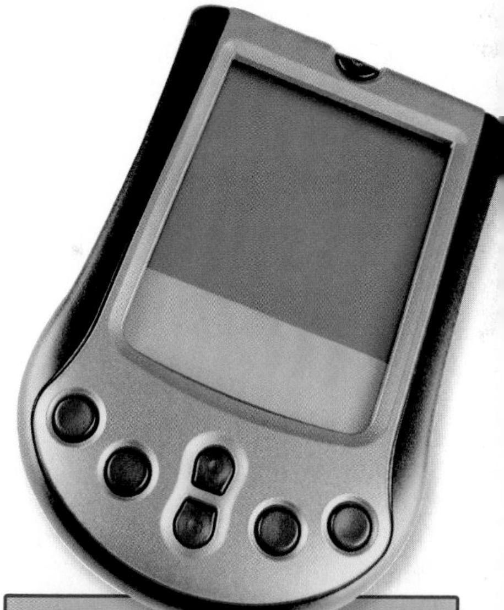

2000
Personal Data Assistant
Electronic devices have become smaller, and wireless communication has become more common. Hand-held computers can store personal data, send e-mails, and even share images.

1925 1950 1975 2000

Computer Programming Computer programmers are the people who program computers. **Computer programmers use computer languages that convert input information into instructions that the CPU can understand.** You may have heard the names of some computer languages, such as Basic, C++, and Java. Each language is designed for a specific purpose. For example, some languages allow users to complete complex calculations. But a program written in such a language may not be practical for word processing.

Programmers create software by using a step-by-step development process. First, they outline exactly what the program will do. Second, they develop a flowchart. A flowchart is a diagram showing the order of computer actions and data flow. Third, they write the instructions for the computer in a particular language. Complicated programs may contain millions of instructions. And finally, they test the program.

Reading Checkpoint **What is a computer language?**

Computer Networks

You have probably traveled on a network of roads and highways that connects cities and towns. A **computer network** is a group of computers connected by cables or telephone lines. **A computer network allows people in different locations to share information and software.**

There are two types of networks. A set of computers connected in one classroom or office building is known as a local area network (LAN). Computers connected across larger distances form a wide area network (WAN). In wide area networks, very powerful computers serve as a support connection for hundreds of less powerful computers.

FIGURE 14
A Global Network
The Internet links together millions of computers around the world.

The Internet The most significant wide area network is the Internet. The **Internet** is a global network that links millions of computers in businesses, schools, and research organizations. The Internet is a network of host computers that extends around the world. You might say that the Internet is a network of networks. The Internet, along with other smaller networks, sometimes is called the information superhighway.

The Internet began in 1969 as a military communications system. Colleges and universities were later added so that scientists could exchange data. Beginning in 1993, businesses were allowed to sell Internet connections to individuals. With easy access available, use of the Internet has grown at a rapid rate.

World Wide Web The World Wide Web (www) was developed in 1989. The **World Wide Web** is a system that allows you to display and view files, called pages, on the Internet. A Web page can include text, pictures, video, or sound. Prior to the development of the World Wide Web, Internet users could only view information in the form of words and numbers. Through the Web, users can look at images similar to those you might see on television or videos. Software programs called search engines allow people to search the Web for information.

Reading Checkpoint **What is the World Wide Web?**

Lab zone **Try This Activity**

What a Web You Weave

Many businesses and individuals have home pages on the World Wide Web. Such pages usually describe the characteristics of the business or person.

Communicating Design your own home page that describes your interests, hobbies, and achievements. A home page usually allows a user to click on certain words to find out more information about a particular topic. Be sure to include text, photographs, and art in your design.

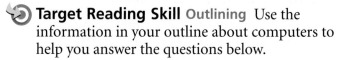

Section 3 Assessment

Target Reading Skill **Outlining** Use the information in your outline about computers to help you answer the questions below.

Reviewing Key Concepts

1. a. **Defining** What is a computer?
   b. **Explaining** How do computers store and process information?
   c. **Applying Concepts** How can electrical off and on switches be combined with numbers to store information?
2. a. **Reviewing** What is the function of computer hardware? Software?
   b. **Comparing and Contrasting** Describe the roles of input and output devices.
   c. **Sequencing** Place the following parts in the correct order for entering, correcting, saving, and then printing a message: CPU, output device, input device, memory storage.
3. a. **Reviewing** What is a computer network?
   b. **Describing** Give an example of a computer network.
   c. **Making Judgments** What are the advantages of computer networks?

Writing in Science

Software Advertisement Write an advertisement for a new software application. The application should be for word processing, graphics, or simulations. In your ad, give your software application's name, explain what the software does, and describe features that will appeal to customers.

Lab zone **Skills Lab**

Computer Programming

Problem

Can you create a model of a computer program?

Skills

observing, forming operational definitions, making models

Materials

- 2 identical sets of 10 interlocking bricks per student
- newspaper
- pencil and paper

Procedure

1. Obtain 2 sets of bricks, a piece of newspaper, and a pencil and paper. Ask your lab partner to do the same.
2. You and your partner should do Steps 3–6 without communicating with each other.
3. Place one brick on a table. On a piece of paper, write the number "1." Next to the number write instructions that someone can follow to place the brick exactly as you did. What you wrote is called a line of instruction. See the example above.

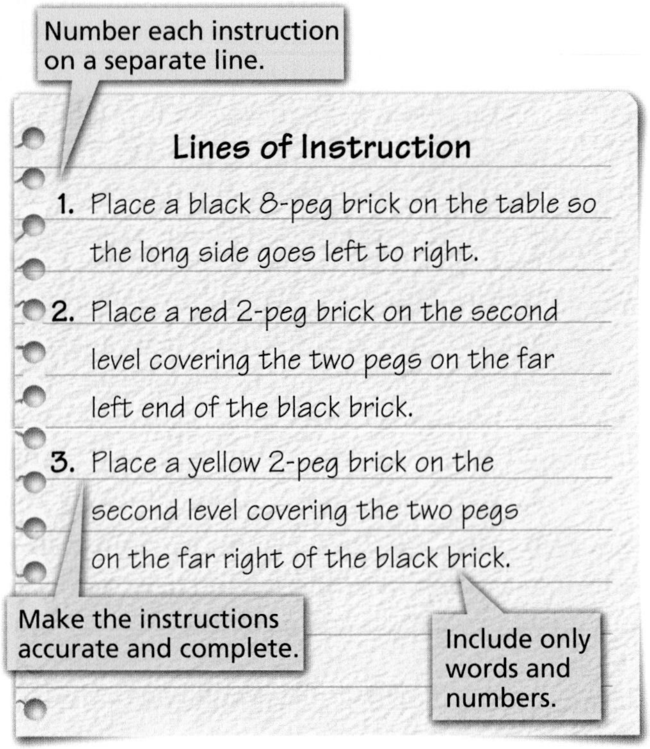

Number each instruction on a separate line.
Lines of Instruction
1. Place a black 8-peg brick on the table so the long side goes left to right.
2. Place a red 2-peg brick on the second level covering the two pegs on the far left end of the black brick.
3. Place a yellow 2-peg brick on the second level covering the two pegs on the far right of the black brick.
Make the instructions accurate and complete.
Include only words and numbers.

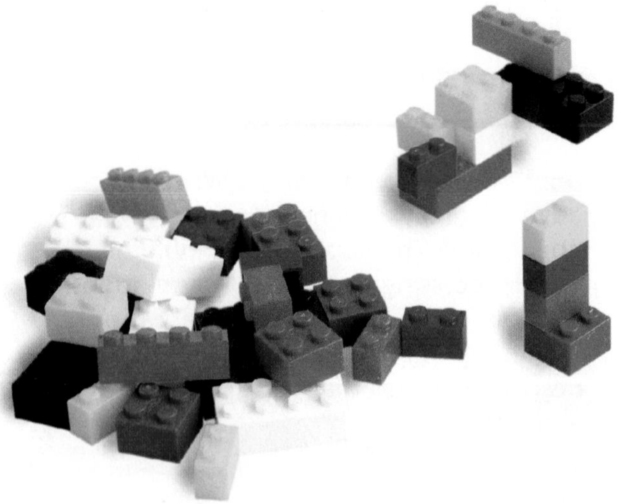

4. Select another brick from the same set and attach it to the previous brick. Write a number "2" on your paper and another line of instruction next to the number.
5. Repeat Step 4 eight more times, using the numbers 3 through 10 in front of your instruction lines. You should have one line of instruction for each brick you placed.
6. Cover your structure with the newspaper. Then, trade your second set of bricks and your instruction sheet with your lab partner.
7. Using your partner's instructions and brick set, build the same structure your partner built. Your partner should do the same using your instructions and brick set.
8. When you both are finished, uncover your partner's structure. Compare the structure with the one you built using your partner's instructions. Note any places where your structure is not identical to your partner's.

9. Together, review Line 1 of your partner's instructions. Determine whether the brick was placed exactly as in the original structure. Identify any problems in the line of instruction. (*Hint:* A line of instruction is a problem if it resulted in a brick being placed incorrectly, or if there is more than one way to carry out the instruction.)
10. If the line of instruction has a problem, work with your partner to rewrite it.
11. Review all the remaining lines of instruction one at a time, following the procedures in Steps 9 and 10.
12. Now review the structure you built using your partner's instructions. Repeat the procedures in Steps 8 –11.
13. When you are finished, discuss what you learned about writing lines of instruction.
14. Take apart your brick structures and place the bricks in their containers. Be careful not to mix up your set of bricks with your partner's set.

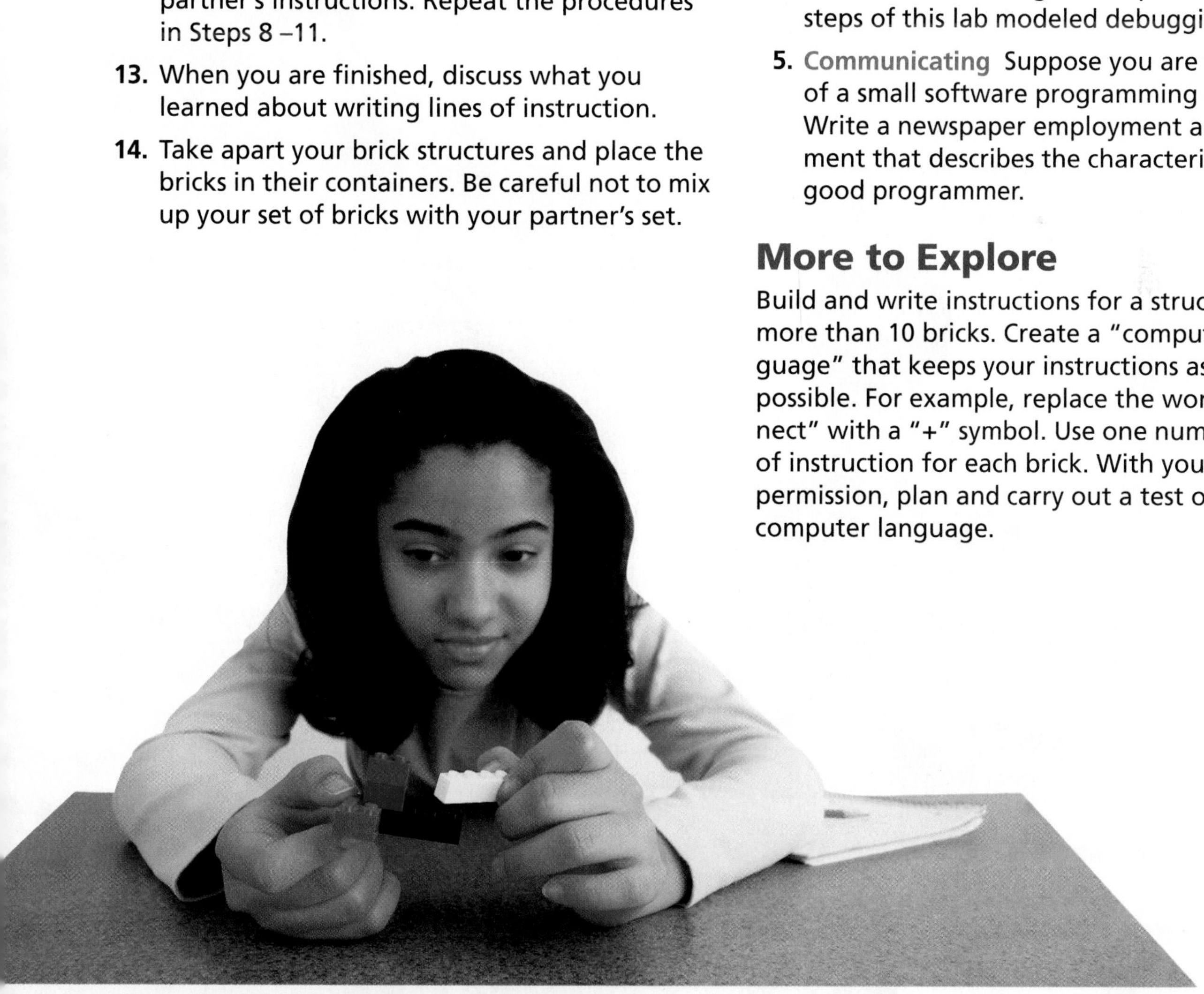

Analyze and Conclude

1. **Observing** Did you have to rewrite any of your instructions in Step 10? If so, explain why.
2. **Forming Operational Definitions** Write an operational definition of a well-written computer program.
3. **Making Models** During which steps of the lab were you modeling the actions of a computer programmer? In which steps were you modeling the actions of a computer?
4. **Making Models** "Debugging" means examining a computer program to identify instructions that might be a problem. Which steps of this lab modeled debugging?
5. **Communicating** Suppose you are the owner of a small software programming company. Write a newspaper employment advertisement that describes the characteristics of a good programmer.

More to Explore

Build and write instructions for a structure using more than 10 bricks. Create a "computer language" that keeps your instructions as short as possible. For example, replace the word "connect" with a "+" symbol. Use one numbered line of instruction for each brick. With you teacher's permission, plan and carry out a test of your computer language.

Science and **Society**

When Seeing ISN'T Believing

Combining photography and computers can produce visual magic. A computer can turn a photo's objects and colors into a code. Then, using a computer to change the codes, a person can change a photo in amazing ways. Changing photos with computers is called digital manipulation.

The Issues

Advantages of Photo Manipulation

Computers allow people to greatly improve a photograph. Images of objects or people can be added, removed, or moved around. Fuzzy pictures can become sharper. Colors can be brightened. Unclear or tiny details can be made easy to see. Old or damaged photos can be made to look like new.

▲ Original image

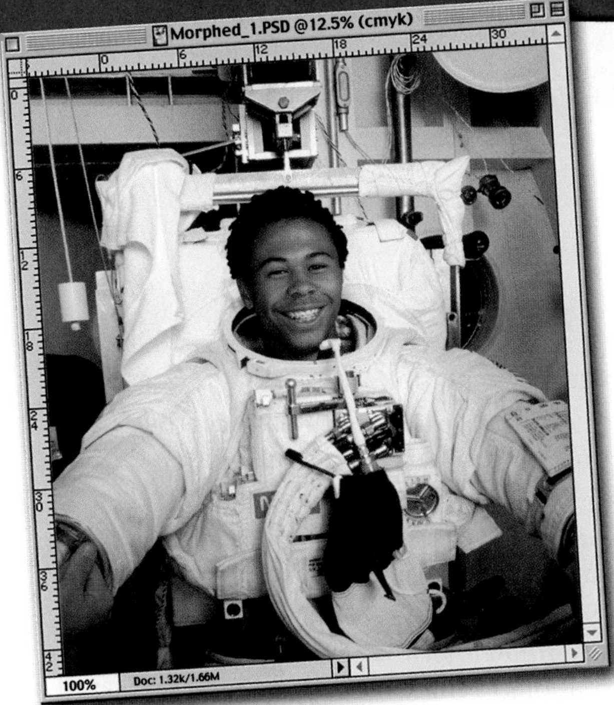

▲ Photos can be combined using digital manipulation.

▲ Digital manipulation can change your image in realistic ways.

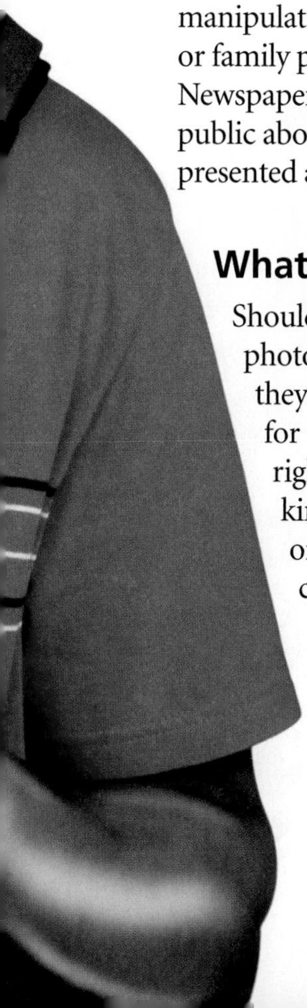

Disadvantages of Photo Manipulation

It's nearly impossible to tell the difference between a changed and unchanged photo. Some people worry that digital manipulation could be used to harm or cheat people. Personal or family photos could be changed to a person's disadvantage. Newspapers, magazines, and TV stations could mislead the public about individuals and stories. Faked photos might be presented as evidence in court cases.

What Safeguards Are Needed?

Should governments pass laws against changing photographs? Such laws would be hard to enforce, and they might make it difficult to use digital manipulation for useful purposes. Such laws might also violate the right of free speech, since the courts consider photos a kind of speech, or expression. Should photographers or organizations police themselves? They could write codes of conduct. For example, it could be considered acceptable to make photos clearer digitally, but not to add, take away, or move around parts of a photo. Some photographers who work for newspapers have suggested such a code. Another safeguard might be to put a symbol on any digitally manipulated photo.

You Decide

1. **Identify the Problem**
   Summarize the problems created by digital manipulation of photos.
2. **Analyze the Options**
   Research this topic further at the library or on the Internet. List additional arguments for and against manipulating photos, and explain possible remedies.
3. **Find a Solution**
   You run a TV station. Your assistants want to use two digitally changed photos, one in a commercial and one in a news story about an individual. Will you let them use one, or both, or neither? Explain.

Go Online
PHSchool.com

For: More on photo manipulation
Visit: PHSchool.com
Web Code: cgh-4040

Chapter 22 Study Guide

1 Electronic Signals and Semiconductors

Key Concepts

- There are two basic kinds of electronic signals: analog signals and digital signals.
- The two types of semiconductors can be combined in different ways to make diodes, transistors, and integrated circuits.

Key Terms

electronics
electronic signal
analog signal
digital signal
semiconductor
diode
transistor
integrated circuit

2 Electronic Communication

Key Concepts

- In a telephone, sound is changed into an electronic signal that is transmitted and then transformed back into sound.
- Sound can be reproduced using an analog device such as a phonograph or a digital device such as a CD player.
- Voices and music on an AM or FM radio station are electronic signals carried by an electromagnetic wave.
- Electromagnetic waves can be used to carry images as well as sound.

Key Terms

transmitter
receiver

3 Computers

Key Concepts

- Computer information is represented in the binary system.
- Computer hardware includes a central processing unit, input devices, output devices, and memory storage devices.
- Software is a set of instructions that directs the computer hardware to perform operations on stored information.
- A computer network allows people in different locations to share information and software.

Key Terms

computer
binary system
hardware
central processing unit (CPU)
input device
output device
software
computer programmer
computer network
Internet
World Wide Web

Review and Assessment

Go Online
PHSchool.com
For: Self-Assessment
Visit: PHSchool.com
Web Code: cka-4220

Organizing Information

Flowcharts Copy the flowchart about telephone communication onto a separate sheet of paper. Then complete it and add a title. (For more on flowcharts, see the Skills Handbook.)

Vocal cords vibrate
↓
a. ______?______
↓
Electronic signal sent to a receiver
↓
b. ______?______
↓
Ear hears sound waves

Reviewing Key Terms

Choose the letter of the best answer.

1. The use of electric current to control, communicate, and process information is called
a. frequency modulation.
b. amplitude modulation.
c. electrical communication.
d. electronics.

2. Current is varied smoothly to represent information in
a. an analog signal.
b. a digital signal.
c. frequency modulation.
d. amplitude modulation.

3. A sandwich of three layers of semiconductor that is used to amplify an electric signal is known as a(n)
a. diode.
b. analog signal.
c. transistor.
d. integrated circuit.

4. An example of an output device is a
a. transistor.
b. printer.
c. keyboard.
d. scanner.

5. A group of computers connected by cables or telephone lines is a
a. microprocessor.
b. CPU.
c. modem.
d. network.

If the statement is true, write *true*. If it is false, change the underlined word or words to make the statement true.

6. In analog signals, pulses of current are used to represent information.

7. A transistor changes alternating current into direct current.

8. Computer information is represented in the base-10 system.

9. Input devices feed data into a computer.

10. Computer programs are also called hardware.

Writing in Science

Sequence of Events Imagine that you are a director in charge of televising a live music concert. Describe the sequence of events through which the images will be transmitted from a camera on stage to the television screens in people's homes.

Discovery Channel School

Electronics
Video Preview
Video Field Trip
▶ Video Assessment

Review and Assessment

Checking Concepts

11. Compare an analog signal with a digital signal.

12. Define each of the following in your own words: diode, transistor, and integrated circuit.

13. Draw an illustration of an electromagnetic wave. Explain how an electromagnetic wave is generated.

14. How is a radio show broadcast and received?

15. How is the World Wide Web different from the Internet?

Thinking Critically

16. Relating Cause and Effect What are some advantages of semiconductors and the electronic components made from semiconductors?

17. Calculating The television pictures people enjoy are composed of images shown very quickly. Each image on a traditional television screen lasts for $\frac{1}{30}$ of a second. How many images appear on the screen during a 30-minute program?

18. Applying Concepts A computer program is a list of instructions that tells a computer exactly how to perform a task. Write a program that describes the steps involved in some small task, such as walking your dog, taking out the trash, setting the table, or playing a game. Reread and revise your description so that a person could use it to correctly perform the task.

19. Comparing and Contrasting How is an electromagnetic wave changed to produce AM and FM waves?

20. Classifying What type of semiconductor device is shown in the diagram below? How can you tell?

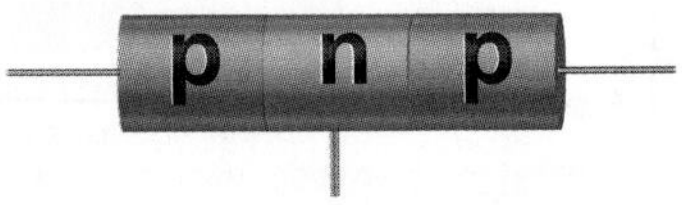

Applying Skills

Use the illustrations below to answer Questions 21–24.

Examine the waves diagrammed below. The diagrams may not all show a variation of the same wave.

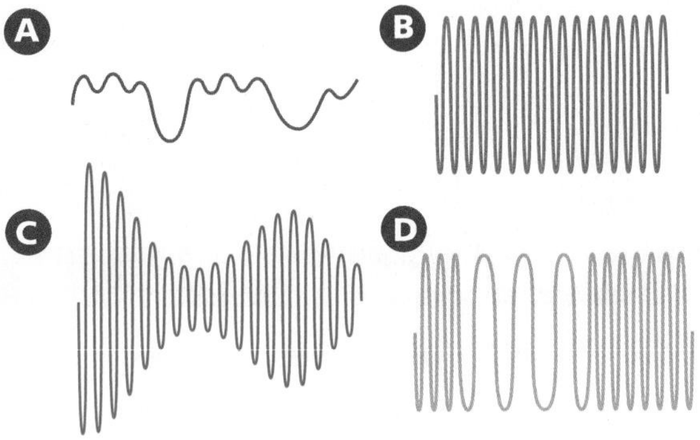

21. Predicting Diagram A represents an audio signal. What would that signal look like if it were converted to an AM radio signal? Draw a sketch to illustrate your answer.

22. Interpreting Diagrams Which of these waves might be a carrier wave? Describe the role of a carrier wave in electronic communication.

23. Classifying Two radio transmitters send out electronic signals shown as diagram C and diagram D. Which represents an AM wave? Which represents an FM wave? How can you tell?

24. Comparing and Contrasting Could the wave in diagram C be a modulated version of the wave in diagram A? Explain how you know.

Lab zone Chapter **Project**

Performance Assessment Present both the existing computer application and the new one you invented to the class. Provide diagrams of each and describe their operation. You might want to pretend to sell your new invention to the class. Prepare a poster describing the task that your new application will accomplish. Show yourself enjoying the benefits!

Standardized Test Prep

Test-Taking Tip

Sequencing Events

Some test questions require you to arrange a series of events in order. You might be asked to arrange events in order, or to identify which event in a series happens first or last. Or a question might ask you which event comes before or after another event. Before looking at the answer choices, first try to recall the correct sequence in which the events occur.

Sample Question

When you speak into a telephone transmitter, which of the following events happens first?

A An electronic signal travels through a series of wires.
B A vibrating disk creates sound waves.
C Sound vibrations are changed into electronic signals.
D Electronic signals are changed into vibrations.

Answer

The correct answer is **C.** The events described in **A, B,** and **D** all happen after sound vibrations are converted into electronic signals.

Choose the letter of the best answer.

1. Each of the events listed below happens in the process of producing an image and sound in a television set. Which event happens last?
A A communication satellite receives electromagnetic signals.
B Electronic signals are converted into sound and light.
C Electromagnetic signals are sent out from an antenna.
D Light and sound are converted into electronic signals.

2. In the binary number system, the number 8 would be written as
F 2.
G 8.
H 100.
J 1000.

Use the graphs and your knowledge of science to answer Question 3.

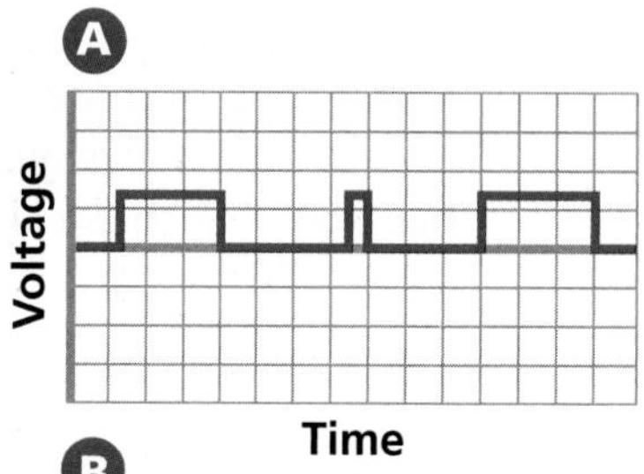

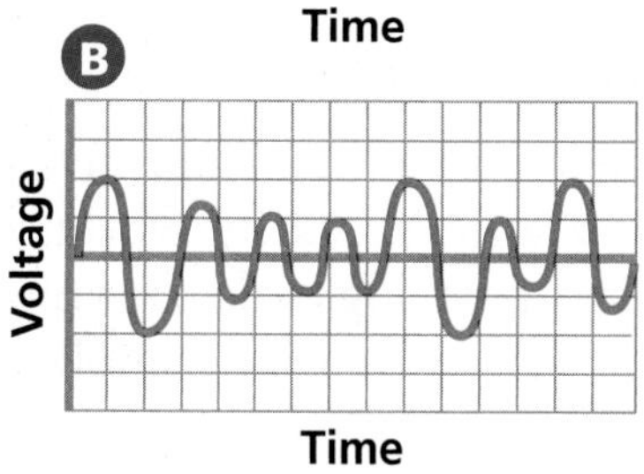

3. Which of the following statements about graphs A and B is correct?
A Graph A shows an analog signal and graph B shows a digital signal.
B Graph A shows a digital signal and graph B shows an analog signal.
C Both graphs show analog signals.
D Neither graph shows an analog signal.

4. A device that can change an alternating current to a direct current is a
F transistor.
G central processing unit.
H diode.
J integrated circuit.

5. Which of the following items is an input device in a computer?
A computer monitor
B printer
C mouse
D central processing unit

Constructed Response

6. Explain what an integrated circuit is. Also explain how integrated circuits are useful devices.

Think Like a Scientist

Scientists have a particular way of looking at the world, or scientific habits of mind. Whenever you ask a question and explore possible answers, you use many of the same skills that scientists do. Some of these skills are described on this page.

Observing

When you use one or more of your five senses to gather information about the world, you are **observing.** Hearing a dog bark, counting twelve green seeds, and smelling smoke are all observations. To increase the power of their senses, scientists sometimes use microscopes, telescopes, or other instruments that help them make more detailed observations.

An observation must be an accurate report of what your senses detect. It is important to keep careful records of your observations in science class by writing or drawing in a notebook. The information collected through observations is called evidence, or data.

Inferring

When you interpret an observation, you are **inferring,** or making an inference. For example, if you hear your dog barking, you may infer that someone is at your front door. To make this inference, you combine the evidence—the barking dog—and your experience or knowledge—you know that your dog barks when strangers approach—to reach a logical conclusion.

Notice that an inference is not a fact; it is only one of many possible interpretations for an observation. For example, your dog may be barking because it wants to go for a walk. An inference may turn out to be incorrect even if it is based on accurate observations and logical reasoning. The only way to find out if an inference is correct is to investigate further.

Predicting

When you listen to the weather forecast, you hear many predictions about the next day's weather—what the temperature will be, whether it will rain, and how windy it will be. Weather forecasters use observations and knowledge of weather patterns to predict the weather. The skill of **predicting** involves making an inference about a future event based on current evidence or past experience.

Because a prediction is an inference, it may prove to be false. In science class, you can test some of your predictions by doing experiments. For example, suppose you predict that larger paper airplanes can fly farther than smaller airplanes. How could you test your prediction?

Activity

Use the photograph to answer the questions below.

Observing Look closely at the photograph. List at least three observations.

Inferring Use your observations to make an inference about what has happened. What experience or knowledge did you use to make the inference?

Predicting Predict what will happen next. On what evidence or experience do you base your prediction?

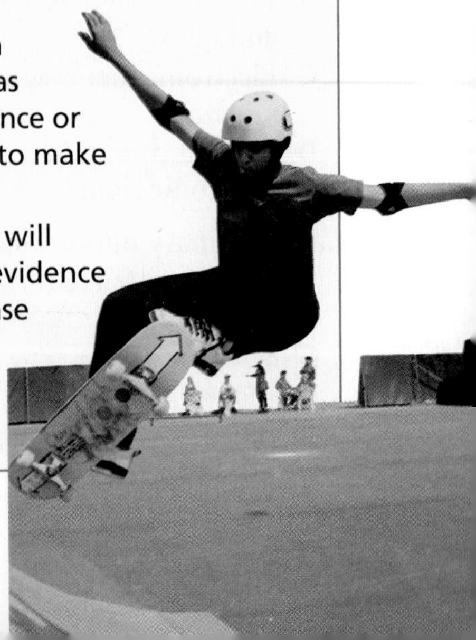

Classifying

Could you imagine searching for a book in the library if the books were shelved in no particular order? Your trip to the library would be an all-day event! Luckily, librarians group together books on similar topics or by the same author. Grouping together items that are alike in some way is called **classifying.** You can classify items in many ways: by size, by shape, by use, and by other important characteristics.

Like librarians, scientists use the skill of classifying to organize information and objects. When things are sorted into groups, the relationships among them become easier to understand.

Activity

Classify the objects in the photograph into two groups based on any characteristic you choose. Then use another characteristic to classify the objects into three groups.

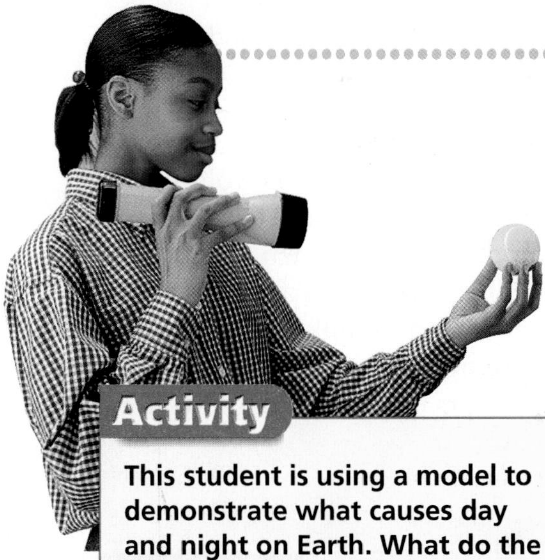

Making Models

Have you ever drawn a picture to help someone understand what you were saying? Such a drawing is one type of model. A model is a picture, diagram, computer image, or other representation of a complex object or process. **Making models** helps people understand things that they cannot observe directly.

Scientists often use models to represent things that are either very large or very small, such as the planets in the solar system, or the parts of a cell. Such models are physical models—drawings or three-dimensional structures that look like the real thing. Other models are mental models—mathematical equations or words that describe how something works.

Activity

This student is using a model to demonstrate what causes day and night on Earth. What do the flashlight and the tennis ball in the model represent?

Communicating

Whenever you talk on the phone, write a report, or listen to your teacher at school, you are communicating. **Communicating** is the process of sharing ideas and information with other people. Communicating effectively requires many skills, including writing, reading, speaking, listening, and making models.

Scientists communicate to share results, information, and opinions. Scientists often communicate about their work in journals, over the telephone, in letters, and on the Internet. They also attend scientific meetings where they share their ideas with one another in person.

Activity

On a sheet of paper, write out clear, detailed directions for tying your shoe. Then exchange directions with a partner. Follow your partner's directions exactly. How successful were you at tying your shoe? How could your partner have communicated more clearly?

Making Measurements

By measuring, scientists can express their observations more precisely and communicate more information about what they observe.

Measuring in SI

The standard system of measurement used by scientists around the world is known as the International System of Units, which is abbreviated as SI (**Système International d'Unités,** in French). SI units are easy to use because they are based on multiples of 10. Each unit is ten times larger than the next smallest unit and one tenth the size of the next largest unit. The table lists the prefixes used to name the most common SI units.

Common SI Prefixes		
Prefix	**Symbol**	**Meaning**
kilo-	k	1,000
hecto-	h	100
deka-	da	10
deci-	d	0.1 (one tenth)
centi-	c	0.01 (one hundredth)
milli-	m	0.001 (one thousandth)

Length To measure length, or the distance between two points, the unit of measure is the **meter (m).** The distance from the floor to a doorknob is approximately one meter. Long distances, such as the distance between two cities, are measured in kilometers (km). Small lengths are measured in centimeters (cm) or millimeters (mm). Scientists use metric rulers and meter sticks to measure length.

Common Conversions		
1 km	=	1,000 m
1 m	=	100 cm
1 m	=	1,000 mm
1 cm	=	10 mm

Activity

The larger lines on the metric ruler in the picture show centimeter divisions, while the smaller, unnumbered lines show millimeter divisions. How many centimeters long is the shell? How many millimeters long is it?

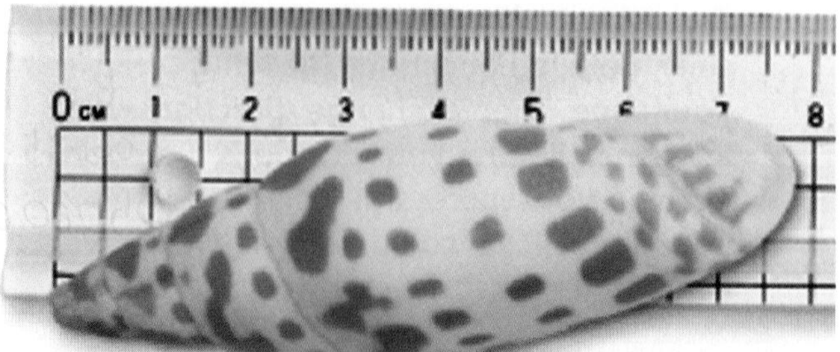

Liquid Volume To measure the volume of a liquid, or the amount of space it takes up, you will use a unit of measure known as the **liter (L).** One liter is the approximate volume of a medium-size carton of milk. Smaller volumes are measured in milliliters (mL). Scientists use graduated cylinders to measure liquid volume.

Activity

The graduated cylinder in the picture is marked in milliliter divisions. Notice that the water in the cylinder has a curved surface. This curved surface is called the *meniscus*. To measure the volume, you must read the level at the lowest point of the meniscus. What is the volume of water in this graduated cylinder?

Common Conversion		
1 L	=	1,000 mL

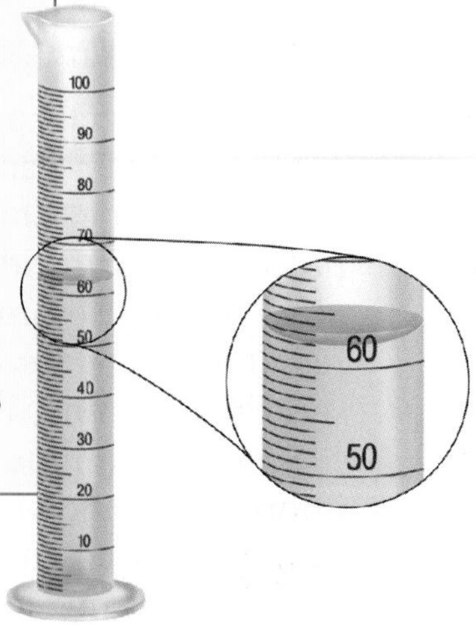

Mass To measure mass, or the amount of matter in an object, you will use a unit of measure known as the **gram (g).** One gram is approximately the mass of a paper clip. Larger masses are measured in kilograms (kg). Scientists use a balance to find the mass of an object.

Common Conversion
1 kg = 1,000 g

Activity

The mass of the potato in the picture is measured in kilograms. What is the mass of the potato? Suppose a recipe for potato salad called for one kilogram of potatoes. About how many potatoes would you need?

Temperature To measure the temperature of a substance, you will use the **Celsius scale.** Temperature is measured in degrees Celsius (°C) using a Celsius thermometer. Water freezes at 0°C and boils at 100°C.

Time The unit scientists use to measure time is the **second (s).**

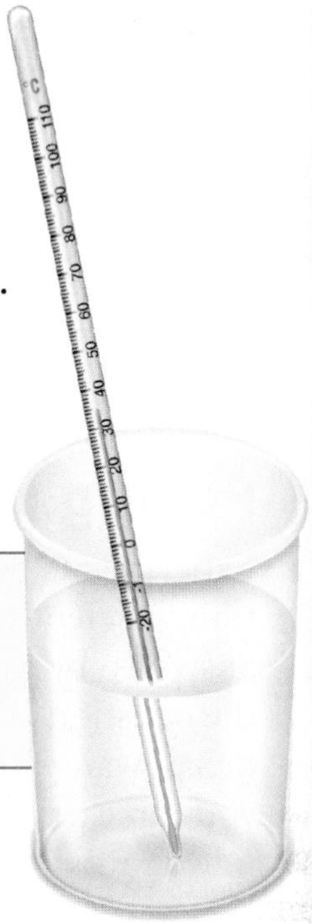

Activity

What is the temperature of the liquid in degrees Celsius?

Converting SI Units

To use the SI system, you must know how to convert between units. Converting from one unit to another involves the skill of **calculating,** or using mathematical operations. Converting between SI units is similar to converting between dollars and dimes because both systems are based on multiples of ten.

Suppose you want to convert a length of 80 centimeters to meters. Follow these steps to convert between units.

1. Begin by writing down the measurement you want to convert—in this example, 80 centimeters.
2. Write a conversion factor that represents the relationship between the two units you are converting. In this example, the relationship is 1 meter = 100 centimeters. Write this conversion factor as a fraction, making sure to place the units you are converting from (centimeters, in this example) in the denominator.
3. Multiply the measurement you want to convert by the fraction. When you do this, the units in the first measurement will cancel out with the units in the denominator. Your answer will be in the units you are converting to (meters, in this example).

Example

80 centimeters = ■ meters

$$80 \text{ centimeters} \times \frac{1 \text{ meter}}{100 \text{ centimeters}} = \frac{80 \text{ meters}}{100}$$

$$= 0.8 \text{ meters}$$

Activity

Convert between the following units.

1. 600 millimeters = ■ meters .6

2. 0.35 liters = ■ milliliters .00035

3. 1,050 grams = ■ kilograms 1,050,000

Conducting a Scientific Investigation

In some ways, scientists are like detectives, piecing together clues to learn about a process or event. One way that scientists gather clues is by carrying out experiments. An experiment tests an idea in a careful, orderly manner. Although experiments do not all follow the same steps in the same order, many follow a pattern similar to the one described here.

Posing Questions

Experiments begin by asking a scientific question. A scientific question is one that can be answered by gathering evidence. For example, the question "Which freezes faster—fresh water or salt water?" is a scientific question because you can carry out an investigation and gather information to answer the question.

Developing a Hypothesis

The next step is to form a hypothesis. A **hypothesis** is a possible explanation for a set of observations or answer to a scientific question. In science, a hypothesis must be something that can be tested. A hypothesis can be worded as an *If . . . then . . .* statement. For example, a hypothesis might be "*If I add salt to fresh water, then the water will take longer to freeze.*" A hypothesis worded this way serves as a rough outline of the experiment you should perform.

Designing an Experiment

Next you need to plan a way to test your hypothesis. Your plan should be written out as a step-by-step procedure and should describe the observations or measurements you will make.

Two important steps involved in designing an experiment are controlling variables and forming operational definitions.

Controlling Variables In a well-designed experiment, you need to keep all variables the same except for one. A **variable** is any factor that can change in an experiment. The factor that you change is called the **manipulated variable.** In this experiment, the manipulated variable is the amount of salt added to the water. Other factors, such as the amount of water or the starting temperature, are kept constant.

The factor that changes as a result of the manipulated variable is called the **responding variable.** The responding variable is what you measure or observe to obtain your results. In this experiment, the responding variable is how long the water takes to freeze.

An experiment in which all factors except one are kept constant is called a **controlled experiment.** Most controlled experiments include a test called the control. In this experiment, Container 3 is the control. Because no salt is added to Container 3, you can compare the results from the other containers to it. Any difference in results must be due to the addition of salt alone.

Forming Operational Definitions Another important aspect of a well-designed experiment is having clear operational definitions. An **operational definition** is a statement that describes how a particular variable is to be measured or how a term is to be defined. For example, in this experiment, how will you determine if the water has frozen? You might decide to insert a stick in each container at the start of the experiment. Your operational definition of "frozen" would be the time at which the stick can no longer move.

Experimental Procedure	
1.	Fill 3 containers with 300 milliliters of cold tap water.
2.	Add 10 grams of salt to Container 1; stir. Add 20 grams of salt to Container 2; stir. Add no salt to Container 3.
3.	Place the 3 containers in a freezer.
4.	Check the containers every 15 minutes. Record your observations.

Interpreting Data

The observations and measurements you make in an experiment are called **data.** At the end of an experiment, you need to analyze the data to look for any patterns or trends. Patterns often become clear if you organize your data in a data table or graph. Then think through what the data reveal. Do they support your hypothesis? Do they point out a flaw in your experiment? Do you need to collect more data?

Drawing Conclusions

A **conclusion** is a statement that sums up what you have learned from an experiment. When you draw a conclusion, you need to decide whether the data you collected support your hypothesis or not. You may need to repeat an experiment several times before you can draw any conclusions from it. Conclusions often lead you to pose new questions and plan new experiments to answer them.

Activity

Is a ball's bounce affected by the height from which it is dropped? Using the steps just described, plan a controlled experiment to investigate this problem.

Technology Design Skills

Engineers are people who use scientific and technological knowledge to solve practical problems. To design new products, engineers usually follow the process described here, even though they may not follow these steps in the exact order. As you read the steps, think about how you might apply them in technology labs.

Identify a Need

Before engineers begin designing a new product, they must first identify the need they are trying to meet. For example, suppose you are a member of a design team in a company that makes toys. Your team has identified a need: a toy boat that is inexpensive and easy to assemble.

Research the Problem

Engineers often begin by gathering information that will help them with their new design. This research may include finding articles in books, magazines, or on the Internet. It may also include talking to other engineers who have solved similar problems. Engineers often perform experiments related to the product they want to design.

For your toy boat, you could look at toys that are similar to the one you want to design. You might do research on the Internet. You could also test some materials to see whether they will work well in a toy boat.

Drawing for a boat design ▼

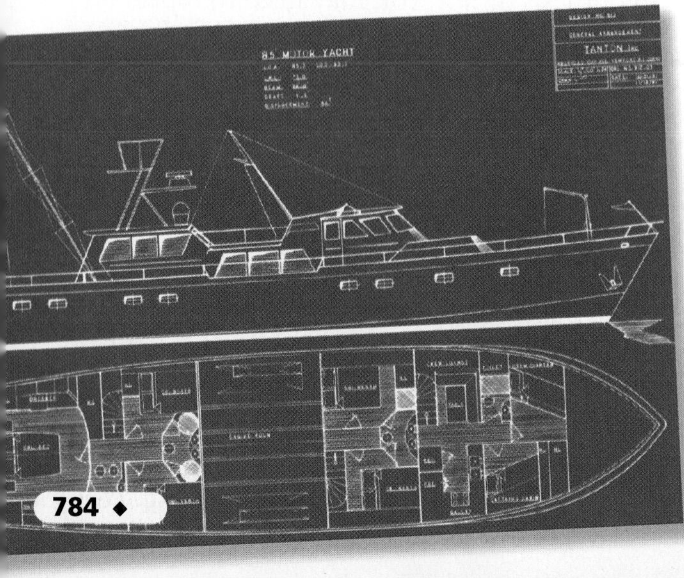

Design a Solution

Research gives engineers information that helps them design a product. When engineers design new products, they usually work in teams.

Generating Ideas Often design teams hold brainstorming meetings in which any team member can contribute ideas. **Brainstorming** is a creative process in which one team member's suggestions often spark ideas in other group members. Brainstorming can lead to new approaches to solving a design problem.

Evaluating Constraints During brainstorming, a design team will often come up with several possible designs. The team must then evaluate each one.

As part of their evaluation, engineers consider constraints. **Constraints** are factors that limit or restrict a product design. Physical characteristics, such as the properties of materials used to make your toy boat, are constraints. Money and time are also constraints. If the materials in a product cost a lot, or if the product takes a long time to make, the design may be impractical.

Making Trade-offs Design teams usually need to make trade-offs. In a **trade-off,** engineers give up one benefit of a proposed design in order to obtain another. In designing your toy boat, you will have to make trade-offs. For example, suppose one material is sturdy but not fully waterproof. Another material is more waterproof, but breakable. You may decide to give up the benefit of sturdiness in order to obtain the benefit of waterproofing.

Build and Evaluate a Prototype

Once the team has chosen a design plan, the engineers build a prototype of the product. A **prototype** is a working model used to test a design. Engineers evaluate the prototype to see whether it works well, is easy to operate, is safe to use, and holds up to repeated use.

Think of your toy boat. What would the prototype be like? Of what materials would it be made? How would you test it?

Troubleshoot and Redesign

Few prototypes work perfectly, which is why they need to be tested. Once a design team has tested a prototype, the members analyze the results and identify any problems. The team then tries to **troubleshoot,** or fix the design problems. For example, if your toy boat leaks or wobbles, the boat should be redesigned to eliminate those problems.

Communicate the Solution

A team needs to communicate the final design to the people who will manufacture and use the product. To do this, teams may use sketches, detailed drawings, computer simulations, and word descriptions.

Activity

You can use the technology design process to design and build a toy boat.

Research and Investigate

1. Visit the library or go online to research toy boats.
2. Investigate how a toy boat can be powered, including wind, rubber bands, or baking soda and vinegar.
3. Brainstorm materials, shapes, and steering for your boat.

Design and Build

4. Based on your research, design a toy boat that
   - is made of readily available materials
   - is no larger than 15 cm long and 10 cm wide
   - includes a power system, a rudder, and an area for cargo
   - travels 2 meters in a straight line carrying a load of 20 pennies
5. Sketch your design and write a step-by-step plan for building your boat. After your teacher approves your plan, build your boat.

Evaluate and Redesign

6. Test your boat, evaluate the results, and troubleshoot any problems.
7. Based on your evaluation, redesign your toy boat so it performs better.

Creating Data Tables and Graphs

How can you make sense of the data in a science experiment? The first step is to organize the data to help you understand them. Data tables and graphs are helpful tools for organizing data.

Data Tables

You have gathered your materials and set up your experiment. But before you start, you need to plan a way to record what happens during the experiment. By creating a data table, you can record your observations and measurements in an orderly way.

Suppose, for example, that a scientist conducted an experiment to find out how many Calories people of different body masses burn while doing various activities. The data table shows the results.

Notice in this data table that the manipulated variable (body mass) is the heading of one column. The responding variable (for Experiment 1, the number of Calories burned while bicycling) is the heading of the next column. Additional columns were added for related experiments.

Calories Burned in 30 Minutes

Body Mass	Experiment 1: Bicycling	Experiment 2: Playing Basketball	Experiment 3: Watching Television
30 kg	60 Calories	120 Calories	21 Calories
40 kg	77 Calories	164 Calories	27 Calories
50 kg	95 Calories	206 Calories	33 Calories
60 kg	114 Calories	248 Calories	38 Calories

Bar Graphs

To compare how many Calories a person burns doing various activities, you could create a bar graph. A bar graph is used to display data in a number of separate, or distinct, categories. In this example, bicycling, playing basketball, and watching television are the three categories.

To create a bar graph, follow these steps.

1. On graph paper, draw a horizontal, or x-, axis and a vertical, or y-, axis.
2. Write the names of the categories to be graphed along the horizontal axis. Include an overall label for the axis as well.
3. Label the vertical axis with the name of the responding variable. Include units of measurement. Then create a scale along the axis by marking off equally spaced numbers that cover the range of the data collected.
4. For each category, draw a solid bar using the scale on the vertical axis to determine the height. Make all the bars the same width.
5. Add a title that describes the graph.

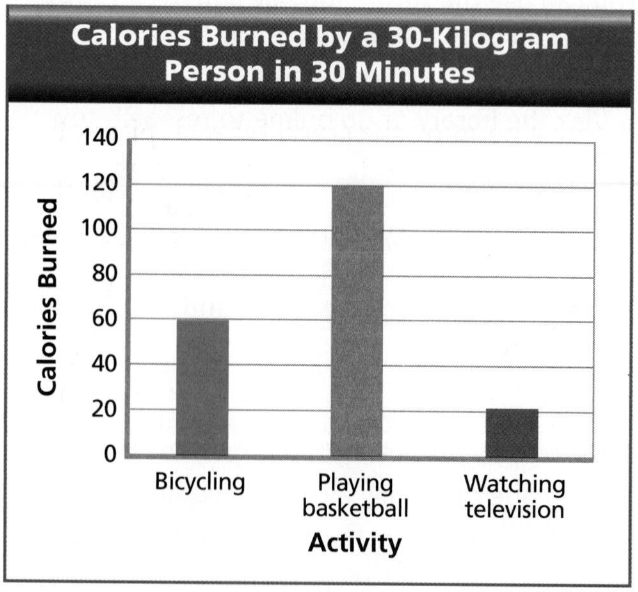

Line Graphs

To see whether a relationship exists between body mass and the number of Calories burned while bicycling, you could create a line graph. A line graph is used to display data that show how one variable (the responding variable) changes in response to another variable (the manipulated variable). You can use a line graph when your manipulated variable is *continuous*, that is, when there are other points between the ones that you tested. In this example, body mass is a continuous variable because there are other body masses between 30 and 40 kilograms (for example, 31 kilograms). Time is another example of a continuous variable.

Line graphs are powerful tools because they allow you to estimate values for conditions that you did not test in the experiment. For example, you can use the line graph to estimate that a 35-kilogram person would burn 68 Calories while bicycling.

To create a line graph, follow these steps.

1. On graph paper, draw a horizontal, or *x*-, axis and a vertical, or *y*-, axis.
2. Label the horizontal axis with the name of the manipulated variable. Label the vertical axis with the name of the responding variable. Include units of measurement.
3. Create a scale on each axis by marking off equally spaced numbers that cover the range of the data collected.
4. Plot a point on the graph for each piece of data. In the line graph above, the dotted lines show how to plot the first data point (30 kilograms and 60 Calories). Follow an imaginary vertical line extending up from the horizontal axis at the 30-kilogram mark. Then follow an imaginary horizontal line extending across from the vertical axis at the 60-Calorie mark. Plot the point where the two lines intersect.

Effect of Body Mass on Calories Burned While Bicycling

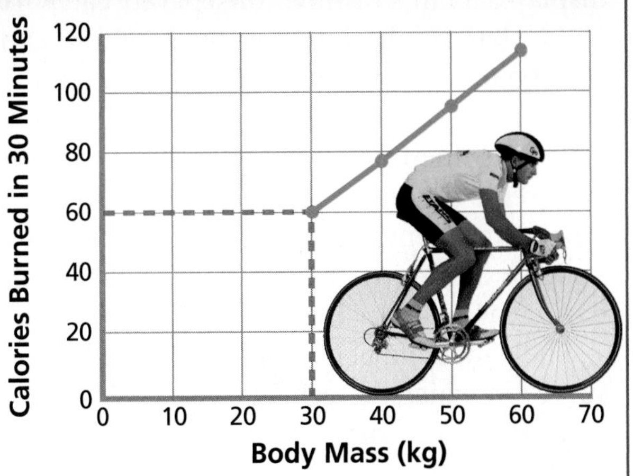

5. Connect the plotted points with a solid line. (In some cases, it may be more appropriate to draw a line that shows the general trend of the plotted points. In those cases, some of the points may fall above or below the line. Also, not all graphs are linear. It may be more appropriate to draw a curve to connect the points.)
6. Add a title that identifies the variables or relationship in the graph.

Activity

Create line graphs to display the data from Experiment 2 and Experiment 3 in the data table.

Activity

You read in the newspaper that a total of 4 centimeters of rain fell in your area in June, 2.5 centimeters fell in July, and 1.5 centimeters fell in August. What type of graph would you use to display these data? Use graph paper to create the graph.

Circle Graphs

Like bar graphs, circle graphs can be used to display data in a number of separate categories. Unlike bar graphs, however, circle graphs can only be used when you have data for *all* the categories that make up a given topic. A circle graph is sometimes called a pie chart. The pie represents the entire topic, while the slices represent the individual categories. The size of a slice indicates what percentage of the whole a particular category makes up.

The data table below shows the results of a survey in which 24 teenagers were asked to identify their favorite sport. The data were then used to create the circle graph at the right.

Favorite Sports

Sport	Students
Soccer	8
Basketball	6
Bicycling	6
Swimming	4

Sports That Teens Prefer

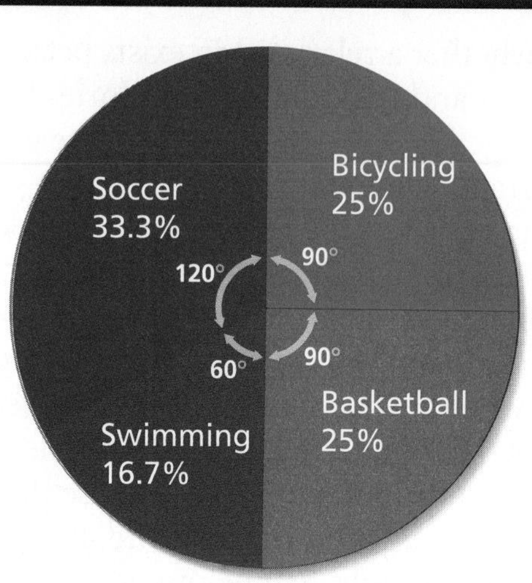

To create a circle graph, follow these steps.

1. Use a compass to draw a circle. Mark the center with a point. Then draw a line from the center point to the top of the circle.
2. Determine the size of each "slice" by setting up a proportion where x equals the number of degrees in a slice. (*Note:* A circle contains 360 degrees.) For example, to find the number of degrees in the "soccer" slice, set up the following proportion:

$$\frac{\text{Students who prefer soccer}}{\text{Total number of students}} = \frac{x}{\text{Total number of degrees in a circle}}$$

$$\frac{8}{24} = \frac{x}{360}$$

Cross-multiply and solve for x.

$$24x = 8 \times 360$$
$$x = 120$$

The "soccer" slice should contain 120 degrees.

3. Use a protractor to measure the angle of the first slice, using the line you drew to the top of the circle as the 0° line. Draw a line from the center of the circle to the edge for the angle you measured.
4. Continue around the circle by measuring the size of each slice with the protractor. Start measuring from the edge of the previous slice so the wedges do not overlap. When you are done, the entire circle should be filled in.
5. Determine the percentage of the whole circle that each slice represents. To do this, divide the number of degrees in a slice by the total number of degrees in a circle (360), and multiply by 100%. For the "soccer" slice, you can find the percentage as follows:

$$\frac{120}{360} \times 100\% = 33.3\%$$

6. Use a different color for each slice. Label each slice with the category and with the percentage of the whole it represents.
7. Add a title to the circle graph.

Activity

In a class of 28 students, 12 students take the bus to school, 10 students walk, and 6 students ride their bicycles. Create a circle graph to display these data.

Math Review

Scientists use math to organize, analyze, and present data. This appendix will help you review some basic math skills.

Mean, Median, and Mode

The **mean** is the average, or the sum of the data divided by the number of data items. The middle number in a set of ordered data is called the **median.** The **mode** is the number that appears most often in a set of data.

Example

A scientist counted the number of distinct songs sung by seven different male birds and collected the data shown below.

Male Bird Songs

Bird	A	B	C	D	E	F	G
Number of Songs	36	29	40	35	28	36	27

To determine the mean number of songs, add the total number of songs and divide by the number of data items—in this case, the number of male birds.

$$\text{Mean} = \frac{231}{7} = 33 \text{ songs}$$

To find the median number of songs, arrange the data in numerical order and find the number in the middle of the series.

27 28 29 35 36 36 40

The number in the middle is 35, so the median number of songs is 35.

The mode is the value that appears most frequently. In the data, 36 appears twice, while each other item appears only once. Therefore, 36 songs is the mode.

Practice

Find out how many minutes it takes each student in your class to get to school. Then find the mean, median, and mode for the data.

Probability

Probability is the chance that an event will occur. Probability can be expressed as a ratio, a fraction, or a percentage. For example, when you flip a coin, the probability that the coin will land heads up is 1 in 2, or $\frac{1}{2}$, or 50 percent.

The probability that an event will happen can be expressed in the following formula.

$$P(\text{event}) = \frac{\text{Number of times the event can occur}}{\text{Total number of possible events}}$$

Example

A paper bag contains 25 blue marbles, 5 green marbles, 5 orange marbles, and 15 yellow marbles. If you close your eyes and pick a marble from the bag, what is the probability that it will be yellow?

$$P(\text{yellow marbles}) = \frac{\text{15 yellow marbles}}{\text{50 marbles total}}$$

$$P = \frac{15}{50}, \text{ or } \frac{3}{10}, \text{ or } 30\%$$

Practice

Each side of a cube has a letter on it. Two sides have *A*, three sides have *B*, and one side has *C*. If you roll the cube, what is the probability that *A* will land on top?

Area

The **area** of a surface is the number of square units that cover it. The front cover of your textbook has an area of about 600 cm^2.

Area of a Rectangle and a Square To find the area of a rectangle, multiply its length times its width. The formula for the area of a rectangle is

$$A = \ell \times w, \text{ or } A = \ell w$$

Since all four sides of a square have the same length, the area of a square is the length of one side multiplied by itself, or squared.

$$A = s \times s, \text{ or } A = s^2$$

Example

A scientist is studying the plants in a field that measures 75 m × 45 m. What is the area of the field?

$$A = \ell \times w$$

$$A = 75 \text{ m} \times 45 \text{ m}$$

$$A = 3{,}375 \text{ m}^2$$

Area of a Circle The formula for the area of a circle is

$$A = \pi \times r \times r, \text{ or } A = \pi r^2$$

The length of the radius is represented by r, and the value of π is approximately $\frac{22}{7}$.

Example

Find the area of a circle with a radius of 14 cm.

$$A = \pi r^2$$

$$A = 14 \times 14 \times \frac{22}{7}$$

$$A = 616 \text{ cm}^2$$

Practice

Find the area of a circle that has a radius of 21 m.

Circumference

The distance around a circle is called the circumference. The formula for finding the circumference of a circle is

$$C = 2 \times \pi \times r, \text{ or } C = 2\pi r$$

Example

The radius of a circle is 35 cm. What is its circumference?

$$C = 2\pi r$$

$$C = 2 \times 35 \times \frac{22}{7}$$

$$C = 220 \text{ cm}$$

Practice

What is the circumference of a circle with a radius of 28 m?

Volume

The volume of an object is the number of cubic units it contains. The volume of a wastebasket, for example, might be about 26,000 cm^3.

Volume of a Rectangular Object To find the volume of a rectangular object, multiply the object's length times its width times its height.

$$V = \ell \times w \times h, \text{ or } V = \ell wh$$

Example

Find the volume of a box with length 24 cm, width 12 cm, and height 9 cm.

$$V = \ell wh$$

$$V = 24 \text{ cm} \times 12 \text{ cm} \times 9 \text{ cm}$$

$$V = 2{,}592 \text{ cm}^3$$

Practice

What is the volume of a rectangular object with length 17 cm, width 11 cm, and height 6 cm?

Fractions

A **fraction** is a way to express a part of a whole. In the fraction $\frac{4}{7}$, 4 is the numerator and 7 is the denominator.

Adding and Subtracting Fractions To add or subtract two or more fractions that have a common denominator, first add or subtract the numerators. Then write the sum or difference over the common denominator.

To find the sum or difference of fractions with different denominators, first find the least common multiple of the denominators. This is known as the least common denominator. Then convert each fraction to equivalent fractions with the least common denominator. Add or subtract the numerators. Then write the sum or difference over the common denominator.

Example

$$\frac{5}{6} - \frac{3}{4} = \frac{10}{12} - \frac{9}{12} = \frac{10-9}{12} = \frac{1}{12}$$

Multiplying Fractions To multiply two fractions, first multiply the two numerators, then multiply the two denominators.

Example

$$\frac{5}{6} \times \frac{2}{3} = \frac{5 \times 2}{6 \times 3} = \frac{10}{18} = \frac{5}{9}$$

Dividing Fractions Dividing by a fraction is the same as multiplying by its reciprocal. Reciprocals are numbers whose numerators and denominators have been switched. To divide one fraction by another, first invert the fraction you are dividing by—in other words, turn it upside down. Then multiply the two fractions.

Example

$$\frac{2}{5} \div \frac{7}{8} = \frac{2}{5} \times \frac{8}{7} = \frac{2 \times 8}{5 \times 7} = \frac{16}{35}$$

Practice

Solve the following: $\frac{3}{7} \div \frac{4}{5}$.

Decimals

Fractions whose denominators are 10, 100, or some other power of 10 are often expressed as decimals. For example, the fraction $\frac{9}{10}$ can be expressed as the decimal 0.9, and the fraction $\frac{7}{100}$ can be written as 0.07.

Adding and Subtracting With Decimals To add or subtract decimals, line up the decimal points before you carry out the operation.

Example

$$\begin{array}{r} 27.4 \\ +\ 6.19 \\ \hline 33.59 \end{array} \qquad \begin{array}{r} 278.635 \\ -\ 191.4 \\ \hline 87.235 \end{array}$$

Multiplying With Decimals When you multiply two numbers with decimals, the number of decimal places in the product is equal to the total number of decimal places in each number being multiplied.

Example

$$\begin{array}{rl} 46.2 & \text{(one decimal place)} \\ \times\ 2.37 & \text{(two decimal places)} \\ \hline 109.494 & \text{(three decimal places)} \end{array}$$

Dividing With Decimals To divide a decimal by a whole number, put the decimal point in the quotient above the decimal point in the dividend.

Example

$$15.5 \div 5$$

$$5\overline{)15.5}\ \ \text{quotient } 3.1$$

To divide a decimal by a decimal, you need to rewrite the divisor as a whole number. Do this by multiplying both the divisor and dividend by the same multiple of 10.

Example

$$1.68 \div 4.2 = 16.8 \div 42$$

$$42\overline{)16.8}\ \ \text{quotient } 0.4$$

Practice

Multiply 6.21 by 8.5.

Ratio and Proportion

A **ratio** compares two numbers by division. For example, suppose a scientist counts 800 wolves and 1,200 moose on an island. The ratio of wolves to moose can be written as a fraction, $\frac{800}{1,200}$, which can be reduced to $\frac{2}{3}$. The same ratio can also be expressed as 2 to 3 or 2 : 3.

A **proportion** is a mathematical sentence saying that two ratios are equivalent. For example, a proportion could state that $\frac{800 \text{ wolves}}{1,200 \text{ moose}} = \frac{2 \text{ wolves}}{3 \text{ moose}}$. You can sometimes set up a proportion to determine or estimate an unknown quantity. For example, suppose a scientist counts 25 beetles in an area of 10 square meters. The scientist wants to estimate the number of beetles in 100 square meters.

Example

1. Express the relationship between beetles and area as a ratio: $\frac{25}{10}$, simplified to $\frac{5}{2}$.
2. Set up a proportion, with x representing the number of beetles. The proportion can be stated as $\frac{5}{2} = \frac{x}{100}$.
3. Begin by cross-multiplying. In other words, multiply each fraction's numerator by the other fraction's denominator.

   $$5 \times 100 = 2 \times x, \text{ or } 500 = 2x$$

4. To find the value of x, divide both sides by 2. The result is 250, or 250 beetles in 100 square meters.

Practice

Find the value of x in the following proportion: $\frac{6}{7} = \frac{x}{49}$.

Percentage

A **percentage** is a ratio that compares a number to 100. For example, there are 37 granite rocks in a collection that consists of 100 rocks. The ratio $\frac{37}{100}$ can be written as 37%. Granite rocks make up 37% of the rock collection.

You can calculate percentages of numbers other than 100 by setting up a proportion.

Example

Rain falls on 9 days out of 30 in June. What percentage of the days in June were rainy?

$$\frac{9 \text{ days}}{30 \text{ days}} = \frac{d\%}{100\%}$$

To find the value of d, begin by cross-multiplying, as for any proportion:

$$9 \times 100 = 30 \times d \qquad d = \frac{900}{30} \qquad d = 30$$

Practice

There are 300 marbles in a jar, and 42 of those marbles are blue. What percentage of the marbles are blue?

Significant Figures

The **precision** of a measurement depends on the instrument you use to take the measurement. For example, if the smallest unit on the ruler is millimeters, then the most precise measurement you can make will be in millimeters.

The sum or difference of measurements can only be as precise as the least precise measurement being added or subtracted. Round your answer so that it has the same number of digits after the decimal as the least precise measurement. Round up if the last digit is 5 or more, and round down if the last digit is 4 or less.

Example

Subtract a temperature of 5.2°C from the temperature 75.46°C.

$$75.46 - 5.2 = 70.26$$

5.2 has the fewest digits after the decimal, so it is the least precise measurement. Since the last digit of the answer is 6, round up to 3. The most precise difference between the measurements is 70.3°C.

Practice

Add 26.4 m to 8.37 m. Round your answer according to the precision of the measurements.

Significant figures are the number of nonzero digits in a measurement. Zeroes between nonzero digits are also significant. For example, the measurements 12,500 L, 0.125 cm, and 2.05 kg all have three significant figures. When you multiply and divide measurements, the one with the fewest significant figures determines the number of significant figures in your answer.

Example

Multiply 110 g by 5.75 g.

$$110 \times 5.75 = 632.5$$

Because 110 has only two significant figures, round the answer to 630 g.

Scientific Notation

A **factor** is a number that divides into another number with no remainder. In the example, the number 3 is used as a factor four times.

An **exponent** tells how many times a number is used as a factor. For example, $3 \times 3 \times 3 \times 3$ can be written as 3^4. The exponent ^{4} indicates that the number 3 is used as a factor four times. Another way of expressing this is to say that 81 is equal to 3 to the fourth power.

Example

$$3^4 = 3 \times 3 \times 3 \times 3 = 81$$

Scientific notation uses exponents and powers of ten to write very large or very small numbers in shorter form. When you write a number in scientific notation, you write the number as two factors. The first factor is any number between 1 and 10. The second factor is a power of 10, such as 10^3 or 10^6.

Example

The average distance between the planet Mercury and the sun is 58,000,000 km. To write the first factor in scientific notation, insert a decimal point in the original number so that you have a number between 1 and 10. In the case of 58,000,000, the number is 5.8.

To determine the power of 10, count the number of places that the decimal point moved. In this case, it moved 7 places.

$$58{,}000{,}000 \text{ km} = 5.8 \times 10^7 \text{ km}$$

Practice

Express 6,590,000 in scientific notation.

Reading Comprehension Skills

Your textbook is an important source of science information. As you read your science textbook, you will find that the book has been written to assist you in understanding the science concepts.

Learning From Science Textbooks

As you study science in school, you will learn science concepts in a variety of ways. Sometimes you will do interesting activities and experiments to explore science ideas. To fully understand what you observe in experiments and activities, you will need to read your science textbook. To help you read, some of the important ideas are highlighted so that you can easily recognize what they are. In addition, a target reading skill in each section will help you understand what you read.

By using the target reading skills, you will improve your reading comprehension—that is, you will improve your ability to understand what you read. As you learn science, you will build knowledge that will help you understand even more of what you read. This knowledge will help you learn about all the topics presented in this textbook.

And—guess what?—these reading skills can be useful whenever you are reading. Reading to learn is important for your entire life. You have an opportunity to begin that process now.

The target reading skills that will improve your reading comprehension are described below.

Building Vocabulary

To understand the science concepts taught in this textbook, you need to remember the meanings of the Key Terms. One strategy consists of writing the definitions of these terms in your own words. You can also practice using the terms in sentences and make lists of words or phrases you associate with each term.

Using Prior Knowledge

Your prior knowledge is what you already know before you begin to read about a topic. Building on what you already know gives you a head start on learning new information. Before you begin a new assignment, think about what you know. You might page through your reading assignment, looking at the headings and the visuals to spark your memory. You can list what you know in the graphic organizer provided in the section opener. Then, as you read, consider questions like the ones below to connect what you learn to what you already know.

- How does what you learn relate to what you know?
- How did something you already know help you learn something new?
- Did your original ideas agree with what you have just learned? If not, how would you revise your original ideas?

Asking Questions

Asking yourself questions is an excellent way to focus on and remember new information in your textbook. You can learn how to ask good questions.

One way is to turn the text headings into questions. Then your questions can guide you to identify and remember the important information as you read. Look at these examples:

Heading: Using Seismographic Data

Question: How are seismographic data used?

Heading: Kinds of Faults

Question: What are the kinds of faults?

You do not have to limit your questions to the text headings. Ask questions about anything that you need to clarify or that will help you understand the content. *What* and *how* are probably the most common question words, but you may also ask *why*, *who*, *when*, or *where* questions. Here is an example:

Properties of Waves

Question	Answer
What is amplitude?	Amplitude is . . .

Previewing Visuals

Visuals are photographs, graphs, tables, diagrams, and illustrations. Visuals, such as this diagram of a normal fault, contain important information. Look at visuals and their captions before you read. This will help you prepare for what you will be reading about.

Often you will be asked what you want to learn about a visual. For example, after you look at the normal fault diagram, you might ask: What is the movement along a normal fault? Questions about visuals give you a purpose for reading—to answer your questions. Previewing visuals also helps you see what you already know.

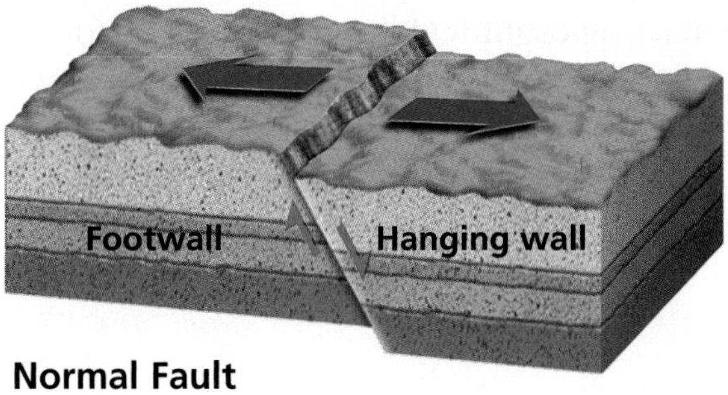

Normal Fault

Outlining

An outline shows the relationship between main ideas and supporting ideas. An outline has a formal structure. You write the main ideas, called topics, next to Roman numerals. The supporting ideas, sometimes called subtopics, are written under the main ideas and labeled A, B, C, and so on. An outline looks like this:

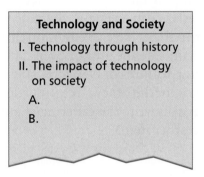

Technology and Society
I. Technology through history II. The impact of technology on society A. B.

When you have completed an outline like this, you can see at a glance the structure of the section. You can use this outline as a study tool.

Identifying Main Ideas

When you are reading, it is important to try to understand the ideas and concepts that are in a passage. As you read science material, you will recognize that each paragraph has a lot of information and detail. Good readers try to identify the most important—or biggest—idea in every paragraph or section. That's the main idea. The other information in the paragraph supports or further explains the main idea.

Sometimes main ideas are stated directly. In this book, some main ideas are identified for you as key concepts. These are printed in boldface type. However, you must identify other main ideas yourself. In order to do this, you must identify all the ideas within a paragraph or section. Then ask yourself which idea is big enough to include all the other ideas.

Comparing and Contrasting

When you compare and contrast, you examine the similarities and differences between things. You can compare and contrast in a Venn diagram or in a table. Your completed diagram or table shows you how the items are alike and how they are different.

Venn Diagram A Venn diagram consists of two overlapping circles. In the space where the circles overlap, you write the characteristics that the two items have in common. In one of the circles outside the area of overlap, you write the differing features or characteristics of one of the items. In the other circle outside the area of overlap, you write the differing characteristics of the other item.

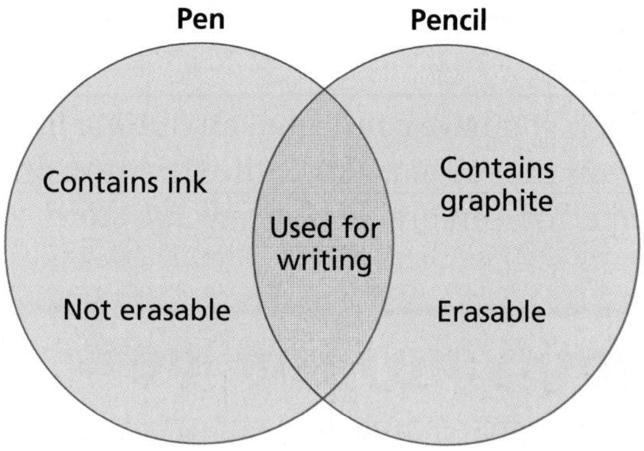

Table In a compare/contrast table, you list the items to be compared across the top of the table. Then list the characteristics or features to be compared in the left column. Complete the table by filling in information about each characteristic or feature.

Blood Vessel	Function	Structure of Wall
Artery	Carries blood away from heart	
Capillary		
Vein		

Sequencing

A sequence is the order in which a series of events occurs. Recognizing and remembering the sequence of events is important to understanding many processes in science. Sometimes the text uses words like *first, next, during,* and *after* to signal a sequence. A flowchart or a cycle diagram can help you visualize a sequence.

Flowchart To make a flowchart, write a brief description of each step or event in a box. Place the boxes in order, with the first event at the top of the page. Then draw an arrow to connect each step or event to the next.

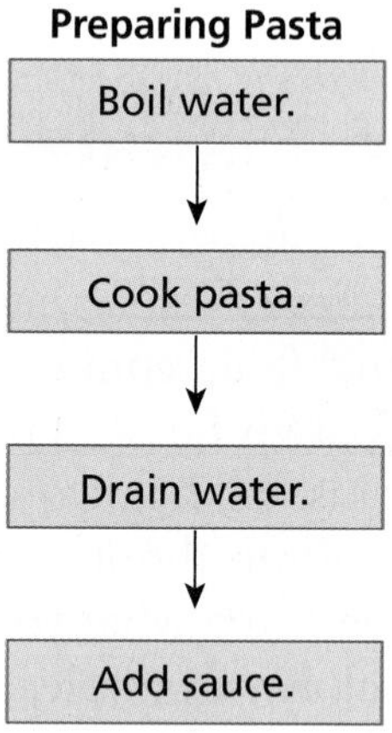

Cycle Diagram A cycle diagram shows a sequence that is continuous, or cyclical. A continuous sequence does not have an end because when the final event is over, the first event begins again. To create a cycle diagram, write the starting event in a box placed at the top of a page in the center. Then, moving in a clockwise direction around an imaginary circle, write each event in a box in its proper sequence. Draw arrows that connect each event to the one that occurs next, forming a continuous circle.

Identifying Supporting Evidence

A hypothesis is a possible explanation for observations made by scientists or an answer to a scientific question. A hypothesis is tested over and over again. The tests may produce evidence that supports the hypothesis. When enough supporting evidence is collected, a hypothesis may become a theory.

Identifying the supporting evidence for a hypothesis or theory can help you understand the hypothesis or theory. Evidence consists of facts—information whose accuracy can be confirmed by testing or observation.

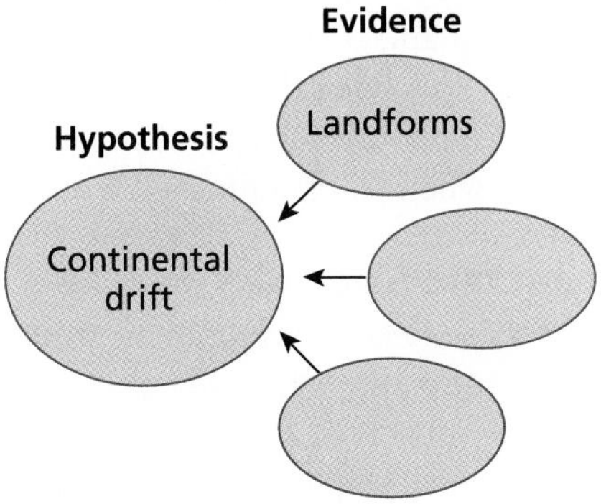

Relating Cause and Effect

Identifying causes and effects helps you understand relationships among events. A cause makes something happen. An effect is what happens. When you recognize that one event causes another, you are relating cause and effect. Words like *cause, because, effect, affect,* and *result* often signal a cause or an effect.

Sometimes an effect can have more than one cause, or a cause can produce several effects. For example, car exhaust and smoke from industrial plants are two causes of air pollution. Some effects of air pollution include breathing difficulties for some people, death of plants along some highways, and damage to some building surfaces.

Science involves many cause-and-effect relationships. Seeing and understanding these relationships helps you understand science processes.

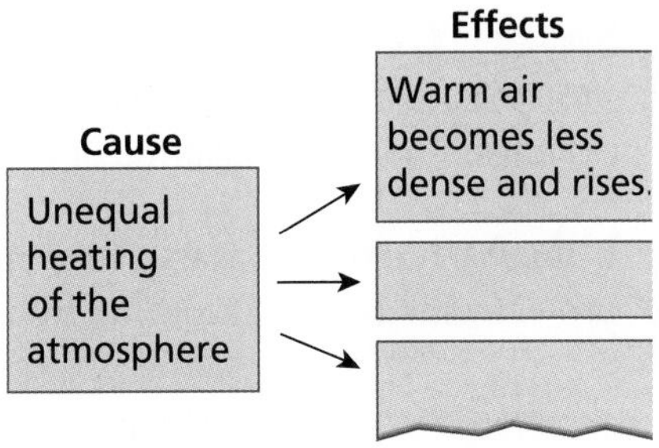

Concept Mapping

Concept maps are useful tools for organizing information on any topic. A concept map begins with a main idea or core concept and shows how the idea can be subdivided into related subconcepts or smaller ideas. In this way, relationships between concepts become clearer and easier to understand.

You construct a concept map by placing concepts (usually nouns) in ovals and connecting them with linking words. The biggest concept or idea is placed in an oval at the top of the map. Related concepts are arranged in ovals below the big idea. The linking words are often verbs and verb phrases and are written on the lines that connect the ovals.

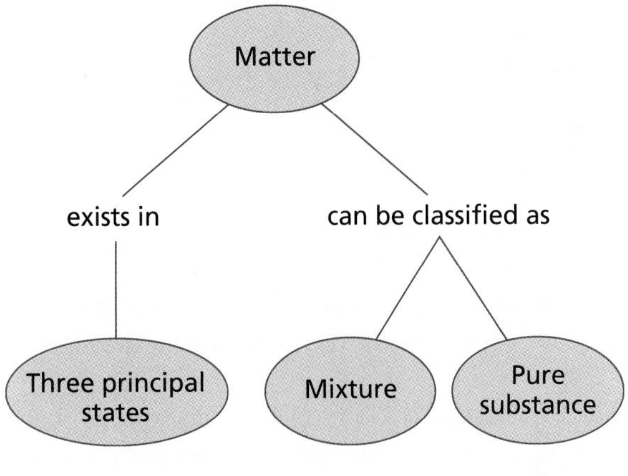

Safety Symbols

These symbols warn of possible dangers in the laboratory and remind you to work carefully.

Safety Goggles Wear safety goggles to protect your eyes in any activity involving chemicals, flames or heating, or glassware.

Lab Apron Wear a laboratory apron to protect your skin and clothing from damage.

Breakage Handle breakable materials, such as glassware, with care. Do not touch broken glassware.

Heat-Resistant Gloves Use an oven mitt or other hand protection when handling hot materials such as hot plates or hot glassware.

Plastic Gloves Wear disposable plastic gloves when working with organisms and harmful chemicals. Keep your hands away from your face, and dispose of the gloves according to your teacher's instructions.

Heating Use a clamp or tongs to pick up hot glassware. Do not touch hot objects with your bare hands.

Flames Before you work with flames, tie back loose hair and clothing. Follow instructions from your teacher about lighting and extinguishing flames.

No Flames When using flammable materials, make sure there are no flames, sparks, or other exposed heat sources present.

Corrosive Chemical Avoid getting acid or other corrosive chemicals on your skin or clothing or in your eyes. Do not inhale the vapors. Wash your hands after the activity.

Poison Do not let any poisonous chemical come into contact with your skin, and do not inhale its vapors. Wash your hands when you are finished with the activity.

Fumes Work in a ventilated area when harmful vapors may be involved. Avoid inhaling vapors directly. Only test an odor when directed to do so by your teacher, and use a wafting motion to direct the vapor toward your nose.

Sharp Object Scissors, scalpels, knives, needles, pins, and tacks can cut your skin. Always direct a sharp edge or point away from yourself and others.

Animal Safety Treat live or preserved animals or animal parts with care to avoid harming the animals or yourself. Wash your hands when you are finished with the activity.

Plant Safety Handle plants only as directed by your teacher. If you are allergic to certain plants, tell your teacher; do not do an activity involving those plants. Avoid touching harmful plants such as poison ivy. Wash your hands when you are finished with the activity.

Electric Shock To avoid electric shock, never use electrical equipment around water, or when the equipment is wet or your hands are wet. Be sure cords are untangled and cannot trip anyone. Unplug equipment not in use.

Physical Safety When an experiment involves physical activity, avoid injuring yourself or others. Alert your teacher if there is any reason you should not participate.

Disposal Dispose of chemicals and other laboratory materials safely. Follow the instructions from your teacher.

Hand Washing Wash your hands thoroughly when finished with the activity. Use soap and warm water. Rinse well.

General Safety Awareness When this symbol appears, follow the instructions provided. When you are asked to develop your own procedure in a lab, have your teacher approve your plan before you go further.

Science Safety Rules

General Precautions
Follow all instructions. Never perform activities without the approval and supervision of your teacher. Do not engage in horseplay. Never eat or drink in the laboratory. Keep work areas clean and uncluttered.

Dress Code
Wear safety goggles whenever you work with chemicals, glassware, heat sources such as burners, or any substance that might get into your eyes. If you wear contact lenses, notify your teacher.

Wear a lab apron or coat whenever you work with corrosive chemicals or substances that can stain. Wear disposable plastic gloves when working with organisms and harmful chemicals. Tie back long hair. Remove or tie back any article of clothing or jewelry that can hang down and touch chemicals, flames, or equipment. Roll up long sleeves. Never wear open shoes or sandals.

First Aid
Report all accidents, injuries, or fires to your teacher, no matter how minor. Be aware of the location of the first-aid kit, emergency equipment such as the fire extinguisher and fire blanket, and the nearest telephone. Know whom to contact in an emergency.

Heating and Fire Safety
Keep all combustible materials away from flames. When heating a substance in a test tube, make sure that the mouth of the tube is not pointed at you or anyone else. Never heat a liquid in a closed container. Use an oven mitt to pick up a container that has been heated.

Using Chemicals Safely
Never put your face near the mouth of a container that holds chemicals. Never touch, taste, or smell a chemical unless your teacher tells you to.

Use only those chemicals needed in the activity. Keep all containers closed when chemicals are not being used. Pour all chemicals over the sink or a container, not over your work surface. Dispose of excess chemicals as instructed by your teacher.

Be extra careful when working with acids or bases. When mixing an acid and water, always pour the water into the container first and then add the acid to the water. Never pour water into an acid. Wash chemical spills and splashes immediately with plenty of water.

Using Glassware Safely
If glassware is broken or chipped, notify your teacher immediately. Never handle broken or chipped glass with your bare hands.

Never force glass tubing or thermometers into a rubber stopper or rubber tubing. Have your teacher insert the glass tubing or thermometer if required for an activity.

Using Sharp Instruments
Handle sharp instruments with extreme care. Never cut material toward you; cut away from you.

Animal and Plant Safety
Never perform experiments that cause pain, discomfort, or harm to animals. Only handle animals if absolutely necessary. If you know that you are allergic to certain plants, molds, or animals, tell your teacher before doing an activity in which these are used. Wash your hands thoroughly after any activity involving animals, animal parts, plants, plant parts, or soil.

During field work, wear long pants, long sleeves, socks, and closed shoes. Avoid poisonous plants and fungi as well as plants with thorns.

End-of-Experiment Rules
Unplug all electrical equipment. Clean up your work area. Dispose of waste materials as instructed by your teacher. Wash your hands after every experiment.

The laboratory balance is an important tool in scientific investigations. You can use a balance to determine the masses of materials that you study or experiment with in the laboratory.

Different kinds of balances are used in the laboratory. One kind of balance is the triple-beam balance. The balance that you may use in your science class is probably similar to the balance illustrated in this Appendix. To use the balance properly, you should learn the name, location, and function of each part of the balance you are using. What kind of balance do you have in your science class?

The Triple-Beam Balance

The triple-beam balance is a single-pan balance with three beams calibrated in grams. The back, or 100-gram, beam is divided into ten units of 10 grams each. The middle, or 500-gram, beam is divided into five units of 100 grams each. The front, or 10-gram, beam is divided into ten major units of 1 gram each. Each of these units is further divided into units of 0.1 gram. What is the largest mass you could find with a triple-beam balance?

The following procedure can be used to find the mass of an object with a triple-beam balance:

1. Place the object on the pan.
2. Move the rider on the middle beam notch by notch until the horizontal pointer drops below zero. Move the rider back one notch.
3. Move the rider on the back beam notch by notch until the pointer again drops below zero. Move the rider back one notch.
4. Slowly slide the rider along the front beam until the pointer stops at the zero point.
5. The mass of the object is equal to the sum of the readings on the three beams.

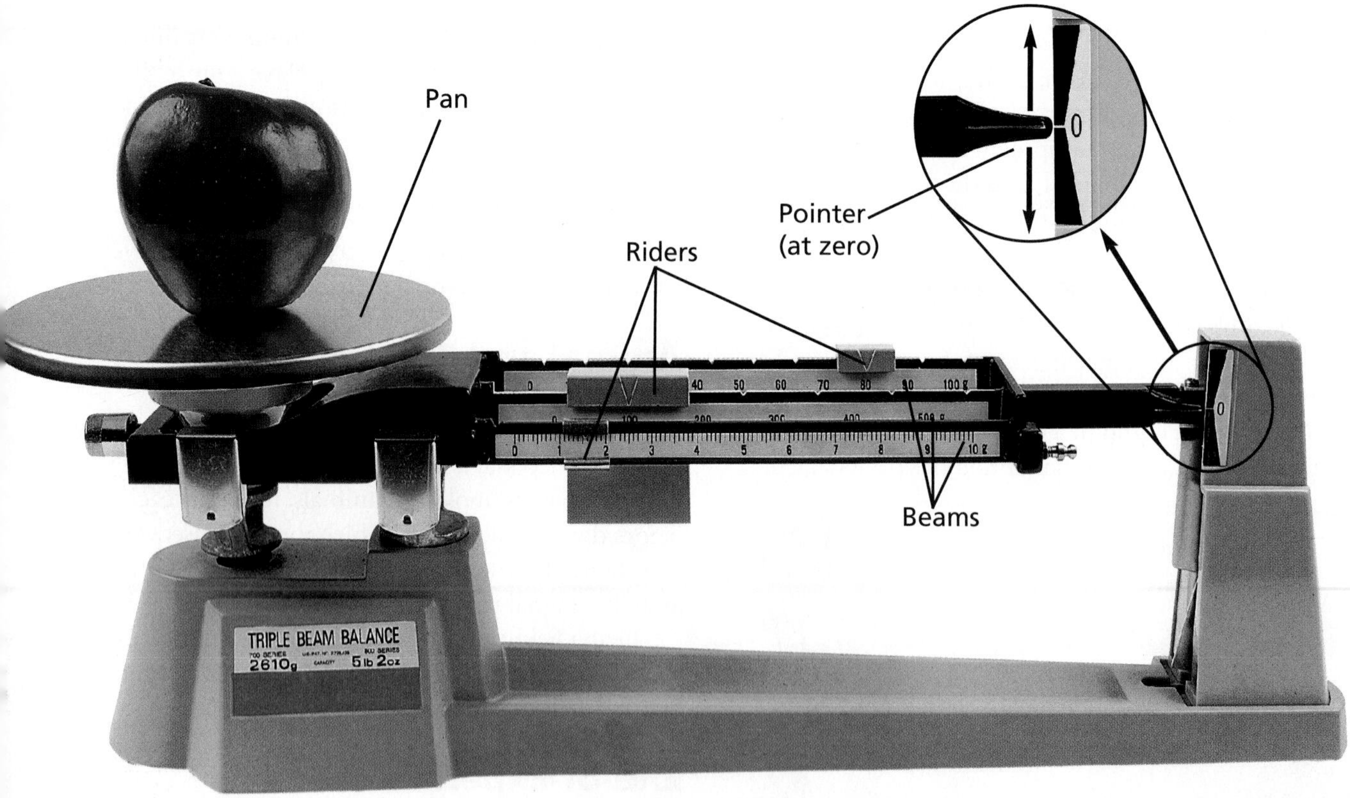

Triple-Beam Balance

Name	Symbol	Atomic Number	Atomic Mass†
Actinium	Ac	89	(227)
Aluminum	Al	13	26.982
Americium	Am	95	(243)
Antimony	Sb	51	121.75
Argon	Ar	18	39.948
Arsenic	As	33	74.922
Astatine	At	85	(210)
Barium	Ba	56	137.33
Berkelium	Bk	97	(247)
Beryllium	Be	4	9.0122
Bismuth	Bi	83	208.98
Bohrium	Bh	107	(264)
Boron	B	5	10.81
Bromine	Br	35	79.904
Cadmium	Cd	48	112.41
Calcium	Ca	20	40.08
Californium	Cf	98	(251)
Carbon	C	6	12.011
Cerium	Ce	58	140.12
Cesium	Cs	55	132.91
Chlorine	Cl	17	35.453
Chromium	Cr	24	51.996
Cobalt	Co	27	58.933
Copper	Cu	29	63.546
Curium	Cm	96	(247)
Darmstadtium	Ds	110	(269)
Dubnium	Db	105	(262)
Dysprosium	Dy	66	162.50
Einsteinium	Es	99	(252)
Erbium	Er	68	167.26
Europium	Eu	63	151.96
Fermium	Fm	100	(257)
Fluorine	F	9	18.998
Francium	Fr	87	(223)
Gadolinium	Gd	64	157.25
Gallium	Ga	31	69.72
Germanium	Ge	32	72.59
Gold	Au	79	196.97
Hafnium	Hf	72	178.49
Hassium	Hs	108	(265)
Helium	He	2	4.0026
Holmium	Ho	67	164.93
Hydrogen	H	1	1.0079
Indium	In	49	114.82
Iodine	I	53	126.90
Iridium	Ir	77	192.22
Iron	Fe	26	55.847
Krypton	Kr	36	83.80
Lanthanum	La	57	138.91
Lawrencium	Lr	103	(262)
Lead	Pb	82	207.2
Lithium	Li	3	6.941
Lutetium	Lu	71	174.97
Magnesium	Mg	12	24.305
Manganese	Mn	25	54.938
Meitnerium	Mt	109	(268)
Mendelevium	Md	101	(258)

†Numbers in parentheses give the mass number of the most stable isotope.

Name	Symbol	Atomic Number	Atomic Mass†
Mercury	Hg	80	200.59
Molybdenum	Mo	42	95.94
Neodymium	Nd	60	144.24
Neon	Ne	10	20.179
Neptunium	Np	93	(237)
Nickel	Ni	28	58.71
Niobium	Nb	41	92.906
Nitrogen	N	7	14.007
Nobelium	No	102	(259)
Osmium	Os	76	190.2
Oxygen	O	8	15.999
Palladium	Pd	46	106.4
Phosphorus	P	15	30.974
Platinum	Pt	78	195.09
Plutonium	Pu	94	(244)
Polonium	Po	84	(209)
Potassium	K	19	39.098
Praseodymium	Pr	59	140.91
Promethium	Pm	61	(145)
Protactinium	Pa	91	231.04
Radium	Ra	88	(226)
Radon	Rn	86	(222)
Rhenium	Re	75	186.21
Rhodium	Rh	45	102.91
Rubidium	Rb	37	85.468
Ruthenium	Ru	44	101.07
Rutherfordium	Rf	104	(261)
Samarium	Sm	62	150.4
Scandium	Sc	21	44.956
Seaborgium	Sg	106	(263)
Selenium	Se	34	78.96
Silicon	Si	14	28.086
Silver	Ag	47	107.87
Sodium	Na	11	22.990
Strontium	Sr	38	87.62
Sulfur	S	16	32.06
Tantalum	Ta	73	180.95
Technetium	Tc	43	(98)
Tellurium	Te	52	127.60
Terbium	Tb	65	158.93
Thallium	Tl	81	204.37
Thorium	Th	90	232.04
Thulium	Tm	69	168.93
Tin	Sn	50	118.69
Titanium	Ti	22	47.90
Tungsten	W	74	183.85
Ununbium	Uub	112	(277)
Ununquadium	Uuq	114	*
Unununium	Uuu	111	(272)
Uranium	U	92	238.03
Vanadium	V	23	50.941
Xenon	Xe	54	131.30
Ytterbium	Yb	70	173.04
Yttrium	Y	39	88.906
Zinc	Zn	30	65.38
Zirconium	Zr	40	91.22

*Newly discovered

English and Spanish Glossary

A

absolute zero The temperature at which no more energy can be removed from matter. (p. 474)
cero absoluto Temperatura a la cual no se puede quitar más energía a la materia.

acceleration The rate at which velocity changes. (p. 320)
acelaración Razón a la que cambia la velocidad.

acid A substance that tastes sour, reacts with metals and carbonates, and turns blue litmus red. (p. 236)
ácido Sustancia de sabor agrio que reacciona con metales y carbonatos, y que vuelve rojo el papel de tornasol azul.

acoustics The study of how sounds interact with each other and the environment. (p. 556)
acústica Estudio de cómo interactúan los sonidos entre ellos y con el medio ambiente.

activation energy The minimum amount of energy needed to get a chemical reaction started. (p. 205)
energía de activación Cantidad mínima de energía que se necesita para que empiece una reacción química.

air resistance The fluid friction experienced by objects falling through the air. (p. 347)
resistencia del aire Fricción de fluido experimentada por los objetos que caen a través del aire.

alcohol A substituted hydrocarbon that contains one or more hydroxyl groups. (p. 270)
alcohol Hidrocarburo sustituto que contiene uno o más grupos hidroxilos.

alkali metal An element in Group 1 of the periodic table. (p. 120)
metal alcalino Elemento en el Grupo 1 de la tabla periódica.

alkaline earth metal An element in Group 2 of the periodic table. (p. 121)
metal alcalinotérreo Elemento en el Grupo 2 de la tabla periódica.

alloy A mixture of two or more elements, one of which is a metal. (pp. 122, 173)
aleación Mezcla de dos o más elementos, uno de los cuales es un metal.

alpha particle A type of nuclear radiation consisting of two protons and two neutrons. (p. 140)
partícula alfa Tipo de radiación nuclear que consiste de dos protones y dos neutrones.

alternating current Current consisting of charges that move back and forth in a circuit. (p. 739)
corriente alterna Corriente que consiste en cargas eléctricas que se mueven hacia adelante y hacia atrás en un circuito.

amino acid One of 20 kinds of organic compounds that are the monomers of proteins. (p. 276)
aminoácido Uno de 20 tipos de compuestos orgánicos que son los monómeros de las proteínas.

ammeter A device used to measure current in a circuit. (p. 710)
amperímetro Aparato usado para medir la corriente en un circuito.

amorphous solid A solid made up of particles that are not arranged in a regular pattern. (p. 72)
sólido amorfo Sólido constituido por partículas que no están dispuestas en un patrón regular.

amplitude The maximum distance the particles of a medium move away from their rest positions as a wave passes through the medium. (p. 516)
amplitud Distancia máxima a la que se separan las particulas de un medio de sus posiciones de reposo, cuando una onda atraviesa el medio.

amplitude modulation A method of transmitting signals by changing the amplitude of a wave.
amplitud modulada Método de transmisión de señales por el cual se cambia la amplitud de una onda. (p. 595)

analog signal An electric current that is varied smoothly to represent information. (p. 751)
señal analógica Corriente eléctrica que varía levemente para representar información.

antinode A point of maximum amplitude on a standing wave. (p. 526)
antinodo Punto de máxima amplitud en una onda estacionaria.

Archimedes' principle The rule that the buoyant force on an object is equal to the weight of the fluid the object displaces. (p. 382)
principio de Arquímedes Regla que enuncia que la fuerza de flotación que actúa sobre un objeto es igual al peso del líquido que desaloja.

atom The basic particle from which all elements are made. (pp. 39, 103, 663)
átomo Partícula básica de la que están formados todos los elementos.

atomic mass The average mass of all the isotopes of an element. (p. 110)
masa atómica Promedio de la masa de todos los isótopos de un elemento.

atomic number The number of protons in the nucleus of an atom. (p. 107)

número atómico Número de protones en el núcleo de un átomo.

aurora A glowing region produced by the interaction of charged particles and atoms in the atmosphere.
aurora polar Área resplandeciente en la atmósfera de la Tierra producida por la interacción de partículas cargadas y los átomos de la atmósfera. (p. 675)

average speed The overall rate of speed at which an object moves; calculated by dividing the total distance an object travels by the total time. (p. 313)
rapidez media Velocidad general a la que se mueve un objeto; se calcula dividiendo la distancia total recorrida por el tiempo total empleado.

B

balanced forces Equal forces acting on an object in opposite directions. (p. 336)
fuerzas equilibradas Fuerzas iguales que actúan sobre un objeto en direcciones opuestas.

barometer An instrument used to measure atmospheric pressure. (p. 378)
barómetro Instrumento que se usa para medir la presión atmosférica.

base A substance that tastes bitter, feels slippery, and turns red litmus paper blue. (p. 238)
base Sustancia de sabor amargo, escurridiza y que vuelve azul el papel de tornasol rojo.

battery A combination of two or more electrochemical cells in series. (p. 704)
pila Combinación de dos o más celdas electroquímicas en serie.

Bernoulli's principle The rule that a stream of fast-moving fluid exerts less pressure than the surrounding fluid. (p. 394)
principio de Bernoulli Regla que enuncia que la corriente de un fluido de rápido movimiento ejerce menor presión que el fluido del entorno.

beta particle A fast-moving electron that is given off as nuclear radiation. (p. 140)
partícula beta Electrón de rápido movimiento que se produce como radiación nuclear.

binary system A number system using combinations of only two digits, 0 and 1. (p. 763)
sistema binario Sistema de números que usa combinaciones de sólo dos dígitos, 0 y 1.

boiling The process that occurs when vaporization takes place inside a liquid as well as on the surface.
ebullición Proceso que se da cuando la vaporización se efectúa dentro de un líquido, además de en la superficie. (pp. 79, 489)

boiling point The temperature at which a substance changes from a liquid to a gas. (p. 79)
punto de ebullición Temperatura a la que una sustancia cambia de líquido a gas.

Boyle's law A principle that describes the relationship between the pressure and volume of a gas at constant temperature. (p. 86)
ley de Boyle Principio que describe la relación entre la presión y el volumen de un gas a temperatura constante.

brainstorming A process in which group members freely suggest any creative solutions that come to mind. (p. 24)
lluvia de ideas Proceso mediante el cual los miembros de un grupo sugieren libremente cualquier solución creativa que se les ocurre.

buoyant force The upward force exerted by a fluid on a submerged object. (p. 381)
fuerza de flotación Fuerza ascendente que ejerce un líquido sobre un objeto sumergido.

C

camera An optical instrument that uses lenses to focus light, and film to record an image of an object. (p. 635)
cámara Instrumento óptico que usa lentes para enfocar la luz, y película para grabar la imagen de un objeto.

carbohydrate An energy-rich organic compound made of the elements carbon, hydrogen, and oxygen.
carbohidrato Compuesto orgánico altamente energético hecho de elementos de carbono, hidrógeno y oxígeno. (p. 285)

carboxyl group A —COOH group, found in organic acids. (p. 271)
grupo carboxilo Grupo —COOH, que se haya en los ácidos orgánicos.

catalyst A material that increases the rate of a reaction by lowering the activation energy. (p. 209)
catalítico Material que aumenta la velocidad de una reacción al disminuir la energía de activación.

cellulose A complex carbohydrate found in plant structures. (p. 286)
celulosa Carbohidrato complejo que se haya en las estructuras vegetales.

Celsius scale The temperature scale on which water freezes at 0 degrees and boils at 100 degrees. (p. 474)

escala Celsius Escala de temperatura en la cual el agua se congela a los 0 grados y hierve a los 100 grados.

central processing unit (CPU) Directs the operation of a computer, performs logical operations and calculations. (p. 765)
unidad central de procesamiento (CPU) Dirige la operación de una computadora, realiza operaciones y cálculos lógicos.

centripetal force A force that causes an object to move in a circle. (p. 363)
fuerza centrípeta Fuerza que causa que un objeto se mueva en círculos.

change of state The physical change of matter from one state to another. (p. 488)
cambio de estado Cambio físico de la materia de un estado a otro.

Charles's law A principle that describes the relationship between the temperature and volume of a gas at constant pressure. (p. 88)
ley de Charles Principio que describe la relación entre la temperatura y el volumen de un gas a presión constante.

chemical bond The force that holds atoms together. (pp. 39, 151)
enlace químico Fuerza que mantiene unidos a los átomos.

chemical change A change in which one or more substances combine or break apart to form new substances. (p. 52)
cambio químico Cambio en el cual una o más sustancias se combinan o se rompen para formar nuevas sustancias.

chemical digestion The process that breaks large molecules in food into smaller molecules. (p. 251)
digestión química Proceso que rompe las moléculas grandes en la comida en moléculas más pequeñas.

chemical energy A form of potential energy that is stored in chemical bonds between atoms. (pp. 60, 450, 703)
energía química Forma de energía potencial almacenada en los enlaces químicos entre átomos.

chemical equation A short, easy way to show a chemical reaction, using symbols. (p. 195)
ecuación química Forma corta y sencilla de mostrar una reacción química, usando símbolos.

chemical formula A combination of symbols that represents the elements in a compound and their proportions. (pp. 40, 161)
fórmula química Combinación de símbolos que representan a los elementos de un compuesto y la razón de los átomos.

chemical property A characteristic of a pure substance that describes its ability to change into a different substance. (p. 37)
propiedad química Característica de una sustancia pura que describe su capacidad para cambiar a una sustancia diferente.

chemical reaction The process in which substances undergo chemical changes that result in the formation of new substances. (pp. 186, 703)
reacción química Proceso por el que las sustancias sufren cambios químicos que dan como resultado la formación de nuevas sustancias.

chemical symbol A one- or two-letter representation of an element. (p. 115)
símbolo químico Representación con una o dos letras de un elemento.

chemistry The study of the properties of matter and how matter changes. (pp. 8, 35, 184)
química Estudio de las propiedades de la materia y de cómo cambia.

cholesterol A waxy lipid in animal cells. (p. 288)
colesterol Lípido ceroso que se haya en las células animales.

circuit breaker A reusable safety switch that breaks the circuit when the current becomes too high.
interruptor de circuito Interruptor de seguridad que se puede volver a usar, que se usa para cortar el circuito cuando la corriente es demasiado alta. (p. 717)

closed system A system in which no matter is allowed to enter or leave. (p. 197)
sistema cerrado Sistema en el cual la materia no puede entrar ni salir.

cochlea A fluid-filled cavity in the inner ear that is shaped like a snail shell. (p. 559)
cóclea Cavidad llena de líquido en el oído interno que tiene forma de caracol.

coefficient A number in front of a chemical formula in an equation that indicates how many molecules or atoms of each reactant and product are involved in a reaction. (p. 198)
coeficiente En un ecuación, número delante de una fórmula química que indica cuántas moléculas o átomos de cada reactivo y producto participan en una reacción.

colloid A mixture containing small, undissolved particles that do not settle out. (p. 224)
coloide Mezcla que contiene partículas pequeñas y sin disolver que no se depositan.

combustion A rapid reaction between oxygen and fuel that results in fire. (p. 213); the process of burning a fuel to produce thermal energy. (p. 464)
combustión Reacción rápida entre el oxígeno y el combustible que produce fuego; proceso de quemado de un combustible para producir energía térmica.

communicating The process of sharing ideas with others through writing and speaking. (p. 14)
comunicar Proceso de compartir ideas con otras personas a través de la escritura o el lenguage hablado.

compass A device with a magnetized needle that can spin freely. (p. 670)
brújula Instrumento con una aguja imantada que puede girar libremente.

complementary colors Any two colors that combine to form white light or black pigment. (p. 614)
colores complementarios Dos colores cualesquiera que se combinan para crear luz blanca o pigmento negro.

complex carbohydrate A long chain, or polymer, of simple carbohydrates. (p. 286)
carbohidrato complejo Cadena larga, o polímero, de carbohidratos simples.

composite A combination of two or more substances that creates a new material with different properties. (p. 278)
material compuesto Combinación de dos o más sustancias que crea un nuevo material con propiedades diferentes.

compound A pure substance made of two or more elements chemically combined. (p. 40)
compuesto Sustancia pura formada por dos o más elementos combinados químicamente.

compound machine A device that combines two or more simple machines. (p. 433)
máquina compuesta Dispositivo que combina dos o más máquinas simples.

compression The part of a longitudinal wave where the particles of the medium are close together. (p. 513)
compresión Parte de una onda longitudinal donde las partículas del medio están muy juntas.

computer An electronic device that stores, processes, and retrieves information. (p. 763)
computadora Aparato electrónico que almacena, procesa y obtiene información.

computer network A group of computers connected by cables or telephone lines that allows people to share information. (p. 768)
red de computadoras Grupo de computadoras conectadas por cables o líneas telefónicas que permite que la gente comparta información.

computer programmer A person who uses computer languages to write programs, or sets of operation instructions, for computers. (p. 768)
programador de computadoras Persona que usa los lenguajes de computación para escribir programas o conjuntos de instrucciones de operaciones para computadoras.

concave lens A lens that is thinner in the center than at the edges. (p. 627)
lente cóncava Lente que es más fina en el centro que en los extremos.

concave mirror A mirror with a surface that curves inward. (p. 620)
espejo cóncavo Espejo cuya superficie se curva hacia dentro.

concentrated solution A mixture that has a lot of solute dissolved in it. (p. 230)
solución concentrada Mezcla que tiene muchos solutos disueltos en ella.

concentration The amount of one material in a certain volume of another material. (p. 208)
concentración Cantidad de un material en un cierto volumen de otro material.

condensation The change from the gaseous to the liquid state of matter. (pp. 80, 489)
condensación Cambio de la materia del estado gaseoso al estado líquido.

conduction The transfer of heat from one particle of matter to another. (p. 480); a method of charging an object by allowing electrons to flow by direct contact from one object to another object. (p. 686)
conducción Transferencia de calor desde una partícula de materia a otra; método para cargar un objeto que consiste en permitir que los electrones fluyan por contacto directo de un objeto a otro.

conductivity The ability of an object to transfer heat or electricity to another object. (p. 119)
conductividad Capacidad de un objeto para transferir calor o electricidad a otro objeto.

conductor A material that conducts heat well. (p. 483); a material through which charges can easily flow. (p. 695)
conductor Material que puede conducir bien el calor; material a través del cual pueden fluir las cargas eléctricas fácilmente.

cones Cells in the retina that respond to and detect color. (p. 630)

conos Células en la retina que responden y detectan el color.

conservation of charge The law that states that charges are neither created nor destroyed but only transferred from one material to another. (p. 686)
conservación de la carga eléctrica Ley que enuncia que las cargas no se crean ni se destruyen, sino que sólo se transfieren de un material a otro.

conservation of mass The principle stating that matter is not created or destroyed during a chemical reaction. (p. 196)
conservación de la masa Principio que enuncia que la materia no se crea ni se destruye durante una reacción química.

constraint Any factor that limits or restricts a design.
restricción Cualquier factor que limita o restringe un diseño. (p. 24)

constructive interference The interference that occurs when waves combine to make a wave with a larger amplitude. (p. 524)
interferencia constructiva Interferencia que ocurre cuando las ondas se combinan para crear una onda con una amplitud mayor.

controlled experiment An experiment in which only one variable is manipulated at a time. (p. 12)
experimento controlado Experimento en el cual sólo una variable es manipulada a la vez.

convection The transfer of heat by the movement of currents within a fluid. (p. 480)
convección Transferencia del calor a través del movimiento de las corrientes dentro de un líquido.

convection current A current caused by the rising of heated fluid and sinking of cooled fluid. (p. 480)
corriente de convección Movimiento circular causado por el ascenso de un líquido calentado y el descenso de un líquido enfriado.

convex lens A lens that is thicker in the center than at the edges. (p. 626)
lente convexa Lente que es más gruesa en el centro que en los extremos.

convex mirror A mirror with a surface that curves outward. (p. 622)
espejo convexo Espejo cuya superficie se curva hacia fuera.

cornea The transparent front surface of the eye. (p. 630)
córnea Superficie frontal transparente del ojo.

corrosion The gradual wearing away of a metal element due to a chemical reaction. (p. 119)
corrosión Desgaste gradual de un elemento metal debido a una reacción química.

corrosive The way in which acids react with some metals so as to eat away the metal. (p. 237)
corrosivo Forma en que reaccionan los ácidos con algunos metales, como si se comieran el metal.

covalent bond A chemical bond formed when two atoms share electrons. (p. 167)
enlace covalente Enlace químico que se forma cuando dos átomos comparten electrones.

crest The highest part of a transverse wave. (p. 512)
cresta Parte más alta de una onda transversal.

crystal An orderly, three-dimensional pattern of ions or atoms in a solid. (p. 162)
cristal Patrón ordenado tridimensional de iones o átomos en un sólido.

crystalline solid A solid that is made up of crystals in which particles are arranged in a regular, repeating pattern. (p. 72)
sólido cristalino Sólido constituido por cristales en los que las partículas están dispuestas en un patrón regular repetitivo.

D

data Facts, figures, and other evidence gathered through observations. (p. 13)
dato Hecho, cifra u otra evidencia reunida por medio de las observaciones.

decibel (dB) A unit used to compare the loudness of different sounds. (p. 548)
decibelio (dB) Unidad usada para comparar el volumen de diferentes sonidos.

decomposition A chemical reaction that breaks down compounds into simpler products. (p. 200)
descomposición Reacción química que descompone los compuestos en productos más simples.

density The ratio of the mass of a substance to its volume. (pp. 47, 383, 544)
densidad Razón de la masa de una sustancia a su volumen.

destructive interference The interference that occurs when two waves combine to make a wave with a smaller amplitude. (p. 525)
interferencia destructiva Interferencia que ocurre cuando dos ondas se combinan para crear una onda con una amplitud más pequeña.

diamond A form of the element carbon in which the atoms are arranged in a crystal structure. (p. 262)
diamante Forma del elemento del carbono en la cual los átomos de carbono están dispuestos en una estructura de cristal.

diatomic molecule A molecule consisting of two atoms. (p. 131)
molécula diatómica Molécula que tiene dos átomos.

diffraction The bending of waves as they move around a barrier or pass through an opening.
difracción Cambio de dirección de las ondas cuando rodean una barrera o pasan por una abertura. (p. 524)

diffuse reflection Reflection that occurs when parallel rays of light hit a rough surface and all reflect at different angles. (p. 618)
reflexión difusa Reflexión que ocurre cuando rayos de luz paralelos tocan una superficie rugosa y se reflejan en diferentes ángulos.

digestion The process that breaks down complex molecules of food into smaller molecules. (p. 251)
digestión Proceso que rompe las moléculas complejas de comida en moléculas más pequeñas.

digital signal Pulses of current used to represent information. (p. 751)
señal digital Pulsaciones de corriente que se usan para representar información.

dilute solution A mixture that has only a little solute dissolved in it. (p. 230)
solución diluida Mezcla que sólo tiene un poco de soluto disuelto en ella.

diode An electronic component that consists of layers of two types of semiconductors. (p. 753)
diodo Componente electrónico que consiste en capas de dos tipos de semiconductores.

direct current Current consisting of charges that flow in only one direction in a circuit. (p. 738)
corriente directa Corriente que consiste en cargas eléctricas que fluyen en una sola dirección en un circuito.

directly proportional A term used to describe the relationship between two variables whose graph is a straight line passing through the point (0, 0).
directamente proporcional Término empleado para describir la relación entre dos variables cuya gráfica forma una recta que pasa por elpunto (0, 0). (p. 92)

DNA DeoxyriboNucleic Acid, one type of nucleic acid.
ADN Ácido desoxirribonucleico, un tipo de ácido nucleico. (p. 289)

Doppler effect The change in frequency of a wave as its source moves in relation to an observer. (p. 550)
efecto Doppler Cambio en la frecuencia de una onda a medida que se mueve su fuente en relación al observador.

double bond A chemical bond formed when atoms share two pairs of electrons. (p. 168)
enlace doble Enlace químico formado cuando los átomos comparten dos pares de electrones.

dry cell An electrochemical cell in which the electrolyte is a paste. (p. 705)
celda seca Celda electroquímica en la que el electrolito es una pasta.

ductile A term used to describe a material that can be pulled out into a long wire. (p. 118)
dúctil Término usado para describir un material que se puede estirar hasta convertirlo en un alambre largo.

E

ear canal A narrow region leading from the outside of the human ear to the eardrum. (p. 558)
canal auditivo Región estrecha que va desde el exterior del oído humano hasta el tímpano.

eardrum A small, tightly stretched, drumlike membrane in the ear. (p. 558)
tímpano Membrana pequeña muy tensa con forma de tambor que está en el oído.

echo A reflected sound wave. (p. 542)
eco Onda sonora reflejada.

echolocation The use of reflected sound waves to determine distances or to locate objects. (p. 565)
ecolocación Uso de ondas sonoras reflejadas para determinar distancias o para localizar objetos.

efficiency The percentage of the input work that is converted to output work. (p. 417)
eficiencia Porcentaje del trabajo aportado que se convierte en trabajo producido.

elastic potential energy The energy of stretched or compressed objects. (p. 446)
energía elástica potencial Energía de los objetos estirados o comprimidos.

elasticity The ability of a material to bounce back after being disturbed. (p. 544)
elasticidad Capacidad de un material para volver a su forma original después de verse alterada.

electric circuit A complete, unbroken path through which electric charges can flow. (p. 694)
circuito eléctrico Camino completo y continuo a través del cual pueden fluir las cargas eléctricas.

electric current The continuous flow of electric charges through a material. (p. 693)
corriente eléctrica Flujo continuo de cargas eléctricas a través de un material.

electric field The region around a charged object where the object's electric force interacts with other charged objects. (p. 684)
campo eléctrico Región alrededor de un objeto cargado en donde su fuerza eléctrica interactúa con otros objetos con carga eléctrica.

electric force The attraction or repulsion between electric charges. (p. 684)
fuerza eléctrica Atracción o repulsión entre cargas eléctricas.

electric generator A device that converts mechanical energy into electrical energy. (p. 740)
generador eléctrico Instrumento que convierte la energía mecánica en energía eléctrica.

electric motor A device that transforms electrical energy to mechanical energy. (p. 732)
motor eléctrico Instrumento que convierte la energía eléctrica en energía mecánica.

electrical energy The energy of moving electrical charges. (pp. 60, 450, 730)
energía eléctrica Energía de cargas eléctricas que se mueven.

electrochemical cell A device that transforms chemical energy into electrical energy. (p. 704)
celda electroquímica Instrumento que convierte la energía química en energía eléctrica.

electrode A metal strip that conducts electricity. (p. 60); a metal part of an electrochemical cell, which gains or loses electrons. (p. 704)
electrodo Tira de metal que conduce la electricidad; parte metálica de una celda electroquímica que gana o pierde electrones.

electrolyte A liquid or paste that conducts electric current. (p. 704)
electrolito Líquido o pasta que conduce la corriente eléctrica.

electromagnet A magnet created by wrapping a coil of wire with a current around a ferromagnetic core.
electroimán Imán creado al enrollar una espiral de alambre con corriente alrededor de un núcleo ferromagnético. (p. 727)

electromagnetic energy A form of energy that travels through space as waves. (pp. 60, 451)
energía electromagnética Forma de energía que viaja a través del espacio en forma de ondas.

electromagnetic induction The process of generating an electric current from the motion of a conductor through a magnetic field. (p. 736)
inducción electromagnética Proceso por el cual se genera una corriente eléctrica a partir del movimiento de un conductor a través de un campo magnético.

electromagnetic radiation The energy transferred through space by electromagnetic waves. (p. 575)
radiación electromagnética Energía transferida por ondas electromagnéticas a través del espacio.

electromagnetic spectrum The complete range of electromagnetic waves placed in order of increasing frequency. (p. 579)
espectro electromagnético Gama completa de ondas electromagnéticas colocadas en orden de menor a mayor frecuencia.

electromagnetic wave Transverse waves that transfer electrical and magnetic energy. (p. 575)
ondas electromagnéticas Ondas transversales que transfieren energía eléctrica y magnética.

electromagnetism The relationship between electricity and magnetism. (p. 725)
electromagnetismo Relación entre la electricidad y el magnetismo.

electron A negatively charged particle that is found outside the nucleus of an atom. (pp. 104, 663)
electrón Partícula con carga negativa que se halla fuera del núcleo de un átomo.

electron dot diagram A representation of the valence electrons in an atom, using dots. (p. 151)
diagrama de puntos de electrones Representación del número de electrones de valencia en un átomo, usando puntos.

electronic signal A varying electric current that represents information. (p. 750)
señal electrónica Corriente eléctrica variable que representa información.

electronics The use of electric current to control, communicate, and process information. (p. 750)
electrónica Uso de la corriente eléctrica para controlar, comunicar y procesar información.

element A pure substance that cannot be broken down into other substances by chemical or physical means. (p. 38); one of about 100 basic materials that make up all matter. (p. 663)
elemento Sustancia pura que no se puede descomponer en otras sustancias por medios químicos o físicos; uno de aproximadamente 100 materiales básicos que componen toda la materia.

endothermic change A change in which energy is taken in. (p. 54)
cambio endotérmico Cambio en el que se absorbe energía.

endothermic reaction A reaction that absorbs energy in the form of heat. (p. 190)
reacción endotérmica Reacción que absorbe energía en forma de calor.

energy The ability to do work or cause change (pp. 54, 443, 511); the ability to move an object some distance. (p. 730)
energía Capacidad para realizar trabajo o causar un cambio; capacidad para mover un objeto una determinada distancia.

energy level A region of an atom in which electrons of the same energy are likely to be found. (p. 105)
nivel de energía Región alrededor del núcleo en la cual es probable que se encuentren los electrones con la misma energía.

energy transformation The process of changing one form of energy to another. (p. 454)
transformación energética Proceso de cambio de una forma de energía a otra.

engineer A person who is trained to use both technological and scientific knowledge to solve practical problems. (p. 22)
ingeniero Persona capacitada para usar conocimientos tecnológicos y científicos para resolver problemas prácticos.

enzyme A biological catalyst that lowers the activation energy of reactions in cells. (p. 209)
enzima Catalítico biológico que disminuye la energía de activación de las reacciones en las células.

ester An organic compound made by chemically combining an alcohol and an organic acid. (p. 271)
ester Compuesto orgánico formado químicamente al combinar un alcohol y un ácido orgánico.

evaporation The process that occurs when vaporization takes place only on the surface of a liquid.
evaporación Proceso que se da cuando la vaporización se efectúa únicamente en la superficie de un líquido. (pp. 78, 489)

exothermic change A change in which energy is given off. (p. 54)
cambio exotérmico Cambio en el que se libera energía.

exothermic reaction A reaction that releases energy in the form of heat. (p. 191)
reacción exotérmica Reacción que libera energía en forma de calor.

external combustion engine An engine powered by fuel burned outside the engine. (p. 492)
motor de combustión externa Motor alimentado por combustible que se quema fuera del motor.

eyepiece A lens that magnifies the image formed by the objective. (p. 634)
ocular Lente que aumenta la imagen formada por el objetivo.

F

Fahrenheit scale The temperature scale on which water freezes at 32 degrees and boils at 212 degrees.
escala Fahrenheit Escala de temperatura en la cual el agua se congela a los 32 grados y hierve a los 212 grados. (p. 474)

farsightedness A condition that causes a person to see nearby objects as blurry. (p. 632)
hipermetropía Condición que causa que una persona vea borrosos los objetos cercanos.

fatty acid An organic compound that is a monomer of a fat or oil. (p. 288)
ácido graso Compuesto orgánico que es un monómero de una grasa o aceite.

ferromagnetic material A material that is strongly attracted to a magnet, and which can be made into a magnet. (p. 665)
material ferromagnético Material que es atraído fuertemente a un imán y el cual puede transformarse en un imán.

fluid A substance that can easily flow. (pp. 73, 374)
fluido Sustancia que puede fluir con facilidad.

fluid friction Friction that occurs as an object moves through a fluid. (p. 342)
fricción de fluido Fricción que ocurre cuando un objeto se mueve a través de un fluido.

fluorescent light Light bulb that glows when an electric current causes ultraviolet rays to strike a coating inside a tube. (p. 590)
luz fluorescente Lámpara que se ilumina cuando una corriente eléctrica causa que los rayos ultravioleta choquen con el recubrimiento interior de un tubo.

focal point The point at which light rays parallel to the optical axis meet, or appear to meet, after being reflected (or refracted) by a mirror (or a lens).
punto de enfoque Punto en el que se encuentran, o parecen encontrarse, los rayos de luz paralelos al eje óptico después de reflejarse (o refractarse) en un espejo (o lente). (p. 620)

force A push or pull exerted on an object. (p. 334)
fuerza Empuje o atracción que se ejerce sobre un objeto.

fossil fuel A material such as coal that forms over millions of years from the remains of ancient plants and animals. (p. 462)
combustible fósil Material, como el carbón de piedra, que se forma durante millones de años a partir de los restos de animales y vegetales; se quema para liberar la energía química.

free fall The motion of a falling object when the only force acting on it is gravity. (p. 346)
caída libre Movimiento de un objeto que cae cuando la única fuerza que actúa sobre el mismo es la gravedad.

freezing The change from the liquid to the solid state of matter. (pp. 78, 488)
congelación Cambio de la materia del estado líquido al estado sólido.

frequency The number of complete waves that pass a given point in a certain amount of time. (p. 517)
frecuencia Número de ondas completas que pasan por un punto dado en cierto tiempo.

frequency modulation A method of transmitting signals by changing the frequency of a wave. (p. 595)
frecuencia modulada Método de transmisión de señales por el cual se cambia la frecuencia de una onda.

friction The force that one surface exerts on another when the two surfaces rub against each other. (p. 341); a method of charging an object by rubbing it against another object. (p. 686)
fricción Fuerza que ejerce una superficie sobre otra cuando se frotan una contra otra; método para cargar con electricidad un objeto que consiste en frotarlo contra otro objecto.

fuel A material that releases energy when it burns. (p. 213)
combustible Material que libera energía cuando se quema.

fulcrum The fixed point around which a lever pivots. (p. 426)
fulcro Punto fijo en torno al cual gira una palanca.

fullerene A form of carbon that consists of atoms arranged in the shape of a hollow sphere. (p. 263)
fullereno Forma del elemento del carbono que consiste en átomos de carbono colocados en forma de esfera hueca.

fundamental tone The lowest natural frequency of an object. (p. 553)
tono fundamental Frecuencia natural más baja de un objeto.

fuse A safety device with a thin metal strip that will melt if too much current passes through a circuit.
fusible Elemento de seguridad que tiene una tira metálica delgada que se derrite si pasa demasiada corriente a través de un circuito. (p. 717)

G

galvanometer A device that uses an electromagnet to detect small amounts of current. (p. 731)
galvanómetro Instrumento que usa un electroimán para detectar pequeñas cantidades de corriente.

gamma radiation A type of nuclear radiation made of high-energy waves. (p. 140)
radiación gamma Tipo de radiación nuclear hecha de ondas de alta energía.

gamma rays Electromagnetic waves with the shortest wavelengths and highest frequencies. (p. 584)
rayos gamma Ondas electromagnéticas con la menor longitud de onda y la mayor frecuencia.

gas A state of matter with no definite shape or volume. (p. 75)
gas Estado de la materia sin forma ni volumen definidos.

glucose A simple carbohydrate; the monomer of many complex carbohydrates. (p. 285)
glucosa Carbohidrato simple; monómero de muchos carbohidratos complejos.

graph A diagram that shows how two variables are related. (p. 90)
gráfica Diagrama que muestra la relación entre dos variables.

graphite A form of the element carbon in which each carbon atom is bonded tightly to three other carbon atoms in flat layers. (p. 262)
grafito Forma del elemento carbono en el cual un átomo de carbono se une estrechamente a otros tres átomos de carbono en capas llanas.

gravitational potential energy Potential energy that depends on the height of an object. (p. 445)
energía potencial gravitatoria Energía potencial que depende de la altura de un objeto.

gravity The force that pulls objects toward each other. (p. 344)
gravedad Fuerza que atrae objetos entre sí.

grounded Allowing charges to flow directly from the circuit into Earth in the event of a short circuit.
conectado a tierra Permitir que la carga fluya directamente del circuito a la Tierra en el caso de un cortocircuito. (p. 716)

group Elements in the same vertical column of the periodic table; also called a family. (p. 114)
grupo Elementos en la misma columna vertical de la tabla periódica; también llamado familia.

H

halogen An element found in Group 17 of the periodic table. (p. 133)
halógeno Elemento que se encuentra en el Grupo 17 de la tabla periódica.

hardware The permanent components of a computer, including the central processing unit and input, output, and memory storage devices.
hardware Componentes permanentes de una computadora, incluyendo la unidad central de procesamiento, dispositivos de entrada y salida, y dispositivos de registro de memoria. (p. 765)

heat Thermal energy that is transferred from matter at a higher temperature to matter at a lower temperature. (p. 475)
calor Energía térmica que se transfiere desde una materia a mayor temperatura a una materia a menor temperatura.

heat engine A device that converts thermal energy into mechanical energy. (p. 491)
motor térmico Máquina que convierte la energía térmica en energía mecánica.

hertz (Hz) Unit of measurement for frequency. (p. 517)
hercio (Hz) Unidad de media de frecuencia.

heterogeneous mixture A mixture in which pure substances are unevenly distributed throughout the mixture. (p. 41)
mezcla heterogénea Mezcla en la cual las sustancias puras están distribuidas desigualmente.

hologram A three-dimensional photograph created using lasers. (p. 638)
holograma Fotografía tridimensional creada usando rayos láser.

homogeneous mixture A mixture in which substance are evenly distributed throughout the mixture. (p. 41)
mezcla homogénea Mezcla en la cual las sustancias químicas están distribuidas uniformemente.

hydraulic system A system that multiplies force by transmitting pressure from a small surface area through a confined fluid to a larger surface area.
sistema hidraúlico Sistema que multiplica la fuerza transmitiendo la presión de un área total pequeña a un área total mayor a través de un fluido confinado. (p. 391)

hydrocarbon An organic compound that contains only carbon and hydrogen. (p. 266)
hidrocarburo Compuesto orgánico que contiene sólo carbono e hidrógeno.

hydrogen ion A positively charged ion (H^+) formed of a hydrogen atom that has lost its electron.
ión hidrógeno Ión con carga positiva (H^+) formado por un átomo de hidrógeno que ha perdido su electrón. (p. 242)

hydroxide ion A negatively charged ion made of oxygen and hydrogen (OH^-). (p. 243)
ión hidróxido Ión con carga negativa formado de oxígeno e hidrógeno (OH^-).

hydroxyl group An —OH group, found in alcohols.
grupo hidroxilo Grupo —OH, que se haya en los alcoholes. (p. 270)

hypothesis A possible explanation for a set of observations or answer to a scientific question. (p. 11)
hipótesis Explicación posible a un conjunto de observaciones o respuesta a una pregunta científica.

I

illuminated Word used to describe an object that can be seen because it reflects light. (p. 588)
iluminado Palabra que se usa para describir un objeto que se puede ver porque refleja la luz.

image A copy of an object formed by reflected or refracted rays of light. (p. 619)
imagen Copia de un objeto formado por rayos de luz que se reflejan y se refractan.

incandescent light Light bulb that glows when a filament inside it gets white hot. (p. 588)
luz incandescente Lámpara que se ilumina cuando un filamento interior se calienta tanto que se pone blanco.

inclined plane A simple machine that is a flat, sloped surface. (p. 423)
plano inclinado Máquina simple que consiste en una superficie plana con pendiente.

index of refraction A measure of the amount a ray of light bends when it passes from one medium to another. (p. 624)
índice de refracción Medida de la inclinación de un rayo de luz cuando pasa de un medio a otro.

indicator A compound that changes color in the presence of an acid or a base. (p. 238)
indicador Compuesto que cambia de color en presencia de un ácido o una base.

induction A method of charging an object by means of the electric field of another object. (p. 686)
inducción Método para cargar un objeto mediante el campo eléctrico de otro objeto.

inertia The tendency of an object to resist any change in its motion. (p. 350)
inercia Tendencia de un objeto a resistir cualquier cambio en su movimiento.

inferring The process of making an inference, an interpretation based on observations and prior knowledge. (p. 7)
inferir Proceso de realizar una inferencia; interpretación basada en observaciones y en el conocimiento previo.

infrared rays Electromagnetic waves with wavelengths shorter than radio waves, but longer than visible light. (p. 581)
rayos infrarrojos Ondas electromagnéticas con longitud de onda menor que las ondas de radio, pero mayor que la de la luz visible.

infrasound Sound waves with frequencies below 20 Hz. (p. 549)
infrasonido Ondas sonoras con frecuencias menores de 20 Hz.

inhibitor A material that decreases the rate of a reaction. (p. 209)
inhibidor Material que disminuye la velocidad de una reacción.

input device A device that feeds data to a CPU
dispositivo de entrada Dispositivo que envía información a una CPU; un teclado es un dispositivo de entrada. (p. 765)

input force The force exerted on a machine. (p. 413)
fuerza aplicada Fuerza que se ejerce sobre una máquina.

input work The work done on a machine as the input force acts through the input distance.
trabajo aportado Trabajo realizado sobre una máquina mientras la fuerza aplicada actúa a lo largo de la distancia de aplicación. (p. 413)

instantaneous speed The speed of an object at one instant of time. (p. 313)
rapidez instantánea Velocidad de un objeto en un instante de tiempo.

insulator A material that does not conduct heat well. (p. 483); a material through which charges cannot easily flow. (p. 695)
aislante Material que no conduce bien el calor; material a través del cual las cargas eléctricas no pueden fluir con facilidad.

integrated circuit A circuit that has been manufactured on a chip (a tiny slice of semiconductor), which can contain thousands of diodes, transistors, and resistors. (p. 754)
circuito integrado Circuito que ha sido fabricado en un chip (una diminuta placa de un semiconductor), que puede contener miles de diodos, transistores y resistores.

intensity The amount of energy per second carried through a unit area by a wave. (p. 547)
intensidad Cantidad de energía por segundo que lleva una onda a través de una unidad de área.

interference The interaction between waves that meet. (p. 524)
interferencia Interacción entre ondas que se encuentran.

internal combustion engine An engine that burns fuel inside cylinders within the engine. (p. 492)
motor de combustión interna Motor que quema el combustible dentro de cilindros, dentro del motor.

International System of Units (SI) The system of units (SI) used by scientists to measure the properties of matter. (pp. 45, 310)
Sistema Internacional de Unidades (SI) Sistema de unidades usado por los científicos para medir las propiedades de la materia.

Internet An international computer network that shares data, information, and news. (p. 769)
Internet Red de computadoras internacional que comparte datos, información y noticias.

ion An atom or group of atoms that has become electrically charged. (p. 159)
ión Átomo o grupo de átomos con carga eléctrica.

ionic bond The attraction between oppositely charged ions. (p. 160)
enlace iónico Atracción entre iones con cargas opuestas.

ionic compound A compound that consists of positive and negative ions. (p. 160)
compuesto iónico Compuesto que tiene iones positivos y negativos.

iris The ring of muscle that controls the size of the pupil and gives the eye its color. (p. 630)
iris Anillo muscular que controla el tamaño de la pupila y da el color al ojo.

isomer Compounds that have the same chemical formula but different structural formulas. (p. 268)
isómero Compuestos que tienen la misma fórmula química pero diferentes fórmulas estructurales.

isotope An atom with the same number of protons and a different number of neutrons from other atoms of the same element. (p. 108)
isótopo Átomo con el mismo número de protones y un número diferente de neutrones que otros átomos del mismo elemento.

J

joule A unit of work equal to one newton-meter. (p. 409)
julio Unidad de trabajo igual a un newton-metro.

K

Kelvin scale The temperature scale on which zero is the temperature at which no more energy can be removed from matter. (p. 474)
escala Kelvin Escala de temperatura en la cual el cero es la temperatura a la cual no se puede quitar más energía de la materia.

kinetic energy Energy that an object has due to its motion. (pp. 59, 443)
energía cinética Energía que tiene un objeto debido a su movimiento.

L

larynx Two folds of tissue that make up the human voice box. (p. 549)
laringe Dos pliegues de tejido que forman la caja sonora humana.

laser A device that produces a narrow beam of coherent light. (p. 636)
láser Aparato que produce un delgado rayo de luz coherente.

law of conservation of energy The rule that energy cannot be created or destroyed. (p. 458)
ley de la conservación de la energía Regla que dice que la energía no se puede crear ni destruir.

law of conservation of mass The principle that the total amount of matter is neither created nor destroyed during any chemical or physical change. (p. 53)
ley de conservación de la masa Principio que enuncia que la cantidad de materia total no se crea ni se destruye durante cambios químicos o físicos.

law of conservation of momentum The rule that in the absence of outside forces the total momentum of objects that interact does not change. (p. 357)
ley de la conservación del momento Regla según la cual en ausencia de fuerzas externas, el momento total de los objetos no cambia en su interacción.

law of reflection The rule that the angle of reflection equals the angle of incidence. (p. 522)
ley de reflexión Regla que enuncia que el ángulo de reflexión es igual al ángulo de incidencia.

lens A curved piece of glass or other transparent material that is used to refract light. (p. 626)
lente Trozo de cristal u otro material transparente curvado que se usa para refractar la luz.

lever A simple machine that consists of a rigid bar that pivots about a fixed point. (p. 426)
palanca Máquina simple que consiste en una barra rígida que gira en torno a un punto fijo.

lift An upward force. (p. 395)
fuerza de elevación Fuerza ascendente.

lipid An energy-rich organic compound made of carbon, oxygen, and hydrogen. Fats, oils, waxes, and cholesterol are lipids. (p. 288)
lípido Compuesto orgánico rico en energía hecho de carbono, oxígeno e hidrógeno; las grasas, aceites, ceras y colesterol son lípidos.

liquid A state of matter that has no definite shape but has a definite volume. (p. 73)
líquido Estado de la materia que no tiene forma definida pero sí volumen definido.

longitudinal wave A wave that moves a medium in a direction parallel to the direction in which the wave travels. (p. 513)
onda longitudinal Onda que mueve el medio en dirección paralela a la dirección en la que viaja la onda.

loudness Perception of the energy of a sound. (p. 546)
volumen Percepción de la energía de un sonido.

luminous Word used to describe an object that can be seen because it emits light. (p. 588)
luminoso Palabra que se usa para describir un objeto que se puede ver porque emite luz.

M

machine A device that changes the amount of force exerted, the distance over which a force is exerted, or the direction in which force is exerted. (p. 413)
máquina Dispositivo que altera la cantidad de fuerza ejercida, la distancia sobre la que se ejerce la fuerza o la dirección en la que se ejerce la fuerza.

magnet Any material that attracts iron and materials that contain iron. (p. 655)
imán Material que atrae hierro o materiales semejantes.

magnetic declination The angle between geographic north and the north to which a compass needle points. (p. 672)
declinación magnética Ángulo entre el norte geográfico y el norte hacia donde a punta la aguja de una brújula.

magnetic domain A region in which the magnetic fields of all atoms are lined up in the same direction. (p. 664)
dominio magnético Área en la que los campos magnéticos de todos los átomos están alineados en la misma dirección.

magnetic field The region around a magnet where the magnetic force is exerted. (p. 657)
campo magnético Área alrededor de un imán en la cual se ejerce la fuerza magnética.

magnetic field lines Invisible lines that map out the magnetic field around a magnet. (p. 657)
líneas del campo magnético Líneas invisibles que representan el campo magnético alrededor de un imán.

magnetic force A force produced when magnetic poles interact. (p. 656)
fuerza magnética Fuerza que se produce cuando interactúan los polos magnéticos.

magnetic pole The ends of a magnetic object, where the magnetic force is strongest. (p. 656)
polo magnético Extremo de un objeto magnético, donde la fuerza magnética es mayor.

magnetosphere The region of Earth's magnetic field shaped by the solar wind. (p. 674)
magnetosfera Área del campo magnético de la Tierra formada por el viento solar.

malleable A term used to describe material that can be pounded into shapes. (p. 118)
maleable Término usado para describir el material al que se le puede dar forma.

manipulated variable The one factor that a scientist changes during an experiment (p. 12)
variable manipulada Único factor que un científico cambia durante un experimento.

mass A measure of how much matter is in an object. (pp. 45, 344)
masa Medida de cuánta materia hay en un objeto.

mass number The sum of protons and neutrons in the nucleus of an atom. (p. 108)
número de masa Suma de protones y neutrones en el núcleo de un átomo.

matter Anything that has mass and occupies space.
materia Cualquier cosa que tiene masa y ocupa espacio. (pp. 34, 184, 459)

mechanical advantage The number of times a machine increases a force exerted on it. (p. 416)
ventaja mecánica Número de veces que una máquina amplifica la fuerza que se ejerce sobre ella.

mechanical digestion The physical process that tears, grinds, and mashes large pieces of food into smaller ones. (p. 251)
digestión mecánica Proceso físico que rompe, tritura y muele grandes pedazos de comida en pedazos más pequeños.

mechanical energy Kinetic or potential energy associated with the motion or position of an object.
energía mecánica Energía cinética o potencial asociada con el movimiento o posición de un objeto. (pp. 447, 730)

mechanical wave A wave that requires a medium through which to travel. (p. 511)
onda mecánica Onda que necesita un medio por el cual viajar.

medium The material through which a wave travels. (p. 511)
medio Material a través del cual viaja una onda.

melting The change from the solid to the liquid state of matter. (pp. 77, 488)
fusión Cambio en el estado de la materia de sólido a líquido.

melting point The temperature at which a substance changes from a solid to a liquid. (p. 77)
punto de fusión Temperatura a la que una sustancia cambia de estado sólido a líquido.

metal A class of elements characterized by physical properties that include shininess, malleability, ductility, and conductivity. (p. 118)
metal Clase de elementos caracterizados por las propiedades físicas que incluye brillo, maleabilidad, ductilidad y conductividad.

metallic bond An attraction between a positive metal ion and the electrons surrounding it.
enlace metálico Atracción entre un ión metálico positivo y los electrones que lo rodean. (pp. 172, 174)

metalloid An element that has some characteristics of both metals and nonmetals. (p. 135)
metaloide Elemento que tiene algunas características de los metales y de los no metales.

meter The basic SI unit of length. (p. 311)
metro Unidad básica de longitud del SI.

microscope An optical instrument that forms enlarged images of tiny objects. (p. 635)
microscopio Instrumento óptico que forma imágenes aumentadas de objetos diminutos.

microwaves Radio waves with the shortest wavelengths and the highest frequencies. (p. 580)
microondas Ondas de radio con la menor longitud de onda y la mayor frecuencia.

mirage An image of a distant object caused by refraction of light as it travels through air of varying temperature. (p. 625)
espejismo Imagen de un objeto distante causado por la refracción de la luz cuando viaja por el aire a temperaturas cambiantes.

mixture Two or more substances that are mixed together but not chemically combined. (p. 41)
mezcla Dos o más sustancias que están mezcladas, pero que no están combinadas químicamente.

molecular compound A compound that is composed of molecules. (p. 168)
compuesto molecular Compuesto que contiene moléculas.

molecule A neutral particle made of two or more atoms joined by covalent bonds. (pp. 39, 167)
molécula Partícula neutral hecha de dos o más átomos que se unen por enlaces covalentes.

momentum The product of an object's mass and velocity. (p. 356)
momento Producto de la masa de un objeto por su velocidad.

monomer One molecule that makes up the links in a polymer chain. (p. 272)
monómero Molécula que forma los enlaces en una cadena polímera.

motion The state in which one object's distance from another is changing. (p. 309)
movimiento Estado en el que la distancia entre un objeto y otro va cambiando.

music A set of tones and overtones combined in ways that are pleasing. (p. 553)
música Conjunto de tonos y sobretonos combinados de manera agradable.

N

nanotube A form of carbon that consists of atoms in the form of a long, hollow cylinder. (p. 263)
nanotubo Forma del carbono que consiste en átomos en forma de un cilindro largo y hueco.

nearsightedness A condition that causes a person to see distant objects as blurry. (p. 632)
miopía Condición que causa que una persona vea borrosos los objetos lejanos.

neon light Glass tube containing neon gas that produces light. (p. 591)
luz de neón Tubo de vidrio que contiene gas neón que produce luz.

net force The overall force on an object when all the individual forces acting on it are added together.
fuerza neta Fuerza total que actúa sobre un objeto cuando se suman las fuerzas individuales que actúan sobre él. (p. 335)

neutralization A reaction of an acid with a base, yielding a solution that is not as acidic or basic as the starting solutions were. (p. 246)
neutralización Reacción de un ácido con una base, que produce una solución que no es ácida ni básica, como lo eran las soluciones originales.

neutron A small particle in the nucleus of the atom, with no electrical charge. (pp. 106, 663)
neutrón Partícula pequeña en el núcleo del átomo, que no tiene carga eléctrica.

newton A unit of measure that equals the force required to accelerate 1 kilogram of mass at 1 meter per second per second. (p. 335)
newton Unidad de medida que es igual a la fuerza necesaria para acelerar 1 kilogramo de masa 1 metro por segundo cada segundo.

noble gas An element in Group 18 of the periodic table. (p. 134)
gas noble Elemento del Grupo 18 de la tabla periódica.

node A point of zero amplitude on a standing wave.
nodo Punto de amplitud cero en una onda estacionaria. (p. 526)

nonmetal An element that lacks most of the properties of a metal. (p. 129)
no metal Elemento que carece de la mayoría de las propiedades de un metal.

nonpolar bond A covalent bond in which electrons are shared equally. (p. 170)
enlace no polar Enlace covalente en el que los electrones se comparte por igual.

nuclear energy The potential energy stored in the nucleus of an atom. (p. 451)
energía nuclear Energía potencial almacenada en el núcleo de un átomo.

nuclear fusion The process in which two atomic nuclei combine to form a larger nucleus, forming a heavier element and releasing huge amounts of energy. (p. 116)
fusión nuclear Proceso en el cual dos núcleos atómicos se combinan para formar un núcleo mayor; forman un elemento más pesado y liberan grandes cantidades de energía.

nucleic acid A very large organic compound made up of carbon, oxygen, hydrogen, nitrogen, and phosphorus; examples are DNA and RNA.
ácido nucleico Compuesto orgánico muy grande hecho de carbono, oxígeno, hidrógeno, nitrógeno y fósforo; ejemplos son ADN and ARN. (p. 289)

nucleotide An organic compound that is one of the monomers of nucleic acids. (p. 290)
nucleótido Compuesto orgánico que es uno de los monómeros de los ácidos nucleicos.

nucleus The central core of the atom. (pp. 105, 663)
núcleo Centro de un átomo.

O

objective A lens that gathers light from an object and forms a real image. (p. 634)
objetivo Lente que reúne la luz de un objeto y forma una imagen real.

observing The process of using one or more of your senses to gather information. (p. 7)
observar Proceso de usar uno o más de tus sentidos para reunir información.

Ohm's law The law that states that resistance is equal to voltage divided by current. (p. 707)
ley de Ohm Ley que enuncia que la resistencia es igual al voltaje dividido por la corriente.

opaque material A material that reflects or absorbs all of the light that strikes it. (p. 611)
material opaco Material que refleja o absorbe toda la luz que llega a él.

open system A system in which matter can enter from or escape to the surroundings. (p. 197)
sistema abierto Sistema en el que la materia puede entrar desde el medio que la rodea o salir hacia él.

optic nerve Short, thick nerve that carries signals from the eye to the brain. (p. 630)
nervio óptico Nervio corto y grueso que lleva señales del ojo al cerebro.

optical axis An imaginary line that divides a mirror in half. (p. 620)
eje óptico Recta imaginaria que divide un espejo por la mitad.

optical fiber A long, thin strand of glass or plastic that can carry light for long distances without allowing the light to escape. (p. 640)
fibra óptica Filamento largo y delgado de vidrio o plástico que puede transportar luz a través de largas distancias sin dejarla escapar.

organic acid A substituted hydrocarbon with one or more of the —COOH group of atoms. (p. 271)
ácido orgánico Hidrocarburo sustituto que tiene uno o más grupos de átomos —COOH.

organic compounds Most compounds that contain carbon. (p. 265)
compuesto orgánico La mayoría de los compuestos que contienen carbono.

origin The (0, 0) point on a line graph. (p. 92)
origen Punto (0, 0) en una gráfica lineal.

output device A device that presents data from a computer. (p. 765)
dispositivo de salida Dispositivo que presenta información de una computadora; un monitor es un dispositivo de salida.

output force The force exerted on an object by a machine. (p. 413)
fuerza desarrollada Fuerza que una máquina ejerce sobre un objeto.

output work The work done by a machine as the output force acts through the output distance.
trabajo producido Trabajo que una máquina efectúa mientras la fuerza desarrollada actúa a lo largo de la distancia desarrollada. (p. 413)

overtone A natural frequency that is a multiple of the fundamental tone's frequency. (p. 553)
armónico Frecuencia natural que es un múltiplo de la frecuencia del tono fundamental.

P

P wave A longitudinal seismic wave. (p. 531)
onda P Onda sísmica longitudinal.

parallel circuit An electric circuit with multiple paths. (p. 711)
circuito paralelo Circuito eléctrico con caminos múltiples.

particle accelerator A machine that moves atomic nuclei at higher and higher speeds until they crash into one another, sometimes forming heavier elements. (p. 124)
acelerador de partículas Máquina que mueve los núcleos atómicos a velocidades cada vez más altas hasta que chocan entre ellas, a veces forman elementos más pesados.

pascal A unit of pressure equal to 1 newton per square meter. (p. 373)
pascal Unidad de presión igual a 1 newton por metro cuadrado.

Pascal's principle The rule that when force is applied to a confined fluid, the increase in pressure is transmitted equally to all parts of the fluid.
principio de Pascal Regla que enuncia que cuando se aplica una fuerza a un fluido confinado, el aumento en la presión es transmitida por igual a todas las partes del fluido. (p. 389)

period A horizontal row of elements in the periodic table. (p. 114)
período Fila horizontal de los elementos en la tabla periódica.

periodic table A chart of the elements showing the repeating pattern of their properties. (p. 111)
tabla periódica Tabla de los elementos que muestra el patrón repetido de sus propiedades.

permanent magnet A magnet made of material that keeps its magnetism. (p. 666)
imán permanente Imán hecho de un material que mantiene su magnetismo.

pH scale A range of values used to express the concentration of hydrogen ions in a solution. (p. 244)
escala pH Rango de valores usados para expresar la concentración de iones de hidrógeno que hay en una solución.

photoelectric effect The ejection of electrons from a substance when light is shined on it. (p. 577)
efecto fotoeléctrico Expulsión de electrones de una sustancia cuando le da la luz.

photon A tiny particle or packet of light energy.
fotón Partícula diminuta o paquete de energía luminosa. (p. 577)

physical change A change in a substance that does not change its identity. (pp. 51, 186)
cambio físico Cambio en una sustancia que no cambia su identidad.

physical property A characteristic of a pure substance that can be observed without changing it into another substance. (pp. 36, 185)
propiedad física Característica de una sustancia pura que se puede observar sin convertirla en otra sustancia.

physics The study of matter and energy and how they interact. (p. 8)
física Estudio de la materia y de la energía, y de cómo interactúan.

pigment A colored substance used to color other materials. (p. 615)
pigmento Sustancia con color que se usa para colorear otros materiales.

pitch Perception of the frequency of a sound. (p. 548)
tono Percepción de la frecuencia de un sonido.

plane mirror A flat mirror that produces an upright, virtual image the same size as an object. (p. 619)
espejo plano Espejo liso que produce una imagen virtual vertical del mismo tamaño que el objeto.

plasma A gas-like state of matter consisting of a mixture of free electrons and atoms that are stripped of their electrons. (p. 116)
plasma Estado de la materia similar al gas que consiste en la mezcla de electrones libres y átomos desprovistos de sus electrones.

plastic A synthetic polymer that can be molded or shaped. (p. 277)
plástico Polímero sintético que se puede moldear o se le puede dar forma.

polar bond A covalent bond in which electrons are shared unequally. (p. 170)
enlace polar Enlace covalente en el que los electrones se comparten de forma desigual.

polarized light Light that vibrates in only one direction. (p. 576)
luz polarizada Luz que vibra en una sola dirección.

polyatomic ion An ion that is made of more than one atom. (p. 159)
ión poliatómico Ión que está hecho de más de un átomo.

polymer A large molecule in which many smaller molecules are bonded together. (p. 272)
polímero Molécula grande en la que muchas moléculas más pequeñas están unidas.

potential energy Stored energy that results from the position or shape of an object. (pp. 59, 445)
energía potencial Energía almacenada que es el resultado de la posición o forma de un objeto.

power The rate at which one form of energy is transformed into another; the rate at which work is done. (pp. 409, 712)
potencia Razón a la que se realiza trabajo.

precipitate A solid that forms from a solution during a chemical reaction. (p. 188)
precipitado Sólido que se forma de una solución durante una reacción química.

predicting The process of forecasting what will happen in the future based on past experience or evidence. (p. 8)
predecir Proceso de pronosticar lo que va a suceder en el futuro, basado en la experiencia pasada o en evidencia.

pressure The force exerted on a surface divided by the total area over which the force is exerted.
presión Fuerza ejercida sobre una superficie dividida por el área total sobre la cual se ejerce la fuerza. (pp. 85, 373)

primary colors Three colors that can be used to make any other color. (p. 614)
colores primarios Tres colores que se pueden usar para hacer cualquier color.

product A substance formed as a result of a chemical reaction. (p. 195)
producto Sustancia formada como resultado de una reacción química.

projectile An object that is thrown. (p. 348)
proyectil Objeto que es lanzado.

protein An organic compound that is a polymer of amino acids. (p. 276)
proteína Compuesto orgánico que es un polímero de aminoácidos.

proton A positively charged particle that is part of an atom's nucleus. (pp. 105, 663)
protón Partícula con carga positiva ubicada en el núcleo de un átomo.

prototype A working model used to test a design.
prototipo Modelo funcional usado para probar un diseño. (p. 25)

pulley A simple machine that consists of a grooved wheel with a rope or cable wrapped around it. (p. 430)
polea Máquina simple que consiste en una rueda con un surco en el que entra una cuerda o cable.

pupil The opening in the center of the iris through which light enters the inside of the eye. (p. 630)
pupila Abertura en el centro del iris a través de la cual entra la luz en el ojo.

Q

qualitative observation An observation that deals with characteristics that are not expressed in numbers. (p. 7)
observación cualitativa Observación que se centra en las características que no se pueden expresar con números.

quantitative observation An observation that deals with a number or amount. (p. 7)
observación cuantitativa Observación que se centra en un número o cantidad.

R

radar A system that uses reflected radio waves to detect objects and measure their distance and speed.
radar Sistema que usa ondas de radio reflejadas para detectar objetos y medir su distancia y velocidad. (p. 580)

radiation The transfer of energy by electromagnetic waves. (p. 480)
radiación Transferencia de energía a través de ondas electromagnéticas.

radio waves Electromagnetic waves with the longest wavelengths and lowest frequencies. (p. 580)
ondas de radio Ondas electromagnéticas con la mayor longitud de onda y la menor frecuencia.

radioactive decay The process in which the atomic nuclei of unstable isotopes release fast-moving particles and energy. (p. 139)
desintegración radiactiva Proceso por el cual los núcleos atómicos de isótopos inestables liberan partículas de rápido movimiento y gran cantidad de energía.

radioactivity The spontaneous emission of radiation by an unstable atomic nucleus. (p. 139)
radiactividad Emisión espontánea de radiación por un núcleo atómico inestable.

rarefaction The part of a longitudinal wave where the particles of the medium are far apart. (p. 513)
rarefacción Parte de una onda longitudinal donde las partículas del medio están alejadas.

ray A straight line used to represent a light wave.
rayo Línea recta que se usa para representar una onda de luz. (p. 618)

reactant A substance that enters into a chemical reaction. (p. 195)
reactante Sustancia que participa en una reacción química.

reactivity The ease and speed with which an element combines, or reacts, with other elements and compounds. (p. 119)
reactividad Facilidad y rapidez con las que un elemento se combina, o reacciona, con otros elementos y compuestos.

real image An upside-down image formed where rays of light meet. (p. 621)
imagen real Imagen invertida formada donde se encuentran los rayos de luz.

receiver A device that receives radio waves and converts them into a sound or light signal. (p. 757)
receptor Aparato que recibe las ondas de radio y las convierte en señales de sonido o de luz.

reference point A place or object used for comparison to determine if an object is in motion. (p. 309)
punto de referencia Lugar u objeto usado como punto de comparación para determinar si un objeto está en movimiento.

reflecting telescope A telescope that uses a concave mirror to gather light from distant objects. (p. 634)
telescopio reflector Telescopio que usa un espejo cóncavo para reunir luz de los objetos distantes.

reflection The bouncing back of an object or wave when it hits a surface through which it cannot pass. (p. 522)
reflexión Rebote de un objeto o una onda cuando golpea una superficie por la cual no puede pasar.

refracting telescope A telescope that uses two convex lenses to form images. (p. 634)
telescopio refractor Telescopio que usa dos lentes convexas para formar imágenes.

refraction The bending of waves as they enter a new medium at an angle. (p. 523)
refracción Cambio de dirección de las ondas cuando entran en un nuevo medio en un determinado ángulo.

refrigerant The substance that absorbs and releases heat in a cooling system. (p. 495)
refrigerante Sustancia que absorbe y elimina calor en un sistema de enfriamiento.

regular reflection Reflection that occurs when parallel rays of light hit a smooth surface and all reflect at the same angle. (p. 618)
reflexión regular Reflexión que ocurre cuando rayos de luz paralelos chocan contra una superficie lisa y se reflejan en el mismo ángulo.

replacement A reaction in which one element replaces another in a compound or when two elements in different compounds trade places. (p. 200)
reemplazo sustitución Reacción en la que un elemento reemplaza a otro en un compuesto o dos elementos de diferentes compuestos se intercambian.

resistance The measurement of how difficult it is for charges to flow through a material. (p. 698)
resistencia Medida de lo difícil que es para las cargas eléctricas fluir a través de un material.

resonance The increase in the amplitude of a vibration that occurs when external vibrations match an object's natural frequency. (p. 527)
resonancia Aumento en la amplitud de vibración que ocurre cuando vibraciones externas se corresponden con la frecuencia natural de un objeto.

responding variable The factor that changes as a result of changes to the manipulated, or independent, variable in an experiment. (p. 12)
variable respuesta Factor que cambia como resultado del cambio de la variable manipulada, o independiente, en un experimento.

retina The layer of cells that lines the inside of the eyeball. (p. 630)
retina Capa de células que recubre el interior del globo ocular.

reverberation The echoes of a sound that are heard after a sound source stops producing sound waves.
reverberación Ecos de un sonido que son oídos después de que la fuente sonora deja de producir ondas sonoras. (p. 556)

RNA Ribonucleic acid, a type of nucleic acid. (p. 289)
ARN Ácido ribonucleico; un tipo de ácido nucleico.

rods Cells in the retina that detect dim light. (p. 630)
bastones Células de la retina que detectan la luz tenue.

rolling friction Friction that occurs when an object rolls over a surface. (p. 342)
fricción de rodamiento Fricción que ocurre cuando un objeto rueda sobre una superficie.

S

S wave A transverse seismic wave. (p. 531)
onda S Onda sísmica transversal.

salt An ionic compound made from the neutralization of an acid with a base. (p. 247)
sal Compuesto iónico formado por la neutralización de un ácido con una base.

satellite Any object that orbits around another object in space. (p. 363)
satélite Cualquier objeto que orbita alrededor de otro objeto en el espacio.

saturated hydrocarbon A hydrocarbon in which all the bonds between carbon atoms are single bonds. (p. 269)
hidrocarburo saturado Hidrocarburo en el que todos los enlaces entre los átomos de carbono son enlaces simples.

saturated solution A mixture that contains as much dissolved solute as is possible at a given temperature. (p. 231)
solución saturada Mezcla que contiene la mayor cantidad posible de soluto disuelto a una temperatura determinada.

science A way of learning about the natural world through observations and logical reasoning; leads to a body of knowledge. (p. 7)
ciencia Estudio del mundo natural a través de observaciones y del razonamiento lógico; conduce a un conjunto de conocimientos.

scientific inquiry The ongoing process of discovery in science. (p. 10)
investigación científica Proceso continuo de descubrimiento en la ciencia.

scientific law A statement that describes what scientists expect to happen every time under a particular set of conditions. (p. 15)
ley científica Enunciado que describe lo que los científicos esperan que suceda cada vez que se la una serie de condiciones determinadas.

scientific theory A well-tested explanation for a wide range of observations or experimental results.
teoría científica Explicación comprobada de una gran variedad de observaciones o resultados de experimentos. (p. 16)

screw A simple machine that is an inclined plane wrapped around a central cylinder to form a spiral.
tornillo Máquina simple que consiste en un plano inclinado enrollado en un cilindro central para formar una espiral. (p. 425)

secondary color Any color produced by combining equal amounts of any two primary colors. (p. 614)
color secundario Color producido al combinar iguales cantidades de dos colores primarios cualquiera.

seismic wave A wave produced by an earthquake. (p. 531)
onda sísmica Onda producida por un terremoto.

seismograph An instrument used to detect and measure earthquake waves. (p. 533)
sismógrafo Instrumento que se usa para detectar y medir ondas de terremotos.

semiconductor A material that conducts current under certain conditions. (pp. 135, 752)
semiconductor Material que conduce la corriente bajo ciertas condiciones.

series circuit An electric circuit with a single path.
circuito en serie Circuito eléctrico con un solo camino. (p. 710)

short circuit A connection that allows current to take an unintended path. (p. 715)
cortocircuito Conexión que permite que la corriente tome un camino no establecido.

sliding friction Friction that occurs when one solid surface slides over another. (p. 342)
fricción de deslizamiento Fricción que ocurre cuando una superficie sólida se desliza sobre otra.

slope The steepness of a line on a graph, equal to its vertical change divided by its horizontal change.
pendiente Inclinación de una recta en una gráfica, igual a su cambio vertical dividido por su cambio horizontal. (p. 316)

software A detailed set of instructions that directs the computer hardware to perform operations on stored information. (p. 767)
software Conjunto de instrucciones detalladas que dirige el hardware de una computadora para que realice operaciones con la información almacenada.

solar wind Streams of electrically charged particles flowing at high speeds from the sun. (p. 674)
viento solar Corrientes de partículas con carga eléctrica que fluyen a gran velocidad desde el Sol.

solenoid A coil of wire with a current that acts as a bar magnet. (p. 726)
solenoide Espiral de alambre con una corriente que actúa como un imán de barra.

solid A state of matter that has a definite shape and a definite volume. (p. 71)
sólido Estado de la materia con forma y volumen definidos.

solubility A measure of how much solute can dissolve in a given solvent at a given temperature.
solubilidad Medida de cuánto soluto se puede disolver en un solvente dada una temperatura determinada. (p. 231)

solute The part of a solution present in a lesser amount and dissolved by the solvent. (p. 222)
soluto Parte de una solución presente en menor cantidad y disuelta por el solvente.

solution A well-mixed mixture containing a solvent and at least one solute that has the same properties throughout. (pp. 41, 222)
solución Mezcla homogénea que contiene un solvente y al menos un soluto que tiene las mismas propiedades en toda la solución.

solvent The part of a solution that is present in the largest amount and dissolves a solute. (p. 222)
solvente Parte de una solución que está presente en la mayor cantidad y que disuelve un soluto.

sonar A system that uses reflected sound waves to detect and locate objects underwater. (p. 566)
sonar Sistema que usa ondas sonoras reflejadas para detectar y localizar objetos debajo del agua.

sonogram An image formed using reflected ultrasound waves. (p. 567)
sonograma Imagen creada usando ondas de ultrasonido reflejadas.

specific heat The amount of heat required to raise the temperature of 1 kilogram of a material by 1 kelvin. (p. 476)
calor específico Cantidad de calor que se requiere para elevar la temperatura de 1 kilogramo de material 1 grado Kelvin.

spectroscope An instrument used to view the different colors of light produced by different light sources. (p. 588)
espectroscopio Instrumento que se usa para ver los diferentes colores de la luz producidos por fuentes de luz diferentes.

speed The distance an object travels per unit of time.
rapidez Distancia que viaja un objeto por unidad de tiempo. (p. 312)

standing wave A wave that appears to stand in one place, even though it is really two waves interfering as they pass through each other. (p. 526)
onda estacionaria Onda que parece que permanece en un lugar, aunque en realidad son dos ondas que interfieren cuando se cruzan.

starch A complex carbohydrate in which plants store energy. (p. 286)
almidón Carbohidrato complejo en la que las plantas almacenan la energía.

state One of the three forms—solid, liquid, or gas—in which matter exists. (p. 487)
estado Una de las tres formas (sólido, líquido o gas) en las que existe la materia en la Tierra.

static discharge The loss of static electricity as electric charges transfer from one object to another.
descarga estática Pérdida de la electricidad estática cuando las cargas eléctricas se transfieren de un objeto a otro. (p. 688)

static electricity A buildup of charges on an object.
electricidad estática Acumulación de cargas eléctricas en un objeto. (p. 685)

static friction Friction that acts on objects that are not moving. (p. 342)
fricción estática Fricción que actúa sobre los objetos que no se mueven.

step-down transformer A transformer that decreases voltage. (p. 743)
transformador reductor Transformador que disminuye el voltaje.

step-up transformer A transformer that increases voltage. (p. 742)
transformador elevador Transformador que aumenta el voltaje.

structural formula A description of a molecule that shows the kind, number, and arrangement of atoms. (p. 267)
fórmula estructural Descripción de una molécula que muestra el tipo, número y posición de los átomos.

sublimation The change in state from a solid directly to a gas without passing through the liquid state. (p. 81)
sublimación Cambio del estado sólido directamente a gas, sin pasar por el estado líquido.

subscript A number in a chemical formula that tells the number of atoms in a molecule or the ratio of elements in a compound. (p. 161)
subíndice Número en una fórmula química que indica el número de átomos que tiene una molécula o la razón de elementos en un compuesto.

substance A single kind of matter that is pure and has a specific set of properties. (p. 35)
sustancia Tipo único de materia que es pura y tiene un conjunto de propiedades específicas.

substituted hydrocarbon A hydrocarbon in which one or more hydrogen atoms have been replaced by atoms of other elements. (p. 270)
hidrocarburo sustituido Hidrocarburo en el cual uno o más átomos de hidrógeno han sido sustituidos por átomos de otros elementos.

supersaturated solution A mixture that has more dissolved solute than is predicted by its solubility at a given temperature. (p. 235)
solución supersaturada Mezcla que tiene más soluto disuelto de lo que se predice por su solubilidad a una temperatura determinada.

surface tension The result of an inward pull among the molecules of a liquid that brings the molecules on the surface closer together (p. 74)
tensión superficial Resultado de la atracción hacia el centro entre las moléculas de un líquido, que hace que las moléculas de la superficie se junten más; hace que la superficie actúe como si tuviera una piel delgada.

surface wave A combination of a longitudinal wave and a transverse wave that travels along the surface of a medium. (p. 532)
onda superficial Combinación de una onda longitudinal con una onda transversal que viaja por la superficie de un medio.

suspension A mixture in which particles can be seen and easily separated by settling or filtration. (p. 224)
suspensión Mezcla en la cual las partículas se pueden ver y separar fácilmente por sedimentación o por filtración.

synthesis A chemical reaction in which two or more simple substances combine to form a new, more complex substance. (p. 200)
síntesis Reacción química en la que dos o más sustancias simples se combinan para formar una sustancia nueva más compleja.

system A group of related parts that work together.
sistema Grupo de partes relacionadas que funcionan en conjunto. (p. 26)

T

technology A way of changing the natural world to meet human needs or solve practical problems.
technología Como la gente modifica el mundo para satisfacer sus necesidades o para solucionar problemas prácticos.

telescope An optical instrument that forms enlarged images of distant objects. (p. 634)
telescopio Instrumento óptico que forma imágenes aumentadas de los objetos lejanos.

temperature A measure of the average energy of motion of the particles of a substance. (pp. 54, 472)
temperatura Medida de la energía promedio de movimiento de las partículas de una sustancia.

temporary magnet A magnet made from a material that easily loses its magnetism. (p. 666)
imán temporal Imán hecho de un material que pierde fácilmente su magnetismo.

terminal A convenient attachment point used to connect a cell or battery to a circuit. (p. 704)
terminal Punto de conexión conveniente que se usa para conectar una celda o batería a un circuito.

terminal velocity The greatest velocity a falling object can achieve. (p. 347)
velocidad terminal La máxima velocidad que puede alcanzar un objeto que cae.

thermal energy The total potential and kinetic energy of the particles in an object. (pp. 54, 449)
energía térmica Energía cinética y potencial total de las partículas de un objeto.

thermal expansion The expansion of matter when it is heated. (p. 490)
expansión térmica Expansión de la materia cuando se calienta.

thermogram An image that shows regions of different temperatures in different colors. (p. 581)
termografía Imagen que muestra regiones de diferentes temperaturas en diferentes colores.

third prong The round prong of a plug that connects any metal pieces in an appliance to the safety grounding wire of a building. (p. 716)
tercero terminal Terminal redondeado de un enchufe que conecta cualquier parte de metal de un artefacto con el alambre a tierra de un edificio.

total internal reflection The complete reflection of light by the inside surface of a medium. (p. 640)
reflexión interna total Reflexión completa de la luz en la superficie interna de un medio.

tracer A radioactive isotope that can be followed through the steps of a chemical reaction or industrial process. (p. 142)
trazador Isótopo radiactivo que se puede seguir mediante los pasos de una reacción química o proceso industrial.

trade-off An exchange in which one benefit is given up in order to obtain another. (p. 24)
trade-off Intercambio en el cual se renuncia a un beneficio para obtener otro.

transformer A device that increases or decreases voltage. (p. 741)
transformador Instrumento que aumenta o disminuye el voltaje.

transistor A solid-state component used to amplify an electronic signal or to switch current on and off.
transistor Componente electrónico que se usa para amplificar una señal electrónica o apagar y encender la corriente. (p. 753)

transition metal One of the elements in Groups 3 through 12 of the periodic table. (p. 122)
metal de transición Uno de los elementos en los Grupos 3 a 12 de la tabla periódica.

translucent material A material that scatters light as it passes through. (p. 611)
material traslúcido Material que dispersa la luz cuando ésta lo atraviesa.

transmitter A device that transfers signals from one form to another. (p. 756)
transmisor Aparato que convierte señales de una forma a otra.

transparent material A material that transmits light without scattering it. (p. 611)
material transparente Material que transmite luz sin dispersarla.

transverse wave A wave that moves the medium in a direction perpendicular to the direction in which the wave travels. (p. 512)
onda transversal Onda que mueve el medio en dirección perpendicular a la dirección en la que viaja la onda.

triple bond A chemical bond formed when atoms share three pairs of electrons. (p. 168)
enlace triple Enlace químico formado cuando los átomos comparten tres pares de electrones.

troubleshooting The process of analyzing a design problem and finding a way to fix it. (p. 25)
solución de problemas Proceso por el cual se analiza un problema de diseño y se halla una forma de solucionarlo.

trough The lowest part of a transverse wave. (p. 512)
valle Parte más baja de una onda transversal.

tsunami A huge surface wave on the ocean caused by an underwater earthquake. (p. 532)
tsunami Gran ola superficial del océano causado por un terremoto subterráneo.

tungsten-halogen bulb Incandescent light bulb containing a tungsten filament and a halogen gas.
lámpara de tungsteno-halógeno Lámpara de luz incandescente que contiene un filamento de tungsteno y gas halógeno. (p. 589)

U

ultrasound Sound waves with frequencies above 20,000 Hz. (p. 549)
ultrasonido Ondas sonoras con frecuencias mayores de 20,000 Hz. (p. 549)

ultraviolet rays Electromagnetic waves with wavelengths shorter than visible light, but longer than X-rays. (p. 582)
rayos ultravioletas Ondas electromagnéticas con longitud de onda menor que la luz visible, pero mayor que la de los rayos X.

unbalanced force Forces that produce a nonzero net force, which changes an object's motion.
fuerza desequilibrada Fuerzas que producen una fuerza neta diferente de cero, lo cual cambia el movimiento de un objeto. (p. 336)

unsaturated hydrocarbon A hydrocarbon in which one or more of the bonds between carbon atoms is double or triple. (p. 269)
hidrocarburo no saturado Hidrocarburo en el que uno o más de los enlaces entre átomos de carbono es doble o triple.

unsaturated solution A mixture that contains less dissolved solute than is possible at a given temperature. (p. 231)
solución no saturada Mezcla que contiene menos soluto disuelto de lo que es posible a una temperatura determinada.

V

valence electrons The electrons that are in the highest energy level of an atom and that are involved in chemical reactions. (p. 150)
electrones de valencia Electrones que tienen el más alto nivel de energía de un átomo y participan en reacciones químicas

Van Allen belt Two doughnut-shaped regions 1,000–25,000 kilometers above Earth that contain electrons and protons traveling at high speed.
cinturones de Van Allen Par de regiones circulares ubicadas de 1,000 a 25,000 kilómetros de la Tierra; están formadas de electrones y protones que viajan a alta velocidad. (p. 674)

vapor light Light bulb containing neon or argon gas along with a small amount of solid sodium or mercury. (p. 590)
luz de vapor Lámpara que contiene gas neón o argón y una pequeña cantidad de sodio sólido o mercurio.

vaporization The change of state from a liquid to a gas. (p. 78)
vaporización Cambio del estado de líquido a gas.

variable A factor that can change in an experiment. (p. 12)
variable Factor que puede cambiar en un experimento.

vary inversely A term used to describe the relationship between two variables whose graph forms a curve that slopes downward. (p. 93)
variar inversamente Término empleado para describir la relación entre dos variables cuya gráfica forma una curva con pendiente hacia abajo.

velocity Speed in a given direction. (p. 314)
velocidad Rapidez en una dirección dada.

vibration A repeated back-and-forth or up-and-down motion. (p. 512)
vibración Movimiento repetido hacia delante y hacia atrás o hacia arriba y hacia abajo.

virtual image An upright image formed where rays of light appear to meet or come from. (p. 619)
imagen virtual Imagen vertical que se forma desde donde parecen provenir los rayos de luz.

viscosity A liquid's resistance to flowing. (p. 74)
viscosidad Resistencia a fluir que presenta un líquido.

visible light Electromagnetic waves that are visible to the human eye. (p. 582)
luz visible Ondas electromagnéticas visibles al ojo humano.

voltage The difference in electrical potential energy between two places in a circuit. (p. 696)
voltaje Diferencia en la energía potencial eléctrica entre dos lugares en un circuito.

voltage source A device that creates an electrical potential energy difference in an electric circuit. (p. 697)
fuente de voltaje Instrumento que crea una diferencia en la energía potencial eléctrica en un circuito eléctrico.

voltmeter A device used to measure voltage, or electrical potential energy difference. (p. 712)
voltímetro Aparato usado para medir el voltaje o la diferencia de energía eléctrica potencial.

volume The amount of space that matter occupies.
volumen Cantidad de espacio que ocupa la materia. (p. 46)

W

wave A disturbance that transfers energy from place to place. (p. 511)
onda Perturbación que transfiere energía de un lugar a otro.

wavelength The distance between two corresponding parts of a wave. (p. 517)
longitud de onda Distancia entre dos partes correspondientes de una onda.

wedge A simple machine that is an inclined plane that moves. (p. 424)
cuña Máquina simple que consiste en un plano inclinado en movimiento.

weight A measure of the force of gravity on an object. (pp. 45, 345)
peso Medida de la fuerza de gravedad sobre un objeto.

wet cell An electrochemical cell in which the electrolyte is a liquid. (p. 705)
celda húmeda Celda electroquímica en la que el electrolito es un líquido.

wheel and axle A simple machine that consists of two attached circular or cylindrical objects that rotate about a common axis, each one with a different radius. (p. 428)
rueda y eje Máquina simple que consiste en dos objetos circulares o cilíndricos unidos, de diferente radio, que giran en torno a un eje común.

work Force exerted on an object that causes it to move. (p. 406)
trabajo Fuerza ejercida sobre un objeto para moverlo.

World Wide Web (WWW) A part of the Internet that allows the displaying and viewing of text, pictures, video, and sound. (p. 769)
World Wide Web (WWW) Parte de la Internet que permite la presentación y visión de texto, fotos, video y sonido.

X

X-rays Electromagnetic waves with wavelengths shorter than ultraviolet rays, but longer than gamma rays. (p. 583)
rayos X Ondas electromagnéticas con longitud de onda menor que la de los rayos ultravioleta, pero mayor que la de los rayos gamma.

Index

Page numbers for key terms are printed in **boldface** type.
Page numbers for illustrations, maps, and charts are printed in *italics*.

Index

Page numbers for key terms are printed in **boldface** type.
Page numbers for illustrations, maps, and charts are printed in *italics*.

D

Index

Page numbers for key terms are printed in **boldface** type.
Page numbers for illustrations, maps, and charts are printed in *italics*.

F

Index

Page numbers for key terms are printed in **boldface** type.
Page numbers for illustrations, maps, and charts are printed in *italics*.

H

I

Index

Page numbers for key terms are printed in **boldface** type.
Page numbers for illustrations, maps, and charts are printed in *italics*.

P

Index

Page numbers for key terms are printed in **boldface** type.
Page numbers for illustrations, maps, and charts are printed in *italics*.

Index

Page numbers for key terms are printed in **boldface** type.
Page numbers for illustrations, maps, and charts are printed in *italics*.